Final Report of the
Attorney General's Commission on PORNOGRAPHY

D1123417

Final Report of the
Attorney General's Commission on PORNOGRAPHY

Introduction by
Michael J. McManus

RUTLEDGE HILL PRESS
NASHVILLE, TENNESSEE

Published in Nashville, Tennessee, by Rutledge Hill Press, Inc., 513 Third Avenue South, Nashville, Tennessee 37210.

Distributed by Word Books, P.O. Box 1790, 4800 W. Waco Drive, Waco, TX 76796

Typography by ProtoType Graphics, Inc.
Printing and Binding by Arcata Graphics

Library of Congress Cataloging-in-Publication Data

United States. Attorney General's Commission on Pornography.
    Final report of the Attorney General's Commission on Pornography.

    Reprint. Originally published: Washington, D.C.: U.S. Dept. of Justice; For sale by Supt. of Docs., U.S. G.P.O., 1986. With new introd.
    Bibliography: p.
    1. Pornography—United States.   2. Pornography—Social aspects—United States.   I. Title.
KF9444.A864 1986   363.4′7′0973   86-21971
ISBN 0-934395-42-X (pbk.)

Printed in the United States of America
1 2 3 4 5 6 7 — 90 89 88 87 86

T A B L E   O F   C O N T E N T S

PART 4: The Commissioners

PART 5: Reference Material

PUBLISHER'S PREFACE

One of the purposes of the Attorney General's Commission on Pornography and its *Report* was to make recommendations concerning how the spread of pornography could be contained in ways consistent with constitutional guarantees. While many of the ninety-two recommendations given in the *Report* are directed to the Attorney General, others are aimed at ordinary citizens who are encouraged to become involved in protecting their communities. Yet the *Report* as published by the Federal Government was unwieldy, expensive, and hard to obtain. A more affordable and available edition was necessary to spur community discussion and action.

While Rutledge Hill Press preferred to publish the entire *Report* as printed by the Federal Government, upon advice of counsel, certain deletions or condensations were made. Most were inconsequential to the purpose of the *Report*, but all deletions are indicated by the symbol ✂.

The two major portions affected are:

1. The appendixes to Chapter 19 on organized crime have been deleted. They have been replaced by a description of the appendixes on page 302.
2. In Chapter 24 extensive quotations and detailed descriptions from paperback books, movies, videos, and a tabloid were abbreviated because necessary copyright permissions could not be secured.

Generally, we have avoided any editing of the *Report*. However, since we felt that the *Report* would be most understandable by beginning it with the Overview and Analysis of Commission Findings, we have moved the three chapters on the Commissioners—their biographies, acknowledgments and notes, and their statements—to the end of the book instead of printing them at the beginning as the U.S. Government Printing Office did. The Commission's Charter was moved to the front and now follows the introduction. We have also numbered the chapters consecutively throughout the *Report*.

The Introduction to this edition of the *Final Report of the Attorney General's Commission on Pornography* was written by Michael J. McManus. It is a summary, analysis, and commentary on the substance of the *Report* on one hand, as well as the story of some of the drama of the Commission and the aftermath of the initial publication of the *Report*. McManus is a syndicated columnist whose two columns, "Ethics and Religion" and "Solutions" appear in 135 and 55 newspapers respectively across the country. McManus covered the Commission's meetings in New York, New York, Scottsdale, Arizona, and Washington, D.C. As one of the few journalists who followed its proceedings at any depth, he has written numerous columns on the Commission, its workings, and the Report. He lives with his wife and three children in Stamford, Connecticut.

Few books have caused as much storm and controversy as has the *Final Report of the Attorney General's Commission on Pornography*. It has been both praised and condemned. It should not, however, be itself censored.

—RUTLEDGE HILL PRESS

INTRODUCTION

by Michael J. McManus

When Attorney General Edwin Meese III announced formation of a Commission on Pornography on May 20, 1985, he asked it to "determine the nature, extent, and impact on society of pornography in the United States, and to make specific recommendations to the Attorney General concerning more effective ways in which the spread of pornography could be contained, consistent with constitutional guarantees."

This Final Report answers that mandate. When it was released, the American Civil Liberties Union (ACLU) called it "censorship . . . a national crusade against dirty pictures." But the Commissioner's Chairman, Henry Hudson, now a U.S. Attorney in Virginia, says "Those looking for censorship in this Report will be gravely disappointed."

More important, the Report could spark a major assault against illegal obscenity in the United States. Commissioner James Dobson, President of Focus on the Family, says in his personal statement, "America could rid itself of hard core pornography in 18 months if the recommendations offered in (the *Final Report*) are implemented. . . . But that will occur only if American citizens demand action from their government. Nothing short of a public outcry will motivate our slumbering representatives to defend community standards of decency" (page 509).

Anyone who studies the *Report* will become equipped to be an effective advocate for enforcement of existing laws against hard core pornography and child pornography. However, it must be acknowledged this book is very long—longer than an average concerned citizen can be expected to read from cover to cover. It is a reference work, more like an *Encyclopaedia Britannica*, which no one needs to read from *A* to *Z*.

Purpose of Introduction

Therefore, one purpose of this Introduction is provide a succinct summary of the *Report's* most important findings. A second goal is to give the interested citizen a quick roadmap into the Commission's analysis and conclusions. Thus, brief quotes from the *Report* will be followed by page numbers so that those who want to read more extensively will know where to turn.

A third purpose is to give this reporter's sense of how the Commission functioned as a group of people. I covered the last three meetings of the Commission—in New York City, Scottsdale, Arizona, and Washington, D.C.— to watch the Commissioners thrash out their conclusions.

Finally, I felt an extra sense of responsibility to write about this unpleasant subject in depth because so few of my peers in journalism are doing so. Frankly, I was shocked to discover that almost the only people I saw at all three sessions were writers for *Playboy*, *Penthouse*, and *Forum* magazines and representatives of the ACLU. The TV networks only showed up to hear a few victims' lurid testimony. Where were the newsmagazines, the Associated Press, or *The New York Times*? They were all absent, except for token appearances. *The Washington Post* did not even cover the final week of meetings in Washington of the first federally-appointed panel to study this issue since 1970. Therefore, it was no surprise that most reporting on the Commission's findings was shallow and quick to quote predictable critics, such as the ACLU or *Penthouse* Publisher Bob Guccione.

For example, on the day the Report was released, NBC-TV had only three sentences on the conclusions of the 1960-page *Report*, plus one sentence each from Meese and the Commission's director. Compared to those five sentences, three critics, including Christie Hefner of *Playboy*, each had 4-5 sentences of dissent.

Many publications repeated the myth that the Commission never defined "pornography." See page 8 where it is plainly defined as material that is "predominantly sexually explicit and intended primarily for the purpose of sexual arousal."

It saddens me, as a former *Time* magazine correspondent, to say it was clear to me that *Time's* July 21, 1986 cover story, "Sex Busters," was written by someone who had not read more than excerpts of the *Report*. It sneers about "a new moral militancy," but cites almost none of the ample evidence backing the *Report's* most important conclusion that some forms of pornography are leading to "an increase in aggressive behavior toward women" and an "increase in the incidence of sexual violence" (page 39–40).

However, the Commission deserves some criticism, too. The Overview and Analysis, which was drafted by Commissioner Frederick Schauer, a professor of law at the University of Michigan, is overly verbose. Yet—despite its length—it contains few of the *Report's* 92 recommendations, which are scattered through Part II.

More important, the Overview asserts that "clinical and experimental research" is "virtually unanimous" that "exposure to sexually violent materials has indicated an increase in the likelihood of aggression." And there is "a causal relationship between exposure to material of this type and aggressive behavior towards women" (page 39).

Yet the Overview does not cite one bit of that evidence to back the *Report's* central new finding! Instead, the reader is directed to Chapter 18, "Social and Behavioral Science Analysis," which is praised as "sensitive, balanced, comprehensive, accurate and current," on which the Commission relied "extensively" (page 39). Much public confusion could have been avoided if the Overview had simply quoted from the evidence. (See its summary below under "Social and Behavioral Science Research Analysis") So *The New York Times* erroneously concludes in an editorial, "The Meese Commission's connection of pornography and crime outruns its own evidence."

Now it is true that a 1970 Presidential Commission on Obscenity and Pornography "found no evidence to date that exposure to explicit sexual materials plays a significant role in the causation of delinquent or criminal behavior." However, the Meese Comission found that conclusuion "starkly obsolete" (page 6). Why? Pornography has changed radically since 1970, and today many new techniques bring it directly into homes.

Pornography More Violent and More Degrading

"Some of this material involves sado-masochistic themes" with "whips, chains, devices of torture, and so on," says the Overview. Another involves "the recurrent theme of a man making some sort of sexual advance to a women, being rebuffed and then raping a woman," who "eventually becomes aroused and ecstatic about the initially forced sexual activity, and usually is portrayed as begging for more." Finally, there's the "slasher film," which has "suggestive nudity coupled with extreme violence, such as disfigurement or murder" (page 39).

To people who think of *Playboy* when they think of pornography, this is shocking. However, this *Report* provides detail in Chapter 24 on pornographic imagery that is even more offensive. Concerned citizens must at least look at this material, for many people have no idea how ghastly it is. One study of magazines sold in adult bookstores found that "Depictions of a woman alone predominanted these covers in 1970 . . . but only constituted 11 percent of the authors' 1980 sample. Bondage and domination imagery was the most prevalent imagery (17 percent) (page 357).

The Commission staff went to sixteen adult stores and listed the titles of 2,323 separate magazine titles, 725 books, and 2,370 films. Read some of them anywhere between pages 387 and 424. Some of the titles on page 387 and 388 are "All Tied Up," "Almost Incest," "Animal Action," "Amputee Times," and "Anal Agony." There are verbal descriptions of the contents of some of them, beginning on page 425. One paragraph suffices:

> Thirteen photographs of a partially clothed and gagged Caucasian female with her arms bound with rope. The rope is tightly looped around the base of each breast causing them to swell to an abnormal size. There are clothes pins pinching each nipple and a vibrator-dildo partially inserted into her vagina (page 427).

In commenting on this material, much of which is legally obscene, one Commissioner, Dr. Park Dietz, a Professor of Law, Behavioral Medicine and Psychiatry at the University of Virginia, wrote in his personal statement:

> The offensiveness of some of the quoted language is nothing when compared to the suffering described by victims whose accounts are quoted in the victimization chapter. This is not bedtime reading. As with the practice of medicine, one must sometimes cause discomfort to effect a cure, and it was our judgment that the public and the truth would best be served by including certain discomforting materials in the report (page 487).

Technology Makes Pornography More Available

While broadcast television has become more sexually explicit, with frequent "themes of adultery, fornication, prostitution, sexual deviation, and sexual abuse. . . ." (page 362), it has rarely included nudity because the Federal Communications Commission (FCC) has traditionally required so-called "decency standards." However, broadcast TV does contain "a significant amount of material . . . that qualifies as the type of sexual violence that the Commission has found to be the most harmful form of pornography." (As noted in more detail below, the Commission found violence is more dangerous than nudity.)

Under the current law, however, Cable TV and satellite broadcasts are not subject to FCC regulations and are often substantially more sexually explicit than anything on broadcast television. "Channels which carry 'R' rated programming reach in excess of 14.5 million homes." Some are unrated films that would be 'X' if given a rating, with explicit sex and violence. Others show such "X–rated" films as *The Devil in Miss Jones* (whose plot is summarized on pages 437–438).

About eighty percent of sexually explicit films and video are made in Los Angeles. "In 1985, approximately 100 full length sexually explicit films were distributed to nearly 700 'adults only' pornographic theaters. These theaters sold an estimated 2 million tickets each week" with $500 million in annual box office receipts, the *Report* says on page 352 in Chapter 23, the "Production and Distribution of Sexually Explicit Materials."

But many X–rated theaters are closing as video cassette recorders (VCRs) become more available. By the end of 1986, thirty-eight percent of homes will have one. Videos are much cheaper to make than films ($4,000 to $20,000 versus $60,000 to $75,000). Some 1,700 new sexually explicit video cassettes were released in 1985; they account for about one-fifth of rentals and sales.

Dial-A-Porn is a totally new form of obscene communication. Some calls involve live conversations with paid performers who will talk to the caller in as sexually explicit terms as desired, billing the customer's credit card for each minute of conversation. More conventional Dial-A-Porn are recorded messages of sex acts described by the performer as though they were occurring during the call. "The acts described may include lesbian sexual activity, sodomy, rape, incest, excretory functions, bestiality, sadomasochistic abuse, and sex acts with children" (page 365). What's alarming is that children make many of the calls!

The volume of these calls is immense. Some companies can handle 50,000 callers per hour without any caller getting a busy signal! "During one day in May of 1983, 800,000 calls were placed to one sexually explicit recorded message service. . . . In California, Dial-A-Porn providers earn $1.26 per call while the telephone company earns 74 cents" (page 366).

The Difference between Pornography and Obscenity

Not all pornography is legally obscene. Some has been held by the courts to be constitutionally protected speech. On the other hand, The Supreme Court has repeatedly said, "Obscene material is unprotected by the First Amendment."

This situation has led to much confusion, of course, and has persuaded many prosecutors to give up on prosecuting pornographers. However, present laws *can* be enforced. No legally obscene material is sold in Cincinnati or Atlanta; the prosecutors there made aggressive use of a three-pronged definition of obscenity outlined by the Supreme Court in a landmark 1973 case, *Miller vs. California*. "Material is obscene if all three of the following conditions are met," says the Overview on pages 17–18.

1. The average person, applying contemporary community standards, would find that the work, taken as a whole, appeals to the prurient interest; and
2. the work depicts or describes, in a patently offensive way, sexual conduct specifically defined by the applicable state (or federal) law; and
3. the work, taken as a whole, lacks serious literary, artistic, political or scientific value.

This test has proven so stringent, that the effect of *Miller* and a number of subsequent court cases "is to limit obscenity prosecutions to 'hard core' material devoid of anything except the most explicit and offensive representations of sex," says the *Report's* Overview on page 18. It continues, "Only the most thoroughly explicit materials, overwhelmingly devoted to patently offensive and explicit representations and unmitigated by any significant amount of anything else, can be and are in fact determined to be legally obscene" (page 316).

It might be added that while this *Report* rarely uses the phrase "hard core," the Supreme Court used that same phrase in *Miller* and defined it as a description of "patently offensive representations or descriptions of ultimate sexual acts, normal or perverted, actual or simulated; and patently offensive representations or descriptions of masturbatory, excretory factions, and lewd exhibition of the genitals" (page 316).

Lawyers will be interested in an extended treatment of this subject in Chapter 20, "The History of the Regulation of Pornography," and the next chapter, "First Amendment Consideration."

The Concept of Harm

"A central part of our mission has been to examine the question of whether pornogrpahy is harmful," begins an important section of the Overview on page 31. While its prose is dense and convoluted, this section through page 48 is must reading for anyone concerned about pornography. The most frequent assertion of those opposed to increased enforcement of obscenity laws is that pornography "isn't harmful."

That point of view was argued on the Commission itself by Dr. Judith Becker, Columbia University associate professor and director of the Sexual Behavior Clinic at the New York State Psychiatric Insitute. During the Commission's meeting in Scottsdale, Arizona, she said, "One of the mandates was to determine the relationship between pornography and antisocial behavior and the commission of sexual crimes . . . I don't think there is in the social science data any conclusive causal relationship between this type of material and the commission of sexual crimes. The data show that in certain experiments attitudes change and I think one makes a quantum leap from attitudinal changes to committing serious crimes.

It was a powerful presentation. Yet, she voted *with* the Commission two months later, in a *unanimous* vote, that "since we believe that an increase in aggressive behavior towards women will in a population increase the incidence of sexual violence in that population, we have reached the conclusion unanimously and confidently, that the available evidence strongly supports the hypothesis that substantial exposure to sexually violent materials as described here bears a causal (not *casual*, as some TV commentators read the word) relationship to antisocial acts of sexual violence, and for some subgroups, possibly to unlawful acts of sexual violence" (page 40).

However, there are some cautionary words on pages 33–35 on the "standard of proofs":

> There will never be *conclusive* proof that such a causal connection exists, if 'conclusive' means no other possibility exists . . . The world is complex, and most consequences are 'caused' by numerous factors . . . We have concluded, for example, that some forms of sexually explicit material bear a causal relationship both to sexual violence and to sex discrimination, but we are hardly so naive as to suppose that were these forms of pornography to disappear the problems of sex discrimination and sexual violence would come to an end." Rather, they simply assert that "if this factor were eliminated while everything else stayed the same then the problem would at least be lessened.

Further, it cited a "wide range" of evidence. First, there was personal testimony of "women reporting on what men in their lives have done to them or to their children as a result of exposure to certain sexually explicit materials." Another type of testimony came from sex offenders themselves "who have told us how they became 'addicted' to pornography, or how they were led to commit sex crimes as a result of exposure to pornographic materials." Other witnesses were clinical experts who treat sex offenders, experimental social scientists, and law enforcement officials.

Victim Testimony

I urge readers to read for at least one half hour in the heart-rending "Victim Testimony" in Chapter 16 that begins on page 197. The first quotes are from Andrea Dworkin, author of *Men Possessing Women*, whose testimony in New York moved Dr. Park Dietz to tears. She said:

> I am a citizen of the United States, and in this country where I live, every year millions of pictures are made of women with our legs spread. We are called beaver, we are called pussy, our genitals are tied up . . . our throats are used as if they are genitals for penetration. . . .
> In this country where I live as a citizen, women are penetrated by animals and objects for public entertainment, women are urinated on and defecated on. . . . Asian women in this country where I live are tied from trees and hung from doorways as a form of public entertainment . . . There are those who say it is a form of pleasure . . . a form of freedom. Certainly it is freedom for those who do

it. Certainly it is freedom for those who use it as entertainment. But we are asked to believe that it is freedom for those to whom it is done. . . .

The women in pornography, 65–70 percent of them we believe, are victims of incest or child sexual assault. . . . They are frequently raped, the rapes are filmed, they are kept in prostitution by blackmail. . . .

I'm asking you to help the exploited, not the exploiters. You have a tremendous opportunity here. I am asking you as individuals to have the courage . . . to actually be willing yourselves to go out and cut that woman down and untie her hands and take the gag out of her mouth, and do something for her freedom."

Linda S. testified:

"The incest started at the age of eight. I did not understand any of it and did not feel that it was right. My dad would try to convince me that it was OK. He would find magazines with articles and/or pictures that would show fathers and daughters. . . . He would say that if it was published in magazines that it had to be all right because magazines could not publish lies."

A former prostitute is quoted on page 222:

"We were all introduced to prostitution through pornography. There were no exceptions in our group, and we were all under eighteen. Pornography was our textbook. We learned the tricks of the trade by men exposing us to pornography and us trying to mimic what we saw."

It is worth noting that dozens of victims are quoted according a wide range of adverse effects suffered as the result of "porn rape": forced sexual performance, battery and torture, murder, imprisonment, VD, suicide, prostitution, and such anguish as fear, shame, guilt, amnesia, nightmares, and frigidity.

One criticism of this sort of testimony came from Judith Becker and Commissioner Ellen Levine, editor of *Woman's Day*, in a jointly signed personal statement (pages 540–546): "To find people willing to acknowledge their personal consumption of erotic and pornography materials and comment favorably in public about their use has been nearly impossible. Since such material is selling to millions of apparently satisfied customers, it seems obvious that the data gathered is not well balanced."

The Commission itself said "Plainly some of these witnesses were less credible or less helpful than others, but many of the stories these witnesses told were highly believable and extremely informative." But it "refused to make invalid statistical generalizations" from subjective accounts about how widespread such harms were (page 36).

However, the Commission adds that it "heard much evidence from law enforcement personnel that a disproportionate number of sex offenders were found to have large quantities of pornographic material in their residences. . . . There is a correlation between pornographic material and sex offenses."

Social and Behavioral Science Research Analysis

More important, sex offenders themselves told social science researchers astounding facts about themselves and the influence of pornography. See Chapter 18 beginning on page 259 for a mass of evidence, some of which is summarized here:

1. Interviews with 411 sex offenders "revealed a staggering number" of victims. In a study conducted partly by Commissioner Becker, each criminal had "attempted an average of 581 sex offenses and completed typically 533 offenses each, with a mean number of 336 victims each" (page 259)!
2. Since 1970, pornographers have quoted a Danish study by Kutchinsky which alleged that the number of reported sex crimes dropped after legalization. Kutchinsky argued that the availability of pornography siphons off potentially dangerous sex impulses—the safety value theory. But many subsequent studies of his work show that he lumped together voyeurism and homosexuality, which police stopped reporting after legalization, with rapes, which actually increased in number (page 260).
3. "Cross-national data from areas as disparate as England, Australia, Singapore and South Africa" found that "rape reports have increased where porn laws have been liberalized while the same steep rise is not in evidence where restrictions exist." (page 260).
4. Rapists are fifteen times as likely as non-offenders to have had exposure to "hard-core" pornography "during childhood or between six to ten years old. They also tended to report an earlier age of 'peak experience' with pornography" (page 265).
5. Even non-violent, soft-core pornography may "legitimate rape." The eight major men's magazines (Chic, Club, Gallery, Genesis, Hustler, Oui, Playboy, and Penthouse) have sales that are five times higher per capita in Alaska and Nevada than in other states, such as North Dakota. And rape rates are six times higher per capita in Alaska and Nevada than North Dakota.

    Some dismiss this latter study as only being "correlational," not conclusive proof that pornography causes rape and the Commission does point out that these correlational "findings do not indicate that men are induced to rape as a result of exposure to these magazines" (page 262). But the Commission also says "this relationship was present even with controls for potential confounding variables such as police practices, propensity to report rape" (page 261).

    Father Bruce Ritter, a Commissioner who runs Covenant House for runaway teenagers at Times Square in New York, in his personal statement suggests comparing the magazine–rape correlation with studies of the Surgeon General linking smoking to cancer. That evidence, he says "was overwhelmingly correlational—showing higher death and illness rates among smokers than in non-smokers" (page 534).
6. Sexually violent films affect "normal" people as well as criminals. What may be surprising is that the most dangerous material is not X–rated

moves of fornication, but R–rated "slasher" films like the "Toolbox Murders" in which a naked woman in a tub masturbates and then is killed by a man with a power drill.

After seeing one such film per day for five days, college males "were asked to participate in what was presented as a different study—a pretest of a law school documentary" of a rape trial. Another group saw X–rated nonviolent films and were asked the same questions about the rape victim. "Those massively exposed to sexual violence judged the victim of the assault to be significantly less injured and evaluated her as less worthy than did the control group" (pages 274–275).

7. One study not mentioned by the Commission is worth noting. The FBI interviewed two dozen sex murderers in prison who had killed multiple numbers of times. Some eighty-one percent said their biggest sexual interest was in reading pornography. They acted out sex fantasies on real people. For example, Arthur Gary Bishop, convicted of sexually abusing and killing five young boys said, "If pornographic material would have been unavailable to me in my early states, it is most probably that my sexual activities would not have escalated to the degree they did." He said pornography's impact on him was "devastating. . . . I am a homosexual pedophile convicted of murder and pornography was a determining factor in my downfall."

In fact, the Commission has two studies in which over half of rapists say they were "incited to commit an offense" by pornography and forty-two percent of child molesters "implicated pornography" in their crimes (pages 268–269).

However, the Comission itself was unsatisfied with its own review of the social science literature. It remembered the testimony of Dr. C. Everett Koop, the U.S. Surgeon General, at its first hearing in June, 1985. Koop expressed concern "that we are not operating in the dark on this matter, as may have been the case a decade or two ago," when the 1970 Presidential Commission was working. He said the earlier commission's conclusions that pornography did not cause "delinquent or criminal behavior" was based "upon a very limited universe of scientific literature." And he offered to pull together the nation's leading researchers to obtain a consensus of their opinions.

Chairman Henry Hudson immediately expressed interest. But Koop estimated that it would cost $100,000 to survey the literature, pay for the conference of the nation's leading experts, and publish a report. That posed a formidable problem for the Commission, because its total budget was only $400,000—compared to $2 million that the Presidential Commission had spent between 1968 and 1970. A budget of the same size in today's dollars would have been $6 million.

However, Hudson made a written request of Attorney General Meese that he appropriate additional money for the Surgeon General's work. The approval was not granted then, or upon two subsequent requests. On Jan. 31, I attended a briefing, first by Surgeon General Koop followed by one with the Attorney General. Koop complained at his meeting that Meese personally refused a request to fund the study he had made only days earlier. So in the session with Meese, I quoted Koop and said, "Why won't you fund this additional research on the impact of pornography? The issue of harm is central to the deliberations of your Commission on Pornography, and the independent analysis that social scientists can offer is important." Meese paused, blinked and then said, "There's no problem about that. The Surgeon General only asked me about that the other day. We can work it out."

However, the funds were not made available until March. And the researchers, many of whom are college professors, could not be freed to gather until June—a full month *after* the Commission's work was scheduled to be completed. At the unanimous request of the Commission, Hudson asked Meese to extend the life of the Commission, so that it might be able to digest the Surgeon General's conclusions. Meese refused.

However, early in August, I obtained a summary of a "consensus" of two dozen leading researchers who were gathered by the Surgeon General, including Professor Edward Donnerstein of the University of Wisconsin, a psychologist who has been quoted in the press as critical of the Pornography Commission's findings. Another critic who was present was Professor Neal Malamuth of UCLA. Yet these are their five major conclusions:

1. Children and adolescents who participate in the production of pornography experience adverse and enduring effects.
2. Prolonged use of pornography increases the belief that less common sexual practices are common.
3. Pornography that portrays sexual aggression as pleasurable for the victim, increases the acceptance of the use of coercion in sexual relations.
4. Acceptance of coercive sexuality appears to be related to sexual aggression.
5. In laboratory settings, measuring short term effects, exposure to violent pornography increases punitive behavior towards women.

How do those conclusions differ in any way from the Pornography Commission's findings? The Commission concluded that "In both clinical and experimental settings, exposure to sexually violent materials has indicated an increase in the likelihood of aggression. More specifically, the research, which is described in much detail later in this *Report*, shows a causal relationship between exposure to material of this type and aggressive behavior towards women" (page 39).

Asked to react to the Surgeon General's findings, Alan Sears, Executive Director of the Pornography Commission, said in an August 9, 1986, interview: "This independent group of social scientists, who gathered on behalf of the Surgeon General, has confirmed some of the findings of the Attorney General's Commission on Pornography. And they have given further credence to the conclusions of the Commission."

Five Classes of Pornography

Perhaps the most useful new analysis of the Commission was its examination of pornography's harm according to five different "classes":

Class I: Sexually Violent Material: Based on the sort of evidence cited above, pulled from many chapters of the *Report*, the Commission said "Exposure to sexually violent materials has indicated an increase in the likelihood of aggression." The research also "shows a causal relationship between exposure to material of this type and aggressive behavior towards women. . . .The evidence says simply that the images that people are exposed to bears a causal relationship to their behavior. That is hardly surprising. What would be surprising would be to find otherwise . . ."

"Sexual violence is not the only negative effect. . . . The evidence is also strongly supportive of significant attitudinal changes on the part of those with substantial exposure to violent pornography. . . . Victims of rape and other forms of sexual violence are likely to be perceived by people so exposed as more responsible for the assault (and the rapist) as less responsible." Also these materials lead to "a greater acceptance of the 'rape myth' that women enjoy being coerced into sexual activity," an attitude which is "pervasive and profoundly harmful" (page 40).

It should be noted that while the Commission voted unanimously on this section at its final meeting, two commissioners changed their minds later. Dr. Judith Becker and Ellen Levine, in a personal statement on page 540 say, "The social science research has not been designed to evaluate the relationship between exposure to pornography and the commission of sexual crimes; therefore, efforts to tease the current data into proof of a causal link between these acts cannot be accepted."

Class II: Nonviolent Materials Depicting Degradation, Domination, Subordination, or Humiliation: Researcher Dolph Zillmann is quoted as defining this class as material which portrays women as "masochistic, subservient, socially non-discriminating nymphomaniacs"—women who "tend to overrespond in serving the male interest." This degrading material constitutes "the largely predominant proportion of commercially available pornography," said the Commission (page 41).

This material's impact is "substantially similar" to that of violent material, although this judgment is made "with somewhat less confidence," because there has been less research done on it. "Substantial exposure to material of this type will increase acceptance of the proposition that women like to be forced into sexual practices, and . . . that the woman who says "no" really means "yes'" (page 41). And "over a large enough sample of population that believes that many women like to be raped," there will be "more acts of sexual violence." However, it added, "We are not saying that everyone exposed to material of this type has his attitude changed" or that everyone with these attitudes "will commit an act of violence" (page 42).

Class III: Non-Violent and Non-Degrading Materials: This was the Commission's "most controversial" category, which it said "is in fact quite small in terms of currently available materials." It would include couples "in consensual and equal vaginal intercourse . . . oral-genital activity" or "two couples simultaneously engaging in the same activity" (page 43).

Asked to give examples of films fitting this category, not one Commissioner could offer any. Commissioner James Dobson said, "I have sat here for 200 hours and I am not sure where the boundary lines are between Class II and III, and if I don't know, it is pot luck for the reader. . . . Is there a difference if the camera is three feet away vs. three inches?"

Commissioner Schauer, who drafted the Overview, replied, "Explicitness does not make for degradation, though it generates concern. It may be very, very explicit and very, very offensive to many without a relationship of inequality or domination."

Dr. Dobson replied, "Explicitness is degrading in and of itself." But he was outvoted on grounds that consensual sex "does not bear a causal relationship to rape and other acts of sexual violence," as the Report puts it. "The harmfulness of these materials turns on a conclusion about the harmfulness of the activity itself."

However, the Report adds "It is far from implausible to hypothesize that materials depicting sexual activity without marriage, love, commitment or affection bear some causal relationship to sexual activity without marriage, love, commitment or affection. There are undoubtedly many causes for what used to be called the 'sexual revolution,' but it is absurd to suppose that depictions or descriptions of uncommitted sexuality were not among these" (page 44).

That, of course, was Dobson's point. In the years since pornography has become widely available, divorces have tripled. Similar data can be found for abortions, teen pregnancies, and so forth.

Class IV: Nudity: "None of us think that the human body or its portrayal is harmful," the Report says. But there are "legitimate questions when "mere" nudity stops being 'mere' nudity and has such clear connotations of sexual activity that it ought at least to be analyzed according the same factors that we discuss with respect to sexually explicit materials containing neither violence nor degradation" (pages 46–47). Clearly, however, the Commission was not going to oppose such nudity as Michelangelo's *David*, or the nudity of children on a beach.

Class V: The Special Horror of Child Pornography: This class of materials is dealt with in a separate section of the Overview, beginning on page 66. "What is commonly referred to as 'child pornography' is not so much a form of pornography as it is a form of sexual exploitation of children," said an outraged Commission. "Actual children are photographed while engaged in some form of sexual activity, either with adults or with other children." It thus "involves sexual abuse of a real child."

Congress has outlawed the practice, and the Supreme Court has upheld the

law. Therefore, little or none can now be found in "adult bookstores." It is produced largely by "child abusers themselves, and then kept or informally distributed to other child abusers." However, there "appears to be commercial
network for child pornography," that is filled by "foreign magazines" that flow
almost untouched through the U.S. Mail.

For example, the Commission cites one magazine called *Lisa, 10 years, and
her dog*, which was published in Denmark. It contains 2.5 pages of ads for
other child pornography magazines. Some of the ads feature girls identified as
ten years old committing fellatio on an adult male. A part of this magazine has
six photographs of a dog "licking the vagina of the partially clothed prepubescent female," as a detective describes the material on page 431–432.

Child pornography creates a "permanent record of sexual practices" which
can "follow the child up to and through adulthood," says the *Report*. There is
"substantial evidence that photographs of children engaged in sexual activity
are used as tools for further molestation of other children." All agree that the
psychological harm of this child abuse can be devastating to a youngster.

The Overview fails to outline the forty-eight recommendations for combatting this plague. I have summarized some of them below in the Law Enforcement section of this Introduction. For more detailed treatment, see Chapter 11
(pages 130–181).

The Lack of Law Enforcement

"With few exceptions the obscenity laws that are on the books go unenforced"
says the Overview of the *Report* on page 53. Cities as big as Miami and Buffalo
have "but one police officer assigned to enforcement of the obscenity laws. Chicago had two. . . . Enforcement of federal laws has been minimal." Only seven
of ninety-four U.S. Attorneys are prosecuting a single case of adult pornography (though more have child pornography cases pending).

What is the record of the U.S. Postal Service in prosecuting adult pornography? If you were to add up all the mail cases, all of the prosecutions for trucking material across state lines, all of the cases involving broadcasting
obscenity, all of the prosecutions of organized crime figures who stand in the
shadows behind the adult bookstores, obscene videos, and films—there was
not one single federal indictment against adult pornographers in all of 1983!
There were only six in 1982, but four of them were brought by a single prosecutor in Kentucky.

The Commission says it is "dismayed at the unwillingness of the states to
assume the bulk of the responsibility for enforcement of the criminal law."
However, it adds, "Most of the material that we find most harmful is distributed
throughout the country by means of large and sophisticated distribution networks" (page 56).

That is a euphemism for "organized crime."

Organized Crime

Fortunately, the *Report* has an "Organized Crime" section, beginning on page
291. The Commission agreed with a 1978 FBI analysis that "organized crime

involvement in pornography . . . is indeed significant, and there is an obvious national control directly, and indirectly by organized crime figures in the United States. Few pornographers can operate in the United States independently without some involvement with organized crime. Only through a *well coordinated all out national effort* from the investigative and prosecutive forces" can pornography be stemmed.

The Commission frankly states, "Organized crime families from Chicago, New York, New Jersey, and Florida are openly controlling and directing the major pornography operations in Los Angeles," where most films and videos are made. Los Angeles Police Chief Daryl Gates told the Commission, "organized crime infiltrated the pornography industry in Los Angeles in 1969 due to its lucrative financial benefits. By 1975, organized crime controlled 80 percent of the industry and it is estimated that this figure is between 85–90 percent today."

Why? A "combination of the large amounts of money involved" and "the incredibly low priority obscenity enforcement had within police departments and prosecutors' offices. . . . Magazines which cost 50 cents to produce wholesale for $5 and the retail price is $10. . . . The well-known pornographic film *Deep Throat* (summarized beginning on page 438) was produced by the members of one organized crime family for $25,000 and is reliably estimated to have grossed $50 million as of 1982. They used profits to build a vast financial empire in the 1970s that included ownership of garment companies in New York . . . 'adults only' pornographic theaters in Los Angeles . . . a motion picture company" (that made *Texas Chain Saw Massacre*). And "they also used profits from *Deep Throat* to finance drug smuggling operations in the Caribbean," says the *Report* (pages 295–296).

Isolated Examples of Enforcement

However, it must be added that some cities and a few U.S. Attorneys have *successfully* enforced the law. Atlanta and Cincinnati were commended by the Commission for their virtual elimination of obscene material. As Lt. Harold Mills of Cincinnati Police (now retired) told the Commission in Chicago, "At present, the city of Cincinnati has no adult bookstores, no X–rated movies, no massage parlors, no adult movies on cable television, and no go-go dancers."

What's more, this crackdown resulted in a dramatic forty-two percent *decrease* in such crimes as assaults, prostitution, and drug dealing in an area where one massage parlor, two X–rated bookstores and a "soft core" theater were closed. More important, there was in the area an eighty-three percent plunge of serious crime such as rapes, robberies, and aggravated assaults (pages 114–115).

North Carolina is also praised by the Commission for its unique federal–state–local joint attack on pornography. In 1985, the state was "No. 1 in porn outlets per capita, No. 3 in availability of child porn, and had not a successful porn prosecution in a decade," Assistant U.S. Attorney Robert Showers, 31, told me. "Nine months ago kids could find hard-core pornography in every convenience store or gas station. And Playboy Channel was in every city. Now, in North Carolina you cannot find hard core pornography in any gas station, convenience store or grocery. The Playboy Channel has been removed from most stations. The 600–700 hard core pornography outlets are down to 125. The only ones fighting us are the syndicate's stores. They bring in lawyers and spend $100,000 to $200,000 on each trial to defend clerks."

A new state obscenity law sparked some of this change. But more important was a North Carolina Task Force on Pornography, chaired by Showers, that was America's first federal–state–local prosecution effort.

Law Enforcement Recommendations

Due to the scale of organized crime's involvement, the most important recommendations in the Pornography *Report* are directed at Attorney General Edwin Meese, III. First, he is urged to "direct the United States Attorneys (federal prosecutors) to identify the major sources of obscene material within their districts and commence prosecutions without further delay."

There is an edge to this section. Clearly, Meese could have gotten more than seven of ninety-four U.S. Attorneys active during his first eighteen months in office without waiting for the Commission to come up with its conclusions. Or he could have announced some initiatives when he was handed the *Report* July 9, 1986. Oddly, however, he simply received the *Report* beneath a semi-nude female statue of the "Spirit of Justice," sparking raucous comments from the press. He said he had "not read" the *Report*, which had been in his staff's hands for two months. And the Government Printing Office printed so few copies that it sold out quickly despite a stiff price of $35.

Of course, Attorney General Meese created the Commission and is bound to respond in some way to it. But last April the Commissioners were clearly worried about how substantial Meese's response would be.

Look at the *Report's* exceedingly frank language on page 97. "If the flow of obscene material is going to be resolved through criminal prosecution, the Attorney General of the United States must take a *significant, ongoing,* and *personal role* in directing a combined federal, state and local effort." (Emphasis added by the Commission.)

The Commission reminds the man who created it that guidelines in the *United States Attorneys Manual* place a "priority on the prosecution of three types of obscenity cases: those involving large scale distributors who realize substantial income from multi-state operations, those where there is evidence of involvement by known organized crime figures, and those involving child pornography."

U.S. Attorney Robert C. Bonner was asked by a District Attorney why he wasn't enforcing the federal law. Bonner's response contained in a 1984 letter was that it would be a "misuse of the limited resources of this office to prosecute so-called adult films" because they would be difficult to prosecute and win. Yet the Commission notes that Los Angeles Police have had 300 successful cases (page 99). (A recent arrest of a Los Angeles pornography producer was on charges of procurement for prostitution, since he was paying actors to have sex! That prompted the Commission to recommend that other prosecutors also utilize "the existing laws including those prohibiting pandering.")

Other recommendations for the Attorney General:

- "Appoint a high ranking official from the Department of Justice to oversee the creation and operation of an Obscenity Task Force." The FBI, Customs, and Postal Service, and attorneys with experience in prosecuting pornography would fashion a national strategy, train U.S. Attorneys, and help them with complex cases. Consider the difficulty of a single local U.S. Attorney in making a case against the person who is allegedly the largest distributor of pornography in America, who operates through a complex network of 200 known businesses in nineteen states and seven foreign countries and who is allegedly closely associated with a member of La Cosa Nostra's Colombo family in New York.
- Create an "Obscenity Law Enforcement Data Based"—profiles of cases prosecuted, information on known offenders, corporate records, and legal briefs used in the past that would be available to federal, state, and local prosecutors. This seems obvious, but the only people who have done it to date are attorneys who defend pornographers.
- "U.S. Attorneys should use federal–state–local teams of prosecutors," like the North Carolina Obscenity Force described above, which developed "a law enforcement blueprint" including a new obscenity law.

In addition to better enforcement of existing laws, the Commission called for some new laws to fill gaps in existing laws. At the federal level, it recommends:

1. "Congress should enact a forfeiture statute to reach the proceeds and instruments of any offense committed under federal obscenity laws," a routine measure in drug enforcement in which cars or buildings used for illegal activity are seized. The loss of such valuable property would have a more significant deterrent effect than the mere imposition of a fine or modest period of incarceration" (page 86).
2. "Congress should amend federal obscenity laws to eliminate the necessity of proving transportation in interstate commerce," to only require proof that it "affects" interstate commerce. Organized crime is expert at covering up the movements of its trucks, with false pickups and deliveries that make it "virtually impossible to detect" which items in a shipment crossed state lines. The new law would be like that for firearms (page 88).
3. "Congress should . . . specifically proscribe obscene cable and satellite television programming." This closes a minor loophole in the law. Conservatives on the Commission were disappointed that they lost a 6–5 vote that would have required the imposition of "decency" standards for cable or satellite broadcasting, that would have eliminated R–rated movies that often feature simulated sex and total nudity from being piped into half of America's homes (page 91).
4. "Congress should enact legislation to prohibit the transmission of ob-

scene material through the telephone." This is a very important proposal designed to make "Dial-A-Porn" illegal. Various attempts by the Federal Communications Commission to issue regulations were knocked out in court (page 92).

At the state or local level:

1. "State Legislatures should amend . . . obscenity statutes to eliminate misdemeanor status for second offenses," making them felonies. In Miami, a corporation with twenty-five prior obscenity convictions was fined only $1,600 for the twenty-sixth offense. In California, where the pornography industry earns $550 million a year, a major distributor is often fined no more than $10,000 (page 95).
2. State forfeiture provisions should be added to obscenity laws (page 96).

Child Pornography Enforcement

Before the first federal child pornography legislation was passed, there were 264 different commercial "over-the-counter" magazines showing children nude or engaged in sexual conduct. One producer and distributor made a profit of between five to seven million dollars. Some children were kidnapped and others sold by parents for the lurid trade. However, after passage of a law in 1977, all "kiddie porn" magazines disappeared from stores and went underground. This illustrates what would happen with all hard core, illegal material if the recommendations of this Report were implemented. The Child Protection Act of 1984 removed the requirement that there be proof of transportation across state lines (as is proposed for adult pornography), said no one under age 18 could be used as a model, and made it possible to prosecute the often noncommercial, clandestine exchange of child pornography among pedophiles (child molesters).

The government finally has begun to enforce the law. The Report notes that in 1985 "the Postal Inspection Service conducted 183 (child) pornography investigations which resulted in 179 arrests and 143 convictions." (page 112).

However, producers continue to exploit underage performers, and prosecution is difficult since a runaway teen is likely to lie about age to make some money or in hopes of "being a star."* Performers do not have to sign any contracts, and producers do not have to keep records.

Therefore, the Commission made two important recommendations:

1. "Congress should enact a statute requiring the producers, retailers, or distributors of sexually explicit visual depictions to maintain records containing consent forms and proof of performers' ages." (page 138).
2. And it proposed that producers be prohibited from "using performers under the age of 21" (page 140).

---

*In July, 1986, tens of thousands of video stores had to pull dozens, if not hundreds of videos from their stock, when they learned that a pornography star named Traci Lords was only fifteen to seventeen years old when she made seventy-five films that feature her, such as "New Wave Hookers" and "Educating Mandy." Tracie was really Norma ✂ , a 1984 runaway. The pornographer knew she was underage and told her, with a wink, "Get a phony ID." Since she is only 18 now, all of the films she made were child pornography.

Commissioners said, "Adolescents are notoriously poor in making sexual choices well into their late teens and twenties. Thus teen use of contraceptives 'approaches an almost random pattern,' with only a third of sexually active teenagers using contraceptives constantly." America's teen pregnancy rate is seven times that of Denmark, and is higher than any nation. Further, the Commissioners heard extensive testimony that the psychological damage of having one's sexual activity permanently available to anyone willing to pay a price can be "severe and even more important, *irreversible*" (page 141). Other key proposals:

- Congress should "prohibit the exchange of information concerning child pornography or children to be used in child pornography through computer networks" (page 142).
- Congress should give "financial incentives for the states to initiate task forces on child pornography" (page 145).
- State Legislatures should amend child pornography statutes to include "forfeiture provisions," to make the "knowing possession," production, giving away, exhibiting, advertising, or exchange of child pornography a felony (page 150–155).
- State Legislatures should "eliminate requirements that the prosecution identify or produce testimony from the child who is depicted." Why should a child, plainly photographed as a victim, be forced to give testimony about abuse that was horrifying enough to live through, or to verify in court that his or her age was, if proof of age can be otherwise obtained? (pages 156–157).
- State Legislatures should "require photo finishing laboratories to report suspected child pornography" (page 157).
- State Legislatures should "permit judges to impose a sentence of lifetime probation" in addition to other sentencing. The recidivist rate for pedophiles is very high, and the threat of future incarceration should remain for life (page 157).
- "State and local law enforcement agencies should use search warrants in child exploitation cases, and ask the child if pictures were taken (page 165).

Victim Assistance

One of the most important concerns of the Commission was to awaken in America's conscience a compassion for the victims of pornography. Up till now, these victims have been forgotten. Pornography has bared their young bodies with no loftier goal than to make money by exciting male readers to the point of masturbation. But those who are portrayed as willing partners in anonymous sex are people, not just sexual objects. When the camera lights go off, what happens to them?

If you read nothing else in this book, survey the ruined lives of those who tell their own stories in the chapter on Victim Testimony beginning on page 197. One who is quoted here is a former Playboy Bunny. *Playboy's* Hugh Hefner, in a column published by the Chicago *Sun-Times*, Dec. 8, 1985 in response to an earlier critical column of mine, decided to ridicule her in print. Here's what he said:

> Another Meese Commission witness almost speaks in tongues: "I am a former *Playboy* Bunny. . . . I was extremely suicidal and sought psychiatric help for the eight years I lived in a sexually promiscuous fashion. There was no help for me until I changed my lifestyle to be a follower of Jesus Christ and obeyed the Biblical truths including no premarital sex. . . . I implore the Attorney General's Commission to see the connection between sexual promiscuity, venereal disease, abortion, divorce, homosexuality, sexual abuse of children, suicide, drug abuse, rape and prostitution to pornography. Come back to God America, before it's too late." For [the] witness . . . , everything from diverse to acid indigestion can be chalked up to pornography. She attempted to blame *Playboy*—the magazine, the clubs and the philosophy—for her sexual downfall. The Meese Commission has trundled out a parade of born-again basket cases, anti-sex feminists and fun-hating fundamentalists. More than anything else, the testimony of these witnesses struck us as sad, misdirected—even pathetic. It was also inflammatory, misinformed scapegoating.

Really? Allow me to insert some of her statements which Mr. Hefner left out in those dotted sections. As a little girl, she found *Playboy* around the house (more than 75 percent of pornography is seen by children).

> What a distorted image of sexuality this gave me. Pornography portrays sex as impersonal and insatiable. It depicts everything from orgies to sadism to incest to bestiality. I never questioned the morality of becoming a *Playboy* Bunny because the magazine was accepted at home.
> I found that premarital sex with single men led me to affairs with married men. I looked on men as power objects and got on casting couches in the attempt to become a movie star. I experienced everything from date-rape to physical abuse to group sex and finally to fantasizing homosexuality as I read *Playboy* magazine. The "Playboy Philosophy" gave me no warning as to the emotional, physical and spiritual devastation that accompanied supposed sexual liberation. In reality, it was an addiction to sexual perversion. I was extremely suicidal and sought psychiatric help for the eight years I lived in a promiscuous fashion.

After her religious conversion this former *Playboy* Bunny remained chaste until her marriage three years later, where she has found "beauty, joy, fulfillment and peace of sex within a loving marriage." And she is no longer depressed or suicidal. "I ask you to judge which philosophy gives freedom?" she asked.

Instead of answering that question, Hefner denigrated her as a "born again basket case." What's more, Hefner was invited to testify before the Meese Commission but did not do so himself. He sent a paid attorney.

Given the problems that the victims of pornography have had, the Commission made two important recommendations to help them:

1. "Legislatures should conduct hearings and consider legislation recognizing a civil remedy for harm attributable to pornography" (page 186).

Laws were proposed by The Minneapolis City Council, and one was enacted in Indianapolis, which concluded that pornography demeaned women as a class. The harm is thus seen as a form of discrimination by sex. The Commission on Pornography was sympathetic to these efforts, even though the one in Minneapolis was vetoed by the mayor and the Indianapolis statute was overturned by a U.S. Court of Appeals. Hearings might suggest better ways to write the law using the Court's guidelines. The Commission felt it is significant that though the Court rejected the definition of pornography in the statute, it did accept the harm of pornography to women, a portion of which follows:

> "Depictions of subordination tend to perpetuate subordination. The subordinate status of women in turn leads to affront and lower pay at work, insult and injury at home, battery and rape on the streets. In the language of the legislature, 'pornography is central in creating and maintaining sex as a basis of discrimination. Pornography is a systematic practice of exploitation and subordination based on sex which differentially harms women. The bigotry and contempt it produces, with the acts of aggression it fosters, harm women's opportunities for equality . . ." (page 188).

2. Local agencies should allocate victims of crimes funds . . . for psychiatric evaluation . . . and medical treatment of victims and their families." (page 174).

New York State has such a law, and the Report gives detail on one proposed by Sen. Arlen Specter, R-Penn. However, since the Report was written, Sen. Charles Grassley, R-IA, got a Senate committee to approve his proposal for a "Child Abuse Victim Rights Act" which would enable any person harmed by child abuse or pornography to sue a pornographer for damages ranging from $50,000 to triple actual costs incurred. The concept of the bill thus differs from the proposal of the Commission, but is worth exploring since no public costs are involved.

Citizen and Community Action

"Suggestions for Citizen and Community Action and Corporate Responsibility," which begins on page 329, is a guide for citizen activism in fighting both legal obscenity and legal but offensive pornography.

"One of the most frequently posed questions of the Commission collectively and to us as individuals is, 'What can I do in my community to make sure that the family environment is not being violated by obscene materials?'" Commission Chairman Henry Hudson said in an interview.

The answers given are clear, succinct, and well-written. In a volume of often impenetrable prose, this chapter stands out for its strong, lucid style. More important, according to Rev. Don Wildmon, Director of the National Federation for Decency in Tupelo, Miss.—the organization which has been perhaps been most effective in mobilizing grass roots citizen involvement—this chapter "is the best thing that I have seen. It spells out in 1-2-3-4 detail what the local citizen can do—and how to do it. It suggests meeting with the Police Depart-

ment, for example, and asking what it has done to enforce the law, how to organize a court watch, etc."

The range of potential citizen action is very wide, but it should be said that
the "Commission did not recommend or encourage acts of public protest or
boycotts," said Hudson. "Once a community has made a threshhold decision
that a problem exists and there is a desire to take affirmative steps to protect the
community, we offered them examples of techniques which had been successful in other places. But it was not meant to be a recommendation for citizen
action," Hudson added. "However, too frequently we lose sight of the fact that
the right of a citizen to engage in public protest is co-existant with the constitutional right of an individual to publish pornographic materials. (There is no
right to publish obscene materials)," he said.

Since the chapter is well-outlined, no attempt is made to summarize it here.
But a few "suggestions" of the Commission may be of general interest:

1. "Since one aspect of the constitutional test of obscenity is the notion of
   contemporary community standards, this is an area of the law which
   presents a significant opportunity for public input" (page 330).
2. "While there are some areas of the law in which this Commission has recommended change, the lack of prosecution of obscenity cases appears to
   be directly attributable to a failure of enforcement. Public expression of
   concern about pornography and a call for redoubled law enforcement efforts will undoubtedly trigger an increase in official action" (page 332).
3. "While citizens have every right to picket, the pickets should not preclude
   others from entering or leaving business premises (page 331). (Even *The
   Washington Post*, which was generally critical of this *Report*, said in an
   editorial dated July 11, "We see nothing wrong with consumer boycotts or
   with making your views known to retailers and advertisers. These are
   classic pressure tactics that have been used by all sorts of groups from unions to the NAACP."
4. "It is important to understand what is *not* obscene as well as what is obscene. . . . Citizens are encouraged to review state and federal case law
   which discusses materials which have been found obscene. . . ." (page
   333).
5. Pages 333–334 contain an excellent series of questions designed to help
   citizens assess the local extent of obscene/pornographic materials ranging
   from the obvious ("adults only" bookstores) to the invisible (Dial-A-Porn).
6. Pages 335–336 list excellent questions to ask the police, local prosecutor,
   and the U.S. Attorney in assessing their commitment to enforcing the law.

Censorship Was Not Recommended

According to *Webster's New Collegiate Dictionary,* a censor is "One who acts as
an overseer of morals and conduct, especially an official empowered to examine written or printed matter, motion pictures, etc., in order to forbid publication if objectionable."

There is absolutely nothing in the *Final Report of the Attorney General's*

Commission on Pornography suggesting the need for censorship as Webster's defines it. Chairman Henry Hudson, now a U.S. Attorney based in Alexandria, Virginia, says, "One of the myths perpetuated by those who have not read the Report, or those who choose not to read it, is that the Report is promotive of censorship. A reading of it would indicate the contrary. We recommended no major changes of the law definitively—only that existing laws be more conscientiously enforced." Or as Commissioner James Dobson puts it "The salient finding emerging from twelve months of testimony before our Commission reflected this utter paralysis of government in response to the pornographic plague" (p. 84).

Of course, if the obscenity laws are enforced, the producers of illegal material could be charged with crimes. The Supreme Court in Paris Theatre v. Slaton (June, 1973) said, "The sum of experience, including that of the past two decades, affords an ample basis for legislatures to conclude that a sensitive, key relationship of human existence, central to family life, community welfare and the development of human personality, can be debased and distorted by crass commercial exploitation of sex."

But there has never been a proposal that some government official sit in each publisher's office or movie production house. Freedom of expression is protected by the First Amendment. But that freedom has never been absolute. Slander and libel have long been illegal, for example. Obscenity is not a First Amendment issue. It is a crime, and the courts have ruled it such. What is proscribed is the depiction or description of specific sexual activity that threatens the common good. Writers and producers are expected to be self-regulating, or to run the risk of being held guilty of obscenity.

In its Paris Theater decision the U.S. Supreme Court said, "We categorically disapprove the theory that obscene films acquire constitutional immunity from state regulation simply because they are exhibited for consenting adults only. Rights and interests other than those of the advocates are involved. These include the interest of the public in the quality of life, the total community environment, the tone of commerce and, possibly, the public safety itself." In other words, in 1973 the Court said that obscene material does, in fact, cause harm to the community, and possibly to the public safety of individuals. This Report provides ample evidence for its unanimous conclusion that "exposure to sexually violent materials has indicated an increase in the likelihood of aggression," and that there is a "causal relationship between exposure to material of this type and aggressive behavior toward women."

Speaking personally, I would argue that the Commission was so afraid of the charge of censorship it did not take its own analysis of "harm" of sexually violent and degrading materials to its logical, legal conclusion. Why did the Commission fail to recommend that obscenity statutes be changed to include the concept of "harm"? Most of the sexually violent films now being made—those for which the evidence of harmfulness is strongest—are not legally obscene because they do not portray ultimate sexual acts. They receive an R–rating and are packed with teenagers who are most vulnerable to what is a subliminal, diabolical message—that murdering nude women is thrilling, especially when done by a power drill while a woman bathes, or by a chain saw.

The Commission heard testimony in Houston from Dr. Victor Cline, Professor of Psychology at the University of Utah, who also cites the work of Dr. James McGaugh at the University of California, Irvine, on memory. The "research suggests that experiences at times of emotional (or sexual) arousal get locked in the brain by the chemical epinephrine and become virtually impossible to erase. These memories, very vivid and graphic in nature, keep intruding themselves back on the mind's memory screen serving to stimulate and arouse the viewer," he said. "This may help explain pornography's addicting effect. These powerfully sexually arousing experiences become vivid memories which the mind 'replays' stimulating the child again and again suggesting the need for further stimulation. . . . Most evidence suggests that all sexual deviations and their variations are learned behavior. I know of no good evidence anywhere suggesting genetic transmission of sexual pathology. In fact Stanley Rachman at the Maudsley hospital in London has repeatedly conditioned young males into sexual deviations (fetishes) using standard conditioning procedures. . . . Many sexual deviations occur (or are learned) through the process of masturbatory conditioning. Vivid sexual memories and fantasies are masturbated to which at the moment of climax further reinforces their linkage in the brain and leads in time to the increased probability of their being acted out in real life behavior," Cline testified.

Put more simply, a certain percentage of adolescents whose first sexual experiences are triggered by pornography of violent sex, will develop a fetish, a conditioning that will associate violence with sex. We are training rapists and murderers with pornography. For more evidence in this Report, see pages 267–268 in the Social Science Chapter, where it documents studies that have distinguished with "predictive validity" who is a rapist and who is not by subjecting both rapists and a control group to two types of pornography—consenting and forced sex. By measuring the penile erection of respondents, researchers found that "Rapists respond to both rape and mutually enjoyable intercourse while nonrapists exhibited arousal only to the latter."

And on page 281 this Report states, ". . . subjects who have demonstrated sexual aggression in the laboratory are also more likely to report using coercion and force in their actual sexual interactions."

Of course, not everyone who sees an R-rated "slasher film" becomes a pornography addict or a murderer. But as Dr. Dobson puts it, in his personal comment, "a small but dangerous minority will . . . choose to act aggressively against the nearest available females. Pornography is the theory; rape is the practice" (page 506).

Why, therefore, did not the Commission recommend that state and federal obscenity laws be changed to proscribe "graphic sexual violence?" I asked Chairman Hudson that question, and he said: "Our mission dealt only with obscenity. If we had meandered into the area of violence, but not sexually explicit materials, it would have opened new vistas for the Commission and was a virtual impossibility with our time constraints."

Mr. Hudson is wrong. His organization was called the Attorney General's Commission on Pornography, not obscenity.

In one other area, the Commission retreated from present obscenity law. See the Overview section on "The Special Prominence of the Printed Word" (pages 58–59) in which the Commission acknowledges that "material consisting entirely of the printed word can be legally obscene"—yet the Commission suggests that "materials consisting of the printed word (i.e. without any photographs) simply not be prosecuted at all, regardless of content." Why? "There is for all practical purposes no prosecution of such materials now. . . . What is lost in the ability to prosecute this material is more than compensated for by the symbolic and real benefits accompanying the statement that the written word has had, and continues to have, a special place in this and any other civilization."

See the personal comments of Chairman Hudson who concluded that this decision, approved by a 6–5 vote was "disturbing," (page 485). Father Bruce Ritter argues the other side in his statement, in which he says, "I thought it very important that the Commission send a strong message to the public that we do not favor a return to times when the repression of unpopular ideas was part of the political landscape" (page 514). Thus, although the logical conclusion of the Commission's findings would have been to recommend that sexually violent and degrading material be classified as obscene—thus legally censoring such material—the Commission's concern to avoid the repression of unpopular ideas caused it not to recommend any censorship.

Who Is Repressing Whom?

But repression is a two-way street and unfortunately, the news media gave much of its attention not so much to the *Report*—which very few have read— but to a letter sent by Alan Sears, the Executive Director of the Commission, to twenty-six companies who were allegedly "involved in the sale or distribution of pornography."

The Commission was considering how to discuss the distribution of pornography in America, and it asked Sears to write to the companies to verify allegations made by Rev. Don Wildmon, Executive Director of the National Federation of Decency. Rev. Wildmon had given testimony that these companies were selling soft-core pornographic magazines in retail outlets.

The language of the letter, dictated on Justice Department stationery by some members of the Commission, was heavy-handed and some companies allegedly saw it as threatening: "The Commission has determined that it would be appropriate to allow your company an opportunity to respond to the allegations prior to drafting its final section on identified distributors." The letter enclosed the Wildmon testimony, but did not identify its source. It asked firms to "advise the Commission . . . if you disagree. Failure to respond will necessarily be accepted as an indication of no objection." The reaction was not what the Commission expected.

"Since the Commission's letter went out, 12,000 retail stores have stopped selling *Playboy*," said Bruce Ennis, an attorney representing *Playboy*. "A substantial number of these outlets saw the letter as a threat to brand them as distributors of obscene material." Since *Playboy* is not legally obscene, "the Commission knowingly and deliberately encouraged and sponsored censorship of constitutionally protected materials," he said and would "blacklist" offenders by listing their names in the *Report*.

Therefore *Playboy, Penthouse, Playgirl*, and other groups in the publishing industry filed suits against the Commission, asking for a letter of apology, for a banning of any list of corporate distributors of pornography, and for dropping the chapter advising citizens how to exercise *their* first amendment rights! Judge John Garrett Penn of the Federal District Court refused to halt publication of the citizen action chapter, but he did ask the Commission to send a letter retracting the implied threat, and he prohibiting publishing the Wildmon list. He said, "It is clear that something has occurred in the marketplace. A deprivation of a First Amendment right, that is, a prior restraint on speech, a right so precious in this nation, constitutes irreparable injury." The list of retailers selling pornography was never intended to be in the *Report*—making that charge moot. And the letter Judge Penn requested was sent to the twenty-six companies.

The accusations of Bruce Ennis do not reflect the intent of the Commission. I was present when the Commission discussed the matter and know that the Commission was trying to be fair to corporations which had been criticized by encouraging them to respond. More important, 7,000 stores had stopped selling pornographic magazines *before* the Sears letter was sent. Sales of adult magazines were already declining. In the April 1986 issue of *CDPDA News*, John Harrington, executive vice president of the Council for Periodical Distributors, said that adult magazine sales had "deteriorated by as much as 25% to 30% in 1985" because of "a major shift in public attitudes toward pornography," and the failure of U.S. distributors to give "financial indemnification to their customers." So prior to when the Commission's letter was sent, stores had "drastically reduced or eliminated space for adult publications."

Only one of six chains of convenience stores which stopped selling adult magazines said the Sears letter was a factor in its decision. 7-Eleven, the largest with 8,100 stores, said the Commissioner's letter was not a factor. A spokesman, Doug Reed, said 7-Eleven was impressed by the evidence presented to the Commission "showing a possible link between pornography and crime, violence and child abuse. . . ." That wasn't the only consideration. Reed said, "Our own research showed a weakening support of the sale of adult magazines." To be specific, polls of their customers taken three years earlier found that almost no one objected to their sale, but in 1986 nearly half do object. Thus, 7-Eleven made an economic decision. In a letter to Sears, 7-Eleven also noted, "Apparently, a very small segment of society employs various tools, including adult magazines, to assist in abuses of children." That's not the family image 7-Eleven wanted to project. Reed told me that 7-Eleven had gotten 61,606 letters and calls, ninety-six percent of which were positive. "We know we made the right decision," he said.

Yet the suit filed by *Playboy* against the members of the Commission and its executive director did not simply seek an apology, which has been given. It is seeking to recover the amount of its "lost sales"—which could be millions of dollars—from the individual Commissioners and Alan Sears *personally*. "I could lose my home and everything I own," one Commissioner told me. "The government did not give us liability insurance—or even tell us that we didn't have any! We received no pay for our work, and had difficulty even recovering our expenses. That's bad enough. But to be personally liable for serving the government in incredible."

Because the suit is pending, the Commissioners cannot give detailed explanations of their position on the matter when asked by the press. That is why many Commissioners have not talked to the press about the *Report*, and why those who do avoid the issue when the *Playboy* charges are mentioned by talk show hosts. So the real question is, Who is intimidating whom? Those who refer to the "chilling effect" of the Commission on Pornography on creative expression are doing a little "chilling" of free expression themselves.

"Censorship" of the *Final Report*

It might be of interest to know of the difficulty in getting the *Final Report of the Attorney General's Commission on Pornography* published.

During the last session of the Commission in late April, I asked Executive Director Sears which commercial publisher was going to reprint the book, noting that in the past major government reports such as that of the Riot Commission in 1968 hit the newsstands the day they were released. Sears replied, "Anyone can re-publish the *Report*, but no one has shown interest. And it is unethical for any of us to approach any of them. But you could do so."

So I took on the task. Since I had no contacts in the book publishing industry, I went to a top book agent in New York who introduced me to the editors-in-chief of the two big publishers within days. And he himself submitted written proposals to every other publisher capable of doing "an instant book."

Because of its wider perspective, I have included a story that appeared July 17, 1986, in the *Boston Globe* by reporter Richard Steward.

Despite predictions that the controversial federal study on pornography in America would become a best seller, the nation's major book publishers have not been titillated.

The publishers have declined to print the report of the Attorney General's Commission on Pornography made public earlier this month.

Some conservative and religious groups, who advocated wide distribution of the report, contend that the publishing firms are censoring the report by refusing to publish it.

When queried on their decision, publicists for several New York publishing firms said they would call back with a response, but failed to do so. Inquiries were made to Vintage, Penguin, Viking and Simon and Schuster.

A spokeswoman for Random House said publisher Howard Kaminsky had rejected publishing the report because 'he felt it was too large and had already found its audience' among those who had bought copies of the government document. At Grove Press, a spokesman said the company had never considered publishing the report. Bantam Books declined comment. . . ."

Mike McManus of Stamford, Conn., a syndicated columnist who closely monitored the pornography commission's year-long inquiry, said he attempted to interest several New York publishers in printing the report but was "turned down by every single commercial publisher in New York."

Said McManus, "They don't want to publish opinions they don't agree with." McManus conceded he also had trouble interesting Christian book publishers in printing the report.

"McManus, who writes two columns, one on urban affairs and the other on moral and religious issues, came up with a publisher after several months of trying. The company, Rutledge Hill Press in Nashville, Tenn., prints regional books about the Southeastern United States, according to it President, Larry Stone.

"I think I got this by default," said Stone, alluding to the refusal of the major national publishing firms to print it. . . .

Rev. B. Edgar Johnson, general secretary in the Kansas City headquarters of the Church of the Nazarene, said . . . he was disturbed by the decision of the book publishers not to reprint the pornography report. "I have a concern, and wonder if by not making the information available that, whatever is said about it will be believed more than what it says about itself."

In Tupelo, Mississippi, Rev. Donald Wildmon of the National Federation for Decency, charged the commercial book publishers with being involved in a "censorship move." Wildman said, "Many of these people are involved in the distribution or are sympathetic" to those who distribute pornographic material.

The article is accurate. An additional point: one publisher told my agent that if we had 100,000 copies sold in advance, that it would publish the "instant book." But when I rounded up the advance commitments—in effect, guaranteeing a profitable book, the editor who made the commitment refused to take calls from me.

The *Globe* reporter was surprised that most publishers contacted had no comment or refused to return calls. "They could have at least said, 'We can't work it into our schedule,'" he told me.

Was the Commission a Stacked Deck? Penthouse Says No!

One widely expressed opinion about this Commission is that it was stacked with right-wingers. For example, here is what Hendrick Hertzberg wrote for *The New Republic's* issue for July 14 & 21, 1986: "The 1986 commission has been stacked to prevent unwelcome surprises. Of its 11 members, six have well-established public records of supporting government action against sexy books and films. . . . The Meese commission lacked the financial staff resources of its predecessor (the 1970 President's Commission on Obscenity and Pornography), but since its conclusions were preordained, it didn't really need them."

But Eric Nadler and Philip Nobile, writers for *Penthouse* who attended every meeting of the Commission and are contemptuous of its conclusions, have written a series of articles that deride the Commission and its conservative members. In doing so they provide credible evidence that the stacked deck was all over the floor at the Commission meeting in Scottsdale, Arizona, in February. They described its "stalemate," its "fierce debate" and near disaster in the August, 1986, issue of *Penthouse*. They point out that the Commission was deeply divided, unable even to agree on whether the nuclear family is the basic unit of society. They say the Commission had such "irreconcilable differences" that it "went into meltdown."

Members of the Commission and Their Roles

The Commission appeared to be composed of four conservatives, three liberals, and four "middle of the roaders." (For official biographies, see pages 477–482.)

In Scottsdale, there were three consistent liberals, as measured by how they voted. They were Dr. Judith Becker, Ellen Levine, and Deanne Tilton-Durfee.

Dr. Judith Becker, is a Columbia University psychologist whose work with sex offenders convinced her that their interest in pornography was a symptom, not a cause, of their deviance. She rarely spoke in the meetings. She attended fewer meetings than anyone, suggested no witnesses, and did not even complete the writing assignments which she accepted as her responsibility. In the final week, when all major recommendations were reviewed a final time, she did not argue against any of them and voted with the Commission on such key issues as the harm of sexually violent material, or of degrading sex, and on the law enforcement proposals. Yet her dissent from the Commission's conclusions, co-written with Ellen Levine, is sweeping (page 540).

Ellen Levine, editor of *Women's Day* and a Vice President of CBS, which owns the magazine, was the media's representative on the Commission. During the Commission's deliberations, she asked *Women's Day* readers in a poll if they thought pornography "encourages violence against women." By 8 or 9 to 1, they said yes, in mailed-in responses. And "one in four reports a personal experience linking sexual abuse to pornography," she told me. Yet in Scottsdale, Ms. Levine said sexually violent material is "not morally troublesome to me." She signed the *Report,* raising no fundamental objections. She later dissented in the statement she co-authored with Ms. Becker.

It should be added that Levine objected to hearing from the victims of pornography (pages 197–223), and tried to eliminate them from the Chicago hearing. Only two of the 208 witnesses who testified were her suggestions.

Deanne Tilton-Durfee is President of the California Consortium of Child Abuse Councils. She is the primary author of Chapter 7, "Child Pornography," which is excellent. In the Committee she spoke with conviction on that subject, but was curiously indifferent to pornography involving adults. In Scottsdale she usually voted with Levine and Becker, perhaps believing adult practices are tolerable.

Only two Commissioners were consistently conservatives: Chairman Hudson and Dr. James Dobson. Two others usually joined in: Diane Cusack, and Judge Edward Garcia.

Henry Hudson was the prosecutor of Arlington County, Virginia, when he was named to the Commission. He recently was promoted to U.S. Attorney. In Arlington he gained a reputation for closing "adult bookstores," and therefore was called "Hang 'Em High Henry" by *Penthouse*. Unfailingly courteous and formal, he avoided first names, calling fellow commissioners "Professor Schauer" or "Ms. Levine." He held his reins of Chairman lightly, always asking others for their opinions, and, as is proper for a chairman, rarely showing his own opinion until he voted. In fact, his respect for the opinions of others was often the only glue that held the Commission together.

James Dobson, Ph.D psychologist, has written books that have sold millions of copies—*Dare to Discipline, The Strong-Willed Child, What Wives Wish Their Husbands Knew About Women*, and others. His film series, *Focus on the Family*, has been seen by 50 million Americans. And his daily radio show, also called *Focus on the Family*, is the most widely syndicated radio program in America. Often he was the only verbal defender of traditional values on the Commission.

Diane Cusack served two terms as a City Councilwoman in Scottsdale, Arizona. She suggested a number of the witnesses. She participated moderately in the dialogue; but when she did, she tended to make a common sense point that the academicians and lawyers needed to hear. She feels the most important conclusion of the Commission was its charge "to all levels of law enforcement they should start committing maximum resources to enforcing the law."

Judge Edward Garcia, appointed by President Reagan a U.S. District Judge, generally voted conservatively and contributed nothing to the dialogue. He did do his homework, however, and sent many written comments to the staff.

The other commissioners were middle-of-the-road, not voting consistently with one group or the other:

Father Bruce Ritter, founder of Covenant House, a home for runaway youth at Times Square and of four similar facilities in other cities, is deeply committed to fighting pornography. His personal statements, while lengthy, are worth reading, particularly his opening statement which begins on page 509. He voted with the liberals on weak standards for cable TV and on not enforcing obscenity laws for materials involving only the printed word. In his personal statements, he explains these votes at length.

Harold "Tex" Lezar, a former speech writer for President Nixon, an assistant to William F. Buckley, Jr., and a former Assistant Attorney General, had a major hand in creating the Commission. With those conservative credentials, one would have thought he would have been an articulate leader of the conservative wing. But he spoke rarely ("I did not view my role as a debater," he said), missed the crucial Scottsdale meeting, and then voted liberal on the key issue on whether cable television should be held to the same "decency" standard as broadcast television forbidding nudity, let alone simulated sex, or simply be forbidden to broadcast legally obscene material. Conservatives lost this vote by 6–5 when Lezar voted against the decency standard. However, on most issues, he voted conservatively, and, in fact says "I would have preferred that the Commission went further" on sexually violent materials and "recommended prosecution" of slasher films, for example, under the Miller standard, though they are not now called legally obscene. But he did not argue the point during the last week when decisions were being made.

On the other hand, Lezar played an important behind-the-scene role in creating the Commission, and in seeing that Hudson and Sears—tough prosecutors with rare achievements in winning obscenity battles—were given key roles on the Commission.

Dr. Park Dietz has earned degrees in medicine (M.D.), public health, and sociology from Johns Hopkins. He is a criminal psychiatrist. His votes in Scottsdale were mostly liberal, where he argued that the bulk of pornographic material had "mixed effects," teaching new "positions and techniques" that he said were helpful, while also prompting some men to have dangerous sexual appetites. However, Dietz underwent a major change of thinking between Scottsdale and the last session in Washington. His personal statement which begins on page 487 is the most powerful indictment of pornography in the Report.

Frederick Schauer a professor of law at the University of Michigan, had the most complex role on the Commission. In Scottsdale, he and Dietz sided with the liberal wing on the "mixed effects" of non-violent and non-degrading material in Class III, and voted that the bulk of available pornography is "predominantly harmless." However, he took on the task of writing the Commission's "Overview and Analysis," which summarizes the Commission's conclusions. In it he says the bulk of pornography falls into Class I or II, either violent or degrading, which is harmful, and that what's left in Class III is "small."

It should be noted that early in his legal career Schauer defended the producers of *Deep Throat*, a film found legally obscene in a number of courts, and one whose content is summarized beginning on page 438. He took a number of such cases, and now says, "To defend somebody in a criminal case is not to say it is good conduct or to say that my client is wonderful. Now I take no paying clients."

Alan Sears, the Executive Director of the Commission, did not have a vote on the Commission, but his influence was substantial. As an Assistant U.S. Attorney in Louisville, he had prosecuted and won several obscenity cases. In the Commission deliberations, he often made a case for the harmfulness of all classes of pornography—whether legally obscene or not—and argued powerfully for the importance of strengthened law enforcement, using existing law. Since completing his work on the Commission for the Department of Justice, he has been promoted to a position in the Interior Department.

The Politics of the Commission

After the Commission met in January, the ACLU wrote a report called "Rush to Judgment." The report criticized the Commission for its votes in New York calling for greater enforcement of existing laws and for additional tools in the battle against pornography, such as the ability to seize personal assets used in the production or distribution of obscenity. Dr. Dobson summarized that session with satisfaction that "The Pornography Commission is going to condemn pornography, condemn the industry that produces and distributes it, and condemn the government—virtually every branch of it—for not enforcing the laws that are on the books."

As it turned out in Scottsdale, both views were premature.

Though this was the next to last session, the Commissioners were just beginning to address the harm of pornography. Why? As a conservative put it at the time, "Henry did not have the votes in New York, with Diane Cusack and Judge Garcia not able to be present." That was my first clue that there was a powerful liberal faction on the Commission.

No clues were needed in Scottsdale. The three women took liberal stands on most issues, and often had Schauer and Dietz on their side. With Lezar absent, key votes were 5–5; and on some, Judge Garcia or Cusack took a neutral stance, resulting in conservative defeats.

At the suggestion of Dr. Dietz, all pornography was put into the five classes mentioned. The Commission was asked to consider the harm of each class of material on three separate grounds: social science evidence, "totality of evidence" in which victim testimony and law enforcement testimony are considered, and moral, ethical, and cultural issues.

Everyone considered social science evidence the most objective and therefore, very important. However, all agreed it would be unethical to expose very young children to this material, to see how many became rapists, for example. Another problem was that the social science evidence seemed more unclear at the time the discussion was taking place than it does now. Dr. Edna Einsiedel, the staff social scientist, had written only about half of the Social Science chapter which begins here on page 246. She could cite studies, such as one on pages 274–275, which showed that college males, after seeing such slasher movies as *Texas Chain Saw Massacre* and *Halloween*, showed less sympathy for victims of rapists in mock trials and were more likely to believe the "rape myth" that women want to be raped than a control group who saw non-violent movies.

After explaining the evidence of harm, Dr. Judith Becker said "I have a difficulty with the word 'harm'" Dr. Becker said. "I'd call it harm if people then went and raped or engaged in violent behavior against someone. What the laboratory experiments demonstrate is a negative impact of exposure to sexually violent material. That's all I'm willing to say."

Levine and Tilton agreed and convinced Schauer and Dietz to vote that the yardstick in looking at sexually violent materials should not be "harm," but simply a "negative" impact. Debate swirled for several hours, and when the weary Judge Garcia was asked to vote, he said "I don't care." which gave the liberals a 5–4 victory.

However, the group did vote unanimously that sexually violent materials had a "predominantly negative" impact—except, incredibly, for its impact on the institution of the family. Father Ritter argued that the "single greatest harm" of violent pornography is its attack on the family. He said pornography "attacks radically the concepts of love, affection, commitment, fidelity. Frankly, it despises them, and literally teaches a contempt for the very glue that holds the family together . . . There is no longer any necessary connection between sex and families, between sex and love, between sex and commitment."

Oddly, this thesis was fought by the Commission's women! Ellen Levine said "We are developing a very vocal and important part of our society which is not traditionally based," that is families headed by single women. She said "only five percent" of today's families were "traditional," with a husband who supports the family, a mother who doesn't work, and two children.

Dobson nearly rose out of his chair, saying her statistics excluded families with one child or three, as well as those with working mothers with traditional values. He retorted, "In fact, four-fifths of families are intact, traditional families."

Levine was unpersuaded. Later she said "Pornography is a symptom, not a cause" of problems in families.

Hudson asked for what amounted to a vote on whether the family is the basic unit of society. The Commission, incredibly, voted 5–5! Dietz and Schauer voted with the three women against the traditional concept of family.

In his personal statement (which begins on page 487), Dietz later took a strong position in the opposite direction. There he outlines eight ways that pornography is a public health menace because it harms those who produce it, those who use such "adult" products as handcuffs and bondage hoods in which people have died, those who engage in homosexual sex in peep show booths that spread AIDS, those who get "sexual disinformation" such as the apparent normality of having sex "with one's children, stepchildren, parents, siblings . . . pets and neighbors," those who are encouraged to be irresponsible in sexual conduct, which leads to "illegitimacy, teenage pregnancy, abortion. . . ."

Therefore, I recently asked him why in Scottsdale he voted that pornography was not harmful to the family. He said, "We were sitting as the government there. I did not think it was the government's business to decide on an ideal form of small group living. Under some circumstances single parents can raise their children successfully. Some of the harms to battered women suggest it would be better for them to leave their battering spouses."

It was Dietz who phrased the motion for the vote on sexually-violent materials: "Sexual violent materials are immoral and unethical and the willing production, distribution, and consumption of them are an offense against humanity." The vote was unanimous. Similarly, they voted together on Class II that degrading pornography is "an offense against humanity."

The problem, however, was that at that point everyone viewed Class II as a narrow category involving only bestiality, defecation, bondage, and so forth. In everyone's mind, that left all commonplace pornography in Class III of non-violent and non-degrading material.

Becker said "I know of no research that indicates the viewing of consensual sexual activity results in anti-social behavior."

Ritter asked if there weren't studies that showed commonplace pornography helped "maintain, if not cause perversions?" Later he said, "So much of the available pornography is homosexual pornography. Is this Commission obliged to say . . . that heterosexual activity is no more normative to society than homosexual behavior?"

Hudson asked for a vote on whether the panel had the mandate to determine "what certain types of sexual behavior (are) normal, abnormal, anti-social?" On this, the vote was 8–2, with only Father Ritter and Schauer voting yes. The rest felt the Commission's job was not to judge particular sexual behavior. With that vote out of the way, Hudson asked the panel whether social science gave evidence of harm of consensual sex. They concluded unanimously that the research showed "predominantly no negative effects" among users of Class III pornography. This was a painful vote for such people as Dobson, but he could not cite studies with evidence.

Sears recalled testimony, such as that by Andrea Dworkin, that Class III pornography showed "women as whores by nature," who accept men that dominate them. Dietz said this was no different than TV shows that made women seem subordinate to men. The rape myth was voted on, and defeated 10–0.

Ritter again tried to make the case that Class III pornography promoted promiscuity, the breakdown of marriage, and homosexuality. Dietz countered that there were "mixed effects" of this material. On one hand, it taught "new positions and techniques" of sex that might be helpful to married couples, thus helping them have better sex lives. On the other hand, it might make some men want forms of sex that their wives would find degrading.

Dobson conceded that sex therapists could use some of this material to help couples with problems, but that pronography was harmful, even if it was not violent or degrading. His thoughts are condensed in his personal statement:

A growing number of children are finding their parents' sexually explicit videos and magazines and are experimenting with what they have learned on younger children. Obviously, obscenity cannot be permitted to flow freely through the veins of society without reaching the eyes and ears of children. . . . Raising healthy children is the primary occupation of families and anything which invades the childhoods and twists the minds of boys and girls must be seen as abhorrent to the mothers and fathers who gave the birth. . . . Until we know that pornography is not addictive and progressive . . . until we are certain that the passion of fantasy does not destroy the passion of reality . . . until we are sure that obsessive use of obscene materials will not lead to perversions and conflict between husbands and wives . . . then we dare not adorn them with the crown of respectability. . . . This is not sexual repression. This is self-preservation.

But when Hudson asked for votes, considering the "totality of evidence" on whether the most widely available pornography was "predominantly harmful," "predominantly not harmful," or had "mixed effects," the winner was "mixed effects" voted for by Cusack, Garcia, Schauer, and Dietz. Ritter, Dobson, and Hudson were three votes for "predominantly harmful;" and Becker said "not harmful." Levine said "no answer." So did Tilton.

"What on earth?" asked *Penthouse*, summing up the vote. "The Meese Commission—conceived by prosecutors and ordained by the legions of decency—had just voted that pornography could actually *help* families."

After a break, the group reconvened, and Ms. Cusack said, "Henry, I want to reconsider my vote to "predominantly harmful." She reconsidered for these reasons: she did not believe the type of pornography considered could "strengthen" the family. Such a vote would be a signal that some legally ob-scene material was legitimate; and she doubted that the effect of pornography "upon one's spouse" would be healthy.

As soon as she changed her vote, Dobson asked if the material covered in this vote could include a depiction of "five women" involved in sexual activities "including cunnilingus and fellatio." Hudson said yes. "So this Commission is going on record saying that obscene material is not harmful to the family?" he asked incredulously.

Hudson said that with Ms. Cusack's switch, the group had voted for the "pre-dominantly harmful category." Ellen Levine immediately said, "I want to change my vote to 'mixed effects.' That deadlocked the panel 4–4–1, with one abstention. Then Ms. Tilton switched her vote, making it 5–4–1, with "mixed effects" winning once again.

A three hour debate ensued. Ritter tried to convince the group to remove "sex education materials" from the category. Levine asked how he would draw the line on what was used for education. Finally, Ritter predicted, "If this Commis-sion is split in this category, we'll be laughed out of existence."

Dobson said, "To whitewash this classification of smut would place a stamp of respectability on some of the most graphic, legally obscene materials most of us have ever encountered."

But everyone was exhausted. The deadlock seemed hopeless. So Hudson asked each person to write his or her own separate statement on Class III, which the staff might be able to "blend." At this point, the "meltdown" of the Commission was complete. A group of people who can only write individual statements is not a Commission at all.

As a columnist, I was depressed. I considered what I could write about the debacle that would be helpful, and could not think of anything. For a month, the disasterous meeting festered in my mind. Then I decided to write two columns. First, for my "Ethics and Religion" column I described the "mud-dled mind" of the Commission and said "The Commission could not agree if it was harmful, for example, for films to depict graphic portrayals of fornication, of orgies involving a number of men and women, of homosexuals doing fellatio on one another, of a man performing oral sex on a woman, or incest involving adults!"

I provided the names and addresses of the "libertarians" and suggested that readers ask them to explain the facts that "Alaska and Nevada residents buy five times as many porn magazines per capita as North Dakota, and have a rape rate that is six times higher. Mere coincidence? Nonsense," I argued. "An FBI study of 37 murderers confessing multiple killings, found 29 used hard and soft-core porn to fuel their anticipatory fantasy." In my political column, "Solutions," I predicted, "The Reagan Administration could be profoundly embarrassed by the final conclusions of the Commission, and suggested that readers write to Chairman Hudson "whether you agree or disagree" with my analysis.

Second Thoughts

According to the staff, my column sparked about 1,000 letters. Park Dietz studied a sample of them, and of the 4,000 other letters sent in by individual citizens without prompting, with some of his students. Reading these letters was a factor in his change of mind from a liberal to a conservative stance. In an interview, he explained why:

> For the last 10 years, my life has been in mental hospitals, prisons, and with police looking at the worst problems we have, extreme cases of incurable disease, mental illness and the most horrifying crimes. I have spent my time with assassins, rapists, and have little contact with people outside of that world or my academic world, where I can see the day to day concerns of ordinary people.
>
> But in the citizen mail the concerns were overwhelmingly in the direction of asking us to "do something about the problem." I was also influenced by Father Ritter and Jim Dobson, who have their eye on a different ball than I've had. And I was moved by the witnesses who came before us as victims, and by the law enforcement people who were almost unanimous in citing a link between porn and crime.

Something similar must have happened in the minds of other Commissioners, because when the group reconvened in Washington for the final set of meetings at which their *Report's* conclusion were to be thrashed out, participants ultimately concluded, as the Overview states, that Class III materials which are non-violent, and non-degrading, "are in fact quite small in terms of currently available materials." Why? After several more days of debate, the group concluded that Class II, which is degrading sexual material, "constitutes somewhere between the predominant and the overwhelming portion of what is currently standard fare heterosexual pornography" (page 42).

The Commission said "To the extent that these materials create or reinforce the view that the woman's function is disproportionately to satisfy the sexual needs of men, then the materials will have pervasive effects on the treatment of women in society far beyond the incidence of identifiable acts of rape or other sexual violence" (page 42).

The pornography of the nation had not changed between February and April, but the mind of the Commission had clearly changed.

The Schauer Draft

The most important new element confronting the Commission in Washington was a 192-page draft of the Commission's *Final Report* by Professor Frederick Schauer. The work was *not* requested by Chairman Hudson or the staff. In fact, by the time the group gathered in April, the Commissioners had only seen forty pages of the new version. Schauer was unhappy with the long draft, more than 1,500 pages written by the staff with different members of the Commission (which constitutes the bulk of this volume—everything that goes after the Overview that was drafted by Schauer.)

He breezed into the initial meeting late, unpacked his briefcase, and handed out thick copies of his draft. And he had allies.

Father Ritter said, "Without this kind of a framing document, the *Report* of the Commission will not be well-received." Levine and Becker agreed. Dietz said, "There is a clarity and consistency here, and we can use it to test ideas and replace materials."

Dobson said, "Fred has done a remarkable job synthesizing" the material, "but I have problems with aspects of its content. Other sections of the Report do not dovetail well with it. I am not in favor of doing anything that relegates the staff document to an Appendix. To negate that would undo the work of four months. The Schauer draft does not have a great deal in the way of suggestions or alternatives that we have voted on and considered at great length."

Only Hudson shared Dobson's reservations.

Many Commissioners asked if it were possible to extend the life of the Commission to study the document with more care. Hudson answered, "This is our last meeting," with the finality of a Chairman who had talked to the Attorney General.

Schauer explained that a key principle he followed in writing the draft, was that, "where societal differences are reflected in the differences among us, to present the strongest, most plausible arguments for the competing points of view." He argued against listing such votes as a 6–5 decision, but "to show through nuanced wording why the majority took a given stand, and why the minority disagreed, paying equal respect to each side." That's the genius of his approach.

That is the reason the Overview can be confusing to read. It is not written for clarity, but to assure the Commission, deeply divided on some issues, that all points of view are included.

The group then adjourned that Monday morning to read his document. They labored for the rest of the week—often till 11 p.m. over parts of it. When they reconvened, it was clear that the effective chairmanship of the Commission had shifted from Hudson, a quiet careful man, to the wiry, bearded, loquacious Schauer at the opposite end of the table.

Levine complained that the Schauer draft "has not included very many specific recommendations. Do we plan to ask that they be in the framework or in the Appendix?"

Schauer briefly replied, "I do not take this as not having made recommendations. . . . I've made them at a different level of specificity." (But try to find one!) However, he said more specific proposals "can be interweaved in the Appendix." Clearly, Schauer considered his draft "THE REPORT," and the rest of it as an Appendix.

The Commission as a whole, however, disagreed. "Tex" Lezar said, "I assume we are going to integrate the two together."

Dobson added, "Fred's section on law enforcement is not compatible with the staff version. If we agree to the Schauer document, all the work, involved debate, and unanimous votes are up for grabs now. In Los Angeles, we voted unanimously to condemn the FCC for the way it handled Dial-A-Porn. We said we were going to condemn all levels of government for its paralysis on enforcing the law. We criticized the way video booths are run. None of those specifics are in this document." *

---

*Ultimately Dobson was the only Commissioner to vote against the Schauer draft, which was passed, 10–1.

Tilton agreed. "This document provides a thread, but we want to be sure the staff recommendations get in. There has to be an integration of the two."

Dietz felt there "is an advantage in having specific recommendations with the chapter" dealing with that subject, such as law enforcement or child pornography."

And the final Report, which is in your hands, does combine both the Schauer draft, as revised with suggestions from the Commission into the "Overview and Analysis," and the rest of the Commission's work—what the Commissioners erroneously kept calling a staff document, but was in reality the Commission's own 92 virtually unanimous proposals for enforcing the laws, or strengthening them (listed on pages 77 through 83), along with a number of "suggestions" on how citizens can assess their own community's situations and do something about them (pp. 329–340)

For the record, Schauer still calls his section "THE REPORT." In July, 1986, in an interview, he said, "It was my intention that the specific material prepared by staff would be integrated in my framing document." On the other hand, he says, "It was not my intention to discuss specific recommendations."

Readers of this Report should ask themselves what it would be if the Schauer draft was the whole report. As noted earlier, it asserts that sexually violent or degrading material is a cause of violence against women—but it fails to provide a scintilla of evidence. Why not? He could at least have pointed readers to this evidence. Surely a law professor should understand the importance of evidence in making a case.

If the Schauer draft were the whole report, there would be few specific law enforcement or child pornography recommendations, and few suggestions for citizen action.

A Strategy to Discredit the Commission on Pornography

As noted at the beginning of this Introduction, I was surprised that so few colleagues in journalism covered the work and conclusions of the Commission. I attributed it to sloppy journalism, or to bias against the subject by the mainstream news media. As an example, Hendrik Hertzberg's slanted article in The New Republic of July 14 & 21, 1986, entitled "Big Boobs," was clearly based solely on the reporting of two writers for Penthouse and Forum magazines, rather than on Hertzberg's own reporting or even his study of what the Commission actually said. The author acknowledges that his information came from this source:

> Not a single major newspaper assigned a reporter to cover the story on a regular basis. The only reporters who turned up for every meeting, and who assiduously collected the chaotic pastiche of hastily written drafts and documents that will make up the final report, were two representatives of what might be called the trade press. Philip Nobile and Eric Nadler of Forum, a kind of journal of sexual opinion put out by the Penthouse empire, will publish their researchers next month in a book, The United States of America vs. Sex: How the Meese Commission Lied About Pornography. . . . It is thanks to an advance reading of their man-

uscript and a collection of documents I have that I have some idea of how the commission went about its work.*

It is unprofessional journalism to report an event from a single, biased source. (Had he talked to the Commission staff or any of the Commissioners, he would have learned that this representative of more than 150 papers did cover three weeks of sessions—those in which decisions were made.) But I would not call Hertzberg's writing sinister.

What *is* sinister is a plan to pay the largest public relations firm in Washington, Gray & Company, up to $900,000 for a "strategy designed to further discredit the Commission on Pornography," to "launch a series of pre-emptive strikes against the Commission's report," and to undertake "quiet efforts . . . to persuade the Attorney General, the White House and the leaders of both political parties that the forthcoming report on the work of the Commission is so flawed, so controversial, so contested and so biased that they should shy away from publicly endorsing the document."

Those are quotes from a proposal made by Gray to the "Media Coalition," which includes magazine and book publishers and their distributors and is chaired by John M. Harrington, Executive Vice President of the Council for Periodical Distributors Association. What is quoted above is a letter to Mr. Harrington by Stephen Johnson, Gray's Senior Vice President. Its date is June 5, 1986—a full month before the Pornography Commission's Report had been released to the public.

What is frightening to me as a journalist is that the public relations campaign outlined in the letter is working. As of August 7, both Attorney General Meese and the President *have* shied "away from publicly endorsing the document." And the major news organizatons have either ignored the Commission's Report or have provided highly biased accounts, such as *Time*'s cover story, "Sex Busters," the title of which reflects its mindset.

And when the leaders of denominations representing 150 million Americans stood on the steps of St. Patrick's Cathedral in New York City on July 25, 1986, and endorsed the Commission's top priorities to focus on hard core, sexually violent or degrading pornography and child pornography, they did not get thirty seconds on the evening news of ABC-TV, NBC-TV, or CBS-TV, nor one paragraph in the three newsmagazines. Among those gathered by the National Coalition Against Pornography endorsing the *Report* that day were three Catholic cardinals, the Orthodox Archbishop of North America, seven bishops of United Methodist, Episcopalian, Orthodox, Catholic, and Free Methodist churches, three rabbis representing all branches of Judaism, and the elected leaders or top staff of Southern Baptists, Nazarenes, Assemblies of God, Church of God (Anderson, Ind.), the National Association of Evangelicals, the National Council of Churches, Presbyterian Church (U.S.A.), and the Church of Jesus Christ of Latter-day Saints (Mormons).

Joseph Cardinal Bernadin of Chicago, who co-chaired the meeting with Rev. Jerry Kirk of Cincinnati, Ohio, said, "As religious leaders, we believe in the

*Hendrik Hertzberg, "Big Boobs," *The New Republic*, July 14 & 21, 1986, page 21.

inherent dignity of each human being. Created in God's image and likeness, the human person is the clearest reflection of God's image and likeness, the human person is the clearest reflection of God's presence among us. Because human life is sacred, we all have a duty to develop the kind of societal environment that protects and fosters its development." He said one "assault on human dignity" was "hard core and child pornography," issues surfaced by "the recently released *Report of the Attorney General's Commission on Pornography*. We are in unanimous agreement that hard-core and child pornography, which is not protected by the Constitution, is an evil which must be eliminated."

However, both he and others emphasized their respect for the First Amendment. Perhaps Episcopal Bishop William Frey of Colorado put that most pungently when he said, "We are not shock troops leading an assault on the First Amendment or on soft core pornography. But we hope by this gathering to raise the consciousness of our constituencies" about its "addictive and corrosive effect."

Rabbi Marc Tanenbaum of the American Jewish Committee, speaking on behalf of liberal, conservative and orthodox Jewish leaders, was eloquent: "No one who walks through the streets of this city or other cities can't but help feel that there is a social pathology at loose, a plague and a pestilence which daily dishonors the dignity of life of our people. There is a moral ecology in the world . . . that is assaulted by the prevalence of drugs, crack, prostitution and the decline of the family and crime. Pornography both contributes to that and is a symbol of moral decadence of our nation. We feel that out of the depth of the Jewish tradition . . . a fundamental obligation" to join other religious leaders "to stand together in a serious, responsible way, not to allow vigilantes or extremists of either side to exploit the issue."

During the press conference, I asked Pornography Commissioner Father Bruce Ritter how he assessed the importance of this unprecedented meeting. He said the meeting was "more important" than the Commission's *Report*, because it "mainstreamed" the conclusion that pornography is harmful. No longer can the issue be dismissed as only a "concern of religious extremists."

Silver-haired George Cornell, who has covered religion for the Associated Press for more than thirty years, witnessed the event and said, "I can not think of a time when this has happened before. The Mormons tend not to be ecumenical. The small pentecostal denominations don't meet with the Catholic hierarchy or mainline Protestants. It is remarkable, a rare phenomenon." Unbelievably, their unprecedented meeting to support the Commission was almost ignored. (AP did do a story, but the network camera crews there might as well have stayed home.)

Yet in the popular mind, theme is an assumption that the only people who support the Commission's basic findings are "a handful of zealots" and "religious extremists." Has this come about as a result of a campaign that would "launch a series of pre-emptive strikes" against the *Report*, "using advertorials in major national newspapers and magazines, placing spokespersons on national and local television and radio news, public affairs and talk shows, holding a series of news cnferences in major cities across the country, and meeting with government leaders and politicians to discuss the biases, misrepresentations, and factual errors contained in the report. . ." as the letter from Gray & Company to John Harrington proposes?

The Gray letter outlines five key components in its proposal to influence public opinion. The goal of this effort is to convince Americans that:

1. "There is no factual or scientific basis" for the assertion that "sexually-oriented" materials cause criminal sexual or violent behavior "in any way";

2. It is a waste of the nation's time, energy, and financial resources to try to contain these materials because "it diverts our attention from real economic and social problems";

3. "This campaign to infringe on all our rights" is the work of "religious extremists";

4. If the effort to stop pornography succeeds, its leaders will be encouraged to force their "narrow and social agenda on the majority"; and

5. One does not have to approve of certain publications to support the right of others to read them.

One does not have to be a professional journalist to recognize these themes in the way the Attorney General's Commission on Pornography, the *Final Report*, and the subject of restraining the most dangerous forms of pornography have been presented in the popular media. All five points of the Gray letter have become conventional wisdom of media reporting and analysis of this subject.

I have interviewed both Mr. Johnson and Mr. Harrington. They acknowledge that the letter is genuine, and that Gray did get the contract to pursue the outlined goals, though the precise plan is somewhat different. A group has been established called "Americans for Constitutional Freedom."

I believe it would have been far wiser if legitimate publishing and distribution companies had joined in a call for getting rid of obscene films and literature, which are not produced or delivered by these companies, but by companies controlled for the most part by organized crime. In taking such a stand, legitimate publishers could have made a clearer case for protecting legal, though pornographic, magazines like *Playboy*.

George Gallup, the nation's leading pollster, said recently, "The American people appear ready to call a halt to the pernicious spread of pornography in our society. A majority of three-fourths now favor a total ban on magazines and movies that show sexual violence, and another one-fifth are in favor of restrictions rather than a ban. Only 4-6 percent think there should be no restrictions whatsoever."

And the margin of support is increasing. In 1985, seventy-three percent favored a ban on sexually violent magazines; in 1986 seventy-six percent do so. In 1985, sixty-eight percent favored a ban on movies depicting sexual violence; seventy-four percent do so in 1986. And another eighteen percent in each case want to prohibit public display of both forms of hardcore sexual material.

Gray & Company may have a big budget. But the people of America are "ready to call a halt to the pernicious spread of pornography."

A Final Word

Pornographers have critized this Report as not having been based on solid social science evidence proving the harm of pornography. However, Commissioner Park Elliott Dietz, who is both a physician with a master's degree in public health and a social scientist with a Ph.D., says in his personal statement on page 487, "Every time . . . president or a parliament or a congress or a legislature or a court has made a judgment affecting social policy, this judgment has been made in the absence of absolute guidance from the social sciences. The Constitutional Convention of 1787 had no experimental evidence to guide its decision-making. When the first Congress proposed the First Amendment in 1789 . . . the empirical social sciences had not yet been conceived." Fortunately, there now is social science evidence backing the Commission's recommendations.

But the issue is also a moral one, says Dr. Dietz. He also cited medical and public health consequences of pornography and he said that when he began serving on the Commission, "the morality of pornography was the farthest thing from my mind. Thus, I was astonished to find that by the final meeting of the Commission, pornography had become a matter of moral concern to me. While other Commissioners may have learned things about the dark side of life that they had never known, I remembered something about the higher purposes of life and of humanity's aspirations that I had forgotten during too many years of working on the dark side. I therefore conclude my remarks with staements on morality and freedom that would have seemed foreign to me not many months ago."

At that final session, Dr. Dietz read a brief statement and suggested that it provide the concluding paragraphs of the Report's Overview.

As a governmental body, we studiously avoided maing judgments on behalf of the government about the morality of particular sexual acts between consenting adults or their depiction in pornography. This avoidance, however, should not be mistaken for the absence of moral sentiments among the Commissioners."

I, for one, have no hesitation in condemning nearly every specimen of pornography that we have examined in the course of our deliberations as tasteless, offensive, lewd, and indecent. According to my values, these materials are themselves immoral, and to the extent that they encourage immoral behavior they exert a corrupting influence on the family and on the moral fabric of society.

Pornography is both causal and symptomatic of immorality and corruption. A world in which pornography were neither desired nor produced would be a better world, but it is not within the power of government or even of a majority of its citizens to create such a world. Nonetheless, a great deal of contemporary pornography constitutes an offense against human dignity and decency that should be shunned by the citizens, not because the evils of the world will thereby be eliminated, but because conscience demands it.

When Dr. Dietz concluded, a cheer erupted around the table. Father Bruce Ritter took off his priest's Roman collar and handed it to him as a trophy. But Commissioner Fred Schauer strenuously objected to incorporating Dietz' words in the Overview, which Schauer himself had drafted. So it was placed in Dietz' personal statement, page 487, and Commissioners Hudson, Dobson, Lezar, Garcia and Cusack asked to be listed as co-signers.

At that point the divisions within the Commission surfaced again, and some of its members objected. "That's not right. Those of us who don't co-sign it don't want to look as if we are against morality." But Dietz and the five co-signers persisted and submitted their burning indictment of the pornography they had viewed.

What is the long term significance of the *Report*? On numerous radio talk shows, Alan Sears makes the same point as Dietz did at the final meeting of the Commission:

> The most important thing in the battle for those who wish to fight the pornographers—those who spew their hostility for billions of profits annually—is education. This Commission Report, though not perfect, provides the single best education about pornography—the legal issues, law enforcement failures, the production and distribution of materials, the content of those materials, and most important, what you as a private citizen can do to prod your officials and local law enforcement officers into action, and to act on your own behalf to create a better world for our children to live.
>
> The Commission recognizes that the elimination of pornography won't eliminate all rape, every child molestation or sex discrimination. But it is confident that there would be, in a society without pornography, fewer rapes, fewer children molested, and less sex discrimination."

It is a vision worth working for!

Mike McManus
Stamford, Connecticut
August, 1986

CHARTER OF THE
ATTORNEY GENERAL'S
COMMISSION ON PORNOGRAPHY

1. *Authority and Official Designation*
   The Attorney General's Commission on Pornography (the "Commission") will operate pursuant to the provisions of the Federal Advisory Committee Act, Pub. L. No. 92–463, 86 Stat. 770 (1972), as amended by the Government in the Sunshine Act, Pub. L. No. 94–409, S 5 (c), 90 Stat. 1241, 1247 (1976) (the "Act"). Pursuant to Section 9(c) of the Act, the following information is provided regarding the Commission.

2. *Objectives and Scope of Activity*
   The objectives of the Commission are to determine the nature, extent, and impact on society of pornography in the United States, and to make specific recommendations to the Attorney General concerning more effective ways in which the spread of pornography could be contained, consistent with constitutional guarantees.
   The scope of the Commission includes: a study of the dimensions of the problem of pornography, particularly visual and graphic pornography, including changes over the last several years in the nature of pornography, its volume, the impact of new technology, and pornography that relates to children; an examination of the means of production and distribution of pornographic materials, specifically including the role of organized crime in the pornography business; a review of the available empirical and scientific evidence on the relationship between exposure to pornographic materials and antisocial behavior, and on the impact of the creation and dissemination of both adult and child pornography upon children, including, as appropriate, the commissioning of new research on these subjects; a review of national, State, and local efforts, whether by the government or others, to curb pornography; and the exploration and, where appropriate, the recommendation of possible roles and initiatives that the Department of Justice and agencies of local, State, and Federal government could pursue in controlling, consistent with constitutional guarantees, the production and distribution of pornography.

3. *Organization and Membership*
   A. *Membership.* The Commission shall be composed of not more than eleven members appointed by the Attorney General. Any vacancy in the Commission shall not affect its powers but may be filled by the Attorney General in his discretion.
   B. *Officers.* The Attorney General shall designate one of the members of the Commission to be the Chairman. The Chairman may appoint, from among the members of the Commission, such other officers as he deems appropriate. The Attorney General shall appoint an individual to serve as the Executive Director of the Commission.
   C. *Designated Government Official.* The Attorney General shall designate one officer or employee of the Department of Justice to serve as the Designated Government Official required by section 10(e) of the Act.

4. *Operations*
   A. *Functions of the Chairman.* In accordance with the Act, and consistent with its provisions regarding participation of the Designated Government Official, the Chairman shall:
   (1) call meetings and set hearings;
   (2) develop the agenda for meetings and hearings;
   (3) preside at meetings and hearings;
   (4) provide for the keeping of detailed minutes of meetings and transcripts of hearings of the Commission;
   (5) provide for the maintenance and retention of records of the Commission; and
   (6) certify the accuracy of the minutes of meetings and transcripts of hearings of the Commission.
   B. *Functions of the Designated Government Official.* The Designated Government Official shall exercise those duties and responsibilities required by the Act.
   C. *Functions of the Executive Director.* The Executive Director shall:
   (1) serve as contact point for the public to provide current information concerning the operations of the Commission;
   (2) under the general direction of the Commission acting through its Chairman, supervise the operations of the staff; and
   (3) perform such other duties and responsibilities as the Commission acting through its Chairman may assign.

3. *Meetings and Hearings of the Commission.* It is estimated that the Commission will hold approximately seven meetings during its term. In addition, the Commission is empowered to hold hearings and take testimony concerning any of the issues within its scope of activity, and may hold as many hearings as it deems necessary to fulfill the objectives of the Commission. A majority of the appointed and qualified members shall constitute a quorum, but a lesser number may conduct hearings.

All meetings and hearings of the Commission shall be open to the public unless a determination has been made by the Attorney General, in accordance with section 10(d) of the Act, that a meeting or hearing, or a portion thereof, should be closed to the public. Timely notice of each meeting or hearing shall be published in the *Federal Register* stating the name of the Commission, the time, place, and purpose of the meeting or hearing and the name, address, and telephone number of the Designated Government Official or other Department of Justice employee, whom members of the public may contact for further information. Other than in exceptional circumstances, such notice shall be published at least fifteen days in advance of the meeting or hearing day. If shorter notice is given, the reason must be stated in the notice.

E. *Records of the Commission.* The Commission's records shall consist of all papers, documents, and other materials pertinent to its establishment and activities, including its charter, agendas of meetings and hearings, determinations for closed meetings and hearings, minutes, reports, and all documents related to its proceedings and those of its subgroups, including working papers, drafts, studies, or other documents made available to or prepared for or by the Commission or its subgroup. These records shall be available for public inspection and copying to the extent required by the Act. These records shall be maintained by the Commission for the term of its operations, and shall be deposited with the Department of Justice upon the termination of the Commission.

F. *Minutes of the Meetings.* Detailed minutes shall be kept of each meeting of the Commission, which shall include a record of the persons present, a complete and accurate description of matters discussed, and conclusions reached, and copies of all reports received, issued, or approved by the Commission. The accuracy of such minutes shall be certified by the Chairman.

G. *Public Participation.* At any meeting of the Commission that is open to the public, but not at a closed meeting, interested persons shall be permitted to attend and to file written statements with the Commission. At any time prior or subsequent to a closed meeting, interested persons shall be permitted to file written statements with the Commission.

5. *Duration*

The Commission shall terminate one year from the date of the first Commission meeting, which will be sufficient time for the Commission to file the report required by Paragraph 6. The term of the Commission may be extended by the Attorney General upon his determination that the Commission requires additional time to complete its work.

6. *Reporting*

Within one year of its first meeting, the Commission shall report its findings and conclusions to the Attorney General. If the Commission determines that more time is required to provide an opportunity to review additional evidence or complete its work, it shall so report.

7. *Support Services*

The Department of Justice shall provide all necessary support services for the Commission.

8. *Duties*

The duties of the Commission are solely advisory; these duties are to carry out the objectives set forth in Paragraph 2.

9. *Remuneration*

Commissioners shall receive no remuneration other than compensation for travel and per diem expenses incurred in connection with the Commission's business.

10. *Estimated Annual Costs*

The Office of Justice Programs and the Office of Legal Policy shall provide the estimated annual cost of $400,000 for the operation of the Commission. Approximately ten work-years of staff support will be required.

11. *Date Charter Filed*

The Commission's Charter was filed on March 29, 1985.

William French Smith
Attorney General

PART

1

Overview And Analysis of Commission Findings

C H A P T E R • 1

Introduction

THE COMMISSION AND ITS MANDATE
The Attorney General's Commission on Pornography (referred to throughout this Report as "The Commission") was established pursuant to the Federal Advisory Committee Act,[1] on February 22, 1985 by then Attorney General of the United States William French Smith, at the specific request of President Ronald Reagan. Notice of the formation of The Commission, as required by Section 9(c) of the Federal Advisory Committee Act, was given to both Houses of Congress and to the Library of Congress on March 27 and March 28, 1985. On May 20, 1985, Attorney General Edwin Meese III publicly announced formation of The Commission and the names of its eleven members, all of whom served throughout the duration of The Commission's existence.

The formal mandate of The Commission is contained in its Charter, which is attached to this Report in Appendix A. In accordance with that Charter, we were asked to "determine the nature, extent, and impact on society of pornography in the United States, and to make specific recommendations to the Attorney General concerning more effective ways in which the spread of pornography could be contained, consistent with constitutional guarantees." Our scope was undeniably broad, including the specific mandate to "study . . . the dimensions of the problem of pornography," to "review . . . the available empirical evidence on the relationship between exposure to pornographic materials and antisocial behavior," and to explore "pos-

sible roles and initiatives that the Department of Justice and agencies of local, State, and federal government could pursue in controlling, consistent with constitutional guarantees, the production and distribution of pornography."

Because we are a commission appointed by the Attorney General, whose responsibilities are largely focused on the enforcement of the law, issues relating to the law and to law enforcement have occupied a significant part of our hearings, our deliberations, and the specific recommendations that accompany this Report. That our mandate from the Attorney General involves a special concern with enforcement of the law, however, should not indicate that we have ignored other aspects of the issue. Although we have tried to concentrate on law enforcement, we felt that we could not adequately address the issue of pornography, including the issue of enforcement of laws relating to pornography, unless we looked in a larger context at the entire phenomenon of pornography. As a result, we have tried to examine carefully the nature of the industry, the social, moral, political, and scientific concerns relating to or purportedly justifying the regulation of that industry, the relationship between law enforcement and other methods of social control, and a host of other topics that are inextricably linked with law enforcement issues. These various topics are hardly congruent with the issue of law enforcement, however, and thus it has been necessarily the case that issues other than law enforcement in its narrowest sense have been

---

1. 5 U.S.C. App.2, 86 Stat.770(1972), as amended by 90 Stat.1241, 1247(1976)

before us. In order that this Report accurately reflect what we thought about and what we felt to be important, we have included in the Report our findings and recommendations with respect to many issues that are related to but not the same as law enforcement.

For similar reasons, we have been compelled to consider substantive topics not, strictly speaking, specified exactly in our charter. A few examples ought to make clear the problems that surround trying to consider an issue that itself has no clear boundaries: We have heard testimony and considered the relationship between the pornography industry and organized crime, and this has forced us to consider the nature of organized crime itself; we have examined the evidence regarding the relationship between pornography and certain forms of anti-social conduct, and this has necessitated thinking about those other factors that might also be causally related to anti-social conduct, and about just what conduct we consider anti-social; we have thought about child pornography, and this has caused us to think about child abuse; and we have, in the course of thinking about the relationship between pornography and the family, thought seriously about the importance of the family in contemporary America. This list of examples is hardly exhaustive. We mention them here, however, only to show that our inquiry could not be and has not been hermetically sealed. But we all feel that what we may have lost in focus has more than been compensated for in the richness of our current contextual understanding of the issue of pornography.

THE WORK OF THE COMMISSION
We have attempted to conduct as thorough an investigation as our severe budgetary and time constraints permitted. The budgetary constraints have limited the size of our staff, and have prevented us from commissioning independent research. We especially regret the inability to commission independent research, because in many cases our deliberations have enabled us to formulate issues, questions, and hypotheses in ways that are either more novel or more precise than those reflected in the existing thinking about this subject, yet our budgetary constraints have kept us from testing these hypotheses or answering these questions. In numerous places throughout this report we have urged further research, and we often recommend that research take place along specific lines. We

hope that our suggestions will be taken up by researchers. Neither this Report nor any other should be taken as definitive and final, and we consider our suggestions for further research along particular lines to be one of the most important parts of this document.

The time constraints have also been significant. We all wish we could have had much more time for continued discussion among ourselves, as the process of deliberation among people of different backgrounds, different points of view, and different areas of expertise has been perhaps the most fruitful part of our task. Yet we have been required to produce a report within a year of our creation as a Commission, and our ability to meet together has been limited by the budgetary constraints just referred to, as well as by the fact that all of us have responsibilities to our jobs, our careers, and to our families that make it impossible to suspend every other activity in which we are engaged for the course of a year.

Despite these limitations, we have attempted to be as careful and as thorough as humanly possible within the boundaries of these constraints. We thought it especially important to hear from as wide a range of perspectives as possible, and as a result held public hearings and meetings in Washington, D.C., from June 18 to 20, 1985; in Chicago, Illinois, from July 23 to 25, 1985; in Houston, Texas, from September 10 to 12, 1985; in Los Angeles, California, from October 15 to 18, 1985; in Miami, Florida, from November 19 to 22, 1985; and in New York City from January 21 to 24, 1986. With the exception of the initial hearing in Washington, each of the hearings had a central theme, enabling us to hear together those people whose testimony related to the same issue. Thus the hearings in Chicago focused on the law, law enforcement, and the constraints of the First Amendment; in Houston we concentrated on the behavioral sciences, hearing from psychologists, psychiatrists, sociologists, and others who have been clinically or experimentally concerned with examining the relationship between pornography and human behavior; in Los Angeles our primary concern was the production side of the industry, and we heard testimony from those who were knowledgeable about or involved in the process of producing, distributing, and marketing pornographic materials; in Miami most of our time was spent dealing with the issue of child pornography, and we heard from people who in either their professional or personal capacities had familiarity with the creation, consequences, or legal control of child pornography; and in New York we heard about organized crime and its relationship with the production, distribution, and sale of pornographic materials.

Although these hearings each had their specific concentration, we also attempted to hear people throughout the country who wished to address us on these and many other issues, and one of the reasons for conducting hearings in different cities in various parts of the country was precisely to give the greatest opportunity for the expression of views by members of the public. Time did not permit us to hear everyone who desired to speak to us, but we have tried as best we could to allow a large number of people to provide information and to express their opinions. The information provided and the opinions expressed represented a wide range of perspectives and views on the issues before us. Many of the people appearing before us were professionals, who because of their training and experiences could enlighten us on matters that would otherwise have been beyond our knowledge. Many people represented particular points of view, and we are glad that varying positions have been so ably presented to us. And many others have been members of the public who only wished to represent themselves, relating either points of view or personal experiences. All of this testimony has been valuable, although we recognize its limitations. These limitations will be discussed throughout this report, although there is one that deserves to be highlighted in this introductory section. That is the distortion that has been the inevitable consequence of the fact that some pornography is illegal, and much pornography is, regardless of legality or illegality, still considered by many people to be harmful, offensive, or in some other way objectionable. As a result, legal as well as social constraints may distort the sample, in that they severely limit the willingness of many people to speak publicly in favor of pornography. This phenomenon may have been somewhat counterbalanced by the financial resources available to many of those from the publishing and entertainment industries who warned us of the dangers of any or most forms

of censorship. But the point remains that various dynamics are likely to skew the sample available to us. In evaluating the oral evidence, we have thus been mindful of the fact that the proportion of people willing to speak out on a particular subject, and from a particular point of view, may not be a fully accurate barometer of the extent that certain views are in fact held by the population at large.

Many of the limitations that surround oral testimony lessen considerably when written submissions are used, and we have made every effort to solicit written submissions both from those who testified before us and from those who did not. We have relied heavily on these, in part because they represent the views of those who could not testify before us, and in part because they frequently explored issues in much greater depth than would be possible in a brief period of oral testimony.

The written submissions we received constitute but a miniscule fraction of all that has been written about pornography. While it would not be accurate to say that each of us has read all or even a majority of the available literature, we have of course felt free to go beyond the written submissions and consult that which has been published on the subject, and much of what is contained in this report is a product of the fact that many thoughtful people have been contemplating the topic of pornography for a long time. To ignore this body of knowledge would be folly, and we have instead chosen to rely on more information rather than less. We could not have responsibly conducted our inquiry without spending a considerable period of time examining the materials that constitute the subject of this entire endeavor. Engaging in this part of our task has been no more edifying for us than it is for those judges who have the constitutional duty to review materials found at trial to be legally obscene.[2] Obviously, however, it was an essential part of our job, and many witnesses provided to us for examination during our hearings and deliberations samples of motion pictures, video tapes, magazines, books, slides, photographs, and other media containing sexually explicit material in all of its varied forms. In addition, when in Houston we visited three different establishments

---

2. "We are tied to the 'absurd business of perusing and viewing the miserable stuff that pours into the Court . . .' *Interstate Circuit, Inc. v. Dallas*, 390 U.S., at 707 (separate opinion of Harlan, J.). While the material may have varying degrees of social importance, it is hardly a source of edification to the members of this Court who are compelled to view it before passing on its obscenity." *Paris Adult Theatre I v. Slaton*, 413 U.S. 49, 92–93(1973) (Brennan, J., dissenting).

specializing in this material, and in that way were able to supplement the oral and written testimony with our own observations of the general environment in which materials of this variety are frequently sold.

In addition to our public hearings, we have also had public working sessions devoted to discussing the subject, our views on it, and possible findings, conclusions, and recommendations. These working sessions occupied part of our time when we were in Houston, Los Angeles, Miami, and New York, and in addition we met solely for these purposes in Scottsdale, Arizona, from February 26 to March 1, 1986, and in Washington, D.C., from April 29 to May 2, 1986. As we look back on these sessions, there is little doubt that we have all felt the constraints of deliberating in public. It can hardly be disputed that the exploration of tentative ideas is more difficult when public exposure treats the tentative as final, and the question as a challenge. Still, we feel that we have explored a wide range of points of view, and an equally wide range of vantage points from which to look at the problem of pornography. As with any inquiry, more could be done if there were more time, but we are all satisfied with the depth and breadth of the inquiries in which we have engaged. When faced with shortages of time, we have chosen to say here less than we might have been able to say had we had more time for our work, but we are convinced that saying no more than our inquiries and deliberations justify is vastly preferable to paying for time shortages in the currency of quality or the currency of accuracy. Thus, given the many constraints we operated under, we believe this Report adequately reflects both those constraints and the thoroughness with which we have attempted to fulfill our mandate.

Finally, we owe thanks to all those who have assisted us in our work. Although in another part of this Report we express our gratitude more specifically, we wish here to note our appreciation to an extraordinarily diligent staff, to numerous public officials and private citizens who have spent much of their own time and their own money to provide us with information, and especially to a large number of witnesses who appeared before us at great sacrifice and often at the expense of having to endure great personal anguish. To all of these people and others, we give our thanks, and we willingly acknowledge that we could not have completed our mission without them.

THE 1970 COMMISSION ON OBSCENITY AND PORNOGRAPHY

Our mission and our product will inevitably be compared with the work of the President's Commission on Obscenity and Pornography, which was created in 1967, staffed in 1968, and which reported in 1970. Some of the differences between the two enterprises relate to structural aspects of the inquiry. The 1970 commission had a budget of $2,000,000 and two years to complete its task. We had only one year, and a budget of $500,000. Taking into account the changing value of the dollar,[3] the 1970 Commission had a budget nearly sixteen times as large as ours, yet held only two public hearings. We do not regret having provided the opportunity for such an extensive expression of opinion, but it has even further depleted the extremely limited resources available to us. In addition to differences in time, budget, and staffing, there are of course differences in perspective. Although the work of the 1970 Commission has provided much important information for us, all of us have taken issue with at least some aspects of the earlier Commission's approach, and all of us have taken issue with at least some of the earlier Commission's conclusions. We have tried to explain our differences throughout this Report, but it would be a mistake to conclude that we saw our mission as reactive to the work of others sixteen years earlier. In sixteen years the world has seen enormous technological changes that have affected the transmission of sounds, words, and images. Few aspects of contemporary American society have not been affected by cable television, satellite communication, video tape recording, the computer, and competition in the telecommunications industry. It would be surprising to discover that these technological developments have had no effect on the production, distribution, and availability of pornography, and we have not been surprised. These technological developments have themselves caused such significant changes in the practices relating to the distribution of pornography that the analysis of sixteen years ago is starkly obsolete. Nor have the

---

3. Taking 1967, the date of creation of the 1970 Commission, as the base year, the dollar at the end of 1984, five months before this Commission commenced work, was worth $0.31.

changes been solely technological. In sixteen years there have been numerous changes in the social, political, legal, cultural, and religious portrait of the United States, and many of these changes have undeniably involved both sexuality and the public portrayal of sexuality. With reference to the question of pornography, therefore, there can be no doubt that we confront a different world than that confronted by the 1970 Commission.

Perhaps most significantly, however, studying an issue that was last studied in the form of a national commission sixteen years ago seems remarkably sensible even apart from the social and technological changes that relate in particular to the issue of pornography. Little in modern life can be held constant, and it would be strikingly aberrational if the conclusions of one commission could be taken as having resolved an issue for all time. The world changes, research about the world changes, and our views about how we wish to deal with that world change. Only in a static society would it be unwise to reexamine periodically the conclusions of sixteen years earlier, and we do not live in a static society. As we in 1986 reexamine what was done in 1970, so too do we expect that in 2002 our work will similarly be reexamined.

We do not by saying this wish to minimize the fact that we are different people from those who studied this issue sixteen years ago, that we have in many cases different views, and that we have in a number of respects reached different conclusions. Whether this Commission would have been created had the 1970 Commission reached different conclusions is not for us to say. But we are all convinced that the creation of this Commission at this time is entirely justified by the difference between this world and that of 1970, and we have set about our task with that in mind.

DEFINING OUR CENTRAL TERMS

Questions of terminology and definition have been recurring problems in our hearings and deliberations. Foremost among these definitional problems is trying to come up with some definition for the word "pornography." The range of materials to which people are likely to affix the designation "pornographic" is so broad that it is tempting to note that "pornography" seems to mean in practice any discussion or depiction of sex to which the person using the word objects. But this will not do, nor will an attempt to define "pornography" in terms of regulatory goals or condemnation. The problem with this latter strategy is that it channels the entire inquiry into a definitional question, when it would be preferable first to identify a certain type of material, and then decide what, if anything, should be done about it. We note that this strategy was that adopted by the Williams Committee in Great Britain several years ago,[4] which defined pornography as a description or depiction of sex involving the dual characteristics of (1) sexual explicitness; and (2) intent to arouse sexually. Although definitions of the sort adopted by the Williams Committee contain an admirable dose of analytic purity, they unfortunately do not reflect the extent to which the appellation "pornography" is undoubtedly pejorative. To call something "pornographic" is plainly, in modern usage, to condemn it, and thus the dilemma is before us. If we try to define the primary term of this inquiry at the outset in language that is purely descriptive, we will wind up having condemned a wide range of material that may not deserve condemnation. But if on the other hand we incorporate some determination of value into our definition, then the definition of pornography must come at the end and not the beginning of this report, and at the end and not at the beginning of our inquiry. Faced with this dilemma, the best course may be that followed by the Fraser Committee in Canada,[5] which decided that definition was simply futile. We partially follow this course, and pursuant to that have tried to minimize the use of the word "pornography" in this Report. Where we do use the term, we do not mean for it to be, for us, a statement of a conclusion, and thus in this Report a reference to material as "pornographic" means only that the material is predominantly sexually explicit and intended primarily for the purpose of sexual arousal. Whether some or all of what qualifies as pornographic under this definition should be prohibited, or even condemned, is not a question that should be answered under the guise of definition.

If using the term "pornography" is problematic, then so too must be the term "hard core pornography." If we were forced to define

4. *Report of the Home Office Committee on Obscenity and Film Censorship* (Bernard Williams, Chairman) (1978)
5. *Report of the Special Committee on Pornography and Prostitution* (Paul Fraser, Q.C., Chairman) (1985)

the term "hard core pornography," we would probably note that it refers to the extreme form of what we defined as pornography, and thus would describe material that is sexually explicit to the extreme, intended virtually exclusively to arouse, and devoid of any other apparent content or purpose. This definition may not be satisfactory, but we all feel after our work on this Commission that the late Justice Stewart was more correct than he is commonly given credit for having been in saying of hard core pornography that although he could not define it, "I know it when I see it."[6] But although we are inclined to agree with Justice Stewart, we regrettably note that the range of material to which witnesses before us have applied this term is far broader than we would like, and we therefore conclude that careful analysis will be served if we use this term less rather than more.

Trying to define the word "obscenity" is both more and less difficult. It is more difficult because, unlike the word "pornography," the word "obscenity" need not necessarily suggest anything about sex at all. Those who would condemn a war as "obscene" are not misusing the English language, nor are those who would describe as "obscene" the number of people killed by intoxicated drivers. Given this usage, the designation of certain sexually explicit material as "obscene" involves a judgment of moral condemnation, a judgment that has led for close to two hundred years to legal condemnation as well. But although the word "obscene" is both broader than useful here as well as being undeniably condemnatory, it has taken on a legal usage that is relevant in many places in this Report. As a result, we will here use the words "obscene" and "obscenity" in this narrower sense, to refer to material that has been or would likely be found to be obscene in the context of a judicial proceeding employing applicable legal and constitutional standards. Thus, when we refer to obscene material, we need not necessarily be condemning that material, or urging prosecution, but we are drawing on the fact that such material *could* now be prosecuted without offending existing authoritative interpretations of the Constitution. Numerous submissions to us have made reference to "erotica." It seems clear to us that the term as actually used is the mirror image of the broadly condemnatory use of "pornography," being employed to describe sexually explicit materials of which the user of the term approves. For some the word "erotica" describes any sexually explicit material that contains neither violence nor subordination of women, for others the term refers to almost all sexually explicit material, and for still others only material containing generally accepted artistic value qualifies as erotica. In light of this disagreement, and in light of the tendency to use the term "erotica" as a conclusion rather than a description, we again choose to avoid the term wherever possible, preferring to rely on careful description rather than terms that obscure more than advance rational consideration of difficult issues.

Various other terms, usually vituperative, have been used at times, in our proceedings and elsewhere, to describe some or all sexually explicit materials. Such terms need not be defined here, for we find it hard to see how our inquiry is advanced by the use of terms like "smut" and "filth." But we have also encountered frequent uses of the term "X-rated," and a few words about that term are appropriate here. As will be discussed in detail in the section of this Report dealing with the production of sexually explicit materials, "X" is one of the ratings of the Motion Picture Association of America (MPAA), a private organization whose ratings of films are relied upon by theaters and others to determine which films are or are not suitable for people of various ages. But the MPAA rating system is not a series of legal categories, and does not have the force of law. Although many films that carry either an "X" rating or no rating might be deemed to be legally obscene, many more would not, and it is plain that many X-rated films could not conceivably be considered legally obscene. Moreover, there is no plain connection between the words "pornographic" and "X-rated," and once again it seems clear that common usage would apply the term "pornography" to a class of films that overlaps with but is not identical to the class encompassed by the "X" rating. As a result, we avoid the term "X-rated," except insofar as we are discussing in particular the category of materials so rated in the context of the purposes behind the MPAA rating system.

---

6. *Jacobellis v. Ohio*, 378 U.S. 184, 197(1964) (Stewart, J., concurring).

C H A P T E R • 2

The History of Pornography

PORNOGRAPHY AS SOCIAL PHENOMENON

Descriptions of sex are as old as sex itself. There can be little doubt that talking about sex has been around as long as talking, that writing about sex has been around as long as writing, and that pictures of sex have been around as long as pictures. In this sense it is odd that historical treatments of pornography turn out to be historical treatments of the *regulation*, governmental or otherwise, of pornography. To understand the phenomenon of pornography it is necessary to look at the history of the phenomenon itself, prior to or at least distinct from the investigation of the practice of restricting it. Some works on the history of sexual behavior, eroticism, or erotic art help to serve this goal, but the history of pornography still remains to be written. Commissioning independent historical research was far beyond our mandate, our budget, and our time constraints, yet we do not wish to ignore history entirely. We feel it appropriate to offer the briefest overview here, but we urge as well that more comprehensive historical study be undertaken.

The use of comparatively explicit sexual references for the purposes of entertainment or arousal is hardly a recent phenomenon. Greek and Roman drama and poetry was frequently highly specific, and the works of Aristophanes, Catullus, Horace, and Ovid, to name just a few, contain references to sexual activity that, by the standards of the time, are highly explicit. Scenes of intercourse have been found on the walls of the brothel at Pompeii, and the Roman sculptural representations of the god Priapus are as bawdy as

Aubrey Beardsley's most explicit drawings. Obviously the explicitness of the past must be viewed in light of the times, and there is no question but that the works of Aristophanes are less shocking to our contemporary vision than are some of the materials currently shown in adult theaters. Yet to ask what the Romans would have thought about "Deep Throat" is akin to asking what the Romans would have thought about helicopters. The more useful historical question is whether highly explicit sexuality for the times was a part of the literature and discourse of the times, and the answer to that question is plainly "yes."

Similar observations can be made about later historical periods and about other cultures. *The Thousand and One Nights* and the *Kamasutra* are but examples of the fact that numerous eastern cultures also have a long history of comparatively explicit depictions and descriptions of sexuality. In western cultures the explicit treatment of sex continued through modern history. Whether in the form of the medieval bawdy ballads and poems of Chaucer, Dunbar, and others, or in the form of the French farces of the fourteenth and fifteenth centuries, or in the form of the art and poetry of Renaissance Florence, or in the form of Elizabethan ballads and poetry, sexuality, and quite explicit sexuality at that, was a recurrent theme in drama, in poetry, in song, and in art.

We can be fairly certain that sexually explicit descriptions and depictions have been around in one form or another almost since the beginning of recorded history, and we can also be fairly certain that its regulation by law in a form resembling contemporary regulation of sexually explicit materials is a comparatively recent phenomenon. It is difficult, however, to draw useful conclusions from this aspect of the history. For one thing, until the last several hundred years, almost all written, drawn, or printed material was restricted largely to a small segment of the population that undoubtedly constituted the social elite. The drama of the classical age was frequently highly sexually explicit, or at least suggestive, but its audience tended to be limited to the wealthiest, best educated, and most powerful members of society. And of course the historical or universal presence of a phenomenon need not justify permitting its continuation. Slavery was a central fixture of much of the past, and warfare and ethnocentricity are as nearly universal as sexually explicit depictions, but the sensitivities of most cultures demand that such practices be discouraged.

In addition, it is a mistake to draw too many conclusions about social tolerance and social control from the presence or absence of laws or law enforcement practices. There is little indication that sexual *conduct* was part of classical drama, and the very fact that many sexual references were veiled (however thinly) rather than explicit indicates that some sense of taboo or social stigma has always been in most societies attached to public discussion of sexuality. Yet although some degree of inhibition obviously attached to public descriptions and depictions of sexual acts, it is equally clear that the extent of these inhibitions has oscillated throughout history. In somewhat cyclical fashion, social tolerance of various practices has been at times limited and at times extensive. To conclude that inhibition, in some form or another, of public discussion and representations of sexual practices is a totally modern phenomenon is to overstate the case and to misinterpret the evidence from earlier times. But to assume that public discussions and descriptions of sexuality were, prior to 1850, always as inhibited as they were in English speaking countries from 1850 to 1950 is equally mistaken.

We have mentioned here the early history of pornography in large part to encourage thinking about sexually explicit material as social phenomenon as well as object of governmental regulation. Although our task is largely to think about laws and law enforcement, we know that thinking about law requires thinking as well about the social foundations of the practice involved. Most historical study to date has not been about the social practice of pornography, but largely about control of that social practice by government. If the use of sexually explicit material is to be understood fully, the scope of thinking about the issue should be broadened substantially.

REGULATION AND THE ROLE OF RELIGION

When earlier social inhibitions about public descriptions and depictions of sexuality and sexual practices came to be enforced by law, it was largely in the context of religious rather than secular concerns. Moreover, the earliest enforcement efforts were directed not against descriptions or depictions of sex itself, but only against such depictions when combined with attacks on religion or religious authorities.

This phenomenon of regulation in defense of religion rather than in defense of decency can be seen by the tolerance, at least in European cultures, of secular bawdiness up to the middle of the seventeenth century. Although many European countries rigidly controlled written and printed works from medieval times through the seventeenth century, this control was exercised only in the name of religion and politics, and not in the name of decency. In one legal form or another, and in secular as well as ecclesiastical tribunals, heresy, blasphemy, treason, and sedition were all severely sanctioned, but sexually explicit representations alone were rarely treated as a matter justifying punishment or restraint. Perhaps the best example of this phenomenon was the action of the Council of Trent in 1573, when it permitted publication of a version of Boccacio's *Decameron* in which the sinning priests and nuns were converted into sinning members of the laity.

If we focus on England, from which our legal system emerged, it is commonly acknowledged that sexuality itself was not treated as a matter for governmental legal concern until 1663. That year saw the conviction in London of Sir Charles Sedley, but the activity for which he was convicted hardly looks like a case involving pornography.[7] Instead, Sedley was convicted of the crime of committing a breach of the peace for getting drunk, removing his clothes, uttering profane remarks, and

7. *King v. Sedley*, 1 Keble 620 (K.B.), 83 Eng. Rep. 1146 (1663).

pouring urine on the crowd below the tavern balcony on which he was standing at the time. Although Sedley's profane remarks included words, there seems little doubt that he would have been convicted even had he remained silent. The significance of this case, therefore, lies in the fact that mere indecent behavior, absent any attack on religion, and absent any challenge to secular authority, was for the first time perceived to be something deserving of governmental involvement. Prior to Sedley's case, government stepped in to protect the person and his property, to protect the authority of the state, and to protect the church. With Sedley's case came the beginning of a broader range of governmental concerns, and thus Sedley's case is properly seen as the precursor of most modern regulation of sexually explicit materials.

Even after Sedley's case, the common law was hardly eager to come to the defense of decency. Throughout the seventeenth and eighteenth centuries, common law courts in England were only occasionally asked to take action against the kind of material that would then have been considered pornographic. Even when asked, the courts were often reluctant to respond. In 1708, for example, James Read was indicted in London for publishing an extremely explicit book entitled *The Fifteen Plagues of a Maidenhead*. The Queen's Bench court, however, dismissed the indictment, and Lord Justice Powell's statement provides an apt summary of the general reaction of the law to sexually explicit materials until very late in the eighteenth century:

> "This is for printing bawdy stuff but reflects on no person, and a libel must be against some particular person or persons, or against the Government. It is stuff not fit to be mentioned publicly; if there should be no remedy in the Spiritual Court, it does not follow there must be a remedy here. There is no law to punish it, I wish there were, but we cannot make law; it indeed tends to the corruption of good manners, but that is not sufficient for us to punish."[8]

Not all of the common law reaction to sexual explicitness absent religious blasphemy was the same. In 1727 Edmund Curll was convicted for corrupting public morals on ac-

count of his publication of *Venus in the Cloister, or the Nun in Her Smock*,[9] and the Crown's attack on John Wilkes, largely on the basis of his activities as political dissident, included prosecution for publishing his highly explicit *Essay on Woman*.[10] Yet at about the same time, in 1748 to be exact, the publication of John Cleland's *Memoirs of a Woman of Pleasure*, better known as *Fanny Hill*, took place without either public outcry or governmental intervention.

The history of the English experience with sexually explicit materials is largely paralleled by the experiences in other European countries, and in the English colonies, including those in North America. As the world entered the nineteenth century, it remained the case that in most of the world there was greater tolerance for sexually explicit writing, printing, and drawing than there would be fifty years later, and that governmental action against spoken, written, or printed materials remained largely devoted to protecting the authority of the state and to protecting the integrity and values of religion.

OBSCENITY LAW—THE MODERN HISTORY

As indicated in the previous section, there were traces of legal concern with decency itself in the eighteenth century, but these were little more than traces. If one is searching for the roots of modern American obscenity law, one must look to the first half of the nineteenth century in both Great Britain and the United States. The impetus in Britain came initially from private organizations such as the Organization for the Reformation of Manners and its successor the Society for the Suppression of Vice. As printing became increasingly economical, printed materials became more and more available to the masses. Thus, the kinds of sexually explicit material that had circulated relatively freely in England among the elite during the eighteenth century and earlier now became more readily available to everyone. With this increased audience came an increase in demand, and with the increased demand came an increased supply. As a result, the early part of the nineteenth century saw much greater production and circulation of material as sexually ex-

---

8. *Queen v. Read*, Fortescue's Reports 98, 92 Eng. Rep. 777 (1708).

9. *Dominus Rex v. Curll*, 2 Str. 789, 93 Eng. Rep. 849 (1727). Because the religious aspects of this book were anti-Catholic, it seems safe to conclude that protection of religion was no part of the governmental desire to indict or to convict.

10. *The King v. John Wilkes*, 2 Wils. K.B. 151, 95 Eng. Rep. 737 (1764), 4 Burr. 2527, 98 Eng. Rep. 327 (1770).

plicit as had been less widely circulated earlier. And because the audience was more broad-based, the material itself became not necessarily more explicit, but certainly briefer, simpler, and more straightforward.

These developments in England came at about the same time as general views about sexual morality, and especially about public sexual morality, were becoming increasingly stern. In an important sense, Victorianism preceded Victoria, and thus the initiatives of organizations like the Society for the Suppression of Vice found a receptive audience in the population at large, in government, and in the judiciary. Because private prosecution for criminal offenses was part of the English system of criminal justice at the time, the Society and others like it were able to commence their own criminal prosecutions, and their efforts from the early 1800s through the 1860s resulted in many prosecutions for obscene libel, as it had by then come to be called. Most of these prosecutions were successful, and by the 1860s there had developed a well established practice of prosecuting people for distributing works perceived as immoral.

The 1800s also saw the development of more effective ways of printing drawings in one form or another for mass circulation, and saw as well the development of photography. Not surprisingly, printed materials with a sexual orientation came to include increasingly large amounts of pictorial material. This development not only increased the impact of the materials, and therefore the offensiveness of many of the materials, but also increased their accessibility. With literacy no longer a requirement for appreciation, the market demand increased, and so, consequently, did the supply. Legal reactions to the proliferation of pictorial materials, again largely inspired by the Society for the Suppression of Vice and similar organizations, included the Vagrancy Act of 1824, which provided criminal penalties for the publication of an indecent picture, as well as legislation enacted in 1853 directed primarily at the increasing importation into England of so-called "French postcards."

American developments were similar. Although prior to 1800 there existed colonial statutes and some common law cases seemingly inclusive of profanity or sexual immorality, again the plain intent of these laws, as well as their universal application, was only to that which was blasphemous or in some other way threatening to religion. Pure sexual explicitness, while often condemned, was not until after 1800 taken to be a matter of governmental concern. After 1800, however, trends with respect to the type of material available and the audience to whom it was directed were quite similar to the trends in England. The reaction was also similar, and in Pennsylvania in 1815 the case of *Commonwealth v. Sharpless*[11] represented the first reported conviction in the United States for the common law crime of obscene libel. Massachusetts followed six years later, in the case of *Commonwealth v. Holmes*,[12] and at about the same time Vermont passed the country's first *statute* prohibiting the publication or distribution of obscene materials. Other states followed, and by the middle of the nineteenth century the production and distribution of obscene materials was a crime throughout most of the United States.

As in England, however, most of the enforcement impetus in the United States came from private organizations. Most prominent among these were the Watch and Ward Society in Boston and the New York Society for the Suppression of Vice. The New York Society for the Suppression of Vice, officially created in 1873, was largely the product of the efforts of Anthony Comstock, who crusaded actively from about that time until his death in 1915 for greater restrictions on indecent materials, and for more vigorous prosecution of the laws against them. Although he was also actively opposed to light literature, pool halls, lotteries, gambling dens, popular magazines, weekly newspapers, contraception, and abortion, most of his energies were directed at sexually explicit magazines, books, and pictures. In large part his most vigorous efforts were directed at magazines like *The National Police Gazette*, and other generally nonartistic works. Although Comstock admitted that artistic or literary merit did not concern him if the material dealt with "lust," most prosecutions of the time were for comparatively unimportant works, a phenomenon that was to change in the early part of the twentieth century. Comstock was largely responsible for the enactment of the federal laws that still, with only comparatively minor modifications through the years, constitute the bulk

---

11. 2 Serg. & Rawle 91 (1815).
12. 17 Mass. 336 (1821).

of the federal laws dealing with obscene materials. And he himself, as a specially appointed agent of the Post Office Department, enthusiastically and vigorously enforced the law. Shortly before his death, he announced with pride that he had "convicted persons enough to fill a passenger train of sixty-one coaches, sixty coaches containing sixty passengers each and the sixty-first almost full. I have destroyed 160 tons of obscene literature."

Although Comstock's efforts were the most vigorous, the most extensive, and the most effective, similar initiatives took place throughout the United States during the latter part of the nineteenth century and the early part of the twentieth. The result of this had a profound effect on the nature of the industry, for throughout the first half of the twentieth century in the United States the market for sexually explicit materials was almost exclusively clandestine. During this period prosecutions and legal developments surrounded the attempted and often successful actions against works now (and even then) commonly taken to be of plain literary or artistic merit. The law concerned itself not only with comparatively explicit works such as D.H. Lawrence's *Lady Chatterley's Lover* and James Joyce's *Ulysses*, but works containing suggestions of sexual immorality no more explicit than that in, for example, Theodore Dreiser's *An American Tragedy*. The Supreme Judicial Court of Massachusetts found this book to be obscene because "the seller of a book which contains passages offensive to the statute has no right to assume that children to whom the book might come would not read the obscene passages, or having read them, would continue to read on until the evil effects of the obscene passages were weakened or dissipated with the tragic denouement of the tale."[13]

With publications such as *An American Tragedy* and *Esquire* magazine[14] constituting the legal skirmishes, it was plain that truly sexually explicit material could not circulate openly, and in fact it did not for much of this century. It still existed, however, despite having been driven rather deeply underground. We discuss the more recent history of the production, distribution, and sale of truly explicit material at greater length later in this

Report dealing with the nature of the industry in general, but it is important to note here that the existence of legal disputes about mainstream literary works did not mean that these works constituted the extent of what was available. So-called "stag films" were produced and distributed in a highly surreptitious fashion. Sales of pornographic pictures, magazines, and eight millimeter films took place through the mails as a result of advertisements in heavily guarded language, or through sales by someone who knew someone who knew someone else, or in some form or another "under the counter" in establishments primarily devoted to more accepted material. Until the 1960s, therefore, the law operated largely in two quite different roles. On the one hand, and more visible, were the prosecutions of books and films that contained substantial merit and were directed to and available to a general audience. But on the other hand were enforcement efforts against much more explicit material, distributed in much more surreptitious fashion, as to which serious constitutional or definitional issues never arose. It was not until the early 1960s, when the Supreme Court began actively to scrutinize the contents of material found to be obscene, that attempted prosecutions of unquestionably serious works largely withered, and that most of the legal battles concerned the kinds of material more commonly taken to be pornographic.

This active Supreme Court scrutiny had its roots in the 1957 case of *Roth v. United States*,[15] discussed at length in Chapter 30 of this Part, in which the First Amendment was first taken to limit the particular works that could be found obscene. By the 1960s, cases such as *Jacobellis v. Ohio*[16] had made this close scrutiny a reality, and by 1966 the range of permissible regulation could properly be described as "minimal." In that year the Supreme Court decided the case of *Memoirs v. Massachusetts*,[17] which held that material could be restricted only if, among other factors, it was "utterly without redeeming social value." The stringency of this standard made legal restriction extraordinarily difficult, and shortly thereafter the Supreme Court made it even more difficult by embarking on a practice of reversing obscenity convictions with

13. *Commonwealth v. Friede*, 271 Mass. 318, 171 N.E. 472 (1930).
14. *Hannegan v. Esquire*, 327 U.S. 146 (1946)
15. 354 U.S. 476 (1957)
16. 378 U.S. 184 (1964).
17. 383 U.S. 413 (1966).

respect to a wide range of materials, many of which were quite explicit.[18] The result, therefore, was that by the late 1960s obscenity regulation became essentially dormant, with a consequent proliferation of the open availability of quite explicit materials. This trend was reinforced by the issuance in 1970 of the Report of the President's Commission on Obscenity and Pornography, which recommended against any state or federal restrictions on the material available to consenting adults. Although the Report was resoundingly rejected by President Nixon and by Congress, it nevertheless reinforced the tendency to withdraw legal restrictions in practice, which in turn was one of the factors contributing to a significant growth from the late 1960s onward of the volume and explicitness of materials that were widely available.

The Supreme Court decisions of 1973, most notably *Paris Adult Theatres I v. Slaton*[19] and *Miller v. California*,[20] by reversing the "utterly without redeeming social value" standard and by making clear once again that the First Amendment did not protect anything and everything that might be sold to or viewed by a consenting adult, tended to recreate the environment in which obscenity regulation was a practical possibility. Since 1973, however, the extent of obscenity regulation has varied widely throughout the country. In some geographic areas aggressive prosecution has ended the open availability of most extremely explicit materials, but more commonly prosecution remains minimal, and highly explicit materials are widely available. Because the current situation is explored throughout this Report, and because it is described in detail in a later part, we will go no further in this Chapter, whose primary purpose has been to put the present into historical perspective.

---

18. E.g., *Redrup v. New York*, 386 U.S. 767 (1967).
19. 413 U.S. 49 (1973).
20. 413 U.S. 15 (1973).

The Constraints of the First Amendment

THE PRESUMPTIVE RELEVANCE OF THE FIRST AMENDMENT

The subject of pornography is not coextensive with the subject of sex. Definitionally, pornography requires a portrayal, whether spoken, written, printed, photographed, sculpted, or drawn, and this essential feature of pornography necessarily implicates constitutional concerns that would not otherwise exist. The First Amendment to the Constitution of the United States provides quite simply that "Congress shall make no law . . . abridging the freedom of speech, or of the press." Longstanding judicial interpretations make it now clear that this mandate is, because of the Fourteenth Amendment, applicable to the states as well,[21] and make it equally clear that the restrictions of the First Amendment are applicable to any form of governmental action, and not merely to statutes enacted by a legislative body.[22]

To the extent, therefore, that regulation of pornography constitutes an abridgment of the freedom of speech, or an abridgment of the freedom of the press, it is at least presumptively unconstitutional. And even if some or all forms of regulation of pornography are seen ultimately not to constitute abridgments of the freedom of speech or the freedom of the press, the fact remains that the Constitution treats speaking and printing as special, and thus the regulation of anything spoken or printed must be examined with extraordinary care. For even when some forms of regulation of what is spoken or printed are not abridg-

ments of the freedom of speech, or abridgments of the freedom of the press, such regulations are closer to constituting abridgments than other forms of governmental action. If nothing else, the barriers between permissible restrictions on what is said or printed and unconstitutional abridgments must be scrupulously guarded.

Thus, we start with the presumption that the First Amendment is germane to our inquiry, and we start as well with the presumption that, both as citizens and as governmental officials who have sworn an oath to uphold and defend the Constitution, we have independent responsibilities to consider constitutional issues in our deliberations and in our conclusions. Although we are not free to take actions that relevant Supreme Court interpretations of the Constitution tell us we cannot take, we do not consider Supreme Court opinions as relieving us of our own constitutional responsibilities. The view that constitutional concerns are only for the Supreme Court, or only for courts in general, is simply fallacious, and we do no service to the Constitution by adopting the view that the Constitution is someone else's responsibility. It is our responsibility, and we have treated it as such both in this Report and throughout our deliberation.

THE FIRST AMENDMENT, THE SUPREME COURT, AND THE REGULATION OF OBSCENITY

Although both speaking and printing are

---

21. *Gitlow v. New York*, 268 U.S. 652 (1925).
22. E.g., *Bantam Books, Inc. v. Sullivan*, 372 U.S. 58 (1963); *Organization for a Better Austin v. Keefe*, 402 U.S. 415 (1971).

what the First Amendment is all about, closer examination reveals that the First Amendment cannot plausibly be taken to protect, or even to be relevant to, every act of speaking or writing. Government may plainly sanction the written acts of writing checks backed by insufficient funds, filing income tax returns that understate income or overstate deductions, and describing securities or consumer products in false or misleading terms. In none of these cases would First Amendment defenses even be taken seriously. The same can be said about sanctions against spoken acts such as lying while under oath, or committing most acts of criminal conspiracy. Although urging the public to rise up and overthrow the government is protected by the First Amendment, urging your brother to kill your father so that you can split the insurance money has never been considered the kind of spoken activity with which the First Amendment is concerned. Providing information to the public about the misdeeds of their political leaders is central to the First Amendment, but providing information to one's friends about the combination to the vault at the local bank is not a First Amendment matter at all.

The regulation of pornography in light of the constraints of the First Amendment must thus be considered against this background—that not every use of words, pictures, or a printing press automatically triggers protection by the First Amendment. Indeed, as the examples above demonstrate, many uses of words, pictures, or a printing press do not even raise First Amendment concerns. As Justice Holmes stated the matter in 1919, "the First Amendment . . . cannot have been, and obviously was not, intended to give immunity for every possible use of language."[23] As described in Chapter 2, both the states and the federal government have long regulated the trade in sexually explicit materials under the label of "obscenity" regulation. And until 1957, obscenity regulation was treated as one of those forms of regulation that was totally unrelated to the concerns or the constraints of the First Amendment. If the aim of the state or federal

regulation was the control of obscenity, then the First Amendment did not restrict government action, without regard to what particular materials might be deemed obscene and thus prohibited.[24] When, throughout the first half of this century, states would determine to be obscene such works as Theodore Dreiser's *An American Tragedy*,[25] or D.H. Lawrence's *Lady Chatterley's Lover*,[26] or Erskine Caldwell's *God's Little Acre*,[27] or Radclyffe Hall's *The Well of Loneliness*,[28] the First Amendment was not taken to constitute a significant barrier to such actions.

In 1957, however, in *Roth v. United States*,[29] the Supreme Court confronted squarely the tension between the regulation of what was alleged to be obscene and the constraints of the First Amendment. After *Roth*, it is not simply the form of regulation that immunizes a prosecution from the First Amendment. The Court made clear in *Roth*, and even clearer in subsequent cases,[30] that the simple designation of a prosecution as one for obscenity does not cause the First Amendment considerations to drop out. If the particular materials prosecuted are themselves protected by the First Amendment, the prosecution is impermissible. After *Roth* mere labels could not be used to justify restricting the protected, and mere labels could not justify circumventing the protections of the First Amendment.

But the Supreme Court also made clear in *Roth* that some materials were themselves outside of the coverage of the First Amendment, and that obscenity, carefully delineated, could be considered as "utterly without redeeming social importance." As a result, the Court concluded, obscene materials were not the kind of speech or press included within the First Amendment, and could thus be regulated without the kind of overwhelming evidence of harm that would be necessary if materials of this variety were included within the scope of the First Amendment. But to the Court in *Roth*, that scope was limited to material containing *ideas*. All ideas, even the unorthodox, even the controversial, and even the hateful, were within the scope of the First

23. *Frohwerk v. United States*, 249 U.S. 204 (1919).
24. *Dunlap v. United States*, 165 U.S. 486 (1897).
25. *Commonwealth v. Friede*, 271 Mass. 318, 171 N.E. 472 (1930).
26. *People v. Dial Press*, 182 Misc. 416 (N.Y. Magis. Ct. 1929).
27. *Attorney General v. Book Named "God's Little Acre,"* 326 Mass. 281, 93 N.E.2d 819 (1950).
28. *People v. Seltzer*, 122 Misc. 329, 203 N.Y.S. 809 (N.Y. Sup. Ct. 1924).
29. 354 U.S. 476 (1957).
30. E.g., *Kingsley International Pictures Corp. v. Regents*, 360 U.S. 684 (1959).

Amendment. But if there were no ideas with "even the slightest redeeming social impor- tance," then such material could be taken to be not speech in the relevant sense at all, and therefore outside of the realm of the First Amendment.

The general *Roth* approach to obscenity regulation has been adhered to ever since 1957, and remains still today the foundation of the somewhat more complex but neverthe- less fundamentally similar treatment of ob- scenity by the Supreme Court. This treatment involves two major principles. The first, reit- erated repeatedly and explained most thor- oughly in *Paris Adult Theatre I v. Slaton*,[31] is the principle that legal obscenity is treated as being either not speech at all, or at least not the kind of speech that is within the purview of any of the diverse aims and principles of the First Amendment. As a result, legal ob- scenity may be regulated by the states and by the federal government without having to meet the especially stringent standards of justification, often generalized as a "clear and present danger," and occasionally as a "com- pelling interest," that would be applicable to speech, including a great deal of sexually ori- ented or sexually explicit speech, that is within the aims and principles of the First Amendment. Instead, legal obscenity may constitutionally be regulated as long as there exists merely a "rational basis" for the regula- tion, a standard undoubtedly drastically less stringent than the standard of "clear and present danger" or "compelling interest."

That legal obscenity *may* be regulated by the states and the federal government pursu- ant to *Roth* and *Paris* does not, of course, mean that the states *must* regulate it, or even that they necessarily *should* regulate it. It is in the nature of our constitutional system that most of what the Constitution does is to estab- lish structures and to set up outer boundaries of permissible regulation, without in any way addressing what ought to be done within those outer boundaries. There is no doubt, for example, that the speed limits on the high- ways could be significantly reduced without offending the Constitution, that states could eliminate all penalties for burglary without violating the Constitution, and that the high- est marginal income tax rate could be in-

creased from fifty percent to ninety percent without creating a valid constitutional chal- lenge. None of these proposals seems a par- ticularly good idea, and that is precisely the point—that the fact that an action is constitu- tional does not mean that it is wise. Thus, al- though the regulation of obscenity is, as a result of *Roth, Paris*, and many other cases, constitutionally permissible, this does not answer the question whether such regulation is desireable. Wisdom or desirability are not primarily constitutional questions.

Thus the first major principle is the con- stitutional permissibility of the regulation of obscenity. The second major principle is that the *definition* of what is obscene, as well as the determination of what in particular cases is obscene, is itself a matter of constitutional law. If the underpinnings of the exclusion of obscenity from the scope of the First Amend- ment are that obscenity is not what the First Amendment is all about, then special care must be taken to ensure that materials, in- cluding materials dealing with sex, that *are* within what the First Amendment is all about are not subject to restriction. Although what is on the unprotected side of the line between the legally obscene and constitutionally pro- tected speech is not protected by the First Amendment, the location of the line itself is a constitutional matter. That obscenity may be regulated consistent with the First Amend- ment does not mean that anything that is per- ceived by people or by legislatures as obscene may be so regulated.

As a result, the definition of obscenity is largely a question of constitutional law, and the current constitutionally permissible defi- nition is found in another 1973 case, *Miller v. California*.[32] According to *Miller*, material is obscene if *all* three of the following condi- tions are met:

1. The average person, applying contem- porary community standards, would find that the work, taken as a whole, ap- peals to the prurient interest [in sex]; and
2. The work depicts or describes, in a pat- ently offensive way, sexual conduct spe- cifically defined by the applicable state [or federal] law; and

31. 413 U.S. 49 (1973).

32. 413 U.S. 15 (1973). Among the most significant aspects of *Miller* was the fact that it rejected as part of the definition of obscenity the requirement that before material could be deemed obscene it had to be shown to be "utterly without redeeming social value." This standard had its roots as part of the test for obscenity in *Memoirs v. Massachu- setts*, 383 U.S. 413.

3. The work, taken as a whole, lacks serious literary, artistic, political, or scientific value.

It is not our function in this Report to provide an exposition of the law of obscenity. In a later part of this Report we do provide a much more detailed treatment of the current state of the law that we hope will be useful to those with a need to consider some of the details of obscenity law. But we do not wish our avoidance of extensive description of the law here to imply that the law is simple. Virtually every word and phrase in the Miller test has been the subject of extensive litigation and substantial commentary in the legal literature. The result of this is that there is now a large body of explanation and clarification of concepts such as "taken as a whole," "prurient interest," "patently offensive," "serious value," and "contemporary community standards." Moreover, there are many constitutionally mandated aspects of obscenity law that are not derived directly from the definition of obscenity. For example, no person may be prosecuted for an obscenity offense unless it can be shown that the person had knowledge of the general contents, character, and nature of the materials involved, for if the law were otherwise booksellers and others would avoid stocking anything even slightly sexually oriented for fear of being prosecuted on account of materials the content of which they were unaware.[33] The procedures surrounding the initiation of a prosecution, including search and seizure, are also limited by constitutional considerations designed to prevent what would in effect be total suppression prior to a judicial determination of obscenity.[34] And the entire subject of child pornography, which we discuss in Chapters 4 and 11 is governed by different principles and substantially different legal standards.

The constitutionally-based definition of obscenity is enforced not only by requiring that that definition be used in obscenity trials, but also, and more importantly, by close judicial scrutiny of materials determined to be obscene. This scrutiny, at both trial and appellate levels, is designed to ensure that non-obscene material is not erroneously determined to be obscene. The leading case here is the 1974 unanimous Supreme Court decision in Jenkins v. Georgia,[35] which involved a conviction in Georgia of the Hollywood motion picture Carnal Knowledge. In reversing the conviction, the Supreme Court made clear that regardless of what the local community standards of that community may have been, the First Amendment prohibited any community, regardless of its standards, from finding that a motion picture such as this appealed to the prurient interest or was patently offensive.[36] Thus, although appeal to the prurient interest and patent offensiveness are to be determined in the first instance by reference to local standards, it is clear after Jenkins that the range of local variation that the Supreme Court will permit consistent with the First Amendment is in fact quite limited.

In the final analysis, the effect of Miller, Jenkins, and a large number of other Supreme Court and lower court cases is to limit obscenity prosecutions to "hard core"[37] material devoid of anything except the most explicit and offensive representations of sex. As we explained in our Introduction to this part, we believe that the late Justice Stewart was more perceptive than he has been given credit for having been in saying of hard-core pornography that he knew it when he saw it.[38] Now that we have seen much of it, we are all confident that we too know it when we see it, but we also know that others have used this and other terms to encompass a range of materials wider than that which the Supreme Court permits to be restricted, and wider than that which

---

33. *Smith v. California*, 361 U.S. 147 (1959). The principle was reaffirmed in *Hamling v. United States*, 418 U.S. 87 (1974), which also made clear that the defendant need not be shown to have known that the materials were legally obscene.

34. See, *Heller v. New York*, 413 U.S. 483 (1973); *Roaden v. Kentucky*, 413 U.S. 496 (1973).

35. 418 U.S. 153 (1974).

36. The third facet of the *Miller* test, that the work lack "serious literary, artistic, political, or scientific value," is never in any event to be determined by reference to local standards. Here the frame of reference must in all cases be national. *Smith v. United States*, 431 U.S. 291 (1977).

37. The Supreme Court in fact uses the term in *Miller*.

38. "I have reached the conclusion . . . that under the First and Fourteenth Amendments criminal laws in this area are constitutionally limited to hard-core pornography. I shall not today attempt further to define the kinds of material I understand to be embraced within that shorthand description; and perhaps I could never succeed in intelligently doing so. But I know it when I see it, and the motion picture involved in this case is not that." *Jacobellis v. Ohio*, 378 U.S. 184, 197 (1964) (Stewart, J., concurring).

most of us think ought to be restricted. But it should be plain both from the law, and from inspection of the kinds of material that the law has allowed to be prosecuted, that only the most thoroughly explicit materials, overwhelmingly devoted to patently offensive and explicit representations, and unmitigated by any significant amount of anything else, can be and are in fact determined to be legally obscene.

IS THE SUPREME COURT RIGHT?

We cannot ignore our own obligations not to recommend what we believe to be unconstitutional. Numerous people, in both oral and written evidence, have urged upon us the view that the Supreme Court's approach is a mistaken interpretation of the First Amendment. They have argued that we should conclude that any criminal prosecution based on the distribution[39] to consenting adults of sexually explicit material, no matter how offensive to some, and no matter how hard-core, and no matter how devoid of literary, artistic, political, or scientific value, is impermissible under the First Amendment.

We have taken these arguments seriously. In light of the facts that the Supreme Court did not in *Roth* or since unanimously conclude that obscenity is outside of the coverage of the First Amendment, and that its 1973 rulings were all decided by a scant 5-4 majority on this issue, there is no doubt that the issue was debatable within the Supreme Court, and thus could hardly be without difficulty. Moreover, we recognize that the bulk of scholarly commentary is of the opinion that the Supreme Court's resolution of and basic approach to the First Amendment issues is incorrect.[40] With dissent existing even within the Supreme Court, and with disagreement with the Supreme Court majority's approach predominant among legal scholars, we could hardly ignore the possibility that the Supreme Court might be wrong on this issue, and that we would wish to find protected that which the Supreme Court found unprotected.

There are both less and more plausible challenges to the Supreme Court's approach

to obscenity. Among the least plausible, and usually more rhetorical device than serious argument, is the view that the First Amendment is in some way an "absolute," protecting, quite simply, all speech. Even Justices Black and Douglas, commonly taken to be "absolutists," would hardly have protected all spoken or written acts under the First Amendment, and on closer inspection all those accused of or confessing to "absolutism" would at the very least apply their absolutism to a range of spoken or written acts smaller than the universe of all spoken, written or pictorial acts. This is not to deny that under the views of many, including Black and Douglas, what is now considered obscene should be within the universe of what is absolutely protected. But "absolutism" in unadulterated form seems largely a strawman, and we see no need to use it as a way of avoiding difficult questions.

Much more plausible is the view not that the First Amendment protects all spoken, written, or pictorial acts, but that all spoken, written, or pictorial acts are at least in some way covered, even if not ultimately protected, by the First Amendment. That is, even if the government may regulate some such acts, it may never do so unless it has a reason substantially better than the reasons that normally are sufficient to justify governmental action. Whether this heightened standard of justification is described as a "clear and present danger," or "compelling interest," or some standard less stringent than those, the view is still that regulating any spoken, written, or pictorial acts requires a particularly good reason. And when applied to the regulation of obscenity, so the argument goes, the reasons supplied and the empirical evidence offered remain too speculative to meet this especially high burden of justification.

Other views accept the fact that not all spoken, written, or pictorial acts need meet this especially high burden of justification. Only those acts that in some way relate to the purposes or principles of the First Amendment are covered, but, it is argued, even the hardest-core pornographic item is within the First Amendment's coverage. To some this is

---

39. We do not in this Report discuss *Stanley v. Georgia*, 394 U.S. 557 (1969), in which the Supreme Court held the mere *possession* of even legally obscene material to be constitutionally protected. We do not discuss *Stanley* because nothing we recommend is inconsistent with it, and no one has suggested to us that we should urge that *Stanley* be overruled.

40. See, e.g., Kalven, *The Metaphysics of the Law of Obscenity,* 1960 Sup. Ct. Rev. 1; Henkin, *Morals and the Constitution: The Sin of Obscenity,* 63 Colum. L. Rev. 391 (1963); Richards, *Free Speech and Obscenity Law: Toward a Moral Theory of the First Amendment,* 123 U. Pa. L. Rev. 45 (1974).

because both the distribution and use of such items are significant aspects of self-expression. And while not all acts of self-expression are covered by the First Amendment, acts of self-expression that take the form of books, magazines, and films are, according to the argument, so covered. These, it is argued, are the traditional media of communication, and when those media are used to express a different world view, or even merely to achieve sexual satisfaction, they remain the kinds of things towards which the First Amendment is directed. As a result, regulation of the process by which an alternative sexual vision is communicated, or regulation of the process by which people use the traditional media of communication to experience and to understand a different sexual vision, is as much a part of the First Amendment as communicating and experiencing different visions about, for example, politics or morals. A variant on this last argument, which takes obscenity to be within a range of First Amendment coverage admittedly smaller than the universe of communicative acts, looks not so much to the act or to the communication but instead to the government's reasons for regulating. If, so the argument goes, government's action in restricting is based on its reaction to a particular point of view, then the action is impermissible. Because it is the purpose of the First Amendment to allow all points of view to be expressed, an attempt by government to treat one point of view less favorably than another is unconstitutional for that reason alone, no matter how dangerous, offensive, or otherwise reprehensible the disfavored point of view may be.

We have heard witnesses articulate these various views intelligently and forcefully, and we have read more extensive versions of these arguments. They are not implausible by any means, but in the final analysis we remain unpersuaded that the fundamental direction of *Roth* and *Paris* is misguided. Indeed, we are confident that it is correct. Although we do not subscribe to the view that only political speech is covered by the First Amendment, we do not believe that a totally expansive approach is reasonable for society or conducive to preserving the particular values embodied in the First Amendment. The special power of the First Amendment ought, in our opinion, to be reserved for the conveying of arguments and information in a way that surpasses some admittedly low threshold of cognitive appeal, whether that appeal be emotive, intellectual, aesthetic, or informational. We have no doubt that this low threshold will be surpassed by a wide range of sexually explicit material conveying unpopular ideas about sex in a manner that is offensive to most people, and we accept that this is properly part of a vision of the First Amendment that is designed substantially to protect unpopular ways of saying unpopular things. But we also have little doubt that most of what we have seen that to us qualifies as hard-core material falls below this minimal threshold of cognitive or similar appeal. Lines are of course not always easy to draw, but we find it difficult to understand how much of the material we have seen can be considered to be even remotely related to an exchange of views in the marketplace of ideas, to an attempt to articulate a point of view, to an attempt to persuade, or to an attempt seriously to convey through literary or artistic means a different vision of humanity or of the world. We do not deny that in a different context and presented in a different way, material as explicit as that which we have seen *could* be said to contain at least some of all of these characteristics. But we also have no doubt that these goals are remote from the goals of virtually all distributors or users of this material, and we also have no doubt that these values are present in most standard pornographic items to an extraordinarily limited degree.

In light of this, we are of the opinion that not only society at large but the First Amendment itself suffers if the essential appeal of the First Amendment is dissipated on arguments related to material so tenuously associated with any of the purposes or principles of the First Amendment. We believe it necessary that the plausibility of the First Amendment be protected, and we believe it equally necessary for this society to ensure that the First Amendment retains the strength it must have when it is most needed. This strength cannot reside exclusively in the courts, but must reside as well in widespread acceptance of the importance of the First Amendment. We fear that this acceptance is jeopardized when the First Amendment too often becomes the rhetorical device by which the commercial trade in materials directed virtually exclusively at sexual arousal is defended. There is a risk that in that process public willingness to defend and to accept the First Amendment will be lost, and the likely losers will be those who would speak out harshly, provocatively, and often offensively against the prevailing order, including the prevailing order with respect to sex. The manner of presentation and distribution of most standard pornography confirms the view that at bottom the predominant use of such material is as a masturbatory aid. We do not say that there is anything necessarily wrong with that for that reason. But once the predominant use, and the appeal to that predominant use, becomes apparent, what emerges is that much of what this material involves is not so much portrayal of sex, or discussion of sex, but simply sex itself. As sex itself, the arguments for or against restriction are serious, but they are arguments properly removed from the First Amendment questions that surround primarily materials whose overwhelming use is not as a short-term masturbatory aid. Whether the state should, for example, prohibit masturbation in certain establishments that are open to the public is a question that some would wish to debate, but it is certainly not a First Amendment question. Similarly, the extent to which sex itself is and under what circumstances constitutionally protected is again an interesting and important constitutional question, but it is not usefully seen as a First Amendment question.[41]

We recognize, of course, that using a picture of sex as a masturbatory aid is different from the simple act of masturbation, or any other form of sex. The very fact that pictures and words are used compels us to take First Amendment arguments more seriously than would be the case if the debate were about prostitution. Still, when we look at the standard pornographic item in its standard context of distribution and use, we find it difficult to avoid the conclusion that this material is so far removed from any of the central purposes of the First Amendment, and so close to so much of the rest of the sex industry, that including such material within the coverage of the First Amendment seems highly attenuated.

Like any other act, the act of making, distributing, and using pornographic items contains and sends messages. For government to act against some of these items on account of the messages involved may appear as problematic under the First Amendment, but to hold that such governmental action violates the First Amendment is to preclude government from taking action in every case in which government fears that the restricted action will be copied, or proliferate because of its acceptance. Government may prosecute scofflaws because it fears the message that laws ought to be violated, and it may restrict the use of certain products in part because it does not wish the message that the product is desirable to be widely disseminated in perhaps its most effective form. So too with reference to the kind of material with which we deal here. If we are correct in our conclusion that this material is far removed from the cognitive, emotive, aesthetic, informational, persuasive, or intellectual core of the First Amendment, we are satisfied that a governmental desire to restrict the material for the messages its use sends out does not bring the material any closer to the center.

We thus conclude not that obscenity regulation creates no First Amendment concerns, nor even that the Supreme Court's approach is necessarily correct. But we do believe the Supreme Court's approach is most likely correct, and we believe as well that arguments against the Supreme Court's approach are becoming increasingly attenuated as we focus on the kind of material commonly sold in "adults only" establishments in this country. We may be wrong, but most of us can see no good reason at the moment for substituting a less persuasive approach for the Supreme Court's more persuasive one.

THE RISKS OF ABUSE

Although we are satisfied that there is a category of material so overwhelmingly preoccupied with sexual explicitness, and so overwhelmingly devoid of anything else, that its regulation does no violence to the principles underlying the First Amendment, we recognize that this cannot be the end of the First Amendment analysis. We must evaluate

41. As this report is being written, the Supreme Court has under advisement after oral argument the case of *Bowers v. Hardwick*, 760 F.2d 1202 (11th Cir. 1985), Sup. Ct. Docket No. 85-140, challenging the constitutionality of the Georgia sodomy statute as applied to the private and consensual acts of two male homosexuals. The arguments rely primarily on constitutional claims of liberty, privacy, and freedom of association. If the Supreme Court strikes down the statute as unconstitutional, arguments other than the First Amendment might be available to challenge certain laws against certain uses of even legally obscene materials. Without such an action, however, such privacy or liberty arguments, which the Supreme Court rejected with respect to exhibition of obscene material to consenting adults in a theater in *Paris*, would be unlikely to succeed. *Doe v. Commonwealth's Attorney*, 403 F. Supp. 1199 (E.D. Va. 1975), *aff'd without opinion*, 425 U.S. 901 (1976).

the possibility that in practice materials other than these will be restricted, and that the effect therefore will be the restriction of materials that are substantially closer to what the First Amendment ought to protect than the items in fact aimed at by the *Miller* definition of obscenity. We must also evaluate what is commonly referred to as the "chilling effect," the possibility that, even absent actual restriction, creators of material that is not in fact legally obscene will refrain from those creative activities, or will steer further to the safe side of the line, for fear that their protected works will mistakenly be deemed obscene. And finally we must evaluate whether the fact of restriction of obscene material will act, symbolically, to foster a "censorship mentality" that will in less immediate ways encourage or lead to various restrictions, in other contexts, of material which ought not in a free society be restricted. We have heard in one form or another from numerous organizations of publishers, booksellers, actors, and librarians, as well as from a number of individual book and magazine publishers. Although most have urged general anti-censorship sentiments upon us, their oral and written submissions have failed to provide us with evidence to support claims of excess suppression in the name of the obscenity laws, and indeed the evidence is to the contrary. The president of the Association of American Publishers testified that to his knowledge none of his members had even been threatened with enforcement of the criminal law against obscenity, and the American Library Association could find no record of any prosecution of a librarian on obscenity charges. Other groups of people involved in publishing, bookselling, or theatrical organizations relied exclusively on examples of excess censorship from periods of time no more recent than the 1940s. And still others were even less helpful, telling us, for example, that censorship was impermissible because "This is the United States, not the Soviet Union." We know that, but we know as well that difficult issues do not become easy by the use of inflammatory rhetoric. We wish that many of these people or groups had been able to provide concrete examples to support their fears of excess censorship.

Throughout recent and not so recent history, excess censorship, although not necessarily prevalent, can hardly be said not to have occurred. As a result we have not been content to rest on the hollowness of the assertions of many of those who have reminded us of this theme. If there is a problem, we have our own obligations to identify it, even if witnesses before us have been unable to do so. Yet when we do our own researches, we discover that, with few exceptions, the period from 1974[42] to the present is marked by strikingly few actual or threatened prosecutions of material that is plainly not legally obscene. We do not say that there have been none. Attempted and unsuccessful actions against the film *Caligula* by the United States Customs Service, against *Playboy* magazine in Atlanta and several other places, and against some other plainly non-obscene publications indicate that mistakes *can* be made. But since 1974 such mistakes have been extremely rare, and the mistakes have all been remedied at some point in the process. While we wish there would be no mistakes, we are confident that application of *Miller* has been overwhelmingly limited to materials that would satisfy anyone's definition of "hard core."

Even without successful or seriously threatened prosecutions, it still may be the case that the very possibility of such an action deters filmmakers, photographers, and writers from exercising their creative abilities to the fullest. Once it appears that the likelihood of actual or seriously threatened prosecutions is almost completely illusory, however, we are in a quandary about how to respond to these claims of "chilling." We are in no position to deny the reality of someone's fears, but in almost every case those fears are unfounded. Where, as here, the fears seem to be fears of phantom dangers, we are hard pressed to say that the law is mistaken. It is those who are afraid who are mistaken. At least for the past ten years, not one remotely serious author, photographer, or filmmaker has had anything real to fear from the obscenity laws. The line between what is legally obscene and what is not is now so far away from their work that even substantially mistaken applications of current law would leave these individuals untouched. In light of that, we do not see their fears, however real to them, as a sufficient reason now to reconsider our views about the extent of First Amendment protection.

---

42. 1974 seems the most relevant date because that was the year in which the Supreme Court, in *Jenkins v. Georgia*, 418 U.S. 153 (1974), made it clear that determinations of obscenity were not primarily a matter of local discretion.

Much more serious, much more real, and much less in our control, is the extent to which non-governmental or governmental but non-prohibitory actions may substantially influence what is published and what is not. What television scriptwriters write is in reality controlled by what television producers will buy, which is in turn controlled by what sponsors will sponsor and what viewers will view. Screenwriters may be effectively censored by the extent to which producers or studios desire to gain an "R" rating rather than an "X," or a "PG" rather than an "R," or an "R" rather than a "PG." Book and magazine writers and publishers are restricted by what stores are willing to sell, and stores are restricted by what people are willing to buy. Writers of textbooks are in a sense censored by what school districts are willing to buy, authors are censored by what both bookstores and librarians are willing to offer, and librarians are censored by what boards of trustees are willing to tolerate.

In all of these settings there have been excesses. But every one of these settings involves some inevitable choice based on content. We think it unfortunate when *Catcher in the Rye* is unavailable in a high school library, but none of us would criticize the decision to keep *Lady Chatterley's Lover*, plainly protected by the First Amendment, out of the junior high schools.

We regret that legitimate bookstores have been pressured to remove from their shelves legitimate and serious discussions of sexuality, but none of us would presume to tell a Catholic bookseller that in choosing books he should not discriminate against books favoring abortion. Motion picture studios are unable to support an infinite number of screenwriters, and their choice to support those who write about families rather than about homosexuality, for example, is not only permissible, but is indeed itself protected by the First Amendment.

Where there have been excesses, and we do not ignore the extent to which the number of those excesses seems to be increasing, they seem often attributable to the plainly mistaken notion that the idea of "community standards" is a carte blanche to communities to determine entirely for themselves what is obscene. As we have tried once again to make clear in this report, nothing could be further from the truth. Apart from this, however, the excesses that have been reported to us are excesses that can only remotely be attributed to the obscenity laws. In a world of choice and of scarce resources, every one of these excesses could take place even were there no obscenity laws at all. In a world without obscenity law, television producers, motion picture studios, public library trustees, boards of education, convenience stores, and bookstores could still all choose to avoid any mention or discussion of sex entirely. And in a world without obscenity laws, all of these institutions and others could and would still make censorious choices based on their own views about politics, morals, religion, or science. Thus, the link between obscenity law and the excess narrowness, at times, of the choices made by private industry as well as government is far from direct.

Although the link is not direct, we are in no position to deny that there may be some psychological connection between obscenity laws and their enforcement and a general perception that non-governmental restriction of anything dealing with sex is justifiable. We find the connection unjustifiable, but that is not to say that it may not exist in the world. But just as vigorous and vocal enforcement of robbery laws may create the environment in which vigilantes feel justified in punishing offenders outside of legal processes, so too may obscenity law create an environment in which discussions of sexuality are effectively stifled. But we cannot ignore the extent to which much of this stifling, to the extent it exists, is no more than the exercise by citizens of their First Amendment rights to buy what they want to buy, and the exercise by others of First Amendment rights to sell or make what they wish. Choices are not always exercised wisely, but the leap from some unwise choices to the unconstitutionality of criminal laws only remotely related to those unwise choices is too big a leap for us to make.

C H A P T E R • 4

The Market and the Industry

THE MARKET FOR SEXUAL EXPLICITNESS

More than in 1957, when the law of obscenity became inextricably a part of constitutional law, more than in 1970, when the President's Commission on Obscenity and Pornography issued its report, and indeed more than just a year ago in 1985, we live in a society unquestionably pervaded by sexual explicitness. In virtually every medium, from books to magazines to newspapers to music to radio to network television to cable television, matters relating to sex are discussed, described, and depicted with a frankness and an explicitness of detail that has accelerated dramatically within a comparatively short period of time. To attempt to isolate the causes of this phenomenon is inevitably to embark on a futile enterprise, for the sexual openness of contemporary America is unquestionably a product of that immense interplay of factors that makes contemporary America what it is in numerous aspects apart from sexual explicitness.

We have spent much of our time investigating the nature of the industry that produces, distributes, and sells sexually explicit materials, for we do not believe we could responsibly have drawn conclusions relating to that industry unless we became familiar with it. The results of this investigation are set out comprehensively and in detail in a later Part of this Report, but we feel nevertheless that a general overview of the market and the industry is necessary here.

The pervasiveness of sexual explicitness in the society in which we live underscores the importance of distinguishing what might plausibly be characterized as "pornographic" from the entire range of descriptions, depictions, and discussions that are more sexually explicit than would have been the case in earlier times, and that, for that reason, engender some or substantial objection from various people within the society. We find it useful in this Report to describe some particularly salient aspects of the pornography industry, but any such discussion must be preceded by a brief survey of some other forms of sexually explicit material that are usefully contrasted with the more unquestionably pornographic.

The Motion Picture Industry

With few exceptions, what might be called the "mainstream" or "legitimate" or "Hollywood" motion picture industry does not produce the kinds of films that would commonly be made available in "adults only" outlets. The films shown in such establishments, the ones containing little if any plot, unalloyed explicitness, and little other than an intent to arouse, are not the products of the motion picture industry with which most people are familiar. Nevertheless, sexuality, in varying degrees of explicitness or, to many, offensiveness, is a significant part of many mainstream motion pictures. One result of this phenomenon has been the rating system of the MPAA. Because those ratings are so frequently used as shorthand, and frequently erroneous shorthand, for certain forms of content, a brief description of the rating system may be in order.

The rating system, established in 1968, has no legal force, but is designed to provide information for distributors, exhibitors, and viewers of motion pictures. At the present time there are five different categories within the rating system. Motion pictures rated "G" are considered suitable for everyone, and people of all ages are admitted when such films are shown. The "PG" rating, which stands for "parental guidance suggested," still allows all to be admitted, but warns parents that some material may not be suitable for children. Films receive a PG rating if there is more than minimal violence, if there is brief nudity, or if there are non-explicit scenes involving sex. A "PG-13" rating is used where more parental caution is suggested, especially with respect to children under the age of thirteen.

Most germane to this Report are the ratings of "R" and "X." An "R" rating indicates a restricted film, and those under the age of seventeen are admitted only if accompanied by a parent or guardian. Motion pictures with this rating may be somewhat, substantially, or exclusively devoted to themes of sex or violence. They may contain harsh language, sexual activity, and nudity. Films with this rating, however, do not contain explicit sexual activity. If a film contains explicit sexual activity, or if, in some cases, it contains particularly extreme quantities and varieties of violence, it is rated "X", and no one under the age of seventeen may be admitted.

Only in rare cases will anything resembling standard pornographic fare be submitted to the MPAA for a rating. More often such material will have a self-rated "X" designation, or will have no rating, or will have some unofficial promotional rating such as "XXX." It is important to recognize, however, that although no motion picture not submitted to the MPAA can have any rating other than "X," and that although standard pornographic items would unquestionably receive an "X" rating if submitted, not all, and indeed, not many *officially* "X" rated motion pictures would commonly be considered to be pornographic. Although the nature of what kind of content will get what rating will change with the times, it remains the case that the "X" rating, especially when applied to the small number of mainstream films that officially receive that rating after submission to the MPAA, is not in every case synonymous with what most people would consider pornography.

Sexually Explicit Magazines

Although the sexual content of large numbers of magazines has increased in recent years, particular attention is often focused on so-called "men's" magazines, commonly referred to within the trade as "male sophisticate" magazines. In recent years variations aimed at a female audience have also appeared, but the genre remains largely directed to men.

Magazines of this variety tend to be produced and distributed in a manner no dissimilar to the production and distribution methods for most mass-circulation magazines. It is almost misleading to consider them as one category, however, for such magazines vary enormously in content and explicitness. A very few magazines of this variety combine their sexual content with a substantial amount of non-sexually oriented, and frequently quite serious, textual or photographic matter. Some magazines have for their photographs little more than suggestive nudity, while a number of others feature significant amounts of simulated or actual sexual activity. From the perspective we adopt and explain in Chapter 5, *all* of the magazines in this category contain at least some material that we would consider "degrading." Some contain a large amount of such degrading material, and some also contain sexually violent material.

With respect to the category of the legally obscene, some of the magazines in this category could not plausibly be considered legally obscene, while others have occasionally been determined to be legally obscene by particular courts. As a purely empirical matter, such determinations of obscenity for even the most explicit and offensive of these magazines seem aberrational, and by and large most of these magazines circulate widely throughout the country without significant legal attack.

Television

Television has become technologically more diverse than in earlier years, and it is no longer possible even to think of television as one medium. Broadcast television, whether network or local, has a frequent explicit or implicit sexual orientation but, with only the rarest exceptions, sexual activity of any explicitness at all, or even frontal nudity, has been largely absent from broadcast television. In part this is explained by rules and regulatory practices of the Federal Communications Commission, and in part this is explained by the practices of stations, networks, and sponsors. But whatever the cause, the amount of nudity, sexual innuendo, and sex itself on broadcast television has traditionally been a far cry from even moderate levels of sexual explicitness, although it is plainly the case that the degree of sexual explicitness in depiction, in theme, and in language on broadcast television has been increasing substantially in recent years.

Cable television, however, by which we include satellite as well, is quite different. Under current law, cable is not subject to the same range of Federal Communications Commission content regulation, and as a result is often substantially more sexually explicit than anything that would be available on broadcast television. This increased explicitness may take the form of talk shows or call-in shows specializing in sexual advice, music videos featuring strong sexual and violent themes, cable channels that specialize in sexual fare, and more general purpose cable channels may offer mainstream motion pictures that would not in uncut form be shown on broadcast television. Although some motion pictures available on cable might be deemed legally obscene in some areas, and although much of this material is highly explicit and offensive to many, by and large the sexually explicit material available on cable would not be of the type likely to be determined to be legally obscene. More often, what is available, and it does vary from area to area and channel to channel, is a degree of sexuality somewhat closer to what is available in a mainstream motion picture theater, but would not be available on broadcast television.

In some sense the video tape cassette ought to be considered a form of television, since the television is the device by which such cassettes are viewed. But the cassettes themselves are so variable in content that generalization is difficult. Much of what people rent or, less frequently, buy to watch at home is standard motion picture theater fare, and therefore can encompass anything from the kinds of films that are rated "G" to the kinds of films that are rated "R," and occasionally the kinds of films that are officially rated "X" by the MPAA. In many video outlets, however, a range of even more sexually explicit material is available, not dissimilar to what might be shown in an "adults only" theater. Although much of this material would commonly be considered pornographic, and although much of it might in some areas be

found to be legally obscene, it has in the past tended to be more on the conventional end of such material, obviously reflecting the desires of patrons of an establishment offering a full range of video material. More recently, however, some less conventional material has become available in some full range of video outlets. Finally, there is the material available either in "adults only" establishments offering many types of materials, or in "adults only" outlets offering video tapes. This material, although viewed at home, is for all practical purposes the same as that which would be shown in "adults only" theaters or peep shows, and the same range of sexual themes and practices is commonly available.

THE PORNOGRAPHY INDUSTRY

In terms of methods of production, methods of distribution, and methods of ultimate sale to consumers, the pornography industry itself must be distinguished from the outlets for some degree of sexual explicitness discussed in the previous section. The true pornography industry is quite simply different from and separate from the industry that publishes "men's" magazines, the industry that offers some degree of sexually oriented material on broadcast and cable television, and the mainstream motion picture industry. In some rare instances there may be some linkages between the two, but in general little more than confusion is served by concentrating on these linkages rather than on the major differences.

The Production of Films, Video Tapes, and Magazines

There can be little doubt that there has within the last ten to twenty years been a dramatic increase in the size of the industry producing the kinds of sexually explicit materials that would generally be conceded to be pornographic. One consequence of this is that the industry is not as clandestine as it was in earlier years. Nevertheless, when this industry is compared to the kinds of industries that produce more mainstream materials, it is still the case that the production of pornographic materials is a practice and a business that remains substantially "underground."

Approximately eighty percent of the American production of this type of motion picture and video tape takes place in an around Los Angeles, California. In part this is a consequence of the location there of technical personnel, such as camera operators, who either are, have been, or wish to be employed in the mainstream motion picture industry. Indeed, this description applies as well to many of the performers in these films, although, unlike technical personnel, the likelihood of a performer who is involved in pornographic materials simultaneously or eventually working in the mainstream motion picture industry is minuscule.

Production of these materials tends to be done on a rather limited budget, usually in temporary locations such as motel rooms or rented houses, and usually in quite a short period of time. Often not only the premises, but the photographic equipment as well, is rented for only the limited time necessary to make the film. It is not uncommon for producer, director, and scriptwriter to be the same person. In many cases the performers are secured through one of a number of agents who specialize in securing performers for highly sexually explicit films. Although there is virtually no overlap between this industry and the mainstream film industry, the method of securing performers for films is largely similar, with agents providing producers with books describing various performers, and with producers often interviewing a number of possible performers before selecting the ones to be used.

As this Report is being written, the technological nature of the industry is in the midst of transition from photographic motion pictures to video tape. The proliferation of the home video tape recorder is in many respects transforming the industry, and in addition the process of producing a video tape tends to be more efficient and less expensive than the process of producing a photographic motion picture. With respect to aspects of production that are not technical, however, this technological development has had little effect on the production side of the industry.

The production of the standard variety of pornographic magazine, the kind likely to be sold in an "adults only" establishment for a rather high price, is in many respects similar to the production of pornographic motion pictures and video tapes. The process again operates in a partially clandestine manner, although it is much more likely here that the production and distribution processes will be combined. When this is the case taking the photographs, assembling them with some amount of textual material, and physically manufacturing the magazine will all take place at the same location.

With respect to the business of producing pornographic paperback books containing nothing but text, the writing, production, and distribution processes are again likely to be combined. Although independent authors are occasionally used, more common is the use of a full-time staff of authors, employed by the producer to write this kind of book at a rapid rate.

Channels of Distribution

The process of distribution of films is rapidly in the process of becoming history. The photographic motion picture film typically shown in "adults only" theaters is rapidly decreasing in popularity, along with the theaters themselves, as the video tape cassette becomes the dominant mode of presentation of non-still material. Many of these video tapes are sold or rented for home consumption, and many are shown in "peep show" establishments. The effect of this is that the "adults only" theater, in any event an expensive operation, and one that is more visible than many patrons would like, is becoming an increasing rarity. Similar trends are apparent with respect to mainstream motion pictures and the theaters in which they are shown as well, although the effect of video tape on the pornographic film industry is much more dramatic, probably owing in large part to the fact that a night out at the movies remains substantially more socially acceptable in contemporary America than a night out at the peep show.

The films that are shown in "adults only" theaters, or that are shown by use of traditional projection equipment in peep shows, tend to be distributed nationally by use of complex and sophisticated distribution networks concentrating exclusively on highly sexually explicit material. There are exceptions to this generalization and one reason for the attention that focused in the early 1970s on films such as "Deep Throat," "The Devil in Miss Jones," and "Behind the Green Door" was that the standard methods of distribution and exhibition were changed so that films such as these were shown in theaters usually showing more mainstream films. But apart from exceptions such as these, most of the chain of distribution involves producers who deal only in this kind of material, distributors and wholesalers whose entire business is devoted to highly sexually explicit materials, and theaters or peep shows catering exclusively to adults desiring access to very sexually explicit material.

With respect to video tapes, most of the distribution is on a national scale, and most of that national distribution is controlled by a relatively limited number of enterprises. These distributors duplicate in large quantities the tapes they have purchased from producers, and then sell them to wholesalers, frequently with some promotional materials, who in turn sell them to retailers specializing in this type of material, or to more generally oriented video retailers who will include some of this material along with their more mainstream offerings. Based on the evidence provided to us, it appears as if perhaps as many as half of all of the general video retailers in the country include within their offerings at least some material that, by itself, would commonly be conceded to be pornographic.

Magazines are also distributed nationally, and again are likely first to be sold to wholesalers who will then sell to retailers. This process, however, likely culminating in a sale at an "adults only" outlet, does not account for as high a proportion of the total sales as it does for films or video tapes. More so than for films or tapes, many of the magazines are sold by mail, usually as a result of advertisements placed in similar magazines, in pornographic books containing text, and even in more mainstream but sexually oriented publications. There is some indication that the video tape has hurt the pornographic magazine industry as well as the pornographic motion picture industry. The retail prices for such magazines, within the recent past commonly in the range of from ten to twenty-five dollars per magazine, are in some geographical areas likely to be substantially discounted, and adult establishments appear to be offering an increasing percentage of video tapes and a decreasing percentage of books and magazines.

The Retail Level

Apart from mail order, and apart from the rental of pornographic video tapes in general use video retail outlets, most pornographic material reaches the consumer through retail establishments specializing in this material. These outlets, which we refer to as "adults only" outlets or establishments, usually limit entry to those eighteen years of age or older, but the strictness of the enforcement of the limitation to adults varies considerably from outlet to outlet. At times these retail outlets will take the form of theaters in which only material of this variety is shown, and at times they will be "adults only" outlets specializing in books and magazine. Increasingly, however, the peep show, often combined with an outlet for the sale of pornographic books and magazines, is a major form of meeting consumer demand.

The typical peep show is located on the premises of an "adults only" establishment selling large numbers of pornographic magazines, along with some other items, such as pornographic text-only books, sexual paraphernalia, sexually oriented newspapers, and video tapes. The peep show is often separated by a doorway or screen from the rest of the establishment, and consists of a number of booths in which a film, or, more likely now, a video tape, can be viewed. The patron inserts tokens into a slot for a certain amount of viewing time, and the patron is usually alone or with one other person within the particular booth. The peep show serves the purpose of allowing patrons to masturbate or to engage in sexual activity with others in some degree of privacy, at least compared to an adult theater, while watching the pornographic material. In a later section of our report describing these establishments we note in detail the generally unsanitary conditions in such establishments. The booths seem rarely to be cleaned, and the evidence of frequent sexual activity is apparent. Peep shows are a particularly common location for male homosexual activity within and between the booths, and the material available for viewing in some of the booths is frequently oriented towards the male homosexual.

There are, of course, establishments offering adult material that do not contain peep shows. Although video tapes and various items of sexual paraphernalia are likely to be sold, the bulk of the stock in these establishments consists of pornographic magazines, frequently arranged by sexual preference. There can be little doubt that the range of sexual preferences catered to by magazines is wider than that of any other form of pornography. As the listing of titles later in this report makes clear, virtually any conceivable, and quite a few inconceivable, sexual preferences are featured in the various specialty magazines, and materials featuring sado-masochism, bestiality, urination and defecation in a sexual context, and substantially more unusual practices even than those are a significant portion of what is available.

THE ROLE OF ORGANIZED CRIME

We have spent a considerable amount of our time attempting to determine whether there is a connection between the pornography industry and what is commonly taken to be "organized crime." After hearing from a large number of witnesses, mostly law enforcement personnel, after reading a number of reports prepared by various law enforcement agencies, and after consulting sources such as trial transcripts, published descriptions, and the like, we believe that such a connection does exist.

We recognize that the statement that there is a connection between the pornography industry and organized crime is contrary to the conclusion reached by the President's Commission on Obscenity and Pornography in 1970. That Commission concluded that:

> Although many persons have alleged that organized crime works hand-in-glove with the distributors of adult materials, there is at present no concrete evidence to support these statements. The hypothesis that organized criminal elements either control or are "moving in" on the distribution of sexually oriented materials will doubtless continue to be speculated upon. The panel finds that there is insufficient evidence at present to warrant any conclusion in this regard.

Caution about jumping too easily to conclusions about organized crime involvement in the pornography industry was further induced by the evidence offered to us by Director William H. Webster of the Federal Bureau of Investigation. Director Webster surveyed the FBI field offices throughout the country, and reported to us that "about three quarters of those [fifty-nine] offices indicated that they have no verifiable information that organized crime was involved either directly or through extortion in the manufacture of pornography. Several offices, did, however, report some involvement by members and associates of organized crime."[43] We reach our conclusions in the face of a negative conclusion by the 1970 Commission, evidence by the FBI, not so much because we disagree, but because we feel that more careful analysis will reveal that

the discrepancies are less than they may at first appear.

One leading cause of conflicting views about organized crime involvement in pornography is that there are conflicting views about what organized crime is. To many people organized crime consists of that organization or network of related organizations commonly referred to by law enforcement personnel and others as La Cosa Nostra. This organization, which we describe in much more detail later in our Report specifically addressing on organized crime, is a highly structured and elaborately subdivided organization in some way involved in an enormous range of criminal activities. It has its own hierarchy, its own formalized system of ranks and methods of advancement, and its own procedures for settling disputes. Commonly, although in our view erroneously, La Cosa Nostra and "organized crime" are synonymous.

To other people organized crime consists of any large and organized enterprise engaged in criminal activity, regardless of any connection with La Cosa Nostra. To the extent that enterprises have continuity and a defined membership and engage in crime, then tis is considered to be organized crime.

Finally, to still others the "best" definition of organized crime lies somewhere in between. For them organized crime consists of a large and organized enterprise engaged in criminal activity, with a continuity, a structure, and a defined membership, *and* that is likely to use *other* crimes and methods of corruption, such as extortion, assault, murder, or bribery, in the service of its primary criminal enterprise.

These differences in definition are especially important with respect to identifying the connection between the pornography industry and organized crime, because much of the evidence supports the conclusion that major parts of the industry are controlled by organizations that fit the second or third but not the first of the foregoing definitions. In particular, there is strong evidence that a great deal of the pornographic film and video tape distribution, is controlled by one ✂
✂   , operating out of the Cleveland area, but with operations and controlled organizations throughout the country. Although we inevitably must rely on secondary evidence, it

---

43. We note, however, that a report prepared by the FBI in 1978, which is included in a later portion of this report, contains detailed information regarding various links between organized crime and the pornography industry.

appears to us that ✂ enterprise is highly organized and predominantly devoted to the vertically integrated production, distribution, and sale of materials that would most likely be determined to be legally obscene in most parts of the country. Of this we are certain, and to that extent we could say that significant parts of the pornography industry are controlled by organized crime. We also have some but less clear evidence that organizations like ✂ but not quite as large, play similar roles, and that all of these various organizations at times have employed other activities that themselves violate the law in order to further the production, distribution, and sale of pornographic materials. In this sense these organizations would fit the third as well as the second definition of organized crime.

We also have strong reason to believe, however, that neither ✂ organization, nor some substantially smaller ones, are themselves part of La Cosa Nostra. In that sense this part of the industry would not fit the first of the above definitions of organized crime. We do not say that there are no connections with La Cosa Nostra. On the contrary, there seems to be evidence, frequently quite strong evidence, of working arrangements, accommodations, assistance, some sharing of funds, and the like, as well as evidence of control by La Cosa Nostra, but nothing that would justify saying that these organizations are La Cosa Nostra or are part of La Cosa Nostra.

Much the same could be said about the relationship between smaller pornography operators and La Cosa Nostra. Again there seems little evidence of direct ownership, operation, or control, but there does seem to be a significant amount of evidence that "protection" of these smaller operators by La Cosa Nostra is both available and required. This applies in some areas to distribution, in some to production, and in some to retail outlets themselves, in much the same way that it applies frequently to many more legitimate businesses. But we are not reluctant to conclude that in many aspects of the pornography business that La Cosa Nostra is getting a piece of the action.

This is not to say that La Cosa Nostra is not itself engaged in pornography. There also seems strong evidence that significant portions of the pornographic magazine industry, the peep show industry, and the pornographic film industry are either directly oper-

ated or closely controlled by La Cosa Nostra members or very close associates. Major portions of these industries seem to be as much a part of La Cosa Nostra as any other of their activities. At times there is direct involvement by La Cosa Nostra even with the day-to-day workings of business, and in many cases there is clear control even when the everyday management is left to others. In many of the reports and other documents we have received there has been evidence to the effect that members of the Columbo, DeCavalcante, Gambino, and Luchese "families" have been actively in as well as merely associated with the production, distribution, and sale of unquestionably pornographic materials. There is much evidence that alleged La Cosa Nostra members such as Robert ✂ and others are or have in the recent past been major figures in the national distribution of such materials. Although we cannot say that every piece of evidence we have received to this effect is true, the possibility that none of this cumulative evidence is true is so remote that we do not take it seriously.

As was the case with many other topics within our mandate, our lack of investigative resources has made it impossible to investigate these matters directly. Moreover, the matters to be investigated with respect to organized crime are, as has been well known for decades, so clandestine that thorough investigation without conflicting information is virtually impossible to accomplish. Nevertheless, there has been much investigation by federal and state authorities, and we have found it important to rely on those investigations. We include as an appendix to the later specific discussion of organized crime a number of those reports prepared by other law enforcement agencies. We are indebted to all of those who have worked on these reports, for without them our investigation would have been much less complete. At times there is information in these reports that we are unsure of, but we have little doubt as to the general truth of the big picture painted by these reports, and we have little hesitancy in relying on them to the extent either of agreeing with the big picture, or of agreeing with specific facts where those facts recur in consistent form in information from a number of different sources. The general picture seems clear, and we invite recourse to those specific reports to fill out this general conclusion that seems most appropriate as a statement from us.

The Question of Harm

MATTERS OF METHOD

Harm and Regulation—The Scope of Our Inquiry

A central part of our mission has been to examine the question of whether pornography is harmful. In attempting to answer this question, we have made a conscious decision not to allow our examination of the harm question to be constricted by the existing legal/constitutional definition of the legally obscene. As explained in Chapter 3, we agree with that definition of principle, and we believe that in most cases it allows criminal prosecution of what ought to be prosecuted and prohibits criminal prosecution of what most of us believe is material properly protected by the First Amendment. In light of this, our decision to look at the potential for harm in a range of material substantially broader than the legally obscene requires some explanation. One reason for this approach was the fact that in some respects existing constitutional decisions permit non-prohibitory restrictions of material other than the legally obscene. With respect to zoning, broadcast regulation, and liquor licensing, existing Supreme Court case law permits some control, short of total prohibition, of the time, place, and manner in which sexually

explicit materials that are short of being legally obscene may be distributed. When these non-prohibitory techniques are used, the form of regulation is still constrained by constitutional considerations, but the regulation need not be limited only to that which has been or would be found legally obscene. To address fully the question of government regulation, therefore, requires that an examination of possible harm encompass a range of materials broader than the legally obscene.

Moreover, the range of techniques of social control is itself broader than the scope of any form of permissible or desirable governmental regulation. We discuss in Chapter 8 many of these techniques, including pervasive social condemnation, public protest, picketing, and boycotts. It is appropriate here, however, to emphasize that we do not see any necessary connection between what is protected by law (and therefore protected *from* law), on the one hand, and what citizens may justifiably object to and take non-governmental action against, on the other. And if it is appropriate for citizens justifiably to protest against some sexually explicit materials despite the fact that those materials are constitutionally protected, then it is appropriate for us to broaden the realm of our inquiry accordingly.[44]

Most importantly, however, we categori-

---

44. With respect to the general issue of condemnation, and especially with respect to the condemnation of specific materials by name, our role as a government commission is somewhat more problematic. At some point *governmental* condemnation may act effectively as governmental restraint (see, *Bantam Books, Inc. v. Sullivan*, 372 U.S.,p. 58 [1963], and we are therefore more cautious in condemning specific publications by name than citizens need be. This caution, however, does not mean that we feel that governmental agencies may not properly condemn even that which they cannot control. We feel that we have both the right and the duty to condemn, in some cases, that which is properly constitutionally protected, but we do so with more caution than is necessary when the condemnation comes from the citizenry and not the government.

cally reject the idea that material cannot be constitutionally protected, and properly so, while still being harmful. All of us, for example, feel that the inflammatory utterances of Nazis, the Ku Klux Klan, and racists of other varieties are harmful both to the individuals to whom their epithets are directed as well as to society as a whole. Yet all of us acknowledge and most of us support the fact that the harmful speeches of these people are nevertheless constitutionally protected. That the same may hold true with respect to some sexually explicit materials was at least our working assumption in deciding to look at a range of materials broader than the legally obscene. There is no reason whatsoever to suppose that such material is necessarily harmless just because it is and should remain protected by the First Amendment. As a result, we reject the notion that an investigation of the question of harm must be restricted to material unprotected by the Constitution.

The converse of this is equally true. Just as there is no necessary connection between the constitutionally protected and the harmless, so too is there no necessary connection between the constitutionally unprotected and the harmful. We examine the harm question with respect to material that is legally obscene because even if material is therefore unprotected by the First Amendment, it does not follow that it is harmful. That some sexually explicit material is constitutionally regulable does not answer the question of whether anything justifies its regulation. Accordingly, we do not take our acceptance of the current constitutional approach to obscenity as diminishing the need to examine the harms purportedly associated with the distribution or use of such material.

We thus take as substantially dissimilar the question of constitutional protection and the question of harm. Even apart from constitutional issues, we also take to be separate the question of the advisability of governmental regulation, all things considered, and the question of the harmfulness of some or all sexually explicit materials. The upshot of all of this is that we feel it entirely proper to identify harms that may accompany certain sexually explicit material before and independent of an inquiry into the desirability and constitutionality of regulating even that sexually explicit material that may be harmful. As a result, our inquiry into harm encompasses much material that would not generally be considered "pornographic" as we use that term here.

What Counts as a Harm?

What is a harm? And why focus on harm at all? We do not wish in referring repeatedly to "harm" to burden ourselves with an unduly narrow conception of harm. To emphasize in different words what we said in the previous section, the scope of indentifiable harms is broader than the scope of that with which government can or should deal. We refuse to truncate our consideration of the question of harm by defining harms in terms of possible government regulation. And we certainly reject the view that the only noticeable harm is one that causes physical or financial harm to identifiable individuals. An environment—physical, cultural, moral, or aesthetic—can be harmed, and so can a community, organization, or group be harmed independent of identifiable harms to members of that community.

Most importantly, although we have emphasized in our discussion of harms the kinds of harms that can most easily be observed and measured, the idea of harm is broader than that. To a number of us, the most important harms must be seen in moral terms, and the act of moral condemnation of that which is immoral is not merely important but essential. From this perspective there are acts that need be seen not only as causes of immorality but as manifestations of it. Issues of human dignity and human decency, no less real for their lack of scientific measurability, are for many of us central to thinking about the question of harm. And when we think about harm in this way, there are acts that must be condemned not because the evils of the world will thereby be eliminated, but because conscience demands it.

We believe it useful in thinking about harms to note the distinction between harm and offense. Although the line between the two is hardly clear, most people can nevertheless imagine things that offend them, or offend others, that still would be hard to describe as harms. In Chapter 6 our discussion of laws and their enforcement will address the question of the place of governmental regulation in restricting things that some or many people may find offensive, but which are less plainly harmful; but at this point it should be sufficient to point out that we take the offensive to be well within the scope of our concerns.

In thinking about harms, it is useful to draw a rough distinction between primary and secondary harms. Primary harms are those in which the alleged harm is commonly taken to be intrinsically harmful, even though the precise way in which the harm is harmful might yet be further explored. Nevertheless, murder, rape, assault, and discrimination on the basis of race and gender are all examples of primary harms in this sense. We treat these acts as harms not because of where they will lead, but simply because of what they are.

In other instances, however, the alleged harm is secondary, not in the sense that it is in any way less important, but in the sense that the concern is not with what the act *is*, but where it will lead. Curfews are occasionally imposed not because there is anything wrong with people being out at night, but because in some circumstances it is thought that being out at night in large groups may cause people to commit other crimes. Possession of "burglar tools" is often prohibited because of what those tools may be used for. Thus, when it is urged that pornography is harmful because it causes some people to commit acts of sexual violence, because it causes promiscuity, because it encourages sexual relations outside of marriage, because it promotes so-called "unnatural" sexual practices, or because it leads men to treat women as existing solely for the sexual satisfaction of men, the alleged harms are secondary, again not in any sense suggesting that the harms are less important. The harms are secondary here because the allegation of harm presupposes a causal link between the act and the harm, a causal link that is superfluous if, as in the case of primary harms, the act quite simply *is* the harm.

Thus we think it important, with respect to every area of possible harm, to focus on whether the allegation relates to a harm that comes from the sexually explicit material itself, or whether it occurs *as a result* of something the material does. If it is the former, then the inquiry can focus directly on the nature of the alleged harm. But if it is the latter, then there must be a two-step inquiry. First it is necessary to determine if some hypothesized result is in fact harmful. In some cases, where the asserted consequent harm is unquestionably a harm, this step of the analysis is easy. With respect to claims that certain sexually explicit material increases the incidence of rape or other sexual violence, for ex-

ample, no one could plausibly claim that such consequences were not harmful, and the inquiry can then turn to whether the causal link exists. In other cases, however, the harmfulness of the alleged harm is often debated. With respect to claims, for example, that some sexually explicit material causes promiscuity, encourages homosexuality, or legitimizes sexual practices other than vaginal intercourse, there is serious societal debate about whether the consequences themselves are harmful.

Thus, the analysis of the hypothesis that pornography causes harm must start with the identification of hypothesized harms, proceed to the determination of whether those hypothesized harms are indeed harmful, and then conclude with the examination of whether a causal link exists between the material and the harm. When the consequences of exposure to sexually explicit material are not harmful, or when there is no causal relationship between exposure to sexually explicit material and some harmful consequence, then we cannot say that the sexually explicit material is harmful. But if sexually explicit material of some variety is causally related to, or increases the incidence of, some behavior that *is* harmful, then it is safe to conclude that the material is harmful.

The Standard of Proof

In dealing with these questions, the standard of proof is a recurrent problem. How much evidence is needed, or how convinced should we be, before reaching the conclusion that certain sexually explicit material *causes* harm? The extremes of this question are easy. Whenever a causal question is even worth asking, there will never be *conclusive* proof that such a causal connection exists, if "conclusive" means that no other possibility exists. We note that frequently, and all too often, the claim that there is no "conclusive" proof is a claim made by someone who disagrees with the implications of the conclusion.

Few if any judgments of causality or danger are ever conclusive, and a requirement of conclusiveness is much more rhetorical device than analytical method. We therefore reject the suggestion that a causal link must be proved "conclusively" before we can identify a harm.

The opposite extreme is also easily dismissed. The fact that someone makes an assertion of fact to us is not necessarily sufficient proof of that fact, even if the assertion remains uncontradicted. We do not operate as a judge sitting in a court of law, and we require more evidence to reach an affirmative conclusion than does a judge whose sole function might in some circumstances be to determine if there is sufficient evidence to send the case to the jury. That there is a bit of evidence for a proposition is not the same as saying that the proposition has been established, and we do not reach causal conclusions in every instance in which there has been some evidence of that proposition.

Between these extremes the issues are more difficult. The reason for this is that how much proof is required is largely a function of what is to be done with an affirmative finding, and what the consequences are of proceeding on the basis of an affirmative finding. As we deal with causal assertions short of conclusive but more than merely some trifle of evidence, we have felt free to rely on less proof merely to make assertions about harm than we have required to recommend legal restrictions, and similarly we have required greater confidence in our assertions if the result was to recommend criminal penalties for a given form of behavior than we did to recommend other forms of legal restriction. Were we to have recommended criminal sanctions against material now covered by the First Amendment, we would have required proof sufficient to satisfy some variant of the "clear and present danger" standard that serves to protect the communication lying at the center of the First Amendment's guarantees from government action resting on a less certain basis.

No government could survive, however, if all of its actions were required to satisfy a "clear and present danger" standard, and we openly acknowledge that in many areas we have reached conclusions that satisfy us for the purposes for which we draw them, but which would not satisfy us if they were to be used for other purposes. That we are satisfied that the vast majority of depictions of violence in a sexually explicit manner are likely to increase the incidence of sexual violence in this country, for example, does not mean that we have concluded that the evidence is sufficient to justify governmental prohibition of materials that both meet that description and are *not* legally obscene.

It would be ideal if we could put our evidentiary standards into simply formulas, but that has not been possible. The standards of proof applicable to the legal process preponderance of the evidence, clear and convincing evidence, and proof beyond a reasonable doubt—are not easily transferred into a nonjudicial context. And the standards of justification of constitutional law—rational basis, compelling interest, and clear and present danger, for example—relate only to the constitutionality of governmental action, not to its advisability, nor to the standards necessary for mere warnings about harm. Thus we have felt it best to rely on the language that people ordinarily use, words like "convinced," "satisfied," and "concluded," but those words should be interpreted in light of the discussion in this section.

The Problem of Multiple Causation

The world is complex, and most consequences are "caused" by numerous factors. Are highway deaths caused by failure to wear seat belts, failure of the automobile companies to install airbags, failure of the government to require automobile companies to install airbags, alcohol, judicial leniency towards drunk drivers, speeding, and so on and on? Is heart disease caused by cigarette smoking, obesity, stress, or excess animal fat in our diets? As with most other questions of this type, the answers can only be "all of the above," and so too with the problem of pornography. We have concluded, for example, that some forms of sexually explicit material bear a causal relationship both to sexual violence and to sex discrimination, but we are hardly so naive as to suppose that were these forms of pornography to disappear the problems of sex discrimination and sexual violence would come to an end.

If this is so, then what does it mean to identify a causal relationship? It means that the evidence supports the conclusion that if there were none of the material being tested, then the incidence of the consequences would be less. We live in a world of multiple causation, and to identify a factor as a *cause* in such a world means only that if this factor were eliminated while everything else stayed the same then the problem would at least be lessened. In most cases it is impossible to say any more than this, although to say this is to say quite a great deal. But when we identify something as a cause, we do not deny that there are other causes, and we do not deny that some of these other causes might bear an even *greater* causal connection than does some form of pornography. That is, it may be, for example, and there is some evidence that points in this direction, that certain magazines focusing on guns, martial arts, and related topics bear a closer causal relationship to sexual violence than do some magazines that are, in a term we will explain shortly, "degrading." If this is true, then the amount of sexual violence would be reduced more by elminating the weaponry magazines and keeping the degrading magazines than it would be reduced by eliminating the degrading magazines and keeping the weaponry magazines.

Why, then, do we concentrate on pornography? For one thing, that is our mission, and we have been asked to look at this problem rather than every problem in the world. We do not think that there is something less important in what we do merely because some of the consequences that concern us here are caused as well, and perhaps to a greater extent, by other stimuli. If the stark implications of the problem of multiple causation were followed to the ultimate conclusion of casting doubt on efforts relating to anything other than the "largest" cause of the largest problem, few of us could justify doing anything in our lives that was not directly related to feeding the hungry. But the world does not operate this way, and we are comfortable with the fact that we have been asked to look at some problems while others look at other problems. And we are equally comfortable with the knowledge that to say that something is one of many causes is not to say that it is not a cause. Nor is it to say that the world would not be better off if even this one cause were eliminated.

When faced with the phenomenon of multiple causation, cause is likely to be attributed to those factors that are within our power to change. Often we ignore larger causes precisely because of their size. When a cause is pervasive and intractable, we look elsewhere for remedies, and this is quite often the rational course. A careful look at the available evidence can give us some idea of where the problems are, what different factors are causing them, which remedies directed at which causes are feasible, and which remedies directed at which causes are futile, unconstitutional, or beyond available means. We acknowledge that all of the harms we identified have causes in addition to the ones we identify. But if we are correct with respect to the causes we have indentified, then we can take confidence in the fact that lessening those causes will help alleviate the problem, even if lessening other causes might very well alleviate the problem to a great extent.

The Varieties of Evidence

We have looked at a wide range of types of evidence. Some has come from personal experience of witnesses, some from professionals whose orientation is primarily clinical, some from experimental social scientists, and some from other forms of empirical science. We have not categorically refused to consider any type of evidence, choosing instead to hear it all, consider it all, and give it the weight we believe in the final analysis it deserves. No form of evidence has been useless to us, and no form is without flaws. A few words about the advantages and disadvantages of various types of evidence may help to put into perspective the conclusions we reach and the basis on which we reach them.

Most controversial has been the evidence we have received from numerous people claiming to be victims of pornography, and reporting in some way on personal experiences relating to pornography. In later portions of this Report concerned with victimization and with the performers in pornographic material we discuss this evidence in more detail. We have considered this firsthand testimony, much of it provided at great personal sacrifice, quite useful, but it is important to note that not all of the first-hand testimony has been of the same type.

Some of the first-hand testimony has come from users of pornography, and a number of witnesses have told us how they became "addicted" to pornography, or how they were led to commit sex crimes as a result of exposure to pornographic materials. Although we have not totally disregarded the evidence that has come from offenders, in many respects it was less valuable than other victim evidence and other evidence in general. Much research supports the tendency of people to externalize their own problems by looking too easily for some external source beyond their own control. As with more extensive studies based on self-reports of sex offenders, evidence relying on what an offender thought caused his problem is likely to so overstate the external and so understate the internal as to be of less value to us than other evidence.

Most of the people who have testified about personal experiences, however, have not been at any point offenders, but rather have been women reporting on what men in their lives have done to them or to their children as a result of exposure to certain sexually explicit materials. As we explained in the introduction, we do not deceive ourselves into thinking that the sample before us is an accurate statistical reflection of the state of the world. Too many factors tended to place before us testimony that was by and large in the same direction and concentrated on those who testified about the presence rather than the absence of consequences. Nevertheless, as long as one does not draw statistical or percentage conclusions from this evidence, and we have not, it can still be important with respect to identification and description of a phenomenon. Plainly some of these witnesses were less credible or less helpful than others, but many of the stories these witnesses told were highly believable and extremely informative, leading us to think about possible harms of which some of us had previously been unaware. Many witnesses have urged us to draw conclusions about prevalence exclusively from anecdotal evidence of this variety, but we have refused to do so. But that we have refused to make invalid statistical generalizations does not mean that we cannot learn from the stories of those with personal experiences. Many of their statements are summarized in the victimization section of this Report, and we urge people to consider those statements as carefully as we did. We can and we have learned from many of these witnesses, and their testimony has provided part of the basis for our conclusions. As in many other areas of human behavior, the most complete understanding emerges when a phenomenon is viewed from multiple perspectives. One important perspective is the subjective meaning that individuals attribute to their own experiences. This perspective and the unique experiences of individuals are less amenable to objective or statistical inquiry than certain other perspectives, and thus can be valuably examined through the kinds of witnesses whose statements we summarize later in this Report.

The evidence provided by clinical professionals carries with it some of the same problems. Although filtering the evidence through a trained professional, especially one who described to us the experience of numerous cases, eliminates some of the credibility problems, the problem of statistical generalization remains. Because people without problems are not the focus of the clinician's efforts, evidence from clinical professionals focuses on the aberrational. Consequently, clinical evidence does not help very much in answering questions about the overall extent of a phenomenon, because it too is anecdotal, albeit in a more sophisticated way and based on a larger sample. Still, clinical evidence should not be faulted for not being what it does not purport to be. What it does purport to be is sensitive professional evaluation of how some people behave, what causes them to behave in that manner, and what, if anything, might change their behavior. Clinical evidence helps us to identify whether a problem exists, although it does not address the prevalence of the problem. We have looked at the clinical evidence in this light, and have frequently found it useful.

The problems of statistical generalization diminish drastically when we look to the findings of empirical social science. Here the attempt is to identify factors across a larger population, and thus many of the difficulties associated with any form of anecdotal evidence drop out when the field of inquiry is either an entire population, some large but relevant subset of a population, or an experimental group selected under some reliable sampling method.

Some of the evidence of this variety is correlational. If there is some positive statistical correlation between the prevalence of some type of material and some harmful act, then it is at least established that the two occur together more than one would expect merely from random intersection of totally independent variables. Some of the correlational evidence is less "scientific" than others, but we refuse to discount evidence merely because the researcher did not have some set of academic qualifications. For example, we have heard much evidence from law enforcement personnel that a disproportionate number of sex offenders were found to have large quantities of pornographic material in their residences. Pornographic material was found on the premises more, in the opinion of witnesses, than one would expect to find it in the residences of a random sample of the population as a whole, in the residences of a random sample of non-offenders of the same sex, age, and socioeconomic status, or in the residences of a random sample of offenders whose offenses were not sex offenses. To the extent that we believe these witnesses, then there is a correlation between pornographic material and sex offenses. We have also read and heard evidence that is more scientific. Some of this evidence has related to entire countries, where researchers have looked for correlations between sex offenses and changes in a country's laws controlling pornography or changes in the actual prevalence of pornographic materials. Other evidence of this variety has been conducted with respect to states or regions of the United States, with attempts again being made to demonstrate correlations between use or non-use of certain sexually explicit materials and the incidence of sex crimes or other anti-social acts.

Correlational evidence suffers from its inability to establish a causal connection between the correlated phenomena. It is frequently the case that two phenomena are positively correlated precisely because they are both caused by some third phenomena.

We recognize, therefore, that a positive correlation between pornography and sex offenses does not itself establish a causal connection between the two. It may be that some other factor, some sexual or emotional imbalance, for example, might produce both excess use of pornographic materials as well as a tendency to commit sex offenses. But the fact that correlational evidence cannot definitively establish causality does not mean that it may not be some evidence of causality, and we have treated it as such. The plausibility of hypothesized independent variables causing both use of pornography and sex offenses is one factor in determining the extent to which causation can be suggested by correlational evidence. So too is the extent to which research design has attempted to exclude exactly these possible independent variables. The more this has been done, the safer it is to infer causation from correlation, but in no area has this inference been strong enough to justify reliance on correlational evidence standing alone.

The problem of the independent variable drops out when experiments are conducted under control group conditions. If a group of people is divided into two subgroups randomly, and if one group is then exposed to a stimulus while the other is not, then a difference in result between the stimulus group and the control group will itself establish causation. As long as the two groups are divided randomly, and as long as the samples are large enough that randomness can be established, then any variable that might be hypothesized other than the one being tested will be present in both the stimulus group and the control group. As a result, the stimulus being tested is completely isolated, and

positive results are very strong evidence of causation.

The difficulty with experimental evidence of this variety, however, is that it is virtually impossible to conduct control group experiments outside of a laboratory setting. As a result, most of the experiments are conducted on those who can be induced to be subjects in such experiments, usually college-age males taking psychology courses. Even a positive result, therefore, is a positive result only, in the narrowest sense, for a population like the experimental group. Extrapolating from the experimental group to the population at large involves many of the same problems as medical researchers encounter in extrapolating from tests on laboratory animals to conclusions about human beings. The extrapolation is frequently justified, but some caution here must be exercised in at least noting that the extrapolation requires assumptions of relevant similarity between college age males and larger populations, as well as, in some cases, assumptions of causality between the effects measured in the experiment and the effects with which people are ultimately concerned.

Perhaps more significantly, enormous ethical problems surround control group experiments involving actual anti-social conduct. If the hypothesis is that exposure to certain materials has a causal relationship with rape, for example, then the "ideal" experiment would start with a relatively large group of men as subjects, would then divide the large group randomly into two groups, and would then expose one of the two groups to the pornographic materials and the other to control materials. Then the experimenter would see if the stimulus groups committed more rapes than the control group. Of course such an experiment is inconceivable, and as a result most experiments of this variety have had to find a substitute for counting sexual offenses. Some have used scientific measures of aggression or sexual arousal, some have used questionnaires reflecting self-reported tendency to commit rape or other sex offenses, some have used experiments measuring people's willingness to punish rapists, and some have used other substitutes. With respect to any experiment of this variety, drawing conclusions requires making assumptions between, for example, measured aggression and an actual increased likelihood of committing offenses. Sometimes these assumptions are justified, and sometimes they are not, but it is always an issue to be examined carefully.

One final point about the experimental evidence presented to us is in order. Even with control group experiments, the ultimate conclusions will depend on the ability of the researcher to isolate single variables. For example, where there is evidence showing a causal relationship between exposure to violent pornography and aggressive behavior, the stimulus as just described contains two elements, the violence and the sex. It may be that the cause is attributable solely to the violence, or it may be that the cause is attributable solely to the sex. Good research attempts to examine these possibilities, and we have been conscious of it as we evaluated the research presented to us.

The Need to Subdivide

Taking into account all of the foregoing methodological factors, it has become clear to all of us that excessively broad terms like "pornography" or "sexually explicit materials" are just too encompassing to reflect the results of our inquiry. That should come as no surprise. There are different varieties of sexually explicit materials, and it is hardly astonishing that some varieties may cause consequences different from those caused by other varieties.

Our views about subdivision as a process, if not about the actual divisions themselves, reflect much of the scientific evidence, and we consider the willingness of scientists to subdivide to be an important methodological advance over the efforts of earlier eras. So too with our own subdivision. We have unanimously agreed that looking at all sexually explicit materials, or even all pornographic materials, as one undifferentiated whole is unjustified by common sense, unwarranted on the evidence, and an altogether oversimplifying way of looking at a complex phenomenon. In many respects we consider this one of our most important conclusions. Our subdivisions are not intended to be definitive, and particularly with respect to the subdivision between non-violent but degrading materials and materials that are neither violent nor degrading, we recognize that some researchers and others have usually employed broader or different groupings. Further research or—thinking, or just changes in the world—may suggest finer or different divisions. To us it is embarking on the process of subdivision that is most important, and we strongly urge that further research and thinking about the question of pornography recognize initially the way in which different varieties of material may produce different consequences.

We cannot stress strongly enough that our conclusions regarding the consequences of material within a given subdivision are not a statement about *all* of the material within a subdivision. We are talking about classes, or categories, and our statements about categories are general statements designed to cover most but not all of what might be within a given category. Some items within a category might produce no effects, or even the opposite effects from those identified. Were we drafting laws or legal distinctions, this might be a problem, but we are not engaged in such a process here. We are identifying characteristics of classes, and looking for harms by classes, without saying that everything that is harmful should be regulated, and without saying that everything that is harmful *may* be regulated consistent with the Constitution.

OUR CONCLUSIONS ABOUT HARM

We present in the following sections our conclusions regarding the harms we have investigated with respect to the various subdividing categories we have found most useful. To the extent that these conclusions rest on findings from the social sciences, as they do to a significant extent, we do not in this part of the Report describe and analyze the individual studies or deal in specifics with their methodologies. For that we rely on our analysis of the social science research which is included later in this Report. Each of us has relied on different evidence from among the different categories of evidence, and specific studies that some of us have found persuasive have been less persuasive to others of us. Similarly, some of us have found evidence of a certain type particularly valuable, while others of us have found other varieties of evidence more enlightening. And in many instances we have relied on certain evidence despite some flaws it may have contained, for it is the case that all of us have reached our conclusions about harms by assimilating and amalgamating a large amount of evidence. Many studies and statements of witnesses have both advantages and disadvantages, and often the disadvantages of one study or piece of testimony has been remedied by another. Thus, the conclusions we reach cannot be identified with complete acceptance or complete rejection by all of us of any particular item of evidence. As a result, we consider the social science analysis, which is much more specific than what we say in this section, to be an integral part of this Report, and we urge that it be read as such. We have not relied totally on that analysis, as all of us have gone beyond it in our reading. And we cannot say that each of us agrees with every sentence and word in it. Nevertheless, it seems to us a sensitive, balanced, comprehensive, accurate, and current report on the state of the research. We have relied on it extensively, and we are proud to include it here.

Sexually Violent Material

The category of material on which most of the evidence has focused is the category of material featuring actual or unmistakably simulated or unmistakably threatened violence presented in sexually explicit fashion with a predominant focus on the sexually explicit violence. Increasingly, the most prevalent forms of pornography, as well as an increasingly prevalent body of less sexually explicit material, fit this description. Some of this material involves sado-masochistic themes, with the standard accoutrements of the genre, including whips, chains, devices of torture, and so on. But another theme of some of this material is not sado-masochistic, but involves instead the recurrent theme of a man making some sort of sexual advance to a woman, being rebuffed, and then raping the woman or in some other way violently forcing himself on the woman. In almost all of this material, whether in magazine or motion picture form, the woman eventually becomes aroused and ecstatic about the initially forced sexual activity, and usually is portrayed as begging for more. There is also a large body of material, more "mainstream" in its availability, that portrays sexual activity or sexually suggestive nudity coupled with extreme violence, such as disfigurement or murder. The so-called "slasher" films fit this description, as does some material, both in films and in magazines, that is less or more sexually explicit than the prototypical "slasher" film.

It is with respect to material of this variety that the scientific findings and ultimate con-

clusions of the 1970 Commission are least reliable for today, precisely because material of this variety was largely absent from that Commission's inquiries. It is not, however, absent from the contemporary world, and it is hardly surprising that conclusions about this material differ from conclusions about material not including violent themes.

When clinical and experimental research has focused particularly on sexually violent material, the conclusions have been virtually unanimous. In both clinical and experimental settings, exposure to sexually violent materials has indicated an increase in the likelihood of aggression. More specifically, the research, which is described in much detail later in this Report, shows a causal relationship between exposure to material of this type and aggressive behavior towards women.

Finding a link between aggressive behavior towards women and sexual violence, whether lawful or unlawful, requires assumptions not found exclusively in the experimental evidence. We see no reason, however, not to make these assumptions. The assumption that increased aggressive behavior towards women is causally related, for an aggregate population, to increased sexual violence is significantly supported by the clinical evidence, as well as by much of the less scientific evidence.[45] They are also to all of us assumptions that are plainly justified by our own common sense. This is not to say that all people with heightened levels of aggression will commit acts of sexual violence. But it is to say that over a sufficiently large number of cases we are confident in asserting that an increase in aggressive behavior directed at women will cause an increase in the level of sexual violence directed at women.

Thus we reach our conclusions by combining the results of the research with highly justifiable assumptions about the generalizability of more limited research results. Since the clinical and experimental evidence supports the conclusion that there is a causal relationship between exposure to sexually violent materials and an increase in aggressive behavior directed towards women, and since we believe that an increase in ag-

---

45. For example, the evidence from formal or informal studies of self-reports of offenders themselves supports the conclusion that the causal connection we identify relates to actual sexual offenses rather than merely to aggressive behavior. For reasons we have explained beginning on page 35 the tendency to externalize leads us to give evidence of this variety rather little weight. But at the very least it does not point in the opposite direction from the conclusions reached here.

gressive behavior towards women will in a population increase the incidence of sexual violence in that population, we have reached the conclusion, unanimously and confidently, that the available evidence strongly supports the hypothesis that substantial exposure to sexually violent materials as described here bears a causal relationship to antisocial acts of sexual violence and, for some subgroups, possibly to unlawful acts of sexual violence.

Although we rely for this conclusion on significant scientific empirical evidence, we feel it worthwhile to note the underlying logic of the conclusion. The evidence says simply that the images that people are exposed to bears a causal relationship to their behavior. This is hardly surprising. What would be surprising would be to find otherwise, and we have not so found. We have not, of course, found that the images people are exposed to are a greater cause of sexual violence than all or even many other possible causes the investigation of which has been beyond our mandate. Nevertheless, it would be strange indeed if graphic representations of a form of behavior, especially in a form that almost exclusively portrays such behavior as desirable, did not have at least some effect on patterns of behavior.

Sexual violence is not the only negative effect reported in the research to result from substantial exposure to sexually violent materials. The evidence is also strongly supportive of significant attitudinal changes on the part of those with substantial exposure to violent pornography. These attitudinal changes are numerous. Victims of rape and other forms of sexual violence are likely to be perceived by people so exposed as more responsible for the assault, as having suffered less injury, and as having been less degraded as a result of the experience. Similarly, people with a substantial exposure to violent pornography are likely to see the rapist or other sexual offender as less responsible for the act and as deserving of less stringent punishment.

These attitudinal changes have been shown experimentally to include a larger range of attitudes than those just discussed. The evidence also strongly supports the conclusion that substantial exposure to violent sexually explicit material leads to a greater acceptance of the "rape myth" in its broader sense—that women enjoy being coerced into sexual activity, that they enjoy being physically hurt in sexual context, and that as a result a man who

forces himself on a woman sexually is in fact merely acceding to the "real" wishes of the woman, regardless of the extent to which she seems to be resisting. The myth is that a woman who says "no" really means "yes," and that men are justified in acting on the assumption that the "no" answer is indeed the "yes" answer. We have little trouble concluding that this attitude is both pervasive and profoundly harmful, and that any stimulus reinforcing or increasing the incidence of this attitude is for that reason alone properly designated as harmful.

Two vitally important features of the evidence supporting the above conclusions must be mentioned here. The first is that all of the harms discussed here, including acceptance of the legitimacy of sexual violence against women but not limited to it, are more pronounced when the sexually violent materials depict the woman as experiencing arousal, orgasm, or other form of enjoyment as the ultimate result of the sexual assault. This theme, unfortunately very common in the materials we have examined, is likely to be the major, albeit not the only, component of what it is in the materials in this category that causes the consequences that have been identified.

The second important clarification of all of the above is that the evidence lends some support to the conclusion that the consequences we have identified here *do not vary with the extent of sexual explicitness so long as the violence is presented in an undeniably sexual context.* Once a threshold is passed at which sex and violence are plainly linked, increasing the sexual explicitness of the material, or the bizarreness of the sexual activity, seems to bear little relationship to the extent of the consequences discussed here. Although it is unclear whether sexually violent material makes a substantially greater causal contribution to sexual violence itself than does material containing violence alone, it appears that increasing the amount of violence after the threshold of connecting sex with violence is more related to increase in the incidence or severity of harmful consequences than is increasing the amount of sex. As a result, the so-called "slasher" films, which depict a great deal of violence connected with an undeniably sexual theme but less sexual explicitness than materials that are truly pornographic, are likely to produce the consequences discussed here to a greater extent than most of the materials available in "adults only" pornographic outlets.

Although we have based our findings about material in this category primarily on evidence presented by professionals in the behavioral sciences, we are confident that they are supported by the less scientific evidence we have consulted; and we are each personally confident on the basis of our own knowledge and experiences that the conclusions are justified. None of us has the least doubt that sexual violence is harmful, and that general acceptance of the view that "no" means "yes" is a consequence of the most serious proportions. We have found a causal relationship between sexually explicit materials featuring violence and these consequences, and thus conclude that the class of such materials, although not necessarily every individual member of that class, is on the whole harmful to society.

Nonviolent Materials Depicting Degradation, Domination, Subordination, or Humiliation

Current research has rather consistently separated out violent pornography, the class of materials we have just discussed, from other sexually explicit materials. With respect to further subdivision the process has been less consistent. A few researchers have made further distinctions, while most have merely classed everything else as "non-violent." We have concluded that more subdivision than that is necessary. Our examination of the variety of sexually explicit materials convinces us that once again the category of "non-violent" ignores significant distinctions within this category, and thus combines classes of material that are in fact substantially different.

The subdivision we adopt is one that has surfaced in some of the research. And it is also one that might explain a significant amount of what would otherwise seem to be conflicting research results. Some researchers have found negative effects from nonviolent material, while others report no such negative effects. But when the stimulus material these researchers have used is considered, there is some suggestion that the presence or absence of negative effects from non-violent material might turn on the nonviolent material being considered "degrading," a term we shall explain shortly.[46] It appears that effects similar to, although not as extensive as that involved with violent material, can be identified with respect to such degrading material, but that these effects are likely absent when neither degradation nor violence is present.

An enormous amount of the most sexually explicit material available, as well as much of the material that is somewhat less sexually explicit, is material that we would characterize as "degrading," the term we use to encompass the undeniably linked characteristics of degradation, domination, subordination, and humiliation. The degradation we refer to is degradation of people, most often women, and here we are referring to material that, although not violent, depicts[47] people, usually women, as existing solely for the sexual satisfaction of others, usually men, or that depicts people, usually women, in decidedly subordinate roles in their sexual relations with others, or that depicts people engaged in sexual practices that would to most people be considered humiliating. Indeed, forms of degradation represent the largely predominant proportion of commercially available pornography.

With respect to material of this variety, our conclusions are substantially similar to those with respect to violent material, although we make them with somewhat less assumption

---

46. For example, the studies of Dr. Zillmann regarding non-violent material, studies that have been particularly influential for some of us, use material that contain the following themes: "He is ready to take. She is ready to be taken." This active/passive differentiation that coincides with gender is stated on purpose." Women are portrayed as "masochistic, subservient, socially nondiscriminating nymphomaniacs." Dr. Zillmann goes on to characterize this material as involving mutual consent and no coercion, but also describes the films as ones in which "women tend to overrespond in serving the male interest."

47. We restrict our analysis in large part to degradation that is in fact depicted in the material. It may very well be that degradation led to a woman being willing to pose for a picture of a certain variety, or to engage in what appears to be a non-degrading sexual act. It may be that coercion caused the picture to exist. And it may very well be that the existing disparity in the economic status of men and women is such that any sexually explicit depiction of a woman is at least suspect on account of the possibility that the economic disparity is what caused the woman to pose for a picture that most people in this society would find embarrassing. We do not deny any of these possibilities, and we do not deny the importance of considering as pervasively as possible the status of women in contemporary America, including the effects of their current status and what might be done to change some of the detrimental consequences of that status. But without engaging in an inquiry of that breadth, we must generally, absent more specific evidence to the contrary, assume that a picture represents what it depicts.

than was the case with respect to violent material. The evidence, scientific and otherwise, is more tentative, but supports the conclusion that the material we describe as degrading bears some causal relationship to the attitudinal changes we have previously identified. That is, substantial exposure to material of this variety is likely to increase the extent to which those exposed will view rape or other forms of sexual violence as less serious than they otherwise would have, will view the victims of rape and other forms of sexual violence as significantly more responsible, and will view the offenders as significantly less responsible. We also conclude that the evidence supports the conclusion that substantial exposure to material of this type will increase acceptance of the proposition that women like to be forced into sexual practices, and, once again, that the woman who says "no" really means "yes."

With respect to material of this type, there is less evidence causally linking the material with sexual aggression, but this may be because this is a category that has been isolated in only a few studies, albeit an increasing number. The absence of evidence should by no means be taken to deny the existence of the causal link. But because the causal link is less the subject of experimental studies, we have been required to think more carefully here about the assumptions necessary to causally connect increased acceptance of rape myths and other attitudinal changes with increased sexual aggression and sexual violence. And on the basis of all the evidence we have considered, from all sources, and on the basis of our own insights and experiences, we believe we are justified in drawing the following conclusion: Over a large enough sample of population that believes that many women like to be raped, that believes that sexual violence or sexual coercion is often desired or appropriate, and that believes that sex offenders are less responsible for their acts, will commit more acts of sexual violence or sexual coercion than would a population holding these beliefs to a lesser extent.

We should make clear what we have concluded here. We are not saying that everyone exposed to material of this type has his attitude about sexual violence changed. We are saying only that the evidence supports the conclusion that substantial exposure to degrading material increases the likelihood for an individual and the incidence over a large population that these attitudinal changes will

occur. And we are not saying that everyone with these attitudes will commit an act of sexual violence or sexual coercion. We are saying that such attitudes will increase the likelihood for an individual and the incidence for a population that acts of sexual violence, sexual coercion, or unwanted sexual aggression will occur. Thus, we conclude that substantial exposure to materials of this type bears some causal relationship to the level of sexual violence, sexual coercion, or unwanted sexual aggression in the population so exposed.

We need mention as well that our focus on these more violent or more coercive forms of actual subordination of women should not diminish what we take to be a necessarily incorporated conclusion: Substantial exposure to materials of this type bears some causal relationship to the incidence of various nonviolent forms of discrimination against or subordination of women in our society. To the extent that these materials create or reinforce the view that women's function is disproportionately to satisfy the sexual needs of men, then the materials will have pervasive effects on the treatment of women in society far beyond the incidence of identifiable acts of rape or other sexual violence. We obviously cannot here explore fully all the forms in which women are discriminated against in contemporary society. Nor can we explore all of the causes of that discrimination against women. But we feel confident in concluding that the view of women as available for sexual domination is one cause of that discrimination, and we feel confident as well in concluding that degrading material bears a causal relationship to the view that women ought to subordinate their own desires and beings to the sexual satisfaction of men.

Although the category of the degrading is one that has only recently been isolated in some research, in the literature generally, and in public discussion of the issue, it is not a small category. If anything, it constitutes somewhere between the predominant and the overwhelming portion of what is currently standard fare heterosexual pornography, and is a significant theme in a broader range of materials not commonly taken to be sexually explicit enough to be pornographic. But as with sexually violent materials, the extent of the effect of these degrading materials may not turn substantially on the amount of sexual explicitness once a threshold of undeniable sexual content is surpassed. The category therefore includes a great deal of what would now be considered to be pornographic, and includes a great deal of what would now be held to be legally obscene, but it includes much more than that. Since we are here identifying harms for a class, rather than identifying harms caused by every member of that class, and since we are here talking about the identification of harm rather than making recommendations for legal control, we are not reluctant to identify harms for a class of material considerably wider than what is or even should be regulated by law.

Non-Violent and Non-Degrading Materials

Our most controversial category has been the category of sexually explicit materials that are not violent and are not degrading as we have used that term. They are materials in which the participants appear to be fully willing participants occupying substantially equal roles in a setting devoid of actual or apparent violence or pain. This category is in fact quite small in terms of currently available materials. There is some, to be sure, and the amount may increase as the division between the degrading and the non-degrading becomes more accepted, but we are convinced that only a small amount of currently available highly sexually explicit material is neither violent nor degrading. We thus talk about a small category, but one that should not be ignored.

We have disagreed substantially about the effects of such materials, and that should come as no surprise. We are dealing in this category with "pure" sex, as to which there are widely divergent views in this society. That we have disagreed among ourselves does little more than reflect the extent to which we are representative of the population as a whole. In light of that disagreement, it is perhaps more appropriate to explain the various views rather than indicate a unanimity that does not exist, within this Commission or within society, or attempt the preposterous task of saying that some fundamental view about the role of sexuality and portrayals of sexuality was accepted or defeated by such-and-such vote. We do not wish to give easy answers to hard questions, and thus feel better with describing the diversity of opinion rather than suppressing part of it.

In examining the material in this category, we have not had the benefit of extensive evidence. Research has only recently begun to distinguish the non-violent but degrading from material that is neither violent nor degrading, and we have all relied on a combination of interpretation of existing studies that may not have drawn the same divisions, studies that did draw these distinctions, clinical evidence, interpretation of victim testimony, and our own perceptions of the effect of images on human behavior. Although the social science evidence is farm from conclusive, we are, on the current state of the evidence, persuaded that material of this type does not bear a causal relationship to rape and other acts of sexual violence. We rely once again not only on scientific studies outlined later in the Report, and examined by each of us, but on the fact that the conclusions of these studies seem to most of us fully consistent with common sense. Just as materials depicting sexual violence seem intuitively likely to bear a causal relationship to sexual violence, materials containing no depictions or suggestions of sexual violence or sexual dominance seem to most of us intuitively unlikely to bear a causal relationship to sexual violence. The studies and clinical evidence to date are less persuasive on this lack of negative effect than they are persuasive for the presence of negative effect for the sexually violent material, but they seem to us of equal persuasive power as the studies and clinical evidence showing negative effects for the degrading materials. The fairest conclusion from the social science evidence is that there is no persuasive evidence to date supporting the connection between non-violent and non-degrading materials and acts of sexual violence, and that there is some, but very limited evidence, indicating that the connection does not exist. The totality of the social science evidence, therefore, is slightly against the hypothesis that non-violent and non-degrading materials bear a causal relationship to acts of sexual violence.

That there does not appear from the social science evidence to be a causal link with sexual violence, however, does not answer the question of whether such materials might not themselves simply for some other reason constitute a harm in themselves, or bear a causal link to consequences other than sexual violence but still taken to be harmful. And it is here that we and society at large have the greatest differences in opinion.

One issue relates to materials that, although undoubtedly consensual and equal, depict sexual practices frequently condemned in this and other societies. In addition, level of societal condemnation varies for different activities; some activities are condemned by some people, but not by others. We have discovered that to some significant extent the assessment of the harmfulness of materials depicting such activities correlates directly with the assessment of the harmfulness of the activities themselves. Intuitively and not experimentally, we can hypothesize that materials portraying such an activity will either help to legitimize or will bear some causal relationship to that activity itself. With respect to these materials, therefore, it appears that a conclusion about the harmfulness of these materials turns on a conclusion about the harmfulness of the activity itself. As to this, we are unable to agree with respect to many of these activities. Our differences reflect differences now extant in society at large, and actively debated, and we can hardly resolve them here.

A larger issue is the very question of promiscuity. Even to the extent that the behavior depicted is not inherently condemned by some or any of us, the manner of presentation almost necessarily suggests that the activities are taking place outside of the context of marriage, love, commitment, or even affection. Again, it is far from implausible to hypothesize that materials depicting sexual activity without marriage, love, commitment, or affection bear some causal relationship to sexual activity without marriage, love, commitment, or affection. There are undoubtedly many causes for what used to be called the "sexual revolution," but it is absurd to suppose that depictions or descriptions of uncommitted sexuality were not among them.[48] Thus, once again our disagreements reflect disagreements in society at large, although not to as great an extent. Although there are many members of this society who can and have made affirmative cases for uncommitted sexuality, none of use believes it to be a good thing. A number of us, however, believe that the level of commitment in sexuality is a matter of choice among those who voluntarily engage in the activity. Others of us believe that uncommitted sexual activity is wrong for the individuals involved and harmful to society to the extent of its prevalence. Our view of the ultimate harmfulness of much of this material, therefore, is reflective of our individual views about the extent to

whether sexual commitment is purely a matter of individual choice.

Even insofar as sexually explicit material of the variety being discussed here is not perceived as harmful for the messages it carries or the symbols it represents, the very publicness of what is commonly taken to be private is cause for concern.[49] Even if we hypothesize a sexually explicit motion picture of a loving married couple engaged in mutually pleasurable and procreative vaginal intercourse, the depiction of that act on a screen or in a magazine may constitute a harm in its own right (a "primary harm" in the terminology introduced earlier in this Chapter) solely by virtue of being shown. Here the concern is with the preservation of sex as an essentially private act, in conformity with the basic privateness of sex long recognized by this and all other societies. The alleged harm here, therefore, is that as soon as sex is put on a screen or put in a magazine it changes its character, regardless of what variety of sex is portrayed. And to the extent that the character of sex as public rather than private is the consequence here, then that to many would constitute a harm.

In considering the way in which making sex public may fundamentally transform the character of sex in all settings, it seems important to emphasize that the act of making sex public is as an empirical matter almost always coincident with the act of making sex a commercial enterprise. Whether the act of making sex public if done by a charitable institution would be harmful is an interesting academic exercise, but it is little more than that. For in the context we are discussing, taking the act of sex out of a private setting and making it public is invariably done for someone's commercial gain. To many of us, this fact of commercialization is vital to understanding the concern about sex and privacy.

We are again, along with the rest of society, unable to agree as to the extent to which making sex public and commercial should constitute a harm. We all agree for ourselves on the fundamental privateness of sex, but we disagree about the extent to which the privateness of sex is more than a matter of individual choice. And although we all to some extent think that sexuality may have in today's society become a bit too public, many of us are

---

48. Nor, of course, do we deny the extent that the phenomenon, in part, also goes the other way. Sexually explicit materials in most cases seem both to reflect and to cause demand.

49. The concerns summarized here are articulated more fully in a statement that expresses the views of a number of individual members of this Commission.

concerned that in the past it has been some-what too private, being a subject that could not be talked about, could not constitute part of the discourse of society, and was treated in some way as "dirty." To the extent that making sex more public has, while not without costs, alleviated some of these problems of the past, some of us would not take the increased publicness of sexuality as necessarily harm-ful, but here again we are quite understand-ably unable to agree.

The discussion of publicness in the pre-vious paragraph was limited to the necessary publicness consequent in making a picture of a sexual act, regardless of whether the picture is made public in the broader sense. But to the extent that this occurs, we are once again in agreement. While some might argue that it is desirable for sexual explicitness to be pub-licly displayed to both willing and unwilling viewers, and while some might argue that this is either a positive advantage for the ter-rain of society or of no effect, we unani-mously reject those conclusions. We all agree that some large part of the privateness of sex is essential, and we would, for example, unani-mously take to be harmful to society a prolif-eration of billboards displaying even the hypothesized highly explicit photograph of a loving married couple engaged in mutually pleasurable and procreative vaginal inter-course. Thus, to the extent that materials in this category are displayed truly publicly, we unanimously would take such a consequence to be harmful to society in addition to being harmful to individuals. Even if unwilling viewers are offended rather than harmed in any stronger sense, we take the large scale of-fending of the legitimate sensibilities of a large portion of the population to be harmful to society.

A number of witnesses have testified about the effects on their own sexual relations, usu-ally with their spouses, of the depiction on the screen and in magazines of sexual prac-tices in which they had not previously en-gaged. A number of these witnesses, *all women*, have testified that men in their lives have used such material to strongly encour-aged, or coerce, them into engaging in sexual practices in which they do not choose to en-gage. To the extent that such implicit or ex-plicit coercion takes places as a result of these materials, we all agree that it is a harm. There has been other evidence, however, about the extent to which such material might for some be a way of revitalizing their sex lives, or,

more commonly, simply constituting a part of a mutually pleasurable sexual experience for both partners. On this we could not agree. For reasons relating largely to the question of publicness in the first sense discussed above, some saw this kind of use as primarily harm-ful. Others saw it as harmless and possibly beneficial in contexts such as this. Some pro-fessional testimony supported this latter view, but we have little doubt that profes-sional opinion is also divided on the issue.

Perhaps the most significant potential harm in this category exists with respect to children. We all agree that at least much, probably most, and maybe even all material in this category, regardless of whether it is harmful when used by adults only, is harmful when it falls into the hands of children. Expo-sure to sexuality is commonly taken, and properly so, to be primarily the responsibility of the family. Even those who would disagree with this statement would still prefer to have early exposure to sexuality be in the hands of a responsible professional in a controlled and guided setting. We have no hesitancy in con-cluding that learning about sexuality from most of the material in this category is not the best way for children to learn about the sub-ject. There are harms both to the children themselves and to notions of family control over a child's introduction to sexuality if chil-dren learn about sex from the kinds of sexu-ally explicit materials that constitute the bulk of this category of materials.

We have little doubt that much of this mate-rial does find its way into the hands of chil-dren, and to the extent that it does we all agree that it is harmful. We may disagree about the extent to which people should, as adults, be tolerated in engaging in sexual practices that differ from the norm, but we all agree about the question of the desirability of exposing children to most of this material, and on that our unanimous agreement is that it is unde-sirable. For children to be taught by these ma-terials that sex is public, that sex is commercial, and that sex can be divorced from any degree of affection, love, commit-ment, or marriage is for us the wrong message at the wrong time. We may disagree among ourselves about the extent to which the effect on children should justify large scale restric-tions for that reason alone, but again we all agree that if the question is simply harm, and not the question of regulation by law, that ma-terial in this category is, with few exceptions, generally harmful to the extent it finds its way into the hands of children. Even those in society who would be least restrictive of sexually explicit materials tend, by and large, to limit their views to adults. The near unanimity in society about the effects on children and on all of society in exposing children to explicit sexuality in the form of even non-violent and non-degrading pornographic materials makes a strong statement about the potential harms of this material, and we confidently agree with that longstanding societal judgment.

Perhaps the largest question, and for that reason the question we can hardly touch here, is the question of harm as it relates to the moral environment of a society. There is no doubt that numerous laws, taboos, and other social practices all serve to enforce some forms of shared moral assessment. The extent to which this enforcement should be enlarged, the extent to which sexual morality is a necessary component of a society's moral environment, and the appropriate balance between recognition of individual choice and the necessity of maintaining some sense of community in a society are questions that have been debated for generations. The debates in the nineteenth century between John Stuart Mill and James Fitzjames Stephen, and in the twentieth century between Patrick Devlin and H. L. A. Hart, are merely among the more prominent examples of profound differences in opinion that can scarcely be the subject of a vote by this Commission. We all agree that some degree of individual choice is necessary in any free society, and we all agree that a society with no shared values, including moral values, is no society at all. We have numerous different views about the way in which these undeniably competing values should best be accommodated in this society at this time, or in any society at any time. We also have numerous different views about the extent to which, if at all, sexual morality is an essential part of the social glue of this or any other society. We have talked about these issues, but we have not even attempted to resolve our differences, because these differences are reflective of differences that are both fundamental and widespread in all societies. That we have been able to talk about them has been important to us, and there is no doubt that our views on these issues bear heavily on the views we hold about many of the more specific issues that have been within the scope of our mission.

Thus, with respect to the materials in this category, there are areas of agreement and areas of disagreement. We unanimously agree that the material in this category in some settings and when used for some purposes can be harmful. None of us think that the material in this category, individually or as a class, is in every instance harmless. And to the extent that some of the materials in this category are largely educational or undeniably artistic, we unanimously agree that they are little cause for concern if not made available to children are foisted on unwilling viewers. But most of the materials in this category would not now be taken to be explicitly educational or artistic, and as to this balance of materials our disagreements are substantial. Some of us think that some of the material at some times will be harmful, that some of the material at some times will be harmless, and that some of the material at times will be beneficial, especially when used for professional or nonprofessional therapeutic purposes. And some of us, while recognizing the occasional possibility of a harmless or beneficial use, nevertheless, for reasons stated in this section, feel that on balance it is appropriate to identify the class as harmful as a whole, if not in every instance. We have recorded this disagreement, and stated the various concerns. We can do little more except hope that the issues will continue to be discussed. But as it is discussed, we hope it will be recognized that the class of materials that is neither violent nor degrading, as it stands, is a small class, and many of these disagreements are more theoretical than real. Still, this class is not empty, and may at some point increase in size, and thus the theoretical disagreements may yet become germane to a larger class of materials actually available.

Nudity

We pause only briefly to mention the problem of mere nudity. None of us think that the human body or its portrayal is harmful. But we all agree that this statement is somewhat of an oversimplification. There may be instances in which portrayals of nudity in an undeniably sexual context, even if there is no suggestion of sexual activity, will generate many of the same issues discussed in the previous section. There are legitimate questions about when and how children should be exposed to nudity, legitimate questions about public portrayals of nudity, and legitimate questions about when "mere" nudity stops being "mere" nudity and has such clear connotations of sexual activity that it ought at least to be analyzed according to the same factors that we discuss with with respect to sexually explicit materials containing neither violence nor degradation.

In this respect nudity without force, coercion, sexual activity, violence, or degradation, but with a definite provocative element, represents a wide category of materials. At the least explicit end of the spectrum, we could envision aesthetically posed, airbrushed photographs of beautiful men or women in a provocative context. The provocation derives from the power of sex to attract the attentions and stir the passions of all of us. Such materials may have, in most uses, little negative effect on individuals, families, or society. But at the other end of the continuum, we see materials specifically designed to maximize the sexual impact by the nature of the pose, the caption, the seductive appearance, and the setting in which the model is placed. For example, consider a woman shown in a reclining position with genitals displayed, wearing only red feathers and high heeled shoes, holding a gun and accompanied by a caption offering a direct invitation to sexual activity. With respect to such more explicit materials, we were unable to reach complete agreement. We are all concerned about the impact of such material on children, on attitudes towards women, on the relationship between the sexes, and on attitudes towards sex in general; but the extent of the harms was the subject of some difference of opinion.

None of us, of course, finds harmful the use of nudity in art and for plainly educational purposes. Similarly, we all believe that in some circumstances the portrayal of nudity may be undesirable. It is therefore impossible to draw universal conclusions about all depictions of nudity under all conditions. But by and large we do not find the nudity that does not fit within any of the previous categories to be much cause for concern.

THE NEED FOR FURTHER RESEARCH

Although we have mentioned it throughout this report, it is appropriate here to emphasize especially the importance of further research by professionals into the potential and actual harms we have discussed in this Chapter. We are confident that the quality and quantity of research far surpasses that available in 1970, but we also believe that the research remains in many respects unsyste-

matic and unfocused. There is still a great deal to be done. In many respects research is still at a fairly rudimentary stage, with few attempts to standardize categories of analysis, self-reporting questionnaires, types of stimulus materials, description of stimulus materials, measurement of effects, and related problems.

We recognize that the ethical problems discussed above will inevitably place some cap on the conclusions that can be drawn from the research in this area. But apart from this inherent and incurable limitation, much can still be done. The research that has led to further subdivision of the large category of sexually explicit materials has perhaps been the most important development in recent years, and we strongly encourage research that will deal more precisely with different varieties of materials. We also believe that many other specific questions are in need of further research. There needs to be more research, for example, about the effect of pornography on the marriage relationship, about the nature of appetites for pornographic material and how those appetites are developed, about the effect of depictions of particular sexual practices on the sexual preferences of those who view them, and about the effects of exposure to pornographic material on children. This list could be much longer, but the point is only to show that much more needs to be done.

Some of the professionals who have provided evidence to us have been quite outspoken in their views about what the government in general or the legal system in particular ought to do about pornography. This phenomenon has been about equally divided between those researchers who have advocated fewer legal controls and those who have advocated more. While we do not deny to citizens the right to speak out on matters of public concern, we ought to note that we have tended to rely mostly on evidence provided by those who seem less committed to a particular point of view beyond their scientific expertise. We deal in an area in which a great deal must be taken on faith, including description of stimulus materials, description of experimental environments, questionnaire design, and description of what may or may not have been told to subjects. At no time have we suspected any scientist of deliberately or even negligently designing an experiment or reporting its results, but it remains nevertheless the case that there is room for judgment and room for discretion. Where a researcher has taken on the role as active crusader, one way or another, on the issue of governmental control of pornography, we are forced to question more than we would otherwise have done, the way in which this judgment and discretion has been exercised. We will not suggest how any researcher should balance the issue of his or her own credibility against his or her own strong feelings about an issue of importance. But we will note that the more that is expected to be taken on trust, the more likely it is that active involvement with respect to what is to be done with the results of the research will decrease the amount of trust.

Laws and Their Enforcement

AN OVERVIEW OF THE PROBLEM

In Chapter 5 we explored the various harms alleged to be caused by certain kinds of sexually explicit materials. We also indicated our conclusions with respect to questions of harm. But as we insisted throughout Chapter 5, the fact that a certain kind of material causes a certain kind of harm, although generally a factor in making decisions about law and law enforcement, does not by itself entail the conclusion that the material causing the harm should be controlled by the law. In some cases private action may be more appropriate than governmental action. In some cases governmental action, even if ideally appropriate, may be inadvisable as a matter of policy or unworkable as a matter of practice. And in some cases governmental action may be unconstitutional. Still, the prevention and redress of harms to individuals and harms to society have long been among the central functions of government in general and law in particular. Although we are sensitive to the space between what is harmful and what harms the government ought to address, at least we start with the assumption that where there is an identified harm, then governmental action ought seriously to be considered. In some cases the result of that consideration will be the conclusion that governmental action is inappropriate, unworkable, or unconstitutional. But so long as we have identified harms, we must consider carefully the possible legal remedies for each harm we have identified.

We have tried to consider as broadly as possible the kinds of legal remedies that might be appropriate to deal with various harms. Although enforcement of the criminal law has long been considered the primary legal tool for dealing with harmful, sexually explicit material, it has not been the only such tool, and ought not to be considered the only possible one. We have tried to be as open as we could be to various options in addition to, or instead of, enforcement of the criminal law. Thus in this Chapter we will consider the appropriateness, as exclusive or supplemental remedies, of zoning, administrative regulation, civil remedies for damages in the form of a civil rights action, civil remedies to obtain an injunction, and other possible legal responses to the harms that have been identified. We do not claim to be exhaustive in our consideration of regulatory options. Some options that have been suggested to us simply do not warrant discussion. And others that we mention briefly could and should be explored more thoroughly by others. But it is important to us to emphasize that approaches other than the traditional criminal law sanctions do exist, and are an integral part of thinking carefully about the issue of pornography.

SHOULD PORNOGRAPHY BE REGULATED BY LAW?

The Question Is Deregulation

Numerous witnesses at our public hearings, as well as many others in written evidence or in various publications, have urged upon us the view that pornography should not be regulated by law. Because such arguments have been around for some time, and because such arguments were substantially accepted by the 1970 Commission, we have very seriously considered them. To a significant extent, however, the arguments remain unpersuasive.

Many of the arguments against regulation, both those made currently and those made earlier, rest on claims of harmlessness that, as we have explained in Chapter 5 are simply erroneous with respect to much of this material. Some of these claims of harmlessness tend either to ignore much of the evidence, or to extrapolate from plausible conclusions about the most innocuous material to conclusions about an entire class. Others start with the assumption that no finding of harm can be accepted unless it meets some extraordinarily high burden of proof, a burden of proof whose rigor often seems premised on an *a priori* assertion that the material being discussed ought not to be regulated.

In addition to erroneous or skewed claims of harmlessness, many of the arguments against regulation depend on claims of unconstitutionality that would require for their acceptance a view of the law strikingly different from that long accepted by the Supreme Court in its rulings on obscenity. As we discuss in Chapter 3, we accept the Supreme Court's basic approach to the constitutional question. To the extent that claims for non-regulation thus rest on constitutional arguments with which neither we nor the Supreme Court accept, we reject those arguments for non-regulation.

To the extent that arguments for non-regulation do not depend on implausible claims of harmlessness or rejected claims of unconstitutionality, however, they deserve to be taken even more seriously. As questions of policy in particular areas or the appropriateness of governmental action in general, serious arguments have been made that go to the most fundamental questions of what governmental action is designed to achieve.

We have thought carefully about these issues explicitly, and in doing so we have found it necessary to recast the question. The question as often presented to us in effect asks whether, if we had no laws dealing with pornography, we would want them. This question is not the same as the question whether, given 180 years of pornography regulation in the United States, we should repeal it. Although virtually every argument for deregulation presented to us has been in the former tone, it is the latter that represents reality. We certainly do not take everything that is to be inevitable, and we deem it important to treat

even that which has been assumed for generations as open for serious and foundational reconsideration. Nevertheless, it remains the case the there are vast real and symbolic differences between not doing what has not before been done and undoing what is currently in place. To undo makes a statement much stronger than that made by not doing. In many cases it may be fully appropriate to make this stronger statement, but we presuppose here that the evidence and our convictions must be stronger to urge dismantling what is now in place than it would have to be to refuse to put in place what did not now exist. Moreover, we recognize that this is an area marked by serious debate, involving plausible arguments both for and against regulation. Where the issues are not all on one side, we have given some weight to the considered judgment of the past. In some sense, therefore, the burden of proof is on those who would urge adoption of a variety of governmental regulation that does not now exist. In a nation founded on principles of limited government, those who would make it less limited have the obligation to persuade. But where there exists a present practice and long history of regulation of a certain variety, the burden is on those who would have government make the necessarily much stronger statement implied by an affirmative act of deregulation.

In light of this, we take the question of the governmental regulation of the legally obscene not to be, whether if we did not have obscenity laws would we want them, but whether given that we have obscenity laws, do we want to abandon them? In many areas the issues before us are not close, and how the question is put does not determine the outcome. But in many other areas the questions are indeed difficult, and how the questions are cast, and where the burden of proof lies, do make a difference. With reference to criminal sanctions against the legally obscene, for example, the burden must be on those who would have us or society make the especially strong statement implicit in the act of repeal. But with reference to certain forms of regulation that do not now exist, the burden is similarly on those who would have us or society make the especially strong statement implicit in urging the totally new.

Law Enforcement, Priority, and Multiple Causation

As we have discussed in Chapter 5, most of the harms that we have identified are not caused exclusively or even predominantly by pornography. In Chapter 5 we discussed this problem of multiple causation in terms of relatively abstract questions of harm. But when the phenomenon of multiple causation is applied to actual problems of laws and their enforcement, the issue gets more difficult. Even if it is the case that a certain form of sexually explicit material bears a causal relationship to harm, the question remains whether some other stimulus has an even greater causal relationship. Except peripherally, we could not be expected to delve deeply into all possible other causes of sexual violence, sex discrimination, and extreme sexual aggression. To the extent that we make recommendations about law enforcement, we make them from a presupposition that others from a larger perspective must make the ultimate determinations about allocation of scarce financial and other societal resources. This task includes not only the allocation of resources among various causes of the harms we have identified, but also involves the even more difficult question of allocating resources among these harms and others. These are difficult questions, and we do not claim that either simple formulas or easy platitudes can answer questions about, for example, apportioning money among countermeasures against poverty, racism, terrorism, and sexual violence. None of us would say that any of these is unimportant, but we recognize that in a world of scarce resources the long term commitment of resources to combat one evil inevitably draws resources away from those available to combat another evil. Even if one assumes that there are currently under-utilized resources that could be allocated to the harms we discuss here, such an allocation still involves a decision to allocate the currently under-utilized resources to combat these harms rather than some others. We have no solutions to these intractable problems of priority in a world in which there is more to do than there are resources with which to do it. Nevertheless, we feel it important to note here that we have not ignored these problems, and we urge that everything we say be considered in light of these considerations.

Although we are sensitive to the difficulty of problems of priority, we still feel confident in concluding that, at the very least, the problems of sexual violence, sexual aggression short of actual violence, and sex discrimination are serious societal problems that have traditionally received a disproportionately

small allocation of societal resources. To the extent that we would be asked the question whether resources should be expended on alleviating these problems rather than dealing with others, we assert strongly that these problems have received less resources than we think desirable, and that remedying that imbalance by a possibly disproportionate allocation in the opposite direction is appropriate.

The conclusion in the previous paragraph does not address the question of priorities of approach once we have decided to treat these problems as high priority matters. With respect to priorities in dealing with the problems of sexual violence, sexual aggression not involving violence, and sex discrimination, people disagree about the optimal priority that dealing in some way with sexually violent pornography and sexually degrading pornography ought to have. But images are significant determinants of attitudes, and attitudes are significant determinants of human behavior. To the extent constitutionally permissible, dealing with the messages all around us seems an important way of dealing with the behavior. We have concluded that the images we deal with here seem to be at the least a substantial cause of the harms we have identified. But common sense leads us to go further, and to suppose that the images are a significant cause even when compared with all of the other likely causes of these same harms. To the extent that this substantial causal relationship has not been reflected in the realities of law enforcement, we have little hesitation in making recommendations about increased priority.

The Problem of Under-inclusiveness.

The problem of multiple causation is addressed to those causes of certain harms other than some varieties of pornographic materials. The problem has another aspect, best referred to as the problem of under-inclusiveness. For even if we restrict our consideration to sexually oriented images, to the various kinds of sexually explicit materials discussed in Chapter 5, it is certainly the case that many of those materials are constitutionally immune from governmental regulation. And to the extent that the material involved becomes less explicit, the immunity from regulation, as a matter of current law, increases. A great deal of sexual violence, for example, is part of less sexually explicit and generally available films and magazines, and because it is presented in less explicit fashion in the context of some plot or theme it remains beyond the realm of governmental control, although non-governmental self-restraint or citizen action seems highly appropriate. And when we include various other sources of sexually oriented messages and images in contemporary society, from prime time television to the lyrics of contemporary music to advertisements for blue jeans, it is even more apparent that much of what people are concerned with in terms of truly pornographic materials might also be a concern with respect to an immense range and quantity of materials that are unquestionably protected by the First Amendment. Many of these materials may present the message in a more diluted form, but certainly their prevalence more than compensates for any possible dilution. As a result, even the most stringent legal strategies within current or even in any way plausible constitutional limitations would likely address little more than the tip of the iceberg.

We thus confront a society in which the Constitution properly requires governments to err on the side of underregulation rather than overregulation, and in which the First Amendment leaves most of the rejection of unacceptable and dangerous ideas to citizens rather than to government. Faced with this reality, it would be easy to note the irremediable futility of being limited only to a thin slice of the full problem, and as a consequence recommend deregulation even as to the material we deem harmful and constitutionally unprotected. But this would be too easy. First, it ignores the extent to which the materials that can be regulated consistent with the Constitution may, because they present their messages in a form undiluted by any appeal to the intellect, bear a causal relationship to the appeal to the intellect, bear a causal relationship to the harms we have identified to a disproportionate degree. And with respect to sexual violence, these materials may disproportionately be aimed at and influence people more predisposed to this form of behavior. For both of these reasons, most of us believe that in many cases the harm-causing capacities of some sexually explicit material may be more concentrated in that which is constitutionally regulable and legally obscene than in that which is plainly protected by the Constitution. This factor of concentration of harm may itself justify maintaining a strategy of

law enforcement in the face of massive underinclusiveness.

More significantly, however, law serves an important symbolic function, and in many areas of life that which the law condemns serves as a model for the condemnatory attitudes and actions of private citizens. Obviously this symbolic function, the way in which the law teaches as well as controls, is premised on a general assumption of legitimacy with respect to the law in general that generates to many people a presumption that the law's judgments are morally, politically, and scientifically correct in addition to being merely authoritative. In making recommendations about what the law should do, we are cognizant of the responsibilities that accompany law's symbolic function. We are aware as well of its opportunities, and of the symbolic function that may be served by even strikingly underinclusive regulation. Conversely, we are aware of the message conveyed by repeal or non-enforcement of existing laws with respect to certain kinds of materials. To the extent that we believe, as we do, that in a number of cases the message that is or would be conveyed by repeal or non-enforcement is exactly the opposite message from what we have concluded and what the evidence supports, we are unwilling to have the law send out the wrong signal. Especially on an issue as publicly noted and debated as this, the law will inevitably send out a signal. We would prefer that it be the signal consistent with the evidence and consistent with our conclusions.

THE CRIMINAL LAW

In light of our conclusions regarding harm, and in light of the factors discussed above, we reject the argument that all distribution of legally obscene pornography should be decriminalized. Even with that conclusion, however, many issues remain, and it is to these that we now turn.

The Sufficiency of Existing Criminal Laws

The laws of the United States and of almost every state make criminal the sale, distribution, or exhibition of material defined as obscene pursuant to the definition set forth by the Supreme court in *Miller v. California*.[50] The enormous differences among states and among other geographic areas in obscenity law enforcement are due not to differences in

---

50. 413 U.S., p. 15 (1973). We discuss *Miller* and other applicable cases in detail in Chapter 3.

the laws as written,[51] but to differences in how, how vigorously, and how often these laws are enforced.

Some witnesses have urged us to recommend changes in the criminal law resulting in laws that are significantly different in scope or in method of operation from those now in force. We have, for example been urged to recommend a "per se" approach to obscenity law that would make the display of certain activities automatically obscene and we have been urged to recommend a definition of the legally obscene that is broader than that of *Miller*. We have thought carefully about these and similar suggestions, but we have rejected them. We have rejected these suggestions for a number of reasons, the most important of which is that it has not been shown that the basic definitions or broad methods of operation of existing laws are in any way insufficient legal tools for those who care to use them. Some witnesses have complained about the uncertainty of the existing legal definition of obscenity, but it has appeared to us that these uncertainty claims have usually been the scapegoat for relatively low prosecutorial initiatives. A substantially larger number of witnesses involved in law enforcement have testified that they do not find excess uncertainty in the *Miller* standard as applied and interpreted, and consequently believe that the existing laws are sufficient for their needs. The success of prosecutorial efforts in Atlanta, Cincinnati, and several other localities, in which vigorous investigation, vigorous prosecution, and stringent sentencing have substantially diminished the availability of almost all legally obscene materials, plainly indicates that the laws are there for those areas that choose the course of vigorous enforcement. We recognize that not all localities will wish to make the commitments of resources that Atlanta and Cincinnati have, but the experiences in such localities persuades us that the desire to have new or more laws, while always appealing as political strategy, is in fact unjustified on the record.

Moreover, a new law incorporating a definition of its coverage different from that in *Miller* would be sure to be challenged in the courts on constitutional grounds. At the moment, the conclusion must be that these pro-posals are constitutionally dubious in light of *Miller*, that they would remain so until there was a Supreme Court decision validating them and in effect overruling *Miller*, and that there is no indication at the present time that the Supreme Court is inclined in this direction. Even assuming a desire to restrict materials not currently subject to restriction under *Miller*, a desire that most of us do not share, we find a strategy of embarking on years of constitutional litigation with little likelihood of success to be highly counterproductive unless the current state of the law is distinctly unsatisfactory in light of the desire to pursue legitimate goals. Because we do not find the existing state of the law unsatisfactory to pursue the goals we have urged, we reject the view that laws incorporating a different and constitutionally suspect definition of coverage are needed or are in any way desirable.

The Problems of Law Enforcement

If the laws on the books are sufficient, then what explains the lack of effective enforcement of obscenity laws throughout most parts of the country? The evidence is unquestionable that with few exceptions the obscenity laws that are on the books go unenforced. As of the dates when the testimony was presented to us, cities as large as Miami, Florida, and Buffalo, New York, had but one police officer assigned to enforcement of the obscenity laws. Chicago, Illinois, had two. Los Angeles, California, had fewer than ten. The City of New York will not take action against establishments violating the New York obscenity laws unless there is a specific complaint, and even then prosecution is virtually non-existent. Federal law enforcement is limited almost exclusively to child pornography and to a few major operations against large pornography production and distribution networks linked to organized crime. From January 1, 1978, to February 27, 1986, a total of only one hundred individuals were indicted for violation of the federal obscenity laws, and of the one hundred indicted seventy-one were convicted.[52]

From this and much more evidence just like it, the conclusion is unmistakable that with respect to the criminal laws relating to obscenity, there is a striking under-

---

51. There are exceptions to this, however. For example, California has until recently employed as a definition of obscenity not the test in *Miller*, but the "utterly without redeeming social value" test from *Memoirs v. Massachusetts*, 383 U.S., p. 413 (1966).

52. Of the remaining twenty-nine cases, only three resulted in acquittals.

enforcement, and that this under-enforce-
ment consists of under-complaining, under-
investigation, under-prosecution, and under-
sentencing. The reasons for this are complex,
and we regret that we have not been able to explore nearly as much as we would have liked
the reasons for this complex phenomenon. We
offer here only a few hypotheses, and hope
that further research by criminologists and
others will continue where we leave off.

With respect to sentencing, the evidence
was almost unanimous that small fines and
unsupervised probation are the norm, with
large fines or sentences of incarceration quite
rare throughout the country. In examining
this phenomenon, we can speculate on a
number of problems. When the prosecution
involves as defendants those with significant
control over the enterprise, the defendant is
likely to appear as very much like the typical
"white collar" criminal nicely dressed, well-
spoken, and with a residence in the suburbs.
A person fitting this description is least likely
in contemporary America to receive jail time,
regardless of the crime. In this respect we
suspect that the problem of under-sentencing
is traceable to the same causes that have produced the same phenomenon with regard to
other crimes. People who have control over
the sale of illegally obscene materials do not
go to jail for many of the same reasons that
price fixers, odometer adjusters, and securities manipulators do not go to jail, and if they
do it is still less often and for less time than do
people committing other crimes that allow
equivalent statutory sentences. Moreover, like
these and other crimes, obscenity offenses often appear to both judges and probation officers as less serious than violent crimes, and
often as even less serious than various crimes
against property. To a significant extent,
those involved in the sentencing process tend
not to perceive obscenity violations as serious
crimes. Whether these judgments of seriousness made by judges and probation officers
are or are not correct is of course debatable,
but the point remains that there seems to be a
substantial interposition of judgment of seriousness between the legislative determination and the actual sentence. As a result,
sentencing usually involves only a fine and

unsupervised probation, and is often treated
by the defendant as little more than a cost of
doing business.[53]

With respect to those without ownership or
managerial control, usually ticket takers or
clerks, many judges and probation officers
seem understandably reluctant to impose periods of incarceration on people who are
likely to be relatively short-term employees
earning little more than the minimum wage.
Although in some cases ticket takers or clerks
are involved with the business itself, more often they are not. With some justification in
fact, therefore, some judges perceive that people who would but for fortune be clerks in
candy stores rather than clerks in pornography outlets should not receive jail time for
having taken the only job that may have been
available to them.

Whatever the causes of under-sentencing, it
is apparent that with the current state of sentencing the criminal laws have very little deterrent effect on the sale or distribution of
legally obscene materials. Although we have
recommended mandatory minimum sentences for second and further offenses, some of
us are not convinced that this will actually
serve as a solution, for in many areas mandatory sentencing may result in plea bargains
for lesser charges, or prosecutorial reluctance
to proceed against someone the prosecutor is
unwilling to see go to jail. None of us are certain about the effects of mandatory sentencing, and mandatory sentencing may be
appropriate if it comports with practices for
crimes of equivalent seriousness within a jurisdiction. But we fear that the problem of
under-sentencing is more complex than simple, and to the extent that mandatory minimum sentencing may in practice be only
cosmetic, it should not blunt efforts to look
further for the roots of the problem of under-
sentencing.

The problem of under-sentencing is likely
to affect the level of prosecution. When the
end result of even a successful persecution is
a fine that is insignificant compared to the
profits of the operation, or at most a period of
incarceration that is so minimal as to have insignificant deterrent effect, the incentive to
prosecute diminishes on the part of both

53. In this connection, we should note our support (and our specific recommendation in that section of this Report)
for use of the Racketeer Influenced and Corrupt Organizations (RICO) Act as a method of requiring many of those
convicted of multiple and substantial obscenity violations to disgorge the profits from their enterprises. Whether in this
form or another, methods of attacking profits, or the assets purchased with those profits, seem likely to be more effective
financial deterrents than substantially smaller fines.

prosecutors and law enforcement personnel. The potentially light sentence magnifies the fact that obscenity prosecutions are likely to be properly perceived as necessitating a high expenditure of time and resources as well as being, in terms of the likelihood of securing a conviction, high risk enterprises. The defendants will usually be represented by sophisticated lawyers with a mandate to engage in a vigorous and extensive defense. It would be a rare prosecutor who did not understand the difference between prosecuting a mugger represented by a young public defender with too many cases and too little time and resources, on the one hand, and, on the other, prosecuting a pornography distributor who has a team of senior trial lawyers at his disposal and who will probably receive only a minimal sentence even if convicted.

In addition to the fact that obscenity prosecutions are seen as high risk and low reward ventures for prosecutors and law enforcement personnel, it is also the case that being involved in obscenity investigation or obscenity prosecution is likely to be lower in the hierarchy of esteemed activities within a prosecutorial office or within a police department. This may stem in part from the extent to which the personal views of many people within those departments are such as to treat these matters as not especially serious. The extent to which this is so, and the extent to which there are other factors we have been unable to isolate, we cannot at this time determine. But we are confident that the phenomenon exists.

The upshot of all of the above is that we are forced to conclude that the problem of under-prosecution cannot be remedied simply by saying that enforcement of the obscenity laws ought to have a higher priority, or simply by providing more money for enforcement, or simply by increasing the amount of community and political pressure on all those involved in the law enforcement effort. We do not discount any of these approaches, as all have proved effective at times when used in conjunction with other techniques of changing law enforcement practices; but it is clear that the dynamics are sufficiently complex

that no one remedy for the problem will suffice. There is a multiplicity of factors explaining the lack of enforcement, and changing that situation will require a multiplicity of remedies. We urge that many of the specific recommendations we suggest be taken seriously.

Federalism

We operate in a nation with dual systems of criminal law. The laws of most states make the sale, exhibition, or distribution of obscene material a crime, but federal law also makes it a crime to use the mails or the facilities of interstate commerce for such purposes. In thinking about law enforcement a recurring issue is the proper sphere of operation for federal law and the proper sphere of operation for state law.

Putting aside the enforcement of federal laws against child pornography, which we discuss in Chapter 7,[54] federal law enforcement efforts are now directed almost exclusively against large nationwide obscenity distribution networks with known connections with organized crime. With few exceptions, there is little enforcement of federal obscenity laws in cases not involving some strong suspicion of organized crime involvement. For example, despite reasonably clear evidence that sophisticated multi-state operations dealing in large quantities of legally obscene material have substantial contacts with localities such as Los Angeles and New York City, there has been essentially no federal prosecution of the obscenity laws in the Central District of California and the Southern District of New York. We mention these particular districts only because they are large and have within them particular concentrations of either production or distribution of legally obscene materials. But the pattern of federal non-involvement is not limited to these districts. The nationwide pattern of little federal prosecution seems to have changed somewhat within the past months, most likely as a result of the publicity associated with this Commission, but it remains a safe conclusion that enforcement of federal law has been minimal.

---

54. In addition to trying to achieve some degree of analytic clarity, we put aside child pornography in this context because we note the extent to which prosecutors and other law enforcement officials have frequently relied on the number of child pornography prosecutions to give a general impression of vigorous enforcement of the obscenity laws in their jurisdiction. On closer examination, it has usually appeared that there was a great deal of activity with respect to child pornography, and virtually none with respect to the obscenity laws. We do not of course deny the importance of allocating large amounts of resources to child pornography. We do not believe, however, that any purpose is served by clouding the existing state of affairs with respect to the enforcement of the obscenity laws.

We note the extent to which it has become common to assume that whenever there is a large problem the solution ought to be a federal one. Witness after witness representing some branch of state law enforcement complained that the real problem was the lack of federal support. Although we sympathize with these witnesses in their attempts to get more support for their efforts, we are dismayed at the unwillingness of the states to assume the bulk of the responsibility for enforcement of the criminal law. Although we do not deny the extent of federal responsibility, and although we do not deny that some states have budgetary crises that approach in seriousness if not in magnitude that of the federal government, there comes a point at which the ready solution of more federal money for even the most worthy endeavors can no longer be the strategy of first resort. We are aware of our responsibilities, now a matter of law as well as good sense, to look for alternatives other than major additional expenditures of federal funds with respect to our own rather than someone else's agenda, and we urge that states consider their law enforcement responsibilities mindful of these considerations. We also note that in our federal system primary responsibility for law enforcement has always been with the states. The police power of the states has commonly been taken to include primary responsibility for dealing with the very types of harms at which the obscenity laws are addressed. And the constitutional commitment to a federal system assumes that state involvement is preferable to federal in areas, such as most of the criminal law, in which local decisions may vary. We see no reason not to make, in general, the same assumptions with respect to the enforcement of obscenity laws.

Despite our view that primary law enforcement responsibilities rest with the states, federal law and federal law enforcement have an essential role to play in the enforcement of the obscenity laws. Most of the material that we find most harmful is distributed throughout the country by means of large and sophisticated distribution networks. It is precisely with respect to this kind of massive and complex interstate (and international) operation that the special skills and resources of federal investigative agencies are most needed, and to which the nature of federal criminal prosecution is most suited. Prosecutions can, as with the MIPORN prosecutions in Miami, join in a single prosecution people from different states who are integral and controlling parts of the same enterprise. And the federal judicial apparatus is often more suited than that of the states where evidence and witnesses must be secured from throughout the country.

Thus, we do not see the scope of federal prosecution as being limited to cases involving demonstrable connections with organized crime. In any case in which the evidence indicates a multi-state operation of substantial size and sophistication, federal rather than or in addition to state law enforcement is most appropriate. By concentrating vigorously on such operations, federal prosecutorial and investigative resources will be reserved for the cases in which federal involvement has the greatest comparative advantage, while still reserving to the states that primary role in more local law enforcement that is at the core of our system of federalism.

What Should Be Prosecuted?

In Chapter 5 we discussed at length the increasing trend in the scientific research and in general discussions of this subject to recognize that not all pornographic items are identical. There are substantial differences in the content of such materials, and we have tried in the rough categorization of Chapter 5 to express our sympathy with these efforts to advance the clarity of thinking about the issue of pornography. Indeed, we hope that we have contributed to those efforts. As the natural consequence of these efforts to recognize the differences among pornographic materials, we urge that thinking in terms of these or analogous categories be a part of the analysis of the total law enforcement effort.

The categories we discussed in Chapter 5 encompass a range of materials far broader than the legally obscene, and thus, in the context of this discussion of the criminal law, a range of materials far broader than what we know can be prosecuted consistent with the Constitution. Nevertheless, these categories, with the exception of nudity not involving the lewd exhibition of the genitals, exist within as well as around the legally obscene, material that has been or could be criminally prosecuted consistent with the Miller standard, there exist materials that are sexually violent, materials that are non-violent but degrading, and materials that, although highly sexually explicit and offensive to many, contain neither violence nor degradation. In light of our conclusions in Chapter 5, we would urge that prosecution of obscene materials that portray sexual violence be treated as a matter of special urgency. With respect to sexually violent materials the evidence is strongest, societal consensus is greatest, and the consequent harms of rape and other forms of sexual violence are hardly ones that this or any other society can take lightly. In light of this, we would urge that the prosecution of legally obscene material that contains violence be placed at the top of both state and federal priorities in enforcing the obscenity laws.[55]

With respect to materials that are nonviolent yet degrading, the evidence supporting our findings is not as strong as it is with respect to violent materials. And on the available evidence we have required more in the way of assumption to draw the connection between these materials and sexual violence, sexual aggression, and sex discrimination.

Nevertheless, these assumptions have significant support on the evidence and in our own logic and experiences, and the causal evidence remains for us strong enough to support our conclusions. None of us hesitate to recommend prosecution of those materials that are both degrading and legally obscene.

If choices must be made, however, prosecution of these materials might have to receive slightly lower priority than sexually violent materials, but this is not to say that we view action against degrading materials as unimportant.

With respect to materials in the third category we have identified, materials that are neither violent nor degrading, the issues are more difficult. There seems to be no evidence in the social science data of a causal relationship with sexual violence, sexual aggression, or sex discrimination. These three harms do not exhaust the possible harms, however, and our disagreements regarding this category reflect disagreements that abound in this society at this time. Many people believe that making sex into an essentially public act is a harm of major proportions, a harm that is compounded by its commercialization. To others legitimizing through this material either a wide range of traditionally prohibited sexual practices, or legitimizing sex without love, marriage, commitment, or even affection is the primary harm with which people should be concerned. Some people have recognized the extent to which material of this variety is likely to wind up in the hands of children, and thus to frighten children or to encourage children to model their behavior on what they have seen, and would take this to be a sufficient condition for serious concern. And some people note the importance to any society of some set of shared moral values, including values relating to sexuality, and look upon the proliferation of the material even in this category as an attack on something that is a precondition for a community. On the other hand, many people see these concerns as less problematic, or matters appropriate for individual choice and nothing more, or see in some of the use of these materials beneficial effects which ought also to be taken into account. We cannot resolve these disagreements among ourselves or for society, but the fact of disagreement remains a fact.

Regardless of who is right and who is wrong about these issues, and we do not purport to have clear, definitive, or easy answers, the substantially lower level of societal consensus about these matters is an empirical fact.[56] To some of us, this substantially lower level of societal consensus, when combined with the absence for these materials of scientific evidence showing a causal connection with sexual violence, sexual aggression, or sex discrimination, leaves a category as to which this society is less certain and as to which one array of concerns, present with the two previous categories, is absent. More than this is necessary to recommend deregulation or even to support a recommendation not to prosecute what has long been taken to be regulable. And we will not so easily discount the substantial arguments that can be made for regulation by recommending a drastic change in what has been general practice for most of the history of this nation. Nevertheless, the factors of lower societal consensus and absence of causal connection with sexual violence, aggression, or discrimination are to some of us germane to the question of priority.

55. In discussing priorities here, we exclude from consideration child pornography. As we explain in Chapter 7, child pornography involves a different range of materials, a different kind of "industry," a different kind of offender, and consequently different approach to the problems of law enforcement. We treat it separately because it is so different. We do not in so doing wish to suggest that the problems are any less. If anything they are greater, but they remain different, and little purpose is served by dealing with child pornography as part of the larger category of pornography.

56. Indeed, all of the survey evidence supports the view that there are substantial disparities between societal views regarding restrictions on materials depicting sexual violence and materials depicting sex alone.

With respect, therefore, to legally obscene material within this category it seems entirely appropriate to some of us, at least in terms of long-term commitment of resources, for prosecutors and law enforcement personnel to treat such material differently from material containing sexual violence or degradation of women. Should a community wish to allocate sufficient resources to obscenity enforcement that material in this category is prosecuted as vigorously as that in the previously discussed category, we find that an entirely legitimate decision for a community to make. But if a community does not wish to devote resources to that extent, or if a community believes that the material in this category, even if legally obscene, is not cause for the stringent sanctions of the criminal law, then it would seem to some of us appropriate for that community to concentrate its efforts on material that is either violent or degrading.

On this issue we are, as would be expected given our differences with respect to the harms associated with this category, deeply divided. Some of us would strongly urge that all legally obscene material be prosecuted with equal vigor, and would not only urge the communities of which we are part to take this course, but would condemn those that did not. Others of us see the prosecution of material within this category as something that should quite consciously be treated as a lower priority matter, and still others of us see the questions with respect to this category as being primarily for the community to make, with community decisions to prosecute vigorously, or not at all, or somewhere in between, as entitled to equal respect.

Although we are divided on this question, the division is likely on the current state of the law to be more philosophical than real. Pursuant to *Miller*, material is obscene only if, among numerous other factors, it offends the community in which it is made available. As a result, in those communities in which material within this category is not considered especially problematic, the material will not be considered legally obscene. And in those communities in which material within this category is condemned, it will offend community standards and thus, if the other requirements of *Miller* are met, will be legally

obscene.[57] As a result, therefore, the existing legal approach incorporates within the definition of obscenity the views of a particular community. The question whether to prosecute material in this category, therefore, assuming that the decision to prosecute is in effect a community decision, will turn into the question, under current law, whether the material is obscene at all.

The Special Prominence of the Printed Word

In oral testimony before us, in written submissions, and in numerous published discussions of the question of pornography, fears have been expressed about the dangers of excess censorship. As we have explained in Chapter 3, we are sensitive to the risks of excess censorship beyond the bounds of what the First Amendment or good sense should allow, but we have found many of these claims to be little more than hyperbole, warning against censorship in the abstract but providing little in the way of real evidence that the possibility exists.

That the evidence presented has been weak, however, does not mean that we should ignore the possibility that in some areas prosecution might be attempted of works of undoubted merit in the name of obscenity law, or that obscenity prosecution might be threatened as a way of exercising impermissible control over works that are not even close to being legally obscene. We heard testimony, for example, about a local prosecutor who, presented with a citizen complaint about a not even plausibly obscene book in the local library, sought out a written statement of a literary justification for the book instead of telling the complaint that the book quite simply was not obscene. And as we have investigated similar incidents, and listened to claims about excess censorship, it has become apparent to us that the vast majority of these concerns have surrounded books consisting entirely of the printed word text only, without photographs or even drawings.

In thinking about these concerns, we note that material consisting entirely of the printed word can be legally obscene, as the Supreme Court held in 1973 in *Kaplan v. California*.[58] And we have seen in the course of

---

57. We emphasize that it is the values of the entire community that are relevant, and we do not suggest here that it is appropriate for a prosecutor or law enforcement official to substitute his or her values for that of the community as a whole.

58. 413 U.S., (1973), p. 115.

our inquiries books that would meet this standard—books consisting of nothing other than descriptions of sexual activity in the most explicit terms, plainly patently offensive to the vast majority of people, and plainly devoid of anything that could be considered literary, artistic, political, or scientific value.

Although many such books exist, and although they constitute part of all the categories of material we have identified, they seem to be the least harmful materials within the various categories. Because they involve no photographs, there need be no concerns with those who are actually used in the process of production. And the absence of photographs necessarily produces a message that seems to necessitate for its assimilation more real thought and less almost reflexive reaction than does the more typical pornographic item. There remains a difference between reading a book and looking at pictures, even pictures printed on a page.

All of us would strongly urge prosecution of legally obscene material containing only text when the material is either targeted at an audience of children or when its content involves child molestation or any form of sexual activity with children. Because of the effect of the child pornography laws, photographic material involving children is becoming less available, and this material, which is likely to encourage acts of child molestation, occupies a significant portion of textual obscenity. There is little prosecution of this material now, and we hope that that situation will change.

Some of us, however, except for material plainly describing sexual activity with minors or targeted to minors, would urge that materials consisting entirely of the printing word simply not be prosecuted at all, regardless of content. There is for all practical purposes no prosecution of such materials now, so such an approach would create little if any change in what actually occurs. But by converting this empirical fact into a plain statement even the possibility of prosecuting a book will be eliminated. If this is eliminated even as a possibility, those of us who take this position believe that the vast majority of potential abuses can be quelled and the vast majority of fears alleviated with what will be at most a negligible reduction in law enforcement effectiveness. Most likely there will be no effect at all on law enforcement, although those who take this position nevertheless de-

plore many of the books, a substantial proportion of which involve violence or degradation. But from this perspective, what is lost in the ability to prosecute this material is more than compensated for by the symbolic and real benefits accompanying the statement that the written word has had and continues to have a special place in this and any other civilization.

Others of us, however, while sharing this special concern for the written word, would not adopt such a rigid rule, and would retain both in theory and in practice the ability to prosecute obscene material regardless of the form in which the obscenity is conveyed. Especially in light of the fact that we have seen many books that are devoted to sexual violence and sexual degradation, some of us fear that giving carte blanche to such material, regardless of current prosecutorial practices, is to send out exactly the wrong signal. Those of us who take this position share the concern for the written word, but believe that that concern can best be reflected in ways other than providing a license for material that, although presented in verbal form, seems substantially similar to the forms of pictorial obscenity that concern us.

Although we are deeply divided on the question of a clear rule prohibiting prosecution (except in cases involving or directed at children), we share each others concerns. Those of us who would adopt a clear rule nevertheless regret some of its consequences, and deplore much of the textual obscenity we have seen. And those of us who reject the idea of a clear rule understand the concerns for purely verbal communication, and urge that prosecution of entirely textual material be undertaken only with extraordinary caution.

REGULATION BY ZONING

For many people the harms caused by pornography relate in part to the effects on communities and neighborhoods of the establishments in which such materials are commonly sold. Whether it be a peep show, an "adults only" pornographic theater, or a so-called "adult bookstore," there seems widespread agreement that virtually all such establishments are largely detrimental to the neighborhoods in which they are located. Some of the negative consequences arise from the style of the establishments themselves, which usually have garish lights and signs advertising the nature of what is to be found within in no uncertain terms. Other consequences flow from the clientele, who are often people that many citizens would just as soon be somewhere else. And such establishments are likely to exist in close proximity to areas in which prostitution exists, and in close proximity to establishments such as bars featuring live, sexually oriented entertainment. As a result, most people would consider such establishments environmentally detrimental, and there is some evidence indicating a correlation between crime rates and the particular neighborhoods in which such establishments exist.

Although some communities have attempted to deal with pornography outlets through criminal prosecution, others have attempted zoning regulation more narrowly tailored to alleviating the consequences discussed in the previous paragraph. These regulations generally take two forms. One is a dispersal regulation, in which zoning ordinances prohibit location of such an establishment within a specified distance of another such establishment. The principle behind dispersal ordinances is that of scattering these establishments throughout a large geographic area, so that no concentration of them can have a major deleterious effect on any one neighborhood. Alternatively, some communities have endeavored to concentrate these establishments, attempting through zoning to limit them to one or just a few parts of the community, usually remote from residential areas, and frequently remote as well from certain business districts.

In order for such ordinances to be effective, they must be able to describe the establishments they regulate in terms at least slightly broader than the Miller definition of obscenity. Were the Miller standard to be used, the administrative enforcement mechanism commonly in force with respect to zoning would become bogged down in the more cumbersome procedures characteristic of full trials.

Most such ordinances, therefore, regulate establishments that specialize in sexually explicit material, and usually the ordinance contains a definition of sexually explicit material that is more precise but more expansive than Miller.[59] Although such ordinances include more than could criminally be prosecuted under Miller, the Supreme Court has approved zoning regulation of this variety, first in 1976 in Young v. American Mini Theaters, Inc.,[60] and then again in February 1986 in City of Renton v. Playtime Theaters, Inc.[61] The most significant qualification imposed by the Court is the requirement that the zoning regulation not have the effect of a total prohibition.[62] The result, therefore, is that if communities wish to restrict the location of such "adults only" establishments, they may do so, but they may not under the guise of zoning banish them altogether.

Witnesses who have testified before us about zoning approaches in their localities have by and large not endorsed these approaches. Most of these witnesses, however, have been law enforcement personnel who would prefer prohibition to relocation. The zoning approach, which is not aimed at prohibition, is not surprisingly a poor tool if prohibition is the desired result.

Moreover, in most localities these ordinances contain "grandfather" clauses, eliminating from the restrictions those establishments already in place on the date of enactment of the ordinance.[63] Thus the result has often been to prevent the problem from growing, but has done little to diminish the extent of an existing problem.

It has been suggested that zoning may be the ideal solution to the problem of pornography, because it allows people who wish access to this material to have such access without having its sale intrude on the lives and sensibilities of the majority of the population who wish to have nothing to do with it.

59. For example, the Detroit ordinance that was before the Supreme Court in the Young case defined as an "adult establishment" any establishment concentrating on offering material emphasizing "specified sexual activities" or "specified anatomical areas." "Specified sexual activities" were defined to include, for example, "Human Genitals in a state of sexual stimulation or arousal," "Acts of human masturbation, sexual intercourse or sodomy," and "Fondling or other erotic touching of human genitals, pubic region, buttock or female breast." The definition of "Specified anatomical areas" was similarly broader than would be permitted by Miller if the aim were total prohibition. To the extent that zoning approaches concentrate on establishments specializing in this material, we note that such approaches may have the effect of providing incentives for attempts to introduce more plainly pornographic material into more mainstream outlets.

60. 427 U.S., (1976), p. 50.

61. 54 U.S.L.W. 4160 (Feb. 25, 1986).

62. On this point, see, Schad v. Mt. Ephraim, 452 U.S., (1981) p. 61.

63. Although such clauses may be required by state law, we note that nothing in the First Amendment, or in federal constitutional law generally, would require such an approach.

This solution is ideal, however, only under the presupposition that the material is not indeed harmful except insofar as it causes offense to non-users. With respect to sexually violent material and degrading material, we have found that the evidence does not support such a modest view of the likely consequences, and thus we reject an equivalently modest remedy for what we take to be harmful material, even when its access is restricted to willing buyers. If indeed the material in these categories is harmful, as we have found it to be, we cannot consistent with that finding urge a remedy of moving it to another part of town.

With respect to materials that are neither violent nor degrading, however, both the evidence of harms and the level of societal consensus are less, and zoning might possibly be more appropriate for establishments restricting their stock to materials in this category. As suggested above (beginning on page 56), the absence of evidence for this material of a causal connection with sexual violence, sexual aggression, or sex discrimination may suggest lower prosecutorial priority within a system of enforcement of the criminal laws. But even for localities that may choose this course, the offensiveness of these materials and the deleterious effects on the neighborhoods in which they are made available may still be seen to justify some restriction. If this is the case, then zoning may be the appropriate way to deal with materials of this variety, although many of us are concerned that in practice such an approach will concentrate such establishments in or near the most economically disadvantaged segments of a locality. Some of us fear that zoning may be a way for those with political power to shunt the establishments they do not want in their own neighborhoods into the neighborhoods of those with less wealth and less political power.

Restrictions on public display, whether through the criminal law or zoning ordinances, are in effect another form of zoning. The concept here is that there may be many materials that, regardless of their alleged harmlessness, and regardless of the fact that they are not legally obscene, ought not to be displayed in a manner that offends unwilling viewers. Moreover, the public display does not differentiate between passersby who are adults and those who are children, and taking into account the likelihood that children will be exposed to this material at inappropriate ages justifies restrictions that might seem harsh in settings involving only adults. Even those most likely to oppose obscenity regulation would, we suspect, have little difficulty in principle with restricting sexually explicit material from billboards. None of us has difficulty with this either, even when extended somewhat beyond the legally obscene. We believe that public display regulations, including but not limited to the control of advertising materials displayed on the exterior of adult establishments, and including but not limited to the display ordinances requiring shielding of the covers of sexually explicit magazines, are fully justifiable measures in a society that has long restricted indecent exposure. If copulating in a public park may be restricted, we are not troubled by regulations prohibiting billboards depicting copulation.

We ought finally to mention in this section the attempts in a number of communities to restrict "adults only" pornographic establishments through the use of nuisance laws and related legal remedies. Nuisance laws, when applied to sexually explicit materials, are attempts to serve many of the interests that generated the zoning approach, but here the aim is prohibition rather than relocation. The desired result in most such legal actions is an injunction against further operation of the establishment. For that reason, all effective uses of this approach have thus far been found unconstitutional. Even where an establishment has been found guilty of a criminal obscenity violation, the law as of this moment does not permit the finding of obscenity with respect to one magazine, or one film, to justify what is in fact a restriction on other films and other magazines not yet determined to be legally obscene, and therefore presumptively protected by the First Amendment. Total prohibition, therefore, on the state of the law right now, seems much more likely to stem from substantial criminal penalties for those involved with such establishments than from civil remedies directed in some way directed against the establishment and not the person.

THE CIVIL RIGHTS APPROACH TO PORNOGRAPHY

Within the last several years a substantial amount of the public discussion of pornography has centered around a proposed antipornography ordinance drafted by two scholars, Andrea Dworkin and Catherine MacKinnon, and proposed in one form or another in a number of localities, most notably Minneapolis, Minnesota; Los Angeles, California; Cambridge, Massachusetts; and Indianapolis, Indiana. The only community actually to adopt such an ordinance was Indianapolis, which on June 11, 1984, drafted an ordinance providing *civil* remedies against pornography. The ordinance defined pornography as:

> The graphic sexually explicit subordination of women, whether in pictures or in words, that also includes one or more of the following: (1) Women are presented as sexual objects who enjoy pain or humiliation; or (2) Women are presented as sexual objects who experience sexual pleasure in being raped; or (3) Women are presented as sexual objects tied up or cut up or mutilated or bruised or physically hurt, or as dismembered or truncated or fragmented or severed into body parts; or (4) Women are presented being penetrated by objects or animals; or (5) Women are presented in scenarios of degradation, injury, abasement, torture, shown as filthy or inferior, bleeding, bruised, or hurt in a context that makes these conditions sexual; [or] (6) Women are presented as sexual objects for domination, conquest, violation, exploitation, possession, or use, or through postures or positions of servility or submission or display.

The ordinance has subsequently been held unconstitutional by the United States District Court for the Southern District of Indiana,[64] and that decision has been affirmed by the United States Court of Appeals for the Seventh Circuit.[65] Recently the Seventh Circuit's decision has been affirmed, on the merits but without opinion, by the Supreme Court of the United States.[66] The basis for the finding of unconstitutionality was the way in which the definition set forth above was substantially more inclusive than that in *Miller*. To the extent that legislation restricts material beyond the legally obscene, that legislation must confront an array of First Amendment-inspired barriers that few if any statutes could meet. This statute could not surmount those obstacles, for much the same reason, according to the courts, that attempted restrictions on members of the American Nazi Party and the Ku Klux Klan could not surmount those obstacles. Once the comparatively narrow realm of *Miller*-tested legal obscenity is left, virtu-

ally no restrictions on communication based on the point of view expressed, no matter how wrong or harmful it may be, are permitted by the First Amendment.

That this ordinance with this definition was properly held unconstitutional, however, should not deflect attention from three other features of the ordinance and of the support it engendered. First, we are in substantial agreement with the motivations behind the ordinance, and with the goals it represents. The harms at which the ordinance is aimed are real and the need for a remedy for those harms is pressing. That we understand both the harm and the urgent need to remedy these harms should be apparent from the discussion in Chapter 5. Moreover, although we feel that the safer and better course is to proceed within existing constitutional boundaries, our recommendations regarding criminal prosecution for legally obscene material containing sexual violence or degradation are largely consistent with what this ordinance attempts to do, although the approach we recommend clearly will reach less material. In effect, this ordinance reaches material containing sexually violent or sexually degrading material when it is sexually explicit. The only constitutionally permissible approach, however, is to reach material containing sexually violent or sexually degrading material when it is legally obscene, and that in effect is what we have strongly urged here.

In addition, the ordinance proposed a civil remedy, rather than a criminal one. We have thought about the issue of a civil remedy, because the question whether there should be a civil or a criminal remedy is analytically distinct from the question of what material will be reached by that remedy. A civil remedy could be combined with all or part of the category of material reached by *Miller*, and we have thought about the possibility of civil rather than criminal sanctions with respect to *Miller*-tested obscenity. Although we recognize that details would remain to be worked out, in large part relating to who would have the ability to bring an action against whom, we endorse the concept of a civil remedy so long as it takes place within existing constitutional limitations. Although we do endorse the concept of a civil remedy, and although we do recognize that much of the material we

---

64. *American Booksellers Ass'n v. Hudnut*, 598 F. Supp. (S.D. Ind. 1984), p. 1316.
65. *American Booksellers Ass'n v. Hudnut*, 771 F.2d (7th Cir. 1985), p. 323.
66. *Hudnut v. American Booksellers Ass'n*, 54 U.S.L.W., (Feb. 24, 1986), p. 3560.

have seen directly implicates in a harmful way the civil rights of women, we do not ignore the deterrent effect on publishers of being forced to defend a wide range of suits that might raise claims that are totally without merit, but which would still require at least a preliminary defense. Although we recognize that occasionally prosecutors might be overzealous, we have no doubt that the average prosecutor is substantially less likely to be overzealous than the *most* zealous potential plaintiff. We have heard from a wide range of people in the course of our work, and some have employed definitions of pornography or have expressed views about what ought to be restricted that are far beyond what any of us would conceivably tolerate. We are unwilling to have each of these people as potential plaintiffs. We are not willing to put a publisher to a defense in every case in which someone thinks that material is obscene or pornographic. If a procedure could be devised that provided for some preliminary determination by a judge or magistrate that the suit was plausible *before the complaint was allowed to be filed*, our fears would evaporate, and with such a procedure we believe that civil remedies available to a wide range of people ought seriously to be contemplated. And in any event, civil remedies that restricted the right of action to, for example, people who were compelled to perform in obscene material or people who were compelled to view obscene material would not have the problems associated with a potentially enormous class of plaintiffs, and ought to be considered even more seriously.

Finally, the ordinance and the support for it properly focused attention on the people who are frequently coerced into performing in sexually explicit films, or into posing for sexually explicit pictures. And even where coercion in the contemporary legal sense is absent, the conditions of employment unquestionably deserve close attention. We agree with these concerns for the participants, and we agree that legal concern for participants need not be limited to the question of child pornography. We believe that civil and other remedies ought to be available to those who have been in some way injured in the process of producing these materials. But we are confident that the remedies of restricting the material itself, at least beyond the category of the legally obscene, permissi-

ble in the case of child pornography, remain constitutionally impermissible with respect to adults. We believe, therefore, that the appropriate remedy in the case of adults is that which is directed at the conduct itself, and we include in a later Chapter of this Report a special report directed exclusively to harms to performers, and possible remedies for those harms.

OBSCENITY AND THE ELECTRONIC MEDIA

Where legally obscene material is transmitted by radio, television, telephone, or cable, the same legal sanctions are or should be available as are available for any other form of distribution or exhibition. Although federal law has long prohibited the transmission of legally obscene materials by radio, television, and telephone, the advent of cable television left a gap in the law. The Cable Communications Policy Act of 1984 attempts to provide criminal penalties for anyone transmitting over any cable system "any matter which is obscene or otherwise unprotected by the Constitution." A number of states have or are on the verge of adopting similar changes in their obscenity laws to include cable transmission, and we support those legislative efforts to ensure that the law keeps up with technological changes. To the extent that obscene material appears on cable television, we urge prosecution to the same extent and with the same vigor as we do with respect to any other form of distribution of obscene material. We note that this has not always been the case, and we urge that enforcement efforts directed to legally obscene material, in whatever regulatory form those enforcement efforts might take, be as aggressive with respect to cable transmission of the legally obscene as with other forms of distribution of the legally obscene.

Under existing law, however, the Federal Communications Commission has the power to impose some sanctions against certain broadcasting of sexually explicit language or pictures over radio and television even where the material is not legally obscene. In *FCC v. Pacifica Foundation*,[67] the Supreme Court upheld the constitutionality of this form of regulation, in the context of sanctions against a radio station for a daytime broadcast of George Carlin's "Seven Dirty Words" monologue, which is in fact about the FCC regula-

---

67. 438 U.S., (1978), p. 726.

tions, and which uses repeatedly the words the FCC prohibits.

As we have explained in Chapter 4 and will do later, there is a great deal available on cable television today that is sexually explicit but which is not legally obscene. Some of this material contains sexual violence, some of it is degrading as we have used that term here, and some of it is, although rather explicit, neither violent nor degrading. In almost all of these cases the films shown have simulated rather than actual sexual activity, most have a rather sustained story line, and many are mainstream and highly acclaimed Hollywood productions.

With respect to these materials that are not legally obscene, they are beyond the reach of the law as it stands today. Nevertheless, we have been urged to recommend changes in the law so that material which is "indecent" as well as legally obscene might be kept from cable television to the same (or greater) extent as it has been kept from broadcast non-subscriber radio and television. We have not adopted these suggestions, however, although it is an issue on which we are deeply divided. Some of us believe that enforcement of obscenity laws with respect to such material, when combined with vigorous enforcement of the "lockbox" requirements so that children may be prevented by their parents from seeing such material, are all that is appropriate at this time. Some of us are persuaded by the fact that the suggestions made to us are all, on the existing state of the law, unconstitutional, with all of the courts that have confronted the issue deciding that cable cannot be controlled by the standards applicable to broadcast non-subscriber television.[68] Some of us are skeptical about *Pacifica* itself, and do not wish to extend to new areas a principle that we find dubious even with respect to broadcast media. In light of the existence of, for example, serious and non-pictorial sexual advice programs as well as serious mainstream motion pictures containing more explicit sexuality than would be available on broadcast television, extension of the limitations of broadcast television to cable seems highly likely to restrict that which simply ought not to be restricted. Some of us

question the current state of the law, but would urge change in the direction of permitting restriction of pure violence rather than indecency. Some of us are also uncomfortable once again about taking on any doubtful causes and courses of constitutional adjudication when existing law seems sufficient for the more extreme cases. And some of us reject all of the above, and feel that cable television, even with lockboxes, is so similar to broadcast television that regulation of more than the legally obscene should be permitted with respect to cable just as it is when the airwaves rather than wires are the medium of transmission. Some of us who hold this view would prefer somewhat broader definitions of what can permissibly be regulated in many areas. And others of us who take this position are comfortable with the existing definition of obscenity, but feel that television is a medium with a special power and a special intrusiveness in contemporary society.

These are difficult questions, going not only to the roots of First Amendment doctrine and theory, but also to the nature of television in American life. As with other fundamental issues, we are unable to agree here, and as a result there is no consensus among us that would justify urging that regulation of cable encompass more than the legally obscene.

Many of the same considerations apply to the regulation of those telephone services, commonly referred to as Dial-a-Porn, that provide sexually explicit messages. As we discuss at length in a later Part, there is no doubt that the number and variety of these services is increasing, and that they have generated substantial citizen concern. Some of the concerns relate to the way in which these services are advertised, and some relate to the messages themselves regardless of who uses the service. Most of the concerns, however, relate to the frequent use of these services by minors, a concern that seems accentuated by the extent to which many of the services seem designed to cater to the particular asexual perceptions of teenagers rather than adults. We have heard a number of these messages, and we have little doubt that the bulk of them could be considered to be legally obscene under existing law.[69] Although they use words

68. *Cruz v. Ferre*, 755 F.2d, (11th Cir. 1985), p. 1415. *Community Television of Utah v. Roy City*, 555 F. Supp. 1164 (D. Utah 1982); *HBO v. Wilkinson*, 531 F. Supp., (D. Utah 1982), p. 987. The Supreme Court has yet to be faced with the question.

69. We believe this to be the case even when the messages are directed at and available only to adults. To the extent that they are directed at and available to minors, the application of the test for obscenity may properly take that into account. *Ginsberg v. New York*, 390 U.S., (1968), p. 629.

rather than pictures, even those of us who would refuse to apply obscenity law to materials containing only the printed word would not apply that principle to these materials. Apart from the fact that many seem implicitly if not explicitly directed at minors, the nature of the spoken voice, especially in this context, contains enough of the characteristics of the visual image that we have no difficulty in saying that such material should be dealt with consistent with our recommendations concerning films, tapes, and pictorial magazines.

Although once again we have been urged to recommend new laws that are substantially more encompassing than the existing definition of the legally obscene, we find such approaches both unnecessary and undesirable. The vast bulk of this material seems to us well within the *Miller* definition, and thus could be prosecuted in accordance with the concerns and the priorities we have urged here. In light of that, we see few advantages and substantial risks in going further. But we also urge that there be laws allowing the prosecution of such legally obscene material, and we urge as well that such laws be enforced. There seems now to be little enforcement, and in light of the frequency with this material is used by minors, we deplore the failure to have and to enforce obscenity laws with respect to material of this type.

ENFORCING BOTH SIDES OF THE LAW

Both in Chapter 3 and in this Chapter we have emphasized our belief that conscientious enforcement of existing obscenity laws and the dictates of the First Amendment are not inconsistent. But our confidence in this conclusion will be increased if all of those with law enforcement responsibilities would recognize their responsibilities to enforce the existing principles of the First Amendment as conscientiously and as vigorously as they enforce the obscenity laws. The Constitution is a law too, and we expect that anyone who has taken an oath to uphold the law will recognize that they must uphold the First Amendment as well.

We make these general observations because we acknowledge that many citizens,

sincerely and for very good reasons, would want the law to do more than it is now constitutionally able to do, and more than we feel it ought constitutionally be able to do. Many of these citizens will find an outlet for their views in the fully legitimate and appropriate private actions that we discuss in Chapter 8. But many others will make requests or demands on law enforcement personnel, sometimes out of ignorance about the constitutional constraints but often out of an understandable frustration that the Constitution, in the name of long-run values, often prevents us from doing what seems quite justifiable in the short run.

When faced with such requests or demands, we hope that law enforcement personnel will recognize their responsibilities to interpose their legal responsibilities at that time. They must refuse to take any action that would in any way be governmentally threatening to those who are exercising their constitutional rights, and they must be willing to explain to their angry constituents why they have not taken action and must not do so. We recognize that this may not always be easy in a world in which the citizens properly expect their elected and appointed officials to be responsive to the desires of the citizenry. But we should point out as well that most of our recommendations about increased or at least maintained law enforcement presuppose this attitude, and presuppose an environment in which the limitations of the First Amendment are enforced by all public officials at the point at which they first matter. To assume that enforcement of the obscenity laws is for law enforcement personnel while enforcement of the Constitution is for the courts is to misunderstand the nature of the system. It may also, ultimately, be to threaten the constitutional underpinnings of what we have urged in this Report. In the long run, the enforcement of the obscenity laws depends on the willingness of those who do the enforcing to respect the appropriate constitutional limitations. If that respect does not take place in practice and at the first instance, neither courts nor commissions such as this one will be able to be as confident of the current accommodation between conflicting goals as we now are.

C H A P T E R • 7

Child Pornography

THE SPECIAL HORROR OF CHILD PORNOGRAPHY

What is commonly referred to as "child pornography" is not so much a form of pornography as it is a form of sexual exploitation of children. The distinguishing characteristic of child pornography, as generally understood, is that actual children are photographed while engaged in some form of sexual activity, either with adults or with other children. To understand the very idea of child pornography requires understanding the way in which real children, whether actually identified or not, are photographed, and understanding the way in which the use of real children in photographs creates a special harm largely independent of the kinds of concerns often expressed with respect to sexually explicit materials involving only adults.

Thus, the necessary focus of an inquiry into child pornography must be on the process by which children, from as young as one week up to the age of majority,[70] are induced to engage in sexual activity of one sort or another, end the process by which children are photographed while engaging in that activity. The inevitably permanent record of that sexual activity created by a photograph is rather plainly a harm to the children photographed. But even if the photograph were never again seen, the very activity involved in creating the photograph is itself an act of sexual exploitation of children, and thus the issues re-lated to the sexual abuse of children end those related to child pornography are inextricably linked. Child pornography necessarily includes the sexual abuse of a real child, and there can be no understanding of the special problem of child pornography until there is understanding of the special way in which child pornography is child abuse.

CHILD PORNOGRAPHY AS A COTTAGE INDUSTRY

In addition to understanding the way in which child pornography is defined by its use of real children engaged in real sexual activity, it is important to understand the way in which the "industry" of child pornography is largely distinct from any aspect of the industry of producing and making available sexually explicit materials involving only adults.

A significant aspect of the trade in child pornography, and the way in which it is unique, is that a great deal of this trade involves photographs taken by child abusers themselves, and then either kept or informally distributed to other child abusers. As we discuss in more detail later, some of these child abusers are situational, abusing children on occasion but not restricting their sexual preferences to children. Others are preferential, not only preferring children as a means for achieving sexual satisfaction, but seeking out children in order to satisfy this desire. We have heard substantial evidence

---

70. A significant amount of sexually explicit material includes children over the applicable age of majority who look somewhat younger. Because people who are actually minors are not used in this type of publication, it would not qualify as child pornography, although it might still be legally obscene. In general, this variety of material does not cater to the pedophile, but instead to those who prefer material with young-looking models.

that both situational and preferential child molesters frequently take photographs of children in some sexual context. Usually with non-professional equipment, but sometimes in a much more sophisticated manner, child abusers will frequently take photographs of children in sexual poses or engaged in sexual activity, without having any desire to make *commercial* use of these photographs. At times the child abuser will merely keep the photograph as a memento, or as a way of re-creating for himself the past experience. Frequently, however, the photograph will be given to another child abuser, and there is substantial evidence that a great deal of "trading" of pictures takes place in this manner.[71] The desire to have collections of a large number of photographs of children seems to be a common, although not universal, characteristic of many pedophiles. Some of this exchange of photographs takes place in person, a great deal takes place through the mails, and recently a significant amount of the exchange has taken place by the use of computer networks through which users of child pornography let each other know about materials they desire or have available.

In addition to the primarily non-commercial trade in child pornography, there appears to be a commercial network for child pornography, consisting to a significant extent of foreign magazines that receive the very kinds of pictures described in the previous paragraph, and then sell in magazine form collections of these non-commercially produced photographs. These magazines will frequently contain advertisements for private exchange of pictures in addition to publishing pictures themselves.[72] Although the publication of the magazines, almost exclusively abroad, is itself a commercial enterprise, it does not appear as if most of the contributors contribute for the purpose of commercial gain. And although the publication of these magazines is largely foreign, there is substantial evidence that the predominant portion of the recipients of end contributors to these magazines are American.

Prior to the late 1970s, when awareness and concern about child pornography escalated dramatically, commercially produced and distributed child pornography was more prevalent than it is now. It was in the late 1970s that this awareness and concern started to be reflected in major law enforcement initiatives, state and federal, against child pornography. When the Supreme Court in 1982 approved of child pornography laws whose coverage was not restricted to the legally obscene, these enforcement efforts accelerated, and the sum total of these enforcement efforts has been to curtail substantially the domestic commercial production of child pornography. This is not to say that it does not exist. There is a domestic commercial child pornography industry, but it is quite clandestine, and not nearly as large as the non-commercial use of and trade in non-commercially produced sexually explicit pictures of children.

Although there now appears to be comparatively little domestic commercial production of child pornography, there remains a significant foreign commercial industry, and much of this material is available in the United States. Some of this material is in magazine form, some are photographic motion picture films, but increasingly, as with much of the adult material, video tapes are dominating the market. None of this material is available openly, however. We received some testimony that commercially produced child pornography was available "under the counter" in some establishments selling adult sexually explicit material. A number of experienced police officers testified to having no actual knowledge that material is available in this way, but others indicated that they had either heard of its availability or had themselves seen its availability in rare circumstances. We have also heard evidence about more surreptitious networks for the distribution of this material, and we have heard some evidence about the way that this material is sold through the mails. We have little doubt that there is some distribution in the United States of commercially produced material, although the extremely clandestine nature of the distribution networks makes it difficult to assess the size of this trade.

Although we note, therefore, that there is some commercially produced material, efforts to deal with the problem of child por-

---

71. There is also evidence that commercially produced pictures of children in erotic settings, or in non-erotic settings that are perceived by some adults as erotic, are collected and used by pedophiles. There is little that can be done about the extent to which, for example, advertisements for underwear might be used for vastly different purposes than those intended by the photographer or publisher, but we feel it nevertheless important to identify the practice.

72. Some of this private exchange is quite informal, but there is evidence that more formal and elaborate underground networks for the exchange of these pictures exist.

nography will fail if they overestimate the extent of the commercial side of the practice, and underestimate the non-commercial side. The greatest bulk of child pornography is produced by child abusers themselves in largely "cottage industry" fashion, and thus child pornography must be considered as substantially inseparable from the problem of sexual abuse of children. That does not make the problem of child pornography unimportant. On the contrary, to the extent that it is an aid to and a part of a problem that is unfortunately prevalent and plainly outrageous, child pornography, in both its creation and its distribution, is of unquestioned seriousness. But it is different, in virtually every aspect of its definition, creation, distribution, and use. Serious consideration of the issue of child pornography must begin with this fact.

CHILD PORNOGRAPHY, THE LAW, AND THE FIRST AMENDMENT

Because the problem of child pornography is so inherently different from the problems relating to the distribution of legally obscene material, it should be no surprise to discover that tools designed to deal with the latter are largely ineffective in dealing with the former. The problems to which child pornography regulation is addressed are numerous, but four stand out most prominently.

The first problem is that of the permanent record of the sexual practices in which children may be induced to engage. To the extent that pictures exist of this inherently nonconsensual act, those pictures follow the child up to and through adulthood, and the consequent embarrassment and humiliation are harms caused by the pictures themselves, independent of the harms attendant to the circumstances in which the photographs were originally made.[73]

Second, there is substantial evidence that photographs of children engaged in sexual activity are used as tools for further molesta-

tion of other children. Children are shown pictures of other children engaged in sexual activity, with the aim of persuading especially a quite young child that if it is in a picture, and if other children are doing it, then it must be all right for this child to do it.[74] As with the problem of the permanent record, we see here a danger that is the direct consequence of the photographs themselves, a danger that is distinct from the harms related to the original making of the picture.

Third, photographs of children engaged in sexual practices with adults often constitute an important form of evidence against those adults in prosecutions for child molestation. Given the inherent difficulties of using children as witnesses, making it possible for the photographs to be evidence of the offense, or making the photographs the offense itself, provides an additional weapon in the arsenal against sexual abuse of children.

Finally, an argument related to the last is the unquestioned special harm to the children involved in both the commercial and the noncommercial distribution of child pornography. Although harms to performers involved would not otherwise be taken to be a sufficient condition for restriction of the photographs rather than the underlying conduct, the situation with children is of a different order of magnitude. The harm is virtually unanimously considered to be extraordinarily serious, and the possibility of consent is something that the law has long considered, and properly so, to be an impossibility. As a result, forms of deterrence of the underlying conduct that might not otherwise be considered advisable may be considered so with respect to photographs of children. If the sale or distribution of such pictures is stringently sanctioned, and if those sanctions are equally stringently enforced, the market may decrease, and this may in turn decrease the incentive to produce those pictures.

As part of the previous justification, it

---

73. We refer in this regard to our specific recommendation regarding possession of child pornography. We do not believe that a photograph of a child engaged in sexual activity should be part of someone else's "collection," even if that collection remains in the home.

74. We note that there seems to be significant use of adult sexually explicit material for the same purpose. Child molesters will frequently show sexually explicit pictures of adults to children for the purpose of convincing a child that certain practices are perfectly acceptable because adults engage in them with some frequency. We are greatly disturbed by this practice, although we do not take the phenomenon as sufficient to justify restrictions we would not otherwise endorse. Many of the materials used for this purpose are not even close to being legally obscene, and, in the words of Justice Felix Frankfurter, we do not want to "burn the house to roast the pig." *Butler v. Michigan*, 353 U.S., pp. 380, 383, (1957). Nevertheless, we have no doubt that the practice exists, and we have no doubt that it is dangerous insofar as it helps break down the resistance of children to sexual advances by adults. At the very least, we strongly urge that children be warned about the practice in the course of whatever warnings about sexual advances by adults are being employed.

ought to be obvious that virtually all child pornography is produced surreptitiously, and thus, even with vigorous enforcement efforts, enforcement will be difficult. Enforcement efforts against the more accessible product of the process rather than or in addition to the less accessible process itself may enable the realities of enforcement to track the magnitude of the problem.[75]

For all of these, as well as other, reasons, a number of states, including New York, enacted around 1980 laws directed at "child pornography" itself. These laws defined child pornography not in terms of the legally obscene, but rather in terms of *any* portrayal of sexual conduct by a child, or in terms that were somewhat similar to this. Under these statutes, the sale or distribution of any photographic depiction of a real child engaged in sexual activity was made unlawful, regardless of whether the photograph, or magazine, or film was or could be determined to be legally obscene pursuant to *Miller v. California*.[76]

Because these new child pornography statutes encompassed material not legally obscene pursuant to *Miller*, and therefore encompassed material presumptively protected by the First Amendment, a constitutional challenge ensued. But in *New York v. Ferber*,[77] the Supreme Court unanimously rejected the constitutional challenges for reasons substantially similar to those discussed just above. The Court noted the undeniably "compelling" and "surpassing" interests involved in protecting children against this variety of exploitation, and also rested its conclusion on the fact that "the value of permitting live performances and photographic reproductions of children engaged in lewd sexual conduct is exceedingly modest, if not *de minimus*. We consider it unlikely that visual depictions of children performing sexual acts or lewdly exhibiting their genitals would often constitute an important and necessary part of a literary performance or scientific or educational work." Given this minuscule amount of First Amendment protection, therefore, the Court determined that

"when a definable class of material, such as that covered (by the New York statute), bears so heavily and pervasively on the welfare of children engaged in its production, we think the balance of competing interests is clearly struck and that it is permissible to consider these materials as without the protection of the First Amendment."

As a result of *Ferber*, virtually every state, as well as the United States, now prohibits by its criminal law the production, promotion, sale, exhibition, or distribution of photographs of children engaged in any sexual activity regardless of whether the material is legally obscene under the *Miller* standards. After *Ferber* these laws are clearly constitutionally sound, and none of us has any quarrel with the constitutionality of these statutes.

ENFORCEMENT OF THE CHILD PORNOGRAPHY LAWS

In Chapter 6 we discussed the enforcement of state and federal obscenity laws, and described what we see as a rather consistent pattern of underenforcement of these laws. We do not reach the same conclusion with respect to the child pornography laws. It is plain to us that every unenforced violation of the child pornography laws is an underenforcement that ought to be remedied. We believe that many cases remain uninvestigated, and we believe that state and federal prosecution of child pornography, commercial and noncommercial, needs to be even more vigorous. Nevertheless, it remains the case that the child pornography laws seem now to be the subject of a substantial amount enforcement efforts on both the state and local levels. The federal statistics are illustrative. From January 1, 1978, to February 27, 1986, one hundred individuals were indicted in the federal system for violation of the federal obscenity laws, and of those indicted seventy-one were convicted.[78] During that same time period, 255 individuals were indicted in the federal system for violation of federal child pornography laws, and of those 215 were convicted. Although these statistics themselves are highly suggestive of a substantial disparity, we be-

---

75. As much as we urge the most vigorous enforcement of child pornography laws with respect both to commercial and noncommerical production, possession, and distribution, we recognize that the problem of child abuse is larger than the problem of child pornography. We urge vigorous enforcement of child pornography laws as an important way of fighting child abuse, but if it is treated as the only weapon, or the major weapon, a great deal that needs doing will remain undone.

76. 413 U.S., (1973), p. 15. *Miller* is discussed extensively above in Chapter 3.

77. 458 U.S., (1982), p. 747.

78. See, *supra* note 52.

lieve that, if anything, the statistics understate the disparity. For one thing it is highly likely that in absolute terms there are more violations of the federal obscenity laws than there are violations of the child pornography laws. In addition, it was not until final adoption of the Child Protection Act of 1984 on May 21, 1984, that federal law, following *Ferber*, finally eliminated the requirement of "obscenity," and of the 255 indictments in fact 183 were secured in the period from May 21, 1984, through February 27, 1986.

This comparatively aggressive approach to enforcement of the federal child pornography laws has been matched by equally vigorous efforts in the vast majority of states. Although we urge even more aggressive enforcement of the child pornography laws at both state and federal levels, we see less systematic under-investigation, under-prosecution, and under-sentencing than seems to exist with respect to enforcement of the obscenity laws.[79] Child pornography seems to be a matter that judges, prosecutors, and law enforcement personnel have, with few exceptions, taken seriously. We are glad that they do, and we urge them to take it even more seriously.

In terms of taking these matters even more seriously, we note again the inseparable relationship between child pornography and child abuse. To take child pornography more seriously is to take sexual abuse of children more seriously, and vice versa. It is apparent that as of the date of this Report the sexual abuse of children is being taken increasingly seriously in this country, and we applaud that increased concern for a problem that has long been both largely unspoken and largely avoided. That situation is changing rapidly, and the increased attention to child pornography is part of the increased attention being given to all forms of sexual abuse of children, whether photographs are part of the act or not. We do not hesitate to support further efforts, in public education, in the education of children, and in law enforcement, to continue to attempt to diminish the sexual abuse of children, regardless of the form it takes.

None of us doubt that child pornography is extraordinarily harmful both to the children involved and to society, that dealing with child pornography in all of its forms ought to be treated as a governmental priority of the greatest urgency, and that an aggressive law enforcement effort is an essential part of this urgent governmental priority. Our unanimity of vigor about child pornography does not surprise us, and we expect that it will not surprise others. We hope that society will respond accordingly.

---

79. There are, however, impediments to investigation and prosecution that are specially related to any prosecution involving sexual abuse of children. One is the difficulty we address in our specific recommendations. Another is the fact that on occasion parents have themselves been involved in the illegal activity. And there seems still to be some reluctance to impose stiff sentences upon people who look and act otherwise "normal." To that extent a significant problem in dealing with sexual abusers of children is the mistaken and dangerous assumption that all or most of those people are self-evidently "weird."

The Role of Private Action

THE RIGHT TO CONDEMN AND THE RIGHT TO SPEAK

We are a government commission, and thus most of what we have to say is addressed to government. Yet it is simply mistaken to assume that citizen concerns need be exclusively or even largely channeled into governmental action. We feel it appropriate, therefore, to spend some time in this Report addressing the issue of how citizens might appropriately and lawfully put into practice their own concerns.

At the outset, it should be clear that citizens have every right to condemn a wide variety of material that is protected, and properly so, by the First Amendment. That governmental action against a certain variety of communication is unwise and unconstitutional does not mean that the communication is valuable, and does not mean that society is better off for having it. Earlier in this Report we used the examples of the Nazis and the Ku Klux Klan to illustrate this point, and we could add many more examples to this list. That the Communist Party is a lawful organization does not prevent most Americans from finding its tenets abhorrent, and the same holds true for a wide variety of sexually oriented material. Much of that material is, as we have explained, protected by the First Amendment, but it does not follow that the material is harmless, or that its proliferation is good for society.

The act of condemnation, of course, is itself central to what the First Amendment is all about. Just as speaking out against government has long been part of what citizens are both entitled and indeed encouraged to do, so

too is speaking out on matters of concern not directly related to the functioning of government. Expressing a point of view about sexually explicit materials in general, or about particular sexually explicit materials, is plainly the very kind of activity that First Amendment properly protects. To the extent that citizens have concerns about the kinds of sexually explicit material that are available in contemporary America, they should not only recognize that the First Amendment protects and encourages their right to express these concerns loudly and often, but should as well appreciate the fact that in many aspects of our lives to keep quiet is to approve. Moreover, communities are made by what people say and do, by what people approve and what people disapprove, and by what people tolerate and what people reject. For communities, and for the sense of community, community acceptance and community condemnation are central to what a community is.

Although we are concerned here primarily with protest or related action against materials that citizens find harmful, immoral, or objectionable, we do not wish to discount the value of protest directed at government when citizens wish government to do something it is not currently doing. Protest and related activities are entirely appropriate if citizens are dissatisfied with the work of their law enforcement officials, their prosecutors, their administrators and executives, their legislators and their judges. It is certainly appropriate for citizens to protest the work of this Commission. We encourage citizens to be actively involved in what their government is doing, and if they feel that the government is not doing enough, or is doing too much, with respect to prosecution of prosecutable materials, then they should make their wishes known to those who have the power to make changes.

THE METHODS OF PROTEST
It should be apparent from the foregoing that citizens need not feel hesitant in condemning that which they feel is worthy of condemnation. Moreover, they need feel no hesitation in taking advantage of the rights they have under the First Amendment to protest in more visible or organized form. They may, of course, form or join organizations designed expressly for the purposes of articulating a particular point of view. They may protest or picket or march or demonstrate in places where they are likely to attract attention, and where they will have the opportunity to persuade others of their views. The right of citizens to protest is of course coextensive with the right of publishers to publish, and we do not suggest that citizens not exercise their First Amendment rights as vigorously and as frequently as do those who publish their views in print, on film or tape, or over the airwaves.

Of some special relevance in this context is the practice of protesting near the premises of establishments offering material that some citizens may find dangerous or offensive or immoral.

We recognize that such forms of protest may at times discourage patrons who would otherwise enter such establishments from proceding, but that, we believe, is part of the way in which free speech operates in the United States. In the context of a labor dispute, picket lines frequently have this very kind of discouraging effect, and the Supreme Court, even outside of the labor context, has recognized the free speech rights of those people who would protest on public streets or sidewalks but in close proximity to business establishments whose business practices they find objectionable.[80] For citizens to protest in the vicinity of a pornography outlet is fully within the free speech traditions of this country, and so too is protest in the vicinity of an establishment only some of whose wares

the protesters would find objectionable. If people feel that businesses, whether a local store or a multinational corporation, are behaving improperly, it is their right and their obligation to make those views known.

Somewhat related to on-site or near-site protesting, in terms of coercive force, is the boycott, in which a group of citizens may refuse to patronize an establishment offering certain kinds of magazines, or tapes, or other material, and may also urge others to take similar action. At times the boycott may take the form of action against an advertiser, where people may express their views about corporate responsibility by refusing to buy certain products as long as the producer of those products advertises in certain magazines, or on certain television shows. Boycotts attempt to take advantage in organized fashion of the needs for business establishments to have customers. They are thus attempts to mobilize consumer power towards controlling the products and services made available in the market.

In a number of purely business contexts, an organized boycott would violate the antitrust laws, whose aim, in part, is to encourage competition by discouraging some forms of organized economic pressure. But consumer boycotts for social and political aims have been determined by the Supreme Court to be protected by the First Amendment,[81] and thus we do not hesitate to note that a consumer boycott, premised on the view that corporations can often do as much, for good or for evil, as government, is well within the First Amendment-protected methods of protesting business activities that citizens may find objectionable.

THE RISKS OF EXCESS
In pointing out the citizen's undoubted right to protest written, printed, or photographic material that he or she finds harmful, objectionable, immoral, or offensive, we are not so naive as to ignore that this right to protest may often be carried to excess. Citizens who protest, or boycott, or picket, or distribute leaflets, or march, or demonstrate are unquestionably exercising their First Amendment rights. But just like the First

---

80. In fact, in Organization for a Better Austin v. Keefe, 402 U.S., (1971), p. 415, the Court prohibited an injunction directed against people who were passing out leaflets in the neighborhood of the residence of a person whose business practices they found objectionable.

81. NAACP v. Claiborne Hardware Co., 458 U.S., (1982), p. 886.

Amendment rights of some of those who deal in sexually explicit materials, these rights may be exercised harmfully or unwisely.

Thus, we have no doubt that a citizen has the right to refuse to shop at a store that sells the *National Review* or *The New Republic* because the citizen disagrees with the political point of view of one of those magazines. And we have no doubt that a citizen who urges his friends and others to do the same is still well within what the First Amendment does and ought to protect. But we also have no doubt that the citizen who exercises his First Amendment rights in this manner could be criticized by most people, and most of us would strongly support that criticism. Apart from the question of governmental interference, there are positive values associated with the free flow of ideas and information, and society is the loser when that process is unduly stifled. Just as with the free speech rights of those who trade in sexually explicit materials, the free speech rights to protest objectionable material may be exercised in a lawful but societally harmful manner.

Thus we have little doubt that in exercising their First Amendment rights to protest material that they find objectionable, some people will protest material that quite simply ought to be encouraged freely to circulate in this society. We also have little doubt that protest activity may very well inhibit this process of circulation. If large numbers of people refused to patronize bookstores that sold Sinclair Lewis' *Elmer Gantry* because it dealt with sexual immorality by a minister, or if people picketed the residences of booksellers who sold James Joyce's *Ulysses* because of its sexual themes and language, this society would, quite simply, be the worse for it. These examples are of course extreme, but the fears that many arguably valuable but sexually frank works of fiction and non-fiction will be stifled not by governmental action but by social pressure is real.

We have no solutions to this dilemma. We believe it fully appropriate for citizens to protest against material they find objectionable, and we know that at times this protest activity will go too far, to the detriment of all of us. This society is a free society not only because of the First Amendment, but also because of generally held attitudes of tolerance. We encourage people to object to the objectionable, but we think it even more important that they tolerate the tolerable.

THE IMPORTANCE OF EDUCATION AND DISCUSSION

By focusing on protests, boycotts, and related activities, we have here emphasized conduct that is largely negative and reactive. Although we see a central place for communicative activities that are negative and reactive, we do not wish to suggest that this is all that can or should be done. In particular, we note the extent to which education is ultimately central to much that we have been discussing. In the broadest sense, not just with respect to the education that takes place in the schools, and with respect to values and awareness as well as to facts, education is the real solution to the problem of pornography.

We have identified harms that seem to be caused by certain sexually explicit material, but many of those harms are the result of how images affect attitudes, and of how images affect behavior. But the ability of an image to affect behavior is not only a function of what that image is saying or doing, but of what other images are part of the array of stimuli received by an individual. We recognize the extent to which an attraction to one sexual stimulus rather than another may significantly be caused by individual characteristics formed at a relatively early age, in many cases before exposure to any highly sexually explicit material. But we recognize as well that if images can cause certain forms of behavior, as we believe they can and as the evidence shows, then images ought as well to be able to prevent behavior, or cause different behavior.

The images that might cause different behavior can, of course, come from numerous sources. So can the messages that would lead people in even greater numbers to reject the view that sexual violence is sometimes appropriate, to reject the view that women enjoy being physically coerced into sex, to reject the view that women's primary sexual role is to satisfy the desires of men, to reject the view that sex ought to be an essentially public act, and to reject the view that sex outside of love, marriage, commitment, or affection is something to be sought. These positive messages might address all of these underlying attitudes. They might also address pornography more explicitly, discussing its dangers to individuals and to society. The messages might come from family members, or teachers, or religious leaders, or political figures, or the messages might come, perhaps especially, from the mass media.

Ultimately, a significant part of the concern with pornography is a concern about negative messages. One way to deal with negative messages is to prevent them from being sent, or to prevent them from being reinforced once they are sent. Action against harmful pornography, whether by law or by social action or by individual condemnation, is in the final analysis a negative approach. It is an attempt to eliminate a harmful message, and such at- tempts are frequently appropriate. But they cannot succeed by themselves. These essen- tially negative and reactive efforts must be ac- companied by positive efforts. If there are certain attitudes that people ought not to have, then what attitudes ought people to have, and how can those attitudes best be in- culcated? What will be taught in the schools? What forms of behavior will be publicly ad- mired? What will the mass media encourage? What will we expect of each other in interper- sonal behavior? The list goes on and on.

We commenced this Report by noting that we were a Commission appointed by the At- torney General of the United States, and there- fore felt a special responsibility to concentrate our efforts towards law and law enforcement. It is appropriate to conclude, however, with this recognition of the limits of law and the limits of law enforcement. A wide range of behaviors, from telling the truth to our friends to eating with knives and forks rather than fingers, is channeled quite effec- tively without significant legal involvement. And another wide range of behaviors, from jaywalking to income tax evasion, persists even in the face of attempts by law to restrict it. To know what the law can do, we must ap- preciate what the law cannot do. We believe that in many respects the law can serve im- portant controlling and symbolic purposes in restricting the proliferation of certain sexu- ally explicit material that we believe harmful to individuals and to society. But we know as well that to rely entirely or excessively on law is simply a mistake. Law may influence be- lief, but it also operates in the shadow of be- lief. And beliefs, of course, are often a product of deeply held moral, ethical, and spiritual commitments. That foundation of values is the glue that holds a democracy, which functions according to the will of the majority, together. Government can and must protect the interests of the minority, to be sure. But law enforcement cannot entirely compensate for or regulate the consequences of bad decisions if the majority consistently chooses evil or error. If there are attitudes that need changing and behaviors that need re- stricting, then law has a role to play. But if we expect law to do too much, we will discover only too late that few of our problems have been solved.

PART

2

Law Enforcement
Recommendations

C H A P T E R • 9

Introduction

Based upon their collective observations, and the information provided through testimony, the following recommendations are advanced by this Commission.

RECOMMENDATIONS FOR THE JUSTICE SYSTEM AND LAW ENFORCEMENT AGENCIES

RECOMMENDATIONS FOR CHANGES IN FEDERAL LAW

Recommendation 1. Congress should enact a forfeiture statute to reach the proceeds and instruments of any offense committed in violation of the Federal obscenity laws.

Recommendation 2. Congress should amend the Federal obscenity laws to eliminate the necessity of proving transportation in interstate commerce. A statute should be enacted to only require proof that the distribution of the obscene material "affects" interstate commerce.

Recommendation 3. Congress should enact legislation making it an unfair business practice and an unfair labor practice for any employer to hire individuals to participate in commercial sexual performances.

Recommendation 4. Congress should amend the Mann Act to make its provisions gender neutral.

Recommendation 5. Congress should amend Title 18 of the United States code to specifically proscribe obscene cable television programming.

Recommendation 6. Congress should enact legislation to prohibit the transmission of obscene material through the telephone or similar common carrier.

RECOMMENDATIONS FOR CHANGES IN STATE LAW

Recommendation 7. State legislatures should amend, if necessary, obscenity statutes containing the definitional requirement that material be "utterly without redeeming social value" in order to be obscene to conform with the current standard enunciated by the United States Supreme Court in Miller v. California.

Recommendation 8. State legislatures should amend, if necessary, obscenity statutes to eliminate misdemeanor status for second offenses and make any second offense punishable as a felony.

Recommendation 9. State legislatures should enact, if necessary, forfeiture provisions as part of the state obscenity laws.

Recommendation 10. State legislatures should enact a Racketeer Influenced Corrupt Organization (RICO) statute which has obscenity as a predicate act.

RECOMMENDATIONS FOR THE UNITED STATES DEPARTMENT OF JUSTICE

Recommendation 11. The Attorney General should direct the United States Attorneys to examine the obscenity problem in their respective districts, identify offenders, initiate investigations, and commence prosecution without further delay.

Recommendation 12. The Attorney General should appoint a high ranking official from the Department of Justice to oversee the creation and operation of an obscenity task force. The task force should consist of Special Assistant United States Attorneys and Federal agents who will assist United States Attorneys in the prosecution and investigation of obscenity cases.

Recommendation 13. The Department of Justice should initiate the creation of an obscenity law enforcement data base which would serve as a resource network for Federal, State, and Local law enforcement agencies.

Recommendation 14. The United States Attorneys should use Law Enforcement Coordinating committees to coordinate enforcement of the obscenity laws and to maintain surveillance of the nature and extent of the obscenity problem within each district.

Recommendation 15. The Department of Justice and United States Attorneys should use the Racketeer Influenced Corrupt Organization Act (RICO) as a means of prosecuting major producers and distributors of obscene material.

Recommendation 16. The Department of Justice should continue to provide the United States Attorneys with training programs on legal and procedural matters related to obscenity cases and also should make such training available to state and local prosecutors.

Recommendation 17. The United States Attorneys should use all available Federal statutes to prosecute obscenity law violations involving cable and satellite television.

RECOMMENDATIONS FOR STATE AND LOCAL PROSECUTORS

Recommendation 18. State and Local prosecutors should prosecute producers of obscene material under existing laws including those prohibiting pandering and other underlying sexual offenses.

Recommendation 19. State and Local prosecutors should examine the obscenity problem in their jurisdiction, identify offenders, initi-

ate investigations, and commence prosecution without further delay.

Recommendation 20. State and Local prosecutors should allocate sufficient resources to prosecute obscenity cases.

Recommendation 21. State and Local prosecutors should use the bankruptcy laws to collect unpaid fines.

Recommendation 22. State and Local prosecutors should use all available statutes to prosecute obscenity violations involving cable and satellite television.

Recommendation 23. State and Local prosecutors should enforce existing corporate laws to prevent the formation, use and abuse of shell corporations which serve as a shelter for producers and distributors of obscene material.

Recommendation 24. State and Local prosecutors should enforce the alcoholic beverage control laws that prohibit obscenity on licensed premises.

Recommendation 25. Government Attorneys, including State and Local prosecutors, should enforce all legal remedies authorized by statute.

RECOMMENDATIONS FOR FEDERAL LAW ENFORCEMENT AGENCIES

Recommendation 26. Federal law enforcement agencies should conduct active and thorough investigations of all significant violations of the obscenity laws with interstate dimensions.

Recommendation 27. The Internal Revenue Service should aggressively investigate violations of the tax laws committed by producers and distributors of obscene material.

RECOMMENDATIONS FOR STATE AND LOCAL LAW ENFORCEMENT AGENCIES

Recommendation 28. State and Local law enforcement agencies should provide the most thorough and up-to-date training for investigators involved in enforcing the obscenity laws.

Recommendation 29. State and Local law

enforcement agencies should allocate sufficient personnel to conduct intensive and thorough investigations of any violations of the obscenity laws.

Recommendation 30. State and Local law enforcement officers should take an active role in the law enforcement coordinating committees.

Recommendation 31. State and Local revenue authorities must ensure taxes are collected from businesses dealing in obscene materials.

Recommendation 32. State and Local public health authorities should investigate conditions within "Adults Only" pornographic outlets and arcades and enforce the laws against any health violations found on those premises.

RECOMMENDATION FOR THE JUDICIARY

Recommendation 33. Judges should impose substantial periods of incarceration for persons who are repeatedly convicted of obscenity law violations and when appropriate should order payment of restitution to identified victims as part of the sentence.

RECOMMENDATIONS FOR THE FEDERAL COMMUNICATIONS COMMISSION

Recommendation 34. The Federal Communications Commission should use its full regulatory powers and impose appropriate sanctions against providers of obscene Dial-A-Porn telephone services.

Recommendation 35. The Federal Communications Commission should use its full regulatory powers and impose appropriate sanctions against cable and satellite television programmers who transmit obscene programs.

RECOMMENDATION FOR OTHER FEDERAL ORGANIZATIONS

Recommendation 36. The President's Commission on Uniform Sentencing should consider a provision for a minimum of one year imprisonment for any second or subsequent violation of Federal Law involving obscene material that depicts adults.

RECOMMENDATIONS FOR THE REGULATION OF CHILD PORNOGRAPHY

RECOMMENDATIONS FOR CHANGES IN FEDERAL LAW

Recommendation 37. Congress should enact legislation requiring producers, retailers, or distributors of sexually explicit visual depictions to maintain records containing consent forms and proof of performers' ages.

Recommendation 38. Congress should enact legislation prohibiting producers of certain sexually explicit visual depictions from using performers under the age of twenty-one.

Recommendation 39. Congress should enact legislation to prohibit the exchange of information concerning child pornography or children to be used in child pornography through computer networks.

Recommendation 40. Congress should amend the Child Protection Act forfeiture section to include a provision which authorizes the Postal Inspection Service to conduct forfeiture actions.

Recommendation 41. Congress should amend 18 U.S.C. S2255 to define the term "Visual Depiction" and include undeveloped film in that definition.

Recommendation 42. Congress should enact legislation providing financial incentives for the states to initiate task forces on child pornography and related cases.

Recommendation 43. Congress should enact legislation to make the acts of child selling or child purchasing, for the production of sexually explicit visual depictions, a felony.

RECOMMENDATIONS FOR STATE LEGISLATION

Recommendation 44. State legislatures should amend, if necessary, child pornography statutes to include forfeiture provisions.

Recommendation 45. State legislatures should amend laws, where necessary, to make the knowing possession of child pornography a felony.

Recommendation 46. State legislatures should amend, if necessary, laws making the sexual abuse of children through the production of sexually explicit visual depictions, a felony.

Recommendation 47. State legislatures should enact legislation, if necessary, to make the conspiracy to produce, distribute, give away or exhibit any sexually explicit visual depictions of children or exchange or deliver children for such purpose a felony.

Recommendation 48. State legislatures should amend, if necessary, child pornography laws to create an offense for advertising, selling, purchasing, bartering, exchanging, giving or receiving information as to where sexually explicit materials depicting children can be found.

Recommendation 49. State legislatures should enact or amend legislation, where necessary, to make child selling or child purchasing for the production of sexually explicit visual depictions, a felony.

Recommendation 50. State legislatures should amend laws, where necessary, to make child pornography in the possession of an alleged child sexual abuser which depicts that person engaged in sexual acts with a minor sufficient evidence of child molestation for use in prosecuting that individual whether or not the child involved is found or is able to testify.

Recommendation 51. State legislatures should amend laws, if necessary, to eliminate the requirement that the prosecution identify or produce testimony from the child who is depicted if proof of age can otherwise be established.

Recommendation 52. State legislatures

should enact or amend legislation, if necessary, which requires photo finishing laboratories to report suspected child pornography.

Recommendation 53. State legislatures should amend or enact legislation, if necessary, to permit judges to impose a sentence of lifetime probation for convicted child pornographers and related offenders.

RECOMMENDATIONS FOR FEDERAL LAW ENFORCEMENT AGENCIES

Recommendation 54. The State Department, the United States Department of Justice, the United States Customs Service, the United States Postal Inspection Service, the Federal Bureau of Investigation and other Federal agencies should continue to work with other nations to detect and intercept child pornography.

Recommendation 55. The United States Department of Justice should direct the Law Enforcement Coordinating Committees to form task forces of dedicated and experienced investigators and prosecutors in major regions to combat child pornography.

Recommendation 56. The Department of Justice or other appropriate Federal agency should initiate the creation of a data base which would serve as a resource network for Federal, State and Local law enforcement agencies to send and obtain information regarding child pornography trafficking.

Recommendation 57. Federal law enforcement agencies should develop and maintain continuous training programs for agents in techniques of child pornography investigations.

Recommendation 58. Federal law enforcement agencies should have personnel trained in child pornography investigation and when possible they should form specialized units for child sexual abuse and child pornography investigation.

Recommendation 59. Federal law enforcement agencies should use search warrants in child pornography and related cases expeditiously as a means of gathering evidence and furthering overall investigation efforts in the child pornography area.

Recommendation 60. Federal law enforcement agents should ask the child victim in reported child sexual abuse cases if photographs or films were made of him or her during the course of sexual abuse.

Recommendation 61. The Department of Justice should appoint a national task force to conduct a study of cases throughout the United States reflecting apparent patterns of multi-victim, multi-perpetrator child sexual exploitation.

RECOMMENDATIONS FOR STATE AND LOCAL LAW ENFORCEMENT AGENCIES

Recommendation 62. Local law enforcement agencies should participate in the Law Enforcement Coordinating Committees to form regional task forces of dedicated and experienced investigators and prosecutors to combat child pornography.

Recommendation 63. State and Local law enforcement agencies should develop and maintain continuous training programs for officers in identification, apprehension, and undercover techniques of child pornography investigations.

Recommendation 64. State and Local law enforcement agencies should participate in a national data base established to serve as a center for state and local law enforcement agencies to submit and receive information regarding child pornography trafficking.

Recommendation 65. State and Local law enforcement agencies should have personnel trained in child pornography investigation and when possible they should form specialized units for child sexual abuse and child pornography investigations.

Recommendation 66. State and Local law enforcement agencies should use search warrants in child sexual exploitation cases expeditiously as a means of gathering evidence and furthering overall investigation effort in the child pornography area.

Recommendation 67. State and Local law enforcement officers should ask the child victim in reported child sexual abuse cases if photographs or films were made of him or her during the course of sexual abuse.

RECOMMENDATIONS FOR PROSECUTORS

Recommendation 68. The United States Department of Justice should direct United States Attorneys to participate in Law Enforcement Coordinating Committee task forces to combat child pornography.

Recommendation 69. Federal, State, and Local prosecutors should participate in a task force of milti-disciplinary practitioners and develop a protocol for courtroom procedures for child witnesses that would meet constitutional standards.

Recommendation 70. Prosecutors should assist State, Local, and Federal law enforcement agencies to use search warrants in potential child pornography and related child sexual abuse cases.

Recommendation 71. State, Local, and Federal prosecutors should ask the child victim in reported child sexual abuse cases if photographs or films were made of him or her during the course of sexual abuse.

Recommendation 72. State and Local Prosecutors should use the vertical prosecution model in child pornography and related cases.

RECOMMENDATIONS FOR THE JUDICIARY AND CORRECTIONAL FACILITIES

Recommendation 73. Judges and probation officers should receive specific education so they may investigate, evaluate, sentence and supervise persons convicted of child pornography and related cases appropriately.

Recommendation 74. Judges should impose appropriate periods of incarceration for convicted child pornographers and related offenders.

Recommendation 75. Judges should use, when appropriate, a sentence of lifetime probation for convicted child pornographers.

Recommendation 76. Pre-sentence reports concerning individuals found guilty of violations of child pornography or related laws should be based on sources of information in addition to the offender himself or herself.

Recommendation 77. State and Federal correctional facilities should recognize the unique problems of child pornographers and related offenders and designate appropriate programs regarding their incarceration.

Recommendation 78. Federal, State, and Local judges should participate in a task force of multi-disciplinary practitioners and develop a protocol for courtroom procedures for child witnesses that would meet constitutional standards.

RECOMMENDATIONS FOR PUBLIC AND PRIVATE SOCIAL SERVICE AGENCIES

Recommendation 79. Public and private social service agencies should participate in a task force of multi-disciplinary practitioners and develop a protocol for courtroom procedures for child witnesses that would meet constitutional standards.

Recommendation 80. Social, mental health and medical services should be provided for child pornography victims.

Recommendation 81. Local agencies should allocate victims of crimes funds to provide monies for psychiatric evaluation and treatment and medical treatment of child pornography victims and their families.

Recommendation 82. Clinical evaluators should be trained to assist children victimized through the production and use of child pornography more effectively and to better understand adult psychosexual disorders.

Recommendation 83. Behavioral scientists should conduct research to determine the effects of the production of child pornography and the related victimization on children.

Recommendation 84. States should support age appropriate education and prevention programs for parents, teachers and children within public and private school systems to protect children from victimization by child pornographers anad child sexual abusers.

Recommendation 85. A multi-media educational campaign should be developed which increases family and community awareness regarding child sexual exploitation through the production and use of child pornography.

VICTIMIZATION

Recommendation 86. State, County and Municipal governments should facilitate the development of public and private resources for persons who are currently involved in the production or consumption of pornography and wish to discontinue this involvement and for those who suffer mental, physical, educational, or employment disabilities as a result of exposure or participation in the production of pornography.

CIVIL RIGHTS

Recommendation 87. Legislatures should conduct hearings and consider legislation recognizing a civil remedy for harms attributable to pornography.

"ADULTS ONLY" PORNOGRAPHIC OUTLETS

Recommendation 88. "Adults Only" pornographic outlet peep show facilities which provide individual booths for viewing should not be equipped with doors. The occupant of the booth should be clearly visible to eliminate a haven for sexual activity.

Recommendation 89. Holes enabling inter-booth sexual contact between patrons should be prohibited in the peep show booths.

Recommendation 90. Because of the apparent health hazards posed by the outlet environment generally, and the peep show booth in particular, such facilities should be subject to periodic inspection and licensing by appropriate governmental agents.

Recommendation 91. Any form of indecent act by or among "Adults Only" pornographic outlet patrons should be unlawful.

Recommendation 92. Access to "Adults Only" pornographic outlets should be limited to persons over the age of eighteen.

C H A P T E R • 1 0

Recommendations For The Justice System And Law Enforcement Agencies

INTRODUCTION

The effective enforcement of obscenity laws necessarily involves a concerted and responsive effort on the part of each facet of the criminal justice system. Personnel involved in each of these components must exhibit some concern and appreciation for its effect of obscene materials on a community. It is unrealistic to expect law enforcement agencies to devote the same attention to obscenity law violations that violent crimes command. This does not imply, however, that obscenity violations should be accorded the lowest priority, as it appears they are in many jurisdictions today. In order to control the flow of materials falling within the legal definition of obscenity, law enforcement officials must develop a reputation for initiating prosecution when violations are detected. Absent such enforcement policy, there is little incentive to observe existing obscenity laws. The consequences of a policy of inaction are compounded by the lucrative nature of obscenity trafficking.

The product of a successful investigation and vigorous prosecution is rendered virtually worthless if courts fail to appreciate the community significance of obscenity cases. Deterrence should be a significant factor in fashioning an appropriate sentence in these types of cases. Only public awareness of firm but fair sentencing practices in obscenity cases can foster an environment conducive to controlling the flow of these materials.

An observation common to much of the testimony heard by the Commission is that there has been a gradual relaxation over the last twenty years in the enforcement of obscenity laws. This trend is undoubtedly attributable to a number of factors, but its most conspicuous symptom was a dramatic loss of prosecutor interest in these cases. This dampened enthusiasm appears not to have been occasioned by any change in principle or philosophy, but instead was spawned by the judicial creation of insurmountable legal obstacles. In *Memoirs v. Massachusetts*,[82] the United States Supreme Court enunciated the requirement that material must be "utterly without redeeming social value" to be obscene.[83] This additional element of proof marked a significant departure from the pre-existing standard of proof. Prosecutors almost uniformly found this burden to be virtually impossible to satisfy[84] and as a consequence de-emphasized the regulation of obscene material.

Seven years later, in *Miller v. California*,[85] the Supreme Court refashioned the "social value" element of the obscenity standard and considerably eased the prosecution's burden of proof. However, according to a 1977 survey of prosecutors, the *Miller* standard neither in-

---

82. 383 U.S. (1966), p. 413.

83. *Id.*, p. 419.

84. Chicago Hearing, Vol. I, Paul McGeady, p. 81; *See also, Miller v. California*, 413 U.S., (1973), pp. 15,22.

85. 413 U.S., (1973), p. 15.

creased the number of obscenity prosecutions nor the conviction rate nationally.[86] The number of jurisdictions actually prosecuting obscenity violations declined while obscene materials became more readily available.[87] It is therefore reasonable to conclude that *Memoirs v. Massachusetts* was only one of a number of factors contributing to the decrease in obscenity prosecutions.

Since 1973, however, the nature and extent of pornography in the United States has changed dramatically. The materials that are available today are more sexually explicit and portray more violence than those available before 1970. The production, distribution and sale of pornography has become a large, well-organized and highly profitable industry.[88] The growth of the pornography industry has been facilitated in large measure by inadequate law enforcement and prosecutorial resources in this area, and the meting out of minimal punishment to those who have been convicted of violating the obscenity laws. This relaxation of public policy has been further ingrained by the absence of any firm expression of citizen concern.

All individuals and agencies responsible for vice enforcement must be committed to giving obscenity violations adequate priority. As with any law enforcement objective, the agencies must use various criteria in determining the degree of attention the problem merits. This process requires an evaluation of the scope of the problem, the cost to the locality both in safety and economic terms and the public demand for increased enforcement efforts. The enforcement of obscenity laws must obviously be balanced against other law enforcement priorities. In some instances, this evaluation may result in a temporary realignment in enforcement attention, but most agencies will be able to effectively increase obscenity enforcement without substantially detracting from other areas of responsibility for significant periods of time.[89] Once a reputation for community intolerance is developed, officials need only perform periodic inspections.

The law enforcement community should recognize fully the magnitude of this multifaceted problem and bring into focus the means necessary to curtail it. Law enforcement agencies must examine the nature of the pornography industry within their respective jurisdictions and take steps to address the situation. Federal, state and local agencies need adequate manpower and the expertise of qualified investigators to conduct thorough investigations of obscenity law violations, especially those involving large scale pornography operations. The use of forfeiture laws to disgorge illicit profits is a potent prosecutorial tool.

The United States Department of Justice should provide the leadership for a coordinated law enforcement effort through the mandate of its highest ranking officials and its ninety-four United States Attorneys. The Justice Department is able to provide valuable training and assistance to state and local prosecutors and law enforcement officials. The policies and practices of the Department of Justice should lend impetus to a national reassessment of the prioritization of obscenity enforcement. Moreover, it can provide some of the impetus for legislative change.

Congress and the state legislatures must examine existing laws and enact the necessary changes to create an effective and precise means of addressing the expansive scope of the obscenity and pornography problem today.

Once an individual is charged with an obscenity violation, a United States Attorney or local district attorney should prosecute aggressively if the investigation and bringing of charges are to have any effect. This includes enforcing the existing laws and fully using other remedies particularly those laws providing forfeitures that could literally put many pornographers out of business.

Finally, when an individual is brought before the court and is convicted, the sentencing judge must have accurate and comprehensive information about the offender and the offense. The courts must impose sentences with the maximum deterrent effect and cease imposing sentences which merely increase the pornographer's cost of doing business.

The recommendations which follow attempt to accomplish these objectives.

---

86. *An Empirical Inquiry Into the Effects of Miller v. California on the Control of Obscenity,* 52 N.Y.U. L. Rev., (1977), pp. 810, 928.

87. Id.

88. See, the discussions of Production, Distribution and Technology of Sexually Explicit Materials found in Part Three of this Report.

89. One witness before the Commission acknowledged the possibility of a decrease in enforcement efforts in certain

RECOMMENDATIONS FOR CHANGES IN FEDERAL LAW

RECOMMENDATION 1:

Congress should enact a forfeiture statute to reach the proceeds and instruments of any offense committed under the Federal obscenity laws.

Discussion

The addition of civil and criminal forfeiture provisions to the existing federal obscenity laws[90] would greatly enhance their deterrent effect. In addition to the penalties already prescribed by statute, a defendant would be subject to forfeiture of any profits derived from or property used in committing the offense. The Child Protection Act of 1984[91] presently contains such forfeiture provisions pertaining to offenses involving child pornography.[92]

The addition of forfeiture provisions in the federal obscenity statutes would have a profound effect on some of the most egregious offenders, especially those who are members of, associated with, or are influenced or controlled by, organized crime families. The forfeiture provision would affect those who profit by their illegal activity and who have created criminal enterprises large enough to own or lease real estate, fleets of motor vehicles, or other valuable assets. The loss of such valuable property would have a more significant deterrent effect than the mere imposition of a fine or modest period of incarceration which the offender may see as merely another "cost of doing business."[93] Forfeiture provisions would also aid law enforcement efforts

by providing the government with property to be used in future undercover operations and perhaps even provide sufficient assets to reimburse a significant portion of investigative and prosecution costs.

According to the federal prosecutor in a series of Miami, Florida, obscenity cases commonly known as MIPORN where many of the defendants had tremendous assets scattered throughout the United States, forfeitures would have made a tremendous contribution toward underwriting the costs of the government investigation.[94]

Under current law even large scale and well-organized distributors of obscene material that have been repeatedly convicted retain their massive profits which they often use to finance other unlawful activity.[95] It is estimated that the film "Deep Throat" cost $25,000 to produce and has made profits of $50,000,000,[96] and few or none of these proceeds were paid to the "star" of the film, Linda Lovelace (now   ✂   ) or others involved in the actual production.[97] The film's profits were used allegedly by the   ✂ reported members of the Columbo organized crime family,[98] to develop   ✂   Films of Hollywood, which distributed the horror film, "The Texas Chainsaw Massacre,"[99] to purchase yachts, airplanes, islands and property in the Bahamas, and as seed money for drug smuggling activities.[100]

In recognition of the need to seize substantial profits gained through unlawful activity and to prevent their use in other crimes, Con-

---

90. See, 18 U.S.C. SS1461–1465 (1985).

91. 18 U.S.C.A. S2251 (West Supp. 1982).

92. See, Recommendations for the Regulation of Child Pornography, *infra.*

93. The precise items subject to forfeiture should be determined by Congress with any constitutional limitations clearly recognized.

94. "MIPORN was a two and a half year undercover investigation into organized crime's influence in the pornography industry." New York Hearing, Vol. II, Marcella Cohen, p. 41; MIPORN is further discussed in Appendix One to the Organized Crime Chapter.

95. New York Hearing, Vol. I, Christopher J. Mega, pp. 166–67.

96. New York Hearing, Vol. I, William Kelly, p. 71.

97. New York Hearing, Vol. I, Linda   ✂   , p. 63.

98.   ✂   are reported members or associates of the Columbo organized crime family, *See,* The discussion of Organized Crime for further information.

99. New York Hearing, Vol. I, William Kelly, p. 74.

100. New Hearing, Vol. I, Christopher J. Mega, p. 162; *See also,* Cong Rec. S433 (daily ed. Jan. 30, 1984) (Statement of Sen. Jesse Helms).

---

areas if obscenity enforcement was given greater emphasis. "I think there is a great deal of time spent on thefts, minor thefts; and yes, they are important. But I think that obscenity has more far-reaching effects on our culture and is important." Miami Hearing, Vol. II, Barbara Hattemer, p. 96.

gress has authorized forfeiture for other crimes.[101] Any new legislation should be drafted and implemented in a manner similar to other present federal laws to insure due process of law to all parties in interest.[102]

The only present authority to permit the forfeiture of profits and instruments derived from the distribution of obscene materials is RICO. Through 1985 no federal RICO cases have been brought to forfeit profits or instru-

---

101. See e.g., 21 U.S.C. S881(a)(1).

((a) The following shall be subject to forfeiture to the United States and no property right shall exist in them:

(1) All controlled substances which have been manufactured, distributed, dispensed, or acquired in violation of this subchapter.

(2) All raw materials, products and equipment of any kind which are used, or intended for use, in manufacturing, compounding, processing, delivering, importing, or exporting any controlled substance in violation of this subchapter.

(3) All property which is used, or intended for use, as a container for property described in paragraph (1) or (2).

(4) All conveyances, including aircraft, vehicles, or vessels, which are used, or are intended for use, to transport, or in any manner to facilitate the transportation, sale, receipt, possession, or concealment of property described in paragraph (1) or (2).

(5) All books, records and research, including formulas, microfilm, tapes, and data which are used, or intended for use, in violation of this subchapter.

(6) All moneys, negotiable instruments, securities, or other things of value furnished or intended to be furnished by any person in exchange for a controlled substance in violation of this subchapter, all proceeds traceable to such an exchange, and all money, negotiable instruments, and securities used or intended to be used to facilitate any violation of this subchapter, except that no property shall be forfeited under this paragraph, to the extent of the interest of an owner, by reason of any act or omission established by that owner to have been committed or omitted without the knowledge or consent of that owner.

(7) All real property, including any right, title and interest in the whole of any lot or tract of land and any appurtenances or improvements, which is used, or intended to be used, in any manner or part, to commit, or to facilitate the commission of, a violation of this title punishable by more than one year's imprisonment, except that no property shall be forfeited under this paragraph, to the extent of an interest of an owner, by reason of any act or omission established by that owner to have been committed or omitted without the knowledge or consent of that owner.

(8) All controlled substances which have been possessed in violation of this subchapter.);

18 U.S.C. S492. (All counterfeits of any coins or obligations or other securities of the United States or of any foreign government, or any articles, devices, and other things made, possessed, or used in violation of this chapter or of sections 331–333, 335, 336, 642 or 1720, of this title, or any material or apparatus used or fitted or intended to be used, in the making of such counterfeits, articles, devices or things, found in the possession of any person without authority from the Secretary of the Treasury or other proper officer, shall be forfeited to the United States);

18 U.S.C. S924 ((d) Any firearms or ammunition involved in or used or intended to be used in, any violation of the provisions of this chapter or any rule or regulation promulaged thereunder, or any violation of any other criminal law of the United States, shall be subject to seizure and forfeiture and all provision of the Internal Revenue Code of 1954 relation to the seizure, forfeiture, and disposition of firearms, as defined in section 5845(a) of that Code, shall so far as applicable, extend to seizures and forfeiture under the provision of this chapter);

18 U.S.C. S1955. (illegal gambling businesses; (d) Any property, including money, used in violation of the provisions of this section may be seized and forfeited to the United States. All provisions of law related to the seizure, summary, and judicial forfeiture procedures, and condemnation of vessels, vehicles, merchandise, and baggage for violation of the customs laws; the disposition of such vessels, vehicles, merchandise, and baggage or the proceeds from such sale; the remission or mitigation of such forfeitures; and the compromise of claims and the award of compensation to informers in respect of such forfeitures shall apply to seizures and forfeitures incurred or alleged to have been incurred under the provisions of his section, insofar as applicable and not inconsistent with such provisions. Such duties as are imposed upon the collector of customs or any other person in respect to the seizure and forfeiture of vessels, vehicles, merchandise, and baggage under the customs laws shall be performed with respect to seizures and forfeitures of property used or intended for use in violation of this section by such officers, agents, or other persons as may be designated for that purpose by the Attorney General).

18 U.S.C.A. S1963 (West Supp. 1985). ((a) Whoever violates any provision of section 1962 of this chapter shall be fined not more than $25,000 or imprisoned not more than twenty years or both, and shall forfeit to the United States, irrespective of any provision of State law—

(1) any interest the person has acquired or maintained in violation of Section 1962;

(2) any—

(A) interest in;

(B) security of;

(C) claim against; or

(D) property or contractual right of any kind affording a source of influence over; any enterprise which the person has established, operated, controlled, conducted, or participated in the conduct of, in violation of section 1962; and

102. See also, The discussion in this Chapter of Recommendations for Changes in State Law, *infra*.

ments used in or derived from obscenity law violations.[103] The RICO statute currently is inadequate to reach the profits and instruments without establishing and relying on proof of two or more predicate offenses. The proposed legislation would allow forfeiture in the many cases where RICO cannot appropriately be used.

RECOMMENDATION 2:

Congress should amend the Federal obscenity laws to eliminate the necessity of proving transportation in interstate commerce. A statute should be enacted to only require proof that the distribution of the obscene material "affects" interstate commerce.

Discussion

Pursuant to provisions of 18 U.S.C. S1462 and 18 U.S.C. S1465 the United States is required to prove that the particular obscene material in question actually was transported in interstate commerce at a particular specified time and to and from particular and specified locations.[104]

This has become an increasingly insurmountable burden for federal prosecutors to meet in obscenity cases. Distributors of obscenity, especially those associated with or members of organized crime families, frequently avoid the mails and common carriers when they ship their wares. With the assistance of their attorneys such persons and or-

---

103. See, Recommendations For State and Local Law Enforcement Agencies, *infra*, for further discussion.

104. 18 U.S.C. S1462 (1982) provides, in part:

"Whoever brings into the United States, or any place subject to the jurisdiction thereof, or knowingly uses an express company or other common carrier, for carriage in interstate or foreign commerce—

   (a) any obscene, lewd, lascivious, or filthy book, pamphlet, picture, motion-picture film, paper, letter, writing, print, or other matter of indecent character; or

   (b) any obscene, lewd, lascivious, or filthy phonograph recording, electrical transcription, or other article or thing capable of producing sound; or

---

   (3) any property constituting, or derived from, any proceeds which the person obtained, directly or indirectly, from racketeering activity or unlawful debt collection in violation of section 1962.
The Court, in imposing sentence on such person shall order, in addition to any other sentence imposed pursuant to this section, that the person forfeit to the United States all property described in this subsection. In lieu of a fine otherwise authorized by this section, a defendant who derives profits or other proceeds from an offense may be fined not more than twice the gross profit or other proceeds.
(b) Property subject to criminal forfeiture under this section includes—
   (1) real property including things growing on, affixed to, and found in land, and
   (2) tangible and intangible personal property, including rights, privileges, interests, claims and securities.
(c) All right, title, and interest in property described in subsection (a) vests in the United States upon the commission of the act giving rise to forfeiture under this section. Any such property that is subsequently transferred to a person other than the defendant may be the subject of a special verdict of forfeiture to the United States, unless the transferee establishes in a hearing pursuant to subsection (m) that he is a bona fide purchaser for value of such property who at the time of purchase was reasonably without cause to believe that the property was subject to forfeiture under this section);

18 U.S.C. S2318. (counterfeit labels; (d) When any person is convicted of any violation of subsection (a), the court in its judgment of conviction shall in addition to the penalty therein prescribed, order the forfeiture and destruction or other disposition of all counterfeit labels and all articles to which counterfeit labels have been affixed or which were intended to have had such labels affixed);

18 U.S.C. S2344. (c) Any contraband cigarettes involved in any violation of the provision of this chapter shall be subject to seizure and forfeiture, and all provisions of the Internal Revenue Code of 1954 relating of the seizure, forfeiture, and disposition of firearms, and defined in section 5845(a) of such Code, shall, so far as applicable, extend to seizures and forfeitures under the provisions of this chapter); and

18 U.S.C. S2513. (Any electronic, mechanical, or other device used, sent, carried, manufactured, assembled, possessed, sold, or advertised in violation of section 2511 of section 2512 of this chapter may be seized and forfeited to the United States. All provisions of law relating to (1) at the seizure, summary and judicial forfeiture, and condemnation of vessels, vehicles, merchandise, and baggage for violations of the customs laws contained in Title 19 of the United States Code, (2) the disposition of such vessels, vehicles, merchandise, and baggage or the proceeding from the sale thereof, (3) the remission or mitigation of such forfeiture, (4) the compromise of claims, and (5) the award of compensation top informers in respect of such forfeitures, shall apply to seizures and forfeitures incurred, or alleged to have been incurred, under the provisions of this section, insofar as applicable and not inconsistent with the provision of this section; except that such duties as are imposed upon the collector of customs or any other person with respect to the seizure and forfeiture of vessels, vehicles, merchandise, and baggage under the provisions of the customs law contained in Title 19 of the United States Code shall be performed with respect to seizure and forfeiture of electronic, mechanical, or other intercepting devices under this section by such officers, agents or other persons as may be authorized or designated for that purpose by the Attorney General.)

ganizations have developed intricate schemes of operation to prevent proof of this necessary element of the present statute.[105] They use their own trucks and sometimes make several stops or simulated deliveries or pickups along the way.[106] This process thwarts extremely expensive and time consuming surveillance by law enforcement officers and makes it virtually impossible to detect which items in a particular shipment actually crossed state lines.

The proposed amendment should take the form of an additional section of Title 18. Such sections should supplement existing sections 1462 and 1465 and include language which prohibits activities that "affect" commerce. The addition of such a statute would facilitate prosecutions while maintaining the integrity of the present statutory structure. In a multiple count indictment, charges could be brought against individuals under both sections, subject to constitutional limitations which exist in any such case. Legislation which creates a separate violation would prevent the effects of the inevitable and lengthy initial constitutional challenges to such new legislation from crippling or stopping all federal prosecutions.

A requirement that the prosecution prove the transaction "affects" commerce is a more realistic burden of proof which would close the technical loopholes these criminals have so successfully exploited. This requirement

would be consistent with other federal statutes such as the Hobbs Act and the firearms laws.[107] An examination of the constitutional ramifications discloses no barrier to this proposed amendment.[108]

Article I, Section 8 of the United States Constitution empowers Congress to regulate commerce.[109] The interpretation and application of the constitutional limits on Congress' power to regulate has been the issue in many cases whose factual bases are widely divergent. The subject of regulation, whether it is production, distribution or consumption, is constitutionally immaterial so long as the activity in question is within the sphere of Congress' regulatory powers.[110] The underlying principles, however, have been applied consistently to a variety of factual situations. The particular subject matter of the statute should not present a barrier to a constitutionally valid amendment.

The distinction between regulating activities "in commerce" and regulating those which "affect commerce" is a valid one and has been maintained. The standards, however, have been recognized by the courts as being within the total ambit of Congress' constitutional regulatory powers.[111] The decision as to the scope of regulatory jurisdiction lies with Congress and is generally made as a matter of public policy rather than a decision dependent purely on legal considerations.

If the activity is other than purely local in

---

105. Los Angeles Hearing, Vol. I, Kenneth Gillingham, p. 114–16.

106. Id.

107. See, e.g., 18 U.S.C. SS844, 1951 and 1202.

108. See, Wickard v. Filburn, 317 U.S. 111(1942).

109. "Section 8. [1] [The Congress shall have Power] [3] to regulate the Commerce with foreign Nations, and among the several States, and with the Indian Tribes." U.S. Const. art. I, S8, cl.3.

110. See, United States v. Wrightwood Dairy Co., 315 U.S. 110 (1942). More recent cases indicate the validity of the Court's earlier decisions and the ultimate expanse of Congress' power to regulate. These cases represent a variety of legal and factual issues, but each one affirms the underlying principals of the preceding cases. See, e.g., Gulf Oil Corp. v. Copp Paving Co., Inc., 419 U.S. 186 (1974); United States v. American Building Maintenance Industries, 422 U.S. 271 (1975); McLain v. Real Estate Board of New Orleans, 444 U.S. 232(1978); Turf Paradise, Inc. v. Arizona Downs, 670 F.2d. 813 (9th Cir. 1982).

111. See, McLain v. Real Estate Board of New Orleans, 444 U.S. 232, 241(1979). "The broad authority of Congress under the Commerce Clause has, of course, long been interpreted to extend beyond activities in interstate commerce to reach other activities that, while wholly local in nature, nevertheless substantially affect interstate commerce." (emphasis added).

(c) any drug, medicine, article, or thing designed, adapted, or intended for producing abortion, or for any indecent or immoral use; or any written or printed card, letter, circular, book, pamphlet, advertisement, or notice of any kind giving information, directly or indirectly, where, how, or of whom, or by what means any of such mentioned articles, matters, or things may be obtained or made; * * *;"

18 U.S.C. S1465 provides, in part:

"Whoever knowingly transports in interstate or foreign commerce for the purpose of sale or distribution any obscene, lewd, lascivious, or filthy book, pamphlet, picture, film, paper, letter, writing, print, silhouette, drawing, figure, image, cast, phonograph recording, electrical transcription or other articles capable of producing sound or any other matter of indecent or immoral character, shall be fined not more than $5,000 or imprisoned not more than five years, or both.

nature it is subject to federal commerce power regulation. It is within this constitutional grant that Congress may exercise discretion in setting the limits of jurisdiction. Since Congress has already Constitutionally chosen to regulate the activity through 18 U.S.C. SS1462 and S1465, it may, if it chooses, expand the regulatory jurisdiction to include activities which "affect" commerce as well as those "in" commerce.

This Commission finds that virtually all distribution of obscene material substantially affects interstate commerce.

Department of Justice Guidelines now in effect for the United States Attorneys preclude federal prosecution of obscenity cases that properly belong in state courts.[112] Existing guidelines require the United States Attorneys to give higher priority to cases involving large scale distributors who realize substantial income from multi-state operations and cases in which there is evidence of involvement by known organized crime figures.[113] These are the types of cases that require the operational resources of the Department of Justice and federal law enforcement agencies and are accordingly beyond the scope of local law enforcement capabilities.[114] The new section would be a substantial aid to federal prosecutors' efforts, but properly applied it would not result in any more federal encroachment on state prosecutors' prerogatives than present federal law permits.

RECOMMENDATION 3:
Congress should enact legislation making it

an unfair business practice and an unfair labor practice for any employer to hire individuals to participate in commercial sexual performances.

Discussion

This Commission does not advocate nor does it condone the use of individuals in commercial sexual practices. The Commission strongly supports enforcement of existing criminal laws against those who violate them by using individuals in commercial sexual performances or in the production of obscene materials. The Commission does, however, recommend imposing fair labor standards on those businesses which engage individuals to perform sexual acts for commercial purposes. This recommendation is made only out of an abiding concern for those persons used in these sexual performances.

The production of obscene material, like many forms of criminal activity, is an enterprise patterned after other legitimate business structures.[115] Producers of obscene material make capital investments, hire employees, and earn sizeable profits. Unlike other businesses, the regulations governing the production of obscenity are largely self-imposed or non-existent. This industry has been called the "last vestige of true laissez-faire capitalism" in the United States.[116] Unlike more conventional businesses and industries, profits from obscene materials go largely untaxed and their employees often suffer varying degrees of mental and physical injury.[117] Seldom, if ever, do employees maintain

---

112. The guidelines provide, "The Federal role in prosecuting obscenity cases is to focus upon the major producers and interstate distributors of pornography while leaving to local jurisdiction the responsibility of dealing with local exhibitions and sales. This role has not met with complete acceptance and understanding by citizens of communities confronted with offensive matters who find their local prosecutor ineffectual in this area. Even so, local prosecutors have been regarded as having the primary obligation to deal with such material on a local level.

* * * * * * * * * * *

Local prosecutors, however willing to prosecute, frequently experience difficulty because of several factors, notably a lack of expertise in the field, lack of support by the community and/or its officials, and lack of necessary funds. In these circumstances the United States may provide assistance through prosecutive efforts not falling precisely within the above guidelines. Conversely, local authorities dealing with obscene material being distributed within their area may develop evidence of interstate distribution useful to a Federal prosecution. Communications between Federal and local prosecutors, and coordination of efforts in such instances, can be highly productive in both Federal and local efforts." United States Department of Justice, *United States Attorneys' Manual*, Ch. 75, p. 9a (June 18, 1981).

113. Chicago Hearing, Vol. II, James S. Reynolds, p. 263.

114. New York Hearing, Vol. II, William Johnson, p. 82.

115. Chicago Hearing, Vol. II, Duncan McDonald, p. 59.

116. *Id.* at 61; The value of society's goods always derives from the values of its people. A democratic society that is unwilling to bar *Hustler* on public newsstands or ban billboards from beautiful views cannot justly blame capitalism for these offenses. It is up to the political, judicial, and religious institutions of the society, not other businesses, to eliminate such opportunities for ugly profit. Capitalists perform a vital role in determining what goods and services are initially offered to the public. But the people and their government determine the limits of what can be marketed. Markets provide the ultimate democracy; democracy, though, defines the marketplace. G. Gilder, *The Spirit of Enterprise*, 91(1984).

117. See, The discussion of performers in the pornography industry for further information.

insurance, pay benefits or provide pension plans to performers or others who work for them.

Congress should enact legislation, as necessary, that would specifically subject the production of obscene materials to the same types of laws and regulations as other businesses. This would not necessarily involve criminal statutes or penalties, but rather it could take the form of civil regulatory statutes. These are not recommended as exclusive remedies, but as a form of regulation that parallels other existing forms of criminal and civil relief. The basis for these statutes is the government's broad powers to regulate commerce.

Legislation also should be enacted that would make it an unfair business practice and an unfair labor practice to hire individuals to participate in certain sexual performances for purposes of producing sexually explicit materials. Included in the prohibited activities should be sexual performances involving children, violence, sado-masochism, or anything which would meet the description of unlawful sexually explicit depictions developed in such federal law.

Congress should prohibit the sale and distribution of any product made as a result of those unfair practices and provide a civil cause of action for any party injured as a result of these practices.[118] The law should also provide protection for individuals who are used as actors or models in obscene material. Such legislation should make any contracts for prohibited performances void, and provide a formula for the determination of damages and payment of attorneys fees. Existing laws and regulations prohibit an employer from imposing dangerous, unhealthy, or unfair conditions of employment on an employee. Employees have a remedy if they are harmed in the course of their employment. None of these requirements have been applied to the pornography industry where these risks are truly pervasive. It is essential that the commercial laws and regulations be applied in a fair and even-handed manner. Business enterprises should be prevented from operating in a manner which jeopardizes the welfare of its employees.

RECOMMENDATION 4:
Congress should amend the Mann Act to make its provisions gender neutral.

Discussion
The Mann Act[119] makes it a federal offense to transport "any woman or girl" in interstate or foreign commerce for the purpose of "prostitution or debauchery, or for any other immoral purpose, or with intent and purpose to induce, entice, or compel such woman or girl to become a prostitute, or to give herself up to immoral practice, debauchery or to engage in any other immoral practice."[120] Men and boys who are used in prostitution and in the production of obscene materials are often transported in commerce for the very purposes proscribed in the present statute.[121] Those who exploit men and boys for illegal and immoral purposes should be subject to the same punishment as those who exploit females.

The proposed amendment would simply afford protection to a class of persons who are without adequate legal redress. While women and girls may continue to comprise the majority of such cases of exploitation these statistics should provide no excuse to exclude men and boys from equal protection purely on the basis of the smaller number of reported cases.[122]

Further, the Act should be amended to prohibit *illegal* acts rather than the current prohibition against immoral acts. This amendment would address and alleviate the concerns of those who suggest an overzealous prosecutor may use the Act to harass individuals engaged in lawful consensual sexual activity. This amendment would not expand the scope of enforcement or prosecution and it should set clear guidelines for the types of activities that are proscribed.

RECOMMENDATION 5:
Congress should amend Title 18 of the United States Code to specifically proscribe obscene cable and satellite television programming.

---

118. This could be in the form of a civil rights type approach.

119. 18 U.S.C. S2421 (1985).

120. *Id.*

121. See, *Comm. v. Richard Kind*, C-19168; *Comm. v. Theodore Dufresne*, C-19608; and *Comm. v. Alfredo Martin*, C-19568 Circuit Court of Arlington County, Virginia.

122. ". . . statistically there appears to be no particular preference on the part of the child molesters for victim. It's about 50 percent of the time boys and 50 percent of the time they are girls. So clearly boys ought to be included under the Mann Act." Washington, D.C., Hearing, Vol. I, Senator Mitch McConnell, p. 56.

Discussion

The United States Code proscribes the utterance of "any obscene, indecent or profane language by means of radio communication."[123] Because cable and satellite television programming is not conveyed by any means interpreted by the courts to be a radio communication, any obscene programming is not covered by the prohibitions of the present statute.

The Cable Communications Policy Act of 1984 attempts to provide another avenue for the prosecution of obscenity shown over cable television.[124] The Act, provides:

> Whoever transmits over any cable system any matter which is obscene or otherwise unprotected by the Constitution of the United States shall be fined not more than $10,000 or imprisoned not more than 2 years, or both.[125]

The provisions of this section may be in conflict with two other sections of the act governing editorial control of programming by cable operators. Section 531(e) of Title 47 provides that:

> Subject to Section 544(d) of this title, a cable operator shall not exercise any editorial control over any public, educational or governmental use of channel capacity provided pursuant to this section.

In addition, Section 544(d) provides, in part:

> (1) Nothing in this subchapter shall be construed as prohibiting a franchising authority and a cable operator from specifying, in a franchise or renewal thereof, that certain cable services shall not be provided or shall be provided subject to conditions, if such cable services are obscene or are otherwise unprotected by the Constitution of the United States.
> (2) (A) In order to restrict the viewing of programming which is obscene or indecent, upon the request of a subscriber, a cable operator shall provide (by sale or lease) a device by which the subscriber can prohibit viewing of a particular cable service during period selected by that subscriber.

Section 544(d) seems to contemplate allowing the operator to provide obscene programming while Section 559 makes it a crime to do so. The apparent conflict should be resolved and legislation should provide clear guidance for cable operations, federal prosecutors and law enforcement officers.[126]

RECOMMENDATION 6:
Congress should enact legislation to prohibit the transmission of obscene material through the telephone or similar common carrier.

Discussion

This Commission has received substantial evidence of the use of the telephone to transmit obscene material.[127] Dial-A-Porn services offer the caller the opportunity to participate in obscene telephone conversations or to receive obscene messages.[128]

Two years ago, the Congress enacted legislation amending section 223 of the Communications Act of 1934.[129] This enactment

---

123. 18 U.S.C. S1464.

124. 47 U.S.C. S559.

125. Id.

126. Senate Bill 1090 sponsored by Senator Jesse Helms (R-NC) would place a specific prohibition against obscene cable programming by amending Section 1464 of Title 18 of the United States Code. The Helms Bill provides in part:

1464. Distributing obscene material by radio or television.

"(a) Whoever utters any obscene, indecent, or profane language, or distributes any obscene, indecent, or profane material, by means of radio or television, including cable television, shall be fined not more than $50,000 or imprisoned not more than two years, or both."

"(b) As used in this section, the term "distributes" means to send, transmit, retransmit, telecast, broadcast, or cablecast, including by wire or satellite, or produce or provide such material for distribution."

The standard language of Title 18 provides several synonyms for the word "obscene". 18 U.S.C. S1461 provides, "Every obscene, lewd, lascivious, indecent, filthy or vile . . ."

Enactment of legislation of this type would enable United States Attorneys to prosecute violators under the criminal code and alleviate the possible conflict under the Cable Communications Policy Act.

127. See, Los Angeles Hearing, Vol. I, William A. Dunkle, p. 248; Los Angeles Hearing, Vol. I, Judith F. Trevillian, p. 263; Los Angeles Hearing, Vol. I, Brent D. Ward, p. 225. The most commercially prolific form of dissemination of pornographic material is through services commonly referred to as "Dial-A-Porn."

128. See, The discussion of the Dial-A-Porn services available for further information.

129. See, 47 U.S.C. S223(b)(1).

prohibited the use of the telephone to make obscene or indecent communications for commercial purposes to anyone under eighteen years of age except where in compliance with regulations issued by the Federal Communications Commission.[130] The FCC promulgated regulations making it an exception for the provider of a recorded message if the message was made available only between the hours of 9:00 p.m. and 8:00 a.m. eastern standard time or if the caller made prepayment by credit card in the case of a "live" message.[131] Carlin Communications challenged the FCC regulation.

On review, the United States Court of Appeals for the Second Circuit found the regulations were invalid.[132] The court found that the government had a compelling interest in protecting minors from salacious material, but that the FCC regulations were not well tailored to meet their objectives, which could be achieved by less restrictive alternatives.[133] In dicta, the court said the FCC should have given more serious consideration to other options such as "blocking" and access codes. Through "blocking" a subscriber can have access to all "976" numbers blocked from his telephone. Access codes could be issued to subscribers over eighteen who would have to dial the code in order to receive the sexually explicit message.[134]

On October 16, 1985, the FCC announced new regulations governing Dial-A-Porn.[135] Under the new regulations, Dial-A-Porn services must require either an authorized access or identification code or they must obtain prepayment by credit card before transmission of a sexually explicit message.[136]

Carlin challenged the new FCC regulations, and on April 11, 1986, the Court of Appeals granted their petition and set aside the regulations as applied to Carlin.[137] The Court of Appeals relied on statements from New York Telephone that access or identification codes are not technologically feasible in NYT's network,[138] and found that "the record does not support the FCC's conclusion that the access code requirement is the least restrictive means to regulate Dial-A-Porn. . . ."[139] The Court again referred to "blocking" as a less restrictive means of regulating Dial-A-Porn.[140] Blocking devices installed on the telephone customer's own terminal equipment could be used to block access to one or more pre-selected telephone numbers.[141] The Court also suggested that the FCC should have considered the feasibility of passing along the cost of customer premises blocking equipment to the providers of Dial-A-Porn and/or the telephone companies.[142]

The latest decision by the Second Circuit leaves the state of the law regarding Dial-A-Porn even more uncertain. The two attempts by the FCC to promulgate regulations in accordance with the federal statute have failed. The Court of Appeals found earlier that limitations on the hours that Dial-A-Porn messages may be offered were not well tailored enough to regulate the problem.[143] Now the Court has ruled that access codes are unduly restrictive as applied to Carlin in New York, but may be permissible elsewhere.[144] The "blocking" option advanced by the Court has serious practical limitations. Blocking may not be available to all telephone customers.[145] Those who obtain the service would either

130. *Id.*

131. 49 Fed. Reg. 24, 996 (June 4, 1984).

132. *Carlin Communications, Inc. v. FCC,* 749 F.2d 113 (2d Cir. 1984).

133. *Id.,* p. 121.

134. *Id.,* pp. 122–23.

135. 50 Fed.Reg. 42699. (October 22, 1985).

136. *Id.*

137. *Carlin Communications, Inc. v. FCC,* No. 85–4158 (2nd Cir. 1986). The Court noted that "the stay, however, is granted only at the behest of the petitioners here . . . and applies only to Dial-A-Porn service providers on the New York Telephone (NYT) system. (Slip opinion, p. 3).

138. *Id.* slip op. at 11 and 19. The Court noted that the access codes are probably technologically possible in most other parts of the country. *See,* slip op., p. 4.

139. *Id.,* p. 23.

140. *Id.,* pp. 23–24.

141. *Id.,* pp. 6–7.

142. *Id.,* p. 23.

143. 749 F.2d, p. 121.

144. *Carlin Communications, Inc. v. FCC, supra,* slip op., pp. 3–4.

145. See, Los Angeles Hearing, Vol. I, William Dunkle, p. 254.

lose access to all "976" numbers,[146] or have to pre-select which numbers they wanted blocked.[147] Few parents would have sufficient knowledge of the multitude of Dial-A-Porn numbers to be able to pre-select them and prevent their children from calling them by use of a blocking device, and minors would still be free to make the calls from telephones not equipped with blocking devices.

The provision of the federal statute permitting Dial-A-Porn messages to be provided in accordance with FCC regulations[148] has proven unworkable in addition to providing a "safe harbor" provision for Dial-A-Porn merchants. Congress should enact legislation that simply prohibits the transmission of obscene material through the telephone or similar common carrier.[149]

RECOMMENDATIONS FOR CHANGES IN STATE LAW

RECOMMENDATION 7:

State legislatures should amend, if necessary, obscenity statutes containing the definitional requirement that material be "utterly without redeeming social value" in order to be obscene to conform with the current standard enunciated by the United States Supreme Court in Miller v. California.[150]

Discussion

A minority of jurisdictions, including the State of California,[151] retain the requirement that material must be "utterly without redeeming social value" in order to be found obscene.[152]

This standard emanates from the case of *Roth v. United States*, and the later case of

---

146. *Id.*

147. *Carlin Communications, Inc. v. FCC, supra,* slip op., p. 6.

148. 47 U.S.C. S223(8)(2).

149. In an attempt to address the Dial-A-Porn issue, Senate Bill 1090 has been introduced by Senators Jesse Helms (R-NC), John East (R-NC) and Jeremiah Denton (R-Ala) to amend Section 223 of the Communications Act of 1934.

The Bill provides:

> Whoever—"(A) in the District of Columbia or in interstate or foreign communications, by means of telephone, makes (directly or by recording device) any comment, request, suggestion, or proposal which is obscene, lewd, lascivious, filthy, or indecent, regardless of whether the maker of such comments placed the call or" (B) knowingly permits any telephone facility under such person's control to be used by any purpose prohibited by subparagraph (A). Shall be fined not more than $50,000 or imprisoned not more than six months, or both."

Additionally, Rep. Thomas J. Bliley (R-Va) has introduced H.R.4439 which would amend section 223 of the Communications Act and eliminate the provision requiring the FCC to issue regulations.

H.R. 4439

> A bill to amend the Communications Act of 1934 to restrict the making of obscene and indecent communications by telephone. Be it enacted by the Senate and House of Representatives of the United States of America in Congress assembled.

SECTION 1. SHORT TITLE.
This Act may be cited as the "Telephone Decency Act of 1986."

SECTION 2. AMENDMENTS.
Section 223(b) of the Communications Act of 1934 is amended—
(1) in paragraph (1)(A), by striking out "under eighteen years of age or to any person without that person's consent";
(2) by striking out paragraph (2);
(3) in paragraph (4), by striking out "paragraphs (1) and (3)" and inserting in lieu thereof "paragraph (1) and (2)"; and
(4) by redesignating paragraphs (3), (4), and (5) as paragraphs (2), (3), and (4), respectively.

150. 413 U.S. 15 (1973).

151. On April 14, 1986, the Governor of California signed into law Senate Bill 139 which amends the California obscenity law. The new law goes into effect in January of 1987, and defines obscene matter as material which

> taken as a whole, the predominant appeal of which to the average person applying contemporary statewide standards, to a prurient interest, meaning a shameful or morbid interest in nudity, sex, or excretion and is matter which taken as a whole goes substantially beyond customary limits of candor in the description or representation of such matters; and is matter which, taken as a whole *lacks significant literary, artistic, political, educational, or scientific value.* (emphasis added)

The new law still does not contain the exact language of *Miller* and thus its constitutionality may be uncertain until any appeals through the individual system are completed.

152. 354 U.S., (1957), p. 476.

Memoirs v. Massachusetts[153] in which a plurality of the Supreme Court held that a book alleged to be obscene cannot be proscribed unless it is found to be utterly without redeeming social value.[154] The court reversed an obscenity conviction involving John Cleland's book Memoirs of a Woman of Pleasure because the work possessed a "modicum" of social value.[155] The Memoirs test made it almost impossible to convict in obscenity cases.[156] When the Supreme Court decided Miller v. California,[157] a new obscenity test resulted.[158] Although the Court remained divided on basic philosphical grounds, not a single member of the Court voted to retain the Memoirs standard. (emphasis added). Writing for the Court in Miller Chief Justice Warren E. Burger said the standard formulated in Memoirs required proof of a negative, "a burden virtually impossible to discharge under our criminal standards of proof." (emphasis added).[159]

The Court also noted that the standard had even been abandoned by Justice William Brennan who authored the Court's opinion in Memoirs. To the extent that the Memoirs standard exists today, it makes prosecution of obscenity cases extremely difficult. To win acquittal on an obscenity charge, a defendant need only demonstrate some miniscule social value as opposed to the serious literary, artistic, political or scientific value required under Miller. The Memoirs standard is still the law in California[160] and has posed a major obstacle to successful obscenity prosecutions. Consequently, the legal problems attendant to prosecution may contribute to factors which the wholesale pornography industry is centered in the Los Angeles area, and produces most of the materials sold in the entire United States. The pornography industry in the area of Los Angeles earns at least $550 million a year[161] and produces eighty percent of the sexually explicit videotapes, eight millimeter films and novelties are produced there.[162]

The principle of Federalism protects the constitutional prerogative of the states to enact obscenity laws which embody standards less stringent than those approved by the United States Supreme Court in Miller. As Chief Justice Burger wrote in Paris Adult Theatre I v. Slaton[163]

The States, of course, may follow such a "laissez faire" policy and drop all controls on commercialized obscenity, if that is what they prefer, just as they can ignore consumer protection in the marketplace, but nothing in the Constitution compels the States to do so with regard to matters falling within state jurisdiction. See, United States v. Reidel, 402 U.S., at 357, 28 L. Ed. 2d 813; Memoirs v. Massachusetts, 383 U.S., at 462. 16 L. Ed. 2d 1(White, J., dissenting). "We do not sit as a superlegislature to determine the wisdom, need, and propriety of laws that touch economic problems, business affairs, or social conditions," Griswold v. Connecticut, 381 U.S. 479, 482, 14 L. Ed. 2d 510, 85 S. Ct. 1678(1965). See, Ferguson v. Skrupa, 372 U.S., at 731, 10 L. Ed. 2d 93, 95 ALR 2d 1347(1963); Day-Brite Lighting Inc. v. Missouri, 342 U.S. 421, 423, 96 L. Ed. 469, 72 S. Ct. 405(1952).[164]

Law enforcement officers in California blame the existing law for severely hampering their effectiveness in eliminating this activity.[165] A Los Angeles Police Department Captain testified, "We have pleaded with the state legislature ever since Miller came into being to adopt it."[166]

If states sincerely wish to provide an effective basis for law enforcement this change in standards is essential.

RECOMMENDATION 8:
State legislatures should amend, if necessary, obscenity statutes to eliminate misdemeanor

153. 383 U.S., (1966), p. 413.
154. 383 U.S., (1966), p. 413.
155. Id., pp. 418–20.
156. See, Miller v. California, 314 U.S. 15 (1973).
157. Id.
158. 413 U.S., (1973), p. 22; See, Chicago Hearing, Vol. I, Paul McGeady, p. 81.
159. 413 U.S., p. 22.
160. See, supra note 151.
161. Chicago Hearing, Vol. I, Donald Smith, p. 31.
162. Id., p. 30.
163. 413 U.S., (1973), p. 49.
164. Id., p. 64.
165. Id., p. 46; Los Angeles Hearing, Vol. I, James Docherty, p. 15.
166. Los Angeles Hearing, Vol. I, James Docherty, p. 15.

status for second offenses and make any second offense punishable as a felony.

Discussion

State obscenity statutes frequently classify a first conviction as a misdemeanor. In some jurisdictions an obscenity violation becomes a felony when the specific offender is convicted a second time. In other jurisdictions an obscenity violation will remain a misdemeanor regardless of the number of prior convictions. This system results in minimal penalties for many offenders and is no deterrent to large-scale criminal enterprise.

State obscenity laws which provide misdemeanor penalties for recidivist offenders produce results which have a minimal deterrent effect. Fines in the amount of thirty to ninety dollars are a common disposition for a first offense in Chicago.[167] Three hundred to five hundred dollar fines are standard in Houston, Texas.[168] In ✄ Florida, a corporation with twenty-five prior obscenity convictions was fined $1,600.[169] In Los Angeles, where the industry earns $550 million a year,[170] a major distributor is often fined no more than $10,000.[171] The amounts of these fines are inconsequential when compared to the profits earned by many producers or sellers of obscene material.[172]

An amendment to state statutes enhancing the penalties for subsequent convictions for obscenity violations would recognize the recidivist nature of the crime and should be directed to management personnel of the wholesale or retail operation. Classifying the crime as a felony would allow judges to impose substantial fines and periods of incarceration for a repeat offender. A conviction for a felony would substantially reduce the incidence of inappropriate sentencing for recidivists.

RECOMMENDATION 9:

State legislatures should enact, if necessary, forfeiture provisions as part of their obscenity laws.

Discussion

The addition of forfeiture provisions to the state obscenity statutes would greatly enhance their deterrent effect and would be an effective tool for law enforcement officers to use against the most egregious offenders. These forfeiture provisions may mirror such provisions found in several federal statutes. The precise scope of the forfeitures should be the decision of each state legislature and subject to judicial interpretation.

Some states already have taken the initiative in implementing forfeiture provisions in their obscenity laws. The Metropolitan Bureau of Investigation (M.B.I.) in Orlando, Florida, provides an excellent example of the effectiveness of forfeiture provisions under state law. Using the forfeiture provisions of the Florida RICO Act, the M.B.I. obtained forfeitures of $80,000 to $100,000 worth of property in a single investigation and prosecution.[173] The forfeited property included two computer systems, two projection screen televisions and a large assortment of films, magazines, and novelties.[174] Forfeiture should be used to uproot the capital of pornography producers and distributors. Used effectively, forfeiture can substantially handicap these businesses.

RECOMMENDATION 10:

State legislatures should enact a Racketeer Influenced Corrupt Organizations (RICO) statute which has obscenity as a predicate act.

Discussion

States which do not have obscenity as a predicate offense for a racketeer influenced corrupt organizations (RICO) violation should consider enacting such legislation. RICO provides an effective means to substantially eliminate obscenity businesses. (See, Recommendations for the United States Department of Justice, Infra.).

---

167. Chicago Hearing, Vol. I, Thomas Bohling, p. 16.

168. Houston Hearing, Vol. II, W.D. Brown, p. 50.

169. Miami Hearing, Vol. I, Mike Berish, p. 66.

170. Los Angeles Hearing, Vol. I, Donald Smith, p. 30.

171. Id., p. 46.

172. See, The discussion of the Production, Distribution and Technology of Sexual Explicit Materials for further information.

173. New York Hearing, Vol. II, Larry Schuchman, p. 52.

174. Id.; See, Recommendations for Changes in Federal Law in this Chapter.

RECOMMENDATIONS FOR THE UNITED STATES DEPARTMENT OF JUSTICE

RECOMMENDATION 11:

The Attorney General should direct the United States Attorneys to examine the obscenity problem in their respective districts, identify offenders, initiate investigations, and begin prosecuting them without delay.

Discussion

If the flow of obscene material is going to be resolved through criminal prosecution, the Attorney General of the United States must take a *significant, ongoing* and *personal role* in directing a combined federal, state and local effort.

The Attorney General should direct the United States Attorneys to identify the major sources of obscene material within their districts and commence prosecutions without further delay. The United States Attorneys should contact their state and local counterparts and identify persons and organizations responsible for manufacturing and distributing obscene material in their districts. The Attorney General must also follow up on his directives and ensure compliance by the United States Attorneys.

The United States Department of Justice, through guidelines contained in the *United States Attorneys' Manual,* places a priority on the prosecution of three types of obscenity cases: those involving large scale distributors who realize substantial incomes from multi-state operations; those where there is evidence of involvement by known organized crime figures; and those involving child pornography.[175] United States Attorneys may also increase the priority for cases involving highly offensive material or cases where obscenity is found to be a particular problem in the jurisdiction.[176]

Former Attorney General William French Smith and Assistant Attorney General Stephen S. Trott have urged the United States Attorneys to follow existing departmental guidelines and to prosecute obscenity cases aggressively. On October 4, 1982, Attorney General Smith sent a memorandum to all United States Attorneys calling attention to the guidelines and encouraging aggressive and proactive prosecution of obscenity cases.[177] Attorney General Smith also suggested using the Law Enforcement Coordinating Committees to determine the nature and extent of the obscenity problem in the individual districts.[178] Despite this directive from the Attorney General not a single indictment alleging a violation of federal obscenity laws was returned in 1983 in any district in the United States.[179]

Assistant Attorney General Trott sent an additional memorandum to the United States Attorneys on August 24, 1983, calling on them to "step up our level of enforcement" of obscenity violations.[180] Assistant Attorney General Trott again called attention to the guidelines and asked the United States Attorneys to set up a meeting with the United States Postal Inspection Service and Federal Bureau of Investigation in their districts to evaluate the need for additional enforcement.[181] He also offered assistance from the Criminal Division of the Department of Justice if an individual United States Attorney needed help in structuring an enforcement program.[182]

This directive has had little effect on most federal prosecutors. The departmental guidelines have been used as "excuses" to decline prosecution of obscenity cases involving adult material. The guidelines have been per-

---

175. Department of Justice, *United States Attorney Manual* (1977).

176. *Id.* (This Commission does not believe these are inappropriate.)

177. Memorandum of Attorney General William French Smith, October 4, 1982. "Proactive prosecution" is a term used to suggest affirmative action taken by law enforcement officers and prosecutors. This term should be contrasted with "reactive prosecution" in which law enforcement officers respond to specific complaints of recently discovered crimes. Obscenity cases generally cannot be developed without proactive investigative efforts.

178. *Id.*

179. See, *infra* note 180.

180. Memorandum of from Stephen S. Trott, Assistant Attorney General, Criminal Division to all United States Attorneys (Aug. 24, 1983) (discussing enforcement of Obscenity Laws).

181. *Id.*

182. *Id.*

ceived as establishing exclusive categories for prosecution rather than minimum criteria.

The Department's guidelines are clear and the United States Attorneys have been instructed by both the Attorney General and the head of the Criminal Division to use these guidelines to prosecute obscenity cases. A Justice Department official told the Commission in Chicago, "These are not declination guidelines, they are priority guidelines."[183]

Since the time of these directives fewer than ten federal districts[184] have brought obscenity prosecutions despite the presence of large scale distributors and organized crime involvement in their jurisdiction.[185]

There is widespread evidence that the stated policy of the Department of Justice and the established guidelines are not being implemented by the United States Attorneys.[186] Very few obscenity cases have been brought by the United States Attorneys. In addition, the Department of Justice and the United States Attorneys have cited the rigorous pursuit of child pornography cases as compliance with the Attorney General's mandate and as a rationale for neglecting obscenity prosecutions.

From May 1, 1984, through July 1985, there were obscenity prosecutions in only seven of the ninety-four federal districts.[187]

---

183. Chicago Hearing, Vol. II, James S. Reynolds, p. 267.

184. Id.

185. The Criminal Division of the United States Department of Justice has compiled and provided the following statistics with respect to recent and current obscenity law prosecutions.

Adult Pornography

	Indicted	Convicted
1978	11	20
1979	1	2
1980	54(*1)	1
1981	2	15(*2)
1982	7	4(*3)
1983	0	2
1984	6	11(*4)
1985	19	14(*5)
1986		2(*6)

(*1) Includes 45 MIPORN defendants.
(*2) Includes 5 MIPORN defendants.
      Convictions of two other MIPORN
      defendants in 1981 were reversed on
      appeal.
(*3) Includes 1 MIPORN defendant.
(*4) Includes 6 MIPORN defendants.
(*5) Includes 2 MIPORN defendants.
(*6) Both are MIPORN defendants.

Districts Which Have Prosecuted Adult Pornography Cases Since January 1, 1978

Northern District of Alabama	Eastern District of New York
Southern District of Alabama	Western District of New York
Central District of California	Western District of North Carolina
Middle District of Florida	Western District of Pennsylvania
Southern District of Florida	Eastern District of Tennessee
District of Kansas	Western District of Tennessee
Eastern District of Kentucky	Western District of Texas
Western District of Kentucky	District of Utah
District of Massachusetts	Eastern District of Virginia
District of Nebraska	

Districts In Which Adult Pornography Cases Are Presently Pending

Southern District of Florida	District of Utah

Statistics have been obtained from several sources. While they are essentially complete, it is possible a few cases may have been omitted. Letter from Donald B. Nicholson to Alan E. Sears (Feb. 28, 1986).

186. Chicago Hearing, Vol. I, Paul McGeady, pp. 82–3.

187. Chicago Hearing, Vol. II, James S. Reynolds, p. 267. In addition it is noted that this Commission invited United States Attorneys from several major districts to attend and testify at its hearings. No United States Attorney whose office does not prosecute obscenity cases accepted the invitation to appear before the Commission to explain their policy.

There were no obscenity prosecutions in the districts encompassing the Southern District of New York (Manhattan) or the Central District of California (Los Angeles)[188] where the majority of obscene materials are now and were then being produced or distributed.[189]

One witness testified before the Commission that he contacted the office of the United States Attorney for the Central District of California in Los Angeles and requested information regarding the number of obscenity prosecutions brought by that office during the period from 1979 to 1982 along with the number of defendants involved and the number of convictions which resulted.[190] The United States Attorney responded that during that period there was only one prosecution and it involved child pornography.[191] In a letter dated February 22, 1984, the United States Attorney for the Central District of California in Los Angeles, said that it would be a "misuse of the limited resources of this office to prosecute so-called adult films" and added that he and his predecessor had concluded that films of this variety could not be prosecuted successfully in that district.[192]

The perception is pervasive among federal law enforcement agents that most United States Attorneys will not prosecute cases involving obscene matter. According to an Assistant Chief Postal Inspector, the Postal Inspection Service presents very few obscenity cases to the United States Attorneys because federal prosecutors will not authorize prosecution.[193] Experiences of Postal Inspectors in which federal prosecutors have declined prosecution of cases have dissuaded them from fully using their existing resources to investigate obscenity cases.[194]

An agent of the United States Customs Service testified that his office had made countless thousands of seizures of adult materials over the last two years, but had presented none of them to the United States Attorneys' offices.[195] The agent said it was his understanding from the Assistant United States Attorneys that the Department of Justice policy was not in favor of prosecuting obscenity cases and presentation would be pointless.[196] Similar statements have been received from federal agents in Minnesota and New York.[197] The same Customs agent testified that he had presented fifty different child pornography seizures to the United States Attorneys for prosecution of which approximately forty-seven were accepted for prosecution.[198]

While the Departmental guidelines make both child pornography and enumerated types of adult material of *equal priority*, there is a practice of prosecuting child pornography ahead of all else and to the virtual exclusion of obscenity cases. A Department of Justice official testified that all child pornography cases "merit priority" while the Department seeks obscenity cases which would have "significant deterrent effect."[199]

Despite stated departmental objectives, in practice, emphasis on child pornography to the exclusion of adult obscenity cases is apparent.[200] While aggressive prosecution of child pornography cases is laudable, it should not be a justification for the failure to prosecute appropriate cases involving obscene material. The small number of obscen-

188. *Id.*, pp. 267, 271.

189. Chicago Hearing, Vol. 1, Donald Smith, pp. 30–31.

190. Chicago Hearing, Vol. I, Paul McGeady, pp. 82–83.

191. *Id.*, p. 83.

192. Chicago Hearing, Vol. I, Paul McGeady, pp. 83–85; During the same period the Los Angeles Police Department was actively involved in the investigation of major obscenity distributors; Chicago Hearing, Vol. I, Donald Smith, p. 33; Since 1973 the Los Angeles Police Department vice division successfully convicted offenders in over three hundred obscenity cases. In addition, it is noted that the Los Angeles Police Department cases were prosecuted in California state courts which use the *Memoirs-Roth* test, a much more difficult legal standard than in the federal courts which apply *Miller*. Los Angeles Hearing, Vol. I, James Docherty, p. 6; *See also*, The discussion of the History of Regulation and First Amendment Considerations for further information.

193. Washington, D.C., Hearing, Vol. I, Jack Swagerty, p. 138.

194. *Id.*, pp. 70–71.

195. *Id.*; Chicago Hearing, Vol. I, Jack O'Malley, pp. 117–18.

196. *Id.*

197. Chicago Hearing, Vol. I, Paul McGeady, pp. 86–86.

198. Chicago Hearing, Vol. I, Jack O'Malley, p. 119.

199. Chicago Hearing, Vol. II, James S. Reynolds, p. 266.

200. From 1978 through February, 1986, 255 persons were indicted and 215 individuals convicted of child pornography law violations. This should be contrasted with one hundred indictments and seventy-one convictions for obscenity law violations during the same period.

ity prosecutions is not a product of the Department's existing guidelines. The lack of obscenity prosecutions is a result of the way in which the guidelines have been interpreted and not implemented by United States Attorneys. The reverse of the Department's stated policy appears to be the actual practice. The guidelines are used as a basis for declination, i.e.: a reason to "get rid of a case presented", and are not used to establish prosecution priorities. This practice has created the perception among federal law enforcement agents that the work necessary to present an obscenity case to the United States Attorney's office is a wasted effort.[201]

The United States Attorneys should make, as the Assistant Attorney General requested in his memorandum, a realistic appraisal of the obscenity problem in their respective jurisdictions. They should identify existing violations of obscenity laws, use Departmental guidelines to create priorities and begin to prosecute offenders aggressively and without further delay.

In implementing the priorities under the Department of Justice Guidelines, the United States Attorneys may consider examining the nature of the obscene materials. This may be done in accordance with this Commission's findings of harm with respect to each class of material.[202]

Only the Attorney General by direct and continuous action and personal supervision can ultimately ensure that these federal officers fulfill their responsibility in this neglected area. This attention and supervision should result in immediate positive results in law enforcement and prosecution efforts. The effects of this action will have long term consequences and will serve as the foundation for a continuing prosecution and enforcement program.

RECOMMENDATION 12:

The Attorney General should appoint a high ranking official from the Department of Justice to oversee the creation and operation of an obscenity task force. The task force should consist of Special Assistant United States Attorneys and federal agents who will assist United States Attorneys in the prosecution and investigation of obscenity cases.

Discussion

The Attorney General should create a task force under the direction of a high ranking official, of no less stature than a Deputy Assistant Attorney General, to investigate and prosecute obscenity law violations. The director of the task force should be included in all pertinent policy and budget decisions. The individual appointed must have a high degree of personal commitment to the objective of this task force which will require countless hours of personal supervision. This task force should attack the obscenity problem in a concerted and organized manner.

The director of the task force should enlist aggressive and well trained prosecutors and investigators. Experienced prosecutors could be detailed from the Department of Justice or the United States Attorneys' offices on a full-time and/or part-time basis. The Federal Bureau of Investigation, the United States Customs Service and the United States Postal Service should all contribute investigators to the task force. All prosecutors should be seasoned trial attorneys familiar with complex obscenity law issues and defense tactics.

The task force members should be brought together by the Department of Justice for intensive training and then begin immediate service. A selected number of prosecutors from each United States Attorney's office including selected United States Attorneys should also participate in this training to enable them to understand and deal with the problem in each and every federal district where violations occur.

The task force should be used to address two major concerns. First, the task force prosecutors would be particularly helpful in jurisdictions in which the United States Attorneys are burdened with heavy caseloads and believe they cannot allocate manpower to prosecute such crimes or where the Assistant United States Attorneys lack expertise in obscenity prosecutions.[203] The task force would play a support role for the United States Attorneys and federal investigators by assisting them with their cases and by serving as a national resource for legal and technical advice as well as a source of information. Second, the task force could be used to assist, or at their request, relieve United States Attorneys

201. See, Chicago Hearing, Vol. I, Jack O'Malley; Washington, D.C., Hearing, Vol. I, Jack Swagerty.

202. See, The discussion of the harms and benefits attributable to each type of material in Part One.

203. Chicago Hearing, Vol. II, James S. Reynolds, pp. 272–73; Chicago Hearing, Vol. I, Paul McGeady, p. 85; Chicago Hearing, Vol. II, Larry Parrish, pp. 216–17.

of these responsibilities during major investigations of a national scope.

The task force would complement the permanent staff of United States Attorneys as needed or when requested completely take over investigation and prosecution in a particular district.

RECOMMENDATION 13:

The Department of Justice should initiate an obscenity law enforcement data base which would serve as a resource for Federal, State and Local law enforcement agencies.

Discussion

There is no government department or agency which presently serves as a centralized source of complete information for prosecutors and investigators involved with obscenity cases.[204] Federal prosecutors and investigators must currently "recreate the wheel" in almost every new case developed. Many cases involve the same corporations and individuals and a duplication of efforts is a substantial waste of precious investigative time and resources. The Obscenity Task Force discussed in the Department of Justice Recommendation should be complemented by the creation of such a data base within the Department of Justice.

The data base should consist of profiles of cases prosecuted, case histories, corporate records, real estate records, a brief bank, information concerning known offenders, individuals associated with organized crime families and any other information pertinent to the investigation and prosecution of obscenity cases. The data base would enable federal, state and local law enforcement personnel to draw on information and expertise gathered nationwide. This data base should also cross-reference the information contained in the data base created for child pornography.[205]

Two experienced Department of Justice Attorneys with adequate support staff could easily administer this project which would result in a substantial reduction of investigative expenses. The information should be readily available to law enforcement agencies in the legitimate investigation of criminal activity, but safeguards should be enacted to avoid the potential abuse of individual civil liberties.

RECOMMENDATION 14:

The United States Attorneys should use the Law Enforcement Coordinating Committees to coordinate enforcement of the obscenity laws and to maintain surveillance of the nature and extent of the obscenity problem in the localities within their districts.

Discussion

The Law Enforcement Coordinating Committees (LECCs) developed under the direction of former Attorney General William French Smith are comprised of the United States Attorney and representatives of federal, state, and local law enforcement agencies within the particular judicial district. The LECC's objective is to improve cooperation and coordination among participating agencies. In addition the LECCs develop law enforcement priorities for the district, target the most serious crime problems and provide a forum for an exchange of information and intelligence.

The United States Attorney for the Northern District of New York arranged a LECC conference on child pornography in his district.[206] The two hundred law enforcement personnel in attendance were addressed by Federal Bureau of Investigation Agents, United States Postal Inspectors, state police, and state and local prosecutors.[207] The New York conference greatly increased awareness of the child pornography problem and contributed to the almost immediate initiation of at least three child pornography prosecutions.[208]

In July 1984, the United States Attorney for the Eastern District of North Carolina established an LECC subcommittee to investigate obscenity, organized crime and child abuse.[209] At that time the North Carolina obscenity law was considered one of the weakest in the United States and the state had the highest number of "adults only" pornographic outlets per capita of any state in the

---

204. Currently the Department of Justice, Criminal Division, General Litigation and Legal Advice Section has one person to assist prosecutors with information and advice in this area of law. It is impossible for one person, with the present mandate, to fulfill the need as described herein.

205. See, The discussion in Child Pornography for further information.

206. Chicago Hearing, Vol. II, Frederick J. Scullin, p. 39.

207. Id.

208. Id., pp. 39–40.

209. New York Hearing, Vol. II, Robert Showers, p. 60.

nation.[210] The North Carolina LECC subcommittee was comprised of federal, state and local law enforcement officials and spent a year developing a law enforcement blueprint.[211] The subcommittee discovered involvement of organized crime members and their associates in the obscenity business in North Carolina.[212] As a result of its investigation the LECC subcommittee drafted and recommended a more effective state obscenity law which was subsequently enacted by the North Carolina legislature.[213] They also recommended continued cooperation between federal and state authorities, and the creation of a statewide "pornography task force."[214] As a result of these efforts by the LECC subcommittee, the distribution of obscenity in North Carolina can now be more effectively controlled.[215] These two examples illustrate the effectiveness of the LECCs when utilized by United States Attorneys who are committed to fighting obscenity and its related organized crime elements.

The Department of Justice guidelines allow United States Attorneys to prioritize obscenity cases where a particular problem has been identified in the district. The LECCs are a means for the United States Attorney to maintain surveillance of the nature and extent of obscenity trafficking in his or her particular jurisdiction and they should be used specifically for that purpose.

RECOMMENDATION 15:

The Department of Justice and United States Attorneys should use the Racketeer Influenced and Corrupt Organizations Act (RICO) as a means of prosecuting major producers and distributors of obscene material.

Discussion

Recent amendments to the Racketeer Influenced and Corrupt Organizations Act (RICO) made obscenity offenses predicate crimes under the statute.[216] To date, no prosecutions against producers or distributors of obscene material have been brought under RICO in any of the ninety-four federal districts. RICO was enacted as part of the Organized Crime Control Act of 1970.[217] Prosecution under RICO arises when an individual demonstrates an established pattern of racketeering activity. Section 1961(5) requires that at least two of the federal or state predicate crimes enumerated in section 1961(1) must have been committed by the individual within a ten year period.[218] Offenses relating to obscenity are included among the predicate of-

---

210. *Id.*, p. 59.

211. New York Hearing, Vol. II, Sam Currin, p. 90.

212. New York Hearing, Vol. II, Robert Showers, p. 61.

213. *Id.*, p. 63.

214. *Id.*, p. 65; New York Hearing, Vol. II, Sam Currin, p. 90.

215. New York Hearing, Vol. II, Robert Showers, p. 64.

216. 18 U.S.C. SS1961–1968 (West Supp. 1985). Section 1961 (5) defines a "pattern of racketeering activity as at least two acts of racketeering activity, one of which occurred after the effective date of this chapter and the last of which occurred within ten years (excluding any period of imprisonment) after the commission of a prior act of racketeering activity. Section 1961 (1) defines "racketeering activity" as (A) any act or threat involving murder, kidnaping, gambling, arson, robbery, bribery, extortion, dealing in obscene matter, or dealing in narcotic or other dangerous drugs, which is chargeable under State law and punishable by imprisonment for more than one year; (B) any act which is indictable under any of the following provisions of title 18, United States Code: Section 201 (relating to bribery), section 224 (relating to sports bribery), sections 471, 172, and 473 (relating to counterfeiting), section 659 (relating to theft from interstate shipment) if the act indictable under section 659 is felonious, section 664 (relating to embezzlement from pension and welfare funds), sections 891–894 (relating to extortionate credit transactions), section 1084 (relating to the transmission of gambling information), section 1341 relating to mail fraud), section 1343 (relating to wire fraud), sections 1461–1465 (relating to obscene matter), section 1503 (relating to obstruction of justice), section 1510 (relating to obstruction of criminal investigations), section 1511 (relating to the obstruction of state or local law enforcement), section 1951 (relating to interference with commerce, robbery, or extortion), section 1952 (relating to racketeering), section 1953 (relating to interstate transportation of wagering paraphernalia), section 1954 (relating to unlawful welfare fund payments), section 1955 (relating to the prohibition of illegal gambling businesses), sections 2312 and 2313 (relating to interstate transportation of stolen motor vehicles), sections 2320 (relating to trafficking in certain motor vehicles or motor vehicle parts), sections 2341–2346 (relating to trafficking in contraband cigarettes), sections 2421–24 (relating to white slave traffic), (C) any act which is indictable under title 29, United States Code, section 186 (dealing with restrictions of payments and loans to labor organizations) or section 501(c) (relating to embezzlement from union funds), (D) any offense involving fraud connected with a case under title 11, fraud in the importation, receiving, concealment, buying, selling, or otherwise dealing in narcotic or other dangerous drugs, punishable under any law of the United States, or (E) any act which is indictable under the Currency and Foreign Transactions Reporting Act; any of those acts or offenses constitute a predicate act under RICO.

217. 18 U.S.C. SS1961–1968 (West Supp. 1985).

218. *Id.*; A predicated crime is one upon which an action under RICO can be based.

fenses.[219] The activities proscribed under RICO are listed in section 1962 as follows:

A. investing proceeds of a pattern of racketeering in an enterprise.
B. acquiring or maintaining an interest in an enterprise through a pattern of racketeering.
C. conducting affairs of an enterprise through a pattern of racketeering.
D. conspiring to violate (a), (b), or (c).[220]

The penalty provisions of 18 U.S.C. S1963 provide for a fine of not more than $25,000 or imprisonment for not more than twenty years or both.[221] The statute also provides for mandatory forfeiture of:

A. a defendant's interest in any enterprise acquired with racketeering income.
B. interests, securities, claims or contractual rights of an illegally controlled enterprise.
C. proceeds or property derived from such proceeds.

Department of Justice guidelines regarding RICO prosecutions appropriately prohibit a United States Attorney from bringing an indictment for a violation of section 1962(c) based upon a pattern of racketeering activity growing out of a single criminal episode or transaction.[222] Thus an individual could not be indicted under RICO based on violations of 18 U.S.C. S1461 (mailing obscene matter) and 18 U.S.C. S1463 (mailing indecent matter on envelope or wrapper) if both arise out of the same mailing. This is a situation which may occur frequently in obscenity cases and thus preclude the United States Attorney from prosecuting under RICO.[223] It should be obvious that the stringent forfeiture provisions under RICO would be one of the strongest weapons in the prosecution arsenal and could, in appropriate cases, virtually eliminate a large scale pornography operation.

RECOMMENDATION 16:

The Department of Justice should continue to provide the United States Attorneys with training programs on legal and procedural matters related to obscenity cases and also should make such training available to state and local prosecutors.

Discussion

The preparation for trial of an obscenity case involves complex legal and procedural issues. An inexperienced prosecutor may often encounter an experienced defense counsel who specializes in obscenity law and travels throughout the country defending these cases. Defenses and issues which are raised in each case are likely to be similar in prosecutions throughout the country. Trial and appellate case law developed in state and federal cases are very similar. Poorly developed case law developed on the state level can have adverse effects on federal prosecutions and vice versa.

Training programs offered by the Department of Justice that prepare attorneys to address these issues will enable federal prosecutors to be more knowledgeable and effective. They would be of similar value to state and local prosecutors if made available to them. These programs should include a familiarization with defense tactics which may include personal attacks or harassment or law suits against prosecutors and investigators.

RECOMMENDATION 17:

United States Attorneys should use all available Federal statutes to prosecute obscenity violations involving cable and satellite television.

Discussion

The contents of some programs shown on cable and satellite television channels have become a matter of increasing public concern.[224] Some of the feature films shown depict sexual themes, sexual acts and materials which may be obscene under *Miller.*

The obscenity standard enunciated by the Supreme Court in *Miller v. California* can be applied to material transmitted over cable television. When the United States Supreme Court declared that obscenity is not protected speech under The First Amendment, no dis-

219. 18 U.S.C. S1961(1)(B).
220. 18 U.S.C. S1962 (West Supp. 1985).
221. 18 U.S.C. S1963 (West Supp. 1985).
222. United States Department of Justice, *United States Attorney's Manual,* Title 9, Chapter 110, p. 4. (June 18, 1981).
223. *See,* Recommendations for Changes in Federal Law in this Chapter.
224. See, The discussion of Child Pornography Regulation for further information.

tinction was made as to the medium of expression.[225] As the United States District Court in Utah found in *Community Television of Utah v. Roy City*,[226]

> The *Miller* standard is applicable. It is a national standard with a core of uniformity which allows for a degree of flexibility at a community level. It may be uniformly applied to almost all forms of publicly available communication. Books, magazines, cassettes, periodicals, movies, and *cable television* are all treated essentially in the same fashion regardless of numbers. (emphasis added)[227]

The court went on to explain, "The Court finds great difficulty in distinguishing (other than the popcorn) between going to the movies at a theatre and having the movies come to me in my home through electronic transmission over wire. The choice is mine. The location is different. The content is the same."[228]

An individual may possess and view obscene materials in the privacy of his own home.[229] Despite popular arguments to the contrary, it is well established in decisions by the United States Supreme Court that there is no correlative right to *receive, import,* or *distribute* the obscene materials. (emphasis added)[230] An argument that in the cable area the obscene materials are exhibited to consenting adults only is not a defense to an obscenity prosecution.[231]

The Court in *Paris Adult Theaters I v. Slaton*,[232] stated,

Finally, petitioners argue that conduct which directly involves "consenting adults" only has, for that sole reason, a special claim to constitutional protection. Our Constitution establishes a broad range of conditions on the exercise of power by the States, but for us to say that our Constitution incorporates the proposition that conduct involving consenting adults only is always beyond state regulation, is a step we are unable to take.[233]

In addition to the federal obscenity laws codified in 18 U.S.C. S1461, the Cable Communication Policy Act of 1984 provides another avenue for the prosecution of obscenity shown over cable television.[234]

The Act, provides:

> Whoever transmits over any cable system any matter which is obscene or otherwise unprotected by the Constitution of the United States shall be fined not more than $10,000 or imprisoned not more than 2 years, or both.[235]

This section should be used by federal prosecutors if potential conflicts within such Chapter are resolved. Prosecutors should also vigorously enforce any new legislation enacted in the area.

The inability of law enforcement officials to control obscene cable programming is compounded by the inaction of the Federal Communications Commission in this entire area and makes enforcement efforts by United States Attorneys in each district essential.

RECOMMENDATIONS FOR STATE AND LOCAL PROSECUTORS

RECOMMENDATION 18:

State and Local prosecutors should prosecute producers of obscene material under the existing laws including those prohibiting pandering and other underlying sexual offenses.

Discussion

Existing state laws provide penalties for pandering. Pandering or "pimping" generally involves the procuring of an individual to commit an act of prostitution for some form of consideration.

---

225. *Kaplan v. California*, 413 U.S., (1973), pp. 115, 118–19.

226. *Id.*, p. 116.

227. 555 F. Supp., p. 1164 (D. Utah 1982).

228. *Id.*, p. 1170.

229. See, *Stanley v. Georgia*, 394 U.S., (1969), pp. 557, 568.

230. See, *United States v. Reidel*, 402 U.S. 351(1971); *United States v. 37 Photographs*, 402 U.S., (1971), pp. 363, 376.

231. See, *Paris Adult Theater I v. Slaton*, 413 U.S., (1973), 49, 57.

232. 413 U.S., (1972), p. 49.

233. *Id.*, p. 68.

234. 47 U.S.C.A. S559 (West Supp. 1985).

235. *Id. See,* The discussion of the difficulties associated with enforcement of this statute.

The production of obscene material almost always involves acts of prostitution. Performers are recruited and paid or otherwise induced (voluntarily or involuntarily) by producers to perform or have performed upon them various sexual acts including intercourse, fellatio, cunnilingus, sodomy and bestiality. These acts are filmed or otherwise recorded for reproduction and commercial distribution. By procuring an individual to commit an act of prostitution the producer of obscene material is acting in the same capacity as a pimp.[236] Like any other pimp he reaps his financial reward from these acts of prostitution.

Pandering laws are an effective law enforcement tool since they present a separate and distinct crime and do not require proof of obscenity.[237] Law enforcement officers should view the pandering which takes place through the production of obscene materials the same as pandering in any other prostitution case. This Commission has heard substantial testimony regarding coercion used in the production of sexually explicit materials. We accordingly suggest that law enforcement officers should use considered judgement and avoid unnecessary charges of prostitution against the performers.

State and local prosecutors should also scrutinize obscene material for evidence of any other underlying criminal offenses such as physical sexual abuse and bring appropriate charges against the persons responsible for the commission of such crimes.

Persons who appear in pornographic materials often may be doing so under threat of force or coercion.[238] Law enforcement officers should be sensitive to claims of sexual assault, sexual imposition, rape or related crimes of violence against performers. While some performers are willing to engage in the sexual activities required during the production of pornographic materials, law enforcement officers should remain aware of the significant possibility that performers who are forced to engage in certain sexual acts are victims of these underlying crimes.

RECOMMENDATION 19:

State and Local prosecutors must make a careful assessment of the obscenity problem in their jurisdictions, identify offenders involving both adult and child material, and commence prosecution without further delay.

Discussion

There is no substitute for an aggressive prosecutor who will vigorously enforce the existing obscenity laws. Prosecutors in Orlando, Florida; Atlanta, Georgia; and Cincinnati, Ohio, have compiled impressive records in enforcing the laws of those states.

For sixteen years[239] the Solicitor for Fulton County, Georgia, aggressively prosecuted any obscenity violation brought to the attention of that office. As a result Atlanta now has no theatres or bookstores which show or sell materials that would be found obscene under *Miller*.[240] Consistent enforcement efforts have had a substantial deterrent effect.[241]

In Cincinnati, there are no bookstores, movies or cable television programs which are sexually explicit and would be found obscene under *Miller*.[242] The chief of the Cincinnati vice squad attributed this result to "a strong prosecutor and a prosecutor willing to accept the cases and go ahead and prosecute."[243]

In Houston, prosecution of pornography cases has been a high priority and the prosecutor has maintained a conviction rate of ninety-two percent while handling over two hundred cases per year.[244]

---

236. See, *People v. Fixler*, 56 Cal. App. 31 321, 128 Cal. Rptr. 363 (1976); *United States v. Roeder*, 526 F.2d 736, p. 739 (10th Cir. 1975), *cert. denied* 462 U.S. 905.

237. An investigator who testified before the Commission recounted the following experience, "Another area that we are presently using for enforcement is in the area of pandering. In one of our recent cases we charged a hard-core film producer with pandering.

It was our contention that this individual by the name of ✂ who runs a company by the name of ✂ Video in Los Angeles, was hiring these girls to commit sex acts for money, which is prostitution, thus he was a pimp." Chicago Hearing, Vol. I, Donald Smith, p. 36.

238. See *also*, The discussion of Child Pornography Regulation.

239. Chicago Hearing, Vol. II, Hinson McAuliffe, p. 177.

240. *Id.*, p. 185.

241. *Id.*, pp. 185–86.

242. Chicago Hearing, Vol. I, Harold Mills, p. 93.

243. *Id.*

244. Houston Hearing, Vol. I, W.D. Brown, p. 49.

For the past fifteen years, only one detective on the Miami, Florida, police department has been assigned to investigate obscenity violations.[245] During that time, this investigator has brought over one thousand cases for prosecution and a conviction was obtained in every case.[246] The number of "adults only" pornographic outlets in Miami has decreased during this same period from twenty-three to eight.[247]

Local law enforcement agents should also seek assistance from federal agencies to effectively combat organized crime involvement in pornography when identified. According to a local law enforcement officer, "Without the mutual exchange of information of the joint task force, local law enforcement cannot and will not be able to cope with the situation of organized crime and the delivery and dissemination of pornography . . ."[248]

State and local prosecutors must accept the challenge and enforce the existing laws stringently and consistently so that purveyors of obscene material will find no haven in their jurisdictions. These efforts should be based upon an evaluation of the relative harmful effects of materials available.[249] This evaluation should include particular consideration of explicitly violent materials and materials which are humiliating or degrading.

RECOMMENDATION 20:
State and Local prosecutors should allocate sufficient resources to prosecute obscenity cases.

Discussion

See, Recommendation 19 for further discussion of resources devoted to obscenity investigation and prosecution.

RECOMMENDATION 21:
State and Local prosecutors should use the bankruptcy laws to collect unpaid fines.

Discussion

Courts frequently impose a monetary fine after a conviction for an obscenity violation. In a number of cases, especially those involv-

ing corporate defendants, these fines may go unpaid. Once conventional means of collecting of such fines have been exhausted these outstanding judgments can be satisfied by the use of bankruptcy laws.[250] When a defendant accumulates two or more outstanding debts the prosecutor can file an involuntary bankruptcy petition and the court can ultimately take custody of any assets and liquidate them to satisfy those debts including unpaid fines. The liquidation should include items of value such as real property, structures and fixtures. The liquidation would not include the sale or distribution of obscene material which may be a part of the inventory. All such material would be disposed of in the manner provided by law.

The prosecutor in Atlanta, Georgia, successfully used the bankruptcy laws to collect fines and made it unprofitable for many dealers in obscene material to stay in business.[251]

The bankruptcy proceedings are also useful in determining the true ownership of the businesses who deal in obscene materials. This is particularly helpful when "sham" or "shell" corporations are used to conceal ownership. The results may also assist prosecutors to target the culpable individuals for subsequent criminal prosecution.

State and local prosecutors also may enlist the assistance of federal investigators and prosecutors when dealing with a major obscenity distributor with substantial resources. These federal agents and prosecutors could assist in identifying the resources and their location for inclusion in the bankruptcy action.

RECOMMENDATION 22:
State and Local prosecutors should use all available statutes to prosecute obscenity violations involving cable and satellite television.

Discussion

State and local prosecutors should prosecute cable and satellite television programmers or operators under existing state statutes for exhibiting any program that is obscene under

245. Miami Hearing, Vol. I, Mike Berish, p. 63.
246. *Id.*, p. 64.
247. *Id.*, p. 63.
248. New York Hearing, Vol. II, William Johnson, p. 82.
249. See, The discussion of Harms, *supra*.
250. 11 U.S.C. S302 (Supp. II 1984).
251. Chicago Hearing, Vol. II, Hinson McAuliffe, pp. 183–84.

the *Miller* test. The Commonwealth's Attorney for the city of Virginia Beach, Virginia, monitored and videotaped fifty hours of programming on a local cable channel, shown in his jurisdiction. Thirteen and one half hours of the videotaped programming were submitted to a grand jury, which returned seven indictments against the cable operator for distributing obscene material. As a result of those indictments, the cable operator eliminated the channel in question from its program offerings.[252] (See, Department of Justice Recommendations and Recommendations for Law Enforcement Officers in this Chapter).

RECOMMENDATION 23:
State and Local prosecutors should enforce existing corporate laws to prevent the formation, use and abuse of shell corporations which serve as shelters for producers and distributors of obscene material.

Discussion

Producers and distributors of obscene material often use multiple corporate entities as a means of concealing the true ownership or nature of their businesses.[253] They typically create layers of corporations to insulate their identities from a claim of actual ownership. Separate corporations may be formed to perform the different operations of a single bookstore. Separate corporations may be formed to control the sale of magazines, operate the bookstore, construct peep show booths, collect coins from peep show booths, and to repair the same booths.[254]

The articles of incorporation and other documents may list as incorporators, shareholders or officers the names of mere employees or even strangers. The names may be on the documents without the named person's konwledge or consent.[255] Some producers and distributors may rely on law enforcement knowledge of such practices to argue they are not the true owners even though listed as such.

Law enforcement officers face difficult burdens in identifying and bringing charges against or collecting taxes from the true owners who hide behind these shell corporations. Often they can locate only low level employees who may be unfamiliar with the identity of the persons who actually own or control the operation of the business.[256]

State laws governing the formation of corporations should be enforced fully to permit the identification of those persons managing and financing the obscenity industry. Corporate charters should be revoked when fraud is proven and the assets seized when permitted.

RECOMMENDATION 24:
State and Local prosecutors should enforce the alcoholic beverage control laws that prohibit obscenity on licensed premises.

Discussion

Establishments that display or sell obscene materials may also be licensed by the state or locality to sell alcoholic beverages. State and local alcoholic beverage control laws often prohibit obscene material and obscene performances on the licensed premises. Enforcement of these laws or ordinances in the courts or through administrative procedures is another tool at the disposal of law enforcement agents to remove pornography from theatres, restaurants and other establishments.

These enforcement measures should be implemented with recognition of the current social and behavioral science conclusions with respect to various types of materials. Law enforcement officers may consider the potential harm which may be attributable to certain types of materials when establishing criteria for enforcement of this aspect of alcoholic beverage laws.

A finding of guilt under the alcoholic beverage control laws could bring suspension or revocation of an establishment's liquor license. The potential of such a loss of revenue to an individual or business would have a significant deterrent effect.

RECOMMENDATION 25:
Government attorneys, including State and Local prosecutors, should enforce all legal remedies authorized by statute.

See, Discussions of nuisance laws, zoning, anti-display statutes, alcoholic beverage control laws.

---

252. National Decency Reporter, Vol. 22, No. 3, p. 1 (May-June 1985).
253. New York Hearing, Vol. II, William Johnson, p. 82.
254. Id.
255. Id.
256. Id.

RECOMMENDATION FOR FEDERAL LAW ENFORCEMENT AGENCIES

RECOMMENDATION 26:
Federal law enforcement agencies should conduct active and thorough investigations of all significant violations of the obscenity laws with interstate dimensions.

Discussion

As recommended elsewhere in this report, the United States Attorneys should begin prosecuting appropriate violations of the federal obscenity laws without further delay.[257] The efforts of federal prosecutors must be based upon and complemented by active and thorough investigations of all violations of the obscenity laws by the federal law enforcement agencies.

The Federal Bureau of Investigation (FBI) derives its investigative jurisdiction in this area from the federal statutes covering obscenity and child pornography.[258] From the beginning of fiscal year 1978 through the second quarter of Fiscal Year 1985, the FBI has conducted 2,484 investigations involving interstate transportation of obscene materials and violations involving child pornography.[259] These investigations have resulted in 137 indictments and 118 convictions. Of these figures forty-five indictments and fourteen convictions were the result of the single investigation known as MIPORN.[260] The FBI has given its highest priority to cases involving organized crime.[261] The Federal Bureau of Investigation recently conducted a two year investigation which resulted in the case *United States v. Guglielmi*.[262] This case grew out of an approximately two-year investigation by the Federal Bureau of Investigation regarding obscene materials, particularly bestiality films shipped in interstate commerce into the Western District of North Carolina. The investigation, which first centered around undercover purchases from a relatively small street-corner outlet for "sexual aids" and pornographic magazines, films and pockets books, expanded after a successful search of those premises and interview of

the personnel, to a cautious undercover investigation involving telephone calls to, and meetings with, the defendant himself. The introduction to the defendant was made by a former "adult" bookstore operator, and various orders of bestiality films and other materials were followed by a successful search of Central Sales, the defendant's multistory Baltimore warehouse for the shipment of obscene materials. The Grand Jury's eleven-count indictment for violations of Title 18, U.S. Code, Sections 2, 371, 1462 and 1465, followed on June 12, 1985.

The trial lasted approximately four days, during which a number of bestiality films were displayed, in titles of which indicated the animals portrayed. The defense called a number of "experts" who were experienced defense specialists in pornography cases, several of whom were affiliated with the Institute for the Advanced Study of Human Sexuality, a San Francisco, California, group that includes among its classes a course on testifying for the defense in pornography cases. Information provided by other prosecutors made possible the effective cross-examination of these witnesses. The defense "experts" testified that the materials did not appeal to the prurient interest of the average citizen in the Western District of North Carolina, since the average person does not have such an interest.

The trial in general was characterized by numerous *voir dire* examinations and arguments on a number of points of law and fact. Pre-trial motions had also been lengthy and had included a Motion of Recuse, by which the defendant sought to have the trial judge, the Honorable Robert D. Potter, to disqualify himself. This motion was denied, and defendant filed a petition for writ of mandamus to the Fourth Circuit, which was also denied.

The jury was similarly unpersuaded by defense arguments and found the defendant guilty of all eleven counts in the indictment. Judge Potter sentenced the defendant to a total

---

257. See, United States Department of Justice Recommendation 1; "Investigation Authority" is the statutory power granted to an agency to initiate and pursue inquiries into criminal activity.

258. 18 U.S.C. SS1462 & 1465; 18 U.S.C. SS2251-2255; Washington, D.C., Hearing, Vol. II, William Webster, p. 76.

259. Washington, D.C., Hearing, Vol. II, William Webster, p. 76.

260. *Id.*

261. *Id.*, p. 77.

262. C-CR-85-59(W.D.N.C. 1986).

of twenty-five years incarceration and a $35,000 fine. The case is now under appeal.

The Director of the FBI told this Commission that while the Bureau does not "downgrade" the seriousness of the problem of obscenity violations involving adult material, "it is simply the implication of our resources."[263] He added that "it will probably mean that there will be less pro-active initiatives on our part" in adult cases that do not involve organized crime.[264]

This Commission received evidence that two of the FBI field offices in one of the nation's most active obscenity distribution centers, New York City, will not investigate cases involving obscene material.[265]

The Federal Bureau of Investigation is encouraged to seriously step up its investigative efforts relating to obscenity law violations.

The jurisdiction of the United States Customs Services extends to all materials entering the United States by land, sea or air.[266] Prior to the signing of the Child Protection Act of 1984 (18 U.S.C. SS2251–2255), the United States Customs Service had received direction from Commissioner William Von Raab to step up efforts to intercept obscene material. Special emphasis was placed on material depicting children in sexual explicit conduct. The Customs Service was responsible for six successful child pornography prosecutions in fiscal year 1983. Five of the convictions were violations various state laws and the sixth was a violation Federal Law, 18 U.S.C. §1462. With the signing of the Child Protection Act, the figures changed to fourteen federal convictions and twenty state convictions in 1984, and nineteen federal and ten state convictions as of August 1985.

Until the early part of 1985, the Customs Service's method for initiating child pornography investigations was fairly static. A mail parcel would be examined at one of the twenty-two customs foreign mail facilities. The package, once discovered to contain child pornography, would be forwarded to the Office of Investigations in the District concerned. The case agent would then match the name and/or address of the addressee with other seizures. A background investigation

on the addressee would be conducted in order to show other criteria as outlined in the *United States Attorneys Manual*. Based on the results of the investigation and a controlled delivery of the seized parcel, a search warrant would be obtained and executed on the address in question. In the majority of the search warrants executed, the suspect would be found to have a large collection of imported and home-made child pornography. Additionally, more and more evidence was found to link child molestation to the importers of the child pornography.[267]

By February 1985, compilations of seizure lists were being made and disseminated throughout the service. Most field offices had assigned at least one, and sometimes several agents to investigate child pornography cases on an exclusive or collateral basis. Foreign mail facilities were targeting the traditional "source" countries of child pornography: Denmark, the Netherlands, and Sweden.

In January 1985, a special delegation representing the United States Customs Service, the United States Postal Inspection Service and the Federal Bureau of Investigation travelled to Europe. Their purpose was to address the issue of foreign cooperative efforts in fighting the child pornography industry.

As a result of these critical contacts, interagency cooperation is expanding. Investigators are beginning to look for the major distributors, producers, and consumers. Increased cooperation with foreign governments had led to two successful undercover operations in 1985. As a result of the increased foreign cooperation, new methods of smuggling, as well as additional source countries and distributors are being identified. Examples include: Transshipment routes through England, France, East Germany, and Southeast Asian countries heretofore not considered source countries, such as France, Italy, Japan, Thailand and the Philippines; and more sophisticated packaging techniques and profiles.

New methods of conducting child pornography investigations are being developed and attempted. These include the adaptation of methods used in narcotics and currency in-

263. *Id.*, p. 90.
264. *Id.*
265. New York Hearing, Vol. IV, Paul McGeady, p. 126.
266. Chicago Hearing, Vol. I, Jack O'Malley, p. 105.
267. In at least one instance, an agent discovered a molestation in progress. (The case resulted in a guilty plea to an information followed by a probationary sentence.)

vestigations, as well as methods used in the investigation of criminal sex offenses. Some bold and innovative undercover operations have been suggested and implemented.

The Customs Service is actively pursuing the enhancement of existing resources and the development of programs to meet the changing needs of the enforcement effort. It is only by such a process of enhancement and development that the Customs Service or any other agency can hope to compete with the ingenuity of those who sexually exploit children.

Future efforts in pornography enforcement will center around the activities of the Child Pornography and Protection Unit (CPPU). Criminal investigations that focus on sexual exploitations which involve other customs violations and other forms of obscene material have and are being developed. Such investigations involve customs fraud, unreported currency transactions, and general smuggling. Currently, all obscene material encountered by the customs foreign mail facilities are processed for forfeiture under civil statute. If at some future time the Customs Service becomes involved in criminal investigation of obscene violations, the data already available through this procedure will provide invaluable investigative leads.

Customs examines all parcels which are suspected of containing contraband.[268] With respect to obscenity law cases particular attention is given to parcels from Denmark, Sweden and the Netherlands. These countries have traditionally been the source of child pornography entering the United States.[269] In 1984, Customs seized forty-three hundred parcels which contained suspected obscene materials.[270] Child pornography was found in 50 percent of those.[271] The other items seized were largely adult materials including some depicting bestiality, urination and defecation.[272]

When a Customs agent seizes obscene material, a notice is sent to the intended recipient of the material. The notice permits the individual to sign a release and forfeit the

material to the government. The material is subsequently destroyed and generally no one is prosecuted for an obscenity violation.[273] If the material is child pornography, a controlled delivery is made to the recipient and a search warrant is subsequently executed on the recipient's premises, often leading to the arrest of that individual.[274] According to one Customs agent assigned to Chicago, "countless thousands" of obscenity cases involving obscene materials have not been presented to the United States Attorney because based upon their experience, agents perceive that these cases will not be prosecuted.[275]

The United States Postal Inspection Service has investigative responsibility over all federal criminal violations involving the mails including the use of the mails to distribute obscenity.[276] Investigations are initiated based on citizen complaints, advertisements in sexually oriented publications and correspondence initiated by a postal inspector.[277] Postal inspectors are responsible for protecting the mails and postal facilities from criminal attack; for protecting the American public from being victimized by fraudulent schemes where use of the mails is an essential part of the scheme; and for keeping postal management informed of the conditions and needs of the Postal Service.

Postal crimes fall within two broad categories: Criminal acts against the Postal Service, such as, armed robberies, burglaries or theft of mail and misuse of the Postal System such as the mailing bombs, use of the mails to defraud the public and the use of the mails to distribute pornography. The Inspection Service is also responsible for the internal audit of Postal Service operations and for the security of postal facilities and employees. In addition, the Inspection Service is responsible for investigating violations of a number of civil statutes relating to the use of the mails including the Postal False Representations Statute.

Title 18, United States Code, Section 1461, enacted in 1865, is the statute by which the Postal Inspection Service restricts use of the

268. Id.
269. Id., p. 106.
270. Id.
271. Id.
272. Id.
273. Id., p. 107.
274. Id., pp. 107–08.
275. Id., p. 118.
276. Washington, D.C., Hearing, Vol. I, Charles Clauson, p. 135.
277. Id., p. 136.

mails to distribute obscene matter. The statute provides for criminal penalties of up to five years in prison, a $5,000 fine, or both, for using the mails to transmit any "obscene lewd lascivious indecent filthy or vile article, matter, thing, device or substance."

Title 18, United States Code, Sections 2251–2255, the *Protection of Children Against Sexual Exploitation Act of 1977* and the *Child Protection Act of 1984* are the statutes by which the Postal Inspection Service investigates trafficking in child pornography through the mails. The statute provides for criminal penalties of up to ten years in prison and/or a $100,000 fine. The offender's property used in or derived from the crime is subject to criminal and civil forfeiture under this section. Most states have laws dealing with the sale, distribution and/or possession of obscenity. When dual jurisdiction is involved, Inspectors assist local authorities in the enforcement of their laws. On the international level, the Inspection Service cooperates with the Department of State, the United States Customs Service, Interpol and certain foreign postal authorities to stem the flow of obscene material and child pornography into or from the domestic sources.

Congress has also enacted three civil statutes designed to curb the mailing of sexually oriented material. Title 39, United States Code, Section 3006, allowed the Postal Service to refuse to deliver mail in response to advertising which sought to obtain money through the mailing of obscene matter.

Sections 3008–3011, allows postal customers to obtain an order prohibiting any future mailings by anyone who mails them an advertisement which the addressee considers sexually provocative. Title 39 United States Code, authorizes the Postal Service to maintain a list of persons who do not wish to receive sexually oriented advertising and prohibits the mailing of such advertising to persons who have asked to have their names listed. Companion criminal statutes, 18 U.S.C. SS1735–1737, authorize the courts to penalize persons who mail sexually oriented advertising and prohibits the mailing of such advertising to the persons whose names are on the list.

The Department of Justice has establishment enforcement priorities with respect to the obscenity statutes and the Postal Inspection Service's investigative activities are determined accordingly. The Inspection Service has currently established the following priorities:

1. *Policy*
   All investigations involving the use of the mail to transmit child pornography are given priority attention. Major domestic and foreign dealers in obscene material also receive prompt investigative attention.

2. *Child Pornography*
   The objective in child pornography cases is to identify and investigate mail order activity. If other offenses such as child abuse are discovered incident to an investigation, this activity is immediately referred to local police or other appropriate authorities.

3. *Obscene Material*
   The objective in the obscenity area is to investigate cases consistent with Department of Justice priorities. These priorities are:
   A. Large scale commercial obscenity distributors involved in multi-state operations.
   B. Cases in which there is evidence of infiltration by known organized crime figures.
   C. Relatively small dealers are occasionally investigated and/or prosecuted, particularly when the material is especially offensive or when numerous customer complaints are present. This provision is maintained to dispel any notion that pornography distributors can insulate themselves from prosecution if their operations fail to exceed a pre-determined size or if they are fragmented into small scale components.

These priorities, supplemented by guidelines Inspectors receive from the Department of Justice in individual cases, form the basis of the Postal Service investigative program. In 1985 the Postal Inspection Service reported activity in the following areas:

Nationwide
- 15,766 criminal investigations completed.
- A total of 5,570 convictions.
- Convictions obtained in 98% of all cases brought to trial.

- Recoveries, restitutions made and fines imposed—$34.2 million.

    Prohibited Mailings
- Obscenity and Child Pornography (18 U.S.C. 1461, 2251, 2252) 183 investigations completed; of these 176 involved "child pornography"
- 141 convictions for "child pornography" were obtained.

Like other federal agents, postal inspectors present evidence of violations of the law to the appropriate United States Attorney.[278] In fiscal year 1985 the Postal Inspection Service conducted 183 pornography-related investigations which resulted in 179 arrests and 143 convictions.[279] These investigations were principally child pornography cases.[280]

The Postal Inspection Service presents very few cases involving obscene material for prosecution because they have been told by employees of the Justice Department that these cases are "not prosecutable."[281] The Chief Postal Inspector has confirmed that "[i]nvestigations in adult pornography cases have declined in recent years . . . ."[282]

These three law enforcement agencies are capable of making significant contributions to the investigation and prosecution of violations of the federal obscenity laws. The FBI's efforts in the MIPORN investigation of organized crime figures involved in obscenity distribution resulted in fourteen convictions as of February 1986.[283] The FBI should also include obscenity and related crimes among its Uniform Crime Statistics report. Similarly the Customs Service and the Postal Inspection Service have had much success in their child pornography investigations.[284]Working with dedicated prosecutors committed to enforcing the obscenity laws, these agencies can have an even greater impact on the reduction of pornography in the United States.

They must commit the manpower and resources necessary to fulfill the task and conduct active and thorough investigations of all violations of the federal obscenity laws.

RECOMMENDATION 27:

The Internal Revenue Service should aggressively investigate violations of the tax laws committed by producers and distributors of obscene material.

Discussion

The Chief of the Internal Revenue Service Criminal Division has compared the production and distribution of obscene material to drug trafficking since both generate staggering profits on an international scale but with only minimal tax reporting.[285] Authorities also project that millions of dollars in profits from obscenity may be escaping taxation through use of international banking channels.[286]

Allen I. Goelman, a Los Angeles associate of ✄ pleaded guilty to tax evasion charges in November of 1985. Goelman concealed personal earnings of more than $270,000 over a four year period when he served as head of "retail operations" for obscenity distribution. The IRS has recently obtained confidential records from banks in Switzerland and Holland in an attempt to locate more hidden obscenity-derived profits.[287]

The frequent use of "cash only" transactions in the pornography industry provides other opportunities for tax evasion.[288] Adult bookstores often fail to report lucrative income earned from cash operated peep shows.[289]

In March of 1986, an IRS official said the current immoral investigation involving obscenity distributors are not an isolated incident and that more income tax prosecutions may be forthcoming.[290] The same official

278. Id.
279. United States Postal Inspection Service Statistics (1986).
280. Id.
281. Id., p. 70.
282. Washington, D.C., Hearing, Vol. I, Charles Clauson, p. 138.
283. Washington, D.C., Hearing, Vol. II, William Webster, p. 77; Letter from Donald B. Nicholson to Alan E. Sears (Feb. 28, 1986).
284. See, Washington, D.C., Hearing, Vol. I, Daniel Mihalko, p. 155–161; Chicago Hearing, Vol. I, Jack O'Malley, p. 110–16; Chicago Hearing, Vol. II, John Ruberti, p. 62–68.
285. IRS Probing Alleged Money Laundering Abroad by Far Flung Pronography Ring, L.A. Times, Mar. 16, 1985, p. 33.
286. Id.
287. Id.; See, The discussion of Organized Crime for further information.
288. New York Hearing, Vol. II, William Johnson, p. 73–74.
289. Id.
290. L.A. Times, supra note 285.

added, "With the unsettled nature of laws defining obscenity, often times the government is forced to deal with people of this type through the tax laws, and in a business this lucrative, if there's a viable tax interest we're going after them."[291] The Commission strongly encourages the IRS to aggressively investigate violations of the tax laws committed by producers and distributors of obscene materials.

RECOMMENDATIONS FOR STATE AND LOCAL LAW ENFORCEMENT AGENCIES

RECOMMENDATION 28
State and Local law enforcement agencies should provide the most thorough and up-to-date training for investigators involved in enforcing the obscenity laws.

Discussion

To ensure that officers assigned to enforce these laws possess the requisite skill, comprehensive training programs should be established in all jurisdictions. This training should include instruction on investigative techniques, prosecution, victim trauma and the particular stress officers must deal with in obscenity law investigations.

Law enforcement officers involved in the investigation of obscenity violations must be thoroughly acquainted with constitutional law including First and Fourth Amendment implications. The legal and procedural aspects are complex and always subject to change. Included in this training should be a working familiarity with the local community standards. This knowledge should serve as the basis for evaluating cases for prosecution. State and local law enforcement officers should be advised continually of judicial interpretations in the obscenity law area.

Law enforcement officers should receive comprehensive training to avoid errors in judgment which can result in civil rights violations as well as potential civil liability for governmental entities and employees. This training should enable the law enforcement officers to perform their duty within constitutional bounds.

Law enforcement officers should be trained to use regional and national information sources in their investigations. The training should emphasize the need to exercise basic investigative techniques and focus on the similarities and patterns in investigation of obscentiy law violations and other investigations.

Investigators will often encounter victims who have been abused or traumatized. A component of the training program should focus on methods to deal with these individuals compassionately and to direct them to the appropriate support services. Training in all areas should be provided by experienced investigators to members of their own department and supplemented with participation by prosecutors and investigators from other law enforcement authorities who specialize in this area.

The training should address the inordinate amount of stress these investigators must endure. The psychological and emotional pressure the officers face often results from prolonged undercover investigations dealing with the material on a long term basis and a lack of peer support. One police officer told the Commission:

> . . . those people who seem to have involved themselves in investigations of these matters generally get ostracized by their own peers. Most police officers make a fool out of those investigators that are charged with investigations of these matters. Macho—I don't know what to say.
>
> I found most of them (obscenity investigators) to be extremely professional, dedicated policemen with a lot of integrity. It's unfortunate that they are characterized as such in their peer group, because they have a lot of integrity. You investigate other types of crimes, gambling and narcotics, you find the seedier aspects of law enforcement in terms of corruption, but for the most part these people have a lot of personal integrity, and surprisingly they have a lot of regard for first amendments rights. That would be a surprise to many people, but they respect it.[292]

It is as important to train officers in methods to deal with stress and peer support as it is in basic investigative techniques.

291. Id.
292. New York Hearing, Vol. I, Carl Shoffler, pp. 227–28.

RECOMMENDATION 29:

State and local law enforcement agencies should allocate sufficient personnel to conduct intensive and thorough investigations of any violations of the obscenity laws.

Discussion

State and local law enforcement agencies in many regions have devoted insufficient manpower to investigation and enforcement of the obscenity laws. This has led to reactive law enforcement where police may respond to citizen complaints made about obscene materials but do not otherwise initiate investigations.[293]

The Los Angeles Police Department has sixty-seven hundred officers, but only eight are assigned to the pornography unit.[294] Los Angeles is the center of production of obscene material in the United States.[295] The Chicago Police Department has twelve thousand officers, but only two are assigned to their obscene matter unit.[296] The Buffalo, New York, police department has one thousand officers with one officer assigned to obscenity law violations.[297] In Chicago, the unit investigating obscenity violations has requested additional manpower but such requests have been denied by higher authorities within their police departments.[298]

Intensive and thorough investigations of possible obscenity violations cannot be conducted unless sufficient manpower is devoted to the task. The need for additional manpower is even more critical in those jurisdictions with large scale pornography operations where investigations are more complex and time consuming.

Chiefs of police and supervisory personnel must also be responsive to requests for additional manpower should the obscenity problem warrant more intensive investigation. These responses may take the form of additional investigative personnel on a temporary or permanent basis.[299] Supervisory personnel also should recognize the complexity of this assignment and be receptive to requests for frequent in-service training programs. Once the obscenity problem has been effectively addressed law enforcement agencies should need only minimal manpower to maintain control.

RECOMMENDATION 30:

State and Local law enforcement officers should take an active role in the law enforcement coordinating committees.

See, The discussion in the Recommendations for the United States Department of Justice in this Chapter.

---

293. See, *supra* note 174 for discussion of proactive and reactive enforcement and prosecution.
294. Chicago Hearing, Vol. II, Donald Smith, p. 46.
295. Los Angeles Hearing, Vol. I, James Docherty, p. 6.
296. Chicago Hearing, Vol. I, Thomas Bohling, p. 13.
297. Chicago Hearing, Vol. II, John Dugan, p. 193.
298. Chicago Hearing, Vol. II, Officer Tom Bohling, p. 14; Miami Hearing, Vol. I, Sergeant Mike Berish, p. 85–86.
299. In Cincinnati, Ohio, the focus on obscenity law violations is reported to have resulted in a significant decrease of reported crimes. Statistics of Reporting Area-14-800 & 900 Block of Vine Street, which had (1) Massage Parlor, (2) X-Rated Bookstores and (1) "Soft Core" Movie Theater in 1974, all closed by 1979.

1974

PART I OFFENSES (MAJOR)	PART II ARRESTS (MINOR)
2—Rapes	14—Assaults
29—Robberies	2—Forgeries
7—Agg. Assaults	3—Frauds
24—Breaking/Enterings	1—Embezzlement
63—Larcenies	2—Vandalism
24—Thefts	7—Weapons Violations
17—Non-Agg. Offense	52—Prostitution Offenses
166—TOTAL	4—Other Sex Offenses
	85—TOTAL

1979

PART I OFFENSES	PART II ARRESTS
8—Robberies	1—Sex Offense
4—Agg. Assaults	10—Drug Abuse
1—Breaking/Entering	1—Gambling Offense
15—Larcenies	31—Disorderly Conduct
28—TOTAL	1—Vagrancy
	5—Other Offenses
	49—TOTAL

RECOMMENDATION 31:

State and Local revenue authorities must insure taxes are collected from businesses dealing in obscene materials.

Discussion

"Adults Only" pornographic outlets often maintain separate business systems for accounting purposes. These operations may be

---

The above statistics represent an 83% decrease in Part I offenses, 42.35% decrease in Part II arrests. Letter from Lieutenant Harold Mills to Alan E. Sears (July 29, 1985).

The Phoenix Ordinance was based on two hypotheses: first, that there are direct impacts which uniquely relate to this class of land use; and second, that there are indirect, but equally potent, attitudinal concerns which result from proximity to an adult business. Examples of the former are possible traffic congestion, unusual hours of operations, litter, noise, and criminal activity. Illustrating the latter is substantial testimony that has indicated that many neighborhood residents dislike living near an area containing an adult business. Also, financial institutions take nearby adult businesses into account when financing residential properties. Finally, people's perceptions of criminal activity is reinforced by a great incidence of sexual crimes in areas of commercial districts containing adult businesses.

This study specifically shows that there is a higher amount of sex offenses committed in neighborhoods in Phoenix containing adult businesses as opposed to neighborhoods without them. In this project three study areas were chosen—neighborhoods with adult businesses, and three control areas—neighborhoods without adult businesses which were paired to certain population and land use characteristics. The amount of property crimes, violent crimes, and sex offenses from the year 1978 are compared in each study and control area.

THE STUDY AND CONTROL AREAS

Three different study areas containing adult businesses were selected to collect crime data. The east side of Central Avenue was chosen for the location of two study areas, while the west side was the third study area.

A control area has no adult business, but generally speaking, has similar population characteristics of a matched study area in terms of:

1. Number of residents
2. Median family income
3. Percentage of non-white population
4. Median age of the population
5. Percentage of dwelling units built since 1950
6. Percentage of acreage used residentially and non-residentially

Adult business locations are based on information furnished by the Department and verified by the Planning Department.

CONCLUSIONS

Table V *Property, Violent, and Sex Crimes in Selected Study Areas—1978* (was derived from information provided by the City of Phoenix Police Department's Crime Analysis unit and Planning and Research Bureau. The data from these two sections was compiled by adding the number by type of crimes committed in police grids, which are quarter mile neighborhoods. Crimes are based on arrest records and do not reflect ultimate convictions. It has been assumed that conviction rates will be proportional to arrest rates.) is a tabulation of the number of crimes committed and the rate of those crimes per 1,000 people living in each area. This table is on the following page.

There appears to be a significantly greater difference between the study and control areas for sex crimes than for either property or violent crimes. The following table illustrates a comparison of the ratio of the crime rate of the study area to the control area:

Table VI

Crime Rates As a Percentage of Study Area to Control Area

Study Area	Property Crimes	Violent Crimes	Sex Crimes	Sex Crimes (Less Indecent Exposure)
I	147%	144%	1135%	358%
II	173	83	277	160
III	108	86	405	178
Average:	143%	104%	606%	232%

It is observed that there are about 40% more property crimes and about the same rate of violent crimes per 1,000 persons in the Study Areas as compared to the Control Area.

On the other hand there is an average of six times the sex crime rate in the Study Areas as compared with the Control areas. Although the majority of sex crimes are Indecent Exposure, the fourth column illustrates that the remainder of the sex crimes also exhibit a significantly higher rate in the study areas. A detective from the police department stated that most indecent exposure crimes were committed on adult business premises. An example of this finding is in Study Area I. In that location, 89% of the reported indecent exposure crimes were committed at the addresses of adult businesses.

Where there is a concentration of adult businesses, such as in Study Area I, the difference in sex offense rates is most significant. As stated earlier in the report this location has four adult businesses which are less than 1,000 feet away from each other and less than 500 feet away from a residential district. There is also a higher number of sex offenses committed—84 more crimes than in Study Area II, and 56 more crimes than in Study Area III. Similarly, when compared to its Control Area, the sex crime rate, per 1,000 residences is over 11 times as great in Study Area I. In the remaining study areas, which each contain a single adult business, their rates are four and almost three times as great.

in the form of a "front room" and a "back room."[300] The front room is usually where books, magazines, films, videos, and sexual devices are sold. The individual running the business usually keeps fairly accurate financial records for this part of the operation because revenues from it are used to pay rent, utilities, and employees' wages as well as purchase merchandise.[301]

The "back room" usually contains peep show booths or video machines which earn substantial profits—often twice that which the "front room" earns. These "back room" earnings are typically excluded from any financial records of the business and can easily go untaxed.[302] While this Commission does not condone the operation of pornography businesses it urges state and local revenue authorities to strictly scrutinize the reporting methods of these businesses and insure that the proper income is reported and subject to taxation.

RECOMMENDATION 32:
State and Local public health authorities should investigate conditions within "Adults Only" Pornographic outlets and arcades and enforce the laws against any health violations found on those premises.

Discussion
Testimony before the Commission has revealed that sexual acts often occur in the peep booths located in many "Adults Only" porno-

graphic outlets and arcades.[303] Acts such as fellatio, sodomy, and masturbation are common.[304] Some of these establishments have "glory holes" drilled through the walls of the peep booths to permit individuals to engage in anonymous sex with the occupant of the adjoining booth.[305] Upon examination of the interior of these booths, police often find evidence of urine, human feces and semen.[306]

The public health risks posed by this anonymous sexual activity are quite obvious. The public health department in Houston, Texas, reported 214 cases of syphilis and gonorrhea during three months of 1985.[307] Of those infected individuals, 10.7 percent reported they had performed sexual acts in "Adult Only" pornographic outlets.[308] Because of the anonymous nature of these sexual encounters, public health officials find it impossible to trace the origin of the disease.[309] Concern about the spread of Acquired Immune Deficiency Syndrome (AIDS) has made this situation even more significant. Similar risks to public health are posed by massage parlors, brothels, and establishments promoting "piercing"[310] and other sado-masochistic sexual activities.

While this Commission does not condone or support the existence of these businesses dealing in obscene materials, it urges state and local public health officials to inspect the premises of adult bookstores and arcades in their jurisdictions and vigorously enforce the law against all public health violations found on those premises.

RECOMMENDATIONS FOR THE JUDICIARY

RECOMMENDATION 33:
Judges should impose substantial periods of incarceration for persons who are repeatedly convicted of obscenity law violations and when appropriate should order payment of

restitution to identified victims as part of the sentence.

Discussion
The Commission has been apprised repeat-

---

300. New York Hearing, Vol. II, William Johnson, p. 72-73.
301. *Id.*, p. 72.
302. *Id.*, p. 72.
303. See, The discussion of the Production, Distribution and Technology of Sexually Explicit Materials in Part Four. Houston Hearing, Vol. 1, W. D. Brown, p. 39; Chicago Hearing, Vol. II, Hinson McAuliffe, p. 181.
304. *Id.*
305. Houston Hearing, Vol. I, W. D. Brown, p. 41.
306. *Id.*, p. 42.
307. *Id.*
308. *Id.*
309. *Id.*
310. "Piercing" is a form of sado-masochistic sexual activity involving the piercing of the skin or genitals with pins, needles or other sharp instruments.

edly of the minimal periods of incarceration and fines which have been imposed on persons who frequently violate obscenity laws.[311] In cases involving significant violations of the obscenity laws or repeat offenders, only a substantial period of incarceration will provide a deterrent effect.[312]

Judges can also enhance basic law enforcement efforts when they impose substantial periods of incarceration for these offenses. Law enforcement officers, prosecutors and society in general view the sentences imposed as a statement of the community attitude toward the crime. When minimal sentences are given, the significance of the crime is diminished.

Recidivist obscenity law violators should be viewed the same as recidivist violators of other criminal laws. Judges also should be apprised of the nature of the materials involved and the offender's affiliation with organized crime, if any. These factors must be considered before a judge can appropriately sentence an offender.

RECOMMENDATIONS FOR THE FEDERAL COMMUNICATIONS COMMISSION

Modern technology pervades virtually every aspect of daily life and it should come as no surprise that these advances are used in the dissemination of pornography. Two of these technological advances, Dial-A-Porn and cable television, have brought with them some very complex questions of law and public policy. In some instances, the course in resolving the issues remains largely uncharted. A complete discussion of pornography in the United States today cannot be addressed without a careful examination of these technologies particularly with reference to the role of the Federal Communications Commission in regulating them.

RECOMMENDATION 34:
The Federal Communications Commission should use its full regulatory powers and impose appropriate sanctions against providers of obscene Dial-A-Porn telephone services.

Discussion

The term "Dial-A-Porn" has been applied to describe two types of obscene statements made over the telephone as a part of a commercial transaction. In the first instance, the caller dials a number and talks to an individual who makes sexual remarks in response to the stated desires of the particular caller.[313] The caller pays a per minute rate and is billed on his or her credit card.[314] The conversation can last up to forty-five minutes.

The second type of transaction involves placing a call to a number with the "976" prefix. These numbers are part of the Mass Announcement Network Service (MANS) and provide the caller with a pre-recorded message similar to those giving the time of day or weather.[315] The message is sexually explicit and the caller is charged on his monthly telephone statement.[316] The provider of the message receives a payment from telephone company revenues calculated according to the local tariff. The telephone company receives the remainder.[317] In some cities, for example, the cost to the caller is two dollars with $1.45 going to the provider of the message and fifty-five cents to the telephone company.[318]

These Dial-A-Porn recordings include graphic descriptions, complete with sound effects, of lesbian and homosexual acts, sodomy, rape, incest, excretion, bestiality, sadomasochism, and other unlawful, violent or dangerous sexual acts involving adults and children.[319] In May of 1983, 800,000 calls a day were placed to Dial-A-Porn numbers in New York.[320] Approximately 180,000,000

---

311. There were several defendants sentenced in a Federal Bureau of Investigation in a Spectra Photo. Even in cases involving severe sexual or physical abuse minimal sentences were imposed.

312. See, Recommendation for Judicial and Correctional Facilities in this Chapter, for a further discussion of the goals of modern penology.

313. Los Angeles Hearing, Vol. I, Brent Ward, p. 227.

314. *Id.*

315. *Id.,* p. 228.

316. *Id.,* pp. 229-30./

317. *Id.,* p. 229.

318. *Id.*

319. *Id.,* p. 231

320. *Id.,* p. 228.

calls were made to the same numbers in the year ending in February 1984.[321]

Carlin Communications, a leading provider of Dial-A-Porn services, earned $3,600,000 in 1984.[322] Pacific Bell reports that sexually explicit messages represent twenty-seven percent of all "976" calls so far in 1985.[323] Telephone companies explain the existence of "976" service as an opportunity to provide subscribers with a wide range of information as well as a source of revenue to keep telephone rates low.[324] The content of the telephone messages is solely within the control of the provider. New Jersey Bell, however, has reserved the right to review program content under their contract with providers.[325] The easy accessability to Dial-A-Porn messages has given rise to a number of problems. Initially it should be noted that the telephone companies have issued numbers, upon the request of the providers, such as 976-FOXX, 976-4LUV, and 976-LUST.[326] Dial-A-Porn advertising is often misleading in that it refers to "free phone sex" when, in fact, the caller is billed either on his or her credit card or is charged as part of their monthly telephone statement.[327]

Since Dial-A-Porn numbers are openly advertised in pornographic magazines, newsstand racks, in convenience grocery stores, on public billboards and other readily available publications they are often discovered and used by minors unbeknownst to their parents. The telephone company may elect to disconnect the customer's service if they do not pay the toll charges.[328] Finally, there is concern over the long-term effects of Dial-A-Porn recordings on children who listen to them and may attempt to model their behavior after them. This is especially worrisome when descriptions of unlawful, violent and incestuous acts are associated with sexual arousal as in many of the Dial-A-Porn messages.

Two years ago, the Congress enacted legislation amending section 223 of the Communications Act of 1934.[329] This enactment prohibited the use of the telephone to make obscene or indecent communications for commercial purposes to anyone under eighteen years of age except where in compliance with regulations issued by the Federal Communications Commission. The FCC promulgated regulations making it an exception for the provider of a recorded message if the message was made available only between the hours of 9:00 p.m. and 8:00 a.m. eastern standard time or if the caller made prepayment by credit card in the case of a "live" message.[330] Carlin Communications challenged the FCC regulations.

On review, the United States Court of Appeals for the Second Circuit found the regulations were invalid.[331] The court found that the government had a compelling interest in protecting minors from salacious material, but that the FCC regulations were not well tailored to meet their objectives, which could be achieved by less restrictive alternatives.[332] In dicta, the court said the FCC should have given more serious consideration to two other options such as "blocking" and access codes. Through "blocking" a subscriber can have access to all "976" numbers blocked from his telephone. Access codes could be issued to subscribers over eighteen who would have to dial the code in order to receive the sexually explicit message.[333]

On October 16, 1985, the FCC announced new regulations governing Dial-A-Porn.[334] Under the new regulations, Dial-A-Porn services must require either an authorized access or identification code or they must obtain prepayment by credit card before transmission of a sexually explicit message.[335]

Carlin challenged the new regulations, and on April 11, 1986, the Court of Appeals granted their petition and set aside the regu-

---

321. Id.
322. Id., p. 229.
323. Los Angeles Hearing, Vol. I, William Dunkle, p. 251.
324. Id., p. 150.
325. Contract between New Jersey Bell and Sundial Productions. #C115185-2, (Dec. 21, 1982).
326. Hollywood Press, Aug. 9, 1985.
327. Los Angeles Hearing, Vol. I, Judith Trevillian, p. 264.
328. Id.
329. See, 47 U.S.C. S223(b)(1) et. seq.
330. 49 Fed. Reg. 24, p. 996 (June 4, 1984).
331. Carlin Communications, Inc. v. FCC, 749 F.2d, p. 113 (2d Cir. 1984).
332. Id.
333. Id.
334. 50 Fed. Reg. 42699 (Oct. 22, 1985).
335. Id.

lations as applied to Carlin.[336] The FCC now finds itself in a dilemma, since the latest set of regulations have been found unduly restrictive as applied to Carlin in New York, but possibly substainable elsewhere.[337]

The Court of Appeals relied on statements from New York Telephone that access or identification codes are not technologically feasible in NYTS network,[338] and found that "the record does not support the FCC's conclusion that the access code requirement is the least restrictive means to regulate Dial-A-Porn. . . ."[339] The Court again referred to "blocking" as a less restrictive means of regulating Dial-A-Porn.[340] Blocking devices installed on the telephone customers' own terminal equipment could be used to block access to one or more pre-selected telephone numbers.[341] The court also suggested that the FCC should have considered the feasibility of passing along the cost of customer premises blocking equipment to the providers of Dial-A-Porn and/or the telephone companies.[342]

The latest decision by the Second Circuit leaves the state of the law regarding dial-a-porn even more uncertain. The two attempts by the FCC to promulgate regulations in accordance with the federal statute have failed. The Court of Appeals found earlier that limi-tations on the hours that Dial-A-Porn messages may be offered were not tailored enough to regulate the problem.[343] Now the court has ruled that access codes are unduly restrictive as applied to Carlin in New York, but may be permissible elsewhere.[344] The "blocking" option advanced by the court has serious practical limitations. Blocking may not be available to all telephone customers.[345] Those who obtain the service would either lose access to all "976" numbers[346] or have to pre-select which numbers they wanted blocked.[347] Few parents would have sufficient knowledge of the multitude of Dial-A-Porn numbers to be able to pre-select them and prevent their children from calling them by use of a blocking device. And minors would still be free to make the calls from telephones not equipped with blocking devices.

The provision of the federal statute permitting Dial-A-Porn messages to be provided in accordance with FCC regulations[348] has proven unworkable in addition to providing a "safe harbor" provision for Dial-A-Porn merchants. Congress should enact legislation that simply prohibits the transmission of obscene material through the telephone or similar common carrier.[349]

The regulations that have been invalidated

---

336. *Carlin Communications, Inc. v. FCC*, No. 85-4158 (2d Cir. Apr. 11, 1986).

337. *Id.*, pp. 3-4.

338. *Id.*, pp. 11, 19. The Court noted that the access codes are probably technologically feasible in most other parts of the country. *See, Id.*, p. 4.

339. *Id.*, p. 3.

340. *Id.*, pp. 23-24.

341. *Id.*, pp. 6-7.

342. *Id.*, p. 23.

343. 749 F.2d, p. 121.

344. *Carlin Communications, Inc. v. FCC, supra,* slip op., pp. 3-4.

345. See, Los Angeles Hearing, Vol. I, William Dunkle, p. 254.

346. *Id.*

347. *Carlin Communications, Inc. v. FCC, supra,* slip op., p. 6.

348. 47 U.S.C. S223(f)(2).

349. In an attempt to address the Dial-A-Porn issue, Senate Bill 1090 has ben introduced by Senators Jesse Helms, (R-NC), John East (R-NC) and Jeremiah Denton (R-Ala) to amend Section 223 of the Communications Act of 1934. The bill provides:

> Whoever—"(A) in the District of Columbia or in interstate or foreign communications, by means of telephone, makes (directly or by recording device) any comment, request, suggestion, or proposal which is obscene, lewd, lascivious, filthy, or indecent, regardless of whether the maker of such comments placed the call or (B) knowingly permits any telephone facility under such person's control to be used by any purpose prohibited by subparagraph (A). Shall be fined not more than $50,000 or imprisoned not more than six months, or both."

Additionally, Rep. Thomas J. Bliley (R-Va.) has introduced H. R. 4439 which would amend Section 223 of the Communications Act and eliminate the provision requiring the FCC to issue regulations:

H. R. 4439

A Bill to amend the Communications Act of 1934 to restrict the making of obscene and indecent communications by telephone.

"Be it enacted by the Senate and House of Representatives of the United States of America in Congress assembled, Section I, Short title.

This Act may be cited as the "Telephone Decency Act of 1986".

Section II, Amendments.

by the Second Circuit were based on the faulty premise that obscene telephone communications are entitled to some measure of protection so long as they occur between or among "consenting adults". The United States Supreme Court rejected this basic argument in *Paris Adult Theatre I v. Slaton*.[350] In *Slaton*, a motion picture theatre was convicted for showing obscene films.[351]

Its defense was that no one under twenty-one years of age was admitted and that showing the films to consenting adults was protected under the right to privacy.[352] The Court affirmed the conviction, with Chief Justice Burger writing for the majority.

We categorically disapprove the theory, apparently adopted by the trial judge, that obscene, pornographic films acquire constitutional immunity from state regulation simply because they are exhibited for consenting adults only. This holding was properly rejected by the Georgia supreme court. Although we have often pointedly recognized the high importance of the state interest in regulating the exposure of obscene materials to juveniles and unconsenting adults, see *Miller v. California*, ante, at 18-20, *Stanley v. Georgia*, 394 U.S. at 567, *Redrup v. New York*, 386 U.S. 767, 769 (1967), this Court has never declared these to be the only legitimate state interests permitting regulation of obscene material.[353]

The Chief Justice went on to cite other legitimate interests which permitted the regulation of obscene material including maintenance of the "quality of life and the total community environment."[354] The Court also cited the statement of former Chief Justice Earl Warren in *Jacobellis v. Ohio*,[355] that, "there is a right of the Nation and the States to maintain a decent society."[356]

The telephone is also uniquely accessible to children. Children have easy and often unsupervised access to telephones in their

homes and learn to use the telephone at an astonishingly early age. A child need only dial seven numbers to reach a recorded message. Additionally, Dial-A-Porn numbers are openly published and advertised in publications which are sold in racks on the public streets and available to purchasers of any age group. Dial-A-Porn numbers may also be passed along from one child to another.

As a final consideration, the telephone industry, like broadcasting industry, is closely regulated. As a condition of its continued existence a carrier must act in the public interest. The FCC, whose entire regulatory scheme is based on serving the public interest could act to protect these same interests against obscene communications over the telephone if it chose to do so. The time is long overdue for the FCC to exercise its full regulatory powers with respect to this lucrative brand of obscenity.

RECOMMENDATION 35:
The Federal Communications Commission should use its full regulatory powers and impose appropriate sanctions against cable and satellite television programmers who transmit obscene programs.

Discussion
The growth of the cable television industry over the last few years has been remarkable. Approximately forty percent of all homes in the country now have access to cable or satellite television, and 250,000 homes are being connected with the services every month.[357] There are currently 6,500 cable television systems serving forty million households.[358]

The concerns over the content of some of cable television programming have increased as the cable industry has grown. Feature film presentations have been one of cable's strongest drawing cards and an increasing number

---

350. 413 U.S., (1973), p. 49.
351. *Id.*
352. *Id.*
353. *Id.*, p. 57
354. *Id.*, p. 58.
355. 378 U.S., (1964), p. 184.
356. *Id.*, p. 199.
357. Citizens for Decency Through Law, Memorandum (Jan., 1985).
358. Los Angeles Hearing, Vol. I, Brenda Fox, p. 284; Letter from James P. Mooney to Henry E. Hudson (May 2, 1986).

Section 223(B) of the Communications Act of 1934 is amended—
    (1) in paragraph (1)(A), by striking out "under eighteen years of age or to any person without that person's consent";
    (2) by striking out paragraph (2);
    (3) in paragraph (4), by striking out "paragraphs (1) and (3)" and inserting in lieu thereof "paragraphs (1) and (2)"; and
    (4) by redesignating paragraphs (3), (4), and (5) as paragraphs (2), (3), and (4), respectively.

of those films shown on cable fall under the MPAA rating "R".[359] These films depict nudity, sexual themes, simulated sex, graphic violence, or offensive language.[360] While a minor under the age of seventeen cannot be admitted into a theatre to view an "R" rated film without an accompanying parent or guardian, the same films are available to a viewer of any age over cable. Some of the premium channels offer movies that are unrated by the MPAA and go far beyond those in the "R" category and would be generally considered as "X-rated".

These films are sometimes the same films shown in pornography movie theatres and include films which federal and state courts have found to be obscene.[361] For example, the movie, "The Opening of Misty Beethoven" appeared over satellite television in Phoenix, Arizona, in 1981.[362] This film was previously found to be legally obscene by the Supreme Court of Alabama.[363]

These more sexually explicit movies earn a much larger profit for the cable channel.[364] It is less expensive for the cable channel to offer these films than it is for them to acquire and show better known but non-sexually explicit feature films.

The cable industry minimizes any problems associated with sexually explicit cable programs. Brenda Fox of the National Cable Television Association (NCTA) testified in Los Angeles that there are only 700,000 subscribers to the "adult" programming offered on cable.[365] Ms. Fox also testified that the industry has taken what it regards as adequate steps to protect minors from viewing sexually explicit programs. These precautions include lockboxes so parents can control channel selection, program guides and notices, transmission of "adult" programs through scrambled signals and the restriction of this programming to later evening hours.[366] The number of hours of sexually explicit programming, however, continues to escalate. There is

no reason that a cable television programmer or operator could not be prosecuted under existing federal and state obscenity laws by the United States Attorneys and State or local prosecutors for transmitting a program that meets the Miller test for obscenity.

As the Supreme Court held in *Kaplan v. California*, "[W]hen the Court declared that obscenity is not a form of expression protected by the First Amendment, no distinction was made as to the medium of the expression."[367]

In *HBO, Inc. v. Wilkinson*, the United States District Court in Utah found the *Miller* standard applicable to cable television. While a Miami, Florida, ordinance prohibiting indecent cable telecasts was found to be unconstitutional, the portion of the ordinance that proscribed obscene programming was not challenged.[368]

The Cable Communications Policy Act of 1984[369] attempts to provide another avenue for the prosecution of obscenity shown over cable television. The Act provides, in part, that, "Whoever transmits over any cable system any matter which is obscene or otherwise unprotected by the Constitution of the United States shall be fined not more than $10,000 or imprisoned not more than 2 years, or both."[370]

This portion of the section may be in conflict with two other sections of the Act governing editorial control of programming by cable operators. Sections 531(e) of Title 47 provides that:

Subject to section 544(d) of this title, a cable operator shall not exercise any editorial control over any public, educational, or governmental use of channel capacity provided pursuant to this section.

Section 544(d) provides in part:

(1) Nothing in this subchapter shall be construed as prohibiting a franchising authority and a cable operator from specifying, in a

---

359. See, Cable Pornography: Problems and Solutions, Citizens for Decency Through Law, p. 2. (Jan. 1985)
360. Los Angeles Hearing, Vol. II, Jack Valenti, p. 55k.
361. Los Angeles Hearing, Vol. II, James J. Clancy, p. 309; Citizens for Decency Through Law, Memorandum, pp. 2-3 (Jan. 1985).
362. Los Angeles Hearing, Vol. II, James Clancy, p. 310.
363. *Trans-Lux Theatre v. People ex rel. Sweeton*, 366 So. 2d, p. 710 (Ala. 1979).
364. Citizens for Decency Through Law, Memorandum, pp. 2-3 (Jan. 1985).
365. Los Angeles Hearing, Vol. I, Brenda Fox, p. 295.
366. *Id.*, pp. 297-88.
367. 413 U.S., pp. 115, 118-19.
368. *Cruz v. Ferre*, 755 F.2d, pp. 1415, 1418 (11th Cir. 1985).
369. 47 U.S.C. S559.
370. *Id.*

franchise or renewal thereof, that certain cable services shall not be provided *or shall be provided subject to conditions,* if such cable services are obscene or are otherwise unprotected by the Constitution of the United States.

(2) (A) In order to *restrict the viewing of programming which is obscene* or indecent, upon the request of a subscriber, a cable operator shall provide (by sale or lease) a device by which the subscriber can prohibit viewing of a particular cable service during periods selected by that subscriber. (emphasis added)

Section 544(d) seems to contemplate the operator providing obscene programming while Section 559 makes it a crime to do so.[371]

Proposed legislation should be drafted to enable United States Attorneys to prosecute violators under the criminal code and alleviate the possible conflict under the Cable Communications Policy Act.

The FCC has shown no interest in taking action regarding the contents of cable programming. Thomas Herwitz, legal assistant to FCC Chairman Mark Fowler, stated the Commission's views at the Los Angeles hearing regarding cable programming. The position the FCC has taken has been to advocate regulation for cable similar to that for the print medium.[372]

The FCC maintains that the cable subscription services can be controlled adequately within the home to assure that minors do not have access. The FCC position is that since the individual can act as his or her own gatekeeper and preclude those signals not desired to be watched, the government has no compelling interest in further intrusion.[373]

The posture adopted by the FCC has enabled cable television to occupy a status afforded no other medium. The policy considerations that support government regulation of broadcasting to serve the public interest also apply to government regulation of cable television. As the United States Court of Appeals for the District of Columbia has ruled,

> [We] do require that at a minimum the [FCC], in developing its cable television regulations, demonstrate that the objectives to be achieved of regulating cable television are also objectives for which the commission could legitimately regulate the broadcast media.[374]

When 250,000 homes are being connected with cable every month, it is readily apparent that cable television's presence is, in fact, as pervasive as that of the broadcast media.

Parents may make the initial decision to subscribe to a cable service with a variety of program choices. The fact that a parent makes a conscious choice to engage the cable service does not impair the accessibility of the selections to minors in the home. Once cable enters the home it becomes the same in this regard as over the air broadcasts. It comes through the same television set and is usually accessed by the same controls. The FCC has recognized that,

> While particular stations or programs are oriented to specific audiences, the fact is that by its very nature, thousands of others not within this 'intended' audience may also see and hear portions of the broadcast.[375]

This rationale is equally applicable to cable and satellite television programs. In many homes, particularly single parent homes or homes where both parents work, close supervision and screening of the selection of television programs in reality may be either minimal or non-existent.

The cable television industry advocates lockboxes as a means of parental control over the programs viewed by children.[376] In their brief before the Supreme Court in *FCC v. Pacifica,* the Pacifica Foundation specifically

---

371. Senate Bill 1090 sponsored by Senator Jesse Helms (R-NC) would place a specific prohibition against obscene cable programming in section 1464 of Title 18 of the United States Code. The Helms bill provides in part:

S1464. Distributing obscene material by radio or television "(a) Whoever utters any obscene, indecent, or profane material by means of radio or television, including cable television, shall be fined not more than $50,000 or imprisoned not more than two years, or both. (b) As used in this section, the term 'distributes' means to send, transmit, retransmit, telecast, broadcast, or cablecast, including by wire or satellite, or produce or provide such material for distribution.

372. Los Angeles Hearing, Vol. I, Thomas Herwitz, p. 347.
373. *Id.,* p. 348.
374. *HBO v. FCC;* 567 F.2d 9, 34 (D.C. Cir. 1977).
375. *In Re, WUHY-FM,* 24 FCC 2d 408(1970).
376. Los Angeles Hearing, Vol. I, Brenda Fox, pp. 287–88.

raised the issue of lockbox controls. They contended that,

> ... the material to which children are exposed on radio and television may be assumed to be subject to parental supervision to a far greater extent than much of the material to which children are likely to be exposed in other media. And, according to *Broadcasting* magazine, technology is now prepared to provide parents with a device which will permit them to "program" their home television set in advance so that it will only receive material selected by the parent, even in the parent's absence. *Broadcasting*, February 27, 1978, at 83.[377]

The addendum to the Pacifica Foundation's brief included a description and photograph of a lockbox device called a "Video Proctor" which is capable of being programmed by a parent to block out any VHF, UHF, cable, or pay television stations.[378] The Supreme Court was obviously unimpressed by the "lockbox" argument and upheld the FCC's authority to regulate broadcast content. Therefore, the availability of lockboxes does not prevent the FCC from regulating obscenity on radio and broadcast television. A lockbox performs the same function whether used to block out a broadcast or cable station. There is no reason why the availability of lockboxes should justify the FCC's failure to regulate obscene cable or satellite programming.

The availability of program guides is also advanced as a means of parental control. However, program guides are also readily available for broadcast television programs in publications ranging from *TV Guide* to the daily newspaper. Programs guides offer no more protection in the context of cable and satellite television than they do in the realm of broadcast television.

While sexually explicit material may be transmitted by scrambled signals, this method is far from foolproof.

For two weeks in November of 1985, Tampa, Florida, residents received all of the "adult" channels whether they subscribed or not. This phenomenon apparently occurred because of a technological anomaly that was triggered by certain weather conditions.[379]

In Colorado Springs, Colorado, the Playboy Channel "slipped through an electronic loophole" and supplemented a "Rin Tin Tin" movie on the Disney Channel.[380] According to a Naples, Florida, resident, "adult" channels, even though scrambled, can still be heard and sometimes seen clearly enough to be watched.[381]

Finally, controls such as lockboxes, program guides, and scrambling are all based on the premise that consenting adults are entitled to observe what they want to. In *Paris Adult Theatre I v. Slaton*,[382] the United States Supreme Court held that obscene materials do not acquire constitutional immunity from state regulation simply because they are exhibited to consenting adults only.[383]

The time is long overdue for the FCC to take an active role in enforcing the laws and regulations against obscene cable programming.

RECOMMENDATION FOR OTHER FEDERAL ORGANIZATIONS

RECOMMENDATION 36:

The President's Commission on Uniform Sentencing should consider a provision for a minimum of one year imprisonment for any second or subsequent violation of Federal law involving obscene material that depicts adults.

Discussion

The Commission has received considerable evidence with regard to the disparity in sen-

---

377. Brief Appelle, *FCC v. Pacifica Foundation*, 438 U.S., (1978), p. 726.
378. Addendum to Brief Appelle, *FCC v. Pacifica Foundation*, 438 U.S., (1978), p. 726.
379. *Tampa Tribune*, Nov. 8, 1985.
380. *The Daily Sentinel*, Aug. 13, 1984.
381. Statement by Rachel Sturdivant, Naples, Florida, submitted by Florida Coalition for Clean Cable.
382. 413 U.S., (1973), p. 49.
383. *Id.*, p. 57.

tences obscenity law violators receive.[384] Congress has enacted the Sentencing Reform Act of 1984. The President's Commission on Uniform Sentencing is a result of this Act.[385] According to the Department of Justice,

The principal goal of the Sentencing Reform Act is to establish a uniform, determinate federal sentencing system that will accomplish the purpose of just punishment, deterrence, incapacitation, and rehabilitation. This goal is to be achieved primarily through the use of sentencing guidelines established by a Presidentially appointed Sentencing Commission, which will be composed of seven full time members and a staff. At least three members must be active federal judges who will not be required to resign from the bench to serve on

the Commission. The initial set of guidelines is to be completed in eighteen months. In the course of its work, the Commission will examine the offense and offender characteristics that judges now consider in making sentencing determinations, and will determine which of those should be reflected in the guidelines, which ones occur so infrequently that they should not be considered in the guidelines but might justify a departure from the guidelines, and which ones should not affect the sentence at all.[386]

In addition, the President's Commission on Uniform Sentencing should specifically consider the problems associated with sentencing obscenity law violations.

384.

DEFENDANTS SENTENCED IN UNITED STATES DISTRICT COURTS
BY MAJOR OFFENSES FOR THE TWELVE MONTH
PERIOD ENDED JUNE 30, 1981

IMPRISONMENT

MAJOR OFFENSE			IMPRISONMENT			
TITLE/SECTION AND LEVEL			DEFEN-DANTS	PRISON MONTHS	PROBATION MONTHS	FINE
18	1461	FELONY	2	60		
18	1461	FELONY	1	120	60	15,000
18	1461	FELONY	1	180	60	20,000
18	1461	9810				
18	1462	FELONY	1	12		
18	1462	9820				
18	1462	FELONY				
18	1462	9910				
18	1465	FELONY	1	18	60	5,000
18	1465	FELONY	1	24		15,000
18	1465	9820				

PROBATION

MAJOR OFFENSE			PROBATION		
TITLE/SECTION AND LEVEL			DEFEN-DANTS	PROBATION MONTHS	FINE
18	1461	FELONY	1	24	5,000
18	1461	FELONY	1	36	
18	1461	FELONY	1	48	
18	1461	FELONY	1	60	
18	1461	9810			
18	1462	FELONY	2	24	500
18	1462	9820			
18	1464	FELONY			
18	1464	9910			
18	1465	FELONY	3	12	
18	1465	FELONY	2	24	
18	1465	9820			

385. United States Department of Justice, *Handbook on the Comprehensive Crime Control Act of 1984 and other Criminal Statutes Enacted by the 98th Congress* 31 (1984).
386. *Id.*

SPLIT SENTENCE

MAJOR OFFENSE			SPLIT SENTENCES			
TITLE/SECTION AND LEVEL			DEFEN- DANTS	PRISON MONTHS	PROBATION MONTHS	FINE
18	1461	FELONY				
18	1461	FELONY				
18	1461	FELONY				
18	1461	FELONY				
18	1461	9810				
18	1462	FELONY	1	6	24	
18	1462	9820				
18	1462	FELONY				
18	1462	9910				
18	1465	FELONY				
18	1465	FELONY				
18	1465	9820				

FINE ONLY

MAJOR OFFENSE			FINE ONLY		
TITLE/SECTION AND LEVEL			DEFEN- DANTS	AMOUNT	OTHER SENTENCES
18	1461	FELONY			
18	1461	FELONY			
18	1461	FELONY			
18	1461	FELONY			
18	1461	9810			
18	1462	FELONY			
18	1462	9820			
18	1462	FELONY			
18	1462	9910			
18	1465	FELONY	3	15,000	
18	1465	FELONY	1	200,000	
18	1465	9820			

DEFENDANTS SENTENCED IN UNITED STATES DISTRICT COURTS
BY MAJOR OFFENSES FOR THE TWELVE MONTH
PERIOD ENDED JUNE 30, 1982

IMPRISONMENT

MAJOR OFFENSE			IMPRISONMENT			
TITLE/SECTION AND LEVEL			DEFEN- DANTS	PRISON MONTHS	PROBATION MONTHS	FINE
18	1461	FELONY	1	60	60	
18	1461	FELONY	1	108		
18	1461	9810				
18	1462	FELONY	1	48		
18	1462	FELONY	1	60	60	12,500
18	1462	9820				
18	1464	FELONY				
18	1462	9910				
18	1465	FELONY	1	18	60	5,000
18	1465	9820				

PROBATION

MAJOR OFFENSE			PROBATION		
TITLE/SECTION AND LEVEL			DEFEN-DANTS	PROBATION MONTHS	FINE
18	1461	FELONY	1	36	
18	1461	FELONY	1	60	
18	1461	9810			
18	1462	FELONY	1	12	
18	1462	FELONY	2	12	1,000
18	1462	9820			
18	1464	FELONY			
18	1464	9910			
18	1465	FELONY	3	12	
18	1465	9820			

SPLIT SENTENCES

MAJOR OFFENSE			SPLIT SENTENCES			
TITLE/SECTION AND LEVEL			DEFEN-DANTS	PRISON MONTHS	PROBATION MONTHS	FINE
18	1461	FELONY	1	3	36	1,000
18	1461	FELONY				
18	1461	9810				
18	1462	FELONY				
18	1462	FELONY				
18	1462	9820				
18	1464	FELONY	1	6	60	
18	1462	9910				
18	1465	FELONY				
18	1465	FELONY				
18	1465	9820				

FINE ONLY

MAJOR OFFENSE			FINE ONLY		
TITLE/SECTION AND LEVEL			DEFEN-DANTS	AMOUNT	OTHER SENTENCES
18	1461	FELONY			
18	1461	FELONY			
18	1461	9810			
18	1462	FELONY	1	5,000	
18	1462	9820			
18	1462	FELONY			
18	1462	9910			
18	1465	FELONY	1	20,000	
18	1465	9820			

DEFENDANTS SENTENCED IN UNITED STATES DISTRICT COURTS
BY MAJOR OFFENSES FOR THE TWELVE MONTH
PERIOD ENDED JUNE 30, 1983

IMPRISONMENT

MAJOR OFFENSE			IMPRISONMENT			
TITLE/SECTION AND LEVEL			DEFEN-DANTS	PRISON MONTHS	PROBATION MONTHS	FINE
18	1461	FELONY	1	60	60	5,000
18	1461	FELONY	1	108		
18	1461	FELONY				
18	1461	FELONY				
18	1461	FELONY				

PROBATION

MAJOR OFFENSE				PROBATION		
TITLE/SECTION AND LEVEL			DEFEN- DANTS	PROBATION MONTHS		FINE
18	1461	FELONY	1	24		1,000
18	1461	FELONY	2	36		
18	1461	FELONY	1	36		1,500
18	1461	FELONY	1	36		2,000
18	1461	FELONY	2	48		

SPLIT SENTENCES

MAJOR OFFENSE				SPLIT SENTENCES		
TITLE/SECTION AND LEVEL			DEFEN- DANTS	PRISON MONTHS	PROBATION MONTHS	FINE
18	1461	FELONY				
18	1461	FELONY				
18	1461	FELONY				
18	1461	FELONY				
18	1461	FELONY				

FINE ONLY

MAJOR OFFENSE				FINE ONLY	
TITLE/SECTION AND LEVEL			DEFEN- DANTS	AMOUNT	OTHER SENTENCES
18	1461	FELONY	1	5,000	
18	1461	FELONY			
18	1461	FELONY			
18	1461	FELONY			
18	1461	FELONY			

DEFENDANTS SENTENCED IN UNITED STATES DISTRICT COURTS
BY MAJOR OFFENSES FOR THE TWELVE MONTH
PERIOD ENDED JUNE 30, 1984

IMPRISONMENT

MAJOR OFFENSE				IMPRISONMENT		
TITLE/SECTION AND LEVEL			DEFEN- DANTS	PRISON MONTHS	PROBATION MONTHS	FINE
18	1461	FELONY	1	36		
18	1461	FELONY	1	60		
18	1461	FELONY				
18	1461	FELONY				
18	1462	FELONY				
18	1465	FELONY				
18	1465	FELONY	1	24		
18	1465	FELONY	1	36		

PROBATION

MAJOR OFFENSE				PROBATION		
TITLE/SECTION AND LEVEL			DEFEN- DANTS	PROBATION MONTHS		FINE
18	1461	FELONY	1	24		
18	1461	FELONY	1	36		
18	1461	FELONY	4	60		
18	1461	FELONY				
18	1462	FELONY				
18	1462	9820				
18	1465	FELONY	1	12		
18	1465	FELONY				
18	1465	9820				

SPLIT SENTENCES

MAJOR OFFENSE			SPLIT SENTENCES			
TITLE/SECTION AND LEVEL			DEFEN-DANTS	PRISON MONTHS	PROBATION MONTHS	FINE
18	1461	FELONY		3		
18	1461	FELONY				
18	1461	FELONY				
18	1461	FELONY				
18	1461	9810				
18	1462	FELONY	1	6	24	
18	1462	9820				
18	1462	FELONY				
18	1462	9910				
18	1465	FELONY				
18	1465	FELONY				
18	1465	9820				

FINE ONLY

MAJOR OFFENSE			FINE ONLY		
TITLE/SECTION AND LEVEL			DEFEN-DANTS	AMOUNT	OTHER SENTENCES
18	1461	FELONY	1	15,000	
18	1461	FELONY			
18	1461	FELONY			
18	1461	FELONY			
18	1461	9810			
18	1462	FELONY			
18	1462	9820			
18	1462	FELONY			
18	1462	9910			
18	1465	FELONY	3	15,000	
18	1465	FELONY	1	200,000	
18	1465	9820			

DEFENDANTS SENTENCED IN UNITED STATES DISTRICT COURTS
BY MAJOR OFFENSES FOR THE TWELVE MONTH
PERIOD ENDED JUNE 30, 1985

IMPRISONMENT

MAJOR OFFENSE			IMPRISONMENT			
TITLE/SECTION AND LEVEL			DEFEN-DANTS	PRISON MONTHS	PROBATION MONTHS	FINE
18	1461	FELONY	1	6		
18	1461	FELONY				
18	1461	FELONY				
18	1461	FELONY				
18	1461	9810				
18	1462	FELONY				
18	1462	9820				
18	1464	FELONY				
18	1464	9910				
18	1465	FELONY				
18	1465	FELONY				
18	1465	9820				

PROBATION

MAJOR OFFENSE			PROBATION		
TITLE/SECTION AND LEVEL			DEFEN-DANTS	PROBATION MONTHS	FINE
18	1461	FELONY	2	24	
18	1461	FELONY	3	36	
18	1461	FELONY	3	48	
18	1461	FELONY	4	60	
18	1461	9810			
18	1462	FELONY	1	36	
18	1462	9820	3	60	
18	1464	FELONY			
18	1464	9910			
18	1465	FELONY			
18	1465	FELONY			
18	1465	9820			

SPLIT SENTENCES

MAJOR OFFENSE			SPLIT SENTENCES			
TITLE/SECTION AND LEVEL			DEFEN-DANTS	PRISON MONTHS	PROBATION MONTHS	FINE
18	1461	FELONY	5			
18	1461	FELONY				
18	1461	FELONY				
18	1461	FELONY				
18	1461	9810				
18	1462	FELONY				
18	1462	9820				
18	1462	FELONY				
18	1462	9910				
18	1465	FELONY	1			
18	1465	FELONY				
18	1465	9820				

FINE ONLY

MAJOR OFFENSE			FINE ONLY		
TITLE/SECTION AND LEVEL			DEFEN-DANTS	AMOUNT	OTHER SENTENCES
18	1461	FELONY			
18	1461	FELONY			
18	1461	FELONY			
18	1461	FELONY			
18	1461	9810			
18	1462	FELONY			
18	1462	9820			
18	1462	FELONY			
18	1462	9910			
18	1465	FELONY			
18	1465	FELONY			
18	1465	9820			

Source: Administrative Offices of the United States Courts.

C H A P T E R • 1 1

Child Pornography

INTRODUCTION

No clearer measure exists of the radical shift in the issues confronted by the Commission on Obscenity and Pornography in 1970 and those facing this one than the problem of child pornography. In its description of "the industries" producing sexually explicit material the 1970 Commission nowhere mentioned or alluded to child pornography,[387] and its Traffic and Distribution Panel reported that "the taboo against pedophilia . . . has remained almost inviolate" even in the hardest of "hard-core" materials.[388] The recommendations of the 1970 Commission included repeal of all laws restraining distribution of sexually explicit materials to children; no exception was stated for materials depicting children engaged in sexual conduct.[389]

This Commission, by contrast, has devoted a very substantial proportion of its time and energy to examining the extent and nature of child pornography. Indeed, one set of the Commission's hearings was devoted almost entirely to the problem, while extensive oral and written testimony on the subject was received throughout the year. No aspect of the pornography industry has more occupied the attention of Congress and the general public during the past decade, and this Commission has made a wide range of recommendations

for further legislative and public action. The very novelty of child pornography as a matter for public concern, however, requires at least a general overview of the rise of the "kiddie porn" industry, the nature of and the rationale for the governmental response to it, the effects on the children involved, and the contours of the industry's surviving components. That overview must begin with attention to what "child pornography" by definition is and what it is not.

Drawings of children engaged in sexual intercourse with adults date at least from ancient Greece,[390] and a graphic written description of child sexual abuse was to be found in seventeenth century France.[391] Yet although these portrayals or accounts might be deemed "obscene," and although they deeply offend modern sensibilities regarding the rearing and protection of children, they are not "child pornography" in the specific legal and clinical sense that term has acquired over the past fifteen years. As defined by the United States Supreme Court in the 1982 decision, *New York v. Ferber*, the category of "child pornography" is "limited to works that *visually* depict sexual conduct by children below a specified age."[392] It is clear from the Court's language, and in all statutory and

---

387. *Report of the Commission on Obscenity and Pornography* 7-23 (1970).

388. *Id.*, p. 139.

389. *Id.*, pp. 57-67.

390. See, Photographic vase drawings in K. J. Dover, *Greek Homosexuality* (1978).

391. See, description of P. Aries, *Centuries of Childhood*, pp. 100-102 (1962) (diary of Heroard, physician to Henri IV, who set down graphic details of sexual "play" with the child Louis XIII).

392. 458 U.S. 474, 746 (1982). The Court also required that the "category of 'sexual conduct' proscribed must also be suitable limited and described," *id.*, and must not include mere "nudity." *Id.*, p. 765 n. 18. The New York statutes in question, Penal Law 263.15, was found to fit these requirements even though it included "lewd exhibition of the genitals" in its definition of proscribed sexual conduct. *Id..* p. 773.

scholarly definitions of the term, that "child pornography" is only appropriate as a description of material depicting *real* children.[393]

The basis for these limitations is evident from the very nature of the outrage child pornography engenders—anger over the sexual abuse of children used in its production. While concern over "pornography" generally has centered on the impact of sexually explicit materials on the *audience*, "child pornography" has been defined, and attacked, in terms of its effects on the children who appear in it. Thus, as the Court found in *Ferber*, the category of "child pornography" is both broader and narrower than that of "obscenity." Broader in that it includes materials which are not "patently offensive," which do not appeal to the "prurient interest of the average individual, "and which show children in sexual conduct even as an incidental part of the work (rather than "taken as a whole").[394] Narrower, however, in that written materials are wholly excluded, as are visual materials which do not show *actual* children engaged in sexual conduct. Thus a rewrite of *Lolita* which included graphic descriptions of sexual activity with a young girl could never be "child pornography," nor could a fully explicit film of the novel which starred an adult actress playing the part of the young girl. Such a film which used a *minor* actress, however, could be "child pornography" even if not "patently offensive" by prevailing community standards, and (although this is less clear) even if it possessed serious artistic, literary, scientific or educational value.[395] In the context of "child pornography," alone among all the issues considered by the Commission, the definition of "obscenity" proclaimed in *Miller v. California*[396] and its progeny is wholly irrelevant. Indeed, the advent of "kiddie porn" in the years after *Miller* provides vivid illustration of the inadequacy of the concept of "obscenity" for protecting the interests of *performers* in sexually explicit material.[397]

The irrelevance of *Miller* to child pornography is loaded with some historic ironies, for it was later in the very year of that decision, 1973, that the first child pornography ring—involving some fourteen adults using boys under age thirteen for sex and production of pornographic materials—was brought to public view.[398] In the four years that followed police and reporters uncovered a wide range of activities involving the sexual exploitation of children, much of it involving child pornography.[399] Early in 1976 two employees of a large Los Angeles corporation publishing sexually explicit magazines were convicted of pandering for hiring a fourteen-year-old girl to engage in numerous acts of photographed sexual intercourse for publication in the company's magazines.[400] Later in that year the Los Angeles Police Department established a special Sexually Exploited Child Unit to combat child pornography and prostitution,[401] and in the spring of 1977 a string of investigative articles in the *Chicago Tribune*, *Time* and other major publications helped prompt a full Congressional investigation of the problem.[402]

What Congress discovered in its

---

393. The *Ferber* Court began its analysis of "child pornography" by noting the judgment of legislators and clinicians that "the use of children as subjects of pornographic materials is harmful to the physiological, emotional, and mental health of the child," a judgment the Court found "easily passes muster under the First Amendment." *Id.*, p. 758. *Ferber* thus rests squarely on the assumption that the materials in question are limited to those in the production of which *actual* children have been used.

394. *Id.*, p. 764.

395. Thus the Court found that "a work which, taken as a whole, contains serious literary, artistic, political, or scientific value may nevertheless embody the hardest core of child pornography." *Compare, id,* pp. 774-775 (O'Connor, J., concurring) (no defense based on "serious value" should be allowed) *with id.*, pp. 775-777 (Brennan, J., concurring in the judgment) (such a defense required by First Amendment).

396. 413 U.S. 15 (1973).

397. For the full discussion of the problem of the use of *adult* performers in commercial pornography, See, Chapter 17.

398. S. O'Brien, *Child pornography*, p. 60 (1983) (arrests by Los Angeles police). In August of 1973 the sexually sadistic murder of twenty-seven young boys by Dean Corll was uncovered, while several other call-boy rings were also exposed that year.

399. *See* R. Lloyd, *For Money or Love: Boy Prostitution in America* (1977); C. Linedecker, *Children in Chains* 212-242 (1981).

400. *People v Fixler*, 128 Cal. Rptr. 363, 56 Cal. App. 3d 321 (2d Dist. 1976).

401. *Sexual Exploitation of Children, Hrgs. Before the Subcomm. on the Judiciary, U.S. House, 95th Cong., 1st Sess.* 63 (1977) (statement of Investigator Lloyd Martin, Los Angeles Police Dep't) (hearings hereinafter referred to as "Subcommittee on Crime Hearings").

402. For a reprint of the most influential articles *See, Subcommittee on Crime Hearings, supra* note 401, pp. 422-443.

hearings—which involved one Senate and two House subcommittees over ten dates and four cities from May to September of 1977[403]—was summarized by the Senate Judiciary Committee in its report:

> Child pornography and child prostitution have become highly organized, multi-million dollar industries that operate on a nationwide scale. . . .[404]

According to evidence at the hearings, those industries were producing some 264 different commercial magazines each month showing children nude or engaged in sexual conduct,[405] and the founder of the Los Angeles Sexually Exploited Child Unit reported that "We have 30,000 sexually exploited children in that city."[406] One producer and distributor was reported to have made five to seven million dollars in his own child-pornography business,[407] while other witnesses before Congress described the kidnapping of small children by pornographers,[408] and even their sale by parents.[409]

Child pornography had, in short, become a part of the commercial mainstream of pornography by 1977, sold "over the counter" and in considerable quantities. While a substantial amount of such material was of foreign origin,[410] much of it was made using American children. This wholly unanticipated by-product of the "pornography boom" prompted an angry legislative response from Congress and nearly all state legislatures—a response that in itself seems to have reshaped completely the nature of the child-pornography industry.

The governmental battle against sexual exploitation of children has been an ongoing, evolutionary one, marked by an extraordinary degree of consensus among legislators on both the federal and state levels. Detailed analysis of the wide array of statutes which have resulted from this shared concern is beyond the scope of this report. Nevertheless, a general review of applicable federal statutes, along with attention to significant features of current states, is a crucial backdrop to the Commission's recommendations, and, more importantly to understanding the substantial changes in the child-pornography industry since 1977.

Federal Statutes. Comparison of the two major Congressional acts designed to fight sexual exploitation, approved six years apart, provides perhaps the best evidence of how a changing child pornography industry has taxed legislative ingenuity:[411]

1. *The Protection of Children from Sexual Exploitation Act of 1977 (the "1977 Act").*[412] The immediate response of Congress to the evidence gathered in its 1977 investagations was this law, approved February 6, 1978.

It categorically prohibited the production of any "sexually explicit" material using a child under age sixteen, if such material is destined for, or has already travelled in interstate commerce.[413] The definition of the phrase "sexually explicit" included any

---

403. Subcommittee on Crime Hearings, supra note 401; Sexual Exploitation of Children, Hrgs. Before the Subcomm. on Select Education, Comm. on Education and Labor, U.S. House, 95th Cong., 1st Sess. (1977) (hereinafter "Select Education Subcommittee Hearings"); (Protection of Children Against Sexual Exploitation, Hrgs. Before the Subcomm. to Investigate Juvenile Delinquency, Comm. on the Judiciary, U.S. Senate, 95th Cong., 1st Sess. (1977) (hereinafter "1977 Senate Hearings").

404. S. Rep. No. 438, 95th Cong., 1st Sess. 5 (1977).

405. Subcommittee on Crime Hearings, supra note 402, p. 43 (testimony of Dr. Judianne Denses-Gerber, Presl, Odyssey Institute).

406. Id., p. 59 (testimony of Lloyd Martin).

407. Id., p. 117 (statement of Michael Sneed, reporter, Chicago Tribune).

408. Select Education Subcommittee Hearings, supra note 403, p. 116. (statement of Robin Lloyd).

409. Id., pp. 42-43 (testimony of Lloyd Martin).

410. For an excellent overview of the production of child pornography in the Netherlands, Denmark and other northern European countries—as well as the repackaging for shipment to the United States of material originally produced in America—see, Child Pornography and Pedophilia, Hrgs. Before the Perm. Subcommittee on Investigations, Comm. on Governmental Affairs, U.S. Senate, 98th Cong., 2d Sess; Part 1 (1984) (especially testimony of Kenneth J. Herrmann, Jr., and Michael Jupp, and Toby Tyler, id., pp. 322-37); and Child Pornography and Pedophilia, Hrg. Before the Perm. Comm. on Investigations, Comm. on Governmental Affairs, U.S. Senate, 99th Cong., 1st Sess., Part 2 (1985) (especially testimony of Elliott Abrams, et al., members of federal interagency group which traveled to Denmark, The Netherlands, and Sweden to discuss problem of child pornography with government officials) (hearing hereinafter referred to as "1985 Hearings").

411. For a more complete discussion and comparison of the relevant federal statutes, see, Loken, The Federal Battle Against Child Sexual Exploitation; Proposals for Reform, Harv. Women's L. J. (1986).

412. P. L. 95-225, 92 Stat. 7 (1978), codified, p. 18 U.S.C.S. SS2251-2253 (1979).

413. 18 U.S.C.S. S2251(a) (1979).

conduct involving sexual intercourse of any variety, bestiality, masturbation, sado-masochistic abuse, or "lewd exhibition of the genitals or pubic area."[414] Stern penalties (10 years imprisonment and/or $10,000 fine) were imposed for violating these provisions,[415] and were made applicable, as well, to parents or other custodians who knowingly permit a child to participate in such production.[416]

With regard to the traffic in child pornography already produced, the 1977 Act took a somewhat different approach. With the evidence gathered at the hearings centering overwhelmingly on the *commercial* character of such traffic, Congress understandably directed its prohibitions against the transportation, shipping, mailing, or receipt of child pornography in interstate commerce *"for the purpose of sale* or distribution *for sale."*[417] Thus bartering or simply giving away child pornography was not prohibited even if conducted through the mail. Further, constitutional concerns led Congress to restrict the application of these provisions to material depicting children engaged in "sexually explicit" activity, which was also "obscene" under the *Miller* test.[418] As under the production provisions, the age limit for children protected was set at sixteen, and the penalties imposed were identical.[419]

2. *The Child Protection Act of 1984 (the "1984 Act")*.[420] Strong as it appeared to be on its face, the 1977 Act was soon found by federal law enforcement officials to be of only limited practical value. The production of child pornography is so clandestine in character that from 1978 to 1984 only one person

had been convicted under that portion of the 1977 Act.[421] As for distribution of the material, the traffic in child pornography went underground after 1978, and commercial magazines such as those shown to Congress in 1977 were no longer available "over-the-counter" in pornography outlets. Rather, as a Postal official told Congress in 1982, the "bulk of child pornography traffic is noncommercial."[422] This meant, as a Federal Bureau of Investigation witness told the same hearing, that federal enforcement of the 1977 Act was "seriously impaired" by its "for sale" requirements.[423] Further, the limitation of the trafficking provision of the 1977 Act to "obscene" child pornography placed substantial obstacles in the path of prosecutors.[424]

Confronted by this evidence, and reinforced by the *Ferber* decision removing any doubt about the necessity of "obscenity" limitations, Congress in May, 1984, approved a broad revision of the 1977 Act. The Child Protection Act of 1984 removed the requirement that interstate trafficking, receipt, or mailing of child pornography be for the purpose of "sale" to be criminal.[425] Further, it wholly eliminated the "obscenity" restrictions of the 1977 Act,[426] and raised the age limit of protection to eighteen.[427] Provisions raising the amount of potential fines were included,[428] along with new sections authorizing criminal and civil forfeiture actions against violators.[429] The definition of "sexually explicit" material was adjusted slightly: the first word in "lewd exhibition of the genitals or pubic area" was changed to "lascivious," and "sadistic or masochistic abuse" was substituted for "sado-masochistic abuse."[430] Written ma-

414. 18 U.S.C.S. S2253 (1979).
415. 18 U.S.C.S. S2251(c) (1979).
416. 18 U.S.C.S. S2251(b) (1979).
417. 18 U.S.C.S. S2252 (1979).
418. *Id.*
419. *Id.*
420. P. L. 98-299, 98 Stat. 204 (1984), *codified at* 18 U.S.C.S SS2251-2255 (1985 Supp.). The constitutionality of this act has recently been sustained by two different federal court. *United States v. Tolczeki*, 614 F. Supp. 1424 (N.D. Ohio 1985).
421. 1985 Hearing, *supra* note 410, p. 104 (statement of Victoria Toensing, Dep'y Asst. Attorney General).
422. *Exploited and Missing Children, Hrg. Before the Subcomm. on Juvenile Justice, Comm. on the Judiciary, 97th Cong.,* 2nd Sess. 47 (statement of Charles P. Nelson).
423. *Id.* at 39 (statement of Dana E. Caro).
424. *Child Pornography, Hrg. Before the Subcomm. on Juvenile Justice, Senate Comm. on the Judiciary, 97th Cong.,* 2nd Sess. (1982) (statement of Robert Pitler, Bureau Chief, Appeals Bureau, District Attorney's Office for New York County).
425. 18 U.S.C.S. S2252(a) (1979).
426. *Id.*
427. 18 U.S.C.S. S2255 (1) (1979).
428. 18 U.S.C.S. SS2251, 2252 (1979).
429. 18 U.S.C.S. SS2253, 2254 (1979).
430. 18 U.S.C.S. S2255 (1979).

terials, finally, were clearly excluded from the law's reach in this area: only "visual depictions" of children are criminally actionable.[431]

The result of these revisions was a dramatic increase in federal prosecutions. In the first nine months after passage of the 1984 Act virtually the same number of people were indicted for federal child pornography offenses as had been indicted during the previous six years.[432] The production provisions, however, continued to produce few indictments, in part because of the extraordinary difficulties of investigation and proof, and in part, perhaps, because the more easily used trafficking provisions often may be invoked against suspected producers instead. It appears, in any case, that the 1977 Act effectively halted the bulk of the commercial child pornography industry, while the 1984 revisions have enabled federal officials to move against the noncommercial, clandestine mutation of that industry.

State Laws. The federal interest in protecting children, of course, is secondary to that of the states, which act as principal guardians against the abuse or neglect of the young. It was indeed a *state* law substantially broader than the 1977 Act which prompted the landmark decision in *New York v. Ferber*.[433] States are not limited, as is the federal government, to regulation of child pornography in or affecting interstate commerce; they have the power to prohibit *all* production and trafficking in such materials.

To a substantial extent the states have exercised that power. Nearly all ban the production of child pornography, and an overwhelming majority prohibit distribution as well.[434] Most prohibit as well parental consent or accession to use of children in sexually explicit materials, and many outlaw

facilitation of sexual exploitation through financing, developing, duplication, or promoting child pornography.[435] Some have prohibited as well the *possession* of child pornography, an extremely effective weapon against child molesters.[436]

Yet it is clear, too, that much remains to be accomplished on the state level. Not all states ban trafficking in child pornography, so that it remains possible in some parts of this country to distribute such materials intrastate without fear of criminal penalty. Further, only about half of the states protect children from use in pornography until their eighteenth birthday; in other states the age limit is set at sixteen or seventeen.[437] (This Commission has determined, indeed, that such protections should, on a somewhat more limited basis, be extended to age twenty-one.)[438] Finally, few states appear to have taken action to provide substantial assistance to *victims* of child pornography—either through direct aid or through encouraging private civil remedies.[439] The primary role of states in caring for children would seem to argue for their assumption of the principal share of the burden of providing such assistance.

The legislative assault on child pornography drastically curtailed its public presence; it has not, however, ended the problem. Sexual exploitation of children has retreated to the shadows, but no evidence before the Commission suggests that children are any less at risk than before. The characteristics of both perpetrators and victims, combined with the extremely limited state of professional understanding, make it unlikely that child pornography is a passing phenomenon.

Those who sexually exploit children do so for a wide range of reasons, and come from an extremely broad array of backgrounds, and occupations,[440] but it seems helpful to group them into two categories: "situational" and

431. 18 U.S.C.S. SS2251, 2252 (1979).
432. 1985 Hearing, *supra* note 410, at 104 (Victoria Toensing). Statitstics provided to the Commission by the Department of Justice indicate that 183 of the 255 indictments under federal child pornography laws from 1978 to February 27, 1986, were obtained *after* passage of the 1984 Act on May 21, 1984.
433. The law in question was N.Y. Penal Law S263.15.
434. National Legal Resources Center for Child Advocacy and Protection, A.B.A., *Child Sexual Exploitation: Background and Legal Analysis* 35 (1984) (49 states as of November 1984) (hereinafter "A.B.A. Analysis").
435. *Id.*, p. 36.
436. Thus Special Agent Kenneth Lanning of the F.B.I. noted in his testimony before the Commission that "pedophiliacs" almost always *collect* child pornography and/or child erotica." Miami Hearing, Vol. I., Kenneth Lanning, p. 232.
437. A.B.A. Anaylsis, *supra* note 434, p. 37.
438. See, The discussion in this Chapter for Recommendations for Federal Legislation, *infra*.
439. As an example of the difficulty of obtaining for children victimized in sexually explicit material *see, Faloona v. Hustler Magazine*, 607 R. Supp. 1341 (D.C. Tex. 1985), *appeal docketed*, No. 85-1359 (5th Cir. 1985).
440. Washington Hearing, Vol. I, Daniel Mihalko, p. 149; Belanger, *et. al.*, *Typology of Sex Rings Exploiting Children*, in *Child Pornography and Sex Rings* 74 (A. Burgess ed. 1984) (hereinafter "Sex Rings").

"preferential" molesters.[441] The former are
people who act out of some serious sexual or
psychological, need, but choose children as
victims only when they are readily and safely
accessible. "Preferential" molesters, on the
other hand, are those with a clear sexual preference for children ("pedophiles" in common
usage) who can only satisfy the demands of
that preference through child victims. "Preferential" abusers collect child pornography
and/or erotica almost as a matter of course. It
is unclear how large each of these respective
categories is, but it does seem apparent that
"preferential" child molesters over the long
term victimize far more children than do "situational" abusers.

The approaches adopted by various perpetrators also vary widely. The most recent research on "child sex rings" indicates that they
range in structure from highly organized,
"syndicated" operations involving several
perpetrators and many children with production of child pornography for sale or barter, to
"solo" operations in which children are
abused and photographed by only one perpetrator for his pleasure.[442] Child pornography,
while serving primarily the perpetrator's own
needs, is also useful for lowering the inhibitions of other children being recruited by the
perpetrator.[443] Wholly commercial operations
appear to be extremely unusual, but are still
not unknown.[444]

The normal absence of commercial motives, and the strong sexual and/or psychological needs which push both situational
and preferential molesters toward sexual
abuse of children in pornography, suggest
that the *demand* for such material may be
somewhat inflexible. While situational abusers may be steered away from children as victims, preferential abusers may not—and they

are prone, moreover, to far more frequent
abuse. However strong the criminal law, sexual exploitation of children seems likely to remain an irresistible temptation for some.

What is worse, the *supply* of potential victims seems inexhaustible as well. Children
used in pornography seem to come from every
class, religion, and family background; a majority are exploited by someone who knows
them by virtue of his or her occupation,[445] or
through a neighborhood, community or family relationship. Many are too young to know
what has happened; others are powerless to
refuse the demand of an authority figure;
some seem to engage in the conduct "voluntarily," usually in order to obtain desperately
needed adult affection.[446] Adolescents used in
pornography are often runaways, homeless
youth or juvenile prostitutes who may feel
with some justice that they have little choice
but to participate.[447] Thus it seems clear that a
large class of children and teenagers *vulnerable* to use in pornography will continue to exist. Even redoubled efforts to teach children to
protect themselves from such involvement
will not wholly blunt the strong social, family, and economic forces creating that vulnerability.

The rise of the child pornography "problem" took medical, social services and legal
communities as much by surprise as it did
Congress and the general public. It is only fair
to note, therefore, that what one witness
dubbed "conceptual chaos" is a serious obstacle to progress against sexual exploitation of
children in pornography;[448] at present only a
tiny quantity of serious scholarship on the
subject has found its way into print.[449] There
are indications, moreover, that researchers
and clinicians attempting to specialize in the
field have faced serious resistance from their
peers.[450]

441. For these categories and the analysis that follow from them the Commission is grateful to Special Agent, Kenneth
Lanning, F.B.I.
442. Belanger, *supra* note 441, p. 51.
443. Lanning, *Collectors,* in *Sex Rings, supra* note 440, p. 86.
444. See, *Sex Rings, supra* note 440, pp. 67-73, 78 (seventeen of fifty-four child sex rings studies were "syndicated",
most of which sold child pornography and used children in prostitution).
445. *Id.,* pp. 74-75 (38.2 percent of offenders studied had access to children through occupation; 27.3 percent
through their "living situation").
446. U. Schoettle, *Report to the United States' Attorney General's Comm'n on Pornography* 11 (Miami Hearing).
447. See, Rabun, *Combatting Child Pornography and Prostitution: One County's Approach,* in *Child Sex Rings,
supra* note 441, pp. 187-200 (fifteen percent of runaways acknowledged involvement in pornography. James Scanlon &
Price *Youth Prostitution,* in *Child Sex Rings,* p. 139 (seventy-five percent of male hustlers aged fourteen to twenty-five
had participated in pornography).
448. Miami Hearing, Vol. I, Roland Summit, p. 210A19.
449. The leading studies seem to be those contained in *Child Sex Rings, supra* note 440, and U. Schoettle, *Child
Exploitation: A Study of Child Pornography,* 19 J. Am. Acad. Child Psych. 289 (1980) (cited by the Court in *New York v.
Ferber,* 458 U.S. at 758 n. 9) [hereinafter "Child Exploitation"].
450. Statement of Roland Summit, *supra* note 448, pp. 8-15.

No profession is more open to the charge of ignorance in this area than the law itself.[451] Court procedures are particularly intimidating for children asked to relate extremely intimate sexual details that they know will be reacted to with horror by family and friends.[452] A criminal proceeding, moreover, creates a double bind for the child: if he is believed, a former "friend" will go to jail; if he is not, he must endure additional guilt from thoughts that perhaps he did not tell enough.[453] The study of novel investigative and courtroom procedures to address these problems is only in its infancy: where the child pornography itself is not sufficient, without use of the victim as a witness, to establish the prosecutor's case, parents are likely to face an excruciating dilemma. Lawyers and judges, like doctors and mental health professionals, remain largely ignorant of how to respond to child pornography victims.

That ignorance is deeply unfortunate because the pain suffered by children used in pornography is often devastating, and always significant. In the short term the effects of such involvement include depression, suicidal thoughts, feelings of shame, guilt, alienation from family and peers, and massive acute anxiety.[454] Victims in the longer term may successfully "integrate" the event, particularly with psychiatric help,[455] but many will likely suffer a repetition of the abuse cycle (this time as the abuser), chronic low self esteem, depression, anxiety regarding sexuality, role confusion, a fragmented sense of the self, and possible entry into delinquency or prostitution.[456] All, of course, will suffer the agony of knowing the record of their sexual abuse is in circulation, its effects on their future lives unknowable and beyond their control.[457] That may well be their most unhealable wound.

Because the trauma inflicted on children by sexual exploitation is so great, it has seemed to the Commission particularly important to examine every possible approach to improving the state of the law and services to victims. While limitations of time and resources placed significant constraints on that effort, it was nonetheless possible to discuss the problem of child pornography from a number of different perspectives, and to develop recommendations where the evidence called for them. The recommendations so conceived follow, along with explanations of the reasons for each.

---

451. The most scathing indictment of the legal system's capacity to bring child pornogarphy cases to justice was supplied to the Commission by Dr. Roland Summit, who said, in part: "Sex crimes, more than 'legitimate' crimes, seem to require criminal conviction to justify public validation. That standard in itself represents another Catch 22 in favor of traditional denial. The insistence of proof beyond reasonable doubt for an invisible and illogical crime almost guarantees suppression and repudiation." Id. pp. 5-6.
452. See generally, Summit & Kryso, Sexual Abuse of Children: A Clinical Perspective, in Children and Sex, pp. 111, 123-124 (L. Constantine & F. Martinson eds. 1981).
453. Child Exploitation, supra note 449, p. 297.
454. Schoettle Statement, supra note 446, p. 10.
455. Burgess, et al., Impact of Child Pornography and Sex Rings on Child Victims and Their Families in Child Sex Rings, supra note 440, pp. 115-117.
456. Schoettle Statement, supra note 446, p. 10.
457. See New York v. Ferber, supra note 392, 458 U.S., p. 759, and studies cited therein.

TABLE 1

Situational Child Molester

	REGRESSED	MORALLY INDISCRIMINATE	SEXUALLY INDISCRIMINATE	INADEQUATE
BASIC CHARACTERISTIC	Poor Coping Skills	User of People	Sexual Experimentation	Social Misfit
MOTIVATION	Substitution	Why Not?	Boredom	Insecurity and Curiosity
VICTIM CRITERIA	Availability	Vulnerability and Opportunity	New and Different	Non-Threatening
METHOD OF OPERATION	Coercion	Lure, Force, or Manipulation	Involve in Existing Activity	Exploits Size Advantage
PORNOGRAPHY COLLECTION	Possible	Sadomasochistic; Detective Magazines	Highly Likely; Varied Nature	Likely

Source: U.S. Department of Justice, Federal Bureau of Investigation, *CHILD MOLESTERS: A Behavioral Analysis for Law Enforcement,* 19, (1986).

TABLE 2

Preferential Child Molester

	SEDUCTION	INTROVERTED	SADISTIC
COMMON CHARACTERISTICS	1. Sexual Preference for Children 2. Collect Child Pornography and/or Erotica		
MOTIVATION	Identification	Fear of Communication	Need to Inflict Pain
VICTIM CRITERIA	Age and Gender Preferences	Strangers or Very Young	Age and Gender Preferences
METHOD OF OPERATION	Seduction Process	Non-Verbal Sexual Contact	Lure or Force

Source: U.S. Department of Justice, Federal Bureau of Investigation, *CHILD MOLESTERS: A Behavioral Analysis for Law Enforcement,* 25, (1986).

TABLE 3

Cycle

One of the most common questions asked from a public that knows very little about child pornography is: "How does child pornography begin?" This diagram explains one of the most common ways a child is introduced to pornographic activity:

(1) Pornography is shown to the child
    for "sex education."

(2) Attempt to convince child explicit
    sex is acceptable, even desirable.

(6) Photographs or movies are taken of
    the sexual activity.

Cycle of Pornography

(3) Child porn used to convince child
    that other children are sexually
    active—it's ok.

(5) Some of these sessions progress to
    sexual activity.

(4) Child pornography desensitizes—
    lowers child's inhibitions.

Source: S. O'Brien, *Child Pornography*, 89, (1983).

RECOMMENDATIONS FOR CHANGES IN FEDERAL LAW

RECOMMENDATION 37:
Congress should enact a statute requiring the producers, retailers or distributors of sexually explicit visual depictions to maintain records containing consent forms and proof of performers' ages

Discussion

Pornographers use minors as performers in films and other visual depictions.[458] The consumer demand for youthful performers has also created a class of pornography referred to as pseudo child pornography.[459] The growth of pseudo child pornography has made it increasingly difficult for law enforcement officers to ascertain whether an individual in a film or other visual depiction is a minor.

Minors deserve special protection from the

---

458. See, The discussion of performers in Part Three.

459. Pseudo child pornography or "teasers" involve women allegedly over the age of eighteen who are "presented in such a way as to make them appear to be children or youths. Models used in such publications are chosen for their youthful appearance (e.g., in females, slim build and small breasts); and are presented with various accoutrements designed to enhance the illusion of immaturity (e.g., hair in ponytails or ringlets, toys, teddy bears etc.).

'Pseudo child pornography' is of concern since it may appeal to the same tastes and may evoke responses similar or identical to those elicited by true child pornography. However, it is distinct from, and is not 'genuine' child pornography in the sense that it is older adolescents or adults who are displayed in these sexually explicit depictions. It is not individual children who have been directly exploited in the making of such materials. Committee on Sexual Offences Against Children and Youth, 2 *Sexual Offences Against Children*, 1192 (1984). [hereinafter cited as *Sexual Offences Against Children*].

risks inherent in the production of pornographic materials.[460] The performers may be subjected to threats and coercion, provided with controlled substances or exposed to a variety of sexually transmitted diseases.[461] The Child Protection Act of 1984[462] is designed to prohibit employing, using, persuading, inducing, enticing, or coercing any minor to engage in any sexually explicit conduct for the purpose of producing any visual depiction of such conduct.[463]

This proposed legislation should afford protection to minors through every level of the pornography industry. The recordkeeping obligation should be imposed on wholesalers, retailers, distributors, producers and anyone engaged in the sale or trade of sexually explicit material as described by the Child Protection Act.

The concern to be addressed through this legislation is the safety and well-being of children. The current law contains gaps which allow the exploitation of minors to continue. Legislation should be drafted to close the gaps and afford children full protection in every phase of the production and distribution of sexually explicit materials.

Producers would be required to obtain proof of the age of the performer and record the same on a signed release form if the performer engages in any sexual act which would be in violation of the Child Protection Act.[464]

Despite the umbrella protection provided by the Child Protection Act of 1984, loopholes remain that permit the continued exploitation of children. For example, experts and law enforcement officers have found it difficult to extend this protection because in many instances, ascertaining the real ages of adolescent performers is impossible. By viewing a visual depiction, how does one decide if the performer is fourteen or eighteen, seventeen or twenty-one? The growth of the category of pseudo child pornography has further confused the issue.

The above legislation will assist officials in assuring the safety and well being of children.

The recommended legislation would require producers to obtain release forms from each performer with proof of age.[465] The forms would be filed at a specified location listed in the opening or closing footage of a film, the inside cover of the magazine or standard locations in or on other material containing visual depictions.[466]

The name, official title and location of the responsible person or corporate agent supervising such records would also be listed to avoid use of corporate shields. The release forms should be available for inspection by any duly authorized law enforcement officer upon demand as a regulatory function for the limited purposes of determining consent and proof of age.[467] The information contained in these records should not be used as evidence of obscenity or related offenses in a grand jury proceeding or by a petit jury or trier of fact, but should only be used for prosecution of this offense. This exception from use in evidence is necessary to secure compliance by the largest number of persons and avoid Fifth Amendment problems.

A producer should be required to maintain these records for a minimum period of five years.[468] Failure to comply with any of these requirements would be punishable as a felony. This legislation would not only protect minors from abuse, but it would also place the burden of ensuring this protection was implemented squarely on the producers of the materials. The proposed legislation would serve a record-keeping purpose comparable

---

460. See, New York v. Ferber, 458 U.S., (1982), p. 758.

461. See, The discussion of performers, infra.

462. 18 U.S.C. SS 2251–2252 (1985).

463. Id.

464. Producers may fulfill the proof of age requirement through obtaining a driver's license, birth certificate or other verifiable and acceptable form of age documentation.

465. The release forms should also include the stage names of the performers as well as any other aliases the performer may use, fingerprints to avoid forgery or fraudulent certification and the last known address and telephone number for the purpose of verification.

466. "I think consent is a very important part of freedom . . . we all want to increase volunteerism and decrease lack of consent whether that be by models or purchasers of magazines." New York Hearing, Vol. II, Alan Dershowitz, p. 312.

467. This inspection requirement would be similar to the inspection provision included in section 3007 of the Resource Conservation Recovery Act of 1976, as amended in that search warrant would not be necessary for routine examination of records.

468. The five-year requirement would commence the date the film was released or the magazine was distributed.

to that found in environmental and similar statutes.[469] Performers in pornography face more risks than just sexual abuse. A decision by young performers to appear in pornographic materials has serious implications for his or her future personal life and career prospects. The existence of the material and its intermittent resurfacing may destroy employment prospects and threaten family stability.[470]

RECOMMENDATION 38:
Congress should enact legislation prohibiting producers of certain sexually explicit visual depictions from using performers under the age of twenty-one.

Discussion

Producers are currently proscribed through the Child Protection Act from using performers under the age of eighteen to engage in various sexually explicit materials. The proscribed acts include actual or simulated:

A. sexual intercourse, including genital-genital, oral-genital, anal-genital, or oral-anal, whether between persons of the same or opposite sex;
B. bestiality;

C. masturbation;
D. sadistic or masochistic abuse; or
E. lascivious exhibition of the genitals or pubic area of any person.[471]

The Act should be amended to protect performers under the age of twenty-one. The amendment should prohibit producers from using persons between the ages of eighteen and twenty-one in visual depictions of certain sexually explicit activities. The proscribed activities should include actual:

A. Sexual intercourse, including genital-genital, oral-genital, anal-genital, or oral-anal, whether between persons of the same or opposite sex;
B. Bestiality;
C. Masturbation;
D. Sadistic or masochistic abuse; or
E. Lascivious exhibition of the genitals or pubic area of any person.

Persons between the ages of eighteen and twenty-one while physically mature still face problems associated with sexually explicit performances. These risks include: pregnancy,[472] sexually transmitted disease,[473]

---

469. Examples of similar recordkeeping legislation and the penalties are: The Federal Insecticide, Fungicide and Rodenticide Act (FIFRA) which provides, "The Administrator may prescribe regulations requiring producers to maintain such records with respect to their operations and the pesticides and devices produced as he determines are necessary for the effective enforcement of this Act." 7 U.S.C. S1361 (3) FIFRA also gives the administrator of the Environmental Protection Agency the authority to inspect the premises to ensure compliance. "(b) Inspection—For the purposes of enforcing the provision of this Act, any producer, distributor, carrier, dealer, or any other person who sells or offers for sale, delivers or offers for delivery any pesticide or device subject to this Act, shall, upon request of any officer or employee of the Environmental Protection Agency or of any State or political subdivision, duly designated by the Administrator, furnish or permit such person at all reasonable times to have access to, and to copy: (1) all records showing the delivery, movement, or holding of such pesticide or device, including the quantity, the date of shipment and receipt, and the name of the consignor and consignee; or (2) in the event of the inability of any person to produce records containing such information, all other records and information relating to such delivery, movement, or holding of the pesticide or device." 7 U.S.C. S 1361; Failure to comply with the provision may result in civil or criminal penalties. "Any registrant, commercial applicator, wholesaler, dealer, retailer, or other distributor who knowingly violates any provision of this Act shall be guilty of a misdemeanor and shall on conviction be fined not more than $25,000, or imprisoned for not more than one year, or both." 7 U.S.C. S136n. The Resource Conservation and Recovery Act of 1976 requires hazardous waste generators, transporters and owners and operators of treatment, storage and disposal facilities to maintain adequate business records. See, 42 U.S.C. SS3002, 3003, 3004. If the records are not maintained, the owner, operator, generator or transporter of hazardous waste may be subject to civil and criminal penalties. "Any person who—" (3) knowingly omits material information or makes any false material statement or representation in any application, label, manifest, record, report, permit or other document filed, maintained, or used for purposes of compliance with regulations promulgated by the Administrator under this subtitle: shall, upon conviction, be subject to a fine of not more than $50,000 for each day of violation, or imprisonment not to exceed two years (five years in the case of a violation of paragraph (1) or (2), or both). If the conviction is for a violation committed after a first conviction of such person under this paragraph, shall be doubled with respect to both fine and imprisonment." 42 U.S.C. S3008.

470. Los Angeles Hearing, Vol. II, Miki ✁ pp. 118-20; Washington, D.C., Hearing, Vol. II, Tom, p. 50.

471. 18 U.S.C. S2255 (1985).

472. Enablers, Inc., *Juvenile Prostitution in Minnesota* 86 (1978) (over one-half of juvenile female prostitutes had been pregnant at least once; thirty percent had been pregnant two or more times).

473. See, e.g., Enablers, Inc., *supra* note 472, at 85. (half of the female prostitutes interviewed indicated they had venereal disease); D.K. Weisberg, *Children in the Night* 167 (1985) [hereinafter cited as *Children in the Night*] (venereal disease "plagues" juvenile prostitutes; and is their "most prevalent health concern"); 2 *Sexual Offences Against Children*, (1984), p. 1024, (majority of juvenile prostitutes studied in Canada had contracted a sexually transmitted disease, and almost a third do not seek regular medical attention).

physical abuse[474] and damage to self-esteem and mental health.[475]

Perhaps because of the inner conflicts common among this age group, adolescents are notoriously poor in making sexual choices well into their late teens and twenties. Thus adolescent use of contraceptives "approaches an almost random pattern,"[476] with only a third of sexually active teenagers using contraception consistently.[477] Likewise women aged sixteen to nineteen were eighty-eight percent more likely than women age twenty-five to twenty-nine to seek an abortion after twelve weeks of gestation—with women aged twenty to twenty-four fully twenty-five percent more likely to wait than the older group.[478]

Partially because of poor maturity, and partially because of economic and social factors, the health risks of teenage sex are significant. Both infant and maternal mortality are higher for women aged fifteen to nineteen.[479] More precisely, the rate of low birth weight among babies born to nineteen-year-old white mothers is twenty-five percent higher than that for babies born to white mothers aged twenty-, to twenty-four.[480] Abortions, too, are riskier for white women in late adolescence than for older women because they tend to seek them at a much more advanced gestational stage.[481]

Teenagers participating in pornography face all the risks attendant upon adolescent sexual activity but face as well one certainty that other teenagers do not. Their sexual activity, played out before a camera and live audience, is "a graphic form of exhibitionism . . . [which] literally makes the child's body 'available' for anyone willing to pay the price anywhere in the world."[482] Without reciting all the adverse consequences which young "models" suffer, it is sufficient to note that they can be severe[483] and, even more importantly, irreversible. Unlike the young prostitute who may be able to leave his or her past behind, the adolescent "porn star" must always live in fear that the film or photograph will surface, once again wreaking havoc in his or her personal and professional life.

Because of the economic and social realities of late adolescence, moreover, it is highly unlikely that a decision to accept these consequences has been made in an atmosphere free of pressure or coercion. Youths aged eighteen to twenty-one as a group suffer extraordinary levels of unemployment and homelessness.[484] The rate of poverty among the sixteen to twenty-one age group is almost half again as high as that among older adults.[485] It is hardly surprising that desperate youths are attracted by the quick money to be made in pornography. In describing why as a young man he made a "skin flick," ✂ said that he was literally starving, and "It was either do that movie or rob someone."[486] Yet it is equally clear that it offers them no future as a

474. Silber & A. Pines, *Occupational Hazards of Street Prostitutes*, 8 Crim. Just. & Behavior 395 (1981) (sixty-five percent of sample of prostitutes had been victims of violence, an average of 9.2 times each; seventy-five percent victimized by "forced perversion"); *Children in the Night, supra* note 473, p. 162 (violence also an occupational problem for juvenile male prostitutes).

475. Washington, D.C., Hearing, Vol. I, David, p. 47; Washington, D.C., Hearing, Vol. I, Jeff, p. 167; Washington, D.C., Hearing, Vol. I, Lisa, p. 61.

476. F. Bolton, *The Pregnant Adolescent: Problems of Premature Parenthood* 35 (1980).

477. Alan Guttmacher Institute, *Teenage Pregnancy: The Problem That Hasn't Gone Away*, (1981), p. 11. [hereinafter cited Alan Guttmacher Inst., *Teenage Pregnancy*] The vast majority of sexually active adolescents, of course, are aged eighteen, nineteen, and twenty. *Id.*, p. 7.

478. Center for Disease Control, *Abortion Surveillance*, (1985), p. 37. [hereinafter cited as CDC, *Abortion Surveillance*]

479. *Id.* pp. 10, 37.

480. Alan Guttmacher Inst., *Teenage Pregnancy, supra* note 477, p. 29.

481. CDC, *Abortion Surveillance, supra* note 478, p. 37.

482. Schoettle, *Child Exploitation: A Study of Child Pornography*, J. Am. Acad. Child Psych., (1980), pp. 289, 296.

483. See, e.g., *Wood v. Hustler Magazine, Inc.*, 736 F. 2d, pp. 1084, 1086 (5th Cir. 1984) (description of anguish and harassment suffered by woman whose nude photo was stolen and published in *Hustler*); Lederer, *Then and Now—An Interview with a Former Pornography Model* in *Take Back the Night: Women on Pornography* 57 (1980); Testimony of George (Los Angeles).

484. Youths aged sixteen to nineteen are 160 percent more likely to be unemployed than older workers. Those aged twenty to twenty-four are still ninety-three percent more likely to be unemployed than older workers. *Stastical Abstract* at 394. At Covenant House's New York program alone last year over 5,500 youths aged eighteen to twenty-one—virtually all of the homeless—sought crisis shelter. Only a small minority could be placed in independent living arrangements, job training or institutional shelters.

485. *Statistical Abstract* p. 456.

486. *Playgirl* p. 39. (Oct. 1985)

career in itself, and may in fact further worsen their prospects for stable, long-term employment.[487]

Much participation in pornography, of course, occurs as part of the "career" of juvenile prostitution,[488] and it is worth noting that a significant percentage of youths involved in prostitution have been coerced into "the life."[489]

Many of the difficulties discussed could be eliminated through a prohibition on the use of persons under the age of eighteen in any sexually explicit depiction as desented in the Child Protection Act. Persons between the ages of eighteen and twenty-one would receive the necessary protection through a prohibition against participation in certain scenes of actual sexual activity.

RECOMMENDATION 39:

Congress should enact legislation to prohibit the exchange of information concerning child pornography or children to be used in child pornography through computer networks.

Discussion

Many pedophile offenders and child pornographers have traditionally used the mails as a mainstay of their psychological base as well as the source of information regarding potential victims.[490] Recently, however, pedophile offenders and child pornographers have begun to use personal computers for communications.[491] A person may now subscribe to an information service whereby he or she can contact other subscribers.[492] The services are private commercial enterprises which sell access codes to subscribing members. These services offer everything from "private" communications accessed through individual code words to conference calls.[493] The communication may also take the form of a "bulletin board" message to which any other subscriber may respond.[494]

Personal computers have instant communication capabilities and have afforded subscribers the opportunity to establish extensive networks.[495] Within these networks one or two pedophile offenders or child pornographers will often assume leadership roles.[496] These individuals will coordinate the conversations and activities with other members of the networks.[497]

Subscribers may identify themselves using a first name and will identify the children with whom they are currently sexually involved.[498] The vast network which may develop enables pedophile offenders who live hundreds of miles apart to communicate about contact with a child known to both.[499] During these computerized conversations the offender may describe his actual and imagined sexual exploits with children.

Investigators have discovered that pedophile offenders use personal computer communications to establish contacts and as sources for the exchange or sale of child pornography.[500] The computer user, after establishing a secure relationship with another subscriber, will arrange for materials to be sent through the mail.[501] The subscribers will identify and describe the types of materials they seek. Respondents will then transmit the materials to the designated address.

---

487. See, C. Hix, *Male Model*, (1979), pp. 1985–86. (In answer to the question "Would you advise anyone to do nude modeling as a steppingstone into a legitimate career?" porn star Jack ✂ said, "Absolutely not. There are a lot of companies, film companies as well, that won't hire you if you have done nude modelling whether it was for *Playgirl* or *Playboy* or whatever." *Id.*, p. 186.)

488. *Sexual Offences Against Children, supra* note 473, (1984), pp. 1198–99; *Children of the Night supra* note 473, pp. 68–69 (1985) (fourteen of fifty-four juvenile prostitutes for whom information was available had been photographed for commercial photography).

489. *Huckleberry Study*, p. 34; *Sexual Offences Against Children, supra* note 473, pp. 992–93. These studies indicate that about one in six female prostitutes under age twenty-one had been physically coerced into their roles.

490. Miami Hearing, Vol. I, Paul Hartman, p. 105.

491. *Id.*, p. 106.

492. *Id.*, p. 106–07.

493. *Id.*, p. 108–10.

494. During his testimony before the Commission, Postal Inspector Paul Hartman stated, ". . . I accessed a computerized bulletin board and found a message rather casually displayed proclaiming another subscriber's interest in photographs of teen and preteen children." *Id.*, p. 108.

495. *Id.*, p. 109.

496. *Id.*, p. 111.

497. *Id.*

498. *Id.*

499. *Id.* 111–12.

500. *Id.*, p. 111.

501. *Id.*, pp. 108–09.

Pedophile offenders and child pornographers may also use personal computer services to identify particular children who can be used in making child pornography.[502] The subscribers may describe the child physically and give a location where the child may be found.[503]

The technologically complex computer systems and networks operated by pedophile offenders and their multijurisdictional nature should prompt federal interest and substantiate jurisdiction.[504] Each of these systems uses an interstate common carrier, the telephone, as its communication medium. The informa-

502. *Id.*, p. 111.

503. *Id.*

504. Hearings before the Senate Judiciary Committee, Subcommittee on Juvenile Justice, Oct. 1, 1985, p. 4; Senator Paul S. Trible, Jr. (R-Va.), and Senator Jeremiah Denton (R-Ala.) have introduced Senate Bill 1305 to amend 18 U.S.C. sections 1462 and 2252 to prohibit the use of computers for the interstate or foreign dissemination of obscene material, child pornography and advertisements for the same and information about minors which can be used for facilitating, encouraging, offering or soliciting sexually explicit conduct with a minor. The legislation provides:

BILL

"To amend title 18, United States Code, to establish criminal penalties for the transmission by computer of obscene matter, or by computer or other means, of matter pertaining to the sexual exploitation of children, and for other purposes.

Be it enacted by the Senate and House of Representatives of the United States of America in Congress assembled. That this Act may be cited as the "Computer Pornography and Child Exploitation Prevention Act of 1985".

Sec. 2 Section 1462 of Title 18, United States Code is amended by—

1. Inserting after subsection (c) the following:

"(d) any obscene, lewd, lascivious, or filthy writing, description, picture, or other matter entered, stored, or transmitted by or in a computer; or "Whoever knowingly owns, offers, provides, or operates any computer program or service is being used to transmit in interstate or foreign commerce any matter the carriage of which is herein made unlawful; or" and

2. inserting at the end thereof the following:

"For purposes of this section—

1. the term 'computer' means an electronic magnetic, optical, electrochemical, or other high-speed data processing device performing logical, arithmetic, or storage functions, and includes any data storage facility or communications facility directly related to or operating in conjunction with such device;

2. the term 'computer program' means an instruction or statement or a series of instructions or statements in a form acceptable to a computer which permits the functioning of a computer system in a manner designed to provide appropriate products from such computer system:

3. the term 'computer service' includes computer time, data processing, and storage function; and

4. the term 'computer system' means a set of related connected, or unconnected computers, computer equipment, devices, and software."

c. Any person who knowingly enters into or transmits by means of computer, or makes, prints, publishes, or reproduces by other means, or knowingly causes or allows to be entered into or transmitted by means of compute, or made, printed, published, or reproduced by other means—

1. any notice, statement or advertisement, or

2. any minor's name, telephone number, place of residence, physical characteristics, or other descriptive or identifying information.

For purposes of facilitating, encouraging, offering, or soliciting sexually explicit conduct of or with any minor, or the visual depiction of such conduct, shall by punished as provided in subsection (d) of this section, if such persons knows or has reason to know that such notice, statement, advertisement, or descriptive or identifying information will be transported in interstate or foreign commerce or mailed, or if such information has actually been transported in interstate or foreign commerce or mailed."

Sec. 4 Section 2252 of Title 18, United States Code, is amended—

tion about these minors is routinely conveyed between or among various states.

A recent example occurred in ✂
✂ where authorities discovered a computer network known as the "Gay Teen Conference" which was operated by a local man. The network could be reached by any computer operator who obtained a special password and it contained descriptions and depictions of various homosexual acts. The operator of "Gay Teen Conference" also operated a religious computer bulletin board known as "Ministry Bulletin Board." A computer operator was able to obtain the password for "Gay Teen Conference" by contacting the "Ministry Bulletin Board."[505] The proposed legislation would provide a useful law enforcement tool in this area of serious concern.

RECOMMENDATION 40:

Congress should amend the Child Protection

Act forfeiture section to include a provision which authorizes the Postal Inspection Service to conduct forfeiture actions.

Discussion

The United States Postal Inspection Service is the investigative arm of the United States Postal Service.[506] It has investigative responsibilities over all criminal violations of federal law relating to the Postal Service including the child pornography laws.[507]

The most common method of circulating child pornography has traditionally been through the mail.[508] The mail provides a clandestine and anonymous form of communication for both parties.[509]

The efforts of the Postal Inspection Service in the investigation of child pornography would be greatly enhanced through an amendment to the Child Protection Act permitting the Postal Inspection Service to engage in forfeitures.[510]

---

505. *Seminary Graduate Charge in Porno Computer Network*, The Fayetteville (N.C.) Times, Feb. 7, (1986), p. 14B.
506. Washington, D.C., Hearing, Vol. I, Charles Clauson, p. 135.
507. Postal Crimes fall within two broad categories: Criminal Acts (1) against the postal service or its employees, such as armed robberies, burglaries or theft of mail, and (2) misuse of the postal system such as the mailing of bombs, use of the mails to distribute pornography. *Id.*
508. Washington, D.C., Hearing, Vol. 1, Daniel Mihalko, pp. 145–146.
509. *Id.*, p. 146.

---

510. The amendment should be as follows:

To amend the Child Protection Act of 1984 to authorize the Postal Service to conduct civil administrative seizures and forfeitures under the Act, and for other purposes.

Sec. 1. Subsection (b) of section 2254 of title 18 United States Code, is amended by inserting "or the Postal Service" after "the Attorney General."

---

1. in subsection (a) by striking out "subsection (b)" and inserting in lieu thereof "subsection (c)"

2. by redesignating subsection (b) as subsection (c);

3. by inserting after subsection (a) the following new subsection:

"(b)Any person who knowingly enters into or transmits by means of computer, or makes, prints, publishes, or reproduces by other means, or knowingly causes or allows to be entered into or transmitted by means of computer, or made, printed, published, or reproduced by other means any notice, statement, or advertisement to buy, sell, receive, exchange, or disseminate any visual depiction, if—
"1. the producing of such visual depiction involves the use of a minor engaging in sexually explicit conduct; and
2. such visual depiction is of such conduct;

shall be punished as provided under subsection (c), of this section, if such person knows or has reason to know that such notice, statement, or advertisement will be transported in interstate or foreign commerce or mailed, or if such notice, statement, or advertisement has actually been transported in interstate or foreign commerce or mailed."

Sec. 5, Section 2255 of Title 18, United States Code is amended by adding at the end thereof the following new paragraph:
"(5) 'computer' means an electronic, magnetic, optical, electrochemical, or other high-speed data processing device performing logical, arithmetic, or storage function, and includes any data storage facility directly related to or operating in conjunction with such device."

Since 1984 there has been an increased enforcement effort against child pornography. From January 1, 1978, to May 21, 1984, only 69 defendants were indicted for child pornography violations.[511] From May 21, 1984, to June 1985, there were 103 defendants indicted for child pornography violations.[512]

In 1984 the Postal Inspection Service spent 50,000 hours and completed 168 pornography investigations which resulted in 69 arrests.[513] During the first eight months of 1985 the Service spent 36,000 hours and completed 99 investigations.[514] These efforts resulted in 114 arrests.[515] In June 1985 there were over 200 open Postal Service investigations of potential child pornography violations.[516]

Under current federal law the Postal Inspection Service is excluded from participation in forfeiture actions. The forfeiture provision would enable inspectors the opportunity to recover items of value which were used in or derived from illegal activities. This provision should be structured to assist in making the Postal Inspection Service investigations self-supporting and assist in defraying the cost of subsequent prosecutions as well as removing resources from the hands of offenders.

RECOMMENDATION 41:

Congress should amend 18 U.S.C. S2255 to define the term "Visual Depiction" and include undeveloped film in that definition.

Discussion

The Child Protection Act prohibits the transportation of certain sexually explicit visual depictions. The predecessor to the present Act specifically defined visual depictions. The language of the current Act has been used successfully by defense attorneys to exclude undeveloped film that has been legally seized.[517] In an effort to curb the continued exploitation of children, it is necessary to define the term "visual depictions" to include images contained on rolls of undeveloped film, video tape and sketches, drawings or paintings of actual persons.[518] This amendment will afford United States Attorneys the opportunity to bring an indictment under the Child Protection Act for offenses depicted on film undeveloped while under the control of an offender.

The current statute creates a dilemma for law enforcement agents and prosecutors in the case of undeveloped film. If the indictment is brought while film if yet to be developed the depictions contained on the undeveloped film are not subject to prosecution. If the film is allowed to remain in the hands of the offender until developed it is virtually impossible to prevent the pictures from entering circulation which is the very harm sought to be eliminated. This amendment would end the dilemma and enable the prosecution of child pornography contained on undeveloped film possessed by the offender.

RECOMMENDATION 42:

Congress should enact legislation providing financial incentives for the states to initiate task forces on child pornography and related cases.

---

511. Chicago Hearing, Vol. II, James S. Reynolds, p. 268.
512. Id.
513. Washington, D.C., Hearing, Vol. I, Jack Swagerty, p. 140.
514. Id.
515. Id.
516. Id.
517. See, Letter from Joyce A. Karlin to Henry E. Hudson (Dec. 20, 1985).
518. Id.

Sec. 2 Section 2003(b) of title 39, United States Code, is amended—

1. in paragraph (b) (5) by striking out "and";

2. in paragraph (b) (6) by striking out the period at the end and inserting in lieu thereof a semicolon and "and";

3. by inserting at the end of subsection (b) the following new paragraph: "(7) amounts from any civil administrative forfeiture conducted by the Postal Service"; and

4. by inserting in the first sentence of paragraph (e) (1), immediately following the word "title" the first time it appears, the following: "including expenses incurred in the conduct of seizures, forfeitures and disposal of forfeited property pursuant to title 18.

Discussion

The responsibility for financial assistance for a task force program does not lie solely with the federal government, but the program should be the product of a coordinated financial effort between federal and state governments.[519] Federal programs and funding should reward state governments which assume their proper role in creating the task forces described below.

The task forces would consist of experts from different fields including the judiciary, law enforcement agents, and health professionals who would be charged with recom-

mending and implementing changes in the court system and methods to more effectively handle cases of child abuse and exploitation which result from the production and use of child pornography. Upon implementation of such task forces, federal funds would be provided to a state. Federal assistance of this nature would enable states to the task force approach more affectively and economically.

Enabling legislation should provide grants to state governments to establish, develop, implement or operate programs directed toward the treatment and prevention of child sexual abuse related to child pornography.[520]

---

519. This Commission does not encourage or promote the concept of federal funding of programs which are properly within the responsibility of state and local governments. The importance of this program, however, calls for a coordinated effort and an initial incentive plan.

520. Senator Paula Hawkins (R-Fla.) has introduced the Children's Justice Act which attempts to facilitate investigations and prevention of child sexual abuse. The bill provides:

SHORT TITLE

SECTION 1. This Act may be cited as the "Children's Justice Act"

CHILDREN'S JUSTICE GRANT

SEC. 2. Section 4 of the Child Abuse Prevention and Treatment Act is amended by—

1. redesignating subsection (d), (e), (f), the first time such subsection appears, and (f), the second time such subsection appears, as subsection (e), (f), (g), and (h), respectively; and

2. inserting after subsection (c) the following:

"d. 1. In addition to grants made to States under subsection (b), the Secretary is authorized to make grants to States for the purpose of assisting States in the developing, establishing, operating, or implementing programs or procedures for—

"A. handling child abuse cases, especially child sexual abuse cases, in a manner which reduces the trauma to child victims;

"B. improving the chances of successful prosecution or legal action against individuals who abuse children, especially individuals who sexually abuse children; or

"C. improving procedures for protecting children from abuse,

in accordance with the eligibility requirements of this subsection. Grants under this subsection may be made to the State agency which administers funds received under subsection (a) or to an appropriate statewide law enforcement agency which has developed a child abuse program which meets the requirements of paragraph (2). The determination as to which agency of a State may apply for a grant pursuant to the preceding sentence shall be made by the chief executive officer of such State.

"2. A. In order for a State to qualify for assistance under this subsection, such State shall, except as provided in subparagraphs (B) and (C)—

"i. establish a multidisciplinary task force as provided in paragraph (3); and

"ii. adopt reforms recommended by the multidisciplinary task force in each of the three categories provided in subparagraphs, (B), (C), and (D) of paragraph (3).

For purposes of clause (ii), reforms may include proof that the State has made substantial improvement in implementing or enforcing State laws or administrative practices in effect on the date of enactment of the Children's Justice Act as recommended by the task force of such State under paragraph (3).

"B. If the Secretary determines, at the request of any State on the basis of information submitted by the State that such State—

"i. has established a multidisciplinary task force within the 3 years prior to the enactment of the Children's Justice Act with substantially the same functions as the multidisciplinary task force provided for under this subsection; and

"ii. is making satisfactory progress toward developing, establishing, operating or implementing the programs or procedures in each of the three categories provided in subparagraphs (B), (C), and (D) of paragraph (#) and will continue to do so,

then such State shall not be required to meet the requirements of Subparagraph (A).

"C. A State may adopt reformed recommended by the task force of such State in less than all three of the categories provided in subparagraphs (B), (C), and (D) of paragraph (3), but in the event that a State fails to adopt any recommendation in a category the State shall submit to the Secretary a detailed explanation of the reasons for the State not planning to carry out any such omitted recommendation.

"3. A. Each State desiring to receive a grant under this subsection shall establish a multidisciplinary task force on children's justice composed of professionals experienced in the criminal justice system and its operation relating to issues of child abuse. The task force shall include representatives of the law enforcement community, judicial and legal officers including representatives of the prosecution and the defense, child protective services, child advocates, health and mental health professionals, and parents. Each State task force shall, for fiscal year 1987, review, analyze, and make recommendations for reforms needed to improve the response of such State to child abuse cases in each of the categories described in subparagraphs (B), (C), and (D).

"B. A State shall provide for the handling of child abuse cases, especially child sexual abuse cases, in a manner which reduces the trauma to the child victim. Administrative procedures consistent with the reduction of trauma may include—

"i. the establishment of interdisciplinary teams of child abuse professionals such as law enforcement officers, child protective service workers, prosecutors, child's advocates, mental health professionals, and medical personnel for handling child abuse cases;

"ii. coordinated court proceedings for handling intrafamily child abuse; or

"iii. providing for specialized training of law enforcement, legal, judicial, and child welfare personnel to deal with child abuse victims and their families.

"C. A State shall establish reforms designed to improve the chances of successful prosecution or legal action against individuals who abuse children, especially individuals who sexually abuse children. Such reforms may include—

"i strengthening the State definition of child sexual abuse;

"ii. modifications of certain evidentiary restrictions such as the corroboration requirement and the qualification of child abuse victims as witnesses to allow for the age of child abuse victims; or

"iii. establishing procedures for the closed-circuit televising or videotaping of victim's testimony under circumstances which ensure procedural fairness while minimizing the trauma to the child abuse victim, especially child sexual abuse victim.

"D. In order to improve procedures to protect children from abuse, especially sexual abuse, a State shall establish administrative reforms by law or, if possible, pursuant to law by administrative action, such as—

"i. providing a guardian ad litem who is assigned to make an independent investigation and report to the court on recommendations regarding what action should be taken that would be in the best interests of the child;

"ii. granting courts authority to grant civil protection orders to protect children from further abuse, or

"iii. providing treatment programs for the individual who abuses children, especially the individual who sexually abuses children, and the abused child.

"4. A grant authorized by this subsection may be made by the Secretary upon application which is made at such time or times and contains or is accompanied by such information as the Secretary may prescribe. Each such application shall—

"A. contain such assurances as may be necessary to evidence compliance with paragraphs (2) and (3);

"B. contain assurances that the State will comply with the requirements of paragraph (2)(A)(ii) during the fiscal year for which the grant is made; and

"C. provide for making such reports, in such form and containing such information as the Secretary may require to carry out his functions under this subsection, and for keeping such records and for affording such access thereto as the Secretary may find necessary to assure the correctness and verification of such reports.

"5. A. In order to assist the States in developing effective approaches to achieve the objectives set forth in paragraph (1), the Secretary, through the National Center on Child Abuse and Neglect established pursuant to section 2(a), shall—

"i. compile, analyze, publish, and disseminate to each State a summary, including an evaluation of the effectiveness or lack thereof, of approaches being utilized, developed, or proposed with respect to improving the investigation and prosecution of child sexual abuse cases in a manner which reduces the trauma to the child victim along with such other materials or information as may be helpful to the States in developing or implementing programs or procedures to satisfy the requirements of this subsection;

"ii. develop and disseminate to appropriate State and officials model training materials and procedures to help ensure that all law enforcement, legal, judicial, and child welfare personnel are adequately trained to deal with child sexual abuse victims; and

"iii. provide for the support of research projects to assist in identifying effective approaches to achieving the objectives of this subsection.

"B. Not later than two years after the date fund are obligated under section 5(b) for the first fiscal year, the Secretary shall—

"I. review and evaluate the effectiveness of the activities carried out with such funds in achieving the objectives of this subsection; and

"ii. report to the appropriate committees of the Congress on the results of such review and evaluation and on the steps taken by the Secretary, through the National Center on Child Abuse and Neglect Center, to assist the States in achieving such objectives.

"C. The summary, information, and materials required under subparagraph (A) shall be made available to appropriate State officials not later than 180 days after the date of the enactment of the Children's Justice Act."

AUTHORIZATION

SEC. 3. Section 5 of the Child Abuse Prevention Treatment Act is amended by—

1. inserting "(a)" after "Sec. 5"; and

2. inserting at the end thereof the following:

"b. There are authorized to be appropriated $12,000,000 for each of the fiscal years 1987 and 1988 for the purposes of making grants under subsection (d) of section 4."

COORDINATION OF FEDERAL PROGRAMS INVOLVING CHILD ABUSE

SEC. 4. Section 7 of the Child Abuse Prevention and Treatment Act is amended by—

1. inserting "(a)" after "Sec. 7."; and

2. inserting at the end thereof the following:

"b. 1. Within 180 days of the date of enactment of the Children's Justice Act and every 6 months thereafter, the Attorney General, the Secretary of Health and Human Services, Secretary of Education, and the head of any other agency or department designated by the President, or their designees, responsible for programs involving child abuse prevention and treatment shall meet for the purpose of coordinating such programs in order to—

"A. prevent the overlap of such programs and the resulting waste of resources; and

"B. assure that such programs effectively address all aspects of the child abuse problem.

"2. Within one year of the date of the enactment of the Children's Justice Act and annually thereafter, the Secretary of Health and Human Services shall report to Congress with respect to the actions carried out by agencies and departments of the United States for the purpose of coordinating programs involving child abuse prevention and treatment as provided in paragraph (1)."

The programs should handle child sexual abuse cases resulting from the production of child pornography in a manner which reduces the trauma for the victims and the programs should implement procedures which lead to an increase in successful prosecutions against pornographers who sexually abuse children. The program should also present methods of protecting children from the sexual abuse associated with children pornography and related offenses. Many states undoubtedly will recognize the merit of this program and will take the initiative in implementing these procedures.

Congressional action should also address the need for an effective information network which is essential to law enforcement and social service agencies. The information should be assembled for immediate access to assist law enforcement officers as they proceed with a child pornography or related case. This information network should have specific connections with the Uniform Crime Reporting System operated by the Federal Bureau of Investigation. This type of legislation would facilitate the investigation of child sexual abuse and child pornography cases and would lead to effective methods to curb the flow of child pornography and the continued sexual abuse of children.[521]

RECOMMENDATION 43:
Congress should enact legislation to make the acts of child selling or child purchasing, for the production of sexually explicit visual depictions, a felony.

Discussion

Federal prosecutors have been frustrated in their attempts to convict child buyers under the existing laws because purchasing or selling a child is not presently a crime.[522] In one case involving the sale of children for use in the production of pornography the only resort was for the Assistant United States Attorney to prosecute the offender for an immigration violation.[523]

---

521. This data base should be coordinated with the information system recommended to law enforcement agencies.
522. Miami Hearing, Vol. II, Joyce Karlin, p. 170.
523. Id.

MODIFICATION OF FBI OFFENSE CLASSIFICATION SYSTEM

Sec. 5. The Attorney General shall modify the classification system used by the National Crime Information Center in its Interstate Identification Index, and by the Identification Division of the Federal Bureau of Investigation in its Criminal File, and its Uniform Crime Reporting System with respect to offenses involving sexual exploitation of children by—

1. including in the description of such offenses by the age of the victim and the relationship of the victim to the offenders; and

2. classifying such offenses by using a uniform definition of a child.

AMENDMENT TO PUBLIC HEALTH SERVICE ACT

Sec. 6 a. Section 523 of the Public Health Service Act (42 U.S.C. 290dd-3) is amended—

1. by striking out "subsection (e)" in subsection (a) and inserting in lieu thereof "subsections (e) and (i); and

2. by adding at the end the following new subsection:

"i. Nothing in this section shall be construed to supersede the application of State and local requirements for the reporting of incidents of suspected child abuse to the appropriate State or local authorities."

b. Section 527 of such Act (42 U.S.C. 290cc-3) is amended—

1. by striking out "subsection (e) in subsection(a) and inserting in lieu thereof "subsections (e) and (i)"; and

2. by adding at the end the following new subsection:

Amend the title so as to read "A bill to amend the Child Abuse Prevention and Treatment Act to establish a program to encourage States to enact child protection reforms which are designed to improve legal and administrative proceedings regarding the investigation and prosecution of the child abuse cases, especially child sexual abuse cases."

Specific legislation would provide additional protection for children and curb the production and distribution of child pornography. Federal prosecutors would have an additional tool available to further the goal of child protection.

RECOMMENDATIONS FOR STATE LEGISLATION

RECOMMENDATION 44:
State legislatures should amend, if necessary, child pornography statutes to include forfeiture provisions.

For a general discussion of the use of forfeiture provisions, see, Chapter 13.

RECOMMENDATION 45:
State legislatures should amend laws, where necessary, to make the knowing possession of child pornography, a felony.

Discussion

The United States Supreme Court has called child pornography "a serious national problem."[524] In *New York v.Ferber*, the Court said that child pornography constitutes a permanent record of the children's participation in sexual activity, and the circulation of the pornography exacerbates the harm to the children. If the sexual abuse of children in pornography is to be curtailed the production and distribution network must be eliminated.[525]

Investigators have identified several uses of child pornography. The first use by pedophiles is for sexual arousal and gratification.[526] While some pedophiles only collect child pornography and fantasize through it, many have used it as a device to aid in the production of their own child pornography.

Child pornography is often used as part of a method of seducing child victims.[527] A child who is reluctant to engage in sexual activity with an adult or to pose for sexually explicit photos can sometimes be convinced by viewing other children having "fun" participating in the activity.[528] From a very early age children are taught to respect and believe material contained in books and will thus have the same beliefs about child pornography.[529]

A pedophile offender will use child pornography in which the children appear to be having a good time.[530] The offender uses this material to lower the inhibitions of the child and entice him or her into a desired activity. Children who view this material are also subject to a certain amount of peer pressure as they see other children engaged in the activity.

Child pornography is also used to illustrate the activities in which the pedophile wishes a child to engage.[531] In such instances a pedophile offender shows the child the pornography and asks the child to imitate the pictures.

Pornographic depictions of a child may be used to blackmail the child.[532] The pedophile offender will use the pictures to intimidate the child. The pedophile offender will threaten the child with showing the pictures to others if the child does not cooperate.

Child pornography is also seen as a valuable commodity among pedophiles. Visual depictions may be traded or sold between collectors.[533] This subjects a child to repeated victimization by countless numbers of pedophiles and makes the child the object of the pedophile's sexual fantasies.[534] Child pornography which may have originated as a homemade item may eventually by sold to a commercial child pornography publication.[535]

---

524. New York v. Ferber, 458. U.S., (1982), pp. 747, 749.
525. Id., pp. 759–60.
526. K. Lanning, Collectors, in Child Pornography and Sex Rings, (A. Wolbert Burgess ed. 1984), p. 86.
527. Id.
528. U.S. Department of Justice, Federal Bureau of Investigation, Child Molesting: A Behavioral Analysis for Law Enforcement, (1986), p. 61.
529. Id.
530. Id.
531. Child pornography magazines frequently include pictures of children viewing child pornography and replicating the poses or scenes depicted therein. Miami Hearing, Vol. I, R.P. "Toby" Tyler, p. 176A4.
532. Miami Hearing, Vol. II, Paul Der Ohannesian II, p. 51; See also, K. Lanning, Collectors, in Child Pornography and Sex Rings, (A. Wolbert Burgess ed. 1984), p. 86.
533. K. Lanning, Collectors, in Child Pornography and Sex Rings, A. Wolbert Burgess ed. 1984), p. 86.
534. Id.
535. Id.

Child pornography has a life of its own. It is a permanent record of the victimization and sexual abuse of the child.[536] The depictions are timeless and may be distributed and circulated throughout the world for years after they are initially created. Each time the pornography is exchanged the children involved are victimized again.[537]

The harms to children from child pornography which the Supreme Court outlined in New York v. Ferber occur as a result of the existence of the material itself.[538] The enactment of criminal penalties for the possession of child pornography is essential if these harms are to be effectively curtailed.

Several states have recently recognized the inherent harm in child pornography and have enacted legislation prohibiting the possession of such material.[539] Only recently has this type of legislation met any constitutional challenge.[540] This challenge has been premised on the Supreme Court's ruling in Stanley v. Georgia.[541]

In Stanley, police executed a search warrant on the defendant's residence seeking evidence of a suspected bookmaking operation.[542] They located three reels of eight millimeter film in a desk drawer and upon viewing the films, they charged the defendant with possession of obscene matter.[543] He was convicted before a jury.[544] The Supreme Court reversed the conviction and held that "the mere private possession of obscene matter cannot constitutionally be made a crime."[545]

The first constitutional challenge to a state statute prohibiting the possession of child pornography came on December 1, 1985. The first appellate district in Ohio found the state law prohibiting possession of child pornography[546] to be unconstitutional.[547] The analysis used in invalidating the statute was based upon the rationale of Stanley v. Georgia.[548] The Ohio statute was declared unconstitutional because the state could not punish the mere private possession of magazines "which depicted minors . . . engaging in sexual activ-

---

536. Miami Hearing, Vol. I, William Dworin, p. 30.

537. Washington, D.C., Vol. II, John, pp. 47–48.

538. 458 U.S., (1982), p. 747.

539. See, e.g., "Sexual exploitation of a minor; classification A. A person commits sexual exploitation of a minor by knowingly:

    1. Recording, filming, photographing, developing or duplicating any visual or print medium in which minors are engaged in sexual conduct.

    2. Distributing, transporting, exhibiting, receiving, selling, purchasing, possessing or exchanging any visual or print medium in which minors are engaged in sexual conduct.

    B. Sexual exploitation of a minor is a class 2 felony." Ariz. Rev. Stat. Ann. S13–3553(1984);

    "A person who has in possession a photographic representation of sexual conduct which involves a minor, knowing or with reasons to know its content and character and that an actor or photographic subject in it, is guilty of a gross misdemeanor." Minn. Stat. S617.247(1984);

    "A person who knowingly and willfully has in his possession any film, photograph or other visual presentation depicting minors engaging in or simulating, or assisting others to engage in or simulate sexual conduct is guilty of a misdemeanor." Nev. Rev. Stat. S200.730(1984);

    "A. No person, with knowledge of the character of the material or performance involved, shall do any of the following:

    5. Possess or control any obscene material, that has a minor as one of its participants. With purpose to violate division (A)(2) or (4) of this section." Ohio Rev. Code Ann. S2907.321(1984).

540. Ohio v. Meadows, No. 84 CRB 25585, Slip op. (1st Dist. Dec. 18, 1985) cert. granted (Ohio Apr. 9, 1986) (No. 86–233).

541. 394 U.S., (1969), p. 557.

542. Id. p. 558.

543. Id.

544. Id. pp. 558–59.

545. Id. p. 559.

546. R.C. 2907.321(a)(5) (1985).

547. Ohio v. Meadows, No. 84 CRB 25585, Slip op. (1st Dist. Dec. 18, 1985), cert. granted, (Ohio Apr. 9, 1986) (No. 86–233).

548. 395 U.S., (1969), p. 557.

ity."[549] *New York v. Ferber*[550] was distinguished on the grounds that it dealt with distribution and not mere possession of child pornography.[551] In finding the statute unconstitutional the Ohio court placed great significance on the language in *Stanley* where the Supreme Court rejected the contention by the state of Georgia that to eliminate the traffic in obscenity, it is necessary to bar mere private possession by an individual.[552]

In *United States v. Miller*,[553] the United States Court of Appeals for the Eleventh Circuit recently upheld the conviction of a defendant who received child pornography from Europe through the mail.[554] The defendant contended that 18 U.S.C. S2252 (a)(a) violated [555] his right to privacy and relied on *Stanley* for his claim that the statute was unconstitutional.[556] The court rejected the defendant's argument that the statute only applies to individuals who intend to distribute child pornography.[557] However, in considering the privacy issue, the court said "prior decisions on the issue of the right to possess obscene materials are controlling in our analysis of this case.[558]

The court relied on several obscenity decisions in which the Supreme Court rejected the argument that *Stanley* created a right to import or receive obscene materials for private use.[559] The court concluded that *Stanley* cannot be expanded to create a right to receive child pornography through the mail.[560]

Any reliance on the rationale of *Stanley* or other obscenity cases with respect to a prohibition against the possession of child pornography is misplaced. *Stanley* upheld an individual's right to privately possess ob-

scene material.[561] The prevailing obscenity standard at the time of the *Stanley* decision was contained in *Roth v. United States*.[562] *Roth* has since been modified in most jurisdictions by *Miller v. California*.[563]

In *New York v. Ferber*,[564] the Supreme Court upheld a New York law prohibiting the promotion of sexually explicit depictions of children that were not obscene under *Miller*.[565] In *Ferber*, the Court reasoned that the *Miller* standard, like all general definitions of what may be banned as obscene, does not reflect the state's particular and more compelling interest in prosecuting those who promote the sexual exploitation of children. The question under the *Miller* test of whether a work, taken as a whole, appeals to the prurient interest of the average person bears no connection to the issue of whether a child has been physically or psychologically harmed in the production of the work. Similarly, a sexually explicit depiction need not be "patently offensive" in order to have sexually exploited a child through its production. In addition, a work which, taken as a whole, contains serious literary, artistic, political or scientific value may nevertheless embody the most grievous form of child pornography. The Supreme Court reasoned in *Ferber*, "It is irrelevant to the child [who has been abused] whether or not the material . . . has a literary, artistic, political or social value. Memorandum of Assemblyman Lasher in Support of S263.15. We therefore cannot conclude that the *Miller* standard is a satisfactory solution to the child pornography problem."[566]

Any analysis concerning the constitutionality of laws prohibiting the possession of

549. *Ohio v. Meadows*, No. 84 CRB 25585, Slip. op. (1st Dist. Dec. 18, 1985); *cert. granted*, (Ohio Apr. 9, 1986) No. 86–233).

550. 458 U.S. 747(1982).

551. *Ohio v. Meadows*, No. 84 CRB 25585, Slip. op. at 9 (1st Dist., Dec. 18, 1985); *cert. granted* (Ohio Apr. 9, 1986) (No. 86–233).

552. *Id.* at 7.

553. 776 F.2d 978 (11th Cir 1985), *cert. denied*. 54 U.S. L.W. 3698 (U.S. Apr. 22, 1986) (No. 85–1177).

554. *Id.*

555. This provision of the Child Protection Act provides penalties for any person who "knowingly receives or distributes any visual depiction . . ."

556. 776 F.2d, p. 980.

557. *Id.*, p. 979.

558. *Id.*, p. 980 n. 4.

559. *Id.* The court of appeals relied on *United States v. Reidel*, 402 U.S. 35191971); *United v. 12 200 Ft. Reels*, 413 U.S. 123(1973); *United States v. 37 Photographs*, 402 U.S. 363(1971); *United States v. Orito*, 413 U.S. 139(1973).

560. *Id.*, p. 981.

561. 394 U.S. p. 559.

562. 354 U.S., (1957), p. 476.

563. 413 U.S., (1973), p. 15.

564. 458 U.S., (1982), p. 747.

565. *Id.*, pp. 760–61.

566. *Id.*, p. 761.

child pornography should not be made as a parallel to obscenity statutes. The Supreme Court has clearly distinguished the standards to be applied to child pornography laws and adult obscenity statutes.[567]

The Supreme Court stated in Ferber that "the nature of the harm to be combatted requires that the state offense be limited to works that visually depict sexual conduct by children below a specified age."[568] The Court went on to clarify its statement by noting that "the distribution of descriptions or other depictions of sexual conduct, not otherwise obscene, which do not involve live performance or photographic or other visual reproduction of live performances, retains First Amendment protection."[569]

The obscenity precedent is clearly inapplicable to a challenge against a statute in which the offense described clearly involved visual depictions of children engaged in sexual activities.[570]

The rationale underlying the Supreme Court's ruling in Stanley is vastly different from that in Ferber. In Stanley, the Court upheld the defendant's right to "read or observe what he pleases—the right to satisfy his intellectual and emotional needs in the privacy of his own home . . . free from state inquiry into the contents of his library."[571] The Court also found, at that time, "little empirical basis" for the assertion made by the state of Georgia that "exposure to obscene materials may lead to deviant sexual behavior or crimes of sexual violence."[572] However, the Court added in a footnote:

What we have said in no way infringes upon the power of the State or Federal Government to make possession of other items, such as narcotics, firearms, or stolen goods, a crime. Our holding in the present case turns upon the Georgia statute's infringement of fundamental liberties protected by the First and Fourteenth Amendments. No First Amendment rights are involved in most statutes making mere possession criminal.

Nor do we mean to express any opinion on statutes making criminal possession of other types of printed, filmed, or recorded materials. See, e.g., 18 U.S.C. S793 (d), which makes criminal the otherwise lawful possession of materials which "the possessor has reason to believe could be used to the injury of the United States or to the advantage of any foreign nation . . ." In such cases, compelling reasons may exist for overriding the right of the individual to possess those materials.[573]

While Ferber admittedly dealt with a statute prohibiting the distribution of child pornography, the decision recognized compelling reasons for overriding the right of an individual to possess child pornography.[574] The Court found that "it is evidence beyond the need for elaboration that a state's interest in safeguarding the physical and psychological well-being of a minor is 'compelling.'[575] While the Court in Stanley found little evidence then existing that exposure to obscene materials may lead to deviant sexual behavior or crimes of violence,[576] the Court clearly states in Ferber that "the legislative judgment, as well as the judgment found in the relevant literature, is that the use of children as subjects of pornographic materials is harmful to the physiological, emotional, and mental health of the child."[577] Child pornography constitutes a permanent record of the sexual abuse of the child and the harm to the child is exacerbated by the circulation of the material.[578] The very existence of child pornography harms the children who are depicted. According to one child psychiatrist quoted in Ferber, "the victim's knowledge of publication of the visual material increases the emotional and psychic harm suffered by the child."[579] With respect to obscene materials in Stanley, the Court found the privacy rights of the individual to be the overriding

567. 458 U.S., (1982), p. 747.
568. Id., p. 764.
569. Id., pp. 764–65.
570. Ohio v. Meadows, supra note 540, p. 24; 18 U.S.C. S2252(a)(2).
571. 394 U.S., p. 565.
572. Id., p. 566. This Commission has found evidence of harm from exposure to pornography based upon evidence produced since the Stanley decision, See, Textual discussion of harms in Chapter 5.
573. Id., p. 568, n. 11.
574. Id., p. 568.
575. Id., p. 756–57.
576. 394 U.S., p. 566.
577. 458 U.S., p. 758.
578. Id., p. 759.
579. Id., p. 759, n. 10.

concern. In *Ferber,* however, the Court clearly found the harm suffered by minors to be of paramount importance. The focus of the protection constitutes a major distinction between these two landmark decisions. The *Ferber* Court's concern for minors included the consideration that when child pornography is produced and distributed, the *child's* privacy interests are violated.[580]

The Court in *Stanley* rejected the argument that prohibition of the possession of obscene materials is a necessary incident to statutory schemes prohibiting distribution.[581] In *Ferber,* the Court recognized that it may be difficult, if not impossible, to stop the sexual exploitation of children by pursuing only those who produce child pornography.[582] Citing the clandestine nature of the child pornography trade, the Court noted that "the only practical method of law enforcement may be to dry up the market for this material . . ."[583] The prohibition of the mere possession of child pornography is a necessary incident to "drying up the market" for a product the Supreme Court has found to be extremely harmful to the youth of the nation. Such laws are also entirely consistent with the objectives sought to be attained by the Court in *Ferber* and should not be confused with other considerations relevant in the obscenity law context.

RECOMMENDATION 46:

State legislatures should amend, if necessary, laws making the sexual abuse of children, through the production of sexually explicit visual depictions, a felony.

Discussion

The sexual exploitation of children is the basis for the production and distribution of child pornography.[584] The production and distribution of child pornography is done in a largely clandestine fashion which makes law enforcement efforts to curb the dissemination more difficult.[585]

The classification of an offense of the sexual abuse of children in connection with child pornography as a felony gives notice to child pornographers and child sexual abusers who produce child pornography that they will be dealt with in a serious manner. An offense classified as a felony receives more attention within the prosecutor's office than the same offense classified as a misdemeanor. The enhanced priority will undoubtedly lead to more effective enforcement and prosecution.

RECOMMENDATION 47:

State legislatures should enact legislation, if necessary, to make the conspiracy to produce, distribute, and give away, or exhibit any sexually explicit visual depictions of children or exchange or deliver children for such purposes a, felony.

Discussion

Individuals involved in the child pornography trade may often form networks with local, national and international connections.[586] A clergyman who operated a farm for wayward boys used the boys who lived on the farm to engage in sexual acts with sponsors of the farm. The sexual activities episodes were filmed and sold as souvenirs to the sponsors.[587]

In another circumstance, a Boy Scout troop of forty boys was created to provide sexual services to the adult men who accompanied them on outings. The troop leaders also filmed the activities.[588]

Pedophile offenders and child pornographers use such networks as a means to trade, exchange, and traffic in child pornography.[589] They may also use the contacts they make through this network to locate potential child victims.[590]

The existence of these networks of pedophile offenders and child pornographers along with the magnitude of the harm they may inflict makes it imperative that state legislatures act, where existing laws are defi-

---

580. *Id.,* p. 758, n. 9.
581. 394 U.S., p. 567.
582. 458 U.S., p. 760.
583. *Id.*
584. Miami Hearing, Vol. I. William Dworin, p. 30.
585. Washington, D.C., Hearing, Vol. I. Daniel Mihalko, p. 145.
586. Miami Hearing, Vol. II. Seth Goldstein, p. 285X6; During an investigation in Los Angeles California, police found a mailing list of 5,000 customers of child pornography distributor   ✂   Miami Hearing, Vol. II, Joyce Karlin, p. 149.
587. *Id.*
588. *Id.* at 285X18.
589. *Id.*
590. *Id.*

cient, to make the conspiracy to produce, distribute, give away or exhibit any sexually explicit visual depictions of children or to exchange or deliver children for such purpose a felony.

RECOMMENDATION 48:
State legislatures should amend, if necessary, child pornography laws, to create a felony offense for advertising, selling, purchasing, bartering, exchanging, giving or receiving information as to where sexually explicit materials depicting children can be found.

Discussion

Many people who produce and exchange child pornography have created intricate networks for information. They may join together for the purpose of trading children or trading information about the children.[591] Some pedophiles and child pornographers have formed associations which have national membership.[592]

Since child pornography is primarily a covert cottage industry, pedophiles who are child sexual abusers may use various underground publications or child pornography publications to place advertisements for children or child pornography.[593] Advertisements often are presented in coded language[594] or they may be explicit and direct.[595] The ability to easily obtain information regarding the location of children and child pornography allows pedophiles and child pornographers who collect child pornography to continue the exploitation of children.

Legislation is needed to prohibit the advertising, selling, purchasing, bartering, exchanging, given or receiving of information as to where children or child pornography may be found. The penalty for a violation of the new legislation should be a felony. Legislation directed at curbing the flow of child pornography and information related to its production and distribution will enable law enforcement agents to attack the methods of child sexual abusers.

It is well recognized that the advertisement of material which is illegal constitutionally may be prohibited.[596] Since child pornography is illegal, states may enact statutes to prohibit the advertising of such material. States may enact legislation which would regulate the exchange of this information and would assist in impeding the flow of child pornography. The Congress addressed this issue on an interstate level in the Child Protection Act of 1984.[597]

RECOMMENDATION 49:
State legislatures should amend, if necessary, laws to make the acts of child selling or child purchasing, for the production of sexually explicit visual depictions, a felony.

Discussion

Participants in international and local child sex tours provide children for pornography and prostitution.[598] Some of these sex rings use child members to recruit new members[599]

---

591. Washington, D.C. Hearing, Vol. I. Daniel Mihalko, pp. 147-48.
592. The North American Man-Love Boy Association is commonly referred to as NAMBLA. NAMBLA publishes the *Bulletin* and supports laws that would abolish the minimum age for consensual sexual acts. This group is recognized as an association of and for pedophiles. The Rene Guyon Society of which Tim O'Hara is founder and president, has the motto of "Sex before eight [years of age], or it's too late." PIE: Pedophile Information Exchange, has a worldwide newsletter which serves as a contact agency for pedophiles.
593. Miami Hearing, Vol. I. R.P. "Toby" Tyler, p. 176A5.
594. Coded advertisements may provide:

"Family man seeks other with similar interest." *Swing.* Issue 45, p. 18. Dawn Media, San Diego, CA (1982);

"Pretty mother with pretty daughters invites inquiries from gentlemen anywhere, who are interested in meeting us or in photography." *Lolita.* Issue 48; *Id.*

595. "Love them young and innocent! Will buy photos, magazines, video tapes of young girls or boys . . . ." (Display advertisement) *Wonderland: Newsletter of the Lewis Carroll Collectors Guild*, No. 6:6(1984). *Id.*
596. See, *Central Hudson Gas & Electric Corp. v. Public Utility Service Commission of New York*, 447 U.S., (1980), p. 557. In addressing the issue of regulating commercial speech, the Court formulated a four-part test:

At the outset, we must determine whether the expression is protected by the First Amendment. For commercial speech to come within that provision, it at least must concern lawful activity and not be misleading. Next, we ask whether the asserted governmental interest is substantial. If both inquiries yield positive answers, we must determine whether the regulation directly advanced the governmental interest asserted and whether it is not more extensive than is necessary to serve that interest. 447 U.S., p. 466.

597. 18 U.S.C. SS2251-2252(1985).
598. Miami Hearing, Vol. I. Kenneth Hermann, p. 119.
599. *Id.*

and involve adults using many different children.[600] Children are purchased or exchanged in the same way the resulting pornography is sold or traded.[601]

Children have been purchased from Mexico and the Dominican Republic.[602] Yakusa, an organized crime entity in Japan, is actively involved in the trading of children.[603] When these children are brought into this country they may be traded further, used in child pornography or tortured for sexual pleasure.[604] For example, a teacher in Los Angeles imported young boys from Guatemala and El Salvador for sexual activity.[605]

RECOMMENDATION 50:
State legislatures should amend laws, where necessary, to make child pornography in the possession of an alleged child sexual abuser which depicts that person engaged in sexual acts with a minor sufficient evidence of child molestation for use in the prosecuting that individual whether or not the child involved is found or is able to testify.

Discussion
Law enforcement officers and prosecutors often are unable to successfully obtain a conviction against an individual on a charge of child molestation because they are unable to locate the child.[606] An amendment to state statutes which recognizes visual depictions of the molestation as sufficient evidence of the molestation, if all other elements of the crime can be proven, will make current law enforcement efforts more effective.

Such visual depictions are nothing more than records of actual child molestation.[607] Law enforcement efforts should not be barred because the children cannot be identified or located.

In New York, law enforcement authorities located photographs of an adult male engaging in numerous sexual acts with children.[608]

The identity of the adult is known to the authorities, but they can take no action against him for those sexual offenses because the child depicted in the photographs cannot be identified.[609]

Police in Columbus, Ohio, seized photographs of an adult male engaged in sexual acts with two young girls aged nine and ten.[610] They could bring no charges for the child sexual abuse offense until the girls could be located.[611]

RECOMMENDATION 51:
State legislatures should amend laws, if necessary, to eliminate requirements that the prosecution identify or produce testimony from the child who is depicted if proof of age can otherwise be established.

Discussion
Prosecutors are often unable to produce the victim of child pornography to testify at trial as to his or her age.[612] The amendment would allow testimony from a third party as to the age of the child depicted. The testimony may come from relatives or friends of the child if the child is identified but he or she is not located. In addition the prosecution may use an expert witness to testify as to the age of the child based upon physiological characteristics.

The testimony based upon the depictions should be used only for proof of age. The depictions, when entered into evidence, should serve as the basis for this testimony from an expert or other qualified person as to the age of the child shown.

Prior to 1985 a child pornography prosecution in Maryland could not go forward unless the child depicted in the material was present to testify that he or she was under the age of sixteen at the time the pornography was produced.[613] Many cases were not prosecuted because this element of proof could not be met

---

600. *Id.*
601. *Id.*
602. *Id.* pp. 124–25.
603. *Id.* p. 131.
604. *Id.* p. 121.
605. *Id.* p. 132.
606. Miami Hearing, Vol. II. William Cassidy, pp. 201–02.
607. See, *New York v. Ferber*, 458 U.S., (1982), p. 747.
608. Miami Hearing, Vol. II, Paul Der Ohannesian, p. 64.
609. *Id.*
610. Miami Hearing, Vol. II, William Cassidy, pp. 201–02.
611. *Id.*
612. *Id.*, p. 204.
613. Miami Hearing, Vol. II. Alfred Danna, p. 283.

when the child victims could not be located.[614] The Maryland legislature enacted a law providing that of a child's age may be proved by:

1. personal inspection of the child.
2. oral testimony of age.
3. expert medical testimony.
4. observation of the child as depicted in the material.
5. any other method authorized by applicable law or rules of evidence.[615]

States may find the approach taken by the Maryland legislature an effective method to overcome the barriers associated with determining the age of a child pornography victim. This approach allows the use of several alternate forms of reliable evidence.

RECOMMENDATION 52:
State legislatures should enact or amend legislation, if necessary, which require photo finishing laboratories to report suspected child pornography.

Discussion

Pedophile offenders privately produce a great quantity of the child pornography.[616] Some child pornographers may have facilities in their homes to develop the photographs, but many producers must use commercial photo finishing laboratories.[617]

Effective law enforcement practices should include efforts to reach the photo finishing process. One Federal prosecutor told this Commission, ". . . there can be little doubt that photo finishers provide a key link in the chain of distribution of child pornography."[618] The photo finishers should be told clearly by law enforcement agencies the type of materials which are sought. The description may mirror the definition found in the Child Protection Act or their respective state laws.[619]

Photo finishers also should be clearly told what responsibilities they have as well as the sanctions they may face for neglect of duty.

In an attempt to address this problem the California legislature amended the Child Abuse Reporting Law.[620] The California law has resulted in an increased effectiveness in law enforcement efforts without a noticeable incidence of spurious reporting.

Although state and local law enforcement officials must be aware of the special problems associated with automated photo finishers these establishments should not be excused from compliance.

RECOMMENDATION 53:
State legislatures should amend or enact legislation, if necessary, to permit judges to impose a sentence of lifetime probation for convicted child pornographers and related offenders.

Discussion

Many people convicted of child pornography and related offenses present unique problems for the judicial and penal systems. The recidivist rate for pedophile offenders who act on their sexual desires is second only to exhibitionists.[621]

An effective method of balancing the needs of the offender and the need to protect society may be the use of a sentence of lifetime probation. The state legislatures may amend their sentencing statutes to provide for supervised as well as unsupervised probation.

This amendment would give judges and probation officers a tool to moniter convicted child pornographers who pose a specific threat to society. The availability of unsupervised probation may become an important tool in the event the offender repeats the crime or a similar offense. Although unsupervised, the probation still holds the threat of future incarceration and allows the state to retain jurisdiction over the person.

---

614. *Id.*
615. Miami Hearing, Vol. II. Alfred Danna, p. 284J.
616. Washington, D.C., Hearing, Vol. I. Daniel Mihalko, p. 145.
617. *Id.*
618. Chicago Hearing, Vol. II. Frederick Scullin, p. 44.
619. 18 U.S.C. S2252(1985).
620. The statute provides in part.

Any person who depicts a child in, or who knowingly develops, duplicates, prints, or exchanges, any film, photograph, videotape, negative or slide in which a child is engaged in an act of obscene sexual conduct, except for those activities by law enforcement and prosecution agencies and other persons described in subdivisions (c) and (e) of Section 311.3. Cal. Penal Code. S11165 (West 1985).

621. American Psychiatric Association, *Diagnostic and Statistical Manual of Mental Disorders* 271(3d ed. 1980).

RECOMMENDATIONS FOR FEDERAL LAW ENFORCEMENT AGENCIES

RECOMMENDATION 54:

The State Department, the United States Department of Justice, the United States Customs Service, the United States Postal Inspection Service, the Federal Bureau of Investigation and other Federal agencies should continue to work with other nations to detect and intercept child pornography.

Discussion

Child pornography and the sexual abuse of children has overwhelming international aspects. While some child pornography originates in Europe many of the children depicted are American citizens.[622] A pedophile offender will put together a collection of photos either for his personal use, or in direct response to solicitations by one or more pornography distributors. The photos are then sent to a commercial distributor where they are compiled into a commercial-type publication.[623]

The pedophile offender may reside anywhere in the world. The countries where consumers have been identified include the United States, Canada, United Kingdom, France, Italy, Federal Republic of Germany, Belgium, Sweden, Denmark, the Netherlands, Czechoslovakia, Poland, Saudi Arabia, Egypt, Thailand, the Philippines, Hong Kong, Singapore, Australia and Japan.

A commercial publication is distributed by mail throughout the world, in addition, photo sets are sold to individual consumers. In one instance, photos were sold in sets of twelve photographs for $100, forty photographs for $300, or six hundred negatives for $5,000.

In another instance, positive photographic images (slides) were sent to a consumer by COQ International. The positives were used to make negatives and the negatives used to print photo sets. The sets were then sold, along with photos of models recruited by the United States producers for fifteen to thirty-five dollars for a set of six to ten. The same producer also offered special photo sets, custom ordered by the consumer, for two hundred to four hundred dollars per set. He called the service "sponsor a model."

In one case, two special agents from the United States Customs Service corresponded with a distributor of child pornography photos from Bangkok. Evidence was purchased by the agents with the intent to forward it to the customs attache in Bangkok, Thailand, and to refer to the case to the Thai authorities. The Thais, however, preferred that the agents travel to Bangkok in the undercover capacities established in the correspondence. The agents would then purchase child pornography leading to an arrest.

While arrangements were being made for the agents to travel to Bangkok, it was discovered that the offender had been indicted in Detroit, Michigan, in 1981 for the distribution of child pornography.

A procedure for establishing undercover identities for agents to travel abroad was nonexistent. After much difficulty appropriate identities were established with Justice Department and State Department assistance.

The offender had been selling sets of photographs to his customers, packaged discretely in letter class mail. In his final letters to the agents before their departure for Bangkok, he offered to sell six hundred negatives for $5,000. The agents and the Thais decided to pursue this purchase. One agent posed as a distributor of child pornography and the other as a pedophile.

Upon meeting the offender, the agents were led through Bangkok to avoid surveillance, the offender checked the agents' passports to ascertain their identities, and to ensure that they lawfully entered Thailand. He turned over the final installment of the last photo set purchased by one of the agents, and arrangements were discussed for the purchase for the negatives, use of the children he had promised in his correspondence, and the availability of heroin and marijuana. A meeting was arranged for the following day.

The offender was subsequently arrested based on the evidence contained in the correspondence to the customs agent prior to the arrest. Agents discovered several volumes of photographs, hundreds of photos and negatives and paperback books, all depicting explicit sexual activity between adults and children in his apartment. In addition, ad-

---

622. Miami Hearing, Vol. I, R.P. "Toby" Tyler, pp. 156–57.
623. These commercial publications include *Lolitot*, and *Lolita*.

dress books, sexual paraphernalia, travel diaries, and a copy of his 1981 indictment in Detroit were also discovered.

The defendant has plead guilty to all counts, and is scheduled to be sentenced in Thailand.

Child pornography magazine publishers and filmmakers obtain photographs and movies of children from offenders and reprint them for commercial sale.[624] The United States is also the largest consumer of internationally produced child pornography.[625]

To break this circle of distribution, agencies empowered to interact with foreign countries should exercise their powers to curb the sexual exploitation of children.

These agencies face an initial hurdle caused by cultural differences and views of child sexuality. In contrast to the laws protecting children under the age of eighteen in the United States the age of majority in Northern Europe is generally sixteen.[626] In 1985 a bill was introduced before the Dutch parliament that would lower the age of sexual consent to twelve.

The State Department, the United States Department of Justice and the United States Customs Service should continue efforts to negotiate with foreign countries to curb the flow of child pornography. In the past, these efforts have taken the form of suggesting legislative reforms. Although legislation which would effectively combat child pornography is still pending in Denmark, a Danish judge recently found child pornography to be offensive to public decency.[627]

To supplement the broad diplomatic efforts of the State Department specific federal agencies should continue their efforts to control the distribution of child pornography.[628]

Because most of the commercial pornography is imported from European sources, much of the burden of intercepting this material falls on the United States Customs Service. The Customs Service has the authority to search persons and items at the borders[629] and Customs officers may detain and search

any person and property entering the United States without the necessity of a search warrant.[630]

The Customs Service has detected a wide variety of obscene and child pornography materials in the mails including materials which depict such acts as sado-masochism, urination, defecation and bestiality.[631]

In January 1985 an inter-agency task force of agents from the United States Postal Inspection Service, the United States Customs Service, Department of State and the Federal Bureau of Investigation visited several European source countries of child pornography. These nations included Denmark, Sweden and the Netherlands. The agencies sought the assistance of the foreign governments to prevent the distribution of child pornography.

The Commission applauds the efforts of these departments and agencies but encourages enhanced cooperation and detection efforts. A united effort is the only means to an effective and lasting remedy for the overwhelming child pornography problem. The agencies must continually increase their efforts to combat the flow of child pornography.

RECOMMENDATION 55:

The United States Department of Justice should direct the Law Enforcement Coordinating Committees to form task forces of dedicated and experienced investigators and prosecutors in major regions to combat child pornography.

Discussion

The Law Enforcement Coordinating Committees (LECCs), as fully discussed in the Recommendations to Law Enforcement Agencies, provide the basis for effective law enforcement efforts. In the area of child pornography violations, LECCs should use information and assistance available from drug and alcohol abuse programs and other social service agencies. The expertise available through the various social service agencies should be tapped to provide law enforcement agencies

---

624. *Id.*
625. *Id.*
626. Washington, D.C., Hearing, Vol. II, John Forbes, p. 278.
627. Washington D.C., Hearing, Vol. I, Daniel Harrington, p. 142.
628. The United States Custom Service should take a leadership role in these efforts. The Customs Service has resources and expertise to conduct international investigations. The Customs Service should take advantage of the resources of the United States Postal Service and the Department of Justice particularly in domestic matters.
629. Washington. D.C., Hearing, Vol. II, Richard Miller, p. 267.
630. *Id.*
631. *Id.*

with a completely effective enforcement effort.

RECOMMENDATION 56:

The Department of Justice or other appropriate Federal agency should initiate the creation of a data base which would serve as a resource network for Federal, State and Local law enforcement agencies to send and obtain information regarding child pornography trafficking.

Discussion

The United States Department of Justice or other appropriate federal agency should create a data base as a source of central and accessible information regarding child pornography. This data base should be integrated into the data base recommended in the Law Enforcement Chapter of this report.[632]

The data base should include photographs obtained from searches, photographs of missing or abandoned children, the names of defendants and their contacts. It should also include records of the declination of prosecution of any case and the reasons therefor. The data base will allow federal, state and local law enforcement officials to draw on information gathered nationwide. The data base should allow an agency to submit as well as retrieve information.

RECOMMENDATION 57:

Federal law enforcement agencies should develop and maintain continuous training programs for agents in techniques of child pornography investigations.

Discussion

The most important factor in the effective enforcement of child pornography and related child sexual abuse laws is well-trained law enforcement personnel. Each law enforcement agency should have at least one member of its staff who is specifically trained to investigate and apprehend individuals involved in child pornography and related cases. At least one officer should be trained and possess the expertise necessary to conduct a thorough child sexual exploitation investigation. This

training may be conducted through the Federal Law Enforcement Training Center.

Law enforcement officers who are assigned to a child pornography or related unit face additional emotional pressures because of the insidious nature of child pornography. Officers may be required to view significant quantities of child pornography or deal with young victims during the course of their investigations. Training programs should emphasize the special psychological needs of law enforcement officers and they should offer assistance to alleviate the emotional stress.

A second area which training programs should address is the alienation an officer may encounter from other law enforcement officers.[633] These officers often receive minimal assistance and virtually no emotional support from their peers. The training programs should be used to educate officers assigned to a child pornography or related unit as to the types of behavior they may encounter. In addition, all officers within a department or agency should be trained with an awareness toward the difficulties encountered by officers who are assigned to child pornography or related cases.

Designated personnel should be required to participate in continuous training programs. These continuing education programs may be conducted through the LECC.[634] These programs have generally resulted in an increased awareness of the problem of child pornography and its relationship to sexual abuse.[635]

RECOMMENDATION 58:

Federal law enforcement agencies should have personnel trained in child pornography investigation and when possible they should form specialized units for child sexual abuse and child pornography investigation.

Discussion

Agencies with large enough field offices in communities with adequate resources should include a specialized unit within the law enforcement agency to specifically investigate and related child pornography and related child sexual abuse cases. These trained

---

632. This data base also should use the resources of the Child Pornography and Protection Unit (CPPU) established by the United States Customs Service. This CPPU data base has been designed to serve as a resource network for federal, state and local law enforcement agencies to store and receive information.

633. New York Hearing, Vol. I, Carl Shoffler, pp. 277–28.

634. Miami Hearing, Vol. II, Paul Der Ohannesian, pp. 61–62.

635. Id.

agents in field offices will be able to actively investigate child pornography cases with an understanding of the particular local or regional problems. The specialized unit allows an officer to acquire and implement expertise in the area and enhance overall law enforcement efforts.

While this approach should not require additional personnel or expense, it will allow the agency to use its existing personnel more efficiently. Trained officers will be able to devote their time to these investigations. Other investigators should reassign the case to an expert within the unit to maintain efficiency and expertise.

The Commission believes that effective and efficient law enforcement is achieved through education, training and experience. These programs would enable law enforcement agencies to extract the maximum expertise from the personnel within their department.

RECOMMENDATION 59:

Federal law enforcement agencies should use search warrants in child pornography and related cases expeditiously as a means of gathering evidence and furthering overall investigation efforts in the child pornography area.

Discussion

One of the most powerful investigative tools available to law enforcement agents is a search warrant. When used in child pornography and related child sexual abuse cases, a search warrant is unique in its ability to "make or break" an investigation.

Pedophile offenders are "collectors" and will retain photographs, magazines, movies, video tapes and correspondence relating to children for many years. Many of the items collected may not be child pornography. Collections often include "child erotica" which will include "innocent" depictions of children.[636] The discovery of these collections has often unlocked the door to a wealth of infor-

mation by providing a record of the life and activities of an offender.

In a child pornography investigation executing a search warrant on the suspect's residence may yield photos of the individual engaged in sex with children thus supporting additional charges for child sexual abuse.[637] Pedophile offenders often maintain diaries recording their sexual encounters with children.[638] When a suspect uses a computer to store information regarding communications with other offenders or as a personal diary the search should also include access to computer equipment and records.[639]

In New York, police executed a search warrant on the residence of a suspected child molester and found he kept a complete folder on each of his victims including photographs and records of the dates the victim was in his home.[640] An experienced prosecutor has reported that in one half of child sexual abuse cases, proper searches recover photos of the defendant engaged in sexual acts with children.[641]

A collection of "child erotica" may help to identify the individual as an offender,[642] and may strengthen the prosecution case. This is especially true when proving intent is critical. A wrestling coach accused of fondling a juvenile who claims he was merely demonstrating a wrestling hold or technique would receive closer attention if a search of his residence yields child erotica in the form of writings about such acts and the pleasure he derived from them.

Law enforcement officers located child pornography consumers in many states as a result of the seizure of ✂ ✂ mailing list.[643] One person on the list was an Episcopal priest living in ✂ .[644] ✂ police were able to execute a search warrant on his home and seize the individual's album of sexually explicit photos of young boys based upon this information.[645] They found "love letters" from the victims and additional pornography.[646] Police subsequently were able to

636. Miami Hearing, Vol. I, Kenneth Lanning, p. 238.
637. Miami Hearing, Vol. I, William Dworin, p. 44.
638. *Id.*, p. 33.
639. Miami Hearing, Vol. I, Paul Hartman, p. 106.
640. Miami Hearing, Vol. II, Paul Der Ohannesian, p. 52.
641. *Id.*, p. 77.
642. *Id.*, pp. 232, 235.
643. *Id.*, p. 240; Miami Hearing, Vol. I, Robert Northrup, pp. 221–22.
644. Miami Hearing, Vol. I, Robert Northrup, pp. 212–13.
645. Miami Hearing, Vol. II, Kenneth Elsesser, p. 147.
646. Miami Hearing, Vol. II, Alfred Danna, pp. 272–73.

locate one of the boys who was molested by the priest.[647]

The United States Customs office, in Ft. Lauderdale, Florida, and United States Postal Inspectors were conducting a joint child pornography investigation in the Ft. Lauderdale area. During the course of the investigation, a business named   ✂   was identified as a producer and distributor of child pornography in the United States.   ✂

      ✂   The owner and operator of   ✂   was identified. Further investigation revealed the   ✂
✂ was also known as   ✂
and   ✂

The investigators made an undercover buy of child pornography from the owner of the business. The child pornography was being sold in sets of six to ten photos for fifteen to thirty-five dollars a set. The owner was also selling "sponsorships" or custom ordered sets. These photos were available from two hundred to four hundred dollars per set, and would be taken of thirteen to eighteen year old males, "posing" in any manner directed by the customer.

Based on the undercover purchase and other evidence, a search warrant was executed on the owner's residence. The investigators discovered a large quantity of child pornography at the residence and were able to obtain a second warrant for a storage facility in which the defendant kept the releases and applications from his models. He had two sets of applications and releases, one set with the actual dates of birth and one set showing the models to be over eighteen.

Also discovered during the search warrants was the defendant's method for printing and distributing the photographs, as well as his foreign source. COQ International of Denmark was selling the defendant's magazines and slides.

In February, 1985, the Contraband Enforcement Team, of the United States Customs Service, intercepted one magazine entitled *Dream Boy No. 6* sent to   ✂   Florida, address. The magazine had been sent from the Netherlands.

The Contraband Enforcement Team forwarded the magazine to the Special Agent in Charge, Tampa, Florida, for investigation. The Special Agent supervised an investigation which showed that the addressee had

two previous seizures of child pornography. The first was a magazine entitle *Lust Boys* and the second was *Child Pornography Advertisements*.

Based on the previous seizures and other investigation, a controlled delivery of the *Dream Boy* magazine was made. Based on the controlled delivery, a search warrant was obtained for the addressee's residence.

United States Customs agents and United States Postal Inspectors surveilled the residence after the delivery of the magazine, while waiting for the warrant to be issued and delivered. While the surveillance was being conducted, the addressee arrived at his residence. Shortly afterward, a thirteen year old boy arrived at the residence on a bicycle and went inside the house. The warrant was delivered about five minutes later, at which time the agents went into the house. Upon entering the house, the agents discovered the offender on the couch with the boy. Although both the defendant and the boy were clothed, it was obvious that the boy had an erection. It appeared the agents had prevented further molestation from taking place.

Although the offender was arrested, he was granted bond with the provision that he had no contact with anyone under eighteen years of age. He was suspended from his place of employment as a guidance counselor at a middle school.

During subsequent investigation, three other children were identified, through seized photographs of them, and that information was turned over to the local sheriff's department. The parents of the children refused to cooperate in the investigation because they did not want their children to testify in court.

In August, 1985, the offender was sentenced to five years in the Middle District of Florida. Four and one-half years of the sentence were suspended.

When making a request for a search warrant investigators should seek to expand the scope of their search beyond child pornography. In one investigator's experience over ninety-five percent of the child pornography cases in which he used search warrants, both adult and child pornography were found in the possession of the child sexual abusers or child pornographers.[648]

Sexually explicit, "adult" material is often

used to lower the inhibitions of child victims and should be an item sought.[649] The scope of the search should include not only the suspect's home but also his or her office, car and any other known place of habitation or storage. Pedophiles who are involved in child sexual abuse are rarely without some portion of their child pornography in close proximity and often keep materials in several different places. Warrants should be drafted to include a wide range of materials under the suspect's control in a variety of locations.[650]

RECOMMENDATION 60:

Federal law enforcement agents should ask the child victim in reported child sexual abuse cases if photographs or films were made of him or her during the course of sexual abuse.

Discussion

As part of expanding a law enforcement agency's investigation into child sexual abuse and child pornography all investigators should determine if children alleging sexual abuse were ever photographed in sexually explicit poses.

The most obvious way to find such information is to uniformly ask the child victim if photographs were taken. This technique should be employed for effective investigation and will undoubtedly highlight the interwoven connections between child sexual abuse and child pornography. An investigation of one offense should not eliminate an examination of related offenses.[651] Law enforcement officers should acknowledge that child sexual abuse is the basis for the production of child pornography.

RECOMMENDATION 61:

The Department of Justice should appoint a national task force to conduct a study of cases throughout the United States reflecting apparent patterns of multi-victim, multi-perpetrator child sexual exploitation.

Discussion

The Commission has heard testimony regarding alleged multi-victim, multi-perpetrator child sexual molestation rings throughout the country. Few of the investigations of these rings have resulted in successful prosecutions. Multitudes of children have related experiences of being photographed by the alleged molesters, and others have commented on the "quick removal" of volumes of photographs prior to law enforcement searches. In the estimated twenty-five investigations throughout the country involving alleged ritualistic molestation of pre-school children not one photograph has been discovered to substantiate the children's stories.

Even in the face of clear medical evidence of sexual molestation of many of these children, the young ages of the children and the procedures in the criminal courts have combined to undermine and destroy effective prosecution. Given the striking similarities in the nature of the alleged sex crimes committed against children in these rings and the consistent inability of the local law enforcement and child protective services systems to effectively investigate and prosecute, it appears likely that future cases could result in similar unsuccessful efforts within the justice system.

A national task force should pursue extensive study for the purpose of establishing or discarding:

a. Possible links between multi-victim, multi-perpetrator child sex rings and pornography;

b. Possible linkages among multi-victim, multi-perpetrator child sex rings throughout the United States;

c. Production and distribution of child pornography through these organized sex rings;

d. Possible links between sex rings, child pornography and organized crime.

The task force should then develop a report including recommendations for more effective investigation of child sexual exploitation cases reflecting these patterns of conspiracy. The task force would include among others, federal agency headquarters representatives. The task force should have the necessary budgetary and personnel resources to allow ongoing investigations in the field.

---

649. Miami Hearing, Vol. I, Kenneth Lanning, p. 225.
650. Miami Hearing, Vol. I, Kenneth Lanning, pp. 233–34.
651. "In 90% of the child sexual exploitation cases . . . the children admit that at one time or another they were photographed." Miami Hearing, Vol. II, Dennis Shaw, p.117.

The task force should include interdisciplinary representatives and investigators with demonstrated skills and experience in multi-

victim, multi-perpetrator child sexual exploitation cases.

RECOMMENDATIONS FOR STATE AND LOCAL LAW ENFORCEMENT AGENCIES

RECOMMENDATION 62:
Local law enforcement agencies should participate in the Law Enforcement Coordinating Committees to form regional task forces of dedicated and experienced investigators and prosecutors to combat child pornography.

Discussion

In recent years, the United States Attorneys have established Law Enforcement Coordinating Committees (LECCs) within each of the ninety-four districts.[652] The LECC is comprised of federal, state and local law enforcement agencies[653] and is designed to improve coordination and cooperation among agencies.[654] The LECC has proved to be an invaluable tool in effective law enforcement efforts. By coordinating the various agencies' efforts, a successful attack can be launched against any form of criminal activity from all sides. Customs can quickly determine a suspect's past involvement with foreign child pornography; the Postal Inspectors and local law enforcement officers can determine whether the suspect has been corresponding with other identified pedophile offenders and whether he is on any known mailing lists; and the FBI can identify the suspect's arrest history, employment history and lifestyle.[655]

New York has provided an example of the effective use of the LECC for the investigation and prosecution of child pornography cases.[656] This example can also be used as a model for the LECC subcommittee specifically designed to address the problem of child pornography. In addition to general enforcement efforts the LECC may serve to make suggestions for regional or statewide programs.

RECOMMENDATION 63:
State and Local law enforcement agencies

should develop and maintain continuous training programs for officers in identification, apprehension, and undercover techniques of child pornography investigations.

Discussion

State and local agencies may participate in LECC sponsored training programs and should also participate in programs conducted through the Federal Law Enforcement Training Center. These agencies should also develop regional or local training programs. These localized programs should address general law enforcement techniques needed in child pornography cases as well as concerns peculiar to the region. These programs will enhance law enforcement efforts through a more coordinated base of communication among agencies within a geographic area.[657]

RECOMMENDATION 64:
State and Local law enforcement agencies should participate in a national data base established to serve as a center for State and Local law enforcement agencies to submit and receive information regarding child pornography trafficking.
See, The discussion in Recommendations for Federal Law Enforcement Agencies in this Chapter.

RECOMMENDATION 65:
State and Local law enforcement agencies should have personnel trained in child pornography investigation and when possible they should form specialized units for child sexual abuse and child pornography investigations.
See, The discussion in Recommendation for Federal Law Enforcement Agencies in this Chapter.

---

652. Chicago Hearing, Vol. II, Frederick Scullin, p. 37; *See also,* Recommendations for Law Enforcement Agencies in Chapter 2 of this Part.
653. Chicago Hearing, Vol. II, Frederick Scullin, p. 37.
654. *Id.*
655. Miami Hearing, Vol. II, Joyce Karlin, p. 177B–C.
656. Chicago Hearing, Vol. II. Frederick Scullin, pp. 38–41.
657. See *Also,* The discussion, Recommendations for Federal Law Enforcement Agencies, in this Chapter.

RECOMMENDATION 66:

State and Local law enforcement agencies should use search warrants in child exploitation cases expeditiously as a means of gathering evidence and furthering the overall investigation efforts in the child pornography area.

See, The discussion in Recommendation for Federal Law Enforcement Agencies in this Chapter.

RECOMMENDATION 67:

State and Local law enforcement officers should ask the child victim in reported child sexual abuse cases if photographs or films were made of him or her during the course of sexual abuse.

See, The discussion in Recommendation for Federal Law Enforcement Agencies in this Chapter.

RECOMMENDATIONS FOR PROSECUTORS

RECOMMENDATION 68:

The United States Department of Justice should direct United States Attorneys to participate in Law Enforcement Coordinating Committee task forces to combat child pornography.

See, The discussion in Recommendation for Federal Law Enforcement Agencies in this Chapter.

RECOMMENDATION 69:

Federal, State and Local prosecutors should participate in a task force of multi-disciplinary practitioners and develop a protocol for courtroom procedures for child witnesses that would meet constitutional standards.

Discussion

Prosecutors must be aware of the special considerations involving a child victim-witness. In many states children of a certain age are presumed incompetent to testify. When the child is the only witness to a crime, such as child pornography and related crimes, prosecutors face special problems.

Prosecutors should work with other professionals including law enforcement agents, medical and mental health professionals and social service personnel, involved in child pornography cases to develop a courtroom protocol which maintains the integrity and emotional well-being of the child as well as preserving the constitutional rights of the defendant.

The task force should specifically address a number of issues. First, the number of repetitive questions asked of a child witness during the trial should be limited. A child may become easily frightened when repeatedly asked questions during the trial. This lengthy process increases the trauma and sense of guilt in victims associated with these crimes. The task force should develop methods of support for the child through this period while insuring the defendant's right to confrontation.

The prosecutor specifically may reduce this trauma by objecting to repetitive questioning on the ground of harassment.[658] The prosecutor should emphasize the special emotional frailty of the child in making the objection.

Prosecutors should develop guidelines to qualify a child as a competent witness. While very young children may be incapable of communication, those who are articulate should be presumed competent until the testimony demonstrates otherwise. In questioning a child witness prosecutors should be permitted to use age-appropriate language and allow the child to respond in terms with which they feel comfortable. Children should be permitted to use anatomically correct dolls, if necessary, to demonstrate the manner in which they were exposed or molested. The determination of credibility should be left to the jury as it is with any other witness.

Prosecutors should attempt to avoid delays in preliminary hearings and trials. Repeated

---

658. Fed. R. Ev. 611 provides:

    (a) Control By Court. The court shall exercise reasonable control over the mode and order if interrogating witnesses and presenting evidence so as to (1) make the interrogation and presentation effective for the ascertainment of the truth, (2) avoid needless consumption of time, and (3) protect witnesses from harassment or undue embarrassment.

delays add to the confusion and trauma of a child witness. Prosecutors may develop a priority calender for child pornography ad related cases. These guidelines should be used to preserve the credibility of the child witness as well as eliminate the extent of the trauma caused by extensive delays in judicial procedures.

Prosecutors may also consider the use of closed circuit television to present the child's testimony. This would eliminate many of the distractions a child witness faces. A child is normally apprehensive in a new environment and will be reluctant to testify forthrightly. The closed circuit television could enable a child to testify and be subjected to cross-examination without being intimidated by the courtroom proceedings or the presence of the defendant.

The task force should also consider developing guidelines to coordinate criminal, civil and family law proceedings. In addition, the protocol should consider the use of grand juries in place of preliminary hearings. These guidelines would maintain the integrity of the judicial proceeding which eliminating any unnecessary trauma for the victims. All task force recommendations should clearly safeguard the constitutional protections afforded the accused.

RECOMMENDATION 70:
Prosecutors should assist State, Local and Federal law enforcement agencies to use search warrants in potential child pornography cases and related child sexual abuse cases.

See, The discussion in Recommendations for Federal Law Enforcement Agencies in this Chapter.

RECOMMENDATION 71:
State, Local and Federal prosecutors should ask the child victim in reported child sexual abuse cases if photographs or films were made of him or her during the course of sexual abuse.

See, The discussion in Recommendations for Federal Law Enforcement Agencies in this Chapter.

RECOMMENDATION 72:
State and Local prosecutors should use the vertical prosecution model for child pornography and related cases.

Discussion
The vertical prosecution system involves a single prosecutor handling a particular criminal case from its inception to its conclusion. In cases involving sexually abused or exploited children the young victims are often very frightened at the prospect of going into court. Sometimes the procedures that the victim must go through such as meeting new people and continuously repeating his or her story add to the trauma. When the same prosecutor handles the case it enables him or her to work with the victim on a continuing basis, gain the child's confidence, and help prepare the child for trial.

The vertical prosecution model also ensures that the case is not passed on to another prosecutor who may be unfamiliar with the facts or law involved in the prosecution. In California Governor George Deukmejian has established a grant program through the Office of Criminal Justice Planning to implement the vertical prosecution in model programs involving child sexual abuse and child pornography case.

RECOMMENDATIONS FOR THE JUDICIARY AND CORRECTIONAL FACILITIES

RECOMMENDATION 73:
Judges and probation officers should receive specific education so they may investigate, evaluate, sentence and supervise persons convicted in child pornography and related child sexual abuse cases appropriately

Discussion
Recognizing the pedophile offenders and

child pornographers pose unique problems in the judicial and penal systems judges and probation officers must be adequately educated. A judge or probation officer can have a significant and positive impact on the offender only if he or she is fully knowledgeable about the situation.

Offenders in child pornography cases rarely go to trial.[659] He or she generally enters

---

659. Miami Hearing, Vol. II, Joyce Karlin, p. 153.

a plea and proceeds to sentencing.[660] The judge does not have the benefit of the evidence obtained through trial before considering an appropriate sentence.

The judge must bear the burden of thoroughly assessing the defendant and the offense. The judge must actually view the child pornography to make this evaluation. The judge should not only be made aware of the nature of the pornography and related sexual abuse, but he or she must be fully aware of the quantity and type of material a defendant may possess. Many judges hold the mistaken belief the child pornography offenders are less insidious because they are professional people within the community.[661] A judge should examine the child pornography and be aware of the abuses attributable to its production in order to fully evaluate the offender before sentencing.

The judges and probation officers should be fully informed about the latest social science and medical information regarding pedophile offenders and child sexual abusers and their susceptibility to treatment or behavior modification. Therapists and other professionals who have studied pedophile offenders currently express a great deal of doubt as to the viability of rehabilitation of pedophiles.[662] Judges and probation officers should focus their attention toward the need to protect society and potential victims in addition to therapeutic efforts for pedophile offenders.[663]

Until an effective treatment method is

---

660. *Id.*

661. Miami Hearing, Vol. I, Kenneth Lanning, p. 251.

662. The Commission has heard testimony from several law enforcement officers, prosecutors and therapist discussing the recidivist pattern of pedophile offenders. See, *e.g.*, Miami Hearing, Vol. I, William Dworin, p. 22.

663. The following is excerpts from a telephone conversation between a pedophile offender and a child victim. Law enforcement agents have stated that discovering and recording an actual conversation between an alleged pedophile and a victim is rarely discovered.

Subject. Oh, okay. Tell us when you're going to be nine.
Victim. May 12.
S. That's pretty soon Angel.

* * *

S. It's remarkable and I'm wondering if she's in her blue jeans?
V. No.
S. You're not in your blue jeans?
V. No, I'm in something like blue jeans.
S. Oh, I see, okay (Pause) blue jeans are falling out of fashion aren't they baby?
V. Yes.
S. They don't wear them too much anymore.
V. Nope, I don't even have any that fit. All I have is pants.
S. In other words you're going out of your blue jeans baby?
V. Uh, hum, I only have two pairs that still fit me.
S. That's amazing she is getting to be so curvy that she doesn't fit her blue jeans anymore. (Pause) I can tell she's grinning.
V. Laughs.
S. You're so sweet. You're just a precious little Angel. Are you still standing on your head baby?
V. No.
S. You know what I'm interested in, right? I'm interested in playing, right?
V. Right.
S. Is it alright if we have all three?
V. Uh, hum.
S. Okay.
V. Uh, hum.
S. Honestly.
V. Yeah.
S. That's great we'll all three play then okay?
V. Okay.
S. In other words we'll tickle ours and you'll tickle yours, right?
V. Right.
S. Okay, that's my girl.
V. You know what would be good?
S. What.
V. If you gave me your phone number because then sometimes I could call you if my Mom's not off on Tuesday or Thursday sometimes she's at work on Tuesday or Thursday.
S. Oh, I see, yes, I understand however sweetheart for a little while would you do me a favor and just bear with me, be patient with me, okay, for a little while?
V. Okay.
S. It'll be a good idea as a matter of fact sometimes if she's not off on Tuesday and Thursdays I could call and

say let me to speak to Sam and all you have to do is say you have the wrong number, right?

V. Right.

S. And that would protect us. Can you take your panties off.

V. What?

S. Can you take your panties off while we're playing.

V. No.

S. Please, pretty please.

V. No.

S. She'll tell you it's alright.

V. Okay, I'm back.

S. Ask her if she thinks it's alright.

V. You ask her.

S. Oh, okay, alright ah, sweetheart we were discussing the possibility of playing while you were gone from the phone and I wanted you to know all three of us to tickle ourselves while we were talking okay, alright, do you understand?

V. Uh, huh.

* * *

S. Let me put it this way, it would make me very happy if you took your panties off, okay?

V. Well, guess what.

S. What.

V. I can't.

S. You're so sweet, thank you so much Angel. Why?

V. Because.

S. Because of what.

V. Well, I'm downstairs and my brother and sister will be coming home. My sister always runs into my room.

S. Hold it now, you're downstairs.

V. Um, hmm.

S. And won't they see you when they first come in?

V. Yeah.

S. So what you need to do is hang up this phone and go upstairs.

V. Okay.

S. Okay, do me a favor go upstairs first and then come back down and hang this phone up.

V. Okay.

S. Or if you want me to hang this phone up and I'll call you back and you can answer upstairs.

V. Okay.

S. Alright, okay.

V. Okay.

S. Why don't we do that you hang up this phone up and I'll call you back and you can answer upstairs.

V. Okay.

S. Alright okay.

V. Okay.

S. Okay, you're going to hang up now . . .

V. (Hangs up).

* * *

(Phone rings)

V. Hello.

S. Now it's safe, isn't it?

V. Right, except for one thing.

S. Except for what.

V. My blinds are open.

S. Your what.

V. Blinds.

S. Oh, we'll hold on while you close them.

V. Okay.

S. Isn't she precious Angel.

* * *

S. She is just adorable and think about how thoughtful she is, how intelligent she is. I mean didn't you think that was remarkable that she would say my blinds are open.

* * *

S. You betcha she's a very intelligent young lady. It's just delights me I'm so proud of her.

V. I'm back.

S. And I'll betcha that you've taken your panties off now.

V. Hmm, okay.

S. Did she take them off.

V. Um, Humm.

S. You're completely unclothed from the waist down you still have your blouse on though.

V. Right.

S. Okay, so when you hear your brother and sister come home you can put your clothes back on real quick, right.

V. Right.
S. That's good, isn't fun to do something sweetheart and know that you can get away with it, that it's perfectly safe.
V. Yes.
S. It is fun isn't?
V. Um, hmm.
S. Have you ever, have you ever wanted to play with someone like this in person?
V. Um, hmm.
S. Tell us about it.
V. Well um you gave me the idea so I tried it.
S. With who?
V. I just called someone I don't know who they were.
S. Oh, you did?
V. But I looked it up in the phone book, I didn't look for any certain name. I just looked for the number.
S. Oh, I see in other words you got numbers out of the phone book.
V. Right.
S. Well, it's not I'll teach you how to make up numbers one of these days Sweetheart, it's really not necessary to go to the phone book. And, however, I want to find out you talked to someone?
V. Um, hmm.
S. And how old a person was it? Could you tell?
V. No.
S. Was it a man or a woman?
V. Man.
S. Did you tell him that you were tickling yours?
V. What?
S. Did you tell him that you were tickling yours?
V. No.
S. Did you get him to tickle his?
V. No.
S. Well, what did you all do Sweetheart?
V. Talked.
S. Talked about what?
V. Something.
S. Tell me about what, come on. About sex?
V. No.
S. What did you all talk about, tell me now.
V. Well, we just talked.
S. I see.

* * *

S. I see, but ah, you didn't talk about sex.
V. No.
S. And he didn't talk about wanting to be with you or to see you or meet you or something.
V. Well, he would like to come over to our house.
S. He did, he said that.
V. Um, hmm.
S. He did.
V. But I said he couldn't.
S. . . . Angel, you didn't give him your address. I hope.
V. No.
S. Okay, golly that worried that kind of thing worries me.

* * *

S. Well, sweetheart its alright for you talk to anyone on the phone anyone but don't give them your phone number and don't tell them your address. And certainly don't tell them you last name. Okay.
V. Okay.
S. Because that way you'll be perfectly safe as long as you don't give them your phone number as long as you don't give them your address and as long as you don't give them your last name. Okay?
V. Okay.
S. That way you'll be perfectly safe. That way you can talk to anyone on the phone you want to as long as you don't tell them your phone number, your name, your address, okay.
V. Okay.
S. Those things ah, are if you gave them anyone of those things it could be dangerous to you sweetheart. It could be I'm not saying it would be normally, it probably wouldn't be but it could be see.
V. Um, hmm.
S. I don't want to make you unnecessarily afraid, I want you to makeup numbers and talk to people that's fine but protect yourself in the process and as long as you don't give them your phone number your address or your name you're safe. You can tell them your first name that's alright. (Pause). Anyway, since you've talked to me, have you tickled yourself when you went to sleep?
V. Um, hmm, yeah.
S. Good. That's a lot of fun isn't it. Sweetheart?
V. Um, hmm.

widely accepted and implemented judges and probation officers must evaluate and supervise pedophile offenders carefully. Pedophile offenders who are incarcerated after an offense simply may use their time of confinement to plan their life and future offenses upon release. One pedophile offender wrote from his prison cell,

> I plan to get into photography in a bigger way when I get out. While I am in here I am studying photography and plan to set up a part-time business. I plan to be very discreet too. I was getting a little careless and look what it got me. This is one area where discretion and caution are absolutely essential.[664]

There are several problems which have prevented this program from being implemented. First, there is a lack of effective treatment plans. An effective treatment plan should be developed which results in a long term behavior modification with a significant reduction in recidivism rates.

A second problem associated with an incarceration and treatment program is a concern of its coercive nature. If a program is structured to make early release contingent upon cooperative participation in a treatment program, a correctional facility may be subject to allegations of coercion and violations of the offender's constitutional rights.

In the absence of an effective treatment program, a judge and a probation officer should be aware of the perpetual threat a pedophile offender poses to society. The only viable alternative in the absence of an effective treatment program is a substantial period of incarceration. The incarceration should effectively remove the offender from society and protect the community for significant period of time.

Incarceration serves several different purposes. It may serve to deter potential offenders, to protect society from this individual and to provide retribution against the offender. Each of these factors need not be the basis for sentencing in every case.

The judges must examine each of these goals and determine which is the appropriate basis for sentencing. As previously discussed there are very few medical facilities that attempt to treat pedophile offenders.[665] In addition, incarceration often does not serve as a deterrent either to the specific offender or to other potential offenders.

The remaining goals of incarceration are the protection of society and retribution against the offender. Child sexual abuse or child pornography is one of the most insidious offenses known and the goal of retribution generally serves to reassure society of its values. Punishment also serves as an emotional support for the victim. This is particularly important in child pornography cases where the victim is left to feel guilty and ashamed.

The primary goal in sentencing should be to remove the pedophile offender so he or she does not present a threat to society. He or she must be removed for a substantial period of time. The Commission fully acknowledges these needs and recommends that a mandatory minimum sentence of two years be imposed on first time offenders. The sentences for recidivists should be substantially increased.

The welfare of the victim should remain the primary focus of the judge during the sentencing process. The sentence must also be sufficient to protect potential victims. The pedophile offender may continue to communicate with other pedophile offenders. One such communication was sent to an undercover police officer.

> "Now I was arrested and all my photographs, books, magazines, slides, films, were confiscated. Since July 19, I have been here in a state hospital that treats men with sex offenses. I was first sent here for observation and commit-

---

664. Miami Hearing, Vol. I, William Dworin, p. 15.
665. One such facility is the Massachusetts Treatment Center in Bridgewater, Mass.; See, Washington D.C., Hearing, Vol. II, Richard Prentke, p. 65.

S. It is. Has it gotten to where it feels real good yet.
V. No.
S. Well, it will you just keep tickling it and it will, and when you go to sleep sometimes when you're tickling it does it get real juicy?
V. Does it get what.
S. Does it get real wet, real juicy?
V. No.
S. Well, it will. And do you know what it means, when it gets real wet and real juicy.
V. No.
S. It means that you're learning how to do it better.

ted here on November 3 for an indefinite period. That is why I was so happy to hear from you, as I no longer have the contacts with young girls I used to. I still have the same interests, but I am temporarily at a standstill. I was into photography quite a bit and managed to take some shots of Lisa and several of my students.[666]

The correction facility must be kept apprised of these types of communiques and they should be considered during parole hearings or evaluations for release.

RECOMMENDATION 75:
Judges should use, when appropriate, a sentence of lifetime probation for convicted child pornographers.

Discussion
Pedophile offenders present a continuing threat to society since there presently is no universally accepted course of treatment for a pedophile offender. In the absence of effective treatment a convicted pedophile offender must be continually monitored subsequent to his or her release. The most effective method of monitoring a pedophile offenders is through the imposition of lifetime probation as a part of the initial sentence.

Lifetime probation gives probation personnel the ability to continually monitor the pedophile offender while he or she is able to attempt to rejoin society as a productive member. The probation should be conditioned upon special factors including prohibition of unsupervised contact with children as contact well as any contacts with other pedophile offenders.

A lifetime supervised probation term will require the dedicated efforts of federal and state probation officers. The officers must devote substantial periods of time to these individuals to ensure compliance with the terms of the probation.

In some situations the judge may impose a term of unsupervised lifetime probation. This would eliminate the enormous burden on the probation officers while maintaining legal control over the offender. The judge should carefully evaluate the offender and se-

lect the terms of probation which would be most effective and least burdensome on the penal and judical systems.

RECOMMENDATION 76:
Pre-sentence reports concerning individuals found guilty of violations of child pornography or related laws should be based on sources of information in addition to the offender himself or herself.

Discussion
Probation officers, psychiatrists and psychologists have extensive contact with defendants and their counsel in the course of preparing presentence reports. Defendants and their counsel often provide court personnel with most of the information used in compiling these reports.

Information supplied by the defendant about himself or herself and the offense may be inaccurate or incomplete and it usually overlooks the victim's perspective. Sources of information other than the defendant must be tapped to give the sentencing judge the most accurate information. Such information should include but need not be limited to: investigative reports, victims' statements and interviews, interviews of witnesses and persons familiar with the offender's habits, a report of any guardian *ad litem* representing the victim; examination of physical evidence such as pornography created or possessed by the offender; a review of diaries, audiotapes, or videotapes created by the offender; and the offender's criminal, correctional, mental health, educational, military, and work records.[667]

Child sexual abusers often move to another city or state after public exposure or when they come under suspicion. The sentencing judge then should obtain records from jurisdictions in which an offender has previously resided. Victims, prosecutors and investigators should provide information at their disposal to those conducting presentence evaluations.

RECOMMENDATION 77:
State and Federal correctional facilities

---

666. Miami Hearing, Vol. I, William Dworin, pp. 14–15.

667. On January 20, 1984 a federal grand jury in the northern district of New York handed down a twelve-count indictment against a child pornographer. He eventually pled guilty to five counts of mailing child pornography and on May 4, 1984, was sentenced to 10-years in prison on each of the five counts, to run concurrently, and ordered to undergo three months of psychiatric examination at a federal facility, due to his suicidal tendencies. The judge in this case later reduced the sentence to two years in prison followed by five years probation as a result of the psychiatric findings that were conducted by the United States Bureau of Prisons. Washington, D.C., Hearing, Vol. I, Daniel Mihalko, pp. 156–57.

should recognize the unique problems of child pornographers and related offenders and designate appropriate programs regarding their incarceration.

Discussion

In the Southern District of California, a defendant was convicted of transporting material involving the sexual exploitation of children and importing obscene merchandise.[668] The trial court sentenced the offender to the maximum punishment and requested a study by the Bureau of Prisons regarding what treatment he might receive.[669] The study was conducted by a Bureau of Prisons psychologist who had never previously treated a pedophile offender.[670] The psychologist found the defendant amenable to treatment, yet could not recommend a federal institution that was capable of providing the treatment.[671] A community treatment proposal was recommended, which in the prosecutor's view, failed to take into account the danger the defendant posed to the community if released.[672] The Federal Bureau of Prisons has acted to prevent a recurrence of this problem. To avoid any misinterpretation by the courts in the future, the Bureau of Prisons has instructed their mental health staff members to go beyond the specific mental health issues and to consider making recommendations for confinement based on factors other than treatment goals in cases where such a sanction is indicated.

Pedophile offenders and child pornographers present a unique and difficult problem

in correction facilities. The nature of the offenses for which they have been convicted make pedophile offenders and child pornographers the lowest class within the prison social system. They may be subjected to verbal and physical abuse by other inmates but this factor should not cause judges to avoid incarceration when necessary.

To provide humane incarceration pedophile offenders and child pornographer should receive specialized attention from correctional officials. Correctional departments may need to provide areas within a designated facility for convicted child sexual offenders to eliminate the threats of harm from other inmates. The facility should also attempt to develop specific therapy programs as they may become known for pedophiles in an attempt to prepare the. ' for their reemergence into society.

The programs will be an attempt to recognize the special problems of pedophile offender or child pornographer encounters during his or her period of incarceration and should focus on safety and prevention problems.

RECOMMENDATION 78:
Federal, State and Local judges should participate in a task force of multi-disciplinary practitioners and develop a protocol for courtroom procedures for child witnesses that would meet constitutional standards.

See, The discussion in Recommendations for Prosecutors in this Chapter.

RECOMMENDATIONS FOR PUBLIC AND PRIVATE SOCIAL SERVICE AGENCIES

RECOMMENDATION 79:
Public and private social service agencies should participate in a task force of multidisciplinary practitioners and develop a protocol for courtroom procedures for child witnesses that would meet constitutional standards.

Discussion

Public and private social service agencies

should lend their expertise to help develop appropriate courtroom procedures. Many of these guidelines should focus on the development of therapy programs for child victims.

In California, a group of preschool children was allegedly molested and photographed by teachers at the Children's Path preschool.[673] Physicians found conclusive medical evidence that fifteen of the children were sexually abused.[674] A two-year-old reported to her

668. Chicago Hearing, Vol. I, Joan Webber, p. 192.
669. *Id.*
670. *Id.*, p. 193.
671. *Id.*, p. 195.
672. *Id.*, p. 196.
673. Miami Hearing, Vol. I, Laura Brennan, p. 93.

parents instances of controlled substance abuse, sodomy, and oral copulation. She also stated that photographs were taken.[675] Since the time the child told her parents of this situation, she has been receiving psychotherapy on a weekly basis. Her parents have also sought therapy.[676] None of the offenders were brought to trial because their victims were too young to be competent witnesses in court.[677]

Social services agencies should develop guidelines to assist child witnesses in the courtroom.[678] The programs which result may take the form of an advocate to assist the child through the judicial process. This person would be assigned to the child and would be concerned only with the welfare of the child rather than a particular judicial outcome.

RECOMMENDATION 80:
Social mental health, and medical services should be provided for child pornography victims.

Discussion

In many cases, the official intervention into child pornography cases involves only legal and prosecutorial action against the perpetrator. Often, the identities of children appearing in pornographic photographs seized from the homes of pedophile offenders or child pornographers are never established. If the child pornographer is not a member of the family, the case will not be referred to a child welfare agency for protective social services. Child victims of pornography are frequently used as witnesses for the prosecution and subsequently abandoned by the social, medical and mental health services systems.

Child victims of pornography and their families should receive a full range of supportive services including competent medical evaluations and treatment, access to family therapy and peer support groups, legal counsel and guardians *ad litem*.

Because child pornography and child sexual abuse are so intrinsically related, certain treatment models for victims of child sexual abuse can be applied to victims of child pornography. Children who are involved in treatment for child sexual abuse often reveal that pornography was used by the perpetrator as a threat to prevent the child from disclosing the sexual relationship.

Model child sexual abuse crisis centers have been developed to integrate social, medical and mental health services for suspected child sexual abuse victims. Child sexual abuse centers can provide medical assessment, psychological, psychosocial evaluation and crisis intervention services to suspected victims of child sexual abuse and their families.[679] Evaluation teams may consist of a physician, nurse practitioner, psychologist, social worker, and children's services worker. The multidisciplinary team approach can be used in the initial evaluation activities of the center and in the development of follow-up plans, including referrals for law enforcement and children's protective services, court action, and psychological treatment.

In addition, many runaway and homeless children are enticed into pornography or prostitution, or resort to theft in order to survive.[680] Early intervention into their lives can provide a viable deterrent against other crimes. Without intervention, these children

---

674. *Id.*, p. 95.
675. *Id.*, pp. 93–94.
676. *Id.*, p. 94.
677. *Id.*, p. 95.
678. For a more complete discussion *see*, Recommendations for Prosecutors in this Chapter.
679. Model Crisis Center Programs include the San Diego Center for Child Protection and the Los Angeles Child Sexual Abuse Family Crisis Center.

Los Angeles County also completed a study on runaway and homeless youths. Under the auspices of the Los Angeles County Board of Supervisors with participation of the Department of Children's Services, the Dependency Courts, law enforcement, and in conjunction with the private sector, a project has been proposed consisting of the following components designed to assist these children to develop meaningful lives:

—Identification of child
—Establishment of referral resource network
—Intake of child into system, including emergency shelter placement
—Expedited court handling
—Development of more suitable placement alternatives, treatment and handling resources, including a new shelter.

680. See, The discussion of Victimization.

may go on to more serious crimes when they are no longer desirable to pimps and pornographers.[681]

RECOMMENDATION 81:

Local agencies should allocate victims of crimes funds to provide monies for psychiatric evaluation and treatment and medical treatment of victims and their families.[682]

Discussion

Sexual exploitation through the production of child pornography leaves a tremendous cost in its wake. This cost is in economic terms as well as human emotional devastation. Many children suffer physical and emotional dam-

age as well as the effects of sexually transmitted diseases.

An effective response to cases of suspected child sexual exploitation requires a sensitive and comprehensive medical examination of the child that will:

1. Accurately diagnose physical evidence of recent or past sexual assault, and
2. Provide substantial documentation for protective or prosecutorial action.

Evidence of child sexual abuse is more difficult to obtain than evidence of other types of physical abuse which results in external bruising, lacerations, scarring or severe mal-

---

681. "Runaway and homeless youth come from highly disorganized families, and, in many cases, their behavior may be the result of past physical or sexual abuse. Fifty percent of the young people have not voluntarily left home but have been pushed out or encouraged to leave by parents. Fewer than half of these youngsters have a realistic prospect of ever returning to their families. Out on the street, these children are exploited by pimps, drug pushers and peddlers of pornography. Their health and emotional problems are severe. Runaways and homeless youth are unable to care for themselves adequately. Published research indicates that they exhibit stress and other psychological difficulties in excess of those experienced by non-runaways.

Although child abuse is generally perceived as a problem of early childhood, this study has uncovered another largely unrecognized abused population—adolescents. They need the community's care and concern just as much as their younger counterparts.

The community survey of experts reveals the lack of appropriate community resources. Agency staff themselves estimate that they are not coping with the situation adequately. The resource deficit is critically hindering a reasonable level of service provision. What scarce resources are available are not being utilized effectively because there is little rational planning, inadequate communication among agencies, and minimal coordination of effort. Each agency and service goes its own way, doing its best, but without reference to others serving the same population. The public and private sectors appear to operate as two separate subsytems, each in its own encapsulated orbit, with only sporadic interaction.

Our studies demonstrate that the runaway and homeless population is made up of different subpopulations with different characteristics, needs and service requirements. For example, there are multiple reasons for self-initiated breaking away from home, and also a variety of forces within the family that push the young person out involuntarily and prematurely. Planning for runaway and homeless youth requires differential diagnosis and specifically targeted patterns of service delivery. The analysis of existing research on program evaluation suggests that there are panaceas, no universally recognized and accepted program designs to solve the problem, although there are useful lessons and helpful ideas to be gleaned from studying the experiences of other communities across the country. Program development on the local level needs to be carefully coordinated, and adequately researched.

The family plays a central, but ambiguous role, according to our studies. Extant research indicates that family intervention is a highly effective strategy for many young people, and indeed might be the strategy of first choice in most siuations. When reconciliation is possible, it should be given priority. However, research also shows that many families are so destructive, abusive and rejecting that children cannot wisely be returned to them. Almost fifty percent of the runaways need other options, including alternative residential care (such as group homes and foster care) for some, transitional services for those ready for emancipation, and basic survival services to nomadic youngsters committed to life in the streets.

This study has uncovered the *intensive* nature of this problem. We have not been able to ascertain the *extensive* nature of the problem, i.e., its numerical dimensions. The panel of approximation of the number of runaway and homeless youth in Los Angeles county. Knowing the dimension of the problem is essential to designing a solution. When society acknowledges a problem and determines to acquire accurate statistics, the numbers become available. This is the time to learn how many troubled youth must be provided for, and to undertake pilot and demonstration projects designed to develop effective programmatic responses." J. Rothman & T. David, *Status Offenders in Los Angeles County, Focus on Runaway and Homeless Youth: A Study and Policy Recommendations*, 3–4 (unpublished study).

682. Senator Arlen Specter has introduced the Pornography Victims Protection Act. This act would allow an injured child the opportunity to recover damages from producers and distributors. This legislation would expand judicial remedies available to a victimized child and his or her family. Counselors and therapists must be qualified to assist the child and the family. This legislation would permit victims of child pornography and adults who are coerced, intimidated, or fraudulently induced into posing or performing in pornography to institute federal civil actions against the producers

and distributors. A victim could recover treble damages and the costs of the action, as well as seek an injunction to prevent further dissemination of the pornography.

The legislation provides:

Be it enacted by the Senate and House of Representatives of the United States of America in Congress assembled. That this Act may be cited as the "Pornography Victims Protection Act of 1985."

Sec. 2 Section 2251 of title 18, United States Code, is amended—

(1) in subsection (a), by striking out "subsection (c)" and inserting in lieu thereof "subsection (d)" and by inserting before the period at the end thereof the following: "or if such person knows or has reason to know that the minor was transported in interstate or foreign commerce for the purpose of producing any such visual depiction of such conduct":

(2) in subsection (b), by striking out "subsection (c)" and inserting in lieu thereof "subsection (d)" and by inserting before the period at the end thereof the following: "or if such person knows or has reason to know that the minor was transported in interstate or foreign commerce for the purpose of producing any such visual depiction of such conduct":

(3) by inserting immediately after subsection (b) the following:

"(c) (1) Any person who coerces, intimidates, or fraudulently induces an individual, 18 years or older to engage in any sexually explicit conduct for the purpose of producing any visual depiction of such conduct shall be punished as provided under subsection (d), if such person knows or has reason to know that such visual depiction will be transported in interstate or foreign commerce or mailed, if such visual depiction has actually been transported in interstate or foreign commerce or mailed, or if such person knows or has reason to know that the individual 18 years or older was transported in interstate or foreign commerce for the purpose of producing any such visual depiction of such conduct.

"(2) Proof of one or more of the following facts or conditions shall not, without more, negate a finding of coercion under this subsection:

"(A) that the person is or has been a prostitute;

"(B) that the person is connected by blood or marriage to anyone involved in or related to the making of the pornography;

"(C) that the person has previously had, or been thought to have had, sexual relations with anyone, including anyone involved in or related to the making of the pornography;

"(D) that the person has previously posed for sexually explicit pictures for or with anyone, including anyone involved in or related to the making of the pornography at issue;

"(E) that anyone else, including a spouse or other relative, has given permission on the person's behalf;

"(F) that the person actually consented to a use of the performance that is changed into pornography;

"(G) that the person knew that the purpose of the acts or events in question was to make pornography;

"(H) that the person signed a contract to produce pornography; or

"(I) that the person was paid or otherwise compensated";

(4) in subsection (c), by striking out "(c)" and inserting in lieu thereof "(d)" and

(5) by amending the heading to read as follows:

S2251. "Sexual exploitation".

Sec. 3 (a) Section 2252 (a) (1) of title 18, United States Code, is amended by adding at the end thereof the following:

"(C) the producing of such visual depiction involved the use of an adult who was coerced, intimidated, or fraudulently induced to engage in sexually explicit conduct and the person knows or has reason to know that the adult was coerced, intimidated, or fraudulently induced; and

"(D) such visual depiction depicts such conduct; or".

(b) Section 2252 (a) (2) is amended by —-

(1) striking out "and" and the semicolon in clause (A) and inserting in lieu thereof "or the production of visual depiction involved the use of an adult who was coerced, intimidated, or fraudulently induced to engage in sexually explicit conduct and the person knows or has reason to know that the adult was coerced, intimidated, or fraudulently induced; and

(c) the heading for section 2252 is amended to read as follows:

S2252. "CERTAIN ACTIVITIES RELATING TO MATERIAL INVOLVING SEXUAL EXPLOITATION."
   Sec. 4. (a) Chapter 110 of part 1 of Title 18. United States Code, is amended by redesignating section 2252 as section 2261.

(b) Chapter 110 of part J of title 18, United States Code, is amended by inserting after section 2254 the following:

S2252. CIVIL REMEDIES.

"(a) The district courts of the United States shall have jurisdiction to prevent and restrain violations of section 2251 or 2252 by issuing appropriate orders, including —-

   "(1) ordering any person to divest himself of any interest, direct or indirect, in any legal or business entity;

   "(2) imposing reasonable restrictions on the future activities or investments of any person including prohibiting such person from engaging in the same type of legal or business endeavor; or

   "(3) ordering dissolution or reorganization of any legal or business entity after making due provision for the rights of innocent persons.

"(b) The Attorney General or any person threatened with loss or damage by reason of a violation of section 2251 or 2252 may institute proceedings under section (a) and, in the event that the party bringing suit prevails, such party shall recover the cost of the suit, including a reasonable attorney's fee. Pending final determination, the court may at any time enter such restraining orders or prohibitions, or take such other actions, including the acceptance of satisfactory performance bonds, as it shall deem proper. For purposes of this section, a violation of section 2251 or 2252 shall be determined by a preponderance of the evidence.

"(c) Any victim of a violation of section 2251 or 2252 who suffers physical injury, emotional distress, or property damage as a result of such violation may sue to recover damages in any appropriate United States district court and shall recover threefold the damages such person sustains as a result of such violation and the cost of the suit, including a reasonable attorney's fee. For purposes of this section, a violation of section 2251 or 2252 shall be determined by a preponderance of the evidence.

"(d) A final judgment or decree rendered in favor of the United States in any criminal proceeding brought by the United States under this chapter shall estop the defendant from denying the essential allegations of the criminal offense in any subsequent civil proceeding.

"(e) Nothing in this section shall be construed to authorize any order restraining the exhibition, distribution or dissemination of any visual material without a full adversary proceeding and a final judicial determination that such material contains a visual depiction of sexually explicit conduct, as defined by section 2262 of this chapter, engaged in by a minor or by a person who was coerced, intimidated, or fraudulently induced to engage in such sexually explicit conduct.

S2256. CIVIL PENALTIES.

"(a) Any person found to violate section 2252 or 2252 by preponderance of the evidence shall be liable to the United States Government for a civil penalty of $100,000 and the forfeiture of any interest in property described in section 2254. The Attorney General may bring an action for recovery of any such civil penalty or forfeiture against any such person. If the Attorney General prevails he may also recover the cost of the suit, including a reasonable attorney's fee.

"(b) If the identity of any victim of an offense provided in section 2251 or 2252 is established prior to an award of a civil penalty made to the United States under this section, the victim shall be entitled to the award. If there is more than one victim, the court shall apportion the award among the victims on an equitable basis after considering the harm suffered by each such victim.

S2257. VENUE AND PROCESS.

"(a) Any civil action or proceeding brought under this chapter may be instituted in the district court of the United States for an district in which the defendant resides, is found, has an agent, or transacts his affairs.

"(b) In any action under section 2252 or 2256 of this chapter in any district court of the United States in which it is shown that the ends of justice require that other parties residing in any other district be brought before the court, the court may cause such parties to be summoned, and process for that purpose may be served in any judicial district of the United States by the marshall of such judicial district.

nutrition. Obtaining any medical evidence of sexual abuse which results from the production of child pornography requires special expertise and special sensitivity to the needs of the child. Such evidence is only a component of the evaluation and interpretation of findings which must be used with caution and understanding.

Sexually exploited children often must also undergo extensive psychotherapy to restore their mental health. Therapy is costly and may often be outside the limits of ordinary medical insurance. Monies available in the state victims of crimes fund should be used to defray the cost of this evaluation and treatment. The distribution of monies from these funds also recognizes the real injury which these children have suffered.

"(c) In any civil or criminal action or proceeding under this chapter in the district court of the United States for any judicial district, a subpoena issued by such court to compel the attendance of witnesses may be served in any other judicial district except that no subpoena shall be issued for service upon any individual who resides in another district at the place more than one hundred miles from the place at which such court is held without approval given by a judge of such court upon a showing of good cause.

"(d) All other process in any action or proceeding under this chapter may be served on any person in any judicial district in which such person resides, is found, has an agent, or transacts his affairs.

S2258. EXPEDITION OF ACTIONS.

"In any civil action instituted under this chapter by the United States in any district court of the United States, the Attorney General may file with the clerk of such court a certificate stating that in his opinion the case is of general public importance. A copy of that certificate shall be furnished immediately by such clerk to the chief judge or in his absence to the presiding district judge of the district in which such action is pending. Upon receipt of such copy, such judge shall designate immediately a judge of that district to hear and determine the action. The judge designated to hear and determine the action shall assign the action for hearing as soon as practicable and hold hearings and make a determination as expeditiously as possible.

S2259. EVIDENCE.

"In any proceeding ancillary to or in any civil action instituted under this chapter the proceedings may be opened or closed to the public at the discretion of the court after consideration of the rights of affected persons.

S2260. LIMITATIONS.

"A civil action under section 2255 or 2256 of this chapter must be brought within six years from the date the violation is committed. In any such action brought by or on behalf of a person who was a minor at the date the violation was committed, the running of such six-year period shall be deemed to have been tolled during the period of such person's minority."

Sec. 5 (a) The section analysis for chapter 110 of part 1 of Title 18, United States Code, is amended to read as follows:

"CHAPTER 110—SEXUAL EXPLOITATION

"See:
"2251. Sexual Exploitation.
"2252. Certain activities relating to material sexual exploitation.
"2253. Criminal forfeiture.
"2254. Civil forfeiture.
"2255. Civil remedies.
"2256. Civil penalties.
"2257. Expedition of actions.
"2259. Evidence.
"2260. Limitations.
"2261. Definitions for chapter.
"2262. Severability.

(b) The chapter analysis for part 1 of title 18, United States Code, is amended by striking the item relating to chapter 110 and inserting in lieu thereof the following:

"110. Sexual Exploitation . . . . 2251".

Sec. 6 Chapter 110 of title 18, United States Code, is amended by inserting after section 2261 the following:

"If the provisions of any part of this Act or the amendments made by this Act, or the application thereof, to any person or circumstances is held invalid, the provisions of the other parts of this Act or the amendments made by this Act and their applications to other persons or circumstances shall not be affected."

RECOMMENDATION 82:

Clinical evaluators should be trained to assist children victimized through the production and use of child pornography more effectively and better understand adult psychosexual disorders.

Discussion

Clinicians should be trained in the types of problems that may be associated with child sexual exploitation which results from the production of child pornography.[683] Problems with children may include generalized withdrawl or assaultive behavior. Child victims may also display specific inappropriate sexual behavior or specific target sources of anxiety (e.g., men with beards).

Counselors treating these children must

---

683. In addition to requiring certain individuals to report known and suspected cases of child maltreatment, California law now requires mental health professionals to complete coursework or training related to child abuse and neglect.

The Bill

ASSEMBLY BILL NO. 141

ADDITION TO BUSINESS AND PROFESSIONS CODE, SECTION 28

The Legislature finds that there is a need to ensure that professionals of the healing arts who have demonstrable contact with child abuse victims, potential child abuse victims, and child abusers and potential child abusers are provided with adequate and appropriate training regarding the assessment and reporting of child abuse which will ameliorate, reduce, and eliminate the trauma of child abuse and neglect and ensure that reporting of child abuse in a timely manner to prevent additional occurrences.

The Psychology Examining Committee and the Board of Behavioral Science Examiners shall establish required training in the area of child abuse assessment and reporting for all persons applying for initial licensure and renewal of a license as a psychologist, clinical social worker, or marriage, family, and child counselor on or after January 1, 1987. This training shall be required on time for all persons applying for initial licensure or for licensure renewal on or after January 1, 1987.

All persons applying for initial licensure and renewal of a license as psychologist, clinic social worker, or marriage, family and child counselor on or after January 1, 1987, shall, in additional to all other requirements for licensure or renewal, have completed coursework or training in child abuse assessment and detailed knowledge of Section 11165 of the Penal code. The training shall:

(a) Be completed after January 1, 1983.

(b) Be obtained from one of the following sources:

(1) An accredited or approved educational institution, as defined in Section 2902, including extension courses offered by those institutions.

(2) An educational institution approved by the Department of Education pursuant to Section 94310 of the Education Code.

(3) A continuing education provider approved by the responsible board or examining committee.

(4) A course sponsored or offered by a professional association or a local, county, or state department of health or mental health for continuing education and approved by the responsible board.

(c) Have a minimum of 7 contact hours.

(d) Include the study of the assessment and method of reporting of sexual assault, neglect, severe neglect, general neglect, willful cruelty or unjustifiable punishment, corporal punishment or injury, and abuse in out-of-home care. The training shall also include physical and behavioral indicators of abuse, crisis counseling techniques, community resources, rights and responsibilities of reporting, consequences of failure to report, caring for a child's needs after a report is made, sensitivity to previously abused children and adults, and implications and methods of treatment for children and adults.

(e) All applicants shall provide the appropriate board with documentation of completion of the required child abuse training.

The Psychology Examining Committee and the Board of Behavioral Science Examiners shall exempt any applicant who applies for an exemption from the requirements of this section and who shows to the satisfaction of the committee or board that there would be no need for the training in his or her practice because of the nature of that practice.

It is the intent of the Legislature that a person licensed as a psychologist, clinical social worker, or marriage, family, and child counselor have minimal but appropriate training in the areas of child abuse assessment and reporting. It is not intended that by solely complying with the requirements of this section, a practitioner is fully trained in the subject of treatment of child abuse victims and abusers.

also be trained to work effectively with families and other caretakers of victims (e.g., foster parent, extended family child care, professionals). Child caretakers need help to understand possible future behaviors of child victims, alleviate anxiety and avoid creating unnecessary abnormal behaviors as a result of adult inappropriate over-reactive expectations. Parents of five year old victims might be more understanding of and more effective in dealing with recurrent bedwetting or sexual behavior if they are prepared.[684]

Clinicians evaluating child pornography victims also need training in legal and judicial procedures to assure that the evaluation and counseling process does not conflict with the proper disposition of the criminal case.

RECOMMENDATION 83:
Behavioral scientists should conduct research to determine the effects of the production of child pornography and the related victimization on children.

Discussion

It is important that victim research examine the short and long-term effects of the sexual victimization of children. Dr. Roland Summit, a leading medical authority, expressed the need for additional research crucial to this Commission.[685] An understanding of the behavioral patterns of child victims is especially lacking. The child may be disbelieved upon disclosure, during investigation, or as a witness in court.[686] Parents or other child advocates may also be attacked for supporting their child's version of the offense.[687]

Behavioral scientists also should learn more of the characteristics of the child pornographer and the pedophile offender. These conclusions will be valuable to law enforcement agents, prosecutors, judges, parents, and therapists. This research will form the basis for a sound program to curb the sexual exploitation of children.[688]

Such research should include a systematic observation of the child pornographic component of an experience separate from other criminal acts in cases that include pornography and other forms of child abuse. Research should also examine the effects of adult pornography on children.

RECOMMENDATION 84:
States should support age-appropriate education and prevention programs for parents, teachers and children within public and private school systems to protect children from victimization by child pornographers and child sexual abusers.

Discussion

The educational programs must inform children while at the same time preserving a child's innocence and basic trust. The program should avoid instilling any unhealthy fear or mistrust in children. It may focus on the difference between positive healthy affection and touching or contact which is harmful to the child. Training for parents and school personnel should center on how to identify cases and how to report the information to the proper agencies.[689]

RECOMMENDATION 85:
A multi-media educational campaign should be developed which increases family and

---

684. Anticipatory guidance as designed by the American Academy of Pediatrics (AAP) Health Care Service is a useful model.

685. Miami Hearing, Vol. I, Roland Summit, p. 209.

686. *Id.*, p. 199, 216A1.

687. *Id.*, p. 200.

688. UCLA has recently received a federal grant to study long-term effects of exploitation on the McMartin Pre-School child victims.

689. California has developed the educational program, *Child Abuse: Recognize and Eliminate* (CARE). A description of the program follows for purposes of illustration.

CARE PROGRAM

STUDENT WORKSHOP DESCRIPTION

Over eighty percent of child molestations are perpetuated by adults known to the child. The majority of incidents of sexual abuse take place in the home of the abuser or the child. Boys are equally as vulnerable as girls. Child molesters cannot be identified easily; they come from all races, religions, professions, and socio-economic classes. Children can be taught to protect themselves from unwanted, uncomfortable and potentially abusive situations.

C.A.R.E. (Child Abuse: Recognize and Eliminate) is the Los Angeles Unified School District's extensive school-based educational program on child abuse prevention. The student component of CARE is an exemplary model of instruction

community awareness regarding child sexual exploitation through the production and use of child pornography.

Discussion

A multi-media program should inform families and communities of the materials and seduction techniques used by child pornographers and pedophile offenders. The child pornographer or pedophile offender may befriend a potential victim, buy him or her gifts, or take the child on trips. Pedophile offenders or child pornographers may also volunteer their services to be near children in activities such as sports, daycare centers, schools or camps. Because of this seduction process, a child victim's sexual encounters with a pedophile molester may never seem traumatic.[690] The subtle manner in which they abuse their victims necessitates a heightened awareness on the part of children and their parent. While parents or other adult caretakers may be uncomfortable in posing questions about sexuality to their child, parents may be more receptive to a trained professional who candidly answers such questions.[691] Each of these programs should list individuals or services in the community where parents or children may seek information or assistance. These facilities should incorporate a variety of social services as well as the availability of legal advice. They should also assemble information as to agencies which provide particular types of assistance.[692]

---

for children in pre-kindergarten through grade six. Based on the concepts of self-esteem and self-protection, this instruction is conducted in small groups at the school by S.C.A.N. (School Child Abuse and Neglect) Team members. A SCAN Team is a group of onsite school personnel who have received intensive training in child abuse prevention and intervention. Student instruction is one component of this extensive school-based child abuse educational program.

The SCAN Team's role in presenting the student lesson is critical. Since all instruction is delivered by the same individuals, there is a strong assurance that consistency in the information presented is maintained and, that all the children receive this information. (The SCAN Team presents the student curriculum to all students every year). In addition, because SCAN Team Members are full-time, on-site certificated staff, any one or all of the team is available on a daily basis to attend to the needs, problems and/or concerns of any child at any time. If a child needs assistance one week, six weeks or six months after the initial presentation, a trained person known to the child is there to help. SCAN Team members return to the classrooms periodically to reintroduce themselves and remind children of their availability and willingness to meet and talk with the child at any time and for any reason.

The initial basic program includes a directed lesson, film, discussion and question/answer period, and an opportunity for immediate private counseling. The follow-up lesson which takes place approximately six weeks later, focuses on reinforcing the central concepts in a discussion and presenting a different film. The primary message of the instruction emphasizes the value of the child as a human being. The concepts are introduced and developed using a self-esteem approach:

> you are valuable
> you are the best person to protect yourself
> you have rights
> you can communicate
> you have power
> you can get help

Specific strategies—say "no," get away and tell someone—are presented in both the lesson and the film, "Better Safe than Sorry, II." The film presents real-life situations in a what-if format; students react with the children in the film to potentially abusive situations involving strangers, a neighbor and someone in the family. They learn to say "no" to an adult who is bothering them and that not all secrets should be kept. Telling how you feel is the best rule to follow even when it is another person making you feel funny, bad or uncomfortable. Children are told who to tell and specifically introduced to those at the school site who are available for help. Students are instructed to keep telling until believed. Children learn they have a right to body privacy and that some parts of the body, "private parts," need special protection. After they practice various ways to say "no," they learn ways to remove themselves from uncomfortable situations. The concepts "It's not your fault" and "It's right to tell" are emphasized throughout.

After the lesson and film, children have an opportunity to ask questions. Strategies for protection are reinforced and private crisis counseling is immediately available. Four to six weeks later, the SCAN Team members review the concepts using another film, "Now I Can Tell You My Secret." At this time strategies are re-taught, and who and how to tell is re-emphasized. If a child discloses or is identified as needing intervention or referral, the SCAN Team members will report to the appropriate agency and coordinate needed services.

The CARE student instruction stresses safety not fear. It maintains a balance between addressing past and current victims, and not scaring other children. It teaches children that they have rights. It emphasizes the child's self-worth and value. The information provides children the skills necessary for self-protection in potentially abusive situations and gain the confidence to apply these skills. The goal of the instruction if that children learn how to respond to any type of threatening situation. A secure child who knows he is valuable and trusts his feelings is better prepared to recognize potentially dangerous situations, react appropriately, and keep himself safe.

C H A P T E R • 1 2

Victimization

RECOMMENDATION 86:
State, county and municipal governments should facilitate the development of public and private resources for persons who are currently involved in the production or consumption of pornography and wish to discontinue this involvement and for those who suffer mental and physical disabilities as a result of exposure or participation in the production of pornography.

Discussion

As described later in Chapters 16 and 17, victims of pornography may suffer a variety of physical and mental damages. The victimization may include coercion, intimidation, negative effects of forced consumption, physical assault and sexual harassment.

Resources currently exist for victims of sexual abuse and other crimes through victim compensation programs, mental health and medical treatment programs. However, if no crime is reported, as is often the case with pornography, the damages cannot be compensated by victims of crime funds. Furthermore, if mental health or medical staff are not aware of the special nature of pornography victimization, treatment may not be effective in rehabilitating the victim. Those currently involved in the production or forced into consumption of pornography are not aware of alternatives available to them, and they may never believe they can escape the victimization.

Resources for victims of pornography should include:

(A) emergency "safe houses" where persons needing short-term refuge from production or forced consumption of pornography, (B) financial assistance for persons damaged by pornography who do not qualify for public assistance or victims of crimes funds, (C) development of public information materials to assist persons escape victimization through awareness of alternatives, (D) provision of job training and educational opportunities to those who have been denied such opportunities because of financial losses, physical or mental damages incurred through production or forced consumption of pornography, (E) provision of specialized training for counselors and therapists to sensitize them to a special nature of pornography and related sexual victimization.

This training should include particular recognition of the correlated problems of substance abuse, and the allocation of resources to study short- and long-term effects of pornography on those who participate in its production and those who are forcibly exposed to it.

APPENDIX A

The following questionnaire now used in New York and other major cities may serve as an example of the types of issues to be discussed.

"Pornography," as referred to in the question below, includes "men's entertainment" magazines such as *Playboy, Penthouse,* and *Hustler,* as well as hard-core publications showing explicit sex between men and women, between two women, between two men, and between adults and children. Such publications may show women or children tied up or hurt, women or children being penetrated by penises, fists, or objects, and women or children having sex with animals. "Pornography" also includes books, films, cable television programs, and video tapes showing these scenarios.

IF THE ASSAILANT LIVED WITH OR WAS KNOWN TO THE VICTIM

1. Did/do you live with the man who assaulted you?
2. If so, what was/is your relationship?
3. If not, how do you know him?
4. Did/does your assailant use or collect pornography?
5. If so, what kind?
6. Do you know the specific names or titles of the magazines, films, programs or video tapes? If so, what are they?
7. Did/does he use pornography for masturbation?
8. Did/does he use it to get aroused before sexual relations?
9. Did he ever ask you to view pornography with him?
10. Did he ever pressure you to view pornography with him?
11. Did he ever force you to view pornography with him?
12. Was pornography used as part of your normal sexual encounters?
13. If so, how was it used?
14. Did he ever ask you to act out scenes from pornography?
15. Did he ever pressure you to act out scenes from pornography?
16. Did he ever force you to act out scenes from pornography?
17. Did he ever mention pornography in your sexual encounters?
18. Did he ever ask you to pose for nude or pornographic photos or films?
19. Did he ever pressure you to pose for nude or pornographic photos or films?
20. Did he ever force you to pose for nude or pornographic photos or films?
21. Did he ever send nude photographs of you to a magazine or "wife-swapping" club newsletter?
22. Did he ever show nude photographs of you to his friends?
23. Did he ever sell nude photographs of you?
24. Did he refer to pornography when he assaulted you? For example, did he say anything like, "This is what women ask for in the magazines I read," or "This is what the woman did in the movie, and she loved it?"
25. During the assault, did he force you to act out scenes from pornography?
26. Did he, or anyone involved in the assault, take nude or pornographic pictures of you before, during, or after the assault?
27. Did he show you pornographic pictures or films prior to, or after the assault?
28. Did/does he use pornography to learn or teach you sexual techniques? To teach you how to dress in a way that turns him on? To learn how to tie you up?
29. Does he use pornography to justify sex acts that you don't want to participate in? For example, does he show you pictures and say, "A lot of couples do this," or "Look how much she likes doing it."
30. Did/does he use "dial-a-porn" services? Frequent X-rated movie theatres? Frequent establishments that have live sex shows and X-rated film loops or topless and/or bottomless bars and clubs?
31. If so, has he ever asked, pressured, or forced you to attend these establishments with him?
32. Did/does he go to massage parlors, use "escort services," or use prostitutes?

IF THE VICTIM DID NOT KNOW HER ASSAILANT(S)

1. Did your assailant refer to pornography when he assaulted you? For example, did he say anything like, "This is what women ask for in the movie, and she loved it?"
2. Did the assailant show you pornography or use pornography during the assault? If so, what kind?
3. Did the assailants(s) take pictures or films of you during the assault?
4. During the assault were you forced to act out scenes that were from pornography described or displayed by the assailant?
5. Did your assault take place in an area in which there are a lot of pornographic establishments, such as X-rated movie theatres, bookstores, etc."
6. Was there pornography in the place in which you were assaulted?

QUESTIONS FOR WOMEN, GIRLS, AND BOYS WHO HAVE BEEN USED IN PORNOGRAPHY

1. Were you a runaway? If so, when did you leave home?
2. Had you been sexually abused before you left home? If so, by whom? How? How old were you

when the abuse took place? How old was the person who abused you? Was that person a family member or friend?

3. If you were abused before you left home, was pornography part of the abuse? How was it used?
4. Were you involved in prostitution? Did you have a pimp? Was there an older man who told you what to do, made you have sex for money, and collected the money afterwards?
5. How did you first become involved in pornography? What were the circumstances of your life? How old were you?
6. What kind of pornography were you used in?
7. Were you forced into the making of pornography by:
   a. Threats?   d. Trickery?
   b. Violence?   e. Pressure by a relative,
   c. Poverty?   friend, or lover?
   Explain.
8. Were you shown magazines such as *Playboy, Penthouse, Hustler, Screw,* or others or were you shown films to convince you to pose for pornography?
9. Do you know other people who have been forced or pressured into posing for pornography?
10. Were you ever beaten, whipped, spanked, or physically hurt in the making of pornography? Were you ever tied up? Did you have to act out violent scenes? Was the sex physically painful?
11. Do you know people who were physically hurt in the making of pornography?
12. Do you know who produced or profited from the pornography you were used in? Do you know if they were involved in organized crime?
13. Do you know about or have you heard about people being murdered in the making of pornography?
14. Were you in prostitution while you were being used to make pornography? Were other women, girls, or boys you know in pornography also in prostitution?
15. How has your experience in pornography affected how you feel about yourself? How has it affected your relationships with others? Your schooling and/or job performance?
16. Do you ever have flashbacks or nightmares about your experience in pornography?
17. Do you suffer from phobias?
18. How do you feel now when you see pornography?
19. Have you had upsetting experiences with pornography outside your experiences in the sex industry?
20. What would you like to see done to help women, girls or boys who have been used/abused in pornography?
21. Would you like to be able to take legal action against the people who abused you? Would you like to be able to sue them? Would you like to be able to stop the pornography used against you from being shown?

QUESTIONS ABOUT SEXUAL HARASSMENT AND PORNOGRAPHY

Victims of sexual harassment through pornography in public places

1. Is pornography displayed in public places in your community?
2. If so, where is it and what kinds of materials?
3. How does this material make you feel about yourself? How does it make you feel about your relationships with others?
4. Have any people you know been upset by pornographic materials they've seen?
5. Have you ever been sexually harassed by men in pornography districts, in front of pornography theaters or bookstores, in front of the pornography sections of newsstand, grocery store, or drugstore?
6. If so, how did this make you feel?
7. Does the pervasiveness of pornography upset you or frighten you?
8. Does pornography make you frightened to perform your daily activities such as traveling to and from your job?
9. Have you every been sexually harassed by men who referred to pornography or made comments to you that seemed to come from pornography?

Victims of sexual harassment involving pornography on the job

1. Is pornography displayed or used at your place of employment?
2. If so, what kind? Where do you see it? Who uses it?
3. Have you ever been sexually harassed on the job? If so, was pornography involved in harassment, i.e., did your boss, co-worker, or customer show you pornography, display pornography, or make verbal references to pornography?

4. Have your co-workers, bosses, or customers ever compared you to models in pornography?
5. How has the presence or use of pornography in your place of work made you feel about yourself and your ability to perform your job?
6. Have you ever complained to anyone about sexual harassment on the job involving pornography? If so, to whom? If not, why not?
7. Were any steps taken about the harassment?
8. Have you ever been forced to leave your job or have you ever considered leaving your job because of sexual harassment involving or related to pornography?
9. Do you think that pornography has contributed to the way your boss, co-workers, or employers view you and relate to you?

Victims of sexual harassment through pornography in schools and other institutions

1. Is pornography displayed or used in your school?
2. If so, what kind? Where do you see it? Who uses it?
3. Has pornography ever been used in your classroom, i.e., in a course on human sexuality? Have any of your teachers or professors ever used pornographic slides or made references to pornography?
4. Have you ever complained about the presence or use of pornography at your school? If so, to whom? Was any action taken? If not, why not?
5. Have your teachers or fellow students ever used pornography to sexually harass you? Have they ever made verbal references to pornography that have made you feel uncomfortable?
6. Have you ever had pornography imposed on you in social situations at school, such as in fraternity parties or during fraternity or sorority initiations?

Victims of sexual harassment through pornography at home

1. Is there pornography in your home?
2. Do any of your relatives or friends use pornography or make verbal references to it?
3. If so, how does it make you feel?
4. Have you ever attempted to remove the pornography from your home? Were you successful?
5. Do your children see or know about pornography that is kept in your home? If so, has it influenced the way they think about women and sexuality?

C H A P T E R • 1 3

Civil Rights

RECOMMENDATION 87:

Legislatures should conduct hearings and consider legislation recognizing a civil remedy for harm attributable to pornography.

Discussion

The Commission heard substantial testimony regarding a civil rights approach as a remedy for harms attributable to pornography.[693] An ordinance encompassing the civil rights approach was originally proposed in Minneapolis, Minnesota, and a similar ordinance was enacted in Indianapolis, Indiana.[694] In 1984, the Indianapolis-Marion County City-County Council found, in essence, that pornography lowers the social standard of treatment of women as a class. The Council found the status of women and the opportunity for equality are undermined by the pornography industry's use of some women to target all women for abuse through making acts of violation into acts of sexual entertainment.[695] The harm of pornography is thus conceived to be a form of discrimination on the basis of sex.[696]

Pornography, in effect, exemplifies inequality in its violation of human rights. It has been defined in the proposed ordinances as sexually explicit pictures or words that subordinate on the basis of sex when those presented are also shown being sexually exploited or brutalized—for example, women

presented as sexual objects enjoying rape, pain or humiliation, being penetrated by objects or animals, in postures of servility, submission or display, or in scenarios of degradation or torture in a context that makes these conditions sexual.[697] Men, children of both sexes, and transsexuals could sue for similar violations under the ordinance.[698]

Victims and trained professionals described the harms associated with and attributable to pornography, as including rape, battery, sexual harassment, sexual abuse of children, and forced prostitution.[699] Women have been coerced into pornographic performances by abduction, threats, drugs, and constant surveillance. Pornography has been forced on unwilling viewers, typically children or women, in homes, in employment, and in public places. Some assaults have been found to be caused by specific pornographic materials providing instigation as well as instruction and legitimization for the acts. Many experiences of pornography-related humiliation, sexual degradation, enforced servility, and physical and mental abuse were substantiated. On the basis of this evidence, civil claims were created for four specified activities: (1) coercion into pornography, (2) forcing pornography on a person, (3) assault directly caused by specific pornography, and (4) trafficking in pornography

---

693. See, Chicago Hearing, Vol. II, Catherine MacKinnon, p. 133; Chicago Hearing, Vol. II, Terese Stanton, p. 168; Houston Hearing, Vol. I, Diana Russell, p. 302; New York Hearing, Vol. II, Andrea Dworkin, p. 129; Washington, D.C., Hearing, Vol. I, Dorchen Leidholt, p. 197.

694.. See, Indianapolis-Marion County, Ind., Ordinance 35, ch. 16 (June 15, 1984).

695. *Id.* S16-1(a)(2).

696. See generally, MacKinnon, *Pornography, Civil Rights, and Speech*, 20 Harv.C.R.-C.L. L. Rev. 1(1985).

697. Indianapolis-Marion County, Ind., Ordinance 35, ch. 16 (June 15, 1984).

698. *Id.*

699. See, Houston Hearing, Vol. I, Diana Russell, p. 285; Miami Hearing, Vol. II, Garrett, p. 19; Washington, D.C., Hearing, Vol. I, Dorchen Leidholt, Vol. I, p. 205; Washington, D.C., Hearing, Vol. I, Sarah Wynter, p. 183.

(production, sale, exhibition, or distribution).[700] Injunctions and damages would be provided under narrowly specified conditions.[701]

The civil rights approach, although controversial,[702] is the only legal tool suggested to the Commission which is specifically designed to provide direct relief to the victims of the injuries so exhaustively documented in our hearings throughout the country. Most of the evidence that establishes the fact that pornography subordinates women and undermines their status and opportunities for equality comes from extra-judicial sources, studies and individual accounts.[703]

The United States Supreme Court has recognized and relied upon social and behavioral science findings in several decisions. In Muller v. Oregon,[704] the Supreme Court upheld the constitutionality of an Oregon law limiting women to a ten hour workday.[705] In support of the law, Louis D. Brandeis filed a brief containing what the Court called "a very copious collection" of "expressions of opinion from other than judicial sources."[706] Brandeis' brief contained evidence about women's reactions to contemporary work conditions gathered from surveys, government statistics, factory reports, and opinions of employers, employees, and physicians.[707] The Court relied on this evidence to sustain the Oregon law providing special protection for women in the workplace.[708] This method of presenting an argument became known as a "Brandeis Brief."[709]

Almost half a century later, the Supreme Court relied on social science evidence in the landmark school desegregation decision of Brown v. Board of Education.[710] In declaring "separate but equal" schools unconstitutional, the Court found that segregated facilities have a detrimental effect on children.[711] The Court agreed that,

> segregation with the sanction of law . . . has a tendency to [retard] the educational and mental developments of negro children and to deprive them of some of the benefits they would receive in a racial[ly] integrated school system.[712]

The Court added that "this finding is amply supported by modern authority,"[713] and cited, among others, Kenneth Clark and Gunnar Myrdal.[714] The Court's reliance on this material as a basis for finding discrimination was subject to some criticism.[715] On one later occasion, the Court heard "a great deal of medical and sociological"[716] evidence about alcoholism, but rejected it as going "too far on too little knowledge"[717] and declined to find criminal sanctions against public drunkenness to be cruel and unusual punishment.[718] However, the Court has relied upon extrajudicial proof in cases dealing with issues as diverse as the death penalty[719] and the

---

700. See, Indianapolis-Marion County, Ind. Ordinance 39, S16–3(g) (4)-(7) (June 15, 1984).

701. Id. S16–27.

702. See, Chicago Hearing, Vol. II, Nan Hunter, p. 101; Chicago Hearing, Vol. II, Burton Joseph, p. 4; Houston Hearing, Vol. II, John Money, p. 34; Washington, D.C., Hearing Vol. II, Barry Lynn, pp. 169–70.

703. See, MacKinnon, Pornography, Civil Rights, and Speech, 20 Harv.C.R.-C.L. L. Rev. 1(1985).

704. 208 U.S. (1908), p.412.

705. Id., p. 416.

706. Id., p. 419, n.1.

707. Levin & Moise, School Desegregation Litigation in the Seventies and the Use of Social Science Evidence—An Annotated Guide, 39 Law and Contemp. Probs. 50, 51 (1975) [hereinafter cited as Levin & Moise, School Desegregation].

708. 208 U.S., pp. 419–21.

709. Levin & Moise, School Desegregation, supra, note 707, p. 51.

710. 347 U.S. (1954), p. 483.

711. Id., p. 494.

712. Id.

713. Id.

714. Id., pp. 494–95, n. 11.

715. See, Cahn, Jurisprudence, 30 N.Y.U. L. Rev. (1955), p. 150; Fiss, The Jurisprudence of Busing, 39 Law & Contemp. Probs. (1975), p. 194.

716. Powell v. Texas, 392 U.S. 514, (1968), p. 537 (Black, J., concurring).

717. Id., p. 521.

718. Id., pp. 521–23.

719. Furman v. Georgia, 408 U.S. (1972), pp. 238, 250–51 n.15 (Douglas, J., concurring) (citing studies that conclude the death penalty is disproportionately applied in cases involving poor or black defendants); p. 307 n.7 (Stewart, J., concurring) (citing studies comparing crime rates in jurisdictions with death penalty provisions).

constitutionality of six member juries.[720] The late Judge J. Braxton Craven of the United States Court of Appeals for the Fourth Circuit noted that "Brandeis briefs" are now standard operating procedure in equal employment, ecology, and school desegregation cases.[721] Judge Craven wrote,

> To give a simplistic answer to a difficult question, the role that the social sciences ought to play in the judicial decision making process is of course the same as the role of any other science whether medical, electronic, or atomic.
>
> In short, all sources of human information and knowledge properly contribute to the determination of the facts.[722]

Judge Craven concluded with respect to the extra judicial proof in *Brown v. Board of Education*,

> Although startling at the time, the decision now rests upon a bedrock of public opinion that school assignments and legal distinctions based on race are unfair and that enforced separation of a minority group stigmatizes them.[723]

James B. McMillan, United States District Judge in the Western District of North Caroline, wrote, "The study of people and their problems is a natural prerequisite of the legal decision of problems among people."[724] It is this very type of evidence that the Commission has found to be persuasive. While the United States Court of Appeals for the Seventh Circuit found the Indianapolis ordinance unconstitutional because of its definition of "pornography,"[725] the court ac-

cepted the premise of the legislation and said,

> Depictions of subordination tend to perpetuate subordination. The subordinate status of women in turn leads to affront and lower pay at work, insult and injury at home, battery and rape on the streets. In the language of the legislature, "pornography is central in creating and maintaining sex as a basis of discrimination. Pornography is a systematic practice of exploitation and subordination based on sex which differentially harms women. The bigotry and contempt it produces, with the acts of aggression it fosters, harm women's opportunities for equality and rights [of all kinds]." Indianapolis code S16–1(a) (2).[726]

The court of appeals recognized that pornography harms women just as the United States Supreme Court found excessive working hours harmful to women in *Muller v. Oregon* and segregated schools harmful to minority students in *Brown v. Board of Education*. As a result of the United States Supreme Court's summary affirmance of the court of appeals in *Hudnut v. American Booksellers Association*,[727] proponents of the civil rights approach to pornography must attempt to fashion a definition of pornography which will pass constitutional muster.

The Commission recommends that any civil rights approach used to address harms attributable to pornography should include an affirmative defense of a knowing and voluntary consent to the acts. This defense would prevent performers who choose to engage in the production of pornographic materials from seeking recovery.

---

720. *Williams, v. Florida*, 399 U.S. (1970), pp. 78, 101–02 n. 49 (citing psychological evidence that twelve member juries are no more advantageous to criminal defendants than six member panels).

721. Craven, *The Impact of Social Service Evidence on the Judge—A Personal Comment*, 39 Law & Contemp. Probs. (1975), pp. 157, 63.

722. *Id.*

723. *Id.*, p. 153.

724. J.B. McMillan, *Social Science and the District Court The Observations of a Journeyman Trial Judge*, 39 Law & Contemp. Probs. (1975), p. 157, 163.

725. *American Booksellers Ass'n v. Hudnut*, 771 F.2d (1985), p. 323, 325.

726. *Id.*, p. 329 In footnote 2, the court added,

> In saying that we accept the finding that pornography as the ordinance defines it leads to unhappy consequences, we mean only that there is evidence to this effect, that this evidence is consistent with much human experience, and that as judges we must accept the legislative resolution of such disputed empirical questions.

See *Gregg v. Georgia*, 428 U.S., pp. 153, 184–87, 196 S.Ct. 2909, 2930–31, 49 L.Ed.2d, p. 859 (1976) (opinion of Stewart, Powell, and Stevens, J.).

727. 54 U.S.L.W. 3548(Feb. 25, 1986).

CONCLUSION

The pattern of harm documented before the Commission, taken as a whole, supports the conclusion that the pornography industry systematically violates human rights with apparent impunity. The most powerless citizens in society are singled out on the basis of their gender—often aggravated by their age, race, disability, or other vulnerability—for deprivations of liberty, property, labor, bodily and psychic security and integrity, privacy, reputation, and even life.

So that pornography can be made, victims have been exploited under conditions providing them a lack of choice and have been coerced to perform sex acts against their will. Public figures and private individuals alike are defamed in pornography with increasing frequency. It is also foreseeable, on the basis of our evidence, that unwilling individuals have been forced to consume pornography, in order to pressure or induce or humiliate or browbeat them into performing the acts depicted. Individuals have also been deprived of equal access to services, employment or education as a result of acts relating to pornography. Acts of physical aggression more and more appear tied to the targeting of women and children for sexual abuse in these materials.[728]

Through these means, the pornographers' abuse of individual members of protected groups both victimizes them and notifies all of society that such abuse of them is permitted. This in turn serves to terrorize others in their group and contributes to a general atmosphere of bigotry and contempt for their rights and human dignity, in an impact reminiscent of the Ku Klux Klan. Respect for law is undermined when such flagrant violations go unchecked—even more so when they are celebrated as liberties protected by government.

We therefore conclude the pornography, when it leads to coerced viewing, contributes to an assault, is defamatory, or is actively trafficked in, constitutes a practice of discrimination on the basis of sex. Any legal protections which currently exist for such practices are inconsistent with contemporary notions of individual equality.

The Commission accordingly recommends that the legislature should conduct public hearings and consider legislation affording protection to those individuals whose civil rights have been violated by the production or distribution of pornography. The legislation should define pornography realistically and encompass all those materials, and only those materials, which actively deprive citizens of such rights. At a minimum, claims could be provided against trafficking, coercion, forced viewing, defamation, and assault, reaching the industry as necessary to remedy these abuses, consistent with the First and Fourteenth Amendments.

---

728. See, Recommendations for Regulating Child Pornography in Chapter 11 and the complete discussion of Victimization in Chapters 12 and 16.

C H A P T E R   •   1 4

Nuisance Laws

The exhibition of obscene materials constitutes "a crime involving the welfare of the public at large, since it is contrary to the standards of decency and propriety of the community as a whole."[729] Thus the exhibition of obscene materials may be enjoined as a public nuisance under applicable state law or local ordinance.[730]

Nuisance abatement suits have successfully been brought to enjoin the exhibition or dissemination of specific books, magazines, or movies.[731] However, the constitutional provisions against prior restraint of presumptively protected speech is an important limitation on the use of nuisance actions.[732]

Plaintiffs in civil nuisance actions should use procedures which include procedural safeguards against invalid prior restraints.[733]

The United States Supreme Court rejected the application of nuisance statutes to enjoin the future exhibition of unnamed films in an "adults only" pornographic theater.[734]

Courts have also been unwilling to enjoin the future operation of "adults only" pornographic outlets or theaters that have exhibited obscene publications or films in the past because of First Amendment concerns regarding prior restraints.[735] Other courts have upheld injunctions closing the offending establishments for a period of one year.[736]

To avoid First Amendment challenges, nuisance actions may also be brought based upon lewd activity, assignation, or prostitution occurring on the premises where the obscene material is sold or exhibited.[737]

---

729. *Evans Theater Corp. v. Slaton*, 180 S.E.2d, (Ga. 1971), pp. 712, 715-16, *cert. denied* 404 U.S., p. 950.

730. See, *Paris Adult Theatre I v. Slaton*, 413 U.S., (1973), pp. 49, 54–55.

731. See, *Trans-Lux Corp. v. State*, 366; So. 2d, (Ala. 1979), p. 710; *Sanders v. State*, 203 S.E.2d, (Ga.), p. 153; *Minor v. Central Ave. News, Inc.*, 308 N.W.2d, (N.D. 1981), p. 851 , *app. dism.* 102 (Okla.); *People ex rel Busch v. Projection Room Theater*, 550 P.2d, (1976), p. 600.

732. See generally, *Freedman v. Maryland*, 380 U.S., (1965), p. 51; *Southeastern Promotions, Ltd. v. Conrad*, 420 U.S., (1975), p. 546.

733. See, *Southeastern Promotions, Ltd. v. Conrad*, 420 U.S. p. 560.

734. *Vance v. Universal Amusement Co.*, 445 U.S., (1980), p. 308.

735. *People ex rel. Busch v. Projection Room Theater*, 550 P.2d, (1976), p. 600; *State v. A Motion Picture Entitled "The Bet"*, 547 P.2d, (Kan.), p. 760.

736. *State ex rel. Cahalan v. Diversified Theatrical Corp.*, 229 N.W.2d, (Mich. App.), p. 389; *City of Tallmadge v. Avenue Book Store*, No. 10038(Ohio App. Summit County, Oct. 28, 1981) *cert. denied* 459 U.S., (1982), p. 997.

737. *People v. Adult World Bookstore*, 108 Cal. App. 3d 404, 166 Cal. Rptr., (1980), p. 519; *People v. Golman*, 7 Ill. App. 3d 253, 287 N.E.2d, (Ill. 1972), p. 177.

C H A P T E R • 1 5

Anti-Display Laws

Anti-display laws regulate the method by which pornographic materials can be publicly displayed. Statutes or ordinances may be enacted to restrict the display of sexually explicit materials to minors. In order to withstand constitutional challenges, such laws should apply only to materials that are obscene as to minors.[738] The regulations also should contain reasonable time, place, and manner restrictions.[739]

In *M.S. News Co. v. Casado*,[740] the United States Court of Appeals for the Tenth Circuit upheld a Wichita, Kansas, ordinance which restricted the display of material "harmful to minors."[741] The Wichita ordinance defined "harmful to minors" as any

> description, exhibition, presentation or representation, in whatever form, of nudity, sexual conduct, sexual excitement, or sado-masochistic abuse when the material or performance, taken as a whole, has the following characteristics:
>
> (a) The average adult person applying contemporary community standards would find that the material or performance has a predominant tendency to appeal to a prurient interest in sex to minors; and
>
> (b) The average adult person applying contemporary community standards would find that the material or performance de-

> picts or describes nudity, sexual conduct, sexual excitement or sado-masochistic abuse in a manner that is patently offensive to prevailing standards in the adult community with respect to what is suitable for minors and
>
> (c) The material or performance lacks serious literary, scientific, educational, artistic, or political value for minors.[742]

The ordinance also provided criminal penalties.

The penalties may be imposed when any person having custody, control or supervision of any commercial establishment shall knowingly:

> (a) display material which is harmful to minors in such a way that minors, as a part of the invited general public, will be exposed to view such material provided; however, a person shall be deemed not to have "displayed" material harmful to minors if the material is kept behind devices commonly known as "blinder racks" so that the lower two-thirds of the material is not exposed to view.[743]

The court of appeals found that the definition of "harmful to minors" properly tracked the standards enunciated in *Ginsberg v. New*

---

738. See, *Ginsberg v. New York*, 390 U.S., (1968), pp. 629, 645–47.
739. See, *Young v. American Mini-Theaters*, 427 U.S., (1976), pp. 50, 63.
740. 721 F.2d, (10th Cir. 1983), p. 1281.
741. Wichita, Kan., Ordinance no. 36–172, S5.68, (1985), p. 156.
742. *Id.*
743. *Id.*

191

York,[744] and *Miller v. California*.[745] The requirement that the lower two-thirds of the material be covered was neither over-broad nor vague.[746] While the ordinance did restrict adult's opportunity to view the materials, it did not prevent an adult from purchasing them.[747] The Court found the ordinance to be a reasonable time, place, and manner restriction justified by the government's interest in protecting minors.[748]

A Minneapolis, Minnesota, ordinance[749] which was more restrictive than the one enacted in Wichita withstood a constitutional challenge in *Upper Midwest Booksellers v. City of Minneapolis*.[750] The Minneapolis Ordinance provided,

It is unlawful for any person commercially and knowingly to exhibit, display, sell, offer to sell, give away, circulate, distribute, or attempt to distribute any material which is harmful to minors in its content in any place where minors are or may be present or allowed to be present and where minors are able to view such material unless each item of such material is at all times kept in a sealed wrapper.

(a) It is also unlawful for any person commercially and knowingly to exhibit, display, sell, offer to sell, give away, circulate, distribute, or attempt to distribute any material whose cover, covers, or packaging, standing alone, is harmful to minors, in any place where minors are able to view such material unless each item of such material is blocked from view by an opaque cover. The requirement of an

opaque cover shall be deemed satisfied concerning such material if those portions of the cover, covers, or packaging containing such material harmful to minors are blocked from view by an opaque cover.[751]

The Booksellers maintained that the requirement of a sealed wrapper was unduly restrictive as to an adult's right to peruse the materials which were harmful to minors but not to adults.[752] The Court concluded that any inconvenience suffered by adult patrons was not sufficient to render the restrictions unconstitutional.[753] If adults wanted to peruse the materials covered by the ordinance, the Court reasoned that they would be able to do so in one of several ways: 1) ask a clerk to remove the wrapper; 2) view an "inspection copy" kept behind the store counter, or 3) view the material in an "adults only" pornography outlet that excludes minors.[754]

Display laws which define "harmful to minors" with language other than the *Ginsberg* standard have been found unconstitutional.[755]

While opaque covers and sealed wrappers are a permissible means of restricting the display of sexually explicit materials to minors, a Virginia statute which simply made it unlawful to display material harmful to minors in a manner "whereby juveniles may examine and peruse it" was found unconstitutional.[756] The Virginia statute contained no provisions for the use of opaque covers and the court found that outlets would face unreasonable burdens in complying with the statute.[757] They would have to deprive adults of the material, remove

744. 390 U.S., (1968), pp. 629, 645–47.
745. 413 U.S., (1973), pp. 15, 24.
746. 721 F.2d, (10th Cir.1983), pp. 1281, 1287.
747. Id. pp. 1288–89
748. Id.
749. Minneapolis, Minn., Ordinances S385.131(1985).
750. 602 F. Supp. 1361(D. Minn. 1985).
751. Minneapolis, Minn., Ordinances S385.131(6)(a)(1985).
752. 602 F. Supp. p. 1370.
753. Id. p. 1372.
754. Id.
755. See, *Hillsboro News Co. v. City of Tampa*, 451 F. Supp. 952(M.D. Fla. 1978) (ordinance restricted display of "offensive sexual material" found unconstitutionally vague); *American Booksellers Ass'n v. McAuliffe*, 533 F. Supp. 50 (N.D. Ga. 1981) (statute prohibiting display or sale to minors of material containing nude figures held overly broad because prohibition extends to material not obscene as to minors); *American Booksellers Ass'n, Inc. v. Superior Court*, 129 Cal. App. 3d 197, 181 Ca. Rptr. 33(1982) (ordinance over-broad because it required sealing material containing any photo whose primary purpose is sexual arousal regardless of whether obscene as to minors); *Calderon v. City of Buffalo*, 61 A.D.2d 323, 402 N.Y.S.2d, (1978), p. 685 (ordinance over-broad because it prohibited sale and exhibition to juveniles of material that was not obscene as to juveniles); *Oregon v. Frink*, 60 Or. App. 209, 653 P.2d, (1982), p. 553 (statute prohibiting dissemination of all nudity to minors over-broad because it does not limit prohibition to material that is obscene as to juveniles).
756. *American Booksellers Ass'n v. Strobel*, 617 F. Supp., (E.D. Va. 1985), p. 699.
757. Id., p. 706.

it from their shelves or ban minors from their stores.[758] The Court also found the idea of outlets restructuring their premises and creating an "adults only" section to be unreasonable.[759] The Court concluded the statute was over-broad as a time, place and manner restriction.[760] A requirement of opaque covers or "blinder racks" would have narrowed the scope of the restriction and could have provided the basis for the court upholding the statute in this case.[761]

---

758. *Id.*, pp. 702–03.
759. *Id.*
760. *Id.*, p. 706.
761. *Id.*, pp. 706–07.

PART

3

Pornography and Society

CHAPTER • 16

Victim Testimony

INTRODUCTION

Women, men, and children who believe they have been harmed by pornography described adverse physical and psychological effects in their public testimony before the Commission and other bodies and in accounts given in writing or in interviews by Commission staff. The Commission heard testimony from thirty witnesses who reported that they or others with whom they had special relationships had been harmed in some manner by or as a result of pornography. More than one hundred persons were interviewed by Commission staff investigators, who were law enforcement personnel with considerable experience in dealing with trauma victims. Although in many instances, facts related by the person interviewed could be verified by reference to treatment records, court records, or law enforcement files, in other instances no independent verification was possible. In addition to the foregoing, a number of other statements were received in letters from persons who reported pornography-related victimization and in exhibits filed by witnesses from hearings before other fact finders, including city councils, courts of record, and the United States Senate. Some of these individuals reported an extensive series of traumatic events in their lives, making it difficult to assess the relationship, if any, between pornography and their suffering.

Witnesses attributed to pornography their having been coerced into pornographic performances, bound and beaten in direct imitation of pornography, and forcibly imprisoned for the purpose of manufacturing pornography. Although this Commission can neither conclusively determine that pornography caused these physical harms nor conclusively determine that it did not, it was the opinion of the witnesses that pornography played a central role in the pattern of abuse within which they were harmed.

Witnesses attributed many different kinds of damage to psychological functioning and sense of self to their having been used in the production of pornographic materials, exposed to pornographic materials, or sexually assaulted by offenders who used pornography as part of the abuse. Many of these psychological injuries correspond to the signs and symptoms of post-traumatic stress disorder.[762] Witnesses also attributed to pornography financial losses due to hospitalization and therapy, damage to family relationships and status in the community caused by defamatory representations in pornography, associations between prostitution and pornography, and sexual harassment through pornography. Many of the women, men, and children who testified reported each of these types of consequences, and some individuals are quoted repeatedly in various sections of this chapter.

---

762. "The essential feature is the development of characteristic symptoms following a psychologically traumatic event that is generally outside the range of human experience. The characteristic symptoms involve reexperiencing the traumatic event; numbing of responsiveness to, or deduced involvement with, the external world; and a variety of autonomic, dysphoric, or cognitive symptoms." American Psychiatric Association, *Diagnostic and Statistical Manual of Mental Disorder* (3d ed. 1980), p. 236 .

Although we have tried in this chapter to allow victims to speak in their own words, without interpretation or commentary, we have in several instances quoted the words of victim's mothers, friends, or therapists. We have done so only because there are instances in which the victims themselves were unavailable for testimony. In the same vein, we quote here pertinent excerpts from the eloquent testimony of Andrea Dworkin on behalf of other victims whose voices were not heard:

My name is Andrea Dworkin. I am a citizen of the United States, and in this country where I live, every year millions of pictures are being made of women with our legs spread. We are called beaver, we are called pussy, our genitals are tied up, they are pasted, makeup is put on them to make them pop out of a page at a male viewer. Millions and millions of pictures are made of us in postures of submission and sexual access so that our vaginas are exposed for penetration, our anuses are exposed for penetration, our throats are used as if they are genitals for penetration. In this country where I live as a citizen real rapes are on film and are being sold in the marketplace. And the major motif of pornography as a form of entertainment is that women are raped and violated and humiliated until we discover that we like it and at that point we ask for more.

In this country where I live as a citizen, women are penetrated by animals and objects for public entertainment, women are urinated on and defecated on, women and girls are used interchangeably so that grown women are made up to look like five- or six-year-old children surrounded by toys, presented in mainstream pornographic publications for anal penetration. There are magazines in which adult women are presented with their pubic areas shaved so that they resemble children.

In this country where I live, there is a trafficking in pornography that exploits mentally and physically disabled women, women who are maimed; there is amputee pornography, a trade in women who have been maimed in that way, as if that is a sexual fetish for men. In this country where I live, there is a trade in racism as a form of sexual pleasure, so that the plantation is presented as a form of sexual gratification for the black woman slave who asks please to be abused, please to be raped, please to be hurt. Black skin is presented as if it is a female genital, and all the violence and the abuse and the humiliation that is in general directed against female genitals is directed against the black skin of women in pornography.

Asian women in this country where I live are tied from trees and hung from ceilings and hung from doorways as a form of public entertainment. There is a concentration camp pornography in this country where I live, where the concentration camp and the atrocities that occurred there are presented as existing for the sexual pleasure of the victim, of the woman, who orgasms to the real abuses that occurred, not very long ago in history.

In the country where I live as a citizen, there is a pornography of the humiliation of women where every single way of humiliating a human being is taken to be a form of sexual pleasure for the viewer and for the victim; where women are covered in filth, including feces, including mud, including paint, including blood, including semen; where women are tortured for the sexual pleasure of those who watch and those who do the torture, where women are murdered for the sexual pleasure of murdering women, and this material exists because it is fun, because it is entertainment, because it is a form of pleasure, and there are those who say it is a form of freedom.

Certainly it is freedom for those who do it. Certainly it is freedom for those who use it as entertainment, but we are also asked to believe that it is freedom for those to whom it is done.

Then this entertainment is taken, and it is used on other women, women who aren't in the pornography, to force those women into prostitution, to make them imitate the acts in the pornography. The women in the pornography, sixty-five to seventy percent of them we believe are victims of incest or child sexual abuse. They are poor women; they are not women who have opportunities in this society. They are frequently runaways who are picked up by pimps and exploited. They are frequently raped, the rapes are filmed, they are kept in prostitution by blackmail. The pornography is used on prostitutes by johns who are expected to replicate the sexual acts in the pornography, no matter how damaging it is.

Pornography is used in rape—to plan it, to execute it, to choreograph it, to engender the excitement to commit the act. Pornography is used in gang rape against women. We see an increase since the release of "Deep Throat" in throat rape—where women show up in emergency rooms because men believe they can penetrate, deep-thrust, to the bottom of a woman's throat. We see increasing use of all elements of pornography in battery, which is the most commonly committed violent crime in this country, including the rape of women by animals, including maiming, including heavy bondage, including outright torture.

We have seen in the last eight years, an increase in the use of cameras in rapes. And those rapes are filmed and then they are put on the marketplace and they are protected speech—they are real rapes. We see pornography in the harassment of women on jobs, especially in nontraditional jobs, in the harassment of women in education, to create terror and compliance in the home, which as you know is the most dangerous place for women in this society, where more violence is committed against women than anywhere else. We see pornography used to create harassment of women and children in neighborhoods that are saturated with pornography, where people come from other parts of the city and then prey on the populations of people who live in those neighborhoods, and that increases physical attack and verbal assault.

We see pornography having introduced a profit motive into rape. We see that filmed rapes are protected speech. We see the centrality of pornography in serial murders. There are snuff films. We see boys imitating pornography.

We see the average age of rapists going down. We are beginning to see gang rapes in elementary schools committed by elementary school age boys imitating pornography. We see sexual assault after death where frequently the pornography is the motive for the murder because the man believes that he will get a particular kind of sexual pleasure having sex with a woman after she is dead.

We see a major trade in women, we see the torture of women as a form of entertainment, and we see women also suffering the injury of objectification—that is to say we are dehumanized. We are treated as if we are subhuman, and that is a precondition for violence against us.

I live in a country where if you film any act of humiliation or torture, and if the victim is a woman, the film is both entertainment and it is protected speech. Now that tells me something about what it means to be a woman citizen in this country, and the meaning of being second-class.

When your rape is entertainment, your worthlessness is absolute. You have reached the nadir of social worthlessness. The civil impact of pornography on women is staggering. It keeps us socially silent, it keeps us socially compliant, it keeps us afraid in neighborhoods; and it creates a vast hopelessness for women, a vast despair. One lives inside a nightmare of sexual abuse that is both actual and potential, and you have the great joy of knowing that your nightmare is someone else's freedom and someone else's fun.

. . . The first thing I am going to ask you to do is listen to women who want to talk to you about what has happened to them. Please listen to them. They know, they know how this works . . . . It has happened to them.

I am also asking you to acknowledge the international reality of this—this is a human rights issue—for a very personal reason, which is that my grandparents came here, Jews fleeing from Russia, Jews fleeing from Hungary. Those who did not come to this country were all killed, either in pogroms or by the Nazis. They came here for me. I live here, and I live in a country where women are tortured as a form of public entertainment and for profit, and that torture is upheld as a state-protected right. Now, that is unbearable.

I am asking you to help the exploited, not the exploiters. You have a tremendous opportunity here. I am asking you as individuals to have the courage, because I think it's what you will need, to actually be willing yourselves to go and cut that woman down and untie her hands and take the gag out of her mouth, and to do something, for her freedom.[763]

ADVERSE EFFECTS

PHYSICAL HARM

RAPE

The Commission received testimony alleging rapes related to pornography. For example, a woman reported that her daughter was forced to engage in sexual acts in the making of pornographic materials.

My daughter attended [a] Pre-school in . . . California. She was three years old when she began attending. During the six months she attended before the school closed, she was sexually molested on multiple occasions, by teachers on the school grounds and also was taken off school property to unknown locations to be molested by persons unknown to me. Photographs were taken on many (if not

---

763. New York Hearing, Vol. II, Andrea Dworkin, pp. 129–51.

all) of these occasions. She was threatened with physical violence with a knife and a gun and was forced to watch animals being killed.[764]

A man who claimed he had participated in over one hundred pornographic films in two and a half years testified:

> I have seen it totally destroy too many lives, but mostly the girls'. It's a lot harder on young ladies. I have seen a lot of producers and directors and photographers, just to get out a product that they have in mind, either badger or almost force the girls into doing things that they would really rather not do. I, myself, have been on a couple of sets where the young ladies have been forced to do even anal sex scenes with a guy which is rather large and I have seen them crying in pain and just totally destroys their personality when they are forced to do things like that.[765]

Other rapes were allegedly stimulated by the viewing of pornography or modeled after particular pornographic materials.

A mother left her ten-year-old daughter for two hours with a very close friend who lived next door. The friend had the girl watch pornographic movies on the Playboy TV channel and then engaged in oral sex with her.[766]

In testimony before another body, one woman reported:

> Over a period of eighteen years the woman was regularly raped by this man. He would bring pornographic magazines, books, and paraphernalia into the bedroom with him and tell her that if she did not perform the sexual acts that were being done in the "dirty" books and magazines he would beat and kill her. I know about this because my bedroom was right next to hers. I could hear everything they said. I could hear her screams and cries. In addition, since I did most of the cleaning in the house, I would often come across the books, magazines, and paraphernalia that were in the bedroom and other rooms of the house. The magazines had pictures of mostly women and children and some men. Eventually, the woman admitted to me that her ex-husband did in fact use pornographic materials to terrorize and rape her.[767]

Another woman wrote:

> When I first met my husband, it was in early 1975, and he was all the time talking about Ms.   ✂   film, Deep Throat. After we were married, he on several occasions referred to her performances and suggested I try to imitate her actions . . . . Last January . . . my husband raped me . . . . He made me strip and lie on our bed. He cut our clothesline up . . . and tied my hands and feet to the four corners of the bedframe. (All this was done while our nine month old son watched.) While he held a butcher knife on me threatening to kill me he fed me three strong tranquilizers. I started crying and because the baby got scared and also began crying, he beat my face and my body. I later had welts and bruises. He attempted to smother me with a pillow . . . . Then he had sex with me vaginally, and then forced me to give oral sex to him.[768]

Another woman alleged that her father had used *Playboy* in connection with his molestation of her when she was a small child:

> . . . This father took a *Playboy* magazine and wrote her name across the centerfold. Then he placed it under the covers so she would find it when she went to bed. He joined her in bed that night and taught her about sex.

According to another source:

> A five-year-old child told her foster mother, "We have movies at home. Daddy shows them when mother is gone. The people do not wear clothes, and Daddy and I take our clothes off and do the same thing the people in the movies do."[769]

Women who had been asked if they had ever been upset by anyone trying to get them to do what they'd seen in pornographic pictures, movies or books, described the following examples:

> Miss D: I was staying at this guy's house. He tried to make me have oral sex with him. He said he'd seen far-out stuff in movies, and that it would be fun to mentally and physically torture a woman.

764. Miami Hearings, Vol. II, p. 285B.
765. Los Angeles Hearing, Vol. I, p. 81.
766. Letter from Oklahomans Against Pornography to the Attorney General's Commission on Pornography.
767. Minneapolis City Council, Session II, (Dec. 1983), p. 14.
768. Anonymous letter to the Pornography Resource Center forwarded to the Attorney General's Commission on Pornography.
769. Letter from Oklahomans Against Pornography to the Attorney General's Commission on Pornography.

Miss G: He forced me to have oral sex with him when I had no desire to do it.

Miss M: Anal sex. First he attempted gentle persuasion, I guess. He was somebody I'd been dating a while and we'd gone to bed a few times. Once he tried to persuade [me] to go along with anal sex, first verbally, then by touching me. When I said, "no," he did it anyway—much to my pain. It hurt like hell.[770]

One rape victim said that her assailants had attacked her after perusing pornographic magazines:

The third man forced his penis into my mouth and told me to do it and I didn't know how to do it, I did not know what I was supposed to be doing. He started swearing at me and calling me a bitch and a slut and that I better do it right and that I wasn't even trying. Then he started getting very angry and one of men pulled the trigger in his gun so I tried harder.

Then when he had an erection, he raped me. They continued to make jokes about how lucky they were to have found me when they did and they made jokes about me being a virgin. They started kicking leaves and pine needles on me and kicking me and told me that if I wanted more, that I could come back the next day.

Then they started walking away and I put my clothes back on and it was not far from where they had set up their camp and I looked down and saw that they had been reading pornographic magazines. They were magazines with nude women on the covers.[771]

Elsewhere a gang rape was attributed to imitation of a specific piece of pornography:

A gang rape of a juvenile girl [was committed] by six adolescent boys who used a pornographic magazine's pictorial and editorial layout to recreate a rape in the woods outside of their housing development.[772]

Another victim of sexual assault during childhood attributed her assailant's behavior to the instruction of pornography:

What this game consisted of was each child

going into a tool shed with this guy. When my turn came I didn't want to go in because I was scared, it was dark in there and it was dirty. There were cobwebs and there was this giant pitchfork.

One of the kids pushed me inside and shut the door. Then this boy grabbed me and pulled down my shorts and sexually abused me. In short, he finger-fucked me and he made me masturbate him. I was really terrified. I thought I was in hell, and I was also in a lot of pain. I started crying really hard and he finally let me go, but I was told that if I told anyone I wouldn't be believed, that it was all my fault and that I would be punished. He also told me that he would hurt me again if I told anyone. His sister told me that this game he had learned from his dirty books. I knew that he had these dirty books because I had seen him with them.[773]

Another witness testified that pornography had been used by a man who had sexually abused her in childhood:

A lot of raping went on in the basement. That is also where the pornography books were. They were magazines that were brought of hiding, out of boxes that were on the top of shelves.

When [he] and I got to the top of the stairs I knew I was going to pay for my little arrangement. He ordered me to take my clothing off and he tried to rape me. He was too big and I was too small. He forced me to go down on him . . . .[774]

Other witnesses testified that men had required of them particular acts that had been seen in pornography:

While imitating the women in the magazines was one result of the material, I have always felt that another consequence was the initiation of oral sex into the abuse. This did not occur until after the pornographic material arrived and I firmly believe that the idea came from the pornographic magazines.

Pornography did not cause the incestuous relationship with my older brother but I have always felt that its use contributed to the different types of abuse that was used.[775]

770. Minneapolis City Council, Session I. (Dec. 1983), pp. 65, 67. (Testimony based on Diana Russell's research).
771. Minneapolis City Council, Session II, (Dec. 1983), p. 42.
772. Pornography Speech presented to the National Women Judges Conference, October 12, 1986, submitted to the Attorney General's Commission on Pornography.
773. Minneapolis City Council, Session II, (Dec. 1983), pp. 48–49 .
774. Washington, D.C., Hearing, Vol. I, p. 222.
775. Chicago Hearing, Vol. II, p. 291B.

Another woman described the same phenomenon within her marriage:

> I had not realized the extent of the harm that pornography had done to me until a year and a half ago when I was working on a photo montage of the kinds of pornography for an educational forum. I came across a picture of a position that my ex-husband had insisted we try. When we did, I found the position painful, yet he was determined that we have intercourse that way. I hemorrhaged for three days. I finally went to my doctor and I recall the shame I felt as I explained to him what had caused the bleeding.
>
> Once we saw an X-rated film that showed anal intercourse. After that he insisted that I try anal intercourse. I agreed to do so, trying to be the available, willing creature that I thought I was supposed to be. I found the experience very painful, and I told him so. But he kept insisting that we try it again and again.[776]

According to a former *Playboy* bunny:

> A Playmate of the Year, also on the Woman to Woman Show, testified that a man attempted to rape her after he recognized her from the magazine.
>
> I experienced everything from date rape to physical abuse, to group sex and finally to fantasizing homosexuality as I read *Playboy* magazines. The group sex held in Hefner's mansion was accompanied by the pornographic movie, *The Devil in Miss Jones* . . .[777]

A woman who said that both of her husbands had subjected her to sexual and other physical abuse testified,

> Often he would be high on drugs or alcohol and force me to do violent sexual acts while he was leafing through the pictures.[778]

Testifying before another body, one woman described forced sexual activity during the screening of pornographic films:

> . . . comments like "That's how real men do it," instructing the handicapped men, teasing them that if they watched enough of these movies they would be able to perform normally. There were constant remarks made

about what normal male sexual experience was. Then the disabled men were undressed by the able men and the woman was forced to engage sexually with the disabled men, there were two weapons in the room. The woman refused and she was forced, held down by the physically able men. Everyone watched and the movies kept going.

> After this, the able-bodied men said they were going to show the handicapped men how "real men" do it. They forced the woman to enact simultaneously with the movie. In the movie at this point a group of men were urinating on a naked woman. All the men in the room were able to perform this task, so they all started urinating on the woman who was now naked. Then the able-bodied men had sex with the woman while the disabled men watched.[779]

Forced Sexual Performance

During the course of the hearings the Commission received reports from individuals who described situations in which they were forced to engage in certain sexual acts. These acts are distinct from and in addition to those acts described as rape above. As with the acts of rape which were described to the Commission, acts of forced sexual performance included those done in the course of making pornographic material and those relating to the use of existing pornography. Examples of the first of these are abundant:

> A mother and father in   ✂
> forced their four daughters, ages ten to seventeen, to engage in family sex while pornographic pictures were being filmed. This mother also drove the girls to dates with men where she would watch while the girls had sex, then she would collect fees of thirty to fifty dollars.[780]

A woman who had been forced into prostitution and participating in the filming of pornography testified:

> He had video equipment in his home long before it was mass-produced. Every time my pimp sent me to him he would take pornographic pictures of me and a second woman. He also made video tapes of the sex that took place under his direction. This continued on the average of once a week for about a year.

776. Chicago Hearing, Vol. II, p. 241F3.
777. Chicago Hearing, Vol. I, pp. 314, 316.
778. Washington, D.C., Hearing, Vol. I, p. 125.
779. Minneapolis City Council, Session II, (Dec. 1983), p. 72.
780. Letter from Oklahomans Against Pornography to the Attorney General's Commission on Pornography.

There was an apartment that I was sent to often. There were usually two to three men there. After I had sex with them, they would take pictures of me in various pornographic poses. When I was a young girl I didn't have the vocabulary to call them pornographers. I used to refer to them as "the photographers."

On another occasion another young girl and myself were taken to an apartment in to meet some men. We were told that they were gangsters and that we should be nice to them. When we arrived we were taken into a room that had a large bed at its center surrounded by lighting and film equipment. We were told to act out a "lesbian scene." After about fifteen minutes we were told to get dressed, that they couldn't use us. We were returned to [our city] unpaid. Again, it was only in retrospect as an adult that I realized I had been used in a commercial pornographic film loop.[781]

Another woman wrote:

My father was my pimp in pornography. There were three occasions, from ages nine to sixteen, when he forced me to be a pornography model. This was in the 1950s and 1960s. . . . I don't know if the pictures and films are still being distributed.[782]

A sixteen-year-old girl who had been molested by two family friends from age seven to age twelve testified:

Viewing the pictures in the magazine seemed to click something for him, for he then wanted his own personal record of all that he had taught me.

He whipped out his Polaroid camera, which was in his briefcase, and then he proceeded to take pictures of me in these various positions, which included using the vibrator.[783]

Another woman described her discomfort in trying to pose as demanded of her:

So I told him that I would try. The first few attempts I failed, he was very disappointed. I failed under the weight and under the heat of the plaster. He wanted me to be in poses where I had to hold my hands up over my head and they would be numb and they would fall. He eventually tied my hands over my head. Finally he succeeded, he ended up getting a plaster cast of my body.

. . . He told me to take off my clothes and to pose in various positions, either draped over the corroded, rusty seats or in positions where I acted as if I was running towards the door. And then he asked me to put my body in contorted different positions, draped down the stairs of the bus, and they were quite jagged, and at that moment I realized that we were depicting a murder. I became very terrified and scared and I was really cold. I told him I didn't want to do this and that I wanted to go home and that I was really scared.

While we were doing this, I would like to backtrack for a minute, I wasn't achieving the right facial expressions for the pictures so he started telling me stories that depicted pursuits during rape so that I would have the right expressions on my face like the women in the magazines. I remember being very distant from him and just wanting to get home. I remember being very scared.[784]

In these instances in which forced sexual performances were said to be modeled after pornography, the individuals stated that they were shown various pornographic materials and forced to recreate the activities depicted. In some cases the imitation required of victims was highly specific, as in the following example:

My father had an easel that he put by the bed. He'd pin a picture on the easel and like a teacher he would tell me this is what you're going to learn today. He would then act out the picture on me.[785]

Another woman wrote:

I was sexually abused by my foster father from the time I was seven until I was thirteen. He had stacks and stacks of *Playboys*. He would take me to his bedroom or his workshop, show me the pictures, and say, "This is what big girls do. If you want to be a big girl, you have to do this, but you can never tell anybody." Then I would have to pose like the women in the pictures. I also remember being shown a *Playboy* cartoon off a man having sex with a child.[786]

781. Washington, D.C., Hearing, Vol. I, p. 180.
782. Brief of Women Against Pornography submitted to the Attorney General's Commission on Pornography.
783. Miami Hearing, Vol. II, pp. 20–21.
784. Minneapolis, Session, II, (Dec. 1983), pp. 59–60.
785. Chicago Hearing, Vol. II, p. 95.
786. Anonymous letter to Women Against Pornography, submitted to the Attorney General's Commission on Pornography (Aug. 1984).

A mother described her discovery of her daughter's abuse:

My daughter explained that the adults would come into the room and announce that [it] was time for a "movie" or a "bath" and then begin to usher the children . . . into the den or the bathroom. When my daughter refused to undress one of the mothers removed my daughter's clothing with hand movement over her entire body. My daughter was seldom allowed to go home until she had at least one bath with one or more children. Upon hearing this I called the mother and gave her emphatic instructions that my daughter was not to take "baths" at her house. One such occasion after that my daughter came home with obvious dried tears on her face. I feared something dreadful had happened.[787]

They confirmed my fear and discovered even more horror. She had been not only sexually abused but over one thousand pornographic photographs were seized in a search of their apartment spanning a period of over two years. My daughter was only twelve years old at the time of the phone call. She had broken up over the events of the previous week.[788]

One woman who was asked if she had ever been upset by anyone trying to get her to do what they'd seen in pornographic pictures, movies or books said:

This guy had seen a movie where a woman was being made love to by dogs. He suggested that some of his friends had a dog and we should have a party and set the dog loose on the women. He wanted me to put a muzzle on the dog and put some sort of stuff on my vagina so that the dog would lick there.[789]

A woman who had been forced into prostitution and participation in the production of pornography testified:

They knew a child's face when they looked into it. It was clear that I was not acting of my own free will. I was always covered with welts and bruises. They found this very distasteful and admonished me about it. It was even clearer that I was sexually inexperienced. I literally didn't know what to do. So they showed me pornography to teach me about sex and

then they would ignore my tears as they positioned my body like the women in the pictures and used me.

My pimp also made me work "stag" parties. These parties were attended by an average of ten to twenty men. These parties took place in catering halls, bars and union halls. I was also forced to work conventions. These were weekend affairs held at major hotels in New York attended by hundreds of professional men. The series of events was the same. Pornographic films followed by myself and other women having sex with the men. The films that were shown most often set the tone for the kinds of acts we were expected to perform.

My last pimp was a pornographer and the most brutal of all. He owned, on the average, three women and girls at any given time. There was always pornography in our apartment. Every night he would set up the projector and run a series of stag films. When he was sufficiently aroused he would choose one of us for sex. The sex that happened always duplicated the pornography. He used it to teach us how to service him. In retrospect the only sex I knew until I was well into my twenties was coercive sex taught to me through pictures of women coerced into pornographic performances.[790]

A sixteen-year-old girl testified:

At about age eleven and a half he started using the magazine again. In these magazines there were pictures of one woman masturbating another woman, two men and a woman having sex, oral, anal, and vaginal sex. It was with these magazines that we started having me act out positions with him.[791]

The mother of two girls testified:

[My daughters] also had an experience with an eleven-year-old neighbor boy. . . . Porno pictures that [he] had were shown to the girls and to the other children on the block. Later that day, [he] invited [my daughters] into his house to play video games, but then tried to imitate the sex acts in the photos with [my] eleven year old [daughter] as his partner; [my other daughter] witnessed the incident.[792]

A woman testified that her husband de-

787. Houston Hearing, Vol. II, p. 178D3.
788. Houston Hearing, Vol. II, Anonymous, p. 178Q2.
789. Minneapolis City Council, Session I, (Dec. 1983), p. 67 (Testimony based on Diana Russell's research).
790. Washington, D.C., Hearing, Vol. I, pp. 179–82.
791. Miami Hearing, Vol. II, p. 21.
792. Washington, D.C., Hearing, Vol. I, p. 128.

manded that she enact behaviors he had found appealing in pornography:

> ... I was coerced into acting out certain sexual fantasies which he had, many times from reading pornographic literature or viewing certain pornographic movies.[793]

Another woman described her father's use of pornography to encourage and legitimize incest:

> He encouraged me by showing me pornographic magazines which they kept in the bathroom and told me it was not wrong because they were doing it in the magazines and that made it o.k. He told me all fathers do it to their daughters and said even pastors do it to their daughters. The magazines were to help me learn more about sex.[794]

Another woman described the same phenomenon:

> The incest started at the age of eight. I did not understand any of it and did not feel that it was right. My dad would try to convince me that it was o.k. He would find magazines with articles and/or pictures that would show fathers and daughters and/or mothers, brothers and sisters having sexual intercourse. (Mostly fathers and daughters.) He would say that if it was published in magazines that it had to be all right because magazines could not publish lies.
>
> He would show me these magazines and tell me to look at them or read them and I would turn my head and say no. He would leave them with me and tell me to look later. I was afraid not to look or read them because I did not know what he would do. He would ask me later if I had read them and what they said or if I looked real close at the pictures. He would say, "See it's okay to do because it's published in magazines."[795]

Battery, Torture

Witnesses who appeared before the Commission and those who submitted statements reported acts of battery and episodes of torture associated with the production or use of pornography. Individuals described acts of battery or torture inflicted upon them during the

course of producing pornographic materials. For example, a woman who reported having been sexually abused since infancy said:

> That night that I was filmed for a pornographic movie, my stepfather tortured me both physically and sexually because I did not perform adequately enough to be convincing.[796]

A young man who had been the victim of a "sex ring" testified:

> I became involved in bondage. I was shown pornography and was bound in various ways and photographed.[797]

Linda   ✄   testified:

> When I decided to head back north and informed Mr.   ✄   of my intention, that was when I met the real Mr.   ✄   and my two and a half years of imprisonment began. He began a complete turnaround and beat me up physically and began the mental abuse, from that day forward my hell began.
>
> During the filming of Deep Throat, actually after the first day, I suffered a brutal beating in my room for smiling on the set. It was a hotel room and the whole crew was in one room, there was at least twenty people partying, music going, laughing, and having a good time. Mr.   ✄   started to bounce me off the walls. I figured out of twenty people, there might be one human being that would do something to help me and I was screaming for help, I was being beaten, I was being kicked around and again bounced off of walls. And all of a sudden the room next door became very quiet. Nobody, not one person, came to help me.[798]

One witness before the Commission described how women and young girls were tortured and suffered permanent physical injuries to answer publisher demands for photographs depicting sado-masochistic abuse. When the torturer/photographer inquired of the publisher as to the types of depictions that would sell, the torturer/photographer was instructed to get similar existing publications and use the depictions therein for instruction. The torturer/photographer followed the publisher's in-

793. Chicago Hearing, Vol. I, pp. 23–26.
794. Anonymous letter to the Attorney General's Commission on Pornography.
795. Letter to the Attorney General's Commission on Pornography.
796. Washington, D.C., Hearing, Vol. II, p. 262.
797. Washington, D.C., Vol. II, p. 49.
798. Public Hearings before Minneapolis City Council, Session I, (Dec. 1983), pp. 47–49.

structions, tortured women and girls accordingly, and then sold the photographs to the publisher. The photographs were included in magazines sold nationally in pornographic outlets.[799]

The Commission also had received several accounts from individuals who described the use of pornography in the course of physical abuse, and who attributed the type and forms of abuse to specific pornographic materials. For example, one woman who reported having been sexually abused by her father from the age of three testified that he would:

> . . . hang me upside down in a closet and push objects like screwdrivers or table knives inside me. Sometimes he would heat them first. All the while he would have me perform oral sex on him. He would look at his porno pictures almost every day, using them to get ideas of what to do to me or my siblings.[800]

Testifying before another body, another woman said:

> He would read from the pornography like a textbook, like a journal. In fact, when he asked me to be bound, when he finally convinced me to do it, he read in the magazine how to tie the knots and how to bind me in a way that I couldn't get out.[801]

A former prostitute testified before another body:

> The man returned with two other men. They burned her with cigarettes and attached nipple clips to her breasts. They had many S and M magazines with them and showed her many pictures of women appearing to consent, enjoy, and encourage this abuse. She was held for twelve hours, continuously raped and beaten. She was paid fifty dollars, or about $2.33 per hour.[802]

Another woman wrote:

> . . . solid charges . . . could be brought forth. Amongst these charges would be sexual deviance due to repeated inflictions of sadomasochistic acts. I was also told I would be entitled to an annulment as the marriage remained unconsummated throughout.

> . . . While doing household chores, I found very pornographic materials which illustrated sadist techniques and answered my questions as to where my husband got these bizarre ideas.[803]

A former prostitute testified:

> He stripped me, tied me up, spread-eagled on the bed so that I could not move and the began to caress me very gently. Then, when he thought that I was relaxed, he squeezed my nipple really hard. I did not react. He held up a porn magazine with a picture of a beaten woman and said, "I want you to look like that. I want you to hurt." He then began beating me, and when I didn't cry fast enough, he lit a cigarette and held it right above my breast for a long time before he burned me.[804]

Another woman testified before another body:

> During the time that I was held captive by that man, I was physically and psychologically abused by him. I was whipped with belts and electrical cords. I was beat with pieces of wood. I was usually forced to pull my pants down before I was to be beaten. I was touched and grabbed where I did not want him to touch me. I was also locked into dark closets and the basement for many hours at a time and I was often not allowed to speak or cry.
>
> The things that this man did to me were also done to the children of the woman, except that they suffered from even worse abuse. I believe that part of the psychological abuse I suffered from was from the pornographic materials that the man used in his terrorization of us. I knew that if he wanted to, he could do more of the things that were being done in those magazines to me. When he looked at the magazines, he could make hateful obscene, violent remarks about women in general and about me. I was told that because I am female I am here to be used and abused by him and that because he is male he is the master and I am his slave.[805]

A women's shelter wrote to the Commission:

> One woman known to us related that her spouse always had a number of pornographic magazines around the house. The final epi-

799. Los Angeles Hearing, Vol. II, p. 65, 77. One such publication was purchased in Washington, D.C.
800. Chicago Hearing, Vol. II, p. 95.
801. Minneapolis City Council Hearings Session II, (Dec. 1983), p. 68.
802. Public Hearings before Minneapolis City Council, Session II, (Dec. 1983), p. 73.
803. Letter to the Attorney General's Commission on Pornography.
804. Public Hearings before Minneapolis City Council, Session II, (Dec. 1983), p. 77.
805. Public Hearings before Minneapolis City Council, Session II, (Dec. 1983), pp. 15–16.

sode that resulted in ending their marriage was his acting out a scene from one of the magazines. She was forcibly stripped, bound and gagged. And with help from her husband, she was raped by a German shepherd. His second wife became known to us when she sought out support because of the magazines and bondage equipment she discovered in their home.

Penthouse and *Hustler* were always a part of the literature in the third woman's home. Occasionally, her spouse would add *Cheri, Oui, Swedish Erotica* to the collection. His favorite form of abuse was bondage. He enjoyed playing what he called a "game" of whipping and slavery. She knows that what he did to her was directly related to articles about bondage and sex [slaves] which he read. He wanted to involve a second woman, her friend, in the scenarios.[806]

A mother of two girls testified:

[My husband] had a large collection of bizarre S&M and bondage pornography that he kept in the nightstand drawer in our bedroom. One one occasion [he] tied me to our bed and sodomized me. This occurred after I refused to agree to be bound and tied as the models appeared in some of [his] pornographic magazines.

Also, the girls told me that [he] sometimes played a game with them in which their feet were tied up tightly with a rope. The molestation included "bad touching" and exhibitionism by [him], but did not involve actual penetration.[807]

In testifying before another body, one man said:

I understand pornography to be a force in creating violence in the gay community. I was battered by my ex-lover who used pornography. The pornography, straight and gay, I had been exposed to, helped convince me that I had to accept his violence and helped keep me in that destructive relationship.

Then one time, he branded me. I still have a scar on my butt. He put a little wax initial thing on a hot plate and then stuck it on my ass when I was unaware.[808]

Women who were asked in a research project if they had ever been upset by anyone trying to get them to do what they'd seen in pornographic pictures, movies or books described experiences similar to those reported by Commission witnesses:

Miss F: He'd read something in a pornographic book, and then he wanted to live it out. It was too violent for me to do something like that. It was basically getting dressed up and spanking. Him spanking me. I refused to do it.

Miss I: It was S&M stuff. I was asked if I would participate in being beaten up. It was a proposition, it never happened. I didn't like the idea of it.

Miss P: My boyfriend and I saw a movie in which there was masochism. After that he wanted to gag me and tie me up. He was stoned, I was not. I was really shocked at his behavior. I was nervous and uptight. He literally tried to force me, after gagging me first. He snuck up behind me with a scarf. He was hurting me with it and I started getting upset. Then I realized it wasn't a joke. He grabbed me and shook me by my shoulders and brought out some ropes, and told me to relax, and that I would enjoy it. Then he started putting me down about my feelings about sex, and my inhibitedness. I started crying and struggling with him, got loose, and kicked him in the testicles, which forced him down on the couch. I ran out of the house. Next day he called and apologized, but that was the end of him.[809]

A woman whose father had sexually abused her from age three testified:

I have had my hands tied, my feet tied, my mouth taped to teach me big girls don't cry. He would tell me I was very fortunate to have a father that would teach me the facts of life. Many of the pictures he had were of women in bondage, with their hands tied, feet tied and their mouth taped.[810]

In testimony before another body, a woman said:

I was hit and punched because I refused to al-

806. Letter from Donna Dunn's Women's Shelter, Rochester, to the Attorney General's Commission on Pornography.
807. Washington, D.C., Hearing, Vol. I, pp. 126–27.
808. Public Hearings before Minneapolis City Council, Session II, (Dec. 1983), p. 57.
809. Public Hearings before Minneapolis City Council, Session I, (Dec. 1983), pp. 65, 66 (Testimony based on Diana Russell's research).
810. Chicago Hearing, Vol. II, pp. 95–96.

low my partner to put his fist in my vagina in the same fashion as in one of his pornography magazines.[811]

Another woman, testifying before the Commission, reported:

> . . . a trick first showed me how to do bondage and discipline acts. I had numerous customers who would have pornographic material with them. I was asked to shave my pubic hairs because it reminded them of a child or engage in specific sex acts they had seen in a magazine. Having me urinate on them, commonly referred to as golden showers, was a popular request.
>
> Again my customers, who were mostly professional types, would bring many examples in magazines or books of the types of bondage they wanted or of other acts they thought would satisfy their sexual desires, like me acting like their mother, enemas, spanking or cross dressing (men dressing in women's undergarments or clothing). I would also get couples (a man and woman) who were into bondage and discipline, with me as the instructor and ultra dominatrix. My customers would want me to dress like women in the magazines or to bind them in some specific way. Urinating on my customer was also not uncommon.[812]

Murder

In addition to the physical harms already mentioned, some evidence was received alleging a connection between murder and pornographic materials. Cases were reported to the Commission in which a murder may have been patterned after a depiction found in a pornographic magazine or film. For example, the *New York Times* reported:

> The December 1984 issue of *Penthouse* carried this eroticized torture into the 'men's entertainment' forum with a series of photographs of Asian women bound with heavy rope, hung from trees, and sectioned into parts. It is not known whether this pictorial incited a crime that occurred two months later wherein an eight year old Chinese girl living in Chapel Hill, North Carolina, was kidnaped, raped, murdered and left hanging from a tree limb.[813]

Witnesses also described the influence they perceived pornography had in their criminal activities or the crimes others had committed:

> The day came when I invited a small neighborhood boy into my apartment, molested him and then killed him in fear of being caught. Over the next few years I kidnapped, sexually abused and murdered four other boys.
>
> Pornography wasn't the only negative influence in my life, but its effect on me was devastating. I lost all sense of decency and respect for humanity and life.[814]

Imprisonment

The Commission received testimony and other evidence from individuals who reported that they had been kidnapped or held captive during the production of pornographic materials. For example, the woman who appeared in *Deep Throat* testified:

> My name today is Linda ✂   . Linda Lovelace was the name I bore during a two and a half year period of imprisonment. For those of you who don't know the name, Linda Lovelace was the victim of this so-called victimless crime. Used and abused by Mr. ✂ , her captor, she was forced through physical, mental, and sexual abuse and often at gunpoint and threats of her life to be involved with pornography.
>
> I literally became a prisoner. I was not allowed out of his sight, not even to use the bathroom. Why, you may ask? Because there was a window in the bathroom.[815]
>
> Well, at night what he would do is put his body over my body so that if I did try to get up he would wake up. And he was a very light sleeper. If I did attempt to move or roll over in my sleep he would awaken.[816]

A women's shelter wrote:

> In another case, a woman was imprisoned in the house by her husband. He had a video cassette recorder. He would bring home pornographic movies, tie her to a chair and force her

---

811. Testimony before Minneapolis City Council on June 7, 1984, submitted to the Attorney General's Commission on Pornography.
812. Washington, D.C., Hearing, Vol. II, p. 312A–1.
813. N.Y. Times, Feb. 4, 1985.
814. Anonymous letter to the Attorney General's Commission on Pornography.
815. Public Hearings before Minneapolis City Council, Session II, (Dec. 1983), pp. 45, 46, 47.
816. Public Hearings before Minneapolis City Council, Session I, (Dec. 1983), p. 56.

to act out what they were seeing on the screen. She was severely injured and came to our Shelter.[817]

Sexually Transmitted Diseases

Witnesses reported various injuries and diseases associated with the production of pornography.[818] The diseases which were reported included a variety of sexually transmitted diseases. For example, a citizen's group wrote to the Commission:

> How does a three and a half year old girl learn to cope with gonorrhea of the throat and a painful vagina, stretched many times its normal size because her father used her for sexual gratification. This father was another pornography addict.[819]

A former *Playboy* bunny testified:

> I heard a bunny I knew had her reproductive organs removed due to a venereal disease left untreated.[820]

A man who had participated in the production of more than one hundred pornographic films testified:

> I decided to get out of the business because I was kind of scared about all the different diseases and stuff going on. I myself was pretty lucky to only have got gonorrhea a couple of times. I never caught herpes or nothing like that. But it was scary. The diseases are really rampant out there, and especially with the AIDS scare. You have one person that has AIDS in the industry and within six months you can really infect about half the industry because there's so much contact; you have so many different jobs, different people, each month.[821]

A woman testified:

> There seemed to be a lot of venereal diseases and other contact diseases going around and I was afraid of catching something.[822]

Masochistic Self-Harm

One person described her son's use of pornography and his resulting death.[823]

> My son, Troy   ✂   , was murdered on August 6, 1981, by the greed and avarice of the publishers of   ✂   Magazine. My son read the article 'Orgasm of Death,' set up the sexual experiment depicted therein, followed the explicit instructions of the article, and ended up dead. He would still be alive today were he not enticed and incited into this action by   ✂   Magazine's 'How To Do' August 1981 article; an article which was found at his feet and which directly caused his death.[824]

A woman testified about her husband, who was a medical professional and an avid consumer of pornography:

> . . . extremely excited about was the story of a man who had fish in an aquarium, stuck his organ in the aquarium and they nibbled on it until he orgasmed. John was so excited that he would go out and buy a fish tank. At that time John was physically abusing me by pulling my hair, slapping me, kicking me, stomping on my feet.[825]

Prostitution

Witnesses who testified before the Commission and individuals who submitted statements reported several connections between pornography and prostitution. One such connection was the use of pornography as instructional manuals for prostitutes.

For example, a former prostitute testified:

> One of the very first commonalities we discovered as a group, we were all introduced to prostitution through pornography; there were no exceptions in our group, and we were all under eighteen.

> Pornography was our textbook, we learned the tricks of the trade by men exposing us to por-

---

817. Letter from Harriet Tubman Women's Shelter to the Attorney General's Commission on Pornography.

818. See, *Chapter 17* in this Part for a further discussion of the injuries and diseases performers in the pornography industry encounter.

819. Letter from Oklahomans Against Pornography to the Attorney General's Commission on Pornography.

820. Chicago Hearing, Vol. I, p. 317.

821. Los Angeles Hearing, Vol. I, p. 82.

822. Washington, D.C., Hearing, Vol. I, p. 82.

823. Commercial "erotica" was found at the death scene of forty-four out of 150 accidental autoerotic deaths in the largest study of this subject. R. R. Mazelwood, P. E. Dietz & A. W. Burgess, *Autoerotic Fatalities* 130–131 (1983).

824. Houston Hearing, Vol. II, p. 178H1; *Herceg et. al. v.*   ✂   *Magazine, Inc.*, C.A. no. H-82-198, S.D. Texas (1985) (case now on appeal).

825. Washington, D.C., Hearing, Vol. I, p. 81.

nography and us trying to mimic what we saw. I could not stress enough what a huge influence we feel this was.[826]

Another connection was the use of pornographic films by pimps to blackmail the participants:

I was the main woman of a pimp who filmed sexual acts almost every night in our home. The dope man, who supplied us with cocaine for free in exchange for these arranged orgies, was a really freaky man who would do anything. They arranged to have women, who I assumed were forced to be there, have sex with dogs and filmed those acts. There were stacks of films all over the house, which my pimp used to blackmail people with.[827]

Yet another connection was the use of magazines to stimulate the clientele:

When I worked at massage studios, the owners had subscriptions to *Playboy, Penthouse, Penthouse Forum* and the like. These magazines were arranged in the waiting area of most of the massage places which I worked in. If a girl was not inside with a trick, she was expected to sit out front with the men who were waiting or who were undecided and to look at the magazines with them in order to get them titillated. They used the soft porn to help them work up the courage to try the acts described in the magazine with the prostitutes at the massage studio.[828]

PSYCHOLOGICAL HARM

Suicidal Thoughts and Behavior[829]

The Commission received testimony from many individuals who reported suicidal thoughts and behavior. These individuals described experiences related to pornographic materials that led them to feel worthless and hopeless, which in turn led to thoughts of suicide or attempts. For example, the mother of an adolescent girl who said she had been molested through the use of pornography testified:

This is not accomplished overnight, nor is it ever undone. She is now sixteen. She tried to

commit suicide at the age of thirteen and a half as her only means of escape. She spent five months in an adolescent psychiatric unit and nineteen months at a residential care facility for twenty-four hour round-the-clock help with her problems. The brunt of the expenses for her care were our responsibility, reaching close to $100,000.[830]

Another witness testified:

By age fourteen, I had attempted suicide three times and had been in three different mental hospitals. Never had I revealed to anyone my childhood nightmare. Finally, in an effort to revive our sex life, we began to use pornography. This had a devastating effect on our lives. I began to become very depressed and suicidal again. Though we did become more sexually active, the quality of our relationship deteriorated almost to the point of divorce. Pornography again had touched my life in a very destructive way.[831]

A former *Playboy* bunny testified:

I was extremely suicidal and sought psychiatric help for the eight years I lived in a sexually promiscuous fashion.

In Los Angeles, my roommate, who was a bunny, had slashed her wrists because she was so suicidal.

Although I received small parts in *Godfather II* and *Funny Lady*, had sex with movie stars and producers, I felt worthless and empty. Out of my despair I attempted suicide on numerous occasions.[832]

Other individuals reported suicidal thoughts and behaviors as a result of being forced to participate in the production or use of pornography. For example, a teenage boy who had run away from home reported having been sexually abused by his uncle. He stated he was shown pornographic materials in the course of sexual abuse and he was used in the production of pornographic films:

He told me they were for him and his friends to view . . . It was a difficult situation for me.

826. Public Hearings before Minneapolis City Council, Session II, (Dec. 1983), p. 70.
827. Id., p. 79.
828. Id., p. 77.
829. In some instances the symptoms described may be characteristic of mood disorders. See, *DSM-III, supra* note 762, pp. 205–224.
830. Miami Hearing, Vol. II, pp. 33–34.
831. Houston Hearing, Vol. II, p. 187R2.
832. Chicago Hearing, Vol. I, pp. 313–14.

And afterwards, I attempted suicide several times.[833]

A woman reported experiences:

. . . which I found very humiliating and very destructive to my self-esteem and my feeling of self-worth as a person. To prevent these I agreed with him to act out in privacy a lot of those scenarios that he read to me. A lot of them depicting bondage and different sexual acts that I found very humiliating. About this time when things were getting really terrible and I was feeling very suicidal and very worthless as a person, at that time any dreams that I had of a career in medicine were just totally washed away. I could not think of myself any more as a human being.[834]

A woman who testified that her former husband of eleven years was an avid consumer of pornography and had attempted to force her to view pornographic materials testified:

. . . [I] was very suicidal throughout my marriage; attempted several times.[835]

Fear and Anxiety Caused by Seeing Pornography

The Commission heard testimony from several witnesses who described fear and anxiety associated with being shown pornography. The anxieties which have been described may be divided into two primary categories: anxiety attributable to memories of prior abuse which are relived through the images portrayed in the pornography being shown; and an overall embarrassment or discomfort in being made to view pornographic materials.

One witness reported being forced by her father to view pornographic materials during the course of an incestuous relationship:

. . . and of course he had booked a double room. He had all kinds of things in his briefcase, and he pulled out a magazine or book and told me to read it. He sat on the bed and watched me and his facial expression frightened me. I did not want to read it. I did not want to look at those pictures. . . . I was emo-

tionally tortured and I didn't know what to do. I did not like my body or my father's body and having to look at those pornographic pictures forced me to visually memorize painful incidents with my father.[836]

Another witness described similar feelings of anxiety and fear of being shown pornography during the course of sexual abuse in her childhood, beginning when she was ten:

. . . I have no memory of there being any pornography in the bungalow where we lived. All nine kids slept in one room. My stepfather had his own room. My mother slept on the couch in the living room. The pornography was at the store. The pornography was also in the garage where Carl had some kind of office. He was involved in some kind of activity that needed to be hidden. I have no idea what that was. I remember the pictures on the wall and I remember boxes of books again. These were books I didn't want to look at. Carl's apartment is the place where I remember he made the pornography of me.[837]

As they would show me this pornography, I would look at the pictures and then I would feel real scared. . . .[838]

Other women have described their feelings about pornography and the pain it recreated from a previous abusive experience. One woman appearing before the Minneapolis City Council reported that she currently experiences anxiety upon viewing pornography because it reawakens the experience of sexual abuse she had earlier suffered:

Two days later, having failed my attempts to keep those images away from me, I was sexually abused in my family. I don't know if the man that abused me uses pornography but looking at the women in those pictures, I saw myself at fourteen, at fifteen, at sixteen. I felt the weight of that man's body, the pain, the disgust. . . . I don't need studies and statistics to tell me that there is a relationship between pornography and real violence against women. My body remembers.[839]

Parents also reported children's lasting fears after abuse. The mother of a girl who re-

---

833. Washington, D.C., Hearing, Vol. I, p. 48.
834. Public Hearings before Minneapolis City Council, Session II, (Dec. 1983), p. 64.
835. Houston Hearing, Vol. I, p. 61.
836. Washington, D.C., Hearing, Vol. II, pp. 132–33.
837. Washington, D.C., Hearing, Vol. I, p. 223.
838. Id., p. 224.
839. Public Hearings before Minneapolis City Council Session II, (Dec. 1983), p. 112.

portedly was molested and used in the production of pornography in a ✂ pre-school testified:

> She has also talked about a lot of lights, big strong lights, and she is also very fearful of having her picture taken. My sister was visiting from overseas and tried to take her picture and she hid under the bed.[840]

The second category of fear and anxiety was described primarily by adult women who during the course of an intimate relationship were forced to view pornography by a spouse or close friend. These women described feelings of embarrassment, disgust, and public humiliation.

> My husband is very knowledgeable about the Marquis de Sade. He was raised by prostitutes. One of his stepfathers had what he called the largest pornography collection he had ever seen. There was pornographic art throughout his stepfather's home. One evening when we went to visit his mother and his stepfather, the evening's entertainment consisted of getting together with the neighbors and their children and watching a pornography film involving sex with children. I got up, left the room to throw up; and my husband came over to tell me that I had embarrassed him.[841]

Other witnesses described feelings of humiliation at being forced to view pornography and being subject to ridicule when they demonstrated a reluctance to participate. For example:

> We would meet together as a group at pornographic adult theaters or live sex shows. Initially I started arguing that the women on stage looked very devastated like they were disgusted and hated it. I felt devastated and disgusted watching it. I was told by those men if I wasn't as smart as I was and if I would be more sexually liberated and more sexy, that I would get along a lot better in the world and they and a lot of other men would like me more. About this time I started feeling very terrified.[842]

The Commission heard testimony from

several women whose husbands requested they accompany them to view pornography. These women reported feelings of embarrassment and humiliation as well as a deterioration of the marital relationship:

> I went with him once. I was disgusted with what I saw. I was also very embarrassed to have been seen in the theater. He continued going by himself and probably never missed a new showing.[843]

Another woman testified:

> He would take me to the pornography stores here in Houston with the intention of going to get a newspaper or going to get a Better Homes and Gardens. Before I knew it, he would kind of lead me back into the second part of the store. I think that only happened twice because I would get so upset and traumatized . . . .[844]

Yet another woman experienced fear and anxiety when she listened to Dial-A-Porn messages that her son had been calling:

> The chilling horror I felt in my kitchen after my first encounter with Dial-A-Porn lingers with me today. After my initial reaction of disbelief subsided, I was overcome with grief. I cried uncontrollably for myself, my son . . . .[845]

Feelings of Shame and Guilt[846]

The Commission heard testimony from many witnesses who described feelings of worthlessness, guilt, and shame which they attributed to experiences involving pornographic materials.

> As an adolescent, I was sexually molested in my own home by a family member who regularly used pornographic materials. I have been threatened at knifepoint by a stranger in an attempted rape. I have been physically and verbally harassed on the street, in other public places, and over the telephone at all hours of the night. I have experienced and continue to experience the humiliation, degradation, and shame that these acts were meant to instill in me.

---

840. Miami Hearing, Vol. I, p. 101.
841. Houston Hearing, Vol. I, p. 62.
842. Public Hearings before Minneapolis City Council, Session II, (Dec. 12, 1983), p. 62.
843. Chicago Hearing, Vol. I, pp. 153–54.
844. Houston Hearing, Vol. I, p. 58.
845. Los Angeles Hearing, Vol. I, p. 265.
846. These symptoms may be reflective of Post-traumatic Stress Disorder. See, DSM-III, supra note 762, p. 238.

This connection became clear to me when I saw a documentary about pornography called *Not a Love Story*. I realized that I was any one of the women in the film, at least in the eyes of those men who have abused me. I saw myself through the abusers' eyes and I felt dirty and disgusting, like a piece of meat. It was the same shame and humiliation as in the other experiences.[847]

The Commission also heard testimony from people who experienced feelings of guilt and shame when shown pornography:

It was important to me to try and stop the feelings of embarrassment because then I thought that they would not be able to see my shame. Somehow I thought they watched me, waited to see my reaction to the pornography and then they would continue holding it up in front of me to make me squirm. I felt humiliated and hollow.[848]

Guilt and shame were also reported by witnesses as feelings associated with the production of pornography. For example, a young man who was used in the production of pornography as an adolescent testified:

A couple of months later I went into the Straight program, and I talked about it a couple of times, why I would do it. Take her money and go down to buy cocaine with it. I just felt it really disgusted me and I shamed myself.[849]

A statement submitted to the Commission by the National Conference of Judges discussed the feelings of guilt and shame that victims experience because of the production and use of homemade pornography:

. . . collections of self-made pornography detailing who their victims were and the acts they committed. This is a particularly traumatic issue for many of the victims that we treat. It is a source of extreme shame and embarrassment for the victims that pictures of the activity between them and the offender exist. We may not have all those pictures, copies of the pictures may have been sold or traded to other collectors, and we may not have found the entire collection. These collections are catalogued at the Bureau of Criminal Appre-

hension and continue to exist long past the time when the crime has been reported. . . .

In many of our incest families, the perpetrators use pornography as tools or guides in order to initiate their family members into sexual behavior. Manuals and books that speak of father-daughter love, father-son sex, or family love have been used to rationalize and validate this kind of behavior.

Many of our child molesters, both juvenile and adults, have utilized both adult and child pornography as a way to initiate their victims into the sexual behavior as well as a tool or guide for the sexual behavior of child molesting. Many of our victims blame themselves and feel a great deal of culpability because they believed the original depiction from pornography as being normal behavior between adults and children.[850]

In a letter presented to the Minneapolis City Council, a woman described her public embarrassment and shame at seeing what seemed to be a photograph of herself:

It was a full-length figure, naked except for high-heeled shoes and stockings, taking off a shirt. Never in my life had I posed for any photograph, drawing or painting remotely similar to this image. The people giving me this laughed, thought it was funny, thought I would find it funny and truly meant no harm—they are all talented, intelligent, nice people, an indication of the extent of the pornographic mind-set we all suffer under. I felt upset, ripped-off, diminished, insulted, abused, hurt, furious and powerless. All of which I concealed from my friends by smiling and saying, "Where did you get this?" (For the moment I thought they had it made up by the art department at the studio.) "From a magazine" was the answer. Added to the aforementioned reactions was horror! I thought, "This has been published! It is publicly available for anyone to see and assume I may have posed for it."

I curtailed my honest reaction because in a few minutes we would all have to begin filming our show—which we did. They, thinking it had been a fun joke, me in a great deal of pain and distress.[851]

847. Public Hearings before Minneapolis City Council, Session III, (Dec. 1983), p. 126.
848. Washington, D.C., Hearing, Vol. I, p. 225.
849. Washington, D.C., Hearing, Vol. I, p. 170.
850. National Conference of Judges, October 12, 1986.
851. Public Hearings before Minneapolis City Council, Session III, (Dec. 1983), p. 4.

Fear of Exposure through Publication or Display of Pornographic Materials

Some witnesses feared the future dissemination of pornography which had been made of them. For example, a woman who had been forced to participate in the filming of pornography testified:

> But there still exists the pornography that was made of me. I know the men who made it, I know where they are, and there is nothing I can do about it. I live knowing that at any time it could surface and could be used to humiliate me and my family. I know that it can be used to ruin my professional life in the future. I know because some of it was produced within months before my eighteenth birthday that it is protected under current law.[852]

Linda ✂ , who appeared in the film *Deep Throat* as Linda Lovelace, testified:

> I have a son who will be ten in April. My daughter Lindsay will be six on the 4th of July. There are times when my phone rings and it's just obscene phone calls and people saying the typical kind of degradation they say on the telephone. And it's hard because, how do you say to these people, come on, you are hurting my six- and my nine-year-old children. That hurts and it does hurt that the film is still being shown.
>
> I mean, we have a video store in our town, and we have a VCR, and I will not go into that store and get my tapes. I will go to the next town to get them. I just don't feel that store should have that film in the town that I live, but there is nothing I can do about it.
>
> I have no rights as a victim. The only right I have is to be able to tell my story and hope that someone listens.[853]

The young man who had been sexually abused by his uncle and used in the production of pornography testified:

> The sexual abuse that was afflicted on me lowered my self-esteem and the films reminded me of that. I was afraid that this would be shown to the world.[854]

A woman who reported that she was forced into prostitution at age thirteen after running away from a sexually abusive home testified that she was forced to participate in the production of pornographic films and tapes:

> It was clear to me that in the years I was in prostitution that all of the women I met were systematically coerced into prostitution and pornography in the same way a prisoner of war is systematically imprisoned, tortured and starved into compliance by his captors. The difference is that prisoners of war are not held responsible for coerced statements and acts but when a girl or woman is coerced in this very manner into prostitution and for use in pornography, she is held responsible.
>
> This pimp made pornography of all of us. He also made tape recordings of us having sex with him and recordings of our screams and pleading when he gave us brutal beatings. It was not unusual for him to threaten us with death. He would later use these recordings to humiliate us by playing them for his friends in our presence, for his own sexual arousal, and to terrorize us and other women he brought home.[855]

According to the submission on behalf of the National Judges Conference, the continuing existence of pornography impedes treatment of victims:

> The therapeutic issue for the victim to complete treatment is the need to put the crime in the past, an impossibility when there is an existing pictorial history.[856]

Amnesia and Denial and Repression of Abuse[857]

The Commission heard accounts from several witnesses who were unable to recall portions of their lives or specific events. These witnesses attributed their amnesia to trauma associated with the production or use of pornography. The woman who had been sexually abused and forced to participate in the production and viewing of pornography from age ten testified:

> I do not remember the exact beginning of my personal war.[858]

---

852. Washington, D.C., Hearing, Vol. I, p. 189.
853. New York Hearing, Vol. I, pp. 54–55.
854. Washington, D.C., Hearing, Vol. I, p. 49.
855. Washington, D.C., Hearing, Vol. II, p. 183.
856. National Judges Conference, October 12, 1986.
857. These symptoms may be reflective of Post-traumatic Stress Disorder (PTSD). See, *DSM-III, supra* note 762, p. 238.
858. Washington, D.C., Hearing, Vol. I, p. 220.

In 1984 is when I started to speak publicly against pornography because it was during that year that I learned and remembered that I was victimized as a child. Prior to that time I had no memory of it.[859]

My upset has to do with not being able to remember exactly the beginning, or for that matter, the lost segments of time such as a year or two of my life.[860]

It is essential, if one is to survive years of physical abuse, whether one is a child or an adult, to distort one's reality and live in denial.[861]

Witnesses described various psychological mechanisms they used to endure the sexual abuse or humiliation associated with pornography:

Sometimes I would make believe I was in a coma and I'd have to lay absolutely still, because people in comas don't move. So I would set about my task by practicing how not to move and how not to make a sound.[862]

. . . and because of what my family life was like, I learned to cope with being shown pornography.

The way I did that was I would behave as if I was looking at the pictures. But I would not directly look at them. I would make believe that I was blind, that I could not see. In my mind I said to myself, I do not see them, but then concentrated on not allowing my body to respond in any way that would be visible to them. I repeated to myself over and over again, don't move any part of your body. Somehow I believed if I denied the feelings that I could forget the experience, which I later translated to it never happened, and I had stayed that way for twenty years.[863]

A woman who said she had been sexually and emotionally abused since childhood through the use of pornography and who said she suffered from multiple personality testified:

In every episode with him are ones I realized that I could not avoid his advances; I would put myself in a trance-like state and pray for it all to be over with as soon as possible.[864]

. . . Then, like an internal sore, the repressed memories began erupting, baring all of my symptoms and anxiety; I looked for the long-term help that I knew I would need.[865]

. . . It has been extremely difficult for me to write my testimony. I am only now, because of the request that I testify today, beginning to remember the pornography to which I was subjected. The memories that I have relived completely have been of a physical nature, the extreme traumas which were responsible for my splitting. I feel that I have been so desensitized that the memories of having been shown pornographic pictures have seemed harmless and therefore, until now, there has been no need to remember them.

* *

. . . trauma of my relationship with my stepfather, and the role pornography played. Each time I have reread what I have written I am so re-appalled, re-horrified and re-traumatized myself that I decided it more important to just tell you that I knew pornographic magazines played a large part in my stepfather's life. I do not remember in detail the magazines he used, but I do know that they were of a sado-masochistic nature.[866]

Nightmares[867]

The mother of an adolescent girl who said she had been sexually abused through the use of pornography testified that her daughter had recurrent nightmares of the abuse:

He used this magazine to get her to do the same type of thing to him and as a tool to instruct her as to how he wanted her to pose for his nude photographs. To this day, she has nightmares and is continually remembering additional details of his assaults.[868]

---

859. *Id.*, p. 219.
860. *Id.*, p. 220.
861. *Id.*, p. 231.
862. *Id.*, p. 230.
863. *Id.*, p. 224.
864. Washington, D.C., Hearing, Vol. II, p. 262.
865. *Id.*, p. 264.
866. *Id.*, p. 258–59.
867. This symptom may be reflective of Post-traumatic Stress Disorder. *DSM-III, supra* note 762, p. 238.
868. Miami Hearings, Vol. II, p. 32.

Compulsive Reenactment of Sexual Abuse and Inability to Feel Sexual Pleasure Outside of a Context of Dominance and Submission[869]

Many witnesses described an inability to engage in healthy sexual relationships, including reports of a seeming need for abuse or unhealthy dominance. One woman whose husband was an avid consumer of pornography testified:

> This obsession and addiction did not enrich our sex life. It robbed me of a loving relationship, and our sex life turned to his masturbating with his pornography.[870]

Another witness testified:

> My unhealthy concept of sex began when I was a child between the ages of seven and nine. At that time I was introduced to both pictorial and written pornography. This was over fifty-five years ago. My entire concept of what sex was all about came from these materials.[871]

A woman who had been forced to participate in the production and viewing of pornography testified:

> So at night in order to go to sleep I would act out scenes in my head of being tortured and I had to practice how to endure extreme pain. This is how I put myself to sleep at nights as a child. As an adult, instead of having to imagine these scenes, John acted out his violent sado-masochistic fantasies on my body.[872]

> * * *

> I lived with [a man]. One day he told me he had fantasies; fantasies of tying up a woman and using whips. I told him I had the same fantasies. In fact I have been having those fantasies since I was at least twelve or thirteen years old. One of the ways I would put myself to sleep at night as a child was I would run skits through my head and the main character I would act out was me. I was always being hurt.[873]

A former *Playboy* bunny testified:

My first association with *Playboy* began in childhood when I found *Playboy* as well as other pornographic magazines hidden around the house. I have since discovered that a great deal of pornography ends up in the hands of the children. This gave me a distorted image of sexuality. Pornography portrays sex as impersonal and insatiable.[874]

Inability to Experience Sexual Pleasure and Feelings of Sexual Inadequacy

A woman whose father had used pornography in his sexual abuse of her from the age of three testified:

> I was nothing but a pornographic tool for his use. I cannot distinguish the difference between sex and pornography. Because of my sexual abuse as a child I am extremely against pornography, and because of pornography I cannot enjoy sex.[875]

Other witnesses attributed feelings of sexual insecurity and inadequacy to experiences with pornography. For example, a woman whose husband attempted to force her to view pornography testified:

> It was at that point, early in our relationship, that I began to think that there was something wrong with me. After all, if I loved this person, why didn't I share his enthusiasm?[876]

Another woman who said her husband had sexually abused her through the use of pornography testified:

> I thought that I was either a frigid, uncaring wife, but that's the idea; I have received messages from my husband.[877]

Another woman whose husband was an avid consumer of pornography testified:

> It finally progressed to the desire for exchanging parties and sex orgies with many partners. He again told me there was something wrong with me because I would not share him with others and I did not enjoy sex.[878]

> * * *

---

869. These described symptoms may be characteristic of Post-traumatic Stress Disorder and Sexual Masochism. See, DSM-III, *supra* note 762, pp. 238, 274.
870. Chicago Hearing, Vol. I, p. 154.
871. Houston Hearing, Vol. II, p. 178BB1.
872. Washington, D.C., Hearing, Vol. I, p. 230.
873. *Id.*, pp. 229–30.
874. Chicago Hearing, Vol. I, p. 312.
875. Chicago Hearing, Vol. II, p. 98.
876. Houston Hearing, Vol. I, pp. 58–59.
877. Chicago Hearing, Vol. I, p. 24.
878. Chicago Hearing, Vol. I, p. 154.

I can still remember when I told him I still loved him and I would not divorce him if he would change. He said I was sexually cold and selfish . . . .[879]

He was convinced there was something wrong with me because I could no longer respond to him. In fact, I felt very uncomfortable whenever he touched me. He continually told me I was cold, even though he had nothing to offer me. And I believe this was justifying his involvement with pornography.[880]

Feelings of Inferiority and Degradation

Some individuals described situations in which pornography had been used to instill feelings of racial inferiority. For example, one women testified before another body:

> In thinking about coming here today to speak, I realized that my life would be in danger. As a women of color these dangers seem many and great, an absolute loss of credibility and respect, wrath and disgust, potential violence both verbal and physical, and ridicule and harassment to name a few. I also realized the dangers to my life if I did not come. These dangers being complacency, letting go of my rage and terror about pornography and its impact on my life, accepting that the shame is mine, accepting that I am the slut and the whore that deserved what was done to me, believing that I am usable. I have no illusions about men not seeing me as a slut, they do.[881]

Witnesses also described the pornography was used to degrade them as women. For example, a woman whose husband used pornography to abuse her testified:

> As a result of this I developed a very low self-esteem. I felt emotionally isolated because of the fear and embarrassment.[882]

Another woman said:

> He showed me art books and also books, magazines of pornography. And as he was showing me these works, he was doing a critique of women's bodies, of their facial expression, of parts of their bodies and of their dress. Following this was a critique of my too athletic,

too muscular body. I was seventeen, it was very devastating to me that my body was being torn apart in this way.[883]

Another woman testified:

> Once he insisted that we go see an X-rated movie at a theater that showed pornography exclusively. I remember feeling humiliated and frightened being the only woman in the room while the men around me sat masturbating openly. I kept my eyes glued to the top of the screen and prayed for it to be over soon. When we got home, he demanded sex.[884]

A witness who appeared before the Minneapolis City Council described feelings of inferiority and inadequacy:

> When we arrived, he informed me that the other men at the party were envious that he had a girl friend to fuck. They wanted to fuck too after watching the pornography. He informed me of this as he was taking his coat off.
>
> He then took off the rest of his clothes and had me perform fellatio on him. I did not do this of my own volition. He put his genitals in my face and he said, "Take it all." Then he fucked me on the couch in the living room, all this took about five minutes. And when he was finished he dressed and went back to the party. I felt ashamed and numb and I also felt very used.
>
> This encounter differed from others previous, it was much quicker, it was somewhat rougher, and he was not aware of me as a person. There was no foreplay. It is my opinion that his viewing of the pornography served as foreplay for him.
>
> * * *
>
> . . . this usual treatment did result in feelings of low self-esteem, depression, confusion and a lot of shame.[885]

The Commission received reports from individuals who described feelings of exploitation through a partner's use of pornography in an intimate relationship:

> He was a lover. He'd go to porno movies, then he'd come home and say, I saw this in a movie.

---

879. *Id.*, pp. 157.
880. *Id.*, pp. 154.
881. Public Hearings before Minneapolis City Council, Session II, (Dec. 1983), p. 47.
882. Chicago Hearing, Vol. I, p. 25.
883. Public Hearings before Minneapolis City Council Session II, (Dec. 1983), p. 58.
884. Washington, D.C., Hearing, Vol. I, p. 186.
885. Public Hearings before Minneapolis City Council, Session II, (Dec. 1983), pp. 54–55.

Let's try it. I felt really exploited, like I was being put in a mold.[886]

A young man who had been forced to engage in sexual acts for the production of pornography testified that he and other boys who had been exploited by a sex ring felt stigmatized by the publicity surrounding the investigation and prosecution of the offenders:

Those of us who were involved in the ring never talked about it. We wanted to forget the experience. But since my name became public I couldn't escape the stigma of being involved in the . . . sex scandal. I started taking drugs heavily at age twelve to try to cope with the situation.[887]

A woman who had herself been forced into prostitution and the production of pornography testified:

My first husband was always withdrawn and had very little self-esteem. He was a sad young man. People often felt sorry for him. He died before his twenty-fifth birthday in a drunken car accident. Just a few months ago I learned something that helped explain his low self-esteem, his alcoholism, and his avid consumption of pornography. I saw a picture of him as an adolescent in a child pornography photograph in a Women Against Pornography display.[888]

Feelings of Frustrations with the Legal System

The Commission heard testimony describing feelings of frustration and problems with the legal system. Some of the witnesses described helplessness and frustration which they thought could have been alleviated if they had been provided guidance in seeking legal redress. For example, one woman wrote:

Please, please, use their experience and knowledge and work with them. They have tried to get legislation passed against the evils of pornography, for instance the Minneapolis ordinance. . . . Lastly, there are many women's organizations which have been working hard against the evils of the ever-growing, and increasingly more violent pornography which is making our society even more sick.[889]

Linda   ✂   testified:

. . . At a grand jury hearing in California after they had watched a porno film, they asked me why I did it. I said, "Because a gun was being pointed at me" and they just said, "Oh, but no charges were ever filed." I also called the Beverly Hills Police Department on my final escape and told them that Mr.   ✂   was walking around looking for me with an M-16. When they first told me that they couldn't become involved in domestic affairs, I accepted that and told them that he was illegally possessing these weapons and they simply told me to call back when he was in the room.[890]

A young man who had been forced to participate in the production of pornography testified:

During the trial the only name to come out in the newspaper was my name. I was eleven years old at the time.[891]

A woman whose memories of abuse and forced participation in the production of pornography had remained buried for many years testified:

If we had the civil ordinance passed, if I had access to something like that, I would be able to pull through the part of me that exists today. I have no means of doing so. All of the statutes of limitations have run out. Most of the time the women that have been abused, statutes of limitations have run out before we even remember we have been sexually abused.[892]

Another woman testified:

When I think that police, attorneys, legislators, jurors, judges, school teachers and doctors of our country can be desensitized to the suffering of a child, it angers me. A child's justice has been thwarted by the preconditioning of emotions. Victims of sexual violence don't get a fair trial. The true emotions that should be felt have been replaced by sexual fantasies. Victims are a curiosity. People come to see us talk about our genitals as if we are some form of entertainment. Our trial becomes an extension of pornography. So much that even nude photos of us are passed around.[893]

886. Public Hearings before Minneapolis City Council, Session I, (Dec. 1983), p. 65.
887. Washington, D.C., Hearing, Vol. II, p. 48.
888. Washington, D.C., Hearing, Vol. I, pp. 186–87.
889. Letter to the Attorney General's Commission on Pornography.
890. Public Hearings before Minneapolis City Council, Session I, (Dec. 1983), p. 49.
891. Washington, D.C., Hearing, Vol. II, pp. 47–48.
892. Washington, D.C., Hearing, Vol. I, pp. 236–37.
893. Houston Hearings, Vol. II, p. 291B3.

Another woman who had been forced into prostitution and the production of pornography alleged that policemen and juvenile facility workers had been among her abusers.

> I don't think that consent was a possibility for a girl who was delivered into the hands of organized crime figures in New Jersey in the dead of night. Others might wonder why I didn't turn to the police for help. As a matter of fact I didn't have to walk all the way to our local headquarters to speak to the police. They were at our apartment every week for their payoff—me.
>
> * * *
>
> When I was sixteen I was sentenced to juvenile detention by the courts. My incarceration was a nightmare of sexual abuse at the hands of the male employees of the facility. One young girl complained to her parents about this on visiting day. That night, after her parents left, she was made an example of. We heard her cries and pleading all night. The official story the next morning was that she had tried to run away, was caught, and was being held in isolation.
>
> * * *
>
> Soon after I was transferred to a facility upstate. When I saw my opportunity I escaped.[894]

Abuse of Alcohol and Other Drugs[895]

Several of the witnesses reported the use of various drugs, including alcohol, in connection with the manufacture of pornographic materials. A former *Playboy* bunny testified:

> Drug abuse is deeply interwoven into the *Playboy* lifestyle. I saw marijuana being used at ✂   on a regular basis, and cocaine as well. I began taking moderate amounts of alcohol and tranquilizers thinking it would do no harm but the lust grows for more drugs and alcohol to desensitize the psyche to the sexual perversion.[896]

Some witnesses stated that drugs were used to induce an individual to participate in the production of pornography. For example, a woman who had run away from sexual abuse at home at age thirteen described the use of drugs and nude photographs to initiate her into prostitution:

> The third night I was away from home I was wondering around the streets in a sort of daze when I was befriended by a man about twenty years my senior.
>
> I confided my problems to him and he offered to take me in. During my stay with him he treated me relatively well. He was kind to me, he fed me, and he said he cared about me. He also kept me drugged, spoke glowingly about prostitution and took nude photographs of me.[897]

A young woman who had suffered years of sexual and emotional abuse testified:

> I recall at time, from age thirteen until fifteen, having been drugged and used in group demonstrations. . . .
>
> Money, grass and alcohol were used as inducements by [two of the men in the sex ring] in their seduction process. [One] would use the school bus to pick us up and take us over to another's house in Revere. We were paid five dollars plus we were given beer and grass.[898]

Another young man testified:

> When I was young, my uncle sexually molested me. He introduced me to alcohol and drugs. He took nude photographs of me with body paint . . . .[899]

A woman who at eighteen became a nude model and posed for pornographic films testified:

> He had me sign contract, so that scared me, because I had to go to the office every day, you know, and he would try to tell me that soon I would be there, I would be famous. He got me involved with drugs and made me service him, and if I didn't he would threaten me.[900]

The Commission also heard testimony from witnesses who used the money received for participation in prostitution and pornography to buy drugs. A young man who had been forced to participate in the manufacture of pornography testified:

> I spent all the money on drugs. While hustling, quite often I would be picked up by a

---

894. Washington, D.C., Hearing, Vol. I, p. 182.
895. These symptoms are characteristic of substance abuse disorders. See, *DSM-III, supra* note 762, p. 163.
896. Chicago Hearing, Vol. I, pp. 315–16.
897. Washington, D.C., Hearing, Vol. I, p. 177.
898. Washington, D.C., Hearing, Vol. II, pp. 46, 48.
899. Washington, D.C., Hearing, Vol. I, p. 47.
900. Los Angeles Hearing, Vol. I, p. 93.

guy and taken to his house where he would show me homosexual porn films to get him and me turned on. Many times I would be photographed in pornographic poses for private collections. Most often I was involved in prostitution with guys.[901]

Other witnesses said that they used alcohol and other drugs to escape mentally from the abuse they were suffering. For example, one woman testified:

I escaped prostitution quite by accident. I became a heroin addict. I had been taking other drugs throughout the time I was in prostitution and pornography. They had been supplied and doled out by my pimp. I accepted them because they numbed my physical and emotional pain.[902]

SOCIAL HARMS

Loss of Job or Promotion/Sexual Harassment

Reports of sexual harassment similar to those described in the "Physical Injuries" section were also submitted as forms of social injuries. The witnesses stated the harassment was attributable to the presence of pornographic materials and served to reduce their social status:

I was working as a telephone repairwoman for Southern Bell in Florida. Porn was everywhere. They use it to intimidate you, to keep women out of their territory. They had pin-ups in the workrooms. Male workers would draw pornographic pictures of women workers in the cross-boxes and write comments about what we would do in bed. One day I went to the supply room to get some tools. The inside of the room was covered with pornography. The guy who ran it shoved a photograph at me of a woman's rear end with her anus exposed and asked, 'Isn't this you?' I was humiliated and furious.[903]

When I got on the job, three of the trades had set up a nice little shack and had lunch there. And it was a real shock when I walked in because three of the four walls in the room were completely decorated with pictures out of various magazines, Hustler, Playboy, Penthouse,

Oui, all of those. Some of them I would have considered regular pinups but some of them were very, very explicit, showing women with their legs spread wide and men and women performing sex acts and women in bondage. It was very uncomfortable for me to go down there and have dinner and lunch with about twenty men and here is me facing all these pictures and hearing all these men talking about all the wonderful things they did on the weekend with all of these women. I put up with it for about a week and it finally got to the point where I could no longer tolerate sitting there and realizing that all of these men were there, I felt totally naked in front of these men.[904]

A working woman called the Pornography Resource Center in May 1984 to report that her employer had called her into his office, pushed her down on the floor, ripped her dress, taken a gun out of his pocket, and stuffed it into her vagina. A pornographic picture on the lunchroom wall showed a woman sucking a gun."[905]

Many of the complaints received by Amici are from women workers in nontraditional jobs. The following is typical:

"I've been a brakewoman for a railroad for almost nine years. . . . I've seen pornographic pictures of a woman with spread thighs being raped by a huge dismembered penis with my name below."[906]

Financial Losses

The Commission heard reports from individuals who encounter financial consequences attributable to experiences with pornography. Many of these witnesses stated they had suffered financial difficulty because of the need to seek medical and mental assistance because of injuries they attributed to pornographic materials:

The tangible costs are real and run over five hundred dollars per month for weekly therapy, monthly consultations and outside testing. The hospitalization was nearly thirty thousand dollars. Most major insurance policies have a lifetime maximum benefit of ten to twenty thousand dollars on this type of problem; after that if the victim needs help guess who pays. This has a real dollar cost of over

901. Washington, D.C., Hearing, Vol. II, pp. 46, 48.
902. Washington, D.C., Hearing, Vol. I, p. 182.
903. Letter to Women Against Pornography submitted to the Attorney General's Commission on Pornography.
904. Public Hearings before Minneapolis City Council, Session II, (Dec. 1983), pp. 85–86.
905. Testimony to Women Against Pornography, Feb. 1985.
906. Letter from Montana woman to Women Against Pornography submitted to the Attorney General's Commission on Pornography.

seventy thousand dollars so far with many months and perhaps years to go.

My oldest daughter has been in therapy for nearly four years receiving help including a two month hospitalization period for evaluation.[907]

Our four year old daughter was sexually molested at-preschool that she attended in ✂ ✂ . She attended the school, . . . for approximately ten months in 1984. She was two years old . . . .

She has spoken on many occasions where she was taken to certain residence and other locations where she was molested by strangers and threatened with guns and knives and also photographed. All of this was being kept secret through the continuous threats to our daughter that we would leave her, or, worse, that she would die if we were told the secret.

We spent the past year trying to help our daughter through the fears and anxiety over this experience. She is, and has been for about a year, undergoing psychotherapy on a weekly basis. I have also been receiving psychotherapy . . . .[908]

Defamation and Loss of Status in the Community

The Commission received testimony from witnesses who reported that pornographic materials were used to place them in a bad light. The witnesses stated that they had been depicted in pornography without knowledge or consent. Although avenues of recourse may have been available, some were advised to avoid further adverse publicity. For example, one woman testified:

The buyer had their choice of seven famous women pictured in the nude; all of our full names were listed and, of course, choice of color of T-shirt. I was appalled and angry and had meetings with a lawyer regarding what action I should take. All my then advisers, this attorney, my personal manager (regarding career) and my business manager (regarding accounting and finances) advised strongly against taking any action whatsoever. They all concurred that it would be extremely costly and would draw attention to and sell more of these shirts.[909]

Other witnesses stated that pornographic materials were used to hinder their standing within the community. This apparently was particularly true for individuals who had at one time been depicted in pornography. For example, Linda ✂ testified:

And the fact that this film is still being shown and that my three children will one day walk down the street and see their mother being abused, it makes me angry, makes me sad. Virtually every time someone watches that film, they are watching me being raped.[910]

Promotion of Racial Hatred

The Commission received statements identifying pornography as a tool to promote racial bias and hatred. Witnesses identified specific pornographic materials which portray persons of color in a derogatory manner. These individuals attributed continued stereotyping and feelings of racial inferiority to the pornographic materials:

They made other comments, "The only good Indian is a dead Indian." "A squaw out alone deserves to be raped." Words that still terrorize me today.

It may surprise you to hear stories that connect pornography and white men raping women of color. It doesn't surprise me. I think pornography, racism, and rape are perfect partners. They all rely on hate. They all reduce a living person to an object. A society that sells books, movies, and video games like "Custer's Last Stand" on its street corners gives white men permission to do what they did to me. Like they said, I'm scum. It is a game to track me down, rape, and torture me.[911]

Loss of Trust within a Family

The Commission heard reports of family problems attributed to pornography that were more subtle than some of the massive family ruptures described earlier in this Chapter. Some individuals stated that when a family member used pornography or was subjected to the use of pornography, other members of the family felt the effects. For example, a woman who had been forced to view and participate in the production of pornography in childhood by family members testified:

907. Houston Hearing, Vol. II, Anonymous, pp. 178Q1–4.
908. Miami Hearing, Vol. I, pp. 93–94.
909. Public Hearings before Minneapolis City Council, Session III, (Dec. 1983), p. 5.
910. Public Hearings before Minneapolis City Council, Session I, (Dec. 1983), p. 56.
911. Public Hearings before Minneapolis City Council, Session II, (Dec. 1983), p. 19.

. . . I am the only member of my family who is speaking out. I am the only member of my family saying "no" to the abuse. It is very, very common that our families lose themselves from us. I have no support with the exception of one younger brother. My family is very angry at me for saying "no" to the abuse. They are very angry about the fact I am identifying it.

My sisters, they are all repeating the cycles of abuse. They are abusing their children and their children are being incested. This is the long-term cycles, the repeating and maintaining of violent life cycles.[912]

Prostitution

Witnesses who testified before the Commission and individuals who submitted statements reported several connections between pornography and prostitution. One such connection was the use of pornography as instructional manuals for prostitutes. For example, a former prostitute testified:

One of the very first commonalities we discovered as a group, we were all introduced to prostitution through pornography; there were no exceptions in our group, and we were all under eighteen. Pornography was our textbook, we learned the tricks of the trade by men exposing us to pornography and us trying to mimic what we saw. I could not stress enough what a huge influence we feel this was.[913]

Another connection was the use of pornographic films by pimps to blackmail the participants:

I was the main woman of a pimp who filmed sexual acts almost every night in our home. The dope man, who supplied us with cocaine for free in exchange for these arranged orgies, was a really freaky man who would do anything. They arranged to have women, who I assumed were forced to be there, have sex with dogs and filmed those acts. There were stacks of films all over the house, which my pimp used to blackmail people with.[914]

Yet another connection was the use of magazines to stimulate the clientele:

When I worked at massage studios, the owners had subscriptions to Playboy, Penthouse,

Penthouse Forum and the like. These magazines were arranged in the waiting area of most of the massage places which I worked in. If a girl was not inside with a trick, she was expected to sit out front with the men who were waiting or who were undecided and to look at the magazines with them in order to get them titillated. They used the soft porn to help them work up the courage to try the acts described in the magazine with the prostitutes at the massage studio.[915]

Women who are or who have been prostitutes identified pornography as a significant factor in prostitution. These individuals reported that pornography was not only used and made of them while engaged in acts of prostitution, but they stated that pornography is used to perpetuate the concept that women are accustomed to being placed in the role of a prostitute.

I am speaking for a group of women, we all live in Minneapolis and we all are former prostitutes. All of us feel very strongly about the relationship between pornography and prostitution. Many of us wanted to testify at this hearing but are unable because of the consequences of being identified as a former whore. This is absolutely incredible to me that prostitution is seen as a victimless activity and that many women are rightly terrified of breaking their silence, fearing harassment to themselves and families and loss of their jobs.

We have started to meet together to make sense of the abuse we have experienced in prostitution and how pornography endorses and legitimizes that abuse.[916]

Sexual Harassment in the Workplace

Several women reported incidents of sexual harassment in the workplace involving the display and use of pornography. For example, one woman said:

I put up with it for about a week and it finally got to the point where I could not longer tolerate sitting there and realizing that all of these men were there, I felt totally naked in front of these men. The only thing they talked about during lunch period was women, their old ladies, their girl friends, and all their conquests of the weekend.

---

912. Washington, D.C., Hearings, Vol. I, p. 241.
913. Public hearings before Minneapolis City Council, Session II, (Dec. 1983), p. 70.
914. Id., p. 79.
915. Id., p. 77.
916. Id.

I got to the point where I couldn't put up with it any more. And being one of the only two women on the job and being rather new at it and not knowing that I had any alternatives, I got pissed off one day and ripped all the pictures off the wall. Well, it turned out to be a real unpopular move to do. I came back in at lunch time and half the pictures were back up again, they pulled them out of boxes and stuck them on the wall and proceeded to call me names. And just basically call me names or otherwise ignore me.[917]

Another woman wrote:

I was working as a telephone repairwoman for Southern Bell in Florida. Porn was everywhere. They use it to intimidate you, to keep women out of their territory. They had pin-ups in the workrooms. Male workers would draw pornographic pictures of women workers in the cross-boxes and write comments about what we would do in bed. One day I went to the supply room to get some tools. The inside of the room was covered with pornography. The guy who ran it shoved a photograph at me of a woman's rear end with her anus exposed and asked, "isn't this you?" I was humiliated and furious.[918]

A woman testified before another body:

When I got on the job, three of the trades had set up a nice little shack and had lunch there. And it was a real shock when I walked in because three of the four walls in the room were completely decorated with pictures out of various magazines, Hustler, Playboy, Penthouse, Oui, all of those. Some of them I would have considered regular pinups but some of them were very, very explicit, showing women with their legs spread wide and men and women performing sex acts and women in bondage. It was very uncomfortable for me to go down there and have dinner and lunch with about twenty men and here is me facing all these pictures and hearing all these men talking about all the wonderful things they did on the weekend with all of these women. I put up with it

for about a week and it finally got to the point where I could no longer tolerate sitting there and realizing that all of these men were there, I felt totally naked in front of these men.[919]

Another woman wrote:

A working woman called the Pornography Resource Center in May 1984 to report that her employer had called her into his office, pushed her down on the floor, ripped her dress, taken a gun out of his pocket, and stuffed it into her vagina. A pornographic picture on the lunchroom wall showed a woman sucking a gun."

"Testimony to Women Against Pornography, Feb. 1985. Many of the complaints received by Amici are from women workers in nontraditional jobs. The following is typical:

"I've been a brakewoman for the railroad for almost nine years. . . . I've seen pornographic pictures of a woman with spread thighs being raped by a huge dismembered penis with my name below."[920]

Similar to the harassment reported above, women identified pornography as a tool to continue sexual harassment. Women stated that pornography continued to perpetuate the harassment and alienation.

After the LEAP Offices and State had written letters to send out to these various employers, my boss, the man who owned the company, called me up one day and said, "Look, I heard you are having a little trouble down there, why don't you just kind of calm down a little bit. Don't make such a mess. We don't need any trouble down there, just calm down, just ignore it." I said, "Hey, I can't ignore it, I don't have to, I can't, it is already done." A couple of days later they got the letter and they were told that this did not comply with the action guidelines.[921]

917. Public Hearings before the Minneapolis City Council, Session II, (Dec. 1983), p. 86.
918. Letter to Women Against Pornography submitted to the Attorney General's Commission on Pornography.
919. Public Hearings before Minneapolis City Council, Session II, (Dec. 1983), pp. 85–86.
920. Letter from Montana woman to Women Against Pornography submitted to the Attorney General's Commission on Pornography.
921. Public Hearings before the Minneapolis City Council, Vol. II, (Dec. 1983), p. 88.

The Use of Performers in Commercial Pornography

The objective nature of photography confers on it a quality of credibility absent from all other picture-making . . . The photographic image is the object itself, the object freed from the conditions of time and space that govern it.

—Andre Bazin[922]

The leap from "picture making" to photography was an event of profound cultural significance; it was, in Bazin's view "the most important event in the history of plastic arts."[923] It was, as well, the single most important event in the history of pornography: images of the human body could be captured and preserved in exact, vivid detail. As with every other visible activity, sex could now, by the miraculous power of the camera, be "freed from the conditions of time and space."

"Sex" in the abstract, of course, remains invisible to the camera; it is particular acts of sex between individual people which photographs, films, and video tapes can record. Unlike literature or drawing, sexually explicit photography cannot be made by one person: there must be a photographer and one or more persons being photographed. This use of an actual person as the object distinguishes such photography from all other types of sexual material. No study of filmed pornography can thus be complete without careful attention to the circumstances under which individual people decide to appear in it, and the effects of that appearance on their lives.

Nor is this an academic or trivial exercise. The evidence before us suggests that a substantial minority of women will at some time in their lives be asked to pose for or perform in sexually-explicit materials.[924] It appears, too, that the proportion of women receiving such requests has increased steadily over the past several decades.[925] If our society's appetite for sexually-explicit material continues to grow, or even if it remains at current levels, the decision whether to have sex in front of a camera will confront thousands of Americans.

After a brief clarification of terms, we begin our examination of the issues surrounding pornographic "performances" by reviewing the extent to which those issues have been faced by previous commissions and by the courts. We then turn to a brief overview of

---

922. *The Ontology of the Photographic Image*, in *Classic Essays on Photography*, (A. Trachtenberg ed. 1980), pp. 237, 241.

923. *Id.*, p. 241.

924. Houston Hearing, Vol. I, Diana Russell, p. 288. In Professor Russell's random survey of San Francisco women, fourteen percent stated that they had been asked to pose for pornographic pictures. *Id.* p. 285. The survey did not examine how many of these women actually posed for such pictures. A national random survey of Canadians revealed that as many as 60,000 people in that country had been used in pornography as children, and perhaps an equal number as adults. 2 *Sexual Offenses Against Children, Report of the Comm. on Sexual Offenses Against Children and Youths, Min. of Justice and Attorney General of Canada*, (1984), p. 1198 (hereinafter the *Badgley Report*).

925. Houston Hearing, Vol. I, Diana Russell, p. 287. (Younger women statistically are far more likely to have been asked to pose for pornography, with twenty-four percent of those aged twenty to twenty-four having been asked as against two percent of those over sixty.) Because "pornographic pictures" may not have been clearly defined in the questions included in the survey, it is possible different generations of respondents interpreted the query differently.

the kinds and quality of available evidence on the subject, and a summary of what that evidence shows. In conclusion, we consider three areas which the record suggests should be of serious concern, along with recommendations for federal, state and local action.

BACKGROUND

TERMINOLOGY AND DISTINCTIONS

Those who appear in sexually-explicit material, from stills to movies to video tapes, have been variously called "actors," "models," "stars," and "sex workers" during the course of our public hearings. None of these terms seems perfectly appropriate as a description of what such activity involves: the first three seem euphemistic, the last derogatory. We adopt the term "model" not only because it seems to have been the one most commonly used during our hearings, but also because it seems to be somewhat less loaded with positive and negative connotations.[926]

It is important to qualify that definition instantly, however, by limiting its range of application to sexually-explicit material that is *commercially* produced. As we will discuss later, a substantial portion of photographic pornography is made informally, with little or no monetary motive and no intention of widespread distribution. While such small-scale productions are of real concern to us, those who appear in them seem to be at least largely distinct from those who perform in glossier, commercial "X" rated material. Where it is important in the following discussion to refer to those appearing in *noncommercial* pornography, we will do so specifically. And where we wish to refer *both* to those appearing in commercial and noncommercial pornography, we will simply use the term "performers."

PREVIOUS COMMISSION FINDINGS

A fierce debate has raged in this country over obscenity and pornography since the 1970 Commission on Obscenity and Pornography announced its findings; a debate mirrored in the bitter internal struggles of the Commission itself.[927] It is perhaps a measure of the passionate as opposed to reflective character of the struggle that the interests of those persons actually photographed for sexually-explicit material was considered by *neither* the majority nor the minority reports of the Commission. Perhaps because "hard-core" material was seen by the Commissioners as being largely of foreign origin,[928] the risks for performers in such materials may have seemed virtually irrelevant. The Commission's Traffic and Distribution Panel merely paused to note that in making a typical "stag film"[929] the 'performers' are paid $100 to $300.[930] The recommendation of the majority for repeal of all laws regulating distribution of obscene material to adults was premised on the belief "that there is no warrant for continued governmental interference with the full freedom of adults to read, obtain or view whatever such material they wish."[931]

The majority did not consider it even a theoretical possibility that such unlimited freedom might conflict with the freedom and well-being of those performing sexual acts in front of a camera for consumption by the masses.[932] So myopic was the Commission on

---

926. In choosing to use the terms "model" and "modeling" in this context we of course mean no disrespect to those engaged in conventional modeling—nor do we mean to imply that appearing as the subject of a sexually-explicit film is more similar to conventional modeling than it is, for example to conventional acting. See, ✂ & ✂ , *Male Model*, p. 181 (1979) ("The disapproval engendered by nude modeling spills over into the world of straight modeling, though to a lesser degree, merely because the root word 'model' is used in both cases. 'Model' is also a euphemism for an entirely different profession [prostitution].")

927. For an overview of the tension between members of the 1970 Commission and problems in its operation, See, *Hill-Link Minority Report* in *Report of the Commission on Obscenity and Pornography*, (1970), pp. 456, 460–463 (hereinafter *1970 Report*).

928. *1970 Report*, p. 22 (source of "picture magazines" depicting sexual intercourse "principally Scandinavia"; "stag films" domestically produced but in "extremely disorganized" fashion with no national distribution).

929. "Stag films" were the only motion pictures on the market at the time of the Panel's report that met its definition of "hard core" or "under-the-counter" pornography—that is, "wholly photographic reproductions of actual sexual intercourse graphically depicting vaginal and/or oral penetration." *Id*. p. 137.

930. *Id.*, p. 140.

931. *Id.*, p. 58.

932. The dissenter, too, failed to perceive performers in sexually-explicit material as needing any special protection.

this issue, indeed, that under the strict terms of its recommendations, neither "snuff" films[933] nor child pornography would have been subject to prohibition.[934]

Neither of the two major national committees which followed the 1970 Commission was quite so blind to the possible risks to performers in sexually-explicit material. Both the Williams Report[935] and the Fraser Report[936] recommended prohibition of pornographic materials which depicted a child[937] in explicit sexual conduct or which were made in such a manner that "physical injury" was inflicted upon a performer. Yet apart from their concern for protecting children from use in pornography, the Williams and Fraser Committees ultimately gave little attention to the circumstances in which sexually-explicit material is produced, and in particular the situation of those who perform in it. The Williams Committee heard some evidence that "there was much misery in the trade and that many of the girls in strip clubs, for example, were disturbed and mentally ill," but did not think it sufficient in the face of vigorous denials from a publisher of magazines "within the trade."[938] Its analysis of the issue did not extend beyond two paragraphs, and focused solely on production of pornography in Great Britain, which at the time did not generally permit production of any "hard core" pornography.[939] The Fraser Committee gave the issue even more cursory treatment after finding that only "a very small number of [sexually-explicit] films are produced within Canada"

and "the production of other forms of pornography, for example, magazines and books is not undertaken for commercial purposes."[940] The Committee supported a ban on material in which "actual physical harm was caused to the person or persons depicted" as an "additional deterrent to the causing of such harm."[941] Without discussing the nature of the evidence before it, the Committee declared that "we know that the relations between the producers of violent pornography and the actors in it are often such that there is little or no respect for the rights and physical welfare of the latter."[942] Like the Williams Report, however, the Canadian report did not explain what level of proof would be required to demonstrate that "actual" as opposed to "simulated" harm had been caused to performers. Unlike the Williams Report, however, the Fraser Report did not devote even a paragraph to consideration of harms to performers other than those resulting from outright violence on the set.[943]

Ultimately, then, it seems fair to say that in this area, at least, we are without clear guidance from our predecessors in examining a possible "harm" of pornography. The nature of the pornography industry has changed so rapidly in this country since the 1960's that it is hardly surprising that the 1970 Commission felt no obligation to examine the situation of performers; because the industry seems so centered in the United States and continental Europe, moreover, it would have been extremely difficult for the Canadian or

---

933. A "snuff" film is one in which there is apparently an actual murder enacted.

934. To prevent production of child pornography the majority apparently relied on the "taboo against pedophilia" which made the "use of pre-pubescent children in stag films . . . almost nonexistent." 1970 Report, p. 139. The 1970 Commission expressed no concern whatsoever over the possible use of young adolescents in pornography.

935. B. Williams, Report of the Commission on Obscenity and Film Censorship, (1979), p. 131 (hereinafter the Williams Report).

936. P. Fraser, Pornography and Prostitution in Canada: Report of the Special Comm. on Pornography and Prostitution, (1984), pp. 272–79, 629–632 (hereinafter the Fraser Report).

937. The Williams Committee set the age limit for protection of children in this area at sixteen, Williams Report p. 131; the Fraser Committee chose eighteen instead. Fraser Report, pp. 627–28.

938. Williams Report p. 91.

939. Id., p. 37. "Foreign" material was the chief target of British obscenity-law enforcement in the late 1970's, Id., and within Britain the "industry" had agreed to restrain itself through self-regulation. Id. p. 42.

940. Fraser Report p. 87. This abrupt dismissal of the problem of pornography production in Canada is in curious tension with the finding of the Badgley Report that tens of thousands of Canadians have at one time or other been "subjects of sexually explicit depictions." Badgley Report, supra note 924, p. 1198.

941. Id., p. 265.

942. Id.

943. The Report's only reference to possible "harms" of pornography which might be associated with effects on performers was its recitation of the allegation by some "that pornography is to be deplored simply for portraying people in an inhuman way. . . ." Id. p. 96. Even in that context, however, the Report immediately tested the allegation with reference only to the effects of such portrayals on viewers. Id.

See, Hill-Link Minority Report, supra note 927, p. 457 (grounding dissent on need for "protection for public morality" rather than demonstrable individual "harms").

British panels to study it in detail. Nevertheless, the failure of these commissions to examine the issue even in the abstract points to what we view as a nagging conceptual flaw in their approaches: they assumed a photographic image of sexual conduct by actual persons to be essentially no different from a written description or drawing of such conduct. As we will explain below, the use and misuse of "models" and other performers makes that assumption at least gravely doubtful.

PERFORMERS AND OBSCENITY LAW

The refusal of previous commissions to consider carefully the situation of performers in sexually-explicit material is hardly unique in this area; indeed, it is a characteristic of virtually all legal analysis of "pornography" until very recently. In this country, of course, the Supreme Court did not squarely address the constitutional issues inherent in suppression of obscenity until the *Roth* decision in 1957.[944] There the Court rested its view that obscene material could constitutionally be suppressed on the failure of such material to have "even the slightest redeeming *social* importance,"[945] and made no distinctions in its analysis among writings, drawings, or photographs.[946] During the following sixteen years of acrimonious judicial debate over the problem of "obscenity" the Court singled out "photographic speech" for special analysis only twice: in *Times Film Corp. v. Chicago*[947] and *Freedman v. Maryland*[948] it laid out rules governing prior review and censorship of motion pictures. Yet in those decisions, the Court's "recognition that films differ from other forms of expression"[949] seemed in no way based on dangers to performers but rather on a largely unexplained concern for the special power of films to corrupt viewers.[950] When in 1973 the Court finally settled on the test and the rationale for regulation of obscenity in, respectively, *Miller v. California*[951] and *Paris Adult Theater v. Slaton*,[952] photographic speech was not discussed separately and possible risks or harms to performers in sexually-explicit films were not mentioned.[953] The decision of the Court on that same day that "words alone" could be suppressed if obscene reinforced implicitly the assumption that constitutional doctrine governing sexually-explicit material was based solely on its effects on viewers and the public.[954]

With minor exceptions[955] that assumption continued to govern judicial pronouncements on sexually-explicit material until the Supreme Court decided *New York v. Ferber*[956] in 1982. There the Court for the first time extended its analysis of such material to encompass the "privacy interests" of the perform-

944. *Roth v. United States*, 354 U.S., (1957), p. 476.

945. *Id.*, p. 484 (emphasis added).

946. Indeed, the Court was strongly criticized by Justice Harlan in his separate opinion for refusing to examine the materials at issue and make "particularized judgments" on the "individual constitutional problem" presented by each of them, *Id.*, p. 497.

947. 365 U.S., (1961), p. 43. In *Bantam Books v. Sullivan*, 372 U.S., (1963), pp. 58, 70 n. 10, the Court distinguished a system of "prior restraint" affecting books from one affecting movies without explaining relevant differences in the character of each mode of speech.

948. 380 U.S., (1965), p. 649.

949. *Freedman v. Maryland, supra*, 380 U.S., p. 61. The initial indication by the Court that motion pictures might present a "peculiar problem" came in its first decision holding films to be constitutionally protected "speech." *Joseph Burstyn, Inc. v. Wilson*, 343 U.S., (1952), pp. 495, 502–03.

950. In *Times Film Corp.*, the Court referred only to Chicago's "duty to protect its people from the dangers of obscenity in the public exhibition of motion pictures" as a basis for distinguishing films from other modes of expression. *Id.* p. 49. In *Freedman* the Court muddied its references to the distinctive qualities of films by ultimately suggesting that Maryland look for guidance to a previously approved prior censorship scheme for books (in *Kingsley Books, Inc., v. Brown*, 354 U.S., (1957), p. 436, 380 U.S., p. 60.

951. 413 U.S., (1973), p. 15.

952. 413 U.S., (1973), p. 49.

953. The Court explained in *Paris Adult Theater* that suppression of obscenity by the States could be justified by the conclusion that "public exhibition of obscene material, or commerce in such material has a tendency to injure the community as a whole, to endanger the public safety, or to jeopardize . . . the States' 'right to maintain a decent society'," 413 U.S., p. 69.

954. *Kaplan v. California*, 413 U.S., (1973), p. 115. In that decision the Court distinguished between "traditional and emotional response" to suppression of words and the tepid defense mounted on behalf of "obscene pictures of flagrant human conduct," 413 U.S., p. 119.

955. See, *Ali v. Playgirl, Inc.*, 447 F. Supp. 723 (S.D.N.Y. 1978) (cartoon depiction of famous boxer in the nude was held actionable because of its effects on him). In *Zacchini v. Scripps-Howard Broadcasting Co.*, 433 U.S., (1977), p. 562, the Court held that a circus performer's "right of publicity" in his act could, consistent with First Amendment, receive protection under state tort law.

956. 458 U.S., (1982), p. 747.

ers[957]—in this case children. Filming children in the midst of explicit sexual activity not only harmed them because of the sexual abuse involved, but also because "the materials produced are a permanent record of the children's participation and the harm to the child is exacerbated by their circulation."[958] In addition, the continued existence of a market for such materials was found to make it more likely that children would be abused in the future thus justifying a ban on distribution as the "most expeditious if not the only practical method of law enforcement. . . ."[959]

Since Ferber, courts have begun to consider problems faced by performers in pornography, including adults as well as children. The Fifth Circuit recently upheld a judgment against Chic magazine for publishing a nude picture of a woman whose consent had been obtained fraudulently.[960] The same court sustained a judgment against Hustler magazine for "reckless" publication of a nude photograph which had been stolen from the subject's home.[961] And in overturning the "Indianapolis Ordinance"—which sought to provide civil remedies against pornography as a form of sex discrimination—the Seventh Circuit declared that "without question a state may prohibit fraud, trickery, or the use of force to induce people to perform in pornographic or in any other films,"[962] and that under the principles of Ferber the state might be able to "restrict or forbid dissemination of the film in order to reinforce the prohibition of the conduct."[963]

In the wake of the Ferber decision, then, it is still difficult to predict the precise constitutional boundaries which govern regulation of photographic "speech" on behalf of performers.[964] That such performers have privacy and other interests worthy of protection, however, now seems clear. In part as a response to these judicial developments and in part as an effort to aid in future legal analysis, we feel compelled to examine with the utmost care the evidence bearing on the situation of performers used in pornographic photographs, video tapes, and films.

USE OF PERFORMERS IN PORNOGRAPHY—THE EVIDENCE

Because no previous commission has fully examined the special problems presented by the use of actual persons to make sexually-explicit material, and because courts have only begun to develop the legal principles which may be applied to resolving those problems, we approach this aspect of our task with extreme caution. To begin with, we comment on the nature and the quality of the evidence before us both in testimony at our hearings and on the public record elsewhere. Then we examine the main outlines of what that evidence reveals about the nature of the performers' reasons for participation in producing pornography, and their experiences once the decision has been made.

957. Id., p. 759 n. 10.

958. Id., p. 759. Circulation of the pornography was found by the Court to violate "the individual interest in avoiding disclosure of personal matters." Id., p. 759 n. 10 (citing Whalen v. Roe, 429 U.S., (1977), p. 589).

959. Id., p. 760.

960. Braun v. Flynt, 726 F. 2d, (1984), p. 245 , cert. denied, 105 S. Ct., (1984), p. 783.

961. Wood v. Hustler Magazine, Inc., 736 F.2d, (1984), p. 1084, cert. denied, 105 S. Ct., (1985), p. 783. Accord, Hustler Magazine, Inc. v. Douglass, 769 F.2d, (7th Cir. 1985), p. 1128, cert. denied, 54 U.S.L.W., (Mar. 31, 1986), p. 3646.

962. American Booksellers Assn. v. Hudnut, 771 F. 2d, (1985), pp. 323, 332, aff'd mem., 54 U.S.L.W., (Feb. 24, 1986), p. 3560.

963. Id. But cf., Faloona v. Hustler Magazine, 607 F. Supp. (D.C. Tex. 1985), p. 1341, appeal docketed, No. 85-1359 (5th Cir. 1985) (children whose nude pictures, including one showing the plaintiff child holding her vagina open facing the camera, Hustler, (Nov. 1978), p. 33, appeared in adult magazine had no right to revoke mother's consent to publication).

964. For an indication of the confusion still remaining compare Braun v. Flynt, supra note 960, with Faloona v. Hustler Magazine, supra note 963. Deference to the parent's "consent" to publication of the nude pictures in the Faloona case is difficult to justify in view of their graphic character, See, note 963 supra, which makes them at least arguably prohibited "child pornography" under state and federal law. But see, Faloona, supra, 607 F. Supp. p. 1343 n. 4 (denying that the pictures constitute child pornography despite inclusion in federal statute of prohibitions directed at "lewd exhibition of the genitals" of children 18 U.S.C. S2255(2) (D) (1984).

THE NATURE OF THE EVIDENCE

In setting forth the types of evidence we have considered on this subject, it is important to note first the limitations which have been imposed on our fact-finding efforts. Above all, we have not had the power to issue subpoenas summoning reluctant witnesses to appear; thus all information at our disposal was presented to us voluntarily or obtained through our review of materials on the public record. In addition, the severe time constraints imposed on our work were particularly damaging in this area because, as discussed earlier, this aspect of the pornography "industry" has received only the scantiest attention in the past. We, therefore, did not have the benefit of knowing from the outset what were the most likely avenues to discovery of pertinent evidence about activities that are largely underground. Finally, both the difficulty of locating witnesses and the pressure of time meant that we were not able to spend substantial time in cross-examination of their testimony or in background investigations to corroborate their statements.

Caution is dictated, too, because there have been to our knowledge almost no "scientific" investigations into the background of participants in pornography or its effects on them afterwards.[965] Such investigations would certainly be extremely difficult—perhaps impossible—to design and conduct given the clandestine character of the pornography industry. Reliable conclusions about the number and characteristics of performers in pornography will likely remain as difficult to reach as, for example, solid estimates of the number and characteristics of illegal aliens.[966]

What we have been able to discover, however, is deeply disturbing, and, we think, based on substantial evidence from a variety of generally credible sources. Somewhat to our surprise, the testimony of law enforcement officers, of current and former performers in pornography, and of those involved with pornography "behind the scenes" has rarely been in conflict. Further,

significant and useful information is available from court cases, from books and "adult" magazines, and from "adult" film industry publications. If on the whole we believe our understanding of the problems faced by performers in pornography is incomplete, and that our findings and recommendations must be largely tentative, we also view the state of the evidence as highly suggestive. And we think it points to the need for action as well as for further study.

THE PERFORMERS

The most basic questions about performers in pornography—who they are, and how they came to appear in sexually-explicit material—are unfortunately the most difficult to answer decisively. For reasons that are largely obvious but will be explored later, anonymity is a valued commodity among pornography performers: apparently even the best known models frequently do not use their real names for their appearances.[967] And in much pornography (such as that shown in video arcades) the performers are not identified at all. Thus it would have been difficult to conduct independent investigations of their backgrounds even if resources permitted it; instead we have relied on testimony and other information in the public record. What that evidence shows about their age range, background, motivations, and path of entry into modeling is a crucial backdrop to examination of what the sex industry demands of them.

Age

Perhaps the single most common feature of models is their relative, and in the vast majority of cases, absolute youth. As one law enforcement officer who has extensively investigated the production of commercial pornography told us, "they [the producers] are looking for models that look as young as possible. They may use an eighteen-year-old model and dress her up to look like she is

---

965. The survey Diana Russell conducted is the only American survey addressing the issue that we have seen. Houston Hearing, Vol. I, Diana Russell, p. 283. See, *Badgley Report, supra* note 924, addressing the issue in Canada.

966. See, *e.g.,* United States General Accounting Office, *Problems and Options in Estimating the Size of the Illegal Alien Population,* Report to the Chmn. of the Subcomm. on Immigration and Refugee Policy of the Comm. on the Judiciary, United States Senate (1982) ("Current estimates of the size of the illegal alien population in the United States are unsatisfactory and it seems unlikely that more precise estimates can be derived soon." *Id.* p. 19.)

967. Models (particularly women) tend to choose short, suggestive names: Linda Lovelace, Desiree Lane, Ali Moore, Dick Rambone. The majority of the witnesses appearing before us who said they had appeared in sexually-explicit material testified under truncated or fictitious names. The use of assumed names seems to be rooted in far more than the longstanding theatrical practice of giving upcoming actors new names for ''box office'' reasons—rather it appears to be closely related to the models' need to conceal their involvement from their families, friends, and future employers.

15."[968] Female models appearing in "mainstream" commercial pornography appear rarely to be over thirty years old or even in their late twenties; indeed, most whose age we have been able to gauge began their careers in their late teens.[969] Indeed, one former model who now works in the front office of an "adult" video company explained her decision to retire thus: "Good roles for women over nineteen years old have become few and far between."[970] William ✖ , a leading figure in the "adult" film industry, described it simply as "essentially an overage juvenile hall."[971] While male models apparently can enter and remain in the industry at a somewhat older age,[972] on the whole we find Mr. ✖ imagery particularly apt.[973]

Personal Background

Along with their youth, models in sexually-

explicit media seem to share troubled or at least ambivalent personal backgrounds. Although many described or implied unhappy experiences during childhood, we are not able to say with scientific certainty whether their family backgrounds were worse or better than "normal."[974] One model recently declared before a Senate subcommittee that it is a "myth" that models have "unhappy childhoods."[975]

Despite this claim, many other models have painted a drastically different picture of their families—broken marriages,[976] early parental death,[977] and intense family conflict.[978] Many—including the model who denied the "myth" of unhappy childhoods reported having suffered early sexual abuse.[979] Professor Russell, moreover, has found a "highly statistically significant relationship between incestuous abuse and being asked to pose for

---

968. Los Angeles Hearing, Vol. I, William Roberts, pp. 64–65. This emphasis on youth apparently took hold in hardcore sex films in the years after World War II. Before then models who appeared in what were at that time known as "stag films" were in their late twenties or early thirties. Sampson, Commercial Traffic in Sexually Oriented Materials in the United States in 3 Technical Report of the Commission on Obscenity and Pornography 1, (1971), p. 186.

969. The ages at which some prominent "X" rated film models apparently began performing are, so far as we can determine from materials on the public record, as follows: Angel (18); Ali ✖ (18); Amber ✖ (19); Jessie ✖ (18 or 19); Mindy ✖ (19); Shauna ✖ (18); Tiffany ✖ (18); Nikki ✖ (18); Ginger ✖ (19 or 20); Richard ✖ (20 or 21); Seka (24); Samantha ✖ (28); Chelsea ✖ ("fortyish"). The ages listed above are largely taken from articles or interviews published in adult film industry trade publications or in commercial, sexually-explicit "guides" to adult films and videos. As a result, it is possible that models or interviewers understated their ages to maintain a desirable public image. Nevertheless, in 1971 Sampson, supra, note 968 found that "many current female performers appear to be in their late teens or early twenties." Id. p. 186. Further, about half of our witnesses who had appeared in sexually-explicit films or photos began such performing in their teens: Lisa (Washington, D.C.); Jeff (Washington, D.C.); George (Los Angeles); Chris (Los Angeles); Harry ✖ (Miami); and Linda ✖ (New York). See also, Lederer, Then and Now: An Interview with a Former Pornography Model, in Take Back the Night: Women on Pornography, pp. 57,58 (began nude modeling immediately after graduation from high school) (hereinafter "Lederer Interview"); People v. Fixler, 128 Cal. Rptr. 363(Ct. App. 2d Dist. 1976) (use of fourteen-year-old model by large scale commercial publisher of sexually-explicit magazines).

970. Where Are They Now?, Adult Video News, (Aug. 1985), p. 52.

971. Los Angeles Hearing, Vol. I, William Margold, p. 411.

972. Bennett, Breaking into X-Rated Films, A Guide for Prospective Porn Stars, Hustler Erotic Video Guide, (May 1986), p. 71. (Interview with William ✖).

973. See, Interview: Cecil Howard, Adult Video News 1 (October 1984) (interview with prominent "adult film" producer) ("AVN: Does it appear to you that we're now seeing younger and younger girls doing films? CH: It's true and I think that's horrible." Id., p. 24.)

974. Thus Professor Russell in her study found no significant difference in measures of "social class" between women who were asked to pose for pornography and those who were not. Houston Hearing, Vol. I, Diana Russell. Unfortunately, her study did not determine which respondents had actually agreed to pose, so provides only suggestive evidence regarding that subgroup.

975. Effect of Pornography on Women, Children, Hearings before the Subcomm. on Juvenile Justice, Comm. on the Judiciary, U.S. Senate, 98th Cong., 2d Sess., (1984), p. 315. (Statement of Veronica ✖) ("I came from a very loving family. That core of love has always been my strength.") (hereinafter cited as 1984 Senate Hearing.)

976. Statement of Valerie ✖ (Washington, D.C.); Lisa (Washington, D.C.); Jeff (Washington, D.C.); Getting Down with Candida ✖ Forum, (April 1986), pp. 42, 45. From Cheerleader to Smut Star, Adult Video, (April 1986), pp. 8–9. (interview with Ali ✖) (hereinafter "Ali ✖ Interview"); Christy ✖ , Best of Erotic X-Rated Film Guide, p. 24(no.8).

977. Amber ✖ : Porn's Busiest Beaver, Hustler, (April 1986), pp. 24, 30.

978. 1984 Senate Hearing, supra note 975, p. 1064. (Testimony of Linda ✖).

979. Vera, "Beyond Kink," Puritan, copy of article submitted with letter of Veronica ✖ dated February 8, 1986, to Commission (abuse by Stranger); Statement of Jeff (Washington, D.C.) (babysitter); Lisa (Washington, D.C.) (uncle); Valerie ✖ (Washington) (stepfather and stepbrothers); Lederer interview, supra note 969, pp. 57–58; See also, Statement of George (Los Angeles) (exposure by father to hard core pornography during childhood and early teens, considered by witness to have been major contributing influence in decision to perform in such material). Joanna ✖ , X-Rated Cinema, (May 1986), p. 63 ("I was a real little nympho until I was about eighteen. I got tired of every man and his brother making a pass

pornography."[980] In her study she found that "girls and women who are being asked to pose for pornography . . . are those who have already been seriously sexually abused by a relative."[981] Sketchy as the evidence is, we are struck by the relative rarity in the material and testimony we have studied of claims regarding positive features of families of models.[982] If anything, the balance of the evidence suggests that models have typically grown up in circumstances of parental deprivation, abuse, or both.[983]

Economic Circumstances

If it is not possible to speak with certainty about the family backgrounds of the young women and men who become "models," it nevertheless seems clear what chiefly motivates their decision to appear in sexually-explicit material: financial need. As one former model put it when asked why most women enter nude modeling:

A lot of women are hurt or crazy women under stress. Yes, most women come in under a lot of stress. They're usually desperate when they first come in—maybe they need money for some emergency, like I did, or they've gone as long as they can doing odds and ends or work-

ing at (menial) jobs, and they finally just have to pay their bills. I met a woman whose kid was in the hospital, and I met lots of women who were financially strapped. There were also many illegal aliens there who couldn't work regular jobs even if they had the skills because they didn't have their green cards. . . . [T]hey certainly know how to get you to do what they want. Some women are so bad off that they just go immediately into hard-core films.[984]

One prominent model recently described her entry into the business in similar though less sympathetic terms.

I had a sugar daddy who was, you know, keeping me. Paying for everything. I didn't need a dime of my own and never had to work. Then I guess his wife found out, and he ran back to her, breaking it off with me. I was out in the cold. Then a friend of his asked me if I was interested in doing some masturbation stuff on video. I needed the money and said okay.[985]

Although not a universal feature of models' accounts,[986] with striking regularity they speak of money and dire financial need as critical factors in their decision to model.[987]

✂   ✂   ✂

980. Houston Hearing, Vol. I, Diana Russell, p. 310I.
981. Id., p. 310M. In Professor Russell's view, men seeking to make pornography are adept at selecting previously victimized women. Id.
982. Of the models who testified before us, or otherwise have discussed their past publicly, only a handful even refer to their families except to describe such problems as divorce, conflict or abuse. Compare, Statement of Dottie ✂ ("My parents raised me in a happy, healthy home"); and testimony of Veronica ✂ , supra note 975; with text to notes 976–979. Many, however, have given interviews or testimony without any reference at all to their families; thus we do not know what they would say about their upbringing. That so high a number were involved with explicit sex modeling by their late teens certainly does not suggest to us that their silence should be construed as evidence of a happy childhood and adolescence. See note 979 supra.
983. We note as well the similarity of the backgrounds of many of these models to those of prostitutes. See, e.g., Silbert & Pines, Early Sexual Exploitation as an Influence in Prostitution, 28 Social Work 285(1983) (in sample of 200 current and former female prostitutes 60 per cent had been sexually abused as juveniles); Silbert & Pines, Entrance into Prostitution, 13 Youth & Society, (1982), p. 471, (in same sample only half came from two-parent homes, Id., p. 475; only nineteen per cent and thirty-two percent had a "positive relationship" with, respectively, their fathers and their mothers. Id., p. 480.
984. Lederer Interview, supra note 969, pp. 58–59.
985. Amber ✂ : Porn's Busiest Beaver, Hustler, (April 1986), pp. 24, 30.
986. See, Interview—Richard ✂ , Adult Video News 1 (1984) (made his first "X" rated film in 1968 at age twenty or twenty-one because "I wanted to know what it was like." Id. p. 22). Some other models do not clearly refer to financial motivation as a factor in their career decision. Thus Veronica ✂ described to a Senate Subcommittee in 1984 then decided, four years before the hearing, to "write or forget my fantasy to become a writer" and finally to enter "X" rated films. Veronica ✂ 1984 testimony represents the only statement by a current or former model of which we are aware which seems flatly to contradict the assertion that financial need is the overriding reason for entering nude modeling; unfortunately, it not only gives no verifiable details of her previous career but also seems at least partially inconsistent with some of her published statements. See, ✂ , Beyond Kink, supra note 975 (describing (1) how, in 1979, she lived in Paris with "Roger" and, in 1980 how (2) "Mistress Antoinette" placed her "in beautiful bondage" on a tree from which she was "bound and suspended" while "her husband silently (took) pictures.")
987. See, e.g., Heather ✂ , Erotic X-Film Guide 28 (May 1986) (former model, "What was I gonna do when the money stopped coming in? I couldn't live. I couldn't survive, because it was the money that kept me going." Id., p. 58);

at me."); Interview with Lynn Ann ✂ , Adult Cinema 64(Vol. 5, No. 2) (1986) (". . . any orgies that even went on were while I was living at home. At the tender age of 16." Id. p. 68.); Ali Moore Interview, supra note 976, p. 54 ("I had a rough childhood. Some things I'd rather not discuss, and it left me kind of gun shy when it comes to sex.")

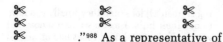

."[988] As a representative of United States Prostitutes Collective put it: "For women working in the sex industry, prostitution and pornography are about money, not sex."[989] Not surprisingly, Professor Russell found that women who had been asked to appear in pornography were significantly poorer than other women in her sample.[990] From what we have learned about the rigors and risks of sex modeling, it is difficult to imagine any overriding motive other than serious economic need for such a momentous decision.[991]

THE JOB

When that decision is made, and for whatever reason, the model enters a world averse to public scrutiny and almost wholly unconcerned with public accountability. In our own examination of the commercial "adult" film and magazine industries we received little information from the industries themselves regarding the position of performers, although we did find at least one industry spokesman, William ✂ , remarkably candid and forthright on the subject. Fortunately, a substantial amount of information in this area is available from knowledgeable law enforcement sources, court cases, and, of course, performers themselves. The view of performers' lives which they provide is invalu-

able and grimly fascinating from the methods of recruitment to the experience of performing to the likely aftermath in personal career directions.

Recruitment

For most young women in commercial pornography, entry into "modeling" seems to occur almost without serious thought. One now famous model described her own initiation in surprisingly casual terms:

> Well, I answered an ad in the paper. It was for a modeling job. It did not say, "adult modeling," or "nude modeling" or anything such as that. I went in and it turned out to be nude modeling. The first day, I took shots for *Penthouse*. So I kept on going and before I knew it, three months later I was doing adult films.[992]

Typically young women and men answer advertisements seeking "models," and only later discover nudity or sexual intercourse is involved in the work.[993] Often, the "model agencies" placing the ads apply strong pressure to convince prospects, as one former model has recently described it:

> The majority of people in this business, they're heartless. They take a little girl off the street, fresh out of high school. They sit there and keep pushing it in her face and asking her

---

988.   ✂

989. Los Angeles Hearing, Vol. II, Margaret Prescod, p. 216. Ms. Prescod pointed out, as did numerous other witnesses, that the "feminization of poverty" had left the sex industry as "one of the few alternatives open to women to get out of, or refuse poverty . . . ." *Id.*, p. 216.

990. Houston Hearing, Vol. I, Diana Russell, p. 310F.

991. One alternative motive advanced by a major male model (Jack   ✂   ) is intriguing: "I was so insecure with [my body] that I wanted to build myself into something that everyone would say was beautiful whether I believed it or not." *Male Model, supra* note 926, p. 183. Obviously the decision to enter sex modeling is an extremely complex one that involves far more than mere economic need. It is likely, for example, that childhood sexual abuse plays a substantial role in predisposing individuals to consider such activity. See, text to notes 974–983, *supra*. Research on the factors influencing such a decision is clearly needed—yet it does seem clear that what the models themselves *say* when asked about their motives is that financial need was paramount. Even Jack   ✂   , when asked why "most" men go into nude modeling replied: "One, because they need some bucks and somebody offers them a hundred bucks or so if they will pose nude for them. The same reason some people might end up in prostitution." *Id.*, p. 186.

992. *Interview: Ginger* ✂ , Adult Video News, (Feb. 1985), p. 30.

993. See, *e.g.*, Los Angeles Hearing, Vol. I, Chris, p. 92; Los Angeles Hearing, Vol. II, Charles Sullivan, p. 65; Los Angeles Hearing, Vol. II, Catherine Goodwin, pp. 78–79.

Ali ✂ *Interview, supra* note 976, p. 9 ("Adult Video: . . . Why do you do it? Ali: Money, money, money. That is the only reason in the world."); Statement of "Lisa" ("The money [offered for nude modeling] wasn't all that great but I was on welfare . . ."); *Interview: Harry* ✂ , Adult Video News (April 1985) ("I was making a whopping $76.00 per week [as a New York actor]. I needed to supplement my income."); letter from Kellie ✂ to United States Department of Justice of March 21, 1986 [former stripper and nude model] stating "the women who get involved in pornography do so not because of a lack of *morals* but because of *economic* necessity"); *Candida* ✂ *Interview, supra* note 976, p. 46 ("Then one summer, it all fell apart . . . I had no support. I got a job in a porn film and thought, why not?"); C. ✂ , *Male Model* 165–86 (among males involved in nude modeling the phrase "At the time, I needed the money" is the "usual explanation" for their initial involvement, *Id.*, p. 179.) Some models, of course, may well have been *coerced* into appearing in sexually-explicit material, See Section B-3-b, *infra;* for them money could not be a factor in their participation.

if she'd like to do porn, and she keeps saying "No" and "No" and they keep on pressing. . . .[994]

Others enter from nude dancing[995] or prostitution.[996]

Whatever their entry route, however, well established, profitable enterprises exist to provide the services of female models to producers of "X" rated material.[997] "Model agents" receive a flat daily fee for each model provided, and provide producers with books containing pictures of those models available.[998] One such agent, William ✂ , described to us the "legitimate ad" he regularly places in a Hollywood publication that, in his words, "lures, literally lures people in on the guise of getting [a legitimate acting] job."[999] After they arrive at his office, Mr. ✂ tells the prospects, who "are all filled with the idea of becoming a star," what his agency actually wants, and then warns them of the hazards of sex modeling.[1000] "Many people," he continued, "years later, would call and thank me for not letting them into the industry, because I would warn them out. I didn't need that on my conscience."[1001] In view of the overall tactics employed by him and other agents, Mr. ✂ "conscience" on this point seems somewhat overnice.

With regard to men involved in "modeling," by contrast, recruitment practices seem far more straightforward. Males have a substantially more difficult time breaking into pornographic modeling; where men are concerned, according to Mr. ✂ , "[t]his is a closed shop" with only a few "superstars" who "end up in all the videos."[1002] Those who are able to enter the business often do so through the good offices of a new or established female performer.[1003] Some male models, on the other hand, drift into pornography in ways similar to women—through nude dancing, prostitution, or clever persuasion.[1004] Recruitment of men may be easier because of what many male performers describe as the ego gratification of working in pornography.[1005]

Coercion

Efficient as it is, the normal recruiting process for pornographic models is apparently not fully adequate to meet producers' needs. It is an unpleasant, controversial, but in our view well established fact, that at least some performers have been physically coerced into appearing in sexually-explicit material, while others have been forced to engage in sexual activity during performances that they had not agreed to beforehand. We heard direct testimony from three unrelated women who each described how brutal force was used to push her into pornography.[1006] The

994. Heather ✂ Interview, supra note 987, p. 30. See, Los Angeles Hearing, Vol. II, Catherine Goodwin, pp. 78–79 (after adolescent had posed for "fashion/glamour" photos, photographer "began to persuade and coerce her to do the S&M type of posing. . . .").

995. Washington, D.C., Hearing, Vol. I, Lisa, p. 61. (nude dancing at age sixteen, then "modeling" at eighteen); Joanna ✂ Interview, supra note 979, pp. 60–61 (nude dancing and stripping at age sixteen, "film career" at age twenty).

996. Chicago Hearing, Vol. II, Terese Stanton.

997. See, People v. Souter, 178 Cal. Rptr. 111(Ct. App., 2d Dist., 1981) (pandering conviction of principal of World Modeling Agency, which provided performers for commercial pornography productions); People ex rel. Van DeKamp v. American Art Enterprises, Inc.; 142 Cal. Rptr. 338(Ct. App., operation which engaged its performers through "model agencies" Id., p. 340).

998. Los Angeles Hearing, Vol. I, William Roberts, p. 64.

999. Los Angeles Hearing, Vol. I, William ✂ , pp. 402–03.

1000. Id., p. 402.

1001. Id.

1002. Bennett, Breaking into "X" Rated Films, Hustler Erotic Video Guide 71 (May 1986) (interview with William ✂). In this article Mr. ✂ seemed to be referring to heterosexual male modeling. With regard to modeling in homosexual publications and films, there appears to be a much broader demand for new and different faces. See generally, Male Model, supra note 926, pp. 172–86.

1003. Id., p. 72. See, Porn Star Confessions, Erotic X-Film Guide 51, (May 1986), p. 60 (story of Marc ✂ , introduced into "Swedish Erotica" through Lisa ✂ , established model).

1004. Los Angeles Hearing, Vol. I, George, p. 86. ("dancing and nude modeling"); Washington, D.C., Hearing, Vol. I, Jeff, p. 168 (prostitution); Male Model, supra note 926, pp. 176–77 (interview with "John ✂ " describing gentle persuasion into nude modeling).

1005. See, Male Model, supra note 926, pp. 182–86 (comments of Jack ✂ , whose "reward" is principally "self-esteem" Id., pp. 182.). But see, Richard ✂ Interview, supra note 986, p. 24 ("AVN: But how much of it do you like? RP: 15% is pleasure and 85% is trauma and hard work for which I'm very well paid.").

1006. See, generally, Washington, D.C., Hearing, Vol. I, Valerie ✂ , p. 217; Washington, D.C., Hearing, Vol. I, Sarah ✂ , p. 175; New York Hearing, Vol. I, Linda ✂ , p. 47; Ms. ✂ testimony was actually a short summary of her full account in L. Lovelace, Ordeal (1980), in which she described her forced introduction and partici-

credibility of that testimony was strongly re-inforced by the testimony of representatives of "sex workers,"[1007] by a victim counselling agency;[1008] and extrinsic evidence on the public record.[1009]

We also find highly credible the assertion of law enforcement officers that models more often face coercion to get them to perform specific sex acts that were not contracted for.[1010] As one of them put it:

Coercion comes in, especially like some of these witnesses have testified, in the area of anal sex, which many of the models don't want to get into. It really comes into a factor in the bondage and S&M type films. I have talked to models and I have seen films where it's quite obvious that the model had no idea as to what they were getting into. Part of an S&M

film, when they start torturing the victim, tying them, whipping them and putting cigarettes out on their body, is the showing of pain. This is what sexually excites some people.

Obviously we are not dealing with people that can act, so they can't act the pain. Therefore the pain is very real. It's quite apparent these people do not realize what they have gotten into once they start the filming.[1011]

Certainly their pain may not be lightly dismissed.

At the same time we may not dismiss the strong assertions of producers, agents, and models in the sex industry that performers are generally safe from physical coercion.[1012] Actual force or threat of force does not, indeed,

1007. Los Angeles Hearing, Vol. II, Priscilla Alexander, p. 229. (Education Coordinator, COYOTE, National Task Force on Prostitution) ("There is certainly evidence that some women have been forced to perform in sexually-explicit productions." Id., pp. 229–30.)

1008. Chicago Hearing, Vol. II, Terese Stanton, (founding member of Pornography Resource Center which provides help to victims of pornography) ("We have gotten calls from both women and men who are currently being forced into the making of pornography—asking us if there is anything we can do for them." Id., p. 6.)

1009. In hearings before the Minneapolis City Council in 1983, one woman related how she was forced into pornographic performance. Public Hrgs. on Ordinance to Add Pornography As Discrimination Against Women (1983), Session II p. 49–52. In those same hearings Professor Kathleen Barry, author of Female Sexual Slavery (1984) submitted a letter describing how some pornography is produced by pimps through the rape of prostitutes, for reasons which "include personal pleasure of the pimp and his friends, blackmailing the victim by threatening to send them to her family, and selling to the pornographers for mass production." Id., Session I, pp. 58–59. A street outreach worker confirmed that young prostitutes are often raped by their pimps, with the rapes photographed, held as a weapon to insure their continued submission, and later "published in pornographic magazines without their knowledge and consent." Id. Session III, p. 77. Because pornography and prostitution are so strongly linked, it may of course be inferred that the coercion which historically and currently afflicts the latter will play some role in the former. See, R. Rosen, The Lost Sisterhood: Prostitution in America, 1900–1918 (about 7.5 per cent of prostitutes at the turn of the century were physically coerced into the profession); Silbert & Pines, Entrance into Prostitution, supra note 987, p. 484 (four per cent of present-day sample of prostitutes listed "physical threat" as the "major reason" they entered prostitution); Badgley Report, supra note 1013, p. 988 (3.6 per cent of juvenile male prostitutes and 15.9 per cent of juvenile female prostitutes were forced into prostitution). Finally, although it has not yet come to trial, we note that a state court in New Mexico has received substantial testimony supporting the existence of a pornography ring which kidnapped a young woman for use in a pornographic film but killed her out of fear of discovery—testimony sufficient for the court to find probable cause and bind the suspects over for trial. See, series of articles from Albuquerque Journal and Tribune, beginning February 15, 1986, on file in Commission Archives. Whether or not a conviction for murder is obtained in that case, we believe the evidence is sufficient to strongly indicate that forcible tactics were used to secure female models for pornography. See also, Jacobs, Patterns of Violence: A Feminist Perspective on the Regulation of Pornography, 7 Harv. Women's L.J. 5, (1984), pp. 20–21.

1010. Los Angeles Hearing, Vol. I, William Roberts, pp. 99–100; Los Angeles Hearing, Vol. II, Catherine Goodwin, pp. 78–79.

1011. Los Angeles Hearing, Vol. I, William Roberts, pp. 99–100. See note 1015, infra.

1012. Los Angeles Hearing, Vol. I, Les Baker, p. 203B–7–8. (President, Adult Film Assn. of America) (describing coercion of Linda ✂ , if it did occur, as "a tragically unfortunate but nevertheless isolated phenomenon."); Los Angeles Hearing, Vol. I, William ✂ , pp. 414–415; Statement of Candida ✂ (denying any coercion used in

pation in pornography by her husband and "manager" Chuck ✂ . Mr. ✂ discounted her testimony on the basis that "if you put a gun to the head of the girl who's performing fellatio on you, what would be left to perform fellatio on." Los Angeles Hearing, Vol. I, William ✂ , p. 414. This view is neither faithful to the actual account of Ms. ✂ experiences nor convincing in its logic. Harry ✂ , who performed with Ms. ✂ in "Deep Throat," has more cogently questioned the validity of her assertions by contradicting certain details of her account of the filming of that movie. Harry ✂ Interview, supra note 987, p. 28. Nevertheless he ultimately conceded that he does not know whether Ms. ✂ was coerced into making "Deep Throat" or other movies, Id., and at least one impartial chronicler of the world in which she moved during the 1970s has apparently found her story fully credible. R. Miller, Bunny: The Real Story of Playboy, (1984), pp. 162–66. Based on their demeanor, their lack of any obvious motive to falsify, and the other evidence we have heard, we can state that we believe the testimony of Linda ✂ , Valerie ✂ and Sarah ✂ to be true, and, in view of their sufferings from continued public exposure in this light, courageous as well.

appear to be a normal part of "mainstream" pornography production.[1013] Rather it seems concentrated in the fringe areas of bondage, sadomasochism, and home-made, noncommercial pornography. Force used to induce young women to enter "mainstream" pornography appears to be applied most often not by filmmakers but by dominating "boyfriends" who in fact play the role of pimp.[1014] All this said, it is nevertheless troubling that the Adult Film Association of America nowhere includes in its "unofficial credo" a pledge to eschew all forms of coercion in recruitment of models.[1015]

Contractual Terms

Those models who enter pornography voluntarily—that is, without having been physically forced—can expect to enter their new employment under contractual terms quite unlike any others we know of. They will by most standards be well paid—from $250 a day for established models[1016]—but they will be paid strictly in cash[1017] and normally by the number and type of sex acts performed.[1018] Fringe benefits such as medical insurance are unknown.[1019] Models sign a standard release form which gives the film producer or the photographer complete ownership of, and unlimited rights to the material produced.[1020] Once they leave the movie set or the film stu-

dio, they have no guarantee of future employment and no ability to control the use of the material in which they appear.

Working Conditions

During a typical day of filming an "X" rated movie or video a performer is expected to engage in at least two sex scenes,[1021] in a manner pellucidly described by Mr. ✂ to prospective male "stars":

> You have to be a machine. You have to get it up, get it in and get it off on cue. You have to be able to completely divorce yourself from your surroundings and be able to function in any situation. For example, if you're working on location for a film shoot and staying at a motel for seven days, you have to cope with being in unfamiliar surroundings, getting irregular sleep and living on McDonald's and Kentucky Fried Chicken, and still be able to perform sexually no matter what else is on your mind.[1022]

Workdays are twelve to fourteen hours long, with videos requiring three and films seven days to shoot.[1023] During the filming of sex scenes it appears to be standard practice to restrict access to the set to the models and film crew; one actor is reported to have "hastily [covered] his private parts" when a reporter could see onto the set.[1024] In mainstream por-

---

1013. See, Los Angeles Hearing, Vol. I, George, p. 87 ("in career of over 100 films, I have never seen a director physically grab [a model] and force her to do a scene.").

1014. See, L. ✂ , Ordeal (1980); Washington, D.C., Hearing, Vol. I, Valerie ✂ , p. 217.

1015. Los Angeles Hearing, Vol. I, Les Baker, p. 203B-3. The A.F.A.A. acknowledges five "responsibilities" which center on protection of children and nonconsenting adults from seeing pornography: none of them relate to problems of adult performers. See, Los Angeles Hearing, Vol. I, George, pp. 86-87. ("I have seen some directors get really violent and have a lot of yelling and throwing things and threatening of the young ladies, they will never work again if they don't want to do a scene. . . . Then, you know, every time I have seen the girls, always regret it afterwards,; there has been a lot of pain involved with doing scenes they didn't want to do".)

1016. Los Angeles Hearing, Vol. I, William Roberts, p. 65; Los Angeles Hearing, Vol. I, Chris, p. 98; Los Angeles Hearing, Vol. I, George, p. 85. (noting that he "would make between $1,000 and $2,000 a week"). William ✂ estimates that male "superstars" earn $80,000 per year, while "newcomers" earn "around $200 per day." Bennett, supra note 972, at 71. The highest salary currently paid—to a female "superstar"—appears to be $17,000 per day. Heather ✂ Interview, supra note 987, p. 58 (statement of Bruce ✂ , prominent X-rated film producer).

1017. Bennett, supra note 972, p. 71; Los Angeles Hearing, Vol. I, George, p. 91.

1018. Los Angeles Hearing, Vol. I, George, p. 85; Los Angeles Hearing, Vol. I, William Roberts, p. 65 ("going rate being about $250 per sex act").

1019. Los Angeles Hearing, Vol. I, George, p. 89.

1020. Los Angeles Hearing, Vol. I, William Roberts, pp. 70-71. For the extraordinary effects of such releases See, Faloona v. Hustler Magazine, 607 F. Supp. 1341(D.C. Tex. 1985) appeal docketed, No. 85-1359 (5th Cir. 1985) (child whose nude pictures appeared in Hustler had no right to revoke mother's consent to publication, even though pictures had been taken for different publication and sold to Hustler by photographer). See also, Shields v. Gross 58 N.Y. 2d 338 (1983) (dismissing Brooke Shields' efforts to stop publication of nude, highly eroticized pictures taken of her at age ten with her mother's consent).

1021. Bennett, supra note 972, p. 72.

1022. Id.

1023. Id.

1024. Goldman, On the Set of An Adult Film. Adult Video News, (1984), p. 10.

---

inducing her to become a model); 1984 Senate Hearing, supra note 976, p. 316 (testimony of Veronica ✂) (denied ever meeting "anyone, man or woman, who was not participating of his or her own free will.").

nography females, but not males, are normally expected to engage in homosexual as well as heterosexual sex,[1025] while in male homosexual pornography women do not perform at all.[1026]

Health Risks

Precisely because sex is their job, models face health hazards of forbidding intensity. Working three to four days a week, with two sex scenes each day,[1027] any one model may have twenty-four to thirty-two different sexual partners every month, just through work. Even though some performers state that they receive regular medical check-ups,[1028] the odds of contracting sexually transmitted diseases are very high—particularly because performers do not even have the option of using condoms or other "safe sex" techniques.[1029] Not surprisingly, even the rumor that a model is infected with a sexually transmitted disease can ruin his or her career,[1030] but just as obviously such a rumor will often fail to spread before the disease has. Further, it is only the established "stars" who can be choosy about their partners.[1031] One of the best known male models described his own experiences in illuminating terms:

When you're a nobody, it doesn't occur to you to be brave and ask, even though you have a lot at stake. I didn't worry too much about that until the Herpes stuff started to become real. Up until 1982, I had one clap scare. I went and received shots for it. I don't know if I ever had it or not. But I had contact with a known carrier. In '82, we got pregnant for the first time, and having Herpes was the difference between a vaginal birth and a Caesarian section

which made a significant difference to us. And I didn't have Herpes and I saw no reason to get it. So I began saying categorically that I wouldn't work with anyone that had Herpes. I had to do this one part with someone who had an active outbreak of Herpes, and we cheated the scene. The person put a towel in her thighs and I ended up f...ing the towel. We had no physical contact. Ironically enough, it turned out to be a beautiful scene."[1032]

When asked who the Herpes carrier was, the model replied that he had "kind of shielded it."[1033]

The advent of Acquired Immune-Deficiency Syndrome (AIDS) might have been expected to produce drastic changes in sex industry practices, but the prevailing attitude seems best reflected in the following, recent comments in a *Hustler* interview of Amber ✀ , a leading "porn star":

Hustler: You're f...ing so many men these days, aren't you afraid of AIDS? Many actors in the business are bisexual.

Amber: There's an incredible fear of AIDS sweeping through the X-rated-film business right now. All of my girlfriends are talking about it. We're scared to death that we'll find out in three years we've only got a few months left.

Hustler: Why do you continue your promiscuous career then?

Amber: I get a blood test regularly and am very careful about the people I work with. Hey, life's a f...ing gamble anyway, and there is where I want to be. I can't think of doing anything else. That's not to say I'm reckless. For

1025. See *generally, Badgely Report, supra* note 924, pp. 1213–21 (analyzing contents of 11 pornographic magazines, with lesbian scenes being "a popular subject" while homosexual male portrayals were nonexistent). In a recent review *Hustler* urged readers to "check out" a film because of the "daring" performance of a male lead as a "bisexual film director." The review continued: "no, he doesn't actually make it with another guy; this flick is daring, but not *that* daring." *Hustler,* (April 1986), p. 18.

1026. A recent video which included bisexual activity involving several men and one woman was dubbed by one "erotica" reviewer as "not, strictly speaking, a gay tape" and "probably different from anything you've ever seen." Review, *Hustler Erotic Video Guide,* (May 1986), pp. 90–91.

1027. The typical work week described by one of the models in testimony before us. Los Angeles Hearing, Vol. I, George, p. 85.

1028. See, *e.g.,* Amber ✀ Interview, *supra* note 977, p. 30; Los Angeles Hearing, Vol. I, George, p. 89.

1029. See, Richard ✀ Interview, *supra* note 986, p. 25 (description by interviewer of "the only time I've seen a rubber being used in a porno movie.")

1030. *Id.,* p. 30; Bennett, *supra* note 972, p. 72.

1031. Richard ✀ Interview, *supra* note 986, p. 30.

1032. *Id.; See also,* Los Angeles Hearing, Vol. I, George, p. 89. (encountered S.T.D. in fellow performers); Lederer Interview, *supra* note 969, p. 66. ("Women who work in the pornography business always have vaginal trichomoniasis or some infection from the working conditions, which run from bad to simply intolerable. At one point there was an epidemic of hepatitis and mononucleosis. The communicable diseases spread quickly." *Id.,* p. 66). That a "sex worker" population would be highly vulnerable to sexually transmitted diseases should hardly come as a shock. See, W. Darrow, *Prostitution and Sexually Transmitted Diseases* in *Sexually Transmitted Diseases,* (K.K.Holmes ed. 1984), p. 109.

1033. *Id.*

instance, I won't f... some guy I know has been f...ing a bunch of other guys not for a lousy thousand dollars. It's not worth it to me, because if I get AIDS, then everyone I come in contact with [will] get it and not just the people I work with, but the people I love and care about too.[1034]

Of course, even an *occasional* sexual contact with a member of a high-risk group carries such a substantial risk of exposure to AIDS[1035] that the gamble Amber ✂ embraces seems a peculiarly misguided one.

Drug Use

Along with the insidious threat of infectious disease, models face a more overt challenge to their physical health: drug use, and in particular, use of cocaine. Few aspects of the world of pornographic modeling seem less free from doubt than the dependence of most performers, at one time or another, on cocaine. The view of one prominent model that in her world "everybody goes through a drug stage"[1036] is perhaps overstated; but involvement of a substantial majority of performers in the use of cocaine seems highly probable.[1037] In the opinion of at least one model, drugs are necessary in her work because "you have to hide, you have to keep your feelings and emotions from being completely destroyed. Each day [in the industry] erodes them away."[1038] It is true that Mr. Les Baker, President of the Adult Film Association of America labelled the problem of drug abuse in his industry a "misconception," contending that such abuse "is a universal problem and we of the A.F.A.A. just a small part thereof."[1039] For him drug usage by pornographic models is simply part of an infection

spreading through the whole "entertainment industry."[1040] William ✂ put it somewhat more positively:

I know that drugs are in my industry. I know that drugs are in almost any form of creative people. Some people seem to need them to do whatever they have to do.[1041]

We of course are in no position to compare the severity of drug abuse in the pornography industry with that in other fields; it is sufficient simply to note that by all accounts such abuse exists and inflicts serious damage on those it touches.[1042]

"Modeling" vs. Acting

The reference of Mr. ✂ to the "creative people" performing in mainstream pornography raises for us, quite apart from the issue of drug abuse, a question of substantial importance in attempting to describe the role and the lot of models. To what extent is their work in fact "creative"? More bluntly, to what extent are they actors as opposed to glorified prostitutes? More than aesthetic judgments hang in the balance: for if the performing in sexually-explicit films can be called truly creative, it is possible to imagine it bringing intangible, subjective benefits to models that scrutiny of contract terms, working conditions and the like could never reveal. Fortunately, it is an issue on which models themselves seem largely in agreement. Mr. ✂ , himself a model, recently was asked, "Is acting ability and training an important factor [in breaking into "X" rated films]?"[1043] His answer was simple and instructive:

1034. Amber ✂ Interview, *supra* note 977, pp. 26–30.

1035. See, Curran, *The Epidemiology and Prevention of the Acquired Immune-Deficiency Syndrome*, 103 Ann. Internal Medicine, (1985), pp. 657, 660 ("the risk of exposure to HTLV-III/LAV infection from a sexual encounter with an occasional partner for a gay man is very high, several times higher than for a heterosexual man or woman.") Blattner, *Epidemiology of Human T-Lymphotropic Virus Type III and the Risk of the Acquired Immune-Deficiency Syndrome*, 103 Ann. Internal Medicine, (1985), p. 665.

1036. Ginger ✂ Interview, *supra* note 982, p. 36.

1037. See, Los Angeles Hearing, Vol. I, William Roberts, p. 98. ("Drugs play a very large part in [the pornography industry]; "George", *supra* note 1013, p. 84 ("eighty to ninety percent of the models do delve into cocaine"); *Interview: Traci Lords*, Adult Video News, (Aug. 1985), p. 34 ("Many girls go through mental breakdowns or get into drugs really bad. They feel so alone because there's just nothing there. So they get into the coke crowd and that's what keeps them going.")

1038. Heather ✂ Interview, *supra* note 987, p. 58, *Accord*, Joanna ✂ Interview, *supra* note 979, p. 60 ("I guess I used [cocaine] to escape.")

1039. Los Angeles Hearing, Vol. I, Les Baker, p. 203B-7.

1040. *Id.*

1041. Los Angeles Hearing, Vol. I, William ✂ , p. 413.

1042. See, Los Angeles Hearing, Vol. I, Les Baker, p. 203B-7 (suicide of young model linked to drugs).

1043. Bennett, *supra* note 972, p. 72.

> No, I don't think so. I think what's most important is being in the right place at the right time, having the right connections and getting the right roles.[1044]

Mr. ✂ went on to explain that the reason some male models "get their foot in the door" but "fail to make it to superstardom" is not for lack of creative drive or talent, but because they "cannot keep functioning reliably shoot after shoot."[1045]

One former model who testified before us was even more careful about distinguishing "modeling" from "acting":

> That also reminds me somehow, what I really wanted to say is when you are paid, to 'act' in these videos and films and stuff, you know, a lot of them say that I am an actor, I am an actress, or something, I am getting paid to act.
>
> When the producer or director pays you, after you leave, and before the shooting, you are paid not by how many lines you have or by what part you have you may have five lines or you may have 107 pages of dialogue, but you are paid per sex scene and that's how they quote it to you. If you have one sex scene a day you get like two hundred to two hundred fifty dollars for that, if you have two sex scenes, there's three or four hundred for two sex scenes. You are paid more for anal or girls are paid more for when they are working with two guys.
>
> So the models that say they are getting paid to act are only doing that to pretty much preserve their job security because, you know, anybody in the industry knows you are paid per sex act and not for acting.[1046]

Several former models have made similar public assessments, declaring flatly that "the market today is just not conducive to anyone who takes their acting seriously."[1047] Adult filmmakers shoot with only the barest of scripts, desperate simply to get the requisite number of sex scenes on film with an alluring title and package.[1048] The result for performers is that, in the words of a leading model:

> You never really forget the sex, you forget the movie. There's a lot of movies on the market that are exactly the same.[1049]

When asked to remember a movie she was proud of, she tellingly replied:

> Yeah, I think one of the films I am most proud of is 'Sex Waves.' There was acting in it, a story to it . . . it wasn't an excuse to have sex.[1050]

As one knowledgeable observer told us, sex scenes are normally shot in one take, and dialogue scenes in two or three:

> They do not spend a lot of time on the dialogue. They do not look for perfection. If they [looked] for perfection, most of the porn movies would still be in production. The people they are using are not well known actors and actresses and they are not very skilled in this area.[1051]

From our limited direct observation of "X"-rated material we must agree: skilled acting seems irrelevant to what is depicted.[1052]

There are, of course, those who disagree. One model speaks of always performing "within the character" he is portraying, even in sex scenes;[1053] another of how "the voice changes" while he plays the character he has portrayed through ninety-seven "features";[1054] a third (more dubiously) of the "ultimate acting challenge" involved in managing to "fool the public" into thinking she enjoys the sex, which she considers pure

---

1044. *Id.*
1045. *Id.*
1046. Los Angeles Hearing, Vol. I, George, pp. 84–85.
1047. *Where are They Now, supra* note 970, p. 52 (statement of Jessie ✂). *Accord, Id.* (statement of Kay ✂) ("Empty plots, with soulless characters"), and *Id.* (statement of Candida ✂) ("An actress has very little say over the creative aspects of the films she's in.")
1048. See, Los Angeles Hearing, William Roberts, Vol. I, pp. 62–72.
1049. Traci ✂ Interview, *supra* note 1037, p. 34.
1050. *Id.*
1051. Los Angeles Hearing, Vol. I, William Roberts, p. 68.
1052. This general distinction between "acting" and pornographic performing seems to have a parallel in the work of fashion modeling:

> Few male centerfold discoveries are fashion model material. Carl ✂ and the select others who have put their clothes back on to forge a career all possess the requisite suit size—40 regular or thereabouts—as well as a special look and a special drive. On the other hand, the requirements for nude modeling, as one auditioner for a male flesh magazine explains, are "body, face, cock," not necessarily in that order.

1053. Richard ✂ Interview, *supra* note 986, p. 24.
1054. *Male Model, supra* note 926, p. 185.

"exploitation."[1055] Clearly it is impossible to draw a bright, unwavering line between legitimate "acting" and pornographic "modeling."

Yet, ultimately we are faced with the simple fact acknowledged even by one of the most partisan of the adult film industry's fans: "Jealousy and most other human emotions (except fear and lust) are rarely expressed in adult films."[1056] Worse, as another sympathetic critic has conceded, "hard-core guarantees realism, . . . yet it remains incapable of showing pleasure."[1057] In a medium where virtually no human emotion (not even sexual pleasure!) can be expressed, and where, moreover, the performers are chosen neither for training in acting nor for natural acting talent, it seems to us all but ludicrous to call them "actors." We do not, therefore, consider it even the mildest paradox that the performers in live or filmed pornography are not treated on an equal footing as other performers by such organizations as Actors Equity and the Screen Actors Guild.[1058] Nor do we consider one of the rising male models to be wholly misguided in describing his job as, simply, f...ing pretty girls for a living."[1059]

Career Prospects

Just as sex modeling appears to offer few opportunities for creative expression, so too it seems to allow only sparse chances for long-term employment and remuneration. The life of a typical model's career is extremely short, usually not more than a few months or years. Of twenty new male "stars" each year in "adult" films, only about half a dozen will remain in the business for over a year.[1060] One of the few women to survive long in the industry, when asked what advice she would give to new female models, replied:

I would tell them not to burn themselves out so fast. What happens is that they become big names and everyone wants them. A couple of years down the line, these girls are going to find people telling them they're overexposed. The typical line is something like we can't pay you a great deal of money because you're not a name yet. Then when they use you in every damn thing around and you become dependent on the income, they tell you we can't pay you very much because you're overexposed. They're setting themselves up for a really bad experience. I had a six year career. I think the reason it was that long is because I would only do three or four films a year. I tried to be choosy. These new stars shouldn't depend on hardcore as a full-time income. The directors are gonna grab them, chew them up, and spit them out real fast.[1061]

Some models manage to remain for longer periods in the "X" rated world, but after they reach the age of forty almost never appear naked, and only rarely appear in sexual intercourse.[1062] Women can almost never expect to hang on in any but minor roles after age thirty,[1063] although a few women have successfully moved into production and management roles.[1064] As for switching to legitimate acting, Mr. ✂ has said bluntly, "if someone thinks he's going to get into mainstream through porn, he's deluding himself."[1065] Whether in films or traditional modeling, his observation seems to hold fast.[1066]

1053. Richard ✂ Interview, *supra* note 986, p. 24.

1054. *Male Model, supra* note 926, p. 185.

1055. Ali ✂ Interview, *supra* note 976, p. 9.

1056. R. ✂ , *The X-Rated Videotape Guide,* (1984), p. 28.

1057. G. ✂ , *Sex on the Screen: Eroticism in Film,* (Jacobs trans. 1985), p. 5.

1058. It is our understanding that at least one prominent pornographic model is a member of Actors Equity, but that his membership depends on work he did in the legitimate theatre. *See,* New York Hearing, Vol. II, Colleen Dewhurst, pp. 190–91.

1059. *Porn Star Confessions, supra* note 1003, p. 61. *See, Joanna* ✂ Interview, *supra* note 979, p. 63 ("Films let me express a lot of my 'extra sexual desire.' If I didn't do films, I'd probably be in bed with the postman.")

1060. Bennett, *supra* note 972, p. 71.

1061. *Interview: Candida* ✂ , Adult Video News, (July 1985), p. 38.

1062. ✂ , *supra* note 1145, p. 28.

1063. *Id.*

1064. One such woman is Candida ✂ , whose written statement is on file with the Commission. *See also,* Candida ✂ Interview, *supra* note 976. Other prominent women who have survived in aspects of the "adult entertainment" business are Dottie ✂ (management position at *Penthouse*), who testified before us; Seka (mail order pornography business), and Veronica ✂ (writing for such "adult publications" as *Puritan* magazine). *See, 1984 Senate Hearing, supra* note 975, pp. 313–22 (statements of Seka and Vera).

1065. Bennett, *supra* note 972, p. 72.

1066. *See, Male Model, supra* note 926, p. 186 (statement of Jack ✂ that "a lot of companies, film companies as well, won't hire you if you have done nude modeling whether it was for *Playgirl* or for *Playboy* or whatever.") *See also,*

As for money, models in the sex industry collect none of the residuals on which professional actors expect to survive through lean years.[1067] One angry former model was quoted at the time she left the business as follows:

> And they deserve it. Do you know what it's like to have somebody pay you five hundred dollars to do two sex scenes, considering the money he's gonna get back? If you want to know something, I've got nothing really to show for it.[1068]

Her experience seems common, and her current dilemma wrenching.

MODELING AND PERSONAL LIFE

As a job, sexually-explicit modeling has dramatically serious defects—from poor working conditions to disease, drugs, economic insecurity, and exclusion from mainstream acting. Modeling, however, appears to have consequences for its participants that extend deeply into their personal lives as well. Limited as our inquiry could be with regard to the world of modeling in general—and to the personal lives of performers in particular—we would be remiss if we failed to take into account what evidence does exist. On the whole, we believe the evidence before us to be highly suggestive in this area—suggestive as much of the attitudes of others as of the feelings of the performers themselves.

A few of the performers in this field, to begin with, speak in glowing terms of the experience. One of them, a former "Pet of the Year" in *Penthouse*, described to us how her marriage had remained strong and happy after her selection for the honor and then during her subsequent career at the magazine in management positions.[1069] Another, speaking before a Senate subcommittee "not only for myself but for every woman that I know in the sex industry," declared:

We do not see ourselves as victims. We do not need to hide in the shelter of being somebody's victim. We accept responsibility for our own lives.[1070]

And a third related how he had maintained a happy marriage and fathered two children during his career adding that, in his words, "I've made the decision that I will abide by the incest taboo, completely."[1071]

Reassuring as these comments are, they stand in a clear minority. William ✄ once again offered the most straightforward summation of what modeling means for the personal relationships of models:

> Whenever I'm interviewing someone who wants to get into porn, I always ask them, "Do you have anybody that you will hurt by doing this?" It would be ideal if someone had no relatives—disenfranchised human being devoid of any past that would haunt them and any kind of present or future that they could destroy. If it's a man, he also better be single because, unless he's married to the most magnanimous of women, it will tear her insides out.[1072]

He went on to point out its effects on the personal reputation of women involved.

> And I'd like to point out that for a woman, there's even more of a stigma than for a man. She'll be called a prostitute and a whore and thought of as sleazy, cheap and slutty. And she has to understand that what she does now will haunt her the rest of her life.[1073]

Mr. ✄ view, bleak as it is, has the weight of his thirteen years' experience in the field behind it; it is, moreover, continually echoed in the testimony and public statements of others who have knowledge of the industry.

1067. In this respect, as to a lesser extent with respect to age limitation, "modeling" in pornography is similar to traditional modeling—which, unlike acting, is not organized in unions and thus has never established residual, retirement, and fringe benefit standards. *See, Male Model, supra* note 926, pp. 109–50.

1068. *Heather* ✄ *Interview, supra* note 987, p. 58. Bruce ✄ , a prominent X-rated film producer, was quoted in the same interview as agreeing with Heather ✄ , listing only four female performers "who made anything out of it." *Id.*

1069. New York Hearing, Vol. II, Dottie ✄ , pp. 301–03. Dottie ✄ , it should be noted, does not appear to have performed in any material depicting actual sexual conduct.

1070. *1984 Senate Hearing, supra* note 975, p. 317 (statement of Veronica ✄). Veronica ✄ , of course, alluded elsewhere to having suffered sexual abuse as a child.

1071. *Richard* ✄ *Interview, supra* note 986, pp. 23–24.

1072. Bennett, *supra* note 972, p. 72.

1073. *Id.*

✄ , *supra* note 1006, pp. 284–86 (discussing death of Dorothy ✄ , whose "death was a cruel blow to *Playboy,* since she was the first Playmate, of all the many Playmates, who looked as if she might become a Hollywood star. . . . One after another, the Playmates disappeared into obscurity. . . ." *Id.*, p. 286).

Personal relationships, to begin with, appear to be severely threatened by modeling in pornography. Romances as well as family ties are often strained or broken.[1074] One young man, who had been lured into making "adult" films at age seventeen, told us about his feelings after leaving modeling and entering a drug rehabilitation program:

> I don't know, I feel scared to have a sexual relationship with a girl. I don't know what it's going to be like or if I am going to be too rough.[1075]

Candida ✂ , a major "star" (and now producer) in the industry, told *Forum Magazine* recently that after her marriage she had ended her performing because "once wed . . . she couldn't quite bring herself to do the sex scenes."[1076] Even that may be of little avail: as one "X" rated film producer put it, "A man getting involved with an ex-porn star will always shove it back in her face."[1077]

What relationships do continue for models are often highly negative. Thus many female models live with highly abusive husbands or boyfriends, whose relationship to them is that of pimp to prostitute.[1078] Others report suffering rape[1079] or demands that they service agents or producers.[1080] Indeed, some may drift directly into "call girl" status.[1081]

> I was never viewed as a human being. . . . Most people, right off the bat, assume I am a piece of meat, a porno star, a floozie.[1082]

"Adult" publications even those which are "soft core," view models as products.[1083] In the midst of that environment a young female performer said that she "just hated [herself] every day"[1084] and a young male told us it "made me feel worthless."[1085] As Andrea Dworkin has explained, that valuation is a central element of contemporary pornographic modeling.[1086] And it is a valuation we strongly reject.

1074. See, e.g., Los Angeles Hearing, Vol. I, Chris, pp. 93–94 (relationship with boyfriend broken); Ginger ✂ Interview, supra note 992, p. 30 (being known as porn star "stops the whole magical process" of romantic attachment, but still accepted by family); Traci ✂ Interview, supra note 1037, p. 34 ("You don't have a personal life."); Ali ✂ Interview, supra note 976, pp. 9–10 (modeling makes relationship with husband "very tough"; family members "know nothing of any porn films"); Heather ✂ Interview, supra note 987, p. 32 (modeling "destroys your sex life," and, according to Bruce ✂ , porn producer, "really screws up relationships.") Los Angeles Hearing, Vol. II, Miki ✂ , p. 116. (*Playboy* "Playmates" suffer alienation from family and friends). But see, Los Angeles Hearing, Vol. I, Mary, p. 78 (husband found "it was very hard for him to adjust . . . to me doing this . . . [and] wasn't very pleased with me," but it "hasn't really affected my married life"; "several relatives stopped speaking to me").
1075. Washington, D.C. Hearing, Vol. II, Jeff, p. 173.
1076. *Candida* ✂ *Interview*, supra note 976, p. 42.
1077. *Heather* ✂ *Interview*, supra note 987, p. 58.
1078. *Lederer Interview*, supra note 969, p. 63; See, Washington, D.C., Hearing, Vol. I, Sarah ✂ ; Washington, D.C., Vol. I, Valerie ✂ ; New York Hearing, Vol. I, Linda ✂ . See also, Heather ✂ Interview, supra note 987, p. 58 ("[Erotic Film Guide]: Actor William ✂ also says that actresses seek out abusive boyfriends and husbands, the dregs of society, because they want to punish themselves. Any comment? ✂ : "It's hard to find a nice man who'd want you. And I guess you figure you wouldn't deserve a nice man.").
1079. *Lederer Interview*, supra note 969, p. 67; Los Angeles Hearing, Vol. II, Miki ✂ , pp. 116, 124.
1080. Los Angeles Hearing, Vol. I, Chris, p. 93; *1984 Senate Hearing*, supra note 975, p. 179 (Linda ✂ statement). The "casting couch" is, unfortunately, apparently not unique to the pornography segment of the entertainment industry.
1081. Los Angeles Hearing, Vol. II, Miki ✂ , p. 117. Ms. ✂ , until 1982 the director of Playmate Promotions, asserted that, among many other abuses, former Playmates "were involved in an international call girl ring with ties to the Playboy mansion." Id. Playboy Enterprises, in a letter from its counsel of November 6, 1985, accused her of "bearing false witness" in "efforts for self-aggrandizement," but offered no specific evidence rebutting her accusations. Until she left Playboy, Miki occupied a position (conceded by all sides) of responsibility and trust. Documents submitted to the Commission by Miki indicate, further that she had received outstanding ratings for performance of her duties at Playboy, and that at least at the time of her resignation had communicated her feelings about the treatment of the Playmates with her superiors. We are, of course, in no position to evaluate the truth of this accusation—or of the others included in her testimony—but we see no clear reason why, as Playboy suggests, Miki's account should be dismissed out of hand. It accords, indeed, with statements submitted by two other former Playmates (Susan ✂ and Brenda ✂), and in significant respects with a recent full scale overview by an outsider. Miller supra note 1006. ("Many girls drawn into this orbit found the world of Playboy was not a pretty place. . . .") Id., p. 160. We can only urge a thorough investigation of Miki's allegations regarding problems faced by the Playmates she supervised, which included sexual exploitation and harassment, rape, murder and attempted murder.
1082. *Interview: Linda* ✂ , Adult Video News, (March 1985), p. 19.
1083. Los Angeles Hearing, Vol. II, Miki ✂ , p. 121.
1084. *Heather* ✂ *Interview*, supra note 1051, p. 58.
1085. Washington, D.C., Hearing, Vol. II, Jeff, p. 171.
1086. A. Dworkin, *Pornography: Men Possessing Women* (1979) ("Contemporary pornography strictly and literally conforms to the word's root [Greek] meaning: the graphic depiction of vile whores, or, in our language, sluts, cows (as in: sexual cattle, sexual chattel). . . ." Id., p. 200.

CONCLUSIONS AND RECOMMENDATIONS

In sum, then, we have found, within the admittedly severe limitations of the evidence, the following propositions to be generally true of commercial pornography's use of performers: (1) that they are normally young, previously abused, and financially strapped; (2) that on the job they find exploitative economic arrangements, extremely poor working conditions, serious health hazards, strong temptations to drug use, and little chance of career advancement; and (3) that in their personal lives they will often suffer substantial injuries to relationships, reputation, and self-image. We acknowledge that exceptions exist to all these findings, and we concede, as well, that extremely thorough investigation might prove one or more of them untrue. Unhappily the power to conduct such an investigation is not in our hands. And the industry itself, which of course knows the full truth of the matter, has shown little interest in sharing that knowledge with us. We are, therefore, left with the unattractive but firm obligation to make recommendations in this area based on what we in our limited way have been able to uncover.

The approach we propose in this area is a cautious but urgent one. Caution we believe to be required from the incomplete character of the evidence currently available. Urgency, however, arises from the extremely serious nature of the harms apparently being inflicted on many young and vulnerable people. Both of these interests will be best served, we believe, if federal and state governments initiate thorough investigations—by agencies or committees possessed of substantial resources and full subpoena powers—of the use of "models." Those investigations should, in our view, proceed from three related, but distinct perspectives: pornographic modeling as (1) a subset of prostitution; (2) a form of sex discrimination; and (3) an invasion of performers' personal rights. Briefly we will consider the parameters of each of these perspectives and possible concrete courses of action available under each.

MODELING AND PROSTITUTION

It seems abundantly clear from the facts before us that the bulk of commercial pornographic modeling (that is, all performances which include actual sexual intercourse), quite simply is a form of prostitution. So much was directly asserted by representatives of prostitutes' organizations who testified before us,[1087] as well as representatives of law enforcement[1088] and effectively denied by no one. Every court which has examined the questions from this standpoint has agreed, reasoning that where persons are paid to have sex it is irrelevant that the act is for display to others.[1089] As prostitution is conduct which the state has a strong interest in regulating, the First Amendment does not preclude that regulation merely because it is labelled "speech" or is filmed.[1090] It is also readily apparent that the interests which have in the past most powerfully justified the state's concern over prostitution—exploitation of the young and the weak, prevention of disease—are just as strongly implicated by pornographic "modeling."

If upon further study our equation of prostitution and "modeling" proves to be true, it is incumbent upon the federal government and the states to consider carefully how to respond. Some of our witnesses have in fact urged *legalization* of pornographic modeling, and of all prostitution, as a means of eliminating its clandestine character and allowing "sex workers" to improve the conditions under which they labor.[1091] Insofar as that proposal would permit the recruitment of men and women into prostitution, the promotion of prostitution, or the living on the avails

---

1087. Los Angeles Hearing, Vol. II, Margaret Prescod, p. 215; Los Angeles Hearing, Vol. II, Priscilla Alexander, p. 224.

1088. Los Angeles Hearing, Vol. I, James Docherty, p. 15. See *also*, Chicago Hearing, Vol. I, Nan Hunter ("some women work in both pornography and prostitution": statement does not contest their overlapping character).

1089. *See, United States v. Roeder*, 526 F.2d 726(10th Cir. 1975), cert. denied 462 U.S. 905(1976); *People v. Sonter*, 178 Cal. Rptr. 111(Ct. App. 2d Dist. 1981); *People ex rel. Van DeKamp v. American Art Enterprises*, 142 Cal. Rptr. 338(Ct. App. 2d Dist. 1977); *People v. Fixler*, 128 Cal. Rptr. 363 (Ct. App. 2d Cist. 1976); *People v. Kovner* 96 Misc. 2d 414 (sup. Ct. N.Y. Co. 1978). *See also, People v. Marta*, 203 Cal. Rptr. 685(Ct. App. 1st Dist. 1984) (defendant convicted of pimping for hiring women to have on-stage sex with customers in a theater).

1090. *Id.; See, United States v. O'Brien*, 391 U.S., (1968), p. 367.

1091. Los Angeles Hearing, Vol. II, Margaret Prescod, p. 215; Los Angeles Hearing, Vol. II, Priscilla Alexander, p. 224; Chicago Hearing, Vol. I, Nan Hunter.

of prostitution—all characteristics, so far as we can tell, of the producers and distributors of commercial pornography—it flies in the face of established international mores,[1092] longstanding national policy,[1093] and simple good sense.[1094] We agree with the International Convention for the Suppression of the Traffic in Persons and of the Exploitation of the Prostitution of Others, adopted by the General Assembly of the United Nations in 1949, that the State should punish any person who "procures, entices or leads away, for purposes of prostitution, another person, even with the consent of that person" or who "exploits the prostitution of another person, even with the consent of that person."[1095] Lifting sanctions against the "employer" seems no more attractive a solution with regard to exploitation in pornography than it would, for example, with regard to child or subminimum-wage labor. "Legalization," if extended to producers and others currently considered "panderers" under state laws, would only make it easier for them to persuade more vulnerable young people to participate in a world that seems to us inherently abusive.

With regard to penalties directed at models themselves, however, the argument for de-criminalization seems much stronger, on several grounds. First, it is not uniform policy in the District of Columbia to make the simple act of prostitution (without accompanying "solicitation") a crime.[1096] Second, those who are misguided, desperate or frightened enough to turn to pornographic modeling are unlikely to be deterred by the relatively light sentences typically imposed on those convicted of prostitution.[1097] Third, models are often so badly harmed by their experience that the addition of criminal penalties to their suffering—which includes a never-ending fear that humiliating photographs or films will be publicly exhibited—may seem superfluous and cruel.[1098] Finally, fear of prosecution may make such models less likely to come forward and provide evidence against those who exploited them.[1099]

While we do not believe, therefore, that prostitution laws are a perfect weapon in every respect for protecting models from procurement and abuse, their application at least to producers and agents seem fully justified. The experience of Los Angeles, where pandering prosecutions and "red-light" nuisance abatement actions have been successfully brought by police and prosecutors, deserves careful study in other jurisdic-

1092. *The International Convention for the Suppression of the Traffic in Women and Children, League of Nations—Treaty Series* (1922) (No. 269), adopted by twenty-eight member nations of the League of Nations in 1921, established the duty of all signatory states to punish the procuring or promoting the prostitution of any women by force, or any woman under age of twenty-one, even with her consent. *See*, V. Bullough, *The History of Prostitution* 184(1964). The United States, which of course refused League membership, never acceded to the Convention. In 1949 the United Nations adopted the Convention for the Suppression of the Traffic in Persona and of the Prostitution of Others, which committed signatory states to punish the procuring or the exploitation of the prostitution of another, without regard to any age limit. *Report of Mr. Jean Fernand-Laurent, Special Rapporteur on the Suppression of Traffic in Persons and the Exploitation of the Prostitution of Others, Economic and Social Council, United Nations* (1983), Annex VII [hereinafter, *United Nations Report*]. At present both international conventions are in effect—although not ratified by the United States and are supplemented by the Convention on the Elimination of All Forms of Discrimination Against Women, adopted by the United Nations in 1979, which also requires (in Article 6) the signatory parties to "suppress all forms of traffic in women and exploitation of prostitution of women." *Id.* Annex IX. On their face these agreements all seem fully applicable to commercial pornography.

1093. The clearest expression of this policy is the White-Slave Traffic Act (the Mann Act), ch. 395, 36 Stat. 825 (codified as amended at 18 U.S.C. SS2421–2424) (1970 & Supp. 1985), which, *inter alia* forbids interstate transportation of women or girls for the purposes of prostitution.

1094. For excellent discussions of the pitfalls of legalized prostitution, *see*, K. Barry, *Female Sexual Slavery*, (1984), pp. 128–134; C. Winick & P. Kinsie, *The Lively Commerce*, (1971), pp. 211–2432; and of course the classic work studying legalized prostitution in 19th century Europe, A. Flexner, *Prostitution in Europe* (1914). For a jolting overview of the pimp-prostitute relationship, *See*, L. Lee, *The Social World of the Female Prostitute in Los Angeles*, Ph.D. Diss. (1982).

1095. *United Nations Report, supra* note 1092, at 60 (Annex VII), quoting resolution 317 (IV) adopted by United Nations on December 2, 1949.

1096. For a listing and analysis of state laws on prostitution, *See*, *Note, Right of Privacy Challenges to Prostitution Statutes*, 58 Wash U.L.Q., (1979), pp. 439, 471–80 (four states and District of Columbia punish solicitation for prostitution but not act itself). The act of prostitution was not an offense under English common law. *Id.* at 443.

1097. *See*, Winick & Kinsie, *supra* note 1094, pp. 218–19.

1098. *See*, *e.g.*, Barry, *supra* note 1094, pp. 125–28; *Fraser Report, supra* note 936, pp. 530–37.

1099. Of course, it is also possible that with no fear of criminal prosecution themselves, models will be impervious to police pressure to give evidence against their employers. On balance the threat of a prostitution charge—in every state no more than a misdemeanor—seems unlikely to persuade many models to betray their colleagues and thereby jeopardize their careers.

tions. There seems little warrant for a state or locality to tolerate the production of commercial pornography that is as exploitative as that discussed above unless its basic approach to prostitution itself is radically different from the national norm.

Quite apart from the use of pandering statutes, however, an approach that seems to us worthy of careful study is imposition of sanctions on any persons trafficking in products or materials which they know or have reason to know were manufactured or marketed through the use of persons engaging in prostitution.

Such legislation would parallel existing legislation which forbids trafficking in products manufactured through child labor or through certain oppressive adult labor practices.[1100] Because not directed specifically at speech,[1101] and because clearly grounded in legitimate governmental interest in controlling prostitution, it would seem likely to survive constitutional attack.[1102] Given the federal government's long commitment to use its powers to regulate interstate commerce to attack prostitution in every form, we are, indeed, somewhat surprised that such a proposal has not been seriously studied before now. Nevertheless, the idea is sufficiently novel and could affect so much commerce not directly within the purview of our charter that we merely offer it for consideration and debate.

SEX DISCRIMINATION
Along similar lines we urge careful study by the Department of Justice of the extent to which producers of sexually-explicit photographs, films, and video tapes are acting in violation of federal civil rights laws, and in particular of Title VII of the Civil Rights Act of 1964.[1103] That law provides, in pertinent part:

> It shall be an unlawful employment practice for an employer . . . to fail or refuse to hire or to discharge any individual, or otherwise to discriminate against any individual with respect to [her] compensation, terms, conditions, or privileges of employment, because of such individual's . . . sex.[1104]

This provision has been interpreted widely to protect employees from having to prostitute themselves to supervisors or submit themselves to sexual intercourse or harassment to keep their jobs.[1105] One court declared flatly, "An employer may not require sexual consideration from an employee as a quid pro quo for job benefits."[1106]

On its face this principle would seem to make illegal the requirements that a performer engage in sexual activity as a condition of his or her employment. There are, however, two limitations on its scope that are at least arguable relevant to production of pornography. The courts have ruled that sexual demands (1) must be "unwelcome,"[1107] and (2) must include disparate treatment of the sexes.[1108] The first of these limitations does not seem a serious one: the overwhelming factor motivating the sexual conduct of pornographic models is financial need, certainly not a desire to have sex with the partner assigned to him or her for the scene.[1109] The sexual act is thus in no way "welcome" in the sense we understand the law to exempt.[1110] With regard to the "disparate treatment": requirement, we note simply that women and

---

1100. See, United States v. Darby, 312 U.S., (1914), p. 100.

1101. A company which hired employees whose duties consisted of providing sexual services to potential clients of the firm could be subject to sanction under such a law.

1102. Cf., New York v. Ferber, 458 U.S., (1982), pp. 747, 761 (advertising and selling child pornography "provide an economic motive for and are thus an integral part of the production of such material, an activity illegal throughout the nation. It rarely has been suggested that the constitutional freedom for speech and press extends its immunity to speech or writing used as an integral part of conduct in violation of a valid criminal statute. Giboney v. Empire Storage 7 Ice Co., 336 U.S., (1949), pp. 490, 498 ."); Wirtz v. Keystone Readers Service, Inc. 282 F. Supp., (S.D. Fla. 1968), p. 971 (magazine subscription service violated federal law prohibiting illegal labor practices by employing high school student at below minimum wage).

1103. 42 U.S.C. S2000(e).

1104. 42 U.S.C. S2000 (e)-2(a)(1).

1105. See, Hensen v. City of Dundee, 682 F.2d 897, 908 (11th Cir. 1982); Bundy v. Jackson, 641 F.2d 934 (D.C. Cir. 1981); Miller v. Bank of America, 600 F.2d 211 (9th Cir. 1979); Tomkins v. Public Service Electric & Gas, 568 F.2d 983 (D.C. Cir. 1979); 29 C.F.R. S1064(1)(a).

1106. Hensen, supra note 1194, 682 F.2d p. 908.

1107. Id., p. 904.

1108. Id., pp. 904, 905.

1109. See, Text to notes 984–991, supra.

1110. Thus Hensen defined "conduct" as "unwelcome" if "the employee did not solicit or incite it" and "regarded the conduct as undesirable or offensive." 682 F.2d p. 903. Model Ali ✄ is a vivid example of an employee finding such

men are normally paid different rates in the industry for the same sex acts,[1111] and that women in mainstream pornography are expected to engage in homosexual activity while men are forbidden to.[1112]

We therefore believe it likely that much of the commercial production of pornography runs afoul of Title VII, even considering the techical limitations on its reach. Further, we believe that Title VII embodies a principle that should not be strangled by technicalities: no one in this country should have to engage in actual sex to get or keep his or her job.[1113] To the extent that Title VII and comparable state statutes do not currently reflect that principle, we urge serious and rapid consideration of proposals to broaden their reach.

INVASION OF PERSONAL RIGHTS

During the course of our review of the position of performers in pornography, we have encountered evidence that they suffer physical coercion, damage to health, serious economic exploitation, and virtually complete loss of reputation. The pornography which they helped create will live on to plague them long after they have extricated themselves from modeling. Its effects subject performers to long-term effects potentially worse than any other form of sexual abuse, a fact noted tellingly by Dr. Ulrich Schoettle in the context of child pornography.

> Pornography is a graphic form of exhibitionism. Unlike prostitution where a degree of "privacy" exists during the sexual acts, pornography literally makes the child's body "available" for anyone willing to pay the price anywhere in the world.

The "privacy interests" of performers in pornography seem to us real and compelling[1114] while the value of the material itself is often indisputably minimal.

It, therefore, seems important for judges and lawmakers to carefully consider how performers may be protected from the unsavory characters who exploit them, and in particular what civil and equitable remedies performers may have in court. There has been disagreement in what we have heard over the current status of the law in this regard;[1115] we know only that they have been exceedingly rare.[1116] If new remedies are needed, as we are inclined to think they are, they should be framed in ways to encourage plaintiffs to come forward: perhaps by providing for treble damages in certain types of cases (such as coercion or fraud) and reasonable attorneys' fees.[1117]

We hope, too, that in studying the availability and desirability of such private remedies, courts and legislatures will be sensitive to the issue of "consent." Because of their youth, their economic desperation, and their troubled backgrounds, we submit that few performers are fully able to appreciate the meaning and the magnitude of their decision to engage in sexual performances—and throw away all control of the resulting material for the rest of their lives. Just as it is appropriate to provide consumers with extensive government protections against the consequences of their ignorance, so every adult needs special safeguards against making a decision which even the pornography industry's strongest booster admits "will haunt her the rest of her life."[1118]

Otherwise she may find that photography's freedom from time and space, so heartily welcomed by Bazin, has become her dungeon.

1111. Los Angeles Hearing, Vol. I, William Roberts, p. 65.

1112. In "gay" pornography, of course, women are excluded altogether. Id.

1113. We emphasize "actual," for the simulated sexual activity regularly engaged in by legitimate actors in their roles does not provoke the same concerns as actual sex. Simulated sexual conduct does not impinge on personal privacy to so enormous a degree; it risks no transmission of venereal disease; it risks no pregnancy; and, finally, it carries no comparable stigma. For a comparison of sex modeling and legitimate acting, see, text to notes 1043–1059, supra.

1114. Cf. New York v. Ferber, 458 U.S. at 759 n. 10.

1115. Compare, 1984 Senate Hearing, supra note 975, p. 249 (statement of Catherine MacKinnon) (Statutes of limitations, single-publication rules, and other technical limitations make actions by performers impractical at present), with Washington, D.C., Hearing, Vol. I, Barry Lynn, pp. 24–25 (such actions are not unknown).

1116. The cases cited in notes 960–963, supra are the only ones we have been able to uncover in this area.

1117. S. 1187, introduced last year by Senator Arlen Specter, essentially contains both these provisions—treble damages and attorney's fees—in seeking to help adult pornography victims obtain compensation for production or distribution of material in which they were coerced or fraudulently induced to appear. We note that consitutional issues may arise if equitable remedies are not carefully tailored to the First Amendment requirements, and that scienter is likely to be of some constitutional relevance in determining how wide the net of liability may be cast.

1118. Bennett, supra note 972, p. 72.

---

conduct "unwelcome": "I'm not going to say all that stuff about how I love to f..k on camera. . . . I guess I really don't like the sex much." Ali ✂ Interview, supra note 976, p. 9.

Social and Behavioral Science Research Analysis

INTRODUCTION

The Commission has examined social and behavioral science research in recognition of the role it plays in determining legal standards and social policy. This role, while notable, is not, nor should it be, the sole basis for developing standards or policy. The lack of funding and the inability under the mandate of the Charter to conduct original research has resulted in the need to rely on existing information. The amount of research conducted in the last fifteen years provides a reasonably sufficient base to reevaluate answers to old questions. Some might argue that given the controversy and heated debate that inevitably surrounds any discussion about pornography, in some ways, we might be better off relying on studies initiated, funded, and presented outside the context of such a milieu.

The major question which frames this research review is: what are the effects of exposure to pornography and under what conditions and in what kinds of individuals are these effects manifested? We also have structured this review with the following considerations in mind: (1) that it provides some input into the policy-making process; (2) that it provides social science information for public consumption and understanding; and (3) that it provides the research community with further questions for investigation.

While the nature of effects is the focus of this section, we have also examined public opinion on pornography to systematically describe the nature of public perceptions of and experiences with such material as well as policy preferences. In terms of effects, correlational as well as experimental studies on sexual offenders as well as on nonoffender populations were examined. For background purposes, we have also presented brief summaries of what some predecessor Commissions have concluded about the social science evidence before them.

Some observations on terminology and on the character of social science evidence are appropriate at this point as guidelines to reading through the rest of this chapter.

We will simply avoid the usual definitional morass by using the term "pornography" to refer to the range of sexually explicit materials used in the various studies reviewed here. In a number of studies, these materials have included sex education materials. In describing specific studies, we also will use the researcher's terminology of choice, but making sure that the stimulus materials are adequately described for the reader.

We also are sensitive to the limitations and strengths of specific research approaches and we have taken special efforts to review these briefly in each major section of this Chapter, if only to underscore the fact that our evaluation of the research recognizes these limitations and indeed proceeds from the assumption that any conclusions must be drawn on the basis of complementary or convergent data.

OVERVIEW OF THE 1970 COMMISSION RESEARCH CONCLUSIONS

The period prior to the creation of the 1970 Commission on Obscenity and Pornography was marked by a paucity of research on the effects of exposure to pornography

(Cairns, Paul and Wishner, 1962). A Commission-sponsored review of the literature in 1970 later concluded that "we still have precious little information from studies of humans on the questions of primary import to the law . . . the data stop short of the 'critical point'". (Cairns, et al, 1970). Much of the Commission-sponsored studies thus constituted some of the earliest investigations on the issue of pornography.

The 1970 Commission funded over eighty studies to examine various aspects of pornography. Surveys included a national in-person survey of public attitudes toward and experiences with pornography (Abelson, et. al., 1970). A number of correlational studies examined social indicators of crime rates (Thornberry and Silverman, 1970; Kupperstein and Wilson, 1970; Ben-Veniste, 1970) while another cluster of studies investigated sex offenders and their previous experiences with erotica, patterns of exposure and self-reported arousal. Finally, another group of studies was commissioned (laboratory experiments) to examine causal links between exposure to pornography and effects (see Technical Reports of the Commission on Obscenity and Pornography, vols. 1, 6, 7, and 8, 1970).

The national survey findings (Abelson, et. al., 1970) showed that between two-fifths to three-fifths of the respondents believed then that sexually-explicit materials provided information about sex, were a form of entertainment, led to moral breakdown, improved sexual relationships of married couples, led people to commit rape, produced boredom with sexually-explicit materials, encouraged innovation in marital sexual technique and led people to lose respect for women (see comparison between 1970 survey findings and 1985 Gallup poll results below).

Experimental findings showed brief increases in sexual activities and fantasies after exposure to sexually-explicit materials but no significant alterations of established sexual behavioral patterns. The Commission further determined that there was no detectable relationship between availability of pornography and crime rates in the United States but suggested that removal of restrictions on pornographic material was correlated with lower sexual crime rates, as determined from Danish data prior to and after the removal of restrictions on pornography (Ben-Veniste, 1970; Kutchinsky, 1970, 1973).

The 1970 Commission concluded:

> . . . In sum, empirical research designed to clarify the question has found no evidence to date that exposure to explicit sexual materials plays a significant role in the causation of delinquent or criminal behavior among youth or adults. The Commission cannot conclude that exposure to erotic materials is a factor in the causation of sex crimes or sex delinquency (p. 223).

The Commission's conclusions were challenged and a number of methodological issues were raised (Cline, 1974; Eysenck and Nias, 1980). At the very least, these conclusions were described as "premature" (see Liebert, 1976). Researchers who have done studies subsequent to the 1970 Report have also consistently identified a major flaw in the 1970 studies: the absence of any investigation of the effects of violent pornography.

On balance, however, the impetus for further research on the effects of exposure provided by the 1970 Commission cannot be overlooked. As the Effects Panel noted in its report,

> One of the contributions of the work of the Panel has been to place the dimensions of human sexual behavior on the agenda for continuing inquiry. By providing resources in terms of funds and technical guidelines, the Panel has helped to legitimate systematic inquiry into an area that heretofore has either been ignored or feared.

It is difficult to quarrel with this observation.

Since the 1970 Commission report, in fact, numerous research studies have been done exploring various aspects of the effects of pornography. Since 1970 the quantity and quality of the research has been impressive. While much remains to be explored, not only has the volume of studies conducted steadily increased, but the programmatic nature of the research conducted by various individuals and research teams has provided a better insight into understanding the various conditions under which certain effects may or may not occur.

Studies done for the 1970 Commission were hampered by time constraints. As the research director for the 1970 Commission pointed out, "most of the researchers had less than nine months in which to establish a research team, arrange a research setting, develop measuring instruments, secure subjects, collect the data, reduce the data, and write a report." (General Preface to Technical

Reports, Commission on Obscenity and Pornography, 1970, p. vii)

Methodological advances in measurement procedures have also enhanced the reliability and validity of research instruments and findings. For example, measures of sexual arousal in some of the 1970 studies were based almost entirely on self-reports (e.g., Cook and Fosen, 1970; Goldstein, et. al., 1970; Davis and Braught, 1970). Since then, the poor correlation between self-reports of sexual arousal to sexually explicit stimuli and physiological measures of arousal has been well documented (Abel, Barlow, Blanchard and Guild, 1977; Blader and Marshall, 1984).

More recent studies have used instruments such as the penile plethysmograph (Malamuth and Check, 1980a), thermography procedures (e.g., Abramson, et. al., 1981) or the vaginal photoplethysmograph (see Sintchack and Geer, 1975; Hatch, 1979) to evaluate arousal (see also Geer, 1975; Heiman, 1977), or have combined physiological measures (e.g., blood pressure readings) with paper-and-pencil tests. Researchers have also attempted to validate paper-and-pencil measures, a critical methodological requirement (see, for example, Burt, 1980; Malamuth, In Press). Finally, more sophisticated statistical techniques have allowed for better data analysis, control, and interpretation. Multiple regression techniques, for instance, have allowed researchers to specify how much each explanatory variable contributes to changes in the variable being measured. Various other statistical techniques have also helped in deciding whether correlational data give any credence at all to the possibility of causal linkages.

A final observation might be made with regard to stimulus differences between the 1970 studies and more recent ones. Stimulus materials used in the 1970 studies were obtained primarily from sex research institutes (the Institutes of Sex Research at Hamburg University in West Germany and at Indiana University) and the Bureau of Customs confiscated contraband collection. One researcher (Tannenbaum, 1970) resorted to producing his own film which he described as showing a young lady "going through the motions of disrobing in a fairly sensuous manner in apparent preparation for the arrival of a lover." These materials were also presented primarily in the form of slides, magazine pictorials, mimeographed passages and film.

It is perhaps as much a function of availability and changing technology that more recent studies have used as stimulus materials films, audiotapes, videos, and material from various "adult men's" magazines, all easily available from outlets as diverse as the neighborhood video store, the corner newsstand, or the local adult bookstore.

OTHER PORNOGRAPHY COMMISSIONS AND SOCIAL SCIENCE RESEARCH

Other organizations which have studied pornography such as the Williams Committee in England and the Fraser Commission on Pornography and Prostitution in Canada have also examined social science research evidence on the effects of viewing pornography. (Report of the Committee on Obscenity and Film Censorship, 1979; Report of the Special Committee on Pornography and Prostitution, 1985).

The Williams Committee, working between 1977 and 1979, commissioned two reviews of the existing literature. One review examined the effects of viewing pornography (Yaffe and Nelson, 1979) and the other examined the effects of exposure to media violence (Brody, 1977). Both reviews highlighted the difficulties of studying human behavior and of understanding human motivations. The review of the effects of viewing sexually-explicit materials concluded that "there is no consensus of opinion by the general public, or by professional workers in the area of human conduct, about the probable effects of sexual material." The review on the effect of exposure to media violence similarly maintained that "social research has not been able unambiguously to offer any firm assurance that the mass media in general, and films and television in particular, either exercise a socially harmful effect, or that they do not."

The long track record of media violence research and antisocial behavior makes the latter conclusion somewhat surprising, particularly since an opposite conclusion was arrived at by a similar commission working under the direction of the United States Surgeon General in 1972, which had examined the effects of exposure to media violence (Surgeon General's Scientific Advisory Committee on Television and Social Behavior, 1972).

The conclusions of the Williams Committee on the effects of viewing pornography may not be as surprising since much of the experimental work was published after 1978. It is not clear, however, how much value these studies would have had for the Williams Committee since its call for more research was predicated on the importance of studying "the human personality as a whole, rather than to specific questions about violent or sexual materials and their supposed effects." (p. 4). The Committee further appeared to give greater attention to correlational studies as it examined in considerable detail studies by Court (1977) and Kutchinsky (1973). The Committee was highly critical of Court's methodology but also pointed out that the Danish data did not lead to the conclusion that the availability of pornography resulted in a decrease in sexual offenses.

The Canadian Fraser Commission similarly sponsored a research review (McKay and Dolff, 1985) and concluded that "the research is so inadequate and chaotic that no consistent body of information has been established. We know very well that individual studies demonstrate harmful or positive results from the use of pornography. However, overall, the results of the research are contradictory or inconclusive." (Report of the Special Committee on Pornography and Prostitution, v. 1, p. 99).

The commissioned review was exceedingly critical of the research, maintaining that the studies in every aspect exhibited "conceptually cloudy thinking," that they were characterized by "blatant silliness" and had no integrating framework, that "the literature is rife with speculation and unwarranted assumptions." The low regard for behavioral science methods is evident throughout the review, with major criticisms focusing on the uselessness of the experimental paradigm (p. 86–87), and the inability to draw conclusions from correlational research. Despite this assessment, the Commission proceeded to recommend criminal sanctions for sexually violent material and child pornography and limits on public display for nonviolent pornography. These recommendations were based on the Commission's observations that these materials were contrary to Canadian values of equality and human dignity.

It is obvious that the contribution of social science findings to policy considerations can vary, from being the sole or primary basis for policy recommendations, as was the case for the 1970 Commission, to being close to irrelevant to such considerations, as seemed to be the case with the Canadian pornography commission.

PUBLIC ATTITUDES TOWARD PORNOGRAPHY

How does the public view pornography and have there been any changes in public opinion in the last fifteen years?

Survey data from a national public opinion poll on the issue of pornography were made available to the Commission by *Newsweek* magazine. The poll was conducted for *Newsweek* by the Gallup organization in March, 1985, and involved a sample size of 1020 respondents interviewed by telephone.[1119]

Comparisons between the Gallup data, where appropriate, will be made with the 1970 Commission survey (see Abelson, et. al., 1970) to examine any observable change.

The 1970 Commission survey used face-to-face interviews from February through April of 1970 with a random sample of 2,486 adults

and 769 persons ages fifteen to twenty (Abelson, et. al., 1970). For purposes of comparison with the 1985 sample, only the data from the adult sample for 1970 will be used. The *Newsweek*-Gallup poll was a telephone survey of 1,020 adults conducted in March, 1985.

The 1970 survey was a far more wide-ranging survey covering a host of areas (including opinions on the effects of sexually-explicit material for which some directly comparable poll data are available from the *Newsweek* poll), the respondents' experiences with sexually explicit materials, opinions on different categories of sexual explicitness, attitudes toward legal and other forms of control, and attitudes toward different categories of sexual explicitness.

1119. Surveys such as this Gallup survey which employ "probability samples" are generally accurate within known limits. That is, the sample results can be applied to the population as a whole within the sampling tolerance ranges for a given sample size. For this survey sample size of 1020 respondents, sampling error is three percent. In practical terms, if we could contact every member of the population being described, the "real" percentage would be within plus or minus three percent of the observed percentage for the sample.

In contrast, the *Newsweek*-Gallup poll was much more limited, consisting of eight questions. For purposes of additional comparison, a 1977 national Gallup poll provides another trend point which allows comparisons with a 1985 question on the applicability of national versus local standards.

Any comparisons between the the 1970 and 1985 findings should be made with caution, given the independence of both surveys and the fact that only a few questions were exactly alike. In those areas where questions were examining similar issues but were not worded the same, only the questions which were more narrowly defined for the 1985 survey were included and any resulting error would be on the side of conservatism. The distinctions between direct and indirect comparisons are carefully noted. A major objective is to note whether patterns observed in 1970 continue in 1985. Comparisons will be made in the three areas: (1) public exposure to sexually explicit materials; (2) perceptions of the effects of pornography; and (3) opinions on the regulation of pornography.

PUBLIC EXPOSURE TO SEXUALLY EXPLICIT MATERIALS

The data from 1970 and 1985 are comparable only in a limited way because of differences in the materials mentioned and changes in technology (e.g., the widespread use of cable and home videos). In 1970, for instance, the respondents were asked if they had "ever seen stag movies or skin flicks." In 1985, respondents were asked whether they had gone to an X-rated movie or bought/rented an X-rated video cassette *in the last year*. The 1985 respondents were asked if they had "ever read" magazines like *Playboy* or *Penthouse*, while 1970 respondents were asked if they had seen or read a magazine "which you regarded as pornographic." Again, we note that this is a loose comparison, only afforded by the fact that the 1985 question is more specific in nature and, therefore, a more conservative estimate.

In response to the question whether they had seen or read a magazine "which you regarded as pornographic," one in five in 1970 said "yes," with twenty-eight percent of the men and fourteen percent of the women responding in the affirmative. However, half of the men and a third of the women in this group were unable to recall the title. Of those titles mentioned, it was clear that the term 'pornographic' embraced a wide variety of

material including *Cosmopolitan*, *Esquire*, *Good Housekeeping* and *Ladies Home Journal* (Abelson, et. al., p. 23).

In contrast, two thirds of the 1985 respondents had read *Playboy* or *Penthouse* at some time. Over a third said they "sometimes buy or read magazines like *Playboy*" (37%) while thirteen percent said they "sometimes buy or read magazines like *Hustler*."

In 1970, fifteen percent of respondents said they had seen a movie they regarded as 'pornographic' in the past year. Again the range of titles mentioned included such films as *Butch Cassidy and the Sundance Kid*, *The Graduate*, *Easy Rider*, and *Bonnie and Clyde*, in addition to titles that could more likely fall in the "adult" movie category. On the other hand, less than ten percent (7%) of the 1985 respondents had been to an X-rated movie in the past year while close to one in ten (9%) had purchased or rented an X-rated video cassette. The marked difference between the questions asked at both time points precludes any conclusion about any increase or decrease in film viewing in the last fifteen years although the media for purveying adult films certainly has increased.

In 1970 as in 1985, men, younger individuals, and those with more education were more likely to have been exposed to sexually explicit material than women, older respondents, and those less educated (Tables 1 and 2). The differences in exposure between men and women are fairly large both in 1970 and in 1985 but are particularly striking in 1970.

At what age is the average person first exposed to sexually explicit materials? Abelson, et. al. (1970) found that about one in five males and about one in ten females had their first exposure by age twelve. By age seventeen, over half of the males (54%) and a third of the females had been exposed (p. 8). Those exposed earlier also tend to differ from those exposed at a later age. "Young adults, college-educated people, those with relatively liberal attitudes toward sex, and people who have experienced the most erotica recently are all disproportionately more likely than others to have had their first experiences with erotica at a young age" (p. 9).

No comparable age-of-first-exposure question was asked in the 1985 *Newsweek*-Gallup Poll. A few other studies have similarly examined these questions and the results may identify any changes which have occurred since 1970.

Gebhard (1980) compared data collected by

the Kinsey Institute between 1938 and 1960 (using only the data from white males and females with at least some college education—a total of 4,388 respondents) to a much smaller nonprobability sample of undergraduate males and females in one university in 1975. By comparing responses to questions on age and source of first knowledge of such topics as coitus, pregnancy, fertilization, menstruation, and venereal disease. Gebhard concluded that "children and young people are learning the basic facts about sex at considerably younger ages than did their parents and grandparents" (p. 168).

For example, over half of each sex in the 1975 sample knew of coitus by age ten whereas only a third of the earlier sample's females and half of the males had this same knowledge at that age. By age eight, thirty-one percent of the males in the Kinsey sample knew of pregnancy compared to sixty-three percent in the 1975 sample; for females, it was thirty-one percent versus seventy-six percent, respectively.

A second finding of this study was that sources of early sex information appeared to have shifted slightly in relative importance. Same-sex peers remained the major source in both samples but to a lesser degree for the more recent sample, with mothers and the mass media becoming more significant (ranked second and third, respectively). These results, however, are simply suggestive because of the difficulty of generalizing beyond these particular groups of respondents and the limited size of the 1975 sample. These data also gave little indication of whether "mass media" includes pornography.

Another more recent set of data based on a national probability sample of 1071 respondents is available from Canada (Check, 1985). The Canadian results show that adolescents, ages twelve to seventeen, report most frequent exposure of sexually explicit fare. As Table 3 shows, two in five twelve to seventeen year olds view such material in movie theaters at least once a month; over a third (37%) see similar material on home videos with the same frequency.

These results should be viewed with caution because of the small numbers in this age group. The 1970 survey data demonstrated a similar pattern. Respondents in the 1970 sample were asked how many times during the past two years they had seen photographs, snapshots, cartoons or movies of a list of sexually explicit items. Adolescents reported more frequent exposure than adults, with three in ten of the adolescents saying they had seen

Table 1

*Previous Exposure to Sexually Explicit Materials, By Age
and Gender: 1970 Commission Survey*

	21–29	30–39	40–49	50–59	60+
Men					
Yes, have seen stag movie	54%	55%	44%	43%	27%
Yes, have seen skin flick	49	28	22	12	6
Women					
Yes, have seen stag movie	17	12	13	5	1
Yes, have seen skin flick	15	10	6	4	1

N = 2482

Question: "There are some movies called stag movies or party movies. These are not shown in regular theaters, but are shown in private homes or private parties or at club meetings. Have you ever seen stag movies or party movies of this kind?"

Question: "Nearly every city has one or more theaters that specialize in showing movies that feature a lot of nudity and suggestions of sexual activity. These movies are sometimes called 'skin flicks.' Have you ever seen these kinds of films?"

(Table 13, Abelson, et al., 1970, p. 17)

such material six or more times in the last two years compared to one in four adult males and one in seven adult females.

In comparing his results to the 1985 American *Newsweek*-Gallup data discussed above for comparable questions, Check found parallel results at least for sexually violent material. Results on nonviolent fare could not be compared because of the differences in question wording. This consistency and the fact that over eighty percent of the sexually explicit material in Canada is from the United States (Special Committee on Pornography and Prostitution, 1985, p. 161) might suggest that the Canadian results may not be dissimi-

lar from what might be found in the United States.

PUBLIC STANDARDS OF ACCEPTABILITY

The 1970 Commission survey examined standards of acceptance for various categories of explicitness in two types of media: movies and print. Table 4 shows that there was slightly greater tolerance for sexual explicitness in the print media than in movies (if one compares the percentages of persons advocating total bans on various categories). The print category presents a problem since it does not distinguish between textual and

Table 2

Exposure to Sexually Explicit Material, By Age, Gender, and Permissiveness: 1985 Newsweek-Gallup Survey

	Men				
	18–20	30–49	50+	Standards Stricter	Standards Less Strict
Ever read *Playboy* or *Penthouse*	91%	92%	70%	77%	88%
Sometimes buy/read magazines like *Playboy*	63	58	29	29	61
Sometimes buy/read magazines like *Hustler*	28	24	11	11	26
Went to X-rated movie in past year	12	9	6	3	12
Bought/rented X-rated video cassette in past year	17	14	4	7	13

	Women				
	18–20	30–49	50+	Standards Stricter	Standards Less Strict
Ever read *Playboy* or *Penthouse*	64	62	28	41	61
Sometimes buy/read magazines like *Playboy*	40	32	5	18	31
Sometimes buy/read magazines like *Hustler*	15	5	0	3	8
Went to X-rated movie in past year	14	4	.3	3	8
Bought/rented X-rated video cassette in past year	12	8	.9	4	10

N = 1020

Table 3

Frequency of Viewing Sexually Explicit Films in
Movie Theaters and on Videos, By Age
(Canadian National Sample)

	Movies			
	12–17	18–34	35–49	55+
Never	28%	34%	48%	74%
1–2 times/yr.	22	44	35	12
1/mo. or more	39	12	7	4
	Videos			
	12–17	18–34	35–49	55+
Never	32	33	50	83
1–2 times/yr.	22	37	25	7
1/mo. or more	37	23	20	5

N = 1071

Note: "Don't Know"/No Response not included
(Check, 1985)

visual or photographic material, which might be found more often in books and magazines, respectively. Restrictiveness also progressively increases the more the behavior departs from what respondents might consider normative. A re-analysis of the 1970 survey data does confirm this observation of acceptability based on perceived normativeness and, in addition, shows that judgments were also related to community size and medium (Glassman, 1978).

In 1985, slightly different distinctions appear to be made (Table 5). Greater tolerance is shown for film (both theater and video tape cassettes) than for print, with the public more likely to suggest no restrictions for the former. While the survey does not use the wider range of distinctions of sexual activities provided 1970 respondents (a limitation imposed no doubt because of the telephone procedure), the three categories used—nudity, sexual relations, and sexual violence—provide a sufficiently diverse range of themes. The data clearly show greater tolerance for nudity, with a majority maintaining that restrictions should only apply to public display. There

was least tolerance for sexual violence, with a majority advocating banning such material. What has been called the "VCR morality" is also very much in evidence here with more than a quarter of the respondents opting for no restrictions on X-rated video tape cassettes. Nearly one in four respondents did not object to the sale or rental of video cassettes featuring sexual violence as long as there is no public display.

These differences are clarified further when one takes into account the respondent's age and gender (Table 5). The young are clearly less opposed than the old, and men more than women, these patterns appearing with fairly high consistency.

There also appears to be some interaction between these demographic characteristics. Greater numbers of older men tend to be more permissive than older women, with about twice as many men over fifty suggesting no restrictions on materials across the board. The gap between men and women narrows significantly among younger respondents (those between eighteen and twenty-nine), with women just as likely as men to favor no

Table 4

Public Permissiveness, by Medium and Content: 1970

	In Movies			In Books, Magazines		
	Total Ban	Some Rest.	No Rest.	Total Ban	Some Rest.	No Rest.
Sex organs showing	45%	46%	5%	41%	47%	7%
Intercourse	50	42	4	48	44	4
Activities with same sex	62	31	3	58	34	4
Oral sex	62	30	3	58	33	4
Whips, belts	65	26	4	60	30	5

Question: On top of this card are descriptions of sexual material sometimes shown in movies in regular theaters (found in printed material). On the bottom of the card are some opinions about who it is all right to admit to movies showing such material. (These could be stories in books, magazines, paperback books, or on typewritten pages.) For each description on top, tell me which, if any, group on the bottom it is all right (to admit to these movies) (for the material to be available).

Key: A—None. There is no one it is all right to admit.
  B—It is all right to admit people like me but not others.
  C—It is all right to admit adults 21 and over but not persons under 21.
  D—It is all right to admit persons 16 or older but not persons under 16.
  E—It is all right to admit anyone who wishes to be admitted.
(Appropriate variations in Key made to Print version)
For categories used above: A = Total Ban
                B, C & D = Some Restrictions
                E = No Restrictions
(Reconstructed from Tables 120 and 122, Abelson, et al., 1970, pp. 102–103)

Table 5

Public Permissiveness, by Medium and Content: 1985
Newsweek-Gallup Survey

	Totally Banned	No Public Display	No Restrictions
Magazines that show nudity	21%	52%	26%
Magazines that show adults having sexual relations	47	40	12
Magazines that show sexual violence	73	20	6
Theater showings of X-rated movies	40	37	20
Theater showings of movies that depict sexual violence	68	21	9
Sale/rental of X-rated video cassettes for home viewing	32	39	27
Sale/rental of video cassettes featuring sexual violence	63	23	13

Question: For each item that I read, tell me if you feel it should be totally banned for sale to adults, sold to adults as long as there is no public display, or should be sole to adults with no restrictions?

restrictions on all materials except magazines with nudity and the sale or rental of videocassettes. Men were more likely to favor no restrictions on these materials than women.

Has there been an increase in permissiveness in the last fifteen years? Again, while some of the categories between 1970 and 1985 are not directly comparable, a reasonable comparison can be made for the category describing depictions of sexual intercourse.

For the 1970 sample, only four percent advocated no restrictions on depicting intercourse in books and magazines and the same percentage advocated no restrictions for movies as well. In 1985, twelve percent advocated no restrictions on "magazines that show adults having sexual relations." Twenty percent favored no restrictions on "theater showings of X-rated movies." The assumption we make here, of course, is that most respondents asso-

Table 6

Medium, Content Type, and Level of Restriction—
Comparisons by Gender and Age:
1985 Newsweek-Gallup Poll

Materials Should be Totally Banned						
	Men			Women		
	18–29	30–49	50+	18–29	30–49	50+
Magazines—nudity	6.6%	9.1%	29.9%	14.8%	20.6%	41.2%
Magazines—adults having sexual relations	26.8	35.6	57.2	31.6	49.6	76.2
Magazines—sexual violence	57.7	73.1	71.7	61.9	81.3	87.2
Theaters—X-rated movies	28.7	22.2	46.7	27.0	39.0	69.0
Theaters—sexual violence	57.7	63.1	68.4	53.3	75.2	85.2
Sale/rental—X-rated video cassettes	17.6	19.1	42.8	20.9	31.5	54.8
Sale/rental video cas. w/ sexual violence	47.8	60.0	62.8	49.2	69.6	78.8

No Public Display of Materials						
	Men			Women		
	18–29	30–49	50+	18–29	30–49	50+
Magazines—nudity	50.7%	59.1%	43.8%	63.9%	54.0%	41.2%
Magazines—adults having sexual relations	52.6	49.7	32.6	53.3	37.9	18.6
Magazines—sexual violence	32.4	17.5	21.1	30.7	13.4	10.1
Theaters—X-rated movies	40.4	48.4	30.3	46.3	40.7	17.7
Theaters—sexual violence	27.9	23.1	18.4	35.7	16.7	8.7
Sale/rental—X-rated video cassettes	39.7	43.8	29.9	50.4	43.2	28.7
Sale/rental video cas. w/ sexual violence	33.1	24.1	18.8	35.7	17.5	13.0

No Restrictions on Materials						
	Men			Women		
	18–29	30–49	50+	18–29	30–49	50+
Magazines—nudity	41.5%	30.0%	25.0%	21.3%	24.0%	16.2%
Magazines—adults having sexual relations	19.1	14.7	9.9	14.3	11.7	4.3
Magazines—sexual violence	7.7	9.1	5.6	7.4	5.6	2.6
Theaters—X-rated movies	25.0	27.8	19.7	23.8	16.2	9.6
Theaters—sexual violence	11.8	12.2	10.2	9.8	6.1	3.5
Sale/rental X-rated video cassettes	40.1	36.6	25.0	28.3	24.5	12.8
Sale/rental video cas. w/ sexual violence	18.4	15.6	15.1	14.3	12.3	6.7

Table 7

Application of Standards to Obscenity/Pornography

National Versus Local Standards:		
	1977 Gallup Poll	1985 Gallup Poll
A national standard	45%	47%
Community set own standard	39	43
Shouldn't be any (volunteered)	9	5
Don't know	7	5

Question: In determining whether a book, magazine or movie is obscene, do you think there should be a single, nationwide standard or do you think each community should have its own standard?

Change in Standards:		
	1977 Poll	1985 Poll
Should be stricter	45%	43%
Should be less strict	6	4
Kept as they are	35	48
Don't know	14	5

Question: Do you think the standards in your community regarding the sale of sexually explicit material should be stricter than they are now, not as strict or kept as they are now?

ciate X-rated movies with depictions of sexual intercourse but these comparisons are made with this caveat in mind. With the exception of sexual violence in magazines, the percentages opting for no restrictions on various categories of materials are also higher in 1985 than in 1970.

Finally, the 1985 sample was asked whether there should be a single nationwide standard or whether local community standards should be applied. Comparable data collected by the Gallup poll in 1977 provides another data point. As Table 7 shows, respondents in 1985 were almost evenly divided on whether a national or community standard should be used (forty-seven percent versus forty-three percent). The numbers who prefer to see local community standards applied have remained about even in 1977 and 1985—about four in ten respondents. There were as many who indicated standards should be stricter in 1977 as in 1985—forty-five percent versus forty-three percent. Additional analysis shows that those who indicated standards should be stricter were

more likely than those who said standards should be less strict to favor application of a national standard (55% to 41%). Six in ten women were also likely to favor a stricter standard compared to four in ten men.

In the last year, this gap between men and women appears to have increased even more on the issue of restrictiveness. A *Washington Post*-ABC News survey in February, 1986[1120] asked the question: "Do you think laws against pornography in this country are too strict, not strict enough, or just about right?" Among men, ten percent said they were about right, forty-one percent said they were not strict enough, and forty-seven percent said they were about right. Among women, on the other hand, only two percent said the laws were too strict, while seventy-two percent—seven in ten women—maintained they were not strict enough. Almost a quarter (23%) said they were just about right.

PERCEPTIONS OF PORNOGRAPHY'S EFFECTS

Respondents are just as likely in 1985 as in

Table 8
Perceptions of Effects of Pornography—1970 and 1985
(Percent Saying "True")

	1970	1985
They provide information about sex	61%	52%
They lead some people to commit rape or sexual violence	49	73
They provide a safe outlet for people with sexual problems	27	34
They lead some people to lose respect for women	43	76
They can help improve the sex lives of some couples	47	47
They provide entertainment	48	61
They lead to a breakdown of morals	56	67
(Base)	(2486)	(1020)

Question for 1985: "Thinking of sexually explicit magazines, movies, video cassettes, and books, tell me if you believe the following are true or not true:"

Question for 1970: "On this card are some opinions about the effects of looking at or reading sexual materials. As I read the letter of each one, please tell me if you think sexual materials do or do not have these effects." Item choices provided the 1970 respondents were worded in the same way or were reasonably similar: "Sexual materials provide information about sex;" ". . . lead people to commit rape; ". . . give relief to people who have sex problems;" ". . . improve sex relations of some married couples;" ". . . provide entertainment;" ". . . lead to a breakdown of morals." The 1970 survey had five additional items not included here since these were not utilized by the 1985 *Newsweek* poll.

1120. The *Washington Post*-ABC News poll was conducted February 6–12, 1986 by telephone among 1,504 men and women nationwide. The margin of error is plus or minus three percentage points.

1970 to perceive both positive and negative effects from exposure to or use of sexually explicit materials (Table 8). However, there is a significant increase in the numbers who perceive negative effects from 1970 to 1985. 1970 and 1985 data in this case were directly comparable since the same categories of effects were used.

The most significant changes were in the areas of violence toward women, with the number of respondents indicating these materials could lead some people to lose respect for women increasing from forty-three percent to seventy-six percent and those believing they lead some people to commit rape or sexual violence increasing from forty-nine percent to seventy-three percent in 1985. Whether this reflects greater sensitivity toward women or greater consciousness of sexually violent material available or both is unclear. A slightly greater number in 1985 than in 1970 were also likely to think that sexually explicit materials provide a safe "outlet

for people with sexual problems" (34% to 27%) while the number of people who agreed that these could help improve the sex lives of some married couples remained the same (47%).

PUBLIC PERCEPTION OF PORNOGRAPHY AS A SOCIAL PROBLEM

1970 respondents were asked to name "what you think are the two or three most serious problems facing the country today?" At the height of the Vietnam War, not surprisingly, more than half named this event the most important issue, followed by racial conflict and civil rights, and thirdly, by the economy (36% and 32%). Only two percent said they were concerned about erotic materials. The 1985 Gallup survey asked the question of perceived importance in a different way: by evaluating the problem relative to other social problems and asking the respondent to judge whether progress was being made to solve these problems (see Table 9).

Table 9
Perceptions of Pornography as a Social Problem
(1985)

	Making Progress	Losing Ground	Staying About Same	Don't Know
a) Preventing violent crime	19%	37%	42%	2%
b) Stopping drug addiction	28	42	26	4
c) Controlling pornography	20	33	38	9
d) Dealing w/air pollution	38	20	36	6

Question: I am going to name a number of problems facing the nation. For each, tell me if you feel this is a problem on which we are making progress, losing ground, or staying about the same.

SUMMARY
There is greater overall public tolerance for sexually explicit materials. However, public opinion on restrictiveness clearly differentiates among different media, content depictions, and public access to such materials. There is a preference for no public display of materials featuring nudity and nonviolent sexual activities whereas a majority favor banning materials that depict sexual violence. There is also a greater willingness to impose restrictions on theater showing and magazine

publication of sexual activities than on home videos.

The most frequent exposure to pornography is reported by adolescents between twelve to seventeen, a finding reported by the Canadian as well as the 1970 Commission survey. While sexual knowledge appears to be acquired at younger ages, it remains unclear what role pornography plays in this "sex education" process.

Finally, the public perceives both beneficial as well as harmful effects from exposure to sexually explicit materials. Some maintain these materials help improve sex lives of some people, that they provide information about sex, and also provide entertainment. A significant number also feel they lead to a loss of respect for women, a breakdown of morals, and the commission of sexual violence. The changes between 1970 and 1985 are most apparent in the increase in the numbers who perceive that exposure to these materials lead to loss of respect for, and the commission of sexual violence against, women.

SEX OFFENDERS AND PORNOGRAPHY

A common contention is that exposure to pornography leads to the commission of sex offenses. There are two ways one can examine this contention: (1) by looking at the relationship between sexual offenses statistics and the availability of pornography, and (2) by examining interview data from sex offenders, investigating the mechanics behind the onset of deviancy and the role of pornography in the commission of sex crimes.

The examination of aggregate social indicators of pornography availability and sexual offense statistics provides another view of the potential relationship between pornography and these offenses. It offers another way of validating results of the laboratory studies or from individual surveys. For example, if the results indicate a higher incidence of sexual aggression in the laboratory studies as a consequence of exposure to particular types of stimuli, and if surveys reveal that individuals who report higher levels of exposure to similar materials also tend to exhibit higher levels of sexual aggression, and if these findings are corroborated with a correlation between aggregate measures of availability and offenses, then we have reason to be more confident in an assertion that exposure to the class of materials in question has a substantial relationship to sexual aggression.

In the case of sex offenders, a comparison of their arousal patterns to those of nonoffender groups is vital, particularly as these patterns correlate with sexual aggression and attitudinal measures. It is reasonable to suggest that findings among nonoffender males who are aroused to coercive sexual themes and who also tend to be more sexually aggressive would be more meaningful if matched by similar patterns among those identified as sex offenders.

From the perspective of the offenders and society as well, understanding their behaviors is crucial because of the social costs in terms of victimization. While the number of sex offenses reported by incarcerated sex offenders appears to be small, results of clinical interviews, conducted with outpatient sex offenders (with great lengths taken to assure confidentiality) reveal that the number of crimes committed by the average sex offender is far greater than generally has been estimated (Abel, Mittelman, and Becker, 1985). Data from two psychiatric clinics obtained from 411 sex offenders revealed a staggering number of multiple victimizations per offender. These offenders attempted an average of 581 sex offenses and completed typically about 533 offenses each, with a mean number of 336 victims each. These attempted or completed offenses were over an average period of twelve years (Abel, Mittelman and Becker, 1985).

AGGREGATE INDICATORS: THE INCIDENCE OF SEX OFFENSES AND PORNOGRAPHY AVAILABILITY:

One of the most frequently cited studies has been the analysis of sex crimes in Denmark before and after the legalization of pornography in the 1960s (see Kutchinsky, 1973; Ben-Veniste, 1970). Kutchinsky's data showed a drop in the number of reported sex crimes after legalization and he argued that the availability of pornography is cathartic as it siphons off potentially dangerous sex impulses—the "safety valve theory" (Kutchinsky, 1970, p. 288; Kutchinsky, 1973). Kutchinsky's work was lauded by the British pornography commission (Williams, 1979) for its thoroughness and the restraint with which he interpreted his findings. It singled out the dramatic reduction in offenses against children coinciding with the availability of pornography and, while the Commission did not endorse the "safety valve" hypothesis, agreed that Kutchinsky's interpretation was plausible, absent any other likely factor (p. 84).

On the other hand, Kutchinsky's study and conclusions did not go unchallenged. First, the weight of empirical evidence amassed in the last two decades by social psychologists, particularly in the area of media violence and aggressive behavior, hardly supports catharsis (see Weiss, 1969; Geen and Quanty, 1977; Bandura, 1973; Bramel, 1969; Comstock, In Press; NIMH, 1982).

Second, a number of problems have been raised with Kutchinsky's analysis and interpretations (see Cline, 1974; Bachy, 1976; Court, 1977; Baron, 1984; Malamuth and Billings, 1985). Some of these problems included the lumping together of sex offenses masked a stable, if not an increased, rape rate (Cline, 1974; Court, 1984). Also, such crimes as voyeurism were no longer recorded by police. Kutchinsky (1973) also noted that other activities such as homosexuality were simply tolerated more and certain social changes such as earlier sexual experiences for females meant reduced reports of intercourse with minors (Bachy, 1976).

The problem of using aggregate social indicators such as crime reports is well illustrated not just with reliability problems in reporting, but also in differential use of the data. For example, by Bachy's (1976) review of Copenhagen rape statistics between 1965 and 1974 which showed increases in rape and attempted rape as a proportion of total sex offenses. These offenses included intercourse with minors and indecent exposure, in addition to rape and attempted rape. Court's (1984) analysis of rape statistics for Copenhagen showed a similar upward trend while a fluctuating pattern was demonstrated by Kutchinsky's figures for the same crime in the same city between 1965 and 1970.

More recently, Kutchinsky (1985) has maintained that the increased availability of "hard-core" pornography in Denmark "may have been the direct *cause* of the real decrease in incidents of peeping and child molestation" (p. 313) and has proposed the "substitution" hypothesis as the most likely explanation. He further cites a similar pattern in West Germany with legalization of pornography in 1973 bringing about a decrease in sex offenses against children. This proposed causal link should be viewed with extreme caution, particularly since pornography availability statistics have not been presented.

Other data are available that allow further cross-cultural comparisons. Abramson and Hayashi (1984), in analyzing pornography in Japan, noted that while it was illegal to show pubic hair and adult genitals in sexually explicit stimuli, pornography appeared to be widely available in this country, including the prevalence of bondage and rape as recurring themes. In terms of rape statistics, however, they concluded that a low incidence of rape appears to be the case and suggested that certain socio-cultural mediating circumstances may be involved. Unfortunately, no data are provided by Abramson and Hayashi on availability or rape rates and at least one study indicates that these rates may actually be increasing. Goldstein and Ibaraki (1983) found that while crime rates have decreased or remained relatively stable among adults, juvenile crime increased from twenty-three percent of all crimes in 1976 to forty-two percent in 1980, occurring mainly in violent crime categories, including rape. The unique character of rape in Japan is also evident from these authors' findings that fifty-seven percent of the total reported rapes are group-instigated and seventy-five percent are committed by juveniles. Finally, an informal survey reported in this study showed that ninety percent of the women interviewed said they would not report the rape to the police if they had been victimized (pp. 317–318).

Other cross-national data from areas as disparate as England, Australia, Singapore, and South Africa were analyzed by Court (1977, 1982, 1984). His studies compared rape rates in countries or areas where pornography is widely available, and those where restrictions exist. On the basis of his findings, Court advanced the propositions that (1) rape reports have increased where pornography laws have been liberalized, while the same steep rise is not in evidence where restrictions exist; (2) intermittent policy changes or changes in the law are temporarily related to changes in the rape rates; (3) the increase in rape reports does not parallel the increase in serious nonsexual offenses.

While Court's data are intriguing, the case he presents is weakened by (a) the selective use of a small number of countries, and (b) the lack of direct correlational analyses between sexual offense statistics and pornography distribution/circulation figures. The Williams Committee in England (Williams, 1981), in fact, took exception with Court's data, pointing out that he did not take into account the rise of crime in general in England (p. 74) and that the rising trend in rape and sexual assaults started well before what Court determined was the date marking the availability of pornography (p. 76; see Court, 1980, 1985 for responses to the Williams Report). Cocrane (1978) has similarly disputed Court's analysis and interpretations.

Kupperstein and Wilson (1970) of the 1970 Commission staff examined the incidence of sex crimes in the United States and reported that the rise in adult sex crimes (using report and arrest data) was not greater than the rise for other offenses between 1960 and 1969, despite the heightened availability of sexually oriented materials. The two indicators used for the latter were the circulation of *Playboy* magazine and the number of complaints reported to the United States Post Office for unsolicited sexually oriented mail. The study employed fairly crude measures, simply examining the percentage increase for various sexual and nonsexual offenses.

On the whole, a number of methodological problems characterize some of these early studies: first, the availability of pornography was simply assumed to have increased or decreased following legal changes. Second, direct correlations between the volume of pornography and sexual offense rates were not investigated. Third, sexual offenses were combined, masking important differences between various categories of offenses. Finally, the mediating effects of other variables which could affect the relationship between the circulation of pornography and sexual offense rates were not systematically investigated.

More recently, correlational evidence using more detailed statistical analyses, presents some additional insight into the pornography-sex crimes relationship on the aggregate or societal level in the United States (Baron and Straus, 1985). A fifty-state correlational analysis of rape rates and circulation rates of adult magazines was conducted, using aggregate circulation rates (subscription and newsstand sales per 100,000 population), for eight magazines (*Chic, Club, Gallery, Genesis, Hustler, Oui, Playboy,* and *Penthouse*). A fairly strong correlation—+.64—was found between these circulation rates and rape rates. This relationship was present even with controls for potential confounding variables such as police practices (measured by police expenditures per capita), propensity to report rape (measured by number of rape crisis centers per 100,000 females; NOW membership per 100,000 females; MS magazine circulation per 100,000 females; and number of battered women's shelters); "southernness" (based on the higher violent crime rates in the South), and "illegitimate opportunities" (referring to greater opportu-

nities to commit crimes in warmer than colder periods; the indicator used was average temperature).

Baron and Straus further found that rape rates are negatively correlated with the status of women when other factors are controlled for. This status-of-women index was measured via economic, political and legal indicators such as women's median income as a percentage of men's; the percentage of female members in the state legislature; and existence of laws giving women the same property rights as men. The study concluded that in a male-dominant society, the lower status of women may be reflected in higher rape rates.

Since it is possible that rape rates also may be a function of the overall culture supporting legitimate violence (that is, the societal endorsement of the use of physical force for socially approved ends, such as crime control or order in schools), the relationship between this factor and rape rates was also examined. Using a twelve-measure index that included such figures as violent television viewing, hunting licenses issued, and use of corporal punishment, no significant association between legitimate violence and rape was found. It is still theoretically possible that rape rates may be influenced indirectly by the level of legitimate violence through the latter's inverse relationship with the status of women; that is, cultural support for violence may contribute to sexual inequality which, in turn, may increase the risk of rape.

Finally, the level of social disorganization was also found to be directly related with rape rates and to affect these rates indirectly through its association with the circulation of pornography and the status of women. Other factors found to correlate with rape rates were the extent of urbanization, economic inequality, and unemployment.

In comparing the relative influence of these various explanatory variables, it was found that the proliferation of sexually explicit magazines and the level of urbanization help explain more of the variation in rape rates than social disorganization. The latter is also "more influential" in predicting rape than are economic inequality, unemployment, or sexual inequality. Together, these six explanatory factors explain eighty-three percent of rape rate variations, certainly a considerable proportion of the variance.

A follow-up study by Jaffee and Straus (1986) examined the impact of a variable called "sexual liberalism" on the relationship between these sexually explicit magazines' circulation rates and rape rates. It was hypothesized that a more liberal sexual climate might explain the relationship between sexually explicit magazines' circulation rate and rape by encouraging men to purchase more of these magazines and also encourage more women to report rape to the police. An index based on twenty-two questions in a national survey measuring attitudes toward a variety of sexual issues was utilized as the measure for "sexual liberalism." Results showed that the original relationship between rape rates and circulation rates of sex magazines was non-spurious and that sexual liberalism played a minor role, accounting for only nine percent of the state-to-state rape rate variations. A problem with this study, however, is that it attempts to match individual-level measures of attitudes with aggregate-level social indicators, using data from forty states for the former (effectively reducing the original sample size of fifty states by a fifth).

Using the Baron and Straus data set, Scott and Schwalm (1985) essentially confirmed the sex magazine-rape rate relationship although their additional analysis showed that when rape rates were correlated with specific magazines, these correlations were higher for Playboy, Penthouse, and Oui than they were for Hustler magazine. Their contention was that sexual content in Hustler magazine was more likely to be associated with rape since this magazine has more sexually violent material than the other three magazines. Since correlations with the other four magazines were not provided, it is difficult to judge the consistency of such a pattern. Furthermore, such a breakdown is again not very helpful since the level of analysis is aggregate rather than individual. Thus, on an individual level, it will be more meaningful to correlate an individual's scores on sexual aggression measures and that individual's readership of specific magazines; on an aggregate level, it is more appropriate to relate the aggregate offense rate with aggregate availability figures for the material in question. And even on the individual level, there may still be some ques-

tion as to the actual separability of individual magazine readership. A readership survey conducted for Hustler magazine among its subscribers shows that on average, the typical subscriber reads 3.6 adult men's magazines (Readex, 1984).[1121]

Scott and Schwalm (1985) also analyzed the effect of three additional variables not investigated by Baron and Straus: the effect of circulation rates on general circulation magazines (e.g., Time, Reader's Digest) and the effect of outdoor men's magazines (e.g., Field and Stream, American Rifleman), the latter using the presumption that an indicator of a "macho" environment could also account for rape rates. Alcohol consumption for each state was also examined. None of these variables was significantly related to rape rates.

Scott (1985) further examined the correlation between adult theaters and rape rates for 1982 and found no relationship to exist. It is quite possible that this finding may be an artifact of the decreasing number of adult theaters in this country as a result of the rise of home videos, as Scott himself pointed out (see also Newsweek, 1985; Knowledge Industries, 1985). He also correlated the number of adult bookstores in each state and rape rates and again, found no relationship. Scott's data may not necessarily be inconsistent with Baron and Straus.' It is quite conceivable that the number of stores may not correlate with rape rates but the actual circulation of the magazines in various outlets do. In any case, Scott's endorsement of the "safety valve" or catharsis hypothesis on the basis of his findings appears premature at the very least.

While Baron and Straus' work is impressive for its methodological care and thoroughness, their findings do not indicate that men are induced to rape as a result of exposure to these magazines. While this is certainly plausible, there are two caveats to their analysis. First, it is a macro-model that is being tested, examining the relationship of various social-cultural factors on rape. Second, given that this is a correlational study, there is always the possibility that there may be some third factor influencing the observed sex-magazine rape rate relationship.[1122] The crucial causal evidence has to come from an examination of

---

1121 The READEX survey was part of the public record as part of a court case involving Hustler magazine (Herceg v. Hustler, Inc.).

1122. Baron and Straus recently conducted additional analyses of their data by introducing a "Violence Approval Index," based on attitude measures from the general Social Survey. By introducing this into their original equation, the relationship between the sale of sex magazines and rape disappeared. While this could offer some tentative support for the authors' contention that a "hypermasculine" climate might be responsible for rape rates, rather than sex magazines

the relationship under controlled conditions, and these studies are discussed below under "Experimental Findings."

On an individual level, some parallel is offered the Baron and Straus data by a recently completed large-scale study on sexual assault among the college student population (Koss, 1986). Correlates of sexual victimization and sexual aggression were examined among 6,000 college students from a probability sample of higher education institutions. This study established a relatively high incidence of sexual assault within this population (336 per 1,000 college women, a rate which includes rape, attempted rape, and forceful sexual contact). The portrait of college men who report behavior that meets legal definitions of rape shows individuals who are sexually experienced, come from homes where family violence was normative, who use alcohol fairly regularly (and reported becoming intoxicated one to three times per month), who regularly discuss with their peers "how a particular woman would be in bed," and who frequently read at least one of the widely available men's magazines.[1123]

While these results offer correlational evidence, again, they do not support any *causal* link between readership of such magazines and sexually aggressive behavior. There are a variety of factors that correlate with sexual aggression as this study and the Baron and Strauss (1986) study demonstrate. Both also provide an important contribution towards our understanding of the types of factors, social, cultural, situational, and individual, which interact to explain sexually aggressive behavior as the theoretical thinking behind it.

In the case of causal relationships, the demonstration of a statistical relationship (that is, that the probability of the observed relationship being due to chance is minuscule) is a first requirement. A second requirement is that other competing or alternative explanations have been controlled in order to establish that X indeed causes Y.

In the case of rape rates and circulation rates of adult magazines, establishing a significant correlation between the two is a first step. That such a relationship may in fact be a spurious one due to the existence of some third factor is a second step in establishing the validity of the relationship. Unlike experimental situations, however, where most "alternative factors" are controlled for, by randomly assigning subjects to experimental conditions, one has to be able to identify every potentially significant "third factor" in correlational research and actually account for these in the analysis. Therefore, we find ourselves, at most, in the position of accepting an observed relationship as being plausible but yet cannot fully preclude the possibility of its being spurious.

EVIDENCE FROM SEXUAL OFFENDERS

There are three levels by which sex offenders' use of pornography can be evaluated: first, what are the patterns of their early exposure to pornography? Second, what is the role of pornography in their fantasy and arousal behaviors? Third and most critical, is the question of the role of pornography in the commission of their sex offenses.

Methodological Considerations

A number of elements need to be considered in the study of sex offender populations.

Nature of the population evaluated. The deviant populations most accessible to researchers in the past were incarcerated sex offenders. This category thus constituted the

---

1123. The question used by Koss (1986) in this survey as a measure of pornography exposure was:

How often do you read any of the following magazines: *Playboy, Penthouse, Chic, Club, Forum, Gallery, Genesis, Oui,* or *Hustler?* (check one):

_____   Never
_____   Seldom
_____   Somewhat frequently
_____   Very frequently

---

per se, they are also appropriately cautious about the severe limitations of this particular finding. They point out that while the Violence Approval Index correlates in expected fashion with the percent males in the population, the percent of the population in the high-violence age group of eighteen to twenty-four, with the Legitimate Violence and Social Disorganization indices, it also has an unexpected negative correlation with the percent single males in the population and has a low correlation (.23) with the rape rate. Second, the data are restricted to forty states which, in combination with the addition of still another variable to the equation, increases the standard error. Until these problems are sorted out, the impact of this variable will have to remain speculative. It is presumably for this reason that these authors included this information in a footnote rather than in their text, and we likewise do so.

samples described in earlier studies, including the significant pioneering surveys done by Gebhard, et al. (1965) and Goldstein, et al. (1970). There is evidence, however, that data provided by incarcerated offenders tends to vary significantly from non-incarcerated groups (Abel, Becker and Skinner, 1985). The demographic profile of incarcerated offenders, for instance, appears to differ from nonincarcerated groups. For example, Goldstein, et al. (1970) found that while forty-two percent of his control sample has some college education, only twenty-six percent of the rapists, twenty percent and five percent of the male-object and female-object pedophiles, respectively, also had similar educational levels. Gebhard, et al. (1965) similarly found lower educational levels among his sexual offender sample compared to controls. Only thirteen percent of heterosexual child molesters, thirteen percent of homosexual child molesters, and twenty-one percent of rapists had a grade eleven or higher education compared to twenty-one percent of other criminal offenders and fifty-two percent of the control sample. Both these studies examined incarcerated samples.

Abel (1985), on the other hand, found that among an outpatient sample of 192 child molesters, forty-six percent had at least one year of college, with a quarter of the total sample completing college or having an advanced degree. Marshall's (1985) comparison of eight-nine outpatient sex offenders with twenty-four control adults showed little difference between the mean IQ's of this group and a comparison control. A mean IQ of 92, 93, 94 and 101 was measured for heterosexual and homosexual child molesters, incest offenders, and rapists, respectively, and 91 for the control sample. It has been estimated that incarceration rates for some sex offenders are low. Only thirteen to sixteen percent of rapists are actually incarcerated, for instance (Abel, Becker and Skinner, 1985; Dietz, 1978), making it likely that an outpatient sample of sex offenders/deviants would more closely resemble the population of deviant cases than an incarcerated one. The representativeness of such an outpatient group still is uncertain, given the fact that these are individuals who, either voluntarily or by court mandate, have sought treatment.

Measurement of Arousal. An important aspect of evaluating sexual deviance in terms of diagnosis, treatment, and projection of future

behavior has been the assessment of arousal patterns. A major weakness in the early studies on sexual deviance was that measures of arousal consisted solely of self-reports. An extensive review of various assessment procedures (Zuckerman, 1971) concluded that the measurement of penis size (penile tumescence) in response to various stimuli provides the most valid indicator of sexual arousal. While the development of the penile transducer provided more accurate assessments of male arousal, problems still exist with this technology. The primary problem is that it is possible for the offender to control his erectile responses (by controlling his attention and sexual fantasies. (See Quinsey and Bergersen, 1976; Laws and Holman, 1978; Abel, Becker and Skinner, 1985; Abel, Rouleau and Cunningham-Rathner, in press). However, it has been possible to identify such faked responses under planned treatment situations and to reduce their occurrence but not to eliminate them entirely (Abel, Mittelman and Becker, 1985).

Ethical Considerations. Clinical researchers are obviously unable to examine sex offenders in laboratory conditions to assess cause-and-effect relationships in the same way their social psychologist counterparts are able to do with non-deviant or "normal" populations. The risks are too great for a group with little or no control over their own behaviors. Furthermore, the notion of informed consent becomes a problem when physiological measures of arousal patterns may reveal interest patterns the patient may not even be aware of (see Able, Rouleau and Cunningham-Rathner, in press). Other ethical considerations further arise out of the occasional conflicting needs of the judicial system, the offender's needs and rights, therapeutic requirements, and even the public interest (see Bohmer, 1983; Abel, Rouleau and Cunningham-Rathner, in press, for an extended discussion).

A number of important advances have been made in the last fifteen years to elucidate the nature of sexual deviancy, particularly as they relate to the measurement of arousal patterns. On the whole, however, certain inherent limitations exist for this particular population that preclude gaining the fullest knowledge about the antecedents of their sexual behaviors. One of the earliest landmark studies based on interviews with sexual offenders was conducted by the Kinsey Institute for Sex

Research (Gebhard, et al., 1965). The study was notable for its scope, including 1365 sex offenders, 888 other criminal offenders, and 477 controls, all white males. The study was conducted during two time periods: 1941 to 1945 and 1953–1955.

Interviews with sex offenders led the authors to conclude that no relation between pornography and sex crimes exists. The researchers, in fact, concluded that the inferior intelligence and education of the average sex offender precludes his deriving sufficient sexual arousal from pornography to lead to overt antisocial activity, a conclusion which has been contradicted much subsequent data.

Some of the other earlier studies on this question were done for the 1970 Commission. On the basis of these early studies (see, for example, Cook and Fosen, 1970; Goldstein, et al., 1970; Walker, 1970; Davis and Braught, 1970), the Commission concluded that (1) sex offenders did not differ from adults in the general population in their reported immediate responses to reading or viewing erotic materials; (2) that sex offenders generally had less adolescent experience with erotica than the general adult population but did not differ from the latter in adult exposure patterns; and (3) erotica was an insignificant factor in the reported likeihood of engaging in sexual behavior during or after exposure.

Since these early studies, much more has been learned about sex offenders in terms of their arousal patterns and efficacies of various treatment approaches.

Early exposure

Do sex offenders differ from non-offenders in their patterns of early exposure to pornography? Goldstein, Kant, Judd, Rice and Green, (1970) found a high level of exposure to pornography during adolescence among sex offenders (categories in this study included rapists, pedophiles, transsexuals, and homosexuals) but these levels were not significantly different from a nonoffender comparison group. In comparing their samples on exposure to pornography during adolescence, Goldstein and his colleagues found that more rapists than controls had never been exposed to particular types of stimuli. Yet, the differences among the various groups were not statistically significant over the total range of stimuli. Significantly less exposure was reported among rapists to photos of partially and fully nude women and to books describing nudity and oral-genital relations. In

fifteen other categories (different themes in different media), the differences were not significant. In their later book elaborating on their findings (Goldstein, Kant and Harman, 1973) Goldstein and his colleagues describe a significantly larger number of rapists as having had exposure to "hard-core" pornography than controls (30% versus 2%) during childhood or between six to ten years old. They also tended to report an earlier age of "peak experience" with pornography, that is, a sexual experience that stood out in their minds the most.

Cook and Fosen (1970) found that among their sample of incarcerated sex offenders and criminal offenders, the latter reported higher rates of exposure to pornography during pre-adolescence and adolescence. Johnson, et al., (1970), on the other hand, found slightly higher rates of early exposure among a sample of convicted sex offenders who were on probation and receiving therapy compared to the control sample consisting of the respondents in the Abelson, et al. (1970) national survey (44% versus 40%).

Walker (1970) interviewed two groups of male sex offenders, one from a maximum security ward of a state hospital and the second who were prisoners in a correctional facility. Two control groups incarcerated in both facilities for reasons other than sex offenses were utilized in addition to another comparison group of male college students and members of a number of men's service clubs. The latter were more closely matched to the sex offender sample in terms of age.

Data on age of first exposure revealed no overall difference between sex offenders and the combined student and men's club controls. However, portrayals of sexual activities for which the sex offenders had earlier exposure than the men's club control group appeared to be of the more unusual variety: bestiality, group sex, and "sex activities with whips, belts or ropes."

While the student and men's club members had significantly greater exposure to a wider range of sexually explicit depictions than the sex offenders, the latter also had collected pornography for a longer period of time than the men's club members.

Another study conducted for the 1970 commission (Davis and Braught, 1970) found that early exposure to pornography was related to greater involvement in deviant sexual practices among groups of criminal offenders and a comparison group of male students. This was particularly true for what they called "serious deviance," primarily rape. The age-of-exposure variable appears to be crucial as these authors found that exposure to pornography was a strong predictor of sexual deviance among the early age of exposure subjects. They also noted that "exposure to pornography in the 'early age of exposure' subgroup was related to a variety of precocious heterosexual and deviant sexual behaviors."

They found a slightly different pattern among those exposed to pornography at a later age, with the amount of exposure correlated with poor character scores and participation in criminal, deviant, and sexually active peer groups. This result suggests that among those later exposed, such exposure to pornography is part of a deviant and highly active sexual life style. Thus, two separate but related factors—pornography and peer pressure—seem to play some interacting role as sexual behavior patterns develop (Davis and Braught, 1973, p. 194). However, because we do not have age-of-commission data for the more deviant sexual behaviors, a hypothesis that gives a causal status to pornography exposure cannot be supported. Among 476 male reformatory inmates between sixteen to twenty-one years old, a similar association was found between early age of exposure to pornography as well as high exposure and sexual deviance.

Because more recent studies (Abel, Rouleau and Cunningham-Rathner, in press) suggest that over fifty percent of various categories of paraphiliacs had developed their deviant arousal patterns prior to age eighteen, it is clear that the age-of-first-exposure variable and the nature of that exposure needs to be examined more carefully. There is also evidence that the longer the duration of the paraphilia, the more significant the association with use of pornography (Abel, Mittelman and Becker, 1985). On the whole, the conclusion of the 1970 study that "both the extent and frequency of sex offenders' experience with erotic material is substantially less than that of non-sex (criminal) offenders and nonoffender adults during preadolescence and during adolescence" needs to be qualified. These data demonstrate relatively lower levels of exposure among sex offenders when the comparison group is criminal offenders. Compared to "normal" adults, however, the differences appear to be more qualitative than quantitative: sex offenders seem to have been

exposed to sexually explicit materials for the first time at earlier ages, and there are some suggestions that the range of material they were exposed to was of the more unusual variety compared to the wider range of materials that control nonoffender groups was exposed to.

It is important to stress that these findings apply specifically to incarcerated samples, particularly groups that were considered serious offenders, given the maximum security facilities housing the Goldstein, et al. sample, the Walker sample and the Davis and Braught sample. A recent study (Carter, Prentky, Knight and Vanderveer, 1985) compared thirty-eight rapists and twenty-six child molesters incarcerated at a state treatment center. No differences were found between the groups in their exposure to pornography in the home (twenty-seven percent of the rapists and twenty-six percent of the child molesters said they had sex materials in their home while they were growing up) and during development (58% of the rapists and 54% of the child molesters had "seen or read sex materials as a teenager"). However, child molesters were found to use pornography more often than rapists in adulthood, were significantly more likely to use these materials prior to and during their offenses, and to employ pornography to relieve an impulse to commit an offense. Because of the absence of a control group of nonoffender adults, it is difficult to determine whether early exposure to pornography in this instance differs significantly from that of a nonoffender sample. The study also does not describe what types of sex materials were involved.

In retrospective interviews with eighty-nine sex offenders (all nonincarcerated and attending an outpatient clinic) and a control sample, Marshall (1985) found that greater numbers in all categories of offenders had been exposed to nonviolent pornography than the comparison group of non-offenders. The term "pornography" in this case was limited to two categories of materials: "hardcore materials," or "those available only in specialized stores and depicting sexual acts with nothing left to the imagination" (p. 14), and materials depicting "forced sex." These were described to the subjects as those portraying "sexual relations between adult males and adult females where the female displayed a clear unwillingness to participate by both her verbal refusals and her physical attempts to prevent the attack, and the male in the depiction was said to recognize this refusal but ignored it by forcefully enacting his sexual wishes."

Marshall found that over a third of the rapists (35%), two in five homosexual child molesters (41%), a third of the heterosexual child molesters, and only a fifth of the control adults (21%) had been exposed to materials that did not depict forced sex. Only four percent of the rapists and eight percent of the controls were exposed to sexually aggressive portrayals (forced sex) during pubescence. Because of the terse description of "hardcore" sex materials used in this study, it is difficult to reconcile these findings with those of earlier ones suggesting early exposure to depictions of more deviant activities.

It is apparent that these studies cover a variety of comparison situations (no non-offender controls, comparison with nonsexual criminal offenders only), populations (incarcerated, non-incarcerated and in therapy) and a range of measures for early exposure. Certainly, the notion that sex offenders have significantly less exposure to sexually explicit materials than normal adults does not appear to hold for nonincarcerated groups (Marshall, 1985; Johnson, et al., 1970) and, for incarcerated groups, appears to be true when the comparison group is nonsexual criminal offenders. Compared to nonoffenders, rapists differ only on specific types of material (Goldstein, et al., 1970). Only one study (Marshall, 1985) shows somewhat higher levels of exposure than non-offender adults.

Fantasies and Arousal

Studies reviewed by and conducted for the 1970 Commission examined differences in arousal patterns for sex offenders and nonoffenders. These studies showed either that sex offenders were somewhat less responsive than other adults to erotic stimuli (e.g., Gebhard, P. H., J. H. Gagnon, W. B. Pomeroy and C.V. Christenson, 1965) or that both groups did not differ in their responses to reading or viewing erotic material (Cook and Fosen, 1970; Walker, 1970; Johnson, W.T., L. Kupperstein, and J. Peters, 1970). The Commission concluded in summary that "the available research indicates that sex offenders do not differ significantly from other adults in their reported arousal or reported likelihood of engaging in sexual behavior during or following exposure to erotica." (p. 284)

Later studies have demonstrated that arousal patterns among sex offenders could in fact differ from non-offenders (Abel, Barlow, Blanchard and Guild, 1977; Barbaree, Marshall and Lanthier, 1979, Quinsey, Chapin and Varney, 1981). The 1970 conclusion can be attributed to a number of factors: first, self-report measures of arousal were used for the most part. The problems with reliance on self-reports as the sole arousal measure have already been discussed. Second, many of the studies used stimuli labeled "erotica" without attempting to discriminate among content cues (stimuli used, for instance, were primarily adult heterosexual activities). Finally, with the exception of the Goldstein, et al. (1970) study, differences among sex offenders categories were not examined.

Subsequent studies have shown the importance of discriminating among various categories of sex offenders, content cues, and utilizing physiological measures of sexual arousal.

While other physiological measures have been used as correlates of sexual arousal (e.g., respiration, galvanic skin response, heart rate), these have been viewed as less desirable than direct erection calibration (Zuckerman, 1971) since increases in these variables have also been recorded for other emotional states not related to sexual arousal.

A key study that attempted to distinguish rapists from nonrapists on the basis of erections was conducted by Abel, Barlow, Blanchard and Guild (1977). This study was also important in its attempt to discriminate responses according to consenting and nonconsenting stimuli. The development of a "rape index" was another important element in this study. The index was the quotient of the mean percent erection to rape cues to the mean percent erection to mutually consenting intercourse, a measure which was found to have predictive validity in this study and subsequent ones (see Abel, et. al., 1976; Quinsey and Chaplin, 1982; Quinsey, Chaplin and Varney, 1981; Barbaree, Marshall and Lanthier, 1979). The results showed that rapists respond to both rape and mutually enjoyable intercourse cues while nonrapists exhibited arousal only to the latter.

Other studies have similiarly found that rapists show sexual arousal to rape cues as well as to depictions of consenting sexual activity compared to nonrapists who are usually more aroused to the latter (Abel, Becker, Blanchard and Djenderedjian, 1978; Barbaree, Marshall and Lanthier, 1979; Quinsey,

Chaplin and Varney, 1981). The nature of sexual cues was further elaborated by Quinsey and Chaplin (1984) who found that rapists did not discriminate among the various sexually explicit narratives used while nonrapists responded most to the consenting sex narratives, less when the sexual partner did not consent, and least when the victim was shown to experience pain.

In comparing these findings to males in the general population, sexual arousal responses have also been found to be indicative of a proclivity to rape but only in combination with other factors will such a tendency be manifested in overtly aggressive behavior (Malamuth, Check and Briere, 1985, Malamuth, In Press).

Child molesters also have demonstrated significantly different arousal patterns with penile circumference measures than a comparison group of non-sex offender patients (Quinsey, Steinman, Bergersen and Holmes, 1975). Twenty male child molesters confined in a maximum security psychiatric institution exhibited significantly higher penile circumference measures when presented with slides featuring children compared to eleven nonsex-offender patients from the same institution and ten control adults from the community.

Marshall (1985) reported that among his sample of eighty-nine sex offenders, two in five of the heterosexual child molesters, two out of three of the homosexual child molesters, and one in two rapists said they used deviant fantasies "usually" or "always" during masturbation. None of the control adults indicated they had these deviant fantasies "usually" or "always" although forty-six percent said they did so "occasionally" or "rarely."

Seven out of eighteen rapists indicated that "consenting pornography" provided a cue to elicit fantasies of forced sex. Similarly, ten of the eighteen who currently used "consenting sex" stimuli used it to elicit rape fantasies.

Abel, (1985) reported that erotica use increased self-reported arousal (i.e., erotica "increased their deviant sexual arousal") more frequently among rapists than among child molesters, with fifty-six percent of the rapists indicating erotica use increased their arousal compared to forty-two percent of the child molesters. Since there were only sixteen rapists compared to 112 child molesters in this report, these findings have to be viewed with caution. In addition, a number of questions can be raised about these data. First, it is unclear what "erotica use" refers to. It could refer to usage for masturbation, for arousal prior to committing an offense, or, perhaps for child molesters, use during the commission of an offense (e.g., to lower the victim's inhibitions). It is also far from clear whether these arousal changes refer to changes in the offender's arousal patterns or whether these are simply their reported reactions to sexually explicit materials. Current evidence suggests a high correlation between deviant fantasies and deviant behaviors (Marshall, 1984; Abel, Rouleau and Cunningham-Rathner, 1985). Some treatment methods are also predicated on the link between fantasies and behavior by attempting to alter fantasy patterns in order to change the deviant behaviors (Davison, 1968; Marquis, 1970; Marshall, 1973). What is unclear, however, is the use of pornographic stimuli as a precondition for the generation of such fantasies.

Commission of Sex Crimes

Goldstein, et al.'s 1970 data on offenders' and a control group's reaction to a "peak experience" with erotica is reproduced below. "Peak experience" in this instance refers to the most memorable depiction of a stimulus, one "which really stood out in your mind the most" (p. 81). Again, keeping in mind that this sample was an incarcerated sample, the results show that as teenagers, deviants did not differ much from controls in terms of trying to enact the behaviors they had seen. As adults, a quarter of the female-object pedophiles did try the behavior depicted shortly thereafter compared to thirteen percent of the controls, fifteen percent of the rapists, six and seven percent of the homosexuals and transsexuals, respectively.

In Marshall's (1985) sample of eighty-nine sex offenders, slightly more than one-third of the child molesters and rapists reported at least occasionally being incited to commit an offense by exposure to forced or consenting pornography. Pornography as an instigator was not deliberately sought out by every offender in this category to arouse them to offend. For some, pornography as an instigator was simply fortuitous. Fifty-three percent of those child molesters who reported being incited to offend by pornography said their use was deliberate in their preparation for committing an offense, as was the case for thirty-three percent of the rapists. Finally, six of the eight rapists who reported being incited to of-

Table 10
Reaction to Peak Experience with Erotica
(Adapted from Goldstein, et al., 1970)

	Control		Rapist		Male Object Pedophile		Female Object Pedophile		User[a]	
	A	T	A	T	A	T	A	T	A	T
Wished to try	30%	48%	35%	80%	35%	65%	25%	40%	58%	66%
Did try	13	28	15	30	15	25	25	20	22	30
N =	46		20		20		20		50	

a. People who were currently avid buyers and consumers of commercially available pornography.

A: Adult   T: Teen

fend by pornography reported occasional use of "consenting" pornography to elicit rape fantasies which in turn led to the commission of a crime. It is unclear whether the use of this type of material was by choice or because it was the only material available.

Finally, Abel, Mittelman and Becker (1985) evaluated the use of erotica/pornography by 256 paraphiliacs undergoing outpatient assessment-treatment. Regardless of paraphiliac activity, those targeting adults were somewhat more likely to use erotica (60%) than those targeting adolescents (43%) or children (46%).

Categorized according to their primary predispositioning, fifty-six percent of their rapists and forty-two percent of their child molesters implicated pornography in the commission of their offenses.

Again, these comparisons have to be viewed with caution. The disparities in the data can, in part, be accounted for by the questions posed to the respondent and the differences in the samples. In terms of the population differences, Abel's and Marshall's samples are non-incarcerated while Goldstein's sample consisted of incarcerated sex offenders in a maximum security prison. The Goldstein sample was questioned about trying the behavior depicted in the stimulus to which the respondent had recently been exposed, a stimulus "which really stood out in your mind the most" (p. 81). This very specific question regarding the imitation of the most memorable depiction (the "peak experience") likely accounts for the lower figures relative to those obtained in the other studies. The other two studies, on the other hand, used more general questions pertaining to the

use of such materials in commission of offenses.

While these figures are suggestive of the implication of pornography in the commission of sex crimes among some rapists and child molesters, the question still remains: is there a difference in the rates of offenses among those who use pornography versus those who don't? The only data available that directly address this issue suggest that these offenses occur regardless of the use of pornography by the offender (Abel, et al., 1985).

Those offenders who did not use pornography did not differ significantly from those who did in frequency of sex crimes committed, number of victims, ability to control deviant urges, and degree of violence used during commission of the sex crime. The longer the duration of paraphiliac arousal, however, the greater the use of pornography.

Based on these data, the authors suggest that sexual deviants appear to come from socially deprived environments which stunt their social and other coping skills. The longer the duration of the paraphilia, or the earlier the onset, the more likely the paraphiliac was to have used erotica. It is difficult to say, however, to what extent this early exposure contributed to the onset of the deviance.

A number of questions are not addressed in the discussion of these data. First, it is not entirely clear what "erotica use" means. Does it mean the offender enjoys viewing the material on a regular basis? Does it mean use for arousal and masturbation? Does it mean use as incitement prior to committing an offense? For a child molester, "use" could refer also to the employment of sexually explicit materials to lower inhibitions of a potential victim and

Table 11

Relationship of Erotica and Paraphilias

Characteristic of Paraphilia	Uses erotica	Does not use erotica	Increased arousal	Decreased arousal
Mean number of sex crimes	302.0	234.0	421.0	189.0
Mean number of victims	139.0	200.0	124.0	153.0
Sex crimes/month	1.7	1.4	2.2	1.3
Victims/month	1.0	0.9	1.0	1.0
Duration of paraphilia (months)	128.0	86.0*	160.0	99.0*
Ability to control behavior[a]	81.0	82.0	75.0	86.0*
Age	33.3	32.2	33.7	32.9
Coercion during crime[b]	3.2	3.2	3.2	3.2
Social skills[c]	3.1	2.6*	3.0	3.2
Assertive skills[c]	2.8	2.7	2.6	2.9
	3.3	3.0	3.2	3.3
		86	82	88

[a]100 = Complete ability

[b]5 = severe coercion

[c]5 = excellent

d   This analysis was conducted on the subgroup that said they "used erotica" (n = 170). The study simply described "increased arousal" in terms of an increase (or decrease) in arousal to their deviant interest.

*p .001 using t-tests

Table reconstructed from Abel, 1985.

to present behaviors that might be imitated (Russell, 1975). There also appear to be a few inconsistencies in the data. For example, the number of sex crimes of those using erotica (302) is considerably higher than those not using it (224), but the mean number of victims shows a difference in the opposite direction (139 vs. 200). Also, the rationale for the use of a criterion value of p = .001 in combination with multiple t-tests remains unclear.

In testimony before this Commission, Abel (1985) suggested on the basis of these data that sexually explicit materials play an important role in the maintenance of these paraphilias. Greater numbers of deviants report current use of erotica, its use is associated with length of the deviancy, and it appears to play some role in maintaining arousal and masturbatory patterns. As Abel (1985) pointed out, while the use of pornography might decrease the likelihood for some offenders to commit sex crimes in the short run, in the long term, "the pairing or association of deviant fantasies with the pleasurable experience of orgasm perpetuates the deviant sexual interest." It is clear that the role of sexually explicit materials in this maintenance of

deviancy needs to be investigated more thoroughly particularly as they relate to repeated offenses.

Summary

While the number of studies on sex offenders has proliferated in the last fifteen years, the etiology of deviancy still remains to be answered.

There is evidence of a correlational relationship between pornography availability and rape offenses in the United States but such evidence remains in need of corroboration by experimental evidence using similar stimuli. Furthermore, correctional data appear inconsistent across cultures. There is little analogous social science evidence on pornography availability and child molestation with the exception of Kutchinsky's recent assertion that increases in availability caused less molestation in Denmark and West Germany (1985). The "causal" assertion here is not only tenuous; clinical evidence of long term use of pornography being correlated with length of the deviancy at least suggests this assertion is debatable.

The contribution of pornography to sexual

deviance remains an open question. At present, "no single, comprehensive theory to explain the development of paraphiliac behavior has yet emerged." (Kilmann et al. 1982). Competing models include a psychoanalytic view which views the paraphilia as a symptom of an underlying psychopathology, with its origins in unresolved conflicts during psychosexual development, a Freudian view; a behavioral model which postulates that the occurrence of sexual variance is a result of classical conditioning processes including modeling, reinforcement, generalization, and punishment, much as "normal" sexual behavior also occurs; and a biological model which suggests genetic influences and emphasizes the control of sexual behavior through biological or hormonal means (e.g., Ball, 1968; Berlin, 1983; Money, 1984).

The 1970 Commission's conclusion that sex offenders have less exposure to pornography may have been applicable only to serious sex offenders (that is, those incarcerated in maximum security institutions). At most, a reevaluation of their evidence and those from subsequent studies suggests that rather than frequency of exposure, it may be the quality of that exposure and the age-of-first-exposure that might help explain subsequent sex behavior differences. Malamuth and Billings (1985) have, in fact, suggested that the effect of pornography on rapists may be more pronounced as a function of their more restrictive home environments, with limited or no information on sexuality and male-female relations.

It is unfortunate that the nature of the first masturbatory experiences and the role of pornography in that experience, if any, also remains a gap in our knowledge for future research to address.

Finally, while self-reports of some offenders appear to implicate pornography in the commission of their sex offenses, the objective data of actual offenses committed which show no significant differences between those who use pornography and those who don't have to be viewed as tentative. It is clear that in addition to investigating developmental sexual behavior patterns among offenders, their arousal patterns as these relate to offenses committed should be investigated more thoroughly.

EFFECTS ON THE "AVERAGE INDIVIDUAL"—THE EXPERIMENTAL EVIDENCE

In order to draw conclusions about whether exposure to pornography leads to or causes certain effects, one would have to look at the experimental evidence for these causal linkages.

The experimental results are presented in terms of effects in the areas of arousal, perceptions, affective states, attitudes, and behavior. Two categories of pornographic stimuli have generally been used to sort out differential effects in these areas: nonaggressive-pornography and aggressive pornography (see, for example, Malamuth and Donnerstein, 1984; Donnerstein, 1983). Some question may be raised about whether in fact these two categories are sufficiently representative of distinctions the average consumer or the public at large might make or whether these two categories afford reasonable conceptual value. Nevertheless, these categories provide a convenient way to organize the results from experimental studies.

The Effects of Violent Sexually Explicit Materials

The findings from studies investigating effects of exposure to sexually violent materials appear to be fairly unequivocal: measures in the areas of attitudes and behaviors have consistently demonstrated changes in attitudes and laboratory-measured behaviors, with the nature of the effect mediated by such additional factors as message cues (e.g., whether the female victim is shown to be abhorring or enjoying the rape) and individual personality differences.

Studies on the effects of exposure to sexually violent material have been conducted primarily in the laboratories of Neal Malamuth (at Manitoba, Canada and University of California, Los Angeles) and Edward Donnerstein at the University of Wisconsin. With the respective colleagues, they have utilized three typical approaches.

The first approach generally has subjects

exposed to stimuli (usually varying consent versus force), with physiological penile tumescence and self-report measures of arousal taken during exposure, followed by questionnaires incorporating dependent variable measures (e.g., likelihood of rape, acceptance of rape myths and interpersonal violence, acceptance of sexual violence against women (see, for example, Malamuth and Check, 1980, 1981, 1983).

A second approach typified by Linz (1985) has subjects exposed to one of several types of stimuli over time (neutral, aggressive, or sexually violent of the "slasher" variety) under the guise of a film evaluation study. Prior to this exposure, measures are generally obtained on psychoticism, in part to eliminate participation by subject who might be especially vulnerable to this type of exposure. The second phase has subjects participate in an ostensibly different study in the law school where they are asked to take part in a mock rape trial. Measures are then obtained at this point which assess punitiveness, rape empathy and similar attitudes.

The third approach has been to expose subjects in the laboratory to sexually violent versus comparison material and assess negative effects by utilizing surrogate measures of aggressive behavior (e.g., shock intensities on an aggression machine. See, for example, Donnerstein, 1980; Donnerstein and Berkowitz, 1981).

All three approaches have different virtues which contribute to our ability to understand various dimensions to the problem. For example, the physiological penile measures of arousal provide an independent and objective means of corroborating self-reports. Surrogate measures of aggression avoid the ethical problems of "inducing" actual anti-social behaviors and at the same time can be validated by actual self-reports of aggression in sexual behavior. Finally, the "massive" exposures afford a first step at our efforts to examine the longer-term effects of exposure to sexually-explicit materials.

Effects on Fantasies

Only one study has examined the effects of sexually explicit materials on fantasies. Malamuth (1981) presented two groups of male subjects with a slide-audio show. One version depicted rape and the other showed a mutually-consenting sexual encounter. Analyses of sexual fantasies which subjects were later asked to create and write down indicated

that those exposed to the rape version were more likely to create aggressive sexual fantasies.

Aggressive sexual fantasies appear to be fairly common among certain groups of offenders. Gebhard, et al., (1965) found that "patterned rapists" or those who raped repeatedly, were significantly more likely than incidental rapists to often engage in sadomasochistic fantasies (twenty percent versus zero percent). Walker and Meyer (1981) found four in five of their rapists to report primarily deviant sexual fantasies while Abel, Becker and Skinner (1985) similarly reported aggressive sexual fantasies among their outpatient sexual assaulters. What role pornography, particularly violent pornography, plays in the construction of these fantasies remains to be answered.

Effects on Arousal, Perceptions, and Attitudes.

Are there differences in effects from exposure to violent versus nonviolent sexually explicit material? An early study (Malamuth, Reisin and Spinner, 1979) had male and female subjects exposed to one of the above stimuli or a neutral one. The materials presented were pictures from Playboy or Penthouse magazines for the sexual exposures and from National Geographic for the neutral exposure. Sexually violent depictions included pictures of rape or sadomasochism whereas the sexually nonviolent material had no aggressive elements. After viewing the materials, subjects filled out a mood checklist. This was followed ten minutes later by an assessment of reactions to rape after the subjects had viewed a videotaped interview with an actual rape victim as well as an assessment several days later in an ostensibly different study. Both types of stimuli were found to reduce the extent to which subjects perceived that pornography may have detrimental effects but neither one affected reactions to rape. Correlational data, on the other hand, showed that sexual arousal to the sexually violent depictions were significantly related with a self-reported possibility of engaging in rape.

Another study (Malamuth, Haber and Feshbach, 1980) examined the effects of written descriptions of a sexual interaction based on a feature from Penthouse magazine and midified to create a violent and nonviolent version for male and female subjects. In this study, males who had been exposed to the sexually violent depiction (sadomasochism) perceived more favorably a rape depiction that was presented to subjects subsequently. Subjects were found to believe that a high percentage of men would rape if they knew they would not be punished and that many women would enjoy being victimized. Finally, of the fifty-three male subjects, seventeen percent said they personally would be likely to act as the rapist did under similar circumstances. Fifty-three percent of these males responded similarly when asked the same question if they could be assured they would not be caught.

In order to draw out the various dimensions in the portrayals of sexual violence which might explain the exhibition or inhibition of sexual responsiveness, Malamuth, Heim and Feshbach (1980) conducted two experiments on male and female students. The first experiment replicated earlier findings that normal subjects seem to be less aroused by sexual violence than by "nonviolent erotica." A second experiment manipulated reactions of the rape victim with one version showing her as experiencing an involuntary orgasm and no pain. The second version had her experiencing an orgasm with pain. Both male and female subjects were aroused to these depictions, with female subjects more aroused by the orgasm with no pain version while the males were most aroused by the orgasm with pain stimulus. The authors postulated in this case that under certain conditions, rape depictions can be arousing, particularly when the rape victim is shown experiencing an orgasm during the assault. According to the authors, subjects may have reinterpreted the events preceding the depiction of the victim's arousal so that the rape is now viewed as one that is less coercive and less guilt-inducing.

Three additional studies (Malamuth and Check, 1980a, 1980b, 1983) provide further evidence that victim reactions have a significant impact on sexual arousal and behavioral intentions. Results from one of these studies showed that both male and female subjects exhibited higher arousal levels when portrayals showed an aroused female, regardless of whether the context was a rape or a mutually consenting situation. The second study (Malamuth and Check, 1980a) similarly showed that male subjects had higher penile tumescence scores when viewing a victim-aroused rape portrayal compared to a portrayal showing victim abhorrence. Significant correlations were also obtained between the reported possibility of engaging in similar behavior, sexual arousal to rape depictions and callous attitudes toward rape.

The effect of sexually violent depictions on attitudes has also been demonstrated with male and female subjects reporting greater acceptance of rape myths after exposure to such material (Malamuth and Check, 1980a; 1985; Malamuth, Haber and Feshbach, 1980).

In an attempt to approximate a "real world" situation, Malamuth and Check (1981) had male and female subjects view full-length features as part of campus cinema showings. The films—*Swept Away* and *The Getaway*—represented sexually violent films whereas control subjects viewed a nonviolent feature film. Dependent measures were obtained after a week in a questionnaire presented as a separate sexual attitudes survey. These measures included rape myth acceptance measures, measures on the acceptance of interpersonal violence as well as adversarial sexual beliefs, measures developed by Burt (1980). Results showed that exposure to sexual violence increased male subjects' acceptance of interpersonal violence against women. A similar trend, though statistically nonsignificant, was found for the acceptance of rape myths. There were nonsignificant tendencies for females in the opposite direction. In addition to the advantage of external validity from this field experiment, the problem of demand characteristics in some laboratory experimental situations is quite effectively dealt with in this study.

Aggressive Behavior

Donnerstein (1980) had male subjects provoked or treated in a neutral manner by a male or female confederate, then had them view one of three films: a sexually explicit film, a film depicting a rape, and a neutral film. Results of this study show that when the target of angered subjects was a male, there was no difference in aggressive behavior (measured by shock intensity on an aggression machine) among males in the erotic and the aggressive-pornographic conditions. However, when the target was a female, aggressive behavior was higher only in the aggressive-pornographic film condition, regardless of provocation.

To account for the impact of victim reactions in a rape portrayal, Donnerstein and Berkowitz (1981) had male subjects angered by a male or female confederate. Following instigation, they then watched one of four films: a neutral film, a non-aggressive pornographic film, an aggressive pornographic film with a positive outcome (where the woman is smiling and offering no resistance, becoming a willing participant in the end) and the last with a negative outcome, where the woman is shown exhibiting disgust and humiliation. Subjects who were angered by a male confederate were not significantly more aggressive towards the male instigator after viewing the pornographic or aggressive-pornographic film; those angered by a female, however, showed significantly higher levels of aggressive behavior in both aggressive-pornographic conditions, that is, those that portrayed a negative and those showing a positive outcome.

What about the effects of positive and negative outcomes on non-angered subjects? The same study (Donnerstein and Berkowitz, 1981) examined this issue using only female confederates. Results showed that for non-angered subjects, only the aggressive-pornographic film with a positive ending elicited higher aggression levels. Subjects exposed to this version also saw the woman portrayed as suffering less, enjoying more, and being more responsible for her situation. These findings suggest the importance of disinhibiting factors that might produce a readiness to respond (e.g., anger or frustration) and message cues (e.g., enjoyment of sexual coercion) as enhancing the likelihood of laboratory aggressive behavior. These are also short-term effects although with appropriate cues, there might be long-term effects as well. This remains speculative at this point (Malamuth and Ceniti, 1986).

A recent study demonstrates that such laboratory aggression is not always manifested when these "enhancing" factors are absent (Malamuth and Ceniti, 1986). Two groups of subjects were exposed to either sexually violent or sexually nonviolent depictions in movies, books and magazines over several weeks and compared to a third no-exposure control group. Several days later, in what was presented as a different study on ESP, measures of laboratory aggression using aversion noise were obtained in the typical aggression paradigm. No differences were found among the three exposure conditions. The authors speculated that a more immediate measure, in

combination with stimuli which "prime" thoughts and feelings relevant to the exhibition of specific behaviors might be more conducive to an individual's performance of such behaviors.

An important study that clarifies the interaction of motivational, message and inhibitory factors as predictors of self-reported sexual aggression (Malamuth, In Press) has demonstrated that (a) such factors as hostility to women, dominance and acceptance of interpersonal violence, arousal to sexual violence, and sexual experience all correlate with sexually aggressive behaviors; (b) the occurrence of these aggressive behaviors is better "explained" or "predicted" by these factors in combination; (c) arousal to sexual aggression correlates with dominance and hostility to women and is also an important predictor of sexual aggression; and (d) these self-reports of sexually aggressive behavior are also correlated with laboratory measures of aggression.

Effects of Massive Exposure

In a study designed to evaluate the effects of massive exposure to sexual violence and to further explore the components of the desensitization process, a series of four studies—all part of a Ph.D. dissertation were conducted. (Linz, 1985). College males were exposed to a series of "slasher films," all R-rated, using a formula of sexual explicitness juxtaposed with much blood and gore. A typical example is a scene from *Toolbox Murders* showing a naked woman taking a tub bath, masturbating, then being stalked and killed with a power drill by a masked male. Comparisons were also made among R-rated nonviolent films and X-rated nonviolent films, both of which included sexually explicit scenes (the former were of the teenage sex films variety).[1124]

After viewing one film per day for five days, subjects were asked to participate in what was presented as a different study—a pretest of a law school documentary—then completed a questionnaire assessing the defendant's intentions, the victim's resistance, responsibility, sympathy, attractiveness, injury and worthlessness.

Among his findings:

1124 The following films were used: R-rated nonviolent "teen sex" films—*Porky's, Fast Times at Ridgemont High, Private Lessons, Last American Virgin,* and *Hots.* X-rated nonviolent films—*Debbie Does Dallas, Health Spa, The Other Side of Julie, Indecent Exposure,* and *Fantasy.* R-rated "slasher" films; *Texas Chainsaw Massacre, Maniac, Toolbox Murders, Vice Squad,* and *I Spit on Your Grave.*

- Those who were massively exposed to depictions of violence against women came to have fewer negative emotional reactions to the films, to perceive them as significantly less violent, and to consider them significantly less degrading to women.
- This desensitization appeared to spill over into a different context when asked to judge a female victim of a rape. Those massively exposed to sexual violence judged the victim of the assault to be significantly less injured and evaluated her as less worthy than did the control group.
- There were no differences between subjects exposed to the teenage sex film or the X-rated film and the control group on either pretrial measures on objectification of women, rape myth acceptance or the acceptance of conservative sex roles or on the post-trial measures (defendant guilt, verdict, victim responsibility).
- Two movies (about three hours viewing time, about twenty to twenty-five violent acts) were sufficient to obtain a desensitization effect similar to the effect obtained after exposure to five movies, suggesting that desensitization can occur fairly rapidly.
- These findings were most pronounced for those subjects high on psychoticism and exposed to the highly sexually violent film. These individuals were significantly more likely to endorse the use of force in sexual relations and to evaluate the victim portrayed in the rape case as less credible, less worthy, and less attractive.

The effectiveness of debriefing procedures was assessed and the measures were found to be generally effective in reducing negative effects observed after film exposure.

Krafka (1985) used these same R-rated "slasher" films in a study similar to Linz's but using female subjects. Krafka also used these films as stimuli for a "violent" condition and contrasted this with exposure to sexual violence and to an X-rated set of films. The effects of massive exposure obtained for male subjects were absent for females.

It is clear that for males, exposure to sexually explicit materials juxtaposed with violence directed at a female target enhances callous attitudes in similar situations involving women as victims.

The Effects of Nonviolent Sexually Explicit Materials

The importance of specifying various contingent conditions under which certain effects may or may not be obtained becomes immediately obvious when one looks at the findings in this area. It is also clear that while there are a greater number of studies that examined the effects of nonaggressive sexually explicit materials, particularly if one includes the 1970 Commission studies, the diversity of dependent variable measures as well as experimental stimuli used is also greater than those in the area of sexual violence.

A number of different effects from a variety of studies have been obtained in the areas of affect, attitudes as well as behavior.

Affective and Perceptual Responses

Wishnoff (1978) exposed sexually inexperienced undergraduate females to explicit erotic films. He found that sexual anxiety decreased while expectations about engaging in intercourse in the near future increased significantly.

Along the same lines, Byrne (1977) and Byrne and Byrne (1977) suggested that initially, exposure to sexually explicit materials may offend and disturb some, or produce apprehension in others. These authors then hypothesized that frequent exposure reduces negative reactions and negative appraisals of these reactions. Once tolerance increases, the stimuli leads to greater pleasurable sexual fantasies and greater enjoyment, a hypothesis generally supported by their data.

Perceptual judgments have also been demonstrably affected by exposure, particularly in the areas of comparative judgments and estimations of reality. Kenrick and Gutierres (1980) found subjects' judgments of the attractiveness of an average female were lowered by exposure to media females. Proposing that such effects could be more significant in the realm of sexually explicit materials, Gutierres, et. al., (1985) did a follow-up recently in which subjects were asked to assess characteristics of others after exposure to slides of Playboy and Penthouse models. In four successive experiments, target persons rated were a stranger and the subject's spouse or long-term live-in partner. Both types of target persons were more negatively rated only by male subjects. Similar results were obtained after males were exposed to "beautiful females in sexually enticing activities" (sexually provocative poses or precoital and coital activities) in contrast to males exposed to less attractive females (Weaver, Masland, and Zillman, 1984).

This perceptual contrasting of aesthetic appraisals is contingent on whether the rated target and the comparison target are associated (Melamed and Moss, 1975; Griffitt, 1971). For example, when an individual is presented in the context of attractive friends, that individual tends to be rated as more "attractive." In the case of comparing media models with a significant other, on the other hand (where presumably there is no association between the target and the comparison), the comparison stimulus, or the media model in this case, "provides an anchor or contrast point for the evaluation of the target stimulus." (Melamed and Moss, 1975, p. 129).

Hatfield and Sprecher (1983) exposed males to "a *Playboy*-type article—a romantic seduction scene designed to be arousing." They predicted that a sexually aroused male would exaggerate a woman's sexual desirability as well as her sexual receptivity. Male subjects were then shown a photograph of "a potential date." Both predictions were confirmed. Aroused men, according to the authors, were more likely to agree that their potential date was "amorous," "immoral," "promiscuous," "willing," "unwholesome," and "uninhibited."

Different results were obtained by Dermer and Pyszcynski (1978) in an investigation of the effects of erotica on males' responses to women they loved. They were particularly interested in whether erotica would enhance "loving" or "liking" responses. Males who read an erotic story (an explicit account of sexual behaviors and fantasies of a college female) reported greater romantic involvement than those in a control condition. That is, they were more apt to report expressing "loving" than "liking" statements to their loved ones when sexually aroused than when not sexually aroused.

In looking at the above studies as a whole, it is quite possible that with "loved ones," could accentuate perceptual judgments while stimuli that primarily enhance arousal reactions (as in the Hatfield and Sprecher, 1983 and Dermer and Pyszcynski, 1978 studies which used textual material) enhance more "love-oriented" responses for loved ones and "lust-oriented" responses in a dating situation.

Effects on Behavior

Initial studies conducted for the 1970 Commission showed that sexually explicit materials had either no effect on sexual behavior or when effects were observed, there were generally slight increases in those sexual activities already in the individual's established repertoire (Amoroso, et. al., 1970; Byrne and Lamberth, 1970; Kutchinsky, 1970). These behavioral effects generally occurred within a short period after exposure. However, as one of the 1970 research investigators observed, it was also possible that,

> the effects of erotica on behavior could have been obscured in the initial body of research because two major components of the influence process were missing from the early investigations: the extended time period necessary for change to occur and the specification of the depicted behavior as well as the relationship between the interactants (Byrne and Kelley, 1984).

While more recent studies examined the impact of nonviolent sexually explicit materials after repeated exposure, others have also examined behavioral effects after short-term exposure. It is in the latter area of behavioral effects from exposure to nonviolent sexually explicit stimuli where apparently conflicting results are found.

Baron and Bell (1977) exposed male students to stimuli that included semi-nude females, nudes, heterosexual intercourse and some explicit erotic passages. The mild erotic stimuli (semi-nudes and nudes) inhibited aggression levels whereas the "stronger" stimuli had no effects. A follow-up study (Baron, 1979), this time on female subjects, using the same stimulus materials found mild stimuli inhibiting aggressive behavior while the stronger stimuli increased aggression. Both these studies measured aggressive behavior via "shocks" delivered on an aggression machine.

In another study, photographs variously depicting "nonerotica," nude females, and couples in sexual activities were shown to male subjects (Zillmann and Sapolsky, 1977). Additionally, subjects were either provoked or unprovoked. For the latter group, no differences in aggression levels by type of stimulus were observed. No differences were observed in aggression levels for subjects who were provoked either, although respondents in this condition also exhibited lower annoyance levels. The authors explained these findings in terms of the aggression-reducing effect of relatively non-arousing but usually pleasant sexually explicit images which act to reduce annoyance or anger and consequently, aggressive behavior.

Along these lines, Sapolsky (1984) has suggested that content characteristics have an impact on affective states (that is, how pleasing or displeasing the stimulus is) as well as on arousal levels. The combination of these factors appear to produce differential responses.

Situational factors such as provocation and the removal of restraints against aggression appear to further mediate the effects of nonviolent pornography on viewers. Donnerstein, Donnerstein and Evans (1975) found that "mild erotica" (semi-nudes and nudes from *Playboy*) inhibited aggressive responses in contrast to "stronger erotica" (frontal heterosexual nudes in simulated intercourse and oral-genital contact) which enhanced aggression, particularly for previously provoked subjects. A subsequent study similarly showed that a pornographic film (black and white stag film depicting oral, anal intercourse and female homosexual intercourse) increased aggression levels among angered males to a significantly greater extent than a neutral film (Donnerstein and Barrett, 1978).

In comparing the effects of both aggressive and erotic films on aggressive behavior of male subjects, Donnerstein and Hallam (1978) found both types of stimuli to increase aggressive behavior against both a male and a female target. However, when these subjects were given a second opportunity to aggress, these responses increased in the pornographic film condition for the female but not for the male target. The second aggression opportunity, the authors suggest, acts to reduce restraints on aggression against women.

In sum, the experimental effects from exposure to nonviolent pornographic material appear to be mediated by a number of conditions: the strength of the stimulus to induce arousal, the affective nature of the stimulus, and situational factors such as the removal of restraints against aggression.

Effects from Longer Term Exposure

A number of studies, both from the 1970 Commission and more recent ones, examined the effects of "massive" exposure to pornography. "Massive exposure" in these studies means exposure over a duration of one to several weeks. Mann, Sidman and Starr (1970) exposed married couples in four consecutive weekly sessions to sexually explicit films or to nonerotic films (for the control group). Sexual activities were recorded in diaries by the subjects during the exposure period and attitudes toward pornography also assessed both prior to and after exposure. Sexual activities increased in frequency during exposure days although these activities were ones these subjects normally engaged in (i.e., they were not related to specific ones portrayed in the stimulus materials). An additional finding was that the reported stimulating effect grew weaker as the weeks progressed. Whether this diminution is attributable to boredom or to habituation is not entirely clear.

Howard, Reifler and Liptzin (1971) similarly exposed male college students to heavy doses of pornographic films, photographs, and reading material during ninety-minute sessions over a three-week period. Experimental subjects could choose from among these materials and other "nonerotic" ones during the first ten sessions. This was followed by three sessions where the original pornographic material was replaced by new ones. During the last two sessions, the "nonerotic" materials were taken away. Control subjects were not exposed to these types of materials. The findings, based on physiologic and attitudinal measures, revealed initial high interest which faded rapidly with repeated exposure. After this period of unrestricted exposure, the provision of new materials failed to revive interest. Decreased penile response was measured as well as concomitant reductions in other responsiveness measures (e.g., heart rate, respiration rate and skin temperature). While the authors interpreted these results in terms of boredom, Zillman and Bryant (1984) suggested that habituation is a potential alternative explanation based on the premise that continued exposure to emotion-inducing stimuli produces declines in the arousal component of the reaction: evidence that habituation effects might be occurring.

To test this hypothesis, Zillman and Bryant (1984) had eighty male and female undergraduates randomly assigned to a massive, intermediate, no exposure or control group. Subjects in the three experimental groups met in six consecutive weekly sessions and watched six films of eight minutes duration each, with varying degrees of exposure to the explicit sex films. Ostensibly, the subjects were to evaluate the aesthetic aspects of these films. All erotic films depicted heterosexual activities, mainly fellatio, cunnilingus, coition, and anal intercourse, none of which depicted infliction of pain. The nonerotic films were educational or entertaining materials, all previously judged as interesting. Experimental subjects returned to the laboratory one week after treatment and were then exposed to three films of varying degrees of explicitness (pre-coitus, oral-genital sex and intercourse, and sadomasochism and bestiality) followed by measurements of excitation levels (heart rate and blood pressure) and affective ratings.

Two weeks after initial treatment, subjects were randomly assigned (within initial exposure treatments) to view one of the following: (a) a film depicting oral-genital sex and heterosexual intercourse; (b) a film depicting sadomasochistic activities; (c) a film featuring bestiality; (d) no film. Measures of aggressive behavior also were obtained at this point.

The results three weeks later indicated that with increasing exposure to various explicit stimuli, arousal responses diminished, as did aggressive behavior. Furthermore, more unusual or "harder" erotic fare appeared to grow increasingly more acceptable with subject evaluations that the material was offensive, pornographic or should be restricted progressively diminishing. Measures of sex callousness suggested further habituation effects as did projective measures of the commonality of these behaviors. According to Zillman and Bryant, these effects were, "evident for both male and female subjects." Similar habituation effects after "massive exposure" were reported by Ceniti and Malamuth (1984) for subjects who were "force-oriented," effects which were most pronounced with exposure to sexually violent depictions. Arousal patterns were not affected, however.

An earlier report on other aspects of the same study (Zillman and Bryant, 1982) showed that subjects also exhibited greater sex-callousness, using measures developed by Mosher (1970). They also showed some cognitive distortion in terms of exaggerated estimates of the prevalence of various sexual activities as a result of massive exposure.

There is contrary evidence from Linz (1985) on the effects of massive exposure to nonviolent sexually explicit materials in a study described earlier under Effects of Massive Exposure to Sexual Violence. Subjects exposed to R-rated "slasher" films, "teen sex" films and "X-rated nonviolent films"[1125] did not show the same effects in a rape-judgment situation as did the "slasher" films which showed perceptual changes described as desensitization to film violence and to violence against women.

Another investigation into the effects of massive exposure to nonviolent sexually explicit materials tested the habituation hypothesis (Zillman and Bryant, in press) using both male and female students and adults from a metropolitan community similarly examined effects of massive exposure. This time, the "behavior" of interest was choice of entertainment material. Two weeks after exposure, subjects were provided an opportunity to watch videotapes in a private situation with G-rated, R-rated and X-rated programs available. This opportunity to view was provided during an ostensible "waiting period" between procedures, with the subject's choice of entertainment and length of viewing unobtrusively recorded. Subjects with considerable prior exposure to common, nonviolent pornography showed very little interest in this type of fare, choosing instead to watch more uncommon materials that included bondage, sadomasochism, and bestiality. These effects, while observable among both males and females, were again more pronounced among the former.

While habituation is certainly a plausible explanation for these findings, choice of entertainment fare on the basis of stimulus novelty cannot be precluded entirely (see Kelley, In Press). An examination of the mean amount of time spent viewing the video tapes shows that for those massively exposed, male students watched an average of three and a half minutes of "uncommon fare" (featuring bondage, S & M, bestiality) while female students watched an average of a minute and a half, with viewing times for their nonstudent

---

1125 Psychoticism measures included such items as the following (Linz, 1985):

(a) The idea that someone else can control your thoughts.
(b) Having thoughts about sex that bother you a lot.
(c) The idea that something is seriously wrong with your body.
(d) Never feeling close to another person.
(e) Feeling lonely when you are with other people.

counterparts only slightly higher. Keeping in mind that subjects had fifteen minutes of viewing time, the graduation to a preference for stronger fare, or habituation, does not seem to be firmly supported by the data. Furthermore, the measurement situation might also be viewed as "permission-granting," with choice of what might normally be considered taboo material being more permissible or socially condoned. One could argue that greater availability of these materials in the real world might also be analogous to an indication of social sanctions being lifted, so to speak, and the laboratory evidence obtained here certainly merits more attention, perhaps through longitudinal studies.

Further measures were obtained from the same samples of subjects in the last study described above in the areas of "sexual satisfaction" and "family values," both through an extensive battery of questions (Zillman and Bryant, 1986a, 1986b). Subjects were asked how satisfied they were with their present sexual partner, their partner's physical appearance, affectionate behavior, commitment and so forth. Their findings showed significantly increased dissatisfaction in these various areas of sexuality after massive exposure.

In the area of "family values," a variety of questions tapped attitudes on pre-marital and extra-marital sex, estimations of occurrences of "sexual faithfulness" in the population, and perceptions of the institution of marriage and divorce. Again, massive exposure appears to have increased acceptance of pre-marital and extra-marital sex and diminished the importance of the institution of marriage. These findings have to be viewed with caution since the large number of statistical tests conducted increases the chances of obtaining false positive conclusions. Because of the complexity of the experimental procedures, the long battery of questions asked, and the absence of a measure validating the effectiveness of the cover story, we must also view these findings as tentative and worthy of further examination.

On the basis of the above findings, it appears that short-term effects have been observed in the laboratory but under very specific conditions. These conditions should be further elaborated on in future research. Massive exposure studies varying the lengths of exposure, on the other hand, suggest that certain types of effects may occur with long-term exposure. The question arises whether this is true of all types of sexually explicit

stimuli that do not have any violent elements.

A recent Canadian study has tried to address this issue (Check, 1985). Four hundred thirty-six college students and nonstudent metropolitan Toronto residents recruited by means of advertisements, were exposed over three videotape viewing sessions to one of three types of materials, or to no material at all. The stimulus materials were constructed (primarily because no materials could be found that exclusively contained the intended manipulations) from existing commercially available entertainment videos to represent one of the following:

1. Sexual violence—Scenes of sexual intercourse which included a woman strapped to a table and being penetrated by a large plastic penis.

2. Sexually explicit and degrading—Scenes of sexual activity which included a man masturbating into a woman's face while sitting on top of her.

3. Sexually explicit—Sex activities leading up to intercourse between a man and woman.

These categorizations were validated in preliminary questionnaires assessing subjects' perceptions of these materials. Results indicated that exposure to both the sexually violent and the nonviolent dehumanizing pornography (1) were more likely to be rated "obscene," "degrading," "offensive" and "aggressive;" (2) tended to elicit more pronounced feelings of anxiety, hostility and depression; and (3) tended to be successfully differentiated from the materials classified as "erotica." The patterns were less clear on reported likelihood of rape measures and reported the likelihood of engaging in coercive sex acts. While those in the violent and in the degrading exposure conditions reported significantly greater likelihood of engaging in these behaviors compared to the control group, an effect more pronounced among those with high pyschoticism scores, those exposed to the "erotica" stimulus did not differ significantly from either the control or both pornography conditions. The findings also have to be viewed with caution as the exposure conditions were not completely equivalent (i.e., the no-exposure control group came in for a single session while the experimental groups came in for four sessions), a caveat Check recognized and discusses. Finally, it is not entirely clear what differential effects on the exposure groups the preliminary instructions to all subjects might have had which included some reference to the study being funded by the Fraser Commission on Pornography.

Similar findings were obtained by Senn (1985) for female subjects exposed over four sessions to slides of "erotica," "nonviolent dehumanizing pornography," and "violent pornography." The first class of materials were discussed as mutually pleasurable sexual expression between two individuals presented as equal in power. The second category was described as having no explicit violence but portraying acts of submission (female kneeling, male standing; female naked, male clothed) while the third included acts of explicit violence in the sexual interaction (e.g., hair-pulling, whipping, rape).

Both violent and nonviolent pornography resulted in greater anxiety, depression and anger than erotica and both were also reliably differentiated from the latter on a number of affective dimensions, with "erotica" consistently rated more positively.

These findings on non-violent, "degrading" pornography are by no means definitive but they do suggest the importance of examining the effects of various content attributes.

Individual Differences

Not everyone reacts in the same way to sexually explicit materials. Researchers have examined various individual explanatory variables which might explain more fully why individuals respond in different ways. We do not intend an exhaustive summary of the variety of individual attributes examined but merely wish to illustrate that observed effects are mediated by a number of factors. Three sets of factors will suffice for discussion.

One characteristic which has been examined is gender. It has often been asserted that females are less interested in sex than males. Some of the early studies in sexual behavior (Kinsey, Pomeroy, Martin and Gebhard, 1953) concluded that females were disinterested in pornography and were less aroused by it. The same sex differences were reported in the national survey of the 1970 Commission (Abelson, et al., 1970).

Experimental findings, however, seem to suggest otherwise. Males and females in laboratory-exposure situations reported the same levels of arousal in response to sexually explicit stimuli (Sigusch, et al., 1970; Byrne

and Lamberth, 1971; Griffit, 1973). Females, however, are also more apt to report negative affect toward erotic stimuli, that is, they report more shock, disgust, and annoyance than males (Schmidt, et al., 1973). These differences, not surprisingly, are even more pronounced when aggressive sexual themes such as rape portrayals are employed (Schmidt 1974). The context of the portrayal is also significant as Stock (1983) demonstrated. Female subjects exposed to an eroticized version of a rape exhibited high arousal levels while a version which emphasized the victim's fear and pain elicited negative affective reactions and lower arousal levels. Krafka's (1985) female subjects did not exhibit the same negative effects that Linz's (1985) males did after exposure to R-rated slasher films which the former attributed to some emotional distancing because the victim in these films was invariably female.

Personality differences also mediate effects. One personality dimension which has been examined is "psychoticism" (Eysenck and Eysenck, 1976) which Barnes, Mamaluth and Check, 1984a, 1984b) found to be positively related to the enjoyment of force and unconventional sexual activities. Linz (1985) and Check (1985) similarly found psychoticism scores to be highly correlated with the acceptance of rape myths.

Finally, experiential factors also help explain response differences. Those with more previous experience with sexually explicit materials also tend to be less inclined toward restrictions (Newsweek-Gallup Survey, 1985) and also tend to exhibit more sex-calloused attitudes (Malamuth and Check, 1985) and more self-reported sexually aggressive behavior (Check, 1985).

Summary for Violent and Nonviolent Sexually Explicit Materials

In evaluating the results for sexually violent material, it appears that exposure to such materials (1) leads to a greater acceptance of rape myths and violence against women; (2) have more pronounced effects when the victim is shown enjoying the use of force or violence; (3) is arousing for rapists and for some males in the general population; and (4) has resulted in sexual aggression against women on the laboratory.

Malamuth's (In Press) research has further demonstrated that such attitudes as rape myth acceptance and acceptance of violence against women are correlated with arousal to such materials and with "real-world" sexual aggression and that subjects who have demonstrated sexual aggression in the laboratory are also more likely to report using coercion and force in their actual sexual interactions. The validation of the measures used in his studies, the use of physiological measures of arousal, and the attempt to systematically examine patterns among different populations with a variety of measures, arousal, attitudinal and behavorial, all tend to provide the type of convergent validation we feel is required of social science evidence.

We are less confident about the findings for nonviolent sexually explicit materials and we hasten to add that this is not necessarily because this class of materials has no effects but because the wide variety of effects obtained needs to be more systematically examined and explained. We can speculate, as have others, about potential explanations regarding some of these differences. For example, Check and Malamuth (1985) have pointed to the differences between Mosher's (1970) lack of effects on sex callousness and Zillmann and Bryant's (1982) finding of greater sex callousness from exposure to nonviolent sexually explicit stimuli (using the same scale developed by Mosher) as possibly attributable to a difference in stimulus characteristics. Mosher's film, based on his own descriptions, depicted "more affection than is typical of much pornography,", while Zillmann and Bryant's (1984) material tended to portray women as "nondiscriminating, as hysterically euphoric in response to just about any sexual or pseudosexual stimulation, and as eager to accomodate seemingly any and every sexual request" (p. 22). Check and Malamuth (1985) maintain that the portrayal in Zillmann and Bryant's study suggests "a dehumanized portrayal of women, which had the effect of generating disrespectful, anti-female attitudes in both male and female subjects" (p. 205).

This explanation could conceivably hold for the differences between Linz's (1985) findings and those of Zillmann and Bryant (1984). Because specific attributes that may characterize these films (other than the fact that they contain no violence) and explain their effects are either confounded (i.e., more than one factor is emphasized, making it difficult to attribute results to a particular one), or are not clearly explicated, it is more difficult to say definitively that this particular class of materials has a particular pattern of effects. There are very tentative suggestions that the manner in which the woman is portrayed in the material (i.e., whether she is portrayed in a demeaning or degrading fashion) might be an important content factor but this is clearly an area that should be investigated. Certainly, the theoretical, (and many will argue the common-sensical) reasons for mediating effects on the basis of content cues are already available from social learning theory (Bandura, 1977; Bandura, et al., 1975).

Some Methodological Considerations

As we have done for previous sections describing different types of data collection procedures with different populations, we need to consider certain issues that pertain to experimental studies that will help clarify our evaluation of research findings. We will consider five issues in particular which are probably most often mentioned: the problem of the ability to generalize the results outside of the laboratory (what researchers call "external validity"); the problem of "the college student" as volunteer subject; the measures used to reflect "anti-social behavior"; ethical issues; and the operationalization of "pornography."

Ability to Generalize Experimental Findings

The problem of the "artificiality" of the experimental situation is an issue not new to social psychologists (see discussions by Berkowitz and Donnerstein, 1982; Littman, 1961). While it is true that the experiment is indeed "artificial," it is so by design. If one wanted to examine if X "causes" Y, a necessary condition for establishing such a casual connection is the elimination or control of other factors which may also affect Y. Such a condition then obviates a "real-world" setting in which numerous factors interact and jointly impinge on the individual. Littman (1961) maintains that systematic experimental designs are designed to test "more universal theoretical propositions that apply to large groups of human beings." That is, they are designed to test theorized relationships about human behavior that makes the issue of representativeness of the experimental setting and subjects of lesser consequence. Berkowitz and Donnerstein, 1982, offer a cogent summary of arguments on this point. (See also Kruglanski, 1975).

The College Student as Experimental Subject

The issue of representativeness has also been raised with regard to the college student as experimental subject, with the implication that the college student hardly represents "real people" in the "real world." To reduce the issue to one of demographics is an oversimplification. If we are interested in the question of human response to sexually explicit materials, why should being in college or being male for that matter be a problem? As Berkowitz and Donnerstein (1982) point out, "The meaning the subjects assign to the situation they are in and the behavior they are carrying out plays a greater part in determining the generalizability of an experiment's outcome than does the sample's demographic representativeness or the setting's mundane realism." (p. 249)

Having said that, we also need to point out that there are, in fact, other attributes of the subject who participates in experiments involving exposure to sexually explicit materials that might have an impact on the interpretations of experimental results. Results from various studies suggest that:

1. Males, more than females, are likely to volunteer for sex-related experiments (Kendrick, et al., 1980).
2. Subjects who are willing to watch sexually explicit materials also tend to be sexually liberal, more sexually experienced, less anxious about sexual performance, and have fewer objections to pornography (Kaats and Davis, 1971; Farkas, et al., 1978; Wolchick Spencer and Lisi, 1983; Wolchick, Braver and Jensen, 1985).
3. Volunteer rates drop for both men and women the more intrusive the experimental conditions. Volunteer rates dropped by two-thirds (from thirty-eight percent to thirteen percent) for women and by over half for men (from sixty-seven percent to thirty percent) with the requirement of partial undressing to accomodate physiological arousal measurements (Wolchick, Braver and Jensen, 1985).

If participants are in fact more liberal, more experienced, and more accepting of sexually explicit materials, then it is certainly plausible that the "error," if there is one, might be in the direction of null findings, while observed effects, particularly in the short term, might be indicative of their robustness (Eysenck, 1984). In any case, it is apparent that these other attributes ought to at least be considered in both the design and interpretation of experimental studies involving sexually explicit materials.

Ethical Considerations

While some bias may be inherent in the volunteer subject in general (Rosenthal and Rosnow, 1969) and in the volunteers for experiments involving sexually explicit materials in particular, we are constrained even more by understandable concerns regarding the more "vulnerable" segments of the population. Sherif's (1980) observations about the lack of evaluation procedures for the effectiveness of debriefing subjects in one particular study (see Malamuth, Heim and Feshbach, 1980 for the study in question and Malamuth, Feshbach, and Heim, 1980 for response to Sherif, 1980) have prompted researchers to measure debriefing effects (Malamuth and Check, 1984; Linz, 1985; Krafka, 1985) and also to eliminate from participation those who might be more vulnerable to the effects of exposure to materials in these studies. For example, Linz (1985) measured potential subjects on a psychoticism scale and eliminated from participation those who had high scores on this measure. Krafka (1985) excluded from her female subject pool those who were sexually inexperienced because of earlier findings (Wishnoff, 1978) that when these types of females were exposed to explicit erotic films, their sexual anxiety diminished while their expectations about engaging in sexual intercourse increased. The trade-off between ethical concerns and representativeness is evident in Krafka's observation: "Although this restricts the population to which the present results generalize, the author was unwilling to show sexually inexperienced females degrading images of sexual behavior and, especially, pornographic rape depictions." (p. 17)

These efforts to protect subjects from potential harm are, of course, laudable and a healthy response to concerns that have been raised. In terms of the final pool of subjects who participate in pornography experiments, however, the self-selection process described above and the researcher-imposed selection process must circumscribe our evaluation of research results.

Measures of Behavioral Effects

The range of dependent variable measures used in these studies is reasonably diverse. The use of similar measures across studies allows for better validation and the use of varied measures also provides the advantage of convergent validation. We will focus on behavioral measures of effects in this discussion and briefly discuss how attitude measures may or may not predict behavior.

Four categories of behavioral measures have been used in these studies:

Measures of aggressive behavior.

The Buss aggression machine, sometimes known as a "shock box," has been widely used in laboratory experiements in the area of media violence and aggressive behavior (see reviews by Andison, 1978; Comstock, In Press). Donnerstein and his colleagues have used this measure to examine similar effects of exposure to violent and nonviolent pornography and aggressive behavior (Donnerstein, et al., 1975; Donnerstein and Barrett, 1978; Donnerstein, 1980; Donnerstein and Berkowitz, 1981).

The procedure usually involves putting the subject in a "learning" situation where the subject's task as "teacher" is to make sure that a "learner" (usually an experimental confederate) masters a given lesson. When the learner makes a "correct" response, the subject is instructed to reward him or her by pressing a button illuminating a light. Whenever the learner makes an error, he is punished by means of an electric shock. The sequence of response has, of course, been preprogrammed. The subject's "aggressive tendencies" are recorded by means of the intensity and the duration of the shock which, in reality, is not received by the confederate (see Baron, 1977b for discussion on this measure).

While this procedure has been criticized (see, for example, Baron and Eggleston, 1972), subsequent procedural modifications have increased its validity and has, in fact, been found to be highly predictive of physical aggression (Baron, 1977b). The question, however, of this measure's predictive validity in the area of sexually aggressive behavior outside of the laboratory still remains open since no efforts have been directed at examining this question.

Other surrogate measures of aggressive behavior have included the infliction of aversive noise (Cantor, et al., 1978; Malamuth, 1983) and infliction of "pain" to an experimental confederate in a retaliation move where the subject has the opportunity to apply too much cuff pressure in a blood pressure reading situation (Zillmann and Bryant, 1984). Some validation is offered by Malamuth (1983) for the use of the aversive-noise measure with evidence that attitudes about real-world aggression (such as wife battering and rape) are clearly correlated with levels of laboratory aggression against females, suggesting some linkage between laboratory aggression and external responses outside the laboratory.

Judgments toward sexual assailants.

In numerous studies, dependent measures have been obtained by having subjects respond to a rape case by evaluating both the victim and the assailant. While perceptual measures are most often used in this instance, one could also presumably consider delivering a verdict or a sentence as "behavior." In these instances, the presentation of a mock trial situation provides an element of mundane realism to the experimental situation. The studies by Linz (1985) and Krafka (1985) are excellent attempts at further diminishing demand characteristics of the experimental situation since the location of this phase of the experiment was conducted at the law school moot court where subjects were asked to evaluate what is purported to be the details of an actual rape case. An earlier study, a field experiment, by Malamuth and Check (1981) provides what may be the best procedure for eliminating demand characteristics and the measurement of effects in a setting that affords both control and realism. In this study, subjects were asked to watch the experimental films which were being shown on campus as part of the regular campus film program. Dependent measures were obtained a week later in what was presented as a public opinion survey. More studies in this area are clearly called for.

Choice and Viewing of Pornographic Fare.

Zillmann and Bryant (In Press) utilized a unique way of measuring behavioral effects of exposure by exxamining subjects' choice of entertainment fare in an unobtrusively measured procedure. In their study of the effects of massive exposure, the following procedure was used to determine subjects' preferences for entertainment fare after they had been repeatedly exposed to pornography or to a neutral stimulus in the control condition: the subjects were met individually by the experimenter and informed of a brief delay caused by equipment problems. The subject was then taken to another waiting area (ostensibly another student's office) with a television set, a video tape recorder, and some video tape cassettes (including general interest and adult tapes ranging from "common erotica to graphic depictions of relatively uncommon sexual practices") and invited to feel free to watch. To ensure the subject knew he could watch in privacy, the subject was told the experimenter would call him on the phone to report to the designated room. Unknown to the subject was the fact that each cassette tape was programmed to emit a unique signal such that when the tape was played, an event recorder also recorded the amount of time spent watching.

The advantage of this procedure is its experimental as well as ecological realism.

Self-reports of Aggressive Sexual Behavior. Two types of measures have been used to describe sexually aggressive behavior: a behavioral inclination measure operationalized by a self-reported likelihood of raping and using force in sexual interactions (see Malamuth, Haber and Feshbach, 1980; Malamuth, 1981; Briere and Malamuth, 1983) and a self-report inventory developed by Koss and Oros (1982) and used in several studies (see Malamuth, 1982; Malamuth, in press; Check, 1985). The latter includes a range of sexual behavior measures from saying things one does not mean to obtain sexual access to using various degrees of physical force.

An instrument developed by Burt to measure attitude (1980) has been used in a number of studies (Koss, 1986; Linz, 1985; Krafka, 1985; Malamuth and Check, 1981; Malamuth, 1981) to tap three dimensions: the acceptance of rape myths, the acceptance of interpersonal violence; and the acceptance of violence against women. The following are examples of the rape myth acceptance measure:

When women go around braless or wearing short skirts and tight tops, they are just asking for trouble.

Women who get raped while hitchhiking get what they deserve.

In evaluating these attitudinal measures and the laboratory measures of sexual behav-

ior, two important questions have been raised to which we have alluded earlier. First, do attitudes predict behavior? And second, do laboratory measures of aggressive behavior predict actual aggression behavior?

On the first question, Malamuth and his colleagues have demonstrated a consistent correlation between Burt's (1980) attitudinal measures and their own measures of behavioral intentions (Briere and Malamuth, 1983; Malamuth, 1981; Malamuth, Haber and Feshbach, 1980; see also Malamuth and Briere, 1986 for a discussion on the attitude-behavior question in the area of sexual aggression). Koss (1986) has similarly demonstrated a high correlation between these sex-stereotyped beliefs and self-reports of sexual aggression. We do not have these same attitudinal data from those members of the population who provide the more extreme measures of sexually aggressive behavior—rapists—which might provide another means of validating the attitude-behavior postulate. However, interviews of incarcerated rapists appear to show similar acceptance of rape myths (Scully and Marolla, 1984). A number of studies are also reviewed in Malamuth and Briere (1986) which support the correlation between attitudes and non-laboratory aggressive behavior.

Operationalizations of Pornography. Researchers, like lay people or the courts, have had some differences in the operationalization of "pornography." Malamuth (1984), for instance, uses the term with the qualifier that "no pejorative connotation is intended" and points out the difficulty of operationalizing the distinction between "aggressive versus positive types of pornography" (p. 29). However, he also relies on Steinem's (1980) separation of "acceptable erotica," in Malamuth's terms, emphasizing the notion of what Steinem called "shared pleasure," from "objectionable pornography," or what Steinem referred to as "sex in which there is clear force, or an unequal power" and describes stimuli in his research as using material belonging to the latter. Others have similarly used the term to refer only to sexually violent material and have used "erotica" to refer to nonviolent sexually explicit material (Abel, 1985). Still others on occasion simply use the term "erotica" and employ subclasses of aggressive and nonaggressive "erotica." (Donnerstein, 1983). Senn (1985) and Check (1985) have operationalized pornography to include both sexually violent and nonviolent but degrading categories and have classified all other sexually explicit portrayals as "erotica."

In examining the types of stimuli used in these studies (Figure 1), it is clear that a wide diversity of research stimuli has been employed. These have ranged from partial nudity (Baron, 1979; Baron and Bell, 1977) to various levels of sexual activity, from "implied" to "explicit," covering a varied range of behaviors—masturbation, homosexual and heterosexual intercourse, oral-genital and oral-anal intercourse, fellatio, cunnilingus, bondage, and bestiality. Sources of materials have also run the gamut from so-called stag films to mainstream sexually explicit magazines, "adult" videos from the neighborhood video store, and even sex education films (Schmidt and Sigusch, 1970; see also the earlier description of stimulus materials used in 1970 experimental studies; Check, 1985). The 1970 Commission found the term "sexually explicit materials" to have greater utility.

Comparison among studies has become hampered by the differences in stimulus materials. A common classification system has been to make use of two subclasses: violent and nonviolent pornography (see Donnerstein, 1983, 1984) and while the stimulus materials representing the former have been relatively consistent (usually a rape scene with variations on victim reactions), the same cannot be said for "violent pornography." The full range of stimuli mentioned earlier, from partial nudity to bestiality (used, for instance, by Zillmann, Bryant, Comisky and Medoff, 1981) falls within the "nonaggressive" pornography category. Perhaps not surprisingly, a full range of results (negative, no effect, and positive) has also been elicited.

Donnerstein (1983) has maintained that differential arousal levels evoke different reactions, with "mild erotica" producing a pleasant distraction and more strongly arousing material resulting in negative effects. However, this differential-arousal attribute has not been pursued in subsequent studies. Zillmann and Sapolsky (1977) have suggested that in addition to arousal, the stimulus' valence property—how pleasing or displeasing it is—also accounts for differential findings.

If the effects from exposure to nonaggressive sexually explicit materials are mediated in part by their affect value, a problem still remains: how do we explain the "pleasing" or

"displeasing" character of a stimulus? Pleasing or displeasing evaluations could arise from a number of factors including the explicitness of the material, the type of activity portrayed (see, for example, Glass' [1978] scale analysis of the 1970 Commission survey data which shows clearly gradations in public perceptions of different activities), or the theme employed. For example, Sherif (1980) raised the possibility of power differentials to explain female subjects' arousal but high negative affect in response to a stimulus portraying a rape victim experiencing an involuntary orgasm in Malamuth, Heim and Feshbach's (1980) study.

Two studies (Check, 1985; Senn 1985) have attempted to reconceptualize nonaggressive sexually explicit materials into two further classes ('sexually explicit and degrading or dehumanizing', and simply 'sexually explicit'). There is theoretical justification for expecting differential effects from these subclasses. Bandura, Underwood and Fromson (1975) have demonstrated that socially reprehensible attitudes or behaviors may be made more acceptable by dehumanization of victims. "Inflicting harm on individuals who are subhuman and debased is less apt to arouse self-reproof than if they are seen as human beings with dignifying qualities." (p. 255). Again, this is clearly a line of research that merits further attention.

The problem of explicating stimulus attributes is complicated with examination of a class of materials categorized by their commercial label: "R-rated slasher films" (see Linz, Donnerstein and Penrod, 1984; Linz, 1985; Krafka, 1985), or "X-rated films." The former "contain explicit scenes of violence in which the victims are nearly always female. While the films often juxtapose a violent scene with a sensual or erotic scene (e.g., a woman masturbating in the bath is suddenly and brutally attacked), there is no indication in any of the films that the victim enjoys or is sexually aroused by violence. In nearly all cases, the scene ends in the death of the victim." (Linz, et al., 1984, p. 137). These studies using this film genre have generally found desensitizing effects among male subjects, after massive exposure.

But the question still remains: what does this class called "R-rated slasher films" mean conceptually? If one were interested in describing potential effects from classes of sexually explicit materials, where does this set of materials fit in? This appears compounded in an examination of effects of sexually violent, violent, and sexually explicit materials on female subjects (Krafka, 1985), where these films are used to operationalize "violent" films, despite allowing that they have "some sexual content."

"X-rated films" pose the same problems. While they appear to be used to represent sexually explicit material without any violence, different themes may be emphasized leading to quite different results.

The need to utilize meaningful classes that go beyond those in current use is important not just for validity requirements. After all, the question which social scientists must ultimately address—with both theoretical and pragmatic or public policy implications—is what types of effects have been demonstrated for what classes of material? Such investigations for some social scientists may have undesirable political or idealogical implications but ignoring the issue also hampers our ability to explain the nature of effects more fully so as to provide for nonlegal policy strategies that are firmly anchored in social science findings (see, for example, Byrne and Kelley, 1984; Kelley, 1985).

Some Theoretical Considerations

In designing research studies to answer particular questions, social scientists do not ordinarily operate in a vacuum. Quite often, the relationships posited, the selection of variables and their operationalizations, the groups of people selected for examination, and the general research procedures are guided by "theory." Quite simply, this is the explanatory framework which rationalizes or justifies why a particular relationship might be expected.

We think it useful to summarize some of the theoretical reasoning that has been applied to the general question of what effects if any might be found from exposure to sexually explicit stimuli.

Social Learning Theory

This approach offers a perspective on human behavior based on the notion that there is "a continuous reciprocal interaction" between environmental factors, an individual's processing of information from his environment and his behavior (Bandura, 1977). This framework assigns a prominent role to the processes of vicarious and symbolic learning (i.e., learning by observing others' behavior and one's own) and a self-regulating process whereby an individual selectively organizes

and processes stimuli and regulates his or her behaviors accordingly.

The generic process of *modeling* is a major component of social learning which many mistakenly interpret as simply imitation, or a one-to-one correspondence between some portrayed novel behavior and the reproduction of such behavior. While this type of effect is not precluded (and there are certainly many anecdotal media accounts of such instances), "modeling" embraces a more complex array of processes which can be subsumed under two categories. First, modeling includes the facilitation of particular response categories ("response facilitation") which assumes that a portrayed behavior functions as an external inducement for similar sets of responses which can be performed with little difficulty. Second, it includes the capacity to strengthen or weaken inhibitions of responses ("inhibition" or "disinhibition") that may already be in the observer's repertoire. If there are restraints on a particular behavior (self-restraints, as in anxiety over a particular behavior, or external restraints, including the possibility of getting caught and punished for some socially disapproved—or illegal—action), such restraints may be lifted when an observer sees a model engage in disapproved acts without any adverse consequences (Bandura, 1973, 1977).

In Check and Malamuth's (1985) application of this theoretical framework, they discuss their findings in terms of Bandura's postulated "antecedent" and "consequent" determinants. The former incorporates symbolic expectancy learning principles exemplified by the symbolic pairing of sex with violence against women and vicarious expectancy learning, or observing others becoming aroused to sexual violence. Consequent determinants include observing seeing a male use force, not getting punished, and, furthermore, finding the experience pleasurable for himself and for his victim.

Two studies based on survey data provide additional information that certain sexually explicit materials may provide "models" for behavior for some individuals.

Russell (1985) reported findings from an earlier study on sexual abuse of women. A probability sample of 930 adult female residents in San Francisco were interviewed. Of this number, about four in ten (389 women) said they had seen pornography and forty-four percent of this group reported being upset by it. Fourteen percent of the total sample reported they had been asked to pose for pornographic pictures and ten percent said they had been upset by someone trying to get them to enact what had been seen in the pornographic pictures, movies or books. An additional finding in this study was that those who were upset by pornographic requests were twice as likely to be incest victims than those who were not upset by similar requests. A similar pattern was found among those who reported being upset at being asked to pose for pornographic pictures, i.e., those who were asked to pose were more than twice as likely to suffer incest abuse in their childhood (thirty-two percent versus fourteen percent). What this suggests, according to Russell, is that women who suffered sexual abuse are significantly more vulnerable to pornography-related victimization, a "revictimization" syndrome.

Silbert and Pines (1986), in a similar study on sexual assault of street prostitutes, came upon unexpected information in the course of their interviews. From detailed descriptions the subjects provided to open-ended questions in regard to incidents of juvenile sexual assault in their childhood and to incidents of rape following entrance into prostitution, it became evident that violent pornography played a significant role in the sexual abuse of street prostitutes. Of the 200 prostitutes interviewed, 193 reported rape incidents and of this number, twenty-four percent mentioned allusions to pornographic material on the part of the rapist. Since these comments were not solicited, it is likely that this figure is a conservative estimate. The authors described the comments as following the same pattern: "the assailant referred to pornographic materials he had seen or read and then insisted that the victims not only enjoyed the rape but also the extreme violence." (p. 12)

Arousal

Arousal has been conceived of as a "drive" that "energizes or intensifies behavior that receives direction by independent means" (Zillmann, 1982, 1978). This model relies on the notion that arousal based on exposure to some communication stimulus can facilitate behaviors which could either be prosocial or anti-social, depending on situational circumstances. Such circumstances could include specific content cues which might elicit either positive or negative affect (Sapolsky, 1984). If arousal levels are minimal and the stimulus evokes pleasant responses (as might be the case when viewing mildly erotic material), the effect might be reduced aggression. If, on the other hand, the stimulus elevates arousal to high levels, then the outcome might be aggressive behavior. This approach has been criticized for its inability to account for the predominance of one response rather than another.

Habituation

The idea of habituation is akin to drug treatment or drug dependency where, over time, one must rely on increasing doses to obtain the same effect. In the area of exposure to explicit sexual stimuli, repeated exposure has resulted in initially strong arousal reactions becoming weaker over time, leading to habituation. (Zillmann, 1982, 1984). One attitudinal manifestation of this effect is callousness, either to victims of aggression or simply to the violent or anti-social behaviors themselves. While this holds promise as an explanatory framework, more research is needed, particularly longitudinal studies, to demonstrate its predictive utility.

Cue Elicitation/Disinhibition

Berkowitz (1974,1984) has proposed a stimulus-response relational model which suggests that an individual (e.g., a film viewer) reacts impulsively to environmental stimuli and this reaction is determined in part by predispositions and in part by stimulus situational characteristics which could function to "disinhibit" such predispositions. Berkowitz has demonstrated that cues associated with aggressive responding such as a situation depicting a female victim, when viewed by an individual predisposed to aggress (one who is provoked or angered), will more likely evoke the aggressive response as a result of the stimulus-response connection already established by previous exposure to the films. (See Donnerstein and Berkowitz, 1981, and Linz, 1985, for applications).

These explanatory-predictive approaches may not necessarily operate independently; they could conceivably complement each other. They stand, however, in contrast and direct opposition to the catharsis theory which is still being promoted in many quarters as the explanation for why exposure to sexually explicit materials has only beneficial effects. Catharsis suggests that exposure to highly arousing material actually leads to a diminution of anti-social effects because relieving the arousal then reduces the instigation to commit any sex crimes in the future. Unfortunately, little evidence exists for this claim and numerous research reviews (primarily in the area of media violence and aggressive behavior) have arrived at this same conclusion (Berkowitz, 1962; Bramel, 1969; Weiss, 1969; Geen and Quanty, 1977; National Institute of Mental Health, 1982; Comstock, 1985). The following observation typifies comments made about the catharsis theory.

> The cause-effect hypothesis that we already described is not supported by the data. Little evidence for catharsis, as we have defined it, exists and much of the evidence that has been adduced in its favor is susceptible to alternative explanations that are at least parsiminious. In fact, when conditions that give rise to such alternative explanations are re-moved from the experimental setting, the reverse [authors' emphasis] of what the catharsis hypothesis predicts is usually found, i.e., aggression begets more, not less, aggression (p. 6).

It is instructive that some have called a moratorium on catharsis (Bandura, 1973), others have proclaimed its demise (Comstock, 1985). Even its major proponent has reformulated his position by explaining why it does not apply to situations involving media exposure (Feshbach, 1980).

OTHER EFFECTS OF SEXUALLY EXPLICIT MATERIALS

If we take the entire potential range of "effects" which could occur as a result of exposure to sexually explicit materials, and if we take the commission of sex offenses to be one extreme of that continuum, then the other end might be represented by beneficial effects. Many have made an argument for such benefits (Tripp, 1985; Wilson, 1978).

Public opinion data both in 1970 and in 1985 show that a majority believe use of sexually explicit materials "provide entertainment," relieve people of the impulse to commit crimes, and improve marital relations.

If they are any indication, the popularity of "How-To" articles on sex in the popular media and in best-sellers such as The Joy of Sex, The Sensuous Woman, and others like them are also testament to the learning that might occur from these materials.

There are also two areas in which sexually explicit materials have been used for positive ends: the treatment of sexual dysfunctions and the diagnosis and treatment of some paraphilias.

In the area of sexual dysfunctions, a common conceptual model views a particular goal as a new response to be learned. The reduction of sexual anxieties or the attainment of orgasm for nonorgasmic individuals might be examples of such objectives. In the process of learning a new response, two steps are implicated: the weakening of response inhibitions and facilitation of the acquisition of new behavior patterns that comprise the steps toward the final objective.

For instance, in teaching nonorgasmic females to achieve orgasm, therapeutic procedures might include desensitization techniques, followed by the modeling of a hierarchy of behaviors such as body exploration, genital manipulation, self-stimulation to orgasm, and the generalization of the response to a partner (Caird and Wincze, 1977; LoPiccolo and Lobitz, 1972; Heiman, LoPiccolo and LoPiccolo, 1976).

A number of controlled experimental studies have demonstrated the efficacy of therapeutic treatments involving video taped modeling, written instructions which implicate principles of observational learning, and information processing. Such procedures have been successful in changing both attitudes and behaviors (Anderson, 1983; Heiby and Becker, 1980; Nemetz, Craig and Reith, 1978; Wincze and Caird, 1976; Wish, 1975).

In the case of diagnosis and treatment of sex offenders, the identification of arousal patterns and the subsequent therapy program (which might involve the inhibition of inappropriate arousal responses such as arousal to a photograph of a child) have involved the use of sexually explicit materials. As part of some treatment methods, the use of aversive techniques might be directed at extinguishing deviant arousal, or they might be combined with positive reinforcement for more appropriate sexual responses. In some treatment programs, the combination of these procedures with social skills training has been found to be effective (Abel, Becker and Skinner, 1985; Whitman and Quinsey, 1981). However, the results have been less conclusive for narrower approaches to treatment (see Quinsey and Marshall, 1983).

On the whole, the learning principles that

include vicarious learning, reinforcement, disinhibition principles that are used in these therapeutic controlled settings are no different from those which have been employed to explain the acquisition of negative attitudes and behaviors.

AN INTEGRATION OF THE RESEARCH FINDINGS

It is clear that the conclusion of "no negative effects" advanced by the 1970 Commission is no longer tenable. It is also clear that catharsis, as an explanatory model for the impact of pornography, is simply unwarranted by evidence in this area, nor has catharsis fared well in the general area of mass media effects and anti-social behavior.

This is not to say, however, that the evidence as a whole is comprehensive enough or definitive enough. While we have learned much more since 1970, even more areas remain to be explored.

What do we know at this point?

• It is clear that many sexually explicit materials, particularly of the commercial variety, that are obviously designed to be arousing, are, in fact, arousing, both to offenders and nonoffenders.

• Rapists appear to be aroused by both forced as well as consenting sex depictions while nonoffenders (our college males) are less aroused by depictions of sexual aggression. On the other hand, when these portrayals show the victim as "enjoying" the rape, these portrayals similarly elicit high arousal levels.

• Arousal to rape depictions appears to correlate with attitudes of acceptance of rape myths and sexual violence and both these measures likewise correlate with laboratory-observed aggressive behaviors.

• Depictions of sexual violence also increase the likelihood that rape myths are accepted and sexual violence toward women condoned. Such attitudes have further been found to be correlated with laboratory aggression toward women. Finally, there is also some evidence that laboratory aggression toward women correlates with self-reported sexually aggressive behaviors.

What we know about the effects of nonviolent sexually explicit material is less clear. There are tentative indications that negative effects in the areas of attitudes might also occur, particularly from massive exposure. The mechanics of such effects need to be elaborated more fully, however, particularly in light of more recent findings that suggest that degrading themes might have effects that differ from non violent, non degrading sexually explicit materials. This is clearly an area that deserves further investigation.

• There are suggestions that pornography availability may be one of a nexus of sociocultural factors that has some bearing on rape rates in this country. Other cross-cultural data, however, offer mixed results as well, so these findings have to be viewed as tentative at best.

• We still know very little about the causes of deviancy and it is important to examine the developmental patterns of offenders, particularly patterns of early exposure. We do have some convergence on the data from some rapists and males in the general population in the areas of arousal and attitudes but again, this remains to be examined more closely.

Clearly, the need for more research remains as compelling as ever. The need for more research to also examine the efficacy of strategies for dealing with various effects is as compelling. If learning—both prosocial and antisocial—occurs from various depictions, and there certainly is clear evidence of both, the need for strategies that implicate the same learning principles must be evaluated. Educational and media strategies have been discussed elsewhere and found to be effective in such disparate areas as health and media violence (see Rubinstein and Brown, 1986; Johnston and Ettema, 1982; American Psychological Association, 1985). Researchers in the area of pornography have no less a responsibility.

SUMMARY OF COMMISSION FINDINGS OF HARM FROM PORNOGRAPHY

The Commission divided pornography into four classifications and then analyzed each classification according to three tiers as set forth below:

Sexually Violent Materials

Social Science Evidence. Negative effects were found to have been demonstrated.

Totality of Evidence. Harm found in all sub-tiers:
1. Acceptance of Rape Myths;
2. Degradation of the Class/Status of Women;
3. Modeling Effect;
4. Family;
5. Society.

Moral, Ethical and Cultural. Harm found.

Sexual Activity Without Violence But with Degradation, Submission, Domination, or Humiliation

Social Science Evidence. Negative effects were found to have been demonstrated.

Totality of Evidence. Harm found in all sub-tiers:
1. Acceptance of Rape Myths;
2. Degradation of the Class/Status of Women;
3. Modeling Effect;
4. Family;
5. Society.

Moral, Ethical and Cultural. Harm found.

Sexual Activity Without Violence, Degradation, Submission, Domination, or Humiliation

All Commissioners agreed that some materials in this classification may be harmful, some Commissioners agreed that not all materials in this classification are not harmful. It was determined that this classification is a very small percentage of the total universe of pornographic materials. See text for further discussion.

Nudity Without Force, Coercion, Sexual Activity, or Degradation

All Commissioners agreed that some materials in this classification may be harmful, some Commissioners agreed that not all materials in this classification are not harmful. See text for further discussion.

C H A P T E R • 1 9

Organized Crime

PREFACE

The Commission has relied heavily on information and intelligence provided by experienced federal, state, and local law enforcement authorities regarding the involvement of organized crime in the pornography industry. This first hand knowledge is based upon years of investigative experience in the highly complex and covert area of organized crime. Many of these law enforcement authorities testified before the Commission on January 21–22, 1986, in New York City, at a hearing devoted primarily to matters relating to organized crime. The Commission has also used investigative reports prepared by the United States Department of Justice, the office of the Attorney General of California, the Middle Atlantic-Great Lakes Organized Crime Law Enforcement Network (MAGLO-CLEN), the Pennsylvania Crime Commission, the Washington, D.C., Metropolitan Police Department and others. Reliance on the investigative reports and the experience of these law enforcement authorities was necessary because the Commission operated without the authority to subpoena witnesses or compel their testimony regarding this sensitive area of inquiry.

INTRODUCTION

Organized crime involvement in the pornography industry has been described by law enforcement officers and by organized crime operatives themselves. A retired veteran Federal Bureau of Investigation agent said of traditional[1126] organized crime members, "you cannot be in the field and distribute pornography without their consent . . . ."[1127] He added that the pornography trade is attractive to organized crime because "it's a fast way of making a buck."[1128] Aladena ✂ , whose involvement in La Cosa Nostra dates back to the late 1940's has reached the same conclusion.[1129] In an interview with a Commission investigator, Aladena ✂ described the connection as he knew it to be in the 1970's as follows:

Interviewer: Is it possible for any person to become a major distributor of pornography in the United States without becoming involved in organized crime?

Aladena: I doubt it. I doubt it.

Interviewer: Okay, why do you doubt it?

Aladena: Well, because there's so much involved and I don't think they would let them.

Interviewer: Okay, so if someone tried to operate without an involvement?

Aladena: Well, somebody would report 'em, they'd say look it, he's taking my business.

1126. For a more complete explanation of traditional organized crime structures and influence see the textual discussion of organized crime, supra.

1127. New York Hearing, Vol. I, Homer Young, p. 40.

1128. Id., p. 41.

1129. New York Hearing, Vol. I, Aladena ✂ interview, Interview by Senior Investigator Edward H. Chapman, Attorney General's Commission on Pornography, p. 112.

Interviewer: . . . what would they do? Shut them down, or take them over?

Aladena: Well, they would do something. I really couldn't answer that. You know, they would do something. They might go so far as killing them, who knows.[1130]

Another individual who was the owner and operator of an "adult" bookstore and spent many years in the pornography business described his experience in dealing with organized crime:

Interviewer: . . . If the mob says, "I do not want this, boy"?:

Subject: You don't sell it. Even if they don't even talk to you. You're not going to sell it nowhere. If you go to the store on 14th street and put it in there, they're gonna bust his ass. Or they're gonna break your legs when you start going through them. There was a man who went from New York City . . . went into Atlanta. Had films to sell . . . They found him at the airport, with a $5,000 Rolex watch on and about eight grand in his pocket, and four rolls of film in his hands, with his head blown up in the trunk of his car. Nobody robbed him, nobody took a dime off him. They didn't even take the film. But he was at the airport with a New York ticket shoved in his coat pocket. Don't come down from New York, selling unless you've been sent down.[1131]

ORGANIZED CRIME INVOLVEMENT IN PORNOGRAPHY

The 1970 President's Commission on Obscenity and Pornography was unable to draw conclusions regarding the role of organized crime in the distribution of obscene and pornographic materials. The 1970 Commission on Obscenity and Pornography found:

Although many persons have alleged that organized crime works hand-in-glove with the distributors of adult materials, there is at present no concrete evidence to support these statements.

The hypothesis that organized criminal elements either control or are "moving in" on the distribution of sexually oriented materials will doubtless continue to be speculated upon. The panel finds that there is insufficient evidence at present to warrant any conclusion in this regard.[1132]

There is some question about how the earlier Commission reached this conclusion.[1133] It is clear that the role of traditional organized crime in the pornography trade has increased substantially since the 1970 report was issued. Until 1970, only one LCN family, the ✁ organization, was known to have been involved significantly in the pornography business.[1134]

The Attorney General's Commission on Pornography has received reports from law enforcement officials, prosecutors, and legislators, describing the substantial role which organized crime, both in traditional (LCN) and non-traditional forms, plays in the pornography business in the United States today.[1135]

In addition to attorneys, many other professional persons assist organized crime families and their associates in the pornography business. Realtors handle land transactions knowing the ultimate purpose of the transaction is to facilitate the sale of obscene material.[1136] Landlords rent property to organized crime families knowing they will be used to warehouse obscene material or to sell, produce, distribute, or display obscene merchandise.[1137] Bankers process accounts and provide all manner of banking services (including the failure to report currency transactions as required by Title 31 United States Code). Printers and film processors develop the visual images taken by pornographers and turn them into finished products for sale or reproduction. Transportation companies and

---

1130. *Id.*, pp. 112–15.

1131. New York Hearing, Vol. I, "Bookstore Operator" interview, pp. 141–44; See *also*, New York Hearing, Vol. II, William Johnson, p. 82A–1 on "16 November 1970, Kenneth Herbert (Jap) Hann's bullet riddled body was found in the trunk of a car at Atlanta International Airport."

1132. *The Report of the Commission on Obscenity and Pornography*, (1970), pp. 141–43.

1133. New York Hearing, Vol. I, Homer Young, p. 10; Former Federal Bureau of Investigation Obscenity Specialist Young reported that a staff member of the 1970 Commission interviewed him for approximately four hours about the role of organized crime in pornography in the 1968/1969 era. Young advised that he furnished the individual with documentation of organized crime involvement which for some unknown reason was not included in the earlier Commission's final report.

1134. New York Hearing, Vol. I, William Kelly, p. 69.

1135. See, Appendix One, *infra*.

1136. New York Hearing, Vol. I, James D. Harmon, p. 14A–5.

1137. ✁

interstate carriers show no discretion in shipping obscene materials to increase organized crime family profits. Academics are paid to act as experts on behalf of organized crime members and associates who are brought to trial and challenged in public debates. Public figures including prosecutors, judges, city, county and state officials, zoning board members, and health department officials may be subjected to monetary and political influence. These people sometimes may ignore the organized criminal activity or impose minimal sanctions when punishment is unavoidable.

Following are highlights of reports provided to this Commission relating to traditional organized crime involvement in and control of the pornography industry.

One report came from a group of law enforcement officers, coordinated through the Investigative Services Division of the Washington, D.C., Metropolitan Police Department, which undertook a study in 1978 to determine the extent of organized crime involvement in the pornography industry.[1138] One reason for the study was, "(knowledge) that organized crime generally involves itself in situations where the gain far outreaches the risk. The pornography industry fits this description."[1139] "An initial probe determined that law enforcement could document Organized Crime control in certain geographic areas. However, it did not appear in 1977 that *any single law enforcement body was in possession of documentation* reflecting the situation on a national level".[1140] (emphasis added)

The project participants determined that traditional organized crime was substantially involved in and did essentially control much of the major pornography distribution in the United States during the years 1977 and 1978. The group further concluded that the combination of the large amounts of money involved, the incredibly low priority obscenity enforcement had within police departments and prosecutors' offices in an area

where manpower intensive investigations were essential for success, and the imposition of minimal fines and no jail time upon random convictions resulted in a low risk and high profit endeavor for organized crime figures who became involved in pornography.[1141] During its seventy-eight year history, the Federal Bureau of Investigation (FBI) has been engaged periodically in investigation of persons and organizations who violate the federal obscenity laws. Though the FBI has not recently been involved in many large scale obscenity related investigations,[1142] Federal Bureau of Investigation director, William H. Webster, along with present and former special agents of the FBI have provided current information about the pornography industry.[1143] In the late 1970's the FBI prepared a report detailing the extent of organized crime involvement in pornography. In preparing that report, the Bureau conducted a survey of the fifty-nine FBI field offices.[1144] Based on the survey and other sources, FBI intelligence analysts concluded:

Information obtained (during the course of the enclosed survey) points out the vast control of the multi-million dollar pornography business in the United States by a few individuals with direct connections with what is commonly known as the organized crime establishment in the United States, specifically, La Cosa Nostra. . . . Information received from sources of this Bureau indicates that pornography is (a major) income maker for La Cosa Nostra in the United States behind gambling and narcotics. Although La Cosa Nostra does not physically oversee the day-to-day workings of the majority of pornography business in the United States, it is apparent they have "agreements" with those involved in the pornography business in allowing these people to operate independently by paying off members of organized crime for the privilege of being allowed to operate in certain geographical areas.[1145]

In 1985, at the request of the Attorney General's Commission on Pornography, Director

1138. *Organized Crime's Involvement in the Pornography Industry,* Investigative Services Division, Metropolitan Police Dept., Washington, D.C. (1978).

1139. New York Hearing, Vol. I, Carl Shoffler, p. 214.

1140. *Id.*, p. 215.

1141. *Id.*

1142. See, Washington, D.C., Hearing, Vol II, William H. Webster, pp. 77–81.

1143. *Id.* at 75; New York Hearing, Vol I, Homer E. Young, p. 16.

1144. Washington, D.C., Hearing, Vol. II, William H. Webster, p. 81.

1145. *Federal Bureau of Investigation Report Regarding the Extent of Organized Crime Development in Pornography,* (1978), p. 6.

Webster conducted a brief survey of the fifty-nine FBI field offices concerning their knowledge of involvement of traditional organized crime in pornography. Director Webster advised this Commission, "About three quarters of those offices indicated that they have no verifiable information that organized crime was involved either directly or through extortion in the manufacturing or distribution of pornography. Several offices, did, however, report some involvement by members and associates of organized crime."[1146]

The FBI reported that on April 30, 1981, Joseph ✂ , a known dealer in pornography in ✂ and ✂ , Massachusetts, met with Gennaro J. ✂ in Boston.[1147] ✂ is the underboss of the New England Organized Crime Family.[1148] Joseph complained that one Carlo ✂ was opening an adult bookstore in the ✂ area to compete with the one jointly owned by Joseph and Carlo. Joseph could not understand why the New York family had authorized Carlo to operate a competing pornography business. Prior to this, Joseph said he had considered Robert ✂ of the New York family to be his "compadre". In response, ✂ became angry because Joseph had first sought an explanation from Robert. ✂ said this prevented him from contacting Robert's boss in New York and he would now have to deal with Sam ✂ , capo of the ✂ family in Massachusetts.[1149]

One former FBI agent told the Commission:

In my opinion, based upon twenty-three years of experience in pornography and obscenity investigations and study, it is practically impossible to be in the retail end of the pornography industry (today) without dealing in some fashion with organized crime either the mafia or some other facet of non-mafia never-the-less highly organized crime.[1150]

The Chicago Police Department has been involved in the investigation of organized crime families who are engaged in the distribution of pornography in the *Midwest*.[1151] Thomas Bohling of the Chicago Police Department Organized Crime Division, Vice Control Section reported, ". . . it is the belief of state, federal, and local law enforcement that the pornography industry is controlled by organized crime families. If they do not own the business outright, they most certainly extract street tax from independent smut *peddlers*."[1152]

An overwhelming majority of obscene and pornographic materials are produced in the Los Angeles, California, area.[1153] Organized crime families from Chicago, New York, New Jersey, and Florida are openly controlling and directing the major pornography operations in Los Angeles.[1154] According to Chief Daryl F. Gates of the Los Angeles Police Department, "Organized crime infiltrated the pornography industry in Los Angeles in 1969 due to its lucrative financial benefits. By 1975, organized crime controlled eighty percent of the industry and it is estimated that this figure is between eighty-five to ninety percent today."[1155]

An investigative report submitted to the California Legislature by the Attorney General of California discussed organized crime infiltration into the pornography industry:

In the early 1970's . . . four organized crime groups moved in on pornography operations in California. They met relatively little resistance because the weak-structured organized crime group of Southern California lacked the necessary strength to deter the infiltration of organized crime from the East.

Organized crime figures first focused on production and retail operations in California. In this effort, they used the influence of their established national distribution network and effectively resorted to illegal and

1146. Letter, William H. Webster, Director, Federal Bureau of Investigation to Henry E. Hudson, chairman, Attorney General's Commission on Pornography, Nov. 15, 1985.
1147. Letter to the Attorney General's Commission on Pornography from the Federal Bureau of Investigation, March 24, 1986.
1148. *Id.*
1149. *Id.*
1150. New York Hearing, Vol. I, William P. Kelly, p. 86.
1151. New York Hearing, Vol. I, Thomas Bohling, p. 178.
1152. *Id.*, p. 189.
1153. See, Los Angeles Hearing, Vol. I, James Docherty, p. 6.
1154. Los Angeles Hearing, Vol. I, Robert Peters, p. 32. Detective Peters estimates that eighty to ninety percent of the pornography in the United States is produced in the Los Angeles area. *See also*, The discussion of production and distribution of sexually explicit materials.
1155. Los Angeles Hearing, Vol. I, Robert Peters, p. 32.

unfair business tactics. The newly arrived organized crime groups formed film duplication companies which illegally duplicated the films of independent producers and displayed them at nationwide organized crime controlled theaters. Faced with continued piracy and loss of profits, many legitimate producers were forced to deal with organized crime controlled distribution companies and film processing labs.

After gaining control or ownership of many California wholesale and retail companies, organized crime forced other independent retailers out of business through price manipulation. Wholesale prices to independent retailers were raised while prices to organized crime controlled outlets were lowered. Independents were undersold by organized crime controlled outlets until lost profits forced them out of business. Many competitors were bought out which allowed the subsequent raising of prices in other parts of the market. Some dealers that openly opposed this takeover were silenced by means of extortion and arson.[1156]

In 1984, California Attorney General John Van De Kamp reported that the arrival of home video cassette recorders on the market in 1979 was accompanied by a growing demand for adult video tapes.[1157] California pornographers, linked to the Gambino, DeCavalcante, Luchese and Columbo organized crime families entered this market through companies that produce, duplicate, distribute and sell adult video tapes.[1158]

Law enforcement agents have described the control of organized crime families in the pornography industry. Organized crime figures and associates are involved in the commerce essential to the pornography business through ownership of the distribution sources of the material. The 1970 Commission on Obscenity and Pornography reported ". . . crime syndicate members reported in in-

terviews that it was not worthwhile for the syndicate to enter the business, primarily because there was no real economic inducement.[1159] In 1986, there are tremendous profits in the pornography industry. These profits are of the type that can be easily hidden from the Internal Revenue Service, because of the cash transactions and the policy of no cash receipts for merchandise.[1160]

Law enforcement officials have described large profit margins in the pornography business today.[1161] Magazines which cost fifty cents to produce wholesale for five dollars and the retail price is ten dollars or more.[1162] A fifty minute eight millimeter film wholesales for three dollars and retails for twenty dollars.[1163] Video cassette tapes which wholesale for fifteen dollars often retail for eighty to ninety-five dollars.[1164]

The well-known pornographic film "Deep Throat" was produced by the ✁ brothers of the Columbo organized crime family for $25,000 and is reliably estimated to have grossed fifty million dollars as of 1982.[1165] The film was ". . . the biggest money maker of any film to that time and possibly since, in the state of Florida."[1166]

Joseph, Anthony, and Louis ✁ all became millionaires as a result of "Deep Throat."[1167] They used profits from the film to build a vast financial empire in the 1970s that included ownership of garment companies in New York and Miami, investment companies, a sixty-five-foot yacht in the Bahamas, "adults only" pornographic theaters in Los Angeles, and record and music publishing companies on both the east and west coasts.[1168] From 1973 to 1976, their corporate empire included ✁ Distributors, Inc., a motion picture company that earned twenty million dollars in its first year of operation.[1169] The ✁ also used profits from

1156. *Investigative Report on Organized Crime and Pornography Submitted to the Attorney General of California,* 2–3.

1157. State of California, Department of Justice, *Organized Crime in California,* (1984), p. 6.

1158. *Id.,* p. 5.

1159. *Investigative Report on Organized Crime and Pornography Submitted to the Attorney General of California* 5.

1160. New York Hearing, Vol. II, William Johnson, p. 82A; See, the discussion of the production and distribution of sexually explicit materials for a detailed explanation of the profitability of the industry.

1161. See, Los Angeles Hearing, Vol. I, James Docherty, p. 6.

1162. New York Hearing, Vol. II, William Johnson, p. 73.

1163. *Id.,* p. 82A–5.

1164. *Id.*

1165. New York Hearing, Vol. I, William Kelly, p. 108A–3.

1166. *Id.*

1167. *Id.,* p. 108A–4.

1168. Cong. Rec., S433 (daily ed. Jan. 30, 1984). (statement of Senator Jesse Helms).

1169. *Id.*

"Deep Throat" to finance drug smuggling operations in the Caribbean.[1170]

Aladena   ✄   , a.k.a., Jimmy ✄ ✄   , a made member of a La Cosa Nostra organized crime family and a former Capo and later acting boss of the Los Angeles crime family, told this Commission that large profits have kept organized crime heavily involved in the obscenity industry.[1171]   ✄ described this involvement to a Commission investigator as follows:

> Interviewer: Could you describe the nature and type of involvement organized crime would have in the pornography industry when you were active in organized crime?

> Aladena: Well, it's very, very big. . . . I'd say, 95 percent of the families are involved in one way or another in pornography. . . . It's too big. They just won't let it go.

> Interviewer: Okay, does organized crime reap a lot of money from their involvement in pornographic industry?

> Aladena: Absolutely. Absolutely.[1172]

The Attorney General's Commission on Pornography concludes that organized crime in its traditional LCN forms and in other forms exerts substantial influence and control over the obscenity industry. Though a number of significant producers and distributors are not members of LCN families, all major producers and distributors of obscene material are highly organized and carry out illegal activities with a great deal of sophistication.[1173]

This influence and control has increased since the report of the 1970 Commission on Obscenity and Pornography and is particularly evident in the distribution of pornographic materials.[1174] Organized crime ele-

ments have found that the large financial gains to be reaped from pornography far outweigh the risks associated with the trade.

RELATED CRIMES AND ACTIVITIES

In addition to the myriad of other harms and anti-social effects brought about by obscenity[1175] there is a link between traditional organized crime group involvement in the obscenity business and many other types of criminal activity. Physical violence, injury, prostitution and other forms of sexual abuse are so interlinked in many cases as to be almost inseparable except according to statutory definitions. Among the crimes known to be interlinked with the pornography industry are:

Murder

One of the largest pornographers in the United States during the 1970's was Michael George Thevis, who headed Peachtree News in Atlanta, Georgia, and 106 other corporations.[1176] In October, 1979 Thevis was convicted in the United States District Court for the Northern District of Georgia for Racketeer Influenced and Corrupt Organnzations Act (RICO) violations including murder, arson, and extortion.[1177]

A leading figure in the national distribution of the film "Deep Throat", Robert DeSalvo, has been missing since January, 1976 and is presumed to have been murdered.[1178] DeSalvo provided evidence on behalf of the United States in the   ✄   trial arising from the "Deep Throat" film distribution.[1179]

During the late 1970s a number of persons involved in the pornography business were murdered in what were believed by law enforcement agents to be pornography turf wars.[1180] The son of Joseph   ✄   , one of the producers of "Deep Throat" along with an in-

---

1170. New York Hearing, Vol. II, Christopher J. Mega, p. 160.

1171. New York Hearing, Vol. I, Interview with James   ✄   by Senior Investigator Edward Chapman, Attorney General's Commission on Pornography, p. 112.

1172. New York Hearing, Vol. I, Interview with Jimmy   ✄   , by Senior Investigator Edward H. Chapman, Attorney General's Commission on Pornography, pp. 115–16.

1173. See, Investigative Report on Organized Crime and Pornography Submitted to the Attorney General of California; State of California, Department of Justice, Organized Crime in California (1984).

1174. See, The discussion of the production and distribution of sexually explicit materials for further information.

1175. See, The sections discussing social and behavioral science research, harms and victimization for a more complete explanation.

1176. New York Hearing, Vol. I, William Kelly, p. 76.

1177. See, United States v.   ✄   , 665 F.2d, (5th Cir. 1982), p. 616.

1178. New York Hearing, Vol. I, William Kelly, p. 75.

1179. Id.; Cong. Rec. S433 (daily ed. Jan. 30, 1984) (Statement of Sen. Jesse Helms).

1180. New York Hearing, Vol. I, Thomas Bohling, pp. 180–87; New York Hearing, William Johnson, Vol. II.

nocent woman, was murdered "gangland style".[1181]

Immediately prior to this Commission's hearing in Chicago, Illinois, in July, 1985, Patsy Ricciardi, owner of the Admiral Theater there, was found murdered. Chicago Police believe his murder was related to his dealings in the pornography business.[1182]

Physical Violence Damage to Property

The damage and injuries range from those sustained by performers[1183] forced to engage in physically harmful acts which can often result in permanent injury,[1184] to damage to property,[1185] "knee-breaking"[1186] and arson.[1187]

A veteran FBI agent told the Commission "Over the years there has been heavy violence associated with the pornography industry. Some of the current well-known names in the industry have reported threats against them or physical brutality."[1188]

A bookstore operator, associated with members of organized crime families, described the "discipline" within the pornography industry for those who choose to disobey rules regarding pricing, territory and other matters.[1189] He said, ". . . Bonjay a year and half ago, took one of the guys held him by his arms up against the wall in the alley, and it's common knowledge, the car ran into him, with the front bumper up against the wall and shattered his knees. That's a pretty good discipline.[1190] This same witness also reported bombs being thrown into stores that were not complying with general price agreements or

failed to pay a street tax to organized crime families.[1191]

Prostitution and Other Sexual Abuse

"Prostitution is the foundation upon which pornography is built. . . . Pornography cannot exist without prostitution. . . . It is impossible to separate pornography from prostitution. The acts are identical except in pornography there is a permanent record of the woman's abuse."[1192]

It is estimated that there are between 400,000 and 500,000 adult women who have been used in prostitution in America.[1193] A recent study found that the average age of the working prostitute was twenty-two; the average age a woman started working as prostitute was seventeen; sixty-three percent of the prostitutes had run away from home; eighty percent were victims of sexual abuse; eighty percent had pimps; and eighty-three percent had no savings or other financial resources.[1194] These women, who have been subject to every form of rape, sexual assault, and battery, and whose lives are totally controlled by their pimps, are used and abused by pornographers for the creation of their wares.[1195] It is impossible for most sexually explicit books, magazines, or films to be produced without acts of prostitution.[1196]

Michael Joseph ✂ , one of the two major pornography distributors in Chicago, and a lieutenant in the Accardo organized crime family, controlled a "strip joint" where numerous persons have been arrested for prostitution related offenses.[1197] Pornographer

---

1181. New York Hearing, Vol. I, Christopher J. Mega, p. 162.; Cong. Rec. S433 (daily ed. Jan. 30, 1984) (statement of Sen. Jesse Helms).

1182. New York Hearing, Vol. II, Thomas Bohling, pp. 182–83.

1183. See, Chapter 2 in this Part for a more complete discussion about performers.

1184. Los Angeles Hearing, Caryl and Brian ✂ , pp. 127–53; New York Hearing, Vol. I, Linda ✂ , p. 51; Washington, D.C., Hearing, Vol. I, Valerie ✂ , pp. 217–41; Washington, D.C., Hearing, Vol. II, Charles Sullivan, pp. 65–77; See also, The discussion of performers and harms attributable to their work.

1185. New York Hearing, Vol. I, Bookstore Operator, p. 152.

1186. Id., p. 141.

1187. New York Hearing, Vol. I, Thomas Bohling, p. 179.

1188. New York Hearing, Vol. I, William P. Kelly, p. 83.

1189. New York Hearing, Vol. I, Bookstore Operator, p. 131; The FBI reported such a territorial dispute in 1981 involving pornography stores in New England. The dispute arose between Joseph ✂ , an operative of New England LCN Boss Gennaro ✂ , and Carlo ✂ , who had been authorized by the New York LCN family to open a competing business in Worcester, Massachusetts. Letter to Attorney General's Commission on Pornography from Federal Bureau of Investigation, March 24, 1986.

1190. New York Hearing, Vol. I, Bookstore Operator, p. 131.

1191. Id.

1192. New York Hearing, Vol. IV, W.H.I.S.P.E.R. Statement, p. 398.

1193. Id.

1194. Id.

1195. Washington, D.C., Hearing, Vol. I, Sarah Wynter, pp. 175–84.

1196. See, Chapter 16 of this Part for a discussion of performers.

1197. New York Hearing, Vol. I, Thomas Bohling, p. 185.

Martin ✄ was identified by his former bodyguard as the one-time owner of a massage parlor and prostitution empire in the northeast.

Narcotics Distribution

Narcotics are often distributed to performers who appear in pornographic materials to lower their inhibitions and to create a dependency.[1198] Profits earned by organized crime from pornography sales have been used to finance drug smuggling.[1199]

Joseph ✄ , a soldier in the Columbo organized crime family, invested proceeds from the movie "Deep Throat" in drug smuggling. New York State Senator Christopher Mega, Chairman of the New York Organized Crime Commission, said, "Few have imagined that the profits of "Deep Throat" may have been part of the capital invested in the development of Norman's Cay into the major drug smuggling base north of the Panama Canal."[1200]

Local police also report that "narcotic transactions are present in these deteriorating neighborhoods (where "adult bookstores" locate) and go hand-in-hand with the rampant criminal activity in those areas."[1201]

Money Laundering and Tax Violations

The nature of the pornography business provides inviting opportunities for skimming on[1202] every level. There is often dishonesty among producers, wholesalers, distributors, retailers and others who attempt to cheat each other.[1203] The often "cash only" business creates immense opportunities to launder money received from other organized crime activity.

Bookstores which primarily sell sexually explicit material have a consistent sales format throughout the United States.[1204] Generally there are two separate operations for accounting purposes, loosely identified as "front room" and "back room" operations.[1205] The front room operation generally consists of a sales area for paperback books, magazines, rubber goods, lotions, stimulants and other materials.[1206] The front room operations profits are generally used to pay for rent, utilities, materials, and employee wages.[1207] The back room operations consist of peep machines which are coin operated and produce substantial income that is usually not reported as taxable income.[1208] A local police officer noted, "The back room operation usually takes in twice the amount as the frontroom operation."[1209] A bookstore operator and associate of known organized crime family members, reported to this Commission that such "skimming" commonly occurs with video cassette rentals and magazines as well as the peep machine coin boxes.[1210]

Organized crime associate Martin Hodas, who was convicted in federal court, Buffalo, New York, in 1985 for obscenity violations has been heavily involved in peep machines.[1211]

Michael Thevis, once a major distributor of pornography in the South, told a meeting of organized crime family members and associates that he owned ninety percent of the movie viewmatic machines in the United States. Michael was interrupted by Robert ✄ , a person alleged to be a member of the Gambino (and/or DeCalvalcante)[1212] organized crime family, who reminded him that

1198. An investigator reported to the Commission that child pornographers use cocaine to lure children, create an addiction and thus a lasting relationship of molestation and pornography production. Miami Hearing, Vol. II, Dennis Shaw, p. 107. Los Angeles Hearing, Vol. I, Chris, pp. 94–95; "I had been taking drugs throughout the time I was in prostitution and pornography. They had been supplied and doled out to me by my pimp." Washington, D.C., Hearing, Vol. I, Sarah ✄ , p. 185.

1199. New York Hearing, Vol. I, Christopher J. Mega, p. 167.

1200. Id.

1201. Los Angeles Hearing, Vol. I, James Docherty, p. 8.

1202. Skimming is the practice of fraudulently reporting income so as to avoid tax liability.

1203. New York Hearing, Vol. I, Bookstore Operator, pp. 146–51.

1204. See, The discussion of production and distribution of sexually explicit materials for a further explanation.

1205. New York Hearing, Vol. I, Bookstore Operator, pp. 146–51; New York Hearing, Vol. II, William Johnson, pp. 73–74.

1206. New York Hearing, Vol. II, William Johnson, pp. 73–74.

1207. Id.

1208. Id.

1209. Id., p. 73. See also, The discussion of the production and distribution of sexually explicit materials for more detailed description of bookstores.

1210. New York Hearing, Vol. I, Bookstore Operator, pp. 124–25.

1211. New York Hearing, Vol. I, Christopher J. Mega, p. 167.

1212. Several law enforcement agencies for years have identified Mr. ✄ as an associate of the de Cavalcante family of New Jersey. However, during the trial of ✄ and ✄ in the Miporn case in June of 1981, a New

though he might have "proprietary rights" the machines were owned by "the family."[1213]

The idea of converting run down theatres in the Midwest into pornographic adult movie houses to launder cash from other illegal rackets was the brain child of Chicago organized crime figure Patsy ✂ who was murdered in July, 1985.[1214]

Myron and Michael Wisotsky were convicted in the United States District Court for the Southern District of Florida in late 1985, for tax evasion which arose from skimming activities at their sexually oriented bookstores.[1215]

A bookstore operator told the Commission:

Subject: 80 percent of the skimming goes on in coin boxes.

Interviewer: Right, how does that happen?

Subject: Because who can tell how many customers come in today, and drop how many quarters, in how many machines. Alright?

Subject: I had a machine. I'm running a hundred stores. I'm doing $1,200 to $1,600 a day in quarters (per store). I'm doing maybe three hundred to five hundred dollars a day in cassette rentals, club memberships . . . if you pay $69.95 per year membership then you also charge $3.95 a day for the rental of each film, right, okay, I'm doing maybe $350 a day in magazines and pocketbook sales. And at the time maybe five or ten rolls or film a day comes to maybe one hundred of five hundred dollars. So we're talking three thousand dollars a day

roughly. Okay. Your magazines and your films and pocketbooks and your straightline pocketbooks. . . . It pays your rent, electric, gas, pays your overhead. If I don't something's happening wrong. Plus, now with the videos coming in, the video rentals go in your pocket too. It's another thing that gets bringing up. It's coming up all the time.

Subject: Alright, the guy who collects the machine is either a manager, or owner, or owner/manager or just somebody like I was in (city) in total control. They know I wouldn't steal they knew I didn't steal.

Subject: The only way you can catch me stealing, is if I got partners, and I'm going to keep those records till the 30th of the month, to the last day of each month. Because of the last day of each month I have been figuring on the coin boxes and the end figure on the coin boxes.[1216]

Copyright Violations

Organized crime elements involved in the production of videocassettes and movies have been known to infringe copyrights by the "pirating" of films produced by legitimate studios and the use of music or other parts of a legitimate enterprise without royalty agreements.[1217]

Fraud

Layers of corporations and hidden transactions of all descriptions are used by organized crime families involved in pornography to conceal true ownership and activities.[1218]

1213. New York Hearing, Vol. I, Homer Young, p. 34.

1214. New York Hearing, Vol. I, Thomas Bohling, p. 182.

1215. New York Hearing, Vol. II, Marcella Cohen, p. 32; United States v. Wisotsky, 83-741-Cr EBD (S.D.Fla.).

1216. New York Hearing, Vol. I, Bookstore Operator, pp. 144–45.

1217. "Arno said he had been previously somewhat reluctant to inform the agents that he was involved in the reproduction of pirated motion pictures as this was a violation of federal copyright statutes. Arno said that there were several problems connected with the production of these video tape cassettes, because there was a lot pressure from the FBI recently in this area and that several producers of pirated films had been busted in the recent past and were now working for the FBI." New York Hearing, Vol. II, Marcella Cohen, pp. 17, 38.

1218. See, The discussion in the Recommendations for Law Enforcement Agencies. "To effectively conceal the full extent of its involvement in the nation's pornography industry, organized crime has developed a maze of organization structures through complex legal maneuvering. Pornography businesses are often represented on corporate papers by persons with no apparent ties to the company's true owner. Business transactions are commonly conducted with hidden corporate affiliates which creates an appearance of legitimate competitive business practices. Foreign corporations and banks have been used to circumvent normal business accounting methods.

For protection purposes, pornographers frequently form several corporations for one operation. They know that law enforcement authorities, when serving search warrants as a result of possible obscenity violation, are restricted to search only the corporation named. The other corporations remain protected from police inspections." Investigative Report on Organized Crime and Pornography Submitted to the Attorney General of California, 5, 6(1978).

"Now, is it possible to be involved with both families?" "I don't know, but that's what the information is, that he is involved with both. It could be right and it might not be right. I don't know." New York Hearing, Vol. I, William P. Kelly, pp. 77–78.

York City FBI agent identified ✂ as a "soldier" of the Gambino family of the Mafia, based upon information provided to the FBI office in New York.

Other crimes associated with organized crime involvement in obscenity include child pornography,[1219] possession, transfer and sale of machine guns and silencers,[1220] and illegal gambling.[1221]

REUBEN ✂

Reuben ✂ , also known as Robert ✂ , Roy C. ✂ , Robert ✂ , Paul ✂ , and Paul ✂ , of ✂ , Ohio, ✂ ✂ , California, and elsewhere, is widely believed to be the largest distributor of pornography in the world.[1222] Law enforcement authorities believe that the ✂ empire has financial control of nearly two hundred businesses in nineteen states, one Canadian province and six foreign countries.[1223] ✂ ✂ is closely associated with known organized crime family members.

James ✂ described ✂ 's connection with Robert ✂ , a member of the LCN Gambino (and/or de Cavalcante) Family: ". . . if he has a problem he goes to ✂ .[1224] ✂ and ✂ have had a long term business relationship, ". . . they were partners, plus . . . if ✂ wanted [✂ ✂] to do something, he [✂] would do it."[1225]

More than twenty years ago ✂ was a small time candy, tobacco and comic book distributor who moved slowly into pornographic magazines.[1226] Avoiding any serious legal problems, he built the business into a mammoth operation encompassing all phases from production to retail sales with a myriad of corporate identities.

One account describes his organization as follows:

[✂] structured his many companies from retail stores to video production firms, in a honeycomb of nominees, false names and dead associates to avoid local obscenity prosecutions. [A 1985 tax case] reveals that the corporate structure has grown hydraheaded over the years, apparently with the more serious intent of avoiding taxes.[1227]

✂ 's influence on the pornography industry is so great because his enterprise produces a very wide range of items and distributes them to retailers through countless disguised channels.[1228] According to Los Angeles police, 580 of the 765 adult video arcade machines there are owned by companies controlled by ✂ .[1229] Police report that ✂ typically installs equipment worth $22,000 to $60,000 at no cost to the store owner.[1230] In exchange, he reaps fifty percent of the income from the peepshows.[1231] A store owner in San Diego, California, described ✂ 's hold on the industry there by saying, "People are afraid of him because of his power. He could just cut people off. You could just die out there. Paranoia sets in and I'm sure he uses it to his advantage."[1232]

Over the past few years, a number of ✂ ✂ associates and corporations have been convicted on obscenity charges and other violations of law.[1233] ✂ , himself however, has evaded any serious consequences for his acts.[1234]

An indictment returned by a federal grand jury in Cleveland in 1985 alleged ✂ conspired to evade millions of dollars in taxes by laundering seven million dollars through foreign bank accounts and also charges that he destroyed records subpoenaed by the grand jury.[1235] One of his co-defendants, Scott

---

1219. New York Hearing, Vol. II, Marcella Cohen, p. 38.
1220. Id.
1221. Pornographer Michael Joseph ✂ , member of ✂ family was reported to the United States Senate Rackets Committee as the number two man in a North Side Chicago numbers racket. New York Hearing, Vol. I, Thomas Bohling, p. 182.
1222. New York Hearing, Vol. I, Marilyn Sommers, p. 199; E. Whalen, *Prince of Porn*, Cleveland Magazine, (Aug. 1985), p. 143.
1223. New York Hearing, Vol. I, Marilyn Sommers, p. 200.
1224. New York Hearing, Vol. I, Interview with Jimmy ✂ , Edward Chapman, p. 115.
1225. Id.
1226. E. Whalen, *Prince of Porn*, Cleveland Magazine, (Aug. 1985), p. 82
1227. Id.
1228. *The Porn Peddlers*, San Diego Reader, Vol. 15, No. 10, Mar. 13, 1986, p. 17.
1229. Id.
1230. Id.
1231. Id.
1232. Id.
1233. See, *e.g.*, *United States v. Sovereign News Co.*, et. al, United States District Court, Western District of Kentucky.
1234. In 1980 ✂ was charged in the MIPORN investigation. The charges were ultimately dismissed. ✂ was also charged with a prior obscenity violation in Cleveland in 1976. He was acquitted.
1235. New York Testimony, Vol. I, Marilyn B. Sommers, pp. 1–15.

Dormen, pled guilty in late 1985 to his part in the conspiracy, admitting that he skimmed money from ✄ 's income and delivered at least $450,000 in cash, to ✄ that went unreported.[1236] When ✄ is the subject of prosecution,

> [he] professes indignity when legally attacked—as he always is—and fights back savagely. He also covers legal fees and fines of associates and gives them bonuses when they face the consequences of arrest.[1237]

Reuben ✄ controls ✄ ✄ (GVA), one of the largest distributors of sexually explicit video tape cassettes in the United States.[1238] GVA recently released and distributed a "White Paper" to video cassette retailers giving them notice of government action to prosecute obscenity violations. The "White Paper" also announced the creation of a legal defense fund for GVA and others involved in the distribution of such video cassettes. In addition, they offer a toll-free number for retailers to call an attorney provided by GVA to advise them on legal matters.[1239]

CONCLUSION
A local law enforcement officer told this Commission, "The industry is very difficult to investigate as a local police officer, as a business in one jurisdiction, in general, is incorporated in another jurisdiction, receives materials from another jurisdiction and is controlled by individuals in another jurisdiction. Federal law enforcement involvement is an absolute necessity to attack the real problem of organized crime influence."[1240] While no known additional organized crime families may live in a particular state, the effect of their production, distribution and sale of obscene material can be readily apparent. Another local law enforcement officer concluded, "Left unchecked, organized crime, in a traditional sense, can suck the lifeblood out of a community. Many times, their enterprises have been viewed as "service" oriented or victimless crimes. However, it tears at the moral fiber of society and through unbridled corruption, it can weaken the government."[1241]

The findings of the 1978 Federal Bureau of Investigation analysis remain essentially correct:

> In conclusion, organized crime involvement in pornography . . . is indeed significant, and there is an obvious national control directly, and indirectly by organized crime figures of that industry in the United States. Few pornographers can operate in the United States independently without some involvement with organized crime. Only through a *well coordinated all out national effort*, from the investigative and prosecutive forces can we ever hope to stem the tide of pornography. More importantly, the huge profits gathered by organized crime in this area and redirected to other lucrative forms of crime, such as narcotics and investment in legitimate business enterprises, are certainly cause for national concern, even if there is community apathy toward pornography.[1242]

1236. *Id.*

1237. E. Whalen, *Prince of Porn*, Cleveland, (Aug. 1985), p. 82.

1238. New York Hearing, Vol. I, Marilyn Sommers, p. 209.

1239. The "White Paper" fails to disclose that some of the video cassettes sold by GVA have been found to be obscene by state and federal courts and that individuals and corporations have been convicted of felonies for their distribution. See, New York Hearing, Vol. II, William Johnson, p. 79.

1240. New York Hearing, Vol. I, Carl Shoffler, pp. 217–18.

1241. New York Hearing, Vol. II, William Johnson, p. 82A–10.

1242. *Federal Bureau of Investigation Report Regarding the Extent of Organized Crime Involvement in Pornography.* (1978).

1243. ✄

1244. ✄

1245. ✄

APPENDIXES TO ORGANIZED CRIME SECTION

PUBLISHER'S NOTE

In the *Final Report of the Attorney General's Commission on Pornography* as printed by the U.S. Government Printing Office, the chapter on Organized Crime was thirty-two pages in length. There also were five appendixes to that chapter totalling 166 pages. In this edition of the Report, we have retained the complete chapter written by the Pornography Commission, but we are merely summarizing the content of the Appendixes. We have done this on the advice of legal counsel. The Bibliography at the Report's conclusion will direct interested readers to the relevant testimony for each of these appendixes.

The first appendix reported on the famous Miami Pornography (MIPORN) investigation which has resulted in forty-five indictments (a third of all federal indictments for violations of federal obscenity law since 1978) and 14 convictions. MIPORN was based on a two-year undercover investigation by the FBI, and testimony to the Commission was given by Marcella Cohen, a Special Attorney in the Criminal Division of the U.S. Department of Justice, who has worked on the case for seven years. Because of the ongoing nature of legal cases growing out of MIPORN and the possibility that at least some of the individuals named in the Report will not stand trial, we have been advised not to print this appendix. We would, however, encourage those wishing to pursue this matter more closely to read the testimony of Ms. Cohen.

The second Appendix reported on the efforts of the Middle Atlantic—Great Lakes Organized Crime Law Enforcement Network (MAGLOCLEN). Marilyn B. Somers, an official of MAGOCLEN, provided testimony of the extraordinary underworld empire of an individual who is allegedly the nation's largest pornographer with a network of 200 companies. He was indicted in 1985 for tax evasion by failing to report his income adequately.

The third Appendix on organized crime in California was very short and is, in fact, quoted in full in the Organized Crime chapter.

The fourth Appendix, which ran ninety-five pages, was prepared by the Metropolitan Washington D.C. Police Department in 1978 to "depict the national distribution flow of pornographic material, the major distributors . . . and the corporate organizational profiles of these major distributors." Much of this appendix is repeated in the other appendixes, or is now out-of-date. This document also provided a summary of the history of obscenity law for Washington police, material more thoroughly presented elsewhere in the Report.

The fifth Appendix is a 1977 report by the Department of Justice on Organized Crime in Pornography. Again, much of this material is dated or repetitive of what can be found elsewhere in this volume.

It is important to note that the distributors mentioned in these appendixes exist for the sole purpose of distributing hard-core sexually explicit pornography. Generally speaking, they are not the people who distribute paperback books and magazines to bookstores and newsstands across the nation. One publisher of explicit materials is quoted in the fifth Appendix as saying in an interview with the *New York Times*, "No legitimate distributor will touch us." In reading the Final Report it is important to keep this distinction in mind.

Regulation of Pornography: An Historical Perspective

Historical discussions with respect to pornography are generally found under two separate topics: one is based in moral doctrines and the other has developed through the legal system. Each of these historical developments will be discussed separately insofar as the concepts are unique and such discussion is warranted.

The legal perspective surrounding pornography has historically taken the form of criminal obscenity laws. The origins of obscenity law can be traced back to the religious doctrines of ancient civilization.[1246] Blasphemy, heresy, and impiety were the basis of charges brought against prominent individuals in Greece during the reign of Pericles.[1247] Plato spoke in favor of restricting writings that told untruths about the gods.[1249] Religious restrictions grew as Christianity became more entrenched, and led to the promulgation of the Index Liborum Prohibitorum by Pope Paul IV.[1250] Works which were prohibited were done so on religious grounds rather than on the basis of any sexual content.[1251]

The development of modern obscenity law as it is recognized in the United States began in England.[1252] The court of Star Chamber reviewed books and theater during the reign of King Henry VIII and continued until 1640.[1253] Restrictions placed on materials were still based largely on religious and political grounds. The focus began to change in 1663 when the British courts were confronted with the situation which arose as the case of King v. Sedley.[1254] This case is widely regarded as the first reported obscenity case. Sir Charles Sedley, in an intoxicated state, stood on a tavern balcony, removed his clothes, and delivered a series of profane remarks. At the conclusion of his tirade, he poured bottles filled with urine on the crowd below. Sedley was convicted, fined, and incarcerated for a week. Sedley's case was thus the first involving an offense to public decency as opposed to one against religion or government.[1255] One hundred and fifty years later, it would also be relied on as precedent by the first American court to find obscenity indictable at common law.[1256]

Public concern over obscenity increased in 17th century England, and in 1708 James Read was indicted for publishing the book The Fifteen Plagues of a Maidenhead.[1257] The

---

1246. See, 2 Technical Report of the Commission on Obscenity and Pornography, (1970), p. 65, (hereinafter cited as Technical Report).
1247. Id.
1248. ✄ Duplicate text and Footnote deleted.
1249. Id.
1250. Id., p. 66.
1251. L. Tribe, American Constitutional Law, (1978), p. 657, [herinafter cited as Tribe].
1252. Id.
1253. Id.
1254. 1 Keble 620 (K.B.), 83 Eng. Rep. (1663), p. 1146, and 1 Sd. 168, 82 Eng. Rep., (1663), p. 1063.
1255. Id.
1256. See, Commonwealth v. Sharpless, 2 Serg. & Rawle, (1815), p. 91.
1257. 11 Mod. Rep. 142, 88 Eng. Rep., (1708), p. 953, and Fotescu's Reports 98, 91 Eng. Rep., (1708), p. 777.

Queens Bench Court dismissed the indictment against Read for obscene libel in *Queen v. Read*.[1258] The court found that Read's work was not a reflection on the government, the church, or any individual, and it rejected the idea that libel included obscenity.[1259] Another case of obscene libel arose in 1727 when Edmund Curll was convicted for publishing *Venus in the Cloister or the Nun in Her Smock*. In *Dominus Rex v. Curll*,[1260] the court rejected the doctrine of *Read* and relied instead on *Sedley's Case*. The court found corruption of morals to be an offense at common law and thereby established obscenity as a crime.[1261]

The crime of obscene libel took root in 19th century England, and was accompanied by the rise of the Society for the Suppression of Vice in 1802.[1262] The Society crusaded against obscene publications, and their work culminated in the passage of two important pieces of legislation. The Vagrancy Act of 1824 made publication of indecent pictures a forbidden act and Lord Campbell's Act of 1857 gave magistrates authority to issue search warrants for obscene material and have it destroyed.[1263] Since the printing of photographs was not prevalent until the late 1800s, the challenged works consisted mainly of writings, sketches, or line drawings.[1264]

The offense of obscene libel was still devoid of any precise definition of what material would be considered obscene. The initial definition was presented in *Regina v. Hicklin*.[1265] The case involved an anti-religious pamphlet called "The Confessional Unmasked," which detailed the sexual nature of questions posed by Catholic priests during confessions. The trial magistrate, Hicklin, ordered the publication destroyed because of references to intercourse and fellatio.[1266] On appeal, the Quarter Sessions Court reversed Hicklin on the grounds that the publisher's motive was an innocent one despite the obscene content of the writing.[1267]

On final appeal, the Queens Bench affirmed Hicklin's initial order and Chief Justice Cockburn fashioned the resulting obscenity standard. Cockburn held that the author's intent was irrelevant as long as the work was obscene.[1268] The work was obscene if it tended to deprave and corrupt minds which are open to such immoral influences and into whose hands the publication may fall.[1269] The determination was based on the impact of certain parts of the writing on susceptible individuals.[1270] The *Hicklin* test remained in force in England for 100 years.[1271] The decision in *Hicklin* also had an effect on American obscenity law.[1272]

American laws concerning pornography also found their origin in sacrilegious works. In 1711, the colony of Massachusetts enacted a statute stating that "evil communication, wicked, profane, impure, filthy, and obscene songs, composures, writings, or prints do corrupt the mind and are incentives to all manner of impieties and debaucheries, more especially when digested, composed or uttered in imitation or in mimicking of preaching or any other part of divine worship."[1273] The law prohibited the "composing, writing, printing, or publishing of any filthy, obscene or profane story, pamphlets, libel or mock sermon, in imitation of preaching or any other part of divine worship."[1274] Despite this enactment, there were no reported obscenity prosecutions until 1815 and the Pennsylvania case of *Commonwealth v. Sharpless*.[1275] Sharpless was charged with showing a drawing depicting a man and woman in a lewd posture.[1276]

1258. *Id.*
1259. *Id.*
1260. 2 Str. 789, 93 Eng. Rep., (1727), p. 849.
1261. *Id.*
1262. *Id.*, p. 72.
1263. *Id.*
1264. Bland, *A History of Book Illustrations*, (1958), p. 272.
1265. L.R. 3 Q.B., (1868), p. 360.
1266. *Id.*
1267. *Id.*
1268. *Id.*
1269. *Id.*
1270. *Id.*
1271. *Technical Report, supra* note 1246, p. 73.
1272. L. Tribe, *supra* note 1250, p. 658.
1273. Ancient Charter, Colony Laws and Province Laws of Massachusetts Bay (1814).
1274. *Id.*
1275. 2 Serg. & Rawle (1815), p. 91.
1276. *Id.*

Like his British counterparts in *Read* and *Curll*, Sharpless contended that there was no statute prohibiting his conduct. The Pennsylvania court relied on *Sedley's Case* and found crimes against public decency to be indictable at common law.[1277]

The first case involving a book alleged to be obscene arose in Massachusetts six years later.[1278] Peter Holmes was charged with publishing a lewd illustration along with the book *Memories of a Woman of Pleasure.*[1279] Relying on both the common law offense and the Massachusetts statute, the Supreme Judicial Court of Massachusetts convicted Holmes.[1280] While the American courts now recognized the common law crime of obscenity, much of the activity which followed was found in the legislative arena. In 1821, Vermont passed the first obscenity statute in the United States. The statute prohibited the printing, publishing, or vending of any lewd or obscene book, picture, or print.[1281] Massachusetts enlarged its colonial statute[1282] and other states soon followed.[1283]

The first federal law concerning obscene materials was enacted in 1842. The focus of the act was to regulate materials imported into the United States.[1284] It prohibited "all indecent and obscene prints, paintings, lithographs, engravings and transparencies."[1285]

The lax enforcement of these statutes after their enactment led citizens and religious groups to take action. Anthony Comstock, a store clerk in New York, took it upon himself to lead the crusade. Comstock and others formed the Committee for the Suppression of Vice and lobbied the Congress to pass tougher obscenity legislation. In 1873, Congress enacted a law governing the mailing of obscene matter.[1286] The Act stated in part that,

> . . . no obscene, lewd, or lascivious book, pamphlet, picture, paper, print, or other publication of an indecent character, or any article or thing designed or intended for the prevention of conception or procuring of abortion, nor any article or thing intended or adapted for any indecent or immoral use or nature, nor any written or printed card, circular, book, pamphlet, advertisement or notice of any kind giving information, directly or indirectly, where, or how, or of whom, or by what means either of the things before mentioned may be obtained or made, nor any letter upon the envelope of which, or postal-card upon which indecent or scurrilous epithets may be written or printed, shall be carried in the mail, and any person who shall knowingly deposit, or cause to be deposited, for mailing or delivery, any of the hereinbefore-mentioned articles or things, or any notice, or paper containing any advertisement relating to the aforesaid articles or things, and any person who, in pursuance of any plan or scheme for disposing of any of the herinafter-mentioned articles or things, shall take, or cause to be taken, from the mail any such letter or package, shall be deemed guilty of a misdemeanor, and, on conviction thereof, shall, for every offense, be fined not less than five thousand dollars, or imprisoned at hard labor not less than one year nor more than ten years, or both, in the discretion of the judge.[1287]

Comstock himself became a federal agent and worked to confiscate prohibited material from the mails. In the year immediately following the enactment of what became known as the Comstock Act, Anthony Comstock claimed to have seized hundreds of thousands of obscene items.[1288] Litigation involving the Comstock Act centered primarily on procedural issues and the authority of Congress to regulate matters as were enumerated in the statute.[1289]

As cases began to arise under the obscenity statutes the question of what items constituted obscene materials was addressed using the English precedent of *Regina v. Hicklin.* In *United States v. Bennett,* [1290] the Court held that a determination of obscenity based on a

---

1277. *Id.*
1278. *Commonwealth v. Holmes,* 17 Mass., (1821), p. 336.
1279. *Id.*
1280. *Id.*
1281. Laws of Vermont, 1824, Ch. XXIII, no. 1, S23.
1282. *Technical Report, supra* note 1246, pp. 74–75.
1283. Mass. Rev. Stat. Chr. 310 S10.
1284. See, L. Tribe, *supra* note 1250, p. 658.
1285. 5 Stat. 556 S28.
1286. *Technical Report, supra* note 1246, p. 77.
1287. 17 Stat. 588, 18 U.S.C. S1461 (1985).
1288. *Technical Report, supra* note 1246, p. 78.
1289. *Id.*
1290. 24 F. Cas. 1093 (C.C.S.D.N.Y. 1879).

portion or excerpt of a work was valid and that its effect would be measured in terms of whether it would corrupt those who might come into contact with it.[1291] In applying *Hicklin*, the American courts reached varying results as to what materials were obscene under the test.[1292]

It was not until the twentieth century that the *Hicklin* rule began to wane. Judge Learned Hand criticized the *Hicklin* test in *United States v. Kennedy*.[1293] He questioned whether the treatment of sexual topics should be reduced to the standard found in a child's library.[1294] He also fashioned a test for implementing community standards, holding that obscenity must be determined in accordance with the present balance between candor and shame at which the community may have arrived here and now.[1295] Twenty years later in *United States v. One Book Entitled Ulysses*,[1296] Judge Augustus Hand rejected *Hicklin* and ruled that excerpts of a work could no longer be used to determine obscenity.[1297] The court noted that the determination of obscenity must be based on an examination of the dominant effect of the material in question.[1298]

The *Hicklin* standard in any form had less than ten years to live when, in 1949, a Pennsylvania state court held that a finding of obscenity must be based on the work's erotic allurement of the *average* reader.[1299]

During the first half of the twentieth century, serious literary efforts were the subjects of obscenity prosecutions. *Ulysses* by James Joyce was one such work, although it was not found to be obscene.[1300] Another was *An*

American Tragedy by Theodore Dreiser. The Supreme Judicial Court of Massachusetts found it to be obscene in 1930.[1301] *Tropic of Cancer* and *Tropic of Capricorn*, by Henry Miller were both found to be obscene.[1302] The United States District Court heard evidence including eighteen published reviews of Henry Miller's works, fifteen letters, and two affidavits of critics, all attesting to the literary merit of the two books.[1303] The court rejected this evidence as "immaterial,"[1304] and held that portions of the books rendered both obscene.[1305] A claimant on behalf of *Tropic of Capricorn* had contended that the portions of the book containing sexual episodes and vernacular expletives with sexual references constituted only thirteen per cent of the total number of pages in the book.[1306] The District Court compared this argument to "the excuse of Midshipman Easy's servant girl that her illegitimate child was such a little one!"[1307] The United States Court of Appeals affirmed, and described Miller's works as practically everything that the world loosely regards as sin is detailed in the vivid, lurid, salacious language of smut, prostitution, and dirt."[1308]

The Appeals Court reasoned that obscenity, though a part of a composition of high literary merit, is not excepted from operation of the statute."[1309]

The Court rejected the evidence of the book's literary merit presented below, which it called "opinions of authors who resent any limitations on their writings."[1310] Erskine Caldwell's *God's Little Acre* was found to be obscene by the Massachusetts Supreme Judicial Court,[1311] which described the work as

---

1291. *Id.*
1292. L. Tribe, *supra* note 1250, p. 658.
1293. 209 F., (S.D.N.Y. 1913), p. 119.
1294. *Id.*
1295. *Id.*
1296. 72 F.2d, (2nd Cir. 1934), p. 705.
1297. *Id.*
1298. *Id.*
1299. *Commonwealth v. Gordon*, 66 Pa. D. & C., (Phila. 1949), p. 101.
1300. *United States v. One Book Called "Ulysses,"* 5 F. Supp. 182 (S.D.N.Y. 1933), aff'd. in. 72 f.2d 705 (2d Cir. 1934).
1301. *Commonwealth v. Friede*, 271 Mass. 318, 171 N.E., (1930), p. 472.
1302. *United States v. Two Obscene Books*, 99 F. Supp. 760 (N.D. Cal. 1951), aff'd. sub nom, *Besig v. U.S.*, 208 F.2d 142 (9th Cir. 1953).
1303. 99 F. Supp., p. 761.
1304. *Id.*
1305. *Id.*, p. 763.
1306. *Id.*
1307. *Id.*
1308. 208 F.2d, p. 145.
1309. *Id.*
1310. *Id.*, p. 147.
1311. *Attorney General v. Book Named "God's Little Acre"*, 326 Mass. 281, 93 N.E. 2d, (1950), p. 819.

abounding in sexual episodes, some of which were portrayed with an abundance of realistic detail.[1312] The trial court heard testimony from literary critics, professors of English literature, and a professor of sociology regarding the literary, cultural, and educational character of the book.[1313] From a sociological perspective, the book was defended as a portrait of poor whites in the old south.[1314] The Massachusetts high court found the book obscene despite this evidence and concluded that "art can flourish without pornography."[1315] In an obscenity prosecution against The Well of Loneliness, by Radclyffe Hall, the prosecution conceded that the book was a "well written, carefully constructed piece of fiction with no unclean words."[1316] It was praised by men of letters, critics, and artists, according to the court.[1317] The New York Magistrate's Court still found that the book's tales of lesbian love affairs tended to "justify the right of a pervert to prey on normal people."[1318] In finding the book obscene, the court stated under the Hicklin standard:

> It pleads for tolerance on the part of society of those possessed of and inflicted with perverted traits and tendencies, but it does not argue for repression or modification of insidious impulses.[1319]

In 1957, the United States Supreme Court struck another blow against Hicklin and began its formulation of a modern obscenity standard. In Butler v. Michigan,[1320] the Court reversed a conviction for a violation of Section 343 of the Michigan Penal Code that prohibited distribution of any material "containing obscene, immoral, lewd, or lascivious language . . . pictures . . . or descriptions tending

to incite minors to violent or depraved or immoral acts, manifestly tending to the corruption of the morals of youth."[1321] Speaking for a unanimous Court, Justice Frankfurter ruled that the statute was overbroad and violative of the Due Process clause of the Fourteenth Amendment of the Constitution.[1322] He stated, "We have before us legislation not reasonably restricted to the evil with which it is said to deal. The incidence of this enactment is to reduce the adult population of Michigan to reading only what is fit for children."[1323]

Butler was significant not only for its specific holding, but it also marked the end of the Hicklin standard. Material was no longer to be determined obscene by measuring the material's effect on susceptible individuals. It also foreshadowed the Supreme Court's landmark pronouncement in Roth v. United States[1324] in 1957.

In Roth v. United States,[1325] the Supreme Court defined the scope of the First Amendment in the context of an obscenity case. Roth had been convicted of mailing obscene circulars and an obscene book in violation of federal law.[1326] Speaking for the Court, Justice Brennan upheld the conviction and found the protection of free speech under the First Amendment was not absolute.[1327] He stated that the First Amendment was not intended to protect every utterance and cited libel, profanity, and blasphemy as examples of unprotected speech. The Court relied on Chaplinsky v. New Hampshire[1328] which had excluded "the lewd and obscene [and] the profane" from the category of protected speech.[1329] Thus obscenity was held to be without First Amendment protection.[1330] Brennan went on to fashion a definition of obscenity, holding that "obscene material is ma-

---

1312. 93 N.E.2d., p. 821.
1313. Id.
1314. Id.
1315. Id.
1316. People v. Friede, 233 N.Y.S., (1929), pp. 565, 567.
1317. Id., p. 569.
1318. Id.
1319. Id.
1320. 352 U.S., (1957), p. 380.
1321. Id., p. 381.
1322. Id., [Reference does not appear in manuscript]
1323. Id., p. 383.
1324. 354 U.S., (1957), p. 476.
1325. Id.
1326. 18 U.S.C. S1461.
1327. 354 U.S., (1957), p. 476.
1328. 315 U.S., (1942), p. 568.
1329. 354 U.S. at 485, quoting Chaplinksy v. New Hampshire, 315 U.S. 268, pp. 511–72.
1330. Id.

terial which deals with sex in a manner appealing to prurient interests."[1331] The *Hicklin* standard was rejected by the Court, with Justice Brennan stating, "The *Hicklin* test, judging obscenity by the effect of isolated passages upon the most susceptible persons, might well encompass material legitimately dealing with sex, and so it must be rejected as unconstitutionally restrictive of the freedoms of speech and press."[1332]

The Supreme Court adopted a test which recognized material as obscene if "to the average person, applying contemporary community standards, the dominant theme of the material taken as a whole appeals to prurient interest,"[1333] For the first time, the Supreme Court had defined obscenity and found it to be without First Amendment protection.

In 1966, the Supreme Court had occasion to reexamine its definition of obscenity in *Memoirs v. Massachusetts*.[1334] The case involved a state court determination that John Cleland's book *Memories of a Woman of Pleasure* was obscene.[1335] Writing for a sharply divided court, Justice Brennan stated that three elements must coalesce in order for a book to be found obscene:

1. the dominant theme of the material taken as a whole appeals to a prurient interest in sex.
2. the material is patently offensive because it affronts contemporary community standards relating to the description or representation of sexual matters.
3. and the material is utterly without redeeming social value.[1336]

In reversing the state court decision, Brennan found that the court had misinterpreted the "social value" part of the obscenity standard.[1337] He said the Massachusetts court "erred in holding that a book need not be worthless before it can be deemed obscene. A book cannot be proscribed unless it is found to be *utterly* without redeeming social value."[1338] Since the Massachusetts court had found that the book possessed a "modicum" of social value, it was therefore not obscene.[1339] The standard enumerated in *Memoirs* reached only what might be referred to as "hard-core" pornography and led to a period of minimal regulation of obscenity during the years leading up to *Miller v. California*.[1340]

By the time *Miller v. California*[1341] reached the Supreme Court in 1973, the composition of the tribunal had changed significantly. Since the *Memoirs* decision in 1966, Warren Burger had become Chief Justice and Justices Black, Fortas, and Harlan had been replaced by Blackmun, Powell, and Rehnquist. *Miller* resulted in the first majority opinion from the Supreme Court on the issue of obscenity since *Roth* in 1957.

Miller had been convicted under the California obscenity statute for mailing unsolicited, illustrated advertisements for "adult" books.[1342] At the outset of his opinion upholding Miller's conviction, Chief Justice Burger said the Court would undertake to formulate more concrete standards for determining obscenity.[1343] Burger pointed out that the standard in *Memoirs v. Massachusetts* was a mere plurality opinion of three Justices, and veered sharply from the test set forth in *Roth*.[1344] He rejected the "utterly without redeeming social value" portion of the *Memoirs* test as requiring proof of a negative, which is "a burden virtually impossible to discharge under our criminal standards of proof."[1345] This pronouncement marked a major change from prior obscenity cases. Burger noted the *Memoirs* test now failed to command the support of a single member of the Court.[1346] The standard the Court announced in *Miller* would

1331. *Id.*, p. 487.
1332. *Id.*, p. 489.
1333. *Id.*
1334. 383 U.S., (1965), p. 413.
1335. *Id.*
1336. *Id.*, p. 418.
1337. *Id.*, p. 419.
1338. *Id.*
1339. *Id.*, pp. 419–20.
1340. 413 U.S., (1973), p. 15.
1341. *Id.*
1342. 413 U.S. 15, (1973), p. 16.
1343. *Id.*, pp. 19–20.
1344. *Id.*, p. 21.
1345. *Id.*, pp. 24–25.
1346. *Id.*, p. 25.

confine the scope of regulation to works that depict or describe sexual conduct. Further, the sexual conduct must be specifically defined by state law.[1347] The three part standard announced in *Miller* requires an examination of,

(a) whether "the average person, applying contemporary community standards" would find that the work, taken as a whole, appeals to the prurient interest, *Kois v. Wisconsin*, *supra*, at 230, quoting *Roth v. United States*, *supra* at 489; (b) whether the work depicts or describes, in a patently offensive way, sexual conduct specifically defined by the applicable state law; and (c) whether the work, taken as a whole, lacks serious literary, artistic, political, or scientific value.[1348]

The Court also gave an example of the types of sexual conduct that state statutes could define for regulation under part two of the standard. The Court noted that prohibited conduct may involve,

a. Patently offensive representations or descriptions of ultimate sexual acts, normal or perverted, actual or simulated.

b. Patently offensive representations or descriptions of masturbation, excretory functions, and lewd exhibition of the genitals.[1349]

Significantly, the Court's opinion in *Miller* also addressed the issue of "contemporary community standards" and found a national standard to be an "exercise in futility."[1350] Burger reasoned that a question of fact is involved in the application of community standards and that "our nation is simply too big and too diverse for this court to reasonably expect that such standards could be articulated for all fifty states. . . ."

A local rather than a national community standard would govern the determinations of "prurient interest" and "patent offensiveness."

The Chief Justice chided the dissenters in *Miller* who favored what he referred to as an "absolutist, anything goes view of the First Amendment because it will lighten our burdens." As to the scope of First Amendment protection, the Court added that "To equate the free and robust exchange of ideas and political debate with commercial exploitation of obscene material demeans the grand conception of the First Amendment and its high purposes in the historic struggle for freedom."[1351]

In a case decided the same day as *Miller*, the Supreme Court rejected the argument that obscene films are constitutionally immune from state regulation simply because they are exhibited to consenting adults only.[1352] However, the mere private possession of obscene matter cannot be proscribed.[1353] The court previously held in *Stanley v. Georgia*[1354] that the Constitution protects the right to receive information and ideas and to be generally free from government intrusion into one's privacy.[1355] The Supreme Court's decision in *Smith v. United States*[1356] clarified that the determination of serious literary, artistic, political, or scientific value is made with reference to a national and not a local standard.[1357] In *Smith*, the court found that only the questions of "prurient interest" and "patent offensiveness" are subject to local community standards under *Miller*.[1358]

In *Jenkins v. Georgia*,[1359] the Supreme Court held that juries do not have "unbridled discretion" in determining questions of "prurient interest" and "patent offensiveness" according to local community standards.[1360] Such determinations are subject to constitutional review.

The concept of pornography as a civil rights violation came to the forefront in 1984 when the city of Indianapolis, Indiana, enacted an ordinance "to prevent and prohibit

---

1347. *Id.*
1348. *Id.*, p. 24.
1349. *Id.*, p. 25.
1350. *Id.*, p. 30.
1351. *Id.*, p. 34.
1352. *Paris Adult Theater I v. Slaton*, 413 U.S., (1973), p. 49.
1353. 294 U.S., (1969), p. 55733.
1354. *Id.*
1355. *Id.*
1356. 431 U.S., (1977), p. 291.
1357. *Id.*, p. 301.
1358. *Id.*
1359. 418 U.S., (1974), p. 153.
1360. *Id.*, p. 160.

all discriminatory practices of sexual subordination or inequality through pornography."[1361] The Indianapolis ordinance defined pornography as "the graphic sexually explicit subordination of women, whether in pictures or in words"[1362] and created a civil remedy for individuals aggrieved by discriminatory practices prohibited by the ordinance.[1363] These practices included trafficking in pornography, coercing a person into a pornographic performance.[1364]

The ordinance was promptly challenged and held unconstitutional in *American Booksellers Assn. v. Hudnut*.[1365] The District Court found that the ordinance regulated speech that was entitled to First Amendment protection.[1366] The court then focused on the issue of whether "the state's interest in protecting women from the humiliation and degradation which came from being depicted in a sexually subordinate context is so compelling as to warrant the regulation of otherwise free speech to accomplish that end."[1367] The court concluded that it was not and reasoned that women are capable of protecting themselves from being harmed by pornography.[1368] The court held that to "deny free speech in order to engineer social change in the name of accomplishing a greater good for one sector of our society erodes the freedoms of all . . . ."[1369]

The United States Court of Appeals for the Seventh Circuit affirmed the District Court's decision.[1370] The Court of Appeals accepted the premise of the ordinance that pornography is a systematic practice of exploitation and subordination based on sex which differentially harms women.[1371] The Court also said in dicta that,

> The Section creating remedies for injuries and assaults attributable to pornography . . . is salvageable in principle, although not by us.[1372]

But the definition of pornography contained in the ordinance was its fatal flaw. The court held,

> The ordinance discriminates on the ground of the content of the speech. Speech treating women in the approved way in sexual encounters "premised on equality" is lawful no matter how sexually explicit. Speech treating women in the disapproved way as submissive in matters sexual or as enjoying humiliation is unlawful no matter how significant the literary, artistic, or political qualities of the work taken as a whole. The state may not ordain preferred viewpoints in this way. The Constitution forbids the state to declare one perspective right and silence opponents.[1373]

The city of Indianapolis appealed to the United States Supreme Court, and on February 24, 1986, the Court summarily affirmed the judgment of the Court of Appeals.[1374]

1361. Indianapolis & Marion County, Ind. Ordinance 24 (May 3, 1984), *amended by* Indianapolis & Marion County, Ind. Ordinance 35 (June 15, 1984), at S16–1 (b) (8). The city Council in Minneapolis, Minnesota, passed a similar ordinance that was vetoed by the mayor.
1362. *Id.* S16–3(9).
1363. *Id.* S16–17.
1364. *Id.* S16–3 (g) (4)–(7).
1365. 598 F. Supp. (S.D. Ind. 1984).
1366. *Id.*, pp. 1331–31.
1367. *Id.*, p. 1335.
1368. *Id.*, pp. 1333–34.
1369. *Id.*, p. 1337.
1370. *American Booksellers Ass'n v. Hudnut*, 771 F.2d 323(7th Cir. 1985).
1371. *Id.*, p. 329.
1372. *Id.*, p. 333.
1373. *Id.*, p. 325.
1374. *Hudnut v. American Booksellers Ass'n* No. 85–1090 Slip op. Feb. 24, 1986.

CHAPTER • 21

First Amendment Considerations

The First Amendment to the United States Constitution mandates that,

Congress shall make no law respecting an establishment of religion, or prohibiting the free exercise thereof; or abridging the freedom of speech, or of the press; or the right of the people peaceably to assemble, and to petition the Government for a redress of grievances.[1375]

Sharp differences exist among legal scholars as to the meaning and scope of the First Amendment. The opinions of Supreme Court Justice William O. Douglas forcefully developed the view that the First Amendment makes the right to free speech absolute. Douglas and other like-minded theorists take the words "Congress shall make no law" at their literal meaning.

In his dissenting opinion in *Roth v. United States*,[1376] Douglas wrote,

The First Amendment, its prohibition in terms absolute, was designed to preclude courts as well as legislatures from weighing the values of speech against silence. The First Amendment puts free speech in the preferred position.[1377]

Thus, in Douglas' view, the courts and legislatures were prohibited from abridging any form of expression, including the most sexually explicit material. In *Roth*, he quoted prominent First Amendment theorists and wrote,

The danger of influencing change in the current moral standards of the community, or of shocking or offending readers, or of stimulating sexual thoughts or desires apart from objective conduct, can never justify the losses to society that result from interferences with literary freedom.[1378]

Justice Douglas concluded that,

. . . if the First Amendment guarantee of Freedom of speech and press is to mean anything in this field, it must allow protests even against the moral code that the standard of the day sets for the community.[1379]

In *Miller v. California*,[1380] Douglas expounded on his theory of broad First Amendment protection. He wrote,

The idea that the First Amendment permits government to ban publications that are "offensive" to some people puts an ominous gloss on freedom of the press. That test would make it possible to ban any paper or any journal or magazine in some benighted place. The First Amendment was designed "to invite dispute," to induce "a condition of unrest," to "create dissatisfaction with conditions as they are," and even to stir "people to anger." *Terminiello v. Chicago*, 337 U.S. 1, 4. The idea that the First Amendment permits punishment for ideas that are "offensive" to the particular judge or jury sitting in judgment is astounding. No greater leveler of speech or literature has been designed. To give the power to the

---

1375. U.S. Const. amend. I.
1376. 345 U.S., (1957), p. 476.
1377. *Id.*, p. 514.
1378. *Id.* pp. 509–10, citing Lockhart and McClure, *Literature, the Law of Obscenity, and the Constitution*, 38 Minn. L. Rev., (1954), pp. 295, 387.
1379. *Id.*, p. 513.
1380. 413 U.S., (1973), p. 15.

censor, as we do today, is to make a sharp and radical break with the traditions of a free society. The First Amendment was not fashioned as a vehicle for dispensing tranquilizers to the people. Its prime function was to keep debate open to "offensive" as well as to "staid" people. The tendency throughout history has been to subdue the individual and to exalt the power of government. The use of the standard "offensive" gives authority to government that cuts the very vitals out of the First Amendment. As is intimated by the Court's opinion, the materials before us may be garbage. But so is much of what is said in political campaigns, in the daily press, on TV, or over the radio. By reason of the First Amendment (and solely because of it) speakers and publishers have not been threatened or subdued because their thoughts and ideas may be "offensive" to some.[1381]

The view that the First Amendment provides absolute protection to sexually explicit materials continues to be espoused by strong and vocal advocates. They contend that unfettered freedom of expression will enable the best and most truthful points of view to prevail in society.[1382] The First Amendment's protection of speech reaches beyond well reasoned discourse. It includes appeals to the human spirit and feelings. One proponent has said "sexually explicit material is usually communication that the activity depicted is pleasurable and appropriate. Frankly, it asserts that it is good and healthy for persons in many places and many positions. Obviously this is a doctrine over which there ought to be profound moral debate."[1383]

Sexually explicit materials depicting children should also be protected speech in the view of many First Amendment absolutists. While they condemn child abuse, some proponents of absolutist First Amendment theory argue that prohibiting expression in the form of child pornography as the Supreme Court did in New York v. Ferber[1384] also does nothing to stop the underlying crimes committed against the children.[1385] Some First Amendment absolutists have adhered so rig-

orously to this principle that they would oppose restrictions on sexually explicit materials even if proof was available to show that the materials promoted sexual violence.[1386] Robert H. Bork, now a judge of the United States Court of Columbia Circuit, has criticized what he calls "the insistence of many very intelligent people that the First Amendment is an absolute."[1387] He writes that,

devotees of this position insist, with a literal respect they do not accord other parts of the Constitution, that the Framers commanded complete freedom of expression without governmental regulation of any kind. The first amendment states: "Congress shall make no law . . . . abridging the freedom of speech . . . ." Those who take that as an absolute must be reading "speech" to mean total absence of governmental restraint.

Any such reading is, of course, impossible. Since it purports to be an absolute position we are entitled to test it with extreme hypotheticals. Is Congress forbidden to prohibit incitement to mutiny aboard a naval vessel engaged in action against an enemy, to prohibit shouted harangues from the visitors' gallery during its own deliberations or to provide any rules for decorum in federal courtrooms? Are the states forbidden, by the incorporation of the first amendment in the fourteenth, to punish the shouting of obscenities in the streets?

No one, not the most obsessed absolutist, takes any such position, but if one does not, the absolute position is abandoned, revealed as a play on words.[1388]

Other constitutional law scholars have offered non-absolutist arguments which would Support First Amendment protection for adult pornography.

C. Edwin Baker has proposed what he calls the "Liberty Model" of First Amendment protection.[1389] According to Baker, this model equates First Amendment protection with the entire realm of individual liberty excluding only coercive or violent action.[1390] Baker rejects as too narrow the notion that sexual protection should be afforded only to speech that

1381. Id., pp. 44-5.
1382. Washington, D.C., Hearing, Vol. II, Barry Lynn, p. 146.
1383. Id., p. 153.
1384. 458 U.S., (1982), p. 747.
1385. Washington, D.C., Hearing Vol. II, Barry Lynn, pp. 185-87.
1386. Chicago Hearing, Vol. I, Jane Whicher, pp. 222-23.
1387. R.H. Bork, Neutral Principals and Some First Amendment Problems, 47 Ind. L. Rev. 1, (1971), p. 21.
1388. Id.
1389. C. Baker, Scope of the First Amendment Freedom of Speech, 25 UCLA L. Rev. 964, (1978), p. 990.
1390. Id., p. 960.

aids in the discovery of truth.[1391] Speech is an important component of self-fulfillment.[1392] Speech that serves to entertain or amuse the speaker or listener has value as a means of self-fulfillment even though it may not communicate significant ideas or advance the search for truth.[1393] Baker finds this value sufficient to merit First Amendment protection.

Vincent Blasi has argued in favor of broad First Amendment protection as a means of ensuring individual autonomy for members of society.[1394] Blasi points to Justice Brandeis statement in *Whitney v. California*[1395] that "those who won our independence believed that the final end of the State was to make men free to develop their faculties . . . they valued liberty both as an end and as a means. They believed liberty to be the secret of happiness."[1396]

According to Blasi,

> The basic idea here is not that speech leads to truth or a stable society or some other social value, but rather that certain speech activities are valuable because they are integral to the process by which persons consciously choose from among alternatives, a process which is regarded as valuable in and of itself because it figures prominently in our vague notions of what it means to be human.[1397]

Blasi asserts that individuals retain a basic minimum of choice making capability, they cease to be individuals any more.[1398] Thus First Amendment protection extends not just to political speech but to speech that appeals to human spirit and feelings.[1399]

Another justification for broad First Amendment protection advanced by Blasi is diversity. If expression is unregulated, individuals may freely receive stimulation from diverse reading and listening fare.[1400] This is essential to human happiness, apart from any search for truth.[1401] Blasi writes,

Even the venerable metaphor of the marketplace of ideas may have continuing force if a market is thought of not so much as a site where prices are determined and purchases made, but rather as a place where people gather to browse, to taste, and to commingle aimlessly.[1402]

Blasi find the social consequences of unregulated expression as likely better than the consequences of regulation.

Geoffrey Stone advances an argument similar to Baker's regarding "self-fulfillment." Stone contends that,

> the very fact . . . that there is a vast market in our society for sexually explicit expression suggests that for many people, this type of speech serves what they believe to be, it may be amusement, it may be containment, it may be sexual stimulation, it may be fantasy, whatever it is, many of us believe that this expression is to our own lives, in some way, valuable. That value should not be overlooked.[1403]

Stone contends that though certain types of speech may seem offensive or immoral to some, the "marketplace" referred to by Blasi is the forum for confronting them as opposed to eliminating them as a matter of law. Stone says,

> What is not appropriate, in our free and democratic society, is for government to prohibit expression because that expression may lead individuals into holding views or morals or attitudes that the majority dislikes. The way to combat that in our society was not to suppress the speech because we don't like the moral standards they may promote. It is rather, to try to convince our citizens, in the marketplace of ideas, that there are better moral standards and there are better modes of moral behavior. That is the tradition of this country and the tradition of the First Amendment. It seems to me any regulation of obscenity on the ground it may be immoral is simply incompatible

---

1391. *Id.*, p. 990.
1392. *Id.*, p. 992–93.
1393. *Id.*
1394. Blasi, *The Checking Value in First Amendment Theory*, 1977 American Bar Foundation Research Journal, (1977), pp. 521, 544.
1395. 274 U.S., (1927), p. 357.
1396. *Id.*, p. 375.
1397. V. Blasi, *supra*, p. 544.
1398. *Id.*, p. 547.
1399. *Id.*, p. 545.
1400. *Id.*, p. 550.
1401. *Id.*
1402. *Id.*
1403. Chicago Hearing, Vol. I, Geoffrey Stone, pp. 163–64.

with our constitutional and non-constitutional positions of free expression.[1404]

Despite the fervent efforts of its advocates, the theory that the First Amendment affords protection to all forms of expression has over the years found favor with only a small minority on the United States Supreme Court. The Court has consistently held that certain types of speech either fall outside the protection of the First Amendment or are protected but subject to regulation. For example, so-called "fighting words" which by their very utterance inflict injury or tend to incite an immediate breach of the peace may be prohibited in the interest of public order.[1405] Defamatory material about public figures is unprotected by the First Amendment if the publisher has either a knowledge of its falsity or a reckless disregard for the truth.[1406]

In addition, commercial speech or advertising may be regulated in order to prevent commercial fraud or deception.[1407] Advocacy of the use of force or violation of the law may be proscribed only where it is "directed to inciting or producing imminent lawless action and is likely to incite or produce such action."[1408] The Supreme Court has emphasized the requirement of imminent lawless action before the speech can be curtailed.[1409]

The question of whether obscenity is protected speech under the First Amendment first reached the Supreme Court in 1957 with the landmark case of Roth v. United States.[1410] In his opinion for the majority, Justice William Brennan said "this Court has always assumed that obscenity is not protected by the freedom of speech and press."[1411] Brennan wrote that,

All ideas having even the slightest redeeming social importance—unorthodox ideas, con-

troversial ideas, even ideas hateful to the prevailing climate of opinion—have the full protection of the guarantees, unless excludable because they encroach upon the limited area of more important interests. But implicit in the history of the First Amendment is the rejection of obscenity as utterly without redeeming social importance.[1412]

The principle that obscenity is excluded from First Amendment protection was restated by the Court in Miller v. California[1413] in 1973. In Miller, Chief Justice Warren Burger wrote, "This much has been categorically settled by the Court, that obscene material is unprotected by the First Amendment."[1414] (emphasis added)

The Supreme Court's rationale in Miller was consistent with earlier precedent regarding the First Amendment value of obscenity. Chief Justice Burger said in Miller that "to equate the free and robust exchange of ideas and political debate with commercial exploitation of obscene material demeans the grand conception of the First Amendment and its high purposes in the historic struggle for freedom."[1415]

In Paris Adult Theater I v. Slaton,[1416] decided the same day as Miller, the Court expounded further on the exclusion of obscenity from constitutional protection. The Court found the right to privacy protects the personal intimacies of the home, family, marriage, motherhood, procreation and child bearing.[1417] It does not encompass the right of an individual to watch obscene movies in a place of public accommodation.[1418] The Court also distinguished the prevention of unlimited distribution of obscenity from exertion of control by the state over reason and the intellect. Chief Justice Burger wrote,

Where communication of ideas, protected by the First Amendment, is not involved, the

---

1404. Id., pp. 167–68.
1405. Chaplinsky v. New Hampshire, 315 U.S., (1942), p. 568; But see, Cohen v. California, 403 U.S., (1971), p. 15; (holding that speech which is merely offensive, i.e. jacket with printed words "Fuck the Draft," is entitled to full First Amendment protection).
1406. New York Times v. Sullivan 376 U.S., (1964), p. 254.
1407 See, Bigelow v. Virginia, 421 U.S., (1975), p. 809.
1408. Brandenburg v. Ohio, 395 U.S., (1969), pp. 444, 447.
1409. See, Hess v. Indiana, 414 U.S., (1973), pp. 105, 109
1410. 354 U.S., (1957), p. 476.
1411. Id., p. 481.
1412. Id., pp. 484–85.
1413. 413 U.S., (1973), p. 15.
1414. Id., p. 23.
1415. Id., p. 34.
1416. 413 U.S., (1973), p. 49.
1417. Id., p. 66.
1418. Id.

mere fact that, as a consequence, some human "utterances" or "thoughts" may be incidentally affected does not bar the state from acting to protect legitimate state interests.[1419]

The Court cited legitimate state interests at stake in stemming the tide of commercialized obscenity.[1420] These include,

The interest of the public in the equality of life and the total community environment, the tone of commerce in the great city centers, and possibly the public safety itself.[1421]

The Court also quoted former Chief Justice Earl Warren's opinion in *Jacobellis v. Ohio*,[1422] where he declared there is a "right of the nation and of the states to maintain a decent society . . . ."[1423]

As early as 1942, the Supreme Court held that lewd and obscene speech "are no essential part of any exposition of ideas, and are of such slight social value as a step to truth that any benefit that may be derived from them is clearly outweighed by the social interest in order and morality."[1424] And in *Roth*, the Court found that historically, "the protection given speech and press was fashioned to assure unfettered interchange of ideas for the bringing about of political and social changes desired by the people."[1425]

Thus the Supreme Court has found that what Chief Justice Burger called "the public portrayal of hard-core sexual conduct for its own sake and for the ensuing commercial gain,"[1426] is far removed from the free and beneficial exchange of ideas that the First Amendment was designed to protect. In *Young v. American Mini-Theaters*,[1427] Justice John Paul Stevens drew the same distinction and said,

Moreover, even though we recognized that the First Amendment will not tolerate the total

suppression of erotic materials that have some arguably artistic value, it is manifest that society's interest in protecting this type of expression is of a wholly different, and lesser, magnitude than the interest in untrammeled political debate that inspired Voltaire's immortal comment. Whether political oratory or philosophical discussion moves us to applaud or to despise what is said, every school child can understand why our duty to defend the right to speak remains the same. But few of us would march our sons and daughters off to war to preserve the citizen's right to see "Specified Sexual Activities" exhibited in the theaters of our choice.[1428]

Obscene materials lack cognitive content and are more closely akin to sexual conduct as opposed to the communicative process. The sole purpose of the material is to provide sexual gratification to the reader or viewer.

Other commentators have gone one step further, and they have contended that constitutional protection should be accorded only to speech that is explicitly political.[1429] One scholar calls the "heart and soul" of the First Amendment the preservation of "our process of self-government from legislative encroachment by guaranteeing to each citizen freedom of political speech and by guaranteeing to the press freedom to publish essentially what it will about the government."[1430] The United States Supreme Court has yet to adopt this interpretation.[1431] To be obscene and without First Amendment protection, material must meet the three-part test enunciated in *Miller v. California*.[1432] The Miller standard involves the determination by the fact finder of whether,

The average person, applying contemporary community standards would find that the work, taken as a whole, appeals to the prurient interest . . . depicts or describes, in a patently offensive way, sexual conduct specifically de-

1419. *Id.*, p. 67.
1420. *Id.*, p. 57.
1421. *Id.*, p. 58.
1422. 378 U.S., (1964), p. 184.
1423. *Id.*, p. 199.
1424. *Chaplinsky v. New Hampshire*, 315 U.S., (1942), pp. 568, 571–72.
1425. 354 U.S., p. 484.
1426. 413 U.S., p. 35.
1427. U.S., (1976), p. 50.
1428. *Id.*, p. 70.
1429. R. H. Bork, *supra* note 1258, p. 20; Washington, D.C., Hearing, Vol. II, Lillian BeVier, pp. 213–14.
1430. Washington, D.C., Hearing, Vol. II, Lillian BeVier, p. 214.
1431. See, *Roth v. United States*, 354 U.S., (1957), pp. 476, 487–88.
1432. 413 U.S., (1973), p. 15.

fined by the applicable state law; and ...whether the work, taken as a whole, lacks serious literary, artistic, political, or scientific value.[1433]

In *Miller*, the court also gave examples of the types of sexual conduct state statutes could define for regulation under the second prong of the test.[1434] They include:

patently offensive representations or descriptions of ultimate sexual acts, normal or perverted, actual or simulated; and

patently offensive representations or descriptions of masturbation, excretory functions, and lewd exhibition of the genitals.[1435]

When the issue of child pornography reached the Supreme Court in 1982,[1436] the justices unanimously upheld the constitutionality of a New York statute which prohibited sexual performances by children that were not obscene under *Miller*.[1437] The Court carefully enunciated the greater leeway it accorded the states in regulating child pornography[1438] and found the value of expression that depicts children engaged in sex acts as "de minimus" and far outweighed by the evils of child abuse and exploitation.[1439] The Court reaffirmed the Miller formulation for obscenity,[1440] but found it inapplicable to child pornography because its standards do not serve to protect minors depicted in pornographic materials.[1441]

Child pornography joined the category of speech that lacks any protection under the First Amendment, and once again the Supreme Court found "speech" whose value was outweighed by other considerations.

The *Miller* test for obscenity has been in existence for thirteen years, giving the Supreme Court, along with federal and state courts, ample opportunity to interpret its component parts.

The Supreme Court has said that "average person" as used in the *Miller* standard "means what it usually means" and is no less clear than "reasonable person" used for generations in other contexts.[1442] Material must be judged by its impact on the average person, "rather than a particularly susceptible or sensitive person—or indeed a totally insensitive one"[1443] and rather than "the most prudish or the most tolerant"[1444] person. Children are not included within the concept of the "average person" unless they are the intended recipients of the material in question.[1445] The Supreme Court has reasoned that a jury trying to define the "average person" by whose standards obscenity is determined "would reach a much lower 'average' when children are a part of the equation than it would if it restricted its consideration to the effect of allegedly obscene materials on adults."[1446]

The Supreme Court found in *Miller* that while First Amendment limitations on the powers of the states do not vary from community to community, there should be no fixed national standards as to what appeals to the prurient interest or what is patently offensive.[1447] The Court said an attempt to ascertain a national community standard would be an "exercise in futility"[1448] and resolved that, "It is neither realistic nor constitutionally sound to read the First Amendment as requiring that the people of Maine or Mississippi accept public depiction of conduct found tolerable in Las Vegas or New York City."[1449] In *Miller*, the

1433. *Id.*, p. 24.
1434. *Id.*, p. 25.
1435. *Id.*
1436. *New York v. Ferber*, 458 U.S., (1982), p. 747.
1437. *Id.*, pp. 750–51.
1438. *Id.*, pp. 756–62.
1439. *Id.*, p. 762.
1440. *Id.*, p. 755.
1441. *Id.*, p. 761.
1442. *Pinkus v. United States*, 436 U.S., (1978), pp. 293, 300.
1443. *Miller v. California*, 413 U.S., (1973), pp. 15, 33.
1444. *Smith v. United States*, 431 U.S., (1977), pp. 291, 304.
1445. 436 U.S. pp. 297–98; See also, *Ginzberg v. New York*, 390 U.S., (1968), p. 629.
1446. *Id.*, p. 298.
1447. 410 U.S., p. 30.
1448. *Id.*
1449. *Id.*, p. 32.

Court upheld the trial Court's instruction that the jury evaluate the material in question with reference to the contemporary standards of the state of California.[1450] While a statewide community standard was approved in *Miller*, it was not mandated.[1451] In ascertaining the community standards, children again are not to be included in the community.[1452] Moreover, the fact that a state law fails to regulate distribution of obscene material to adults is not a conclusive determination of community standards for that jurisdiction.[1453] The "local community standards" formulation of *Miller* is applicable to all federal prosecutions for obscenity.[1454]

The prosecution is not normally required to offer evidence of the contemporary standards of the community in their jurisdiction at trial.[1455] The materials, if "hard-core," may speak for themselves.[1456] However, prosecutors have encountered some problems in bench trials when they offered no evidence of the relevant community standards.[1457] The trial judge may rely on his own experience to decide what the community standards are and whether the material in question violates them. If the judge possesses little or no knowledge of the community's views, he may turn to the government's evidence and if none has been offered, he or she may be relegated to a finding that the prosecution has failed to sustain its burden.[1458]

Contemporary community standards may be proven by expert testimony based upon properly conducted public opinion polls taken in the relevant areas.[1459] Evidence of the availability or lack of availability of comparable materials may also be used to show that the material in question enjoys a reasonable degree of community acceptance or that it does not.[1460] One state court has admitted lay opinion testimony as to community standards, where the witness was properly qualified based on knowledge of and experience with community attitudes.[1461]

The federal appeals courts have upheld geographic definitions of "community" to include the state,[1462] federal judical district[1463] or county.[1464] When the issue of which community's standard applies in a given case arises, the federal appeals courts have applied the standards of the situs of the trial[1465] and the site from which the material in question was mailed.[1466] The fact that distributors of obscene materials may be subjected to different community standards in the various federal judicial districts does not render any of the federal obscenity statutes unconstitutional.[1467]

Finally, state courts have upheld geo-

1450. *Id.*, pp. 33–34.

1451. See, *Hamling v. United States*, 418 U.S., (1974), p. 87; *Jenkins v. Georgia*, 418 U.S., (1974), p. 153.

1452. See, *Pinkus v. United States*, 436 U.S., (1978), p. 293; *United States v. Bush*, 582 F.2d, (5th Cir. 1978), p. 1016.

1453. *Smith v. United States*, 431 U.S., (1977), p. 291.

1454. *Hamling v. United States*, 418 U.S., (1974), p. 87.

1455. *Id.*

1456. See, *Paris Adult Theatre I v. Slaton*, 413 U.S., (1973), pp. 49, 56.

1457. See, *United States v. Obscene Film, Cards, & Magazine*, 541 F.2d, (9th Cir. 1976), p. 810; *United States v. 2200 Paperback Books*, 565 F.2d, (9th Cir. 1977), p. 566; *United States v. Various Articles*, 709 F. 2d, (2d Cir. 1983), p. 132 ; and *United States v. Various Articles*, 750 F.2d, (7th Cir. 1984), p. 596.

1458. *United States v. Various Articles*, 709 F.2d, (2d Cir. 1983), pp. 132, 136.

1459. See, *United States v. Various Articles*, 750 F.2d, (7th Cir. 1984), p. 596; *Carlock v. Texas*, 609 S.W.2d, (Tex. Crim. App. 1980), p. 787; *Commonwealth v. Trainor*, 374 N.E.2d, (Mass. 1978), p. 1216. *People v. Thomas*, 346 N.E.2d, (Ill. 1976), p. 190; *People v. Nelson*, 410 N.E.2d, (Ill. 1980), p. 476; See generally, *Zippo v. Rogers*, 216 F. Supp., (S.D.N.Y. 1963), p. 670; *Randy's Studebaker v. Nissan*, 533 F.2d, (10th Cir. 1976), p. 510.

1460. *United States v. Manerite*, 448 F.2d, (2d Cir. 1971), p. 583; *United States v. Various Articles*, 750 F.2d, (7th Cir. 1984), p. 596; *United States v. Battista*, 646 F.2d, (6th Cir. 1981), p. 237; *United States v. Petrov*, 747 F.2d, (2d Cir. 1984), p. 824.

1461. *Louisiana v. Short*, 368 S. 2d, (La. 1979), p. 1078.

1462. *United States v. Danley*, 523 F.2d, (9th Cir. 1975), p. 369.

1463. *United States v. Dachsteinter*, 518 F.2d, (9th Cr. 1975), p. 20

1464. *United States v. Bagnell*, 679 F.2d, (11th Cir. 1982), p. 826 cert. denied 103 S. Ct. 1449.

1465. *United States v. Sandy*, 605 F.2d, (6th Cir. 1979), p. 210.

1466. *United States v. Thomas*, 613 F.2d, (10th Cir. 1980), p. 787; *United States v. Langford*, 688 F.2d, (7th Cir. 1982), p. 1088.

1467. *Hamling v. United States*, 418 U.S., (1974), p. 87; *United States v. Bagnell*, 679 F.2d, (11th Cir. 1982), p. 826.

graphic definitions of "community" to include the state,[1468] county,[1469] city,[1470] or "local community."[1471]

While the application of local community standards is an important component of the *Miller* standard, juries do not have "unbridled discretion" in determining questions of "prurient interest" or "patent offensiveness."[1472] The Supreme Court has stated emphatically that,

> It would be wholly at odds with this aspect of *Miller* to uphold an obscenity conviction based upon a defendant's depiction of a woman with a bare midriff, even though a properly charged jury unanimously agreed on a verdict of guilty.[1473]

In *Jenkins v. Georgia*,[1474] the Court reversed an obscenity conviction based upon the motion picture "Carnal Knowledge." The Court found that, despite the jury determination, the movie did not depict sexual conduct in a patently offensive way.[1475] The Court restated the principle enunciated in *Miller*, that "no one will be subject to prosecution for the sale or exposure of obscene materials unless these materials depict or describe patently offensive, 'hard-core' sexual conduct . . . ."[1476]

The "prurient interest" prong of the *Miller* test has caused considerable confusion. In *Roth v. United States*,[1477] the Supreme Court held that "obscene material is material which deals with sex in a manner appealing to prurient interest."[1478] In the lengthy footnote which followed, the Court cited the following definitions of "prurient interest":

> i.e., material having a tendency to excite lustful thoughts. *Webster's New International Dic-*

tionary (Unabridged, 2d e., 1949) defined *prurient*, in pertinent part, as follows:

> " . . . Itching; longing; uneasy with desire or longing; of persons, having itching, morbid, or lascivious longings; of desire, curiosity, or propensity, lewd. . . ."

Pruriency is defined, in pertinent part, as follows:

> " . . . Quality of being prurient; lascivious desire or thought. . . ."

See also, Mutual Film Corp. v. Industrial Comm'n, 236 U.S. 230, 242, where this Court said as to motion pictures: " . . . They take their attraction from the general interest, eager and wholesome as it may be, in their subjects, but a *prurient interest may be excited and appealed to . . . .* " (emphasis added)

We perceive no significant difference between the meaning of obscenity developed in the case law and the definition of the A.L.I., Model Penal Code, ©207.10(2) (Tent. Draft No. 6, 1957), viz.:

> " . . . A thing is obscene if, considered as a whole, its predominant appeal is to prurient interest, i.e., a shameful or morbid interest in nudity, sex or excretion, and if it goes substantially beyond customary limits of candor in description or representation of such matters . . . ." See Comment, *id.*, at 10, and the discussion at page 29 *et seq.*[1479]

In *Miller*, the Court reaffirmed the prurient interest requirement without further elaboration or definition.[1480]

The Supreme Court has also ruled that when materials are intended for a clearly defined deviant sexual group prurient interest

---

1468. *Pierce v. State*, 296 Se. 2d, (Ala. 1974), p. 218; *People v. Better*, 337 N.E.2d, (Ill. 1975), p. 272; *Commonwealth v. 767 Main Corp.*, 357 N.E.2d, (Mass. 1976), p. 753; *People v. Colgud, Inc.*, 402 N.E.2d, (N.Y. 1980), p. 1140 (held error to instruct on county standards); *LaRue v. State*, 611 S.W.2d, (Tex. Cr. App. 1980), p. 63; *Slaton v. Paris Adult Theater I*, 201 S.E.2d, (Ga. 1973) p. 456; *State v. Motion Picture*, 547 P.2d Cal. App. 2d 789, 73 Cal. Rptr., (1968), p. 587.

1469. *State v. DePiano*, 375 A.2d, (N.J. 1977), p. 1169; *Davison v. State*, 288 So. 2d, (Fla. 1973), p. 483; *Brazelton v. State*, 282 So., (Ala. Cr. App. 1973), p. 342; *Sedelbaner v. Indiana*, 428 N.E.2d, (Ind. 1981), p. 206, *cert. denied* 455 U.S. 1035.

1470. *People v. Ridens*, 321 N.E.2d, (Ill. 1974), p. 264 *cert. denied* 421 U.S. 993; *City of Belleville v. Morgan*, 376 N.E.2d, (Ill. 1974), p. 704.

1471. *Price v. Commonwealth*, 201 S.E.2d, (Va. 1974), p. 798 *cert. denied* 419 U.S. 902.

1472. *Jenkins v. Georgia*, 418 U.S., (1974), pp. 153, 160.

1473. *Id.*, p. 161.

1474.. 418 U.S., (1974), p. 153.

1475. *Id.*, p. 161.

1476. *Id.*, p. 160, citing 413 U.S., (1973), p. 15, 27.

1477. 354 U.S., (1957), p. 476.

1478. *Id.*, p. 487.

1479. *Id.*, p. n.20.

1480. 413 U.S., (1973), pp. 15, 24.

may be measured by the appeal of the material to that particular group.[1481]

The federal appeals courts have not strayed far from the definitions cited in the Roth footnote.[1482] State court interpretations have also used very similar language to define "prurient interest."[1483] The Supreme Court's most recent pronouncement on the prurient interest standard was in Brockett v. Spokane Arcades, Inc.,[1484] in June of 1985. A Washington state statute[1485] regarding "moral nuisance" defined "lewd matter" in a manner synonymous with "obscene matter."[1486] The statute's definition of "obscene matter" tracked the Miller standard,[1487] but included a definition of "prurient" as "that which incites lasciviousness or lust."[1488] The United States Court of Appeals for the Ninth Circuit found the entire statute unconstitutional.[1489] The Appeals Court ruled that a definition of the word "lust" necessarily encompassed "healthy, wholesome, human reaction common to millions of well adjusted persons in our society, not shameful or morbid desire."[1490] The Court therefore found the statute prohibited material protected by the First Amendment.[1491]

The United States Supreme Court reversed and remanded. The Court reaffirmed the definition of "prurient interest" contained in Roth.[1492] In his opinion for the Court Justice Byron White stated,

> The Court of Appeals was aware that Roth had indicated in footnote 20 that material appealing to the prurient interest was "material having a tendency to excite lustful thoughts" but did not believe that Roth had intended to characterize as obscene material that which provoked only normal, healthy sexual desires. We do not differ with that view.[1493]

Justice White went on to conclude that the Court was "quite sure that by using the words 'lustful thoughts' in footnote 20, the Court was referring to sexual responses over and beyond those that would be characterized as normal."[1494]

While the Supreme Court agreed with the Appeals Court's construction of the prurient interest standard, the Court found that the Court of Appeals erred in declaring the Washington statute facially invalid.[1495] The Supreme Court found partial rather than fa-

---

1481. Mishkin v. New York, 383 U.S., (1965), p. 502; See also, Hamling v. United States, 418 U.S., (1983); p. 87 Jenkins v. Georgia, 418 U.S., (1973), p. 153; United States v. Petrov, 747 F.2d, (2d Cir. 1984), p. 824; Sedelbauer v. State, 455 N.E. 2d, (1983), p. 1159.

1482. See, Flying Eagle Publications v. United States, 273 F.2d, (1st Cir. 1960), p. 799 (unwholesome or unhealthy interest in sex, it is material which portrays sex with a looselipped sensuous leer.); United States v. 35 MM Motion Picture Film, 432 F.2d, (2d Cir. 1970), p. 705 (characterized by the "leer of the sensualist," debasing, shameful or morbid quality in expression or depiction of human sexuality); United States v. Keller, 259 F.2d, (3d Cir. 1958), p. 54 (itching, longing, uneasy with desire for longing, lascivious thoughts, lustful desires.); Penthouse International Ltd. v. McAuliffe, 610 F.2d, (5th Cir. 1980), p. 1353 (shameful or morbid interest in nudity, sex or excretion.); United States v. Langford, 688 F.2d, (7th Cir. 1982), p. 1088 (appeal to a morbid interest as distinguished from a candid interest.); Eastman Kodak Co. v. Hendricks, 262 F.2d, (9th Cir. 1958), p. 393 and Childs v. State of Oregon, 431 F.2d, (9th Cir. 1970), p. 272 (inciting lascivious thoughts, arousing lustful thoughts.)

1483. See, State v. LeWitt, 22 A.2d, (Ct. App. Conn. 1966), p. 579; City of Chicago v. Universal Publishing and Dist. Corp., 34 Ill. 2d 250, 215 N.E.2d, (1966), p. 251; Attorney General v. Book Named John Cleland's Memoirs of a Woman of Pleasure, 349 Mass. 69, 206 N.E.2d, (1965), p. 403, rev'd on other grounds, 383 U.S., (1966), p. 413; People v. Speer, 52 Ill. App. 203, 367 N.E.2d, (1977), p. 372 (shameful, morbid interest in nudity, sex, or excretion); City of Phoenix v. Fine, 4 Ariz. App, 303, 420 P.2d, (1966), p. 26 and Andrews v. State, 639 S.W. 2d, (Tex. App. 1982), p. 4 (morbid or shameful interest in nudity, sex or lewdness going substantially beyond customary limits of candor in description or representation of such matters)l State v. Little AA Corp., 191 Neb. 448, 215 N.W.2d, (1974), p. 853 and People v. Ciampa, 394 N.Y.S.2d, (1977), p. 727 (tending to arouse sexual desires); State v. Great American Theater Co., 327 Kan 633, 608 P.2d, (1980), p. 951 (an unhealthy, unwholesome, morbid, degrading and shameful interest in sex.); Spry v. State, 156 Ga. App. 74, 274 S.E.2d, (1983), p. 2 (material which appeals to prurient interest is material which has tendency to excite lustful thoughts.); State v. Barrett, 292 S.E.2d, (S.C. 1982), p. 590 (shameful or morbid interest in nudity, sex or excretion and is reflective of an arousal of lewd and lascivious desires.)

1484. 105 S. Ct., (1985), p. 2794.
1485. Wash. Rev. Code S7.48A 010 et seq.
1486. Id., p. S7.48A 020(2) (a).
1487. Id.
1488. Id., p. 7.48A.010(8).
1489. J.R. Distributors, Inc. v. Eikenberry, 725 F.2d, (9th Cir. 1984), p. 482.
1490. Id., p. 492.
1491. Id.
1493. 105 S.Ct pp. 2798-99.
1493. Id., p. 2799.
1494. Id.
1495. Id., p. 2801.

cial invalidation to be the proper course and held that the statute should have been invalidated only insofar as the word "lust" be understood as reaching protected materials.[1496] The extent to which *Brockett v. Spokane Arcades*, clarified the meaning of "prurient interest" may be debated. The Court seems to have excluded normal, healthy sexual desires—whatever they are—from the definition of "prurient interest."

Material must also lack serious literary, artistic, political or scientific value in order to be obscene.[1497] In *Kois v. Wisconsin*,[1498] the Supreme Court reversed the obscenity conviction of a publisher of an underground newspaper. The newspaper contained an account of the arrest of a photographer for possession of obscene material, and criticized law enforcement officials for their handling of the case.[1499] Included in the article were two pictures described as similar to those seized from the photographer. The picture depicted "a nude man and nude woman embracing in a sitting position."[1500]

The requirement of serious value necessitates the court review the material as a whole. If the material, as a whole, conveys a literary, artistic, political, or scientific idea or message, it possesses the requisite value.[1501] If it appears that the publisher of the material has tried to redeem or "dress up" otherwise obscene matter, sold and distributed for its obscene contents rather than for its ideas or message, then the value is not serious.[1502] As the Supreme Court reasoned in *Kois* "a quotation from Voltaire on the flyleaf of a book will not constitutionally redeem an otherwise obscene publication."[1503] In *Kois*, the Court

found the publication was not a "mere vehicle for the publication of the pictures," and that the pictures were rationally related to the article about the photographer.[1504]

The courts have distinguished cases involving "sham" publications which include some form of literature in an attempt to save the rest of the material in them from being declared obscene.[1505] The determination is not difficult to make in cases of hard-core pornography.[1506] On two occasions, federal courts have found that *Penthouse* magazine lacks serious value.[1507] The same result was reached in a case involving the movie "Deep Throat."[1508] Federal courts have found serious value contained in *Playboy* Magazine[1509] and in the movie "Last Tango in Paris."[1510]

The determination of serious literary, artistic, political, or scientific value is not made with reference to local community standards.[1511] This prong of the *Miller* test embodies thee First Amendment protection of unpopular or distasteful opinions or ideas, and is thus "particularly amenable to appellate review."[1512] This is in contrast to the determination of "appeal to the prurient interest" and "patent offensiveness." In *Miller*, the Supreme Court found that there can be no "fixed, uniform national standards of precisely what appeals to the 'prurient interest' or is 'patently offensive.'"[1513] The Court clearly found these elements of the *Miller* standard subject to local community standards, leaving the question of serious literary, artistic, political, or scientific value to be determined by a national standard.[1514]

California retains a standard that requires a court to find material "utterly without re-

---

1496. *Id.*, p. 2802.

1497. U.S. p. 25.

1498. 408 U.S., (1972), p. 229.

1499. *Id.*, pp. 229–30.

1500. *Id.*, p. 230.

1501. 413 U.S. p. 24.

1502. 408 U.S. p. 231.

1503.. *Id.*

1504. *Id.*, pp. 230–31.

1505. See, *United States v. Merrill*, 746 F.2d, (9th Cir. 1984), p. 458; *United States v. Various Artlicles*, 536 F. Supp., (S.D.N.Y. 1981), p. 50.

1506. See e.g., *State v. J-R Distributors*, 512 P. 2d, (Wash. 1973), p. 1049 (Bedplay and E-Jac Magazines).

1507. *Penthouse International v. McAuliffe*, 610 F.2d, (5th Cir. 1980), p. 1353 (January, 1978 issue); *Penthouse International v. Webb*, 594 F. Supp., (N.D. Ga. 1984), p. 1186 (September, 1984 issue). But see, *State v. Walden Book Co.*, 386 So.2d, (La. 1980), p. 342 (finding the June, 1980 issue of *Penthouse* had serious value).

1508. *United States v. One Reel of Film*, 481 F.2d, (1st Cir. 1973), p. 206.

1509. *Penthouse International v. McAuliffe*, 610 F.2d, (5th Cir. 1980), p. 1353 (January, 1978 issue).

1510. *United States v. Gladwell*, 373 F.Supp., (N.D. Ohio 1974), p. 247.

1511. *Smith v. United States*, 431 U.S., (1977), pp. 291, 301.

1512. *Id.*, p. 305.

1513. *Miller v. California*, 413 U.S., (1973), pp. 15, 30.

1514.. 4331 U.S., p. 301, citing F. Schauer, *The Law of Obscenity*, (1976), pp. 123–24.

deeming social value" in order to be obscene.[1515] Under the formulation the material need only possess a modicum of social value to be protected speech.[1516]

Under either *Memoirs* or the *Miller* standard, expert testimony may be used to demonstrate the value of a given publication or film.[1517]

In the thirteen years since the *Miller* standard was announced by the Supreme Court, federal and state courts have consistently followed the mandate expressed in *Miller* that

no one will be subject to prosecution for the sale or exposure of obscene materials unless these materials depict or describe patently offensive 'hard-core' sexual conduct.[1518]

1515. See, *People v. Enskat*, 109 Cal. Rptr. 433, 33 Cal. 3d, (1973), p. 900, U.S. *cert. denied* 418 U.S., p. 937. The Governor of California has signed Senate Bill 139 which amends the state obscenity statute as of January 1987. The new law contains a requirement of "significant literary, artistic, political, educational, or scientific value."

1516. See, *Memoirs v. Massachusetts*, 383 U.S., (1966), p. 413.

1517. See, *United Artists v. Gladwell*, 373 F.Supp., (N.D. Ohio 1974), p. 247; *Commonwealth v. 707 Main Corp.*, 357 N.E. 2d, (Mass. 1976), p. 753.

1518. U.S. p. 27; See, *Hamling v. United States*, 418 U.S., (1974), p. 87 (advertising brochure containing full page of pictures portraying heterosexual and homosexual intercourse, sodomy and a variety of sexual acts); *United States v. Gower*, 503 F.2d, (D.C. Cir. 1974), p. 189 (photos and films which showed nude males and females engaged in explicit sexual intercourse, fellatio, cunnilingus and masturbation); *United States v. Alexander*, 498 F.2d, (2d Cir. 1974), p. 934 (photos with no text that depicted fellatio, cunnilingus and sodomy); *McKenzie v. Butler*, 398 F.Supp., (W.D. Tex. 1975), p. 1319 (movie "Deep Throat"); *United States v. Various Articles*, 460 F.Sup., (S.D. N.Y. 1978), p. 826 (film of two naked teenage boys engaging together in oral and anal intercourse and masturbation, which had no plot, point or message and displayed no acting or directoral skills.); *Penthouse v. McAuliffe*, 610 F.2d, (5th Cir. 1980), p. 1353 (January, 1978, "Penthouse" including "2 photos in which the naked woman has her finger inserted in the lips of her genitals so that it contacts her clitoris . . . [an] expression consistent with masturbation. . ." also letters with descriptions of "hard-core" sexual acts.); *United States v. Friedman*, 506 F.2d, (8th Cir. 1974), p. 511 (magazine with photos depicting men and women in heterosexual and homosexual acts including intercourse with penetration, oral intercourse, fellatio, cunnilingus, and masturbation); *Miller v. United States*, 507 F.2d, (9th Cir. 1974), p. 1100, *cert. denied*. 95 S.Ct., (1975), p. 2620 (magazine "The Name is Bonnie" with 45 nude photos depicting and emphasizing female sex organs); *United States v. Miller*, 455 F.2d, pp. 899, 505 F.2d, (9th Cir. 1972, 1974), p. 1247 (photos of male genitals and close-ups of female genitals, descriptions of bestiality, lesbian activities, incest and sodomy between man and woman); *United States v. Pryba*, 502 F.2d, (D.C. Cir. 1974), p. 391 *cert. denied*. 95 S.Ct., (1975), p. 815, (film of nude men and women engaged in homosexual and heterosexual acts); *United States v. Womack*, 509 F.2d (D.C. Cir. 1974), *cert. denied*. 95 S. Ct., (1975), p. 2644 (magazines containing photographs showing young boys posed in a manner which highlights and emphasizes their exposed genitalia in full or partial erection . . . in many instances the position of the boys indicates that oral or anal sodomy is imminent); *Weissbaum v. Hannon*, 439 F.Supp., (N.D. Ill. 1977), p. 873 (S & M photos of naked people whipped and bound; women in chastity belts with invitations for sex; ads for cock rings and humiliation collar, detailed articles about 15-year-old boy initiating 12-year-old girl to sex and bondage); *United States v. American Theater Corp.* 526 F.2d, (8th Cir. 1975), p. 48 (movie depicting men and women engaging in heterosexual and homosexual intercourse, cunnilingus, masturbation and depicting semen spread on women's bodies) *Penthouse Int. Ltd. v. Webb*, 594 F.Supp., (N.D. Ga. 1984), p. 1186 (Sept. & Oct. 1984 "Penthouse," including photos of women in varying degrees of nudity, photos of lesbian sexual activity and masturbation, columns "Penthouse Forum," "Women's Forum" and "Call Me Madam" detailing various sexual acts.); *Pierce v. State*, 244 S.E. 2d, (Ga 1978), p. 589 (magazine pictures of persons exhibiting genitalia and engaging in various forms of sexual activities both homosexual and heterosexual.); *State v. American Theater Corp.* 230 N.W. 2d, (Neb. 1975), p. 209 "Deep Throat." heterosexual intercourse, group sex, explicit penetration, fellatio, cunnilingus, female masturbation and sodomy, seminal ejaculation, sex scenes with only minot interruption.); *Slaton v. Paris Adult Theater I*, 201 S.E. 2d, (Ga. 1973), p. 456 (movies depicting simulated intercourse and fellatio.); *Dyke v. State*, 209 S.E.2d, (Ga. 1974), p. 166 (movie "Devil in Miss Jones." Individual and group acts of intercourse, fellatio, cunnilingus with camera focusing on genitals.); *New York v. Buckley*, 307 N.E.2d, (N.Y. 1973), p. 805 "Screw" magazine. (Photos of heterosexual and homosexual sex with genitals prominently and lewdly displayed, movie review with worth being determined by degree of male erection is it likely to induce, ads for sex paraphernalia and personal ads.); *Harlow v. City of Birmingham*, 296 S.2d, (Ala. Ct. Cr. App. 1974), p. 202 (magazines with every page depicting nude males and females in intercourse, fellatio, cunnilingus, sodomy, including group sex. Lurid stories including "I was Raped by a Black and Now Refuse Abortion," "I Carried My Father's Child," "Smoking Pot Changed My Sex Life."); *Herman v. Arkansas*, 512 S.W.2d, (Ark. 1974), p. 928 (magazine photos of nude female involved in heterosexual and homosexual oral breast manipulation with others. Photos of sex acts with no less than three nor more than eight persons depicted in each photo.); *Kaplan v. United States*, 311 A.2d, (D.C. App. 1973), p. 506 (Peep show depicting naked female shamelessly displaying genitals and breasts and close-up shots with use of banana to simulate sex and oral sex.); *Trans-Lux Corp. v. State ex. rel. Sweeton*, 366 So. 2d, (Ala. 1979), p. 710 (film "The Opening of Misty Beethoven." Numerous scenes of explicit sexual conduct between members of the same sex and members of the opposite sex including cunnilingus, intercourse, masturbation and fellatio in repetitive displays.); *McKinney v. City of Birmingham*, 296 So.2d, (Ala. 1973), p. 197 (films graphically depicting nude men and women with their genitals fully exposed in poses and activities involving actual sexual intercourse, fellatio and cunnilingus between both males and females and other sexual activities); *Illinois v. Ridens*, 282 N.E.2d, (Ill. 1972), p. 691, *cert. denied*. 95 S.Ct., (1975), p. 2000 (magazines showing nude men and women in seductive embraces, posed with their legs spread so as to focus on their genitals); *North Carolina v. Horn*, 203 S.E.2d, (N.C. 1974), p. 36, *cert. denied*. 95 S. Ct. 238 (films showing actual acts of sexual intercourse, fellatio and cunnilingus performed by and between human male and human females); *Washington v. J-R Distributors Inc.*, 512 P. 2d, (Wash. 1973), p. 1049, *cert. denied*. 418 U.S., (1974), p. 949 (magazines "Bed-

In *Ward v. Illinois*, 1519 the Court upheld obscenity convictions based on two publications depicting sadomasochistic sexual acts. The defendant had contended that these types of acts were not enumerated in *Miller* as possible patently offensive depictions of specifically defined sexual conduct.[1520] The Court ruled in *Ward* that the sexual acts mentioned in *Miller* were merely examples and not intended as an exhaustive compilation of the sexual acts whose depiction, if patently offensive, is subject to regulations.[1521]

While the overwhelming majority of cases finding material to be obscene have dealt with depictions of patently offensive "hard-core" sexual conduct, descriptions of the same conduct by words alone may also be legally obscene. In *Kaplan v. California*,[1522] the Supreme Court upheld an obscenity conviction based on a book called *Suite 69* which had a plain cover and contained no pictures.[1523] The Court described the book as consisting,

entirely of repetitive descriptions of physical, sexual conduct, "clinically" explicit and offensive to the point of being nauseous.[1524]

The content of the book was "unvarying" and included "almost every conceivable variety of sexual contact, homosexual and heterosexual . . . ."[1525] Chief Justice Burger wrote in *Kaplan*:

When the Court declared that obscenity is not a form of expression protected by the First Amendment, no distinction was made as to the medium of the expression.[1526]

The Court concluded that "obscenity can, of course, manifest itself in . . . the written and oral description of conduct."[1527]

Materials found not to be obscene under *Miller* frequently depict nudity without explicit sexual activity or merely contain some sexually explicit language.[1528] In *Jenkins v. Georgia*,[1529] the Supreme Court reversed an obscenity conviction involving the motion picture "Carnal Knowledge." The Court noted that the film appeared on many "Ten Best" lists for 1971 and received generally favorable reviews from critics.[1530] One of the actresses in it received an Academy Award nomination.[1531] The Court quoted one review of the film which described the plot as the story "of two young college males, roommates and lifelong friends, forever preoccupied with their sex lives."[1532] The Court cautioned that under *Miller*, juries do not have "unbridled discretion" in determining what is patently offensive or appeals to the prurient interest, and restated the proposition that obscenity under *Miller* only encompasses materials that "depict or describe patently offensive 'hard-core' sexual conduct . . . ."[1533] The Court went on to describe "Carnal Knowledge," finding that,

While the subject matter of the picture is, in a broader sense, sex, and there are scenes in which sexual conduct including "ultimate sexual acts" is to be understood to be taking place, the camera does not focus on the bodies of the actors at such times. There is no exhibition whatever of the actors' genitals, lewd or otherwise, during these scenes. There are occasional scenes of nudity, but nudity alone is not enough to make material legally obscene under the *Miller* standards.[1534]

1519. 431 U.S., (1977), p. 767.
1520. *Id.*, p. 773.
1521. *Id.*
1522. 413 U.S., (1973), p. 115.
1523. *Id.*, p. 116.
1524. *Id.*, pp. 116–17.
1525. *Id.*, p. 117.
1526. *Id.*, p. 119.
1527. *Id.*
1529. 418 U.S., (1974), p. 153.
1530. *Id.*, p. 158.
1531. *Id.*, p, n.5.
1532. *Id.*, p. 158.
1533. *Id.*, p. 160, quoting 413 U.S., (1973), pp. 15, 27.
1534. *Id.*, p. 161.

play" and "E-Jac" containing photos graphically depicting unclothed males and females engaged in acts of masturbation, sexual intercourse, fellatio and cunnilingus.); *Garcia v. State*, 633 S.W.2d, (Tex. App. 1982), p. 611 (magazine entitled "Best of Cum." Front and back covers displaying full page photographs of male ejaculating onto nude females and containing 100 pages of photographs depicting nude males ejaculating onto females.).

The Court held that "Carnal Knowledge" was "simply not the public portrayal of hard-core sexual conduct for its own sake, and for the ensuing commercial gain'" which *Miller* proscribes.[1535] As a matter of constitutional law, the film did not depict sexual conduct in a patently offensive way.[1536]

In *Erzoznik v. City of Jacksonville*,[1537] the Supreme Court found unconstitutional a Jacksonville, Florida, ordinance prohibiting the showing of films containing nudity by a drive-in movie theater where the screen is visible from a public street or place. The ordinance specifically proscribed any motion picture depicting "the human male and female bare buttocks, human female bare breasts, or human bare pubic areas. . . ."[1538] In *Erzoznik*, the Court concluded that,

The ordinance is not directed against sexually explicit nudity, nor is it otherwise limited.

Rather, *it sweepingly forbids display of all films containing any uncovered buttocks or breasts, irrespective of context or pervasiveness.* Thus it would bar a film containing a picture of baby's buttocks, the nude body of a war victim, or scenes from a culture in which nudity is indigenous. The ordinance also might prohibit newsreel scenes of the opening of an art exhibit as well as shots of bathers on a beach. *Clearly all nudity cannot be deemed obscene even as to minors.*[1539](emphasis added)

However, the *Miller* standard may be adjusted to prohibit materials on the basis of their appeal to minors even if they are not obscene to adults.[1540] In *Ginzberg v. New York*,[1541] the Supreme Court considered whether it was constitutionally impermissible for the state of New York to accord to minors under age seventeen a more restricted right than that assured adults to determine for themselves what sexual material they may read or see.[1542] The defendant was convicted of selling two "girlie" magazines to a sixteen-year-old boy.[1543]

The Court found that these magazine were not obscene for adults.[1544] The Court upheld the constitutionality of New York statute recognizing both the authority of parents to direct the upbringing of their children and the state's interests in the well-being of its youth.[1545] As of 1970, forty-one states had enacted some type of special prohibition regarding the distribution of sexual materials to minors. Eighteen of these statutes were either identical or similar to the New York law upheld in *Ginsberg*.[1546]

Pandering is the "business of purveying textual or graphic matter openly advertised to appeal to the erotic interest of [its] customers."[1547] in *Ginzburg v. United States*, the Supreme Court held that "where the purveyor's sole emphasis is on may be decisive in the determination of obscenity."[1548]

Pandering is neither a separate crime nor an element of the offense of obscenity. It need not be included in the indictment for obscenity.[1549] It is, however, relevant evidence to considered.[1550] In *Ginzburg*, the defendant sought mailing privileges in Intercourse and Blue Ball, Pennsylvania, on the basis of the salacious appeal of these names.[1551] The Court noted that "advertisements for the publication in question openly boasted that the publishers would take full advantage of what they regarded [as] an unrestricted license allowed by law in the expression of sex and sexual matters."[1552] The Court found that this evidence reinforced the government's claim that

1535. Id.
1536. Id.
1537. 422 U.S., (1975), p. 205.
1538. Id., p. 207.
1539. Id., p. 213.
1540. Ginzburg v. New York, 390 U.S., (1968), p. 629.
1541. Id.
1542. Id., pp. 636–37.
1543. Id., p. 631.
1544. Id., p. 634.
1545. Id., pp. 639–40.
1546. 2 Technical Report of the Commission on Obscenity and Pornography, (1970), pp. 45–52.
1547. Ginzburg v. United States, 383 U.S., (1966), pp. 463, 467, quoting Roth v. United States, 354 U.S., (1957), pp. 476, 495–96 (Warren, C.J., concurring).
1548. 383 U.S., (1966), pp. 463, 470.
1549. United States v. Palladino, 475 F.2d, (1st Cir. 1973), p. 65; United States v. Ratner, 502 F.2d, (5th Cir. 1974), p. 1300.
1550. Hamling v. United States, 418 U.S., (1974), p. 87; Pinkus v. United States, 436 U.S., (1978), p. 293.
1551. 383 U.S., p. 467.
1552. Id., p. 468.

the magazine was obscene.[1553] The courts generally have found various types of evidence to constitute pandering including sensational advertising,[1554] the name of the theater showing the movie in question,[1555] motion picture previews,[1556] the use of indiscriminate mailing lists,[1557] the types of books available in the store where the publication in question was purchased,[1558] and the use of a peep show booth to show a motion picture.[1559] Courts have also found some evidence does not constitute pandering, including mere advertising,[1560] a lewd or enticing cover on a publication,[1561] references to other books by the same publishers,[1562] a high price[1563] and warnings concerning the sexually explicit nature of the material.[1564] Evidence of pandering is relevant to the "literary, artistic, political or scientific" value prong of the *Miller* standard.[1565] In *Ginzburg*, the the Supreme Court found that "The circumstances of presentation and dissemination of material are equally relevant to determining whether social importance claimed for material in the courtroom was, in the circumstances, pretense or reality—whether it was the basis upon which it was traded in the marketplace or a spurious claim for litigation purposes."[1566] The circumstances of sale, distribution and commercial exploitation of a work for prurient appeal may thus be considered in determining whether a work has serious value.[1567]

Aside from consideration of the *Miller* standard, there are several other important facets of obscenity law.

Obscenity statutes must contain a requirement of scienter or guilty knowledge on the part of the violator.[1568] The defendant need not possess actual knowledge that the material is legally obscene,[1569] nor must he be of the opinion that it is obscene.[1570] It is only necessary that the individual have knowledge of the general nature or character of the material.[1571] Scienter may be proved by circumstantial evidence[1572] and it may be sufficient that the accused had reason to know of the contents of the material or that the circumstances were such that would put him on inquiry.[1573]

The Supreme Court has recognized that,

Eyewitness testimony of a bookseller's personal knowledge of a book hardly need be a necessary element in proving his awareness of

1553. *Id.*, p. 471.

1554. *United States v. Ratner*, 502 F.2d, (5th Cir. 1974), p. 1300; *United States v. Dost*, 575 F.2d, (10th Cir. 1978), p. 1303; *United States v. Gundlach*, 345 F. Supp., (W.D. Pa. 1972), p. 709.

1555. *People v. Sarnblad*, 26 Cal. App. 3d 801, 103 Cal. Reptr., (1972), p. 211 (movie shown at the "Por-No" Theater).

1556. *State v. Boyd*, 300 N.E. 2d, (Ohio App. 1972), p. 752; *New Riviera Arts Theater v. State*, 412 S.W.2d, (Tenn. 1967), p. 890.

1557. *Miller v. U.S.*, 431 F.2d, (9th Cir. 1970), p. 655.

1558. *Orito v. State*, 191 N.W. 2d, (Wisc. 1972), p. 763.

1559. *Sanza v. State Bd. of Censors*, 226 A.2d, (Md. 1967), p. 317; *Hewitt, v. State Bd. of Censors*, 254 A.2d, (Md. 1969), p. 203.

1560. *People v. Bloss*, 201 N.W. 3d, (Mich. 1972), p. 806; *People v. Mature Enterprises, Inc.*, 343 N.Y.S.2d, (1973), p. 911; *Luros v. United States*, 389 F.2d., (8th Cir. 1968), p. 200 (nudist magazines not advertised as erotica); *United States v. Pelligrino*, 467 F.2d, (9th Cir. 1972), p. 41 (book "Woman: Her Sexual Variations and Functions" with explicit color photos of female genitalia advertised as containing knowledge of female sexual response for benefit of adults).

1561. *Books Inc. v. United States*, 388 U.S., (1967), p. 449 *reversing* 358 F.2d, (1st Cir. 1969), p. 935; *United States v. Baranov*, 418 F.2d, (9th Cir. 1969), p. 1051; *Childs v. Oregon*, 401 U.S., (1971), p. 1006 *reversing per curium* 431 F.2d (9th Cir. 1970); *Redrup v. New York*, 386 U.S., (1967), p. 767 (covers "Lust" and "Shame Agent").

1562. *Aday v. United States*, 388 U.S., (1967), p. 447 *reversing* 357 F.2d, (6th Cir. 1966), p. 855.

1563. *Potomac News Co. v. United States*, 389 U.S., (1967), p. 47 *reversing* 373 F.2d, (4th Cir. 1967), p. 635.

1564. *United States v. Stewart*, 377 F.Supp., (E.D. Pa. 1971), p. 299; *City of Rochester v. Carlson*, 202 N.W.2d, (Minn. 1972), p. 632; *State v. Lebovitz*, 202 N.W.2d, (Minn. 1972), p. 648.

1565. *Splawn v. California*, 431 U.S., (1977), p. 595.

1566. 383 U.S., p. 470.

1567. *Splawn v. California*, 431 U.S. U.S., (1977), p. 595.

1568. *Smith v. California*, 361 U.S., (1959), p. 147.

1569. See, *Henley v. Wise*, 303 F.Supp., (N.D. Ind. 1969), p. 62; *People v. Tannahill*, 38 Ill. App. 3d 767, 348 N.E.2d, (1976), p. 847; *People v. Finkelstein*, 9 N.Y.2d 342, 174 N.E.2d, (1961), p. 470.

1570. See, *Hamling v. United States*, 418 U.S., (1974), p. 87; See also, *United States v. Marks*, 364 F.Supp., (E.D. KY. 1073), p. 1022, *aff'd* 520 F.2d, (6th Cir. 1975), p. 913, *rev'd on other grounds*, 403 U.S., (1977), p. 188.

1571 *Rosen v. United States*, 161 U.S., (1969), p. 29.

1572. *Hamling v. United States*, 418 U.S., (1973), p. 87; *Mishkin v. New York*, 383 U.S., (1966), p. 502; *People v. Finkelstein*, 9 N.Y.2d 342, 174 N.E.2d, (1961), p. 470; *State v. Burgun*, 384 N.E.2d, (Ohio 1978), p. 255 (knowledge of character or nature of obscene material is constitutionally adequate indication of scienter and precise knowledge is not required).

1573. *Smith v. California*, 361 U.S., (1954), p. 147; *People v. Rode*, 57 Ill. App. 3d 649, 373 N.E.2d, (1968), p. 605; *Peters v. State*, 449 N.E.2d, (Ind. App. 1983), p. 311.

its contents. The circumstance may warrant the inference that he was aware of what a book contained, despite his denial.[1574]

In *Mishkin v. New York*,[1575] the Court found the following circumstantial evidence of scienter to be sufficient:

... appellant's instructions to his artists and writers; his efforts to disguise his role in the enterprise that published and sold the books; the transparency of the character of the material in question, highlighted by the titles, covers, and illustrations; the massive number of obscene books appellant published, hired others to prepare, and possessed for sale; the repetitive quality of the sequences and formats of the books; and the exorbitant prices marked on the books[1576] "amply show(s), that appellant was 'aware of the character of the material' and that his activity was not innocent but [a] calculative purveyance of filth."[1577]

Two recent state court decisions provide further insight into the type of evidence that is sufficient to prove scienter. In *Beier v. State*,[1578] the Court upheld the conviction of an "adults only" pornographic outlet manager where the evidence showed that he removed money from the cash register, that the store was stocked with large quantities of sexually explicit films and magazines, and that he had in his possession a memorandum instructing store clerks to or not to cooperate with vice officers.[1579] And, in *Commonwealth v. Croll*,[1580] the court found that the jury could reasonably infer that the defendant was aware of the character of the material sold to police officers where he was seen instructing another individual on the use of the cash register, acted in a supervisory capacity during

sales transactions, and was able to answer specific questions about the availability of various items in the stores.[1581] The evidence also showed that placards posted on the doors to the peep show booths gave notice of the nature of the films shown inside.[1582]

Use of fictitious names or destruction of records also may be evidence of scienter.[1583] Moreover, if the defendant is a corporation, scienter may be established by proof of knowledge on the part of officers or directors.[1584] Proof of scienter may be difficult where "sham" corporations are used and corporate records contain names of individuals who actually possess no knowledge of the business or its operations. Similar problems also may be encountered in prosecutions brought against absentee owners or other individuals not observed on the business premises.

Obscenity statutes must be carefully drafted to avoid encompassing protected speech. A statute which prohibits both protected and unprotected speech will be struck down for being overbroad.[1585] In *Butler v. Michigan*,[1586] the Supreme Court reversed a conviction under a Michigan statute prohibiting the distribution of materials "tending to incite minors to violent or depraved or immoral acts, manifestly tending to the corruption of the morals of youth."[1587] These materials were unlawful even if sold to an adult. The Supreme Court found the statute to be overbroad because it prohibited the dissemination of materials to adults that may be harmful to minors but not to adults.[1588]

A New York statute governing the licensing of motion pictures was struck down as overbroad by the Supreme Court in *Kingsley International Pictures Corp. v. Regents*.[1589] The

1574. *Smith v. California*, 361 U.S., (1959), pp. 147, 154.
1575. 383 U.S., (1966), p.502.
1576. *Id.*, pp. 511–12.
1577. *Id.*
1578. 681 S.W.2d, (Tex. Cr. App. 1984), p. 124.
1579. *Id.*, pp. 126 and 128.
1580. 480 A.2d, (Pa. 1984), p. 266.
1581. *Id.*, p. 271.
1582. *Id.*
1583. *United States v. Battista*, 464 F. 2d, (6th Cir. 1981), p. 237.
1584. *States v. American Theater Corp.*, 244 N.W.2d, (Neb. 1976), p. 56.
1585. See, *Ginzburg v. New York*, 390 U.S., (1968), p. 629; *United States v. Thevis*, 484 F.2d, (5th Cir. 1973), p. 1149; *Volkland v. State*, 510 S.W.2d, (Tex. App. 1974), p. 585; *State v. Hull*, 86 Wash. 2d 527, 546 P.2d, (1976), p. 912; (statute's definition of scienter including a situation where person has information or circumstances that would lead prudent person to form belief as to subject matter and if followed by inquiry would disclose its character, meets the constitutional requirement of scienter).
1586. 352 U.S., (1957), p. 380.
1587. *Id.*, p. 381.
1588. *Id.*, pp. 382–3.
1589. 360 U.S., (1959), p. 684.

statute prohibited the licensing of any motion picture "which portrays acts of sexual immorality, perversion or lewdness or which expressly or impliedly presents such acts as desirable, acceptable, or proper patterns of behavior."[1590] A motion picture version of *Lady Chatterly's Lover* was denied a license on the grounds that it presented adultery as appropriate behavior.[1591] The Supreme Court found that the statute prohibited the advocacy of constitutional protected ideas—in this case, the idea that adultery may sometimes be proper—and was thus unconstitutionally overbroad in its reach.[1592]

Closely akin to overbreadth is the concept of vagueness. A statute that does not give adequate notice of what it prohibits is void for vagueness.[1593] This concept is especially important in the area of obscenity where the distinction between protected and unprotected speech may be incomplete or unclear absent a court determination.[1594] A vague statute may also permit law enforcement authorities to exercise too much power to prosecute individuals based on their individual interpretations of the law.[1595] Therefore, the Supreme Court has found obscenity statutes unconstitutional when they lack "ascertainable standards or guilt" or are uncertain "in regard to persons within the scope of the act" or uncertain "in regard to the applicable tests to ascertain guilt."[1596]

The Supreme Court has rejected challenges based on vagueness made against both the language of 18 U.S.C. S1461 and the California state statute containing the words "obscene or indecent."[1597] In *Roth v. United States*, the Court noted that the terms of obscenity statutes are not always precise.[1598] A statute must convey a "sufficiently definite warning as to the proscribed conduct when measured by common understanding and practices."[1599] The Court concluded that the existence of "marginal cases in which it is difficult to determine the side of the law on which a particular fact situation falls is not a sufficient reason to hold the language too ambiguous to define a criminal offense."[1600]

The law governing search and seizure of materials presumptively protected by the First Amendment was the subject of a recent decision by the United States Supreme Court in *New York v. P.S. Video, Inc.*[1601] The Court reaffirmed the proposition that any such seizure must be made pursuant to a warrant and that there must be an opportunity for a prompt postseizure judicial determination of obscenity.[1602] The Court noted that there is no requirement that the magistrate personally view the allegedly obscene material before issuing a warrant.[1603] However, the search warrant must be supported by affidavits containing specific facts so that the magistrate may "focus searching on the question of obscenity."[1604] The Court found that the New York Court of Appeals erred in upholding the suppression of five video tape cassette movies seized by police from a video store pursuant to a warrant in the case at bar because,

> The New York Court of Appeals construed our prior decisions in this area as standing for the additional proposition that are application for a warrant authorizing the seizure of books or films must be evaluated under a "higher" standard of probable cause than that used in other areas of Fourth Amendment law. But we have never held or said that such a "higher" standard is required by the First Amendment.[1605]

The Court held that,

1590. *Id.*, p. 685, quoting N.Y. Education Law S122-1 (McKinney 1958).
1591. *Id.*, p. 685.
1592. *Id.*, pp. 688–89.
1593. F. Schauer, *The Law of Obscenity*, (1976), p. 159.
1594. *Id.*
1595. See, *Joseph Burstyn, Inc. v. Wilson*, 343 U.S., (1952), pp. 495, 504–05.
1596. See, *Winter v. New York*, 333 U.S., (1949), pp. 507, 515–16 (holding statute prohibiting "massing stories to incite crime" unconstitutionally vague); See also, *Gelling v. Texas*, 343 U.S., (1952), p. 960 (holding statute prohibiting licensure of motion picture "of such character as to be prejudicial to the best interest of the people of the city;" to be void for vagueness).
1597. *Roth v. United States*, 354 U.S., (1957), pp. 476, 491–92.
1598. *Id.*, p. 491.
1599. *Id.* citing *U.S. v. Petrillo*, 332 U.S., pp. 1,7,8.
1600. *Id.*, pp. 491–2.
1601. 54 U.S.L.W., (April 22, 1986), p. 4396.
1602. *Id.*, p. 4398, citing *Heller v. New York*, 413 U.S., (1973), p. 483.
1603. *Id.*, p. n.5.
1604. *Id.*, citing *Marcus v. Search Warrant*, 367 U.S., (1961), pp. 717, 732 and *Lee Art Theater, Inc. v. Virginia*, 392 U.S., (1968), p. 636.
1605. *Id.*

An application for a warrant authorizing the seizure of material presumptively protected by the First Amendment should be evaluated under the same standard of probable cause used to review warrant applications generally.[1606]

The use of municipal zoning ordinances to restrict the location of "adult" theaters was upheld by the Supreme Court in *Young v. American Mini Theaters*.[1607] The Detroit ordinance challenged in *Young* prohibited "adult" theaters from being located within 1000 feet of any two other "regulated uses" or within 500 feet of any residential area.[1608] A theater was classified as "adult" if it presented "material distinguished or characterized by an emphasis on matter depicting, describing, or relating to 'specified sexual activities' or 'specified anatomical areas' as defined elsewhere in the ordinance."[1609] The Court found that Detroit enacted the zoning ordinance based on the opinions of urban planners and real estate experts who believed that,

the location of several such business in the same neighborhood tends to attract an undesirable quantity and quality of transients, adversely affects property values, causes an increase in crime, especially prostitution, and encourages residents and business to move elsewhere.[1610]

In a plurality opinion, the Court rejected challenges to the ordinance based on vagueness and prior restraint.[1611] The Court found that the only vagueness question related to the quantum of sexually explicit activity that must be portrayed in order for the material to be "characterized by an emphasis" on such matter.[1612] The Court reasoned that for most films the question was "readily answerable" and in doubtful cases, the ordinance was

"readily subject to a narrow construction by the state courts."[1613] The ordinance did not amount to a prior restraint of speech since the theaters were not prevented from showing the movies and views were not prevented from seeing them.[1614] The Court stated that,

The mere fact that the commercial exploitation of material protected by the First Amendment is subject to zoning and other licensing requirements is not a sufficient reason for invalidating these ordinances.[1615]

The separate zoning classification for adult theaters was also not violative of the equal protection clause of the Fourteenth Amendment to the Constitution.[1616] The classification established by the Detroit ordinance was adequately supported by the city's interest in the present and future character of its neighborhoods.[1617]

The Supreme Court recently affirmed the validity of zoning ordinances that restrict the location of adult theaters in *Renton v. Playtime Theaters*.[1618] Relying on *Young v. American Mini-Theaters*, a seven-member majority of the Court upheld an ordinance enacted by the city of Renton, Washington, that prohibited adult movie theaters from locating within 1000 feet of any residential zone, single- or multiple family dwelling, church, park, or school.[1619] The definition of adult theaters was almost identical to that in *Young* but also included showings of video tape cassettes, cable television, and any other such visual media.[1620] The Court analyzed the Renton ordinance as a "content neutral" time, place, and manner regulation of speech, since it was not aimed at the content of the speech but it was directed at the secondary effects of the theaters on the surrounding community.[1621] The ordinance was designed to,

1606. *Id.*
1607. 427 U.S., (1976), p. 50.
1608. *Id.*, p. 52.
1609. *Id.*, p. 53.
1610. *Id.*, p. 55.
1611. *Id.*, p. 61.
1612. *Id.*, p. 61.
1613. *Id.*
1614. *Id.*, p. 62.
1615. *Id.*
1616. *Id.*, pp. 70–71.
1617. *Id.* p. 72.
1618. Slip. op. No. 84–1360 (Feb. 25, 1986).
1619. *Id.*, p. 1.
1620. *Id.*, p. 2.
1621. *Id.*, pp. 4–5.

prevent crime, protect the city's retail trade, maintain property values, and generally protect and preserve the quality of [the city's] neighborhoods, commercial districts, and the quality of urban life . . . .[1622]

The Court went on to analyze whether the ordinance was designed to serve a substantial governmental interest and whether it allowed for reasonable alternative avenues of communication. The city of Renton had relied heavily on the experience of and studies produced by the neighboring city of Seattle.[1623]

The Court ruled that,

The First Amendment does not require a city, before enacting such an ordinance, to conduct new studies or produce evidence independent of that already generated by other cities, so long as whatever evidence the city relies upon is reasonably believed to be relevant to the problem that the city addresses.[1624]

Reasonable alternative avenues of communication were found to be available in that 520 acres or more than five percent of the land area of Renton was left open for use as adult theater locations.[1625]

Justice William Rehnquist wrote for the majority,

That respondents must fend for themselves in the real estate market, on an equal footing with other prospective purchasers and lessees, does not give rise to a First Amendment violation.[1626]

He added that the First Amendment does not compel the government to "ensure that adult theaters or any other kinds of speech-related businesses . . . will be able to obtain sites at bargain prices."[1627]

These two decisions make it very clear that the Supreme Court will uphold what Justice Rehnquist called "the essence of zoning" and enable local jurisdictions to preserve the quality of life in their communities by restricting the locations of adult movie theaters.[1628]

The law of obscenity encompasses a myriad of legal issues. As Chief Justice Burger wrote in *Miller v. California*,[1629] consideration of these issues does not present "an easy road, free from difficulty."[1630] The Chief Justice resolutely declared that "no amount of 'fatigue' should lead us to adopt a convenient 'institutional' rationale—an absolutist, 'everything goes' view of the First Amendment—because it will lighten our burden."[1631]

1622. *Id.*, p. 6.
1623. *Id.*, p. 8.
1624. *Id.*, pp. 9–10.
1625. *Id.*, p. 11.
1626. *Id.*, p. 12.
1627. *Id.*
1628. *Id.*
1629. 413 U.S., (1973), p. 15.
1630. *Id.*, p. 29.
1631. *Id.*

Suggestions
for Citizen and Community Action
and Corporate Responsibility

PREFACE

Our legal framework has developed in many respects into a system where citizens have delegated their right to redress certain harms to government officials. Government, in turn, is charged with the responsibility of providing appropriate remedies for its citizens, including the investigation and prosecution of individuals and corporations.

A preliminary analysis of governmental responsibilities is significant for several reasons. First, the Constitution of the United States and the Amendments thereto, delineated and apportion the powers delegated the federal, state, and local governments. Each of these levels of government have restrictions on the type of activity it can regulate as well as the manner of such regulation. Some activities can be regulated at all levels of government, while others are the sole responsibility of a single level.

Second, government has been created to act on behalf of and in the best interests of its citizens. The citizens, therefore, have every right to request and expect that the laws developed by the community (whether at the federal, state or local levels) will be enforced by it elected and appointed government officials.

Third, the law is not so simplistic that individual and collective rights are mutually exclusive. Often, there are competing rights. It is this competition which ultimately must be reconciled by both government and citizens alike.

While citizens should and must rely heavily on official government action to ensure that obscenity and pornography-related laws are enforced, there are also a number of alternative remedies available to them in their effort to control the proliferation of pornography in their community. The private actions initiated by groups or individuals are often as effective as a government-initiated action. For example, citizens can organize pickets and economic boycotts against producers, distributors and retailers of pornographic materials. They can also engage in letter writing campaigns and media events designed to inform the public about the impact of pornographic materials on the community.

A citizen's right to free speeh is guaranteed under the First Amendment to the United States Constitution.[1632] This right entitles individuals to organize and speak out even against those offensive materials that are not proscribed by law or cannot under the Constitution be regulated. While such action is permissible and often desirable, there are social if not legal risks of going too far in mandating social conformity in this area. To avoid these pitfalls, citizens are encouraged to be vigorous, well-informed, but responsible advocates and to exercise self-restraint so that in exercising their rights they do not prevent other citizens from exercising theirs.

1632. "Congress shall make no law respecting an establishment of religion, or prohibiting the free exercise thereof; or abridging the freedom of speech, or of the press; or the right of the people peaceably to assemble, and to petition the Government for a redress of grievances." U.S. Const. Amend. I.

INTRODUCTION

Citizen interest in pornography control is a vital component of any local law enforcement program. Since one aspect of the constitutional test for obscenity is the notion of contemporary community standards, this is an area of the law which presents a significant opportunity for public input.

Citizens concerned about pornography in their community should initially determine the nature and availability of pornographic materials in their community, existing prosecution policies, law enforcement practices and judicial attitudes in the community. They should inquire whether these enforcement mechanisms are adequately utilized. They should determine whether the official perception of the current community standards is truly a reflection of public opinion. If enforcement mechanisms appear inadequate or ineffective, if legislative change is necessary to enhance the effectiveness of the criminal justice system, or if the volume of pornography or offensive material is a particular problem in the community, citizens should consider developing a community action program.

A successful community action program should contain the following components:

1. Sincere citizen interest in controlling the proliferation of pornographic material in their community;
2. A police department that is willing to allocate a reasonable portion of its resources to obscenity enforcement;
3. A prosecutor who, in keeping with his or her oath of office, will aggressively pursue violations of obscenity statutes with due regard for the right to distribute constitutionally protected material;
4. A judiciary that is responsive to obscenity violations and will sentence offenders appropriately.

Additional methods by which community action organizations can express their concern about pornography in their community include.

1. Citizen involvement in educating legislators, law enforcement officials and the public at large as to the impact of pornography on their particular community;
2. Citizen action in the area of lawful economic boycotts and picketing of establishments which produce, distribute or sell sexually explicit materials in the community;
3. If the techniques of anti-display and nuisance laws as well as zoning ordinances are determined to be appropriately tailored to the pornography problem in their community, citizens are encouraged to advocate any measures to their local legislators; and
4. A business community that exercises sound judgment as to the effect on the community they serve of material offered in their establishment.

In the area of pornography regulation it is important that the above items be seriously addressed and effectively coordinated. The best written laws will be ineffective if prosecutors do not enforce them or if judges fail to recognize the extent of citizen concern when sentencing offenders. The goals of the community effort against pornography should be to establish constitutionally sound obscenity laws that meet their particular needs, to encourage adequate enforcement of these laws and to use private action to curb the flow of pornography and obscenity in their community.

At the same time, citizens should be aware of the risks of an overzealous approach. First, citizens should recognize that there are a diversity of views as to what, if any, regulations should be imposed on pornographic material. The United States Supreme Court has established definitional guidelines for obscenity, which are discussed elsewhere in the Report, but not without considerable division of opinion. Undoubtedly, diversity of views regarding regulations, enforcement priorities and appropriate community action will exist to varying degrees in each community. These views should be recognized and addressed by citizen advocates.

In maintaining a balanced approach, citizens should be aware of the legal criteria for distinguishing material which is obscene from that which is merely distasteful to some. However, citizen groups may wish to focus on materials which are not legally obscene and which are constitutionally protected from government regulation. Citizens may pursue a variety of private actions with respect to this non-obscene but offensive pornographic material.

It is also important for citizen activists to recognize the rights of other individuals and organizations when exercising their own. Advocates of strict enforcement of pornography laws should recognize the rights of individuals with opposing views. Moreover, while citizens have every right to picket, the pickets should not preclude others from entering or leaving business premises.

Finally, community action groups should guard against taking extreme or legally unsound, positions or actions, such as unfounded attacks on the content of school reading lists, library shelves and general discussions of sex-related topics. With respect to their communications with a public official,

members of citizen action groups should also be aware that such officials keep duty bound to determine the legality of material without regard to that official's personal opinion.

The decision to form or support a citizen action group is one that must be made by each community and participating individuals. If a decision is reached to establish such a group, its members should become involved in advocating, establishing and maintaining community standards related to pornography. The following discussion highlights ways in which citizens can maximize their efforts in this regard while recognizing competing constitutionally protected interests. The suggestions which have been developed were prompted by hundreds of telephone calls and tens of thousands of letters from concerned citizens seeking advice on how to address the pornography issue.

SUGGESTIONS

METHODS BY WHICH CITIZENS CAN EXPRESS CONCERN ABOUT PORNOGRAPHY AND OTHER OFFENSIVE MATERIALS IN THEIR AREA (COMMUNITY)

SUMMARY

Suggestion 1. Citizens concerned about pornography in their community can establish and maintain effective community action organizations.

Suggestion 2. Community action organizations can solicit support from a broad spectrum of civic leaders and organizations.

Suggestion 3. Community action organizations can gather information about pornography in their community.

Suggestion 4. Commmunity action organizations can educate the public about the effect pornography has on their community.

Suggestion 5. Community action organizations can communicate with law enforcement officials and prosecutors about the pornography in their jurisdiction.

Suggestion 6. Citizens can file complaints, when appropriate, with the Federal Communications Commission about obscene broadcasts.

Suggestion 7. Community action organizations can conduct a "Court Watch" program.

Suggestion 8. Community action organizations are encouraged to remain informed of developments in obscenity and pornography-related laws and may wish, when appropriate, to lobby for legislative changes and initiatives.

Suggestion 9. Community action organizations can provide assistance and support to Local, State and Federal officials in the performance of their duties.

Suggestion 10. Citizens can use grassroots efforts to express opposition to pornographic materials to which they object.

Suggestion 11. Citizens can exercise their economic power by patronizing individual businesses and corporations which demonstrate responsible judgment in the types of materials they offer for sale.

Suggestion 12. Parents should monitor the music their children listen to and the recording artists and producers should use discretion in the fare they offer to children.

Suggestion 13. *All institutions which are taxpayer funded should prohibit the production, trafficking, distribution or display of pornography on their premises or in association with their institution to the extent constitutionally permissible.*

Suggestion 14. *Businesses can actively exercise their responsibility as "corporate citizens" by supporting their community's effort to control pornography.*

EXPLANATION OF SUGGESTIONS

Suggestion 1:

Citizens concerned about pornography in their community can establish and maintain effective community action organizations.

Informed and vocal citizen action and community involvement are the cornerstones of an aggressive program for enforcement of obscenity laws. Presently some form of obscenity law exists at the federal level and in all but a few states. While there are some areas of the law in which this Commission has recommended change,[1633] the lack of prosecution of obscenity cases appears to be directly attributable to a failure of enforcement. Public expression of concern about pornography and a call for redoubled law enforcement efforts will undoubtedly trigger an increase in official action.

In organizing a plan of community action, a reasonable objective should be identified. This objective may take the form of increased prosecution, tougher sentencing or private action against merchants. Citizens should also acquaint themselves with the fundamental elements of obscenity law and the principal judicial decisions in this area. It is equally vital that concerned citizens work together to establish a community standard which reflects the collective view of the community.

Citizens can become effective advocates by acting as role models both within their families and their community. To this end, they can choose (1) not to consume pornography; (2) not to patronize individual businesses or corporations which produce, distribute or sell pornography, while patronizing those that do not; (3) to voice their concerns to other citizens and government officials about the pornography problem in their community;

and (4) to organize with other concerned individuals toward a common goal.

In establishing and maintaining a community standard, citizens can engage in a variety of activities. Perhaps the best way to establish and maintain a community standard is through educational campaigns. These can take the form of letter writing campaigns, telephone banks, picketing and lawful boycotts. The end product of the information gathering and disseminating process should be the emergence of a solid collective community standard. It is important that in taking these actions citizens be respectful of the constitutional rights of persons or businesses engaged in the marketing of materials thought to be offensive by citizen group members.

Suggestion 2:

Community action organizations can solicit support from a broad spectrum of civic leaders and organizations.

A community action organization should solicit membership and support from religious, charitable, educational, political, parent-teacher, civic, and other community organizations. Citizens should also seek the endorsement of public officials for their activities. Moreover, the group should select responsible citizens as organizational leaders. In this way, the community action organization will reflect a cross section of civic leaders and organizations and maintain diverse and broad based support.

Suggestion 3:

Community action organizations can gather information about pornography in their community.

The mainstay of any effective advocacy process is complete information. Citizen action groups must be informed as to which local, state and federal officials are responsible for the enforcement of obscenity laws. These groups must also determine the nature and extent of the pornography problem in their community and have a working knowledge of the laws governing this material.

There are basically three law enforcement tiers in each of the federal, state and local government systems. The first is the investigative tier. At the state and local level, the police or other law enforcement agency investigates alleged violations of the law. At the federal

---

1633. See, Recommendations for Law Enforcement Agencies in Chapter 10.

level, the investigative agencies which have jurisdiction over obscenity violations include: the Federal Bureau of Investigation (interstate transportation of obscene material), the Postal Inspection Service (illegal use of the mail to send obscene material), and the United States Customs Service (importation of obscene material).

The second tier involves the prosecutorial function. In some jurisdictions the local prosecutor may bring criminal actions as well as civil suits[1634] on behalf of the citizens they represent, against those individuals and corporations who have allegedly violated the law.[1635]

There are prosecutors at the local and state levels who are responsible for enforcing local and state ordinances and statutes respectively. There are also prosecutors at the federal level which are part of the United States Department of Justice and are located throughout the nation in regional United States Attorneys Offices. There are ninety-four such offices in the United States.

The third tier is the judiciary. The judicial branch is responsible for offering a forum for the resolution of civil disputes and criminal allegations. The judge is also responsible for sentencing those convicted of criminal offenses. There are judges at each level of government who are responsible for interpreting and upholding the laws in their jurisdiction.

It is important to note that the same illegal act may in some instances give rise to both civil and criminal actions. Moreover, some offenses may be actionable under local, state and federal law. It is equally important to remember that many of the officials responsible for law enforcement are elected or appointed for a term of years. These individuals are sensitive to citizen input, but in the final analysis are obligated to base their prosecutorial decision on their interpretation of the law.

With this law enforcement structure in mind, there are four basic steps citizens should follow in gathering information on pornography in their community.

The first step in this information gathering process is to review local, state and federal obscenity and pornography-related laws. Second, citizens should also familiarize themselves with the pertinent legal decisions governing the control of obscene material. It is important to understand what is not obscene as well as what is obscene. In order to develop this understanding citizens are encouraged to review state and federal case law which discusses materials which have been found obscene as well as cases where sexually explicit materials have been found to be constitutionally protected. Citizens are also encouraged to consult with attorneys or other knowledgeable persons on the laws in this area.

Third, concerned citizens should survey pornography producers, distributors, retailers and the actual materials available in the market place. The following is a breakdown of the types of media and establishments that often offer pornographic material in most communities in the United States. The series of questions listed below each heading should facilitate a thorough survey of these establishments and media.

ESTABLISHMENTS AND MEDIA SURVEY QUESTIONS

1. "Adults Only"[1636] Pornographic Theaters
   a. How many pornographic theaters are there in the community? Where are they located?
   b. What movies are shown?
   c. Are sexually explicit advertisements in full public view?
   d. Are any of the theaters of the drive-in type?
   e. What precautions, if any, are taken to prevent minors from gaining access to these establishments?
2. "Adults Only" Pornographic Outlets
   a. How many pornographic outlets are there in the community and where are they located?
   b. What materials are sold? Magazines? Paperbacks? Sexual devices? Videos? Films?
   c. Are there peep show booths where movies are shown?
   d. Are there live peep shows?

1634. Civil laws include nuisance laws and may include zoning.

1635. In some jurisdictions a civil action brought on behalf of the community is done through the city attorney's office, in other jurisdictions the civil action is purely private in nature.

1636. The term "Adults Only" is meant only to describe the nature of the material presented and not necessarily the age of the patrons.

    e. Is sexual activity taking place in these establishments?
    f. Are these pornographic outlets serving as a solicitation point for prostitution?
    g. Are these pornographic outlets adequately inspected for public health violations?
3. Retail Magazine Outlets
    a. How many retail magazine outlets in the community offer pornographic material?
    b. Where are they located?
    c. What magazines and paperbacks do they stock?
    d. Are they displayed on the counter?
    e. Behind the counter?
    f. In racks with general magazines?
    g. In blinder racks?
    h. What precautions, if any, are taken to keep minors from being exposed to these materials?
4. Video Tape Cassette Retailers
    a. How many of the video tape cassette stores, and convenience stores selling and renting videos in the community, stock sexually explicit or sexually violent videos?
    b. Where are the sexually explicit or sexually violent videos displayed?
    c. What precautions, if any, are taken to keep minors from purchasing, renting and being exposed to these videos?
5. Cable, Satellite and Over-the-Air Subscription Television
    a. Is there a cable franchise or over-the-air subscription service in your community?
    b. Are sexually explicit or obscene programs being distributed? When?
    c. What precautions, if any, are taken to keep minors from being exposed to these services?
6. Dial-A-Porn
    a. Does a telephone company in your community have a Dial-A-Porn service available through its MANS Announcement Network Service (976 prefix)?
    b. What is the nature of this service?
    c. Are there pre-recorded sexually explicit conversations?
    d. Are there live telephone conversations?
    e. Are children in the community calling this service?
    f. How are the Dial-A-Porn services advertised and are these advertisements directed to the attention of minors?
    g. What precautions, if any, are being taken to shield minors from exposures to Dial-A-Porn?
7. Hotels
    a. How many hotels in the community advertise and provide sexually explicit or sexually violent movies for their guests?
    b. Where are these hotels located?
    c. What precautions, if any, are taken to preclude minors from viewing these movies?
    d. Are these hotels used for prostitution or other related crimes?
8. Computer Pornography
    a. Are pornographic computer services available in your community?
    b. What is the nature of the service?
    c. Are conversations pre-programmed?
    d. Are conversations live?
    e. Are children in the community using this service?
    f. What precautions, if any, are being taken to keep minors from gaining access to this system?

OFFICIALS

Concerned citizens should also acquaint themselves with the names of the elected and appointed officials responsible for undertaking enforcement action against obscenity. At the local level, these officials include the mayor, city council members, county prosecutor, zoning officials and the chief of police. In the case of a military community, citizens should contact the Base Commander to inform him of the pornography problem present in the community and the distribution of material on the military base.

    The community action leaders may also contact the state attorney general, state legislators, public health officials and the governor, if local efforts prove unsuccessful.

    In addition, if inadequate federal enforcement is a matter of concern, citizen action groups should consider contacting such federal officials and agencies as Members of Congress, United States Senators, the Department of Justice through its United States Attorneys, the Federal Bureau of Investigation, the United States Postal Inspection Service and the United States Customs Service.

Suggestion 4:

Community action organizations can educate the public about the effect pornography has on their community.

Citizen interest in the pornography issue is a vital component of any community action program. In order to instill such interest, community action groups should disseminate information concerning the nature and extent of pornography in the community. This should include an assessment of the current enforcement effort and the rationale for that policy. Citizen groups can provide this invaluable educational service by not only sharing their concerns about pornography, but by sharing their knowledge. This information will encourage other citizens to focus on the pornography issue and make an evaluation of its effect on their community based on a factual analysis.

Suggestion 5:

Community action organizations can communicate with law enforcement officials and prosecutors about the pornography in their jurisdiction.

Citizens and community action organizations should determine whether laws relating to obscenity are being adequately enforced in their area. Officials should be alerted to violations of laws relating to obscenity and unlawful sexual activity within their [jurisdiction].

The section below entitled *Police* contains a detailed series of questions concerning (1) investigations conducted, complaints filed and arrests made, (2) indictments, prosecutions and convictions, (3) citizen complaints, (4) problems faced by law enforcement officials and (5) law enforcement priorities, which can be used when discussing the pornography issue with any law enforcement agency official.

QUESTIONS FOR LAW ENFORCEMENT AGENCIES

Police. If it appears that inadequate police resources are being devoted to enforcement of obscenity and pornography-related laws, citizens should meet with police officials and voice their concern. The following questions may serve as a foundation for an analysis of the police role in enforcing laws in this area.

a. In the past year, how many obscenity and pornography-related complaints were filed with the police department? How many actual investigations were conducted? How many obscenity and pornography-related arrests did the department make? Did those arrests involve child pornography? Did the arrests involve adult obscenity violations? Other? Did those arrests evolve as a result of investigation or through some other circumstance?

b. How many obscenity and pornography-related cases did the police department present to the local prosecutor for prosecution during the preceding year? How many cases have been presented to the local prosecutor for prosecution in the current year? How many of the cases did the prosecutor present for indictment? What type of cases were these? How many cases did the prosecutor decline to prosecute? What types of cases were these? What was the basis for the prosecutor's decision not to prosecute these cases?

c. In what types of cases have obscenity convictions been obtained in past year? Of the cases prosecuted, how many resulted in convictions? Of the convictions obtained, how many resulted in incarceration? How many resulted in fines? In how many cases was the charge reduced by negotiation?

d. How many citizens' complaints concerning pornography were received in the preceding year? How many in the current year? What action was taken on these complaints?

e. What problems do the law enforcement agents encounter in making obscenity and pornography-related arrests? What problems do law enforcement agents face in presenting these cases for prosecution?

f. What is the police department's general policy concerning obscenity and pornography-related law enforcement? What does the police department perceive as the community standard?

Local Prosecutor. The local prosecutor may be the district, county, city, state or commonwealth's attorney, depending upon the jurisdiction. Community action groups should arrange a meeting with their local prosecutor and express their interest in the pornography problem in their area. The line of questions listed under *Police* above should provide a framework for questions for the local prosecutor. Citizens should specifically inquire about the prosecutor's assessment of the community standard in their area and the basis for the opinion.

United States Attorney. Violations of federal obscenity laws should be referred to the United States Attorney in the jurisdiction where the violation occurred. The Office of the United States Attorney is a division of the United States Department of Justice and is guided in its prosecutorial decision making by Departmental Guidelines. Prosecutorial priorities are established on the basis of the United States Attorney's assessment of a particular problem in his or her district. If pornography appears to be a major concern in a geographical area, the United States Attorney should be made aware of the severity of the problem. The United States Attorney, upon confirmation of this fact, should contact the other members of the Law Enforcement Coordinating Committee (LECC's) in his or her jurisdiction[1637] to devise a coordinated approach to this problem.

In addition to those questions suggested under *Police*, the following are a list of questions which community action leaders might wish to ask the United States Attorney:

a. How many obscenity cases were referred to the office of the United States Attorney by the Federal Bureau of Investigation, United States Customs Service, United States Postal Inspection Service or Federal Communications Commission during the past five years?

b. How many of those cases were prosecuted?

c. In how many cases was organized crime a factor?

d. How many citizens' complaints concerning obscenity were referred to the United States Attorney's office during the past five years for investigation by (1) The Postal Investigation Service when the United States mails were used illegally to send obscene material, (2) The United States Customs Service when the importation of obscene material was involved, (3) The Federal Bureau of Investigation where interstate transportation of obscene material was involved, or (4) The Federal Communications Commission where violations pertaining to cable pornography, obscene or indecent broadcasting or dial-a-porn were involved?

Local Offices of the Federal Bureau of Investigation, the United States Postal Inspection Service and the United States Customs Service. The local offices of the Federal Bureau of Investigation, the United States Postal Inspection Service and the United States Customs Service are the investigatory arms of the federal government for obscenity violations. Pornographic materials found in the community which may violate federal obscenity laws should be referred to these agencies for further investigation. These agencies should then refer all confirmed violations of federal law to the United States Attorney for prosecution, or may if appropriate, be referred to the local or state prosecutor. Community action organizations may wish to visit the local offices of these agencies and inquire about the level of obscenity enforcement in their area.

Suggestion 6:

Citizens can file complaints, when appropriate, with the Federal Communications Commission about obscene broadcasts.

See the indepth discussion of the Federal Communications Commission (FCC) and its legal responsibility in the obscenity area in Part Three. If the FCC is unresponsive to citizen complaints, citizens should advise their state and federal legislative representatives of such inaction and request their intervention.

Suggestion 7:

Community action organizations can conduct a "Court Watch" program.

A "Court Watch" program has the two-fold purpose of informing citizens about the court disposition of significant obscenity cases and expressing the citizen's view about the handling of these types of cases. Citizens involved in a "Court Watch" program will often sit through a court hearing or trial. They will write to the prosecutor, judge, or police officer and relay their opinions of the investigation, prosecution and disposition of the case.

"Court Watch" participants will also relay their findings to other interested parties, the media and legislators. In addition, these individuals will often publicly disseminate the information they have gathered when officials come up for re-appointment or re-election.

"Court Watch" programs have been conducted by Mothers Against Drunk Driving (MADD) for the past several years. Through their efforts, MADD has not only increased community awareness about drunk driving but has also been successful in influencing legislators and the law enforcement community. As a result, penalties for drunk driving have been significantly increased in many states.

In sum, a "Court Watch" program will inform the judiciary and other law enforcement officials of the community's concern about obscenity in their area.

Suggestion 8:

Community action organizations are encouraged to remain informed of developments in obscenity and pornography-related laws and may wish, when appropriate, to lobby for legislative changes and initiatives.

1637. *See,* The discussion in Recommendations for Law Enforcement Agencies about LECC's.

In many, if not most jurisdictions, the unfettered flow of obscenity is a direct product of the laxity of enforcement, rather than the inadequacy of law.

Citizens are urged to encourage the enforcement of existing laws before they attempt to introduce new legislation. If the laws themselves prove to be inadequate, then the community should identify and adopt more effective statutes. Citizens should, therefore, carefully assess the obstacles to enforcement.

See Chapter 27 for examples of state statutes which have been determined to be constitutional by state and federal courts. Chapter 27 also contains possible amendments to federal statutes which reflect Commission recommendations. As with state laws, federal statutes should be updated as the pornography industry moves into new areas of technology and consumption not presently addressed by existing laws.

Suggestion 9:

Community action organizations can provide assistance and support to Local, State and Federal officials in the performance of their duties.

Community action organizations can be a valuable resource to legislators and law enforcement agencies, by providing assistance and support. Such support can be evidenced in many ways, including letter writing campaigns, petition drives, attendance at public hearings, testimony at legislative hearings and electoral support.

Suggestion 10:

Citizens can use grassroots efforts to express opposition to pornographic materials to which they object.

Some types of pornographic materials may be harmful, offensive and incompatible with certain community values, but nonetheless fall short of the legal standard for prosecution as obscenity. In these instances grassroots efforts may be an effective countermeasure. Grassroots actions are measures initiated and coordinated privately by citizens, without governmental intervention.

Grassroots measures may include picketing and store boycotts, contacting cable casting companies to protest sexually explicit programs, contacting sponsors of television

and radio programs with pornographic or offensive content and the use of the media to express public concern through letters to the editor and audience participation programs.

A number of community action organizations have confronted retailers of pornography with the magnitude of public concern about the display and sale of this material and have experienced positive results. Some stores have been persuaded to store the material in blinder racks behind the counter. Other merchants have elected to discontinue the sale of material altogether.

When discussions with retailers prove ineffective, pickets and economic boycotts are an alternative method of citizen action. Pickets and boycotts serve to publicly identify merchants which sell this type of materials. If utilized appropriately, they can be an effective means of communicating public opposition to such material and alerting retailers that every option available will be exercised to discourage their circulation.

It is well established that citizens have a constitutional right to boycott for political purposes. In *Missouri v. National Organization for Women,*[1638] the state of Missouri brought an action against the National Organization For Women (N.O.W.) when they organized a campaign for a convention boycott of states which had not ratified the Equal Rights Amendment. The court held that such boycotts were a legitimate means of petition, protected by the First Amendment.[1639]

This issue was later addressed by the Supreme Court in *NAACP v. Claiborne Hardware Co.*[1640] In this case, a local branch of the NAACP launched a boycott of white merchants in Claiborne County, Mississippi, to secure compliance by both civic and business leaders with a list of demands for racial equality. In 1969, those merchants filed suit against the NAACP for injunctive relief and damages. The Supreme Court upheld the NAACP's actions stating:

In sum, the boycott clearly involved constitutionally protected activity. The established elements of speech, assembly, association and petition, though not identical, are inseparable. (citation omitted). Through exercise of these First Amendment rights, petitioners sought to bring about political, social, and economic change.[1641]

1638. 620 F.2d, (8th Cir. 1980), p. 1301.
1639. *Id.*, p. 1319.
1640. 458 U.S., (1982), p. 886.
1641. *Id.*, p. 911.

While pickets and boycotts are constitutionally permissible, and in some instances socially desirable, citizens exercising these practices should be sensitive to the competing rights of others who adopt an opposing viewpoint. This approach is not only socially responsible but is effective advocacy.

Moreover, the visibility of pickets and lawful boycotts will undoubtedly attract both media and corporate attention. It is important, therefore, that the community action organization carefully articulate their concerns. A rational and logical discussion of these issues is the best method to evoke constructive debate geared toward an acceptable resolution of the pornogrpahy problem in the community.

Most importantly, retailers are in business to make money. They realize that their success is a direct product of consumer satisfaction and community patronage. Citizen pickets and boycotts are a sign of community dissatisfaction. Therefore, retailers are unlikely to view organized pickets and lawful economic boycotts lightly.

These types of citizen initiatives can also be effective against cable and satellite television companies who show offensive or sexually explicit programs. Cable operators are not required to offer sexually explicit subscription services.[1642] The economic realities of consumer dissatisfaction with such programming may be felt when customers cancel subscriptions or potential subscribers notify the cable company that they are not subscribing to the basic service because sexually explicit programming is offered on the system. Citizen groups should also actively participate in the cable franchising process by informing local officials and cable company representatives what type of cable programming the community is willing to patronize.

Advertisers may also be influential in furthering grassroot initiatives. Advertisers are in the business of promoting positive public relations. If an advertiser believes that sponsoring a program, advertising in a particular magazine, or using provocative advertisements will have a negative impact on sales, it may reconsider this advertising program.

Community action organizations can also utilize numerous outlets for public comment offered by the media. Newspapers and magazines usually have "letters to the editor" columns which invite comment on current or topical issues. Radio and television talk shows may offer audience participation. These outlets offer a means of reaching large segments of the community.

Another important grassroots measure is organized involvement in the legislative process. Citizen action is essential to the enactment of local pornography-related legislation. Citizens should determine if their community has nuisance, zoning and anti-display laws and if said laws would serve the particular needs of the community.[1643] Nuisance laws prohibit certain illegal activities from taking place in pornographic establishments and often result in closing down the operation if a violation is found. Zoning laws regulate the way land can be used in the community.

Finally, anti-display laws regulate the method by which pornographic materials can be publicly displayed. Statutes or ordinances may be enacted to restrict the display of sexually explicit materials to minors. In order to conform to constitutional requirements, such laws should apply only to materials that are obscene as to minors[1644] and should also contain reasonable time, place, and manner restrictions.[1645]

In light of the legislative options available, communities can constitutionally exercise control over the location of pornographic establishments as well as the display of pornographic materials by retailers.

Citizens should contact their legislators, law enforcement officials, community leaders and media representatives to discuss the role such statutes might play in controlling the distribution of pornography in their community. Citizen action groups should educate these individuals and organizations as to how such laws could ease the circulation of pornography in their community. Only by making the control of pornography a community objective, and endorsing legislation toward that end, will the citizen action group realize its goals.

Suggestion 11:

Citizens can exercise their economic power by

1642. See, Chapter 10 for a discussion of the regulation of cable and satellite systems.
1643. See, Chapters 15 and 21 for a detailed legal discussion of the use of effectiveness of these laws.
1644. See, Ginsberg v. New York, 390 U.S., (1968), pp. 629, 645–47.
1645. See, Young v. American Mini-Theatres, 427 U.S., (1976), pp. 50, 63.

patronizing individual businesses and corporations which demonstrate responsible judgment in the types of materials they offer for sale.

Citizens should recognize individual businesses and corporations which exercise sound judgment in the selection of their book, magazine and video tape inventory. Businesses which elect not to produce, or distribute pornography in an effort to uphold or reinforce community standards should be commended. The same logic applies with equal force to radio and television stations which offer pornographic or offensive programming. Citizens can use their economic power by patronizing those businesses and corporations which support a standard of quality in the community. Such patronage and subscription will serve as further evidence to merchants that the local community has set its standard with respect to such material.

Suggestion 12:

Parents should monitor the music their children listen to and the recording artists and producers should use discretion in the fare they offer to children.

Concern has been expressed over many of the lyrics heard in contemporary rock music. Many popular idols of the young commonly sing about rape, masturbation, incest, drug usage, bondage, violence, homosexuality and intercourse. Given the significant role that music plays in the lives of young people, and considering the fact that even pre-teenagers often listen to such material several hours a day,[1646] this issue was considered carefully by the Commission. Two conclusions ensued.

First, it is recommended that parents closely monitor the music heard by their children. An effort should be made by parents to evaluate the lyrics expressed on radio and television, in rock videos and on pornographic records. Considerable concern has also been expressed about the violence and sexual explicitness portrayed on the covers of such albums. Some of the album covers displayed to the Commission appeared to exhibit depictions satisfying the legal standard for obscenity.

Second, in order to facilitate this parental involvement, the Commission endorses the agreement reached in November, 1985, between the Parents Music Resource Center and the Recording Industry Association of America. By the terms of this voluntary arrangement, the recording industry agreed to label albums containing explicit sex, violence, drug or alcohol abuse with the words, "explicit lyrics" or "parental advisory," or else the actual lyrics would be printed on the album jackets.

The Commission strongly recommends that the recording artists and producers use greater discretion in the music they offer to juveniles. As a first step, however, this voluntary agreement will help parents and teachers take a more active role in limiting their children's exposure to this material.

Suggestion 13:

All institutions which are taxpayer funded should prohibit the production, trafficking, distribution, or display of pornography on their premises or in association with their institution to the extent constitutionally permissible.

Federally funded or assisted institutions should be prohibited from producing, trafficking, distributing, or displaying pornography except for certain well defined legitimate purposes. These institutions include, but are not limited to, hospitals, schools, universities, prisons, government office buildings, military installations and outposts, and mental health facilities. We recognized that in many areas governmental action may, as a matter of constitutional law, be taken only with respect to materials that are legally obscene, and we do not suggest that institutions go beyond their constitutional limitations. In other cases, however, of which schools are the most obvious example, content-based restrictions of the material available in the institutions need not be limited to the legally obscene, and we recognized not only the right but the responsibility of such institutions to control content consistent with the needs of the institution.

Suggestion 14:

Businesses can actively exercise their responsibility as "corporate citizens" by supporting their community's effort to control pornography.

As "corporate citizens," businesses should be responsive to community sentiment regarding the production and distribution of pornographic materials. Many different types

1646. Washington, D.C., Hearing Vol. I, Kandy Stroud, pp. 243–44.

of businesses are involved in the various stages of production and retail distribution including film processors, typesetting and printing services, delivery services, warehouses, commercial realtors, computer services, cable and satellite companies, recording companies, hotels, credit card companies and numerous others. These businesses have a responsibility to exercise due care to insure that they are not contributing to the moral detriment of their community. Businesses can be encouraged to insure that they are not being unknowingly used as an instrument for the spread of obscene or pornographic material which the community has requested not be produced or sold on moral, social or other legitimate grounds.

Corporations are encouraged to conduct site inspections of their facilities and to conduct quality of content examinations of their inventory to safeguard against the sale of materials which offend the community standard. In the case of credit card companies, a review of the types of businesses that their "merchant" members are conducting might be useful. Information and entertainment companies such as cable and satellite systems, computer network services and recording companies should monitor their systems for obscene or other material which offends the community they serve. Broadcasters, advertisers and retailers should diligently protect children and unwilling adults from exposure to sexually explicit communications.

A second rule for corporations, as members of local communities, is to actively support citizen action efforts to curb the proliferation of pornography in the community.

Moreover, corporations, as part of their more general social responsibility, are encouraged to establish and participate in pornography "victim" assistance programs.[1647] They can do this by contributing to social service agencies who specialize in or deal with sexual abuse.[1648] They can also provide direct financial assistance, in the form of scholarships and vocational programs, to "victims" of pornography.[1649]

Finally, corporations can sponsor local educational programs on pornography and its effects on the community. These programs could then be provided to schools, businesses, legislators, law enforcement officials, churches, and other interested groups.

Corporations can and do have an impact on community standards and law enforcement practices. It is up to corporations to act as responsible citizens to ensure that their community is not just a location for another retail outlet, but a worthwhile place to live.

CONCLUSION

Citizen and community involvement in law enforcement and the formulation of legal initiatives is an age-old tradition. Citizens create laws through their elected officials and delegate enforcement of these laws to police, prosecutors and judges.

When the law enforcement mechanism inadequately addresses a particular problem, citizens and communities must explore other avenues. Many times citizens must on their own publicly advocate a community environment which reflects their view of an ideal place to live.

This Commission encourages citizen and community involvement. Examples abound of where citizens have made a difference in the quality of life in their community. "Neighborhood Watch" programs, where citizens protect each others' homes is a prime example of positive citizen efforts. Mothers Against Drunk Driving is another example in which citizen action has made communities across the country a safer place to live. This Commission applauds such efforts and encourages others to improve the quality of life in their community.

1647. See, Chapters 16 and 17 for a discussion of victimization.
1648. See, Chapters 16 and 17 which discusses the numerous forms of victimization associated with pornography.
1649. Id.

Production and Distribution
of Sexually Explicit Material

HISTORICAL OVERVIEW OF THE INDUSTRY

The pornography industry has grown considerably over the last thirty years by continually changing and expanding to appeal to new markets.[1650] In the last several decades, the industry has gone from a low yield, covert business to a highly visible multi-billion dollar industry.[1651] Over five hundred fifty million dollars of this may be attributed to retail sales in the Los Angeles area alone.[1652] The remaining billions of dollars worth of materials are distributed throughout the United States and abroad. In the 1950s, "adults only" pornographic establishments[1653] were dark and dingy stores and theatres located in the less desirable parts of urban areas.[1654] The sex-related materials of this period generally depicted scantily-clad women in seductive poses and were not readily available to the public.[1655] The most graphic publication of this era was the *Tijuana Bible*, a book with illustrations of various sexual acts.[1656]

Magazines were usually produced in black and white and were grainy in quality.[1657] The photographs depicted were mostly of provocatively posed nudes.[1658] Generally, the model's pubic area was not shown in these photographs.[1659] As a result, nudist magazines were extremely popular.[1660]

The films available during this period were also of very poor technical quality.[1661] The film containers were also plain. Usually, the films did not have titles but were given numbers for identifying purposes.[1662] These films showed mostly females in "strip tease"[1663] activities.[1664]

The females depicted in the films were often partially exposed in the breast area and the males, for the most part, were fully dressed.[1665] The first of these films to be a major economic success was produced in 1959 for $24,000 and was about a man who was unable to see clothing on women.[1666] This

1650. Los Angeles Hearing, Vol. I, Robert Peters, p. 32 and 60A.
1651. *Id.* p. 32, 60C; Chicago Hearing, Vol. I, Donald Smith, p. 30.
1652. *Id.*
1653. See, The discussion of "adults only" pornographic outlets.
1654. *Id.* p. 38.
1655. *Id.* pp. 38 and 60A.
1656. *Id.* p. 38.
1657. *Id.* p. 60A.
1658. *Id.* p. 39, New York Hearing, Vol. I, Bruce Taylor, pp. 240–41.
1659. *Id.*
1660. Los Angeles Hearing, Vol. I, Robert Peters, p. 39. Nudist magazines were put out by members of nudist organizations and often depicted pictures of nudists and their families.
1661. *Id.* pp. 38 and 60A.
1662. *Id.*
1663. "Strip tease" refers to the slow and seductive disrobing of a woman usually to music while on stage.
1664. *Id.* p. 38.
1665. *Id.* pp. 38–39. Some films did depict males undressing. *Id.* p. 39.
1666. *The Report of the 1970 Commission on Obscenity and Pornography*, (1970), p. 94.

film ultimately grossed $1,000,000.[1667]

While the above descriptions represent mainstream sexually oriented materials during the 1950's, some more explicit materials were also available.[1668] In some "adults only" pornographic outlets in major cities in the United States, sexually explicit materials depicting individuals with clearly visible pubic hairs could be purchased.[1669] Some "stag films,"[1670] mail order operations and underground connections, were the source for sexually explicit materials in which actual penetration was clearly visible.[1671]

In the 1950's the distribution of sexually oriented materials often took place on an informal basis through "trunk sales".[1672] During this time, Los Angeles had five "adults only" pornographic outlets, all of which were supplied in this way.[1673] The stores selling this material fronted as general newsstands and kept the sexually oriented materials in the back.[1674]

The early 1960's saw the emergence of sexually explicit materials into the public eye. Simulated sex acts with no exposed genitalia constituted the majority of sexually explicit materials and an exposed genital was an obscenity violation in almost any jurisdiction.[1675] Between 1960 and 1965, "adults only" pornographic outlets and theatre locations in Los Angeles alone increased from five to eighteen.[1676] These outlets were primarily located in the central and "Skid Row" sections of downtown.[1677] The "adults only" pornographic outlets were small and in some cases provided other publications in addition to the sexually explicit fare.[1678]

The "adults only" pornographic theatres also began to emerge in small vacated business locations.[1679] These premises were often rundown and conducive to lewd activity.[1680]

During the 1960s, magazine print quality improved.[1681] Magazines were generally four-color publications which continued to depict female nudes.[1682] Nudist magazines also remained popular.

The 1970 Commission on Obscenity and Pornography described the sexually explicit magazines of this period in detail.

"Adult" Magazines Until the Late 1960's. Court decisions overruling obscenity convictions of sexually oriented magazines have affected the market almost as profoundly as similar court decisions dealing with textual material. In 1958, the Supreme Court reversed an obscenity conviction involving two nudist magazines containing pictures clearly revealing the genitalia of men, women, and children. During the early 1960's, nudist magazines slowly broke down the practice of segregating the sexes in photographs which had been observed earlier. Publishers remained very restrained about the situations portrayed in the photos. Any scene implying sexual activity was scrupulously avoided, and body contact was allowed only in situations of a wholly non-sexual nature. Nudist magazines of the early 1960s contained numerous articles extolling nudism and portrayed nudists only at work and play.

By the mid-1960s, secondary publishers had become much bolder in pictorial nudity. Implied erotic activity became an integral part of pseudo-nudist magazines. The so-called "legitimate" nudist magazines, which attempted to reproduce candid shots of nudist camp activities, passed nearly into oblivion because they could not compete in the marketplace with magazines which copied the nudist format, but contained more erotic pictures and more attractive models. By 1967 or 1968, a whole new group of magazines featured nude females posed in a manner which empha-

---

1667. *Id.*
1668. New York Hearing, Vol. I, Bruce Taylor, pp. 240–41.
1669. *Id.* p. 240.
1670. Stag Films was an actual film production label made in Nashville, Tennessee. Los Angeles Hearing, Vol. I, Ted McIlvenna, p. 206.
1671. New York Hearing, Vol. I, Bruce Taylor, p. 241.
1672. Los Angeles Hearing, Vol. I, Robert Peters, pp. 39, 60A. "Trunk sales" refers to the distribution of materials out of the trunk of the seller's car.
1673. *Id.*
1674. *Id.*, p. 39.
1675. *Id.*, p. 60A.
1676. *Id.*
1677. *Id.*, pp. 60A–60B.
1678. *Id.*, p. 60B.
1679. *Id.*, p. 39.
1680. *Id.*, p. 60B.
1681. *Id.*, p. 40.
1682. *Id.*

sized their genitalia in complete detail (known in the industry as "spreader" or "split beaver" magazines). Most contained little, if any, text.

At the same time, male homosexual magazines developed along the same lines, also assisted by favorable Supreme Court decisions which overturned previous obscenity convictions. Homosexual magazines through the late 1960s consisted primarily of posed pictures of nude males. The genitals of the models, the focal points of the photographs, were flaccid. Photographs were usually of a single model, although group scenes were not unusual. There was little or no physical contact between models, and sexual activity was generally not even implied.

Relatively small quantities of fetish books and magazines were produced featuring uses of items such as rubber and leather wearing apparel, lingerie, high heeled boots, etc. Sadomasochistic depictions or descriptions of bondage, spanking, and "domination" by clubs, whips, etc. were also available in limited quantities. Sexual explicitness in these materials was usually far less than in typical "girlie" magazines. Although quite a number of titles were produced, these magazines were not a major factor in the marketplace.

Sexual Content of "Adult" Magazines— 1969-1970. Through June, 1970, there have been few dramatic innovations in the sexual content of "adults only" magazines. Additional female models have been added to the photographs, and many magazines have integrated male and female models. This has led to considerable implied sexual activity in the photographs. Actual sexual activity, or arousal of the male models is seldom depicted.

Magazines aimed at male homosexuals have changed somewhat in the last year or two, and self-imposed restrictions on implied sexual activity are eroding slowly. Most homosexual magazines, however, are considerably less graphic than magazines featuring females.

Fetish magazines continue to be a rather insignificant part of the total production, and have changed relatively little from the mid-1960s.[1683]

During the 1960's, the pocketbook emerged and replaced the *Tijuana Bible*.[1684]

While the pocketbooks were not illustrated, extremely graphic language was used in the text.[1685]

The 1970 Commission on Obscenity and Pornography described the sexually explicit paperback book of this period as follows:

"Sex Pulp" Books Until the Late 1960's. The sexual content of paperback books published for the "adults only" market has become progressively "stronger" in the past decade, primarily because of court decisions involving books such as *Tropic of Cancer* and *Fanny Hill* (See, Legal Panel Report [of the 1970 Commission]).

Until the mid-1960s, most paperback books published for the secondary market were knkown as "sex pulps". These followed a rather rigid set of ground rules: vulgar terms describing sexual acts, genitalia, excretion, etc., were not used, but rather euphemistic or symbolic language was substituted; the books consisted of a series of sexual adventures tied together by a minimal plot; sexual foreplay was described in great detail, but the mechanics of the sex act was not; and much of the sexual content was left to the imagination of the reader.

By the late 1960s, however, the "sex pulp" formula had become relatively passe. A new breed of sexually oriented secondary books came onto the market, in which all restraints upon both language and descriptions of sexual activity were eliminated. In many there was little more than a compilation of non-stop sexual activity.

Some paperback novels of the "sex pulp" type of the early 1960s are still published, probably because a portion of the market prefers less explicit material. However, the industry's criteria for "sex pulp" books has been broadened; this classification now includes any paperback which is badly written, edited, and typeset, and is apparently aimed at relatively poorly educated readers, irrespective of the degree of explicitness of its language or descriptions of sexual activity.

Wholly Textual Sex Oriented Paperback Books in the Secondary Market, 1969-1970. Virtually every English language book thought to be obscene when published, and many similar books translated into English, have been reissued by secondary publishers. The entire stockpile of "classic erotic litera-

---

1683. *The Report of the 1970 Commission on Obscenity and Pornography,* (1970), pp.115–16.
1684. Los Angeles Hearing, Vol. I, Robert Peters, p. 40. Pocketbooks were paperback books which fit into your pocket. They were the forerunner of today's paperbacks.
1685. *Id.*

ture" (e.g., The Kama Sutra, Frank Harris, De Sade, etc.) published over centuries has thus come onto the market. Another type of sexually oriented book has become popular in the last few years—pseudo-medical, alleged case-study analysis of graphic descriptions of sexual activity. Although such books purport to be written by medical doctors or Ph.D.'s, they primarily consist of graphic descriptions of sexual activity.

As of 1970, publishers of sex-oriented, wholly textual paperback books are convinced that there are no legal restrictions on the content of any wholly textual publication. As a result, "adults only" paperback books published and sold in the United States cannot possibly be exceeded in candor, graphic description of sexual activity or use of explicit language. The overwhelming majority of these books are intended for a heterosexual male readership. Almost no such books are written for a female audience. Perhaps 10% or more are directed at the male homosexual market, and less than 5% are specifically written for any of the various fetishes.

Illustrated Paperback Books, 1969–1970. In the past two or three years, some secondary publishers have included photographs in their books. Initially, such paperbacks included photographs in which young females posed with the focus of the camera directly upon their genitalia. In 1968 and 1969, however, two additional types came onto the market which revolutionized the sexual content of illustrated paperback books. One was the illustrated "marriage manual" containing photographs of couples engaging in sexual intercourse "for an educational purpose". The most recent marriage manual of this type depicts fellatio and cunnilingus in addition to vaginal intercourse (penetration shown in detail). The second "breakthrough" occurred in 1969 with the publication of books purporting to be serious studies of censorship and pornography. These books contain illustrations ranging from Oriental and European erotic art to reproductions of "hard-core" photographs taken from Danish magazines, which graphically depict sex activities such as vaginal and anal penetration, fellatio, and cunnilingus. Following this lead, a number of publications containing "hard-core" photographs with textual commentary have been published and are in circulation in many major metropolitan areas.

To some extent, therefore, the pictorial content of a number of paperbacks published and sold in the United States has reached the level of sexual explicitness found in Danish materials. However, Danish-type "pornographic" magazines (consisting entirely of photographs of sexual activity) have yet to be published and sold openly in this country; domestic publishers apparently believe that the inclusion of text is required to provide a legal defense in the event of an obscenity prosecution.[1686]

During the 1960s, the technical quality of sexually explicit films remained poor, but the content began to change.[1687] In the early 1960s, the majority of films involved simulated sexual acts with the focus on female genitalia.[1688] By the end of the 1960s, sexually explicit films showing oral and genital copulation were more readily available.[1689] The packaging of the films also changed. The boxes were more colorful and some had a photograph on the cover depicting a scene from the film.[1690]

The 1970 Commission on Pornography and Obscenity described the sexually explicit films during this period as follows:

> Between 1964 and 1968, exploitation films moved in a variety of directions. Some producers dropped all pretense of a plot and substituted nudity for a story line. Others produced "roughies," a mixture of sex and violence. Some films depicted women as aggressors (nymphomaniacs, lesbians, and prostitutes); others portrayed them as victims. A few films were self-styled "documentaries" dealing with sexual mores and aberrations. Still others were known as "kinkies" (dealing with fetishes) and "ghoulies" (minimizing nudity and maximizing violence).

> In 1969, and continuing into 1970, exploitation films dealt with the same themes often found in general release motion pictures: perversion, abortion, drug addiction, wayward girls, orgies, wife-swapping, vice dens, prostitution, promiscuity, homosexuality, transvestism, frigidity, nymphomania, lesbianism, etc. Almost all of the popular movie-making formulas have been utilized as settings for presenting these themes, including westerns and historical epics, although contemporary settings are still the most widely used.

1686. *The Report of the 1970 Commission on Obscenity and Pornography,* (1970), pp.112–14.
1687. Los Angeles Hearing, Vol. I, Robert Peters, p. 40.
1688. *Id.*
1689. New York Hearing, Vol. I, Bruce Taylor, p. 292A.
1690. Los Angeles Hearing, Vol. I, Robert Peters, pp. 40–41.

The vast majority of exploitation films are directed at the male heterosexual market. Relatively few films are produced for a male homosexual audience, but the number of these films has increased in the past year or two. A small number of theaters exclusively exhibit male homosexual films and a few exhibit such films on occasion. This market is quite small at present, and is included in the estimate for the entire exploitation film market, although "male" films are developing their own producers and theaters.

Full female nudity in exploitation films has become common in the last year or two, although male genital exposure is almost unknown except in those films directed at the male homosexual market. Sexual activity covering the entire range of heterosexual conduct leaves almost nothing to the imagination. Actual sex acts, however, are not shown, only strongly implied or simulated. Self-imposed restrictions on the use of "vulgar" language have also disappeared in many films.[1691]

During the 1960s the distribution of sexually explicit pornographic materials expanded significantly.[1692] Although "trunk sales" remained the major method of distribution, large wholesale warehouses began to emerge.[1693] The wholesalers used small storefront businesses and older commercial buildings for storage and dissemination of materials.[1694] The channels of distribution also became more complex with producers and wholesalers providing a variety of materials to outlets which now stocked several different types of sexually explicit materials.[1695]

The real proliferation of sexually explicit materials in the United States took place in the 1970s.[1696] During this period, distribution locations for sexually explicit materials in Los Angeles alone increased from eighteen to over 400.[1697]

In the 1970s, producers of sexually oriented materials depicted sexually explicit and varied acts and continuously tested the bounds of existing obscenity laws.[1698] While most of these materials consisted primarily of simulated sexual acts, materials depicting actual sexual intercourse and oral copulation were increasingly available.[1699] Sexually explicit magazines like Swedish Erotica were distributed widely and focused on depictions of actual sex acts.[1700] Most of the materials designed to appeal to paraphilias became prevalent during this period, including those showing harmful homosexual acts, sadomasochism, bondage and discipline, children and animals as well as visuals of ejaculation, urination and defecation.[1701]

Child pornography was more commonly available in the 1970s and appeared in commercially produced magazines such as Moppets and Where the Young Ones Are.[1702] Child pornography and materials with depictions of bestiality were openly available at some "adults only" pornographic outlets,[1703] sold under-the-counter in others and also available through mail-order sales.[1704]

"Adults only" pornographic theaters became more noticeable as they advertised and showed films of better technical quality.[1705] Many of the mainstream theaters went out of business in the 1970s and were purchased to show sexually explicit films.[1706] The most widely circulated of these films in the history of the industry, "Deep Throat"[1707] and "The Devil in Miss Jones," were produced and marketed during this period.

In the late 1970s, the industry expanded to include much larger "adults only" pornographic outlets, complete with peep show booths.[1708] The number of independently owned stores declined and were replaced by

---

1691. The Report of the 1970 Commission on Obscenity and Pornography, (1970), pp. 94–95.
1692. Los Angeles Hearing, Vol. I, Robert Peters, pp. 41, 60B.
1693. Id.
1694. Id., p. 60B.
1695. Id., p. 41.
1696. Id., p. 41 and 60B; New York Hearing, Vol. I, Carl Shoffler and Ledra Brady, p. 238A–5.
1697. Los Angeles Hearing, Vol. I, Robert Peters, p. 60B.
1698. Los Angeles Hearing, Vol. I, Robert Peters, pp. 44–45.
1699. Id., pp. 43, 44, 60B.
1700. Id., p. 44.
1701. Id., pp. 44, 45, 60B.
1702. Id., p. 48.
1703. Child pornography was sold over the counter in New York City during this period.
1704. Id., p. 60B.
1705. Id., p. 42.
1706. Id.
1707. "Deep Throat" cost twenty-five thousand dollars to produce and has earned over fifty million dollars.
1708. Los Angeles Hearing, Vol. I, Robert Peters, pp. 41, 42, and 51; See, The detailed discussion of "adults only" pornographic outlets and peep show booths.

stores owned by producers and distributors of sexually explicit materials who wanted to enter the retail business.[1709] The company-owned "adults only" pornographic outlet became prevalent in the 1970s and has continued to dominate the retail market.[1710]

The distribution of sexually explicit materials in the 1970s became a sophisticated business.[1711] Not only were distributors investing in retail outlets, but they began to operate out of more modern facilities with some distributors constructing their own buildings to accommodate their growth.[1712]

The Industry Today

Southern California is the production capital of the world for sexually explicit materials.[1713] At least eighty percent of the sexually explicit video tapes, eight millimeter films and sexual devices and paraphernalia that are produced in the United States are produced and distributed within Los Angeles County.[1714]

Southern California has become the center of the sexually explicit film and film-related industries for the same reasons that it is the center of the mainstream film industry: the availability of resources and the temperate climate.[1715] Processing facilities and equipment, as well as film technicians, camera operators and performers are readily accessible for local operations producing sexually explicit material.[1716]

The 1980s have seen the complete transformation of the industry into a big business with large scale distributors,[1717] theater chains,[1718] and technological advances such as home videos,[1719] subscription television,[1720] Dial-A-Porn[1721] and computer sex subscription services.[1722] Distribution locations have become large complexes operating out of modern industrial centers.[1723] The major distributors own their own buildings and have incorporated all aspects of production into their businesses.[1724]

The following portions of this chapter are devoted to an in depth discussion of the industry today. These portions describe the various sexually oriented materials and services and how and where these products and services are produced and distributed.

It should be noted that compiling information on the production and distribution aspects of this industry was a very difficult task. Much of the detailed information is closely guarded by industry representatives and was thus unavailable to the Commission.

PRODUCTION, DISTRIBUTION, AND TECHNOLOGY OF SEXUALLY EXPLICIT MATERIALS

MOTION PICTURES

Production

The average cost of producing a feature length sixteen or thirty-five millimeter[1725] sexually explicit movie for theatrical release is seventy-five thousand dollars. The costs may range from thirty to one hundred fifty thousand dollars.[1726] A sixteen millimeter film

---

1709. *Id.*, p. 42.
1710. *Id.*
1711. *Id.*, p. 51.
1712. *Id.*, pp. 51, 60B.
1713. Los Angeles Hearing, Vol. I, James Docherty, p. 6.
1714. *Id.*
1715. *Id.*, p. 7.
1716. *Id.*
1717. *Id.*, p. 60D.
1718. *Id.*, p. 52.
1719. *Id.*, pp. 52–53.
1720. See, Section D, *infra.*
1721. See, Section E, *infra.*
1722. See, Section F, *infra.*
1723. *Id.*, pp. 54, 60D.
1724. *Id.*
1725. Thirty-five millimeter films are more expensive to produce than sixteen millimeter films.
1726. Los Angeles Hearing, Vol. I, William Roberts, p. 72. John Weston, Counsel, Adult Film Association of America, estimates that a feature length film costs between $75,000 and $125,000 to produce. Interview with John Weston, Counsel, Adult Film Association of America (Mar. 8, 1986).

that will be marketed on video tape costs between ten and thirty thousand dollars to produce.[1727]

The sexually explicit film industry is presently in a state of transition from a theater centered base to one dominated by video tape cassettes viewed in the home.[1728] Not surprisingly, the most rapidly growing method of production is to shoot a sexually explicit movie directly on video tape.[1729] A sixty minute video can be produced in two days at a cost of between four and eight thousand dollars.[1730] A ninety minute video is often taped within three days at a cost between ten and twenty thousand dollars.[1731] The costs primarily consist of performer and crew fees.[1732]

Most sexually explicit movies begin by the producer[1733] choosing a title.[1734] The producer attempts to choose a title that will attract the customer's eye and make the movie more marketable. One current trend is to take popular general release movies and develop sexually explicit "takeoffs" based on the titles and plots of the general release movies.[1735]

After a title has been selected, the script is written to suit the title. Sometimes, however, the script has no relationship to the title.[1736] In addition, it is not uncommon for producers to use the same script for more than one movie.[1737]

Once a title is chosen and a script written, the producer finds a location at which to shoot the movie.[1738] Films may be shot in motel rooms, private homes or on sound stages.[1739] The primary consideration for the type of location used is often the budget allotted to the particular film.[1740]

After a location is selected, the producer chooses the performers.[1741] Producers sometimes contact performers through agents.[1742] The producer usually looks through the agent's book listing performers along with their photographs.[1743] The producer may choose a performer on the basis of appearance alone or on the basis of previous performances.[1744] The producer may select performers by using a "cattle call," in which ten or fifteen performers are asked to appear at his location for an interview.[1745] In Los Angeles there are two agents who specialize in providing performers for sexually explicit films.[1746] The agent receives forty-five to fifty dollars a day for each performer that he provides.[1747]

The producer is looking for several things when choosing the performers. The most important factor is appearance.[1748] Producers may want performers who have certain anatomical characteristics or who look particularly youthful.[1749] The second criterion is that the performer must be able to do the sexual acts called for in the script.[1750] These acts may include sadomasochistic activities, anal sex, group sex, urination and defecation.[1751]

Female performers earn $350 to $500 per

1727. Los Angeles Hearing, Vol. I, William Roberts, p. 73.
1728. Los Angeles Hearing, Vol. I, Les Baker, pp. 203B-2-3.
1729. Los Angeles Hearing, Vol. I, William Roberts, p. 73.
1730. Id.
1731. Id.
1732. Id.
1733. The term "producer" is used to include the producer, writer and director as one individual, since this is usually the case. Id., p. 62.
1734. Id.
1735. Id., p. 63 (e.g., Romancing the Stone, Romancing the Bone; On Golden Pond, On Golden Blonde; the Wizard of Oz, the Wizard of Ahas; the Cotton Club, the Cotton Tail Club).
1736. Id.
1737. Id.
1738. Id.
1739. Id.
1740. Id., pp. 63-64.
1741. See, Chapter 17 for a detailed discussion of performers.
1742. Id., p. 64.
1743. Id.
1744. Id.
1745. Id.
1746. Id.
1747. Id.
1748. Id.
1749. Id.
1750. Id., p. 65.
1751. Id.

day of performance.[1752] Male performers earn $250 to $450 per day of performance.[1753] Better known "stars" of sexually explicit movies earn from $1,000 to $2,500 per day of performance.[1754] Performers may also be paid on the basis of the number and type of sex acts in which they engage.[1755] Some performers receive $250 per sex act.[1756]

As with any filming, the producer must own or rent lights, cameras and props.[1757] The necessary equipment costs five hundred to one thousand dollars per day to rent.[1758] Larger production companies usually own their own equipment.[1759]

The technicians used in sexually explicit movies also may work in the general release film industry.[1760] Others work in the sexually explicit film industry when they are unemployed or need to supplement their income. Still other technicians began and remain exclusively in the sexually explicit film industry.[1761]

When the producer is ready to begin filming, he will often contact the agent and instruct the agent to have the performers meet the producer at a designated location.[1762] The producer sometimes transports the performers to the shooting location to avoid attracting the attention of the police or others.[1763] The police often learn of sexually explicit movie shootings when a neighbor complains about activities next door.[1764] The producer may also have security personnel check for police surveillance while the shooting is in progress.[1765]

Once on site, the performers go through make-up and wardrobe, and have a script review.[1766] The script is usually minimal and is rewritten during the filming.[1767]

Dialogue scenes are usually shot in the first two or three takes.[1768] The sex scenes are usually filmed in one take.[1769] The director will usually tell the performers exactly what he wants them to do.[1770] The director will tell them which way to turn their heads and what positions to use while they engage in sexual activity.[1771]

The most important part of the movies considered by the trade to be the male ejaculation scene.[1772] This scene is always filmed when the male's penis is outside the partner's body.[1773] The male usually ejaculates on the buttocks, breast, or face of his partner.[1774]

Still photographs may also be taken during the shooting[1775] and are used for promotional material such as fliers, film or video package covers, posters, as well as unrelated magazine layouts.[1776]

It is also common for two versions of a movie to be produced during the filming.[1777] One version contains more sexually explicit scenes than the other.[1778] The less sexually explicit film is sometimes introduced into the subscription television market.[1779]

A day's shooting may last from seven in the morning until two o'clock the following

---

1752. Id.
1753. Id.
1754. Id.; The War Against Pornography, Newsweek, (Mar. 18, 1985), p.62.
1755. Los Angeles Hearing, Vol. I, William Roberts, p. 65.
1756. Id.; See, Chapter 17 which discusses performers.
1757. Los Angeles Hearing, Vol. I, William Roberts, pp. 65–66.
1758. Id., p. 66.
1759. Id.
1760. Id.; Interview with John Weston, Counsel, Adult Film Association of America (Mar. 8, 1986).
1761. Los Angeles Hearing, Vol. I, William Roberts, p. 66.
1762. Id., p. 67.
1763. Id.
1764. Id.
1765. Id.
1766. Id., p. 68.
1767. Id.
1768. Id.
1769. Id.
1770. Id.
1771. Id., pp. 68–69.
1772. Id., p. 69.
1773. Id.
1774. Id.
1775. Id.
1776. Id., pp. 69–70.
1777. Id., p. 70.
1778. Id.
1779. Id.

morning.[1780] During this time, the performers and crew are literally locked into the location.[1781] The meals are prepared or brought in and lunch and dinner breaks are taken on site.[1782]

At the conclusion of the shooting the performers are asked to sign a "Model Release."[1783] The performers are then paid for their work. Payment is generally made in cash.[1784] After the shooting is complete, the producer prepares a master print to be sold to the distributor.[1785]

The distributor first edits the movie and then adds the soundtrack.[1786] There are basically three types of sexually explicit films marketed: eight millimeter, sixteen millimeter and thirty-five millimeter.[1787] The eight millimeter films are usually made into loops.[1788] A "loop" is a seven to eight minute excerpt of a feature length film.[1789] A film may be purchased or viewed as several different loops such as "Swedish Erotica One to Six." "Swedish Erotica Two" is actually a continuation of "Swedish Erotica One."[1790]

While eight millimeter film was a popular medium of production in the past, it is no longer widely used.[1791] One law enforcement officer estimated that by 1990, eight millimeter sexually explicit movies will be a thing of the past.[1792] This prediction was based on the fact the eight millimeter films are usually of poor technical quality, lack audio sound, and the fact that lower cost video tapes of improved technical quality are replacing eight millimeter films in peep show booths nationwide.[1793]

Most of the feature length films shown in "adults only" theaters across the country are shot on sixteen millimeter film.[1794] Sixteen millimeter is a popular medium because, through film processing technology, it can be easily converted into eight millimeter or thirty-five millimeter.[1795] Few sexually explicit films are made on thirty-five millimeter because production costs are prohibitive.[1796]

Distribution

Motion Picture Association of America's Rating System. An overview of the Motion Picture Association of America's (MPAA) rating system provides an initial perspective as to the content of some sexually explicit films. The rating system was established on November 1, 1968, by the MPAA, the National Theater Owners and the International Film Importers and Distributors of America.[1797] The rating system evolved because the motion picture industry recognized that it had an obligation to the parents and children of America to provide information about its films in advance of their viewing.[1798]

The Motion Picture Association of America has established five rating categories:

G: "General Audiences—All ages admitted."[1799]

PG: "Parental Guidance suggested; some material may not be suitable for children."[1800]

PG-13: "Parents are strongly cautioned to give special guidance for attendance of children under 13. Some material may be inappropriate for younger children."[1801]

1780. *Id.*, p. 69.
1781. *Id.*, p. 70.
1782. *Id.*
1783. *Id.*
1784. *Id.*, p. 71.
1785. *Id.*
1786. *Id.*
1787. Interview with Don Smith, Los Angeles Police Department (Mar. 9, 1986).
1788. *Id.*
1789. *Id.*
1790. *Id.*
1791. *Id.*
1792. *Id.*
1793. *Id.*; See, The discussion of peep show booths for further information.
1794. *Id.*
1795. *Id.*
1796. *Id.*
1797. Los Angeles Hearing, Vol. II, Jack Valenti, p. 55B.
1798. *Id.*, p. 55C.
1799. *Id.*, p. 55H.
1800. *Id.*
1801. *Id.*

R: "Restricted, under seventeen requires accompanying parent or guardian."[1802]

X: "No one under seventeen admitted."[1803]

Some of the language in "G" rated movies may go beyond polite conversation. The violence in these films is minimal and there are no nudity or sex scenes.[1804] In a "PG" film, there may be some profanity and violence. There are no explicit sex scenes but brief nudity may be present.[1805]

The film's use of one of the harsher sexually derived words, though only as an expletive, will require the rating board to initially issue that film at least a "PG-13" rating.[1806]

If the same sexually derived word is used in a sexually explicit context, the film will receive an "R" rating.[1807] More than one expletive in a film results in an initial "R" rating.[1808] An "R" rated film contains some explicit material relating to language, violence, nudity, sexuality, drug use, or other content.[1809] However, explicit sex is not found in "R" rated films.[1810]

No children are admitted to an "X" rated movie. "X" rated films may contain brutal or sexually related language, explicit sex or excessive and sadistic violence.[1811] A film which is not submitted for a rating by the MPAA cannot, without authorization, use any rating except "X".[1812]

Some producers of sexually explicit movies attach an "X" rating to their product without every submitting the film to the MPAA. In the opinion of MPAA President, Jack Valenti, this is because the producers have assured themselves of the character of their movie and feel the rating is unnecessary.[1813] Moreover, many of these films are produced for the "X" rated movie consumer market.

All advertisements and publicity material must also be submitted to the MPAA for approval prior to the public release of the film.[1814] This includes, but is not limited to, newspaper, magazine, radio and television advertisements, as well as previews of coming attractions.[1815] Once a rating is determined and assigned, it must then appear on all approved advertisements.[1816] The MPAA ratings may be displayed only on versions of the film, video or advertising that are identical to the one rated by the MPAA board.[1817] Any violation of this rule will be met with "cease and desist" demands and, if necessary, legal action by the MPAA.[1818]

The scope of the rating system has recently expanded.[1819] In 1984, the fourteen major home video companies announced that the MPAA ratings given to films for theatrical release will automatically appear on video cassette and disc versions identical to the rated theater version.[1820] This agreement formalized the procedures most home video companies have used since the beginning of the industry.[1821]

Since its inception through September 30, 1985, the MPAA rating board had rated 7,036 feature films.[1822] Table 1 sets forth the number of films which have been rated in each category.

The sexually explicit film industry has established its own structure and guidelines. The Adult Film Association of America (AFAA) represents two hundred of the pro-

1802. *Id.*, p. 55K.
1803. *Id.*
1804. *Id.*, p. 55H.
1805. *Id.*, p. 55I.
1806. *Id.*
1807. *Id.*
1808. *Id.*
1809. *Id.*, p. 55K.
1810. *Id.*
1811. *Id.*
1812. *Id.*, p. 55M.
1813. *Id.*, pp. 12–13.
1814. *Id.*, p. 55N.
1815. *Id.*
1816. *Id.*
1817. *Id.*, p. 55M.
1818. *Id.*
1819. *Id.*, p. 55P.
1820. *Id.*
1821. *Id.*
1822. *Id.*, p. 55L.

Table 1

Rating	Number	Percentage
G	900	12.9
PG	2523	35.9
PG–13**	60	.8
R	3190	45.2
X***	363	5.2

*This Table covers the period from the beginning of the MPAA to September 30, 1985.

**Introduced in July, 1984.

***This number represents a small portion of films advertised as "X" rated. The remaining "X" rated films are self-designated and are not reflected in the 363 figure.

ducers, distributors and exhibitors of the sexually explicit film and video industries.[1823] The AFAA credo states:

1. That films of adult subject matter will be produced for and exhibited to adult audiences and that persons not of legal age will not be admitted.
2. That the definition of an "adult" is that designation set by the constituted authorities of the community, but in no event any person under the age of eighteen years.
3. That we will produce and exhibit only films that are in conformity with the Free Speech provisions of the Constitution of the United States of America.
4. That we will respect the privacy of the general public in our advertising and public displays.
5. That we in no manner will condone, produce, or exhibit child pornography in any form.[1824]

John Weston, counsel to the AFAA, testified that films made with unconsenting adults and children, as well as material depicting bestiality and excrement would be considered off limits by the AFAA.[1825] Unlike the MPAA, there is presently no enforcement mechanism to ensure that the above procedures are followed.[1826]

Sexually Explicit Motion Pictures. Independent of the rating systems, there are several steps involved in the distribution of a sexually explicit motion picture. Once a film is completed, the master print is sold to a distributor at a one hundred percent profit to the producer. The sexually explicit film distribution process is similar to that used for general release films. The sexually explicit film distributor reproduces the movie and packages it. Advertising and promotional materials are prepared by the distributor to announce the new movie. The distributor then markets the movie to wholesalers.

The wholesaler carries hundreds to thousands of titles. The quality, genre and type of film may influence the wholesale and retail prices. The retailers realize a sizeable profit for the sexually explicit films. While eight millimeter sexually explicit films are not the major influence in today's market that they were five years ago, they continue to have a large profit margin.[1827] Both general release and sexually oriented eight millimeter films are processed at the same cost, but there is a significant difference in cost at the retail level. A general release film has a four hundred percent markup as compared to an eight hundred to one thousand percent markup for the sexually oriented film.[1828] The sexually explicit eight millimeter films are mainly distributed to "adults only" pornographic outlets across the country.

At present, there are approximately twelve to twenty-four production companies involved in making sexually explicit theatrical release sixteen millimeter or thirty-five milli-

1823. Los Angeles Hearing, Vol. I, Les Baker, p. 203B–2.

1824. Id. at 203B–3.

1825. Los Angeles Hearing, Vol. I, John Weston, pp. 174–75. See also, Los Angeles Hearing, Vol. I, Les Baker, pp. 203B–4–203B–5.

1826. Los Angeles Hearing, Vol. I, John Weston, pp. 182–83.

1827. Los Angeles Hearing, Vol. I, Robert Peters, p. 60C.

1828. Id.

meter films.[1829] These films are sold to distributors who in turn sell or rent the films to "adults only" pornographic movie theaters across the country.

In 1985, approximately one hundred full length sexually explicit films were distributed to nearly seven hundred "adults only" pornographic theaters in the United States.[1830] These theaters sold an estimated two million tickets each week to their sexually explicit movies.[1831] The annual box-office receipts were estimated at five hundred million dollars.[1832]

Sexually explicit motion pictures are advertised on theater marquis and posters. These films are also advertised in sexually explicit tabloids and magazines. Many major city daily newspapers also advertise "X" rated movies alongside general release films.

John Weston, Counsel for the Adult Film Association of America, stated that the "adults only" pornographic theater business has been declining and will be virtually nonexistent by 1990.[1833] He believes this will occur for a variety of reasons. First, the theaters themselves are expensive to maintain and operate. Second, with the advent of video tape cassettes, Americans are choosing not to go out to movie theaters for their movie entertainment. Weston bases this latter statement on the fact that theater admission costs are higher than video rentals, as well as his belief that an increasing number of people would rather watch movies in the comfort of their own home.[1834] He predicts these same trends will hold true for general release movies as well.[1835]

VIDEO TAPE CASSETTES

Production

Video cassette recorders (VCRs) were first introduced into the American market in 1975 and are now used in approximately twenty-eight percent of all American homes.[1836] It has been estimated that VCRs will be in thirty-eight percent of American homes with televisions by the end of 1986[1837] and eighty-five percent of these homes by 1995.[1838]

Most consumers initially used their VCRs for recording broadcast and cable programming that they were unable to view at its scheduled hour.[1839] In the late 1970s, "X" rated video tapes, which were retailing for over one hundred dollars, constituted over half of the pre-recorded industry sales.[1840] It was uncertain during this beginning stage of the VCR industry what consumer demand would be for purchase and sale of pre-recorded tapes. It was equally uncertain what type of programming, aside from "X" rated films, would appeal to the public.[1841]

As evidenced in the following Table prepared by the Video Software Dealers Association, a wide range of video programming is consumed by the public.

Table 2[1842]

Type	Percent of Market
Action/Adventure	25.2%
Science Fiction	19.6%
Adult	13.0%
Children's	10.4%
Comedy	8.8%
Drama	8.6%
Horror	8.0%
Music Video	2.9%
How–To	2.7%
Foreign	0.8%

1829. Interview with John Weston, Counsel, Adult Film Association of America (Mar. 8, 1986).
1830. *The War Against Pornography,* Newsweek, (Mar. 18, 1985), p. 62.
1831. Id.
1832. Id.
1833. Interview with John Weston, Counsel, Adult Film Association of America (Mar. 8, 1986).
1834. Id.
1835. Id.
1836. The Abernathy/MacGregor Group, Press Release entitled "Home Video Cassettes to Become Dominant Entertainment Medium by 1990's," (1986), p. 2.
1837. Id., p. 3.
1838. Id.. p. 1.
1839. Merrill Lynch, *The Home Video Market: Times of Turbulence and Transition,* (Jan. 6, 1986).
1840. Id.
1841. Id.
1842. Video Software Dealers Association, *1984 VSDA Annual Survey* 1; Current estimates place the figure for "Adult" video tape cassettes at no more than nine percent. Interview with Ronald Siegal, The Fairfield Group (Mar. 6, 1986).

The thirteen percent of the video market identified by the industry as "Adult" *excludes* most of the sexually violent material that the Commission found to be the most harmful form of sexually explicit material. The categories labeled "Action/Adventure," "Science Fiction," and "Horror," which together comprise more than half the market, include many films that contain scenes of rape, sexual homicide, and other forms of sexual violence. The harmfulness of these materials is not lessened by the fact that the breasts and genitals are covered in some scenes, nor the fact that these films are not given an "X" rating by the Motion Picture Association of America, nor the fact that the industry does not consider them "Adult" materials. Indeed, all of these features increase the availability of these materials to minors. Moreover, the "music video" category, which includes many sexually violent depictions, is specifically marketed to young people.

The sexually explicit pre-recorded video tape industry has provided a new means of growth for the sexually explicit film market.[1843] Sexually explicit films were first put on video tape around 1977, a year before general release features appeared on the home video market.[1844] Presently, seventy-five percent of the sexually explicit videos are being made by independent producers.[1845] Of the forty-five identified major producers in the United States, thirty-nine are located in Los Angeles.[1846]

There are thousands of different video titles currently on the market.[1847] *Adult Video News*, a publication about sexually explicit videos, estimates that 1,700 new sexually explicit videos were released in 1985.[1848] It projects this high growth trend will continue.[1849]

While the steps necessary to produce a sexually explicit movie on video are basically the same as for a film,[1850] producers are making more movies available on video primarily for three reasons.[1851] First, the cost of producing a movie on video is substantially less than shooting the same movie on film. Producing a movie on film is expensive because of the high costs of film and equipment.[1852] The average cost of making a sixty to ninety minute feature length movie on film is seventy-five thousand dollars.[1853] The same movie shot directly on video tape costs between $4,000 and $20,000.[1854]

Second, those productions made on video tape can be viewed immediately.[1855] In the film industry, there is a necessary time delay while the film is being processed.[1856] If, after processing, more filming is needed, the entire production operation including crew and performers must be reconvened.[1857] Finally, it may take several weeks to edit a film. Video tapes can be edited by computer in a matter of days.[1858]

When the producer has completed the video, it is ready to be sold to a distributor. The producer often sells his film at a one hundred percent profit.[1859] Generally, if it costs a producer fifteen thousand dollars to make a ninety minute video, he will sell it to a distributor for twenty-five to thirty thousand dollars.[1860]

Distribution

The distribution network for sexually explicit video tape cassettes is similar to that for sexually explicit films. Once the distributor re-

1843. Los Angeles Hearing, Vol. I, Robert Peters, p. 35.
1844. Stricharchuk, *Selling Skin: "Porn King" Reuben Sturman Expands His Empire With the Help of a Businessman's Skills*, Wall St. J., (May 8, 1985). p. 24, col. 1.
1845. Los Angeles Hearing, Vol. I, William Roberts, pp. 62, 74A.
1846. Chicago Hearing, Vol. I, Donald Smith, p. 31; Los Angeles Hearing, Vol. I, James Docherty, p. 7.
1847. Los Angeles Hearing, Vol. I, Robert Peters, p. 53.
1848. Los Angeles Hearing, Vol. I, William Roberts, p. 61.
1849. *Id.*
1850. See, The detailed description of how a typical sexually explicit movie is produced in this chapter.
1851. Interview with John Weston, Counsel, Adult Film Association of America (Mar. 8, 1986).
1852. *Id.*
1853. *Id.*
1854. Los Angeles Hearing, Vol. I, Robert Peters, p. 73.
1855. Los Angeles Hearing, Vol. I, William Roberts, p. 72; Interview with John Weston, Counsel, Adult Film Association (Mar. 8, 1986).
1856. *Id.*
1857. *Id.*
1858. *Id.*
1859. Los Angeles Hearing, Vol. I, William Roberts, pp. 71, 74D.
1860. *Id.*

ceives the video tape, he duplicates it. The master tape is used to produce thousands of video tapes in order to supply the thousands of "adults only" pornographic outlets and general video tape retailers across the country.[1861] The distributor also packages the video tape and prepares his advertising and promotional material. The cost to the distributor for the purchase, reproduction, packaging and advertising of a video tape is on average between eight and fifteen dollars.[1862] The distributor then sells the video tape to a wholesaler for about thirty-one dollars.[1863] Generally, the distributor's profit margin is between one hundred percent and four hundred percent for a video tape.[1864]

Recently, the major sexually explicit film distributors have rapidly entered the national video tape market.[1865] Some of these distributors have completely discontinued eight millimeter films and are focusing on video tape distribution.[1866] This is not surprising in light of the fact that the sexually explicit video industry's profits are in the hundreds of millions of dollars annually.[1867]

The wholesalers sell the video tapes to retailers across the country. Each wholesaler may carry thousands of titles from different distributors and sell the video tapes to retailers at a two to six dollar profit.[1868]

Many times the distributor and the wholesaler are one and the same.[1869] Sometimes, the producer, distributor and wholesaler are the same individual or corporation.[1870]

It has been estimated that there are at least twenty thousand home video retail outlets nationwide.[1871] Many general convenience stores now carry pre-recorded cassettes for sale or rental.[1872]

More specifically, it has been estimated that in 1985 there were approximately nineteen thousand video specialty stores in the United States. A video specialty store is a retail outlet which derives more than fifty-one percent of its gross revenues from the sale or rental of video products.[1873] It has also been estimated that in the United States there will be approximately twenty-four thousand video specialty stores in 1986 and twenty-seven thousand in 1987.[1874]

Sexually explicit video tapes can be purchased in "adults only" pornographic outlets as well as a significant number of general video retail outlets.[1875] One source estimated that at least twelve thousand of the over twenty thousand general video retail outlets across the United States distribute sexually explicit video tapes.[1876]

Once the tapes are in the stores, they are either rented or sold.[1877] In 1985 it was estimated that one in five pre-recorded video tapes was purchased.[1878] The average price of all pre-recorded video tapes was forty-two dollars,[1879] while the average price of sexually explicit video tapes ranged from sixty to eighty dollars.[1880] The sexually explicit video tapes also rented for between four and seven dollars a day.[1881] The retailers of these sexually explicit video tapes often realize a profit of twenty-three to twenty-eight dollars on each video tape sold.[1882]

The proportion of sales to rentals is ex-

1861. Los Angeles Hearing, Vol. I, William Roberts, p. 73.
1862. Id., p. 72.
1863. Id.
1864. Id.
1865. Los Angeles Hearing, Vol. I, Robert Peters, p. 35.
1866. Id.
1867. Id.
1868. Los Angeles Hearing, Vol. I, William Roberts, p. 72.
1869. Id.
1870. Id.
1871. Merrill Lynch, The Home Video Market: Times of Turbulence and Transition, (Jan. 6, 1986), p. 5.
1872. Id.
1873. Interview with Ronald Siegel, The Fairfield Group (Mar. 6, 1986).
1874. Id.
1875. New York Hearing, Vol. I, Gerald Piazza, p. 294.
1876. Los Angeles Hearing, Vol. I, John Weston, pp. 203A–13 citing, VCRs: Coming on Strong, Time, (Dec. 24, 1984), p. 47.
1877. Merrill Lynch, The Home Video Market: Times of Turbulence and Transition, (Jan. 6, 1986), p. 9.
1878. Id.
1879. Id., p. 3; Video Software Dealers Association, 1984 VSDA Annual Survey 3.
1880. Miami Hearing, Vol. I, Mike Berish, p. 91; Los Angeles Hearing, Vol. I, William Roberts, p. 72.
1881. Los Angeles Hearing, Vol. I, William Roberts, p. 74E.
1882. Id.

pected to increase as the price of pre-recorded video tapes declines.[1883] In 1985, at the retail level there were approximately $3.5 billion in sales of pre-recorded video tapes as compared to approximately $3.8 billion spent on theater tickets.[1884] An estimated eighty percent of the $3.5 billion spent on pre-recorded video tapes was on general release movie programming.[1885]

It has also been estimated that VCR playback will account for twenty-five percent of total television set usage in 1995.[1886] In evening prime time hours in 1995, VCR playback may command seventeen percent of total television set usage.[1887]

The Video Software Dealers Association (VSDA)[1888] conducted a survey of its members on September 6, 1985 regarding the retail of "adult" video tapes. Table 3 is a reproduction of the survey the VSDA sent to the Commission.

Sexually explicit video tapes are advertised on posters inside "adults only" pornographic outlets as well as trade magazines such as Adult Video News. These videos are also advertised in sexually explicit tabloids, magazines and paperback books. In addition, some video clubs advertise "X" rated videos in their publications and some general video retailers also advertise these sexually explicit videos.

MAGAZINES

Production

Mainstream sexually explicit magazines have grown in number since the arrival of the first of this genre, Playboy, in 1953. These magazines generally follow a formula of sexually explicit photographs featuring primarily nude females in a variety of sexual activities interspersed with textual content that is either also sexually oriented or covers general interest topics.

The content of the April, 1986 issues of twelve of the most widely circulated of these magazines was examined and analyzed to more systematically portray this material. The magazines examined were: Cheri, Chic, Club International, Gallery, Genesis, High Society, Hustler, Oui, Penthouse, Playboy, and Swank.

To get a better understanding of the range of material available in one issue of these magazines, frequency counts were obtained of the advertising, editorial and pictorial content.

Each advertisement was counted regardless of whether it was a display or a classified advertisement. In terms of the percentage of sexually oriented advertising, the amounts ranged from 100 percent of the advertising being sex-related as was the case with Club International and High Society, to twenty percent in Penthouse and ten percent in Playboy.

Phone sex was the product/service most heavily advertised across these magazines, with forty-nine percent of the advertising featuring this service. This was followed by sexually explicit video (sixteen percent) and sexually oriented magazine (ten percent) advertisements.

Editorial content in these magazines similarly varied from being totally or almost totally sex-related (Club International had one hundred percent sex-oriented content, followed by Cheri, with ninety-four percent, Club with ninety-three percent, and High Society with ninety-one percent), to having a greater proportion of general interest topics (sixty-seven percent in Playboy and sixty percent in Penthouse were on nonsex-related topics).

Pictorial matter generally consisted of a "centerfold," other photographs of females posed alone, with other females, or with one or two males, and featured a variety of sexual activities. The most common of the acts portrayed was that of a nude female in what the jargon of the trade calls the "split beaver" shot, a shot of a female with her legs spread apart and in many instances, also spreading open her vaginal lips with her fingers. One in five of the acts portrayed in these magazines were of this variety. Nineteen percent of the

1883. Merrill Lynch, The Home Video Market: Times of Turbulence and Transition (Jan. 6, 1986), p. 9.
1884. Id.
1885. Id.
1886. The Abernathy/MacGregor Group Press Release entitled "Home Video Cassettes to Become Dominant Entertainment Medium by 1990s," p. 4.
1887. Id., p. 5.
1888. The Video Software Dealers Association is a national trade association whose regular membership consists of approximately two thousand retailers and wholesalers of video software throughout the United States and whose associate members include a number of motion picture companies, independent video producers and manufacturers of various products related to the video industry. Letter from Charles B. Ruttenberg, Counsel, Video Software Dealers Association to Alan E. Sears, Executive Director, Attorney General's Commission on Pornography (Jan. 16, 1986).

Table 3
"Adult" Survey[1889]

*Number of individual stores that responded to survey: 2279
*Number of companies that responded to survey: 705
*Stores which carry "adult" product: YES NO
          Number of stores   965 1314
          % of respondents   42% 58%

---

*The following questions were answered by retailers who carry "adult" product:

What percentage of your gross dollar volume is in "adult" product?

% of "Adult" Product	% of Respondents
0–5%	13%
6–10%	23%
11–15%	25%
16–20%	19%
21–25%	8%
26–35%	11%
36–90%	1%

What percentage of your daily transactions are in "adult" product?

% of "Adult" Product	% of Respondents
0–5%	18%
6–10%	25%
11–15%	25%
16–20%	16%
21–25%	6%
26–35%	9%
36–90%	1%

What percentage of your total inventory is in "adult" product?

% of "Adult" Product	% of Respondents
0–5%	15%
6–10%	45%
11–15%	19%
16–20%	11%
21–25%	5%
26–35%	4%
36–90%	1%

1889. The term "adult" was not explained or defined in the survey. It is therefore somewhat uncertain what participants included in this category. Interview with Charles Ruttenberg, Counsel, Video Software Dealers Association
(May 9, 1986).

activities depicted showed some type of touching or fondling, followed by oral-genital (twelve percent) and sexual activities between two women (nine percent).

In 1983, a similar content analysis was carried out on one issue of eleven of these magazines by Canadian National Commission studying sexual offenses against children.[1890] Included in this analysis were Playboy, Penthouse, Hustler, Gallery, Cheri, Playgirl, Forum, Oui, Club, Swank, and Genesis. The results showed that

- A large majority of the photographs depicted partially dressed females.
- The largest category of photographic depictions was for female body parts, primarily breasts, nipples (17%), followed by genitals (14%).
- The most common sexual act depicted in the text was masturbation (21%) followed by oral-genital contact (14%).
- The use of force in these textual depictions (anal penetration, bondage equipment, weapons, rape and murder) accounted for 10% of the sexual acts depicted.
- Sexually oriented products featuring children were most heavily advertised in Hustler magazine.

In 1980, Malamuth and Spinner conducted a more specific study that analyzed the content of all Playboy and Penthouse cartoons and pictorials from 1973 through 1977.[1891] Pictorial violent sexuality was found to have increased significantly over the five years analyzed both in absolute numbers and as a percentage of the total number of pictorials. However, pictorials rated sexually violent were still a small percentage of the total pictorial material, reaching about five percent in 1977. Throughout this period, Penthouse was also found to have a greater percentage of sexually violent cartoons than Playboy (thirteen percent versus six percent).

The sexually explicit magazines which are not included in the studies discussed above and are primarily available at "adults only" pornographic outlets portray masturbation as well as group, lesbian, gay, and transvestite sexual activities. Actual anal and vaginal intercourse as well as fellatio, cunnilingus and sodomy are also prevalent.[1892] There are depictions of rape, incest, bondage and discipline, sadomasochism, urination and defecation, bestiality, and simulated sexual activity with juveniles.[1893] Additionally, they cater to every type of paraphilia which has currently been identified.[1894]

In 1982, Dietz and Evans classified 1760 heterosexual pornographic magazines according to the imagery portrayed on the cover photographs.[1895] Four shops were randomly selected from the 42nd Street district in New York City and every magazine-format publication with a female or cross-dress male on the cover was categorized. Depictions of a woman posed alone predominated these covers in 1970, according to the authors, but only constituted eleven percent of the authors' 1980 sample. Bondage and domination imagery was the most prevalent imagery (seventeen percent of the covers) while smaller proportions of material were devoted to group sexual activity (10%). The authors suggested that pornographic imagery is an unobtrusive measure of the relative prevalence of those paraphilias associated with preferences for specific types of visual imagery.

1890. Committee on Sexual Offenses Against Children and Youths, Sexual Offenses Against Children (1984).

1891. Malamuth and Spinner, A Longitudinal Content Analysis of Sexual Violence in the Best-Selling Erotic Magazines, 16 The Journal of Sex Research 226 (1980). See also, Miami Hearing, Vol. II, Judith Reisman, p. 242; A Content Analysis of Playboy, Penthouse, and Hustler Magazines With Special Attention to the Portrayal of Children, Crime and Violence (The Institute for Media Education, Judith Reisman 1986); The Playboy Cartoon Information Delivery System and Client Sexual Exploitation By Health Professionals, Sexual Exploitation of Clients by Health Professionals (Accepted for publication, A.W. Burgess ed. 1985).

1892. See, The Imagery Found Among Magazines, Books, Films in "Adults Only" Pornographic Outlets discussed in this Part. Los Angeles Hearing, Vol. II, Joseph Haggerty, pp. 16–66.

1893. Chicago Hearing, Vol. I, Jack O'Malley, pp. 106, 111.

1894. Paraphilias are psychosexual disorders where "unusual or bizarre imagery or other acts are necessary for sexual excitement. Such imagery or acts tend to be insistently and involuntarily repetitive and generally involve either: (1) preference for use of a nonhuman object for sexual arousal; (2) repetitive sexual activity with humans involving real or simulated suffering or humiliation, or (3) repetitive sexual activity with nonconsenting partners. In other classifications these disorders are referred to as "Sexual Deviations." American Psychiatric Association, Diagnostic and Statistical Manual of Mental Disorders, (3d ed. 1983), p. 266.

1895. Dietz and Evans, Pornographic Imagery and Prevalence of Paraphilia, 139 American Journal of Psychiatry, (1982), p. 1493.

In 1985, Dietz, Harry and Hazelwood[1896] analyzed the content of nineteen detective magazines representing eighteen different titles from six publishers. The study found that covers tended to juxtapose erotic images with images of violence, bondage, and domination. Sadistic imagery accounted for twenty-eight percent of the covers and women were most often shown as dominated by men. Bondage was depicted in thirty-eight percent of the covers, with all the bound subjects females.

The layout of these magazines varies. Most sexually explicit magazines are four color and usually undated. Some magazines contain all photographs and others have less photographs and a few editorials.[1897] Some magazine contents are tailored to consumers who prefer less sexually explicit material and others are produced with predominantly graphic ultimate sexual acts or specific paraphilias depicted.[1898] Advertising is generally sexually related and includes advertisements for mail order sales, sexual devices and paraphernalia, sexually explicit videos and telephone sex.[1899]

Law enforcement sources have stated that most of the production work associated with these magazines is done in-house.[1900] The models are hired, the film is shot and processed, the pictorial layout is completed and the magazine is printed all within the corporate network.[1901] They believe that this is particularly the case with two major producers of the magazines: Star Distribution, Inc., and Parliament News.[1902]

In order to determine the extent and nature of pornographic magazines available, the Commission staff conducted a survey of pornographic outlets in six major cities in the eastern United States. The results of the survey indicated that there were over 2,300 different magazine titles available in these 16 stores alone. For a further discussion of the types of magazines and other material surveyed see the discussion of specific material in Chapter 27.

Distribution

Since the arrival of *Playboy* magazine in 1953, the market for mainstream sexually explicit magazines has expanded.[1903] The growth of these magazines was evident through the early 1980s after which time circulation appears to have declined significantly.[1904] Table Four sets forth the thirteen top-selling mainstream sexually explicit magazines audited by the A.B.C. and the average monthly circulation for each from 1975–1984.

1896. Dietz, Harry and Hazelwood, *Detective Magazines: Pornography for the Sexual Sadists?* (1985) (available from Dr. Dietz, School of Law, University of Virginia).

1897. Telephone interview with Sergeant Donald Smith, Los Angeles Police Department (Mar. 9, 1986).

1898. *Id.*

1899. Telephone interview with Detective Robert Peters, Los Angeles Police Department (Mar. 9, 1986).

1900. *Id.*

1901. *Id.*

1902. *Id.*

1903. Chicago Hearing, Vol. I, Peter Petruzzellis, 288G; In conducting our analysis of the most widely circulated sexually explicit magazines, the Commission received substantial assistance from the Audit Bureau of Circulation (A.B.C.) which is a repository possessing factual information concerning the audited circulation of major magazine publications. The information made available by the A.B.C. provides the basis for estimated changes in the extent, volume and regional distribution of sales from 1975 to 1984. The information also describes the minimal market value of a significant portion of the pornographic magazine business in the United States.

The A.B.C. prepares and issues standardized statements of circulation, geographical analysis, and other information reported to it by its membership. It also verifies the figures contained in the members' statements by means of an annual auditor's examination of the publisher's records. Finally, it distributes the above information, without editorial comment.

The A.B.C. publishers' reports are prepared twice annually. Publishers submit figures indicating their total sales for each month as well as their average circulation for a given six-month period. The publishers also submit geographical analyses for their total paid circulation based on a one-month period.

The A.B.C. records only provide circulation figures for sexually explicit magazines which are part of its membership. A.B.C. records, therefore, are not a comprehensive listing of the circulation of all sexually explicit magazines. In addition, the list of sexually explicit publications whose circulation is reported by the A.B.C. has changed from time to time. Not all sexually explicit magazines surveyed in this section have consistently been members of the A.B.C. However, A.B.C. figures were available for nine of the surveyed sexually explicit magazines in 1975, for thirteen in 1980 and for ten in 1984. Audit Bureau of Circulation Brochure, *This is the ABC*; Interview with Jackie Kid, Audit Bureau of Circulation (Feb. 10, 1986).

1904. See, Table Four.

Table 4

Top Selling Sexually Explicit Magazines Audited by the Audit Bureau of Circulation***
Average Circulation Per Month for 1975–1984

	1975	1976	1977	1978	1979	1980	1981	1982	1983	1984
Cheri					*362,572	395,805	443,034	409,958	388,497	360,993
Chic			*282,221	22,952	294,331	268,340	212,356	164,507	**N/A	**N/A
Club Magazine	*255,146	543,010	738,152	579,648	529,834	528,192	539,783	518,463	486,776	463,605
Club International						*241,761	254,768	242,152	217,214	185,532
Forum	*318,728	466,295	637,416	728,028	805,624	721,233	581,917	523,163	500,313	438,132
Gallery Magazine	647,173	688,612	700,491	661,077	660,302	583,123	541,065	481,186	484,506	475,321
Genesis	*342,589	368,508	373,399	382,802	414,506	361,481	333,588	311,178	273,720	284,897
High Society						*443,142	448,767	414,729	377,033	360,723
Hustler	554,559	1,681,889	1,826,156	1,517,011	1,639,284	1,531,855	1,309,473	1,147,181	1,075,141	**N/A
Oui	1,276,498	1,166,784	994,737	882,066	862,488	780,420	731,166	480,615	**N/A	**N/A
Penthouse	3,966,109	4,235,021	4,599,903	4,367,094	4,429,911	4,542,910	4,248,554	4,017,853	3,596,758	3,275,677
Playboy	5,663,149	5,388,522	4,914,381	4,978,490	5,378,069	5,308,553	5,091,266	4,619,572	4,187,452	4,209,824
Playgirl	1,061,010	921,061	747,230	625,252	727,259	772,406	670,721	650,605	602,499	562,778
Total	14,084,961	15,450,702	15,814,086	14,984,420	16,104,180	16,479,221	15,406,458	13,981,162	12,189,909	10,617,482

*Indicates an initial report. The report is based on the second half of the year, starting July 1 of the reported year and ending on December 30 of the same year.

**Indicates information not available due to resignation of the client or temporary suspension of service.

***The average monthly circulation is based on annual reports made by the Audit Bureau of Circulations (ABC), 123 North Wacker Drive, Chicago, Illinois 60606. Annual reports were not available for the publications listed below for the years indicated:

Club Magazine—1984
Club International—1984
High Society—1984
Hustler—1983
Playboy—1984

The last entries for these publications were calculated by taking the average of two six month reports for the year in which the final entries were made. The two six month periods were from January 1 through June 30, 1984 and from July 1 through December 30, 1984.

Of the three top selling magazines, *Playboy, Penthouse* and *Hustler, Penthouse* and *Hustler* experienced a significant increase in monthly circulation from 1975 to 1980. In 1975, *Penthouse* had a monthly circulation of 3,966,109 and in 1980 this number had risen to 4,542,910. In 1975, *Hustler* had a monthly circulation of 554,559 and in 1980, that figure had risen to 1,531, 855. *Playboy*, on the other hand, experienced a slight decrease in monthly circulation between 1975 and 1980. In 1975, 5,663,149 *Playboy* magazines were circulated each month and in 1980 that figure had decreased to 5,308,555. However, by 1983, all had experienced a decrease in average monthly circulation; *Playboy* sold 4,187,452, *Penthouse* sold 3,596.758 and *Hustler* sold 1,075,141. Moreover, between 1984 and 1985 most of these magazines again experienced a significant decline in circulation.[1905]

The A.B.C.'s Magazine Publisher's Statements provide the per issue single copy and subscription prices for the magazines. In calculating a total dollar value for these thirteen magazines, we used the 1982 figures and single copy prices. 1982 was the last year that all thirteen magazines were represented by the ABC and a vast majority of these magazines are single copy sales. The dollar value of each magazine was calculated by multiplying the number of magazines sold by the per issue single copy price. In 1982, the estimated monthly sales value in the United States alone for these thirteen magazines was approximately $38,602,502.25.

Besides the thirteen magazines discussed above, it has been estimated that there are currently between fifty thousand and sixty thousand different sexually explicit magazine titles available in the United States.[1906] In fact hundreds of new titles come out each month.[1907] As discussed above, these magazines depict a variety of sexual themes and acts.[1908]

Sovereign News and Star Distributors, Inc. are major distributors of many of these magazines.[1909] These companies distribute magazines to "adults only" pornographic outlets and mail order operations across the country through a sophisticated nationwide network.[1910] In those areas of the country not serviced by Sovereign News or Star Distributors, smaller subdistributors are used to transport the magazines to "adults only" pornographic retail outlets.[1911]

At least half of the retail sales of sexually explicit magazines are made by pornographic outlets and the remainder of these magazines are sold by mail order.[1912]

The profit margin for producers and distributors of sexually explicit magazines remains high.[1913] The cost of producing both sexually explicit and non-sexually explicit magazines is similar at the processing level.[1914] The processing costs range from only sixty cents to one dollar per issue,[1915] but the profit margins are vastly different. The non-sexually explicit magazines are often marked up 240 percent from the wholesale to retail levels, while the sexually oriented publications are marked up more than four hundred to five hundred percent.[1916] Retailers in turn mark up the magazines based on consumer supply and demand.[1917] Usually the maximum markup at the retail level is one hundred percent.[1918]

Sexually explicit magazines are advertised in sexually explicit paperbacks, tabloids and other magazines. Some of the more mainstream magazines, for example *Playboy*, also advertise through direct mail, television and in many major city daily newspapers and magazines.

1905. Media Industry Newsletter, (Mar. 5, 1986) Vol. 39, No. 9.
1906. Interview with Sergeant Donald Smith, Los Angeles Police Department (Mar. 9, 1986).
1907. Id.
1908. See, The Imagery Found Among Magazines, Books, Films in "Adults Only" Pornographic Outlets, *infra.*
1909. Interview with Sergeant Donald Smith, Los Angeles Police Department, (Mar. 9, 1986).
1910. Id.; Mail order companies can be found in most large cities such as Los Angeles, New York and Chicago as well as some smaller cities. Id.
1911. Id.
1912. Id.
1913. Los Angeles Hearing, Vol. I, Robert Peters, pp. 33–34.
1914. Id.
1915. Id.; Some magazines cost as much as two dollars to produce. Miami Hearing, Vol. I, Mike Berish, p. 91.
1916. Id.
1917. Interview with Detective Robert Peters, Los Angeles Police Department (Mar. 9, 1986); Interview with Washington, D.C., Metropolitan Police Department Detectives (Mar. 10, 1986).
1918. Id.

CABLE AND SATELLITE TELEVISION

Production

Cable television is a subscription service that first appeared in the United States in the 1940s to serve areas where broadcast television signals could not be received.[1919] The cable television industry expanded slowly until the 1970s, when the Federal Communications Commission (FCC) adopted a deregulatory philosophy to allow cable services to offer a greater number of channels and to foster program diversity.[1920] Cable subscriptions also increased when satellites were used by cable programming networks to distribute programming to local cable operators across the country.[1921] As a result of these developments, cable operators were able to offer programming from a wide variety of sources.

Today there are over sixty-five hundred cable television systems in the United States serving over forty million subscribing households.[1922] Cable television is currently available to seventy percent of the eighty-five million television households in the country.[1923]

Programs offered by cable companies are distributed to subscribers through a closed circuit wire system.[1924] The cable wire is strung along utility poles or buried in an underground conduit and enters the subscriber's home in the same way as a telephone line.[1925] This differs from broadcast television which transmits its signals through the airwaves to anyone in the vicinity with a television.[1926]

While broadcast television stations are required to be licensed by the Federal Communications Commission (FCC) cable systems are not. They operate based on a contractual agreement or franchise with a state or local government body.[1927] The Cable Communications Policy Act of 1984[1928] establishes a national policy regarding the areas of the cable television industry which are subject to federal, state and local regulation.[1929]

In addition to cable, there are several other types of television services including Satellite Master Antenna Television (SMATV), Over-the-Air Subscription Television (STV), Backyard Satellite Receiving Dishes (TVRO) and Multipoint Distribution Service (MDS).[1930]

SMATV signals are received by a large antenna and delivered to individuals in multiple unit dwellings by wire. The service is usually provided without charge to occupants of apartment buildings and to hotel and motel guests.[1931] STV signals are transmitted over the airwaves in a scrambled mode by a broadcast station. Viewers in the service area who desire the programming must rent a decoding device for their televisions.[1932] The FCC has preempted most state and local regulation of the SMATV and STV services.[1933] Backyard satellite receiving dishes (TVROs) are large antenna discs used by individuals to receive satellite transmitted programming. Often these discs are used to intercept programming that is transmitted via satellite from the cable programers to the local cable operators.[1934] MDS signals provide one to eight channels of programming to subscribers.[1935] Subscribers must have a special antenna and signal to receive and convert the transmitted signal into a frequency compatible with a standard television.[1936] MDS is used most commonly in multiple unit dwell-

---

1919. Los Angeles Hearing, Vol. I, Brenda Fox, p. 283.
1920. Id.
1921. Id.
1922. Letter from James P. Mooney, President and Chief Executive Officer, National Cable Television Association to Henry E. Hudson, Chairman, Attorney General's Commission on Pornography (May 2, 1986).
1923. Los Angeles Hearing, Vol. I, Brenda Fox, p. 306-R.
1924. Id., pp. 306-N-306-0.
1925. Id., pp. 306-8.
1926. Id., p. 282.
1927. Id.
1928. 47 U.S.C. S521 et seq.
1929. Los Angeles Hearing, Vol. I, Brenda Fox, pp. 306-0-306-P. See, The discussion of FCC regulatory responsibilities in the Recommendations for Law Enforcement Agencies.
1930. Id., pp. 306S-306U.
1931. Id., pp. 306S-306T.
1932. Id., p. 306T.
1933. Id.
1934. Id., p. 306U.
1935. Id., p. 306-T.
1936. Id., p. 306-T-306-U.

ings and to a lesser extent in single family residences.[1937]

Individual local cable operators control what programming will be offered on their systems.[1938] One of the basic attributes of cable television is "narrowcasting" or presenting programming designed for a particular audience, such as children's programs, educational programs, "adults only" programs, and foreign language programs.[1939] Most cable systems offer a basic service package consisting of local broadcast channels and other nationally or regionally distributed channels such as Cable News Network (CNN), Christian Broadcasting Network (CBN), and the sports channel (ESPN).[1940] Cable systems usually offer at least one of the "pay television" channels such as Home Box Office (HBO), Cinemax, Showtime or the Disney Channel. These channels usually carry unedited movies without commercial interruption and are sold to subscribers on a per channel or per program basis.[1941] The subscriber pays a monthly fee for the basic service and an additional fee for the "pay television" channels.[1942]

Distribution

An analysis of the various forms of television transmission discloses that most of the sexually explicit programs appear on "pay television." This programming includes movies that have been given an "R" rating by the Motion Picture Association of America (M.P.A.A.) and self-designated "triple X" films.[1943] Movies in the "R" category may depict violence, nudity, or sexuality, and contain sexually explicit or profane language.[1944] Unedited programs with these ratings are generally not shown over regular broadcast television, therefore, cable and satellite television programs often contain more sexually explicit scenes than those shown over broadcast television. The difference in fare offered over regular broadcast television and cable and satellite television is due in part to the different legal restriction placed on each. Under current law, regular broadcast television cannot offer either indecent or obscene programs. Cable and satellite programs cannot offer obscene programs, but have been permitted to show material that would meet the criteria for indecency.

Nevertheless, a significant amount of material appears on network television that qualifies as the type of sexual violence that the Commission has found to be the most harmful form of pornography. Although the sexually violent material aired on network television is probably never legally obscene the covering of breasts and genitals does not render the material any less harmful.

The Commission also recognizes that the nonviolent sexual content of network television is offensive to many Americans. Sexually suggestive and provocative attire and performances, sexual humor and innuendo, and themes of adultery, fornication, prostitution, sexual deviation, and sexual abuse are all prevalent in broadcast television and treated with varying degrees of sensitivity.

Channels which carry "R" rated programming reach in excess of 14.5 million homes over sixty-nine hundred cable and SMATV systems.[1945] Instances have been reported where movies represented as having an "R" rating were actually unrated films or even milder versions of "X" rated movies shown in "adults only" pornographic theatres throughout the country.[1946] In addition to the sexual activity, the violence depicted in "R" rated movies can also be very explicit. Many times the violence depicted is of a sexual nature.

Other "pay television" channels carry programming that is exclusively "adult oriented" or sexually explicit.[1947] One such channel began in December of 1980 and currently has over seven hundred thousand subscribers

---

1937. *Id.*, p. 306-U.

1938. *Id.*, p. 291. The exception to this rule occurs when, under the terms of the cable franchise agreement, cable operators are required to indiscriminantly lease channels to the public.

1939. *Id.*, pp. 284–85.

1940. *Id.*, pp. 283–84.

1941. *Id.*, p. 284.

1942. *Id.*, p. 286.

1943. *Id.*, pp. 285, 306-X; Los Angeles Hearing, Vol. II, Charles Dawson, p. 173.

1944. Los Angeles Hearing, Vol. II, Jack Valenti, p. 55EE; theater goers under seventeen must be accompanied by a parent or guardian.

1945. Los Angeles Hearing, Vol. I, Brenda Fox, p. 289.

1946. Citizens for Decency Through Law, *Cable Pornography: Problems & Solutions* 2(Jan. 1985).

1947. Los Angeles Hearing, Vol. I, Brenda Fox, p. 306-Y.

over five hundred-eighty cable television systems.[1948] The channel's sexually explicit programs are shown during the hours of 8:00 p.m. and 6:00 a.m. In addition to "R" rated movies, the channel programming includes original adult programs and unrated movies.[1949] For example, this channel has shown a version of the movie "The Opening of Misty Beethoven," which, in at least one version, has been declared legally obscene.[1950]

In addition to this channel, there are two satellite delivered networks which distribute sexually oriented programs to cable and satellite systems. One of the networks began operations in January of 1985 and delivers sexually explicit movies over both cable and satellite television. Its programs are shown between 11:00 p.m. and 4:00 a.m. over six cable systems.[1951]

Another network shows "triple X," unedited adult programming.[1952] A "triple X" rating is attached by the movie producer and generally covers the same material as the "X" rating but is meant to connote very explicit fare.[1953] This network has been in existence sine 1983 and its programs are shown to 26,400 subscribers over eleven cable and satellite systems.[1954]

There are two other potential sources of sexually explicit programming over cable: local origination and access channels. Cable industry representative Brenda Fox, testified before the Commission that the National Cable Television Association (NCTA) knows of only one system that locally originates "X" rated movies on a pay-per-view basis.[1955] However, she recognized that there may be other systems that locally originate sexually oriented programs on a per-channel or per-program basis.[1956]

In the area of leased access channels, Ms. Fox stated that the cable operators have no editorial control over the lessees' programming.[1957] For example, pursuant to federal, state and local laws, Manhattan cable is required to set aside a number of channels for use by the public on a first-come, first-served basis.[1958] The cable operator must offer the "access" channels to all applicants on a nondiscriminatory basis.[1959] This requirement has resulted in late night sexually explicit programs which are available to all cable subscribers.[1960] One program, Midnight Blue, shows sexually explicit fare over the Manhattan cable television system owned by Time, Inc. Midnight Blue is produced by Al Goldstein, publisher of *Screw* magazine.[1961] Ralph P. Davidson, Chairman of the Board of Time, Inc., addressed the Commission:

"Midnight Blue." Although Midnight Blue appears on Manhattan Cable Television, a subsidiary of Time, Inc., we would like the record to be clear and unambiguous— Midnight Blue is not now nor has it ever been a program of Manhattan Cable. It is a program created locally by an unaffiliated third party which is carried on one of Manhattan Cable's commercial "access" channels.

There should be no misunderstanding— Manhattan Cable would not carry Midnight Blue in the absence of state, local and federal requirements that it do so. Manhattan Cable is required by federal, state and local law to set aside a number of channels for use by the public on a first-come, first-served basis. Further, Manhattan Cable is prevented by law from exercising any editorial control over the content of commercial access programming, unless such programming is legally "obscene." The current obscenity law in New York is based on the "community standards" criterion set forth by the United States Supreme Court in *Miller*. It should be noted that Manhattan Cable operates in a community (the southern half of

1948. *Id.*
1949. *Id.*
1950. Los Angeles Hearing, Vol. I, James Clancy, p. 345-I. See, *Trans-Lux Theater v. People ex rel. Sweeton* 366 So. 2d 710 (Ala. 1979) (finding "The Opening of Misty Beethoven" to be obscene).
1951. Los Angeles Hearing, Vol. I, Brenda Fox, p. 306-Z.
1952. Los Angeles Hearing, Vol. II, Charles Dawson, p. 173.
1953. Los Angeles Hearing, Vol. II, Jack Valenti, pp. 12–13.
1954. Los Angeles Hearing, Vol. I, Brenda Fox. p. 306-Z.
1955. Los Angeles Hearing, Vol. I, Brenda Fox. p. 306-Z.
1956. *Id.*
1957. *Id.*, p. 306-AA.
1958. Letter from Ralph P. Davidson, Chairman of the Board, Time, Inc. to Alan E. Sears, Executive Director, Attorney General's Commission on Pornography, (Mar. 14, 1986), pp. 3–4.
1959. Los Angeles Hearing, Vol. I, Brenda Fox, p. 306-AA.
1960. *Id.*
1961. Los Angeles Hearing, Vol. II, Al Goldstein, p. 263. While the NCTA believes that Midnight Blue is an isolated case, there is no guarantee that a similar situation will not occur in other cable systems.

Manhattan) which is generally regarded as among the most tolerant in the country of adult material.

As you are undoubtedly aware, Section 612(h) of the Cable Communications Policy Act of 1984 imposes responsibility for policing the content of commercial access programming on the franchising authority, which in the case of Midnight Blue is New York City. Time Inc., would welcome any Commission recommendations that would enable cable operators to exercise full editorial discretion over such access programming. We can assure you that, if this were done, Midnight Blue would be removed from Manhattan Cable.[1962]

As mentioned above, in addition to the cable-transmitted pay television channels, "X" rated and other sexually explicit movies are also available on direct satellite channels. Some of the "X" rated movies shown over satellite television[1963] include "The Opening of Misty Beethoven,"[1964] "Sex Wish," "Easy," "Talk Dirty to Me," "Vista Valley PTA," "Insatiable," "Taboo," "Insatiable II," and "The Devil in Miss Jones."[1965] Although citizen complaints about obscene programming have been filed with the Federal Communication Commission, no action has yet been taken to regulate this programming.[1966]

Cable television operators have taken some precautions regarding the showing of sexually explicit programs.[1967] Some cable programmers and operators offer detailed program guides giving specific information about the content of upcoming programs.[1968] Some provide on-screen notices or warnings before sexually explicit programs are shown.[1969] Most operators limit such programming to the late evening hours and transmit the material in a scrambled mode to ensure against inadvertent reception by non-

subscribers.[1970] Finally, all cable systems are required by federal law[1971] to provide lockboxes, upon request, for either lease or sale. This device enables a subscriber to lock out a particular channel or channels during certain periods.[1972]

DIAL-A-PORN

Production

In the 1920s, the Bell Telephone Company began providing recorded messages which gave the time of day and weather to its customers. The technology developed for such message services enabled Bell to provide these services at reduced costs because an operator did not have to handle the calls and give the information.[1973] Such recorded messages were called "Dial-it" services.

By the 1970s, this service had expanded and included recordings such as dial-a-joke and sports score lines.[1974] The telephone company was solely responsible for the content, distribution and advertising of the recorded messages.[1975]

In the early 1980s, the Federal Communications Commission ruled that providing information by recorded messages was a service beyond the permissible scope of the telephone companies' authority.[1976] As a result of this ruling, the entire telephone Dial-it service network was transformed.

Today, the delivery of all recorded message services involves two entities: the information provider, which is responsible for the content, distribution, and advertising of the message; and, the telephone company, which is responsible for transmitting the calls and billing the caller.[1977]

The recorded messages referred to as "Dial-A-Porn" began in 1982 after the deregulation

1962. Letter from Ralph P. Davidson, Chairman of the Board, Time, Inc., to Alan E. Sears, (Mar. 14, 1986), pp. 3–4.
1963. See, Film World, X-Rated Movie Handbook, (1986) Vol. 2, No. 8.
1964. See, Trans-Lux Theatre v. People ex rel. Sweeton, 366 So. 2d 710(Ala. 1979) (this movie was found legally obscene).
1965. Los Angeles Hearing, Vol. I, James Clancy, p. 345-H.
1966. Id., p. 314.
1967. Los Angeles Hearing, Vol. I, Brenda Fox, p. 287.
1968. Id.
1969. Id.
1970. Id.
1971. 47 U.S.C. S544 (d)(2)(A).
1972. Los Angeles Hearing, Vol. I, Brenda Fox, pp. 287–88.
1973. Los Angeles Hearing, Vol. I, William Dunkle, p. 248.
1974. Id., p. 249.
1975. Id.
1976. Id.
1977. Id.

of the Dial-it service.[1978] With the advent of telephone deregulation, some telephone companies began holding lotteries to select providers of recorded messages or Dial-it services. One provider or Dial-A-Porn Services was a winner in the lottery conducted in New York State and by February of 1983 was offering Dial-A-Porn services over three telephone lines. It had acquired the lines either through the lottery process or by leasing them from other lottery winners.[1979] While this company has become one of the leading providers of Dial-A-Porn services, there are now many other Dial-A-Porn providers in the market.[1980]

There are two types of Dial-A-Porn calls.[1981] The first, involves the customer dialing a number and carrying on a live conversation with a paid performer on the other end of the line. The performer who answers the call will talk to the caller in terms as sexually explicit as the caller desires and may encourage him to perform sexual acts during the course of the phone conversation.[1982] The call may last up to forty-five minutes and the caller is billed on his credit card for an amount usually between fifteen and thirty dollars.[1983]

The second type of Dial-A-Porn call involves the receipt of a pre-recorded message when the caller dials the designated number.[1984] These calls are a part of the Mass Announcement Network Service (MANS) and all begin with the prefix "976."[1985] MANS recorded messages provide other information such as prayers, racetrack results, weather forecasts, sports scores, time of day, and childrens' stories.[1986] The caller is charged for each call to this service on his other monthly telephone bill.[1987]

The Dial-A-Porn recorded messages often consist of verbal illustrations of sex acts. These acts are frequently described by the performer as though they were actually occurring during the call with the caller and the performer was an actual participant in the acts.[1988] The acts described may include lesbian sexual activity, sodomy, rape, incest, excretory functions, bestiality, sadomasochistic abuse, and sex acts with children.[1989] One Dial-A-Porn number in California,[1990] offers the caller a choice of five "pleasures" including descriptions of sadomasochistic abuse, urination, and anal intercourse.[1991]

Distribution

Dial-A-Porn recordings are now available locally in New York, Los Angeles, San Francisco, Philadelphia, Denver, Pittsburgh, Baltimore, Washington, D.C., and other major cities across the country.[1992] These services generate large numbers of calls.

Many Dial-it providers can communicate fifty-seven second messages to a maximum of 50,000 callers per hour without any caller receiving a busy signal.[1993] During one day in May of 1983, eight hundred thousand calls were placed to one sexually explicit recorded message service.[1994] In the year ending February 28, 1984, 180 million calls were made to the same numbers.[1995]

In 1984, Dial-A-Porn recordings represented forty-four percent of the twenty-seven million messages on the "976" exchanges of-

1978. Los Angeles Hearing, Vol. I, Brent Ward, p. 228. Brent Ward has been the United States Attorney for Utah since 1981. He recently represented the United States in *FCC v. Carlin Communications*. In this case, an investigation was conducted which resulted in a judicial proceeding. Witnesses and evidence were subpoened regarding the Dial-A-Porn industry in general and the defendant in particular.

1979. Id.

1980. Los Angeles Hearing, Vol. I, Teresa Hillman, pp. 379, 388A-6; Los Angeles Hearing, Vol. I, Brent Ward, p. 227.

1981. Id.

1982. Id.

1983. Id.

1984. Id., p. 228.

1985. Id., p. 228.

1986. Id.

1987. Id., p. 230.

1988. Id., p. 231.

1989. Id.

1990. The telephone companies have issued such numbers as 976-FOXX, 976-4LUV, 976-SLUT and 976-LUST upon the request of a Dial-A-Porn provider. These numbers indicate that nature of the 976 service.

1991. Los Angeles Hearing, Vol. I, Teresa Hillman, p. 381; *Flesh Fantasy News Paper*, Vol. XIII, No. 23, Issue, No. 612 (Aug. 9. 1985).

1992. Los Angeles Hearing, Vol. I, Teresa Hillman, p. 380; Los Angeles Hearing, Vol. I, Brent Ward, p. 229.

1993. Los Angeles Hearing, Vol. I, Brent Ward, p. 228.

1994. Id.

1995. Id.

fered by Pacific Bell.[1996] This figure dropped to twenty-seven percent in 1985, but was due to an increase in the volume of other "976" offerings.[1997]

Dial-A-Porn providers and the telephone companies realize significant revenues from the Dial-A-Porn services. When a caller is charged on his monthly telephone bill for prerecorded Dial-A-Porn messages, the provider of the message and the telephone divide the revenues according to local tariffs.[1998] The telephone company generally earns from two to nineteen cents for a one-minute call[1999] with the remainder going to the Dial-A-Porn provider.

In New York, one Dial-A-Porn provider earns two cents per call and the telephone company earns 9.4 cents.[2000] In California, Dial-A-Porn providers earn $1.26 per call while the telephone company earns seventy-four cents.[2001] In some other areas, Dial-A-Porn providers earn $1.45 per call while the telephone companies receive fifty cents.[2002] At two cents per call in New York City, one major Dial-A-Porn provider earned sixteen thousand dollars a day and a total of $3.6 million for the year ending February 28, 1984.[2003] The telephone company for the state of New York has earned as much as thirty-five thousand dollars a day from Dial-A-Porn calls.[2004] Pacific Bell estimates that their company earned twelve million from Dial-A-Porn calls between October 1984 and October 1985.[2005]

Not all Dial-A-Porn calls are local calls. Eighty percent of the calls made to Dial-A-Porn recordings provided by one major service in New York are local calls and twenty percent are long distance.[2006] A direct long distance call from Michigan to a Dial-A-Porn

number in New York costs the caller fifty-eight cents per message during the day, thirty-four cents per message after five o'clock in the evening and twenty-three cents per message after eleven o'clock at night.[2007]

Telephone companies face a dilemma as a result of the rapid rise of Dial-A-Porn. The telephone companies support the MANS concept as a means of providing information to the public and earning revenues to help keep basic telephone rates down.[2008] However, they have been subjected to mounting public criticism for helping to provide sexually explicit messages to anyone who can dial the assigned number.[2009]

In response, some companies have taken legal action against Dial-A-Porn providers. For example, one telephone company has refused to offer Dial-A-Porn services at an estimated revenue loss of five hundred thousand dollars per year.[2010]

One telephone company recommended to the Commission several steps to alleviate the growing Dial-A-Porn problems. It proposed that all advertising clearly and plainly disclose the cost of the telephone call.[2011] If an individual is unaware of the charge or if a child makes an unauthorized call, the company should offer a one-time adjustment of the telephone bill to delete the charges.[2012] They also suggested that a telephone subscriber could have "976" access "blocked" from his or her lines.[2013]

The advertising of Dial-A-Porn numbers has become pervasive. In the San Francisco area, Dial-A-Porn numbers are listed in the white pages of the telephone directory under "Dial-It" and in the yellow pages under "Recorded Announcements."[2014] Listings under

1996. Los Angeles Hearing, Vol. I, William Dunkle, p. 251.
1997. Id.
1998. Los Angeles Hearing, Vol. I, Brent Ward, p. 229.
1999. Id.
2000. Id.; Los Angeles Hearing, Vol. I, Teresa Hillman, p. 380.
2001. Los Angeles Hearing, Vol. I, Teresa Hillman, p. 380.
2002. Los Angeles Hearing, Vol. I, Brent Ward, p. 229.
2003. Id.
2004. Los Angeles Hearing, Vol. I, Judith Trevillian, p. 271.
2005. Los Angeles Hearing, Vol. I, William Dunkle, p. 259.
2006. Los Angeles Hearing, Vol. I, Brent Ward, p. 229.
2007. Los Angeles Hearing, Vol. I, Judith Trevillian, pp. 273–74.
2008. Los Angeles Hearing, Vol. I, William Dunkle, p. 250.
2009. See generally, Los Angeles Hearing, Vol. I, Teresa Hillman; Los Angeles Hearing, Vol. I, Judith Trevillian.
2010. Los Angeles Hearing, Vol. I, Judith Trevillian, p. 276.
2011. Id., p. 253.
2012. Id., p. 254.
2013. Id.; See, The discussion in recommendations for Law Enforcement Agencies for more information about the legal issues surrounding Dial-A-Porn.
2014. Los Angeles Hearing, Vol. I, Teresa Hillman, p. 383; Los Angeles Hearing, Vol. I, Brent Ward, p. 229.

the San Francisco yellow pages heading include "Adult Fantasy," "Gay Phone" and "High Society."[2015]

In addition to telephone directories, the numbers are also openly advertised in sexually explicit magazines and tabloids. For example, the June 1985 issue of one leading sexually explicit magazine contained ten pages of Dial-A-Porn advertisements.[2016] Many of these publications are sold on the public streets with the Dial-A-Porn numbers openly displayed.[2017]

Dial-A-Porn numbers have also been advertised in a major California newspaper, although many newspapers have now discontinued the advertisements.[2018] In addition, Dial-A-Porn numbers are found in magazines in convenience stores and newsstands and are passed around among children and even written on walls.[2019]

Moreover, some Dial-A-Porn advertising is deceptive. Advertisements often refer to "free phone sex" or "free love" when in fact the caller is charged on their telephone bill if they make the call.[2020] This misapprehension is especially common among younger callers and minors.[2021]

COMPUTERS

Production

The personal home computer provides individuals with an extraordinary new form of communication and information access. Providers of sexually explicit materials have taken advantage of this new technology by making computer subscription services the most recent advance in "sexually explicit communications."

In order to set up a computer information service, the information provider must have a computer facility with the capability of handling a number of incoming calls to the information service. The computers used by information providers can cost from twenty to thirty thousand dollars for a micro-computer (which can handle approximately ten calls at one time) to timeshare computers costing one hundred thousand dollars or more (which can handle significantly more calls). The basic cost of providing an information service of any type depends on the magnitude and complexity of the service offered. Computer services offering sexually explicit communications run the gamut from small bulletin board operations to large scale multifaceted services.

The types of information provided also vary. The computer services are similar to Dial-A-Porn telephone services[2022] in that some offer live conversations with an employee of the service, pre-recorded messages or an open line where individuals can communicate with other subscribers. Sexually explicit services may offer one or all of these features. Other, general information providers may offer open "adult" channels where subscribers can carry on sexually explicit conversations with others on the system.

Distribution

Communicating by personal computer requires standard computer equipment. Computer communications require a personal computer (PC), a modem[2023] and access to a standard telephone line.[2024] The computer operator needs only a rudimentary knowledge of

2015. Los Angeles Hearing, Vol. I, Teresa Hillman, p. 388A–6.

2016. Los Angeles Hearing, Vol. I, Brent Ward, p. 230.

2017. Los Angeles Hearing, Vol. I, Teresa Hillman, p. 383.

2018. Los Angeles Hearing, Vol. I, Teresa Hillman, p. 383.

2019. Los Angeles Hearing, Vol. I, Brent Ward, p. 231; Los Angeles Hearing, Vol. I, Judith ✂ , p. 264, Teresa Hillman, p. 377.

2020. Id., pp. 384–85; Los Angeles Hearing, Vol. I, Brent Ward, p. 230; Los Angeles Hearing, Vol. I, Judith Trevillian, p. 264.

2021. Los Angeles Hearing, Vol. I, Brent Ward, p. 230. In 1985 Dr. Victor Cline conducted research involving fourteen children (eleven boys and three girls) and their parents on the effects of Dial-A-Porn on children. He found that each of the children displayed an addictive behavior toward the Dial-A-Porn recordings. Cline reported that none of the children stopped placing the calls until they were admonished by their parents upon discovery of the practice. The research also concluded that the children retained very vivid and recurring memories of the Dial-A-Porn recordings. Cline observed that the children exhibited characteristics of embarrassment, guilt and shame about their involvement with Dial-A-Porn. Cline suggested that the long-term effects of the Dial-A-Porn experiences may be the most alarming.

2022. See, Section E for a complete discussion of Dial-A-Porn.

2023. A modem is an inexpensive device which connects the computer to the telephone system and allows the personal computer access to computer information systems. A modem can be a separate device that sits alongside your computer, or it can be an electronic board built inside the machine.

2024. Miami Hearing, Vol. I, Paul Hartman, p. 117A4.

the equipment for effective communication.[2025]

The computer operator may subscribe to the services of one of many computer information firms. These firms provide access to their computer system for a fee.[2026] Once a computer firm is selected, the operator must acquire a working knowledge of the systems commands to operate the computer effectively. These firms provide a manual which explains the system's commands to the operator following his or her subscription to their service.[2027]

The computer firms offer a wide variety of communication services and provide varying degrees of privacy and security.[2028]

The firms may offer subscribers access to electronic "bulletin boards" where individuals have the opportunity to publicly place and read messages.[2029] These messages are accessible to all subscribers.

Firms may also offer a feature which permits one subscriber to send a confidential message to another subscribers.[2030] This service is similar to mailing a letter directly to another person. The message is sent by computer and received only by the person for whom the message is intended. The sender directs the messages to the recipient by routing them to the recipient's assigned identification number.[2031]

Many computer companies offer a "conference" feature which enables three or more subscribers to engage in a conversation.[2032] Conferences can be monitored by any subscriber to the service and afford no measure of privacy to participants in the dialogue.[2033] This is analogous to the Citizens Band radio network that can be monitored by anyone with a CB radio.

Computer services generally charge an initial subscription fee and a users' fee based upon the time of day and amount of computer time the subscriber uses.[2034] The initial fee is usually between thirty-five and one hundred dollars and user fees range from fifteen to twenty-five dollars per hour.[2035]

Sexually explicit computer subscription services are now available. One sexually explicit magazine, in January of 1985, began what they advertise as an "uncensored erotic" service called SEXTEX.[2036] This service offers an array of features including: (1) a conference calls with unlimited parties; (2) a

---

2025. Id.; the owner's manual is supplied by the computer company and explains the mechanics of operations in detail. Id.

2026. Id.

2027. Id.

2028. Id., pp. 117A4–A5.

2029. Id., p. 117A4.

2030. Id., p. 117A5.

2031. Id.

2032. Id., p. 117A6.

2033. Id.

2034. The two largest home computer information services, CompuServe and The Source, operate in this manner. Telephone interview with CompuServe and The Source sales representatives. (March 6, 1986).

2035. Bane, X-Rated Computers, Genesis (Jan. 1984), pp. 76, 80.

2036. SEXTEX is the only service offered by CVC Online in New York. SEXTEX is synonymous with "COMPUSEX." Interview with Chris Rogers, sales representative, CVC Online (Mar. 6, 1986).

In the July 1985 issue of High Society an article discussing SEXTEX described the following as examples of SEXTEX communications.

"Here's just a taste of the kinds of carnal conversations that go on every night with SEXTEX":

Phone: How about sitting on my face?
Ultima: First tell me how really great you are at eating pussy.
Phone: I like to take things slow, I start by rimming around your pussy with long strokes.
'Ultima: That sounds great, I'm already getting wet.
Phone: I like to tease until I see the sweet juice start to run out of your pussy.

Slick: You said a mouthful? While you've got your big shaft between my beautiful knockers you can stick the head of it in my mouth. Will you let me suck it and swallow the cream?
Lust: I sure will! I'm going to blow a load any minute. How's your pussy? I'll hold off for you.
Slick: I've got my fingers working on it frantically, but I wanna hold out a little longer.
Lust: Do you wanna come in my mouth?
Slick: Do you wanna come all over my titties and pretty face? Maybe I should get out my instant camera so I can take a picture of your cum shooting out.
Lust: Do you really have a camera? I think the keyboard would look great covered with your cum.

Getting User Friendly with Computer Sex, High Society (July 1985), p. 7.

"sex shop" that allows the operator to purchase sexual devices, sexually explicit magazines and video tapes by computer; (3) bulletin boards where the operator can post related messages for other subscribers to read and/or respond to; (4) an electronic mail service which allows one subscriber to send personal notes to other SEXTEX users and to other computer information services; (5) A "Guide" which features articles on sex and travel; (6) the opportunity to place or answer a personal ad or seek some sexual advice.[2037]

The privacy of all communications is stressed by SEXTEX in their advertisements:

Your privacy is of paramount importance to us. SEXTEX has a password system that prevents unauthorized access, and you can change your password anytime you want. Your real identity need never be revealed; you will be known only by a user-name you select. Each SEXTEX transaction is strictly confidential. Information is used only to process the transaction and cannot be monitored even by us. The name SEXTEX will never appear on any bill. Your credit card statement will simply read "Video-tex Services."[2038]

SEXTEX subscribers are asked to sign a written contract when they apply for the service. This contract states that the applicant is eighteen years of age or older and that he will not let anyone under eighteen use the service.[2039] However, there is no indication that the computer services engage in any independent age verification for users and subscribers.[2040] The lack of verification permits young computer users and computer hackers easy access to the system.

Billing for SEXTEX services is currently done on the subscriber's credit card account.[2041] Alternate forms of payment (i.e. cash and checks) may be accepted in the future.[2042]

There are also a number of sexually oriented national and local bulletin boards systems.[2043] GENDERNET describes itself as an "information source for the transvestite and transsexual."[2044] ODYSSEY II is designed for nudists and swingers.[2045] SYSLAVE is known as "the kinkiest in L.A."[2046]

Sexually explicit computer subscription services and bulletin boards are often advertised in sexually explicit tabloids and magazines. Some are advertised through newsletters or direct mail.

Sexually oriented computer communications are not limited to subscription services offered by pornographers. Any two computer operators with compatible systems can carry on a sexually oriented conversation. Moreover, one of the largest personal home computer information networks with over 250,000 subscribers, offers its own "Adult Channel."[2047] This designated channel is one of several conference channels offered by the computer network.[2048] Subscribers may use the "Adult Channel" as an introduction and then continue private conversations elsewhere in the network by a simple system command.[2049]

Computers have also emerged as a method of communication between pedophiles about child victims.[2050]

OTHER MATERIALS SOLD IN PORNOGRAPHIC OUTLETS

Production

There is a wide variety of sexual devices and sexually oriented paraphernalia available in the United States. The Institute for the Advanced Study of Human Sexuality, in an attempt to collect and catalogue these devices,

---

2037. Id., pp. 6–7.

2038. SEXTEX Brochure received by Commission February 12, 1986 (July 1985), p. 7.

2039. Id.

2040. CVC Online representative Chris Rogers stated that the application asks for the date of birth but no independent verification is sought. They rely on the fact that credit cards are needed for billing as a deterrent to under age subscribers. Interview with Chris Rogers, sales representative, CVC Online (Mar. 6, 1986).

2041. SEXTEX Brochure received by Commission February 12, 1986 by CVC Online, Inc.

2042. CVC Online Representative Chris Rogers stated that some time in the future alternative methods of payments may be available. Interview with Chris Rogers, CVC Online sales representative (Mar. 6, 1986).

2043. Type Dirty to Me, Playboy (Mar. 1985) p. 174.

2044. Id.

2045. Id., p. 175.

2046. Id., p. 176.

2047. "X"-Rated: The Joys of CompuSex, Time (May 14, 1984).

2048. Id.

2049. Id.

2050. This issue is specifically addressed in Chapter 11, discussing child pornography.

estimated that there were at least five thousand different "sexual enhancers" that had been marketed in the United States.[2051]

Sexual devices and paraphernalia which can be purchased in many "adults only" pornographic outlets or through mail order include: dildos, penis rings, stimulators, french ticklers, aphrodisiacs, inhalants, inflatable dolls with orifices and police and detective equipment.[2052] Some are purchased for internal use while others are bought for external stimulation.

There are also sexual devices and paraphernalia designed for specific types of sexual activity. For example, there are products specifically designed for sadomasochistic sexual activity. Such products include masks, whips, chains, manacles, clamps and paddles.[2053]

The majority of sexual devices and paraphernalia are produced offshore at the request of suppliers in the United States.[2054] The manufacturers of these products is often subcontracted out to locations in the Orient because labor is available at a substantially reduced cost.[2055] After the products are made, they are shipped to suppliers in the United States.

The largest supplier of sexual devices and paraphernalia in country is alleged to be ✂ through his "Doc Johnson" line of products.[2056] "Doc Johnson" products account for seventy to seventy-five percent of the sexual device and paraphernalia market.[2057] The remainder of the market is mostly made up of smaller specialty companies.[2058]

Distribution

The ✂ News Company, which is owned and operated by ✂ and headquartered in Cleveland, allegedly distributes the majority of "Doc Johnson" and other sexual device and paraphernalia products.[2059] ✂ News has eighty-five to ninety major "news agencies" or distributorships nationwide.[2060] Each distributorship has a different company name and handles a designated region of the country.[2061] Often, they are operated by a local person who has been formally trained at the ✂ News facility in Cleveland.[2062]

These distributors provide approximately 12,000 of the 14,000 to 15,000 pornographic outlets within the United States with "Doc Johnson" and other products.[2063] In those few areas of the country that the ✂ News network does not cover, the products are sold to sub-distributors who then sell to retailers in their area.[2064] Most of the distributors use trucks or trains to transport the materials.[2065]

In essence, the supplier and the distributor are one in the same for this product line at pornographic outlets. Moreover, ✂ owns numerous pornographic outlets across the country.[2066] In some instances, then, he supplies, distributes and sells his own products.

Most of the "adults only" pornographic outlets in the United States carry sexual devices and paraphernalia as part of their general stock and account for approximately fifty percent of total sales of these products.[2067] Sexual devices and paraphernalia are sold along with sexually explicit magazines, pa-

2051. Los Angeles Hearing, Vol. I, Ted McIlvenna and Loretta Haroian, p. 224E.

2052. *Id.* The Commission received reports regarding individuals that used such "police" equipment to assist in obtaining access to victims of sexual abuse and/or rape; See, The Imagery Found Among Magazines, Books, Films in "Adults Only" Pornographic Outlets in Chapter 24.

2053. Other sadomasochistic sexual devices include orifice spreaders, testicle harnesses, body harnesses, branding irons, penis stretchers, crosses, enema bags, hand cuffs, rubber hands for anal insertion, underwear with openings for sexual usage, hoists, horse penises, leather straight jackets, lock restraints, mace, pins, racks, rectal catheters, restraining tables, stocks, breast chains, and nipple clamps. See, The Imagery Found Among Magazines, Books, Films in "Adults Only" Pornographic Outlets in Chapter 24.

2054. Interview with Ted McIlvenna, President, The Institute for the Advanced Study of Human Sexuality (Feb. 28, 1986); Interview with Sergeant Don Smith, Los Angeles Police Department (Mar. 9, 1986).

2055. Some small scale manufacturing of these products still goes on in the United States. *Id.*

2056. Interview with Sergeant Don Smith, Los Angeles Police Department (Mar. 9, 1986). ✂ .

2057. *Id.*

2058. *Id.*

2059. For further information ✂ , See, The discussion of organized crime in Chapter 19.

2060. *Id.*

2061. *Id.*

2062. *Id.*

2063. *Id.*; Some sources estimate the number of "adults only" pornographic outlets to be sixteen thousand. Los Angeles Hearing, Vol. II, Dennis Sobin, p. 259.

2064. Interview with Sergeant Donald Smith, Los Angeles Police Department (Mar. 9, 1986).

2065. Interview with Ted McIlvenna, President, Institute for the Advanced Study of Human Sexuality (Mar. 8, 1986).

2066. Interview with Detective Robert Peters, Los Angeles Police Department (Mar. 9, 1986).

2067. Interview with Ted McIlvenna, President, Institute for the Advanced Study of Human Sexuality (Mar. 8, 1986).

perback books, periodicals, videos and films.

The remainder of these products are distributed through mail order operations.[2068] Advertisements for such goods are found in sexually explicit paperback books, magazines and tabloids nationwide.[2069] Sometimes, these products are advertised through direct mail.

PAPERBACK BOOKS

Production

The volume of sexually explicit paperback books which have been published is tremendous. The 1970 President's Commission on Obscenity and Pornography estimated that approximately five thousand new "adult" titles were published each year.[2070] Recent studies of this segment of the industry suggest that while it is doubtful that five thousand sexually explicit paperbacks are still published each year, the actual number published is still large.[2071]

Two major publishers or sexually explicit paperbacks are Star Distributions, Inc., and Greenleaf Classics.[2072] Star Distributors, Inc., is located in New York and is alleged to be controlled by ✂ .[2073] Greenleaf Classics is located in California.[2074] William ✂ , Greenleaf's director in 1971, was convicted of obscenity violations for publishing the *Illustrated Report of the President's Commission on Obscenity and Pornography*.[2075]

The content of sexually explicit paperback books is similar to the content of any other sexually explicit medium.[2076] Incest, sado-masochism, bondage and discipline, bestiality and sexual acts involving children are all common themes in these books.[2077] Current paperbacks available include titles such as: *Suckalot Wife, Grandma's Horney Visit, Daddy's Sweet Slut, Hot, Wet Nun, Transvestite in Chains, Vietnamese Pleasure Girls, Rape High School, Rhonda's Trained Dobermans, Pony for Daughter* and *Tying up Rebecca*.[2078]

Paperback books often are developed as part of a series.[2079] Such series include: *Siren Slavegirls, Tales of Terror, Pedophilia in the American Family, Incest Tales,* and *Forbidden Fantasies*.[2080]

The cover of these paperbacks is often illustrative of their contents.[2081] *I Want All Night Abuse* pictures a kneeling man about to whip a partially nude, large-breasted woman who is bound, gagged and crying.[2082] *Naughty Family Urges* depicts two nude men and two nude women involved in orgy-like sexual activity.[2083] *Kneeling for Daddy* depicts the back view of a muscular man from the waist down including the buttocks and genitals. A pigtailed girl with one breast exposed and holding a lollypop can be seen through his legs.[2084]

The paperback books are very detailed in their descriptions of sex-related themes and acts and are often written at an elementary school reading level.[2085] The books are usually between one hundred and two hundred pages long and have retail cover prices of $2.95 to $4.95.[2086]

2068. Cook, *The "X"-Rated Economy,* Forbes (Sept. 18, 1978), p. 81; Interview with Ted McIlvenna, President, Institute for the Advanced Study of Human Sexuality (Mar. 8, 1986).

2069. See, The Imagery Found Among Magazines, Books, Films in "Adults Only" Pornographic Outlets in Chapter 24.

2070. Sampson, *Commercial Traffic in Sexually Oriented Materials in the United States (1969–1970),* in 3 Technical Report of the Commission on Obscenity and Pornography (1971), p. 98.

2071. Eisenberg, *Toward a Bibliography of Erotic Pulps,* 15 J. of Popular Culture (1982), pp. 175, 176; See, The Imagery Found Among Magazines, Books, Films in "Adults Only" Pornographic Outlets, *infra.*

2072. Interview with Daniel Eisenberg, Modern Languages and Linguistics Department, Florida State University (Apr. 10, 1986).

2073. See, The discussion on organized crime influence in the pornography industry for more information ✂ .

2074. Eisenberg, *Toward a Bibliography of Erotic Pulps,* 15 J. of Popular Culture (1982), pp. 175, 179.

2075. *Id.* at 180.

2076. See, The Imagery Found Among Magazines, Books, Films, in "Adults Only" Pornographic Outlets in Chapter 24.

2077. *Id.*

2078. *Id.*

2079. *Id.*

2080. *Id.*

2081. *Id.*

2082. *Id.*

2083. *Id.*

2084. *Id.*

2085. *Id.*

2086. *Id.*

These books generally do not provide specific information about the authors of the books.[2087] Many books do not even include the name of the author.[2088] And, when the author's name is given, many times this name is fictitious.[2089]

The majority of publishers care little about the literary quality of these paperbacks and pay authors small lump sum amounts of five hundred dollars per book or employ in-house authors on salary who write these paperbacks full time.[2090]

Many sexually explicit paperback books contain advertisements on the back cover or the inside flap.[2091] The advertisements may be for sexually explicit paperbacks, magazines, or sexual devices and paraphernalia.[2092] Some paperbacks also have personal advertisements.[2093] Personal advertisements often contain names and addresses or may use a confidential number postal exchange system for correspondence with the individual described in the advertisement.[2094]

These paperbacks also contain order forms for the sex related products shown in the advertisement.[2095] When ordering, the purchaser is required to sign a release on the form that states he or she is over the age of eighteen.[2096] The product or personal advertisement orders may be paid for by cash, check, money order, or credit card.[2097]

Distribution

Star Distributor is not only a major publisher, but also a major distributor of sexually explicit paperbacks.[2098] These sexually explicit paperback books are distributed through "adults only" pornographic outlets across the country. These paperbacks are also sold through mail order operations advertised in sexually explicit magazines, tabloids and other paperback books.

Sexually explicit paperback books are advertised in sexually explicit magazines, tabloids and other paperbacks. These books are also advertised in some Book Club publications and publisher's catalogs.

TABLOIDS

Production

There are few nationally distributed sexually explicit tabloids.[2099] The vast majority of sexually explicit tabloids are regional publications.[2100] Some of these tabloids are published by a swinger or sex club.[2101] Others are established by individuals or regional corporations.[2102] Most of the tabloids are independently owned.[2103]

Sexually explicit tabloids vary in their sexual explicitness and content diversity. Some contain all photographs. Others contain text and photographs. The photographs depicted in some of these tabloids include sadomasochistic activities, sexual acts between two women, masturbation, oral-genital contact, and vaginal and anal intercourse. The text may be sexually oriented or of a general interest nature.

The advertisements in these tabloids are mostly regional and for sexually related goods and services. The tabloids often con-

2087. Interview with Daniel Eisenberg, Modern Languages and Linguistics Department, Florida State University (Apr. 10, 1986).

2088. *Id.* This is particularly true with ✂ . *Id.*

2089. Eisenberg, *Toward a Bibliography of Erotic Pulps*, 15 J. of Popular Culture, (1982), pp. 175, 176.

2090. *Id.*, p. 181.

2091. See, The Imagery Found Among Magazines, Books, Films in "Adults Only" Pornographic Outlets in Chapter 24.

2092. *Id.*

2093. *Id.*; One such advertisement read: "Animal of Action Sexy Model has those hard to find and elaborate poses available! Tell her what you want to see, from golden showers, slaves, master, animals and action or bi-scenes, I ah, should I say I can pose anyway you want, live or in person or by mail. Send $10 in cash with your order."

2094. *Id.*

2095. *Id.*

2096. *Id.*

2097. *Id.*

2098. See, The Imagery Found Among Magazines, Books, Films in "Adults Only" Pornographic Outlets in Chapter 24.

2099. The best known of these tabloids is *Screw Magazine*. Even *Screw Magazine* is predominantly regionally circulated (seventy percent in New York). Interview with Dennis Sobin, President, First Amendment Consumer and Trade Society (FACTS) (Apr. 11, 1986).

2100. *Id.*

2101. *Id.*

2103. *Id.*

2203. *Id.*

tain advertisements for sexually explicit video tapes, films, photo sets, magazines and paperback books. [2104] Sexual paraphernalia, aphrodisiacs, and sadomasochistic devices are also advertised. The majority of the advertisements in tabloids are for escort services, prostitution, massage parlors, sexually explicit telephone messages, and classified listings. Advertisements comprise a significant portion, if not the majority, of the tabloids.

The following examples of advertisements are from the *Hollywood Press*. The *Hollywood Press* is published weekly and sold predominantly in California. [2105] Two advertisements for escort agencies included:

International Escorts Featuring Beautiful Blondes, Brunettes, Blacks and Orientals. Master Charge & Visa Accepted. 24 Hours at Your Location for Your Convenience & Pleasure . . .

And,

Gourmet Treats Escort Agency Menu (Take Out) Entrees
 -Blondes, Brunettes and Redheads (long, shoulder-length, straight or curly)
 -Busty or Slender, Classic Builds (38-25-36; 34-23-34; 36-24-36, etc.)
 -International & American Beauties
 -Tall to Petite
 -Novices to Mature "Experts"[2106]
Each Dish: Available individually or in any combination . . . Prepared to order . . . Served for Short but Satisfying Meal or Full Course. Delivered: ANYTIME. Checks & All Major Credit Cards Accepted. Delicious Dolls Interviewed. [2107]

Other advertisements for sex-related services included:

CLINIC specializing in Special Specialties.
 -Bondage and Discipline
 -Two Completely Equipped Dungeons
 -Enemas—Give & receive

-T.V.'s—Complete Wardrobes, Maids Outfits
-Infantilism—Diapers, Rubber pants
-Spankings—The Best in Town
-Wrestling—Mats and Showers Available
-Videos & Slides—For Your Viewing Pleasure
5 Dominants
5 Submissives
Open 7 Days a Week, Visa, Mastercharge . . .[2108]

GOLDEN RAIN. Drips & Drips, Golden Showers, Cum Down My Crotch, Let Me Stand Over You & Give You My "Golden Juices! Call . . .[2109]

SHE MALE. Exceptionally attractive transsexual, flawless complexion, refined features, cock intact. Cauc. brunette, 24 yrs, $100 cash for 1/2 hour. In call. Clean cut, muscular athletes 18–30 free. . . .[2110]

The classified advertisement section of the *Hollywood Press* edition surveyed also had help wanted advertisements. These included advertisements for nude models, escorts, nude dancers, performers and masseuses. [2111] Many of these tabloids are produced in-house. This has been made possible by the advent of inexpensive machines which have typeset and photo screening capabilities. [2112] These machines can now be purchased for approximately six thousand dollars. [2113]

Distribution

Sexually explicit tabloids are generally published and distributed on a regional basis. These tabloid publishers exercise several options in distributing their products. A few sell their tabloids to conventional distributors who sell to newsstands. [2114] Many publishers sell their tabloids to distributors who specialize in sexually explicit products and sell to "adults only" pornographic outlets. [2115] Others sell directly to newsstands and "adults

---

2104. See, The Imagery Found Among Magazines, Books, Films in "Adults Only" Pornographic Outlets in Chapter 24.

2105. *Hollywood Press*, July 5, 1985, p. 2.

2106. *Id.*, p. 11.

2107. *Id.*

2108. *Id.*, p. 21.

2109. *Id.*

2110. *Id.*

2111. It should be noted that the fact that a publication has advertisements for prostitution does not make it a sexually explicit publication. Sexual explicitness refers to the publication as a whole, not simply its advertisements.

2112. Interview with Dennis Sobin, President, First Amendment Consumer and Trade Society (FACTS) (Apr. 11, 1986).

2113. *Id.*

2114. *Id.*

2115. *Id.*

only" pornographic outlets in their area.[2116] Still others sell their tabloids from street vending machines.[2117] The selling of these tabloids through street vending machines is particularly problematic because children can view and purchase these publications.

Sexually explicit tabloids are also offered through subscription and mail order sales.[2118] The tabloids advertise through direct mail, other regional tabloids and magazines, and even some radio stations.[2119]

The cost of these tabloids ranges from one to four dollars.[2120] Some cost as much as eight dollars.[2121] The majority, however, cost two dollars.[2122]

PHOTO SETS

Production

There is a market among consumers of sexually explicit materials for individual custom made photographs and photo sets.[2123] This portion of the industry can best be described as a "cottage industry" since the product is often homemade or made by very small scale commercial producers.[2124]

Individuals who produce these photos sets can do so with minimal overhead. The necessary costs for producing photo sets include renting or buying a camera, purchasing film, photo processing, location and model fees

and mailing. Models are often found by the photographer placing advertisements for "models" in newspapers.[2125] The photographer's home is often used as a studio.[2126]

These photo set photographers must find photo processors who will develop their sexually explicit film. Some photographers use general commercial photo processors including one hour photo services.[2127] Others use mail order services which advertise "confidential and uncensored" photo processing in sexually explicit publications.[2128] One such photo processing lab was ✂ .[2129] ✂ was the focus of a Federal Bureau of Investigation undercover operation in 1981 and 1982.[2130] The sexually explicit photographs knowingly processed by ✂ included depictions of bestiality, excretion, homosexuality, examples of extreme mutilation, castration, torture and child pornography.[2131] These types of photos were processed on a regular basis.[2132]

Individual photographs or photo sets often depict sex related activities not generally represented in commercially produced pornography. These activities include piercing,[2133] scat,[2134] castration and extreme sadomasochism.

The photo set business enables a producer to offer "custom" service.[2135] Often the customer writes or telephones his or her requests

2116. Id.
2117. Id.
2118. Id.
2119. Dennis Sobin states that sexually explicit magazines sell their mailing lists. These lists are extremely useful to these small publications. Id.
2120. Id.
2121. Id.
2122. Id.
2123. See, Los Angeles Hearing, Vol. II, Charles Sullivan, p. 66; Los Angeles Hearing, Vol. II, Caryl Cid, p. 127; Los Angeles Hearing, Vol. II, Brian Cid, p. 134. See also, The discussion of advertisements in tabloids for these photo sets.
2124. Sexually explicit magazines include solicitations for photographs through amateur photograph contests. See, Dominatrix Domain, No. 17, p. 33.
2125. Los Angeles Hearing, Vol. II, Charles Sullivan, pp. 65, 76B.
2126. Id., p. 66.
2127. Id.
2128. Los Angeles Hearing, Vol. II, Caryl Cid, p. 127.
2129. Id.
2130. Id., pp. 127–29; United States v. Petrov, 747 F.2d (2nd Cr. 1984), p. 824.
2131. Id., p. 129. In a different case in Colorado a "search resulted in the seizure of approximately five thousand photographs, negatives and video cassettes depicting young men and women in their late teens and early twenties in various sadomasochistic and other types of pornographic poses. Various props for these photographs such as wooden stocks, wooden racks, a jail cell, ropes, boards with nails protruding from then and other torture devices were located." Los Angeles hearing, Vol. II, Charles Sullivan, p. 66. See also, The Imagery Found Among Magazines, Books, Films in "Adults Only" Pornographic Outlets, infra. for a description of depictions from the Spectra Photo case which appeared in the magazine Big Tit Dildo Bondage.
2132. Chicago Hearing, Vol. II, Frederick Scullin, p. 56E.
2133. "Piercing" is a slang term for a paraphilia in which sexual arousal requires piercing the skin, and often the genitals, with pins, needles, and other sharp instruments.
2134. "Scat" is a slang term describing sexual conduct in which feces are either used or ingested by one of the participants.
2135. "Love to model in person or by mail. Custom poses. Any position, any attire, any partners. Nothing too radical.

and photographs are taken of the described activity.[2136] The photographs may be ordered through contacting the individual photographer directly or through a mail order service.

Sexually explicit photo sets are a lucrative endeavor for photographers and photo processors alike. Photo sets usually include six to ten photographs and sell for nine to twenty-five dollars to individual consumers.[2137]

Some film processors have made substantial revenues from processing and duplicating sexually explicit photo sets. ✂ mentioned above, earned approximately six hundred thousand dollars from April 1, 1981, until March 31, 1982, through its mail order pornographic photo processing business.[2138] Federal Bureau of Investigation agents were able to identify that the volume of business attributable to one individual producer, ✂ , accounted for thirty thousand dollars of the six hundred thousand dollar total.[2139]

Moreover, some of these photo set photographers sell their photos to sexually explicit commercial publications. These publications often offer the photographer hundreds of dollars for a few rolls of film.[2140]

Distribution

Once the photo set photographer has taken the photographs and had the film processed he has several options. He may sell the final product to commercial publishers for reprint in their publications or he may sell them to individual consumers.[2141] The photo sets sold for individual consumption are available at "adults only" pornographic outlets[2142] and through mail order operations offering sexually explicit products. Often, the photographers advertise their photo sets in sexually explicit publications.[2143]

AUDIO TAPES

Production

In order to commercially produce a sexually explicit audio cassette tape the producer needs a cassette recorder and performers. He must duplicate and package the tape in-house or through an outside firm, or sell the master to a distributor who will handle this process for him. These tapes look and are packaged like general music cassette tapes.

The commercially produced audio tapes contain sexually explicit conversations and acts. Audio tapes are similar to pre-recorded Dial-A-Porn recordings.[2144] Both are audio recordings of sexually oriented conversations or activities. The activities described in these tapes include sadomasochistic acts and sexual relations with children, among others.

The Commission also heard testimony about homemade non-commercial audio tapes. One ex-prostitute testified how her pimp made recordings of sexual activities and brutal beatings.[2145] Another woman testi-

---

2136. A Federal Bureau of Investigation agent testified before the Commission, ". . . the actual order from the customer was located in his or her handwriting. Some of these orders were for custom shots with a customer actually describing the poses that the models should effect and naming particular models they wanted to see in these photographs." Los Angeles Hearing, Vol. II, Charles Sullivan, pp. 68–69; See, Washington Hearing, Vol. II, Ken Lanning, pp. 30-31.

2137. Los Angeles Hearing, Vol. II, Charles Sullivan, p. 69.

2138. Los Angeles Hearing, Vol. II, Caryl Cid, p. 127; See also, Chicago Hearing, Vol. II, Frederick Scullin, p. 45.

2139. Special Agent Brian Cid stated, ". . . from 1978 until 1982 ✂ did thirty thousand dollars worth of business with ✂ , doing business as ✂ , operated a mail order company from his apartment in ✂ , Pennsylvania. He specialized in photographs depicting the bondage and torture of women. He sold the photographs in color set packages of ten for eight dollars and black and white set packages for six dollars. His mailing list consisted of over three hundred customers nationwide." Los Angeles Hearing, Vol. II, Brian Cid, p. 134.

2140. Los Angeles Hearing, Vol. II, Charles Sullivan, p. 72.

2242. Id., p. 68.

2142. See, The detailed discussion of "adults only" pornographic outlets in this Chapter.

2143. The advertisements often accompany a photograph. The following are a few examples of these advertisements.

"Ten photos of this faceless slave. She is bound onto a metal chair. Rope is wrapped around her neck and chest. Great fantasy set." *Fundgeon Times*, Vol. 1, No. 4, p. 10.

"Tim's slave girl is bound upside down hand and foot. Clips on her nipples and pussy. See her twist and turn. Ten good shots." *Id.*

"This is one of the best selling photo sets. Debbie was bound to the bed and a riding crop as well as several nipple clamps were used on her. The marks are real!!" Id., p. 12.

2144. See, The discussion of Dial-A-Porn in this Chapter.

2145. Washington, D.C., Hearing, Vol. I, Sarah Wynter, p. 183.

Try me. Send a $5 bill for 3 gorgeous color photos or send a $20 bill for 10 mind-shocking photos and private phone. You won't be disappointed." *Trained Teen Slave and Over Daddy's Knee* (1984), p. 174. See also, *Dominatrix Domain*, No. 17, p. 34; *Fundgeon Times*, Vol. 1, No. 4, p. 15.

fied that her husband wanted to record her domination of him in a sadomasochistic scenario:[2146]

> There was another time when he wanted to record on a cassette tape recorder the sounds of him being spanked and me being the dominant female giving him a punishment. He wanted the tape so he could listen to it on his own later for pleasure.[2147]

While these non-commercial audio tapes are generally produced for private consumption, they may be, and have been, shared with or distributed among close friends and associates.

Distribution

Audio tape recordings of sexually explicit conversations and activities are available in "adults only" pornographic outlets and mail order operations throughout the United States. The mail order audio tape dealers often advertise their product in sexually explicit magazines and tabloids.

PEEP SHOWS

Production

The average peep show booth has dimensions of about three by five feet.[2148] The booths are partitioned four-sided cubicles generally made out of wood or plastic.[2149] Often, a bench is built onto one of the walls. On the wall next to the bench is the coin or token-operated box.[2150] A customer places coins or tokens into the box and the movie inside the booth is activated.

If a film is shown, the booth is equipped with a movie projector.[2151] If a video is shown, the peep show booth is wired so that a selected video appears on the television screen.[2152] Sometimes, the video system in the booths is computer operated.[2153] If the peep show involves live performances, there is usually a clear partition between the performer and viewer.

Peep show movies come in eight millimeter, sixteen millimeter or VHS format.[2154] The eight millimeter films do not have sound and are shorter in length than the videos. The movies include homosexual, heterosexual and sadomasochistic sexual activities between two women, coprophilia, bestiality or simulated juvenile sexual activities.[2155]

Distribution

Some "adults only" pornographic outlet owners buy their peep show booths outright while others rent their booths.[2156] The initial cost of purchasing a peep show booth is between twenty and thirty thousand dollars.[2157] If booths are rented, the store owner usually shares the profits of the booths with the lessors in exchange for the lessor's installation and maintenance of the booths.[2158]

Inside the booths the viewer may see approximately two minutes of the movie for twenty-five cents.[2159] As the number of sexually explicit scenes or diversity of sexual acts increase, the viewing time decreases.[2160] Tokens or quarters are needed to operate the peep shows and can be obtained at the outlet's sales counter.

The average peep show booth has enough room for two adults to stand shoulder to shoulder. The inside of the booth is dark, when the door is closed, except for the light which emanates from the screen or enters from the bottom of the door.

The inside walls of the peep show booths are often covered with graffiti and messages.[2161] The graffiti is generally of a sexual nature and consists of telephone numbers, names, requests and offers for homosexual

---

2146. Chicago Hearing, Vol. I, Diann, p. 29N.
2147. Id.
2148. Washington, D.C., Hearing, Vol. II, Dennis DeBord, p. 9; Some booths are as large as four feet by eight feet. New York Hearing, Vol. I, Bookstore Operator, p. 127.
2149. Washington, D.C., Vol. II, Dennis DeBord, p. 99.
2150. Id., p. 97.
2151. Id., p. 99.
2152. Id.
2153. New York Hearing, Vol. I, William Kelly, p. 84.
2154. Washington, D.C., Hearing, Vol. II, Dennis DeBord, pp. 97–98.
2155. Id., p. 98
2156. New York Hearing, Vol. I, Bookstore Operator, p. 145.
2157. Los Angeles Hearing, Vol. I, Robert Peters, p. 105.
2158. Id., p. 149.
2159. Washingon, D.C., Hearing, Vol. II, Dennis DeBord, pp. 98–99.
2160. New York Hearing, Vol. I, Bookstore Operator, p. 128.
2161. Washington, D.C., Hearing, Vol. II, Dennis DeBord, p. 99–100.

acts, anatomical descriptions and sketches.[2162] The booth may also contain a chart which is used to schedule appointments and meetings in that particular booth.[2163] In some cases, this arrangement has been used for the solicitation of prostitutes.

After purchasing tokens from the store clerk,[2164] the patron selects the type of movie he wishes to view. A brief description of the film is usually posted on the outside of the peep booth door.[2165] A number or letter is assigned to each film and indicates which coin box inside the booth corresponds with the selected movie.

The film or video tape[2166] is operated by placing one quarter, coin, slug or token into the coin box, which, in turn, activates the movie projector or video tape player to begin the movie.[2167] Quarters or tokens must be repeatedly inserted to continue viewing the movie[2168] which may last from ten to ninety minutes.[2169]

In addition to movie viewing, the booths also provide places for anonymous sexual relations.[2170] Many booths are equipped with a hole in the side wall between the booths to allow patrons to engage in anonymous sex.[2171] The holes are used for oral and anal sexual acts.[2172] Sexual activity in the booths involves mostly males participating in sexual activities with one another.[2173] However, both heterosexual and homosexual men engage in these activities.[2174] The anonymity provided by the "glory holes" allows the participants to fantasize about the gender and other characteristics of their partners.[2175]

The booth is sometimes equipped with lock on the door.[2176] Many patrons intentionally leave the door unlocked. Some patrons look inside the booths in an attempt to find one already occupied.[2177] It is commonplace for a patron to enter an occupied booth, close the door behind him, and make advances toward the occupant.[2178] He may grab the occupant's genitals in an effort to invoke sexual activity[2179] or attempt to arrange a later sexual encounter.[2180] The sexual activities reported in peep show booths include masturbation, anal intercourse, and fellatio.

Inside the booths, the floors and walls are often wet and sticky with liquid or viscous substances, including semen, urine, feces, used prophylactics, gels, saliva or alcoholic beverages.[2181] The soles of a patron's shoes may stick to certain areas of the floor.[2182] The booths are also often littered with cigarette butts and tobacco.[2183] The trash and sewage and the application of disinfectants or ammonia on occasion create a particularly nauseating smell in the peep booths.[2184]

It has been estimated that peep shows are the biggest moneymaking portion of this industry.[2185] Annual net profits for peep show booths alone have been projected at two billion dollars.[2186]

2162. Id.
2163. An appointment schedule may indicate a person's name, age, penis size, sexual preference, age and description of the sexual partner being sought, such as "young boy looking for . . ." and the date, time and location of a future meeting. Id.
2164. Some stores impose a minimum number of tokens which must be purchased.
2165. Washington, D.C., Hearing, Vol. II, Dennis DeBord, p. 97.
2166. Some peep booths are equipped with closed circuit television. Houston Hearing, Vol. I, W. D. Brown, p. 41.
2167. Id.; Washington, D.C., Hearing, Vol. II, Dennis DeBord, p. 98.
2168. Washington, D.C., Hearing, Vol. II, Dennis DeBord, pp. 98–99.
2169. Interview with Detective Robert Peters, Los Angeles Police Department (Mar. 10. 1986).
2170. Houston Hearing, Vol. I, W. D. Brown, p. 36.
2171. The holes are commonly referred to as "glory holes." Id.
2172. Interview with detectives, Washington, D.C., Metropolitan Police Department, in Washington, D.C. (Feb. 21, 1986).
2173. Washington, D.C., Hearing, Vol. II, Dennis DeBord, pp. 101–03.
2174. Id., p. 103; Houston Hearing, Vol. II, W. D. Brown, p. 39.
2175. Houston Hearing, Vol. I, W. D. Brown, p. 39.
2176. Washington, D.C., Hearing, Vol. II, Dennis DeBord, p. 101.
2177. Id., pp. 101–02.
2178. Id., p. 101.
2179. Id., pp. 101-02.
2180. Id., p. 102.
2181. Id.
2182. Id.
2183. Id.
2184. Id., pp. 100–01.
2185. New York Hearing, Vol. I, William Kelly, p. 85.
2186. Id.

OUTLETS

"ADULTS ONLY" PORNOGRAPHIC OUTLETS

"Adults only" pornographic outlets can be found in both large metropolitan areas and many small towns throughout the United States. Although these "adults only" pornographic outlets are frequently located in downtown metropolitan areas, they have also appeared in business and residential sections of suburban communities.[2187]

The windows of "adults only" pornographic outlet storefronts are usually opaque to prevent the general public from looking into the store from the outside.[2188] Prominently displayed on the outside facade of the outlets may be large signs such as "adult books, movies and magazines" and "$.25 movies" to entice patronage.[2189] These signs are sometimes accompanied by neon and flashing lights designed to attract attention and arouse public curiosity. Sometimes, there are also signs displayed which say "no one under 18 is permitted inside."[2190] Although most states require patrons to be at least eighteen years old to enter these establishments, few, if any, stores have employees at the point of entry to verify ages and enforce this law.

The inside of a "adults only" pornographic outlet can be divided into distinct display and sales areas. The display areas include sections devoted to sexual devices and paraphernalia, reading materials and peep show booths.[2191] In the typical pornographic outlet it is not uncommon to see anywhere from 1,000 to 2,000 different items for sale.[2192]

In some "adults only" pornographic outlets, patrons are required to pay a nominal fee to get into the sexually explicit material and peep booth areas. This fee is sometimes deducted from a future purchase.[2193]

The "novelty section" of the average pornographic outlet contains numerous sexual devices and paraphernalia such as dildos, rubber vaginas, tools used to simulate sodomy, medical appliances to spread anal and vaginal orifices, "love" creams, blow-up dolls with orifices, stimulants, inhalants,[2194] whips, leather harnesses, edible panties and rubber clothing articles.[2195]

The "magazine section" is often divided into categories such as heterosexuality, homosexuality, lesbianism, sadomasochism, bondage and discipline, excretion, bestiality and simulated child pornography.[2196] There are many other types of magazines which are meant to appeal to specific sexual interests.[2197] For example, *Mother's Milk*[2198] depicts women who have milk in their breasts engaged in various sexual acts that include squirting milk. *Poppin' Mamas*[2199] depicts pregnant women engaged in various sexual acts including lesbian activities.[2200] The magazines are often wrapped in cellophane to prevent customers from thumbing through the magazines, to restrict law enforcement officers from examining the magazines, and to

---

2187. Houston Hearing, Vol. I, W. D. Brown, p. 35.

2188. Washington, D.C., Hearing, Vol. II, Dennis DeBord, p. 95.

2189. *Id.*

2190. *Id.*, p. 96.

2191. Houston Hearing, Vol. I, Brown, p. 37.

2192. Houston Hearing, Vol. I, W. D., Brown, p. 37.

2193. *Id.*

2194. It has been found that most of these chemical agents contain volatile nitrites which are schedule D drugs. These chemical agents are primarily used for the alleged stimulation of sexual desires and sexual arousal, although many are marketed under the pretext that they have other purposes such as room deodorizing or for use as perfume. "The Spanish fly," a prominent chemical product on the market, has a high concentration of caffeine. Houston Hearing, Vol. I, W. D. Brown, pp. 38–39.

2195. *Id.*; Washington, D.C., Hearing, Vol. II, Dennis DeBord, p. 96.

2196. Washington, D.C., Hearing, Vol. II, Dennis DeBord, p. 96.

2197. *Id.*, pp. 96–97.

2198. *Id.*, p. 96.

2199. *Id.*

2200. For a more thorough discussion and description of magazines, See, The Imagery Found Among Magazines, Books, Films in "Adults Only" Pornographic Outlets in Chapter 24. One expert has advised the Commission Staff that the American Psychiatric Association could rewrite its Diagnostic Statistical Manual Sections on psychosexual disorders based on the various subjects of sexually explicit magazines.

provide arguments in the event of prosecution as to "lack of knowledge" by outlet personnel.[2201]

The "paperback book" section contains paperbacks with a variety of themes including incest, child sex,[2202] bestiality, [2203] group sex,[2204] and sadomasochism.[2205] *A Pony for Daughter, Teen Sex Slaves of Saigon, Family Lovers,* and *Whipped Wives* are among current paperback titles.[2206]

The "movie section" of these "adults only" pornographic outlets contain mostly eight millimeter films and video tape cassettes. There are thousands of titles on the market today on subjects running the gamut of sexual behaviors with some appealing to specific paraphilias.[2207]

Eight millimeter films retail for approximately eighty dollars in these stores.[2208] Video tape cassettes sell for sixty to eighty dollars depending on the type and quality of the product.[2209]

In addition, an "adults only" pornographic outlet may contain anywhere from five to one hundred "peep show booths".[2210] These booths are usually located in a secluded section near the rear of the establishment.

Some pornographic outlets also have live sex acts.[2211] "Show World" in the Times Square District of New York City, has booths where patron can watch nude dancers and observe live sex acts.[2212] Some booths are equipped with telephones so that the patron can engage in a conversation with the nude performer.[2213] Some booths have glass between the patron and the performer while others are constructed with holes in the glass to permit physical contact between the patron and the performer.[2214]

Most "adults only" pornographic outlets advertise their services and products on their storefronts. Some of these establishments advertise in local phone directories like any other business establishment. Some also advertise through sexually explicit tabloids and magazines, flyers and business cards.

Pornographic outlets generally, and peep shows in particular, are a primary focus of organized crime involvement.[2215] These outlets are primarily a cash business and as such, it is relatively easy to "launder" or hide actual profits.[2216] One witness who had operated numerous "adults only" pornographic outlets, advised, that the daily receipts for his stores were sixteen hundred dollars a day in quarters from peep shows and three hundred fifty dollars a day from magazine sales.[2217]

The store operator also stated it was common practice in this industry, like many other businesses, to keep two sets of financial records: one for the Internal Revenue Service and a second personal set.[2218] The witness observed that it was also commonplace to state no more than one hundred dollars as daily gross revenue for an "adults only" pornographic outlet,[2219] although he estimated that his stores would gross between sixty and eighty thousand dollars a month.[2220]

The impact of sexually explicit videos on "adults only" pornographic outlets is uncertain. Videos are being increasingly used in the outlets' peep show booths. In addition,

2201. Houston Hearing, Vol. I, W. D. Brown, p. 37. Some of these outlets also have a list of vice squad officers so they can be identified and not sold sexually explicit materials. *Id.*, p. 39.

2202. Washington, D.C., Hearing, Vol. II Dennis DeBord, p. 96.

2203. *Id.*

2204. *Id.*

2205. *Id.*

2206. See, The discussion of paperback books observed in "adults only" pornographic outlets in The Imagery Found Among Magazines, Books, Films in "Adults Only" Pornographic Outlets in Chapter 24.

2207. Washington, D.C., Hearing, Vol. II, Dennis DeBord, p. 96.

2208. *Id.*, p. 97.

2209. Los Angeles Hearing, Vol. I, William Roberts, p. 71; Miami Hearing, Vol. I, Mike Berish, p. 91; See, The discussion and description of the sexually explicit video industry for further information.

2210. New York Hearing, Vol. I, William Kelly, p. 84; See, The detailed discussion of peep show booths in this Chapter.

2211. Houston Hearing, Vol. I, W. D. Brown, p. 42.

2212. Commission staff survey of "adults only" pornographic outlets, New York City Times Square District, October, 1985.

2213. *Id.*

2214. *Id.*

2215. See, The discussion of organized crime involvement in the pornography industry for further information.

2216. New York Hearing, Vol. I, Bookstore Operator, pp. 142–55.

2217. *Id.*, p. 149.

2218. *Id.*, pp. 146–47.

2219. *Id.*, p. 144.

2220. *Id.*, p. 149.

the stores sell and rent videos as part of their general business. In this way, the proliferation of sexually explicit video tape cassettes has become a positive revenue source.

In addition, some individuals patronize "adults only" pornographic outlets primarily for the atmosphere and potential for sexual activity. Others go to these outlets to purchase sexually explicit magazines, books or sexual devices. These patrons will undoubtedly not be significantly influenced by the availability of video.

At the same time, however, the "adults only" pornographic outlet is no longer the exclusive source for an individual who wants to buy or rent a sexually explicit video tape cassette. He may rent sexually explicit videos at general video retail outlets which also stock general release and children's videos. He may then view them in the privacy of his own home.

In sum it is unclear at this point what long term effects sexually explicit videos will have on these "adults only" pornographic outlets.[2221]

Nearly all of the general information stated above regarding the typical outlet and peep show booth, except financial information, was observed first hand by the members of the Commission. As part of the public hearings conducted in Houston, Texas, the Attorney General's Commission on Pornography toured three of the fifty "adults only" pornographic outlets operating in that city. The Commissioners were accompanied on this tour by several detectives from the Houston City Police Department. The three locations visited were Mr. Peepers, ✂ ; Hillcroft News, ✂ and Talk of the Town, ✂ .

During this tour, the Commissioners observed the materials available in the outlets, the peep show booths—complete with patrons engaging in explicit sexual activity— and the generally unhealthy environment posed by the sexual activity and debris in the store.

Each of the outlets viewed by the Commission, which were described as representative of those in Houston generally, were divided into two areas. An entering patron initially encountered a room well stocked with sexually explicit publications with covers depicting a variety of homosexual as well as heterosexual activities. A number of materials portraying sodomy and sadomasochistic acts were also conspicuous. Several of the stores had glass cases displaying an assortment of sexual devices and paraphernalia. The rear portion of each store contained peep show booths in which patrons could observe segments of sexually explicit movies for twenty-five cents per minute or two of film footage. Some outlets charged admission to the peep booth area, typically one dollar.

The peep show booth area of each of the outlets toured had minimal illumination, stark decor and a pervasive darkness. The peep show booths were equipped with holes in the wall to enable genital contact with patrons in other booths. Uniformly the walls and floors of booths were stained with substances identified by the accompanying vice detectives as semen, urine, saliva and feces.

In addition, individual Commissioners took private tours of the New York Times Square area and Washington, D.C., pornographic retail establishments.

GENERAL RETAIL OUTLETS

"Adults only" pornographic outlets are by no means the exclusive retailers of sexually explicit materials in the United States. Sexually explicit magazines rely heavily on single issue sales in convenience stores and general bookstores and newsstands across the country.[2222] Some of these mainstream stores now also sell "X" rated video tapes.[2223]

Sexually explicit magazines and tabloids are also sold at newsstands. Newsstands often place these magazines in racks alongside non-sexually explicit magazines. This often means that such magazines are in full view of passersby and children.

Vending machines are also used as a retail outlet for sexually explicit tabloids.[2224] These unmonitored machines pose serious problems because anyone can purchase a tabloid from these machines and anyone can view the exposed portions of the tabloid.

2221. See, Section B in this Chapter for a detailed discussion of sexually explicit video tapes.

2222. For example, of the three top selling sexually explicit magazines at least fifty percent or more of their total sales in 1982 were attributed to single copy sales. Audit Bureau of Circulation, ABC Audit Report—*Playboy, Penthouse,* and *Hustler,* 1982.

2223. The Commission heard testimony regarding of convenience stores nationwide which sell pornographic magazines and video tapes. Thousands of such retail outlets have stopped selling sexually explicit magazines in recent months.

2224. See, The discussion of newspaper distribution for further information.

MILITARY BASES

The Commission contacted Army, Air Force and Navy Base Exchange representatives to determine what, if any, regulations exist which govern (1) the types of pornographic materials base exchanges, located on federal property, can purchase and sell and (2) the method of display of pornographic materials in the exchanges.

ARMY AND AIR FORCE BASE EXCHANGES

The individual exchange managers, in coordination with the base commander, make the decision as to which magazines are sold in the Army and Air Force base exchanges.[2225] These managers are instructed in the Army and Air Force Exchange Service Manual to tailor the magazine assortment at the exchange to the demand of customers in the local military community.[2226]

Regulations require magazines which have been classified by the Army and Air Force as "adult-oriented"[2227] to be displayed in a specified manner.[2228]

Once the magazine has been classified as adult-oriented it must be put on the top shelf of the self-service magazine display racks in the exchanges.[2229] The magazine front must be completely covered so that only the title is visible to the public.[2230]

In the case of video cassette films, it is the policy of these military exchanges to offer "G," "PG," "PG-13" and "R" rated videotapes for sale or rent.[2231] No "X" rated videos should be available at the exchanges.[2232] The exchanges feel they can draw this line based on a widely accepted MPAA rating system.[2233]

MARINE BASE EXCHANGES

The Marine Base Exchange regulations require that "books, periodicals, and recordings sold in exchanges should conform to generally accepted moral standards."[2234] The base commander is required to establish an offensive literature review board which periodically reviews "adult" publications and recordings and submits a report to the commander for his consideration.[2235] The base commander then determines what material will be made available at the base.[2236] Those "adult" publications which are sold are to be made available for sale in a manner

---

2225. *Army and Air Force Exchange Service Manual*, (Jan.. 1985), pp. 40–11, Ch. 10, Sec. 2.
2226. *Id.*
2227. The "adult-oriented" classification is determined as follows:

Army installations: The installation commander should use the consumer advisory council to decide which magazines stocked by the exchange should be classified as adult-oriented for display purposes. The council will meet, when necessary, to review new magazines offered for sale, and to review the entire assortment every 2 years . . . .

Air Force installations: The exchange manager, in coordination with the installation commander, should decide which magazines stocked by the exchange should be classified as adult-oriented . . . .

On both Army and Air Force installation, departmental policies define magazines to be classified as adult-oriented as those that: (1) When considered as a whole, are patently offensive under contemporary standards of the local military community as to what is suitable material for children, and (2) If openly displayed or with portions of their contents exposed to unconsenting customers or other patrons, would invade those persons' right to privacy. *Id.*, Sec. 3(a)–(c).

2228. *Id.*, Sec. 3–4.
2229. *Id.*, Sec. 4.
2230. *Id.*
2231. Interview with Phil Alsup, Washington Legal Counsel, Army and Air Force Exchange Service in Washington, D.C. (Mar. 7, 1986).
2232. *Id.*
2233. See, The discussion of the MPAA rating system in this Chapter for further information.
2234. *Marine Corps Exchange Manual*, Ch. 2, Sec. 11, p. 21108.
2235. *Id.*
2236. *Id.*; *SALE OF "ADULT" TYPE LITERATURE.* Commanders will ensure that "adult" type literature sold in Marine Corps exchanges is made available for sale in a manner which reduces public exposure and discourages browsing by patrons who are minors. One method of reducing public exposure to "adult" literature would be to place all such material behind the sales counter, posting notice to "inquire at the sales counter for adult literature." Another method would be to display the literature on to shelf exposing only the titles.
Marine Corps Exchange Manual, (May 1983), Ch. 2.

which reduces public exposure and discourages browsing by patrons who are minors.[2237] Display methods consistent with this policy include behind the counter sales and display racks which only expose the title of the publication.[2238]

NAVAL BASE EXCHANGES

The Naval Base Exchanges operate much the same way as the Army, Air Force, and Marine Exchanges. The individual Base Commander directly decides what, if any, sexually explicit materials will be available at his Base.[2239] The Naval Regulations generally prohibit printed or visual matter which is considered offensive.[2240] The types of magazines offered at the Navy exchanges is based on consumer demand and subject to the approval of the Commanding Officer or his representatives.[2241] Sexually explicit materials which are offered at the exchanges must be stocked and displayed so that they are not accessible to children.[2242] In addition, no "X" rated video tapes are sold or rented at the Navy exchanges.

The Commission received testimony with respect to the manner in which some military commanders have dealt with the proliferation of "adults only" pornographic outlets in the communities adjacent to their bases.[2243] In North Carolina, the commanding generals of two large military bases at Camp LeJeune and Fort Bragg declared a number of these pornographic outlets off limits to military personnel.[2244] The action of the commanding officers had the effect of closing these establishments. This result was praised by the citizens in the nearby communities.[2245] The off limits order was later challenged vigorously in the courts.[2246]

In its decision dismissing the North Carolina action, the District Court concluded that a military commander has an overriding duty to safeguard the morals, welfare and discipline of his men and that the military commander may exercise this legitimate and important responsibility to place establishments selling sexually explicit materials off limits.[2247] The order by the Chief District Judge in North Carolina upholding the Commanding General's order was affirmed by the Fourth Circuit Court of Appeals.[2248]

2237. Id., p. 21109.
2238. Id.
2239. Interview with Estelle Shenkler, Counsel, Navy Resale Services Support Office (Mar. 6, 1986).
2240. Literature and Recordings:

   (1) Policy on Offensive Literature: The sale of magazines, comics, pocket-size books and other periodicals that are considered offensive is prohibited. Magazines, comics, pocket-size books and other periodicals as well as their covers will be screened by the commanding officer or his/her designated representative(s) and those that are considered offensive will not be sold.

   (2) Policy on Offensive Recordings: The sale of phonograph records and other recordings (including video tape recordings) deemed offensive is prohibited. Phonograph records and other recordings as well as their package covers will be screened by the commanding officer or his/her designated representative(s). Those items considered to be offensive will not be placed on sale . . . .

   4. Screening Program: Using the suggested guidelines, a continuing program which requires regular screening of all adult reading material and adult recordings before they are placed on sale will be maintained by the commanding officer or his/her designated representative. Any material which is considered offensive will not be sold. An exchange's physical location and patronage are factors to be considered. When a determination is made to sell adult type material, it will not be put on open display. Magazines may be offered from racks in which only the title portion of the magazines is visible. Adult type literature and recordings which by virtue of the title or package design are not suitable for open display will be made available, upon request, at such locations as checkout counters, customer service desks or other similar areas where a clerk is in attendance. A sign will be placed on the appropriate racks or counters informing customers that the adult type material is located at designated counters and is available upon request. Counters designated as appropriate to the sale of adult type material will be identified with an informative sign.

Navy Exchange Manual, Ch. 4, Part A, Sec. IV, p. 4134, 2.f (Nov. 1984); Id. at f(1), f(2), and f(4).
2241. Interview with Estelle Shenkler, Counsel, Navy Resale Services Support Office (Mar. 6, 1986).
2242. Navy Exchange Manual, Ch. 4, Part. A. Sec. IV, p. 4134, 2.f (Nov. 1984).
2243. New York Hearing, Vol. I, Sam Currin, p. 85.
2244. Id.
2245. Id.
2246. Enslin v. Fulham, No. 83-137-Civ.-4 (E.D.N.C. 1984).
2247. New York Hearing, Vol. I, Sam Currin, p. 127A–11.
2248. Id., p. 86; See also, Hustler v. Gsell, Civil Action No. R-79-1482. In 1979, Hustler Magazine, Inc., Chic Magazine, Inc. and Flynt Distributing Company, Inc. filed a legal action against Army and Air Force Exchange Service

PRISONS

Seventeen prison systems were polled regarding their policies for the admission of sexually explicit material into their penal institutions for consumption by inmates.[2249] Fifteen of the systems had written policies. All of those with such policies cited state or federal law as the basis for the policies.

The United States Bureau of Prisons (BOP), Arizona, California and Wisconsin all use pertinent state or federal statutes solely as the basis for their written policy. No attempt appears to have been made to interpret or apply the statutes.

Alabama and Nevada have no written policies regarding sexually explicit material distribution in their penal institutions. However, Alabama does not allow the sale of sexually explicit materials within the system, and will allow only *Playboy* magazine to be received by the inmates. Alabama keeps ten other sexually explicit magazines in the prison libraries. The sole basis for rejection of a publication or materials in the Alabama system is the judgment of the reviewer of this material. The reviewer was not specified in the correspondence from Alabama.

Nevada, on the other hand, indicated that no review of materials occurs because there is no written or unwritten policy on the subject. Prison officials are not allowed to conduct censorship of any type. Anything is acceptable, and no provision is made for restricting obscene or unlawful materials.

All the other systems that had a written policy named either the warden, superintendent or a designee, or a review committee appointed by the warden or other chief administrator, as the reviewing authority. Alabama, Arizona, Michigan, Texas, and Wisconsin do not specify the reviewing authority, but indicate that a review does take place.

In most cases criteria for rejection of sexually explicit material is based on its propensity to be prejudicial to good order and conduct (BOP's only criterion) or if the material is obscene or unlawful. In the case of material being prejudicial to good order and conduct, the decision is made by the reviewing body without much in the way of guidelines.

In the case of material being obscene or unlawful, a variety of definitions arose. "Unlawful" is either left undefined or references state or federal law. The definition of obscene is less consistent among the systems. Where obscenity is defined (in seven out of the seventeen), the *Miller* definition is either used verbatim or is paraphrased in total or in part. Ten of the seventeen states define the type of material to be restricted by describing the *Miller* test and/or citing examples. Five of them do both. Washington state is a notable example because the *Miller* definition of obscenity is used, examples are cited, and, by law, the material in question must not be protected by the United States or Washington State Constitutions.

The sex acts defined by the eight systems which chose to specifically describe sexually explicit depictions prohibited in their institutions were fairly consistent. These acts were generally: intercourse, normal or perverted, anal or oral; interest in excretory functions in a sexual context; or masturbation. Some provisions were also made for the lewd exhibition of genitals.

Michigan appeared to have the most restrictive policy. The restrictions pertain to photos of persons in "see through" garments and provides for a list of restricted publications. However, testimony from a Michigan inmate, named Grant H. Hendrick as part of a

---

2249. The seventeen systems included Alabama, Arizona, the United States Bureau of Prison, California, Florida, Illinois, Kentucky, Massachusetts, Michigan, Nevada, New Jersey, New York, Tennessee, Texas, Virginia, Washington, and Wisconsin.

---

representatives. The suit charged that the base exchanges in the Capitol Exchange Region refused to sell *Hustler* and *Chic* although similar magazines published by their competitors were sold in the exchanges. The plaintiffs claimed that this decision was arbitrary and a violation of their First and Fifth Amendment rights. The base exchange operators argued that they stocked their exchanges based on customer demand and sales potential. the plaintiffs asserted that all of the three base exchanges in question sold *Playboy* and *Penthouse*, the two most widely circulated sexually explicit magazines for men; *Playgirl*, the highest selling sexually explicit magazine directed toward women, and *Players*, another widely circulated sexually explicit magazine.

The Court in entering a judgment in favor of defendants based its decision on defendants' testimony that the decision to stock merchandise was a business decision. *Hustler* and *Chic* were not excluded because of content.

Walter H. Annenberg Foundation Criminology Study,[2250] indicates that sexually explicit materials are readily available, sold in prison commissaries, and shown on prison closed-circuit television.

There were three other systems which had a list of permissable publications: Florida, Illinois and New York.[2251] New York's list is the most comprehensive and approves large quantities of sexually explicit materials. The United States Bureau of Prisons and Kentucky expressly forbid the compilation of a restricted publication list.

The only states which stated that sexually explicit materials are provided in prison libraries were Alabama and New York. Six other states specifically said such publications were not provided in the libraries. The rest of the states surveyed did not respond to that question. Finally six of the states responded that no sexually explicit publications were sold in prison commissaries. The remaining states did not comment.

2250. Affidavit of Grant H. Kendrick, Michigan State Prisoner #131851 (Sept. 9, 1984).
2251. New York also has a list of disapproved publications.

CHAPTER • 24

The Imagery Found Among Magazines, Books and Films in "Adults Only" Pornographic Outlets

Among the most common inquiries made to the staff of the Attorney General's Commission on Pornography was a request for information on the content of currently available pornography in the United States. The only pertinent data available to the Commission was a single report in the *American Journal of Psychiatry*,[2252] and brief descriptions which have appeared in current periodicals and other works.[2253] In order to provide data concurrent with the deliberations of the Commission, the Commission through its staff investigated the content of currently marketed materials.

METHOD

Six major cities were selected for inclusion in the investigation, based in part on their proximity to the Commission offices in Washington, D.C. The six cities selected were Washington, D.C.; Baltimore, Maryland; Miami, Florida; Philadelphia, Pennsylvania; New York, New York; and Boston, Massachusetts. In each city, "adults only" pornographic outlets were selected randomly by listing all of the identifiable outlets and selecting specific outlets for investigation using a table of random numbers.[2254] The investigative instruments were designed to identify the city, outlet, type of material (magazine, book, or film), and a variety of specific details about the forms of conduct portrayed and the participants portrayed. In addition to a coding form which was completed for each item included in the investigation, the other materials available for sale in each outlet were also recorded. In each outlet, the total number of magazine titles, film titles and book titles was recorded.

Completion of the coding forms was done by trained investigators.[2255] In addition to their investigative experience and training, the coders were trained specifically for this project in a uniform training session in which all were instructed on the forms to be used, the manner of completing the forms, the technique for random selection, and the distinctions necessary to complete the forms (e.g., the distinction between whipping and spanking) and the specific selection procedures to be used. These selection procedures included selecting every magazine sold as

---

2252. Dietz and Evans, *Pornographic Imagery and Prevalence of Paraphilia*, 11 American Journal of Psychiatry, p. 139 (1982).

2253. See for example, *The Report of the Commission on Obscenity and Pornography*, (1970), pp. 115-37.

2254. In New York, the random selection had been made at the time of the earlier study referred to in footnote 2309. Of the four stores studied earlier, three were identified. The fourth was no longer found at the previous location, thus, three of the four stores selected previously were investigated.

2255. Investigators included an Arlington County, Virginia, Police Department detective, Edward H. Chapman; a Washington, D.C., Metropolitan Police Department detective, Joseph B. Haggerty; a United States Postal Service inspector, Daniel L. Mihalko, and special agents of the United States Customs Service, David H. Borden, and Ramon Martinez.

new merchandise which had one or more photographs on the front cover, every fifth book going from left to right and from top to bottom which had one or more visual depictions on the front cover, and every fifth film with one or more photographs on the box front. Pamphlets, packets of photographs, and tabloid newspapers were excluded. For magazines, books and films, duplicate titles were eliminated so that a particular issue of a magazine was only coded once. If multiple copies were available for sale, that item was only coded once.

The following number of outlets were investigated in each city: Washington, D.C., four (4); New York, New York, three (3); Baltimore, Maryland, three (3); Boston, Massachusetts, three (3). An effort to study outlets in Miami, Florida was aborted when an individual requested that the investigators discontinue their work. Eighty-five forms were coded in Miami, before the investigation was halted and these specific items are noted in Miami are contained within the list of specific titles observed. Likewise, an effort to study two outlets in Philadelphia had to be terminated because the investigators were asked to leave the premises by a person purporting to "represent the owner." In neither Philadelphia outlet was data collection completed. A total of 350 magazines, 115 books, and 105 films had been coded in Philadelphia before data collection was halted. The specific titles observed in Philadelphia are, however, included in the list of titles which follow.

RESULTS

In all stores surveyed magazines and bookstores with depictions of vaginal intercourse between one female and one male were in a minority among the types of sexual activity depicted.

There was geographic difference in only a very few types of sexual activity depicted on the covers of books and magazines displayed for consumer purchase. Films and magazines which depicted actual photographs of sexual encounters between humans and animals were seen in New York, New York, Philadelphia, Pennsylvania and Miami, Florida, but not in Washington, D.C., Boston, Massachusetts, or Baltimore, Maryland. Stores in at least two cities, Boston and Baltimore, had magazines which depicted and featured sexual activities involving one or more persons with amputated limbs. Materials depicting actual scenes of urination and/or defecation were present in some of the locations but not in others. All outlets, with the exception of one store in Baltimore and one in New York, had paperback books which featured the preceding themes as well as incest and child molestation. Every store surveyed featured magazines with photographs depicting bondage, simulated child pornography[2256] and various other paraphillic activity[2257] in significant percentages.[2258]

In addition to visual and written materials, every store surveyed sold dildos, vibrators, "aphrodisiac" pills, lotions or cremes for sexual use and condoms. Many of the stores sold other devices such as knives, throwing stars, "police" badges, whips, handcuffs, vials of "poppers" anylnitrite or butylnitrite, lingerie, restraints, penis rings, odorizers, studded collars and leashes, blow up dolls, artificial vaginas, penis "enlargers" and a variety of other items.

These findings are supplemented by observations, by the same investigative team members, of the types of materials sold at outlets in Houston, Texas,[2259] New York, New York, Miami, Florida,[2260] Los Angeles, California, and Chicago, Illinois, that determined similar types of materials were sold in each city reviewed.

In the sixteen stores specifically surveyed the following number of titles of written and visual material were found:

2256. For a discussion of simulated child pornography, see, the discussion found in the Recommendations for Child Pornography.

2257. The essential feature of disorders in this subclass (Paraphilias) is that unusual or bizarre imagery or acts are necessary for sexual excitement. American Psychiatric Association, *Diagnostic and Statistical Manual of Mental Disorders*, (3d ed. 1980), p. 266.

2258. Full formal results were not completed at the time of printing of this final report. The Commission, through its archives, will make such information available to persons conducting future research on this subject.

2259. The Attorney General's Commission on Pornography toured three pornography outlets in Houston, Texas.

2260. An informal survey of stores was conducted in Miami after the unsuccessful formal survey attempt described hereinafter.

CITY	MAGAZINES	BOOKS	FILMS
Baltimore (BA)	938	196	796
Boston (BN)	1,372	1,365	290
Miami (MI) (partial)	85	0	0
New York (NY)	454	320	1,700
Philadelphia (PA) (partial)	350	115	105
Washington, D.C. (DC)	1,145	1,920	680
Totals	4,644	3,916	3,571

Of the totals listed above 2,325 separate magazine titles, 725 book titles and 2,370 film titles were found. The titles of the magazines, books and films found follow:

MAGAZINES

A COCK BETWEEN FRIENDS (DC)
A DATE WITH PUSSY (BN)
A FEW GOOD MEN (BN)
A GOOD FUCK (DC)
A HOLE LOT OF FUCKING #1 (DC, BN)
A LUST SO DEEP (BA)
A PIECE OF CANDY (DC)
A SIERRA DOMINO DICTIONARY (DC)
A THING FOR GETTING BUTT FUCKED (BN)
AC/DC BISEXUAL SWINGERS (DC, BN)
ACCU JACKING (PA)
ACE IN THE HOLE (PA)
ACTS OF LOVE (NY)
ADAM (DC, BN)
ADAM #1 #30 (DC)
ADAM #2 #30 (BN)
ADAM FILM WORLD (BN)
ADAM FILM WORLD #5 #11 (BA)
ADAM GIRLS (DC)
ADAM GIRLS #1 #12 (DC, BN)
ADULT CINEMA (BN)
ADULT CINEMA #4 #11 (DC)
ADULT CINEMA REVIEW #5 #1 (BN)
ADULT EROTICA (DC)
ADULT VIDEO (DC)
ADULT VIDEO NEWS (DC)
ADVOCATE (DC)
ADVOCATE MEN 3-86 (BN)
AEROBIC ORGASM (BA)
AGGRESSIVE BLONDES (PA, BN)
AGGRESSIVE WOMEN (DC)
ALL ABOUT BALLS (BA)
ALL AMERICAN SUPER BITCHES (BA)
ALL BLACK (DC)
ALL DAY FUCKERS (BN)
ALL MUSCLE (DC)
ALL THOSE JUICY YOUNG PUSSIES #1 (DC)
ALL TIED UP (PA, BN)
ALL WAYS CARA (BN)
ALMOST INCEST (NY)
AMATEUR BONDAGE (BA, DC)
AMATEUR BONDAGE #3 (DC)
AMATEUR PHOTOGRAPHER'S GUIDE TO AVAILABLE
    MODELS #4 #5 (DC)

AMAZON (DC, NY)
AMBUSHED (PA)
AMERICAN EROTICA (DC, NY)
AMERICAN EROTICA #2 (DC, BN)
AMERICAN EROTICA, TAMMY'S TRIO (BN)
AMERICAN EROTICA #102 (NY, BN)
AMERICAN EROTICA #133 (NY)
AMERICAN EROTICA #134 (NY, BN)
AMERICAN EROTICA #137 (NY)
AMOUR (PA)
AMPUTEE TIMES (BA, BN)
AN ANAL FLIGHT (BN)
ANAL (NY, BN)
ANAL ACTION (DC, PA, BN)
ANAL AGONY (DC, PA)
ANAL BIKER (BN)
ANAL BLONDES (BA, AC/DC)
ANAL BLONDES #2 (BN)
ANAL CLIMAX (BA, DC, PA, BN)
ANAL CUM (BA, OC, PA, BN)
ANAL DREAMS (DC, PA, BN)
ANAL ENDING (BN)
ANAL ERUPTIONS (BA, DC, PA, BN)
ANAL EXPLOSION (MI, PA, BN)
ANAL FANTASY (NY)
ANAL FUCK (BA)
ANAL GIRLS (DC)
ANAL GIRLS THAT LIKE BLACK COCK (BA)
ANAL GRADUATES (NY)
ANAL HUMP (BA)
ANAL JOCK (BN)
ANAL LEATHER (NY, BN)
ANAL MAGIC (DC)
ANAL MASTURBATION (DC, BN)
ANAL MISTRESS (BA)
ANAL NEIGHBORS (NY, BN)
ANAL NYMPHO (BA, DC)
ANAL PERSUASION (NY, BN)
ANAL SECRETARY (DC)
ANAL SEX (BA)
ANAL SQUEEZE (DC, BN)
ANAL STUD (DC)
ANAL SWEAT (DC, BN)
ANAL SWEAT #1 #2 (BN)

ANAL THREESOME (BA, NY, BN)
ANAL THRUST (PA)
ANAL TREAT (NY)
ANAL VIRGINS (BA)
ANAL VIRGINS #2 (NY)
ANAL WEEKEND (DC, BN)
ANALESE (PA, BN)
ANALISM (PA, BN)
ANALLY YOURS AMAZON #14 (DC)
AND JEREMY MAKES 3 (BA, DC)
ANGIE, MY SISTER AND ME (NY)
ANIMAL ACTION (DC, PA, BN)
ANYTHING GOES #2 (DC)
APPRENTICE (BN)
ARAS HOURI (DC, BN)
AROUND THE WORLD (PA)
ASIAN AFFAIR (NY)
ASIAN ANAL GIRLS (DC)
ASIAN ASS (BA)
ASIAN SLUT (DC, NY)
ASIAN SUCK MISTRESS (BA)
ASKING FOR IT (DC, BN)
ASS ATTACK #1 #2 (PA)
ASS BUSTERS #1 #2 (BN)
ASS FUCKING BI-SEXUAL 3-WAY (DC, NY)
ASS IS NICE (BN)
ASS MASTERS (BA, DC, PA, BN)
ASS MASTERS #3 (NY)
ASS MASTERS #5 (NY)
ASS MASTERS #7 (DC, NY)
ASSAULT (PA)
ASSES AND ANKLES (BN)
ASSES UP (BA, NY)
ASSHOLE FUCKIN (BA, NY)
ASSHOLES & PUSSIES (BN)
ART SUCKO (DC)
ASS BANDITS (BA, DC, BN)
ASS FUCKED (DC)
ASS IN THE GRASS (DC, NY, BN)
ASS LOVER (NY, BN)
ASS MASTERS #2 (NY)
ASS MASTERS #4 (NY)
ASS MASTERS #6 (DC, NY)
ASS PARADE (BA, NY)
ASSES (BN)
ASSES IN BONDAGE (DC, BN)
ASSHOLE BUDDIES (DC, PA, BN)
ASSHOLE IN HEAT #1 (BN)
ASSTRAVAGANZA (DC)
AURORA FUCKS (BA)
AUTO BUNS (BN)
B & D GUIDE (DC, BN)
B & D REVIEW (BN)
B & D REVIEW #1 #3 (BN)
B & D SEX DEVICES (DC)
BABE (BA)
BABY DOLL FUCKER (DC)
BABY DOLLS (BA, DC, BN)
BABY DOLLS #30 (BA)
BACK ALLEYS (PA)
BACK DOOR AFFAIRS (BA, DC, PA, BN)
BACK DOOR FUCK (PA)
BACK DOOR NURSE (NY)
BACK ROOM BLOOD (BN)
BACKS (DC)
BACKSEAT BULLMEAT (PA)
BN BACKYARD BOY (BA)
BAD GIRLS (DC)
BAD MAMA JAMA (NY)
BALL GAMES (BA, DC, BN)
BALLIN ANGEL (DC, BN)

BALLIN BIG BEAR (DC)
BALLIN BLONDS (DC, BN)
BANG ME (BA, DC)
BANZAI ASS (MI)
BAR BACKS (BN)
BARGAIN PUSSY (PA)
BASIC SLEAZE (MI, DC, NY, BN)
BATHHOUSE B/J (PA, BN)
BEACH BALLING (DC)
BECKY CLAY (BA)
BEG FOR COCK (BN)
BELATED BIRTHDAY (BA, BN)
BEST OF CLUB (DC)
BEST OF CLUB INTERNATIONAL (DC)
BEST OF HUSTLER #11 (DC)
BEST OF PURITAN (DC)
BI BI LOVE (PA)
BI THE WAY (DC, BN)
BI-LIFESTYLES #1 #2 (BN)
BIANCA (PA)
BIFF #1 (PA)
BIG BAZOOMS (PA)
BIG BEAUTIFUL BOSOMS (DC)
BIG BELLIES (BA)
BIG BLACK BAZOOMS (BA)
BIG BLACK BITCH (PA)
BIG BLACK COCK (BN)
BIG BLACK JUGS (NY)
BIG BLACK TITS & TWATS (BA)
BIG BLONDE DOUBLE FUCK (BA)
BIG BOOBS (DC, BN)
BIG BOOBS #1 #2 (DC)
BIG BOOBS BONANZA (BN)
BIG BOYS AND THEIR BUDDIES (BA)
BIG BUST BONDAGE (DC, NY, BN)
BIG BUSTED (DC)
BIG BUSTED BALL BUSTER (DC, BN)
BIG BUSTY BABE (PA)
BIG BUTTHOLE BUDDIES (BN)
BIG DICKS AND LITTLE CUNTS (NY)
BIG FUCKIN TITS (NY)
BIG FUCKIN TITS #2 (NY)
BIG JOHN'S ORGY (DC)
BIG JUICY JUGS (BA)
BIG MAMA JAMA (BA)
BIG MAMA (PA)
BIG MEN ON CAMPUS (DC, PA)
BIG TIT #1 #6 (BN)
BIG TIT BALLERS (BA, NY)
BIG TIT BLACK BITCH (BN)
BIG TIT BLACK MILK (MI)
BIG TIT DILDO BONDAGE (DC)
BIG TIT PHOTOS (DC)
BIG TITS (DC, BN)
BIG TITS & BARE CLITS (BA)
BIG TITS & HEAVY FUCKING (NY)
BIG TITS #3 (DC, BN)
BIG TITTED LEZZIES (BA)
BIG-O-HOE (NY)
BISEXUAL DESIRES (DC, PA)
BISEXUAL LUST (NY)
BISEXUAL THREESOMES (BA)
BISEXUAL TRIOS (DC)
BITCHIN' BLACK ASS (BA)
BITCHIN BRUNETTE ASSES (BA)
BITCHY MAMA (BN)
BIZARRE BETTY BANG (PA)
BIZARRE BITCHES (BN)
BIZARRE CONTACTS (BN)
BIZARRE DREAMS (BN)
BIZARRE FANTASIES (BN)

BIZARRE FANTASIES #1 #2 (BN)
BIZARRE PEOPLE (PA, BN)
BIZARRE SEX (BN)
BIZARRE TRENDS (BA, BN)
BIZARRE TRENDS, LEATHERS & BOOTS (DC)
BIZERK (BN)
BLACK & KINKY (NY)
BLACK & LUSTY (BA, MI, DC, NY)
BLACK & MILKY (BA)
BLACK & NASTY (BA)
BLACK & PROUD (NY)
BLACK NURSE (NY)
BLACK & SLICK (PA)
BLACK & TAN (PA)
BLACK & WHITE & HORNY (DC, PA, NY)
BLACK & WHITE BALLERS (BA, DC)
BLACK & WHITE DYNAMITE (BA)
BLACK & WHITE FETISH EXCHANGE (BA)
BLACK & WHITE LUST (NY)
BLACK & WHITE SHAVED PUSSY (BA)
BLACK AND BITCHIN (PA)
BLACK AND BLONDE LESBIANS (BN)
BLACK AND BLONDE LESBIANS #2
BLACK BABES (DC)
BLACK BALLED (NY)
BLACK BALLED #2 (NY)
BLACK BALLED BROADS (DC)
BLACK BALLER (PA)
BLACK BAZOOMS & BEAVERS (BA)
BLACK BEAUTIES (BA)
BLACK BEAVER FEVER (NY)
BLACK BIRDS (PA)
BLACK BITCH (PA)
BLACK BOOB & BODY BONDAGE (BA)
BLACK BOOBS (PA)
BLACK BOX (BA)
BLACK BUSH FUCKERS (DC, PA, NY, BN)
BLACK BUST (BA, DC, BN)
BLACK BUTT (BA)
BLACK CHIX (PA)
BLACK COCK (BN)
BLACK DICK (PA)
BLACK DICK FOR TWO (DC)
BLACK DRAGONS (DC, BN)
BLACK ECSTASY (PA)
BLACK FANTASY #1 (NY)
BLACK GIRL REVIEW (PA, BN)
BLACK GIRL REVIEW #19 (BA)
BLACK GOLD (BA, DC, BN)
BLACK HAIRY BEAVERS (BA)
BLACK HEAT (NY)
BLACK HOT HONEY (BA, PA)
BLACK HUSTLER (NY)
BLACK IMPACT (PA)
BLACK IN WHITE #1 (DC)
BLACK JUMBO JUGS (DC)
BLACK LASSES #1 #2 (BA)
BLACK LESBO (BA)
BLACK LOVER (BA, PA)
BLACK LUST (BA)
BLACK MAGIC (DC)
BLACK MAMA (DC, NY)
BLACK MAMBA (PA)
BLACK MEAT FUCKED RAW (BA)
BLACK MEAT/BLACK HEAT (BN)
BLACK MILKER (PA)
BLACK & NASTY #2 (BA)
BLACK & SEXY (PA)
BLACK NURSE, WHITE COCK (BA, PA)
BLACK ON BLACK (NY)
BLACK ORIENTAL (NY)

BLACK PIMP (NY)
BLACK PUSSY (DC)
BLACK PUSSYPALS (BA)
BLACK PUSSYRAMA (BA, DC, PA)
BLACK SAPPHO #1 (NY)
BLACK SATIN (BN)
BLACK SCORPI (PA)
BLACK SEXERCISE (BA, PA)
BLACK SHAVED PUSSY (BA, BN)
BLACK SHAVERS (DC)
BLACK SNACK (DC, PA)
BLACK SNATCH, TITS & BUTTS (BA)
BLACK SUGAR (DC, NY)
BLACK TIT & BODY TORTURE
BLACK TIT BLACK BITCH (BA, DC)
BLACK TITS & TWATS (PA)
BLACK TOWERS (BA)
BLACK WHOPPERS (NY)
BLACK WHORE (BA)
BLACK WITH CREAM (NY)
BLACK ZINGERS (PA)
BLACK, BALD & BEAUTIFUL (PA)
BLACKS & BLONDES (DC, NY)
BLACKS & BLONDES #2 (NY)
BLACKS & BLONDES #3 (NY)
BLACKS & BLONDES #4 (BN)
BLADE (PA)
BLAZING COCKS (BN)
BLAZING RUSSIES (MI)
BLINDMAN'S BOFF (DC)
BLOND STALLIONS (BN)
BLONDE ASS FUCKER (NY)
BLONDE BELLY BUSTER (PA, BN)
BLONDE BITCHES (BA, DC, BN)
BLONDE CANNIBALS (DC, PA)
BLONDE HEAT (BN)
BLONDES (PA)
BLONDES CUM HARD (NY)
BLONDES HAVE MORE CUM (DC, PA, NY)
BLONDES HAVE MORE CUM #3 (BA, NY)
BLONDES HAVE MORE CUM #5 (DC)
BLONDES LOVE TO FUCK (BN)
BLONDES RIPE FOR FUCKING (BA, DC, BN)
BLONDIE (MI)
BLOW JOB (BA)
BLOWN BY THE BUTLER (NY)
BLUE CLIMAX (BA, DC)
BLUE CLIMAX #8 (NY)
BLUE CLIMAX #10 (BN)
BLUEBOY (BA, DC, BN)
BLUEBOY 3-86 (BN)
BLUEBOY COLLECTION (BA)
BOBBY SOX AND TENNIS SHOES (DC)
BODY FUCKERS (DC)
BODY HEAT (DC)
BON APPETITE (MI)
BOND MAID (PA)
BONDAGE (DC)
BONDAGE ANNUAL #6 (BN)
BONDAGE ARTWORK (BN)
BONDAGE BEAUTIES (DC)
BONDAGE BY EUROPA (BN)
BONDAGE CABIN (BA)
BONDAGE EXCHANGE (DC, BN)
BONDAGE IN THE BUFF (BA)
BONDAGE LATEX CATALOG (BN)
BONDAGE LIFE (BA, DC, NY)
BONDAGE MOODS (DC, BN)
BONDAGE MOODS #2 (DC)
BONDAGE PARADE (NY)
BONDAGE PHOTO TREASURES #1 (DC)

BONDAGE PRISONERS (BA)
BONDAGE SCENES (DC, PA)
BONDAGE VIDEO (MI)
BONDS OF LOVE (DC)
BONERS (PA)
BOOB & BODY BONDAGE (DC)
BOOB & BODY BONDAGE #1 #2 (BN)
BOOB GAME (BN)
BOOBS & BALLS (DC)
BOOBS & BEAVERS (DC, BN)
BOOBS & BEAVERS #1 #2 (BN)
BOOBS & BUNS (DC, BN)
BOOBS & MILK (BA)
BOOBS, BUSTS & BAZOOMS (BA)
BOOK OF BLACKS II (NY)
BOOK OF BLACKS III (PA)
BOOTS (PA)
BORDELLO STUDS (PA, BN)
BOSS LADY #3 (BN)
BOSSLADY (BN)
BOTTOM (BA, PA, BN)
BOTTOMS UP (MI)
BOUND PLEASURES (BA)
BOUND RESTRAINT (DC)
BOUND TO OBEY (BA, DC, BN)
BOUND TO PLEASE (DC, BN)
BOUND TO PLEASE #3 #12 (DC)
BOX LUNCH (BA,DC)
BOY CHICKS (BN)
BOY ON GIRL (BN)
BOY TOYS (PA, BN)
BOYS FROM MAN-AGE (DC, BA, BN)
BOYS IN THE BROTHEL (DC, PA, BN)
BOYS OUT OF UNIFORM (BN)
BOYS TOWN (BN)
BOYS WILL BE GIRLS (BA, DC)
BOYS WITH TOYS (BA)
BRENTWOOD (PA)
BROADS & BOOBS (BA, BN)
BROWN BABY DOLLS (DC)
BROWN DOLLS (BA, DC)
BROWN JUICY BITCH (BA, DC, PA)
BROWN SUGAR BUNS (NY)
BUCK SHOTS (PA)
BUDDY BLAST (PA, BN)
BUDS (PA)
BUILT TO THE HILT (PA)
BULL (MI)
BUMS GESCHICHLEN IS GERMAN FOR FUCKSTONES
  (BA, DC)
BUOYS UP (PA)
BUSHWACK (BN)
BUST OUT (BN)
BUSTER & BILL (PA)
BUSTY (DC)
BUSTY & SHAVED (BA)
BUSTY CUM SUCKERS (DC, PA)
BUSTY MILKER (DC, BN)
BUSTY MOMS (DC)
BUTT FUCKED (DC, BN)
BUTT FUCKED AGAIN (BN)
BUTT FUCKED SCRIPT GIRL (DC)
BUTT FUCKERS (MI)
BUTT FUCKIN' WITH SOUL (BA)
BUTT FUCKING (BA)
BUTT LOVER (DC)
BUTT PLUGGED (BN)
BOUND TO TEASE (DC)
BOUND TO TEASE #3 #1 (BN)
BOX LUNCH (BA, DC)
C.O.D. (DC, BN)

CALIFORNIA BOYS (BN)
CALIFORNIA COCK (PA)
CALIFORNIA HARDCORE (BN)
CALL-A-GIRL #2 #6 (BA)
CANDY SAMPLES (PA)
CANDY SAMPLES GIVES GREAT HEAD (DC)
CAPTURED (BA)
CAREER GIRLS
CARNAL CARA LOTT (NY)
CASTING COUCH (DC, BN)
CATALOG OF TRAINERS & GAGS (BN)
CATFIGHTS GALORE (BA)
CAUGHT BETWEEN TWO COCKS (BN)
CELEBRITY FUCKERS (BA, DC, PA, BN)
CENTURIAN (PA, BN)
CHAIR BONDAGE (BA, DC, BN)
CHAIR BONDAGE #1 #2
CHAMPS (BN)
CHAMPS GOING FOR THE BIG ONE (BN)
CHASTISEMENT (BN)
CHEATING WIVES (PA)
CHEEKS (PA)
CHERI (DC)
CHERRY PIE (PA)
CHERRY TARTS (BN)
CHESAPEAKE SWINGING MODERNS (DC)
CHESAPEAKE SWINGING MODERNS #3 (BA)
CHIC 2-86 (DC)
CHINA LADY (PA)
CHOCOLATE BOOBS & CUNTS (NY)
CHOCOLATE BOX (DC)
CHOCOLATE CUPCAKE (MI)
CHOCOLATE MILK (PA)
CHOCOLATE PUSSY (BA, BN)
CHOCOLATE TEEN (DC)
CHRISTOPHER STREET (DC)
CHRISTY CANYON (BA)
CHUBBY CHEEKS (BA)
CHUBBY CHEEKS #9 (BN)
CHUNKY ASSES (BA, DC)
CIAO (PA)
CINEMA BLUE (DC)
CINEMA BLUE 2-86 (BN)
CINEMA BLUE 3-86 (BA)
CINEMA BLUE 4-86 (BA)
CLASS ERECTIONS (PA, BN)
CLASSY BITCH (NY)
CLASSY BLACK (BA, PA)
CLEAN PUSSY (DC)
CLEAN UP CREW (DC)
CLIMAX (NY)
CLIMAX CORNER (PA)
CLINIQUE (PA)
CLOSE-UP (DC)
CLUB (DC)
CLUB CONTACT (BA)
CLUB GOLDEN ROD (BN)
CLUB GOLDEN ROD #17 (BN)
CLUB INTERNATIONAL (DC)
CLUB INTERNATIONAL 1-86 (DC)
COAST TO COAST CONNECTION (BA, DC)
COCK BITE (BN)
COCK BITER (PA)
COCK CRAMMED (BN)
COCK CRAVING BLONDES (PA)
COCK CRAZY (DC)
COCK FOR DESSERT (DC)
COCK FOR LUNCH (DC)
COCK HARD (BN)
COCK HOLD (DC, BN)
COCK HOUNDS (DC)

COCK HUNGRY STEWARDESS (NY)
COCK HUNGRY WOMEN (DC)
COCK MATES (PA)
COCK ON DELIVERY (BN)
COCK RING (DC)
COCK SHOTS (DC)
COCK SMITH (BA, MI, DC, NY, BN)
COCK STRUCK BRUNETTES (NY, BN)
COCK STUFFED SLUTS (BN)
COCK SUCK (PA)
COCK SWALLOWING ASS FUCKERS (DC, NY)
COCK TEASER'S DELIGHT (BA)
COCK THROBS (BA, DC)
COCK THROBS ANNUAL #1 (DC)
COCKEY GIRLS (DC, NY)
COCKEYE (DC, NY)
COCKPIT CUNT (NY)
COCKSUCKERS (BA, DC)
COCKSUCKING GUYS (DC)
COCKSUCKING JOGGER (DC, PA, BN)
COCO CUPS (BA, DC)
CODI'S FUCK FEAST (DC)
COLLECTION TODAY #2 (NY)
COLOR CLIMAX (BA)
COLOR CLIMAX #115 (DC)
COLOR CLIMAX #94 (BN)
COLT MEN (DC)
COLT MEN #2 (PA)
COMING ON AT 5 (BN)
COMPANION (DC)
CONNEXION (DC)
CONSENTING ADULTS (DC, BN)
CONSENTING ADULTS #4 (DC)
CONSENTING ADULTS #5 (BA)
CONSENTING COUPLES (BA, DC, BN)
CONTINENTAL SPECTATOR #168 (DC, BN)
COOKIES & CREAM (NY)
CORNHOLED BLONDES #2 (BN)
CORPORAL (DC, BN)
CORPORAL QUARTERLY #1 #3 (DC)
CORPORAL REVIEW (BA)
CORPORAL VIDEO LETTERS TO SANDY (BN)
COUNTRY CUNT (NY, BN)
COUPLES (DC)
COUPLES IN HEAT (BA, DC)
COVER TO COVER CUM (NY, DC)
COVERBOYS OF THE EIGHTIES (PA)
COWBOYS (PA)
COZY CUNT (DC)
CREAM OF COCOA (NY)
CREAMY BLACK (DC)
CREAMY PUSSIES (DC, BN)
CROSSFIRE (PA)
CROTCH (BA)
CROTCH EATERS (PA)
CRUDE (DC)
CULT OF SODOMY (BN)
CUM AND GET IT (DC, PA)
CUM CLEAN (BN)
CUM COATED LIPS #2 (NY)
CUM CRASED BABES (BN)
CUM DRIPPING BLOW JOBS (DC)
CUM FREAKS (DC)
CUM FUCKERS (DC, NY)
CUM HUNGRY GIRLS (DC)
CUM IN ME (DC. PA)
CUM ON MY NIPPLES (NY)
CUM ON STRONG (DC, BN)
CUM SHOTS (MI)
CUM SHOTS II (DC, BN)
CUM SOAKED THREEWAY (DC, BN)

CUM SUCKING VIXENS (DC)
CUM 4 EVER (DC)
CUMMING OUT (BA, BN)
CUMMING TRIOS #1 (BA, DC)
CUNT SUCKING COCK FUCKING (DC)
CUNTS & COCKS #3 (NY)
CUNTS AND COCKS (NY)
CUNTS OUT OF TOWN (BN)
CYCLE STUDS (PA)
DANNY COMBS, COCKSMITH (BN)
DARK & DIRTY (NY)
DARK & SWEET #2 (NY)
DARK & SWEET #3 (NY)
DART (DC)
DAUGHTERS OF SODOM (DC, NY)
DAUGHTERS OF THE ORIENT (PA)
DEEP FUCK (NY)
DEEP PENETRATION (BN)
DEEP PLUNGE (BA)
DEEP THROAT DUDES (PA)
DEEP WITHIN GINGER LYNN (NY)
DEEP WITHIN STACEY DONOVAN (BA)
DELUX HARDCORE INTERNATIONAL (BA)
DE SADE'S WORLD (NY)
DESIRES WITH ASIAN GIRLS (BA)
DEVIATIONS (PA, BN)
DEVIATIONS DIRECTORY 86-87 (BN)
DIAL YOUR MISTRESS (BA)
DIAL YOUR MISTRESS #1 #9 (BA)
DIAMOND #2 (BA, BN)
DIAMOND COLLECTION #14 (DC)
DIAMOND COLLECTION #15 (DC)
DIAMOND COLLECTION #18 (DC)
DIAMOND FEVER (BN)
DIAMOND FEVER #2 (BN)
DICK ADDICTS (BA, DC)
DICK EXAM (DC)
DICK FIX (DC, BN)
DIFFERENT KIND OF LOVING (DC)
DIFFERENT LAYS (NY)
DILDO BABES (DC, PA)
DILDO BABIES (BA)
DILDO DAZE (BA)
DILDO FEVER (BN)
DIRECT CONTACT (DC)
DIRECT LINE (DC)
DIRTY BLONDES #2 (BN)
DIRTY BLONDES #3 (BA)
DIRTY BOYS (DC)
DIRTY SHARY (NY)
DISCREET SWINGERS (BA, DC)
DO NOT DISTURB (BN)
DOC BLACK COCK #1 (BN)
DOCTORS & VAMPIRES (MI, DC, BN)
DOMINA (BN)
DOMINA #2 #3 (BN)
DOMINA IN LEATHER (BN)
DOMINANT BLACK BITCH (PA, BN)
DOMINANT MISTRESS (DC)
DOMINANT TVs (BA)
DOMINATRIX CONNECTION (BA)
DOMINATRIX DOMAIN (DC)
DOMINIQUE #3 (BN)
DOMINO AND HER MEN (PA)
DOUBLE ACTION (MI)
DOUBLE BLONDE DYNAMITE (DC, BN)
DOUBLE COCKED (DC)
DOUBLE DIP (DC, PA, BN)
DOUBLE DOUBLE ORGY (DC)
DOUBLE DYKES (DC, PA, BN)
DOUBLE DYNAMITE (PA, BN)

DOUBLE FUCKED GAL (BN)
DOUBLE FUCKED SPECIAL (PA, BN)
DOUBLE FUCKED SPECIAL #2 (DC, NY)
DOUBLE FUCKED SPECIAL #3 (BN)
DOUBLE JAM FUCKED (DC)
DOUBLE LICKERS (BA, DC, BN)
DOUBLE ORGY (DC)
DOUBLE SUCKED STUD (DC, NY, BN)
DRACULA FUCKS (DC)
DRAG DESIRES (BN)
DRAG FANTASIES #1 #1 (BN)
DRAG FANTASIES #2 #1 (BN)
DRAG QUEENS #4 #3 (BA)
DREAM (DC)
DREAM FUCK #2 (BN)
DREAM SUCK (NY)
DREAMER (DC)
DRESDEN DIARY JOURNAL (DC)
DRIVE SHAFT (PA)
DRIVE SHAFT VIDEO (BN)
DRUMMER (BA, DC, PA, BN)
DUSHCA (DC)
DUSHCA'S LESBIAN AFFAIRS (BA)
DYNAMIC DUOS (BA, DC, PA, BN)
DYNAMIC DUOS #2 (BN)
DYNAMIC DUOS #4 (BN)
DYNAMIC DUOS #5 (DC, BN)
DYNAMITE TITS (DC, PA, BN)
E/Z SPREADERS (DC, BN)
EAGER BEAVERS #1 (DC, PA, BN)
EAGER TO PLEASE (PA, BN)
EASTERN CONNECTION (PA, BN)
EASY ACCESS (DC)
EASY ACTION (BN)
EASY PIECES (DC, PA, NY, BN)
EASY PIECES #1 #3 (BA)
EASY'S SWINGERS CONNECTION (BA, DC)
EAT OUT MY HOLE (BA, DC)
EATING GIRLS (BA)
EATING PUSSY #2 (DC)
EAU D'ANAL (PA)
ENDLESS ORGIES (BA, BN)
ENEMA ADVENTURES (DC)
ENEMA EROTICA (BA)
ENEMA EROTICA #8 (BA)
ENEMA FANTASIES (BN)
ENEMA THRILLS (DC)
ENGLISH TANNING (BA, BN)
ENGLISH TANNING #2 #3 (BN)
ENGLISH TANNING #3 #1 (BA)
ENSLAVE (BN)
ENSLAVE #3 #2 (BA)
ERO (BA, BN)
ERO 11 (BA)
EROS 3-86 (DC, BN)
EROTIC AND HOT (BA, DC, BN)
EROTIC ASS (PA, NY)
EROTIC FANTASIES (DC)
EROTIC VIDEO (NY)
EROTIC WORLD OF SEKA (PA)
EROTIC X-FILM GUIDE 2-86 (DC)
EROTICA PIERCING & SLAVE PIERCING (BN)
EROTICON #1 #3 (BA)
EROTOMIC (DC)
EUROPE ON 5 FUCKS A DAY (DC, PA)
EUROPEAN HEAT (BA, PA)
EUROPEAN HEAT #2 (BN)
EUROPEAN PUSSY (DC)
EUSI NA EUPI (BA, DC, BN)
EUSI NA EUPI #6 #4 (BA)
EVERY DOG HAS HIS DAY (PA)

EXCITING #9 (DC)
EXECUTIVE LOAD (BA, BN)
EXOTIQUE (BN)
EXOTIQUE #2 #3 (BN)
EXPERIENCED SLUTS (NY)
EXPOSE (DC)
EXPRESS (DC)
EXQUISITE (BN)
EXTAS (DC, BN)
EXTAS #4 (BN)
EXTAS #6 (DC)
EXTAS #11 (DC)
F.M.I. (DC, PA)
FANNY (DC, PA)
FANTASY (DC)
FANTASY #18 (DC, BN)
FANTASY #19 (BA, DC, BN)
FANTASY FUCK (BA)
FANTASY REGISTER (DC, BN)
FANTASY WORLD #2 #4 (BN)
FAR EASTERN PUSSY (DC, NY, BN)
FAT FUCKS (DC, BN)
FEEL THE HEAT (DC)
FEM-DOM VIDEO (BN)
FEMALE MIMICS INTERNATIONAL (BN)
FEMALE MODELS (DC)
FEMALE MODELS #8 (DC, BN)
FEMALE SEXUAL FANTASIES (BN)
FEMALE SWINGERS (DC, BN)
FEMME FATALE #3 #3 (BN)
FETISH ACTION (BA)
FETISH BIZARRE (BN)
FETISH FANTASIES (DC, BN)
FETISH FILMS QUARTERLY (BN)
FETISH PHONEBOOK (DC, BN)
FETISH WORLD (BN)
FETISHIST (DC)
FETTERS IN LONDON (BN)
FIESTA WIVES SPEC. #3 (BA)
FIFTEEN (BA)
FIGHTING HELLCATS (DC)
REVIEW #1 (DC, NY)
FILM FUCKS (BA)
FILM WORLD (DC, BN)
FILTHY WOMEN (PA, BN)
FINAL ACTION #1 (NY)
FINGER FRIGGIN' (BA, DC, BN)
FINGER FRIGGIN' #2 (BA)
FINGER FUCKING FEMMES (DC, PA, BN)
FINGER FUCKING FEMMES #2 (DC, BN)
FINGER IN (BA)
FIREMAN'S FANTASIES (PA)
FIRESIDE 3 WAY (BN)
FIRST FUCK (NY)
FIRST TIME ANAL SEX (BN)
FIZZ BANG (BA)
FLAIR (DC, BN)
FLASHBACK 3 (PA)
FLASHBACKS (BN)
FLESHTONES (PA)
FLICK TRICK (PA, BN)
FOOT LOVERS #1 #3 (DC)
FOOT PHOTOS (BA)
FOOT PLAY (BN)
FOOT PLAY #1 #2 (BN)
FOOT WORSHIP (DC, BN)
FOR ADULTS ONLY (DC)
FOR GUYS WHO LOVE BIG TITS #3
FOR RENT (PA)
FOR THE LOVE OF BLACK COCK (DC)
FOR THE LOVE OF CUM (NY)

FORBIDDEN LUST (DC, BN)
FOREIGN COCK (BA, DC)
FOREST FUCK (PA, BN)
FOREVER ANAL (BN)
FORTUNA #2 (DC)
FORTUNE NOOKIE (NY)
FOUR PLAY (BA)
FOX HUNT (DC)
FOXY (BA)
FOXY #5 (DC)
FOXY #6 (DC)
FOXY BLACK (DC, PA)
FOXY HARDCORE GIRLS (NY)
FOXY HARDCORE GIRLS #4 (DC)
FOXY HARDCORE GIRLS #5 (DC)
FOXY HARDCORE FIRLS #6 (DC)
FOXY LADY (BA, DC)
FRATHOUSE FUCK (PA, NY)
FREAKS CUM (NY)
FREE SEX (BA, DC, NY)
FRENCH CIMENA & VIDEO
FRENCH FIREWORKS (PA)
FRESH HOT PUSSY (DC, BN)
FRESH MILK & BIG TITS (PA, BN)
FUCK ALLEY (DC)
FUCK BUDDIES (PA)
FUCK DANCERS (BN)
FUCK FEAST (BA, DC)
FUCK FRENZY (BA, DC, BN)
FUCK GAMES (BA)
FUCK HER IN THE ASS (DC, BN)
FUCK JUNKIES #1 (NY)
FUCK LICKERS (BA)
FUCK LOVING COUPLES (BA, DCC, BN)
FUCK MASTERS (NY)
FUCK ME DEEP (DC)
FUCK MY HOT WET CUNT (BA)
FUCK'N'SUCK (BA)
FUCK POKER (BA)
FUCK QUEEN (BA, DC, NY)
FLOPPERS (BA, DC, PA)
FOOT & BODY BONDAGE (NY, BN)
FOOT & BODY BONDAGE #1 #2 (BN)
FOOT LIGHTS #1 #1 (BN)
FOOT LOVERS (BA, BN, DC)
FUCK-A-LOTTA HOT PUSSY #1 (BN)
FUCK SUCKING TRIOS (DC)
FUCK THIS JOB & SUCK IT (PA)
FUCK TOY (BN)
FUCKATASH (BN)
FUCKATHON (PA)
FUCKED BUTT FUCKED AGAIN (BA, BN)
FUCKFACE (PA)
FUCKIN' AROUND (DC, BN)
FUCKIN' HARD (BN)
FUCKIN' HEFTY (BN)
FUCKIN' PREGNANT (DC, BN)
FUCKIN' WILD (BN)
FUCKING & SUCKING (BN)
FUCKING BY THE BOOK (PA)
FUCKING COUPLES (DC)
FUCKING HOUSEWIVES (BA)
FUCKING POWER (DC)
FUCKING REDHEAD (BA)
FUCKING SEX STARS (DC)
FUCKING SUPERSTARS (DC)
FUCKING SUPERSTARS OF SEX (DC, BN)
FUCKING SWINGERS (DC, BN)
FUCKING VIRGIN ASS (DC)
FULL SERVICE SALON (BA)
FULL THROTTLE (PA, BN)

FUN & GAMES
FUNG-U (BA)
GALLERY (DC)
GALLERY 1-86 (DC)
GALS GALORE (DC)
GAME (BN)
GANG BABES (BA)
GANG BANG (DC, PA, BN)
GANG BANG BIRTHDAY (BN)
GAY COCKSUCKER #3 (BA)
GAY IS BEAUTIFUL (DC, BN)
GAY SEX (DC, NY)
GEISHA (DC)
GEISHA GIRLS (DC, BN)
GEISHA TWAT (BA)
GENTLEMAN'S COMPANION 1-86 (DC)
GENTLEMAN'S COMPANION 3-86 (BA)
GET IT WHILE IT'S HOT (DC, PA)
GET KINKY (BN)
GETTING OFF
GETTING THE SHAFT (BA, DC, BN)
GINGER LYNN (DC)
GIRL NEXT DOOR (DC)
GIRL ON GIRL (BN)
GIRLS (DC)
GIRLS #1 (BN)
GIRLS #5 (BA)
GIRLS GALORE (DC, BN)
GIRLS GALORE #4 #4 (BN)
GIRLS JUST WANNA GET FUCKED (BA)
GIRLS JUST WANNA HAVE SEX (PA, BN)
GIRLS LOVING GIRLS (BA, DC, PA, BN)
GIRLS OF GREECE (PA)
GIRLS OF LONDON (DC, PA, BN)
GIRLS OF X-RATED MOVIES #8 (DC)
GIRLS THAT LOVE IT FROM BEHIND (BA)
GIRLS THAT LOVE IT SLICK (BA, PA, BN)
GIRLS THAT LOVE TO SIT ON IT (BA)
GIRLS WHO ARE BLACK & JUICY (PA)
GIRLS WHO CRAVE BIG COCKS (NY)
GIRLS WHO EAT CUM (BA)
GIRLS WHO EAT DARK MEAT (DC)
GIRLS WHO EAT GIRLS (DC)
GIRLS WHO EAT HOT CUM (DC)
GIRLS WHO FUCK AROUND (BA)
GIRLS WHO LIKE TO SIT ON IT #2 (DC)
GIRLS WHO LOVE GIRLS (NY, BN)
GIRLS WHO LOVE GIRLS #4 (DC, NY)
GIRLS WHO LOVE IT FROM BEHIND (DC, BN)
GIRLS WHO LOVE IT FROM BEHIND #2 (DC, BN)
GIRLS WHO LOVE IT SLICK (PA, NY, BN)
GIRLS WHO LOVE IT SLICK #2 (BN)
GIRLS WHO LOVE THEIR TOYS #55 (DC)
GIRLS WHO LOVE TO SIT ON IT (DC)
GIRLS WHO LOVE TO SIT ON IT #2 (DC)
GIRLS WHO LOVE TO SIT ON IT #115 (BA)
GIRLS WHO LOVE UNCUT DICKS (DC)
GIRLS WHO SUCK EACH OTHER (MI)
GIRLS WHO TAKE IT DEEP (PA, BN)
GIRLS WHO TAKE IT UP THE ASS (DC, PA)
GIRLS WHO TAKE IT UP THE ASS #5 (NY, BA)
GLORY HOLE GANG (PA)
GOIN DOWN (DC, NY)
GOLDEN GIRLS (BA, BN, DC)
GOLDEN GIRLS #13 (NY)
GOLDEN GIRLS #14 (NY)
GOLDEN GIRLS #15 (NY)
GOLDEN GIRLS #16 (NY)
GOLDEN GIRLS #17 (NY)
GOLDEN GIRLS #15 (NY)
GOLDEN GIRLS #19 (NY)

GOLDEN GIRLS #2 (BA)
GOLDEN GIRLS #20 (NY)
GOLDEN GIRLS #21 (NY)
GOLDEN GIRLS #22 (NY)
GOLDEN GIRLS #23 (DC, NY, BN)
GOLDEN GIRLS #24 (NY)
GOLDEN GIRLS #25 (NY)
GOLDEN GIRLS #26 (NY)
GOLDEN GIRLS #27 (NY)
GOLDEN GIRLS #28 (NY)
GOLDEN GIRLS #29 (DC, NY)
GOLDEN GIRLS #30 (DC)
GOLDEN GIRLS #31 (BA)
GOLDEN ROD (BA)
GOLDEN SEKA (DC)
GOOD GIRLS, BAD GIRLS, WOMEN AT PLAY (DC)
GORGEOUS GIRLS WHO GOTTA HAVE COCK (DC)
GORGEOUS GIRLS WHO LIKE TO GIVE ASS (DC)
GOURMET ANAL COLLECTION (DC, NY)
GOURMET ANAL COLLECTION #2 (DC, BN)
GOURMET COLLECTION #5 (DC)
GRADE A SQUIRTS (DC)
GREEK & DEEP (BN)
GREEK BONUS (DC, PA, BN)
GREEK BROTHERS (BA)
GREEK LETTERMAN (DC)
GROUP FUCKING (DC)
GROUP LOVE (DC)
GULP (DC)
GUYS WHO FUCK TIGHT BLACK PUSSY (BA, BN)
GUYS WILL BE GIRLS (DC)
GYM #2 (BN)
GYM JOCKS (BN)
GYM NASTY (NY)
HAIRY & HORNY (PA, NY, BN)
HANGING BREASTS (DC, PA, BN)
HANGING TITS SPECIAL (DC)
HARD & HORNY (BA)
HARD & WET (BN)
HARD BLASTING (PA)
HARD BOUND (BN)
HARD COCK ASTERN (PA)
HARD DICK WORKOUT (BA)
HARD EDGE HUNKS (BN)
HARD FACTS (PA)
HARD FUCK BODIES (BA)
HARD FUCKIN' BUDDIES (BN)
HARD KNOTS (DC)
HARD LEATHER (BA, DC)
HARD MEAT (DC)
HARD ON (DC)
HARD ONS IN SEX WEAR #1 (BN)
HARD OUTTAKES (NY, BN)
HARD PLEASURES (NY)
HARD RIDERS (DC)
HARD RIDERS #2 (BN)
HARD S & M (DC)
HARD S & M #2 (PA)
HARD SHOTS (BN)
HARD SUCKER #1 (BN)
HARD THROBS (DC)
HARD TIMES (DC, BN)
HARD TO CUM BY (PA)
HARD TO GET (BA)
HARD TV (BA, PA, NY)
HARD TV #2 (BA, DC)
HARD TV #3 (BA)
HARD TV #6 (BA)
HARD TV #8 (BA, DC, NY)
HARD TV #9 (DC)
HARD, FAST & DEEP (DC, BN)

HARDBALL (BA, NY)
HARLEQUIN AFFAIR (BA, DC)
HARVEY (DC)
HAYRACKER (PA)
HEAD OF THE CLASS (BN)
HEAD OR BUST (DC, PA)
HEAD TO HEAD (PA)
HEAD WAITER (PA)
HEADMAN (PA)
HEAT (PA)
HEATHER IRONS BONDAGETTE IN LOVE (BA, DC)
HEAVY CARE LOAD (PA)
HEAVY TRAFFIC (DC, PA, BN)
HEEL TO TOE (DC)
HEELS & TOES #2 (DC)
HEFTY MAMAS (BA, DC)
HERE WE CUM (DC, BN)
HERE'S LOOKING AT YOU (BN)
HERE'S LOOKING AT YOU #113 (BN)
HERE'S THE BEEF (MI, PA)
HEY YOU, FUCK MY ASS #1 (BN)
HIGH HEELED & DOMINANT (BN)
HIGH HEELED SLUTS #1 #2 (BN)
HIGH HEELS (BA)
HIGH SCHOOL MEMORIES (DC, BN)
HIGH SCHOOL MEMORIES #64 (BN)
HIGH SOCIETY 2-86 (DC)
HIGH VOLTAGE (PA)
HIRED COCK (BN)
HOGTIE (BN)
HOGTIE #4 #8 (BN)
HONCHO (BA, DC, BN)
HONCHO 2-86 (BN)
HONCHO 4-86 (BA)
HOOKER 2-86 (DC)
HORNY (PA)
HORNY HARD ON (BA)
HORNY MAMA (NY)
HORNY TRIO (NY)
HORNY UNDERGRADS (DC)
HOT & GETTIN HOTTER (PA)
HOT & HORNY (NY, BN)
HOT & HUNG LATINOS (BN)
HOT & HUNGRY HOLE (BN)
HOT ANAL ORGASMS (DC, PA)
HOT ANUS (BN)
HOT ASS #1 (BA, DC, NY)
HOT BABES MASTURBATING (BA, BN)
HOT BITCHES IN HEAT #2 (BN)
HOT BLACK (PA)
HOT BLACK PUSSY (NY)
HOT BLONDE CUNT, BIG BLACK COCK (DC)
HOT BODIES (DC)
HOT BOX (DC, BN)
HOT BRUNETTES (BA, BN, MI)
HOT BRUNETTES #2 (DC)
HOT CHOCOLATE #1 (DC, NY)
HOT CUM (DC)
HOT DICK LICKER #1 (BN)
HOT DOG (DC)
HOT ENCOUNTERS (DC)
HOT FLESH (BA)
HOT FOR CUM (BA, DC)
HOT FUCKER (PA)
HOT FUCKING CUNTS (DC, NY)
HOT FUCKING SHE MALE (NY)
HOT FUSES (BA, DC, PA, NY)
HOT GOODS (BA)
HOT HARD MEAT (DC, BN)
HOT JUICES (DC, PA, NY, BN)
HOT LASHES (BN)

HOT LEGS (DC, BN)
HOT MALE REVIEW (DC)
HOT MALE REVIEW #2 #3 (PA)
HOT MALE REVIEW #2 #5 (BA)
HOT MECHANICS (DC, NY, BN)
HOT MOMENT (BA)
HOT PIECES OF ASS (DC, BN)
HOT PUSSY (BN)
HOT RODDERS (BA, DC, BN)
HOT SHAVES (BA)
HOT SHOT GUNSLINGERS (BN)
HOT SHOTS #1 (PA, BN)
HOT SPELL (DC, BN)
HOT STRIPPER (BN)
HOT STUFF #3 (BN)
HOT SUCKER (DC, NY)
HOT SWINGING COUPLES (DC)
HOT SWINGING COUPLES #4 (BA)
HOT TITTIES & TWAT (DC)
HOT TO POP (PA, BN)
HOT TRICKS (MI, DC, BN)
HOT TUB ORGASM (DC)
HOT TYPE (PA)
HOT WET PUSSY (DC)
HOT YOUNG SLUTS (PA)
HOT, KNOCKED-UP & HORNY (NY)
HOTTEST X-RATED FILM SCENES OF 80s (DC)
HOUSE MASTER (DC)
HOUSEWIFE HOOKERS (BA, BN)
HOW I FUCKED MY BUDDY (BN)
HOW TO PLAY AN ORGAN (PA)
HUMBLY YOURS (BN)
HUNK (DC)
HUNKY & FUNNY (PA)
HUSTLE (BA)
HUSTLER #10 (DC)
HUSTLER HUMOR (DC)
HUSTLER 2-86 (DC)
HUSTLING PUSSY (NY)
I LOVE TO FUCK COWBOYS (DC)
IF IT MOVES FUCK IT (MI, DC, BN)
IMPULSE (PA)
IN CROWD (DC)
IN STYLE (DC)
IN STYLE FOR MEN 3/4-86 (BA)
IN THE PINK (BN)
IN TOUCH FOR MEN (DC, PA)
IN TOUCH FOR MEN #110 (BN)
IN TOUCH FOR MEN #112 (BA)
INCH FOR INCH (PA, NY)
INCHES (BA, DC, PA)
INCURABLY ANAL (BA)
INSATIABLE PUSSY (BA, DC, NY, BN)
INSATIABLES #20 WEEKEND PASS (DC)
INSIDE GINGER LYNN (NY)
INSIDE LESBIAN LIFESTYLES (BA, BN)
INSIDE MARILYN (DC)
INSIDE SHAUNA GRANT (NY)
INSTANT PORN (DC, BN)
INTERRACIAL SEX DIRECTORY (DC)
INTIMATE (BA, DC, BN)
INTIMATE #1 #11 (DC)
J/O BUDDIES (BN)
JACKIN OFF (DC, BN)
JACKS ARE WILD (DC)
JAILHOUSE ROCK (BN)
JANEY ROBBINS SENSUALLY KINKY (BA)
JETS OF JIZZ (NY)
JEWELS OF THE ORIENT (BA, PA)
JIGGLE (PA)
JIZZ TITS (BN)

JOCK (BA, DC)
JOCKSTRAP (PA)
JOCKSTRAP, ONE TO ONE (BN)
JOHN HOLMES (DC)
JOHN HOLMES & URSULA (DC)
JOHNNY HARDEN & FRIENDS (PA)
JOY JUICE (BA, BN)
JOYS OF MASTURBATION (NY)
JUG JUICE (BA)
JUGGS (DC)
JUGS (PA)
JUICY BLACK NURSE (NY)
JUICY JASMINE (BA)
JUNIOR CADETS (PA)
JUST FOR LUST (BA, DC)
JUST FOR YOU (BA, PA)
JUST FUCK ME (DC, NY)
JUST ME AND TWO DICKS (PA)
JUST MEN (BA, DC, PA)
KAREN SWALLOWS CUM (BA, DC, BN)
KEYHOLE (PA)
KIDNAPPED GIRLS AGENCY (DC)
KING OF THE THOROUGHBREDS (PA)
KINGSIZE (BA, PA)
KINKY ACTION (DC)
KINKY ANAL (NY)
KINKY CONTACTS (PA)
KINKY COUPLES (BN)
KINKY COUPLES #9 (BA)
KINKY KICKS (BA)
KINKY PUSSY (DC, PA, BN)
KINKY SEX (BN)
KINKY THREE WAYS (MI)
KINKY WAYS (MI)
KINKY WORLD (BN)
KINKY WORLD #2 #3 (BN)
KINKY WORLD #2 #4 (BN)
KNOCKED UP BLACK MAMA (BA, DC)
KNOCKED UP MAMA (DC, PA, BN)
KNOCKED UP TITTERS (DC, BN)
KNOTS & KINKS #3 (BA)
KUM #1 (DC)
L.A. LADIES (DC, BN)
L.A. LA DIES #1 #2 (BN)
L.A. DIFFERENCE #1 #2 (BN)
L.A. DIFFERENCE #1 #3 (BN)
L.A. DIFFERENCE #1 #4 (BN)
LADIES IN LACE (NY)
LADIES IN LACE #1 #2 (NY)
LADIES NIGHT (DC, BN)
LADIES OF THE ORIENT #13 (BN)
LADIES OF THE ORIENT #9 (NY)
LADIES ROPED (BA)
LADY DOMINA (DC, BN)
LADY FUCK (BA, DC)
LADY WITH A DICK (BA, DC)
LADY YOU NEED TO GET DICKED (DC, NY)
LASHES (BA, DC)
LASHES #6 (BA)
LATENT IMAGE (DC)
LATEX ANNUAL (BN)
LATEX CATALOG #4 (BN)
LATIN BABES (DC, PA, BN)
LATIN LANCES (DC, BN)
LATIN LANCES #1 #2 (BN)
LATINO LUST (BN)
LAUREL BLAKE BY MARK MAR (BA)
LAYOVER (DC)
LEATHER BOUND (DC)
LEATHER HOODS (BN)
LEATHER LIPS #1 (DC, BN)

LEATHER PUSSIES (DC)
LEATHER SLEASE (DC)
LEG PARADE (BA)
LEG SHOW (DC)
LEG SHOW 5-89 (BA)
LEGS (BA)
LEGS & ASSES (DC, NY)
LEGS & LACE, LOVE & LUST (BN)
LEGS, LACE & LINGERIE (BA, BN)
LEGS, LEGS, LEGS (PA, BN)
LESBI (BA)
LESBIAN AFFAIR (NY)
LESBIAN CUNT SUCKERS (NY, BN)
LESBIAN DESIRE (BA)
LESBIAN FOOT LOVERS, THE MOVIE (BN)
LESBIAN GIRLS (DC, BN)
LESBIAN GIRLS #3 #1 (NY)
LESBIAN GIRLS #3 #2 (NY)
LESBIAN GYMNASIUM (PA, BN)
LESBIAN LIFESTYLES (PA, BN)
LESBIAN LOVE (BA)
LESBIAN LOVERS (DC, BN)
LESBIAN LUST (NY)
LESBIAN MELTING POT (BA)
LESBIAN PUSSIES (DC)
LESBIAN SEDUCTION (BA, PA, BN)
LESBIAN SEDUCTION #3 #1 (BN)
LESBIAN TRIO (DC)
LESBIANS (BN)
LESBO TRIO (NY)
LESBOS LIFE (BN)
LET'S CUM TOGETHER (BA, DC)
LET'S HAVE A FUCK PARTY (DC, BN)
LET'S HAVE A THREEWAY (PA, BN)
LETTERS TO CORPORAL (DC)
LETTERS TO CORPORAL #2 #2 (BN)
LETTERS TO GOURMET (DC, NY)
LETTERS TO GOURMET #2 (NY)
LEWD (DC, NY)
LEZ (DC)
LEZ ACTS (BA, PA, BN)
LEZ BITCHES IN HEAT (NY)
LEZ LOVERS (NY, BN)
LEZ LOVERS #2 #4 (BN)
LEZ LOVERS #3 #1 (BN)
LEZ LUST #1 (BN)
LEZ LUV (DC)
LEZ MILKER (DC, PA, NY)
LEZ MOUTH (BA)
LEZ SNATCH, TITS & ASS (BN)
LEZ URGENT DESIRES (PA, BN)
LEZ URGENT DESIRES #2 (MI, BN)
LEZGO CRAZY (DC, BN)
LIBERATED LOVERS (DC)
LIBERATED LOVERS #12 (BA, DC)
LIBERATED LOVERS #13 (BA, BN)
LICK A DICK (BA, NY)
LICK MY BALLS (DC)
LICKABLE LOVELIES (DC)
LICKED INTO SHAPE (NY)
LICKIN LEZ (DC)
LICKING LESBIANS (BA, DC, NY)
LIKE A HORSE (PA, NY)
LIKE LARGE (PA)
LIKE TO GIVE ASS (DC, BN)
LIL' SHAVERS (BA)
LIMITED EDITION CATALOG FILMS 1-208 (BA)
LIP SERVICE (DC)
LISA DELEEUW RAUNCHY REDHEAD (NY)
LISA'S WORLD (BN)
LITTLE MILK (PA)

LIVE WIRE (DC, NY, BN)
LOADS OF LUST (DC)
LOCAL SWINGERS (BN)
LOCAL SWINGERS (BN)
LONG BLACK SUPER COCK (BA)
LONG HARD SUMMER (DC)
LOOKING GLASS (MI, DC)
LOOKING GOOD (DC)
LOVE (DC)
LOVE #15 (DC)
LOVE GIRLS (PA)
LOVE GREEK STYLE (BA, DC, BN)
LOVE MAKERS #1 #1 (BN)
LOVE MUSCLE (BN)
LOVE SLAVES (DC, PA)
LOVE SUCKER (NY)
LOVE TOO (BA, NY)
LOVING LASHES (BN)
LUST (BA, NY)
LUST BISEXUAL (DC)
LUST FLOOD (PA)
LUST FOR BLACK FLESH (BA)
LUST FOR LEATHER (MI, PA)
LUSTFUL ACTION (DC)
LUSTY BLACK MEAT (DC)
LUSTY LADIES (PA, NY)
LUSTY LADIES #2 (NY)
LUSTY LATIN, VANESSA DEL RIO (DC)
LUSTY YOUNG LADIES (BN)
LOCKER ROOM (BN)
LOCKER ROOM LUST (BN)
MACHO MOTEL (DC, PA)
MADE FOR ANAL (DC)
MADE IN EUROPE (DC, BN)
MADE IN EUROPE #2 (BN)
MAGNUM GRIFFIN (BN)
MAKE MINE A DOUBLE (NY)
MAKING CONTACT WITH LIVE MODELS (DC, BN)
MALE CALLS (DC)
MALE FILE (BA, DC, BN)
MALE FILE #3 (DC, BN)
MALE FILE #4 (BA)
MALE STARS (BA, DC)
MAMA MILKED (PA)
MAN-AGE JOY STICKS #1 #2 (BN)
MANDATE (BA, DC, BN)
MANDATE 2-86 (BN)
MANHOOD RITUALS (BA)
MANPOWER (DC, BN)
MAN'S BEST FRIEND (PA)
MANSCAPE (DC)
MARATHON LEZZIES (BN)
MARATHON LEZZIES #2 (BN)
MARTINET (BN)
MASTURBATION FANTASY (DC, PA, BN)
MATCHED PAIR (DC)
MAX (DDC)
MAX BIG BUSTY BEAUTIFUL (DC)
MEAN BITCH (DC, NY, BN)
MEAT PACKERS (DC, NY, BN)
MEN (DC, BN)
MEN OF ARENA (BN)
MEN OF ARENA #9 (BA, BN)
MEN OF MEN (DC)
MEN OF REVOLT (DC)
MEN WHO CRAVE TIGHT PUSSIES (BA, DC)
MEN 5-86 (BN)
MENAGE-A-TWAT (DC)
MENTOR #2 (PA)
MILITARY 3 WAY (PA)
MILK & HONEY (NY)

MILK MAMA (DC, PA, BN)
MILK SHOOTERS (DC)
MILKIN' MOMS (DC)
MILKY MAMAS (BA, BN)
MILKY MELONS (BA)
MILKY MISS (DC)
MILKY SQUIRTS (DC)
MILKY WAY (PA, NY)
MISTRESS (BN)
MISTRESS ANTOINETTE'S COLL. #4 (BA)
MISTRESS ANTOINETTE'S KINKY CONTACTS (DC)
MISTRESS OF PAIN (PA)
MOMS (PA)
MORE CALIFORNIA BOYS (BA)
MORE FAT FUCKS (BN)
MORE THAN GIRLFRIENDS (BN)
MORE THAN TWO #37 (BA)
MORE THAN 2 (BN)
MOTEL MENAGE-A-TROIS (BN)
MOTHER JUGS (BN)
MOTHER JUGS #4 #1 (BN)
MOUNDS (BA)
MOUTHPIECE (NY)
MR. FIX-IT, FUCKS IT (BA)
MUD (PA)
MUD CATS (BN)
MULATTO #3 #2 (BN)
MULATTO SPLITS & TITS (BA)
MULTIPLE ORGASMS (DC, BN)
NANA'S FAREWELL 3-WAY (BN)
NATIONAL CONNECTIONS (DC)
NATIONAL CONNECTIONS #22 (DC)
NATIONAL CONNECTIONS #23 (BA)
NATIONAL EXCHANGE (MI, DC)
NATIONAL EXCHANGE #20 (BN)
NATIONAL SEX HOTLINE (BA)
NATIONAL SWINGERS QUARTERLY (DC)
NATIONWIDE SWINGERS YELLOW PAGES #15 (DC)
NAUGHTY BABIES (BN)
NAUGHTY BABIES #2 (BA, BN)
NAUGHTY DAUGHTER IN HEAT (DC)
NAUGHTY NANCY (BA, NY)
NAUGHTY NIKHO (DC)
NAUGHTY NIKHO #2 (BA)
NAVED SNATCH (NY)
NEW BREED #1 (PA, BN)
NEW BREED #2 (DC)
NEW CUMMERS #1 (BN)
NEW NATIONAL NEWS (BA)
NEW TRICKS (BA, DC)
NEW WAVE HOOKERS (NY)
NEW WAVE SEX (PA, NY, BN)
NEW YORK SWINGING MODERNS #6 (DC)
NIGHT LUST (PA, BN)
NIGHT OF THE WANG #1 (BN)
NIGHT SHIFT (BN)
NIGHT STARS (DC)
NIKHO'S REVENGE (BA)
NIPPON NOOKIE THE SUCKIN' COOKIE (BN)
NIPPON NOOKIES (BN)
NO HOLES BARED (BN)
NOT JUST ANOTHER BUTT FUCK (NY)
NOW DARLING (DC)
NUDE TOUCH (PA)
NUMBERS (DC)
NUMBERS & SON OF DRUMMER (BA)
NUMBERS ANNUAL #1 #4 (BA)
NUMBERS ANNUAL #3 (BA)
NUMBERS 2-86 (BN)
NUTS & BOLTS (PA)
NYMPHO TAKES TWO (BN)

OBEAH (BA, DC)
OBEISANCE (NY)
OBEY ME (BN)
ODYSSEY (DC, PA, BN)
ODYSSEY 3-86 (BA)
ODYSSEY EXPRESS (DC)
OFTY #10 (DC)
OFTY #2 (BA, DC)
OFTY #4 (BA, DC, NY)
OFTY #5 (BA, DC)
OLYMPUS (DC)
ONE HOT TIME (DC)
ONE ON ONE (PA)
ONE SIZE FITS ALL (DC, BN)
ONE SIZE FITS ALL #2 (BN)
OOO-AAH (BA)
OPEN INVITATION (BN)
OPEN THROAT (DC)
ORAL LOVER (NY, BN)
ORAL LUST (BA, DC)
ORAL ORGASMS (DC)
ORAL SUCKERS (PA)
ORGY (DC, BN)
ORGY IN CUM (BN)
ORIENTAL CALLGIRLS (MI)
ORIENTAL COCK (DC)
ORIENTAL DELIGHT (BN)
ORIENTAL DELIGHT #17
ORIENTAL DELIGHT #5 (NY)
ORIENTAL DISHES (BN)
ORIENTAL DOLL'S EROTIC FANTASIES (BN)
ORIENTAL DREAMS (BA)
ORIENTAL EROTICA (MI, DC, PA)
ORIENTAL EROTICA #3 (NY)
ORIENTAL FETISHES (DC)
ORIENTAL LOVERS (BA)
ORIENTAL LOVERS #2 (BN)
ORIENTAL MYSTIQUE (DC, BN)
ORIENTAL MYSTIQUE #2 (PA)
ORIENTAL NYMPHS (NY)
ORIENTAL ORGASMS (DC, PA, BN)
ORIENTAL
ORGASMS #5 (BN)
ORIENTAL ORGIES (BA, MI)
ORIENTAL ORGIES #2 (BN)
ORIENTAL SEXPOT (DC)
ORIENTAL SQUEEZE (DC, NY)
OSO ASS (NY)
OUI (DC)
OUI, DAZZLING BLONDES & REDHEADS (DC)
OUI, FANTASY FEMALES (DC)
OUI, SUN & FUN (DC)
OUR BOYS IN UNIFORM (DC, BN)
OUTTAKES (DC)
OVER 200 PICTURES OF COCK SHOTS (DC)
OVER 289 PREGNANT & MILK MAMAS #1 #1 (BN)
OVER 289 BIG TIT PHOTOS (DC, BN)
PAIN BY LANA (DC, BN)
PAIN IN THE ASS (MI)
PAINFUL PLEASURE (BN)
PAINFUL PLEASURES #1 #3 (BN)
PANTY BABES (NY)
PANTY PASSIONS #4 (BN)
PARTNER (BN)
PARTNER 3-86 (BN)
PARTY FUCK (PA, BN)
PARTY FUCKIN' (MI)
PARTY PEOPLE'S DIRECTORY #7 (BA)
PASSION FOR BLACK (BA, DC)
PASSION PARTY (DC)
PEACH FUZZ PUSSIES (BN)

PEEK-A-BOO PUSSY (PA, BN)
PENNSYLVANIA CONNECTION (BA)
PERFECTING EROTIC PASSION (BN)
PERSON TO PERSON (DC)
PERSONAL BONDAGE (BA, DC)
PETER PILLOW (PA)
PHOTO SLUT (BA, DC, BN)
PICTORIAL (BN)
PIECE OF CAKE (DC)
PINK HOLE (BA)
PINK SNAPPER (DC)
PLATINUM PLAY DUDES (PA)
PLAY GUY (BA, DC, BN)
PLAY GUY 2-86 (BN)
PLAY GUY 4-86 (BA)
PLAYERS (DC)
PLAYERS #12 #9 (DC)
PLAYERS GIRLS PICTORIAL #6 #7 (DC)
PLEASE ME (BN)
PLEASURE (BA, DC)
PLEASURE MOUNTAIN (DC)
PLEASURE READER #1 #2 (DC)
PLEDGE SUCK (DC, BN)
POCKET JOURNAL #1 (BN)
POCKET JOURNAL #2 (BN)
POCKET JOURNAL #3 (BN)
POOL FUCK (BN)
POOL TOOLS (BN)
POOLSIDE PRICKS (PA, BN)
POPPIN MAMAS (PA, BN)
PORN (PA)
PORN PUSSYS (BA)
PORN STAR 1986 ANNUAL (BA)
PORNOBOY #12 (DC, BN)
PORNOBOY #19 (DC)
PORNORAMA (BA)
PREGNANT COCK FUCKERS (PA, BN)
PREGNANT COCK FUCKERS #2 (BN)
PREGNANT DILDO BONDAGE (DC)
PREGNANT LESBIANS (DC, BA)
PREGNANT PUSSIES (DC, BA, MI)
PRESCRIPTION FOR PASSION (DC)
PRETTY GIRLS (BA, DC, PA, BN)
PRETTY GIRLS #3 (DC)
PRETTY GIRLS #4 (DC)
PRETTY GIRLS #53 (DC)
PRETTY GIRLS OF THE ORIENT (BA, NY)
PRETTY YOUNG GIRLS (DC, BN)
PRICK PLEASERS (PA)
PRIDE (MI)
PRIMA (BA)
PRIMA #8 (BA)
PRIMA II (DC)
PRIMA III (DC)
PRIME TIME TV (BN)
PRINCE (DC, BN)
PRINCE #11 (DC)
PRINCE #13 (BN)
PRINCE #14 (DC, BN)
PRINCE #17 (DC)
PRINCE #18 (DC)
PRIVATE (DC)
PRIVATE #38 (DC)
PRIVATE HAREM (DC)
PRIVATE PLEASURES OF JOHN HOLMES (BA, DC)
PRIVATE X-POSURE (DC)
PRO ASS FUCKER (NY, BN)
PROD #4 (PA)
PRUDISH PEOPLE (DC, PA)
PRUDS (PA)
PUMPING ASS (NY)

PUMPING IRON (BN)
PUNISHED (PA, NY, BN)
PUNISHED #2 #4 (BN)
PUNK FUCK (DC)
PURITAN #11 (BA)
PURITAN #7 (BA, DC)
PURITAN #8 (DC, BN)
PURPLE (BA)
PUSSIES & LACE (PA)
PUSSY #1 (BA, BN)
PUSSY CREAM (PA)
PUSSY MASTERS (MI, DC)
PUSSY MASTERS #2 (BN)
PUSSY ON A STICK (PA, BN)
PUSSY PAGEANT (BN)
PUSSY PALS (DC)
PUSSY POKING (NY)
PUSSY PUMPING, COCK SUCKERS, ASS FUCKERS
   (DC)
PUSSY RAMMER (BA)
PUSSY SANDWICH (DC)
QUADRAFUCK (NY)
QUEENS OF ANAL SEX (NY)
QUEENS OF DOUBLE PENETRATION (DC)
QUEENS OF DRAG (BA, DC)
QUEST (DC)
RAM (DC)
RAMMIN' PUSSY (BA)
RANCHLAND
RAUNCH (PA)
RAVEN (BA)
RED CHEEKS BONANZA (BN)
REAM-O-RAMA (DC, BN)
REAR ENDED (BN)
REAR GUARD (PA, BN)
RED CHEEKS (BN)
RED HOT (BN)
RED HOT PUSSY (DC, BN)
RED HOT RUSSIAN (DC)
RED JOY STICK (PA)
REFLECTIONS (BA, DC)
RENAULT AND JASON MEET ROSE (BA, PA)
RENE'S FUCK BOOK (BA, NY, BN)
RIDIN' THE HUMP (BN)
RIM IT (NY)
RIPE AND EAGER (DC, BN)
RIPE NIPPLES (DC, PA, BN)
ROADSIDE CHERRY'S REVENGE (PA)
ROCK SUCKER (BN)
RODOX (BA)
ROGER'S BOYS OUT OF UNIFORM (BN)
ROGER'S YOUNG LEATHER HOODS (BN)
ROMANCING THE BONE (BA)
ROOM MATES (BA, DC)
ROPE DISCIPLINE (DC, BN)
ROPED & TIED (BA)
ROPED LADIES (BA)
ROUGH & READY ANNUAL (BA)
ROUGH BOYS (DC)
ROUGHTRADE (PA, BN)
ROUND 1 (PA)
ROXANNE (DC)
RUBBER QUARTERLY (DC)
RUBBER QUARTERLY #1 #6 (BN)
RUBBER TV (DC, BN)
RUMPBUSTERS (DC, BN)
SABRINA (DC)
SABRINA RETURNS (BA)
SAILOR'S DELIGHT (DC)
SAINTS & SINNERS (DC, BN)
SAINTS & SINNERS #25 (BN)

SAINTS & SINNERS #26 (BN)
SAINTS & SINNERS #28 (BN)
SALES AGENT (DC)
SANDBLAST (PA)
SAPPHO (PA)
SARAH FOSTER TATE IN BONDAGE (DC, BA, BN)
SAVAGE SUCKER (NY, BN)
SAY BI BI (BA, BN)
SCALP HAPPY (BN)
SCREWIN' & COCK FUCKIN (DC)
SCREWTIME (BA, DC)
SEKA (BA)
SELECT (DC)
SELECTRA #18 (DC)
SELECTRA #21 (DC)
SELECTRA #5 (DC)
SELEXION (MI, DC)
SEVEN HARD MEN (BA)
SEX SISTERS (BN)
SEX DANCER (BN)
SEX FREAKS (BA, DC, PA, BN)
SEX GODDESSES #9 (DC)
SEX MANIA (DC)
SEX MASTER (PA)
SEX SCENES (PA)
SEX SISTER #3 #4 (BN)
SEX STARS FAVORITE POSITION (NY)
SEX TAPES (PA)
SEX TOYS (DC)
SEX WEAR (DC)
SEX WORKOUT (BA)
SEXIEST MOUTHS IN X-FILMS (DC)
SEXTRAVERTS (DC, BN)
SEXTRAVERTS #12 (BA)
SEXUAL EXCESS (DC)
SEXUAL POSITIONS (NY)
SEXUAL POSITIONS #2 (BN)
SEXY BLACK (PA)
SEXY SENORITAS (BN)
SHAFTED (DC)
SHAUNA
SHAVE ME & FUCK ME (NY)
SHAVED (DC)
SHAVED BOX, WILD TITS, TIGHT ASS #1 (BN)
SHAVED BUTT FUCK (BN)
SHAVED PUSSIES (DC)
SHAVED REVIEW (DC)
SHAVED SLITS (MI)
SHAVED SLUTS (PA)
SHE (BN)
SHE MALE FUCKERS (BA, DC, BN)
SHE MALE SEX & SANDWICH (BA)
SHE MALE SUPERSTAR #4 (BA)
SHE MALES (DC, NY)
SHE'S AT THE END OF HER ROPE
SHIPPING STUDS (BA, BN)
SHOOT OUT (DC, BN)
SHOOTING PUSSY (DC)
SHOW GIRL SUPERSTARS #2 (NY)
SHOW GIRL SUPERSTARS #5 (NY)
SHOWER MALE (BA)
SHOWGIRL (PA)
SHOWTIME (PA)
SINFUL SWINGERS (BN)
SINFUL SWINGERS #3 (DC)
SINGLE HANDED (PA)
SINGLE SWINGERS (BA)
SINGLE SWINGERS #24 (BA)
SISTER TRIO II (BN)
SISTERS (BA)
SIT ON IT (NY)

SIT ON MY COCK (DC, NY, BN)
SIXTY NINERS (DC, BN)
SIZZLING CLITS (DC)
SIZZLING REAR (NY)
SKI MEAT (BN)
SKIN (DC)
SKIN #2 (PA)
SKIN FLICKS #1 (BA, DC, PA)
SKIN GAME (DC)
SKIN GAME #8 (DC)
SKIN SIN (PA)
SKIN TIGHT (BN)
SKIRTS UP-PANTS DOWN (PA)
SKY FUCK (NY, BN)
SLAP & SWAT (BN)
SLAP BAM (DC)
SLAP SHOTS (PA)
SLAP SHOTS #2 #2 (BN)
SLAVE (NY)
SLAVE EXCHANGE (BA)
SLAVE EXCHANGE #3 #2 (BA)
SLICK GETS A FREEBIE (PA)
SLIPPERY LOVE (BN)
SLIPPERY ONE (DC)
SLIT SUCKING SLUTS (DC, PA)
SLIT SUCKING SLUTS #1 #3 (BN)
SLURP EZE (BA, DC)
SLUT FROM SHANGHAI (BA)
SLUTS (DC)
SLUTS IN UNIFORM (BA)
SMOOTH CHIX (BN)
SMOOTH MOVES (DC, PA)
SNATCH (PA, NY, BN)
SNATCH #1 #2 (BN)
SNOB (BA)
SNOB #2 (BA)
SO BIG, SO THICK, SO BLACK #1 (BA, NY)
SO BLACK (NY)
SOCIAL SWINGER (DC, PA, BN)
SOCK IT TO ME (PA)
SOMETHING DIFFERENT (DC)
SOMETHING WILD (MI, DC, BN)
SOUL BUTTS (PA)
SPANK (BA, DC, PA, BN)
SPANK #2 #1 (BN)
SPANK #3 #2 (BA)
SPANKING (BN)
SPANKING GAZETTE (BA)
SPANKING LETTERS (DC, BN)
SPANKING VIDEO #1 (DC)
SPIKES DOMINATION (BN)
SPIKES DOMINATION #1 #4 (BN)
SPIKES DOMINATION #2 #1 (BN)
SPLIT BEAVERS (BN)
SPREAD'EM (BN)
SPURS (DC, PA)
SPURTER (BA)
SQUEEZE (BA, DC, BN)
SQUIRT 'EM (DC)
STAG (DC)
STAG 1-86 (DC)
STALLION (BA, DC)
STALLION 1-86 (PA, BN)
STAR CHIX (DC, BN)
STARLIGHT (BA)
STARS (DC, NY)
STEAM HEAT (DC, PA. BN)
STICK IT IN (DC)
STILETTO (DC, BN)
STILETTO #5 (DC, BN)
STING (PA)

STOCKROOM STUDS (BN)
STREET GIRL FROM TAIWAN (BA, DC, NY)
STRIP (DC, BN)
STRIP DOWN (BN)
STRIPTEASE (BA, DC, BN)
STROKE (BA, DC)
STROKE-SAFE SEX (BA)
STUD #5 (BN)
STUD ALLEY (PA, BN)
STUD FLIX (BA, DC, BN)
STUD FLIX #3 (BA)
STUD SERVICE (PA)
STUD SUCKER (BA, DC, BN)
STUDENT LOVERS (BN)
STUFFED PUSSY (DC)
SUBMIT (BA)
SUCK (DC, PA, BN)
SUCK IT (NY)
SUCK ME, FUCK ME (DC)
SUCK MY BALLS (MI, DC)
SUCK OFF (BA, DC)
SUCK THROAT (DC)
SUCK 2 DICKS (BA)
SUCKERS #1 (NY)
SUCKIN' CANDY (DC, BN)
SUCKIN' MEAT (DC)
SUCKING SENIORS (PA, NY)
SUCKLE (DC, BN)
SULTRY BLACK DOLLS (BA, BN)
SUMMER DAY, SUMMER LOVERS (DC)
SUMMER FANTASY (BN)
SUMMER FANTASY #2 (BN)
SUMMER ROSE FOREVER (PA, BN)
SUMMER'S ANAL PASSION (BA)
SUNSTROKES (BN)
SUPER BIG (PA)
SUPER BITCH (BN)
SUPER BLACK MILK (DC)
SUPER BOOBS & BEAVERS (PA, BN)
SUPER GIRLS (BA)
SUPER GOURMET REVIEW #2 (NY)
SUPER GOURMET REVIEW #8 (NY)
SUPER GOURMET REVIEW #9 (NY)
SUPER HARD SHOTS (PA, BN)
SUPER HARD SHOTS #2 (BN)
SUPER HEAD #5 (DC)
SUPER HOT SHORTS (DC)
SUPER HOT SHOTS (DC, BN)
SUPER HOT SHOTS #18 (DC, BN)
SUPER HOT SHOTS #5 (BN)
SUPER INTENSE (PA)
SUPER SEKA (DC, NY)
SUPER SEX STAR (DC)
SUPER SLUTS (NY)
SUPER SNATCH (DC)
SUPER SPIKES (BN)
SUPER STUDS #2 (BN)
SUPER STUDS IN DRAG (BN)
SUPER SUCKERS (DC, NY, BN)
SUPER TITS (DC, BN)
SUPERSTAR (DC)
SUPERSTAR STUDS (BN)
SUPERSTAR STUDS #2 (BN)
SUPERSTAR STUDS #3 (BN)
SUPERSTAR TITS & TWATS (DC)
SUPERSTARS OF EROTICA #2 (BA, PA)
SUPERSTARS OF EROTICA #3 (DC)
SUPERSTARS OF FILM (DC)
SURFER BLUE (DC)
SURRENDER TO THE BEAVER (PA, BN)
SUSHI (DC, PA, BN)

SUSHI CUNTS (BA)
SWALLOW HARD (PA)
SWALLOW PARTY (NY)
SWANK (DC)
SWANK LETTERS #9-1985 (DC)
SWANK 2-86 (DC)
SWEAT #1 #1 (PA)
SWEDISH EROTICA (DC, BN)
SWEDISH EROTICA #10 (DC)
SWEDISH EROTICA #100 (DC)
SWEDISH EROTICA #101 (DC)
SWEDISH EROTICA #102 (DC)
SWEDISH EROTICA #103 (BN)
SWEDISH EROTICA #2 (DC)
SWEDISH EROTICA #3 (DC)
SWEDISH EROTICA #33 (BA)
SWEDISH EROTICA #4 (DC)
SWEDISH EROTICA #45 (DC)
SWEDISH EROTICA #49 (NY)
SWEDISH EROTICA #54 (DC)
SWEDISH EROTICA #6 (DC)
SWEDISH EROTICA #60 (DC)
SWEDISH EROTICA #63 (DC)
SWEDISH EROTICA #7 (DC)
SWEDISH EROTICA #74 (DC)
SWEDISH EROTICA #75 (DC)
SWEDISH EROTICA #78 (DC)
SWEDISH EROTICA #79 (DC)
SWEDISH EROTICA #8 (DC)
SWEDISH EROTICA #80 (DC)
SWEDISH EROTICA #85 (BN)
SWEDISH EROTICA #87 (DC, BN)
SWEDISH EROTICA #88 (BN)
SWEDISH EROTICA #89 (DC, BN)
SWEDISH EROTICA #90 (DC, BN)
SWEDISH EROTICA #91 (DC, BN)
SWEIDSH EROTICA #92 (DC)
SWEDISH EROTICA #93 (DC)
SWEDISH EROTICA #96 (DC)
SWEDISH EROTICA #97 (DC)
SWEDISH EROTICA #98 (DC)
SWEETIES (DC, PA, BN)
SWING WOMEN (DC)
SWINGER'S ADVERTISER (DC)
SWINGER'S ALMANAC (BA)
SWINGER'S ALMANAC #2 (BN)
SWINGER'S BIBLE #1 #4 (DC)
SWINGER'S CONNECTIONS #1 (DC, BN)
SWINGERS IN ACTION (DC)
SWINGER'S NATIONAL REGISTER (DC, BN)
SWINGER'S NATIONAL REGISTER #7 #2 (DC)
SWINGERS PARTICIPATION (DC)
SWINGERS PHONEBOOK (DC)
SWINGERS SATISFACTION (DC)
SWINGERS TODAY (PA, BN)
SWINGING CONTACTS (DC)
SWINGING GALS (DC)
SWINGING GALS #30 (BN)
SWINGING LADIES (PA)
SWINGING LADIES #1 #4 (BN)
SWINGING NYMPHOS (BA)
SWINGING PLAYMATES (MI)
SWINGING SINGLES (DC)
SWINGING SINNERS (DC, BN)
SWINGING SINNERS #28 (DC)
SWINGING WOMEN (BN)
SWINGING WOMEN #3 #3 (DC)
SWINGING/GROUP SEX (BA)
SWITCH HITTERS (DC, PA, BN)
SWEET CHOCOLATE (NY, BN)
SWEET COCKS (BN)

SWEET CREAM (PA)
SWEET STARLETS (BA)
SWEET YOUNG FOXES & FINGER TALKIN' (PA)
TABOO (BA, DC, BN)
TABOO #3 #3 (DC)
TABU (BA, DC)
TAKE IT ALL OFF (DC, BN)
TAKE 3 (PA)
TAMI'S INCREDIBLE ASSHOLE (BA, NY)
TAN TIGERESS (NY)
TAN TIGERESS, A COCKSUCKING SLAVE (PA, NY)
TARGET #2 (DC)
TASTE OF LUST (NY)
TAUT ADVENTURE (DC, BN)
TEACHER'S PET (DC)
TEASER'S COLLECTION #1 (NY)
TEEN (DC)
TEEN BOOBS & TWATS (BA, DC, PA, BN)
TEEN HOLES (DC)
TEEN MOMS (BA)
TEEN PLAYMATES (PA)
TEEN SPLITTERS (PA, BN)
TEEN TITS & TWATS (NY)
TEEN TWATS, TITS & ASS (DC, BN)
TEENAGE MASTURBATION (BN)
TEENAGE TRAMP (BN)
TEENAGERS (BN)
TEENY TITS (DC, PA)
TEN INCH TOOLS (PA, BN)
TENDER LOVING CARE (BA, DC, BN)
TENDER SHAVERS (BA, BN)
TENDER TWAT (PA, BN)
TENDER YOUNG TITS (DC, PA, BN)
TENDER YOUNG TITS #2 (BN)
TENDRES VOYEUR (PA)
THE ADVENTURES OF DICK RAMBONE (DC, PA, BN
THE ADVENTURES OF LUNA (NY)
THE ADVENTURES OF MARC NOLL (PA)
THE ADVOCATE 1-86 (BN)
THE ASSMAN COMETH (PA, BN)
THE BANK DICK (PA)
THE BELLHOP MEETS THE BULL (BN)
THE BEST LITTLE STUDHOUSE IN TOWN (PA)
THE BEST OF CUM (NY, BN)
THE BEST OF CUM #2 (NY)
THE BEST OF F.I. NEWS (DC)
THE BEST OF FETISH TIMES (BN)
THE BEST OF FOOT WORSHIP (BA)
THE BEST OF HUSTLER #11 (DC)
THE BEST OF LESBIAN GYMNASIUM (BN)
THE BEST OF NOVA ANNUAL I (MI)
THE BEST OF PRETTY GIRLS (DC)
THE BIG 3-WAY FUCK OFF (NY)
THE BITCH GODDESSES (BN)
THE BITCH GODDESSES #4 (BN)
THE BOILER ROOM (PA)
THE BOYS (BA)
THE BOYS FROM MAN-AGE #4 (BN)
THE BOYS OF MARDI GRAS (DC, PA)
THE BOYS OF RIO (NY)
THE CONTINENTA SPECTATOR (DC, NY)
THE DIGEST (DC, BN)
THE DIGEST #3 (BN)
THE DOOMED COURIER (BN)
THE DRESDEN DIARY (DC)
THE EROTICA WORLD OF CARA (NY)
THE FABULOUS SHANNON (BN)
THE FALCON FILE (DC, BN)
THE FALCON FILE #15 (BN)
THE FARMER'S DAUGHTERS (BA)
THE FOUR THURSDAYS (BN)

THE FOXIEST BLONDE OF ALL, SEKA (NY)
THE FUCKING SURPRISE (PA)
THE GOURMET BOOK OF 69
THE GOURMET TREASURY OF CUM (NY)
THE HONEY INTERN (PA)
THE HOT RODDERS (BA, DC)
THE JOY OF BONDAGE #1 (DC)
THE JOY OF SCREWING (DC)
THE LEGEND OF JENNIE LEE (BN)
THE MALE (BA)
THE MAN WHO FUCKED
TWO CUNTS #1 (BN, BA)
THE MANY FACES OF RENE (BN)
THE MARRIAGE BED (DC)
THE MEET MARKET (MI, BN)
THE MEETING PLACE (DC)
THE NEW SWEDISH EROTICA #80 (BN)
THE NEW SWINGING SINNERS #19 (DC)
THE ORIGINAL SWEDISH EROTICA #90 (BN)
THE OTHER SIDE OF VANESSA (BN)
THE PAINTER (PA)
THE PRINT MASTERS APPRENTICE (BN)
THE RIGHT SQUIRTING STUFF (BA)
THE SEEKERS (BA, DC, BN)
THE SEEKERS #67 (DC)
THE SEEKERS #68 (BA)
THE SEEKERS 1986 (DC, BN)
THE SENSUOUS GIRLS OF SWANK (DC)
THE SINNERS (MI)
THE TASTE OF LUST (DC)
THE WIDE WORLD OF LICORICE DICK (NY)
THE WONDERFUL WORLD OF FEET (PA)
THE WONDERFUL WORLD OF HARVEY #1 (BN)
THE WONDERFUL WORLD OF LESBIANS (BN)
THESE GALS NEED DEEP PENETRATION #2 (DC, BN)
THESE GIRLS NEED DEEP PENETRATION (BN)
THIS BUTT'S FOR YOU #1 (BN)
THIS STUD FOR HIRE (MI, DC, BN)
THREE DAY PASS (BN)
THREE SCORE (BN)
THREE SCORE #3 (DC, BN)
THREE THE HARD WAY (DC, BN)
THREE WAY BLOW-OUT (DC)
THREE WAY CRAM (DC)
THREE WAY CUM (BA)
THREE WAY CUM #5 (DC)
THREE WAY HEAT (DC)
THREE WAY LAY (PA, BN)
THREE WAY ORGIES (BA, DC)
THREE WAY SEX #2 (NY, BN)
THREE WAY SPREADS (MI, BA)
THRILL FUCKING (BA)
THROBBING 3-WAY #2 (BA)
THUNDERTITS (BA)
TIE DOWN (NY, BN)
TIED & TICKLED (DC)
TIED & TORMENTED (DC, BN)
TIED & TORMENTED #1 #3 (DC, BN)
TIED & TORTURED (DC, NY, BN)
TIGHT BLACK PUSSY (BA, NY, BN)
TIGHT GRIP (BN)
TIGHT HOLE (NY)
TIGHT RUBBER (PA)
TIGHT-N-ANAL (DC)
TIGHTROPES (DC)
TINY TITS #3 (BN)
TIP TOP (BA, DC)
TIT FUCKERS (BA, PA, BN)
TIT HANGERS (BN)
TIT PARADA (PA TUBS (BN)
TIT STARS (BA)

TITANIC TITS (PA)
TITANS (PA)
TITORAMA #4 #1 (BA)
TITS (DC)
TITS & TIGHT TWATS (DC)
TITS 4 EVER (NY)
TITS 4 U (BA)
TITTERS (DC)
TITTIE MILK (BA, DC, BN)
TITTY FRUITY (PA, BN)
TNT (PA)
TONGUE (PA)
TONGUE TWISTERS (DC, PA)
TOOL #2 (BN)
TOOL JOB (NY)
TOP TO BOTTOM (DC)
TORRID TV'S (BA, BN)
TORSO 1-86 (PA)
TORSO 2-86 (PA)
TORSO 3-86 (BA)
TOTAL TITS (DC, PA)
TOTALLY ANAL (NY)
TOUCH ME (BN)
TOUGH COMPETITION (DC)
TOURIST ATTRACTION (PA)
TRACI LORDS SUPERSTARS (NYY)
TRACEY & CHRISTY (DC)
TRAINERS & GAGS (BN)
TRANSEXUAL TEMPTATION (DC, BA)
TRANSIT STOP (PA)
TRANSSOUL (BA)
TRANSVESTITE (NY)
TRAPPED (DC)
TRASHY LADIES (DC)
TRI-SUCK (NY)
TRIANGLE (DC, BN)
TRIANGLE #2 (BN)
TRIANGLE #3 (MI, DC, PA, BN)
TRICKING AT THE OFFICE (BN)
TRICKING OFF THE STREET (BN)
TRICKING OFF THE STREET #5 (BN)
TRICKS (BA, BN)
TRICKS OF THE TRADE (DC, NY)
TRIPLE ACTION (DC, BN)
TRIPLE ACTION-2 CUNTS AND A BIG COCK (NY)
TRIPLE CUM (DC, BN)
TRIPLE FUCKED (BA)
TRIPLE LICKS (PA)
TRIPLE TONGUE (NY)
TRIPLE TRACTION (PA, BN)
TRIPLE TROUBLE (MI)
TRUCKERS (PA, BN)
TUB STUDS (BN)
TUBS (BN)
TURNABOUT (NY, BN)
TURNABOUT #1 #2 (BN)
TURNED ON II (DC)
TURNED ON TO BLACK DICK (BA)
TV CUM (BA, DC, NY)
TV DINNER (BA)
TV HOT DREAMS (BA)
TV HOUSE PARTY (NY)
TV QUEENS (DC, BN)
TV QUEENS #3 #1 (BA, BN)
TV QUEENS #3 #2 (BA)
TV SAMPLER (BN)
TV SEX #1 #4 (NY)
TV TIMES (BA, DC)
TV TRICKS (BA)
TV TRIPLE PLAY (DC)
TV'S GETTING TOGETHER (NY)

TV'S TOP TO BOTTOM (BA, DC)
TWAT EATING GIRLS (BA, DC, BN)
TWIN 44'S (BA, DC, BN)
TWO COCKS IN HEAT (DC, BN)
TWO CUNTS (BN)
TWO GIRLS (DC)
TWO WAY SWINGERS (MI, BN)
TORSO (DC)
ULTRA (PA)
UNCUT (MI)
UNDERFOOT (DC)
UNDERGRADS (DC)
UNISEX SHOES & BOOTS (BN)
UNITE (BA, DC, BN)
UNITE #23 (BA)
UNREAL PEOPLE (DC)
UP AND COMING (BA, NY)
UP CLOSE & PERSONAL (BN)
UP CLOSE & PERSONAL #7 (BN)
UP HER ASS (BA, PA, BN)
UP HER ASS (BN)
UP MY ASS #3 (DC)
UP THE ASS (NY, BN)
UPDATE #37 (DC, BN)
URGE (BA, DC)
URGENT DESIRES (DC)
URSULA'S LESBIAN LUST (DC, BN)
URSULA (DC, NY)
URSULA'S ANAL FRIENDS (BA, DC, NY)
VANESSA (DC, NY, BN)
VELVET (DC, BN)
VELVET TALKS (DC)
VELVET 2-86 (DC)
VELVET 3-86 (BN)
VERY UNCUT (PA)
VICKIE'S VICES (BA)
VIDEO VIEW (DC)
VIDEO X (BN)
VIDEO X #7 #3 (BA)
VIRGIN LOVE (NY)
VIRGIN PUSSY (BA, DC, BN)
VOLCANIC LOADS (BN)
VOYEUR (BN)
VULGAIRE (DC, BA)
WANNA FUCK (NY, BN)
WATCH ME MASTURBATE (BN)
WATCHING TURNS ME ON (DC, PA)
WATER WORKS #4 #2 (BA)
WAVE RIDERS (BA, DC, BN)
WELCOME HOME FUCKER (BA)
WET BLACK (PA)
WET CUNTS (BA, NY, BN)
WET DREAM (PA)
WET DREAM COME TRUE (BA)
WET LIPS (BA)
WET PUSSY (BN)
WET SHOTS #1 #1 (NY)
WET SNATCH WET TO THE SKIN (BN)
WET, WILD AND BLACK (BA)
WHAM BAM (PA)
WHAM BAM WINDOW WASHERS (PA)
WHAT THE FUCK #1 (BN)
WHIPS & ROPE #10 (BA)
WHITE CHICKS LOVE BLACK DICK (BA, NY, BN)
WHITE COCK, BLACK PUSSY (NY)
WHITE IN BLACK (PA, BN)
WHITE MEAT (NY)
WHITE MEAT FOR A BLACK STUD (DC, PA)
WHOPPER KINGS III (PA)
WHOPPERS WORKOUT (BN)
WICKED WOMEN (BN)

WICKED WOMEN #2 #4 (BN)
WICKED WOMEN #3 #1 (BN)
WILD BLACK (BA, PA)
WILD CATS (PA)
WILD IN THE WOODS (NY)
WILD MENAGE (BA, BN)
WILD SCREW (BN)
WILD SCREW AND ANAL TOO (BN)
WILD TEEN (DC)
WILD WEST BOYS (DC, BN)
WILD WEST FUCKERS (DC)
WILD, WET & BLACK (PA)
WILDE WOOD (BN)
WISH (BA)
WOMEN ON WOMEN (PA)
WOMEN TO WOMEN (DC)
WOMEN WHO CRAVE HOT DICK (BA, DC)
WOMEN WHO LOVE BLACK COCK #1 (DC, NY)
WOMEN WHO LOVE BLACK COCK #2 (DC)
WOMEN WHO LOVE CUM (DC, BN)
WOMEN WHO LOVE TO SUCK COCK (DC, NY)
WORKING GIRLS (BA)
WORKING GIRLS NEED LOVE TOO (DC, NY)
WORKLOAD (PA, NY)
WORKOUT BENCH (BN)
WRESTLING MEAT (PA)
X-FILMS (DC)
X-RATED CINEMA (DC)
X-RATED CINEMA 1-86 (DC)
X-RATED COUPLES (DC)
X-RATED COUPLES #5 (BA)
X-RATED FANTASIES (BA)
X-RATED STARS IN ACTION #5 (DC)
X-RATED SWINGERS (DC)
X-RATED VIDEO 10-85 (DC)
XMAS GOODIES (DC)
XXX MOVIE III (DC)
YEARLING (DC)
YEARLING 8 (PA)
YOUNG & BLACK (BA)
YOUNG & HORNY (BN)
YOUNG & HUNGRY TO FUCK (DC, NY)

YOUNG & SHAVED (BN)
YOUNG & VERY HUNG (PA)
YOUNG AND LONELY (BN)
YOUNG BEAVERS #1 (DC, PA, BN)
YOUNG BLACK BEAUTIES (BA)
YOUNG BOX (DC)
YOUNG BUNS, TWATS & TITS (BN)
YOUNG CHINA DOLLS (BA, DC, NY, BN)
YOUNG GIRLS (DC)
YOUNG LOVE (BA)
YOUNG LOVE #17 (BN)
YOUNG LOVE #18 (BA)
YOUNG LOVE #2 (BA)
YOUNG LOVE #9 (BA)
YOUNG MILKY (PA)
YOUNG PUSSY (NY, BN)
YOUNG SHAVERS (BN)
YOUNG SNATCH (NY)
YOUNG, TIGHT AND READY TO FUCK #1 (NY)
YOUR COCK UP MY ASS (DC, PA, BN)
YUMMY BLACK (PA)
100 PAGES OF BIG BEAUTIFUL BOSOMS (DC, BN)
100 PAGES OF EATING PUSSY (DC, NY, BN)
100 PAGES OF EATING PUSSY #2 (NY)
100 PAGES OF FUCKING & SUCKING (PA, BN)
100 PAGES OF URSULA (DC, BN)
13-1/2 (DC)
19 AND BOUND (BN)
1986 DIRECTORY OF ADULT FILMS (BN)
1986 DIRECTORY OF ADULT FILMS #2 #10 (BA)
2 DICKS FOR TERRY (DC)
200 PICTURES OF COCK SHOTS (DC)
230 PICTURES OF EROTIC LUSTFUL LOVERS (DC)
250 PAIRS OF LEGS (DC)
299 SHAVED PUSSYS (NY)
3 ON 1 (PA)
300 YOUNG DARLING (NY)
301 BIG TITS (BN)
4 WAY SEX FESTIVAL (BN)
69 (BA)
69 HOT PANTIES (BA, BN)
69 LESBIANS MUNCHING (DC, BN)

PAPERBACK BOOKS

ABBIE'S LESBIAN LOVE (DC)
A BEDSIDE ODYSSEY (DC)
ABNORMAL YOUTH (DC)
ABUSED, DEFILED AND DEGRADED (BA)
ABUSED RUNAWAY (BN, DC)
ABUSED SLAVE (BN)
ABUSED TV (BN)
ABUSED VIETNAMESE VIRGINS (BC)
ABUSING THEIR SERVANTS (BN)
AC/DC PARTY SWINGER (DC)
ACTION ON THE STREET (BA)
ADULTERY—A TURN ON (PA)
AFTER DINNER NYMPH (DC)
A GIRL & HER DOG (BN)
ALICE—SEX CRAZED RUNAWAY (DC)
ALL NIGHT ABUSE (BN)
ALL THE WAY IN (DC)
ALL THE WAY IN MOM (BA)
A MOTHER'S LOVING SON (DC)
AMY THE HAPPIEST HOOKER (DC)
AN ADULTERER'S GUIDE (NY)
ANAL COMPULSIVES NEEDING REAR SERVICE (BN)
ANAL REUNION (DC)
ANAL SLAVE (DC)
ANDREW'S BALL SUCKING MOUTH (DC)

APARTMENT HOUSE SWAPPERS (BA)
A PONY FOR DAUGHTER (DC)
ARAB CAPTIVES (BN, DC)
ARMY COCK (BN)
A SIDE ORDER OF SEX (DC)
ASS FUCKING COWBOY (BN)
AUNT BRENDA SEX TUTOR (DC)
A VIRGIN'S SHAME (BN)
A WIFE USED (PA)
BACK DOOR HOUSEWIFE (BN)
BACK DOOR TEEN (BN)
BACK ROW TRAMPS (BN)
BACKSEAT TEASE (DC)
BACK WOODS ANIMAL FUN (BN)
BAD LITTLE GOOD GIRL (BN)
BALL BUSTER (DC)
BALLING AUNT (PA)
BARBARA (BN)
BARRY'S NEW BRA (DC)
BATTERED BRIDE (BN)
BEACH BOY STUDS (BN)
BED TO BED BONNIE (DC)
BED TO BED DEBBIE (DC)
BETTY'S ANIMAL LOVER (DC)
BIG BUTCH BROTHER (DC)

BIG RIG BALL LICKER (DC)
BIG TITS, HOT COCK (DC)
BIKER BRUTES (BN)
BIKER'S HOT OIL BOY (BN)
BISEXUAL NYMPHO (PA)
BISEXUAL SISTER (BN)
BIZARRE SISTERS IN SUBMISSION (BN)
BLACK HEAT (BN)
BLACK LEATHER BIKER (DC)
BLACK LEATHER DOLL (DC)
BLACK LESBIAN TEACHER (BN)
BLACK MARINE D.I. (BN)
BLACK STEPFATHER (BN)
BLOW HARD SECRETARY (DC)
BONDAGE BRAT (DC)
BONDAGE FETISH (BN)
BONDAGE FOR THREE WIVES (BA)
BOSS TRUCKER (BN)
BOTH WAYS BABY DOLL (DC)
BOUND FOR SEX (BN)
BOUND LESBIAN (BA)
BOUND TO PAIN (DC)
BOUND, WHIPPED & RAPED SCHOOLGIRLS (BN)
BOY CONVICT (DC)
BOYS AT SEA (BN)
BOYS GANG ORGY (DC)
BOYS IN BEIRUT (BN)
BOY SLAVES FOR SHERRY (DC)
BOYS ON THE BEACH (DC)
BRAWLING CUNTS (BN)
BREAKING IN A RECRUIT (DC)
BREAK MY CHERRY (DC)
BRENDA'S EAGER SURRENDER (DC)
BRENDA'S LUST FULFILLED (DC)
CALDWELL HIGH—LUST FACTORY (DC)
CAMPAIGN GIRL (DC)
CAMPING SEX CLUB (BN)
CAMPUS GANG BANG (BN)
CANDY KANE (DC)
CARNAL ECSTASY (DC)
CAT GIRL IN HEAT (DC)
CATHY'S SORE BOTTOM (DC)
CELEBRITY SEX SCANDALS (DC)
CENTER FIELD CATCHER (DC)
CHAIN WHIPPED BRIDE (DC)
CHAINED SLAVE SECRETARY (PA)
CHAINED UP BABYSITTER (DC)
CHAINED YOUTH: GIRLS IN BONDAGE (DC)
CHEERLEADER GANG BANG (BN)
CHEERLEADER'S LOVING PET (BN)
CHEERLEADER WITH HOT PANTS (BN, NY)
CHICKEN FARM (BN)
CHILD BRIDE (BN)
CLIMBING THE RANKS (DC)
COCK STARVED NYMPHO (BN)
COCK SUCKIN' WIFE (DC)
COME JOIN THE FUN (DC)
COME WITH SISTER (DC)
COMING OUT TOGETHER (BN)
CONFIDENTIAL SEX SURVEY (DC)
CONVENT OF SATAN (BN)
CONVICT LESBIAN (DC)
CORALIE CAMELOT (NY)
COUNTRY GIRL (PA)
COUSIN BLEW THEM ALL (DC)
COUSIN IN CHAINS (DC)
COWBOY CHICKEN (BN)
CRAZY FOR ROPE (BN, DC)
CREAMY VIRGIN NYMPH (BN)
CULT OF LUST (BN, DC)
CUNT SUCKING GIRLS (BN)

DADDY'S HOT DAUGHTER (DC)
DADDY TASTES SO SWEET (BN)
DAD GOES DOWN (BN, DC)
DAD + DAUGHTER = ECSTASY (NY)
DAMIEN: THE YOUNG YEARS (DC)
DAMIEN II: THE YOUTH (BN)
DANNY DOES (DC)
DARLING, DARLING NIECE (DC)
DAUGHTER LEARNS FAST (BA)
DAUGHTER LEARNS HOW (DC)
DAUGHTER LOVES DOGGY FUN (MI)
DAUGHTER LOVES IT (DC)
DAUGHTER'S FIRST TIME (BN)
DAUGHTER'S HOT URGES (DC)
DAUGHTER'S NEW HOT FAMILY (BN, DC)
DAUGHTER'S PEEPING FUN (DC)
DEBBIE'S DINGE BINGE (DC)
DECK THE BITCH (BA)
DEEP THROAT DAUGHTER (DC)
DEEP THROAT ECSTASY (NY)
DESERT GANG BANG (BN)
DESPERATELY SUCKING TEACHER (BN)
DEVIL WOMAN'S WHIP (NY)
DINER DOLL (DC)
D.I.'S BIG STICK (DC)
DISCIPLINE LUST (DC)
DOCKSIDE DICKS (NY)
DOG ACT (BN, DC)
DOGGIE GOES DOWN (BN)
DOG HOUSE DAUGHTER (BN)
DOG LOVING DAUGHTER (DC)
DOING WHAT SHE DOES BEST (NY)
DONNA'S SECRET (DC)
DORIS' OLDER LOVER (DC)
DOROTHY: SLAVE TO PAIN (DC)
DOWN ON DAD (DC)
DRAG QUEEN MARINE (DC)
DRIPPING DYKES (DC)
EAGER HOT BUTT (DC)
EAGER NAKED DAUGHTER (BN, DC)
EASY COME, EASY FLOW (NY)
EASY OFFICE GIRLS (BN, DC)
ECSTASY BETWEEN YOUNG & OLD (BN)
ENRICHING HER DESIRE (NY)
EROTIC LINGERIE: SATIN, LEATHER & LACE (BN)
EVER READY RANDI (DC)
FACTORY SWAPPER (NY)
FAMILY CAPTIVES (DC)
FANNY LOVING GIRLS (DC)
FINDING TRUE LUST (DC)
FIREBALLER (DC)
FOOT LOOSE & SEXY (DC)
FORCED INTO SPANKING (DC)
FRANK'S OVERSIZED AUNT (DC)
FRATHOUSE INITIATION (BN)
FRAT HOUSE LOVERS (BN)
FRESHMAN CLASS STUD (BN, DC)
FRESHMAN CLASS VIRGIN (BN)
FRESHMEN ON THE FLOOR (BN)
FUCK CRAZY WIVES (DC)
GAG THE BITCH (BN, NY)
GANG BANG BROTHERS (DC)
GANG BANG TEENS (BN)
GANGS ALL HERE (MI)
GARY & SHEILA (DC)
GAS JOCKEY STUDS (BN, DC)
GHETTO GIRLS (BN)
GHETTO SHE MALE (BN)
G.I. BLOW (DC)
GINNY'S DESIRE FOR LUST (DC)
GIRLS WHO CAN'T SAY NO (DC)

GIRLS WHO SUBMIT (DC)
GIRLS WITH KINKY NEEDS (DC)
GLORIA'S NEW CONQUEST (DC)
GOING ALL THE WAY (BN)
GOING DOWN ON HER DAD (DC)
GOLDEN GIRLS (DC)
GOOD GIRL GONE BAD (DC)
GRETA'S DUNGEON ORDEAL (BN)
HARD AT WORK (DC)
HARD BLACK STUD (DC)
HARD COCK KILLERS (DC)
HARDCORE HUSTLER (DC)
HARD TO PLEASE (DC)
HARD TRAINING (DC)
HARRY GETS THE SISTERS (BN)
HEATHER IS A NYMPHO (BN)
HEAVY HUNG RECRUIT (BN, DC)
HELD FOR SEDUCTION (NY, DC)
HELEN'S HIDDEN URGE (DC)
HE-MAN SISSY (DC)
HER FLAIR FOR AFFAIRS (BA)
HER HIDDEN TREASURES (BN)
HER HOT TITS (BN)
HER HUSBAND CRAWLS (BN)
HER KINKY NEEDS (DC)
HER MEAN STEPMOTHER (DC)
HER NEIGHBOR'S SEXY WAYS (DC)
HER SENSUOUS SEARCH (DC)
HER STRANGE AUNT (BN)
HIGH SCHOOL BUDDIES (BN)
HIGH SCHOOL COMERS (BA)
HIGH SCHOOL NYMPHS (DC)
HIGH SCHOOL TRANSVESTITES (DC)
HIGH SOCIETY SLUT (DC)
HIS DAUGHTER'S BIG TITS (BN, NY)
HIS GIRLFRIEND'S FATHER (NY)
HITCHHIKING BOY (BN)
HOLDING WENDY DOWN (BN, DC)
HOLLYWOOD BALL BUSTER (BN)
HOLLYWOOD HUSTLER (BN)
HOLLYWOOD TRANSVESTITE (BN)
HOOKER IN PIGTAILS (DC)
HORNY BALLING BABYSITTER (DC)
HORNY BIG SISTER (PA)
HORNY CHEATING WIFE (NY)
HORNY DARLING NIECE (DC)
HORNY FAMILY SUCKERS (NY)
HORNY HOLY ROLLER FAMILY (BN)
HORNY LITTLE NIECES (BN)
HORNY NEWLYWEDS (DC)
HORNY PEEPING FAMILY (DC)
HORNY SCHOOLGIRLS (PA)
HORNY WIDOWED SISTER (BN, NY)
HOSPITAL ORGY (BN)
HOSTAGE NURSE (BN)
HOT & WILLING DAUGHTER (DC)
HOT ASSED COACH (DC)
HOT BED LIBRARIAN (DC)
HOT CHAINS, COLD WIFE (DC)
HOT CHEERLEADERS (PA)
HOT CHICKEN TAKE ONE (DC)
HOT COCK NAZI MASTER (BN)
HOT COMING NIECE (DC)
HOT CROTCH KATHY (DC)
HOT DEAN HUNG HUNK (NY)
HOT EASY SIS (BN, DC)
HOT FAMILY LOVERS (DC)
HOT FOR BLACK FLESH (BN)
HOT FUN SCHOOLGIRL (DC)
HOT HUNK JOCK (BA)
HOT IN THE HAMPTONS (DC)

HOT LIVE-IN BABYSITTER (PA)
HOT MODEL (BN)
HOT MOUTH DEB (BN)
HOT MOUTHED VIRGIN (DC)
HOT NEW DAUGHTER (BN)
HOT SCHOOLGIRL SISTER (BN, DC)
HOT SHORTS (BN)
HOT STUFF (DC)
HOT TO TROT BETSY (DC)
HOT WIDE SPREAD DAUGHTER (DC)
HUMILIATE ME (DC, NY)
HUNGRY TEEN (DC)
HUNKY CRUISER (DC)
I AM CURIOUS BLUE (DC)
ILLICIT PLEASURE (DC)
INCEST MOMMY (NY)
IN HOT PURSUIT (DC)
INITIATION NIGHT (DC)
IN PAIN (PA)
IRON ROD LUKE (BN)
ISLAND OF INCEST (BA)
ISLAND OF LUST (PA)
IT'S ALL OVER (DC)
I WANT ALL NIGHT ABUSE (BN, DC)
JAKE GETS EVERYTHING (NY)
JANET (BN)
JANICE'S SENSUAL DELIGHTS (NY)
JAPANESE SADIST DUNGEON (BN)
JAP SADIST'S VIRGIN CAPTIVES (BN)
JAP SADIST'S VIRGIN SLAVE (BN)
JIM & SUSAN (DC)
JOCK IN A G-STRING (DC)
JOCK RAPE (BN)
JODIE'S LUST (DC)
JOHN'S KINKY MOM (BN)
JOSEPHINE'S SUBMISSION (BN)
JUICY HOT MOM (DC)
JUVENILE SLUTS (BN)
KAREN A LOVING DAUGHTER (DC)
KATHY'S CONFESSION (DC)
KATHY'S DARK DESIRES (NY)
KAY WANTON WIFE (DC)
KINKY CALL GIRL (BN)
KINKY SEX (MI)
KNEEL ASSHOLE (NY)
KNEELING FOR DADDY (DC)
LADY HAS BALLS (DC)
LARRY SEX MASTER (BA)
LAURIE'S HORNY SCHEMES (NY)
LAVENDER TRIANGLE MURDERS (DC)
LAWFULLY WEDDED NYMPH (NY)
LEATHER LICKING SLUT (DC)
LEATHER MASTER (DC)
LEE'S EASY TO EXCITE (NY)
LEFT ON HER OWN (DC)
LERAE'S WHITE TRICKS (BN)
LESBIAN DILDO SLAVE (BN)
LESBIAN IN LEATHER (BN)
LESBIAN JOURNAL: THE MAKING OF A LESBIAN
   (BN, DC)
LESBIAN JOURNAL: XZ (DC)
LESBIAN LIEUTENANT (DC)
LESBIAN MOTHER (BN)
LET'S GO LUST (DC)
LETTING HERSELF GO (NY)
LEWD INTERLUDES (DC)
LIBERTEENS—JANET (BN)
LIBERTEENS—LUCY (DC)
LIBERTEENS—MARY (BN)
LICKING HER BALLS (DC)
LICK IT, SIS (DC)

LIMITED EDITION (DC)
LORINDA (BN)
LORI'S ANGUISH (DC)
LOVERS IN PARADISE (DC)
LOVERS ON THE SIDE (NY)
LOVING HER BROTHER (DC)
LOVING IT (DC)
LOVING THE COACH (BN)
LOW LIFE BRUTES (NY)
LUMBERJACKS LITTLE BROTHER (BN)
LUST AROUND THE CLOCK (DC)
LUST AT SCHOOL (NY)
LUST FOR BLACK FLESH (BN)
LUSTFUL PLEASURES (DC)
LUST IN THE WILD (BA)
LUST KNOWS NO RULES (BA)
LUST LOVERS (DC)
LUST UNLEASHED (NY, DC)
LUSTY PAULA (DC)
MACHO MAN IN HEELS (BA)
MADAME MADE HIM CRAWL (BN)
MADE TO YIELD (DC)
MAKE HER YELL (DC)
MAKING MOTHER SUCK (DC)
MANY LOVES (DC)
MASSAGE PARLOR SECRETS (DC)
MELANIE'S TORMENT (DC)
MIKE'S DOMINATING WAYS (DC)
MISS LEE EASY LAY (DC)
MOIST FOR ANY MAN (DC)
MOIST FOR BLACK COCK (BN)
MOIST LITTLE RICH GIRL (DC)
MOM AND ME (BA)
MOM AND THE TWINS (NY)
MOM, DAD AND BECKY (BN)
MOM DOES IT BEST (DC)
MOM LOVES HOT DOGS (PA)
MOMMA'S SLAVE BOY (BN)
MOMMY'S BOY LOVERS (DC)
MOM MY TEACHER (DC)
MOM'S DOGGY DAYS (BN)
MOM'S GOLDEN SHOWER NIGHTS (DC)
MOM'S HOT & HORNY KIDS (DC)
MOM'S HOT SUCKER (DC)
MOM'S INCEST URGES (DC)
MOM'S SWEET THIGHS (BN)
MONEY MAKES THE LUST GO AROUND (NY)
MOTEL MAIDEN (DC)
MOTHER READY FOR ALL (DC)
MOTHER'S HOT SUCKING (PA)
MOTHER'S LAP DOG (BN)
MOTHER'S LOVING BEAT ALL (DC)
MOTHER'S PRIVATE NEED (NY)
MOTHER'S SPECIAL NEEDS (DC)
MRS. BARRETT'S BLACK BOYS (BN)
MUSCLE BEACH BRUTES (BN)
MUSCLE MEN (BN)
MY COUSIN, MY WIFE (BA)
MY SISTER, MY LOVER (DC)
MY WIFE THE NYMPH (DC)
NAKED HORNY WIFE (DC)
NAKED NAUGHTY NIECE (DC)
NAKED TEEN ON A LEASH (BN, DC)
NAKED WET WIFE (PA)
NAM RECRUIT (BN, DC)
NAUGHTY FAMILY ORGY (DC)
NAUGHTY FAMILY URGES (BN)
NAUGHTY SISTER IN HEAT (DC)
NAUGHTY SPREAD SISTER (DC)
NAZI ABUSE (BN)
NAZI DUNGEON SLAVE (BN)

NAZI LUST (DC)
NAZI MASTERS (BN)
NAZI SEX SLAVE (BN)
NAZI SLAVE (BN, DC)
NEEDING BLACK COCK (DC)
NEW BOY ON THE STREET (BN, DC)
NEW KID IN PRISON (BN)
NIECE WITHOUT PANTIES (DC)
NIGHT OF AGONY (DC)
NIGHTS OF MALTA (DC)
NIGHTS WITH DADDY (BN)
NIGHT TIME NYMPH (PA)
NINA'S BREAK IN (BN, DC, MI)
NO HOLDING OUT (DC)
NO HOLES BARRED (DC)
NOTHING SHORT OF PASSION (DCC)
NURSE IN DISTRESS (DC)
NURSES' BEDSIDE SKILLS (DC)
NYMPH IN FULL GLORY (DC)
NYMPHO HUNGER (DC)
NYMPHO MOTHER'S INCEST OBSESSION (BN)
NYMPH'S LOVE NEST (NY)
OFF CAMERA ACTION (DC)
OF THEE I SWING (DC)
OIL RIG RAMROD (BN, DC)
ONE FINAL ORGY (DC)
ONE MORE FOR THE ROAD (DC)
ON THE MAKE (NY)
OPEN BUTT WELDER (BA)
ORGY AFTERNOON (DC)
ORGY IN UNIFORM (DC)
ORGY NIECE (PA)
OVER DADDY'S KNEE (DC)
OVERHEATED MOTHER (NY)
PANIC IN PRISON (DC)
PANTHOLOGY TREE (DC)
PANTIES FOR DADDY (DC)
PARK AVENUE BITCH (BN)
PASS AROUND PLAYGIRL (DC)
PASSION AND TEACHER (PA)
PEEPING MOTHER & DAUGHTER (DC, NY)
PEEPING SISTERS (DC)
PENTHOUSE SHIT (BN)
PIANO BAR PICKUP (BN)
P.I.'s BIG STICK (BN)
PILAR'S FRENCH TOUCH (BN, DC)
PLAYING THE FIELD (NY)
PLEASURE FOR EVERYONE (DC)
PLEASURES REVEALED (NY)
POPPING NANCY'S CORK (DC)
PORNO PUSSIES (MI)
POUND THAT PUSSY (BN, DC)
P.O.W. SEX SLAVE (BN)
PRESCRIPTION FOR PUSSY (DC)
PRETTY PANTY MARINE (BN)
PROWLING HOUSEWIFE (DC)
PUNISHED NAUGHTY SCHOOLGIRL (BN)
PUNISHING HIS WIFE & DAUGHTER (BN)
PUNK HUSTLER (BN)
PUSSY RAMMERS (NY)
PUSSY SLAVES (BN)
RAMMED, CRAMMED SISTER (PA)
RAPED BY ARAB TERRORISTS (BN)
RAPED STEPDAUGHTER (BN)
RAPE FANTASY (BN)
RAPE HEAT (BN)
REAR ATTACK (BN)
REAR END TEACHER (DC)
REBEL RAPE (DC)
RENT A NUDE MODEL (DC)
RICH BITCH'S NIGGER (BN)

RICH BITCH'S WET SLIT (BN, DC)
RICH GIRL'S BLACK STUD (BA)
RICH TRASHY BITCH (DC)
RICK'S BIG STICK (BN, DC)
RITA'S BLACK FETISH (BN)
ROMEO & ROMEO (BN, DC)
RUB A BIG STUD (BN, DC)
RUTH'S WILD ORGY (DC)
SALLY'S ANAL PUNISHMENT (DC)
SALLY'S BIG BROTHERS (BN, NY)
S & M BIKE STUD (BN)
S & M CLUB RAID (NY)
SAN QUENTIN SLAVEBOY (DC)
SCAT BOY (DC)
SCAT SLAVERS (PA)
SCHOOLGIRL SUGAR DADDIES (BN)
SCHOOL SUGAR DADDIES (BN)
SCHOOL YARD SLUT (BN)
SCRATCHING SLUTS (BN)
SEA WEARY, SEX HUNGRY (BN)
SECOND HONEYMOON (DC)
SENSUAL RELATIONS (NY)
SENSUOUS STUDENT COUNSELOR (BA)
SENTENCED TO SEX (DC)
SERVING HER DAD (DC)
SEX BEHIND THE BARN (DC)
SEX FILLED DAYS (NY)
SEX GUIDE FOR THE SINGLE GIRL (DC)
SEX MARKS THE SPOT (DC)
SEX SHARING PAIRS (DC)
SEX SLAVE DAUGHTERS (BN)
SEX SWAMP CAMP (DC)
SEX TOY DAUGHTER (BN)
SEX WITH A NURSE (DC)
SEXY STUDENT BODIES (NY)
SHARON (BN)
SHEER TORTURE (DC)
SHE MADE HIM DO IT (BN)
SHE-MALE IN BONDAGE (DC)
SHE-MALE M.D. (DC)
SHE-MALE SLUT (BN)
SHE MARRIED FOR LUST (DC)
SHERRY (BN)
SHIPBOARD SWING-FEST (DC)
SHOWER ROOM ORGY (BN)
SIBLING SEX SWING (NY)
SISTER BLOWS BIG ONES (DC)
SISTER'S HOT SECRET (DC)
SLANT-EYED SAVAGES (NY)
SLAVE BROOD FARM (BA)
SLAVE GIRL & THE LASH (BN)
SLAVE OF DESIRE (DC)
SLAVE TO A SADIST (BN)
SLAVE TO THE S.S. (BN)
SLAVE TO THE WHIP MISTRESS (DC)
SLAVE WIFE SUCKS (BN)
SLUTTY LITTLE SUSAN (BN)
SLUTTY STREET BITCH (DC)
SMALL TOWN AFFAIR (DC)
SMALL TOWN'S BAD GIRL (BA)
SMALL TOWN SISTERS (BN)
SOCCER FIELD STUDS (DC)
SOCIETY SUCKER (BN)
SOFT SUCKING LIPS (BN)
SOMEWHERE OVER THE ORGY (BA)
SOVIET SADIST'S SLAVE (BN)
SOVIET SEX SLAVES (PA)
SPANKED DAUGHTER (BN)
SPANKED DAUGHTERS (BN)
SPANKED SON (BN)
SPECIAL REPORTS—TWISTED TWINS (DC)

SPREAD ANGEL (BN)
SPREAD ASS SURFER (DC)
SPREAD BLACK BEAUTY (BN)
SPREAD FOR HER PET (BN)
SPREAD SCHOOLGIRL (BN)
SPREAD WIDER MOM (DC)
SPUNKY LAD (BN)
STACKED HOT MOM (DC)
STARS IN THEIR EYES (BN)
STEPFATHER'S SLAVE (BN)
STOCK CAR (BN)
STOCK CAR SADIST (DC)
STOCK CAR STUD (BN)
STRADELLA (DC)
STREET BOY (BN)
STUDENT VICTIMS OF RED TORTURE (BN, DC)
STUDLORN COLUMN (DC)
STUD REPAIRMAN (NY)
STUD SISSY (DC)
SUBMISSIVE MISS (DC)
SUCK EAGER DAUGHTER (DC)
SUCK HARDER COUSIN (PA)
SUCKIN' AMY (BN)
SUCKING BALLING WIFE (BN)
SUCK LOVING MOTHER (BN)
SUE'S SEX NEEDS (DC)
SUNSET STRIP RUNAWAY (BN, DC)
SUPER STUD FOR HIRE (DC)
SUPER SUCKER (DC)
SWAP FEST GALORE (BN)
SWAPPER (MI)
SLURPING PUSSY (BN)
SLUTS OF TUCKERVILLE HIGH SCHOOL (BN)
SLUTTISH DAUGHTER (BN)
SWAPPING SLUTS (NY)
SWAPPING SURFERS (DC)
SWEDISH SEX TRIP (DC)
SWEET SPREAD TEEN (DC)
SWITCH HITTER SUMMER (BN)
SWITCH HITTING PITCHER (BN, NY)
TAKE IT, WIMP (DC)
TAKE ME HARD (DC)
TAKING IT ALL (DC, NY)
TAKING TANYA'S CHERRY (BN)
TANYA'S TOUCH (DC)
TAUGHT SEX AND REMEMBERING (DC)
TEACHER & THE TEAM (DC)
TEACHER LOVES IT ALL (DC, NY)
TEACHER'S BAD BOY (BN)
TEACHER'S RAPE ATTACK (BN)
TEAM CIRCLE JERK (DC)
TEEN D.J. (BN)
TEEN FETISH FANTASIES (DC)
TEEN IN TERROR (DC)
TEEN NYMPHOS: NEEDING IT MORE (BN)
TEEN RAPE ORGY (BN, DC)
TEENS BRUTAL ORDEAL (MI)
TEEN SEX HUNGER (DC)
TEEN SEX SLAVES OF SAIGON (DC)
TEENS IN BONDAGE (BN)
TEENS IN HEAT: TAKING ALL COMERS (BN)
TEENS IN RESTRAINT (BN)
TEEN STREET SLUTS (BN)
TEEN SWINGER (BN)
TEEN TEASES SHOWING ALL (BN)
TEEN WHIP MISTRESS (DC)
THE BOYS AND MABEL (DC)
THE CAPTAINS HOT ROD (BN, DC, NY)
THE DOBERMAN NEXT DOOR (BN)
THE EROTIC INSTRUCTOR (DC)
THE FAMILY'S HOT NIGHTS (DC)

THE GOVERNOR'S WILD WIFE (BN)
THE JAGGED EDGE (DC)
THE KID NEXT DOOR (BN)
THE LANDLADY GETS HERS (BN)
THE LUXURIES OF LUST (DC)
THE MASTER'S REVENGE (BN)
THE MIRROR CHRONICLES (DC)
THE NEIGHBOR'S KIDS (MI)
THE NUNS ANIMAL FUN (NY)
THE ORAL URGE (DC)
THE PASSION PAGEANT (DC)
THE PAYOLA GAME (DC)
THE PRIDE & POWER (DC)
THE RAVISHED COED (BN)
THE SCHOOLGIRL'S RAPE NIGHT (BN)
THE SCHOOL TEASE (BN)
THE SMALL ROOMS OF PARIS (DC)
THE SPEED BUNNIES (DC)
THE UNFULFILLED HOUSEWIFE (DC)
THE WANDERING WIVES (DC)
THE WAYWARD TEENAGER (BA)
THE WILLING HOUSEWIFE (DC)
THEY ALL MAKE MOTHER (DC)
THE YOUNG COACH (BN)
THREE CHEERS FOR SEX (DC)
THRUST INTO PLEASURE (NY)
TIED & TORMENTED (DC)
TIED UP TITS (BN, DC, NY)
TIGHT END (DC)
TIM'S LOVING MOTHER (DC)
TONGUE FUCKED ASSHOLE (DC)
TOO YOUNG (DC)
TOO YOUNG TO BE WED (BN)
TOP NOTCH NYMPH (DC)
TORTURE HUNGER (BA)
TOTAL SURRENDER (BN, DC, NY)
TOUGH CHICKEN (BA)
TRAINED TEEN SLAVE (DC)
TRAINED TO BE CHAINED (DC)
TRAINING THEIR MEN (BN)
TRANSVESTITE ATHLETE (DC)
TRANSVESTITE BRIDEGROOM (BN)
TRANSVESTITE LESBIAN (BN)
TRANSVESTITE MANIA (BN)
TRANSVESTITE NEXT DOOR (BN)
TRANSVESTITE QUARTERBACK (DC)
TRANSVESTITE SECRETARY (BN)
TRANSVESTITE SEDUCTRESS (BN)
TRANSVESTITE TORMENT (BN)
TRANSVESTITE TV STAR (NY)
TRANSVESTITE BONDAGE PLAYMATE (DC)
TREAT ME ROUGH (DC)
TRIAL OF THE VIRGIN CAPTIVE (BN)
TRUCKER'S ALL NIGHT SLUT (BN, DC)
TRUCKER STUD (BN)
TURKISH JAIL TERROR (NY)
TURNED ON DOCTORS (DC)
TWIN BROTHERS IN LOVE (BN)
2 HORNY SISTERS (DC)

TWO HOT HORNY BABYSITTERS (DC)
TWO NAUGHTY HORNY MOMS (DC)
TWO SUCKING NIECES (DC)
TYING UP REBECCA
UMMM! MOM'S A HOT ONE (BN)
UNCLE DON'S SECRET (DC)
UNCLE'S DESIRES SATISFIED (DC)
UNWILLING SEX SLAVE (BN)
UP ALL NIGHT (NY)
UP THE YING YANG (DC)
USED BY THE GESTAPO (BN)
VERY HORNY DAUGHTER (PA)
VICKY'S COCK FUCKING THROAT (DC)
VIRGIN CHEERLEADER'S LUST (BN)
VIRGIN STUDENT NURSE (DC)
VIRGIN'S BLACK STUD (BN)
VIRGIN SLAVE'S TORMENT (BN, DC)
VIRGIN STUDENTS (BN)
VOYEUR WIFE ON VACATION (DC)
WANDA (DC)
WANDA AND THE WHIP (BN)
WET BLACK SLITS (BN, DC)
WET HORNY MOM (DC)
WET, SPREAD & READY (DC)
WET SPREAD SHOW OFF (DC)
WET TEEN LEZZIE (BN)
WHIPPED & CHAINED COUSIN (DC)
WHIPPED COUSINS (BN)
WHIPPED WIVES (PA)
WHITE MASTERS: BLACK SLAVE GIRLS (BN)
WICKED LITTLE BITCH (DC)
WIDOW KAREN (DC)
WIDOW ON THE PROWL (BN)
WIFE PUNISHERS (DC)
WIFE'S PUPPY LOVE (BN)
WIFE'S SEX SEARCH (DC)
WILD & KINKY RN (DC)
WILD EASY DAUGHTER (DC, NY)
WILD HOT BRIDE (DC)
WILD SCHOOL GIRLS (BN)
WILD SIN PARK (DC)
WILD TEEN FOR HIRE (DC)
WILD VIRGIN BABYSITTER (DC)
WILLING STUDENT (BN)
WINDY'S STRAYING LUST (DC)
WITH THIS RING I THEE LUST (NY)
YOUNG & HORNY WIDOW (BN)
YOUNG & IN LOVE (NY)
YOUNG ASS LOVERS (DC)
YOUNG EASY & WILLING (BN)
YOUNG GIRLS WHO LIKE IT KINKY (BN)
YOUNG LEGS WIDE OPEN (DC)
YOUNG MOIST & BLACK (BN)
YOUNG MOIST LESBIAN (DC)
YOUNG SLIT SLURPERS (BN)
YOUNG TRACY GETS IT (BA)
YOUNG WIFE, HOT WIFE (BN)
YOU'VE COME A LONG WAY BARBARA (DC)

FILMS

A COMING OF ANGELS (DC)
A FEW GOOD MEN (DC)
A GIRL LIKE THAT (DC)
A LACY AFFAIR (DC)
A LICENSE TO THRILL (DC, PH, BA)
A LITTLE DYNASTY (DC)
A LITTLE SEX IN THE NIGHT (DC)
A MARRIED MAN (DC)
A MATTER OF SIZE (DC)

A NIGHT AT HALSTEAD'S (DC)
A NIGHT FOR LOVERS (DC)
A NIGHT TO REMEMBER (DC)
A STAR IS BORN (DC)
A TASTE OF CHERRY (DC)
A TOUCH OF SEX (DC, BA)
A WINTER STORY (DC)
A WINTER'S TALE (DC)
A WOMAN'S TORMENT (DC)

A.W.O.L. (DC)
ABDUCTED AND TRAINED (DC)
ADAM & CO—MODERN MEN/MODERN TOYS (DC)
ADAM/FORESKIN FANTASY #1 (DC)
ADAM/FORESKIN FANTASY #2 (DC)
ADULT MOVIE BLOOPERS (DC)
ADULT 45 (DC)
ADVENTURE IN SAN FENLEU (DC)
AEROBISEX GIRLS (DC)
AFTERNOONER (DC)
AGE OF CONSENT (DC)
ALEXANDRIA (DC)
ALEXIS' SLAVE LESSONS (DC)
ALL AMERICAN BOYS (DC)
ALL AMERICAN GIRLS (DC)
ALL AMERICAN GIRLS IN HEAT (DC)
ALL AMERICAN SUPERBITCHES (DC)
ALL OF ME (DC)
ALL THE ACTION (DC, MI)
ALL THE DEVIL'S ANGELS (DC)
ALL THE RIGHT BOYS (DC)
ALL THE WAY IN (DC)
ALL TIED UP (DC)
ALLEY CATS (DC)
ALWAYS READY FOR FOUR (DC)
AMANDA BY NIGHT (DC)
AMATEUR COED (DC)
AMBER AROUSED (DC)
AMERICAN BABYLON (DC)
AMERICAN CREAM (DC)
AMERICAN DESIRE (DC)
AMOUR (DC)
AN UNNATURAL ACT (DC, MI)
ANAL ANNIE & THE WILLING HUSBANDS (DC)
ANAL ANNIE JUST CAN'T SAY NO (DC)
ANAL ANNIE/BACKDOOR HOUSEWIVES (DC)
ANAL PHABATEN (DC)
ANGEL IN BONDAGE (DC)
ANGEL IN DISTRESS (DC)
ANGEL ON FIRE (DC)
ANGELA THE FIREWORKS WOMAN (DC)
ANIMAL (DC)
ANIMAL IMPULSE (DC)
ANNA OBSESSED (DC)
ANOTHER ROLL IN THE HAY (DC)
ANYTIME/ANYPLACE (DC)
ANYWHERE/ANYTIME (DC)
ARCADE (DC)
AROUND THE WORLD WITH JOHNNY WADD (DC)
AROUSED (DC)
AUNT PEG (DC)
ASIAN KNIGHTS (DC, BA)
AUDRA'S ORDEAL (DC)
AUNT PEG GOES HOLLYWOOD (DC)
AURORA'S SECRET DIARY (DC)
AUTOBIOGRAPHY OF A FLEA (DC)
AVALON CALLING (DC)
AWAKENING OF SALLY (DC)
B.Y.O.B. (DC)
BABE (DC)
BABY BLUE (DC)
BABY CAKES (DC)
BABY DOLL (DC)
BABY FACE (DC)
BABY LOVE AND BEAU (DC)
BABYLON BLUE (DC)
BABYLON GOLD (DC)
BABYSITTER (DC)
BACK ROAD TO PARADISE (DC)
BACK TO SCHOOL (DC)
BACKDOOR ROMANCE (DC)

BAD BAD BOYS (DC)
BAD GIRLS 3 (DC)
BAD MAMA JAMA #3 (DC)
BAD MAMA JAMA #2 (DC)
BAD PENNY (DC)
BARBARA BROADCAST (DC)
BARELY LEGAL (DC)
BATHHOUSE FANTASIES (DC)
BATTLE OF THE STARS (DC)
BAVARIAN CREAM (DC)
BEACHED (DC)
BECOMING MEN (DC)
BEDTIME TALES (DC)
BEDTIME VIDEO #1 (DC)
BEFORE SHE SAYS I DO (DC)
BEHIND THE GREEK DOOR (DC)
BEHIND THE SCENES (DC)
BENEATH THE PALM (DC)
BENEATH THE ULTRA VIXENS (DC)
BEST LITTLE WAREHOUSE IN L.A. (DC)
BEST LITTLE WHOREHOUSE IN SAN FRANCISCO
   (DC, NY)
BEST OF ALEX DERENXY (DC)
BEST OF ATOM (DC)
BEST OF BIZARRE #3 (DC)
BEST OF BIZARRE #4 (DC)
BEST OF BUCKSHOT (DC)
BEST OF DIAMOND #1 (DC)
BEST OF STALLION #1 (DC)
BEST OF STALLION #2 (DC)
BEST OF STALLION VOLUME #3 (DC)
BEST OF STALLION VOLUME #4 (DC)
BEST OF XXX (DC)
BETRAYED (DC)
BETWEEN LOVERS (DC)
BETWEEN THE CHEEKS (DC)
BETWEEN THE SHEETS (DC)
BEVERLY HILLS #6 (DC)
BEVERLY HILLS COP (DC, PH)
BEVERLY HILLS WIVES (DC)
BEYOND DE SADE (DC)
BEYOND HAWAII (DC)
BEYOND TABOO (DC, BA)
BEYOND YOUR WILDEST DREAMS (DC)
BI-COASTAL (DC)
BI-SEXUAL FANTASY (DC)
BIG BABY GAMES (DC)
BIG BAD BERTHA (DC)
BIG BROTHER (DC)
BIG BUSTY BABES VOL. 2 (DC)
BIG BUSTY VIDEO #5/UNCLE GEORGE
BIG BUSTY VIDEO NO. 3 (DC)
BIG MELONS #4 (DC)
BIJOU (DC)
BIMBO HOT BLOODED #1 (DC, BA)
BIRDS AND BEADS (DC, PH)
BIRTHDAY BALL (DC)
BISEXUAL SOLO (DC)
BITCH BUSTERS (DC)
BIZARRE BONDAGE #1 (DC)
BIZARRE BONDAGE #2 (DC)
BIZARRE BONDAGE #3 (DC)
BIZARRE ENCOUNTERS #9 (DC)
BIZARRE FANTASIES (DC)
BIZARRE LIFESTYLES (DC)
BIZARRE MARRIAGE COUNSELOR (DC)
BIZARRE MOODS (DC, NY)
BIZARRE PEOPLE (DC)
BIZARRE SORCERESS (DC)
BIZARRE VIDEO #4 (DC)
BIZARRE WOMEN (DC)

BIZARRE WRESTLING WOMEN (DC)
BIZARRE WRESTLING WOMEN #5 (DC)
BLACK AND WHITE AFFAIR (DC)
BLACK BI-SEXUALS IN L.A. (DC)
BLACK BABY DOLLS (DC)
BLACK BROTHERS (DC)
BLACK BUN BUSTERS (DC)
BLACK DYNASTY (DC)
BLACK FORBIDDEN FANTASIES (DC)
BLACK GARTER (DC)
BLACK HEAT (DC)
BLACK JAILBAIT (DC)
BLACK JAW BREAKERS (DC, BA)
BLACK LESBIAN ORGY (DC)
BLACK LUST (DC, BN)
BLACK LUST #1 (DC)
BLACK LUST #2 (DC, NY)
BLACK LUST #3 (DC, BN)
BLACK LUST #4 (DC, BN)
BLACK LUST #5 (NY)
BLACK MAGIC (NY)
BLACK ON BLACK (DC)
BLACK ON WHITE (DC)
BLACK ORIENT EXPRESS (DC, BA)
BLACK SISTER/WHITE BROTHER (DC)
BLACK TABOO (DC)
BLACK THROAT (DC)
BLACK WORKOUT (DC)
BLACKBALLED (DC)
BLACKS & BLONDES (DC, NY, BA)
BLACKS & BLONDES #2 (DC)
BLACKS & BLONDES #3 (DC)
BLACKS & BLONDES #4 (DC)
BLACKS & BLONDES #6 (DC)
BLACKS & BLONDES #9 (DC)
BLACKS & BLONDES #13 (DC)
BLACKS & BLONDES #14 (DC)
BLACKS & BLONDES #15 (DC)
BLACKS & BLONDES #16 (DC)
BLACKS & BLONDES VOL. #8 (DC)
BLACKS HAVE MORE FUN (DC)
BLONDE ON BLACK (DC)
BLONDE GODDESS (DC)
BLONDE HEAT (DC)
BLONDES DO IT BEST (DC)
BLONDES LIKE IT HOT (DC)
BLONDIE (DC)
BLOOD SUCKING FREAKS (DC)
BLOWN AWAY (DC)
BLUE DREAM LOVER (DC)
BLUE ICE (DC)
BLUE INTERVIEW (DC)
BLUE JEANS (DC)
BLUE RIBBON BLUE (DC)
BLUE VOODOO (DC)
BODACIOUS TATS'S (DC)
BODIES BY JACKIE (DC)
BODIES IN HEAT (DC)
BODY AND FINDER (DC)
BODY HEAT (DC)
BODY LOVE (DC)
BODY SCORCHERS (DC)
BODY TALK (DC)
BOLD OBSESSION (DC)
BONDAGE AT EMITYVILLE (DC)
BONDAGE CLASSICS #3 (DC)
BONDAGE CLASSICS #4 (DC)
BONDAGE CLASSICS #7 (DC)
BONDAGE CLASSICS #8 (DC)
BONDAGE INCEST (DC)
BONDAGE INTERLUDES #1 (DC)

BONDAGE INTERLUDES #2 (DC)
BONDAGE JOB INTERVIEW (DC, BA)
BONDAGE VIDEO #1 (DC)
BONDAGE VIDEO #2 (DC)
BONDAGE VIDEO #3 (DC)
BONDAGE 101 (DC)
BONDAGE 201 (DC)
BONDAGE 301 (DC)
BONDAGE-GRAM (DC)
BOOTS AND SADDLES (DC)
BOOTSIE (DC, MI)
BORDELLO (DC)
BORE 'N' STROKE (DC)
BOTH WAYS (DC)
BOUND (DC)
BOUND & PUNISHED (DC, NY)
BOUND FOR SLAVERY (DC)
BOUND IN LOVE (DC)
BOUND IN WEDLOCK (DC)
BOUND PAIN BY LANA (DC)
BOX ENCOUNTER (DC)
BOYNAPPED (DC)
BOYS CAN'T HELP IT/TOBY ROSS (DC)
BOYS FROM RIVERSIDE DRIVE (DC)
BOYS IN THE BATH (DC, BA)
BOYS IN THE SAND (DC)
BOYS OF MARDI GRAS '84 (DC)
BOYS OF SAN FRANCISCO (DC)
BOYS OF VENICE (DC)
BREAKER BEAUTIES (DC)
BREAKING AND ENTERING (DC)
BREAKING IT (DC)
BREEZY (DC)
BRIAN/GOLDEN BOY VS. CATHERINE THE GREAT
   (DC)
BRIAN'S BOYS (DC)
BRIAN PATCH DOLLS (DC)
BROADCAST BABES (DC)
BROADWAY BOYS (DC)
BROOKE WEST/THE VICIOUS SIDE (DC)
BROTHER LOAD (DC)
BUCKSHOT'S BECOMING MEN (DC)
BUDDING OF BRIE (DC)
BULLET #1 (DC)
BULLET #3 (DC)
BUNNY'S OFFICE FANTASIES (DC)
BURNING DESIRE (DC)
BURNING SNOW (DC)
BUSTER/THE BEST YEARS (DC)
BUTTER ME UP (DC)
C-HUNT (PH)
CABALLERO COLLECTION (NY)
CABALLERO COLLECTION #7 (NY)
CABALLERO PREVIEW #1 (DC)
CAFE FLESH (DC)
CASH ON THE LINE (DC)
CALIFORNIA BOYS (DC)
CALIFORNIA GOLDEN BOYS (DC)
CALIFORNIA SUMMER (DC)
CALIFORNIA SURFER GIRLS (DC)
CALIFORNIA WET (DC)
CALICULA (DC)
CALIVISTA PREVIEW PART 1 (DC)
CALL GIRL (DC)
CALL ME ANGEL SIR (DC)
CANDI STORE (DC)
CANDIDA ROYALE'S FANTASIES (DC, NY)
CANDY LIPS (DC)
CANDY SHIELDS (DC)
CANDY STRIPERS II (DC, BA)
CAPTIVE A STORY OF BONDAGE (BA)

CAPTIVE COEDS (DC)
CAPTIVES (DC)
CARESSES (DC)
CARIBBEAN CRUISING (DC)
CARNAL FANTASIES (DC)
CARNAL OLYMPICS (DC)
CARA LOTT (NY)
CARRIE (DC)
CASEY (DC)
CATHOUSE FEVER (DC)
CAUGHT (DC, NY)
CAUGHT FROM BEHIND II (DC)
CAUGHT FROM BEHIND III (DC)
CELEBRATION (DC)
CENTERFOLD CELEBRITIES #1 (DC)
CENTERFOLD CELEBRITIES #4 (DC)
CENTERFOLD CELEBRITIES #5 (DC)
CENTERFOLD FEVER (DC)
CENTERSPREAD GIRLS (DC)
CENTURION (DC)
CENTURY MINING (DC)
CEREMONY (DC)
CHAIN REACTIONS (DC)
CHAINED (DC, NY)
CHANGING PLACES (DC)
CHAPTER THREE (DC)
CHASTITY JOHNSON (DC)
CHEAP THRILLS (DC)
CHEATING WIVES (NY)
CHEERLEADERS '85 (DC)
CHEROKEE STATION (DC)
CHERRY (DC)
CHERRY BUSTERS (DC)
CHERRY CHEESCAKE (DC)
CHERRY HUSTLERS (DC)
CHICKEN LOVER (NY)
CHINA AND SILK (DC)
CHINA DE SADE (DC, BA)
CHINA GIRLS (DC)
CHINA SISTERS (DC)
CHIP OFF THE OLD BLOCK (DC)
CHOCOLATE CREAM (DC)
CHOCOLATE CANDY (DC)
CHOCOLATE CHERRIES (DC)
CHOCOLATE DELIGHTS (DC)
CHRISTOPHER STREET BLUES (DC)
CISSY (DC)
CITY OF SIN (DC)
CLASS OF '84/PART 2 (DC)
CLASS REUNION (DC)
CLASSICAL ROMANCE (BA)
CLASSICS OF IRVING KLAW #2 (DC)
CLEOPATRA'S BONDAGE REVENGE (DC)
CLIMAX #301 (NY)
CLIMAX #316 (NY)
CLOSE UP (DC)
CO-ED TEASERS (DC)
COCK LUST #2 (NY)
COCK TALES (DC)
COED FEVER (DC)
COFFEE TEA OR ME? (DC, MI)
COLLECTION (PH)
COLLEGE GIRLS IN BONDAGE (DC)
COLOR CLIMAX #282 (NY)
COLOR CLIMAX #284 (NY)
COLOR CLIMAX #303 (NY)
COLOR CLIMAX #313 (DC, NY)
COLOR ME AMBER (BA)
COLT VT-303 (DC)
COLT VT-308 (DC)
COLT VT-311 (DC)

COLT VT-312 (DC)
COME AGAIN DOCTOR (DC)
COME AS YOU ARE (DC)
COME GET ME (DC)
COMING ATTRACTIONS (DC)
COMING SOON (DC)
COMING THROUGH THE WINDOW (DC)
COMING TOGETHER (DC)
COMPANIONS (DC, NY)
COMPUTER GIRLS (DC)
CONFESSIONS OF A CANDYSTRIPER (DC)
CONFESSIONS OF A NYMPH (DC)
CONFESSIONS OF A TEENAGER (DC)
CONFIDENTIAL CASE HISTORIES (DC)
CONSENTING ADULTS (DC)
CORPORAL (DC)
CORPORATE ASSETS (DC)
CORRUPTION (DC)
COTTONTAIL CLUB (DC)
COUNTRY GIRL (DC)
COUPLE ON A LEASH (DC, NY)
COUPLES (DC)
COUSIN BUCK (DC)
COUSINS (DC)
COVER GIRL (DC, BA)
COVERBOY (DC, BA)
COWGIRLS IN CHAINS (DC)
CRACKED ICE (DC)
CRAM COURSE (DC)
CREAM PUFF (DC, BA)
CREME DE BANANA (DC)
CREME DE COCOA (BA)
CREME D'FEMME/VOL 1 (DC)
CRIME DOES PAY (DC)
CRY FOR CINDY (DC)
CUM SHOT (NY)
CUMMING LOVERS (DC)
CUMMING OF AGE (DC)
CUNT II (BA)
CUPIDS ARROW (DC)
CURIOSITY EXCITED THE KAT (DC)
CURIOUS (DC)
DADDY DEAREST (DC)
DADDY DOESN'T KNOW (DC)
DADDY'S DAY OF RECKONING (DC)
DADDY'S GIRLS (DC)
DADDY'S LITTLE GIRLS (DC)
DAISY CHAIN (DC)
DALLAS-SIX BALL SIDE POCKET (BN)
DAMES (DC)
DANCE FEVER (DC)
DANGEROUS (DC)
DANGEROUS PASSION (NY)
DANGEROUS STUFF (DC)
DANICA RHAE/STAR CUTS VOL 2 (DC)
DANIELLE (DC)
DANIELLE'S GIRLFRIENDS (NY)
DARK PASSIONS (DC)
DAUGHTER OF DARKNESS (DC)
DAUGHTER OF EMMANUELLE (DC, NY)
DAUGHTERS OF DISCIPLINE PT. 2 (DC)
DAY AND NIGHT (DC)
DEAR FANNY (DC)
DEAR THROAT (DC)
DEBBIE DOES DALLAS (DC)
DEBBIE DOES DALLAS 3 (DC)
DEBBIE DOES 'EM ALL (DC, MI)
DEBBIE'S FANTASY (DC)
DEBBI'S CONFESSION (DC)
DEEP CHILL (DC, BA)
DEEP PASSAGE (DC, NY)

DEEP ROOTS (DC)
DEEP THROAT (DC, NY, BN)
DEEP THRUST (DC)
DELICIOUS (DC)
DELIVERIES IN THE REAR (BA)
DELIVERY BOYS (DC)
DER LANG FINGER (NY)
DER PERVERSE ONKEL (NY)
DER SEX-SPION (NY)
DESIRE FOR MEN (DC)
DESIREE (DC)
DESIREE LANE (DC, NY)
DESIRES OF THE DEVIL (DC)
DESPERATELY SEEKING SUZIE (DC, BA)
DEVIATIONS (DC)
DEVIL'S ECSTASY (DC)
DEVIL'S PLAYGROUND (DC)
DEVINE ATROCITIES (DC, NY)
DIAMOND #69 (DC)
DIAMOND #70 (DC)
DIAMOND #52 (DC)
DIAMOND #56 (DC)
DIAMOND #57 (DC)
DIAMOND #61 (DC)
DIAMOND COLLECTION (NY, BN, DC)
DIAMOND COLLECTION #64 (NY)
DIAMOND COLLECTION #67 (NY)
DIAMOND COLLECTION #89 (NY)
DIAMOND COLLECTION-DESIREE LANE (NY)
DIAMOND LITTLE GEMS VOL 8 (DC)
DIAMOND LITTLE GEMS VOL 10 (DC)
DIAMOND LITTLE GEMS VOL 11 (DC)
DIAMOND LITTLE GEMS VOL 12 (DC)
DIAMOND LITTLE GEMS VOL 7 (DC)
DIAMOND LITTLE GEMS VOL 9 (DC)
DIAMOND LITTLE GEMS VOL 1 (DC)
DIAMOND LITTLE GEMS VOL 5 (DC)
DIANNA'S DESTINY (DC)
DIAPER TIME (DC)
DICK CASSIDY AND THE SUNDANCE GIRLS (NY)
DICK OF DEATH (DC, BA)
DIFFERENT STROKES (DC)
DILDO #1 (BA)
DILDO LUST #1 (NY, BN)
DILDO LUST #2 (NY)
DIRTY BLONDE (DC)
DIRTY GIRLS (DC)
DIRTY LETTERS (DC)
DIRTY OLD MAN (NY)
DIRTY SHARY (DC)
DIRTY SUSAN (NY)
DIRTY WASH (NY)
DISCO LADY (BA)
DISHONORABLE DISCHARGE (DC)
DISROBICS (DC)
DO ME EVIL (DC)
DOCTOR DESIRE (DC)
DOCTOR YES (DC)
DOCTOR'S ENEMA (DC)
DOG FUCKERS (NY)
DOG IN LOVE (NY)
DOG SEX (NY)
DOING IT (DC)
DOMINA LADY HELL (NY)
DOMINATED BY DESIRE (BN)
DON'T TELL DADDY (DC)
DOOGAN'S WOMAN (DC)
DORMITORY DAZE (DC)
DOUBLE WHIPPING (DC)
DOUBLE YOUR PLEASURE (DC)
DOWNSTAIRS/UPSTAIRS (DC)

DR. BIZARRO (DC)
DR. STORM (DC)
DR. STRANGESEX (DC)
DRACULA EXOTICA (DC)
DREAM BOYS (DC)
DREAM GIRL (DC)
DREAMER (DC)
DREAMS OF MISTY (DC)
DREAMS OF PLEASURE (DC)
DREAMS OF SULKA (NY)
DRESSING LESSON (DC)
DRILLER (BA)
DUTCHESS OF PORNO-HOT PANTS (NY)
DUTY AND DISCIPLINE (DC)
DYNAMITE (DC)
E-3/THE EXTRA TESTICLE (DC)
EAGER BEAVER (DC)
EARTHMAN (DC)
EASY (DC)
EASY ALICE (DC)
EAT AT THE BLUE FOX (DC)
EAT IN EAT OUT (DC)
EBONY EROTICA II (DC, NY)
EBONY LUST (NY)
EDUCATING EVA (DC)
EDUCATING MANDY (DC)
EDUCATING TRICIA (BA)
EDUCATING WANDA (DC)
EDUCATION OF VELVET (DC)
EIGHTEEN AND ANXIOUS (DC)
EL BIMBO (DC)
ELEVEN (DC, NY)
ELIZABETH AND HER AUNTY (DC)
EMBASSY AFFAIR (DC)
ENEMA AFFAIR (DC)
EROTIC DREAM HOUSE (DC)
EROTIC EXPRESS (DC)
EROTIC FANTASIES (DC)
EROTIC FANTASIES #3 (DC)
EROTIC GOLD (DC)
EROTIC INTERLUDE (DC)
EROTIC MOMENTS (DC)
EROTIC REFLECTIONS (DC)
EROTIC WORLD OF RENEE SUMMERS (DC)
EROTIC ZONES #1 (DC)
EROTIC ZONES #2 (DC)
EROTICA #6 (DC)
EROTICA COLLECTION #10 (DC)
EROTICA COLLECTION #6 (NY)
EROTICA COLLECTION #9 (DC)
EROTICA JONES (DC)
EROTICA VOL #7 (DC)
ESCAPE ME NEVER (DC)
ESP (DC)
ESSEX PREVIEW #2 (DC)
EVERY MAN'S FANTASY (DC)
EVERY WHICH WAY (DC)
EVERYTHING BUT THE KITCHEN SINK (DC)
EXCHANGE STUDENT (DC)
EXHAUSTED (DC)
EXPENSIVE TASTE (DC)
EXPERIMENTS IN BLUE (DC)
EXPOSE ME LOVELY (DC)
EXPOSE ME NOW (DC)
EXPOSED (DC)
EXQUISITE AGONY (DC)
EXTRA LARGE (DC)
EYES OF A GAY STRANGER (DC)
'F' (DC)
FACES (DC, BA)
FADE IN (DC)

FADE OUT (DC)
FADE TO RED (DC, MI)
FALCON #41/NIGHT FLIGHT (DC)
FALCON PAC #10 (DC)
FALCON PAC #11 (DC)
FALCON PAC #12 (DC)
FALCON PAC #14 (DC)
FALCON PAC #15 (DC)
FALCON PAC #16 (DC)
FALCON PAC #17 (DC)
FALCON PAC #19 (DC)
FALCON PAC #2 (DC)
FALCON PAC #21 (DC)
FALCON PAC #23 (DC)
FALCON PAC #24 (DC)
FALCON PAC #25 (DC)
FALCON PAC #26 (DC)
FALCON PAC #27 (DC)
FALCON PAC #28 (DC)
FALCON PAC #29/HUGE 1 (DC)
FALCON PAC #3 (DC)
FALCON PAC #30 (DC)
FALCON PAC #38 (DC)
FALCON PAC #4 (DC)
FALCON PAC #5 (DC)
FALCON PAC #8 (DC)
FALCON PAC 20 (DC)
FALCON PAC 22 (DC)
FALCON PAC 30 (DC)
FALCON PAC 31/HUGE 2 (DC)
FALCON PAC 37 (DC)
FALCONHEAD I (DC)
FALCONHEAD II (DC)
FALCONPAC/THE BROTHERS (DC)
FALCONPAC 18 (DC)
FALCONPAC 32 (DC)
FALCONPAC 33/SPOKES (DC)
FALCONPAC 36 (DC)
FALCONPAC 39 (DC)
FALCONPAC 40/SPLASH SHOTS (DC)
FLACONPAC 42 (DC)
FALCONPAC 43 (DC)
FALCONPAC 44 (DC)
FALCONPAC 45 (DC)
FALCONPAC 46/SPRING TRAINING (DC)
FALCONPAC 6 (DC)
FAMILY AFFAIR (DC, NY)
FAMILY SECRETS (DC)
FANTASIES UNLTD (DC)
FANTASIZE (DC)
FANTASY (NY)
FANTASY CLUB (NY, DC, BA)
FANTASY CLUB #53 (NY)
FANTASY CLUB #58 (NY)
FANTASY CLUB-DIKE DREAMS (NY)
FANTASY CLUB-QUICK LICKS (BA)
FANTASY CLUB-REAP CANAL (NY)
FANTASY FOLLIES #1 (DC)
FANTASY LAND (DC)
FANTASY MANSION (DC)
FANTASY WEEKEND (DC)
FANTASY WORLD OF NICOLE (DC)
FANTISEX ISLAND (DC)
FAREWELL SCARLET (DC)
FARMERS DAUGHTER (DC)
FASCINATION (DC)
FAST CARS/FAST WOMEN (DC)
FAST TIMES AT CHERRY HIGH (DC)
FC #25 (DC)
FEELS LIKE SILK (DC)
FEMME (DC)

FEMME FATALE (DC)
FEMMES DE SADE (DC)
FIGHTING FEMMES (DC)
FILM #170 (DC)
FINGER LICKIN' GOOD (DC)
FIONA ON FIRE (NY)
FIREFOXES (DC)
FIRST TIME AROUND (DC)
FIRSTS (DC)
FIST & FIRE (DC)
FINING WHITES WAGON (NY)
FLAMING TONGUES (DC)
FLASH/CAUGHT IN THE ACT (DC)
FLASHBACKS (DC)
FLASHTRANCE (DC)
FLESH AND ECSTASY (DC)
FLESH AND LACE PART 2 (DC)
FLESH AND LACE PART 1 (DC)
FLESH 1995 (DC)
FLESHDANCE (DC)
FLESHDANCE FEVER (DC)
FLESHTONES (DC)
FLYING SKIRTS (DC)
FLYING SIX MAN (DC)
FOOT SHOW (DC)
FOOT WORSHIPPERS (DC)
FOR ME LOVE OF PLEASURE (BA)
FOR MEMBERS ONLY (DC)
FOR RICHER FOR POORER (DC)
FOR SERVICES RENDERED (DC)
FOR THE LOVE OF PLEASURE (DC)
FORBIDDEN (DC)
FORBIDDEN ENTRY (NY)
FORBIDDEN FANTASIES (NY)
FORBIDDEN FRUIT (DC)
FORBIDDEN PORTRAIT (DC, NY)
FORBIDDEN WAYS (DC)
FORGIVE ME I HAVE SINNED (DC)
FORMAL FAUCETT (PH)
FOUR O'CLOCK (DC)
FOUR WAY STUD (NY)
FOXHOLES (DC)
FOXY LADY (PH)
FOXY LADY #1/L.A. VIDEO (DC)
FOXY LADY/CALVISTA (DC)
FRAT HOUSE FROLICS (DC)
FRAT HOUSE MEMORIES (DC)
FREEWAY HONEY (DC)
FRENCH CLASSMATES (DC)
FRENCH EROTICA (DC)
FRENCH FANTASIES (NY)
FRENCH FLESH (NY)
FRENCH HEAT (NY)
FRENCH LETTERS (DC)
FRENCH LIEUTENANT'S BOYS (DC)
FRENCH POSTCARD GIRL (NY)
FRENCH SCHOOLGIRLS (DC)
FRENCH TOUCH (DC)
FRENCH WIVES (DC)
FRISKY BUSINESS (DC)
FRITZ THE CAT (DC)
FROM HOLLY WITH LOVE (DC)
FROM RUSSIA WITH LUST (DC)
FURY IN ALICE (DC)
FUTURE SEX (DC)
FUTURE VOYEUR (DC)
G THEY ARE BIG (NY)
G.G. VOL 26 (DC)
GAMES (DC)
GAMES WOMEN PLAY (DC)
GANG BANG LUST (NY)

GANG BANGS (DC)
GARAGE GIRLS (DC)
GARTERS AND LACE (DC)
GAYRACULA (DC)
GEISHA GIRLS (BA)
GEISHA SLAVES (DC)
GETTIN' READY
GETTING AHEAD (DC)
GETTING IT (DC)
GETTING OFF (DC)
GETTING OFF CAMPUS (DC)
GG #15 (DC)
GG #16 (DC)
GG #20 (DC)
GG #7 (DC)
GIANTS PT. 2 (DC)
GINGER LYNN (NY, BN)
GINGER LYNN VOL 1/STAR CUTS (DC)
GINGER ON THE ROCKS (DC)
GINGER VIVID (DC)
GINGER'S LUST (NY)
GIRL FROM S.E.X. (DC)
GIRL WITH HUNGRY EYES (DC)
GIRLFRIENDS (DC, NY)
GIRLS & DOGS (NY)
GIRLS AND GUYS AND GIRLS OR GUYS (BA)
GIRLS FROM THE CANDY STORE (NY)
GIRLS OF HOLLYWOOD HILLS (DC)
GIRLS OF KLIT HOUSE (DC)
GIRLS OF THE NIGHT (DC)
GIRLS ON CELLBLOCK F (DC)
GIRLS ON FIRE (DC)
GIRLS ON GIRLS (DC)
GIRLS ON THE RUN (DC)
GIRLS THAT LOVE GIRLS (DC)
GIRLS USA (DC)
GIVE IT TO ME (DC)
GLADYS THE PLUMBER (DC)
GLITTER (DC)
GLORY HOLE-THE SUNSHINE BOYS (BN)
GLORY HOLE #104-BATHING BEAUTIES (BN)
GO FOR IT (DC)
GOING BOTH WAYS (DC, NY)
GOING DOWN (DC)
GOLD RUSH BOYS (DC)
GOLDDIGGERS (DC)
GOLDEN BOYS OF THE SS (DC)
GOLDEN GEISELL VIDEO (NY)
GOLDEN GIRLS (DC, PH, BA)
GOLDEN GIRLS (WRESTLING VOL. 10) (DC)
GOLDEN GIRLS (WRESTLING) #13 (DC)
GOLDEN GIRLS #11 (NY)
GOLDEN GIRLS #14 (NY)
GOLDEN GIRLS #2 (BA)
GOLDEN GIRLS #24 (NY)
GOLDEN GIRLS #25 (NY)
GOLDEN GIRLS WRESTLING #14 (DC)
GOLDEN GIRLS WRESTLING #17 (DC)
GOLDEN GIRLS WRESTLING #2 (DC)
GOLDEN GIRLS WRESTLING #39 (DC)
GOLDEN GIRLS WRESTLING #7 (DC)
GOLDEN GIRLS WRESTLING #9 (DC)
GOOD GIRL/BAD GIRL (DC)
GOOD HOT STUFF (DC)
GOODBYE GIRLS (DC)
GOURMET #3 (DC)
GOURMET #5 (DC)
GOURMET QUICKIE—CHRISTY CANYON (NY)
GOURMET QUICKIE—MAI LIN (NY)
GOURMET QUICKIE—PAM JENNING (NY)
GOURMET QUICKIES (DC)

GOURMET VIDEO #9 (DC)
GOURMET VIDEO 102/PARTY GIRLS (DC)
GRABBER (NY, DC)
GRANADA AFFAIR (DC)
GRAND OPENING (DC, BN)
GREASE MONKEY/MISTRESS RENATA (DC)
GREASE MONKEYS (DC)
GREAT SEXPECTATIONS (DC)
GREATEST LITTLE CATHOUSE OF VEGAS (DC)
GREEK LADY (DC, NY)
GREY HANKY LEFT (DC)
GROWING UP (DC)
GUYS WHO DO (DC)
GVC #138/BROADCAST BABES (DC)
GVC 109 (DC)
GVQ #706 (DC)
GVQ #709 (DC)
GWEN'S TIT TORMENT (DC)
GYM COACH BONDAGE (DC)
HALF THE ACTION (DC)
HALF-TERM PUNISHMENT (DC)
HANDFUL OF DIAMONDS (DC)
HANDY RANDY GUYS (DC)
HARD DISK DRIVE (DC)
HARD FOR MONEY (DC)
HARD FOR THE MONEY (DC, BA)
HARD LUCK NUMBER (DC)
HARD MEN AT WORK (NY)
HARD MONEY (DC, BN)
HARD SOAP (DC)
HARD TO SWALLOW (DC, MI)
HARD TO SWALLOW/LITTLE ORAL ANNIE (DC)
HARD WORKER (DC)
HARDY GIRLS (DC)
HAREM GIRLS IN BONDAGE (DC)
HARLEQUIN AFFAIR (DC)
HEAD (DC)
HEAD AND TAILS (DC)
HEAD OR TAILS (DC)
HEAD TRIPS (DC)
HEALTH SPA (DC)
HEARTBREAKER (DC, BA)
HEAT (DC)
HEAT OF THE MOMENT (DC)
HEAT WAVES (DC)
HEAVENLY DESIRE (DC, NY)
HEAVENLY NURSE (DC)
HEAVEN'S TOUCH (DC, BA)
HEAVY EQUIPMENT (DC)
HEAVY LOAD (DC)
HELLFIRE WEST (DC)
HER NAME WAS LISA (DC, MI)
HER TOTAL RESPONSE (DC)
HERMAPHRODITE (DC)
HEROS (DC)
HIGGINS/PIZZA BOYS (DC)
HIGH SCHOOL BUNNIES (DC)
HILL STREET BLACKS (NY)
HIS LITTLE BROTHER (DC)
HOLE (DC)
HOLLY MCCALL'S FANTASIES (NY)
HOLLYWOOD AT LARGE (DC)
HOLLYWOOD CONFIDENTIAL #1 (DC)
HOLLYWOOD CONFIDENTIAL #2 (DC)
HOLLYWOOD CONFIDENTIAL #3 (DC)
HOLLYWOOD CONFIDENTIAL #4 (DC)
HOLLYWOOD COWBOY (DC)
HOLLYWOOD GAY (DC)
HOLLYWOOD HEARTBREAKERS (DC)
HOLLYWOOD PINK (DC)
HOLY ROLLING (DC)

HOME FOR UNWED MOTHERS (NY)
HOMETOWN GIRLS (DC)
HONEY DRIPPER (DC)
HONEY PIE (DC)
HONG KONG DONG (BA)
HONORABLE JONES (DC)
HOOKED UP HOOKER (NY)
HOOKER'S HOLIDAY (DC)
HORNY HOUSEWIFE (DC)
HORROR IN THE WAX MUSEUM (DC)
HORSE (DC)
HORSE LOVER (NY)
HORSE POWER (NY)
HOSTAGE GIRLS (DC, BA)
HOT ACTION (DC)
HOT BLOODED (DC)
HOT BODIES (DC)
HOT CARS NASTY WOMEN (MI)
HOT CHOCOLATE (DC)
HOT CIRCUIT (DC)
HOT CLOSE UPS (DC)
HOT COUNTRY (DC)
HOT CUNT SERVICE (NY)
HOT DALLAS NIGHTS (DC)
HOT DOGS (DC, NY)
HOT DREAMS (DC)
HOT FOR CASH (DC)
HOT FUDGE (DC)
HOT GIRLS IN LOVE (DC)
HOT GYPSY LOVE (DC)
HOT HIGH AND HORNY (DC)
HOT JOBS (DC)
HOT LEGS (DC)
HOT LINE (DC)
HOT LUNCH (DC)
HOT MERCHANDISE (DC)
HOT NIGHTS & HARD BODIES (BA)
HOT NUMBER (DC)
HOT NURSES (DC)
HOT OFF THE PRESS (DC)
HOT PANTS (NY)
HOT PURSUIT (DC)
HOT PINK (DC)
HOT ROCKERS (DC)
HOT ROOMERS (DC)
HOT SCHOOL REUNION (DC)
HOT SHOTS (DC)
HOT SHOTS/VOL 1 (DC)
HOT SPA (DC)
HOT SPANKING (BA)
HOT SPOTS (DC)
HOT SPUR (DC)
HOT TAILS (DC)
HOT TEENAGE ASSETS (DC)
HOT TOUCH (DC)
HOT WIRE (DC, BA)
HOT WIRED VANESSA (DC, BA)
HOTEL HOOKER (DC, NY)
HOTLINE (DC)
HOTTER THAN HELL (DC)
HOTTEST HUNKS (DC)
HOUSE OF ILL-REPUTE (DC)
HOUSE OF LUST (DC)
HOUSE OF PLEASURE (DC)
HOUSE OF SIN (DC)
HOUSE OF STRANGE DESIRES (DC)
HOUSESALE DISCIPLINE (DC)
HOW DO YOU LIKE IT? (DC, BA)
HOW I GOT THE STORY (DC)
HOW TO ENLARGE YOUR PENIS (DC, NY)
HOW TO PERFORM FELLATIO (DC, NY)

HUGE #1 (NY)
HUGE BOOBED BABY (NY)
HUGE BRAS (DC, BA)
HUGE BRAS VOL 3 (DC)
HUGE BRAS #4 (NY)
HUGE LADIES #1 (NY)
HUNGRY HOLE (DC)
HUNGRY HOLES (BA)
HUNK (DC)
HUSTLER #17 (DC)
HUSTLER VIDEO MAGAZINE #1 (DC)
HUSTLER VIDEO VOL. 2 (DC)
HUSTLERS (DC)
HYAPATIA LEE—SWEET YOUNG FOXES (NY)
HYPERSEXUALS (DC)
HYPNOTIC SENSATIONS (DC)
I DREAM OF GINGER (DC)
I WANT TO BE A MISTRESS (DC)
I WANT TO BE BAD (DC)
I WANT WHAT I SEE (DC)
ICE CREAM (TUESDAY'S LOVER) (DC)
ICE CREAM/NAKED EYES (DC)
ILLUSIONS OF ECSTASY (DC)
ILLUSIONS OF EXTASY (BA)
IMMORAL MISTER TEAS (DC)
IMPULSE (BA)
IN A WEEK (DC)
IN LOVE (DC)
IN SARAH'S EYES (DC)
IN SEARCH OF THE PERFECT MAN (DC)
IN THE HEAT OF THE KNIGHT (DC)
IN THE NAME OF LEATHER (DC)
IN THE PINK (DC)
INCEST DELIGHT (NY)
INCEST/BROTHER LOVE (DC)
INCH BY INCH (DC)
INCH BY INCH/MATT STERLING (DC)
INCHES (DC)
INDECENT EXPOSURE (DC)
INDECENT PLEASURES (DC)
INDECENT WIVES (DC)
INDIAN LADY (DC)
INFLAMED (DC)
INITIATION OF A MARRIED WOMAN (DC)
INITIATION OF CYNTHIA (DC)
INNOCENTS FROM HELL (DC)
INPUT (DC)
INSANE LOVERS (DC)
INSATIABLE (DC)
INSIDE CANDY SAMPLES (DC)
INSIDE CHINA LEE (DC)
INSIDE DESIREE COUSTEAU (NY)
INSIDE GEORGINA SPELVIN (DC)
INSIDE JENNIFER WELLES (DC, NY)
INSIDE LITTLE ORAL ANNIE (NY)
INSIDE MARILYN (DC)
INSIDE SEKA (NY)
INTEGRATED (NY, BA)
INTENSIVE CARE (DC)
INTERLUDE OF LUST (DC)
INTERLUDES (DC)
INTERNATIONAL INTRIGUE (EMBASSY GIRLS) (DC)
INTERNATIONAL SKIN (BA)
INTIMATE COUPLES (DC)
INTIMATE DESIRES (DC, BA)
INTIMATE REALITIES #2 (DC)
INTIMIDATION (DC)
INTRODUCTIONS (DC)
INTRUDERS (DC)
IRA'S ORDEAL (DC)
IRRESISTABLE (DC)

ISLAND OF PASSION (DC)
IT'S INCREDIBLE (DC)
IT'S MY BODY (DC)
I'VE NEVER DONE THIS BEFORE (DC)
IVY LEAGUE (DC)
JACK N JILL #2 (DC)
JACK'N'JILL (DC)
JACKS ARE BETTERS (DC)
JACQUETTE (DC)
JADE PUSSY CAT (DC)
JAILHOUSE GIRLS (DC)
JAILMATES (DC)
JANE BONDA'S WORKOUT (DC)
JAP/VOL 23 (DC)
JAP/VOL 24 (DC)
JAPANESE EROTICA #1 (DC)
JAPANESE EROTICA #2 (DC)
JAPANESE EROTICA #25 (DC)
JAPANESE EROTICA #26 (DC)
JAPANESE EROTICA #27 (DC)
JAPANESE EROTICA #28 (DC)
JAPANESE EROTICA #3 (DC)
JAPANESE EROTICA #4 (DC)
JAPANESE EROTICA #5 (DC)
JAPANESE EROTICA #6 (DC)
JAPANESE EROTICA #7 (DC)
JAPANESE EROTICA #8 (DC)
JAWBREAKERS (DC)
JOCK EMPIRE (DC)
JEFF NOLL'S BUDDIES (DC)
JESSIE ST. JAMES' FANTASIES (DC)
JOB SITE (DC)
JOCKS (DC)
JOE GAGE'S (DC)
JOE GAGE'S CLOSED SET #2 (DC)
JOE GAGE'S HEATSTROKE (DC)
JOE ROCK (DC)
JOHNNY DOES PARIS (DC)
JOINT VENTURE (DC)
JOSEPHINE (DC)
JOY (BA)
JOY TOYS (DC)
JOYS OF EROTICA (NY, BA)
JOYS OF EROTICA-RAVEN-SERIES 107 (NY)
JOYS OF EROTICA-RENEE-SUMMERS-SERIES 112
    (NY)
JUANITA (NY)
JUBILEE OF EROTICISM (DC)
JUDGE FOR YOURSELF (DC)
JUDGEMENT DAY (DC)
JUDI'S B & D SCHOOL (DC)
JUGGS (DC)
JUICE (DC)
JUNIOR CADETS (DC)
K-KUM (BA, DC)
K-SEX (NY)
KAKTEEN FREUND (NY)
KANSAS CITY TRUCKING CO. (DC)
KAREN'S B & D PHONE SEX (DC)
KEPT AFTER SCHOOL (DC)
KIDNAPPED GIRLS' AGENCY (DC)
KIMONO (DC)
KING SIZE (DC, NY)
KINKORAMA (DC)
KINKY BUSINESS (DC)
KINKY COUPLES (DC)
KINKY LADIES OF BOURBON STREET (DC)
KIP NOLL AND THE WESTSIDE BOYS (DC)
KIP NOLL SUPERSTAR (DC)
KIP'S CASTING COUCH (DC)
KISS AND TELL (DC)

KISSIN COUSINS (DC)
KNEEL BEFORE ME (DC)
KNOCKOUT (DC)
KRISTARA BARRINGTON #1 (BN)
L.A. BOILING POINT (DC)
L.A. PLAYS ITSELF (DC)
L.A. TOOL & DIE (DC)
LADIES IN LACE (DC)
LADIES NIGHT (DC)
LADIES OF THE EIGHTIES (DC)
LADIES THREE (DC)
LADIES WITH BIG BOOBS (DC)
LADY DOG (NY)
LADY CASANOVA (DC)
LADY MADONNA (DC)
LAS VEGAS EROTICA (DC, MI)
LASSIE (NY)
LAST TABOO (DC)
LAYOVER (DC)
LE VOYEUR (DC)
LEATHER LOVER (DC)
LEATHER MISTRESS (DC)
LEATHER PERSUASION (DC)
LEATHER REVENGE (DC)
LEATHERS BOND (DC)
LECHER (DC)
LEGACY OF LUST (DC)
LEGEND OF LADY BLUE (DC)
LEO AND LANCE (DC)
LESBIAN DESIRES (DC)
LESBIAN FOOT LOVERS (DC, BN)
LESBIAN PASSION (DC)
LESBIAN REVENGE (DC)
LESLIE BOREE'S FANTASIES (BA)
LET ME TELL YA 'BOUT BLACK CHICKS (DC)
LET MY PUPPETS COME (DC)
LETS PLAY DOCTOR (DC)
LET'S TALK SEX (DC)
LICKEN GOOD (NY)
LICORICE TWISTS (DC)
LIKE A HORSE (DC)
LIKE A VIRGIN (DC)
LIMITED EDITION (DC, BA)
LINDA WONG (DC)
LINGERIE (DC)
LIPPS AND MACAINE (DC)
LIQUID ASSETS (DC)
LISA THATCHER'S FANTASIES (DC)
LISA'S RUBBER SEDUCTION (DC)
LITTLE BLUE BOX (DC)
LITTLE BROTHER'S COMING OUT (DC)
LITTLE FRENCH MAID (DC)
LITTLE GEMS—BIG SISTER (NY)
LITTLE GEMS—PILE DRIVER (NY)
LITTLE GEMS #2 (DC)
LITTLE GEMS #3 (DC)
LITTLE GEMS #4 (DC)
LITTLE GEMS #6 (DC)
LITTLE GIRL (NY)
LITTLE GIRL LOST (DC)
LITTLE GIRLS BLUE PART II (NY)
LITTLE GIRLS OF THE STREET (DC)
LITTLE GIRLS TALKING DIRTY (DC)
LITTLE KIMMIE JOHNSON (DC)
LITTLE MUFFY JOHNSON (DC)
LITTLE OFTEN ANNIE (DC)
LITTLE ORAL ANNIE TAKES MANHATTAN
LITTLE ORPHAN DUSTY PART 2 (DC)
LITTLE ORPHAN SAMMY (DC)
LITTLE SCHOOL GIRL (DC)
LOADSTAR (DC)

LOCKERROOM FEVER (DC)
LOG JAMMIN' (DC)
LOLITA RAPE (NY)
LOLLIPOP PALACE (DC)
LONG HARD NIGHTS (DC, MI)
LONG JEAN SILVER (DC)
LONG JOHN (DC)
LONG RUSH (DC)
LOOKING FOR LOVE (DC)
LOOSE ENDS (DC)
LOOSE MORALS (BA)
LOOSE TIMES AT RIDLEY HIGH (DC)
LOSING CONTROL (DC)
LOST IN LUST (DC)
LOTTERY LUSTY (BA)
LOVE BUTTONS (DC)
LOVE DREAMS (DC)
LOVE NOTES (DC)
LOVE THEATER (DC)
LOVE TO MOTHER (DC)
LOVE UNDER SIXTEEN (DC)
LOVES OF LOLITA (DC)
LUSCIOUS (DC)
LUST AMERICAN STYLE (DC)
LUST AT FIRST BITE (DC)
LUST BUG (DC)
LUST CAMERA ACTION (NY)
LUST FLIGHT 2000 (DC)
LUST IN SPACE (DC)
LUST IN THE FAST LANE (DC)
LUST OF LESBIAN SEDUCTION (NY)
LUST WEEKEND (DC)
LUST-SEX SERVANT (BA)
LUSTFULLY SEEKING SUSAN (DC)
LUSTY ADVENTURES (DC)
LUSTY BUSINESS (NY)
LUSTY COUPLES (DC)
LUSTY LADIES (PH)
MACHO WOMEN (DC)
MAD JACK, BEYOND THE THUNDERBONE (BA)
MADE IN THE SHADE (DC, NY)
MADE TO ORDER (DC)
MAGIC GIRLS (DC)
MAGNUM GRIFFIN COLLECTION MALE EROTICA
  (NY)
MAGNUM GRIFFIN VOL 2 (DC)
MAGNUM-GRIFFIN #1 (DC)
MAGNUM-GRIFFIN #3 (DC)
MAGNUM-GRIFFIN #4 (DC)
MAID IN MANHATTAN (DC)
MAID TO BE SPANKED (DC)
MAKE IT HARD (DC)
MAKE IT HURT (DC)
MAKE ME FEEL IT (DC)
MAKE MY NIGHT (DC)
MAKING IT BIG (DC, BA)
MAKING IT HUGE (DC)
MAKING PORNO MOVIES (DC)
MALE STAMPEDE (DC)
MALES IN MOTION (DC)
MALIBU DAYS/BIG BEAR NIGHTS (DC)
MALIBU SWINGERS (BA)
MAMA'S BOY (DC)
MAMAS IN BONDAGE (DC)
MAMED WOMEN (BA)
MAN HUNT (DC)
MANDY'S EXECUTIVE SWEET (DC, MI)
MANHATTAN MISTRESS (DC)
MAN'S COUNTRY (DC)
MANSON (DC)
MARATHON (DC)

MARILYN CHAMBERS (DC)
MARILYN CHAMBERS' PRIVATE FANTASIES #2 (DC)
MARILYN CHAMBERS' PRIVATE FANTASIES #6 (DC)
MARILYN CHAMBERS' PRIVATE FANTASY #1 (DC)
MARILYN CHAMBERS' PRIVATE FANTASIES #5 (DC)
MARILYN MY LOVE (DC, MI)
MARINA HEAT (DC)
MARINE FURLOUGH (DC)
MARQUISE MARIE (DC)
MASCARA (DC)
MASTER AND MS. JOHNSON (DC)
MASTER CONTROL (DC, NY)
MASTER OF DISCIPLINE (DC)
MATINEE IDOL (DC)
MEN & STEEL (DC)
MEN COME FIRST (DC)
MEN OF THE MIDWAY (DC)
MENAGE-A-TROUX (NY)
MEN'S VIDEO MAGAZINE (DC)
MIAMI VICE (PH)
MID-SUMMER'S NIGHT DREAM (DC)
MIDNIGHT HEAT (DC)
MIDNIGHT HUSTLE (BA)
MIDNIGHT LADY (DC)
MIDNIGHT SPECIAL #1 (DC)
MIDNIGHT SPECIAL #2 (DC)
MIDNIGHT SPECIAL #3 (DC)
MIDNIGHT SPECIAL #4 (DC)
MIDNIGHT SPECIAL #6 (DC)
MILK CHOCOLATE (DC)
MIND GAMES (DC)
MISS AMERICAN DREAM (DC)
MISS PASSION (DC, BA)
MISS SEPTEMBER (DC)
MISSING PIECES (DC, BA)
MISTRESS (DC)
MISTRESS CANDY (NY)
MISTRESS ELECTRA (DC)
MISTRESS MARIANNE'S SLAVE OF LOVE (DC)
MISTRESS MICHELLE (DC)
MISTY BEETHOVEN (DC)
MODE DE SADE (DC)
MODERN MEN MODERN TOYS (DC)
MOMMA'S BOY (DC)
MONDO FETISH (DC)
MOONSHINE MAMA (NY)
MORE MIND GAMES PART TWO (DC)
MOST VALUABLE SLUT (DC)
MOVE OVER JOHNNY (DC)
MOVIE STAR (DC)
MOVING (DC)
MR. DRUMMER 1984 (DC)
MR. GOODSEX (BA)
MRS. SMITH'S EROTIC HOLIDAY (DC)
MRS. WINTER'S LOVER (DC)
MUDHONEY (DC)
MUSCLE BOUND (DC)
MUSCLE UP (DC)
MUSICAL SEDUCTION—TEEN SEX (NY)
MUSTANG (DC)
MY PRETTY GO BETWEEN (DC)
MY SISTER SEKA (DC)
MY STRAIGHT FRIENDS (DC)
MY TONGUE IS QUICK (DC, BA)
MATING SEASON (DC)
MAXIMUM (DC)
MAXIMUM I (DC)
MELANIE'S HOT LINE (DC)
MEMBERS ONLY (DC)
MEMORIES WITH MISS ANGIE (PH)
MEMPHIS CATHOUSE BLUES (DC)

NAKED CITY NIGHTS (DC, NY)
NAKED LUST (DC)
NAKED NIGHT (DC)
NASTY (DC)
NASTY LADY (DC)
NASTY LADY LUST #1 (NY)
NASTY NURSES (DC)
NATIONAL BAD TASTE COMEDY FINALS (DC)
NAUGHTY GIRLS NEED LOVE TOO (DC)
NAUGHTY NANETTE (DC)
NAUGHTY NIECES #1 (DC, NY)
NAUGHTY NIECES #2 (DC, NY)
NAUGHTY NURSES (DC)
NAUGHTY SUZANNE (DC)
NAVY BLUE (DC)
NEON NIGHTS (DC)
NETWORK SEX (DC)
NEVER A TENDER MOMENT (DC)
NEVER BIG ENOUGH (DC)
NEVER ENOUGH (DC)
NEVER SO DEEP (DC)
NEW CUMMERS (DC)
NEW KID IN TOWN (DC)
NEW WAVE HOOKERS (DC)
NEW WAVE HUSTLERS (DC)
NEWCOMERS (DC)
NICE 'N' TIGHT (DC)
NICOLE/STORY OF (DC)
NIGHT AT HELLFIRE (DC)
NIGHT CALLER (DC)
NIGHT HUNGER (DC)
NIGHT MOODS (DC)
NIGHT MOVES (DC)
NIGHT OF LOVING DANGEROUSLY (BA)
NIGHT OF SUBMISSION (DC)
NIGHT OF THE HEADHUNTER (DC)
NIGHT PROWLERS (DC)
NIKKIE CHARM (NY, BN)
NINE LIVES OF A WET PUSSYCAT (DC)
NO HOLES BARRED VOL 2 (DC)
NON-STOP (DC)
NOONER (DC)
NOSEY NURSE (DC)
NOSTALGIA BLUE (DC)
NOTHING BUT THE BEST (DC)
NOVA VOL 26 (DC)
NOVA VOL. 20 (DC)
NOVA/MADE TO ORDER (DC)
NOW THE CANE (DC)
NURSE LUST (NY)
NURSE WITH A CURSE (DC)
NURSES'S LUST NUTCRACKER (DC)
OBEDIENCE SCHOOL (DC)
OBSESSION (DC)
ODDS & ENDS (NY)
ODYSSEY (DC)
OFFICE DISCIPLINE (DC)
OH BROTHER (DC)
OH DOCTOR (DC)
OH FANNEY (DC, BA)
OH THOSE NURSES (DC)
OIL RIG #99 (DC)
OIL WELL WORKER (DC)
OLD RELIABLE VT-13 (DC)
OLD RELIABLE VT-18 (DC)
OLD RELIABLE VT-20 (DC)
OLD RELIABLE VT-29 (DC)
OLDER MEN WITH YOUNGER GIRLS (DC, BA)
OLDER WOMEN WITH YOUNG BOYS (DC)
OLINKA/GRAND PRIESTESS OF LOVE (DC)
OLYMPIC FEVER (DC)

OLYMPIC AFFAIR (DC)
ONCE AND FOR ALL (DC)
ONCE UPON A MADONA (DC)
ONCE UPON A SECRETARY (DC)
ONE IN A BILLION (DC)
ONE LAST FLING (DC)
ONE NIGHT IN BANGKOK (MI)
ONE NIGHT OF PASSION (DC)
ONE SIZE FITS ALL (DC)
ONE-TWO-THREE (DC)
OPEN FOR BUSINESS (DC)
OPEN NIGHTLY (DC)
OPENING NIGHT (DC, NY)
OPPOSITES ATTRACT (DC)
ORANGE HANKY LEFT (DC)
ORGY II (BA)
ORGY LUST #1 (BN)
ORGY OF THE DOLLS (DC, BA)
ORIENTAL DICK (DC)
ORIENTAL ENCOUNTERS (DC)
ORIENTAL LESBIAN FANTASIES (DC)
ORIENTAL LUST (DC)
ORIENTAL MADAM (BA)
ORIENTAL SEXPRESS (DC)
ORIENTAL TABOO (DC)
ORIENTAL TECHNIQUES OF PAIN & PLEASURE (DC)
ORIFICE PARTY (DC)
OTHER SIDE OF LIANNA (DC)
OUR MAJOR IS SEX (DC)
OUTLAW LADIES (DC)
OUTLAW WOMEN (DC)
OUTRAGE (DC)
OZARK VIRGIN (DC)
P.M. PREVIEW #1 (DC)
P.M. PREVIEW TAPE #3 (DC)
PACIFIC (DC)
PAIN & PLEASURE (DC, NY)
PAIN & PUNISHMENT (DC)
PAIN BY LANA (DC)
PAIN DANCE (DC, BN)
PAIN MANIA (DC)
PAINFUL REUNION (DC)
PAINMANIA/DAUGHTERS OF DISCIPLINE (DC)
PALACE OF PLEASURES (DC)
PAPER DOLLS (DC)
PARIS CONNECTION (DC)
PARTY GIRL (DC, NY)
PARTY STRIPPER (DC)
PARTY OF SYMPHONY (NY)
PASSAGE TO ECSTASY (DC)
PASSING STRANGERS (DC)
PASSION FOR BONDAGE (DC)
PASSION NO SHAME REGRETS (DC)
PASSION PIT (DC, BA)
PASSION TOYS (DC)
PASSIONATE LEE (DC)
PASSIONATE PISSING (NY)
PAULA'S PUNISHMENT (DC)
PAYING FOR IT (DC)
PEACHES AND CREAM (DC)
PEEK-A-BOOK GANG (DC)
PEEP HOLE POKER (NY)
PEEP SHOW/YMAC (DC)
PEEPHOLES (DC)
PEGASUS (DC)
PLEASURE PRODUCTIONS #4 (NY)
PENETRATION (DC, BA)
PENETRATION #6 (DC)
PENETRATION 5 (DC)
PERFECT WEEKEND (DC)
PERFECTION (DC)

PERFORMANCE (DC)
PERILS OF PRUNELLA (DC)
PERSONAL TOUCH 2 (DC)
PERVERSE (DC)
PERVERSION (DC)
PET OF THE MONTH (DC)
PETER GALORE (DC, BA)
PHADRA GRANT'S FANTASIES (NY)
PHOENIZ #1 (DC)
PHONE SEX FANTASIES (DC)
PHYSICAL ATTRACTION (DC)
PHYSICAL II (DC)
PIGGY'S (DC)
PIMMLICHE TOCHTER (DC)
PINK CHAMPAGNE (DC)
PINK LIPS (DC)
PIPE DREAMS (DC)
PIPELINE (DC)
PISS & CHAMPAGNE (NY)
PISS SERVICE (NY)
PLATINUM-TICKLED PINK (BN)
PLAYGIRL (DC)
PLAYING WITH FIRE (DC)
PLAYMATE (DC)
PLEASE MR. POSTMAN (DC)
PLEASURE #1 (DC)
PLEASURE #2 (DC)
PLEASURE BEACH (DC)
PLEASURE CHANNEL (DC, BA)
PLEASURE ISLAND (BA)
PLEASURE MASTERS (BA)
PLEASURE MOUNTAIN (DC)
PLEASURE OF INNOCENCE (DC)
PLEASURE PARTY (DC)
PLEASURE PRODUCTION (NY, BA)
PLEASURE PRODUCTIONS #3 (NY)
PLEASURE PRODUCTIONS #8 (NY)
PLEASURE SEEKERS (DC)
PLEASURE SO DEEP (DC)
PLEASURES IN THE SUN (DC)
POINT ME TOWARD TOMORROW (DC)
POLITICAL PARTY (PH)
PONY GIRLS (DC, NY)
POOL SERVICE (DC)
POPULAR MECHANICS (DC)
PORKY'S PEEKERS (NY)
PORN STARLET CONTEST (DC)
PORNBIRDS (DC)
PORNO SHOW (NY)
PORTRAIT OF DESIRE (DC)
PORTRAIT OF LUST (DC)
POWER OF NICOLE (DC)
PRACTICE MAKES PERFECT (DC)
PREGNANT BABYSITTER (DC)
PREPPY SUMMER (DC)
PRETTY GIRL #2 (NY)
PREVIEW #2 (DC)
PRISONER OF PARADISE (DC)
PRISONER OF PLEASURE (DC)
PRIVATE AFFAIRS OF PAMELA MANN (DC)
PRIVATE COLLECTION (DC)
PRIVATE COLLECTION OF LARRY BRONCO (DC)
PICK UP (DC)
PIERCING OF JAMIE (DC)
PIERCING OF LAURA (DC)
PRIVATE NURSES (DC, NY)
PRIVATE PARTY (DC)
PRIVATE PARTY/BUCKSHOT (DC)
PRIVATE PLEASURES OF JOHN C. HOLMES (DC)
PRIVATE PRACTICE (DC)
PRIVATE TEACHER (DC)

PRIZED POSSESSION (DC)
PRO BALL CHEERLEADER (DC)
PROBATION OFFICER'S DISCIPLINE (DC)
PROGRAMMED FOR PLEASURE (DC)
PROJECT: GINGER (DC, MI)
PRUNELLA (DC)
PUBLIC AFFAIR (DC)
PUNISHED #2 (DC, BN)
PUNISHED #3 (DC, NY)
PURELY PHYSICAL (DC)
PUSS N BOOTS (DC)
PRIVATE FANTASIES (DC)
PRIVATE LESSONS (DC)
PRIVATE MOMENTS (DC)
QUEEN OF WRESTLING PART II (DC)
QUEEN OF WRESTLING PART I (DC)
QUICK LICKS (DC)
RAM ROD (NY)
RAMBONE—THE FIRST TIME (DC)
RAMBONE THE DESTROYER (BA)
RANDY THE ELECTRIC LADY (DC)
RAVAGED (DC, NY)
RAVEN (DC, NY, MI)
RAVEN VOL 1/STAR CUTS (DC)
RAW COUNTRY (DC)
RAW TALENT (DC, BA)
RAWHIDE (DC)
REAL ESTATE (DC)
REAR ACTION GIRLS #1 (DC)
REAR ACTION GIRLS #2 (DC)
REAR ENDED (DC, BA)
REBECCA'S DREAM (DC)
RED ALL OVER (DC)
RED BALL EXPRESS (DC)
REDWOOD ROMANCE (DC)
REEL PEOPLE (DC)
REFLECTIONS (DC)
REFLECTIONS OF YOUTH (DC)
REGAL VOL 3 (DC)
REGAL VOL 5 (DC)
REGENCY (DC)
REGENCY #14 (DC)
REGENCY #18 (DC)
REGENCY #4 (DC)
REINCARNATION OF SERENA (DC, NY)
REN SAKATA (DC)
RENDEZVOUS WITH DESTINY (DCC)
RETURN TO ALPHA BLUE (DC)
REVENGE (DC)
REVENGE AND PUNISHMENT (DC)
REVENGE BY LUST (BA)
REVENGE OF THE NIGHTHAWK (DC)
REVOLUTION (DC)
RHINESTONE COWGIRLS (DC)
RHODA JO (DC)
RIBU 039 (NY)
RICH BITCH (DC)
RICH QUICK/PRIVATE DICK (DC)
RIDING MISTRESS (DC)
RIKKI BLAKE (NY)
RIPPLE WRINKLE (NY)
RIPPLES AND WRINKLES (DC)
RIVERMAN ROBIN'S NEST (DC)
RODEO (DC, BA)
ROLLERBABIES (DC)
ROMANCING THE BONE (DC)
ROMP AROUND (DC)
ROOM SERVICE PLUS (DC, NY)
ROOM 2-D (DC)
ROOMMATES (DC, NY)
ROPE BURN (BN)

ROPE THAT WORKS (DC)
ROSE MARIE (NY)
ROSEMARIE VOL 2/STAR CUTS (DC)
ROUGH RIDERS #3-HELPER (BN)
ROUTE 89 (DC, BA)
ROXBURY VOL #1 (DC)
RUB DOWN (DC)
RUBBER PARTY (DC)
RUMP HUMPERS (BA)
RUNNING WILD (DC)
RUSHING (DC)
S & M NEW ENGLAND STYLE (DC)
S & M DOUBLE FEATURE (DC)
S & M PARTY AT MIDNIGHT (NY, BN, DC)
SADDLE HORNY (DC)
SADIE (DC)
SADISTIC SWEETHEART (DC)
SAILOR IN THE WILD (DC)
SALLY ROBERTS IN BONDAGE #1 (DC)
SALLY ROBERTS IN BONDAGE #3 (DC)
SALLY ROBERTS IN BONDAGE #4 (DC)
SALLY'S FIRST LESSON (DC, BN)
SALON FOR SEDUCTION (DC)
SALT AND PEPPER (DC)
SALT AND PEPPER BOYS (DC)
SAME TIME EVERY YEAR (DC)
SAMURAI DICK (DC)
SAN FRANCISCO (NY)
SAN FRANCISCO GENERAL HOSPITAL (DC)
SANTA COMES TWICE (DC)
SAPPHO SEXTET (DC)
SATIN DOLLS (DC)
SATIN FINISH (DC)
SATIN VIDEO WALL TO WALL SEX #1 (NY)
SATISFACTIONS (DC)
SATISFIERS OF ALPHA BLUE (DC)
SAURE GURKEN (NY)
SAVAGE BUNS (DC)
SAVAGE SADISTS (DC)
SAVAGED AND RAVAGED (DC)
SCANDAL IN THE MANSION (BA)
SCANDAL MANSION (DC)
SCANDALOUS SIMONE (DC)
SCATMAN (DC)
SCENT OF HEATHER (DC)
SCHOOL CHUMS (NY)
SCHOOL GIRL REUNION (DC)
SCHOOL REPORTS #1 (DC)
SCHOOL REPORTS #2 (DC)
SCHOOL TEACHERS (DC)
SCHOOLDAZE (DC)
SCHOOLGIRL BY DAY (DC)
SCHOOLMATES II (DC)
SCHWARZE GIER (DC)
SCOTT MADSEN'S AEROBIFLEX (DC)
SCOUNDRELS (DC)
SCREEN PLAY (DC)
SCREEN TEST (DC)
STORY OF BOBBY (DC)
STORY OF JOANNA (DC)
STORY OF PRUNELLA (DC)
SECRETS OF SEKA (PH)
SEDUCE ME TONIGHT (DC)
SEDUCTION OF CINDY (DC)
SEDUCTION OF SEKA (DC)
SEDUCTRESS (DC)
SEKA'S FANTASIES (NY, DC)
SEKA'S LACY AFFAIR/PART 2 (DC)
SENSATIONS (DC)
SENSUAL ENCOUNTERS OF EVERY KIND (DC)
SENSUAL EROTICA (DC)

SENSUOUS DETECTIVES (DC)
SENSUOUS TALES (DC, BA)
SENSUOUS MOMENTS (DC)
SERENA-ADULT FAIRY TALE (DC)
SERVICE ENTRANCE (DC)
SERVICED WITH A SMILE (DC)
SEVEN INTO SNOWY (DC)
SEVEN SEDUCTIONS (DC)
SEVEN SEDUCTIONS OF MADAME LAU (DC)
SEX AND THE CHEERLEADERS (DC)
SEX APPEAL (DC)
SEX AS YOU LIKE IT (DC)
SEX BAZAAR (DC)
SEX CLINIC GIRLS (DC)
SEX CRIMES 2084 (DC)
SEX DREAMS ON MAPLE STREET (DC)
SEX DRUGS AND ROCK AND ROLL (DC)
SEX FIFTH AVENUE (DC)
SEX GAMES (DC)
SEX IN THE COMICS (DC)
SEX ON THE SET (DC)
SEX SEX ORGY #236 (NY)
RITUALS OF THE OCCULT (DC)
SEX ROMANCE (DC)
SEX SHOOT (DC)
SEX SHOWS OF PARIS (BA)
SEX STARS (DC)
SEX STEWARDESSES (DC)
SEX TOYS (DC)
SEX TRICKS (DC)
SEX U.S.A. (DC)
SEX-A-VISION (MI)
SEX-ED WITH LITTLE RED (DC)
SEXAHOLIC (DC)
SEXAVISION (DC)
SEXBUSTERS (DC)
SEXCALIBUR (DC)
SCREW #1 (DC)
SCREWPLES (DC)
SEA CADETS (DC)
SECLUDED PASSION (DC)
SECRET DREAMS OF MONA (DC)
SECRET TABLETS OF RAMA (DC)
SWEET NIGHTMARES (DC)
SWEET SISTER (DC)
SWEET SURRENDER (DC, BA)
SWEET TASTE OF HONEY (DC)
SWEET YOUNG FOXES (DC, BA)
SWING SHIFT (DC)
SEXDRIVES (DC)
SEXEO (DC)
SEXERCISE GIRLS (DC)
SEXORCIST DEVIL (DC)
SEXPERT (DC)
SEXSATIONS (DC)
SEXTASY (DC)
SEXTOOL (DC)
SEXUAL POSITIONS (DC)
SEXUAL WITCHCRAFT (DC)
SEXY (DC, MI)
SEXY BLACKMAIL (NY)
SEXY SHAVERS (NY)
SGT. SWANN'S PRIVATE FANTASIES (DC)
SHACKING UP (DC)
SHADES OF ECSTASY (BA)
SHAMEFUL DESIRES (DC)
SHANA (DC)
SHANA GRANT'S FANTASIES (DC)
SHANGHAI GIRLS (DC)
SHAPE UP FOR SENSATIONAL SEX (DC)
SHARON IN THE ROUGH HOUSE (DC)

SHAUNA (DC)
SHAUNA GRANT (NY)
SHAVED (NY, BA)
SHAVED BUNNIES (DC, NY)
SHAVED PINK (BA)
SHAVETAIL (DC)
SHE DID WHAT HE WANTED (DC)
SHE MALE (NY)
SHE-MALE COLLECTION #3 (DC)
SHE-MALE CONFIDENTIAL (DC)
SHE-MALE ENCOUNTERS #1 (DC)
SHE-MALE ENCOUNTERS #5 (DC)
SHEER DELIGHT (DC)
SHE'S A BOY TOY (DC, BA)
SHOE SHINE (DC)
SHOOTING STARS (BA)
SHOPPE OF TEMPTATIONS (DC)
SHORE LEAVE (DC)
SHOW YOUR LOVE (DC)
SHOWGIRLS (MI)
SIGHS (DC)
SILHOUETTE—INNOCENT GIRLS (NY)
SILK/SATIN & SEX (DC)
SINDEROTICA (DC)
SISTER DEAREST (DC)
SISTER EVE (DC)
SIX EASY PIECES (BA)
SIX FACES OF SAMANTHA (DC)
SIZING UP (DC)
SIZZLE (DC)
SIZZLING SUBURBIA (DC)
SKI HUSTLERS (DC)
SKIN DEEP (DC, PH)
SKIN ON SKIN (DC)
SKINTIGHT (DC)
SKY PIES (DC, BA)
SLAVE OF PLEASURE (DC)
SLAVE PIERCING (DC)
SLAVE THERAPY (DC)
SLAVES FOR SALE PART ONE (DC)
SLAVES FOR SALE PART TWO (DC)
SLAVES OF MISTRESS MONIQUE (DC)
SLEAZE (DC)
SLEAZE/C. RAGE (DC)
SLEEPLESS NIGHTS (DC)
SLICE OF LIFE (DC)
SLIP INTO SILK (DC)
SLIP UP (DC)
SLIT SKIRTS (DC)
SLUTS IN HEAT (DC)
SMALL TOWN BOY (DC)
SMALL TOWN GIRLS (DC)
SNACK TIME (DC)
SNAKE FUCKERS (NY)
SOFT STROKE (DC)
SOMETHING WILD (DC)
SONG OF THE LOON (DC)
SOPHISTICATED PLEASURE (DC)
SORE THROAT (DC)
SOUND OF LOVE (DC)
SOUNDS OF SEX (DC)
SOUTH OF THE BORDER (DC, BA)
SOUTHERN COMFORT (NY)
SPACE VIRGINS (DC)
SPACEMAN (DC)
SPANKING TUTOR (DC)
SPANK ME DADDY (DC, NY)
SPANKING SALESMAN (DC)
SPECIAL REQUEST (DC)
SPERMA (NY)
SPITFIRE (DC)

SPLIT IMAGE (DC)
SPORTS EROTICA 2 (DC)
SPREAD SCHOOL GIRL (BN)
SQUALOR MOTEL (DC)
STACY'S HOT ROD (DC)
STALAG 69 (DC)
STAND BY YOUR WOMAN (DC)
STAR CUTS—ALI MOORE #1 (BA)
STAR '85 (DC, BA)
STARLET NIGHT (DC)
STARVED FOR AFFECTION (DC)
STEAM HEAT (DC)
STEAMIN' HOT (DC)
STEPHANIE'S LUST STORY (DC)
STICKY FINGERS (DC, BA)
STIFF COMPETITION (DC)
STRANGE BEDFELLOWS (DC)
STRANGE FAMILY (DC)
STRANGE LUST #1 (NY)
STRANGE LUST #3 (BA)
STRANGE PLACES STRANGE THINGS (DC)
STRAY CATS (DC)
STREET BOYS (DC)
STREET HEAT ORGY (DC)
STREET KIDS (DC)
STREET STAR (DC)
STRICTLY FOR LADIES ONLY (DC)
STRICTLY FORBIDDEN (DC)
STRICTLY FUCKING BUSINESS (DC)
STRIPTEASE (DC)
STUD HUNTER (DC)
STUD WARS (DC)
STUDENT BODIES (DC)
STUDHUNTERS 1 (DC)
STUDHUNTERS 2 (DC)
SUBMISSION OF SERENA (DC)
SUBURBAN LUST (DC)
SUBWAY (DC)
SUE PRENTISS R.N. (DC)
SULKA (NY)
SULKA'S DAUGHTER (DC)
SULKA'S WEDDING (DC)
SUMMER BEACH HOUSE (NY)
SUMMER BREAK (BA)
SUMMER DAYS/SUMMER LOVERS (DC)
SUMMER IN HEAT (DC)
SUMMER OF LAURA (DC)
SUMMER OF SCOTT NOLL (DC)
SUNNY DAY (NY)
SUPERBOWL BONDAGE (DC)
SUPERCHARGER (DC)
SUPERGIRLS DO GENERAL HOSPITAL (DC)
SUPERSTUDS (DC)
SURGE STUDIOS/RANGERS (DC)
SUSAN HART #1 (BN)
SUSAN HART VOL 2/STAR CUTS (DC)
SUSI 1ST BONDAGE (BA)
SUZE'S CENTERFOLD (DC)
SUZE'S CENTERFOLDS #7 (DC)
SUZY ALBERT VS. LITTLE JIMMY (DC)
SUZY'S BIRTHDAY BANG (DC)
SWAP MEAT (NY)
SWAPMEET (DC)
497
SWEATBOX (DC)
SWED. EROTICA #2 (NY)
SWED. EROTICA #11 (BN)
SWED. EROTICA #14 (BN)
SWED. EROTICA #16 (BN)
SWED. EROTICA #12 (NY)
SWED. EROTICA #18 (BN, BA)

SWED. EROTICA #20 (NY)
SWED. EROTICA #22 (BN)
SWED. EROTICA #23 (BN)
SWED. EROTICA #24 (BN, BA)
SWED. EROTICA #25 (BN, NY)
SWED. EROTICA #26 (BN)
SWED. EROTICA #27 (NY, BN)
SWED. EROTICA #28 (BN)
SWED. EROTICA #29 (BN)
SWED. EROTICA #30 (BN)
SWED. EROTICA #31 (BN, DC)
SWED. EROTICA #32 (BN)
SWED. EROTICA #33 (BN)
SWED. EROTICA #34 (BN)
SWED. EROTICA #35 (BN)
SWED. EROTICA #36 (BN)
SWED. EROTICA #37 (BN)
SWED. EROTICA #38 (BN)
SWED. EROTICA #39 (NY, BN)
SWED. EROTICA #10 (NY, BN)
SWED. EROTICA #41 (BN)
SWED. EROTICA #42 (BN)
SWED. EROTICA #43 (NY, BN)
SWED. EROTICA #44 (NY, BN)
SWED. EROTICA #45 (BN)
SWED. EROTICA #46 (BN)
SWED. EROTICA #47 (NY, BN, BA)
SWED. EROTICA #48 (BN)
SWED. EROTICA #49 (BN)
SWED. EROTICA #5 (NY)
SWED. EROTICA #50 (BN)
SWED. EROTICA #51 (BN)
SWED. EROTICA #52 (BN)
SWED. EROTICA #53 (BN)
SWED. EROTICA #54 (BN)
SWED. EROTICA #55 (BN, BA, DC)
SWED. EROTICA #56 (NY, BN)
SWED. EROTICA #57 (BN)
SWED. EROTICA #58 (BN)
SWED. EROTICA #59 (BN)
SWED. EROTICA #60 (BN, DC)
SWED. EROTICA #61 (BN, DC)
SWED. EROTICA #62 (NY, BN)
SWED. EROTICA #64 (BN, DC)
SWED. EROTICA #111 (BA)
SWEDISH EROTICA ALL YOU CAN EAT
SWEDISH EROTICA VOL. 63 (DC)
SWEDISH SORORITY GIRLS (DC)
SWEET ALICE (DC)
SWEET CHASTITY (DC)
SWEET DOMINANCE (DC)
SWEET DREAMS (DC)
TABOO (DC, NY)
TABOO AMERICAN STYLE (DC)
TABOO II (DC)
TABOO III (DC, NY)
TABOO IV THE YOUNGER GENERATION (BA, DC)
TAIL ENDERS (DC, NY)
TAILHOUSE ROCK (DC)
TAKE MY BODY (DC)
TALK DIRTY OF ME ONE MORE TIME (DC, BA)
TALK DIRTY OF ME PART II (DC, BA)
TALK DIRTY TO ME (DC)
TALK DIRTY TO ME III (DC)
TALL TIMBER (DC)
TAMING OF REBECCA (DC)
TAO PREVIEW TAPE (DC)
TAROT TEMPTRESS (DC)
TASKMASTER (DC)
TASTE OF CANDY (DC)
TASTE OF MONEY (DC)

TASTE THE LASH (DC)
TATTOOED LADY (DC)
TAXI GIRLS (DC, NY)
TAYLOR EVANS FANTASIES (DC)
TEACH ME (DC)
TEACHER TEACHING (DC)
TEACHER'S PET (DC)
TEACHER'S WEEKEND VACATION (DC)
TEASE ME (DC)
TEASERS (DC)
TEEN CLIMAX (NY)
TEENAGE CLIMAX-ANAL CLIMAX (NY)
TEENAGE CYCLE SLUTS (DC)
TEENAGE DESSERT (DC)
TEENAGE DEVIATE (DC)
TEENAGE DOG ORGY (NY)
TEENAGE HUSTLER (DC)
TEENAGE MADAM (DC)
TEENAGE SEX (NY)
TEENAGE SEX #778 (NY)
TEENAGE SEX #788 (NY)
TEENAGE SEX-GREEDY GIRLS (NY)
TEENAGE SEX-LUST LESSON (NY)
TEENAGE SEX-SALESMAN'S LUST (NY)
TEENAGE STEPMOTHER (DC)
TEMPLE OF LOVE (BN)
TEMPTRESS (DC)
TEN LITTLE MAIDENS (DC, BA)
TENNIS WITHOUT BALLS (DC)
TENNYBUNS (DC)
TERMS OF EMPLOYMENT (BA)
TERRI'S LESSON IN BONDAGE (DC)
THAT BOY (DC)
THAT BOY NEXT DOOR (DC)
THAT LADY FROM RIO (DC)
THAT LUCKY STIFF (DC)
THAT'S MY DAUGHTER (DC)
THE ANALYST (DC, BA)
THE ANIMAL IN ME (DC, BA)
THE AROUSERS (BA)
THE ARRANGEMENT (DC)
THE AWAKENING OF EMILY (DC)
THE AWAKENING OF SALLY (DC)
THE BACK ROW (DC)
THE BAD BRIDE (DC)
THE BEST OF RICHARD RANK (NY)
THE BIG E—VOL. #2 (DC)
THE BIG E—VOL. #4 (DC)
THE BIG E—VOL. #5 (DC)
THE BIG E REVIEW TAPE (DC)
THE BIG FANTASY (DC)
THE BIG SPENDER (DC)
THE BIG SURPRISE (DC)
THE BIG SWITCH (DC)
THE BIG THRILL (DC)
THE BIGGER THE BETTER (DC)
THE BIGGEST ONE I EVER SAW (DC)
THE BITE (DC, BA)
THE BLONDE (DC)
THE BLONDE NEXT DOOR (DC)
THE BOARDING HOUSE (DC)
THE CLUB (DC)
THE COMING OF JOYCE (DC)
THE COMPANY WE KEEP (DC)
THE DANCERS (DC)
THE DESTROYING ANGEL (DC)
THE DEVIL IN MISS JONES (DC)
THE DIRTY PICTURE SHOW (DC)
THE DRESDEN DIARY (BA)
THE EIFFEL TOWER (DC)
THE EMBASSY GIRLS/OPEN FOR BUSINESS (DC)

THE ENCHANTRESS (DC)
THE EROTIC WORLD OF LINDA WONG (DC)
THE EX-WIFE (DC)
THE EXPERIMENT (DC, NY)
THE EYES OF EDDIE MARS (NY, BA, DC)
THE FALCONHEAD COLLECTION-GOLDEN BOYS (BN)
THE FILTHY RICH (DC)
THE FINE ART OF ANAL INTERCOURSE (DC)
THE FINE ART OF CUNNILINGUS (DC)
THE FIRE IN FRANCESCA (DC)
THE FISHERMAN (BN)
THE GINGER EFFECT (DC)
THE GIRL FROM CHINA (DC)
THE GIRLS FROM SEX (DC)
THE GIRLS WITH THE HUNGRY EYES (BA)
THE GIRLS OF KLIT HOUSE (DC)
THE GIRLS OF THE A TEAM (DC)
THE GOOD THE BAD AND THE HORNY (DC)
THE GRAFENBERG SPOT (DC)
THE HEARTBREAK GIRL (DC)
THE HEAT IS ON (DC)
THE HORNY DOG (NY)
THE HOT ONES (DC)
THE HUNG AND THE RESTLESS (DC)
THE IDOL (DC)
THE INTERVIEW (DC)
THE IRVING CLAW CLASSICS #1 (DC)
THE JANITOR (DC)
THE JOY STICK GIRLS (NY, DC)
THE JUNK YARD (DC)
THE LADY VANESSA (DC, NY)
THE LAST SUPPER (DC)
THE LEATHERMEN (NY)
THE LOVE SCENE (DC, MI)
THE LOVER GIRLS (DC)
THE LUSTY ADVENTURER (BA)
THE MAIN ATTRACTION (DC)
THE MILLIONAIRE (DC)
THE ORGY MACHINE (DC)
THE OTHER SIDE OF ASPEN (DC)
THE PEEK A BOO GANG (DC)
THE PERFECT FIT (DC)
THE PERFECT GIFT (DC)
THE POONIES (DC)
THE PROSTITUTE (DC)
THE PUNISHMENT OF GARY WILDE (DC)
THE RETURN OF ALCATRAZ (DC)
THE SEX GODDESS (DC)
THE SHOE STORE (DC)
THE SISTER'S PUNISHMENT (DC)
THE SLAVE EXCHANGE (DC)
THE SPERMINATOR (DC)
THE STORY OF JOANNA (NY)
THE STORY OF O (NY)
THE T & A TEAM (DC)
THE THERAPIST (DC, NY)
THE TONGUE (DC)
THE TOTAL WOMAN (DC)
THE TRAINERS (DC)
THE TRAINING OF JULIA (DC)
THE TRAP (DC)
THE ULTIMATE IN X-RATED #6 (NY)
THE ULTIMATE O (DC)
THE UNTAMED (DC, NY)
THE VIRGIN AND THE LOVER (DC)
THE WHORE'S PORT (BA)
THE WIZARD OF AHHHS (DC)
THE WOMEN IN PINK
THE X FACTOR (DC)
THE YOUNG AND THE HUNG (DC)
THESE BASES ARE LOADED (DC)

THEY ALL CAME (DC)
THEY GAVE A PARTY AND EVERYONE CAME (BA)
THEY LAY IT ON THE LINE (BA)
THEY WORK HARD FOR THEIR MONEY (DC)
THINKING BIG (DC)
THOROUGHLY AMOROUS AMY (DC)
THREE DAY PASS (DC)
THRILL STREET BLUES (PH)
THRILLING DRILLING (DC)
THROAT/TWELVE YEARS AFTER (DC)
THRU THE LOOKING GLASS (DC)
THRUST (DC)
THUNDER THIGHS (NY)
TIED AND TICKLED (DC, BN, NY)
TIFFANY MINX (DC)
TIGHT AND TENDER (DC)
TIGHT DELIGHT (DC)
TIGHT END (DC)
TIGHT OF TENDRE (BA)
TIGHT THAI CUNT 67S (NY)
TIMES SQUARE STRIP (DC)
TINA MAKES A DEAL (DC)
TINA'S PARTY (DC)
TIT #1 (BA)
TITILLATION (DC)
TNT TITALATORS (NY)
TO RIDE A TIGER (DC)
TODAY TOMORROW YESTERDAY (DC)
TOILET ORGY (NY)
TOMBOY (DC)
TONGUE IN CHEEK (BA)
TONIGHT (DC)
TONS OF BUNS (BA)
TONS OF BUNS #2 (NY)
TONY'S INITIATION (DC)
TOO GOOD TO BE TRUE (DC)
TOO HOT TO TOUCH (DC)
TOO MANY PIECES (DC)
TOO MUCH TOO SOON (DC)
TOO NAUGHTY TO SAY NO (BA)
TOO YOUNG TO KNOW (DC)
TOP SECRET (DC)
TOPLESS WAITRESS WANTED (NY)
TORTURE DUNGEON (DC)
TOTALLY AWESOME (DC)
TOUCH ME IN THE MORNING (DC)
TOWER OF POWER (DC)
TRACI LORDS (DC)
TRACY DICK (DC)
TRACY IN HEAVEN (DC)
TRADING PARTNERS (DC)
TRAINING ACADEMY (DC)
TRANSEXUAL ENCOUNTERS (NY, BA)
TRANSFORMATION OF SULKA (DC)
TRANSVESTITES IN BONDAGE (DC)
TRASH (DC)
TRASHY LADY (DC)
TREASURE CHEST (DC)
TRI-SEXUAL ENCOUNTERS #1 (DC)
TRICK OR TREAT (DC)
TRICK TIME (DC)
TRILOGY OF THE BIZARRE (NY, BA)
TRINITY BROWN (DC, BA)
TRIPLE TREAT (DC)
TRIPLETS (DC)
TRIPPLE CROSS (BN)
TRIPS (DC)
TRISEXUAL (DC)
TRISEXUAL #2 (DC)
TRISEXUAL ENCOUNTERS #2 (DC)
TROPHY #1 (DC)

TROPHY #2 (DC)
TROPHY #4 (DC)
TRPOHY #5 (DC)
TROPHY #7 (DC)
TROPHY #8 (DC)
TROPHY #9 (DC)
TROPHY/SCREEN PLAY (DC)
TROPIC OF DESIRE (DC)
TRUCK STOP (DC)
TRUE CONFESSIONS (DC)
TRUE CRIMES OF PASSION (DC)
TUB TRICKS (DC)
TUESDAY MORNING WORKOUT (DC)
TUESDAY'S LOVER (BA)
TWELVE AT NOON (DC)
TWO TIMER (DC)
TWO VS. ONE (DC)
TOUCH OF MISCHIEF (DC)
TOUGH AND TENDER (DC)
TOUGH COMPETITION (DC)
TOUGH GUYS (DC)
TOURIST TRAP (DC)
TOWER OF LOVE (DC)
ULTIMATE MOMENTS (DC)
UNDER CONSTRUCTION (BA)
UNDERCOVERS (DC)
UP (DC)
UP & IN (DC)
UP DESIREE LANE (DC, BA)
UP IN THE AIR (DC)
UP UP AND AWAY (DC)
UPSIDE DOWN (DC)
URBAN COWGIRLS (DC)
URBAN HEAT (DC)
URGED IN YOUNG GIRLS (DC)
URGENT DESIRES (DC)
USDA CHOICE (DC)
VALLEY BOYS (DC)
VALLEY GIRL'S REVENGE (DC)
VALLEY VIXENS (DC)
VAMP'S BLACKMAIL (DC)
VANESSA—MAID IN MANHATTAN (DC)
VANESSA #2 (DC, NY)
VANESSA'S BED OF PLEASURE (DC, BA)
VANESSA'S HOT NIGHT (DC)
VARIATIONS (DC)
VCA PREVIEW #2 (DC)
VCX PREVIEW #1 (DC)
VELVET HIGH (BA)
VELVET TONGUE (DC)
VICTORIA'S SECRET DESIRES (DC)
VIDEO ENCOUNTERS (DC)
VIDEO GIRLS (DC)
VIOLATED (DC)
VIVA VANESSA THE UNDRESSER (DC)
VIXEN (DC)
VIXENS OF KUNG FU (PH)
WALL TO WALL (DC)
WALL TO WALL #2 (DC)
WALL TO WALL SEX #2 (NY)
WANDA WHIPS WALL STREET (DC)
WANTED—BILLY THE KID (DC)
WATERMELON BABES (DC)
WEEK-END COWGIRLS (DC)
WEEKEND FANTASY (DC)
WET (DC)
WET AND WILD #1 (BA)
WET DREAMS (DC, BA)
WET LUST (BN)
WET RAINBOW (DC)
WET SEX (DC)

WET SHORTS (DC)
WET WIDE AND WICKED (DC)
WHAT BOTTOMS ARE FOR (DC)
WHAT'S MY PUNISHMENT? (DC)
WHEN SHE WAS BAD (DC)
WHITE CHICKS (NY)
WHORES POINT (DC)
WHORESMAN (DC)
WICKED SCHOOLGIRLS (DC)
WICKED WAYS (DC)
WICKED WHISPERS (DC)
WILD ABOUT HORSES (NY)
WILD BILL'S HUGE LADIES (NY)
WILD DALLAS HONEY (DC, PH)
WILD OATS (DC)
WILD SIDE (DC)
WILD TOGA PARTY (BA)
WILD WEEKEND (DC)
WILDE HOUSE (DC)
WILDSIDE (DC)
WINDOWS (DC)
WINGS OF PASSION (DC)
WISH YOU WERE HERE (DC)
WITH LOVE ANNETTE (DC)
WITH LOVE LONI (DC)
WOLLUST IN LEADER (NY)
WOMEN AND ANIMALS DOG-LOVERS (NY)
WOMEN AND ANIMALS (NY)
WOMEN AT PLAY (DC)
WOMEN IN LOVE (DC)
WOMEN WHO LOVE WOMEN (DC)
WOMEN WHO SEDUCE MEN (DC, NY)
WOMEN WITHOUT MEN (DC)
WOMENS DESIRES (DC)
WOMEN'S FANTASIES (DC, NY)
WORKING GIRLS (DC)
WORKING IT OUT (DC)
WORKING MEN (DC)
WORKING OVERTIME (NY)
WORKLOAD (DC)
WORLD OF SUPERSTARS (DC)
WRECKED 'EM (DC)
WRESTLING MEAT (DC)
X TEAM (DC)
X-RATED BLOOPERS (DC, MI)
XRCO (DC)
YAMA HAMA MAMAS (NY)
YANK MY DOODLE (DC)
YELLOW FEVER (DC)
YES MY LADY (DC)
YOUNG AND INNOCENT (DC)
YOUNG AND RESTLESS (DC)
YOUNG GIRLS DO (DC)
YOUNG OLYMPIANS (DC)
YOUNG ONES (DC)
YOUNG PREY (DC)
YOUNG SEKA #1 (BN)
YOUNG SEKA VOL 1/STAR CUTS (DC)
YOUNG SEKA VOL 2/STAR CUTS (DC)
YOUNG STAR GAZER (DC)
YOUNG YANKEES (DC)
YOUNGBLOODS (DC)
YOU'RE THE BOSS (DC)
YOUTHFUL LUST (DC)
1001 NIGHTS (DC)
18 CANDLES (DC)
4 IN HAND (DC)
5 DAYS WITH PHIL/OLD RELIABLE (DC)
69 PARK AVENUE (DC)
7-CARD STUD (DC)
800 FANTASY LANE (DC)

SPECIFIC MATERIALS

In addition to the quantitative data presented above, Commission staff members also reviewed specific materials and prepared descriptions of selected materials as contained hereinafter.

Materials were rented, purchased or obtained from the United States Postal Inspection Service, the United States Customs Service and state and local police agencies that had been seized or otherwise obtained during the course of official investigations of commercial obscenity sales and distribution. The Kentucky State Police provided numerous exhibits purchased in a recent investigation and obscenity prosecution involving video cassettes and other items in the Western District of Kentucky.[2261]

No claim is made that the materials described are the most representative sample that could be found in there is no existing source of information to identify such materials. The materials that were selected however were not to be rare, one-of-a-kind items or the "worst" representative materials found. All items selected from stores were from an identifiable class of material in the display areas of the store and were representative of that class. In addition to the foregoing, all materials had to be for sale to the general public, over the counter or through mail order at addresses that could easily be obtained from materials in pornography outlets in the districts obtained. Videocassette films were rented, or available for rental, at "neighborhood" video dealers and were also required to be available in pornography outlets in nearby locations. Some of the materials were specifically selected because they had been found to be obscene in a federal or state criminal proceeding and/or because of their virtual nationwide availability.[2262] Each description identifies the staff member preparing the description, the source from which the material was obtained and other relevant information.

MAGAZINE DESCRIPTIONS

Tri-Sexual Lust[2263] is a 32 page, four-color magazine, measuring 8-1/2x11 inches, containing 63 four-color photographs. The magazine shows no copyright and identifies itself as a "Visions of Fantasy" publication with no address listed. It lists a retail price of $15.00. There is one full page of advertisements for a hardcore magazine. The cover features an apparently naked caucasian-female lying on her back with two male caucasian erect penises touching her cheek, next to her wide open mouth. A limited written text accompanies the photographs. The magazine contains photographs of one or more of the following acts:

1. One photograph of an apparently naked caucasian-female lying on her back. There are two erect penises lying on her cheek next to her wide open mouth.

2. Two photographs of two clothed caucasian males with a clothed female.

3. One photograph of a partially clothed female holding the penis of a naked male. The male is massaging her vagina through her underwear. A partially clothed male is holding one of the female's breasts in his hand.

4. Six photographs of a partially clothed female performing fellatio on a male while the other naked male is performing cunnilingus on the female.

5. Three close-up photographs of the partially clothed female performing fellatio on a naked or partially clothed male.

6. One photograph of the partially clothed female performing fellatio on a naked male while the other male holds one of her breasts in his hand and licks her arm with his tongue.

7. Eighteen photographs of the partially-clothed female performing fellatio on one of the naked males while the other naked male enters her vaginally from the rear with his penis.

8. Six photographs of the partially clothed female performing fellatio on a naked male while the other naked male enters her vaginally with his penis from the front.

2261. *United States v. Sovereign News Company, General Video of America*, No. Cr84-00149-L(A), Western District of Kentucky (1985).

2262. Three films were selected because of their substantial history of litigation. A summary of cases relating to the three films follows.

2263. Description of Senior Investigator Chapman. This magazine was seized by Kentucky State Police and found obscene in *U.S. v. Sovereign News Co., General Video of America, et al.*, No. CR 84-00149-C(A) (W.D. KY).

9. Three photographs of the naked female performing fellatio on what appears to be an ejaculating naked male while the other naked male is next to her.

10. Three photographs of a naked male vaginally entering from the rear a partially clothed female with his penis while the other naked male kisses one of her breasts.

11. Three photographs of the partially clothed female performing fellatio on a naked male while holding the penis of the other naked male in her hand.

12. One photograph of the partially clothed female performing fellatio on a naked male while the other naked male holds one of her breasts in her hand.

13. One photograph of a partially clothed male kissing a partially clothed female while the other naked male is performing cunnilingus on the female.

14. Five photographs of a partially clothed female performing fellatio on a male while the other naked male holds her breasts and places his erect penis on the back of her neck.

15. One close-up photograph of the female performing fellatio on one male while the other male's erect penis rests on her cheek.

16. One photograph of the female performing fellatio on the two males at the same time. The heads of the penises are touching, forming a 180 degree line.

17. Two photographs of a female performing fellatio on an ejaculating penis.

18. One photograph of the male vaginally entering the partially clothed female with his penis while the other naked male kisses her mouth.

19. One photograph of the partially clothed female being vaginally penetrated by one of the naked male's penis while the other naked male is licking her buttocks.

20. One photograph of one naked male vaginally penetrating the partially clothed female with his penis while she performs fellatio on the ejaculating penis of the other male.

Teeny Tits, Big Boobs to Chew & Suck On #1,[2264] is an eighty-eight page four-color magazine, measuring 8x10-1/2 inches, containing 123 photographs. Sixteen photographs are four color photographs. The magazine indicates a copyright and identifies itself as an "Oakmore Enterprises, Inc.," publication of 1779 W. Adams St., Los Angeles, California. It has a listed retail price of $7.50. There are three full pages of advertisements for hardcore, sexually explicit magazines, videos and films. The cover of the magazine features two photographs of partially clothed caucasian females with their hair in pigtails and their breasts exposed. A written text accompanies the photographs throughout the magazine describing several scenarios. These include an abduction and sexual assault with the female ultimately becoming a willing partner and a female encountering a number of strange men, becoming engulfed in group sex with those men and engaging in acts of sexual intercourse, fellatio and cunnilingus. The magazine contains photographs of one or more of the following poses:

1. Thirty-four photographs of a partially clothed caucasian female exposing her breasts.

2. Thirteen photographs of a partially clothed caucasian female licking her breasts.

3. Five photographs of a partially clothed caucasian female licking her breasts and exposing her vagina.

4. Eighteen photographs of a partially clothed caucasian female exposing her breasts and spreading open her vagina with her fingers.

5. Thirty-seven photographs of a partially clothed caucasian female exposing her breasts and her vagina.

6. Twelve photographs of a partially clothed caucasian female exposing her breasts and inserting a finger or fingers into her vagina.

7. Four photographs of a partially clothed caucasian female exposing her breasts and her buttocks.

8. Three close-up photographs of a caucasian female's vagina spread open with her fingers.

Big Tit Dildo Bondage Vol. #1, Number 1[2265] is a 44 page, four-color cover magazine measuring 8-1/2x11 inches, containing 123 photographs. Ten photographs are four-color photographs. The magazine indicates a copyright date of 1985, by Holly Publications, 12011 Sherman Rd, North Hollywood, California 91605. It has a listed retail price of $7.00. There are two full pages of advertisement for sado-masochistic magazines and video-tapes involving foot worship and torture. One video-tape entitled "Foot Torture" is described as follows:

A pretty jogger is taken to a man's apartment and made to remove her outfit right down to her panties and sweat socks. After smelling her socks he licks her bare feet, ties them up and places them over a Hibatchi. Then he tickles them and. . . .

The cover of the magazine features four, four color photographs. Each photograph depicts a naked female bound with rope, gagged and displaying a vibrator-dildo partially inserted into her vagina. A written text accompanies the photographs throughout the magazine. It graphically describes how women enjoy being bound, gagged and humiliated even though they may at first resist engaging in such activity. The magazine contains photographs of one or more of the following depictions:

1. Two photographs of a naked caucasian female with her mouth gagged and her arms and legs tightly bound with rope. The rope is tightly looped around the base of each breast causing them to swell to an abnormal size. There is a vibrator-dildo partially inserted into the vagina.

2. Seven photographs of a naked black female with her mouth gagged and her arms and legs tied to two posts. Rope is tightly looped around the base of each breast causing them to swell to an abnormal size. There is a vibrator-dildo partially inserted into the vagina.

3. Sixteen photographs of a naked-caucasian-female with her mouth gagged. Her arms are tightly bound to

her legs causing them to spread apart. A vibrator-dildo is partly inserted into the vagina. She is wearing a wide leather collar around her neck. A metal ring is attached to the front of the collar through which the restraining ropes are passed.

4. Five photographs of a partially-clad or naked female inserting a vibrator-dildo into her vagina.

5. One close-up photograph of a caucasian female's vagina with a vibrator-dildo held in close proximity.

6. Thirteen photographs of a partially clothed and gagged caucasian female with her arms bound with rope. The rope is tightly looped around the base of each breast causing them to swell to an abnormal size. There are clothespins pinching each nipple and a vibrator-dildo partially inserted into her vagina.

7. Three close-up photographs of a naked caucasian female bound with rope, a vibrator-dildo is partially inserted into her vagina.

8. Two photographs of a naked black-female blindfolded and gagged with her arms tied to two posts. The rope is tightly looped around the base of each breast causing them to swell to an abnormal size.

9. One photograph the same as #8 without the blindfold.

10. One photograph of a naked and gagged black female with her arms and legs bound with rope to two posts. The rope is tightly looped around the base of each breast causing them to swell to an abnormal size.

11. One photograph the same as #10 with a pipe wrench affixed to her left nipple.

12. Two close-up photographs of the wrench affixed to the left nipple.

13. Three photographs of a partially-clothed caucasian female with rope tightly looped around the base of each breast causing them to swell to an abnormal size.

14. Three close-up photographs of a gagged and naked caucasian female with rope looped tightly around the

2265. Description of Senior Investigator Chapman. This magazine was purchased from an adult bookstore in Washington, D.C.; photographs appearing in this magazine were part of a collection which were the subject of a Federal Bureau of Investigation inquiry resulting in a prosecution and conviction. See, Los Angeles Hearing, Vol. II, Charles Sullivan, p. 65.

base of each breast causing them to swell to an abnormal size. Clothes-pins are pinching each nipple.

15. Five close-up photographs of a dildo-vibrator partially inserted into the vagina of a partially clothed caucasian female.

16. One photograph of a partially clothed caucasian female with her feet tied to the ends of a pole spreading her legs. A dildo-vibrator is partially inserted into her vagina.

17. Three photographs of a naked and gagged caucasian female bound with ropes and her arms to her side. The ropes are attached to a hoist.

18. Four close-up photographs of ropes looped around the base of a caucasian female's breasts causing them to swell to an abnormal size.

19. A close-up photograph of a bound and naked caucasian female's buttocks exposing her vagina.

20. One photograph of a naked caucasian female on her knees with her arms bound with rope to a pole behind her back.

21. Five photographs of a gagged and naked caucasian female with her arms bound with rope to a pole behind her back. Rope is tightly looped around the base of her breasts causing them to swell to an abnormal size. A dildo-vibrator is partially inserted into the vagina.

22. One photograph of a partially clothed caucasian female with her arms bound with rope behind her back. Her wrists are attached to a rope hoist causing her to bend over.

23. One photograph of a partially clothed caucasian female with her arms apparently bound over her head. Her breasts are being tightly squeezed in a vise-like instrument.

24. Three close-up photographs of a naked caucasian female's buttocks with a dildo partially inserted into her vagina and a long douche-like hose partially inserted into her rectum.

25. One extremely close-up photograph of a dildo partially inserted into a caucasian female's vagina.

26. One photograph of a partially clothed

caucasian female secured with ankle and wrist restraints to a rack mounted on a wall.

27. One photograph of a partially-clothed caucasian female her wrists are tied together and hoisted over her head. Her legs are attached to the ends of a pole spreading her legs apart.

28. One photograph of a gagged and naked caucasian female with a dildo-vibrator partially inserted into her vagina.

29. Eight photographs of a gagged and naked caucasian female. Her arms are bound and hoisted over her head. Her ankles are tied to the ends of a pole spreading her legs apart. A dildo-vibrator is partially inserted into her vagina.

Squirt 'Em[2266] has a retail list price of $6.95. It is a four color cover magazine measuring 8-1/4x11 inches. There are 48 pages containing 69 photographs, 12 of which are four color photographs. The magazine is identified as a Golden State Publication, copyrighted by Oakmore Enterprises, Inc., 1779 W. Adams Blvd, Los Angeles, California. The magazine contains three full pages of ads for adult magazines and video cassettes. The cover of the magazine features four photographs of two caucasian females, apparently naked, manually expressing a stream of milk from their engorged breasts. One of the photographs involves a close-up view of a breast expressing milk into a glass. A written text which accompanies the photographs throughout the magazine describes the sexual fantasies and activities in graphic detail of the two featured caucasian females. The 69 photographs depict one or more of the following acts:

1. Seventeen photographs of a naked caucasian female manually expressing a stream of milk from her engorged breasts with her fingers.

2. Five close-up photographs of an engorged breast expressing a stream of milk into a glass.

3. Four photographs of a naked caucasian female who while lying on her back manually expressed a stream of milk into the air from her engorged breast

2266. Description by Senior Investigator Chapman. This magazine was purchased from an adult bookstore in Washington, D.C.

causing the stream of milk to fall back onto her chest.

4. Six photographs of a partially clothed female manually expressing a stream of milk from her engorged breast.
5. Three photographs of a naked female caressing her engorged breasts.
6. Two photographs of a partially clothed female with engorged breasts displaying full frontal nudity.
7. One photograph of a partially clothed female squeezing her engorged breast with what appears to be her milk dripping from her hand.
8. Eleven photographs of a partially clothed female exposing her vagina to the camera.
9. One photograph of a partially clothed female exposing her vagina to the camera while eating a banana.
10. Eight photographs of a partially clothed female displaying full frontal nudity with what appears to be her own milk covering her from her chest to her vagina.
11. One close-up photograph of an engorged breast being manually expressed with what appears to milk dripping from the fingers and inside a glass being held close to the breast.
12. Two photographs of a partially clad female, lying on her back with what appears to be her milk on her chest.
13. Three close-up photographs of a female manually expressing her engorged breast showing milk on her nipple.
14. One photograph of a partially clothed female apparently drinking her own milk from a glass.

Al Parker and Sky Dawson in Turned On II[2267] is an 8½x11 inch four-color cover magazine containing 76 photographs, 19 of which are four-color photographs. It lists a retail price of $10.00. There is no statement of copyright nor any publishing information. The magazine features one full page ad for *Turned On #1* displaying two photographs of fellatio and one of oral-anal contact. The cover of *Turned On II* features two four color photographs. The large one consists of a close-up photograph of a caucasian male licking the flaccid head of a black male's penis.

The smaller photograph depicts a caucasian male licking the head of another caucasian male's penis. The male performing fellatio has what appears to be semen dripping from his lip and chin. There is no written text accompanying the photographs. The 76 photographs depict one or more of the following acts:

1. Two close-up photographs of a caucasian male licking the flaccid head of a black male's penis.
2. Four photographs of a caucasian male licking the head of another caucasian male's penis. The male performing fellatio has what appears to be semen dripping from his tongue, lip and chin.
3. Three photographs of a group of naked males masturbating in the presence of a large figure of a penis.
4. Twenty-two close-up photographs of a naked caucasian male performing fellatio on another naked caucasian male with or without others present.
5. One photograph of a naked caucasian male with his hand on the buttocks of a naked black male.
6. One close-up photograph of a naked caucasian male with the testicles of another naked caucasian male in his mouth.
7. One photograph of a naked caucasian male biting and pulling on the lower rear straps of another caucasian male's athletic supporter.
8. Five photographs of a naked caucasian male engaged in oral-anal contact with another naked caucasian male with or without others present.
9. One photograph of a naked caucasian male holding in his hand the flaccid penis of another caucasian male.
10. Four photographs of a naked caucasian male engaged in fellatio with another naked caucasian male.
11. Two close-up photographs of a naked caucasian male with his mouth close to the erect penis of another caucasian male.
12. One photograph the same as #11 with the caucasian male holding in his hand the erect penis of the other caucasian male.

2267. Description by Senior Investigator Chapman. This magazine was purchased from an adult bookstore in Washington, D.C.

13. One close-up photograph of a caucasian male engaged in fellatio with a black male.

14. One photograph of a naked caucasian male bending over, exposing his anus and testicles to the camera.

15. Eleven photographs of a naked caucasian male penetrating the anus of another naked caucasian male.

16. Two photographs of a naked caucasian male bent over with another naked caucasian male standing behind and over him, masturbating.

17. One photograph of two naked caucasian males standing together kissing.

18. One photograph of one naked caucasian male engaged in fellatio with another caucasian male while a third caucasian male stands nearby masturbating.

19. One photograph of one naked caucasian male engaged in fellatio with two other naked caucasian males at the same time.

Bizarre Climax No. 9[2268] is a 36 page, four-color magazine measuring 6¹/₂x9 inches, containing 64 four-color photographs. There is no list price. The magazine indicates a copyright date of 1979, and identifies itself as a "Viola-Press" publication, 6000 Frankfurt Postfach 700734, Printed by ZBF-Vertriebs Gmbh, Schossbergstrasse 23, 6200 WI-Schierstein. There are two full pages advertising adult 8mm movies and magazines. The cover features four photographs. The large one depicts 3 adult caucasian females wearing constrictive latex and leather S&M outfits. One female is bound, gagged and blindfolded. She is restrained to a rack-like apparatus and is being dominated by the other two females. The 3 smaller photographs depict the same females; one female receives an enema from a douche then expels the contents from her rectum into a chamber pot.

The 3rd photograph depicts one of the females with her buttocks spread exposing her anus and vagina. She is urinating into a chamber pot held by another female. A trilingual text (English, German and French) accompanies the photographs throughout the magazine, describing in graphic and nauseating detail the use of urine and feces in sadomasochistic sexual activity. Unless otherwise

indicated, the caucasian females are wearing leather or latex constrictive S&M attire which at times exposes their breasts and vaginas. The 64 photographs depict one or more of the following acts.

1. Three photographs of a caucasian female bound, gagged, blindfolded and restrained to rack-like apparatus. She is being dominated by two other caucasian females.

2. One photograph the same as #1 with a dildo inserted into the vagina of the bound and gagged female.

3. Four photographs depicting the administration of an enema with a douche-like appliance, fully exposing the caucasian female's anus and vagina.

4. Eight close-up photographs of a caucasian female expelling the liquid enema and fecal matter from her rectum into a chamber pot.

5. Two close-up photographs of a caucasian female's buttocks spread to expose her anus and vagina, urinating into a chamber pot held by another white female.

6. One photograph of a caucasian female wearing a constrictive full head and face latex mask. She is supporting a black dildo between her breasts with the head of the dildo in her mouth.

7. One close-up photograph of a caucasian female inserting a dildo into the shaved vagina of another caucasian female.

8. One photograph of two caucasian females kissing in a clear glass bathtub, half-full of a yellowish liquid which appears to be urine.

9. One photograph of two caucasian females standing and facing the camera exposing their vaginas.

10. One photograph of a caucasian female with the hose of the douche inserted into her nose. She is sitting with her legs spread exposing her vagina. Another caucasian female is behind the first holding the hose.

11. One photograph of two caucasian females; one with a dildo inserted into her rectum and the other female with the end of the dildo in her mouth.

2268. Description by Senior Investigator Chapman. Seized by the United States Postal Inspection Service. This magazine is available by mail order.

12. One photograph of a caucasian female sitting on a chair toilet seat inserting a black dildo into her vagina while another caucasian female is apparently holding the chair off the ground.

13. One photograph of a caucasian female sitting on a chair toilet seat urinating. Another caucasian female is apparently holding the chair off of the ground.

14. Two photographs of a caucasian female sitting on the chair toilet urinating onto the masked face of a caucasian female under the chair.

15. One close-up photograph of the caucasian female's buttocks on the chair toilet seat urinating, with a black dildo inserted in her vagina.

16. One close-up photograph of a caucasian female sitting on the chair toilet seat defecating.

17. One close-up photograph of a caucasian female with a douche hose inserted in her nose, spreading her legs and exposing her vagina and anus.

18. A series of five photographs showing a clothed caucasian male encountering two clothed caucasian female prostitutes.

19. One photograph of a naked caucasian male being fellated by one of two caucasian females who are attired in S&M apparel exposing their breasts and vaginas.

20. One photograph of one caucasian female straddling a naked caucasian male on his hands and knees while the second caucasian female masturbates on a couch nearby.

21. One photograph of one of the caucasian females sitting on the face of the other caucasian female who is performing cunnilingus.

22. Two close-up photographs of a penis penetrating a vagina.

23. One photograph of a caucasian female with her mouth open and tongue protruding. Semen is dripping from her face.

24. A series of four photographs showing a caucasian female servant preparing her caucasian female mistress for defecation.

25. Three close-up photographs of the caucasian mistress defecating into a silver plated dish.

26. Two photographs of two caucasian females wearing school uniforms. One is sucking and fondling the breast of the other while masturbating.

27. One photograph of a caucasian female teacher wearing a fullbody constrictive latex outfit holding a switch in front of the two caucasian female students.

28. One photograph of the teacher spanking the exposed buttocks of one of the students while the other looks on.

29. One photograph of the teacher wearing the fullbody latex outfit standing next to the two naked students.

30. One photograph of the teacher sitting on top of a desk urinating onto one of the students.

31. One close-up photograph of one of the students with her legs spread exposing her anus and vagina while kissing the teacher on her mouth.

Lisa, 10 years, and her dog[2269] is 32 page two-color magazine measuring 5 3/4x8 1/4 inches, containing 29 two-color photos. There is no list price. The magazine indicates a copyright and identifies itself as a "Exim Training" publication of Blagardsgade 36, dk 2200, Copenhagen-N-Denmark. The magazine contains 2-1/2 pages of advertisements for other child pornographic magazines. The ads features photographs of naked prepubescent females indentified as 10 years-old and committing fellatio on an adult male, there is also an advertisement for S&M magazines feature adults and children. The cover of Lisa, 10 years, and her dog, features a photograph of a naked prepubescent caucasian female identified as 10 years old, holding a male dachshund in her arms. A tri-lingal written text (English, German and French) accompanies the photographs throughout the magazine describing in graphic detail bestial acts involving cunnilingus and masturbation. The 29 photographs depict one or more of the following acts including the child identified as Lisa.

1. Three photographs of a naked prepubsent female holding a male dachshund in her arms.

2269. Description by Senior Investigator Chapman. Seized by the U.S. Postal Inspection Service in cooperation with the U.S. Customs Service. This magazine is available by mail order.

2. Two photographs of a partially clothed prepubesent female exposing her vagina.

3. One photograph of a partially clothed prepubescent female exposing her buttocks.

4. Four photographs of a partially clothed prepubescent female posed with the dog.

5. Four photographs of a naked prepubescent female posed with the dog.

6. Six photographs of the dog licking the vagina of the partially clothed prepubescent female.

7. One photograph of the naked prepubescent female masturbating the male dog.

8. Five photographs of the dog licking the vagina of the naked prepubescent female.

9. One photograph of a naked prepubescent female lying on her stomach with the dog straddling her back in a position commonly referred to as "Doggie Style."

10. Two photographs of a naked prepubescent female exposing her vagina to the camera and posed with the dog.

Every Dog Has His Day, 13 has a list price of $10.00. It is a 48-page magazine, measuring 8-1/2x11 inches displaying a four-color cover. It contains one hundred and eleven photographs, eleven of which are in color, and the remainder in black and white. There is no statement of copyrights or publishing rights. The cover features two photographs. The large photograph depicts a naked caucasian male fellating a large dog, described in the text as a cross between a German shepherd and a collie. The smaller photograph depicts one naked caucasian male licking the anus of the other naked caucasian male who is masturbating.

The written text, continuing throughout the entire magazine, describes two men who after meeting in a bar go home together and ultimately become involved in homosexual acts and bestiality. The one hundred and eleven photographs depict one or more of the following acts in a living room setting, many of which involve close-up photography.

1. Four photographs of a naked male licking the anus of another naked male.

2. Five photographs of a naked male masturbating.

3. Eleven photographs of a naked male engaged in fellatio with a dog.

4. Two photographs of two naked males masturbating each other.

5. Twelve photographs of one naked male licking the testicles of another naked male.

6. Eighteen photographs of a naked male engaged in fellatio with another naked male.

7. One photograph of a naked male squeezing his testicles.

8. Seven photographs of a naked male engaged in anal intercourse with another naked male.

9. Two photographs of a naked male masturbating a dog.

10. Two pictures of a dog licking a naked male's penis.

11. One photograph of a naked male kissing the dog's mouth.

12. Seven photographs of a dog licking the anus of a naked male.

13. Three photographs of a dog licking the compressed testicles of a naked male.

14. Four photographs of a naked male licking the dog's testicles.

15. Three photographs of a naked male engaged in fellatio with another naked male who is engaged in fellatio with the dog.

16. Four photographs of one naked male standing and one naked male kneeling in front of him with what appears to be semen dripping from the kneeling male's face.

17. Three photographs of a naked male posing with an erect penis.

18. Four photographs of two naked males kissing.

19. Three photographs of a naked male licking the body of the other naked male.

20. Three photographs of naked males posing.

21. Three photographs of a naked male engaged in anal intercourse with the other naked male with the dog in the picture.

22. One photograph of the dog straddling a naked male lying on his back.

23. One photograph of a naked male engaged in fellatio with another naked male while having his testicles licked by the dog.

24. One photograph of the naked males kissing while the dog licks the testicles of one of the males.

25. One photograph of a naked male engaged in fellatio with the other naked male while the dog licks the knee of one of the males.

Pregnant Lesbians No. 1[2270] is a 8-1/4"x10-3/4", 32-page four-color magazine. It contains 46 four-color photographs and lists a retail price of $11.95. There is no statement of copyright, "Graficolor Productions" is the only publishing information provided. The cover features 3 photographs. The large one shows two obviously pregnant, partially clothed, caucasian females, kissing with their tongues, and their distended abdomens touching. The two smaller photographs show the same females inserting their tongues into the vagina of the other. A written text accompanies the photograph and continues throughout the magazine graphically describing what is occuring in the photographs. The 46 photographs depict one or more of the following acts:

1. Six photographs of two partially clothed, obviously pregnant caucasian females kissing with their tongues and with their abdomens touching.

2. Seven close-up photographs of the same females with one inserting her tongue into the vagina of the other.

3. Three photographs of one of the females licking the abdomen of the other while inserting a finger into the other female's vagina.

4. Nine photographs of one female licking or sucking the breast of the other female.

5. One photograph of one female lying on top of the other female with their abdomens pressed together.

6. Two photographs of one female lying on her back while the other female touches the first female's vagina with her fingers.

7. Three photographs of one female inserting her tongue into the vagina of the other.

8. Two photographs of one female kissing the buttocks of the other female while

inserting her finger into the other female's vagina.

9. Two photographs of one female touching the other female's breast with a vibrator.

10. Two photographs of one female inserting her tongue and a vibrator into the vagina of the other.

11. One photograph of one female kissing the buttocks of, and inserting a dildo into the vagina of the other female.

12. Two photographs of one female on her hands and knees with the other female on her knees behind her. There appears to be a dildo inserted into their vaginas between them.

13. One close-up photograph of the same dildo inserted in both females' vaginas.

14. Three close-up photographs of one female inserting her finger into the vagina of the other.

15. One photo of the two females sitting together. One touches the other's breast. while one touches the abdomen of the other.

Asian Slut[2271] is an 8-1/4x10-1/4 inch, 32 page four-color magazine. It contains 42 four-color photographs and lists a retail price of $12.50. There is no statement of copyright or publishing information. The cover features a close-up photograph of the face of an Asian female with the penis of a caucAsian-male in her mouth. There appears to be semen dripping down her face and hands. A written text, accompanying the photographs and continuing throughout the magazine, graphically describes what is occuring in the photographs. The 42 photographs depict one or more of the following acts occuring in a bedroom setting:

1. Two close-up photographs of the face of an Asian female with the penis of a caucasian male in her mouth. What appears to be semen is dripping down her face and hands.

2. One photograph of a partially clothed Asian female masturbating.

3. One photograph of a partially clothed Asian female with a clothed caucasian male licking her breast and inserting one of his fingers into her vagina.

2270. Description by Senior Investigator Chapman. Purchased in an adult bookstore in the Washington, D.C. area.
2271. Description by Senior Investigator Chapman. Purchased from an adult bookstore in the Washington, D.C. area.

4. One photograph of a partially clothed Asian female with the penis of a partially clothed caucasian male in her mouth.
5. Six photographs of a partially clothed Asian female with the penis of a naked caucasian male in her mouth.
6. Three photographs of a naked caucasian male inserting his tongue into the vagina of the Asian female.
7. Nineteen photographs of a caucasian male inserting his penis into the vagina of the partially clothed Asian female.
8. Seven close-up photographs of the caucasian male's penis inserted into the Asian female's vagina.
9. Two photographs of the naked caucasian male holding his penis in his hand while ejaculating onto the abdomen of the partially clothed Asian female.

PUBLISHER'S NOTE

The *Final Report of the Attorney General's Commission on Pornography* as printed by the U.S. Government Printing Office contained extensive quotations and detailed descriptions from paperback books, movies, videos, and a tabloid. Because necessary copyright permissions could not be secured, material on pages 1647–1744 and 1787–1802 of the first printing of the *Report* have been replaced by the descriptions on pages 434–439 and 451–453.

PAPERBACK BOOKS

Tying Up Rebecca[2272]

The following is a description of a paperback book entitled *Tying Up Rebecca*. On the cover the title is above an illustrated picture of a red-haired female who is nude from the waist up. She has one rope around her neck, another around her body & arms, and her ankles are tied to a bar, spreading her legs apart. She is standing but is bent at the waist from the pull of the rope. She has a ball gag in her mouth, and is wearing a garter belt, stockings and shoes. The illustration is framed in black. At the bottom of the picture is printed "ADULTS ONLY." Printed in the upper left hand corner at the cover is "SIREN SLAVE GIRLS." Printed in the upper right hand corner is the price, $3.95. Across the binding of the book is printed the title and SS–110. The back of the book is an advertisement for a sexual device called the "Deep Stroker," from ✄ . The packaged device is shown with a narrative describing what it does and its price, $19.95.

Inside the cover is another advertisement for Stallion Slo-Cum Spray. A photograph of the product is on this page and printed below the photograph is "Get it up and keep it up! with ✄ spray!" A three-paragraph narrative explains its application and why it's needed. The price is $10.00 and an order

form has been supplied. On the inside of the back cover is another advertisement for an Anal Ecstasy kit. A photograph of the products is shown and beneath the photo is printed "For Sophisticated Sensualists." The Anal Ecstasy Kit, according to its narrative contains a heavy-duty variable-speed vibrator with assorted sleeves and extensions, including two called "prickly knob" and "prickly sleeve." The extensions are 8 inches—"Big Bummer," and 7 inches—"Skinny Finger." The kit includes a "butt plug" and batteries and costs $22.95.

The next page the book contains disclaimers and copyright information.

The foreword describes a male gymnastic coach's fantasy of having sex with his most talented female gymnast, a thirteen-year-old girl named Becky. The story is ten chapters. The following is a description of that story as printed in the book.

Chapter One introduces thirteen-year-old gymnast Becky Mingus and her middle-aged coach Vern Lawless—who hasn't had sex in seven years. In the locker room a 15-year-old cheerleader named Patty begins to masturbate, but mistakenly sticks her fingers in Becky's vagina. Patty then goes into the boys' locker room, discards her towel, rubs her breasts, and exposes her genitals. A boy forces Patty to her knees; Patty tongues his anus; he shoves her face in the drain; Becky

---

2272. Original description was completed by Senior Investigator Joseph B. Haggerty. This paperback book was purchased from an "adults only" pornographic outlet in the Boston, Massachusetts, area.

masturbates; the boy performs cunnilingus; Patty performs fellatio; the boy has vaginal intercourse with Patty.

Chapter Two. At home, Vern's wife wants to make their marriage better, and has bought a skimpy bra and crotchless panties from a girl in the lingerie store who had submitted to Vern's wife's uncontrollable sucking on her breasts and fingering her vagina. Lawless is aroused and masturbates when he sees his wife lying on the rug in the lingerie, but he loses his erection when he spots a picture of Becky. Vern explains his problem, and his wife says she understands and goes to the bathroom to masturbate.

Chapter Three. Becky's father, Henry, sits at home remembering a teenage encounter with a girl and masturbates. He accidentally ejaculates on Becky's face just as she comes in the room. Her face dripping with semen, Becky sees her father's erection and runs to her room crying. The next day, Louise decides to tell Henry, Becky's father, about Vern's lust for Becky. They go to a room upstairs that is equipped with leather clothing, ropes, chains, metal sheaths. Henry unbuttons her blouse, pulls up her skirt, pulls down her panties. His erect penis splits his pants. He performs cunnilingus and analingus. She performs fellatio.

Chapter Four. Louise and Henry continue various sexual activities for much of the chapter. For instance, he calls her slave, slut, bitch, and makes her act like a dog. He chains her wrists and ankles to four corners of the bed with iron cuffs, sticks his finger up her anus, stuffs panties in her mouth, calls her slut and bitch, tears off her bra, and sucks her breasts. Meanwhile Becky goes skinny dipping, and because she is a Girl Scout, helps a boy who has been kicked in the groin by masturbating him and licking his semen after he ejaculates.

Chapter Five. Becky goes swimming again, masturbates, and exposes her genitals to a little boy who is watching her. Meanwhile, Vern and his wife invite Patty to their house, where they all engage in various sexual activities.

The next page was an advertisement. The top of the page reads, "We interrupt this story to bring you a special money-saving offer!" Offered was a series of books categorized as "Strange Tales" and entitled, "Wife's Puppy Love." All were books which described acts of bestiality. They were described as erotic best sellers with savings of up to sixty percent.

Chapter Six. The little boy has taken Becky's clothes, and she gets cramps and cries for help. Patty hears her, pulls her out and tries to revive her with mouth-to-mouth resuscitation, only she mistakenly blows into Becky's vagina instead of her mouth. Becky revives and performs cunnilingus on Patty; Patty performs analingus; Becky urinates in Patty's mouth; Becky performs analingus; Patty defecates; Patty ties Becky to a tree, calls her names ("pubescent scumbag," "douchebag"), penetrates her with a penis-shaped piece of wood, and orders Becky to beg for it. Becky yells "fuck me, fuck me, fuck me;" Patty refuses, kicks her, and tells her to leave. Becky goes home, kisses her sleeping father's penis, and falls asleep.

Chapter Seven. Vern takes his gymnast team to international trials, but because of inadequate facilities, he is forced to share the girls' locker room. Various sexual activities take place including masturbation, fellatio, cunnilingus, intercourse, and analingus. The Russian coach, Svetlana, walks in, sees what is going on, and announces that the trials are cancelled and that Vern must appear before the committee.

Chapter Eight. Vern arrives at Svetlana's suite, and she is wearing nothing but crossed bands of bullets across her breasts and silk over her pubic area. Her assistant, Porkch, is wearing only bracelets of razor blades. Svetlana orders Porkch to "get him hard;" Svetlana whips Vern; Porkch bites hairs from Vern; Porkch performs cunnilingus on Svetlana. Vern grabs the whip, orders Porkch to lash Svetlana to the radiator; Vern performs cunnilingus on Svetlana; Porkch kisses Vern's testicles; Vern pushes his penis in Porkch's mouth and shoves the silk into Svetlana's anus; Vern ejaculates in Porkch's mouth. Room service arrives with spaghetti and olive oil; Vern unties Svetlana, covers her with oil, and ties her to the tub. Vern pulls the boy into the room, ties him, strips him, and commands Porkch to perform analingus on him. The boy ejaculates; Vern urinates on all of them; urine splashes into Svetlana's mouth; the boy performs cunnilingus; Vern gets dressed and leaves.

Chapter Nine. The former wife of Henry Mingus returns to him and says she divorced her second husband, and was shipwrecked with black natives. Henry and wife masturbate, perform cunnilingus, analingus, and fellatio. Becky walks in; mother and daughter hug each other; the mother performs cunnilingus on her daughter; the father wants to have anal intercourse with his daughter; Becky escapes.

Chapter Ten. Becky goes to the gym to practice; Vern follow, attacks her, takes off her clothes, they fight and he forces her to perform fellatio. She gags and spits out the semen; he orders her to swallow it; he puts a wooden peg in her anus and ejaculates again and again in her mouth. He takes out the peg and performs anal intercourse; he ejaculates; she faints; Vern unstraps her and carries her off.

The next few pages contain advertisements for paperback books and for magazines. The first is a series called *Incest Tales*. The next series of paperbacks is called *Trisexual Books*. Each of the books on these two pages sells for $3.95 and the covers of four books in each series are shown. The next two pages show the covers of ten different magazines. The covers show bondage, infantilism, enemas, an engorged breast being milked, a magazine about anal sex showing the bare buttocks of a female in a parochial uniform with her hair in pigtails, three magazines emphasizing female breasts and one showing a foot between a female's breasts. Six of these magazines cost seven dollars each, four cost six dollars each. The last page before the back cover is the order form for any of the items advertised in this book. A form certifying that the purchaser is over the age of twenty-one must be completed.

MOTION PICTURES AND VIDEO TAPE CASSETTES

Forgive Me—I Have Sinned[2273]

Forgive Me—I Have Sinned is available in 8mm and VHS formats. The credits appear. The film represents that it was produced and directed by Phil Princ and presented by Avon Productions.

The "confessor" mails letters to three persons whom he summons for confession. As they discuss their "sins," he is enveloped by smoke behind a cross-stripped screen.

Ingrid, a young girl who, while sleeping on a camping trip, was undressed and fondled by an oriental girl, Serena, in the sleeping bag next to her. Ingrid woke and asked Serena what she was doing. Serena played with Ingrid's nipples, then performed cunnilingus. They kissed and performed cunnilingus on

each other. Ingrid, dressed in a school uniform, tells the confessor that she couldn't help herself.

Brad was curious about the size of his sister's "tits" and sneaked a peek while she was undressing. Becoming excited, Brad began to masturbate when his sister, Maria, caught him in the act. She commanded him to do as she said, handcuffing him, striking him, making him crawl, forcing him to perform cunnilingus and call her "mistress." Brad tells the confessor that maybe he's "an animal or something."

Vicki Jones, is sent to Jason Burke's office from the secretarial pool. Jason thought that she was a "primp faced iceberg" and that she needed "a good fucking." Burke threatened her job and forced her to take dictation with his "cock" as the pen. He told her, "You girls are all the same. You act like you don't like it but you really do. You want a good stiff dick right in your mouth. . . . Oh, suck on it, suck." Jason pulled her by the hair and made her perform fellatio; she cried and his penis fell out; he ordered her to open her mouth, and he shoved her mouth on his penis. He ripped off her panties and penetrated her vagina. She cried, "Let me go. Please, let me go." He responded, "Say 'I like it,' say it, say it." She yelled, "I like it. You're hurting my pussy, ow. Don't, don't."

The confessor moves away from the screen, has her lie down, and straps her wrists. "Now you must be touched and cleansed by me, your confessor. Now you must taste the rod," he tells Vicki. He masturbates, and Vicki licks his penis. "Be cleansed, sinner," the confessor says. Vicki performs fellatio; the confessor masturbates; the confessor penetrates her but withdraws to ejaculate on her buttocks. He tells her that she will be forgiven.

After the confessor's separate encounters with Ingrid, Brad, and Vicki, he assures them that they are not the guilty parties—that Serena, Maria, and Jason are guilty—and that Ingrid, Brad, and Vicki will get their revenge by bringing the guilty ones with them Saturday night.

In preparation for Saturday's cleansing, the confessor fills six glasses with wine, and puts a powder in the three intended for the guilty ones. After the six people arrive, Serena, Maria, and Jason are given the wine with powder; they pass out. When they wake,

2273. Original description By Senior Investigator Haggerty. This nationally distributed film was rented from a neighborhood video store. It was found obscene in *U.S. v. Sovereign News Co., General Video of America, et al.*, N. CR84-00149–L(A) (W.D. KY.).

Jason's hands are tied and Vicki is over him; Maria is in a stock; the confessor is holding Serena by the neck while masturbating himself. Jason, Maria, and Serena are in reverse positions from their previous experiences with Vicki, Brad, and Ingrid. Vicki forces Jason to do her will; Brad forces Maria to do his will; the confessor forces Serena to "suck the rod" while yelling, "You like sucking on little young tits." As Vicki makes Jason perform cunnilingus on her and Brad paddles Maria, the confessor commands Serena to perform fellatio. Serena asks Ingrid to let her perform cunnilingus on her, but Ingrid says she belongs to the confessor. The confessor has intercourse with Ingrid from the rear and says to Serena, "My holy fluid from the rod that baptizes you will cleanse thee." The confessor masturbates and ejaculates on Serena's breast.

Before the film ends, Ingrid is performing cunnilingus with Serena; Vicki is performing fellatio on Jason, and Brad is having intercourse from his sister's rear while she is still in the stock.

The Taming of Rebecca[2274]

Rebecca goes to a school for sexually abused children after her father beat her and forced her to have sex with him. She tells Ms. Zorda what happened:

Masturbating himself while sitting on the toilet, Rebecca's father called for Rebecca and told her to perform fellatio on him. When Rebecca did as she was asked, he said, "That's it, bitch, suck on it hard. That's why your mommy and I made you—to make Daddy feel good." He made her sit on his penis while he played with her nipples. Rebecca said that he was hurting her, but he continued. Then he said, "Allright, bitch, I want to taste a little bit of your cunt." When he finished he commanded her to bend over the tub; he spanked her and then had intercourse with her from the rear. He made her perform fellatio again and then do what he "likes best"—urinate on his penis.

Ms. Zorda advises Rebecca to stay at the school, and she introduces her to the other students and staff members, including Mr. Minindao, the "Dean of Discipline," and his secretary, Linda. Later in their office, Minindao and Linda discuss what a difficult job

they have, and Linda performs fellatio on him, then Minindao performs cunnilingus on her, then they have intercourse. He asks her, "You want my cum? . . . Say please, Daddy, beg me to cum in your face."

Meanwhile various students are talking about "the cave." The last girl who had been taken there and talked to the police had disappeared afterward. One boy says he wants some "serious action," and students begin to strip and masturbate, perform fellatio and cunnilingus, and have intercourse. One boy puts his fist in a girl's vagina.

The dean calls Rebecca into his office and scolds her for participating in an orgy; he orders her to raise her skirt and bend over. When Rebecca refuses, he tells her that he beat one girl until she threw up and then made her eat it. He beats her and then has intercourse with her from the rear. He makes her perform fellatio.

The dean calls in two other students, a boy (John) and a girl. He commands John to undress the girl and stick a pin in her breast. John says no, but complies when the dean threatens to do it to him if he doesn't. John pushes the point through her nipple as she struggles; blood runs down her breast; the girl urinates. Feigning sympathy, the secretary takes her to the cave. Once there, the secretary tells her that she will give her more "pain and pleasure" and makes her perform cunnilingus. The secretary threatens to turn the pin in her nipple if she refuses. The secretary turns the pin; the girl screams. The dean comes in and makes the girl perform fellatio on his "black rod" because she "pissed" on his floor. The secretary removes the pin from the girl's swollen breast. The dean says if she's good he'll put his fist up her "ass." He has intercourse with her, and the girl says, "I won't ever do it again, Daddy D. Oh, please fuck me."

Rebecca tells Ms. Zorda what is going on, and they enter the cave. The dean laughs when he sees them, but Ms. Zorda points a gun at the dean. He laughs again. The sound of a shot is heard.

The Devil in Miss Jones[2275]

The film is available in 8mm and VHS formats. The film begins with an acknowledge-

---

2274. Original description by Senior Investigator Haggerty. This film was seized in the District of Columbia, where it was playing at an (adults only) theater. Prosecution was declined by the U.S. Attorney's Office of Superior Court, 1984.

2275. Original description by Senior Investigator Haggerty. This nationally distributed film was rented from a neighborhood video store.

ment to Arrow films. The film is represented to be produced by Piere Productions.

Miss Jones undresses, fills a tub with water, and slashes her wrists. The water in the tub turns red. When the scene changes, she thinks she is applying for a job. Mr. Abaca tells her she has been confused since her "accident" and apologizes for not being prepared since she took her life prematurely. She was scheduled to go to heaven, but because of her suicide, she won't be allowed to go. Miss Jones, a virgin, says she has never done anything wrong, but since she's going to hell anyway, she'd like to go back for a while to commit lust. Mr. Abaca agrees since she died earlier than expected anyway. He instructs her to go through a door.

Miss Jones meets a man who tells her he is her teacher. Her first lesson is to be cured of her inhibitions. After motioning for her to undress, he puts a dildo in her anus and tells her he will punish her if it falls out. She performs fellatio and says, "I love the taste of it. . . . Please, I want to know what it feels like in my cunt." Excited, she asks her teacher to take out the dildo and put his fingers in her anus. When he does, she sucks on the dildo. "I want to feel your cock, your hard cock spreading me wide apart and tearing me apart. . . . Oh, God, let me have it please. . . . oh, it hurts so. . . . Hurt me, hurt me, hurt me."

The teacher continues to teach Miss Jones. She squirts water in her vagina, squirts water in her anus, performs fellatio on her teacher, and moves her head to catch his semen on her face. Miss Jones rubs an apple on her labia then licks it; she pushes grapes into her vagina then eats them; she sucks a banana then puts it between her legs before sucking it again. A snake crawls on her body, and Miss Jones puts its head in her mouth several times.

Miss Jones and another woman perform fellatio with a man; when the man ejaculates in the woman's mouth, Miss Jones licks her tongue and mouth. Miss Jones is next seen with two men; one man has vaginal intercourse with her, the other anal. "Can you feel your cocks together?" she asks. "Can you put your prick further in my ass, and further in my cunt . . . oh, fuck me, faster, harder, faster."

Mr. Abaca informs Miss Jones that her time is up and assures her that she needn't fear "the fiery furnace," that she'll be comfortable.

Mr. Abaca tells her to touch his hand; she finds herself in another room with a man. He is looking around for a fly. Miss Jones wants him to perform cunnilingus; she wants to perform fellatio; she begs him to touch her, to penetrate her with his penis. The man ignores her; he continues talking about the fly. Miss Jones begs him to touch her; she says she can't do it herself. She masturbates. "Just stick your cock in me and then I can get off, damn you. . . . Please help me, damn you, damn you."

Deep Throat[2276]

Deep throat is available in 8 mm and VHS formats. As the video begins the captions state that the film is presented by Arrow.[2277]

A woman, played by Linda Lovelace, goes home and finds her friend Ellen sitting on a table while a man performs cunnilingus. Linda and Ellen speak to each other, but the man doesn't stop; Ellen asks him if "he minds if she smokes while he's eating."

Later, Ellen and Linda talk by the pool. Linda says she doesn't enjoy sex and has never had a bell-ringing orgasm. Ellen suggests that they invite some men over so Linda can experiment and possibly find the excitement she's looking for.

When the men arrive, Ellen gives the men numbers so that "everybody gets a little piece of this action." Two men arriving are shown receiving numbers eleven and twelve. Ellen and Linda perform cunnilingus and fellatio and have vaginal intercourse with one or two men at a time. Numbers eleven and twelve decline their turns with Linda because they're physically spent from being with Ellen.

When Ellen and Linda talk next about Linda's problem, Ellen says that Linda should see a psychiatrist. Linda takes her advice and goes to see Dr. Young. After determining that her problem is not caused by some childhood trauma, Dr. Young decides that her problem may be physical. An examination proves him right—Linda's clitoris is in her throat. He tells her that the solution is to relax her muscles and take a penis "all the way down." Linda tries fellatio with Dr. Young, taking the entire length of his penis into her mouth. Linda is so grateful that she offers to marry Dr. Young and be his slave. Dr. Young rejects her offer because his blonde nurse wouldn't like

---

2276. Original description by Senior Investigator Haggerty. This nationally distributed film was rented from a neighborhood video store.

2277. Deep Throat is reported to be the most widely sold and distributed pornographic film in history.

it, but he offers her a job making house calls as a "psycho-therapist."

Linda's duties include fellatio, vaginal intercourse, and anal intercourse. One man inserts a jar in her vagina and sucks from a tube attached to the jar. Another man needs Linda to help relieve his pain caused from not having had sex for three years. He wants Linda to come back three times a week—and he says that he can afford it because he has "Blue Cross." Even Dr. Young requires Linda's help because he tried to "ball" two women at the same time. Throughout the action, Dr. Young, his nurse, and Linda engage in fellatio and cunnilingus with each other.

Linda's next case is Wilbert Wayne, who enjoys acting like he's raping women. Linda gets excited by his mask and says she wants to have sex with him. "Okay, but remember, I'm raping you and you have to do everything I say or I'll shoot you," he says. Wilbert asks Linda to marry him, but Linda turns him down. "The man I marry has to have a nine-inch cock," she tells him. Wilbert lacks four inches of measuring up, and Linda suggests silicone injections. Dr. Young is able to fix the length of Wilbert's penis, and when Linda sees the new version, she immediately performs fellatio on Wilbert. When he ejaculates in her mouth and on her face, bells ring and fireworks go off. Linda smiles.

Debbie Does Dallas[2278]

Debbie Does Dallas is a motion picture available in all formats. The film is purportedly presented by School Day Films.

Debbie has been chosen to go to Dallas and become a "cowgirl," but she has to raise the money herself since her parents are opposed to it. Debbie has only two weeks, but her cheerleader friends offer to help raise the money. In fact, they plan to raise enough money so that they all can go.

As the girls start looking for jobs, they gather in the locker room to discuss their progress and their problems. When the last girl leaves, four males and two females go in. They engage in intercourse, cunnilingus, fellatio; the males ejaculate on the females' buttocks and faces; the females lick the semen.

Debbie gets a job in Greenfield's store, and on the third day he suggests that "There are other jobs girls can do." He says he'll pay her ten dollars if she shows him her breasts, and

another ten if he can touch them. He starts to suck her breasts, but Debbie stops him. He says he'll pay ten dollars for "a little suck on each one." Debbie negotiates for twenty and lets him do it.

Debbie tells her friends that she's found a way to make money. After telling them what she just experienced with Greenfield, they decide to ask each other about techniques that are special enough that they can keep their virginity and still make money.

While one girl is working, the telephone rings. She talks to a man named Tom and plays with her breast. When she hangs up, she penetrates her vagina with a candle, but its discovered by the boss's wife, Mrs. Hardwick. Mr. Hardwick comes in and strips; Mrs. Hardwick puts her fingers in the girl's wet vagina while her husband masturbates. Mrs. Hardwick exposes her breast, and Mr. Hardwick has intercourse with the girl while Mrs. Hardwick masturbates. Mrs. Hardwick tongues the girl's breasts; when her husband ejaculates, Mrs. Hardwick licks his penis.

Meanwhile, two other girls accept Mr. Bradley's offer to pay them twenty-five dollars to let him kiss them. He licks their breasts, performs cunnilingus, and both girls perform fellatio. Mr. Bradley has anal intercourse with one of them; then one girl masturbates him until he ejaculates on the other's backside. She rubs her face in his semen.

Another girl accepts money from a Mr. Biddle who wants to spank her on her bare bottom. Still another girl lets two men fondle her at the same time; then one has intercourse with her while she performs fellatio on the other.

Mr. Greenfield wants more from Debbie, but she tells him that she's saving herself. Greenfield says he doesn't want anyone else—he wants Debbie—and that he's ready to pay all the expenses for her and her friends to go to Dallas if she agrees.

Debbie dresses as a Dallas Cowboy Cheerleader; Greenfield dresses like a football player, because he always wanted to be captain of the team. He licks her breasts; she licks his penis; he rubs her clitoris and performs cunnilingus; she performs fellatio; they have intercourse, first with her on top then him; she masturbates him; he ejaculates. As the film ends, she turns her head away, and the word "next . . ." appears on the screen.

2278. Original description by Senior Investigator Haggerty. This nationally distributed film was rented from a neighborhood video store.

LEGAL CASES

The following chart and accompanying material identify cases in which the movie "Deep Throat," "The Devil in Miss Jones," or "Debbie Does Dallas" was named as part of a criminal prosecution or civil action. The list is not exhaustive as unreported decisions are not included.

	The Devil in Miss Jones	Debbie Does Dallas	Deep Throat	TOTALS
STATE CRIMINAL PROSECUTIONS	8[A]	1[G]	17[K]	26
STATE CRIMINAL CONVICTIONS UPHELD ON APPEAL	3[B]	0	9[M]	12
FEDERAL PROSECUTIONS	0	1[H]	9[L]	10
FEDERAL CRIMINAL CONVICTIONS UPHELD ON APPEAL	0	0	4[N]	4
STATE CIVIL ACTIONS	8[C]	0	9[O]	17
STATE CIVIL ACTIONS AFFIRMED ON APPEAL	3[B]	0	6[Q]	9
FEDERAL CIVIL ACTIONS	1[D]	1[I]	10[P]	12
FEDERAL CIVIL ACTIONS AFFIRMED ON APPEAL	1[F]	1[J]	4[R]	6

NOTES

A

See, *Colbert v. State* No. 01–82–0943–CR, Slip. Op. (Ct. of App. Texas. Aug. 9, 1984); *Commonwealth v. Capri Enterprises, Inc.*, 365 Mass. 179, 310 N.E. 2d 326(1974) (found guilty of exhibiting an obscene motion picture; conviction was reversed: statute was unconstitutional under *Miller* standard); *People v. Llewellyn*, 401 Mich 314, 257 N.W. 2d 902(1977) (convicted for exhibiting obscene films; reversed on appeal on the basis that the city standard was preempted by state law); *State v. XLNT Corp.*, 536 S.W.2d 836(Mo. App. 1976) (conviction of possession with intent to circulate obscene film); *State v. Riggins*, 645 S.W.2d 113(Mo. App. 1983) (conviction for promotion of pornography in the second degree); *City of Sioux Falls v. Mini-Kota Art Theaters, Inc.*, 247 N.W.2d 676(S.D. 1976) (convicted of violating city obscenity ordinance); *Circle Cinema, Inc. v. Town of Colonie*, 82 Misc. 2d 527, 371 N.Y.S.2d 344(1975) (seizure procedure did not meet constitutional standards); *Commonwealth v. MacDonald*, 464 Pa. 435, 347 A.2d 390(1975) (criminal complaint quashed for failure to meet *Miller* constitutional standards).

B

See, *State v. XLNT Corp.*, 536 S.W.2d 836(Mo. App. 1976) (conviction for possession with intent to circulate was affirmed); *State v. Riggins*, 645 S.W.2d 113(Mo. App. 1983) (conviction for promotion of pornography in second degree was affirmed); *City of Souix Falls v. Mini-Kota Art Theaters, Inc.*, 247 S.W.2d 676(S.D. 1976) (conviction for violation of city obscenity stature was affirmed).

C

See, *Fairvilla Twin Cinema II v. State ex rel. Eagan*, 353 So.2d 909(Fla. App. 1977) (enjoined further showing of allegedly obscene films); *State ex rel. Gerstein v. Walwick Theater Corp.*, 298 So. 2d 406(Fla. 1974) (petition to enjoin showing of film denied by trial court; reversed on appeal and complaint reinstated); *Miller v. Robert Emmett Goodrich Corp.*, 53 Mich. App. 267, 218 N.W.2d 771(1974) (order granting injunction was vacated on appeal); *State ex rel. Cahalan v. Diversified Theatrical Corp.*, 59 Mich. App. 223, 229 N.W.2d 389(1975) (nuisance action brought against theater for exhibiting obscene films); *Kent City Prosecutor v. Robert Emmett Goodrich Corp.*, 396 Mich. 253, 240 N.W.2d 242(1976) (civil obscenity statute could not be brought to prohibit the exhibition of a film); *State ex rel. Cahalan v. Diversified Theatrical Corp.*, 396 Mich. 244, 240 N.W.2d 460(1976) (statute deeming places of lewdness, assignation or prostitution to be public nuisances did not apply to motion picture houses); *Lazarus v. Yorkview Theater Corp.*, 74 Misc. 2d 729, 345 N.Y.S.2d 413(1973) (court enjoined the sale or distribution of film); *Vergari v. Pierre Production, Inc.*, 42 A.D. 950, 352 N.Y.S.2d 34(1974) (trial court denied preliminary injunction to prohibit exhibition of film; reversed and injunction granted on appeal).

D

See, *United States v. Various Articles of Obscene Merchandise*, 536 F. Supp. 50(S.D. N.Y. 1981) (forfeiture and condemnation).

E

See, *Fairvilla Twin Cinema II v. State ex rel. Eagan*, 353 So. 2d 909(Fla. App. 1977) (affirmed order enjoining further showing of allegedly obscene films); *State ex rel. Cahalan v. Diversified Theatrical Corp.*, 59 Mich. App. 223, 229 N.W. 2d 389 (1975) (nuisance action brought against theater owner; order enjoining exhibition of films affirmed); *Vergari v. Pierre Productions, Inc.*, 42 A.D. 950, 352 N.Y.S.2d 34(1974) (preliminary injunction granted on appeal).

F

See, *United States v. Various Articles of Obscene Merchandise*, 536 F. Supp. 50(S.D.N.Y. 1981) (forfeiture of obscene materials).

G

See, *People v. P.J. Video, Inc. d/b/a Network Video and James Erhardt*, No. 270, Slip. Op. (N.Y. Ct. App. July 5, 1985) (motion to suppress granted).

H

See, *United States v. Various Articles of Obscene Merchandise*, 709 F.2d 132(2d Cir. 1983) (seized items found not obscene).

I

See, *United States v. Various Articles of Obscene Merchandise*, 536 F. Supp. 50(S.D.N.Y. 1981) (forfeiture and condemnation of obscene materials).

J

See, *United States v. Various Articles of Merchandise*, 536 F.Supp. 50 (S.D.N.Y. 1981) (forfeiture and condemnation of obscene materials).

K

See, *Dexter v. State* case number 223,343 (Boxer Co. Tex. Nov. 11, 1974) (film found obscene); *Circle Cinema Inc., Town of Colonie*, 82 Misc. 2d 527, 371, N.Y.S.2d 344(1975) (continued seizure procedure found unconstitutional); *Commonwealth v. MacDonald*, 464 Pa. 435, 347 A.2d 290(1975) (criminal complaint quashed for failure to meet *Miller* constitutional standards); *State v. Auippa*, 293 So. 2d 391(Fla. 1974) (on certification, state supreme court upheld constitutionality of state standards); *Menefee v. City and County of Denver*, 190 Colo. 163, 544 P.2d 382(1976) (conviction for possession and promotion of obscene film revised; statute was found unconstitutionally vague); *People v. Tabron*, 190 Colo. 149, 544 P.2d 372(1976) (Conviction for promoting obscenity reversed; statute was unconstitutional); *Pussycat Theater v. State*, 355 So. 2d 829(Fla. App. 1978) (found guilty of contempt of an order requiring legends "Revised Version" or "Edited Version" on film); *Western Corp. v. Commonwealth;* 558 S.W.2d 605(Ky. 1977) (convicted of exhibiting an obscene film); *People v. Thomas*, 37 Ill. App. 3d 320, 346 N.E. 2d 190(1976) (conviction for exhibiting obscenity was reversed); *People v. Mature Enterprises, Inc.*, 35 N.Y.2d 520, 323, N.E 2d 704(1974) (convicted of distributing obscene material); *Commonwealth v. 707 Main Corp.*, 371 Mass. 374, 357 N.E. 2d 753 (1976) (convicted of violating obscenity statute by exhibiting the film); *People v. Mature Enterprises, Inc.*, 73 Misc. 2d 749, 343 N.Y.S.2d 911 (1971) (found guilty of promotion or possession with the intent to promote obscene material); *People v. Mature Enterprises, Inc.*, 76 Misc. 2d 660, 352 N.Y.S. 2d 346(App. Div. 1974) (conviction for promoting obscene material affirmed); *People v. Hausman*, 82 Misc. 2d 1032, 372 N.Y.S.2d 503 (1975) (conviction for exhibiting obscene film reversed for failure to apply appropriate community standards); *Smith v. State*, 530 S.W. 2d 955(Crim. App. Tx. 1976) (conviction for exhibition of obscene materials was reversed on the basis there was insufficient evidence to establish a commercial purpose); *State v. Runions*, 654 S.W.2d 407(Tenn. App. 1983) (conviction for distributing obscene material).

L

See, *Butler v. Dexter*, 425 U.S. 262(1975) (charges were never presented to grand jury); *United States v. Various Articles of Obscene Merchandise*, 709 F.2d 132(2d Cir. 1983) (not patently offensive under contemporary standards in the New York area); *United States v. Battista*, 646 F.2d 237(6th Cir. 1981) (convictions for conspiracy to violate obscenity statutes); *United States v. Peraino*, 645 F.2d 548(6th Cir. 1981) (found guilty of violating federal obscenity statute, convictions reversed on appeal); *United States v. Cohen,* 583 F.2d 1030(8th Cir. 1978) (convicted of mailing obscene materials); *United States v. Marks,* 585 F.2d 164(6th Cir. 1978) (convictions for transportation of obscene materials was reversed upon application of Bruton rule); *United States v. Marks,* 520 F.2d 913(6th Cir. 1975) (convictions for transporting obscene materials for sale and distribution); *United States v. Pinkus* 551 F.2d 1155(9th Cir. 1977) (convicted of eleven counts of mailing obscene materials); *United States v. Defalco,* 509 F. Supp 127 (S.D. Fla. 1981) (Motion to suppress was granted).

M

See, *Dexter v. State,* case number 223, 343, (Boxar Co. Tex. Nov. 11, 1974) (film found to be obscene); *State v. Auippa,* 298 So. 2d 391(Fla. 1974) (State obscenity statute upheld) *Pussycat Theater v. State,* 355 So. 2d 829(Fla. App. 1978) (affirmed finding of contempt for failure to provide legends "Revised Version" or "Edited Version" on films); *Western Corp v. Commonwealth,* 558 S.W.2d 605(Ky. 1977) (convictions for exhibiting an obscene film affirmed); *People v. Mature Enterprises, Inc.,* 35 N.Y.2d 520, 323 N.E.2d 704(1974) (conviction for showing obscene film affirmed as modified—excessive fine imposed); *State v. American Theater Corp.,* 194 Neb. 84, 230 N.W.2d (1975) (conviction for distribution of obscene material was affirmed); *Commonwealth v. 707 Main Corp.,* 371 Mass. 374, 357 N.E.2d 753(1976) (conviction for exhibiting obscene films was affirmed); *People v. Mature Enterprises, Inc.,* 76 Misc. 2d 660, 352 N.Y.S.2d 346(App. Div. 1974) (conviction for promoting obscene material affirmed); *State v. Runions,* 654 S.W.2d 407(Tenn. App. 1983) (conviction for distributing obscene materials was affirmed).

Cases.

Colbert v. State. No. 01-82-0943-CR, Slip Op., (Ct. of. App. Tex. Aug. 9, 1984) (The Devis in Miss Jones).

Defendant was charged with selling an obscene video, "The Devil in Miss Jones." He pled not guilty. After a trial before a jury, he was found guilty, fined $2,000 and sentenced to 10 days confinement.

On appeal, judgement of conviction was reversed. Two of the assignments of error were sustained:

1. The trial court erred by charging the jury that a person who promotes obscene material or possesses the same with intent to promote it in the course of his business, is presumed to know the character and content of the material;
2. The evidence was insufficient to support the conclusion.

People v. P.J. Video, Inc. d/b/a/ Network Video and James Erhardt. No. 270, Slip. Op. (Ct. of App. N.Y. July 5, 1985) (Debbie Does Dallas)

Defendants were charged with six counts of obscenity in the third degree based upon their possession of allegedly obscene video cassette movies. Defendants moved to suppress the seized films on the grounds that the warrant was not based upon probable cause. The Justice Court sustained the motion to suppress. The state took an appeal from the ruling. The appellate court affirmed the lower court decision. ". . . the statements relied upon are conclusory and patently ambiguous. They may be interpreted as alleging that

sexually explicit acts are pervasive in the two films described but they may also be interpreted in other, less inculpatory ways. That being so, the magistrate was required to require and clarify the affidavits' meaning and the record does not establish that he did so." Slip. Op. at 7.

United States v. Various Articles of Obscene Merchandise. Schedule No. 2102, No. 81 Civ. 5295, Slip. Op. (S.D. N.Y. Nov. 4, 1981) (Deep Throat).

United States sought forfeiture and condemnation of items of allegedly obscene materials. Found the materials were not patently offensive to the average person in that community. The complaint was dismissed.

Hicks v. Miranda. 422 U.S. 332(1974) (Deep Throat).

Four copies of the film "Deep Throat" were seized. The Superior Court declared the movie to be obscene and ordered all copies at the theater to be seized. (No appeal was taken from this judgement). Subsequent action brought to enjoin enforcement of the order. Court ordered the complaint should be dismissed.

Butler v. Dexter. 425 U.S. 262(1975) (Deep Throat).

Charged with commercial obscenity and use of a criminal instrument (16-mm movie projector). Felony complaints were lodged and bond was posted, but the charges were not presented to the grand jury. Supreme Court vacated and remanded.

United States v. Various Articles of Obscene Merchandise. 709 F.2d 132(2d Cir. 1983) (Deep Throat) (Debbie Does Dallas).

Southern District of New York court found items seized were not obscene. United States appealed. Appellate court affirmed the decision. "Having reviewed a representative sample of these works and in the absence of contrary evidence of prevailing community standards, we cannot say that the trial court abused its discretion in finding that the articles on Schedule 2102 were not patently offensive under contemporary standards in the New York area." 709 F.2d at 137.

Young v. Abrams. 698 F.2d 131(2d Cir. 1983) (Deep Throat).

Petition for habeus corpus from a conviction for obscenity in second degree. The district court found guilt beyond a reasonable doubt. Appellate court affirmed.

United States v. Battista. 646 F.2d 237 (6th Cir. 1981) (Deep Throat).

Conviction of conspiracy to violate the obscenity statutes, 18 U.S.C. S1462 and S1465 by transporting the obscene film Deep Throat in interstate commerce. Convictions were affirmed on appeal.

United States v. Peraino. 645 F.2d 548 (6th Cir. 1981) (Deep Throat).

Indicted in Western District of Tennessee for conspiracy to violate federal obscenity statute by transporting "Deep Throat" in interstate commerce. Found guilty and sentenced to eighteen months, twelve months suspended and a $10,000 fine. Raised issues of due process concerning lack of venue. Court held:

One who has no connection with the district of venue at the time of the venue-setting act may not be convicted there for subsequently transporting the materials into other communities whose standards were not established. Merely joining the conspirators in their lawful distribution efforts in other communities after the film was no longer being shown in Memphis does not evidence intent to futher or advance the illegal purpose of the conspiracy to ship the film into Memphis. Absent any evidence of adherence to the criminal purposes of the conspiracy, defendants Joseph Peraino and Plymouth Distributors cannot be held to have become members of the conspiracy. 645 F.2d at 551.

Convictions of Peraino and Plymouth Distrib-

utors were reversed and indictments dismissed.

Universal Amusement Co. v. Vance. 559 2d 1286(5th Cir. 1977).

Application of Texas nuisance statute. The statute only restrains such expression as is not constitutionally protected and is not prohibited by state law.

United States v. Pinkus. 579 F.2d 1174(9th Cir. 1978) (comparison of Deep Throat and the Devil in Miss Jones to the named firm).

On remand from the Supreme Court. Supreme Court reversed on two grounds: 1) holding the jury instructions improper insofar as they permitted children to be included in the community by whose standards obscenity was to be judged; 2) held improperly invoked the concurrent sentences doctrine in declining to address the court's rejection of the defendant's offers of sexually explicit films allegedly "comparable" to the charged film "No. 613" as evidence of community standards.

Court stated:

. . . A defendant must meet a two-pronged test to establish that the proffered comparable materials are admissible as probative of community standards. First, there must be a reasonable resemblance between the proffered comparable and the allegedly obscene materials. Second, the proponent must establish a reasonable degree of community acceptance of the profferred comparables.

* * *

We held that the assertedly comparable films, "Deep Throat" and "The Devil in Miss Jones," satisfied the first prong of the *Jacobs* test because they bore resemblance to the film "No. 613." *Id.*, we did not decide whether the second prong had been satisfied, but that is another question. 579 F.2d at 1175.

United States v. Cohen. 583 F.2d 1030(8th. Cir. 1978).

Defendants were charged with violations of 18 U.S.C. SS1461 and 1462 alleging the mailing, use of common carriers for the carriage in interstate commerce, from California to Iowa of obscene materials, and advertisements informing how obscene materials might be obtained. Convictions were affirmed.

United States v. Marks. 585 F.2d 164(6th Cir. 1978).

Convicted of two counts of transporting obscene materials in interstate commerce and one count of conspiracy to commit that offense. Court applied rule in *Bruton v. United States* and found statements made by the codefendant were inadmissible. Reversed and remanded on this issue. Court also stated with respect to the issue of first amendment protection for the films as not being obscene, "we observe that neither in this nor in the prior appeal have the appellants specifically pointed to any virtues of the films in question which might characterize them as other than classic examples of hard core pornography, nor did our view of the films reveal any."

United States v. Battista. 646 F.2d 237(6th Cir. 1981) (Deep Throat).

Convicted of conspiracy to violate obscenity statute, 18 U.S.C. S514 and S1465 by transporting the obscene film "Deep Throat" in interstate commerce.

[Anthony Novello, Angelo Miragliotta and Mano DeSalvo were found not guilty; Louis Peraino was found guilty, sentenced to 3 years (30 months suspended) and $10,000 fine; Gerard Damison Film Production, Inc. fined $10,000; T. Anthony Arnone sentenced to 2 years (19 months suspended) and fined $3,000; Anthony Battista sentenced to 2 years (22 months suspended) and fined $2,000; Carl R. Carter, suspended sentence, 5 years probation and $1,500 fine; Mell Friedman sentenced to 4 months, 1 year probation and $3,000 fine; Michael Cherubino, mistrial and charges were dismissed.] Convictions were affirmed.

United States v. One Reel of Film. 481 F.2d 206(1st Cir. 1973) (Deep Throat).

Forfeiture proceeding under 19 U.S.C. S1305(a) for the film "Deep Throat." Affirmed the order of forfeiture. The court found the film obscene stating:

"We are thus left with a rarity: a film so single-minded as to fail even the older *Roth-Memoirs* test—unless one is tempted, as plainly a majority of the Supreme Court is not, to find redeeming social value in the explicit portrayal without more, of sexual congress itself." 481 F.2d at 209.

United States v. Marks. 520 F.2d 913(6th Cir. 1975).

Convicted of transporting obscene, lewd, lascivious and filthy films and film previews for the purpose of sale and distributions in interstate commerce and conspiracy to commit the act. Conviction affirmed.

United States v. Pinkus. 551 F.2d 1155(9th Cir. 1977).

Convicted of eleven counts of mailing obscene material in violation of 18 U.S.C. S1461. Convictions were affirmed.

United States v. Various Articles of Obscene Merchandise. 536 F. Supp 501 S.D.N.Y. 1981) (The Devil in Miss Jones, Deep Throat, Debbie Does Dallas).

Action under 19 U.S.C. S1305(a) for forfeiture and condemnation of certain materials. Condemned as obscene: The Health Spa; Disco Lady; Cry for Cindy; Pizza Girl; Many, Many!; Finishing School; The Devil In Miss Jones; Swedish Erotica; Dr. Feel Good; excerpts from The Untamed; Deep Throat; The Devil In Miss Jones; The Defiance; Reflections; Teenage Madam; Devil's Playground; The Other Side of Julie; Cherry Truckers; China Lust; For Love of Money; The Possession; Pink Lips; Like Mother-Like Daughter, Lacey Bodine, Sheila's Payoff; All the Senator's Girls, Blackmail for Daddy, And Then Came Eve; The Blonde In Black Lace; Kowloon Connection; House of Kristina; Super Rod; Bedroom Athlete; What Kind of Girls Do You Think We Are; Taxi Girls; The Opening of Misty Beethoven; Honeysuckle Devine; Juke Joint; Guns of Novocaine, Superstar; Inside Jennifer Welles; Exploring Young Girls; AWOL; Never a Tender Moment; Hot Nazis; Southern Belles, New York Babes; The Pony Girls; Seven Into Snowy; Pool of Pleasures; The Wish; Dream Goddess; The Anniversary; Suzie's Hot Reels; Women in Uniform; Flip Chicks; Teenage Deviate; Jail Bait; Barbara; Broadcast; and Debbie Does Dallas.

United States v. Defalco. 509 F. Supp. 127(S.D. Fla. 1981) (Deep Throat).

Heard motion to suppress. The court found "that the warrants gave the searching agents abundant authority, but insufficient guidance. . . . the warrants fail to meet the requirements of particularit." 509 F.Supp. at 135. Motions to suppress were granted.

McKenzie v. Butler. 398 F. Supp 1319(W.D. Tex. 1975) (Deep Throat).

Cites *Dexter v. State*, Case Number 223,343. (Boxar Co., Tex. Nov 11, 1974).

The film "Deep Throat" was declared obscene.

Exhibitors sought return of the seized copies of the film "Deep Throat." Court denied motion and dismissed the cause.

Miranda v. Hicks. 338 F. Supp. 350(C.D. Cal. 1974).

Declaratory relief as to the constitutionality of California obscenity statute. Court found: 1) the California obscenity statute as written does not meet the specificity test of *Miller* and 2) the California courts interpreting the statute may have liberalized it beyond its wording but have not specifically construed it so as to give fair notice as to what is constitutionally prohibited.

Inland Empire Enterprises, Inc. v. Morton. 365 F.Supp. 1014 (C.D. Cal. 1973) (Deep Throat).

Sought to enjoin any further searches and seizures involving the film "Deep Throat." Court stated, "Upon the doctrine of Federal abstention from invidious interference with state prosecutions for obscenity and upon the failure of Plaintiff to show any irreparable injury or violation of any consititutional or other rights, the complaint . . . is hereby dismissed with prejudice." 365 F.Supp. at 1019.

United States v. One Reel of Film. 360 F.Supp. 1067(D. Mass. 1973) (Deep Throat).

Action for forfeiture of the film "Deep Throat" pursuant to 18 U.S.C. S1305. Court entered an order for forfeiture. In reaching its judgment the court noted,

> Whatever claims may be made about *Deep Throat*, it was designed to have impact only through the sexual scenes. These dominant in tedious succession, and tend to arouse a prurient interest in sex.
>
> Thus, the court reaches the conclusion that the dominant theme of the film, taken as a whole, appeals to a prurient interest in sex; that the film is patently offensive in that it affronts contemporary community standards with respect to description and representation of sexual matters; and that it is utterly without redeeming social value. It is therefore obscene and not protected by the Constitution. (360 F.Supp at 1073).

Commonwealth v. Capri Enterprises, Inc. 365 Mass. 179, 310 N.E.2d 326(1974) (The Devil in Miss Jones).

Indicted and found guilty of knowingly having in their possession for the purpose of exhibition, an "obscene, indecent and im-

pure" motion picture film entitled "The Devil in Miss Jones." Each defendant was fined $5,000. The individual defendants were sentended to 2 years in jail.

Conviction reversed. The court held, "Section 32, therefore, fails to meet the standard of specificity required by the *Miller* decision, and for the same reasons expressed in our decision in the *Horton* case, *ante*, we decline to reinterpret S32 to provide judicially the description of specific sexual conduct which must exist to satisfy the First Amendment requirements as now defined."

Fairvilla Twin Cinema II v. State ex. rel. Eagan. 353 So.2d 909(Fla. App. 1977) (Deep Throat, The Devil in Miss Jones).

Complaint issued seeking an injunction and temporary restraining order, alleging that three obscene films were being exhibited. "Deep Throat," "The Devil in Miss Jones," and "Gladys and Her All Girl Band." Court issued order restraining any further showing of the films. Court held, "It is necessary only that the sworn complaint describing the alleged obscenity personally observed by the affiant provide a sufficient basis upon which the judicial officer issuing the restraining order can make an independent determination that the material is obscene."

State ex rel. Gerstein v. Walwick Theater Corp. 298 So.2d 406(Fla. 1974).

Individual employee and corporation were indicted for exhibiting obscene material. The individual was found not guilty and the jury was unable to return a verdict as to the corporation. State then began legal proceedings to enjoin exhibition of the film. That court dismissed the injunction proceeding on grounds of due process and double jeopardy. Court held:

> The civil injunction provision is not unconstitutional on its face as denying due process or as violating double jeopardy principles. The State is not precluded from persuing an alternative and cumulative remedy of injunction which was available even had there been no criminal proceeding or had the prior criminal proceeding resulted in a verdict of not guilty. Judgement was reversed with instructions to reinstate the complaint.

Miller v. Robert Emmett Goodrich Corporation. 53 Mich. App. 267, 218 N.W.2d 771(1974) (The Devil in Miss Jones).

Defendant-theater operator was enjoined

from showing the film "The Devil in Miss Jones." The court concluded that "the injunction was improperly granted since there is no state law, either statutory or judicial, which specifically defines the definition of sexual conduct which the state may regulate." The judgement was reversed and the injunction vacated.

State ex rel. Cahalan v. Diversified Theatrical Corporation. 59 Mich. App. 223, 229 N.W.2d 389(1975) (The Devil in Miss Jones, Deep Throat).

Action brought against defendant-motion picture theater operators alleging a public nuisance for exhibiting lewd motion pictures. The jury found the four films introduced, "The Devil in Miss Jones. "Deep Throat," "It Happened in Hollywood" and "Little Sisters" to be lewd. The order enjoining the showing of the four named films was affirmed.

Kent City Prosecutor v. Robert Emmett Goodrich Corporation. 396 Mich. 253 240 N.W.2d 242(1976) (The Devil in Miss Jones).

Issue was whether or not a civil obscenity statute could be used to prohibit the showing of the film "The Devil in Miss Jones." The court found that the civil obscenity statute was not directed to the exhibition of a film.

State ex rel. Cahalan v. Diversified Theatrical Corp. 396 Mich. 244, 240 N.W.2d 460(1976).

Issue was whether a statute which provides that a place of lewdness, assignation or prostitution is a public nuisance can be applied to motion picture houses. The court found the statute did not apply to motion picture houses and did not reach the question of obscenity.

People v. Llewellyn. 401 Mich. 314, 257 N.W. 2d 902(1977).

Convicted of exhibiting two allegedly obscene films. The convictions were reversed on appeal on the basis that the city standard used for obscenity was invalid under the theory of state preemption. The question of whether the films were obscene under *Miller* was not addressed.

State v. XLNT Corp. 536 S.W.2d 836(Mo. App. 1976) (The Devil in Miss Jones.)

Conviction of possessing an obscene film. "The Devil in Miss Jones," with intent to circulate it. The conviction was affirmed. There was no question regarding the factual or legal

determination that the "The Devil in Miss Jones" was obscene.

State v. Reggins. 645 S.W.2d 113 (Mo. App. 1985) (The Devil in Miss Jones).

Defendant was convicted of promotion of pornography in the second degree. He received a six-month suspended sentence and was placed on two years probation. The films were "The Devil in Miss Jones" and "Hot and Saucy Pizza Girls." The conviction was affirmed. There was no question raised on appeal as to the pornographic material of the film.

City of Sioux Falls v. Mini-Kota Art Theaters, Inc. 247 N.W. 2d.676(S.D. 1976) (The Devil in Miss Jones).

Convicted of violating the Sioux Falls obscenity ordinance by showing the movie, "The Devil in Miss Jones." The defendant was fined three hundred dollars.

Judgment was affirmed.

Lazarus v. Yorkview Theater Corp. 74 Misc. 2d 729, 345 N.Y.S.2d 413(1973).

Action was brought to enjoin the defendants from the sale or distribution or further distribution or acquisition or possession within the State of New York of the film "The Devil in Miss Jones" and specifically to enjoin the exhibition of the film in Monroe County. The court denied the motion to dismiss and continued the preliminary injunction.

Circle Cinema, Inc. v. Town of Colonie. 82 Misc. 2d 527, 371 N.Y.S. 2d 344(1975) (Deep Throat, The Devil in Miss Jones).

Police seized six films, "Deep Throat," "The Devil in Miss Jones," Marriage Manual," "Climax," "Feel" and "Kitty's Pleasure Palace." The court found the continued seizure procedure did not meet constitutional standards.

Vergari v. Pierre Productions Inc. 42. A.D. 950, 352 N.Y.S. 2d 34(1974) (The Devil in Miss Jones).

State sought to enjoin defendants from exhibiting the film "The Devil in Miss Jones." The trial court found a preliminary injunction was not an available remedy under the statute. The appellate division reversed and granted the preliminary injunction. The defendant was also convicted of obscenity in the second degree.

Commonwealth v. MacDonald. 464 Pa. 435, 347 A.2d 290(1975) (Deep Throat, The Devil in Miss Jones).

Defendants were charged with exhibiting the films, "Deep Throat" and The Devil in Miss Jones." The trial court quashed the criminal complaint on the basis that the statute did not meet the constitutional standards of Miller. In affirming the trial court judgment, the court stated, "We therefore conclude that section 5903(a) fails to satisfy the Miller standard and therefore may not constitutionally be applied unless it is amended to specifically define the sexual conduct whose depiction or description is to be regulated thereby."

State v. Auippa. 298 So. 2d 391(Fla. 1974) (Deep Throat).

Defendant was charged with distributing an obscene film, "Deep Throat" by exhibition. Trial court certified questions to the Florida Supreme Court. The court found:

1. The definition of what material is obscene under Florida statutes was sufficient under the Miller standards;
2. Florida Statute requires a standard of proof that the material is utterly without redeeming social value; and,
3. Florida Statutes set forth what specifically defined conduct is prohibited.

Roberts v. State. 373 So. 2d 672(Fla. 1979).

Court ordered destruction of obscene materials after seizure. The court reversed on the grounds that no seizure had occurred within the meaning of the statute. The court did not reach the issue of obscenity.

Menefee v. City and County of Denver. 190 Colo. 163, 544 P.2d 382 (1976) (Deep Throat).

Menefee was found guilty of possession and promotion of obscene material, "Deep Throat." The convictions were reversed. The court found the Colorado statute was unconstitutionally vague and overbroad.

People v. Tabron. 190 Colo. 149, 544 P.2d 372(1976).

Defendant was found guilty of promoting obscenity. He was fined $1,000 and sentenced to a twelve month jail term. The convictions were reversed. The court found the statute was unconstitutional under the Miller standard.

Pussycat Theater v. State. 355 So. 2d 829(Fla. App. 1978) (Deep Throat)

Theater was found in contempt of an order requiring it to advertise "Deep Throat" with the legends "Revised version" or "Edited version." The finding of contempt was affirmed, but the fine was reduced from $3,000 to $500.

Gayety Theaters, Inc. v. State ex. rel. Gerstein. 359 So. 2d 915(Fla. App. 1978) (Deep Throat).

Theater was held in civil contempt for violating an order enjoining it from showing the film "Deep Throat." The court affimed the order as applied to the Theater, but reversed as it was applied to individual defendants not named in the original order.

Western Corp. v. Commonwealth. 558 S.W. 2d 605(Ky. 1977) (Deep Throat).

Western and two employees were charged with four counts of exhibiting an allegedly obscene film, "Deep Throat." The jury found Western guilty on all counts and it was fined $1,000 on each count. The jury was unable to reach a verdict as to the charges against the two employees and the charges were dismissed. The conviction was affirmed. The court stated:

The movie 'Deep Throat' was introduced in evidence and has been viewed by this court. It contains repeated scenes of actual sexual intercourse, anal sodomy, fellatio and cunnilingus. The story line consists entirely of the sexual activities of Miss Linda Lovelace. We failed to find any serious literary, artistic, political or scientific value in this motion picture. We, therefore, agree with the jury's conclusion that this exhibited material was obscene and violative of contemporary community standards under the tests prescribed in Miller . . . .

Mangum v. State's Attorney for Baltimore City. 275 Md. 450, 341 A.2d 786(1975) (Deep Throat).

Theater was permanently enjoined from showing the film, "Deep Throat," by the Maryland State Board of Censors. The license was denied on the basis that the film was found to be obscene. The order was affirmed. The court noted,

. . . the trail judge as trier of the facts viewed the film "Deep Throat" and found that it was obscene under the Miller test. The court found that it was hard-core pornography and "was nothing more or less than a so-called 'stag' film . . . ." On the basis of our viewing the film, it is clear that this is an accurate categorization.

The film "Deep Throat" is for the most part a series of explicit depictions of sexual acts, including cunnilingus, fellatio, masturbation, normal and anal intercouse, and group sex. Effort was obviously made by the film makers to concentrate on the actors' genitals during the scenes of sexual activity. Well over half of the length of the film was devoted to displaying these explicit sexual acts. The satirical scenes referred by some of petitioner's witnesses were brief and sophomoric, serving as little more than introductions to the scenes of explicit sexual activity.

This case is the first case in which the question of hard-core pornography has been considered by this Court since the Miller definition was formulated by the Supreme Court. The film is clearly within the Miller definition of obscenity or hard-core pornography. In fact, "Deep Throat" would probably be deemed obscene under any meaningful definition of that term, including that set forth by the plurality opinion in Memoirs. It is noteworthy that in other jurisdictions where the matter has arisen, "Deep Throat" has consistently been found to be obscene.

People v. Thomas. 37 Ill. App. 3d 320, 346 N.E. 2d 190(1976) (Deep Throat).

Defendant was convicted of obscenity violation for exhibiting, for public patronage, the film "Deep Throat." He was sentenced to sixty days in jail and fined $1,000. The conviction was reversed. The court stated that the elements of the offense in Illinois must include the requirement that the prosecution prove the subject material to be utterly without redeeming value.

People v. Mature Enterprises, Inc. 3 N.Y.S.2d 520, 323 N.E.2d 704(1974) (Deep Throat).

Defendant was convicted of two counts of obscenity for showing the film, "Deep Throat." It was fined $100,000. The judgement was modified on the grounds of an excessive fine imposed. The defendant did not dispute the finding that the film was obscene within the meaning of the statute.

State v. American Theater Corp. 194 Neb. 84, 230 N.W.2d 209(1975).

Defendant was found guilty of distributing obscene material and was fined $500. The judgement was affirmed on appeal. After quoting from United States v. One Reel of Film, the court concluded, "We find that the film is hard-core pornography and is obscene under both the Roth-Memoirs test and the more recent and less stringent Miller test."

Houston v. Hennessey. 534 S.W.2d 52(Mo. App. 1975) (Deep Throat).

Petitioner, Houston, had been enjoined from exhibiting the film, "Deep Throat." The order was violated and he was held in contempt. The movie had been found to be obscene. The court quashed the writ of habeus corpus it had issued earlier.

Commonwealth v. 707 Main Corp. 371 Mass. 374, 357 N.E.2d 753(1976) (Deep Throat).

Defendant was found guilty of two counts of violating the obscenity statute by exhibiting the film, "Deep Throat." The judgment was affirmed. The defendant made no contention that the jury was not warranted in finding that the motion picture "Deep Throat" was obscene, "and the uncontroverted summary in the record as to the content of the motion picture confirms the correctness of this approach."

Coleman v. Wilson. 123 N.J.Super. 310, 302 A.2d 555(1973).

Prosecutor sought to enjoin the further showing of two films, "Deep Throat" and "Love for Sale." The court found the statute constitutional and found both films obscene. In reviewing the film, the court noted,

"Deep Throat" is a one hour and five minute motion picture portraying a young woman whose clitoris is in her throat. Early in the film there is an extended exhibition of cunnilingus. This is soon followed by a scene of group sex between two women and a number of men showing explicit acts of intercourse, fellatio, cunnilingus and sodomy. . . . The young woman consults a buffoon psychiatrist who diagnoses her amazing deformity and prescribes fellatio to achieve an orgasm. The balance of the film deals with the young woman serving as the doctor's assistant by engaging in sexual acts with him and his patients. Long detailed scenes of fellatio, cunnilingus and sodomy are repeatedly shown.

State v. Spoke Committee University Center. 270 N.W.2d 339(N.D. 1978) (Deep Throat).

Three-judge district court found the film, "Deep Throat" obscene and issued a state-wide injunction prohibiting further showing of the film. The judgement was reversed on the basis of a defective search warrant and illegal seizure of the film.

People v. Mature Enterprises, Inc. 73 Misc. 2d 749, 343 N.Y.S.2d 911(1971) (Deep Throat).

Defendant was found guilty of promotion, or possession with intent to promote, obscene material, knowing the contents and character of the material namely, "Deep Throat." In finding the defendant guilty, the court stated,

> The film runs 62 minutes. It is in color and in sound, and boasts a musical score. Following the first innocuous scene ("heroine" driving a car), the film runs from one act of explicit sex into another forthrightly demonstrating heterosexual intercourse and a variety of deviate sexual acts, not 'fragmentary and fleeting' as to be de minimus . . . but here it permeates and engulfs the film from beginning to end.

People v. Mature Enterprises, Inc. 76 Misc. 2d 660, 352, N.Y.S.2d 346(App. Div. 1974) (Deep Throat).

On appeal court found "Deep Throat" constitutionally obscene. Affirmed the conviction.

People v. Hausman. 82 Misc. 2d 1032, 372 N.Y.S.2d 503(Cty. Ct. 1975) (Deep Throat).

Defendant was found guilty of a violation of the obscenity statute by exhibiting the film, "Deep Throat." The conviction was reversed and a new trial was ordered on the grounds that the court needed to apply the appropriate community standards.

Smith v. State, 530 S.W. 2d 955(Ct. Crim. App. Tx. 1976) (Deep Throat).

Convicted of commercial exhibition of obscene material (Deep Throat). The judgement was reversed on the basis that there was insufficient evidence to establish a commercial purpose. The court noted,

> If the appellant had been charged with the possession of obscene material for the purpose of commercial exhibition, the evidence in the record might have supported a conviction for that offense.

PEEP SHOWS

The following is a description of a film

loop.[2279] The segments may overlap as the film is continually played. The title of the film, according to an advertisement on the outside of the peep show booth, is "Angel Gets Raped."

The film begins by showing a female dressed in a short red dress and knee high socks playing with some dolls. Two men, one black, one white, enter her room and grab the girl. They rip off her clothes. The girl at first struggles with them quite convincingly. The white male holds her down, fondles and kisses her breasts. The black male holds her legs and rips off her panties. He then performs cunnilingus on her. Her pubic area is either shaved or hairless. The black male is then shown pulling down his pants. The white male continues to lick the girl's body. The black male again performs cunnilingus on the girl. A close up is shown. The white male is now nude and the female performs fellatio on him while laying on the floor between his legs. He rubs his penis on her face and she continues fellatio. The black male is shown continuing cunnilingus and with his fingers in the girl's vagina. The two men then change positions. She performs fellatio on the black male while the white male engages in intercourse with her with him on the top. The white male is then shown ejaculating with the semen running down her crotch and in between her buttocks. She is shown continuing fellatio on the black male until he ejaculates in her mouth. The semen is shown on her cheek and running down her chin. The white male is then shown with his finger in her vagina and wiping what appears to be blood from around her labia. She is then shown kissing both men.

Next is a description of a film loop which is made up of film clips titled on the outside of the peep show booth "Wild Lesbians," "Bad Girls."[1280]

The first segment observed was of two white females nude performing cunnilingus on each other. One of the females is shown inserting a dildo in the anus of the other female while continuing cunnilingus. She's shown spreading the female's labia with her fingers. The two females are then shown breaking apart and one female inserting a dildo in the other's anus and performing cunnilingus on

---

2279. Description was completed by Senior Investigator Joseph B. Haggerty. The film was viewed in a peep show booth in an "Adult Only" pornographic outlet in the Washington, D.C., area. An affidavit for seizure had previously been prepared and presented the U.S. Attorney's office of Superior Court but was declined in 1984.

2280. Description was completed by Senior Investigator Joseph B. Haggerty. The film was seized from a pornographic outlet in Washington, D.C. An affidavit for seizure was submitted three times before it was finally approved by the U.S. Attorney's office of Superior Court, but was later declined for prosecution in 1983.

her at the same time. Then she's shown just moving the dildo in the other female's anus. Then the two females are shown positioning themselves so their vaginal areas are touching each other. They move against each other and with their fingers on their own labias, one fondles her own breasts at the same time.

Another film clip is shown, showing a black female inserting her fingers in a white female's vagina.

The next segment shows the black female continuing to move her fingers in and out of the white female's vagina. There are three females in this segment, two white and one black. The black female is then shown inserting her fist in the white female's vagina as she fingers her labia and performs cunnilingus. Then the brunette white female is shown inserting her fist in the black female's vagina. The two white females are shown kissing the black female. A close up is shown of the brunette white female inserting her fist into the black female. The black female's face is shown and appears to be yelling. The brunette white female is shown inserting her fist into the blonde white female. Then she's shown inserting her fists into both the blonde white female and the black female at the same time.

The next segment shows the faces of both females being fisted. The blonde white female appears to be yelling. Then the brunette white female performs cunnilingus on the blonde white female, while the black female licks the blonde white female's breasts. Then the brunette white female places her fingers in the blonde white female's vagina, as she continues cunnilingus. The blonde white female is now performing cunnilingus on the black female at the same time. The females change positions. The blonde white female and the black female both perform cunnilingus on the brunette white female.

The next segment shows the black female and the blonde white female continuing to perform cunnilingus on the brunette white female. The black female also places her fingers in the brunette white female's vagina as she continues cunnilingus on the brunette white female. Then the black female and the blonde white female flick their tongues together. Then they both place their fingers in the brunette white female's vagina at the same time. Then both kiss the brunette white female.

Another film clip begins, showing a white female lying on a bed. Her face is shown with her mouth open grimacing. Shown between her legs is a black female.

The next segment shows the white female's face again. The black female is shown inserting a dildo in the white female's vagina. Then with the dildo inserted in both their vaginas moving together. Then the white female pulls away and reinserts the dildo in the black female's vagina. As she moves the dildo in the black female's vagina the white female licks the other end of the two-headed dildo. Then the white female is shown inserting three fingers in the black female's vagina.

The next segment shows the white female continuing to have her fingers in the black female's vagina. The white female then is shown inserting her fist in the black female's vagina. The black female holds the wrist of the white female as she continues to fist the black female's vagina.

Another film clip is shown, showing a white female (represented to be known porno star Marlene ✂) inserting one finger in the vagina of another female (represented to be known porno star Vanessa ✂). Then Marlene inserts two fingers in Vanessa's vagina. One finger has a large ring. A close up is shown of the insertion. Then Marlene uses her left hand and inserts one finger in Vanessa's vagina, then two fingers are inserted, then three fingers are inserted. Then she inserts her fist in Vanessa's vagina, twisting it around.

The next segment shows Marlene removing her fist from Vanessa's vagina then inserting it again. Vanessa holds Marlene's wrist as she continues to fist her vagina. Marlene is wearing a gold colored bracelet on her left wrist. A close up is shown of the insertion with Marlene twisting her fist around in Vanessa's vagina. Then Marlene removes her fist from Vanessa's vagina and reinserts one finger from her right hand in Vanessa's vagina and performs cunnilingus on her at the same time. A close up is shown of Marlene performing cunnilingus on Vanessa spreading her labia and inserting her tongue.

The next segment shows Vanessa inserting a finger in Marlene's vagina as Marlene fondles her own breasts. Then Vanessa inserts one end of a two-headed dildo in Marlene's vagina. She then inserts the other end in her own vagina. They move together. Marlene grabs a camera to take a picture of them. Then Marlene moves and reinserts the dildo in Vanessa's vagina and performs cunnilingus on her at the same time. Another close up is shown of Marlene performing cunnilingus on Vanessa with her mouth on her clitoris.

The next segment is another film clip showing two white females nude. A close up is shown of one performing cunnilingus on the other. Then spreading of the labia she continued cunnilingus. Then a dildo is shown being inserted in one of the female's anus as she fingers her own labia. The dildo is shown being moved in and out of the female's anus and continued cunnilingus. The other female is shown with the first female performing cunnilingus and inserting fingers in both her vagina and anus. A dildo is inserted in her anus as cunnilingus is continued.

The next segment is a repeat of the first.

TABLOID
(See Publisher's Note on page 434)

The following is a description of a newspaper-like publication entitled *ALL PLEAZURE*.[2281] It is thirteen inches x twelve inches and retails for $1.50. A female on the cover is drawn in a black slip which is pulled off her right shoulder exposing her right breast. She is not wearing panties, but has on dark colored boots or stockings that go up to her thighs. She is in a standing position with one foot on an object with her legs spread open. Her forearms and hands are gloved. She has her right hand on her genital area. Her left hand is around her own throat. In smaller print at the bottom of the cover page is "ADULT TYPE MATERIAL NOT TO BE SOLD OR READ BY PERSONS UNDER 21 YEARS OF AGE."

The first inside page has six photographs of nude females, exposing themselves in various ways.

The next page repeats the title of the publication with a photo of a nude caucasian female in the background. She is bent over showing her buttocks. On this page is the mast head, some disclaimers, and the copyright.

Page four contains three photographs, one of a close-up of a female's labia being spread by fingers and two of nude females.

Pages five through eight contain three photos of a nude caucasian female spreading legs and her labia with her fingers and a story about Margaret Manners. After a description of Margaret and her fantasies of having sex with a black male, there is a conversation between her and her boyfriend while they engage in intercourse. The story talks of Margaret's orgasms and how she feels. The text ends with her boyfriend reaching orgasm.

Page nine is a full page advertisement of eleven Bondage Magazines.

Pages ten through fourteen contain three photos and a story entitled, "FUCK ME, TUFF." Two of the photos are of females spreading their labias, the other is of a nude caucasian female lying on her stomach smiling at the camera. Her hair is in pigtails and she's hugging a stuffed animal. The story is about a woman and a female neighbor who visit the woman's husband's office. The husband won't talk to his wife. The neighbor tells the husband's secretary it is because the husband and the wife got into some bondage and discipline and the husband was upset because the wife had been the dominatrix. The secretary tells the wife that she has had sex with the husband for the last year and it always begins with bondage and discipline. She tells the wife that she should be the one being dominated. She instructs the wife. The wife goes into the husband's office and insults him. He becomes mad, strips her, binds her wrists, puts a dog leash on her and forces her to peform fellatio on him which she does willingly. He ejaculates into her mouth. She swallows it. He throws her on the carpet and slides a dildo into her vagina. She climaxes. He becomes aroused again and has vaginal intercourse with her. They tell each other how much they love each other and she asks if she can dominate sometimes.

On page fifteen are twenty-seven different ads. The largest ad is for a penis enlarger. Following is a description of the remaining twenty-six ads: "Cherry Popper": personal polaroids shot at home by swinging "families." *Piddly Diddlers Getting Off*: secretary shot pictures of girls doing it with boys. *Free Lifesize Sex Doll*: with large breasts and hairy vagina. *30 Dirty Sex Comics*: all 30 for $2.95. *Suck-Off Films*: in color: "Sucking Orgy," "Forced to Suck," "Cream Licker," "School Suck-Off," "Deep Throat Sister," *Wet Videos*: "Golden Showers," "Wet Sex Party," "'P' For Pleasure," "Little Wet Panties." *Save You Money! Free Hardcore Samples! "Little Porno" Magazines*: The Hard-To-Get-Kind. "Nasty Playmate,"

2281. Original description by Senior Investigator Haggerty. This publication was purchased from a pornographic outlet in the District of Columbia, March 1986.

"Cherry Suckers," "Tight Pussies," "Lollipop Pet." Free! Free! 16 glossy photos from new films made especially for "young stuff" collectors. Forbidden Porno: Nasty subjects quietly imported from Danish smut Centers. Free Magazines: Illustrated Forbidden Hardcore. Pictures of My 4 Girls: magazines. Your Name & Address Is Worth $20: Buy direct & enjoy the best in explicit hardcore viewing. Act now & receive authentic rubber dildo free. Women Who Seduce: Drawing of woman and young boy accompanies the ad. Four videos. New Stuff/Hardcore 60 Min. Video: "Cum Covered Cherries," "Peach Fuzz Playmates," "Virgin Ass Fucking," "The Dirty Daughters," "Bound in Bobbysox." Free We'll Give You $25 worth of colorfully illustrated HARD-CORE MAGAZINES for your name and address. Women Who Fuck Anything Magazines: Four magazines offered. A drawing of a female bent over with a dog's snout near her crotch accompanies this ad. 12 Suck Mags: Genuine "Swedish Erotica" Series. Featuring lads & lassies of unusual oral talent. Free Hardcore Magazine Offer: Six bizarre sex subjects: *ASS FUCKING *FORCED VIRGIN *DOUBLE SUCKER *BARN BALLING *YOUNG STUFF *INCEST ORGY. Bizarre sex acts by perverse sex freaks. I'll Make Us Both Come!! When I spread it wide open, rub it, finger it & Masturbate just for you! I also do sucking pictures and other home sex with my husband & 2 girls. Little Porno Pictures: The Forbidden kind. Over 600 Hardcore pictures of cute and tempting fucking & sucking secretly imported from Europe. Forbidden Video: Five videos offered. Part-Time Prostitutes: Housewives, Schoolgirls, Secretaries. Available for all kinds of wild and unusual sex. Knock Out Formula: No prescription—Safe to use. Allows uninhibited sex with any girl. She'll never know you used it. Gay Porno: Hetero dealer has selected hardcore gay material in all media. 8 Inches in 8 Weeks: Penis enlarger.

Pages sixteen and seventeen contain seven photographs of caucasian women. Page sixteen has four photos all with the women nude or partially clothed with their legs spread. Page seventeen contains three photographs of the same girl, two fully clothed and one completely nude with her left hand on the underside of her left thigh near her pubic area. Her right hand is next to her head. Her finger is in her mouth.

Page eighteen also displays several photographs, two of the same female.

Page nineteen is the beginning of another story, entitled, "Uncle's Incestuous Bung-holein." An Uncle Bobby performs cunnilingus on his sixteen-year-old niece, Joanie. Then she wants him to penetrate her anally but first she wants him to perform analingus on her.

Pages twenty and twenty-one contain advertisements for forty different dildos and electric vibrators, two artificial vaginas, a device to tighten the vagina, and an adjustable universal harness. Also there are advertisements for twelve different inflatable dolls: Big John with realistic penis, Big John with vibrating penis, Big John with vibrating and ejaculating penis, Sweet Sexteen deluxe Teenage Greek Doll with vibrating vagina, Sweet Sexteen Teenage Greek Doll with young breasts, Miss Greek, Electronic Greek, Virgin Greek with intact hymen and Natural Hair.

Page twenty-two contains an advertisement for eight more dildos and vibrators, three different butt plugs, two artificial vaginas, and two masturbators.

Page twenty-three is an advertisement for Pleazure Personals and a form to write an advertisement. Accompanying this ad are photographs of two females partially clothed.

Page twenty-four and twenty-five contain forty-four personal ads.

Page twenty-six contains two photographs of the same female that appears on page eighteen. One photo shows two hands spreading the female's labia. The other photo shows the female inserting the small vibrator in her vagina.

Pages twenty-seven through thirty contain the continued text of "Uncle's Incestuous Bung-holein" and a series of three photographs, each showing a woman's labia being spread open. One photo also shows a spread-open anus. Uncle Bobby penetrates his niece anally with his fingers and then his penis. This is her first time. At first there is great pain, but it subsides. Joanie has an orgasm and so does Uncle Bobby as they continue anal intercourse. Joanie performs fellatio on Uncle Bobby to clean him off. Later Joanie is taking a shower. Her father enters and washes her breasts, thighs and pubic area. They go into the master bedroom where Joanie fondles her father's penis and testicles. He then has an erection. Her father then has vaginal intercourse with her, breaking her hymen.

Page thirty-one contains two photos of the

same white caucasion female exposing her labia.

The last page, page thirty-two is called *ALL PLEAZURE MARKET* and contains five different ads: for a swingers club in New Jersey, for an aphrodesiac that produces hard long lasting erections, for free brochures offering "erotic books and magazines for every taste," for male and female actors for "XXXX movies," and for learning how to fly: "F.A.A. certified & A.T.P. jet rated flight instructor."

Sample Forms

OBSCENITY STATUTE UTILIZING *MILLER* STANDARD

Material is obscene if:

1. to the average person, applying contemporary community standards, taken as a whole, it predominantly appeals to a prurient interest in nudity, sex or excretion;
2. the material taken as a whole, lacks serious literary, artistic, political or scientific value, and
3. the material depicts or describes, in a patently offensive way, sexual conduct specifically defined in subparagraphs *a* through e below:
   a. acts of sexual intercourse, heterosexual or homosexual, normal or perverted, actual or simulated;
   b. acts of masturbation;
   c. acts involving excretory functions or lewd exhibition of the genitals;
   d. acts of bestiality or the fondling of sex organs of animals;
   e. sexual acts of flagellation, torture or other violence indicating a sadomasochistic sexual relationship.

FORFEITURE STATUTES (WITH POSTAL SERVICE AMENDMENT)

Possible Criminal Forfeiture Provision:

(a) A person who is convicted of an offense under section 1461, 1462, 1463, 1464, or 1465 of this title shall forfeit to the United States such person's interest in—
   (1) any property constituting, or derived from, gross profits or other proceeds obtained from such offense; and

(2) any property used, or intended to be used, to commit such offense.

(b) In any action under this section, the court may enter such restraining orders or take other appropriate action (including acceptance of performance bonds) in connection with any interest that is subject to forfeiture.

(c) The court shall order the forfeiture of property referred to in subsection (a) if the trier of fact determines, beyond a reasonable doubt, that such property is subject to forfeiture.

(d) (1) Except as provided in paragraph (3) of this subsection, the customs laws relating to disposition of seized or forfeiture property shall apply to property under this section, if such laws are not inconsistent with this section.

(2) In any disposition of property under this section, a convicted person shall not be permitted to acquire property forfeited by such person.

(3) The duties of the Secretary of the Treasury with respect to dispositions of property shall be performed under paragraph (1) of this subsection by the Attorney General, unless such duties arise from forfeitures effected under the customs laws.

Possible Civil Forfeiture Provision:

(a) The following property shall be subject to forfeiture by the United States:
   (1) Any material or equipment used, or intended for use, in producing, reproducing, transporting, ship-

ping, or receiving any visual depiction in violation of section 1461, 1462, 1463, 1464, or 1465 of this title.

(2) Any visual depiction, production, transported, shipped, or received in violation of section 1461, 1462, 1463, 1464, 1465 of this title, or any material containing such depiction.

(3) Any property constituting or derived from, gross profits or other proceeds obtained from a violation of section 1461, 1462, 1463, 1464, or 1465 of this title except that no property shall be forfeited under this paragraph, to the extent of the interest of an owner, by reason of any act or omission established by that owner to have been committed or omitted without the knowledge or consent of that owner.

(b) All provisions of the customs law relating to the seizure, summary and judicial forfeiture, and condemnation of property for violation of the customs laws, the disposition of such property or the proceeds from the sale thereof, the remission or mitigation of such forfeiture, and the compromise of claims, shall apply to seizures and forfeitures incurred, or alleged to have been incurred, under this section, insofar as applicable and not inconsistent with the provisions of this section, except that such duties as are imposed to seizures and forfeitures or property under this section by such officers, agents or other persons as may be authorized or designated for that purpose by the Attorney General or the Postmaster General except to the extent that such duties arise from seizures and forfeitures effected by any customs officer.

Amended Title 39 S2003

S2003. The Postal Service Fund

(a) There is established in the Treasury of the United States a revolving fund to be called the Postal Service Fund which shall be available to the Postal Service without fiscal-year limitation to carry out the purposes, functions, and powers authorized by this title.

(b) There shall be deposited in the Fund, subject to withdrawal by check by the Postal Service—

1. revenues from postal and nonpostal services rendered by the Postal Service;
2. amounts received from obligations issued by the Postal Service;
3. amounts appropriate for the use of the Postal Service;
4. interest which may be earned on investments of the Fund;
5. any other receipts of the Postal Service;
6. the balance in the Postal Service Department Fund established under former section 2202 of title 39 as the commencement of operations of the Postal Service; and
7. amounts from any civil administrative forfeiture conducted by the Postal Service.

(c) If the Postal Service determines that the moneys of the Fund are in excess of current needs, it may request the investment of such amounts as it deems advisable by the Secretary of the Treasury in obligations of, or obligations guaranteed by, the Government of the United States, and, with the approval of the Secretary, in such other obligations or securities as it deems appropriate.

(d) With the approval of the Secretary of the Treasury, the Postal Service may deposit moneys of the Fund in any Federal Reserve bank, any depository for public funds, or in such other places and in such manner as the Postal Service and the Secretary may mutually agree.

(e) The Fund shall be available for the payment of all expenses incurred by the Postal Service in carrying out its functions under this title and, subject to the Postal Rate Commission. Neither the Fund nor any of the funds credited to it shall be subject to apportionment under the provisions of section 665 of title 31.

(1) The Fund shall be available for the payment of all expenses incurred by the Postal Service in carrying out its functions under this title including expenses incurred in the conduct of seizures, forfeitures, and disposal of forfeited property pursuant to title 18 and subject to the provisions of section 3604 of

this title, all of the expenses of the Postal Rate Commission. Neither the Fund nor any of the funds credited to it shall be subject to apportionment under the provisions of subchapter II of chapter 15 of title 31.

(2) Funds appropriated to the Postal Service under section 2401 and 2004 of this title shall be apportioned as provided in this paragraph. From the total amounts appropriated to the Postal Service for any fiscal year under the authorizations contained in sections 2401 and 2004 of this title, the Secretary of the Treasury shall make available to the Postal Service 25 percent of such amount at the beginning of each quarter of such fiscal year.

(f) Notwithstanding any other provision of this section, any amounts appropriated to the Postal Service under subsection (d) of section 2401 of this title and deposited into the Fund shall be expended by the Postal Service only for the purposes provided in such subsection.

SEARCH WARRANTS

The following search warrants have been provided as examples of warrants which have been successfully used in criminal proceedings with only minor editorial changes. Blanks are left to protect the identity of the victims, agency, or officer. Each law enforcement agency should modify the warrants as needed given the constraints of available information, expertise of the affiant and particular legal requirements of respective jurisdictions.

AFFIDAVIT FOR SEARCH WARRANT—CHILD PORNOGRAPHY

_____(name of affiant)_____, being sworn, says that on the information contained within this affidavit, he/she has probable cause to believe and does believe that the property described below is seizable pursuant to (Penal Code Section _____) in that it: (CHECK APPROPRIATE BOX OR BOXES)

_____ tends to show that sexual exploitation of a child has occurred or is occurring.

_____ was used as the means of committing a felony

_____ is possessed by a person with the intent to use it as a means of committing a public offense or is possessed by another to whom he may have delivered it for the purpose of concealing with or preventing its discovery.

_____ is evidence which tends to show that a felony has been committed or a particular person has committed a felony; (or appropriate statutory requirements)

and that he/she has probable cause to believe and does believe that the described property is now located at and will be found at the locations set forth below and thus requests the issuance of a WARRANT TO SEARCH. _____(location)_____, described as a, _____, _____ and identified from _____, as _____(name)_____, _____(address)_____. 2. _____(name)_____, female/male, further description with a home address of _____(address)_____.

For the following property: 1. Phone books, address books, notations, identifying a male/female juvenile(s), "name and/or other juveniles or adults who are being sexually exploited or who are exploiting children. 2. Photographs and/or undeveloped film depicting (name), and or other juveniles nude or in sexual activity. 3. Movies and/or magazines depicting juveniles in sexual activity. 4. Identification including but not limited to _____.

Your affiant says that the facts in support of the issuance of the search warrant are contained in the attached STATEMENT OF PROBABLE CAUSE which is incorporated as it is fully set forth herein. Wherefore, your affiant prays that a search warrant be issued for the seizure of said property or any part thereof, at any time of the day or night, good cause therefore having been shown.

_____
SIGNATURE OF AFFIANT

Subscribed and sworn to before me
this _____ day of _____, 19_____.

_____
Signature of Magistrate

Judge of the _____   _____
Superior/Municipal   Judicial District

Prepared with the assistance of, or reviewed by:

_____
Deputy District Attorney

Your affiant is _____(name)_____. I am a (detective) for the (city) of _____(name)_____, and have been so employed for the past _____ years. For the past _____ years, I have been assigned to the (Sexually Exploited Child Unit of Juvenile Division). I have been assigned to said Division for the past _____ years. I have participated in an excess of _____ investigations involving the sexual exploitation of minors and children. I have personally conducted in excess of _____ investigations resulting in felony charges of child molestation and exploitation. I have received extensive training and have read numerous publications dealing with the sexual exploitation of children. I have talked to in excess of _____ sexually exploited children and in excess of _____ admitted child molesters. I have read and examined in excess of _____ letters between pedophile offenders describing their admitted sexual conduct with children and the manner in which they exploited said children for sexual gratification. I have examined in excess of _____ photographs during these investigations which depict children engaged in sexual activities with the offenders, with other children, with animals and with adults. I have examined and read publications distributed from foreign countries and in the United States which describe in detail sexual activities between adults and children. I am familiar with the manner in which pedophile offenders entice and encourage children to engage in sexual conduct and the manner in which they exchange children with each other, and make contact with other adults who engage in such conduct. From my training and experience, I am aware that pedophile offenders have a specific age preference for the juvenile victim and that when the victim surpasses this age, the pedophile offender, no longer having sexual interest in her or him, will seek out a younger juvenile to take the victim's place sexually. It has been my experience that pedophile offenders will not stop or remain with one juvenile victim but will constantly seek out new victims, using the same method of seduction that had been successful for him. It has been my personal experience and knowledge of pedophile offender from other officers that a pedophile offender has never stopped with one juvenile victim but has continued to molest juveniles whenever the opportunity arises. From interviewing and speaking with pedophile offenders, both in an official capacity and during undercover operations, I am aware that pedophile offenders will retain photographs, magazines, movies and correspondence. This retention will span many years and the material is used by the pedophile offenders to lower the child's inhibitions and to relive the pedophile offender's experience. From the prior investigations that I had conducted and from talking to other detectives involved in pedophile investigations worldwide, I am aware of pedophile offenders retaining their pedophilic and pornographic material in excess of twenty years, and that this material has been shown to juveniles to lower the victims' inhibitions. I am aware that, depending upon the age of the juvenile victims, that pedophile offenders will often furnish drugs and alcohol to lower their inhibitions. A pedophile offender will frequently seek out employment or volunteer his or her service to be close to children and to use and to use the authority over the children and to victimize them. I have testified as an expert in both the (Municipal and Superior) Courts in the field of the sexually exploited child and have assisted the United States Attorney's Office in formulating procedures in the federal prosecution for the importation and non-commercial distribution of child pornography.

Your affiant received intelligence that a _____(name)_____ of _____(address)_____, has had contact with pedophiles in the _____(name)_____, area and traveled to _____(name)_____ to engage in sexual activity with juveniles. This intelligence was received from _____(name)_____, _____(address)_____, who had interviewed a child pornographer suspect and had seized evidence indicating _____, activities.

Your affiant began an undercover investigation of _____(name_____ corresponding with him under the alias of _____(name)_____, In the first letter _____(name)_____ stated that a trusted friend supplied _____(name)_____ and that _____(name)_____ was a firm believer in the liberal upbringing of children and had raised and photographed his ten year old daughter. Enclosed in the letter was an unmounted color slide depicting a female juvenile, approximately eight to ten years old. (Copy of letter incorporated herein as Attachment 1.) On July 12, 1983, your affiant received a letter with a return address of _____(name)_____, _____(address)_____.

The letter, dated July 7, 1983, stated in part: "Thanks for your letter and its absolutely charming enclosure. The enclosures are photos of young ladies with whom I have had extensive personal contacts in recent years. I do have some slides of the two of them engaged in educational activities that probably are similar to some that you had in mind when mentioning your daughter's liberal training. It is a good many years now since I participated directly in the educational games of my two eldest daughters, _____(name)_____ , and _____(name)_____ , or even their young half sisters.

There is also a granddaughter but even she is well into her teens. For a few years, though, she was one of the most uninhibited and enthusiastic preteen I've ever known! Her constant responses were, Can we do it again Grandpa? and Teach me something else! I'll be in _____(name)_____ the last week of July and the first one in August. I'll arrive in _____(name)_____ the 23rd or 24th. Write soon, _____(name)_____," (Copy of letter incorporated herein as Attachment 2.)

Enclosed in this letter were three color photographs of preteen females nude. One photograph depicts a juvenile nude with body paint on her chest, the second photograph depicts a juvenile nude, eating watermelon. She is crouched down, her legs slightly apart and her vagina exposed. The third photograph depicts a female juvenile nude from her waist down her buttocks toward the camera and her vagina exposed. (Copy of photographs incorporated herein as Attachment 3.)

On July 12, 1983, your affiant responded to _____(name)_____ letter suggesting that they could meet when _____(name)_____ arrives in _____(name)_____ (copy of letter incorporated herein as Attachment 4). On July 20, 1983, your affiant received a second letter from _____(name)_____ addressed to _____(name)_____. Enclosed were two black and white photographs and three color photographs all depicting preteen families in nude or semi nude poses. _____(name)_____ stated in part: "The two B&W's of each clowning around are from color negs. . . . I have quite a few. I have about 30 ektachromes of each and _____(name)_____ in action together doing most of the things two little girls can do to each other. Presently I am cultivating the daughters nine and six of an American-Vietnamese couple here in _____(location)_____. I plan to arrive in _____(location)_____ next Sunday afternoon, the 24th, to check into a meeting at the Hilton at the park in _____(location)_____, then to the _____(location)_____. Friday night a friend is driving me to _____(location)_____ for some little girl photos at Black's Beach and a kiddy porn movie festival. Time is running short. If you'd like to phone, the number is _____(number)_____." (Copy of letter incorporate herein as Attachment 5.) The two black and white photographs depict the same female juvenile with her vagina exposed and in one, her legs are wide apart. Two of the three color photographs depict two female juveniles nude laying on the beach with their legs apart. The third photographs depicts a female juvenile nude bending over with her legs spread with her vagina and buttocks to the camera. (Copy of photographs incorporated herein as Attachment 6). On July 21, 1983, your affiant contacted _____(name)_____ at his residence and recorded the conversation. _____(name)_____ indicated that _____(name)_____ is a girl living in _____(name)_____ with whom he had extensive sexual contact beginning when she was six till two years ago at age ten. He also indicated that he was going with a friend from _____(location)_____ to a child porn film festival given by some other friends in _____(location)_____. He indicated that he would bring some undeveloped film to get developed. He also identified himself as an engineer who worked for the _____(name)_____.

On July 25, 1983, your affiant contacted the Hilton-at-the Park in _____(name)_____ and determined that _____(name)_____ had registered on July 24, 1983, and that he gave his home address as _____(address)_____ , _____. Your affiant then contacted the _____ and learned that _____(name)_____ has reserved a room for July 27/29, 1983. This registration had _____(name)_____, return address _____(address)_____.

Based on the photographs sent and the letters indicating _____(name)_____'s sexual interest in juveniles, your affiant is of the opinion that _____(name)_____ engaged in child sexual exploitation. The photographs sent are exhibiting the pubic and rectal areas of juveniles under fourteen years of age for the purposes of sexual stimulation of the viewer.

Based upon your affiant's experience, expertise and all of the information contained above, your affiant is of the conclusion that the property listed in the warrant will be found at the locations to be searched for the following reasons:

1. That the person listed is a pedophile offender,
2. That such persons do not destroy photographs and any other reproductions depicting sexual conduct,
3. That such persons retain these materials for the purposes of personal gratification, to gain the acceptance, confidence, and trust of other pedophiles, to exchange such materials from other pedophiles, to receive monetary gains for the furnishing of such material, to ensure protection from exposure to police authority from other persons,
4. That correspondence from other persons is kept with the same full allegiance,
5. That such persons gain a certain pride from the exhibition of such material,
6. Such materials are kept secure in residence, vehicles, storage facilities and bank deposit boxes to protect themselves against seizure by police authorities; and,
7. That all of the other materials requested for seizure will identify other children being sexually exploited and other adults who are engaging in such exploitation.

Your affiant therefore says that there is probable and reasonable cause to believe that items requested to be seized are items which tend to show that a violation of Section _____ of the (Penal Code) has occurred or is occurring. Your affiant has reasonable cause to believe that grounds for the issuance of a search warrant exists as set forth in Section _____ of the _____ code based upon the fact and the attachments.

AFFIDAVIT FOR SEARCH WARRANT—CHILD PORNOGRAPHY

_____(name)_____, being sworn, says that on the basis of the information contained within this affidavit, he has probable cause to believe and does believe that the property described below is seizable pursuant to (Penal Code) Section _____ in that it: (CHECK APPROPRIATE BOX OR BOXES)

(MODIFY FOR JURISDICTION)

_____ tends to show that sexual exploitation of a child has occurred or is occurring

_____ was stolen or embezzled

_____ was used as the means of committing a felony

_____ is possessed by a person with the intent to use it as a means of committing a public offense or is possessed by another to whom he may have delivered it for the purpose of concealing it or preventing its discovery

_____ is evidence, which tends to show that a felony has been committed or a particular person has committed a felony; and that he has probable cause to believe and does believe that the described property is now located at and will be found at the locations set forth below and thus requests the issuance of a WARRANT TO SEARCH

1. _____(location)_____, described as a two story woodframe house covered with brown asphalt shingles. The numerals _____ are attached to the door frame. 2. _____(name)_____, male caucasian, black hair, brown eyes, _____(description)_____. For the following property: 1. Photographs, negatives, slides, depicting juveniles including, but not limited to _____(name) (and description)_____, undressed, nude and/or engaged in sexual activity. 2. Magazines and/or movies depicting nudity and/or sexual activity used to lower the inhibition of juveniles. 3. Cameras and camera equipment including, but not limited to camera, enlargers, developing equipment, projectors. 4. Items of identification including but not limited to, utility bills, cancelled mail tending to identify the person or person in control of the premise. 5. Address books, notations, records, phone books tending to identify the juveniles.

Your affiant says that the facts in support of the issuance of the search warrant are contained in the attached STATEMENT OF PROBABLE CAUSE which is incorporated as if fully set forth herein. Wherefore, your affiant prays that a search warrant be issued for the seizure of said property or any part thereof, at any time of the day or night, good cause therefore having been shown.

_____
SIGNATURE OF AFFIANT

Subscribed and sworn to before me
this _____ day of _____, 19_____.

_____
Signature of Magistrate
Judge of the _____ Court _____
Superior/Municipal   Judicial District
Prepared with the assistance of, or reviewed by:

_____
Deputy
Your affiant is _____(name)_____.
I am a detective for the _____(location)_____, and have been so employed for past _____ years. For the past _____ years, I have been assigned to the (Sexually Exploited Child Unit of the Juvenile Division). I have been assigned to said (Juvenile Division) for the past _____ years. I have participated in an excess of _____ investigations involving the sexual exploitation of minors and children. I have personally conducted in excess of _____ investigations resulting in felony charges of child molestation and exploitation. I have participated in training and have read numerous publications dealing with the sexual exploitation of children. I have talked to in excess of _____ sexually exploited children and in excess of _____ admitted child molesters. I have read and examined in excess of _____ letters between pedophiles describing their admitted sexual conduct with children and the manner in which they exploited said children for sexual gratification. I have examined in excess of _____ photographs during these investigations which depict children engaged in sexual activities with themselves, with other children, with animals and with adults. I have examined and read publications distributed from foreign countries and in the United States which describe in detail sexual activities between adults and children. I am familiar with the manner in which pedophiles entice and encourage children to engage in sexual conduct and the manner in which they exchange children with each other and make contact with other adults who engage in such conduct. From my training and experience, I am aware that pedophiles have a specific age preference for the juvenile victim and what when the victim surpasses this age, the pedophile, no longer having sexual interest in her or him, will seek out a younger juvenile to take the victim's place sexually. It has been my experience that pedophiles will not stop or remain with one juvenile victim but will constantly seek out new victims, using the same method of

seduction that had been successful for him. It has been my personal experience and knowledge of pedophiles from other officers that a pedophile has never stopped with one juvenile victim but has continued to molest juveniles whenever the opportunity arises. From interviewing and speaking with pedophiles, both in an official capacity and during undercover operations, I am aware that pedophiles will retain photographs, magazines, movies and correspondence. This retention will span many years and the material is used by the pedophiles to lower the child's inhibitions and to relive the pedophile's experience. From the prior investigations that I had conducted and from talking to other detectives involved in pedophilic investigations worldwide, I am aware of pedophiles retaining their pedophilic and pornographic material in excess of twenty years, and that this material has been shown to juveniles to lower the victim's inhibitions. I am aware that, depending upon the age of the juvenile victims, that pedophile will often furnish drugs and alcohol to lower their inhibitions. A pedophile will frequently seek out employment or volunteer his or her service to be close to children and to use the authority over the children and to victimize them. I have testified as an expert in both the (Municipal and Superior) Courts in the field of the sexually exploited child and have assisted the United States Attorney's Office in formulating procedures in the federal prosecution for the importation and non-commercial distribution of child pornography. On March 25, 1983, _____(name)_____, _____(address)_____, went to Police Station and reported that _____(name)_____, had been molesting their son, _____(name)_____. Your affiant was contacted by _____(name)_____ detectives and advised of the complaint. Your affiant contacted _____(name)_____, had never been married and has always had an interest in boys. On March 24, 1983, _____(name)_____, told his father _____(name)_____, had sexual relations with him between the age of twelve to sixteen. _____(name)_____, is aware that _____(name)_____ is a _____(name)_____ school teacher and a Boy Scout Leader. In addition, he was a Big Brother and a Parks Director. _____(name)_____, is frequently with young boys, taking them on trips and having them in his home. On March 25, 1983, your affiant interviewed _____(name)_____, stated that he is nineteen years old. When _____(name)_____ was twelve he would frequently visit _____(name)_____, at his residence, _____(address)_____, _____(name)_____, had items such as trains and clay that was of interest to _____(name)_____. While there _____(name)_____ would encourage _____(name)_____, to be photographed and as this photography continued, _____(name)_____, was convinced to be photographed nude. _____(name)_____ then began to molest _____(name)_____. The majority of the molestation being oral copulation. The victim stated that _____(name)_____ did try to sodomize him on some occasions. _____(name)_____, stated that _____(name)_____ is a photographer and had a darkroom set up in the attic. Most of the photographs were done in black and white and _____(name)_____ observed photographs of himself, nude and being orally copulated by _____(name)_____. _____(name)_____ stated that he also saw photographs of other male juveniles, taken inside _____(name)_____, house and these photographed depicted juveniles nude and engaged in sexual activity. _____(name)_____, stated that _____(name)_____ had movies depicting sexual activity and that _____(name)_____ would show _____(name)_____ these movies to get him excited. _____(name)_____ stated that _____(name)_____ kept many of the photographs under his bed or in other parts of his bedroom and in the attic with the darkroom equipment. Based upon your affiant's experience, expertise and all of the information contained above, your affiant is of the conclusion that the property listed in the warrant be found at the locations to be searched for the following reasons:

1. That the person listed is a pedophile,
2. That such persons do not destroy photographs and any other reproductions depicting sexual conduct,
3. That such persons retain these materials for the purposes of personal gratification, to gain the acceptance, confidence, and trust of other pedophiles, to exchange such materials from other pedophiles, to receive monetary gains for the furnishing of such material, to ensure protection from exposure to police authority from other persons.
4. That correspondence from other persons is kept with the same full allegiance.
5. That such persons gain a certain pride from the exhibition of such material.
6. That such materials are kept secure in residence, vehicles, storage facilities, and bank deposit boxes to protect themselves against seizure by police authorities, and
7. That all of the other materials requested for seizure will identify other children being sexually exploited and other adults who are engaging in such exploitation.

Your affiant therefore says that there is probable and reasonable cause to believe that items requested to be seized are items which tend to show that a felony has been committed. To wit Section _____ of the (Penal Code). Your affiant has reasonable cause to believe that grounds for the issuance of a search warrant exists as set forth in Section _____ of the (Penal Code), based upon the facts and the attachments.

AFFIDAVIT FOR SEARCH WARRANT—CHILD PORNOGRAPHY

_____(name)_____ swears or affirms that he believes and has good cause to believe that photographs and film projectors, movie machines, and various documents, including: diaries, phone records, maps, receipts, ledgers, letters of correspondence and other documents used for the purpose of permitting and facilitating the sexual exploitation of children, and the distribution of obscene matter are being kept and concealed by (name and locations)_____ .

Said apartment is within an apartment building and the entrance is located the 6th Door South from _____(street)_____ that has the letter "F" next to the entranceway, with the building being made of red brick, two story structure with a basement, and flat roof. Said above building is located in _____(county, state)_____. Affiant makes the above allegations on the basis of the fact that:

1. Affiant for a fact that: I, _____(name)_____ , am a detective assigned to the vice branch of the _____(name)_____ Police Department for the past fifteen months and have investigated pornography and deviate sexual conduct.

2. On August 8, 1977, the _____(name)_____ Police Department received from _____(name)_____ Police Department a brochure (see attached #1) concerning photography, conducted by _____(name and address)_____. Included in the brochure were offerings concerning male homosexual activities including masturbating and mutual male sex.

3. On June 16, 1978, Detective _____(name)_____ assigned to pornography investigations, interviewed _____(name)_____ , age seventeen years who advised _____(name)_____ he had been approached by _____(name)_____ who had furnished _____(name)_____ sample photographs and had discussed the making of sexually explicit films with _____(name)_____ as a participant. Thereafter on June 17, 1978, _____(name)_____ advised Detective _____(name)_____ that he had been informed by _____(name)_____ that sexually explicit films made by _____(name)_____ were not marketed in _____(location)_____ but were sent out of state for distribution. _____(name)_____ further advised _____(name)_____ that he could make extra money by modeling at the rate of $5.00 an hour with clothes on, $10.00 an hour for sexually explicit photographs and $15.00 an hour for the making of sexually explicit films.

4. On September 19 and 20, 1978, _____(name and location_____ was interviewed by Detective _____(name, sex offense branch, (name)_____ Police Department who advised that she had found among the personal effects of her son _____(name)_____ , _____(D.O.B.)_____ a series of seventeen photographs as well as a business card of _____(name)_____ , copies of which are attached 2–19.

5. A review of the attachments reveals that they are photographs of a young caucasian male removing underwear and thereafter while in a nude condition, entering a small body of water, the foregoing series consisted of seven photographs. In addition the remaining ten photographs consisted of the same young white male also removing underwear thereafter photographed nude in various positions within the interior of an apartment type dwelling.

6. On September 25, 1978, during a surveillance of _____(name)_____ , Detective _____(name)_____ observed _____(name_____ to be the operator of a 1973 Brown Mercury Comet.

7. On May 1, 1979, I interviewed _____(name)_____ , a young white male, _____(D.O.B.)_____ who advised me that the following events occurred during the summer of 1978.

   A. That he was engaged as a male model by _____(name)_____ for the purpose of fashion modeling following a presentation to his mother by _____(name)_____ that he would be utilized as a model for fashion type photography.

   B. That in regards to this photography he was identified as being fifteen years of age in a consent form executed by his mother.

   C. That thereafter _____(name)_____ enticed him to pose while nude at _____(name)_____ apartment located at _____(name)_____ by promising him and thereafter paying him the sum of $10.00 per hour for each service.

   D. That during some of the nude photography sessions at _____(name)_____ apartment, _____(name)_____ also appeared in the nude and engaged in touching activity around the torso of _____(name)_____ .

   E. That as a part of the nude modeling, he was requested to strip nude by removing one article of clothing at a time and thereafter being placed in various positions.

   F. That on one occasion he was introduced to _____(name)_____ , last name unknown, described by _____(name)_____ as a homosexual. Thereafter, during a nude modeling session at _____(name)_____ residence arranged by _____(name)_____ , _____(name)_____ , last name unknown displayed to him numerous photographs of nude males. _____(name)_____ continued that _____(name)_____ requested him to attain penial erection for purposes of additional photography.

G. That as a result of the nude photography sessions _____(name)_____ was remunerated with checks bearing the logo "Filmakers" and as well was furnished copies of prints of himself appearing in the nude.

H. That _____(name)_____ maintained complete darkroom facilities at his apartment includng developing trays, lights and an enlarger. _____(name)_____ continued that he was personally handed folios of correspondence related to _____(name)_____ photo activities and had continued that such folios were maintained in kitchen cabinets as well as a desk located in an entryway in _____(name)_____ apartment.

I. That on one occasion in August 1978 he was transported in a brown Comet automobile regularly used by _____(name)_____ to a park located in _____(name)_____ County. _____(name)_____ continued that he was directed against to disrobe in a piecemeal manner and enter a small body of water. _____(name)_____ advised that he was photographed and while nude, by _____(name)_____ .

J. That _____(name)_____ suggested to him that they visit a Y.M.C.A. for the purpose of additional photography.

K. That during the nude photo sessions _____(name)_____ solicited his participation in sexually explicit homosexual and heterosexual motion pictures.

L. That in March, 1979 he was again contacted by _____(name)_____ who reconfirmed the earlier proposal concerning sexually explicit photography and who offered him $15.00 an hour for his participation.

8. On May 1, 1979, I spoke with _____(name)_____ . _____(name)_____ states that he had obtained from discarded wastepaper, a package of papers relating to "Filmakers" attached to correspondence directed to _____(name)_____ . The foregoing papers were provided to the affiant and are attachments 20 thru 23. _____(name)_____ verified that _____(name)_____ is currently a resident at _____(location)_____ .

9. Thereafter the papers were reviewed and revealed a duplicate copy of a check drawn on the _____(name)_____ National Bank bearing the logo "Filmakers." In addition was a note-o-gram dated March 28, 1979, addressed to _____(name)_____ , as well as two pages of handwritten notes containing words "Call—Res Rm at Y" as well as "Model Session 1 Hour. $5.00 B & W my bed . . ."

10. On this date I spoke with _____(name)_____ the wife of the individual mentioned above who advised on April 27, 1979, she observed a young white male exit _____(name)_____ car, a brown 1973 Comet and enter the apartment building with _____(name)_____ .

11. On May 1, 1979, I observed a 1973 brown Mercury Comet parked in front of the apartment building where _____(name)_____ resides.

12. Affiant for a fact states that: I, _____(name)_____ , based upon my experience in past investigations related in this area, and based upon numerous search warrants conducted personally or with my assistance, I know that persons who distribute or deal in pornography maintain business records, checks, receipts, correspondence, invoices, and accounting records reflecting orders, sales, payments and distribution of sexually explicit materials for distribution.

Based on my experience, I believe that presently concealed at _____(location)_____ are the previously set forth photographs, and or picture film, projectors, movie machines, receipts, ledgers, letters of correspondence, and other documents used for the purpose of permitting and facilitating sexual exploitation of children and the distribution of obscene matter. Search to include but not limited to all rooms and any passageways into which they may open, all furnishings, cabinets, closets, containers, desks and drawers contained therein: special compartments in floors/walls and the personal property of persons controlling the premises. To include all other areas of said premises where photographs and other above described articles could be kept and concealed.

AFFIDAVIT FOR SEARCH WARRANT—OBSCENITY

_____(name)_____ —swears or affirms that he believes and has good cause to believe: From my investigation I learned from reliable persons the following facts and attending circumstances that: On January 20, 1986, at approximately 1:00 p.m., myself and _____(name)_____ entered _____(store name and location)_____ . We observed a white, male, later identified as _____(name)_____ , sitting behind a display counter. I looked at the movies in the display case and bought a VHS video entitled Biker Slave Girls. The front of the box showed a bound female lying on the floor next to a male crouched down next to her with some type of stick. The paragraph on the back of the box gave a synopsis of the storyline including nipple torture and fisting, the act of shoving a human fist all the way into the vagina or anus of another.

We took the video back to the vice office at _____(location)_____ and viewed this same video. The video opens with the title Biker Slave Girls against a black background. The first scene opens with a white female putting a videotape into a VCR and watching it on TV. This video depicts a white male performing intercourse on a white female while she is bent over a table.

The scene switches back to the female who put the videotape on, lying on her bed and fondling her breast and masturbating. She opens a box containing a set of two round metal balls, commonly referred to as ben wa balls, and inserts them into her vagina and starts masturbating again.

The scene switches back and forth form the television screen to the female on the bed.

Another female enters the room and they both begin to watch the television while the first female starts talking about a "guy" she had previously been with.

The scene changes to a male who opens a matchbook cover which has printing on the inside cover that says "I have cocaine—I want your body."

The next scene shows the female being handcuffed and getting onto the back of motorcycle behind the male.

They ride along until their destination is reached. The male and female get off the motorcycle and the female, still handcuffed, stands on some type of platform, the male tells the female to take her clothes off and he then starts fondling her breasts. He then starts kissing her buttocks.

During the course of this particular scene, the male exposes the female's vagina and inserts his fingers into her vagina. This continues until the female starts masturbating and eventually reaches climax.

The scene changes to the male nailing the handcuffs the female is wearing to a beam above her head. The male runs the claw hammer over the female's breasts and vagina. The female kicks the hammer out of the male's hand. The male slaps the female and tears her underwear off. He starts kissing her and then performs cunnilingus. The male tells the female she's enjoying it too much, takes her out to his motorcycle, and handcuffs her to the wheel. At this point, the male attempts to force the female to perform fellatio. She refuses. The male gets what appears to be a cat-o-nine tails and starts whipping the female across the back and buttocks.

The scene changes to the female, who has been released from the motorcycle, performing fellatio. The male is now wearing a pair of black leather chaps exposing his genital area.

The male has the female turn over onto her knees while he puts a leather ring onto his penis. The male begins anal intercourse with the female who is crying and in apparent pain. This continues for several minutes until the male pulls his penis out and ejaculates onto the back of the female.

The scene changes back to the two females on the bed kissing and fondling each other.

The next scene has females nude inserting a double-headed dildo into each other.

The scene changes again to both females performing cunnilingus on each other.

The next scene shows one female asleep while the other female turns out the light. The movie ends.

The retail merchant's certificate is in the name of _____(name)_____ from previous investigations, it has been discovered that _____(name)_____ is, in fact, the owner of said premises and business.

The above events occurred in _____(county & state)_____ .

SEARCH WARRANT EXAMPLE

On _____, the affiant met Detective _____(name)_____ learned that Detective _____(name)_____ has been employed as a Police Officer by the Metropolitan Police Department, of the _____(location)_____ for the past 18 years. For the past 15 years, Detective _____(name)_____ has been assigned to the Sex Offense Branch, Criminal Investigations Division of the Metropolitan Police Department. During the tenure of his experience in the Sex Offense Branch, Detective (name) has participated in more than 1,500 investigations involving the sexual exploitation of minors and children. Detective _____(name)_____ has personally conducted more than 900 investigations resulting in the arrest of defendants on felony charges of Child Molestation and Exploitation. Detective (name) has received extensive training and has read numerous publications dealing with the sexual exploitation of children. Detective _____(name)_____ has interviewed more than 2,000 sexually exploited children, and more than 1,300 admitted child molesters. Further, Detective _____(name)_____ has read and examined more than 1,000 letters exchanged between pedophiles, describing their admitted sexual conduct with respect to children for the purpose of sexual gratification. Further, Detective (name) has examined more than 2,000 photographs, during the course of his experience, which photographs depict children engaged in sexual activities with offenders, with other children, with animals, and with adults.

Detective _____(name)_____ is familiar with the manner in which pedophiles entice and encourage children to engage in sexual conduct, and the manner in which they exchange children with each other and make contact with other adults who engage in such conduct.

On _____(date)_____ Detective _____(name)_____ whose experience in the investigation of the activities of pedophiles has been herein set forth, provided the affiant with certain of his observations regarding pedophiles, as based upon his personal experiences in the investigation of persons who exhibit pedophilic behavior. Detective _____(name)_____ related to the following information:

1. Pedophiles are persons whose sexual objects are children. They receive sexual gratification and satisfaction from actual physical contact with children, as well as from fantasy involving the use of pictures or other photographic or art media.

2. Pedophiles collect sexually explicit materials, including but not limited to photographs, magazines, motion pictures, video tapes, books, and photographic slides, which materials are used for personal sexual gratification.

3. Pedophiles employ sexually explicit materials, including the types of material listed above, for the purposes of lowering the inhibitions of children, and sexually stimulating both themselves and children, as well as for demonstrating desired sexual acts before, during, and after sexual activity with children.

4. Pedophiles rarely, if ever, dispose of sexually explicit material, particularly when it is used in the seduction of victims.

5. Pedophiles frequently correspond and/or meet with one another for the purpose of sharing information and identities of victims, as a means of gaining status, trust, acceptance and psychological support.

6. Pedophiles rarely destroy correspondence received from other pedophiles.

7. Pedophiles engage in activities and/or gravitate to programs which will be of interest to the type of child victims they desire to attract, which activities and/or programs will provide the pedophile with easy access to children.

8. Pedophiles obtain, collect, and maintain photographs of the children with whom they are or have been involved. Such photographs may depict children fully clothed, in various stages of undress, or totally nude. Pedophiles rarely, if ever, dispose of such photographs, which photographs are considered by pedophile to be treasured possessions.

9. Pedophiles employ such photos, as described in Item 8, as a means of reliving actual encounters and/or fantasies with the depicted children. Pedophiles also employ such photographs as a means of gaining acceptance, status, trust, and psychological support from other pedophiles.

10. Pedophiles remove pictures from magazines, newspapers, books, and other publications, around which photographs pedophiles fabricate fantasy relationships.

11. Pedophiles collect books, magazines, newspapers, and other writings on the subject of adult-child sexual activities, which writings pedophiles maintain to justify an understanding of their specific feelings towards children, as well as their illicit behavior and desires.

12. Pedophiles, who are generally afraid of discovery, often maintain and operate their own photographic production and reproduction equipment, including but not limited to photocopy equipment, "instant" photo equipment, video equipment, and photo processing equipment.

13. Pedophiles exercise great caution to conceal and protect their collections of illicit materials from discovery, theft, and damage.

14. Pedophiles frequently collect and maintain lists of names, addresses, and phone numbers of persons who have similar sexual interests.

15. Pedophiles frequently retain the names of children with whom they currently have or formerly have had sexual contact.

16. Pedophiles frequently employ sexual aids in the seduction of their victims. These sexual aids, such as dildos, serve as a means of exciting and arousing the curiosity of the pedophile's victims.

17. Pedophiles frequently maintain diaries of their sexual encounters with children, which accounts are used as a means of reliving sexual encounters with children.

18. Pedophiles frequently collect and maintain books, magazines, articles, and other writings on the subject of sexual activity. Such books and materials may bear on the topic of human sexuality, sexual education or consist of instructional material. Such books and materials are used by the pedophile as means of seduction of the victim by arousing curiosity, demonstrating the propriety of acts desired, explaining or demonstrating what the pedophile desires from the victim, and a means of sexual arousal on the part of the pedophile, particularly when naked children are depicted within the materials.

19. Pedophiles frequently employ alcohol and narcotic drugs to induce a child to a particular location, such as the pedophile's home, and to lower the child's inhibitions with respect to sexual involvement with the pedophile.

Witnesses Testifying Before the Commission

The Commission wishes to express its gratitude and appreciation to the following people who have appeared in person before us and rendered testimony. The information these people have provided the Commission is invaluable and serves as a substantial data base for this report.

Washington, D.C.—June 19, 1985

Lois H. Herrington, Assistant Attorney General for Justice Programs in the Department of Justice.

Kenneth Lanning, Supervisory Special Agent with the Federal Bureau of Investigation assigned to the behavioral sciences unit at Quantico, Virginia. He has been involved in the study of deviant sex crimes and sexual victimization since 1972.

David, 17 years old, participated in Straight, Inc., a drug rehabilitation program, and the victim of sexual abuse.

Senator Mitch McConnell, Kentucky. Senator McConnell serves on the Senate Judiciary Committee, the Senate Agriculture Committee and the Senate Select Committee on Intelligence. He has served as chairman of the Kentucky Task Force on Exploited and Missing Children.

Lisa, 21 years old, a resident of Baltimore. She was once a nude dancer and has been involved in video pornography.

Representative Frank R. Wolf, 10th District of Virginia, serves on the Appropriations Committee and the House Select Committee on children, Youth and Families.

Sharon, formerly married to a medical professional who is an avid consumer of pornography.

Dr. Dennis M. Harrison, psychologist who practices in the area of forensic and clinical psychology. He has been engaged in private practice for eleven years.

Senator Arlen Specter, Pennsylvania, is chairman of the Subcommittee on Juvenile Justice of the Senate Judiciary Committee and is the co-chairman of the Senate Children's Caucus.

Senator Jeramiah Denton, Alabama, is a member of the Committee on Veterans' Affairs, the Armed Services Committee and the Judiciary Committee. He serves as chairman for the Subcommittee on Terrorism.

Patricia Foscato, social worker and coordinator of a sex abuse prevention project for St. Anne's Institute in Albany, New York. She also maintains a private practice in psychotherapy for adolescents and young adults.

Bonnie, 31, mother of two daughters. She has been sexually abused by each of her two husbands who consumed pornography.

Michelle, 11, sexually abused by her father and her stepfather who were pornography consumers.

Debbie, 13, sexually abused by her father and her stepfather who were pornography consumers.

Charles R. Clauson, Chief Postal Inspector, United States Postal Inspection Service.

Jack Swagerty, Assistant Chief Postal Inspector, United States Postal Inspection Service.

Daniel Harrington, General Manager, United States Postal Inspection Service.

Daniel Mihalko, Postal Inspector, New York, United States Postal Inspection Service.

Jeff, 20 years old, was sexually molested and is currently a participant in Straight, Inc., a drug rehabilitation program.

Sarah ✂ , former prostitute and victim of sexual abuse who was forced to participate in pornographic films.

Dorchen Leidholt, a founder of Women Against Pornography.

465

Valerie Heller, victim of sexual abuse as a child. She is currently affiliated with the organization, Victims of Incest Can Emerge as Survivors (VOICES).

Kandy Stroud, journalist and has been chief diplomatic correspondent for Cable News Network and a concerned parent.

Reverend Jeff Ling, Associate Pastor at New Covenant Fellowship in Manassas, Virginia, serves as consultant to the Parent's Music Resource Center.

Dr. Harry N. Hollis, Jr., Associate Executive Director of Family and Special Moral Concerns of the Christian Life Commission of the Southern Baptist Convention.

Washington, D.C.—June 20, 1985

Dr. C. Everett Koop, Surgeon General of the United States Public Health Service in the Department of Health and Human Services.

Bill, convicted of the sexual molestation of two adolescent females.

Ann Wolbert Burgess, Ph.D., University of Pennsylvania School of Nursing and the Department of Health and Hospitals in Boston, Massachusetts.

John, victim of child sex ring in Boston, Massachusetts.

Tom, brother of child sex ring victim.

Dr. Robert Prentke, Chief Psychologist and Director of Research at the Massachusetts treatment center of sexually dangerous persons.

Judge William H. Webster, Director of the Federal Bureau of Investigation.

Dennis DeBord, Investigator with the vice section of the Fairfax County, Virginia Police Department.

Patricia Powers, Psychiatric Nurse Clinician and Director of an in-processing unit of Psychiatric patients in a large private hospital.

Betty Berneman, News Director for a major radio station WWDB, in Philadelphia.

Reverend Richard C. Halverson, Chaplain of the United States Senate.

Ingrid Horton, President of Society's League Against Molestation in Washington, D.C., and Baltimore, Maryland.

Barry Lynn, Legislative Counsel for the American Civil Liberties Union.

Isabelle Pinzler, Director of the Women's Rights Project to the American Civil Liberties Union Foundation.

Lillian BeVier, the Dougherty Foundation Professor of Law at the University of Virginia.

Senator Dennis DeConcini, Arizona, a member of the Judiciary Committee and ranking member of the Constitution Subcommittee.

Senator William V. Roth, Delaware, Chairman of the Committee on Governmental Affairs and the Permanent Committee on Investigations.

Cora Lynn Goldsborough, Psychologist specializing in the treatment of sexual abuse.

Susan, victim of sexual abuse.

Richard W. Miller, Associate Commissioner of the United States Customs Service.

John Forbes, Special Agent, Customs Attache Office in Bonn, Germany.

Townsend Hoopes, President of the Association of American Publishers.

George, former psychiatrist convicted of sexually molesting three juvenile patients.

Deborah Chalfie, District of Columbia Feminists Against Pornography.

Martha Langelan, District of Columbia Feminists Against Pornography.

Dr. Fern Waterman, family physician specializing in psychiatry with an emphasis on the psychotherapy of children in high crime or high stress communities.

Chicago, Illinois—July 24, 1985

Thomas Bohling, Detective, Chicago Police Department, organized crime division, vice control section.

George Bizek, Lieutenant, Chicago Police Department.

Diann, Homemaker, Minnesota, married to an avid consumer of pornography.

Donald Smith, Sergeant, Los Angeles County Police Department, Supervisory Investigator of Pornography Unit.

Duncan McDonald, vice-president of Citicorp and general counsel for retail services division.

Paul McGeady, General Counsel for Morality in Media and Director of the National Obscenity Law Center.

Harold Mills, Lieutenant, Cincinnati, Ohio, Police Department, Commander of Vice Section.

Jack O'Malley, Special Agent, United States Customs Service.

Andrew P. Weisner, Lieutenant, Allentown, Pennsylvania, Police Department, Vice-President of Eastern States Vice Investigators Association.

David Techter, member, Lewis Carroll Collectors Guild.

Evelyn, Mother and homemaker, Wisconsin, formerly married to an avid customer of pornography.

Geoffrey Stone, Harry Kalven, Jr., Professor of Law at the University of Chicago Law School.

Beverly Lynch, President, American Library Association.

Joan Weber, Assistant United States Attorney for the Southern District of California in San Diego.

Jane Whicher, Staff Counsel, American Civil Liberties Union of Illinois.

Thomas Blee, Attorney, a member of Citizens for Decency Through Law, Indianapolis, Indiana.

Cass Sunstein, Professor, University of Chicago Law School.

Pam Dorres, Chicago Feminist Ad Hoc Pornography Group.

Nettie Sabin, Feminist Community Activist in Chicago, Illinois.

Peter Petruzzellis, Sergeant, Toronto, Canada, Metropolitan Police Department.

Robert Sklodowski, Judge, Criminal Division of the Circuit Court of Cook County, Illinois.

Jeremy Margolis, Inspector General of the State of Illinois.

Brenda ✂ , former Playboy Bunny.

Brad Curl, President, National Christian Organization.

Chicago, Illinois—July 25, 1985

Burton Joseph, Special Counsel with Playboy Enterprises, Inc.

Frederick J. Scullin, United States Attorney for the Northern District of New York.

Bernard J. Malone, United States Attorney for the Northern District of New York in Albany.

John Ruberti, Inspector, United States Postal Service.

Jack Swagerty, Assistant Chief Postal Inspector for Criminal Investigation.

Raymond Oldham, Regional Chief Postal Inspector for the Central Region.

Dr. Frank Osanka, President of Behavioral Consultants and Therapists, Naperville, Illinois.

Mary ✂ , sexual abuse victim.

Nan Hunter, Founder of the Feminist Anticensorship Task Force.

Steve Goldsmith, District Attorney, Indianapolis, Indiana.

Catherine MacKinnon, Professor of Law, University of Minnesota and former Visiting Professor of Law at the University of California at Los Angeles.

Terese Stanton, co-founder of the Pornography Resource Center in Minneapolis, Minnesota.

Hinson McAuliffe, former Solicitor General for Fulton County, Georgia.

John Dugan, Detective, Buffalo, New York, Police Department.

Larry Parrish, Attorney, former Assistant United States Attorney from the Western District of Tennessee in Memphis.

H. Robert Showers, Assistant United States At-

torney for the Eastern District of North Carolina in Raleigh.

Paul McCommon, Legal Counsel for Citizens for Decency Through Law, in Phoenix, Arizona.

James S. Reynolds, Principal Deputy Chief of the General Litigation and Legal Advice section of the Criminal Division, United States Department of Justice.

Michael G. Krzewinski, Detective, Milwaukee, Wisconsin, Police Department.

Houston, Texas—September 11, 1985

Edward Donnerstein, Professor of Communication Arts at the University of Wisconsin at Madison.

W. D. Brown, Sergeant, Houston, Texas, Police Department, Obscenity Division of the Vice Squad.

S. R. Andrews, Houston, Texas, Police Department, Vice Squad.

D. E. Elder, Houston, Texas, Police Department, Vice Squad.

W. W. Bollier, Houston, Texas, Police Department Vice Squad.

Linda, resident of Texas, formerly married to avid consumer of pornography.

Neil Malamuth, Professor and Chair of the Communications Studies Program at University of California at Los Angeles.

Jennings Bryant, Professort and Chair of the Department of Radio and Television, School of Communications at the University of Houston.

Dr. Richard Green, Professor, Department of Psychiatry and Behavioral Science at the State University of New York at Stony Brook.

Wendy Stock, Assistant Professor at Texas A & M University and sex therapist.

Don Byrne, Professor and Chairman of the Department of Psychology at the State University of New York at Albany.

Kathryn Kelley, Associate Professor of Psychology at the State University of New York at Albany.

Donald Mosher, Professor of Psychology at the University of Connecticut.

Diana Russell, Professor of Sociology, Mills College, Oakland, California.

Victor Cline, Professor of Clinical Psychology at the University of Utah.

Paul Abramson, Associate Professor of Psychology at University of California at Los Angeles.

Houston, Texas—September 12, 1985

John Court, Clinical Psychologist and Director of Spectrum Psychological Counseling Center.

John Money, Professor of Medical Psychology and Pediatrics, The Johns Hopkins University and Hospital.

Diana Scully, Associate Professor, Department of Sociology and Anthropology at Virginia Commonwealth University.

Dan, former consumer of pornography.

Dr. Gene Abel, Professor of Psychiatry, Emory University, Atlanta, Georgia.

William Marshall, Professor, Department of Psychology at Queens University in Ontario, Canada.

Dr. Mary Calderone, co-founder, Sex Information and Education Council of the United States.

Ann Welbourne-Moglia, Executive Director of the Sex Information and Education Council of the United States.

Larry Baron, Lecturer, Department of Sociology at Yale University.

Dr. C. A. Tripp, New York Psychotherapist and contributor to Forum magazine.

Los Angeles, California—October 16. 1985

James Docherty, Captain, Los Angeles Police Department, Commanding Officer of the Administrative Vice Division.

Robert Peters, Detective, Los Angeles Police Department, Administrative Vice Division.

William Roberts, Detective, Los Angeles Police Department.

Mary, actress and performer in pornography industry.

George, performer in pornography industry.

Chris, performer in pornography industry.

Ken Gillingham, Detective, Kentucky State Police, Special Investigations Unit.

Randall Gibbs, Detective, Kentucky State Police, Special Investigations Unit.

John Weston, Attorney, Adult Film Association of America.

Dr. Ted McIlvenna, President, Institute for Advanced Study of Human Sexuality.

Dr. Loretta Haroian, Dean of Professional Studies, Institute for Advanced Study of Human Sexuality.

Brent D. Ward, United States Attorney, Utah.

William Dunkle, General Manager for the Information Services Business Unit of Pacific Bell.

Judith Trevillian, Citizens Against Pornography, Linden, Michigan.

Brenda Fox, Vice-President and General Counsel, National Cable Television Association.

James J. Clancy, Attorney, Citizens for Decency Through Law.

Thomas R. Herwitz, Legal Assistant to the

Chairman of the Federal Communications Commission.

Teresa L. Hillman, Parents Opposed to Pacific Bell's Exploitation of Children.

Monica Hill, Los Angeles Radical Women.

William ✄ , actor, agent, critic, director and scriptwriter of sexually explicit films.

Los Angeles, California—October 17, 1985

Jack Valenti, President and Chief Executive Officer of the Motion Picture Association of America.

Michael Antonovich, member, Los Angeles County Board of Supervisors.

Charles Sullivan, Special Agent, Federal Bureau of Investigation.

Catherine Goodwin, Assistant United States Attorney, District of Colorado in Denver.

Dibri Beavers, former editor of Cleveland-based Connection Magazines.

Miki ✄ , Playboy Playmate, January 1973, former director of Playmate Promotions.

Caryl Cid, Special Agent, Federal Bureau of Investigation.

Brian Cid, Special Agent, Federal Bureau of Investigation.

Donal E. Wildmon, Executive Director, National Federation for Decency.

Joseph Haggerty, Detective, Washington, D.C., Metropolitan Police Department, Vice Investigation.

Charles Dawson, founder and Chairman, Fantasy Unrestricted Network.

G. Albert Howenstein, Executive Director of the Governor's Office of Criminal Justice Planning for California.

Margaret Prescod, member, United States Prostitutes Collective.

Priscilla Alexander, member, COYOTE, National Task Force on Prostitution.

Matthew Tekulskeywell, American Society of Journalists and Authors, Inc.

Angus McKenzie, National Writers Union.

Dennis Sobin, President, First Amendment Consumer and Trade Society.

Al Goldstein, President, Milky Way Production, Inc., publisher, Screw Magazine.

Miami Florida—November 20, 1985

William Dworin, Detective, Los Angeles Police Department, Sexually Exploited Child Unit.

Harry ✄ , convicted child pornography producer and distributor.

Mike Berish, Sergeant, Miami Police Department, Vice Unit.

Laura and James ✄ , parents of two-and-a-half-year-old daughter who was sexually exploited at a pre-school.

Paul Hartman, Inspector, United States Postal Service.

Kenneth J. Herrmann, Jr., President, Defense for Children International.

John Michael Jupp, Executive Director, Defense for Child Internationa.

Toby Tyler, Deputy Sheriff, San Bernadino, California.

Richard Lane, Trustee, American Sunbathers Association.

Dr. Roland Summit, Psychiatrist and founder of the Los Angeles County Child Sexual Abuse Project.

Robert Northrup, Inspector, United States Postal Service.

Kenneth Lanning, Special Agent, Federal Bureau of Investigation.

Dr. Lore Stone, Psychotherapist, Los Angeles, California.

William Phelps, Detective, Newark, Ohio, Police Department.

Miami Florida—November 21, 1985

Tom Rodgers, Lieutenant, Indianapolis, Indiana, Police Department.

Garrett ✂, child victim of sexual exploitation through the use of pornography.

Judy ✂, mother of child exploited through the use of pornography.

Paul Der Ohannesian, Assistant District Attorney, Albany County, New York.

Barbara Hattemer, Coordinator, Florida Coalition for Clean Cable.

Dennis Shaw, Lieutenant, Metro Dade Police Department.

William ✂, former consumer of child pornography.

Ken Elsesser, Inspector, United States Postal Service.

Joyce Karlin, Assistant United States Attorney, Los Angeles.

Dr. Simon Miranda, Clinical Psychologist, Miami, Florida.

Larry ✂, former consumer of pornography.

William Cassidy, Law Director, North Ridgeville, Ohio.

Dr. Ulrich Schoettle, Psychiatrist and Clinical ⁄Professor at the University of Washington in Seattle.

Judith Reisman, Research Professor, School of Education, American University, Washington, D.C.

Al Danna, Detective, Baltimore, Maryland Police Department, Criminal Investigation Division, Sex Offense Unit.

New York, New York—January 21, 1986

James D. Harmon, Jr., Executive Director and Chief Counsel of the President's Commission on Organized Crime.

Homer E. Young, retired Special Agent with the Federal Bureau of Investigation, specializing in investigating pornography and organized crime.

Linda ✂, principal performer in the film "Deep Throat."

William Kelly, retired Special Agent with the Federal Bureau of Investigation and special consultant for Broward County, Florida, Sheriff's Office.

Edward Chapman, Detective with the Arlington County Police Department assigned to the sex offense unit and detailed to the staff of the Attorney General's Commission on Pornography.

Christopher Mega, New York State Senator and Chairman of the New York Senate Crime and Correction Committee.

Thomas Bohling, Detective with the Chicago, Illinois, Police Department.

Marilyn B. Sommers, Administrative and Technical Services manager for the Middle Atlantic Great Lakes Organized Crime Law Enforcement Network (MAGLOCLEN).

Carl Shoffler, Detective with the Washington, D.C., Metropolitan Police Department assigned to the organized crime section of the Intelligence Division.

Ledra Brady, Supervisor of the Analytical Section of the Intelligence Division of the Washington, D.C., Metropolitan Police Department.

Bruce Taylor, General Counsel for Citizens for Decency Through Law.

Jerome Piazza, Captain and Commanding Officer for the Manhattan South Public Morals Division of the New York City Police Department.

New York, New York—January 22, 1986

Marcella Cohen, Special Attorney in the Criminal Division of the United States Department of Justice, organized crime and racketeering section, assigned to the Strike Force in Miami, Florida.

Larry Schuchman, investigator with the Orlando, Florida, Police Department, detailed to the Task Force on Narcotics, Vice and Racketeering.

Sam Currin, United States Attorney for the Eastern District of North Carolina in Raleigh.

H. Robert Showers, Assistant United States Attorney and Special Prosecutor for the Eastern District of North Carolina in Raleigh.

William Johnson, Captain and Commander of the Major Crimes Investigation Division of the Fayetteville, North Carolina, Police Department.

Andrea Dworkin, author of *Men Possessing Women* and co-author of legislation recognizing pornography as a violation of the civil rights of women.

Colleen Dewhurst, performing artist and vice president of the Actor's Equity Association.

Heather Grant Florence, vice-president and general counsel for Bantam Books, Inc., and chairperson of the Freedom to Read Committee of the Association of American Publishing, Inc.

J. D. Landis, Bantam Book author.

Patrick F. Fagan, Executive Vice-President of the Free Research and Education Foundation.

Most Revered Edward Egan, Auxiliary Bishop of the Archdiocese of New York and the Vicar for Education.

Ardeth Kapp, President of the Young Women Program, Church of Jesus Christ of Latter Day Saints.

Harriet Pilpel, General Counsel for Planned Parenthood Foundation of America, Inc., and General Counsel to the American Civil Liberties Union.

Alan Dershowitz, Professor of Law at Harvard Law School and columnist with *Penthouse* Magazine.

Dottie ✄ , former Penthouse model and coordinator involved with circulation and Pet productions.

Loring Mandel, Writer, representing the Writers Guild of America, East, Inc.

Corrine Jackson, representative of Writers Guild of America, East, Inc.

June Griffin, Christian Missionary with the Cumberland Missionary Society.

David Cohen, Executive Officer of the Academic Freedom Committee of the American Civil Liberties Union and member of the New York Library Association.

Father Val J. Peter, Executive Director of Boys Town.

Lane Sunderland, Associate Professort of Political Science at Knox College specializing in Constitutional Law and Political Theory.

Daniel Cohen, Chairman of the Jewish Community Affairs Committee of the Philadelphia Chapter of the American Civil Liberties Union.

Reverend Stephen J. Mathew, member of the Interfaith Coalition of the Philadelphia Chapter of the American Jewish Committee.

Jeremiah Gutman, Past president of the New York Civil Liberties Union and vice president of the American Civil Liberties Union.

Jerry Kirk, Pastor of the College Hill Presbyterian Church in Cincinnati, Ohio, founder of Citizens Concerned about Community Values in Cincinnati, and president of the National Coalition Against Pornography.

NOTE: All biographical information is current as of the date of the individual's testimony.

Witnesses Invited But Unable to Appear Before the Commission

The Commission would like to acknowledge the following persons who were extended a formal invitation to personally appear during a scheduled hearing, but were unable to do so. Many other people were informally invited, but declined before a written invitation was issued.

William von Raab, Commissioner, United States Customs Service

Albert Bandura, Stanford University

Senator William L. Armstrong, Colorado

Senator John Stennis, Mississippi

Representative Ralph M. Hall, Fourth District, Texas

Senator Paula Hawkins, Florida

Senator Edward Zorinsky, Nebraska

*Senator Paul S. Trible, Virginia

Robert Pitler, New York District Attorney

Robert Reynolds, District Attorney, Albany, Georgia Tim O'Neal, Attorney

Dennis Nixdorf, President, Western States Vice Investigators Association, Inc.

Charles J. Cooper, Deputy Assistant Attorney General Civil Rights Division, United States Department of Justice

Marty Reddish, Northwestern University School of Law

*Jeanette Boone

Rudolph W. Guiliani, United States Attorney, Southern District of New York

Raymond J. Dearie, United States Attorney, Eastern District of New York

Richard C. Stiener, INTERPOL

Jack E. Yelverton, Executive Director, National District Attorney's Association

C. Raymond Marvin, Executive Director, National Association of Attorneys General

Gerald Robertson, President, Eastern States Vice Investigators Association, Inc.

Douglas Paluschak, Attorney

Sherman Block, Sheriff, Los Angeles County

Danny Goldberg, Gold Mountain Records

Jack Chapman, Detective, Las Vegas Metropolitan Police Department

Kay Parker, Cabellero Control Corporation

Gloria Leonard, *High Society Magazine*

*Candida ✂ , FEMME Productions

Mickie Granberg, Video Software Dealers Association

*Seth Goldstein, Inspector, Office of the District Attorney, Santa Clara County, California

Dr. Judianne Densen-Gerber

James A. Baker, III, Secretary of the Treasury

G. A. Dexter, Inspector, United States Postal Service

*Tim O'Hara, Rene Guyon Society

*Dr. D. James Kennedy, Fort Lauderdale, pastor of Coral Ridge Presbyterian Church

Richard H. Bloser, Director of Film Security, Motion Picture Association of America

Charles Gurtsack, Lieutenant, Organized Crime Field Intelligence Unit, Cleveland, Ohio, Police Department

Richard Phinney, Security Director, Western States-ARA Services

Robert Coles, Harvard University Health Services

Richard M. McIntosh, Lieutenant, Cleveland, Ohio, Police Department

Dr. James Q. Wilson, Harvard University

Dr. Christopher Lasch

Norman Lear

Bridgette Berger, Professor, Sociology Department, Wellesley College

Dr. Bruno Bettleheim

Catherine R. Stimpson, Acting Dean, Graduate School—New Brunswick

Ernest Van Den Haag, *National Review*

David E. Warren, Department of the Treasury, United States Customs Service, Philadelphia, Pennsylvania

Edward Gallen, Department of the Treasury, United States Customs Service, Philadelphia, Pennsylvania

Marie Winn

Erick Homburger Erikson

*Provided a written statement

Persons Submitting Written Statements

The Commission would like to express its sincere appreciation to the following people for their written statements and recognize the submission of other additional information. This testimony was given substantial consideration and the time and effort which went into such submissions was clearly evident. The Commission regrets that it did not have the resources available to hear each person as they appeared.

Karen
Rex A. Cuff
William B. Randolf, Vice-President, Buckingham Chapter, Prison Atheist League of America
Senator Paul S. Trible, Virginia
Debbie H. C. Williamson
Don J. Lewittes, Ph.D.
Anonymous, September 9, 1985
Jeanne Fleming, Ph.D.
Melvin Anchell, M.D.
Ann, October 21, 1985
Jane Doe
Grant Henderick
Anonymous
Eileen McGinley
Florida Coalition for Clean Cable
Candida ✂ , FEMME Productions
Rene Guyon Society
Los Angeles County Commission for Women
John Dentinger
Dr. D. James Kennedy
Anonymous, October 10, 1985
Anonymous
Don Miller
Susan Miller
Anonymous

Gayla Deathrage
James P. Check
Brad Blackmun
Dale Young
Deborah Sheldon
Richard and Deborah Podgurski
Anonymous, October 25, 1985
Wallace P. Hay
Fedenic Schroeder
Marion Douglas
Anonymous
Ruth Harmen/Crew
Tim O'Hara
Seth Goldstein
Maxwell J. Lillienstein, Counsel, American Booksellers Association
Nicholas D'Antonio, Bishop, Archidiocese of New Orleans
Philip M. Hannon, Archbishop of New Orleans
R. Donald Shafer, General Secretary, Brothers in Christ Church, Upland, California
Victor H. Balhe, Bishop, Crookston, Minnesota
James T. Draper, Jr.
Robert M. Blackburn, Resident Bishop, United Methodist Church, Richmond, Virginia
The Right Reverend Peter E. Gillquist, The Evangelical Orthodox Church, Goleta, California
Paul. A Tanner, Executive Secretary, Executive Council, Church of God, Anderson, Indiana
Most Reverend John L. May, Archbishop of St. Louis, Missouri
William K. Cober, Executive Director, National Ministries, American Baptist Home Mission Society

Most Reverend Timothy J. Harrington, Bishop of Worcester, Massachusetts

Ernest E. Mosley, Executive Director, Illinois Baptist State Association

Karen De Crow, Attorney-at-Law, Jamesville, New York

Geraldine Darrow

E. Harold Jansen, Bishop, Eastern District, The American Lutheran Church

Lloyd Klein, Department of Sociology, Brooklyn College

Patricia Gmerek, New York State Pro-Family Coalition

Joan McCain

Barbara Hattemer, Florida Coalition for Clean Cable

Edward Donnerstein, Professor, University of Wisconsin, Madison

Roger W. Libby

James Alleva, Assistant Director of the Morality in Media, National Obscenity Law Center

Anonymous, Madison, Wisconsin

Martin S. Raffel, Executive Director, Pennsylvania Region of the American Jewish Congress

W. Thomas Larkin, Bishop of St. Petersburg, Florida

Robert E. Craig, President, Union University, Jackson, Tennessee

Sidney Westbrook, South Central District, International Church of The Foursquare Gospel

Edward A. McCarthy, Archbishop of Miami, Florida

Most Reverend L. T. Matthiesen, Bishop of Amarillo, Texas

Sean A. Fanelli, President, Nassau Community College

Bill Weber, Pastor, Prestonwood Baptist Church

Jeffery Smith, American National News Service

Eber B. Dourte, Executive Director, Board for Brotherhood Concerns, Brethren in Christ Church

The Right Reverend William C. Wantland, Bishop of Eau Claire, Wisconsin

Most Reverend Stanislaus J. Brzana, Bishop of Ogdensburg, New York

Robert Hess, General Superintendent, Eastern Region, Evangelical Friends Church

Reverend L. T. Charter, Great Lakes District of the International Church of The Foursquare Gospel

Most Reverend Edward D. Head, Bishop of Buffalo, New York

W. B. Tichenor, Missouri Baptist Convention

Douglas A. Houck, Director, Metanoia Ministries, Seattle, Washington

Mike Weldon, Executive Director, The Association of Independent Methodists

Feminists Fighting Pornography

Leanne Katz, Executive Director, National Coalition Against Censorship

Diana Ronald, New York-Connecticut Americans for Morality

Paul A. Duffy, Bishop, The United Methodist Church, Louisville, Kentucky

Don Moore, Executive Director, Arkansas Baptist State Convention

His Eminence Archbishop Iakovos, Primate of the Greek Orthodox Church of North and South America

Gerald L. Stow, Executive Director, Tennessee Baptist Children's Homes, Inc.

Reverend Dr. K. Gene Carroll, General Secretary, The Primitive Methodist Conference

Martin Doorhy

Joyce A. Karlin, Assistant United States Attorney, Major Narcotics Violators Unit, Los Angeles, California

Mrs. J. Solembrino

Mike Douglas

Kurt Vonnegut, National Coalition Against Censorship

William H. Webster, Director, Federal Bureau of Investigation

Skeek Frazee, The Family Crisis Shelter, Community Response Program, Portland, Maine

Most Reverend John R. Roach, Archbishop, Saint Paul and Minneapolis, Minnesota

Billy A. Melvin, Executive Director, National Association of Evangicals

C. L. Gustafson, Pastor, Berean Fundamental Church, Ogallala, Nebraska District

Gloria Morgan

Detective Donald Smith, Administrative Vice Division, Los Angeles, California, Police Department

Thomas J. Webb, Bishop, Allentown, Pennsylvania

Women Hurt in Systems of Prostitution Engaged in Revolt (W.H.I.S.P.E.R.)

Anonymous

Judy Perkins, Bath Area Citizens for Decency

Mrs. Kermit S. Edgar, President, National Woman's Christian Temperance Union

Reverence Monsignor Ronald C. Bill, Vicar

for Community Services, Syracuse, New York

Andrew J. McDonald, Bishop, Little Rock, Arkansas

Leonard W. DeWitt, President, Missionary Church, Fort Wayne, Indiana

Paul E. Jones, Supervisor, Southern California District Headquarters, International Church of The Foursquare Gospel

William R. Houck, Bishop, Jackson, Mississippi

Susie Hoeller, Advisory Board Member, Dallas Association for Decency

Mike Weldon, Executive Director, The Association of Independent Methodists

June B. Griffin, Cumberland Missionary Society

Paul J. McGeady, Morality in Media *United States v. Ralph Borello,* 84-CR-249, (E.D.N.Y. 1984)

Response of the United States of America in Opposition to Defendant Reuben Sturman's Motion to Reduce Bail, *United States v. Reuben Sturman,* Case No. CR-85-133 (E.D. Ohio, Dec. 17, 1985)

Defendant Reuben Sturman's Motion to Amend Conditions of Release by Reduc-

ing Bail, *United States v. Reuben Sturman,* Case No. CR-85-133 (E.D. Ohio Dec. 17, 1985).

Response of the United States In Opposition to Defendent Sturman's Motion For Security, U.S. v. Reuben Sturman, Case No. CR-85-133 (E.D. Ohio Dec. 17, 1985).

Motion For Security, *United States v. Reuben Sturman,* Case No. CR-85-133 (E.D. Ohio Dec. 9, 1985)

Affidavit for Search Warrants, Richard N. Rosfelder, Jr., Cleveland, Ohio.

John Rinck

Jerome J. Hastrich, Bishop, Gallup, New Mexico

Dr. Walter A. Maur, Concordia Theological Seminary, Fort Wayne, Indiana

Mrs. Bob L. White, Baptist Missionary Association of America

Jim Norwood, Tate Springs Baptist Church

Reverend J. R. McArley III, St. James United Methodist Church, Manchester, Georgia

Gerald E. Free, President, Nebraska District, Wisconsin Evangelical Lutheran Synod

PART

4

The Commissioners

Commissioner Biographies

HENRY E. HUDSON

Henry E. Hudson served as chairman of the Attorney General's Commission on Pornography. Henry Hudson was born in Washington, D.C. He was awarded a bachelor of arts degree from American University, School of International Service, Washington, D.C., in 1969. In 1974 Mr. Hudson received his juris doctor from American University, Washington, D.C.

Mr. Hudson is currently serving his second term as Commonwealth Attorney in Arlington County, Virginia. Mr. Hudson recently has been appointed to serve as the United States Attorney for the Eastern District of Virginia. Prior to his election, Mr. Hudson was the Assistant United States Attorney for the Eastern District of Virginia, Criminal Division in Alexandria. Mr. Hudson has also served as the Assistant Commonwealth Attorney in Arlington County, Deputy Clerk of the Circuit Court of Arlington County and Deputy Sheriff.

Chairman Hudson enjoys membership in several professional organizations including the Virginia State Bar, Virginia Commonwealth Attorneys Association, Criminal Law Section of the Virginia State Bar, Virginia Trial Lawyer Association, Arlington County Bar Association, and the National District Attorneys Association. In addition, Mr. Hudson has made significant contributions through his work with various community service organizations including the Arlington County Volunteer Fire Department, the Arlington County Police Trial Board, the American Red Cross, and the Task Force on Substance Abuse and Youth.

In 1981, President Reagan appointed Mr. Hudson to the National Highway Safety Advisory Committee. Mr. Hudson enjoys membership on the Congressional Award Council for the Tenth Congressional District.

JUDITH VERONICA BECKER

Dr. Judith Becker received a bachelor of arts degree in Psychology from Gonzaza University in Spokane, Washington, in 1966. She was awarded a masters of science degree in Clinical Psychology from Eastern Washington State College, Cheney, Washington, in 1968. Dr. Becker received her Ph.D. from University of Southern Mississippi, Hattiesburg, Mississippi, in Clinical Psychology in 1975. Dr. Becker completed her internship at the University of Mississippi Medical School in 1974. Dr. Becker is currently licensed to practice in New York, New Jersey and Tennessee.

Dr. Becker is an Associate Professor of Clinical Psychology in Psychiatry at Columbia University, College of Physicians and Surgeons. She is also the director of the Sexual Behavior Clinic at the New York State Psychiatric Institute. Previously, Dr. Becker has served as Assistant Professor at the University of Tennessee Medical School, an Instructor in Psychiatry and Human Behavior at the University of Mississippi Medical School, and Intern at the University of Mississippi Medical Center.

Dr. Becker's major research interests are in the field of sexual aggression, rape victimization, human sexuality and behavior therapy. She has researched and written numerous papers. Presentations of her research have included those before the Association for the

Advancement of Behavior Therapy, the annual meeting of the Southern Psychological Association, the annual meeting of the Southeastern Psychological Association, the International Academy of Sex Research and the Society for Sex Therapy and Research.

DIANE D. CUSACK

Diane Cusack has recently completed her second term on the Scottsdale City Council. Mrs. Cusack came to Scottsdale in 1957 and since that time has been very active in community affairs.

Mrs. Cusack's involvement with Scottsdale began in 1964 and led to service on the Planning and Zoning Commission for thirteen years, five as Chairman. Mrs. Cusack has participated as a speaker and panelist at numerous meetings of the Arizona Planning Association, and is recognized statewide for her expertise in the planning field.

Presently, Mrs. Cusack is serving her seventh term as President of the Maricopa County Board of Health. Long active in the health field, she is also Chairman of the City's Emergency Medical Services Committee and in the past has served as a member of the Board of the local Hospital.

After receiving a bachelor of arts degree in economics from Rosary College, Mrs. Cusack became one of the first women to attend the Harvard Business School, receiving a Special Certificate in 1954. A market research analyst, Mrs. Cusack has devoted herself to community affairs since residing in Scottsdale.

While raising her family, Mrs. Cusack was active in scouting. She initiated and managed a school library, and served as a Red Cross School Nurses' Assistant at Tonalea School. She also was president of the Scottsdale League of Women Voters and President of the Scottsdale Symphony Guild, and is a member of the Arizona Academy.

Mrs. Cusack and her husband, Joseph, a Senior Engineer with Motorola, have three grown children and remain active members of their church and community.

PARK ELLIOTT DIETZ

Dr. Park Dietz received an A.B. from Cornell University with honors in Psychology and Distinction in All Subjects in 1970. He earned degrees in medicine (M.D.), public health (M.P.H.), and sociology (Ph.D.) from the Johns Hopkins University. While a Robert Wood Johnson Foundation Clinical Scholar, he served psychiatric residencies at the Johns Hopkins Hospital and the Hospital of the University of Pennsylvania, where he was Chief Fellow in Forensic Psychiatry. He is board certified in psychiatry by the American Board of Psychiatry and Neurology. As an Assistant Professor of Psychiatry at the Harvard Medical School he served as Director of Forensic Psychiatry at the maximum security hospital at Bridgewater operated by the Massachusetts Department of Correction.

Dr. Dietz is Professor of Law, of Behavioral Medicine and Psychiatry and Medical Director of the Institute of Law, Psychiatry and Public Policy at the University of Virginia in Charlottesville. At the University of Virginia, he teaches courses in Law and Psychiatry, Psychiatry and Criminal Law, and Crimes of Violence, provides training in forensic psychiatry, conducts research on sexual offenses, violence, and threats and directs the Forensic Psychiatry Clinic, which conducts evaluations on behalf of attorneys and courts in criminal and civil cases. He also serves as a Lecturer in the Department of Health Policy and Management at the Johns Hopkins School of Hygiene and Public Health, as a psychiatric consultant to the Behavioral Science Unit, Federal Bureau of Investigation Academy, Quantico, Virginia, and as a consultant to attorneys, courts and public agencies throughout the United States.

Dr. Dietz is a member of Phi Beta Kappa, Phi Kappa Phi, Alpha Epsilon Delta, and Alpha Omega Alpha honor societies. He was the recipient of the 1975 John P. Rattigan Award of the American Society of Law and Medicine, the 1977 Wendell Muncie Award of the Maryland Psychiatric Society and Maryland Association of Private Practicing Psychiatrists, and the 1986 Psychiatry Section Krafft-Ebing Award of the American Academy of Forensic Sciences.

Dr. Dietz has served on the editorial boards of the *Johns Hopkins Medical Journal*, the *Bulletin of the American Academy of Psychiatry and the Law*, the *Psychiatric Journal of the University of Ottawa*, the *Journal of Forensic Sciences*, and *Behavioral Sciences and the Law*. He has served as Chairman of the Psychiatry Section of the American Academy of Forensic Sciences; Vice President of the American Academy of Psychiatry and the Law; Vice President of the Board of Trustees of the Forensic Sciences Foundation; a member of the Committee on Federal Trauma Research of the National Research Council and National Academy of Sciences; Chairman of the Committee on Abuse and Misuse of Psychiatry and Psychiatrists in the United States and a member of the Advisory Committee on the Paraphilias, Task Force on Nomenclature and Statistics (DSM-III-R), of the American Psychiatric Association; and a member of the Committee on Psychiatry and Law of the Group for the Advancement of Psychiatry. He is also a member of the American Society of Criminology, the American Society of Law and Medicine, the Forensic Science Society (Great Britain), and the Society for the Study of Social Problems.

Dr. Dietz's writings have appeared in the *American Journal of Public Health*, the *Archives of General Psychiatry*, the *Bulletin of the American Academy of Psychiatry and the Law*, *Behavioral Sciences and Law*, the *International Journal of Psychiatry and Law*, the *Journal of the American Medical Association*, the *Journal of Forensic Sciences*, the *Journal of Police Science and Administration*, the *Journal of Public Health Policy*, *Medicine and Law*, *Pharmacology, Biochemistry and Behavior*, *Victimology*, and other professional journals and in more than a dozen books. He has addressed medical, psychiatric, psychological, forensic science, and law enforcement audiences throughout the United States and in Canada, Mexico, Australia, and the Federal Republic of Germany.

JAMES C. DOBSON

Dr. James Dobson received a bachelor of arts degree in psychology from Pasadena College in 1958. He was awarded a master of science degree from the University of Southern California in 1962. He earned a Ph.D. from U.S.C. in 1967 in Child Development and Research Design.

Dr. Dobson served for fourteen years as Associate Clinical Professor of Pediatrics at the University of Southern California School of Medicine, and simultaneously, for seventeen years on the Attending Staff of Children's Hospital of Los Angeles, in the Division of Medical Genetics. He was also Director of Behavioral Research in the Division of Child Development during a portion of this time.

More recently, Dr. Dobson has been President of Focus on the Family, a non-profit organization dedicated to the preservation of the home. In this capacity, he hosts a thirty minute daily radio program heard on more than eight hundred stations in seventeen countries. He is a licensed psychologist in the State of California and a licensed Marriage,

Family and Child Counselor also in California. A six-film series featuring Dr. Dobson has been seen by fifty million people to date.

Dr. Dobson has been active in governmental activities since 1980. He received a special commendation from President Jimmy Carter for his work on the Task Force for the White House Conferences on the Family. He was appointed by President Ronald Reagan in 1982 to the National Advisory Commission for the Office of Juvenile Justice and Delinquency Prevention. He also served on the Citizens Advisory Panel for Tax-Reform, in consultation with President Reagan and currently serves on the Army Science Board as a family consultant for General John Wickham, Chief of Staff, United States Army.

He has published extensively both in professional journals and for individual families. His ten books for parents have sold more than four million copies. His first graduate textbook, co-edited with Dr. Richard Koch, was entitled *The Mentally Retarded Child and His Family* and was designated the best book in its field by the Menninger Clinic. Dr. Dobson was the principal investigator on a $500,000 grant from the National Institute of Health, studying phenylketonuric children and those with related metabolic disorders. This medical directed research was funded by the Department of Health and Human Services.

EDWARD J. GARCIA

Judge Edward Garcia was born in Sacramento, California. He received an associate of arts degree in pre-law from Sacramento City College in 1951. In 1958 he was awarded his LL.B. degree from the University of Pacific-McGeorge School of Law.

In 1984, President Reagan appointed Judge Garcia as United States District Court Judge for the Eastern District of California. Previously, he has served as judge of the Sacramento Municipal Court.

Judge Garcia has served as Deputy District Attorney, supervisory Deputy District Attorney, and Chief Deputy District Attorney for the Sacramento County District Attorney's office. He has also enjoyed membership in the Sacramento and California State Bar Associations. Judge Garcia has been a member of the Board of Directors of the Legal Aid Society for Sacramento and Yolo Counties, a member of the Board of Directors for the University of Pacific-McGeorge Alumni Association, a charter member of the Board of Directors of the Mexican American Educational Association, a member of the Catholic Charities Advisory Board for the Diocese of Sacramento, a member of the Board of Directors of the St. Frances Corporation, a non-profit corporation for the construction of housing for the elderly and needy. In addition, Judge Garcia has served as vice chairman for the Governing Board of the California Center for Judicial Education and Research and a lecturer at the California Judge College and as vice president of the California Judges Association.

ELLEN LEVINE

Ellen Levine, editor-in-chief of *Woman's Day* and a vice president of CBS Magazines, joined CBS in 1982. Previously, Mrs. Leviie was the editor-in-chief and creator of *Cosmopolitan Living*, a lifestyle magazine published by the Hearst Corporation; and at the same time the decorating and food editor of *Cosmopolitan*. Mrs. Levine joined *Cosmopolitan* in 1976. She began her journalism career as a reporter in women's news for *The Record* in Hackensack, New Jersey. In addition to her editorial work, she has been published in many publications, including *The New York Times*.

During her career, Ellen Levine has been cited by many organizations, including receiving the Writers Hall of Fame award for her coverage of lifestyle news in 1981. A year later she was elected to the YMCA's Academy of Women Achievers; and in 1984 she was honored by the Girl Scout Council of Bergen County for outstanding professional achievement. Similar citations as a woman of achievement were also given by the New Jersey State Federation of Women's Clubs and Douglass College of Rutgers University.

Mrs. Levine is a trustee of the Elisabeth Morrow School in Englewood, New Jersey, and on the board of directors of the New Jersey Bell Telephone Company. She is also a member of Senator Bill Bradley's executive committee.

Ellen Levine is a graduate of Wellesley College, where she majored in political science and edited the college newspaper. She lives with her husband, a physician, and two sons in Englewood, New Jersey.

TEX LEZAR

Tex Lezar was born in Dallas, Texas. He received a Bachelor of Arts degree from Yale College and was awarded his juris doctor degree from the University of Texas where he was editor-in-chief of the *Texas Law Review*.

Mr. Lezar was admitted to the practice of law in Texas in 1977.

Currently in private practice in Dallas, Texas, Mr. Lezar is a partner in the firm of Carrington, Coleman, Sloman & Blumenthal. Prior to joining the firm, he had most recently served concurrently as counselor to Attorney General William French Smith and Assistant Attorney General for Legal Policy. In addition to engaging in the private practice of law, Mr. Lezar has previously served as Assistant to William F. Buckley, Jr.; Staff Assistant and Speech Writer to President Richard M. Nixon; Special Counsel to the Honorable John B. Connally, Jr.; and General Counsel to the Texas Secretary of State.

Mr. Lezar is a Fellow with the Institute of Judicial Administration. In addition, Mr. Lezar was a member of the United States Delegation to the International Conference on African Refugee Assistance II and he is a member of the Federal Judiciary Evaluation Committee of Senator Phil Gramm and a member of the American Law Institute.

BRUCE RITTER

The Reverend Bruce Ritter was born in Trenton, New Jersey. Father Ritter studied at St. Francis Seminary and then he went to Our Lady Queen of Peace in Middleburgh, New York. He studied philosophy at the Assumption Seminary in Chaska, Minnesota. Father Ritter began his course work in theology at St. Anthony-on-Hudson in Rennsalaer, New York, and completed his studies at St. Bonauenture's Theoligate in Rome. He was ordained in Rome in 1956 and received his doctorate in medieval dogma in 1958. Father Ritter is the founder and President of Covenant House, an international child care agency that operates short-term crisis centers in New York City, Houston and Toronto, as well as a long-term residential program in Antigua, Guatemala.

Father Ritter has taught at St. Anthony-on-Hudson in Renssalaer, New York, St. Hyacinth Seminary in Granby, Massachusetts, and at Canevin High School in Pittsburgh, Pennsylvania. In 1963, he was assigned to Manhattan College in the Bronx, New York as campus chaplain and professor of theology.

Father Ritter has received national recognition for his extensive work with the homeless and runaway youth. He has received the National Jefferson Award from the American Institute of Public Service in Washington, D.C., the Service to Youth award from the New York

State Division for Youth, and the International Franciscan Award. Father Ritter has received honorary degrees from Amherst College, Villanova University, Boston College, and Fordham University.

FREDERICK SCHAUER

Frederick Schauer is Professor of Law at the University of Michigan Law School. He received A.B. and M.B.A. degrees from Dartmouth College, and a J.D. from the Harvard Law School in 1972.

Professor Schauer was formerly Cutler Professor of Law at the College of William and Mary. He has also been a Visiting Scholar at Wolfson College, Cambridge University, and a member of the law faculty in West Virginia University. Prior to entering academic life, Professor Schauer practiced law with the firm of Fine & Ambrogne in Boston, Massachusetts. He is a member of the Bar of the Commonwealth of Massachusetts, and is certified to practice before the Supreme Court of the United States.

Professor Schauer has written extensively about the law of obscenity, the First Amendment, and constitutional law generally. In addition to numerous articles on these subjects, he is the author of the annual supplements to Gunther, *Constitutional Law,* and has written two books, *The Law of Obscenity,* published by BNA Books in 1976, and *Free Speech: A Philosophical Enquiry,* published by the Cambridge University Press in 1982. The latter book was awarded the Certificate of Merit by the American Bar Association in 1983. Professor Schauer currently serves as Chair of the Section on Constitutional Law of the Association of American Law Schools, and has previously been Vice-Chair of the Section on Law and the Arts of the same organization. Among his other honors and awards is receipt of a National Endowment for the Humanities Fellowship and selection as Professor of the Year at the School of Law of the College of William and Mary. Professor Schauer has also lectured at universities, conferences, and other gatherings throughout the world on constitutional law, legal and political philosophy, freedom of speech, and the legal and philosophical aspects of the regulation of pornography.

DEANNE TILTON–DURFEE

Deanne Tilton–Durfee is President of the California Consortium of Child Abuse Councils (CCCAC), a Statewide network of child abuse organizations including public and privately based inter-disciplinary councils, agencies, and individuals. The Consortium provides broad-based networking, training and technical assistance to programs and agencies providing child abuse prevention and treatment in both urban and rural communities. The Consortium has also sponsored major legislation in the area of child abuse prevention, providing over 15 million in direct funding to community programs Statewide. The California Consortium of Child Abuse Councils is the State Chapter of the National Committee for Prevention of Child Abuse.

Ms. Tilton–Durfee is Administrative Director of the Los Angeles County Inter-Agency Council on Child Abuse and Neglect (ICAN). ICAN is one of the largest child abuse councils in the Country, including the heads of 18 major City, County, and State departments, professional experts in every human services field, and nine community child abuse councils in Los Angeles County. In 1979, Ms. Tilton–Durfee organized a private sector partnership between ICAN and ICAN Associates, a private non-profit charity comprised of influential corporate and media representatives. This partnership has attracted National attention for its cooperative efforts and for the development of the ICAN Neighborhood Family Center Project. This project includes the development and networking of comprehensive multi-service community-based child abuse programs.

Ms. Tilton–Durfee is a member of the Board of Directors of the National Committee for the Prevention of Child Abuse (NCPCA). She also serves as a Commissioner on the California Attorney General's Commission on the Enforcement of Child Abuse Laws. In July, 1985 she was appointed by the California Governor to the Child Abuse Prevention Committee of the State Social Services Advisory Board. Ms. Tilton–Durfee has been in the field of children's services since 1964, beginning as a Los Angeles County Social Worker. She was the County liaison between the Department of Public Social Services and the Juvenile Court when child abuse cases were initially transferred from the Probation Department to DPSS. She also served as a Supervising Children's Services Worker and later as Deputy Regional Services Administrator before being selected to administer ICAN. Ms. Tilton–Durfee has been awarded commendations for her work by the National Association of Counties, the Los Angeles County Board of Supervisors, the ICAN Associates, the Los Angeles Latino Community, the Children's Legislative Organization United by Trauma (CLOUT) and numerous other public and private organizations concerned with the welfare of children and families. She is married to Child Psychiatrist, Michael J. Durfee, M.D.

EXECUTIVE DIRECTOR
Alan E. Sears served as the Executive Director for the Attorney General's Commission on Pornography. Mr. Sears previously served as the Chief of the Criminal Division and as As

sistant United States Attorney for the office of United States Attorney in the Western District of Kentucky. He has extensive trial experience which includes supervision of investigations and prosecution of several obscenity law cases. Mr. Sears is admitted to the practice of law in Kentucky and before the United States district courts for the Western District of Kentucky, the Eastern District of Kentucky, United States Tax Court, the United States Courts of Appeal for the Sixth Circuit and the District of Columbia and the United States Supreme Court.

C H A P T E R • 30

Acknowledgements and Notes

One of the most difficult tasks at the conclusion of a project such as this Commission's work is in properly expressing appreciation to the countless persons who contributed to the success of the project. The Commission wishes to thank everyone who assisted in this work. The Commission also recognizes and commends the following persons and agencies for their extraordinary contributions of personnel and support.

Arlington County Police Department
    Chief William K. Stover

Metropolitan Police Department
    Washington, D.C.
    Chief Maurice Turner

United States Postal Inspection Service
    Chief Postal Inspector Charles R. Clauson

United States Customs Service
    Commissioner William von Raab

Los Angeles County Department of Childrens
    Services
    Robert Chaffee, Director
    Stephen Fox, Director of Governmental
    Relations

Los Angeles County Sheriff's Department
    Child Abuse Unit
    Lt. Richard Willey

Los Angeles City Attorney's Office
    Deputy City Attorney
    Mary House

Los Angeles County Counsel
    Chief of Juvenile Division
    Larry Cory, Esquire

The Police Departments and officers of:
    The City of Los Angeles, California
    The City of Houston, Texas
    The City of Chicago, Illinois
    The City of Buffalo, New York
    The City of Miami, Florida

We also express special appreciation to support work and research performed by the Federal Bureau of Investigation, Director William Webster, support personnel at the United States Department of Justice, the many persons and entities in the United States Courts, General Services Administration, Federal Protective Services and with the City of Scottsdale, Arizona, who provided hearing sites and support for our public hearings and meetings.

Commissioner Statements

STATEMENT OF HENRY E. HUDSON, CHAIRMAN

With the reservations expressed herein, I concur in principle with the conclusions drawn by the majority. The findings contained in our report reflect a balanced assessment of the evidence heard. Ideally, I would have preferred that our condemnation of materials directly affecting behavior be couched in more forceful language, and that our recommendations for enhanced law enforcement, particularly with respect to violent and degrading materials, be likewise more pronounced. The reluctance of some Commissioners to adopt more potent language in these areas was undoubtedly attributable to the scarcity of definitive research on negative effects. While the existing body of research, particularly when coupled with the totality of the other evidence heard, well supports our findings, more corroborative research may warrant firmer control measures. Hopefully these issues will be addressed by behavioral scientists in future years.

Undoubtedly the most divisive task which confronted the Commission has been an analysis of those materials contained in Category III. This group encompasses a wide spectrum of imagery depicting sexual activity without violence, submission, degradation or humiliation. More than any other class evaluated, each Commissioner's personal value assessment of the activity portrayed encumbered objective analysis. The lack of consensus among the American people as to the morality of certain acts was quite evident among our cross-sectional composition.

From a purely social scientific perspective there is no cogent evidence that materials in this class have a predominately negative behavioral effect. There is, however, a scarcity of research material squarely within the definitional boundaries of this Category.

Much of the research touching material representative of this group also includes publications in other categories. The scarcity of significant research in this area adds a definite element of caution in assessing the behavioral effects of this class, particularly with respect to children and adolescents.

Despite the absence of clinical evidence linking Class III materials to anti-social behavior, several correlational connections are disturbing. First, it would appear that imagery comprising this Class may tend to encourage and promote the activity depicted. To the extent that the activity portrayed may be morally offensive, its literary propagation could be a social problem. At least one study has indicated that prolonged exposure to material in this category may cause a desensitized attitude toward the sexual abuse of women. This evokes considerable concern, especially with respect to the effect on individuals with predispositions for antisocial behavior.

Turning next to an assessment of the social effects of Class III materials as determined from all sources of evidence, it is useful to weigh the evidence relating to each category of potential harm identified by the Commission. Aside from attitudinal desensitization, there appeared to be no evident connection between items in this Class and the contention that women enjoy being raped. Several witnesses alluded to the possibility that a behavioral nexus may exist, but no persuasive evidence was introduced. However, depictions in this class do tend to promote the notion that women are inherently promiscuous and enjoy sexual exploitation. This type of imagery conveys the impression that women are fundamentally immoral and hedonistic.

The depictions featured in Category III material appear to de-emphasize the significant natural bond between sex and affection in their portrayal of adultery, fornication and sodomy. Therefore, in the final analysis, Class III material appears to impact adversely on the family concept and its value to society.

On balance, it would appear that materials in Class III have mixed effects depending on their nature and purpose. Those items which tend to distort the moral sensitivity of women and undermine the values underlying the family unit are socially harmful.

Aside from the type of harm which lends itself to a clinical degree of proof, obscenity impacts on society in a number of ways which defy scientific standards of assessment. The visible availability of obscene materials and performances in a community derogates from the family atmosphere normally fostered by local governmental policy. As Chief Justice Earl Warren noted in *Jacobellis v. Ohio*, 373 U.S. 184, 199, "(t)here is a right of the Nation and States to maintain a decent society." The right to preserve a wholesome community atmosphere conducive to family development in itself warrants the control of offensive and obscene materials. Chief Justice Warren E. Burger observed in *Paris Adult Theater I v. Slayton*, 413 U.S. 49, 58, that the desire to maintain "the quality of life and the total community environment" is an adequate legal basis for the regulation of obscene material. Justice Harlan in his dissenting opinion in *Roth v. United States*, 354 U.S. 476, 505, described this governmental obligation as a "responsibility for the protection of the local moral fabric." Inherent in the comments of Chief Justice Burger, as well as those of his predecessors, is the acknowledgement of the existence of a moral and cultural texture in our society, worthy of legal protection. Toward that end, I join Commissioner Park Elliott Dietz in his introductory comments.

Turning to the issue of law enforcement as developed in the text, my concern focuses more on the manner of expression than the underlying conclusion. Initially, the decision to adopt or enforce obscenity laws should re-side, within constitutional limits, with the citizens of each community. Our recommendations are predicated on the assumption that a community seeking to implement these suggestions has made this threshold decision. From the evidence heard and correspondence received, it would appear that most communities desire some degree of obscenity enforcement. However, if law enforcement officials in those communities adopt a policy of conscious oversight or neglect of obscenity cases, as has apparently happened in many jurisdictions, this may spawn a spectre of condonation. In time, an attitude of tolerance will evolve to the level of normal, and often fossilized, public policy. The necessity for reversing this course and employing our suggestions for citizen action deserves more prominence in our report.

The suggested prioritization of obscenity cases, which places the greatest emphasis on violent and degrading materials, seems appropriate. Of greater concern is the possible implication that enforcement with respect to Category III items should be de-emphasized. While prioritization of resources, like other obscenity law enforcement policy, is a matter within the prerogative of each individual jurisdiction, I do not support the suggestion that any items within the current definition of obscenity should not be prosecuted if deemed appropriate by that community. To the extent that prioritization of resources entails the commitment of personnel to long-term, complex investigations, a policy of concentration on violent and degrading materials is logical. On the other hand, the policy distinction between *legally obscene* materials of that type (Category I and II), and those in Category III is less persuasive when applied to cases developed by routine periodic surveys of materials on display in commercial areas. Under the latter circumstances, all materials within the legal definition of obscenity, as established by the standards of that community, should be prosecuted upon discovery.

Our suggestion that publications consisting entirely of the printed word and without imagery be exempted, except for those relating to child abuse, is disturbing. While I have never personally initiated a prosecution of a publication of that type, and cannot envision circumstances warranting such action in my community, I will not unilaterally impose my view on other jurisdictions. To the extent that our text may appear to condone a relaxation of existing obscenity laws with respect to materials comprised solely of the printed work, I depart from the majority. A decision to disregard existing law must in my view be made by the individual community affected.

I am also of the opinion that our report understates the connection between the pornography industry and organized crime. The evidence which I heard revealed more than a mere association. In my view, most elements of the pornography industry, particularly with respect to books and magazines, is directly controlled by the La Cosa Nostra, through its members or associates.

In the final analysis, I believe our final report represents as intensive an examination of the multi-faceted topic of pornography as could be conducted within our time and budgetary constraints. Every issue presented to us was considered from all points of view. Each member of our Commission made a valuable contribution of time and talent to our final product. I am proud to sign the resulting report.

Henry E. Hudson
Chairman

STATEMENT OF DIANE D. CUSACK

At the conclusion of our year-long effort to assess the impact of pornography on American society, it seems appropriate to add my personal thoughts on just a few aspects of deliberations and the report.

Although sometimes with the majority and other times with the minority on certain points, I believe the report fairly states both sides of any divided issues and I am proud to sign this report and to have been a part of a most intensive and intelligent look into a troublesome aspect of our society today. Our chairman, Henry Hudson, and Staff Director, Alan Sears, deserve the gratitude of the country for so keenly perceiving and discharging their uniquely important responsibilities. I know they have my admiration and thanks.

Those who seize upon our divisions do the report a great disservice. Rather, they should credit the high degree of consensus—and frequently unanimity—as a strong statement of our concern for society. Our 92 recommendations are sound and sure, and must be implemented at all levels of government if there is to be any hope of "stemming the tide" of obscenity which is flooding our environment.

There is no doubt among us that the quantity of pornography available today in America is almost overwhelming. In addition, that large portion of it which would be obscene under the Miller test is shockingly violent, degrading and perverted. It is my personal opinion that there is no one who is a consistent user of this material who is not harmed by it. And who, in turn, may harm others because of it. This obscene material should be prosecuted vigorously under the laws and ac-

cording to our recommendations, whether pictorial, film, or written works.

But let us not ignore that body of material which is sexually explicit but not obscene under the Miller test. This material can also be harmful—but in a somewhat different way. Although not prosecutable, nor recommended to be so, it nonetheless presents a cause for concern. Our report clearly states a concern for material that is objectionable but is and should be protected by the First Amendment freedoms. The fact that it is "protected speech" does not automatically remove its objectionable character. For 2500 years of western civilization, human sexuality and its expressions have been cherished as a private act between a loving couple committed to each other. This has created the strongest unit of society—the family. If our families become less wholesome, weaker, and less committed to the fidelity that is their core, our entire society will weaken as well. People who consistently use the materials we have studied—and children who inadvertently are exposed to them—are not made better persons for it. No pornographer has ever made that claim. And those who insist that these materials do no harm had better be right, for the risks to our future are substantial. These materials, whose message is clearly that sexual pleasure and self-gratification are paramount, have the ability to seriously undermine our social fabric. It is the individuals in our great nation who must see this, and reverse the trend—not the government. Chapter 4 of Part One of the Report addresses this issue quite well.

Aristotle has taught us for years that a society must concern itself with virtue. "Otherwise . . . law becomes a mere contract or mutual guarantee of rights, and quite unable to make citizens good and just, which it ought to do. . . ." It is this "good and just" society which America has enjoyed from its beginning. It became so because its people had a shared respect, a unifying vision, a common understanding of man's place in the world. We have a phenomenon today, in the pervasive presence of sexually explicit materials, that challenges one of those understandings held by society for thousands of years—that sex is private, to be cherished within the context of love, commitment, and fidelity. We can use this wondrous gift to create or destroy, to rule or be ruled, to honor each other or debase each other. This Report provides an abundance of information, and the conclusions of a community of eleven citizens. The American people must now decide what to do with it.

STATEMENT OF PARK ELLIOTT DIETZ, M.D., M.P.H., PH.D.[1]

In recent decades there has been a desirable trend toward using empirical evidence to test long-held assumptions underlying legal doctrine and procedure and to rely on social science evidence to make better-informed judgments about difficult questions of law and social policy. Social science has given good service in answering questions about adequate jury size, in determining public perceptions of trademark products, in profiling skyjackers, in sentencing convicted criminals, and in limiting the exclusionary rule. But social science is too new on the historical scene to have developed adequate data on every important social problem, too little funded to have amassed all the data desired, and too positivistic to tell us what we should do, particularly when competing interests are at stake.

The 1970 Commission on Obscenity and Pornography went so far in attempting to rely on social science evidence that a majority of its members took the absence of experimental evidence of causation of antisocial behavior or sexual deviance as a basis for urging the deregulation of obscenity. The present Commission did not limit its inquiry to the products of social science research. While in this respect we depart from the tradition of one predecessor Commission, we do not depart from the tradition of those who have been charged with formulating social policy for the whole of human history. Every time an emperor or a king or a queen or a president or a parliament or a congress or a legislature or a court has made a judgment affecting social policy, this judgment has been made in the absence of absolute guidance from the social sciences. The Constitutional Convention of 1787 had no experimental evidence to guide its decision making. When the First Congress proposed the First Amendment in 1789 and when it was ratified by the states in 1791 and made a part of the Constitution, the empirical social sciences had not yet been conceived.

As in public policy, decision makers in medicine must exercise their best judgment in the face of uncertainty, being guided by science as far as it takes us, being guided by a commitment to the well being of individuals and of society, and being guided by sensitivity toward those situations in which the best interests of an individual conflict with the best interests of society. It is within this framework that I have tried to make my own best judgments about pornography while serving on the Commission. At every step in our joint decision making, the medical and public health consequences have been in the forefront of my concerns. These consequences are not widely recognized, for which reason I devote most of my personal statement to an overview of these.

Before the Commissioners had even met one another, the press had begun to suggest bias among the Commissioners and to wave red flags of censorship. Now, before our report has even gone to the printer, there have already been claims that we are too liberal, that we are too conservative, that we have

---

1. Commissioner Cusack concurs in this statement.

gone too far, that we have not gone far enough, that we have ignored evidence showing how innocuous pornography is, and that we have ignored evidence showing how destructive pornography is. In short, there are those who have rejected our findings before the report has even been issued, and I have no doubt many more will do so in the future without having read it. Likewise, but for somewhat different reasons, there will be those who accept our findings without having read our report. This is equally risky. Our report is meant to be read, and I encourage every adult in America to do so before accepting or rejecting our findings.

The reader should be forewarned, however, that our report contains offensive materials. Some readers will be offended by quoted language, particularly the titles of magazines, books, and films that we considered. But the offensiveness of some of the quoted language is nothing when compared to the suffering described by victims whose accounts are quoted in the victimization chapter. This is not bedtime reading. As with the practice of medicine, one must sometimes cause discomfort to effect a cure, and it was our judgment that the public and the truth would be best served by including certain discomforting materials in the report.

I came to the Commission with personal views on pornography which were based on intellectual and humanitarian concerns and on certain noncontroversial ethical principles; the morality of pornography was the farthest thing from my mind. Thus, I was astonished to find that by the final meeting of the Commission, pornography had become a matter of moral concern to me. While other Commissioners may have learned things about the dark side of life that they had never known, I remembered something about the higher purposes of life and of humanity's aspirations that I had forgotten during too many years working on the dark side. I therefore conclude my remarks with statements on morality and on freedom that would have seemed foreign to me not many months ago.

Pornography And Health

Abuse of Persons Used in Production. Pornography is a medical and public health problem because people, particularly women and children, are abused in the production of certain pornographic materials. People have

been beaten, forced to engage in sexual acts, held prisoner, bound and gagged, and tortured for purposes of producing pornography. In the course of these events they have been exposed to the risk of acquiring sexually transmitted diseases. Some have been supplied with narcotics. Of course, these crimes could have been prosecuted in their own right, even if there were no obscenity or child pornography laws. Moreover, the market for pornography is, after all, but one of several motives for the commission of these crimes, all of which also occurred before the invention of photography. If these were the only adverse health consequences of pornography, the most straightforward remedy would be regulation of the pornography industry to assure safe and fair labor practices. But these are not the only adverse health consequences of pornography.

Injurious Products. Pornography is a medical and public health problem because pornographic retail outlets of the "adults only" variety sell products under the pretext of health and recreation that are the instruments of injury, both intentional and unintentional. People have suffocated in bondage hoods. People have asphyxiated and burned to death in handcuffs and bondage restraints. People have been raped and lacerated with dildos. People have had "sexual aid" devices entrapped in body cavities, requiring extraction at hospital emergency wards. People have died from orally ingesting volatile nitrites and have suffered cerebrovascular injury from inhaling these same chemicals, sold as aphrodisiacs under various pretext labels in these establishments. People have been abducted and have been conned into exiting their vehicles or allowing strangers into their homes when offenders have shown them phony police badges, sold as "novelties" in some of these establishments. People have been robbed and put in fear of their life by offenders who have wielded phony guns, also sold as "novelties" in some of these establishments. If these were the only adverse health consequences of pornography, the most straightforward remedies would be public education, regulation of some of these products through food and drug law and others through criminal sanctions, and tort actions by the injured against producers and distributors of inherently dangerous products and products that were negligently designed, marketed, labeled, and sold. But these are not the only adverse health consequences of pornography.

Vice Centers. Pornography is a medical and public health problem because pornographic retail outlets of the "adults only" variety are the most visible service stations of the vice industry. The peep-show booths, with their locking doors, are the self-service pumps, as evidenced by the body fluids on their floors and walls. The openings in the walls of the booths allow anonymous and casual sexual contact, making it impossible to trace the donors and recipients of sexually transmitted diseases. These establishments draw muggers to a pool of victims who are somewhat disinclined to report a robbery to the police. These establishments signal members of the community and visitors that full vice services may be available nearby through prostitutes and drug dealers and, if not so directly available, are a phone call away through the advertisements found in tabloids, periodicals, and sex-for-sale guides. If these were the only adverse health consequences of pornography, the most straightforward remedy would be to prohibit retail sales except through the mail. But these are not the only adverse health consequences of pornography.

Sexual Disinformation. Pornography is a medical and public health problem because so much of it teaches false, misleading, and even dangerous information about human sexuality. A person who learned about human sexuality in the "adults only" pornography outlets of America would be a person who had never conceived of a man and woman marrying or even falling in love before having intercourse, who had never conceived of two people making love in privacy without guilt or fear of discovery, who had never conceived of tender foreplay, who had never conceived of vaginal intercourse with ejaculation during intromission, and who had never conceived of procreation as a purpose of sexual union. Instead, such a person would be one who had learned that sex at home meant sex with one's children, stepchildren, parents, stepparents, siblings, cousins, nephews, nieces, aunts, uncles, and pets, and with neighbors, milkmen, plumbers, salesmen, burglars, and peepers, who had learned that people take off their clothes and have sex within the first five minutes of meeting one another, who had learned

to misjudge the percentage of women who prepare for sex by shaving their pubic hair, having their breasts, buttocks, or legs tattooed, having their nipples or labia pierced, or donning leather, latex, rubber, or child-like costumes, who had learned to misjudge the proportion of men who prepare for sex by having their genitals or nipples pierced, wearing women's clothing, or growing breasts, who had learned that about one out of every five sexual encounters involves spanking, whipping, fighting, wrestling, tying, chaining, gagging, or torture, who had learned that more than one in ten sexual acts involves a party of more than two, who had learned that the purpose of ejaculation is that of soiling the mouths, faces, breasts, abdomens, backs, and food at which it is always aimed, who had learned that body cavities were designed for the insertion of foreign objects, who had learned that the anus was a genital to be licked and penetrated, who had learned that urine and excrement are erotic materials, who had learned that the instruments of sex are chemicals, handcuffs, gags, hoods, restraints, harnesses, police badges, knives, guns, whips, paddles, toilets, diapers, enema bags, inflatable rubber women, and disembodied vaginas, breasts, and penises, and who had learned that except with the children, where secrecy was required, photographers and cameras were supposed to be present to capture the action so that it could be spread abroad. If these were the only adverse health consequences of pornography, the most straightforward remedy would be to provide factually accurate information on human sexuality to people before they are exposed to pornography, if only we could agree on what that information is, on who should provide it to the many children whose parents are incapable of doing so, and on effective and acceptable means by which to ensure that exposure not precede education. In the absence of such a remedy, the probable health consequences in this area alone are sufficient to support recommendations that would reduce the dissemination of that pornography which teaches false, misleading, or dangerous information about human sexuality. And these are not the only adverse health consequences of pornography.

Encouraging Social Behavior with Adverse Health Consequences. Pornography is a medical and public health problem because it encourages patterns of social behavior which have adverse health consequences. The person who follows the patterns of social behavior promoted by pornography is a person for whom love, affection, marriage, procreation, and responsibility are absolutely irrelevant to sexual conduct. We do not need research to tell us that such persons on the average contribute more than other persons to rates of illegitimacy, teenage pregnancy, abortion, and sexually transmitted diseases. If these were the only adverse health consequences of pornography, the most straightforward remedy would be to more effectively encourage responsible sexual behavior, if only we knew how. In the absence of such a remedy, the probable health consequences in this area alone are sufficient to support recommendations that would reduce the dissemination of pornography. And these are not the only adverse health consequences of pornography.

Fostering Attitudes with Adverse Health Consequences. Pornography is a medical and public health problem because it increases the probability that members of the exposed population will acquire attitudes that are detrimental to the physical and mental health of both those exposed and those around them. The social science evidence adequately demonstrates that even in experimental samples of mentally stable male college students, exposure to violent pornography leads to measurable, negative changes in the content of sexual fantasies, attitudes toward women, attitudes toward rape, and aggressive behavior within the experimental setting. Analogous results of exposure to nonsexual media violence have been well-documented for even longer. Although too few experiments have clearly tested the effects of degrading pornography, there are suggestions in the few existing studies that exposure to degrading pornography has negative effects in the experimental setting, including eliciting anxiety, depression, and hostility. Biographical accounts of individuals go beyond the experimental evidence in attributing changes in male sexual attitudes and demands to pornography, including nonviolent pornography, and in documenting adverse consequences to women and children of the behavior of these men. Some of these accounts include persuasive examples of direct and immediate imitation and of long-term modeling effects. Moreover, the existing population-based evidence for the United States shows a correlation between circulation rates of magazines

containing pornography (primarily of a nonviolent type) and rates of reported rape in the fifty states during the same time period, even after many other factors were statistically controlled. In my opinion, we know enough now to be confident in asserting that a population exposed to violent pornography is a population that commits more acts of sexual brutality than it otherwise would and to suggest somewhat less confidently that the same is probably true of a population exposed to degrading pornography. Even if these were the only adverse health consequences of pornography, there would be no straightforward remedies for these consequences short of reducing the exposure of the population to violent and degrading pornography. And these are not the only adverse health consequences of pornography.

Instruments of Sexual Abuse. Pornography is a medical and public health problem because it is used as an instrument of sexual abuse and sexual harassment. Pornography of all types is used in the sexual abuse of children to instruct them on particular sexual acts and to overcome their resistance by showing them what adults do and by intimidating them about the painful things that might be done to them if they fail to comply. Pornography of all types is used to instruct women in the sexual behaviors that men desire of them but which they have "failed" to provide, forcing women who have or see no other options to choose between the feelings of inadequacy that accompany refusal and the feelings of self-loathing that accompany compliance. Pornography of all types is used to harass women in the workplace and to remind them into whose world they are intruding, leading to feelings of shame, disgust, and powerlessness. Even if these were the only adverse health consequences of pornography, there would be no straightforward remedies for these consequences short of reducing the quantity of pornography in circulation. And these are not the only adverse health consequences of pornography.

Presumed Corruption of Children. Pornography is a medical and public health problem because it falls into the hands of children, who must be assumed vulnerable to adverse mental health consequences unless and until proved otherwise. Although experiments to test this assumption pose potentially insurmountable ethical dilemmas, it should be possible to design studies to examine the responses of children who have been exposed to pornography in other ways, such as negligent parental storage. Such studies would require safeguards to protect the child against any further harm and a suitable control group, such as children whose parents possess pornography to which the children were not exposed. To date, the effects of exposure on young children are unknown, but it would be as imprudent to assume no negative health consequences of pornography as it would to make such an assumption about a drug that had not been properly tested. Even if the assumed harms to exposed children were the only adverse health consequences of pornography, there would be no straightforward prevention or remedy for these consequences short of reducing the quantity of pornography in circulation. And these are not the only adverse health consequences of pornography.

The Limits of Obscenity and Child Pornography Laws in Reducing the Adverse Health Consequences of Pornography. The adverse health consequences of pornography are not limited to a single class of pornographic materials, though the various classes have differing health consequences. Most importantly perhaps, the adverse health consequences of pornography are not limited to materials that are legally obscene or that violate child pornography law. Thus, existing laws, even if enhanced and enforced as recommended in this report, are insufficient to prevent the adverse health consequences attributable to pornography. Obscenity law is designed to suppress the offensive, but on medical and public health grounds it would be more desirable to suppress the harmful. To the extent that the obscene and the harmful overlap, obscenity law is a powerful tool of health promotion. But if the adverse health consequences of pornography are to be minimized, strategies other than effective enforcement of obscenity law and child pornography law will be necessary. In addition to the strategies that increase the effectiveness and enforcement of existing law, the nation's health requires a creative search for countermeasures against the adverse health consequences of non-obscene, non-child pornography, which will inevitably survive law enforcement efforts directed against obscenity and against child pornography. In this search, we must inevitably come to terms with the need for appropriate sex education.

The Commission report endorses citizen actions that could help reduce the adverse health consequences of non-obscene, non-child pornography, but the report is necessarily unclear on the nature and extent of this class of materials. This lack of clarity carries with it the risk that citizen action will be misdirected. To the extent that citizens care to base their actions against non-obscene material on its medical and public health consequences, they will do more to promote health if they insure that their efforts encompass violent and degrading images, especially sexually violent and degrading images. Unhealthy as some nonobscene pornography may be, it is not as unhealthy as detective magazine covers depicting violence toward a woman whose sexual characteristics are emphasized, horror films depicting girls or women undressing moments before the villain pounces upon them, or televised depictions of violence toward alluring, glamorous, and wanton women. Like rape itself, violent pornography is not so much about sex as about violence. It is no distortion of the language to refer to violence that is not sexually explicit as pornography. The word "pornography" derives from the Greek for the writings of prostitutes, and the life of the prostitute is as much a life of violence as it is a life of sex. If sexually stimulating materials that are nonviolent, nondegrading, and nonobscene have beneficial health consequences, the most important among them must be that they distract attention from materials that are violent and degrading.

Pornography And Morality[2]

Acting as a whole, the Commission attempted to provide a reasoned analysis of the permissible and desirable relationships between government and the regulation of sexually explicit materials, including the rights of citizens to take private action. As a governmental body, we studiously avoided making judgments on behalf of the government about the morality of particular sexual acts between consenting adults or their depiction in pornography. This avoidance, however, should not be mistaken for the absence of moral sentiment among the Commissioners.

I, for one, have no hesitation in condemning nearly every specimen of pornography

---

2. Chairman Hudson, Commissioners Dobson, Lezar, Garcia and Cusack concur in this section.

that we have examined in the course of our deliberations as tasteless, offensive, lewd, and indecent. According to my values, these materials are themselves immoral, and to the extent that they encourage immoral behavior they exert a corrupting influence on the family and on the moral fabric of society.

Pornography is both causal and symptomatic of immorality and corruption. A world in which pornography were neither desired nor produced would be a better world, but it is not within the power of government or even of a majority of citizens to create such a world. Pornography is but one of the many causes of immorality and but one of its manifestations. Nonetheless, a great deal of contemporary pornography constitutes an offense against human dignity and decency that should be shunned by the citizens, not because the evils of the world will thereby be eliminated, but because conscience demands it.

Pornography And Freedom

When Andrea Dworkin challenged us to find the courage "to go and cut that woman down and untie her hands and take the gag out of her mouth, and to do something, to risk something, for her freedom," I cried. And I still cry at that image, even as I write, because if we do not act with compassion and conviction and courage for the hostages and victims of the pornographers we do not deserve the freedoms that our founding fathers bequeathed us. It has been nearly two centuries since Phillipe Pinel struck the chains from the mentally ill and more than a century since Abraham Lincoln struck the chains from America's black slaves. With this statement I ask you, America, to strike the chains from America's women and children, to free them from the bonds of pornography, to free them from the bonds of sexual slavery, to free them from the bonds of sexual abuse, to free them from the bonds of inner torment that entrap the second-class citizen in an otherwise free nation.

Appendix

To elucidate one example of the types of material that are probably not obscene under the Miller test but which should be high on any list of media depictions posing risks to health, I append an article that I coauthored, with appreciation to the *Journal of Forensic Sciences* in which it was published and the American Society for Testing and Materials which holds the copyright for permission to include it here.

Park Elliott Dietz, M.D., M.P.H., Ph.D.; Bruce Harry, M.D.; and Robert R. Hazelwood, M.S.

Detective Magazines: Pornography for the Sexual Sadist?

REFERENCE: Dietz, P. E., Harry, B., Hazelwood, R. R., **"Detective Magazines: Pornography for the Sexual Sadist"** *Journal of Forensic Sciences*, JFSCA, Vol. 13, No. 1, Jan. 1986, pp. 197–211.

ABSTRACT: The origins of detective magazines can be traced to 17th and 18th century crime pamphlets and to 19th century periodicals that Lombroso called "really criminal newspapers." Content analysis of current detective magazines shows that their covers juxtapose erotic images with images of violence, bondage, and domination; that their articles provide lurid descriptions of murder, rape, and torture; and that they publish advertisements for weapons, burglary and car theft tools, false identification, and sexual aids. Six case histories of sexual sadists illustrate the use of these magazines as a source of fantasy material. We postulate that detective magazines may contribute to the development of sexual sadism, facilitate sadistic fantasies, and serve as training manuals and equipment catalogs for criminals. We recommend that detective magazines be considered during policy debates about media violence and pornography.

KEYWORDS: psychiatry, criminal sex offenses, deviant sexual behavior, detective magazines, sexual sadism, pornography, criminal behavior, sexual homicide.

A class of popular periodicals known as "detective magazines" has apparently eluded the attention of researchers and commentators concerned with media violence and pornography. These magazines provide factual accounts of crimes and criminals, and are thereby distinguished from mystery fiction. They rarely contain photographs of nudes, and are thereby distinguished from those publications that most individuals casually refer to as erotic, pornographic, or obscene.

In this paper, we review the historical roots of these detective magazines, report data on the content of current detective magazines, present six case histories in which detective magazines were a source of fantasy material, and discuss the possible psychiatric and criminologic significance of detective magazines.

We postulate that detective magazines serve as pornography for sexual sadists. The works of the Marquis de Sade and his literary disciples, though known outside the literati, are too erudite and too remote in setting from everyday life to appeal to the sexual sadist of average intelligence and educational level. In contrast, detective magazines depict and describe sadistic acts in familiar settings, using the imagery and language of tabloid newspapers. This class of periodicals receives little commentary in comparison with those that are considered obscene or pornographic on the basis of their explicit use of erotic imagery. Detective magazines characteristically pair violent and sadistic images with erotic images, yet are more accessible for purchase by young persons than are magazines that depict naked bodies.

The Origins and Readership of Detective Magazines

Periodicals reporting crime are thought to have originated in 17th century England.[1] Crime pamphlets and related publications appeared at a time when oral renditions of crime were still provided by street merchants for a fee. Around 1864, Mayhew described "death hunters" and "running patterers" who were paid to shout out stories of crimes.[2] Death hunters went to the scenes of murders and reported on the details of the killings; running patterers fabricated or embellished the stories of infamous crimes. Mayhew also described "caravan shows," a form of "peep show" in which carts containing a miniature stage, curtains, and scenery were used by puppeteers to reenact infamous murders.[3]

Crime pamphlets flourished throughout 18th century England and appeared in America during the last half of that century. By the middle of the 19th century, as British and American journalists embraced sensationalism,[4] the chaotic relationship between crime and law enforcement[5] found its natural literary outlet. Gradually, newspapers and crime magazines began to replace other forms of information about crime.

The first financially successful American crime magazine was The National Police Gazette, which appeared in 1845.[6] This magazine was highly celebrated, and at least 22 related magazines followed in its wake.[7-9] The Gazette survived well into the 20th century. We examined all issues of the National Police Gazette from its first year of publication. Initially, it featured stories of actual crimes and made modest use of woodcut illustrations. There were many advertisements for home remedies, sexual enhancement and augmentation preparations, trusses, clothing, hats, boots, jewelry, guns, and "cheap" books. By the late 19th century, the Gazette was printed on pink paper and had detailed illustrations of shootings, stabbings, hangings, and debauchery, as well as graphic descriptions of bareknuckle boxing, wrestling, and cockfights. Advertisements offered revealing photographs of women; treatments for veneral diseases, impotence, and "self abuse"; and the services of lawyers and detectives. The Gazette was "for some years the most widely circulated of weekly journals".[10]

The Gazette's decline began around 1920, and "modern" detective magazines appeared by 1924. They were quickly assessed as having virtually no cultural value,[11/12] and they proliferated. More than 20 are currently published on a regular basis. Four detective magazines for which data were available had a combined monthly circulation of 996,000 issues in about 1980.[13]

Otto examined eleven detective magazines as part of a larger study of newsstand magazines in the 1960s and found that they offered the most sexual and nonsexual violence of all general circulation magazines, even though his data excluded advertisements and covers.[14] Reporting on the content of two detective magazines, Lyle noted that "the stories in general are fairly explicit in describing what kind of violence was committed, how it was done, and to what effect".[15] Beattle studied one issue each of Official Detective and True Detective as part of his study of mass market magazines and concluded that detective magazines were among those with the most violent content.[16]

The readership of detective magazines has not been identified. Lazarsfeld and Wyant included one detective magazine in their study of reading habits in 90 American cities,[17] but their statistical analysis excluded the genre. Freidman and Johnson surveyed media use among "aggressive" and "nonaggressive" eighth and ninth grade boys, 20% of whom read "crime and detective magazines"; differences between the two groups in amount and type of magazine reading were not significant.[18] In contrast, Lyle and Hoffman reported that 9% of a sample of sixth grade boys and girls, and 6 and 7%, respectively, of a sample of tenth grade boys and girls, preferred to read "detective/mystery" magazines.[19] Whether these data refer to such magazines as Alfred Hitchcock's Mystery Magazine and Ellery Queen's Mystery Magazine or to the detective magazines considered here is not known. Thus, there is no audience whose rate of use of detective magazines is known.

The Content of Detective Magazines

Detective magazines are readily available at newsstands, drugstores, supermarkets, convenience stores, and elsewhere. One copy of each detective magazine issue available on a single day at ten suburban Boston stores was purchased and studied in detail. The mean purchase price was $1.11; the range was from $0.95 to $2.50. These magazines generally were displayed along with women's, "confession," and children's magazines, usually adjacent to adventure and gun magazines, and always on a different rack from espousedly erotic men's magazines. We have subsequently confirmed these observations regarding display patterns in stores in Charlottesville, VA; Chicago, IL; Columbia, MO; Houston, TX; Kansas City, MO; Los Angeles, CA; New York, NY; St. Louis, MO; Washington, DC; Toronto, Ontario, Canada; and Melbourne, Victoria, Australia.

Nineteen detective magazine issues, representing eighteen different titles from six publishers, were studied. They were: *Detective Cases. Detective Diary, Detective Dragnet, Detective Files, Detective World, Front Page Detective, Guilty! The Best from True Detective, Headquarters Detective, Homicide Detective, Inside Detective, Master Detective, Official Detective Stories, Police Detective* (two issues), *Real Detective, Startling Detective, True Detective, True Police Cases,* and *True Police Yearbook.*

We analyzed several aspects of the content of these 19 issues. First, we analyzed the violent and sexual imagery in photographs used for front covers, article illustrations, and commercial advertisements. Second, we analyzed the words expressive of violence and sexuality used in the titles of articles promoted on the front covers and listed in the tables of contents. Third, we analyzed the textual content of articles for descriptions of violent and sexual behavior. For this third purpose, a stratified, random sample of 38 articles was selected (two articles randomly selected from the signed articles in each issue). The results of these content analyses are presented in the following sections.

Illustrations

The covers of the 19 magazines bore 21 photographs. The most common image on front covers was that of a woman in an inferior or submissive position. Seventy-six percent of the cover photographs showed domination and submission imagery. Men dominated women in 71% of cover pictures, while women dominated men in 5%. Some pictures showed a woman alone in a submissive or subjugated position. Bondage was depicted in 38% of the cover pictures, and all of the bound subjects were women. Ropes, chains, handcuffs, and cloth were used to achieve this bondage with equal frequency. In order of decreasing frequency, other repetitive cover imagery included violent struggles, brassieres, guns, accentuated breasts, strangulation, corpses, blood, and knives or other cutting instruments. Table 1 shows the percentages of each type of image in covers, articles, and advertisements.

In contrast to the cover photographs, the illustrations accompanying articles most often pictured buildings or other settings and conventionally dressed people. Law enforcement personnel were often shown processing a crime scene or working at a desk; they were always men. Violent and erotic imagery was much less prevalent in article photographs than in cover photographs. When it did occur, the most prevalent form was domination and submission imagery. Men dominated women in 5% of the article pictures, and women dominated men in less than 1%. Individuals were most often bound with ropes or handcuffs, less commonly with leather, chains, or cloth.

TABLE 1—*Percentages of photographs depicting particular types of images in detective magazine covers, articles, and advertisements.*

Images	Covers (N = 19)	Articles (N = 891)	Advertisements (N = 926)
Bondage and domination imagery			
bondage	38	5	0.1
domination	76	36	0
Struggles			
strangulation	14	0.6	0
other violent struggles	29	2	3
Weapons			
guns	29	4	6
knives or other cutting instruments	14	0.7	2
blunt instruments	5	0.8	2
bombs	5	.01	0
saws	5	0	3
other weapons[a]	0	1.5	0.1

TABLE 1 (Continued)

Images	Covers (N = 19)	Articles (N = 891)	Advertisements (N = 926)
Sadistic imagery			
corpses	14	3	0
blood	14	1	0
mutilation/slashing	0	0.3	0
Body parts			
breasts accentuated	24	1	3
buttocks accentuated	5	0.2	2
genitals	0	0	2
Clothing			
brassiere	29	1	3
negligee	5	2	0
panties	0	2	4
other "erotic" clothing[b]	0	1.5	3.1
Sexual behaviors			
intercourse[c]	0	0.1	3.2
masturbation	0	0	1
crossdressing	0	0.2	0.1

[a]Includes fire, whips, gas chambers, gallows, and brass knuckles.

[b]Includes stockings, garters, hoods, exaggerated shoes and boots, and constrictive waist garments.

[c]Includes heterosexual and homosexual genital intercourse, fellatio, cunnilingus, and anal intercourse.

Men dominated women in 5% of the article pictures, and women dominated men in less than 1%. Individuals were most often bound with ropes or handcuffs, less commonly with leather, chains, or cloth.

In illustrated, commercial advertisements (that is, excluding classified advertisements), potential weapons such as guns, knives, blunt instruments, or saws were depicted slightly more often than body adornments such as panties, brassieres, or stockings. The guns, knives, and blunt instruments were for sale. The saws appeared in advertisements offering instruction in sharpening saws. Undergarments most often appeared in the illustrations of advertisements for other merchandise.

Seventy-three advertisements in our sample promoted enhancement of sexual control, appeal, or function. Detective or law enforcement training was advertised in 68. Fifty-nine promoted "official" photographic identification cards, police badges, or other means of certifying identity. Mind control techniques were offered in 35 advertisements. Female wrestlers were depicted in 18, and male wrestlers in 9. Most issues had advertisements for mail-order brides, lonely hearts clubs, "locksmith training," and equipment for picking locks, opening car doors, duplicating keys, and building handgun silencers.

Titles and Text

The titles of articles are similar in construction and terminology among detective magazines. Compare, for example, the titles from two magazines published two years apart by two different publishers: "A TRUNK-FULL OF FLESH"; "CANADA'S NUMBER 1 MURDER MYSTERY"; "MURDER BY FREIGHT TRAIN"; "ANNA TOOK THE BLADE 90 TIMES!"; "SEX COP'S DEATH CHAMBER"; "IT TAKES A COP"; "OLD FRIENDSHIPS DIE EASY WITH A .38"; "PORTLAND'S BLOODY SUMMER"; and "TORTURE-SLAYER OF EL TORO" (*Startling Detective*, Vol. 73, No. 3, May 1983, published by Globe Communications Corp.); "SATANIST SMILED AS HE SNUFFED THE SNITCH!"; "ROAST A FAMILY OF SIX!"; "BULLET BARRAGE KO'D THE BOXING REF!"; "WHO LEFT THE NAKED MAN'S HEAD SOAKED IN GORE?"; "THE HOLY VAMPIRE DRANK HIS VICTIM'S BLOOD!"; "WHO BLEW THE BICKERING COUPLE AWAY?"; "WEIRD FETISHES OF WASHINGTON'S RAPE-SLAYER!"; "'HE WAS PLAYING HERO, SO I SHOT THE S.O.B.!'"; "ORDEAL OF THE KIDNAPPED GIRL IN THE PIT!"; and "LETHAL LESSON: NEVER MESS WITH A MARRIED MAN!" (*Front Page Detective*, Vol. 48, No. 5, May 1985, published by RGH Publishing Corp.).

The magazine covers gave the titles of 77 of the 186 articles listed in the tables of contents. Table 2 shows the percentages of words about particular themes on the covers and in article titles. Words describing various forms of killing were most prevalent and included "kill," "murder," "execute," "slay," and "hit-man." Roles described included "stranger," "lover," "victim," "bride," "dame," "whore," "slut," "gigolo," and "mistress." Descriptors of mental states and traits included "crazy," "mad," "maniac," "greed," "treachery," "lust," and "hang-ups." Death-related words included "dead," "body," "corpse," "graveyard," "cemetery," "coffin," and "bloodthirsty." While law enforcement words such as "detective," "police," "crime," "case," and "cop" appeared in the names of every magazine, they were less commonly used in article titles. Sexual terms such as "rape," "gay," "drag," and "sex" made up the next most prevalent category. As can be seen in Table 2, the rank order of themes identified in article titles in the tables of contents was nearly identical to that for articles listed on covers.

TABLE 2—Percentages of detective magazine article titles mentioning particular themes.

Theme	On Cover (N = 77)	In Table of Contents (N = 186)
Killing	38	32
Roles	36	24
Mental state	34	16
Death	30	15
Law enforcement	25	10
Sex	19	14
Strangulation	9	5
Weapons	9	5
Mutilation	6	4
Relentless pursuit	6	3
Secret location	5	3
Life	3	2

In the 38 articles sampled for analysis, there were 40 killings. Fifteen involved torture, and the other 25 were less protracted murders of helpless victims. There were 44 episodes of sexual violence (including 13 sexual mutilations), 14 robberies, and 3 burglaries. The incidents described included 50 shootings, 40 stabbings, 14 strangulations, 10 episodes of being bound and gagged, 7 bludgeonings, 3 burnings, 1 poisoning, and 1 electrocution.

Personal characteristics of victims and perpetrators were usually specified, adding to the credibility of the articles. Forty-seven perpetrators acted against ninety-eight victims. The offenders included 43 males and 4 females; the victims were 42 males and 56 females. When age was mentioned, offenders were usually between 15 and 35, while their victims were usually either 15 to 25 years old, or older than 46. Of the cases identifying race, 12 of 35 offenders and 4 of 44 victims were black. Twenty perpetrators were described as having been previously engaged in criminal activity, and seven were noted to have a history of psychiatric disorder. Five of the offenders were killed during gun battles with police, and all others went to trial. The insanity defense was raised in 13 trials, but only 1 defendant was acquitted by reason of insanity. The death sentence was given five times; three prisoners had been executed when the articles were written. Twenty-two victims were strangers, twelve were friends or acquaintances, and nine were lovers. Two male victims were noted to have been homosexual, and at least seventeen female victims were prostitutes. Men were killed, but virtually never sexually molested; women were almost always sexually attacked before being killed.

Many of the articles contained detailed descriptions of violent acts. Colorfully explicit descriptions of wounds and crime scenes were universal. Stalking or surveillance of the victim, methods of investigation, investigative reconstruction of the events, and crime laboratory work were commonly described. Networks of informants played a pivotal role in almost all investigations, and extensive media publicity was emphasized. Arrests tended to be rapid and overpowering. Extensive coverage was afforded to trials, verdicts, and sentences. Many articles ended by reporting a substantial prison sentence and reminding the reader that the offenders, or others like them, were still at large or might soon be.

Case Reports

The following six case histories illustrate how detective magazines are used as a source of fantasy material. The facts are drawn from investigative files submitted to the FBI Academy Behavioral Science Unit (Cases 1, 5, and 6) or from case files developed in the course of forensic psychiatric evaluations (Cases 2, 3, and 4). Cases 1 and 2 depict multiple murderers who enjoyed detective magazines. The offender in Case 3 used detective magazines during masturbation, but reportedly never acted out his most extreme fantasy scenarios. The pedophile in Case 4 used detective magazines to facilitate his masturbation fantasies and may have begun to act out those fantasies. The offender in Case 5 used detective magazines in the commission of his offense. Case 6 describes the victim of an autoerotic fatality, who used detective magazines in the course of acting out his fantasies.

Case 1

A multiple murderer of the late 1950s had a collection of the covers of detective magazines. He told police investigators that he liked detective magazines "sometimes for the words, sometimes for the covers."

He approached two of his victims on the pretext that he wished them to model bondage scenes for detective magazines. In his statement to the investigating officers he said:

> I told her that I wanted to take pictures that would be suitable for illustrations for mystery stories or detective magazine stories of that type, and that this would require me to tie her hands and feet and put a gag in her mouth, and she [was] agreeable to this, and I did tie her hands and feet and put a gag in her mouth and I took a number of pictures, I don't remember exactly how many, of various poses and changing the pose from picture to picture.

He acknowledged that he never had any intention of submitting the photographs for publication, and added that he was impotent in the absence of bondage.

Case 2

A 35-year-old, married, white man was charged with approximately a dozen murders in several states.

He had never known his father, who had been executed for murdering a police officer and who also had killed a correctional officer during an escape. Shortly before being executed the father wrote: "When I killed this cop, it made me feel good inside. I can't get over how good it did make me feel, for the sensation was something that made me feel elated to the point of happiness . . . " He recalled his grandmother showing him a picture of his father and telling him that his father had been a heroic firefighter. Later, he learned that the photograph was from a detective magazine article about his father's murders and execution. Often told of his resemblance to his father, he came to believe that his father lived within him.

His mother was married four times and also had a series of short-term extramarital sexual partners. She frequently told her son that she had been raped by her father when she was nine. She ridiculed her son's bedwetting, which persisted to age 13, by calling him "pissy pants" in front of guests; he was also beaten for the bedwetting and for night terrors. For as long as he could recall he had had recurrent nightmares of being smothered by nylon similar to women's stockings and being strapped to a chair in a gas chamber as green gas filled the room. One of his stepfathers beat him relentlessly. For leaving a hammer outside, he was awakened by this stepfather burning his wrist with a cigar, which left a permanent scar. For playing a childish game while urinating, he was forced to drink urine. On the one occasion when his mother intervened, the stepfather pushed her head through a plaster wall. From then on she also actively abused her children from the earlier marriages.

Knocked unconscious on multiple occasions, he was once briefly comatose at age 16 and for over a week at approximately age 20. A computed tomography (CT) scan of the brain showed abnormally enlarged sulci and slightly enlarged ventricles. Results of the Halstead-Reitan Neuropsychological Battery and the Luria-Nebraska Neuropsychological Battery were interpreted as showing damage to the right frontal lobe.

As a juvenile, he had police contacts for vandalism, malicious acts, running away, and multiple burglaries (beginning at age seven in the company of an older brother). Apprehended for lewd contact with a 7-year-old girl at age 13, he was sent to reform school for a year. He was suspended from high school for misconduct and poor grades. At age 16, he was arrested for armed robbery, escaped, and later turned himself in to authorities.

At age 18, two weeks after the birth of his first child, he married the child's mother. Despite subsequent arrests for armed robbery, beating his wife, assault, burglary, auto theft, theft, parole violation, and other offenses, he was awarded custody of his daughter after divorcing his first wife. His second and third marriages ended in divorce after he beat his wives, and his fourth marriage ended in divorce for unknown reasons.

After many more arrests and a jail escape, he was eventually sentenced to prison on an armed robbery conviction. He initiated sexual contact with his seven-year-old daughter during a conjugal visit on the prison grounds. Prison records from his early 20s documented a psychotic episode with paranoid delusions and suicidal ideation following the death of a brother. After he was paroled from prison he impregnated one woman and married another (his fifth wife). He separated from her after he was released from parole. His second through fifth wives appeared young enough to pass as teenagers.

In his early 30s, he lived as husband and wife with his 13-year-old daughter, whom he impregnated. The pregnancy was aborted. He continued to molest his daughter, who reported one of his rapes. He also sexually assaulted one of her girlfriends. He celebrated one of his birthdays by sodomizing his then 14-year-old daughter. Eventually she moved to her grandparents' home, and he began living and traveling with another woman, who became his sixth wife and his partner in a two-year series of rapes and murders.

His wife knew of his fantasies of torturing young girls and his desire for women he could control and abuse, and she assisted him in each of his known murders by selecting the victim, orchestrating the abduction, and concealing the evidence. He beat, tortured, and raped his victims, whom he forced to play the role of his daughter in fantasy scenarios that he directed. Available data suggest that he killed his victims to avoid detection and not because the killing gave him sexual pleasure.

His early victims were all teenage girls; his later victims included adults. After his initial murders, he again raped his daughter and her friend. They reported these offenses, and an arrest warrant was issued. The offender changed his identity, as he had on previous occasions, using false identification papers. A gun enthusiast, he bought and sold various firearms; shortly before his last arrest, he possessed two revolvers, an automatic pistol, a derringer, and a semiautomatic assault rifle. Those victims' bodies that have been located showed death by gunshot wounds or blows to the head. Some of the bodies were still bound.

Masturbation he regarded as shameful, dirty, and unmanly. The first sexually explicit pictures he could recall having seen were photographs of his mother with a man he did not recognize. Although familiar with sexually explicit men's magazines, he had never been to an adult book store or an X-rated movie "because I didn't want anybody to think I was in that category." He considered The Exorcist and Psycho influential in his life. In speaking of sexual deviations, he referred to "sadism-maschotism" [sic], but noted that this did not apply to him: " . . . sadism-masochism is where you like to be hurt while you hurt, and I don't think that's it. Maybe one-half of it, cause I think I've been hurt enough." The imagery characteristic of bondage and domination pornography disgusted him: "That ain't me . . . . The ball in the mouth, the excess rope, I think what they've done is taken a fantasy and overdo it. The mask makes somebody look like out of Mars . . . . You're in a room and a girl walks out with a rubber suit or whip and she's subject to get shot." Asked about the covers of detective magazines, he responded by saying that they are what he really likes and that the interviewer seemed to read his mind, asking questions that allowed him to say what he was already thinking.

When he was 14, he learned that his fugitive father had been caught because his mother had told the police his whereabouts. After reporting this, he stated: "Sometimes I [think] about blowin' her head off . . . . Sometimes I wanta' put a shotgun in her mouth and blow the back of her head off . . . ." For years, his favorite sexual fantasy was of torturing his mother to death:

> I was gonna' string her up by her feet, strip her, hang her up by her feet, spin her, take a razor blade, make little cuts, just little ones, watch the blood run out, just drip off her head. Hang her up in the closet, put airplane glue on her, light her up. Tatto "bitch" on her forehead . . .

This fantasy gradually changed and he came to include forced sexual activity and other forms of abuse and torture. After his first wife left him, she replaced his mother in the fantasy; eventually their daughter replaced her.

Case 3

A 35-year-old, single, white man was charged with unarmed robbery. He had had several psychiatric hospitalizations, each time receiving a diagnosis of chronic undifferentiated schizophrenia. He was suspected to have committed the current act to gain readmission.

He left school after the ninth grade and never worked. He admitted to bouts of heavy alcohol consumption, but denied using other drugs. He had been arrested previously for threatening the President, attempted strong-arm robbery, and attempted bank robbery. He admitted several indecent exposures and burglaries for which he had not been arrested. During the burglaries he had taken food and women's underclothing, searched bureau drawers, and torn up clothes. He also admitted to "peeping" and several episodes of crossdressing, donning panties, slips, dresses, and lipstick. On several occasions he had entered houses when the occupants were away and left notes threatening to kill them if they did not leave things for him to take. He denied urinating or defecating in these houses, although he had once thrown a litter box containing cat feces. He had also once tried to steal explosives.

At age ten he had engaged in sexual play with his sister and a niece; there had been at least one episode of intercourse. After he quit school at age 16, he lived briefly with a 14-year-old girl who became pregnant and miscarried. At some point thereafter he began having fantasies of forced vaginal intercourse, sucking and biting on breasts, and mutual oral sexual activity. He described subsequent enchantment with pornography depicting these activities and dated his first contact with detective magazines to approximately the same time.

By his mid-20s, his masturbatory fantasies were of lying on a woman, tying her with heavy, electrical wire, having intercourse with her, killing her by blows and strangulation, and then attacking her genitalia. He said that the detective magazines had not caused these fantasies, adding, "I had 'em before but the [detective] magazines bring them out." By his late 20s, he was having fantasies of mutilation, smearing and drinking blood, and continuing intercourse after his victim's death. He also had recurrent dreams of being a "bloodthirsty murderer."

He stated that he preferred masturbating while looking at the covers and contents of detective magazines. He regarded detective magazine photographs as the best match to his current sexual fantasies and as his most important source of sexual pleasure. He said he masturbated in his bathroom with detective magazine covers and pictures from explicitly erotic magazines so positioned that he could see himself and the pictures in a mirror. He particularly liked pictures in which women "look like whores," and he masturbated to orgasm while fantasizing about "killing whores."

He claimed never to have acted out his most extreme fantasies, but he believed that he might be "losing control over them." He admitted to having had intense "sexual thoughts" during the unarmed robbery, to "enjoying touching, feeling panties and bras," and to excitement at thoughts of women struggling.

A detailed review of his records uncovered no documentation of symptoms or signs of schizophrenia. He admitted to having feigned mental illness so that he could be stopped from acting out his fantasies.

Case 4

A 20-year-old, single, black man with no previous criminal record but several psychiatric evaluations was incarcerated for sexually molesting children. At least three complaints had been lodged previously against him without formal charges being filed.

He stood charged with two sexual assaults against prepubescent girls. In the first incident he asked a girl to go with him, claiming that a friend wanted to speak with her. He grabbed the girl, pulled her pants down, and fondled her genitals until someone appeared, when he fled. The second incident was similar, although reportedly more forceful, with the victim resisting more aggressively. He fled when the victim bit him. He denied any sexual contact with his victims, but did say that in one offense against a girl he "kept hitting until she was unconscious; I thought she was dead."

His father had been rarely present, and the family was on welfare. One of his brothers was said to be mentally retarded and institutionalized. He claimed to have had good relationships with family members and to have had friends. He completed ninth grade with below average grades; the school authorities had wanted him placed in special education classes, but his mother had refused. He was never married, had no military history, and worked intermittently in unskilled jobs. He acknowledged moderate use of alcohol and marijuana, but denied using other drugs.

During the screening psychiatric interview he denied any symptoms suggestive of a psychotic illness. He claimed his present offenses occurred because he was "too scared to ask out women." Fearing that older women might reject him and tell him he was "too young, just a kid, and I can't handle that," he felt anger toward older women, "like I want to kill them." He admitted to daydreams about "beating them up" followed by intercourse. His masturbatory fantasies involved bondage in which the hands of the women were tied behind their backs, their mouths gagged, and their legs tied to bedposts. He denied masturbatory fantasies involving other physical injury. He also denied crossdressing. He believed he would never act on his masturbatory fantasies: "I just couldn't see myself doing something like that; not if she don't do as I tell her. If I get mad I start tearing up stuff, but not kids; I like kids. If I had kids I wouldn't want someone doing that to them." He claimed his fantasies involved "mostly white girls" ages 12 to 13.

He said that he frequently used visual media to stimulate his masturbatory fantasies. His favorite images involved women wearing undergarments, such as brassieres and panties, or two-piece bathing suits, which he commonly found on detective magazine covers, but added that he found detective magazines less appealing than traditional pornography.

Case 5

A 34-year-old, white woman received a telephone call from a man claiming to represent a manufacturing firm that had developed a new line of brassieres and was conducting a marketing survey in her area. She was invited to participate in the survey. She would be sent six free bras to wear for six months, when she would be asked to complete a questionnaire as to their comfort, durability, and washability. She agreed and provided her bust measurements to the caller.

Approximately seven months later, the same man called the second time and said that he would like to deliver the bras to her home. She asked that he call back in a few days as she wanted to discuss the matter with her husband. When he rang, she told him that she had decided not to participate in the survey. He responded, "I don't want to have intercourse with you, I just want to deliver the bras." She hung up immediately.

Five months later, upon receiving a package in the mail which contained four sketches depicting her bound, in various stages of undress, she notified the police. Shortly thereafter, the man called again, asking for her opinion of the sketches.

A second package containing four sketches similar to the first ones arrived about four months later, again followed by a telephone call. During this conversation, the man requested that she meet him and said he would call again to arrange the meeting. He also described the wallpaper pattern in her bathroom. He used no profanity in the telephone conversations.

Approximately four months later he called for the sixth time, requesting a meeting. She hung up on him. Within days came another call during which she agreed to meet him at a shopping center near her home. She notified the police, who arranged surveillance. After waiting in vain for 45 min. at the appointed location, she talked with the surveilling officers and drove home.

The following month, the man called and accurately described her movements at the rendezvous and her return home. He requested that she deliver two of her bras to a designated Salvation Army clothes bin. Again she notified the police and a surveillance of the drop site was arranged; however, the offender was able to pick up the bras undetected by entering the clothes bin from an opening in the rear. Shortly thereafter, she received a third package containing her bras, two pictorial pages, an advertisement page, and a cover from a detective magazine. The bras had semen stains and handwriting on them. The magazine cover and the pictorial pages each showed a woman being threatened by a man holding a knife; her name was written above the women and the word "me" was written above the men. The advertisement was for Nazi paraphernalia. One month later he rang to ask what she thought about the package.

That same month, she received a letter containing polaroid photographs of a white male, nude except for a ski mask, masturbating in a hotel room. The letter said that he had rented the room, intended to kidnap her, and had brought rope with which to bind her and a camera with which to take pictures of her performing various sexual acts. He called her again shortly after she received the letter. The eleventh and final call came one month later.

From the photographs the police were able to identify the hotel, where they found that he had registered under his real name. He was later arrested, convicted, and sentenced to one year in jail. At the time of his arrest, the police seized a folder containing 30 detective magazine covers that depicted women in potentially lethal situations.

Case 6

A 30-year-old white man was discovered dead in his apartment. He was partially suspended in a doorway by a length of plastic clothesline which encircled his neck twice with a knot on the right. The clothesline went up to and through an airspace above the door and was affixed to a hinge beside the victim. His arms hung at his sides, and his feet touched the floor. A pair of wire cutters and more clothesline were found on a washing machine in the apartment. He wore eyeglasses, a brassiere, jockey shorts, and black calf-length socks.

Propped up on a stand directly in front of him was a detective magazine cover which depicted a man strangling a young woman who wore a black brassiere. Two lingerie advertisements taped to a nearby wall showed a woman from the waist up who wore only a brassiere and a woman wearing a brassiere and a panty girdle. A nearby phonograph was on, and the first song on the record was "Barbie Ann." An album cover lying beside the phonograph had a picture of a man with two young women wearing halter tops.

The decedent's wife, Barbara, had been separated from him for four months; she and their only child had moved to another state. He had appeared to be in normal spirits during a visit with his parents six days earlier. A friend with whom he had played pool on the evening before his death and who was the last person to see him alive described him as having been in good spirits at the time of their parting.

The death was ruled to be an accident occurring during autoerotic activity. The decedent's attire and visual props suggest a brassiere fetish, while the detective magazine cover in front of him depicting the sexual murder of a woman wearing a brassiere suggests that he entertained a sadistic fantasy that he had been enacting with his own body. The object of his fantasies may have been his wife. (This case has been reported in less detail elsewhere.[20]

Discussion

Detective magazines juxtapose conventionally erotic images (for example, pictures of scantily clad women or descriptions of sexual acts) with images of violence and suffering. Detective magazines are not the only source for this combination of images; many recent horror films, crime films, and rock video productions have similar characteristics. One study found that bondage and domination was the primary theme of 17% of the magazines sold in "adults only" bookstores.[21] Unlike these magazines, however, detective magazines, being inexpensive and available on many newsstands, have a large circulation. They are always openly displayed, unlike magazines showing nonviolent nudity, and there is no effort to discourage sales to minors.

The cases reported in this paper show that some readers who use detective magazines as sources of sexual fantasy material also act on their fantasies. MacCulloch et al[22] have described men who progress from sadistic masturbation fantasies to crimes that enact portions of the fantasy sequence, and thence to more serious offenses based on an elaborated fantasy sequence. A similar pattern can be recognized in Cases 3 and 4 above.

At least two previously published case reports mention the use of detective magazines as a source of sexual fantasy imagery. Graber et al.[23] reported the history of a 36-year-old man who forced a woman to fellate him at knife-point in a women's restroom of a public park. This attack was followed several weeks later by "an abortive attack on a woman that ended when she was cut by his knife." The offender had no prior criminal record. He reported a lack of sexual experience, including masturbation, until marriage at age 23. The frequency of intercourse with his wife decreased after he experienced a business failure. About a year before his arrest he had begun masturbating while reading the sex crime articles in a detective magazine, which thereafter became his preferred sexual outlet. The offense for which he was arrested was inspired by a detective magazine article.

Wesselius and Bally[24] recorded the history of a 24-year-old man who practiced autoerotic asphyxia by self-hanging for ten years. He first masturbated at age ten while suspended from the bar of a swing set. He began using the pictures in True Detective magazine while masturbating around age 14. The authors report: "From this magazine he developed the idea of dressing in female clothing which he would take from the family laundry hamper . . . ." Within months, he became sexually aroused while watching a hanging scene in a cowboy film, and was particularly excited by the man's struggle and kicking feet. He then began masturbating while hanging himself. The authors noted that "he continued to use True Detective magazines with only occasional use of other more common soft pornography publications." He would become most aroused by dressing in soiled women's undergarments and hanging himself. He also became aroused by wearing such clothing and binding his limbs and neck. He fantasized strangling a woman and was particularly aroused by imagining her helpless struggling and her kicking feet.

Goldstein and Kant[25] quoted a rapist as saying:

I can remember looking through True Detective and stuff like this and seeing articles about women that had been murdered or something . . . . I remember partially nude bodies. There was a lot of magazines on the stands I used to buy all the time, these horror stories, "trips of terror," weird stories, stuff like this. Soon after this, they banned 'em from the newsstands. I used to like to read them all the time.

While there is no doubt that detective magazines provide a rich source of sexually sadistic imagery, the role that these magazines play in the development of sexual sadism, if any, is unknown. To the extent that paraphilic responsiveness is acquired by repeatedly associating sexual arousal with particular images, the availability of sexually sadistic imagery may be important. Detective magazines are one source of such imagery.

The cases we have described do not prove that detective magazines "cause" sexual sadism or sadistic offenses. Only unethical experiments could prove or disprove such causation, and we do not encourage that they be contemplated. Tests of the arousal of normal men and of sexual sadists to the cover imagery we describe could, however, tend to support or refute our postulate and could be conducted in an ethical manner that minimizes the risk of harming the subjects.

We assume that conventionally erotic elements in detective magazines would arouse many males and that responsiveness to particular stimuli can be learned. We postulate that repeated pairing of arousal with the unconditioned stimuli in these magazines, such as depictions of bondage, domination, weapons, strangulation and other struggles, blood, and corpses increases the probability that the viewer will subsequently be aroused by exposure to these stimuli, whether or not they are presented in an erotic context.

We know that some boys and men repeatedly use detective magazines to achieve sexual arousal and that at least some of these individuals are sexual sadists. Of these latter, however, we do not know what proportion were sexual sadists before their exposure to detective magazines. We consider it plausible that some boys and young men turn to detective magazines for such conventional sexual imagery as scantily clad women or descriptions of sexual interaction, and through repeated exposure learn to be aroused by elements of the photographs and articles that otherwise would have had no sexual associations. We recognize, however, that horror movies and other films probably expose more boys and young men to the pairing of erotic and violent images.

Detective magazines might affect the established sexual sadist by reinforcing his paraphilia (particularly if he masturbates to orgasm while looking at or reading the magazines), by adding details to his fantasies and preferred imagery, and by providing consensual validation that lessens the extent to which he considers his preference abnormal or unacceptable.

Beyond their significance with respect to sexual sadism, detective magazines have other potentially criminogenic effects. None of these potential effects is unique to detective magazines, but each should be considered in assessing the social value of these magazines.

Detective magazines publicize particularly serious crimes. In an era in which many value fame more highly than esteem or freedom, the prospect of publicity serves as an inducement to crime. While detective magazines reach a smaller audience than network television, national news magazines, wire services, or the most widely read newspapers, they reach an audience with greater average interest in crime, provide lengthier and more detailed accounts of particular offenders and offenses, and emphasize the degree of publicity received by the offender.

Detective magazines are an unsurpassed source of public information on techniques for committing crimes, on the errors of unsuccessful offenders, and on the methods available to law enforcement agencies for preventing crimes and apprehending offenders. We have examined and studied offenders who have sought out, filed, and used such information to commit crimes, but we also know law enforcement officers who use such information as a source of continuing education.

The advertisements in detective magazines provide access to information and paraphernalia that are sometimes used to commit crimes, including weapons, burglary tools, and car theft equipment. Police badges and other false identification obtained through these advertisements have been used by offenders to gain entry to dwellings or to stop motorists. Cases have been documented of persons murdered or otherwise victimized by persons whom they met through lonely hearts advertisements such as those appearing in detective magazines.[26]

Conclusions

Detective magazines have a lengthy heritage and generate substantial sales. No doubt some readers examine detective magazines out of curiosity or casual interest. Sexual sadists, however, are particularly drawn to detective magazines, and some of these individuals translate their fantasies into action. Clinicians should learn to ask their patients about reading preferences and should also have sufficient knowledge of popular publications to be able to interpret the responses. Since few patients spontaneously mention sadistic sexual fantasies in the course of assessment or psychotherapy, inquiries about reading habits provide an important route through which to explore a patient's fantasy life.

Patients with a particular interest in detective magazines may have problems other than sexual sadism. In our experience, many individuals who are paranoid or preoccupied with violence read or collect detective magazines, mercenary magazines (such as *Soldier of Fortune, Commando,* and *Gung Ho*), and hunting and gun magazines. Peterson[27] noted that "the market of a medium [usually] coincides with that of its advertisements" and that advertisements generally reflect consumer needs and desires. Some of the advertisements in detective magazines cater to those with pronounced feelings of inadequacy by offering greater sexual control, appeal, or function; techniques of mind control; and certification of identity.

Our view that the harmful effects of detective magazines probably outweigh whatever contributions they may make to law enforcement, entertainment, and the economy is, of course, not entirely original. Writing at the end of the 19th century, Cesare Lombroso considered newspaper reports of crime the source of many imitative ("copycat") crimes, of which he gave multiple examples. He concluded:

> This morbid stimulation is increased a hundred-fold by the prodigious increase of really criminal newspapers, which spread abroad the virus of the most loathsome social plagues, simply for sordid gain, and excite the morbid appetite and still more morbid curiosity of the lower social classes. They may be likened to those maggots which, sprung from putrefaction, increase it by their presence.[28]

We suppose that Lombroso put it too strongly, as was his custom. Nonetheless, we are concerned that detective magazines—today's equivalent of "really criminal newspapers"—may contribute to the development and persistence of sexual sadism; facilitate sadistic fantasies; and encourage crime by rewarding it with publicity, disseminating technical information, and easing access to criminal equipment.

We therefore urge policymakers to consider detective magazines in their deliberations concerning violence in the media and pornography. We recommend that the new national commission on pornography[29] include detective magazines and other sources of sexually sadistic imagery among the classes of materials that it studies. Whatever definition of pornography or obscenity emerges from the ongoing public policy debate should surely be formulated to encompass those materials that present the greatest risk of promoting the erotization of violence.

References

[1] Peterson, T., "British Crime Pamphleteers: Forgotten Journalists," *Journalism Quarterly*, Vol. 22, 1945, pp. 305–316.

[2] Mayhew, H., *London Labour and the London Poor. Volume I:London Street-Folk*, Charles Griffin and Company, London, ca. 1864, pp. 227–350.

[3] Mayhew, H., *London Labour and the London Poor. Volume III*, Charles Griffin and Company, London, ca. 1864, pp. 51–167.

[4] Jowett, G. S., Reath, P., and Schouten, M., "The Control of Mass Entertainment Media in Canada, the United States and Great Britain: Historical Surveys," in *Report of the Royal Commission on Violence in the Communications Industry. Volume 4: Violence in Print and Music*, J. C. Thatcher, Toronto, 1977, pp. 3–104.

[5] Monkkonen, E. H., *Police in Urban America, 1860-1920*, Cambridge University Press, Cambridge, 1981.

[6] Mott, F. L., *A History of American Magazines. Volume I: 1741-1850*, Belknap Press, Cambridge, 1937, p. 481.

[7] Mott, F. L., *A History of American Magazines. Volume II: 1850-1865*, Harvard University Press, Cambridge, 1938, pp. 185–187.

[8] Mott, F. L., *A History of American Magazines. Volume II: 1850-1865*, Harvard University Press, Cambridge, 1938, pp. 325–337.

[9] Mott, F. L., *A History of American Magazines. Volume IV: 1885-1905*, Belknap Press, Cambridge, 1957, pp. 199–200.

[10] Smith, G. and Smith, J. B., *The Police Gazette*, Simon and Schuster, New York, 1972.

[11] Morgan, W. L. and Leahy, A. M., "The Cultural Content of General Interest Magazines," *Journal of Educational Psychology*, Vol. 25, 1934, pp. 530–536.

[12] Kerr, W. A. and Remmers, H. H., "The Cultural Value of 100 Representative American Magazines," *School and Society*, Vol. 54, 1941, pp. 476–480.

[13] Hagood, P., *The Standard Periodical Directory*, 7th ed., Oxbridge Communications, Inc., New York, 1980.

[14] Otto, H. A., "Sex and Violence on the American Newsstand," *Journalism Quarterly*, Vol. 40, 1963, pp. 19–26.

[15] Lyle, J., "Contemporary Functions of the Mass Media," in *A Report to the National Commission on the Causes and Prevention of Violence. Volume XI: Mass Media and Violence*, D. L. Lange, R. K. Baker, and S. J. Ball, eds., U.S. Government Printing Office, Washington, DC, 1969, pp. 187–216.

[16] Beattie, E., "Magazines and Violence," in *Report of the Royal Commission on Violence in the Communications Industry. Volume 4: Violence in Print and Music*, J. C. Thatcher, Toronto, 1977, pp. 161–221.

[17] Lazarsfeld, P. F. and Wyant, R., "Magazines in 90 Cities—Who Reads What?," *Public Opinion Quarterly*, Vol. 1, 1937, pp. 29–41.

[18] Friedman, H. L. and Johnson, R. L., "Mass Media Use and Aggression: A Pilot Study," in *Television and Social Behavior. Volume III: Television and Adolescent Aggressiveness*, G. A. Comstock and E. A. Rubinstein, eds., U.S. Government Printing Office, Washington, DC, 1972, pp. 336–360.

[19] Lyle, J. and Hoffman, H. R., "Children's Use of Television and Other Media," in *Television and Social Behavior. Volume IV: Television in Day-to-Day Life: Patterns of Use*, E. A. Rubinstein, G. A. Comstock, and J. P. Murray, eds., U.S. Government Printing Office, Washington, DC, 1972, pp. 129–256.

[20] Dietz, P. E., Burgess, A. W., and Hazelwood, R. R., "Autoerotic Asphyxia, the Paraphilis, and Mental Disorder," in *Autoerotic Fatalities*, R. R. Hazelwood, P. E. Dietz and A. W. Burgess, Lexington Books, Lexington, MA, 1983, pp. 77–100.

[21] Dietz, P. E. and Evans, B., "Pornographic Imagery and Prevalence of Paraphilis," *American Journal of Psychiatry*, Vol. 139, 1982, pp. 1493–1495.

[22] MacCulloch, M. J., Snowden, P. R., Wood, P. J. W., and Mills, H. E., "Sadistic Fantasy, Sadistic Behavior, and Offending," *British Journal of Psychiatry*, Vol. 143, 1983, pp. 20–29.

[23] Graber, B., Hartmann, K., Coffman, J. A., Huey, C. J., and Golden, C. J., "Brain Damage Among Mentally Disordered Sex Offenders," *Journal of Forensic Sciences*, Vol. 27, No. 1, Jan. 1982, pp. 125–134.

[24] Wesselius, C. L. and Bally, R., "A Male with Autoerotic Asphyxia Syndrome," *American Journal of Forensic Medicine and Pathology*, Vol. 4, 1983, pp. 341–345.

NOTE: An earlier version of this paper was presented by the authors in a panel entitled "Bloody Instructions: Intolerable Crimes in Mass Market Magazines" at the Annual Meeting of the American Academy of Psychiatry and the Law, New York, NY, 24 Oct. 1982. Received for publication 6 May 1985; accepted for publication 31 July 1985.

1. Associate professor of law and of behavioral medicine and psychiatry and medical director, Institute of Law, Psychiatry and Public Policy, University of Virginia Schools of Law and Medicine, Charlottesville, VA.

2. Assistant professor of psychiatry and adjunct assistant professor of law, University of Missouri—Columbia, Columbia, MO.

3. Supervisory special agent and instructor, Behavioral Science Unit, FBI Academy, Quantico, VA.

[25] Goldstein, M. J. and Kant, H. S., *Pornography and Sexual Deviance*, University of California Press, Berkeley, 1973, p. 71.

[26] Brown, W., *Introduction to Murder: The unpublished facts behind the notorious lonely hearts killers—Martha Beck and Raymond Fernandez*, Greenberg, New York, 1952.

[27] Peterson, T., "Why the Mass Media are That Way," in *Mass Media and Communication*, 2nd ed., C. S. Steinberg, ed., Hastings House, New York, 1972, pp. 56–71.

[28] Lombroso, C. (Horton, H. P., trans.) *Crime: Its Causes and Remedies*, Little, Brown, and Co., Boston, 1912, p. 211.

[29] "Child Pornography Law Signed; U.S. Study Commission Created," *New York Times*, 22 May 1984, p. A20.

Address requests for reprints or additional information to:
Park Elliott Dietz, M.D., M.P.H., Ph.D.
School of Law
University of Virginia
Charlottesville, VA 22901

PERSONAL COMMENTS BY COMMISSIONER JAMES DOBSON

Now that the work of the Attorney General's Commission on Pornography has come to an end, I look back on this fourteen month project as one of the most difficult, and gratifying, responsibilities of my life. On the down side, the task of sifting through huge volumes of offensive and legally obscene materials has not been a pleasant experience. Under other circumstances one would not willingly devote a year of his life to depictions of rape, incest, masturbation, mutilation, defecation, urination, child molestation and sadomasochistic activity. Nor have the lengthy and difficult deliberations in Commission meetings been without stress. But on the other hand, there is a distinct satisfaction in knowing that we gave ourselves unreservedly to this governmental assignment and, I believe, served our country well.

I now understand how mountain climbers must feel when they finally stand atop the highest peak. They overcome insurmountable obstacles to reach the rim of the world and announce proudly to one another, "we made it!" In a similar context, I feel a sense of accomplishment as the Commission releases its final report to the President, the Attorney General, and the people. For a brief moment in Scottsdale last month, it appeared that our differing philosophies would strand us on the lower slopes. And of course, we were monitored daily by the ACLU, the pornographers, and the press, who huddled together and murmured with one voice, "they are doomed!" But now as we sign the final document and fling it about to the public, it does not seem pretentious to indulge ourselves in the satisfaction of having accomplished our goals. By George, I think we made it!

Let me indicate now, from the viewpoint of this one Commissioner, what the final report is and is not. First, it is not the work of a biased Commission which merely rubberstamped the conservative agenda of the Reagan administration. A quick analysis of our proceedings will reveal the painstaking process by which our conclusions were reached. If the deck were stacked as some have suggested, we would not have invested such long, arduous hours in debate and compromise. Serving on the Commission were three attorneys, two psychologists, one psychiatrist, one social worker, one city council member, one Catholic priest, one federal judge and one magazine editor. Some were Christians, some Jewish, and some atheists. Some were Democrats and some Republicans. All were independent, conscientious citizens who took their responsibility very seriously. Our diversity was also evident on strategic issues about which society itself is divided. Our voting on these more troublesome matters often split 6–5, being decided by a swing member or two. Some whitewash! So the characterization of this seven man, four woman panel as an ultraconservative hit squad is simply poppycock. Read the transcripts. You will see.

Second, the final report does not do violence to the First Amendment to the Constitution. The *Miller* standard, by which the Supreme Court clearly reaffirmed the illegality of obscene matter in 1913, was not assaulted during any of our deliberations. No suggestion was made that the Court had been too lenient . . . or that a Constitutional Amendment should lower the threshold of obscenity . . . or that the Justices should reconsider their position. No. The *Miller* standard was accepted and even defended as the law of the land. What *was* recommended, to the consternation of pornographers, was that government should begin enforcing the obscenity laws that are already on the books . . . criminal laws that have stood constitutional muster! Considering the unwillingness of our elected representatives to deal with this issue, that would be novel, indeed.

Third, the hearings on which this report was based were not manipulated to produce an anti-pornography slant. *Every* qualified libertarian and First Amendment advocate properly requesting the right to testify was granted a place on the agenda, limited only by the constraints of time. A few individuals and organizations on *both* sides of the issue were unable to testify because the demand far exceeded available opportunities. However, objective procedures were established to deal fairly with those wishing to be heard, and complaints alleging bias were, I believe, unfounded. In fact, several organizations were asked to speak on behalf of sexually explicit materials but either declined or failed to appear. It is true that more witnesses testified against pornography than those who favored it, but that was a function of the disproportionate requests that were received by the executive director. Furthermore, I think it also reflects a disproportionate number of American citizens who oppose the proliferation of obscenity.

Looking now at the other side of the coin, let me express what the final report is and what I believe its impact is likely to be. First, the Commission expressed an unmistakable condemnation of sexually explicit material that is violent in nature. We were unanimous in that position throughout our deliberations. There is no place in this culture for material deemed legally obscene by the courts which depicts the dismemberment, burning, whipping, hanging, torturing or raping of women. The time has come to eradicate such materials and prosecute those who produce it. There was no disagreement on that point.

Second, we were also unanimous in our condemnation of sexually explicit materials which depict women in situations that are humiliating, demeaning and subjugating. I can still recall photographs of nude young women

being penetrated by broom handles, smeared with feces, urinated upon, covered in blood or kneeling submissively in the act of fellatio. Most American citizens have no idea that such gruesome scenes are common in the world of obscene publications today. When asked to describe pornography currently on the market, they think in terms of airbrushed centerfolds in the popular "men's magazines." But steady customers of pornography have long since grown tired of simple heterosexual nudity. Indeed, a visit to an adult bookstore quickly reveals the absence of so-called "normal" sexuality. The offerings today feature beribboned 18–to–20 year old women whose genitalia have been shaved to make them look like little girls, and men giving enemas or whippings to one another, and metal bars to hold a woman's legs apart, and 3-foot runner penises and photographs of women sipping ejaculate from champagne glasses. In one shop which our staff visited on Times Square, there were 46 films for sale which depicted women having intercourse or performing oral sex with different animals . . . pigs, dogs, donkeys and horses. This is the world of pornography today, and I believe the public would rise up in wrath to condemn it if they knew of its prominence.

Finally, our Commission was unanimously opposed to child pornography in any form. Though categorically illegal since 1983, a thriving cottage industry still exists in this country. Fathers, step-fathers, uncles, teachers and neighbors find ways to secure photographs of the children in their care. They then sell or trade the pictures to fellow pedophiles. I will never forget a particular set of photographs shown to us at our first hearing in Washington, D.C. It focused on a cute, nine-year-old boy who had fallen into the hands of a molester. In the first picture, the blond lad was fully clothed and smiling at the camera. But in the second, he was nude, dead and had a butcher knife protruding from his chest. I served for 14 years as a member of a medical school faculty and thought I had seen it all. But my knees buckled and tears came to my eyes as these and hundreds of other photographs of children were presented . . . showing pitiful boys and girls with their rectums enlarged to accomodate adult males and their vaginas penetrated with pencils, toothbrushes and guns. Perhaps the reader can understand my anger and disbelief when a representative for the American Civil Liberties Union testified a few minutes later. He advocated the free exchange of pornography, *all* pornography, in the marketplace. He was promptly asked about material depicting children such as those we had seen. This man said, with a straight face, that it is the ACLU's position that child pornography should not be produced, but once it is in existence, there should be no restriction on its sale and distribution. In other words, the photographic record of a child's molestation and abuse should be a legal source of profit for those who wish to reproduce, sell, print and distribute it for the world to see. And that, he said, was the intent of the First Amendment to the Constitution!

Speaking personally, I now passionately support the control of sexually explicit material that is legally obscene, whether it relates to children or adults. Though the Commission has dealt at some length in its report with specific "harms" associated with pornography, I would like to list the dangers here from my own point of view. Our critics have alleged that the Commission wishes to usher in a new era of sexual repression . . . that we favor governmental interference in America's bedrooms and even in our thoughts. That is nonsense. On the other hand, I have seen enough evidence in the past year to convince me of the devastation inflicted on victims of pornography. It is on their behalf that we must intervene. Here, then, are the harms as I perceive them:

1. Depictions of violence against women are related to violence against women everywhere. Though social research on this subject has been difficult to conduct, the totality of evidence supports the linkage between illustration and imitation. Furthermore, pornography perpetuates the so-called "rape myth" whereby women are consistently depicted as wanting to be assaulted even when they deny it. They are shown as terrified victims in the beginnings of rape scenes, but conclude by begging for more. Men who want to believe that women crave violent sex can find plenty of pornographic evidence to support their predilections.

2. For a certain percentage of men, the use of pornographic material is addictive and progressive. Like the addiction to drugs, alcohol or food, those who are hooked on sex become obsessed by their need. It fills their world, night and day.

And too often, their families are destroyed in the process.

3. Pornography is degrading to women. How could any of us, having heard Andrea Dworkin's moving testimony, turn a deaf ear to her protest? The pornographic depictions she described are an affront to an entire gender, and I would take that case to any jury in the land. Remember that men are the purchasers of pornography. Many witnesses testified that women are typically repulsed by visual depictions of the type therein described. It is provided primarily for the lustful pleasure of men and boys who use it to generate excitation. And it is my belief, though evidence is not easily obtained, that a small but dangerous minority will then choose to act aggressively against the nearest available females. Pornography is the theory; rape is the practice.

4. It appears extremely naive to assume that the river of obscenity which has inundated the American landscape has not invaded the world of children. This seven billion-dollar industry pervades every dimension of our lives. There are more stores selling pornographic videos than there are McDonald hamburger stands. More than 800,000 phone calls are made each day to dial-a-porn companies in New York (180,000,000 in 1984), many placed by boys and girls still in elementary school. Furthermore, recent clinical observations by Dr. Victor Cline and others have indicated that a growing number of children are finding their parents' sexually explicit videos and magazines, and are experimenting with what they have learned on younger children. The problem is spreading rapidly. Obviously, obscenity cannot be permitted to flow freely through the veins of society without reaching the eyes and ears of our children. Latchkey kids by the millions are watching porn on Cable TV and reading their parents' adult magazines. For 50 cents, they can purchase their own pornographic tabloids from vendor machines on the street. Or they can hear shocking vulgarities for free on their heavy metal radio stations. At an age when elementary school children should be reading Tom Sawyer and viewing traditional entertainment in the spirit of Walt Disney,

they are learning perverted facts which neither their minds nor bodies are equipped to handle. It is my belief, accordingly, that the behavior of an entire generation of teenagers is being adversely affected by the current emphasis on premarital sexuality and general eroticism seen nightly on television, in the movies, and in the other sources of pornography I have mentioned. It is not surprising that the incidence of unwed pregnancy and abortions has skyrocketed since 1970. Teens are merely doing what they've been taught—that they should get into bed, early and often. And to a large degree, pornography has done this to them.

5. Organized crime controls more than 85 percent of all commercially produced pornography in America. The sale and distribution of these materials produces huge profits for the crime lords who also sell illegal drugs to our kids and engage in murder, fraud, bribery and every vice known to man. Are we to conclude that the 7 billion (or more) tax-free dollars that they receive each year from the pornography industry is not harmful to society? Is malignant melanoma harmful to the human body?

6. Pornography is often used by pedophiles to soften children's defenses against sexual exploitation. They are shown nude pictures of adults, for example, and are told, "See. This is what mommies and daddies do." They are then stripped of innocence and subjected to brutalities that they will remember for a lifetime.

7. Outlets for obscenity are magnets for sex related crimes. When a thriving adult bookstore moves into a neighborhood, an array of "support-services" typically develops around it. Prostitution, narcotics and street crime proliferate. From this perspective, it is interesting that law enforcement officials often claim they do not investigate or attempt to control the flow of obscenity because they lack the resources to combat it. In reality, their resources will extend farther if they first enforce the laws relating to pornography. The consequent reduction in crime makes this a cost-effective use of taxpayers' funds.

The City of Cincinnati, Ohio has demonstrated how a community can rid itself of obscenity without inordinate expenditures of personnel and money.

8. So-called adult bookstores are often centers of disease and homosexual activity. Again, the average citizen is not aware that the primary source of revenue in adult bookstores is derived from video and film booths. Patrons enter these 3 by 3 foot cubicles and deposit a coin in the slot. They are then treated to about 90 seconds of a pornographic movie. If they want to see more, they must continue to pump coins (usually quarters) in the machine. The booths I witnessed on New York's Times Square were even more graphic. Upon depositing the coin, a screen was raised, revealing two or more women and men who performed live sex acts upon one another on a small stage. Everything that is possible for heterosexuals, homosexuals or lesbians to do was demonstrated a few feet from the viewers. The booths from which these videos or live performers are viewed become filthy beyond description as the day progresses. Police investigators testified before our Commission that the stench is unbearable and that the floor becomes sticky with semen, urine and saliva. Holes in the walls between the booths are often provided to permit male homosexuals to service one another. Given the current concern over sexually transmitted diseases and especially Acquired Immune Deficiency Syndrome (AIDS), it is incredible that health departments have not attempted to regulate such businesses. States that will not allow restaurant owners or hairdressers or counselors or acupuncturists to operate without licenses have permitted these wretched cesspools to escape governmental scrutiny. To every public health officer in the country I would ask, "Why?"

9. Finally, pornography is a source of significant harm to the institution of the family and to society at large. Can anything which devastates vulnerable little children, as we have seen, be considered innocuous to the parents who produced them? Raising healthy children is the primary occupation of families, and anything which invades the childhoods and twists the minds of boys and girls must be seen as abhorrent to the

mothers and fathers who gave them birth. Furthermore, what is at stake here is the future of the family itself. We are sexual creatures, and the physical attraction between males and females provides the basis for every dimension of marriage and parenthood. Thus, *anything* that interjects itself into that relationship must be embraced with great caution. Until we *know* that pornography is not addictive and progressive . . . until we are *certain* that the passion of fantasy does not destroy the passion of reality . . . until we are *sure* that obsessive use of obscene materials will not lead to perversions and conflict between husbands and wives . . . then we dare not adorn them with the crown of respectability. Society has an absolute obligation to protect itself from material which crosses the line established objectively by its legislators and court system. That is not sexual repression. That is self-preservation.

If not limited by time and space, I could describe dozens of other harms associated with exposure to pornography. Presumably, members of Congress were also cognizant of these dangers when they drafted legislation to control sexually explicit material. The President and his predecessors would not have signed those bills into criminal laws if they had not agreed. The Supreme Court must have shared the same concerns when it ruled that obscenity is not protected by the First Amendment—reaffirming the validity and constitutionality of current laws. How can it be, then, that these carefully crafted laws are not being enforced? Good question! The refusal of federal and local officials to check the rising tide of obscenity is a disgrace and an outrage. It is said that the production and distribution of pornography is the only unregulated industry remaining today . . . the last vestige of "free enterprise" in America. Indeed, the *salient* finding emerging from 12 months of testimony before our Commission reflected this utter paralysis of government in response to the pornographic plague.

As citizens of a democratic society, we have surrendered our right to protect ourselves in return for protection by the State. Thus, our governmental representatives have a constitutional mandate to shield us from harm and criminal activity . . . including that associated with obscenity. It is time that our leaders

were held accountable for their obvious malfeasance. Attorney General Meese, who has courageously supported other unpopular causes, has been reluctant to tackle this one. He is reportedly awaiting the final report from the Commission before mobilizing the Department of Justice. We will see what happens now. But his predecessors have no such excuse for their dismal record. Under Attorney General William French Smith, there was not a single indictment brought against producers of adult pornography in 1983. None! There were only six in 1982, but four of those were advanced by one motivated prosecutor. In 1981 there were two. Of the 93 United States Attorneys, only seven have devoted any effort to the prosecution of obscenity. Obviously, the multi-billion dollar porn industry is under no serious pressure from federal prosecutors.

Considering this apathy, perhaps it is not surprising that the Department of Justice greeted our Commission with something less than rampant enthusiasm. For example, the first Presidential Commission received two million dollars (in 1967 money) and was granted two years to complete their assignment. Our Commission was allocated only $500,000 (in 1985 money) and was given one year in which to study an industry that had expanded exponentially. Repeated requests for adequate time and funding were summarily denied. Considering the Presidential mandate to establish the Commission, the Department had no choice but to execute the order. But it did very little to guarantee its success or assist with the enormous workload. Quite frankly, failure would have been inevitable were it not for the dedication of eleven determined Commissioners who worked under extreme pressure and without compensation to finish the task. We were also blessed with a marvelous staff and executive director who were committed to the challenge.

Other branches of government must also be held accountable for their unwillingness to enforce the criminal laws. The United States Postal Service makes virtually no effort to prosecute those who send obscene material through the mail. Attorney Paul McGeady testified that there are conservatively 100,000 violations of 18 USC 1461 every day of the year. Likewise, the Federal Communications Commission and Interstate Commerce Commission do not attempt to regulate the interstate transportation of obscene material. Eighty percent of all pornography is produced in Los Angeles County and then shipped to the rest of the country. It would not be difficult to identify and prosecute those who transport it across state lines. The Federal Communications Commission does not regulate obscenity on cable or satellite television. The Customs Service makes no effort to prevent adult pornography from entering this country, and catches only five percent of child porn sent from abroad. The Internal Revenue Service permits organized crime to avoid taxes on the majority of its retail sales, especially the video booth market. The Federal Bureau of Investigation assigns only two of 8700 special agents to obscenity investigation, even though organized crime controls the industry. And on and on it goes.

Local law enforcement agencies are equally unconcerned about obscenity. The City of Miami has assigned only two of 1,500 policemen to this area, neither of which is given a car. Chicago allocates two of 12,000 officers to obscenity control. Los Angeles assigns 8 out of 6,700, even though Los Angeles is the porn capital of the country. Very few indictments have been brought against a pornographer in Los Angeles County in more than ten years, despite the glut of materials produced there. Another serious concern is also directed at the court system and the judges who have winked at pornography. Even when rare convictions have been obtained, the penalties assessed have been pitiful! Producers of illegal materials may earn millions in profit each year, and yet serve no time in prison and pay fines of perhaps $100. One powerful entrepreneur in Miami was convicted on obscentiy charges for the 61st time, yet received a fine of only $1600. The judge in another case refused to even look at child pornography which the defendant had supposedly produced. He said it would prejudice him to examine the material. That judge had never sentenced a single convicted pornographer to

a day in prison. Is there any wonder why America is inundated in sexually explicit material today?

So we come to the bottom line. We've looked at the conditions that have led to the present situation. Now we must consider the mid-course maneuvers that will correct it. I believe the suggestions offered in the Commissioner's final report, herein, will provide an effective guide toward that end. We have not merely attempted to assess the problem; we have offered a proposed resolution. The testimony on which it is based make it clear that we are engaged in a winnable war! America could rid itself of hard core pornography in 18 months if the recommendations offered in the following report are implemented. We have provided a road-map for fine tuning federal and state legislation and for the mobilization of law enforcement efforts around the country. Accordingly, it is my hope that the effort we invested will provide the basis for a new public policy. But that will occur only if American citizens demand action from their government. Nothing short of a public outcry will motivate our slumbering representatives to defend community standards of decency. It is that public statement that the pornographers fear most, and for very good reason. The people possess the power in this wonderful democracy to override apathetic judges, uninterested police chiefs, unmotivated U.S. Attorneys, and unwilling federal officials. I pray that they will do so. If they do not, then we have labored in vain. If wisdom more often than not results from the simultaneous practice of several key virtues—among which must surely be numbered prudence, justice, temperance and fortitude—then the eleven members of the Attorney General's Commission on Pornography were no more likely or qualified than any other group of eleven Americans to undertake the study of this most complex and divisive subject.

STATEMENT OF FATHER BRUCE RITTER

Eleven Solomons we are not!

Eleven Americans, not Solomons therefore, sat down together over the course of a year to listen and to learn, to argue and to debate. At the end we are able to present this modest report of our conclusions to the American

people—a report in which, on most key issues, we were able to achieve virtual or at least substantial unanimity.

We are proud of the result. Or to speak for myself and not the Commission—the purpose of this "personal statement"—I am proud of the result and quite proud that I had this opportunity to serve with my fellow citizens on this Commission.

That we could not agree on all issues is hardly surprising. Indeed that kind of total unanimity is simply not to be found in the real world of a culturally and religiously pluralistic society and it would be dangerously disingenuous to criticize the Commission for memorializing in this Report its differences of perception, of logic, of background, of personal conviction.

At bottom, the creation of this Commission was an inescapably political act—we are, after all, a government body, convened to give advice to the government of the United States, and specifically, to the Justice Department.

More important still, we have been asked to put our eminently fallible judgments at the service of the American people, who are the final arbiters of political power. Our every word, in every hearing and meeting, has been subject to—and has received—rigorous public scrutiny, and may be used and misused in future political debates.

It would be an egregiously self-serving mistake, however, to assume that the work of this Commission was therefore dominated by political considerations. I think it fair to state that we attempted, as best we could, within the short life span of this Commission, to reach our conclusions based on a diligent and serious study of the evidence brought before us.

In the final analysis, however, every thinking adult is a walking-around collection of *a priori* assumptions that influence his thinking on all serious issues. These assumptions, in part the product of education and life experience, in part the rigorous conclusions of reason and logic, are, on balance, the "givens" each of us brings to every debate, to every effort to find the truth of a particular matter. These "givens" are tested, challenged, refined and sometimes repudiated in the elastic give-and-take of serious argument. Eleven Commissioners, perforce, brought such assumptions and convictions to our deliberations. It is my hope that we were able to transcend the limitations necessarily intrinsic to any personal view of the world and human behavior—and for that matter, to transcend the limits of any supposed allegiance to the political and religious ideologies of the Right or Left.

Given the severe time and budgetary constraints under which the Commission la-

bored we were neither able, nor should we have been expected, to treat all aspects of our charge with that degree of thoroughness many readers of this Report might have desired. Nor is it possible within the limits of this necessarily brief personal reflection on the work of the Commission to do more than touch upon those areas of more personal concern or those issues where my decision to vote one way rather than another might require elaboration, *viz.*, the absolutely central debate over Category III materials, the Printed Word controversy, the very thorny issue of the Indecency Standard for cable television—and the hugely controversial and largely shunned as too-hot-to-handle subject of sex education for our children.

The Category III Debate

I think the Commission was quite correct in its general approach to our study of pornography, not only by refusing to establish hasty *a priori* definitions of what pornography is or is not, but also in attempting some delineation and distinction of the various categories of the sexually explicit materials examined by us. The rationale for this approach is, I think, stated quite lucidly and cogently in this Report. That is not to say that other approaches might not have been equally fruitful or to say that there were no serious limitations to this approach. I shall discuss below what I consider the major and perhaps in retrospect, a significantly unacknowledged and even crippling flaw, of this methodology.

Nonetheless, this particular approach greatly facilitated our difficult and time-consuming discussions of the real or potential "harms" ascribed to pornography and the identification of these harms with the various categories of sexually explicit materials. In addition, our chosen approach enabled the Commission to understand better the various kinds of evidence or "proof" needed to draw reasonable conclusions about the kinds of harms "caused" by pornography.

As Commissioners, therefore, based on the evidence presented to us, we had little difficulty reaching the firm conclusion that violent, or even non-violent but degrading pornography represented a significant harm to individuals and to society as a whole and that these two categories of sexually explicit designed-to-arouse materials should be condemned unhesitatingly. The Commission was again unanimous in asserting that to the extent that such materials met the *Miller* standard they should be prosecuted and, if possible, proscribed.

Is there a third category of sexually explicit designed-to-arouse material that is neither violent nor degrading and for which no real harm can be demonstrated that therefore does not merit such condemnation and possible legal proscription under the *Miller* standard? Because the Commissioners became hopelessly deadlocked on this issue it was resolved that each reserve the right to compose a personal statement outlining his or her thinking on the matter.

In my view, and perhaps in that of other Commissioners as well, this is the central theoretical issue of our year's debate. We were not able to resolve this question successfully and for me it represents a major failure of the Commission—not because we were unable to agree on the merits of the issue, or much less, that that other Commissioners did not agree with my own views, but because as a group we were unwilling, or perhaps unable, to confront or to correct or perhaps merely to adjust to the inherent limitations of our approach to the study of pornography.

This inherent and deceptive weakness in our approach—its fatal flaw in my view—also proved to be for us a fatal temptation, permitting the Commission to rely quite heavily—indeed almost exclusively—on evidence of harms drawn from the empirical and social sciences to the virtual exclusion of other kinds of "evidence". While this methodology perhaps proved useful enough when we examined the potential consequences of exposure to Category I and II materials, this over reliance on such evidence did not serve the Commission well in its examination of the allegedly more innocuous materials contained in our so-called Category III.

I say "allegedly more innocuous" because implicitly an assumption began to grow among many Commissioners that sexually explicit materials that were neither violent nor degrading somehow had to be less harmful than materials not obviously so—and indeed, in many important aspects that is quite indisputably true. As a result the focus of our discussions centered more and more, and sometimes almost exclusively, on the harms to be ascribed to sexually violent and degrading materials and the evidence we considered almost exclusively that drawn from the empirical and social sciences—testimony and evidence that in and of itself necessarily lacks

the probative force and authority some, when convenient, wish to ascribe to it.

The weakness of our approach, and one that in my judgment we refused as a body to deal with adequately—and that was the basis for much of the overt and covert disagreement among Commissioners—lay in the easy temptation not to examine the underlying sexual behavior depicted in all classes of pornography and to make fundamental ethical and moral judgments about this behavior.

Pornography is, after all, nothing more than the depiction of certain kinds of human sexual behavior. Quite apart, however, from any depiction in words or in photographs, it is incumbent upon society to make certain ethical and moral judgments about certain kinds of human behavior, not excluding sexual behavior. For example rape is not merely a crime, it is decidedly immoral quite apart from any depiction of it. Sexual behavior that degrades women—or men—is immoral quite apart from the photographic record of it that may exist to memorialize it.

At the heart of our disagreement over the existence, the nature and the extent of Category III materials, in my view, was the inability and quite specific reluctance of the Commission to come to terms with the necessity of making ethical and moral judgments about the underlying behavior depicted in materials that would be contained in Category III materials, e.g., certain sexually explicit solely designed-to-arouse depictions of heterosexual or homosexual behavior, or of group sex that were clearly neither violent nor obviously degrading, in the precise meaning of this term as used in our discussions concerning Category II materials. I think it fair to say that by its refusal to take an ethical or moral position on pre-marital or extra-marital sex, either heterosexual or homosexual, the Commission literally ran for the hills and necessarily postulated the existence of a third category of sexual materials designed to arouse that was neither violent nor degrading, and, that was in some vague and unspecified sense, permissable to some extent—even though much of it would have been judged obscene under the *Miller* standard.

A much larger issue is at stake here than the individual harm or degradation of a particular man or woman, or even of society itself caused by materials commonly and confidently ascribed to Categories I and II. The question may be posed: does pornography, of any category, so degrade the very nature of human sexuality itself, its purposes, its beauty, and so distort its meaning that society itself suffers a grave harm?

The message of pornography is unmistakably and undeniably clear: sex bears no relationship to love and commitment, to fidelity in marriage, that sex has nothing to do with privacy and modesty and any necessary and essential ordering toward procreation. The powerful and provocative images proclaim universally—and most of all to the youth of our country—that pleasure—not love and commitment—is what sex is all about. What is more, that message is proclaimed by powerfully self-validating images, that carry within themselves their own pragmatic self-justification.

To pose the question in another way: is the imaging, the message-conveying power of sexually explicit, designed-to-arouse pornography so great that society must be concerned when that perniciously convincing message becomes well nigh universal among us? I think the answer to that question must be an unequivocal resounding yes!

Speaking for myself, and representing a view that perhaps could not carry the majority of the Commission, I would affirm that all sexually explicit material solely designed to arouse in and of itself degrades the very nature of human sexuality and as such represents a grave harm to society and ultimately to the individuals that comprise society. I find it very difficult therefore to affirm the existence of a third category of pornography that is neither violent nor degrading and not harmful.

To a certain but limited extent I have outlined my convictions further in two documents submitted to this Commission that can be found immediately following this statement. The first, entitled: Nonviolent, Sexually Explicit Materials and Sexual Violence, purports to show how an argument might be drawn from social science itself that the widespread consumption of sexually explicit materials found in universally disseminated male magazines may well lead inevitably to increased rape rates. I think my conclusions, although I am no social scientist, while certainly not apodictic, are at the very least plausible.

The second, entitled: Pornography and Privacy, attempts to make a strong argument against all pornography based on its (pornography's) total and inadmissable invasion of a personal privacy so sacred and so inalienable that it must always remain inviolate. There are, in sum, certain rights so intrinsic, so foundational to the integrity of the human personality and our duties as citizens that they may never be surrendered. One of them is our personal liberty. Another is our sexual privacy.

For these reasons, and for others, I have concluded that for all practical purposes Category III does not exist, viz., that sexually explicit materials designed to arouse that are neither violent nor degrading per se, nonetheless profoundly indignify the very state of marriage and degrade the very notion of sexuality itself and are therefore seriously harmful to individuals and to society, indignifying both performers and viewers alike in ways ethically and morally reprehensible.

If in fact such a category does exist, then I am persuaded that it is so limited as to be totally inconsequential and certainly not represented by the sexually explicit materials studied by this Commission.

To conclude otherwsie, I fear, is to legitimate the existence of a group of materials that some would call "erotica" and would in effect license as permissible and presumably non-prosecutable, a large class of sexually explicit materials designed to arouse that would all too easily send the clear message that the primary purpose of sex is for hedonistic, selfishly solipsistic satisfaction.

To me, the greatest harm of pornography is not that some people are susceptible to or even directly harmed by the violent and degrading and radically misleading images portrayed all too graphically by mainstream pornography. Rather pornography's greatest harm is caused by its ability—and its intention—to attack the very dignity and sacredness of sex itself, reducing human sexual behavior to the level of its animal components.

In a certain sense the Commission was hoisted by its own petard. In its need to describe carefully and to delineate accurately the possible harms of pornography it adopted an approach and methodology and a system of proof quite suitable to establish the—if I may say—the self-evident, the per se nota, harms of violent and degrading pornography. When all is said and done, do the careful conclusions of the Commission with regard to violent and degrading pornography surprise anyone, or does any rational man or woman seriously question the legitimacy of these conclusions—quite apart from any "evidence" thought to establish such harms? The fact is that the Emperor doesn't have any clothes on and he—as far as violent and degrading pornography is concerned—never did and it didn't need four national Commissions (two American, one Canadian, and one British) to "prove" it.

The fatal weakness—fatal because largely unacknowledged—of our approach, however, betrayed and undercut and sadly misdirected the Commission's efforts and prevented us from, in my view, considering adequately the more profound harms to individuals and society caused by pornography as a total genre. The unmistakable consequence for the Commission, in my judgment, was to ascribe more harm to the less harmful and to discount substantially and even to discredit the far graver and more pervasive harms caused by pornography not evidently violent or obviously degrading.

To put it in another way: the greatest harm of pornography does not lie in its links to sexual violence or even its ability to degrade and to indignify individuals. Pornography, all three categories of it—if indeed a third category exists at all—degrades sex itself and dehumanizes and debases a profoundly important, profoundly beautiful and profoundly, at its core, sacred relationship between a man and a woman who seek in sexual union not the mere satisfaction of erotic desire but the deepest sharing of their mutual and committed and faithful love.

This being said, however, I hope no one will dispute the fact that while we did not succeed in resolving the major theoretical dispute before us, the approach and methodology adopted by the Commission did enable us to deal successfuly with matters of great practical importance and concern to the American people.

The "Printed Word" Debate

One of the most difficult and controversial issues that sharply divided the Commission was the special nature and especially protected character of the printed word. Simply put, the issue was this: does the printed word—including printed and non-pictorial pornography—deserve special consideration because of the unique relevance the printed word bears for First Amendment considerations and the precious right of political dissent in the United States, the almost exclusive burden of which is carried by the printed and spoken word?

I voted with the bare majority on this issue, upholding the special preeminence of the printed word and holding that, despite the fact that printed pornography can be declared legally obscene under the *Miller* standard, printed depictions merit special protection unless they involve the degradation and abuse of children.

Because my vote in particular seemed somewhat out of character in light of other government intervention with which I agree, and because it was virtually incomprehensible to some thoughtful people on the Commission and elsewhere, I take this opportunity to at least put on the public record the rationale for my vote.

It was abundantly clear from our discussions that virtually no current prosecution, on grounds of obscenity, of the printed word occur in the United States, and that furthermore, none are realistically contemplated because of the great difficulty and complexity of these prosecutions. Indeed, the Chairman of this Commission, Henry Hudson, conceded on the record that he could not conceive of ever undertaking a prosecution of the printed word.

The problem is of course that among this genre of printed pornography there exists a large body of materials that describe the sexual abuse of children and indeed, advocate for it. It is a particularly noisome and repellent body of literature that in effect is nothing less than "cook book" and how-to-do-it manuals, guides for the sexual exploitation of children.

I expressed to the Commission my strong conviction that unless these particular printed materials involving children were singled out for special and vigorous prosecution—excerpted as it were from the broad mass of printed pornography—the general reluctance to ever prosecute the printed word would prevent any attempt to proscribe these maleficent materials. It is my further conviction that the unanimous action of the Commission recommending the vigorous prosecution of obscene printed materials involving or advocating the sexual exploitation of children will, in fact, spur and aid prosecutors in the vigorous enforcement of the obscenity law, at least in regard to those materials depicting children. The hope of a total prosecution of obscene printed materials is disingenuous and futile—the crying need to prosecute to the full extent of the law those materials depicting the prurient sexual abuse of children is an urgent necessity.

A second reason led me to vote that special consideration be accorded the printed word. Fear of censorship was a constant theme of many witnesses who appeared before this Commission. I do not think we are entitled to judge that concern lightly, or to consider that those who express such anxiety are motivated by self interest. First Amendment values are crucial to American life and the virtual sanctity and integrity of the printed word central to the absolute freedom of political debate and dissent.

I do not agree with those who hold that efforts to regulate and proscribe sexually explicit materials according to the *Miller* standard signal a return to or adoption of a censorship mentality. In short I think that those possessed by such fears, while for them the fear may seem real, are quite simply wrong.

At the same time I thought it very important that the Commission send a strong message to the public that we do not favor a return to times when the repression of unpopular ideas was part of our political landscape. By the barest of margins, the majority of Commissioners adopted this view. I am proud to be among them.

The Indecency Standard

This was another issue that sharply divided the Commission and one that only eleven Solomons could have reached consensus on. Once again I voted with the bare majority and would like to put on record my reasons for so doing.

The issue was, once again, central to the charge of this Commission and could be framed this way: millions of American families are concerned about the virtual invasion of their homes by increasing amounts of increasingly explicit sexual depictions they find offensive and even dangerous to their families, most especially to their children.

The issue is fairly simple and straightforward for broadcast, noncable television. The FCC under its broad powers to regulate what can be transmitted over the air waves prohibits the dissemination of "indecent" words and images. The Supreme Court upheld this right in its *Pacifica* decision on the ground that citizens had a right to expect some regulation of broadcast materials com-

ing into the home over which individual parents had no control.

The matter is not so simple with regard to cable television and other forms of satellite-transmitted programming. At least four court decisions, one of them in federal appeals court, have clearly established the essential diversity of broadcast and cable television and decreed that the "indecency" standard used to regulate broadcast materials could not and must not apply to cable television. In fact, the courts have so far declared, unanimously, that the application of the indecency standard to cable television is unconstitutional.

The issue is complex, not only by reason of the constitutional ambiguities that surround it, but also because, from a broader perspective, citizens have a right to be concerned about who and what are going to regulate what they may see on cable television.

Many witnesses who appeared before this Commission, for example, have pointed out, that if the "indecency" standard currently in force with regard to broadcast television were also imposed on cable television, most of the mainline Hollywood films currently on view in theaters across the country could not be shown on home television served by cable. It is hardly likely, even inconceivable, that the courts on any level, including the Supreme Court, would uphold such an extension of the indecency standard to cable television.

Indeed it is just as unlikely, regardless of an individual's particular ethical or moral persuasion, that such a blanket prohibition would be tolerated by the vast majority of the American people or the Congress that represents them.

There is still another compelling reason why many thoughtful people in this country would actively oppose any attempt to apply the same standards of broadcasting television to cable. Indeed, almost all of the principal religious denominations and religious broadcasters unanimously fought such an equation of broadcast and cable television on the grounds that it might seriously impede their own religious freedom to control their programming as they saw fit and might compel them to grant equal time to atheist or agnostic or anti-religious presentations.

Whatever one thinks of their argument, no one could plausibly accuse these religious leaders of not being sensitive to the import of their position or that they thereby were in favor of indecency on television. The fact is, however, that unless we equate broadcast and cable television, the FCC has no constitutional right to regulate programming on cable using the indecency standard upheld by the *Pacifica* decision.

For all these reasons therefore, and for others, I voted with the bare majority not to recommend the current indecency standards for cable television.

I would strongly support, however, new legislation by Congress that could thread its way successfully through the Scylla of unconstitutionality and the Charybdis of over regulation of this medium by government.

It seems to me that Congress should look to the principles of *New York v. Ginsberg*—which allowed lower obscenity standards to apply if children are recipients of pornography—as a beginning toward unraveling this conundrum. *Ginsberg* allows the government to declare some pornographic material "obscene as to children" and to make its sale to children a criminal act. Is it not possible then, that certain material may be judged "obscene as to the home"—that is, judged by a standard that takes into account the special problems of parents in preventing access by their children to cable television or the telephone, and so be subjected to special regulation when it appears in those settings?

I am certain that all the Commissioners, regardless of how they voted on this narrow issue, deplore the increasing appearance on our home television screens, whether broadcast or cable, of sexually explicit and frequently violent and degrading materials. We differ only on how to achieve the laudable end of protecting our children from this unwanted and dangerous incursion into the sanctity of our families.

Sex Education for Our Children

Few problems have produced more genuine concern among more Americans than the sexual awareness, behavior, and victimization of children. Few, if any, dispute the need of children for knowledge about their sexual natures—its dangers and its promise, its mystery and its power. Yet few areas of public discussion have engendered more bitter, if often legitimate, debate over the means appropriate to achieving a desired end.

This Commission found itself in the middle of that debate, not out of choice but of necessity. We have seen and heard massive quantities of evidence concerning the abuse and exploitation of children by adults, both in the making and in the consumption of sexually explicit material. We have learned, as well, of the extraordinary extent to which sexually explicit magazines, films, video tapes, telephone recordings, and books are a part of the life of our country's children and adolescents. It has become increasingly clear to us that many children who escape actual sexual abuse are nevertheless receiving their primary education in human sexuality from a graphically inappropriate source, one which describes sexual fulfillment as conditioned upon transience, dominance, aggression or degradation.

We have seen, too, that in a society flooded with sexual imagery it is virtually impossible fully to "protect" children from becoming victims of misleading information about sex. Nor is it possible to expect that criminal and civil sanctions, however vigorously applied, will wholly end sexual abuse. Teenagers, and to a great extent even younger children, must learn to protect themselves—both from exploitation by others and from the consequences of their own ignorance and immaturity.

At the same time, however, they deserve an understanding of the beauty of sexuality, and its role as the foundation of family and indeed of human civilization itself. While our charge is limited to examining the nature and effects of pornography, we would be remiss if we failed to note our passionate desire for careful, humane, and explicit instruction of children regarding the nature and effects of sexuality itself.

Unfortunately that desire only leads us directly to a central dilemma of our nation's pluralistic democracy. The very importance of sexuality makes it a central focus of almost every system of religious and ethical values. Teaching children about sex inevitably involves instruction about its relationship with morality and human relationships. Any attempt to evade such instruction or underlying values only results in teaching one specific moral assumption—that no relationship exists between sex and morality. Presenting instruction on sex combined with discussion of the full array of opinions discussed would largely dilute the importance of all of them. While these problems could be wholly avoided if full instruction on sexuality were provided to children by their parents, it is a sad fact that many, if not most, parents ignore or fail seriously in this responsibility.

This dilemma is unfortunate in part because I think we all believe that there is a core group of values which can and should form the basis of instruction on sexuality. Above all, it seems to me we could agree that such instruction should be presented as one important, but not dominant, part of instruction on the family—its history, nature, and importance. The most important institution in human society, the family, is virtually ignored in modern education. That failing is particularly tragic because it is only within the context of exploring the meaning of the family that the meaning and role of sexuality can be understood.

The particular values that almost all of us think it important to emphasize in "sex education"—responsibility, commitment, fidelity, understanding, and tenderness—are precisely those which underlie our society's legal, social and moral assumptions about the family, and can only be effectively conveyed if the two topics are inextricably linked.

If a belief in the necessity of teaching those values with respect to sexuality were in fact shared by all Americans, it would be possible, I think, to devise a mandatory curriculum on human sexuality in the elementary and secondary public schools. Because it seems clear that no such consensus exists I have been forced, in thinking on this subject, to consider only the appropriate minimum action which is necessary and possible for federal, state, and local governments to take. As mandatory, explicitly value-laden age appropriate education in affective sexuality seems at present a task beyond the capacity of public schools, we can only center our hopes for providing such education on the willingness of families to undertake it. Within a voluntary framework, however, perhaps even within a released time context, we can urge the public schools to provide extensive opportunities for students to explore all the issues surrounding the creation and maintenance of families in the United States, with instruction on sexuality forming a substantial part of such a curriculum.

Finally, where children and youth need to learn how to protect themselves from exploitation by adults or manipulation by the media, we can ask the schools to take a strong, mandatory role in providing them the facts.

If this year confronting the products of the pornography industry has taught me anything, it is that we are all profoundly ignorant of the way electronic and photographic images can be used to manipulate viewers. We continue, quite rightly, to insist that our children learn how our novelists and poets use language to shape and redirect emotions and values. Yet with regard to powerful graphic visual images designed to produce handsome profits through sexual arousal of viewers, we have allowed our schools to remain almost completely silent. Teenagers should be taught not only how their emotions and instincts are manipulated by viewing pornography, but also how the pornography industry exploits and abuses the persons used in making it. Such instruction would present none of the religious or moral quandaries of sex education generally, and seems to me a vital protective measure for our young—who are simultaneously the biggest consumers of pornography and the most vulnerable to its vicious effects.

A Priest on the Commission

A decent respect for the wholly creditable, almost entirely unspoken but perhaps genuine anxiety felt by some that my role as priest, my training and background as Roman Catholic theologian might somehow unfairly or unconsciously skew my thoughts and feelings on the issues before the Commission compels this word of assurance.

I do not think that I was invited to join this Commission because I was a priest theologian but rather because of almost 18 years of close personal experience and professional involvement with literally thousands of sexually exploited children, many but not most of whom had been victimized in the actual production of pornography in which they were the hapless performers and "stars."

For this reason I asked a member of my staff, Gregory Loken, a gifted attorney and scholar in his own right as well as a noted advocate for the rights of children and Director of the Youth Advocacy Institute of Covenant House, to make a special study of the question regarding harms to performers in pornography. The Commission has made this statement its own and I consider it an important and original contribution to the research in this field. It is found in Part Four of the Report.

I freely admit to a certain bias in this regard. Nothing, absolutely nothing justifies the sexual abuse of children, and nothing, absolutely nothing—including the most perfervid defense of the First Amendment justifies the recording of this loathsome abuse on film. The Supreme Court of the United States in its unanimous 9—0 *Ferber* decision affirmed this special horror and declared that child pornography did not merit constitutional protection.

But when all is said and done I am who I am. I cannot exit from my personal skin, I can-not divest of myself, any more than any other citizen, of that "walking around collections of a *priori* assumptions" that in part help constitute who and what I am.

I am certain that despite some unfair prior assumptions to the contrary the Commission tried as fairly and honestly and objectively as it could to reach their conclusions as a result of honest and open debate. My position on the Commission carried for me an added important symbolic responsibility. Since I was the only member of the Commission that could be ever thought to "represent" a major religion in the United States, I felt a special obligation to my fellow Commissioners and the people of this country not to adopt or impose a particular theological or sectarian slant on my contribution to the work of this Commission.

In short, I tried not to react as a Roman Catholic priest but as a citizen with a broader mandate and constituency. I hope therefore that my views represent a wide spectrum of the current American experience. At the same time I am proud to be what I am and would have it no other way.

The Writing of this Document

The difficulties and complexities of this subject could hardly be exaggerated. One man's nudity is another man's erotica is another man's soft core pornography is another man's hard core obscenity is another man's boredom!

When, at the end of our public sessions it came time to synthesize the import of our debates and discussions in this report it became abundantly clear to the great majority of Commissioners that this report could not be a "staff document"—that is, a document compiled and assembled by the staff of this Commission could not represent fairly the differing opinions and conclusions of the Commissioners. This is not to denigrate the

enormous contribution of the Commission staff. They merit the highest praise, especially its Director Alan Sears, for their round-the-clock effort to provide the Commission with the materials and support they needed. The staff worked with great diligence and zeal to perform their duties and much of this final report is a product of that diligence.

In the final analysis however, this report could neither be compiled nor assembled. It demanded single authorship. Quite simply this report could not have been written by Committee.

Professor Fred Schauer provided to this Commission the grace of single authorship and it is largely due to his wholly admirable effort in providing the "framing document" for this report that, in my view, we can present to the Attorney General and the American people a product of which I think we can all be proud.

Conclusion

The Chairman of this Commission deserves the gratitude of every member of this body. His was an unenviable and awesome task—to oversee the taking of public testimony and to guide the public debate over the issues with fairness and objectivity. I think Henry Hudson acquitted himself of this responsibility in a wholly admirable way.

His unfailing courtesy to the members of this Commission and its staff was particularly noteworthy, especially when too many late-night sessions over-stressed us all.

To the other Commissioners I can only say thank you. It has been a privilege and rare honor to have served with them. I hope they share with me that pride of accomplishment as we submit this report to the American people for judgment.

I speak for myself yet I am certain the other ten Commissioners would echo my concern over the well nigh universal eroticization of American society. I am convinced, too, that the vast majority of Americans either intuitively or by rational conviction share our concern.

I urge therefore that our fellow Americans examine and debate our logic and conclusions carefully.

PORNOGRAPHY AND PRIVACY

Submitted by: Father Bruce Ritter

> An American has no sense of privacy. He
> does not know what it means. There is no
> such thing in the country.
> —George Bernard Shaw

If there is one single lesson we have learned from studying the "problem of pornography," it may simply be that Mr. Shaw's acid observations on American privacy may finally be coming true. Commercially produced material, regularly distributed to millions of Americans, shows other Americans, in explicit photographic detail, engaged in every variety of sexual intercourse. What might have been considered at one time the most private of human activities is now a matter not simply for public discussion but for graphic public display.

We have not fully agreed among ourselves whether this aspect of "pornography"—one which cuts across all the categories we have used in discussing other issues—should be deemed a "harm." Some of us have viewed the end of the taboo on public sex as at least an ambivalent event, with its possible benefits including an end to ignorant repression of knowledge and dialogue about sexuality. For the rest of us, however, the issue is a clear one, and, with limited exceptions explained below, we consider the assault of pornography on sexual privacy to be one of its most direct and corrosive harms. Because that view has not often been articulated in the debate over sexually explicit materials, however, we feel bound to explain it fully.

That explanation must begin by acknowledging that a concern for "sexual privacy" does not arise in every type of material considered "pornographic." That it arises at all is the result, as we attempt to explain, of deep cultural, moral, and even biological norms that are generally taken for granted, but not generally discussed. Finally the extent to which those norms represent values important to America and Americans—and the extent to which sexually explicit material offends those values—is a matter we believe deserving of substantial consideration by scholars, legislators, and the general public.

The Material in Question. That the debate over "pornography" has traditionally been carried on with only limited reference to questions of privacy is hardly surprising. Not until the last fifteen years—that is, *after* the 1970 Commission Report—did substantial quantities of material appear on the general market which depict full, highly provocative genital nudity and actual (rather than simulated) sexual intercourse. Many of the great "obscenity" debates of this century—on, for example, *Lady Chatterly's Lover* and *Tropic of Cancer*—in fact centered solely on the printed word.

Simulated activity, *drawings* of sexual conduct, and the printed word may cause concern on other grounds but they are largely tangential to discussion of sexual privacy. It is true, as Warren and Brandeis so eloquently explained almost a century ago, that grave damage may be done when "to satisfy a prurient taste the details of sexual relations are spread broadcast in the columns of the daily papers."[1] Nevertheless it is also true that the process of such "broadcast" is a largely indirect one: for damage to occur the writer must be regarded as credible and the reader must exercise his imagination. Photographic representations as we explained in discussing the role of performers in modern commercial pornography, can show actual sexual relations in such a way that those who are shown cannot deny what happened, and those who view the depictions cannot avoid the full force of the images presented.

We thus limit our discussion of "pornography" in this section to that specific form of it which seems to have most urgent and clear-cut effects on sexual privacy—that is, photographic (or live) portrayals of *actual* sexual intercourse or of full genital nudity designed *solely* to excite sexual arousal.[2] The direct,

---

1. Warren & Brandeis, *The Right to Privacy*, 4 Harv. L. Rev. 193 (1890).
2. Thus not only "mere" nudity, but any form of nudity which is used for purposes—artistic, scientific, political, or educational—other than simple sexual provocation are outside the scope of our analysis. We do not deny that privacy concerns may be implicated even in these displays, see, *New York v. Ferber*, 458 U.S., pp. 747, 774–75 (O'Connor, J., concurring), but we do not believe the evidence suggests they represent nearly as substantial a threat to sexual privacy as the material we include.

unmediated public display of human beings in graphic sexual conduct is a new phenomenon in the history of culture, and it represents, in our view, a development harmful to both individuals and society at large.

Anthropological Perspective. While acutely aware of the limitations of anthropological evidence for arguing "what ought to be" for modern industrial society, we think it at least worth nothing two propositions which are widely accepted by anthropologists and which seem of real importance for our inquiry: (1) public display of genitalia is extremely rare among human cultures; and (2) sexual intercourse universally occurs under conditions of privacy. Both have relevance as indicating basic taboos which are more often explained in moral or religious terms.

Genital Nudity. In their still standard overview of 191 human cultures, Ford and Beach found that, "There are no peoples in our sample who generally allow women to expose their genitals under any but the most restricted of circumstances."[3]

In those few societies where women occasionally expose their genitals—e.g., the Lesu, Dahomeans and Kurtatchi—it is a deliberate gesture to invite sexual advance.[4] Conversely the social controls imposed by primitive, semi-primitive and advanced cultures appear to be founded in "the prevention of accidental exposure under conditions that might provoke sexual advances by men."[5] A number of societies, however, place no restrictions on display of male genitals, and in a few nudity in both sexes is accepted.[6] Even in those few which allow such nudity—e.g., the Australian aborigines—strict rules forbid staring at genitals.[7] It is therefore possible to say, in the words of one anthropologist, that "some form of sexual modesty is observed in all societies."[8] That modesty distinguishes humans from all other primates.[9]

Sexual Intercourse. If the privacy of genitalia is the subject of limited variation among cultures, the privacy of sexual intercourse is not. Every human culture is characterized by an insistence on seclusion for sexual union, although physical conditions may make absolute privacy difficult to achieve.[10] Thus when more than one family shares a dwelling, couples will generally copulate in a secluded place outdoors.[11] Children are strictly admonished to ignore their parents' sexual behavior where it is possible they might see it.[12] Among humans, according to one scholar, "sexual privacy, like the incest taboos, is virtually pancultural."[13] Only chimpanzees among all animals have the same absolute regime of sexual privacy—a fact suggesting that this impulse is biological in nature.[14]

Margaret Mead's famous study of Samoan culture—widely regarded as a plea for more sexual openness—provides powerful evidence for the extraordinary impulse toward sexual privacy even in a society with sexual practices far different than our own. There she found married couples sharing large rooms, but careful to preserve some sense of privacy even within the house by means of "purely formal walls" of mosquito netting.[15] *Outside* the house the urge to privacy is extraordinary, as she discussed in describing the sexual knowledge of Samoan children:

> In matters of sex the ten-year-olds are equally sophisticated, although they witness sex activities only surreptitiously, since all expressions of affection are rigorously barred in public. . . . The only sort of demonstration which ever occurs in public is of the horseplay variety between young people whose affections are not really involved. This romping is particularly prevalent in groups of women, often taking the form of playfully snatching at the sex organs.[16]

---

3. C. Ford and F. Beach, *Patterns of Sexual Behavior,* p. 94 (1952), p. 945; W. Davenport, *Sex in Cross Cultural Perspective* in *Human Sexuality in Form Perspective,* pp. 115, 127–129 (F. Beach, ed. 1976).

4. Ford and Beach, pp. 93–94.

5. *Id.* p. 94.

6. *Id.* p. 95.

7. Davenport, *supra* note 1, p. 128.

8. *Id. See also* A. Kinsey, *et al., Sexual Behavior in the Human Female,* (1953), pp. 283–285 (finding anthropological data showing acceptance of nudity only of children before adolescence).

9. Ford and Beach, *supra* note 1, pp. 95, 105.

10. Davenport, *supra* note 1, p. 148; Ford and Beach, *supra* note 1, pp. 68–71. Ford and Beach do list two partial exceptions to this rule—"some Formosan natives" who in the summertime "copulate out of doors and in public, provided there are no children around," and "Yapese couples" who, "though generally alone when they engage in intercourse, copulate almost anywhere out of doors and do not appear to mind the presence of other individuals." *Id.* at 68. Neither of these exceptions, on close inspection, applies to more than "some" members of what amounts to 1 percent of Ford and Beach's sample of 191 cultures.

11. Davenport, p. 150. Ford and Beach pp. 69–71.

12. Davenport, pp. 149–150.

13. G. Jensen, *Human Sexual Behavior in Primate Perspective* in *Contemporary Sexual Behavior: Critical Issues in the 1970's,* (1973), pp. 17, 22. *Accord,* D. Symms, *The Evolution of Human Sexuality* 67 (1979).

14. Jensen, *supra* note 12, p. 67; Symms, *supra* note 12, p. 67, n. 4.

15. *Coming of Age in Samoa,* p. 135 (1928, 1961 ed.).

16. *Id.* pp. 134–35.

Even in a culture she found to be so free of "stress and strain,"[17] the pancultural norms of sexual privacy were strictly observed.

Western and American Traditions. Margaret Mead's disdain for the "Puritanical self-accusations" which characterize Western attitudes toward sexual freedom did not extend to the insistence of our culture on the private nature of sexual conduct. And indeed, any such disdain would be impossible for an anthropologist, for sexual privacy is at the very heart of our own culture—assumed in every major strand of Western thought, and incorporated now in American common and constitutional law. So clear, indeed, is the strength of the traditional belief in sexual privacy, that we view only a brief discussion as necessary. The historical pedigree of that belief is traceable at least to the customs of the ancient world. One historian has found that for ancient Jews nudity was "barbaric and indecent," and that "in Biblical times, it seems, the Hebrews did not come in contact with tribes that were *not* sensitive to the shame of nakedness."[18] In the ancient Hellenic world "nakedness was a vulgarity" that was publicly permitted only in such specialized settings as the gymnasium.[19] Indeed, Plato went so far as to urge shame and *complete secrecy* in all matters related to sexual liaisons.[20] And even the most graphic Greek paintings of sexual conduct used "formula" faces that were not meant to reproduce the features of specific persons.[21] Exposing the naked body of another person, in the ancient world, was a means of humiliation reserved for slaves and war captives.[22]

Developments in Western culture from its Judaic and Hellenic roots until only very recently were all in the direction of *strengthening* the already strict taboos of sexual privacy. Subsequent Western attitudes toward the subject were perhaps best summarized by St. Augustine, himself no stranger to sexual excess, even before the fall of Rome:

> And rather will a man endure a crowd of witnesses when he is unjustly venting his anger on someone than the eye of one man when he innocently copulates with his wife.[23]

Social conditions—in particular, housing consisting of one room for an entire family—even through the early modern and industrial periods of Western history made it difficult to maintain absolute sexual privacy in the home, particularly in the presence of family members.[24] But the first impulse of every class as it obtained the power to do so has been to obtain more personal privacy, particularly in respect to sexual matters.[25] By the beginning of this century sexual privacy had assumed so important a role in Western thought that Freud could suggest, with some force, that the awakening of sexual modesty was a crucial event in the founding of human civilization itself.[26]

Whatever its relation to civilization generally, privacy in sexual matters has long been a deeply ingrained part of American culture. From the often strict religious repression of the colonial period[27] through the more freewheeling nineteenth century,[28] sexual modesty was highly esteemed. Mark Twain and Henry James would have disputed the value of almost every social restriction of late Victorian society; on the need for sexual reticence, however, they stood shoulder to shoulder.[29]

---

17. *Id.* pp. 234.

18. L.M. Epstein, *Sex Laws and Customs in Judaism*, (1948), pp. 26–27 (emphasis added).

19. *Id.*, p. 27. Romans did allow men and women to bathe together in the nude, *id.*, p. 29.

20. Plato *Laws*, p. 841 a-e.

21. A. J. Dover, *Greek Homosexuality* (1978), p. 71.

22. Epstein, *supra* note 19, at 31. "The male slave and the female slave had no sex personalities in the eyes of the ancients. They were considered as having no shame and incapable of causing the sense of shame in others." *Id.*, p. 29.

23. *City of God*, Book XIV, p. 468 (M. Dods trans. 1950). See J. Boswell, *Christianity, Social Tolerance and Homosexuality*, p. 188 (1980) (discussing monastic proscriptions against nudity); Jewish traditions proscribing nudity continues well into this century. Epstein, *supra* note 19, pp. 29–37 (noting reluctance even in twentieth century to approve modern bathing suits for women).

24. P. Aries, *Centuries of Childhood*, p. 106 (1962) (children in ancient regime believed to be wholly "unaware of or indifferent to sex"; "gestures and physical contacts . . . freely and publicly allowed [to children] . . . were forbidden as soon as the child reached the age of puberty").

25. Stone, *supra* note 25, p. 253–257.

26. *Civilization and Its Discontents*, (J. Strachey ed 1961), p. 46 n 1. .

27. For a full discussion of the "essential" quality of sexual privacy in the colonial period, *see* D. Flaherty, *Privacy in Colonial New England*, (1972) p. 79–84. *See also* F. Henriques, *Prostitution in Europe and the Americas*, (1965) pp. 230–45 .

28. *See generally, Note: The Right to Privacy in Nineteenth Century America* 94 Narv. L. Rev. 1892 (1981). The great exception to the America's Victorian sense of sexual shame was the cavalier treatment of slaves' privacy in the Old South. F. Henriques, *supra* note 27, pp. 245–63. That exception is in line with long established notions about the unimportance of sexual privacy for slaves. *See, supra* note 22.

29. *Compare*, for example, the treatment of sexual tension in *Tom Sawyer* with that of *Washington Square*. *See also, The Secret Life I* and *The Secret Life II* in S. Marcus, *The Other Victorians* (1964) (describing as "unique" a memoir describing in detail the sex life of a Victorian gentleman).

The Law. That commitment has firm, if only recently developed, expression in American law. After the Warren and Brandeis article of 1890[36]—which was provoked by the outrage of a Boston matriarch over the smarmy treatment by the newspapers of her daughter's wedding[37]—the right of Americans to be free from publicity about the graphic details of their sex lives became enshrined as a fundamental principle of the common law.[38] As we discussed in our review of the use of performers in pornography, the courts have recently recognized that this principle may be applied to protect those who are photographed while nude or engaged in sexual relations.[39] The Supreme Court, in *New York v. Ferber,* seemed recently to imply that the "privacy interests" of those depicted in pornography may have, as well, constitutional weight even on the strongly-tipped scales of First Amendment analysis.[40] The special importance of sexual relations has for more than two decades been crucial to the development by the Court of the whole concept of a constitutional "right of privacy."[41]

Pornography and the Harm to Privacy. Simply stating what is does not resolve what ought to be. Finding that sexual privacy is pancultural, that it has been a stable feature of western civilization for as long as we have knowledge, and that it currently remains highly valued by Americans in their attitudes, practices and laws, does not ineluctably require a finding that the taboo of sexual privacy ought to *continue* to be held in such high esteem. But we think that these findings, while not constituting a form of "proof" themselves, are nevertheless crucial in assessing where the *burden* of proof ought to rest. In all fairness, we believe, it should rest on those seeking to sweep away the taboo.[42] Does current, photographic pornography offend that taboo? And if so, what is the harm? The answer to the first question is obvious to anyone who views the wholly graphic, undiluted sexual exhibitionism inherent even to "consenting pornography." Nothing is left for the viewer to imagine; no attempt is made to conceal either the face or the genitals of the performers. The consumer of "standard" pornography in the 1980's, unlike the consumers of the materials generally available at the time of the 1970 Commission Report, is a full witness to the most intimate, the most private activity of another human being.

That this is a "harm" we think undisputable, on several grounds. First, those who "perform" in current pornography are, as a group, extremely young, ignorant, confused and exploited; as we have discussed in our examination of their situations, they very frequently cannot be said to have given an informed consent to their use. Second, even when such consent exists, such performances, where they are given in exchange for money, are inseparable from prostitution, and degrade the performers in exactly the same ways as prostitutes are injured by their profession. Neither of these concerns applies, by contrast, to the making of noncommercial, sexually explicit films for use in education or sex therapy—arenas where the reputations of performers are unlikely to be damaged.

Quite apart from injury to performers, though, we believe that injury occurs to society as a whole from such performances, injury that may best be described as the blurring of legitimate boundaries for public dialogue on sexuality. Where no reticence is allowed, where only the act of sex is regarded as an authentic statement about its meaning, most citizens can be expected to withdraw, rather than enter the discussion. Reducing the general sense that some aspects of every person's sexual life are so unique as to deserve special deference means, we think, that many will all the more militantly seek to shut out any dialogue on sexuality altogether. The virulent, devastating divisiveness over sex education in the public schools is, we think, a symptom of the fears that can arise from this destruction of the sense of boundaries.

Now against all of this, what proof is offered that the taboo of sexual privacy should be dismissed with regard to filmed pornography?

Some argue, convincingly enough, that such pornography expresses an idea, if no more elaborate an idea than an attack on sexual privacy itself. Yet that is hardly an argument against the "harm" we have discussed, for ideas can be as harmful as, indeed more harmful than a wide variety of more concrete afflictions. Others contend that the extreme reticence on sexual matters practiced by our society in the past was repressive of and injurious to healthy sexuality. That is also, so far as it goes, true enough. But do we need to pay other people to copulate for us on film in order to discuss sexuality freely?

Surely the case for that need has not been made with even minimal rigor. And even if it had been

---

36. *See, supra* note 1.

37. Prosser, Privacy, p. 48 Cal. L. Rev. 383 (1960).

38. *See,* Restatement (Second) of Torts 652D, Comment L (1977); *Wood v. Hustler Magazine, Inc.,* 736 F. 2d 1084 (1984), *cert. denied* 105 S. Ct. 783; *Melvin v. Reid* 112 Cal. App. 285, 297 91 (Dist. Ct. App. 1931).

39. *See,* Use of Performers in Commercial Pornography, *supra,* in Part Four.

40. 458 U.S. 759 n. 10; *See also, Bell v. Wolfish* 441 U. S. 520, 558–60 (1979) (recognizing "privacy interests" of prisoners implicated by strip searches).

41. *See especially, Griswold v. Connecticut,* 381 U.S. 479 (1965). *See also, Carey v. Population Services Int'l,* 431 U.S. 678 (1977); *Roe v. Wade,* 410 U.S. 113 (1973).

42. Likewise we believe that the critics of sexual taboos regarding incest or child molestation, *see e.g.,* L. Constantini, *The Sexual Rights of Children: Implications of a Radical Perspective,* in *Children and Sex* 4, (1981), p. 255, must bear a similar burden of proof in arguing their cause.

Sexual Privacy in Modern America. The gap between our novelists and the author of *Portrait of a Lady* is indeed a great one, and it is clear that our more liberal notions of sexual reticence form a substantial part of the difference. Yet before simply conceding that privacy in sexual conduct has been relegated to a minor role in modern American life, it would be well to consider two important facts. First, for all their changing mores, Americans still appear to assert strongly their need for privacy in matters sexual. Second, American law in this century has recognized that need ever more forcefully. The combination of these facts, along with evidence from anthropology and history, forms for us the basis on which the "harms" and "benefits" of pornography may, in this area, be assessed.

Attitudes and Practice. In launching their seminal investigation of American sexuality Alfred Kinsey and his colleagues had this to say about their subjects' need for privacy:

> Our laws and customs are so far removed from the actual behavior of the human animal that there are few persons who can afford to let their full histories be known to the courts or even to their neighbors and their best friends: and persons who are expected to disclose their sex histories must be assured that the record will never become known in connection with them as individuals.[30]

In the nearly four decades that have followed, many of Kinsey's hopes for greater sexual tolerance have been realized, but the acute need for sexual privacy has remained. One of the best indicators of that need has been in fact a wrenching problem for researchers attempting to conduct scientific study of pornography: the extraordinarily low volunteer rate for such experiments. In one careful study specifically designed to measure differences between volunteers and nonvolunteers in a sex-film experiment, less than one third of the males and only one in seven of the females agreed to participate if they would be required to be "partially undressed [from the waist down]."[31]

Indeed, no more than half of another group agreed to participate even when told only that they would be watching "erotic movies depicting explicit sexual scenes," with no references to undressing and with assurances that they would be wholly unobserved and that all data would be completely confidential.[32]

Two interesting pieces of evidence from Canada, for which no comparable data for the United States exist, offer a parallel to these laboratory observations. The Badgley Committee surveyed 229 juvenile prostitutes and found that almost 60 percent of both males and females had been asked at least once by clients to be the subjects of sexually explicit depictions. Yet among those requested—teenagers desperate for money who regularly sold their sexual favors to strangers—less than a third agreed to be photographed.[33] Of equal significance, the Fraser Committee conducted a national survey to determine the attitudes of Canadians toward pornography, and found that while 66 percent of their sample declared private viewing of sexually explicit material to be acceptable, only 32 percent could approve of the production of such material, even if no one is "hurt" in the process.[34] Apparently pornography previously produced with someone else's son or daughter is tolerable to Canadians; material which might be produced with one's *own* child is not.

In reaching our conclusion that current American mores continue tightly to embrace sexual privacy, we note that American psychiatrists adhere to their longstanding view that exhibitionism and voyeurism are clear and saddening personality disorders. One overview of their effects finds that they:

> are accompanied by an inconspicuous but real alteration in character, with chronic anxiety beyond the immediate fear of being caught, guilt, fear of losing one's mind, shame, and, usually, inhibition of normal sexual responses. Relief after arrest is common.[35]

Pornography aside, healthy Americans simply do not attempt to peek into other people's bedrooms, and have no interest in showing off their sexual organs to strangers. The "chronic anxiety" attending exhibitionism and voyeurism is thus a reflection of our society's deeply shared commitment to preserving the privacy of sex.

---

30. *Sexual Behavior in the Human Male*, (1948), p. 44.

31. Wolchik, Braver & Jensen (1985). *See also,* Wolchik, Spencer & Lisi (1983).

32. Wolchik, Braver & Jensen (1985).

33. Badgley Report p. 104.

34. Fraser Report p. 104.

35. A Stanton *Personality Disorders* in *The Harvard Guide to Modern Psychiatry,* (1980), 283, 292 . *See* Riley, *Exhibitionism: A Psycho-Legal Perspective,* 16 San Diego L. Rev., (1979), 853, 854–57.

made, we remain convinced, as we said above, that as many of us are silenced in the resulting dialogue as are given voice. Indeed, after a year of witnessing the grotesque sexism of commercial pornography, we now have begun to understand what Catherine MacKinnon, Andrea Dworkin, and others meant when they told us that pornography "silences" women.

Photographic pornography silences it and also degrades.[43] With the exception of noncommercial material produced for educational or therapeutic purposes, it exploits some human beings in violation of some of mankind's deepest instincts about the privacy of sexual conduct. The "right of the Nation and of the States to maintain a decent society,"[44] recognized in dissent by Chief Justice Warren and by a majority of the Supreme Court since 1973,[45] largely means only this: some aspects of American life, and of American sexual behavior, deserve special protection from intrusion, public display, and commercial mass-marketing. Mr. Shaw—and the sex industry—to the contrary notwithstanding, Americans do know the value of privacy. And it is a value that commercial pornography deeply offends.

NONVIOLENT, SEXUALLY EXPLICIT MATERIAL AND SEXUAL VIOLENCE

Submitted by: Father Bruce Ritter

Background

The alleged relationship of sexually explicit material and sexual violence has long been a subject of acrimonious but compelling debate. The "Effects Panel" of the 1970 Commission, often accused of denying such a link, instead stated a relatively moderate view of what was then an almost entirely new area of inquiry: "On the basis of the available data . . . it is not possible to conclude that erotic material is a significant cause of sex crime."[1] Recognizing the impossibility of ever proving "conclusively" the existence of such a casual connection, the 1970 Commission nevertheless determined that the evidence did not, at the time, suggest a "substantial basis" for such a proposition.[2]

The findings of our predecessors, though beleagured in this area by extensive professional criticism,[3] are entitled to significant deference, especially because the 1970 Commission took pains to explain the basis of its conclusions. Rape, however, is among the most violent and damaging of crimes: not only inflicting deep injury on its victims, but also standing as a powerful obstacle to the fight for sexual equality in a democratic society. It is, further, an evil which has increased at shocking rates over the last fifteen years. We thus have the grave, and undeniably unpleasant, duty to examine again the possibility that consumption of sexually explicit materials and some rapes are causally linked—and to report, on the basis of the evidence available *now*, whether a "substantial basis" exists for believing in such a link.

We have with little trouble concluded that circulation of materials which themselves portray graphic sexual violence is a probable "cause" of rape—at least in the sense of being one factor among many (and not necessarily the most important) which increases the likelihood of rape. With regard to sexually explicit materials which do not include depictions of violence our task is more difficult because so many of our witnesses, so many professionals, and so many of our fellow citizens disagree vehemently on the issue. Tempting as it is simply to wash our hands of the question by noting the existence of the dispute and refusing to "take sides" in it, we cannot avoid sifting through the evidence and attempting to come to our own conclusions on the matter. Even if we cannot ultimately agree on the purport of each piece of evidence, or the meaning of all the data collectively, our views should be fully, and publicly, explained.

Problem of Definitions. One serious obstacle to such explanations, unfortunately, arises immediately in the guise of defining the material under examination. For purposes of general discussion about the possible "harms" of sexually explicit material we have found it useful to divide that material into three somewhat imprecise, but nonetheless useful categories: that which is (1) violent; (2) "degrading" but not violent; and (3) neither violent nor "degrading". Unhappily our scheme was not anticipated in advance by researchers and, though a useful blueprint for future scientific inquiry, has not formed the basis for research conducted in the past. The only distinction adhered to with some consistency in the past re-

---

43. *Compare,* Williams Report 138 (live sex shows considered "especially degrading to audience and performers because of their "being in the same space" during performance of intercourse; no account taken of the fact that photographic pornography can only be made if cameraman or photographer is "in the same space" as the performers), *criticized* in Dworkin, *Is There a Right to Pornography?* 3 Oxford J. Legal Stud., (1981), 177, 180–183.

44. *Jacobellis v. Ohio,* 378 U.S., pp. 184, 199 (1964).

45. *Paris Adult Theater I v. Slaton,* 413 U.S., (1973), pp. 49, 59–60, (quoting Warren).

1. 1970 Commission Report, at 287. See, Fraser Report, p. 99; Williams Report, p. 6186.

2. 1970 Commission Report, pp. 286–87.

3. For a review of many of those criticisms see Donnerstein & Malamuth (1984).

search has been that between those materials which depict violence and those which do not. Obviously that distinction is a crude one given the wide range of nonviolent "pornographic" materials, yet it may in some sense correspond with popular perception: thus public opinion seems strongly opposed to free circulation of materials "that depict sexual violence," but sharply divided over the fate of materials that "show adults having sexual relations," with no further explanation of whether the materials in question are "degrading" or not.[4]

For purposes of examining the evidence regarding sexually explicit materials and sexual violence, then, it seems useful to begin, at least, without clearcut distinctions based on the "degrading" character of particular items. Rather, the case for linking nonviolent materials and rape should be examined on its own terms—that is, on the basis of definitions contained in the relevant research—with attention, ultimately, to those pieces of evidence which bear on the question of distinctions among various categories of nonviolent materials. Until we sort through the evidence on this issue we cannot, after all, be certain that boundaries useful for distinguishing among materials on observable *attitudinal* effects are equally valuable with regard to *behavioral* impacts.

Evidence and Standard of Proof. The assumption that consumption of sexually explicit material "causes" sexual violence is one that some 73 percent of Americans would accept as true,[5] but it is unclear what evidence they would point to as crucial to their judgment. From our standpoint some forms of evidence are clearly more persuasive than others, but no one is useless and nondispositive. Evidence from the social sciences—correlational, clinical and experimental—seems by a wide margin the most important tool of analysis in this area, in part, paradoxically, because its *limitations* are most apparent. The results of individual experiments or studies can be rigorously challenged on terms universally accepted by social scientists, and can be examined as carefully for what they do *not* "prove" as for what they do. Anecdotal evidence, even that presented by skilled professionals, has an unfortunate tendency to touch on a wide range of questions without furnishing the basis for answering any single one of them.

Particularly on an issue as bitterly fought and important as this one, therefore, reliance primarily on data from the social sciences seems appropriate and quite possibly imperative. That does not mean, however, that we are bound by the standards of "proof" which govern the work of social scientists. Our task after all, is to recommend policy based on existing knowledge in an area that will always be plagued by uncertainty. Because of limitations on the capacity of social science to measure events outside the laboratory, and because of clear ethical boundaries on what research can be conducted in this area even in the laboratory,[6] it seems wholly unlikely that the extremely high standards for "scientific proof" can ever be satisfied one way or the other on this issue.

The standard more appropriate for our purposes is suggested by the phrase used by the 1970 Commission: is there a "substantial basis" for believing that nonviolent but sexually explicit material is causally linked to sexual violence? If so, what evidence suggests the opposite conclusion—that no such link exists? Finally, which evidence on balance is more persuasive? (This standard was used by us as "the totality of the evidence" in our discussions.) Because rape is so widespread and so dangerous an evil, government action against constitutionally unprotected material might be appropriate if a "substantial basis" for believing in a causal link between such material and sexual violence exists, and might seem imperative if the evidence allows a stronger assessment. Just as government action against cigarette advertising could not await final, irrebuttable "scientific proof" of the causal link between cigarette smoking (let alone cigarette advertising!) and lung cancer, so the government may not be able to await scientific consensus on the pornography/rape connection—even if such consensus were imaginable.

The Evidence

Because direct experimental research on the alleged causal relationship between sexually explicit materials and sexual violence is impossible, or at least unthinkable, we are unhappily left to examine evidence of an indirect nature. That evidence, when it comes from the work of social scientists, tends to take one of two forms: correlational studies and laboratory experiments. The former is a useful launching point for an overview of the issue, because it measures statistical relationships between actual violence and actual consumption of sexual materials. Were no significant relationship found to exist between those two phenomena even on a statistical level, any causal connections between that be extremely difficult to demonstrate through work in the "artificial" setting of a laboratory. Such a setting is useful, however, for exploring possible causal relationships between statistically correlated events; and that is the sense in

---

4. 1985 *Newsweek* Poll. Forty-seven percent of respondents would ban magazines showing adults having sexual relations, but only 21 percent favored such a ban for magazines depicting "nudity". Because many current popular magazines are clearly "degrading" in their portrayals, the difference in views seems more related to sexual explicitness than to the positive or negative portrayal of the person depicted.

5. *Id.*

6. *See, e.g.,* Linz (1985) (excluding subjects from experiment if "psychoticism" or "hostility" score exceeded 1.0 on Symptom-checklist 90); Check (1985).

which experimental evidence is relied on here. Before either correlational or experimental evidence is examined, however, it is crucial to consider first whether sexual violence is a problem which might ever be affected by social change, and whether, in fact, as an aggregate phenomenon it has increased during the period in which sexually explicit materials have been widely available.

Changes in Rape Rates. That first question is easily answered. Rape rates do seem to be related to social change, for they have increased alarmingly during the past 25 years. From 1960 to 1970 the rate of reported forcible rape rose by 95 percent, but that increase seems to have been no more than part of an explosion of violent crime generally, which rose fully 126 percent during the 1960's.[7] Since the report of the 1970 Commission, however, the rate of reported rape has risen almost twice as fast as violent crime generally;[8] from 1970 to 1983 the rape rate virtually doubled, while the rate of reported homicides, for example, remained constant.[9] In 1970 one out of every 20 violent crimes was a forcible rape; by 1983 the proportion had become one out of 16.[10]

Was this extraordinary rise in rape a "real" occurrence, or merely a product of increased reporting of rape? The possibility that increased sensitivity to rape—fueled by movements for women's equality—led to increases in the willingness of individuals to report rapes is not one that can lightly be dismissed,[11] for rape is highly underreported crime.[12] Nevertheless at least three pieces of evidence suggest that the increase of reported rape is not tied to increased willingness-to-report. The National Crime Survey, to begin with, which attempts to gauge actual (as opposed to reported) crime figures through a scientific public survey, showed no significant change in the percent of rapes reported to police from the period 1973–1977 to that of 1978–1982.[13] Yet between those two periods the average number of estimated actual rapes increased substantially.[14]

Second, the 1978 survey by Professor Diana Russell found an increase in the "true rape rate" throughout most of this century;[15] thus historically no serious misrepresentation of trends in this area is found in police data. Finally, correlational data from recent studies of state-by-state rape rates and measurements of the status of women indicate only a small, although significant, relationship between the two.[16]

Rape appears, therefore, to be a phenomenon subject to fluctuation, and during the period that sexually explicit materials have come into general circulation it has been a phenomenon on the rapid increase. That last fact, however, in no sense "proves" or even substantially "suggests" a relationship between the two events; only detailed correlational analysis can begin to do that.

Correlational Evidence. Our predecessors on the 1970 Commission had no sophisticated "correlational" data before them. Indeed, the only "correlational" data which they considered was of the sort discussed above—general trends in the sex-crime rates measured for time periods in which sexual materials were becoming more available. Unfortunately, for reasons discussed below, that sort of evidence is far too crude to be of significant value, and points, in any case, in no particular direction. Far superior correlational data has in the meantime come to the fore, and it shows that a statistical relationship does appear to exist between consumption of certain types of sexual materials and rape rates. Both types of data invite the most careful attention.

---

7. *Sourcebook of Criminal Justice Statistics*, (1984), p. 380, hereinafter *Sourcebook*).

8. *Id.* The high point of both general violent crime rates and reported forcible rates came in 1980, the former having risen 60 percent and the latter 95 percent from 1970 levels. From 1980 to 1983 the rate of all violent crime fell 9 percent, while reported forcible rape rates dropped by 7.5 percent. *Id.*

9. *Id.*

10. *Id.*

11. Rapid social change associated with "women's liberation" may also be viewed, of course, as making rape itself more likely—through setting up more possibilities of "acquaintance rape". *See* Geis & Geis, *Rape in Stockholm: Is Permissiveness Relevant?* 17 Criminology, (1979), p. 311. Women raped by "friends" may be less willing to involve criminal sanctions against their attackers. Thus it is at least arguable that "women's liberation" may in some respects have had a *dampening* effect on rape reporting rates.

12. National Crime Survey figures indicate that no better than half of all rapes are reported. *Sourcebook, supra* note 6, pp. 274–275.

13. Between 1973 and 1977 an average of 46.2 percent of all rapes went unreported according to the Survey; between 1978 and 1982 the average percentage of unreported rapes stood p. 48.2. *Id.*

14. Between 1973 and 1977 the average estimated number of actual rapes per year was 152,877; between 1978 and 1982 the average stood at 173,353, an increase of 13 percent. *Id.*

15. D. Russell, *Sexual Exploitation*, (1984), pp. 52–57. Professor Russell's survey was conducted in 1978, and so is of little value for determining recent trends in rape reporting. It does attest, however, to the fact that, historically, upward trends in police reports of rape have been consistent with *actual* incidence of the crime.

16. Baron and Strauss (1984), for example, found that every change of one standard deviation in the Status of Women Index in a given state is associated with a change in the rape rate of only 0.43 rapes per 100,000 population. By contrast, such a change in the homicide rate would result in a swing of 1.70 rapes, and a one-standard-deviation change in the Sex Magazine Circulation Index would cause a swing of 6.99 rapes (the highest of any variable studied). *Id.*, p. 200.

Danish and Other Cross-Cultural Data. The 1970 Commission was impressed, as was the Williams Committee later, by studies on Denmark conducted by Berl Kutchinsky in which he found that relaxation of Danish pornography laws coincided with a decrease in reported sex crimes. Since that time Kutchinsky's work has been repeatedly criticized, and he himself has been forced to concede that, at least with regard to rape, liberalization of pornography laws was followed ultimately by increases in reports of rape to police.[17] Further, Kutchinsky's approach fails to be even minimally persuasive for two crucial reasons. First, he does not account in any meaningful way for other social forces which might have affected Danish sex crime rates independently of pornography consumption. He fails to note, for example, that sex crime rates in Denmark might have been artificially high during the 20 years after the German occupation of World War II, a conflict described by one historian of Scandinavia as "shattering physically as well as emotionally."[18] A drop in sex crimes during the late 1960's and after would thus be the result simply of recovery from social disintegration wrought by war. Second, and substantially related, Kutchinsky fails to consider the case of Norway—a country with a similar culture and a similar war experience—which has maintained far stricter laws against pornography,[19] and has apparently enjoyed even greater success in combatting sex crimes.[20] In the end Kutchinsky's analysis seems shallow and almost completely without value for analysis of the American experience and American policy.

A more appealing cross-cultural approach, but one with only marginally greater usefulness for our purposes, is that taken by Dr. John Court (1984). His research has examined the temporal changes in rape rates in a wide variety of countries in periods of greater or lesser legal control of pornography. His conclusion, presented with considerable cogency, is simply that greater legal control of pornography appears to hold down rape rates as well. Yet for all its resourcefulness Court's work fails, like that of Kutchinsky, to place the changes studied in careful historical and cultural perspective: thus Singapore, South Africa, Australia and Hawaii are all compared with little contextual information. An additional, related limitation on the helpfulness of his findings arises from his inability to show, like Kutchinsky, whether *actual* consumption patterns fit neatly into the patterns of changing *legal* regulation of sexually explicit materials. Our experience of American enforcement of obscenity laws indicates that such laws are often honored as much in the breach as in the observance.

Sex-Magazine Circulation. Interesting as the work of Kutchinsky and Court is, we have had the benefit of receiving a body of correlational evidence of far greater power. The research of Baron and Strauss (1984, 1985) supplemented by others, has shown a strong statistical relationship between state-by-state circulation rates for the most widely read "men's magazines" and state-by-state reported-rape rates. That relationship persists even when every other factor theoretically associated with rape is controlled for: indeed, they found that the Sex Magazine Circulation Index has a consistently stronger statistical relationship with rape rates than *any* other factor tested.[21] Further, in the model developed by Baron and Strauss other variables theoretically expected to be related to rape rates in fact met expectations: those factors (e.g., percent urban, percent poor) together with the Sex Magazine Circulation Index explain 83 percent of state-to-state variation in rape rates.[22] Two independent studies, by Scott (1985) and Jaffee and Strauss (1986) have not only replicated the Baron and Strauss results for different years, but have cast

---

17. Kutchinsky (1984), pp. 24–25. Kutchinsky attempts to limit the damage of this concession by noting that the increase in rape reports did not substantially begin until 1977, several years after liberalization. He is not, however, able to rule out the possibility that Danish *consumption* of pornography took some time after legalization to reach substantial proportions.

18. F.D. Scott, *Scandanavia*, (1975), p. 247.

19. *See*, General Civil Penal Code of 22 May, 1902, Para. 211, as amended by Law of 24, May, 1985 (received in translated form from Jan Farberg, Norwegian Information Service).

20. According to the Public Information Office of Interpol the rate of reported sexual offenses in Denmark dropped 14.2 percent from 1970 to 1981. In West Germany, another country with liberal obscenity laws used by Kutchinsky in support of his argument, the rate dropped 19.8 percent during that span. In Norway, however, the drop was 33.7 percent in reported sex offenses from 1970 to 1981. These figures are not necessarily computed in the same manner from country to country and should thus be considered only with extreme caution. Nevertheless they do suggest the grave problems in Kutchinsky's selective use of sex-crime figures from one or two locations unembarrassed by historical or cross-cultural analysis.

21. *See* note 16, *supra*.

22. Scott (1985a). In another study Scott (1985b) found that no significant statistical relationship existed between rape rates in the states and the number of "adult theaters" per 100,000 residents in each state. That finding, however, is of almost no value on several grounds: (1) the study did not use multiple regression analysis to examine possible interdependence of the variables; (2) the number of "adult theatres" is an almost completely meaningless figure in view of the fact that each such theatre will sell a different quantity of sexually explicit materials, and no account is taken of that variation; and (3) "adult theatres" are so restricted by zoning, obscenity laws, and the need for urban or semi-urban locations that they cannot be assumed to measure exposure to sexually explicit materials among males who can, if necessary, purchase such materials through the mail.

In their joint statement Commissioners Becker and Levine attempt to discount the importance of this correlational evidence by pointing to a letter from one of the researchers involved, Murray Strauss, which states (1) the correlational research does not "demonstrate" that pornography causes rape," and (2) "the scientific evidence clearly indicates that

doubt on potential "third factors" which would make the sex-magazine/rape association spurious. Baron and Strauss offered two such factors as possibilities: (1) a cultural pattern emphasizing "compulsive masculinity"; and (2) the degree of "sexual openness" within states. The first of those suggestions was undercut by Scott's finding that circulation of men's "outdoor magazines" is *not* associated with state-by-state rape rates. In addition, Baron and Strauss found that controlling for the "index of legitimate violence" and the general violent-crime rate—both seemingly plausible measures of a culture of "compulsive masculinity"—in no way lessened the sex-magazine/rape correlation. Nor did controlling for measures of the status of women—a plausible inverse measure of the degree of "compulsive masculinity" within a given state. Finally, the recent work of Check (1984) and Zillman and Bryant (1984, 1985) indicates that under experimental conditions, massive exposure to mainstream pornography may cause male viewers to become more callous and domineering in their attitudes toward women. Thus pornography may itself be a causal factor in creating a culture of "compulsive masculinity," and even if a correlation could be shown between such a culture and the incidence of rape, the association of the latter with sex-magazine circulation would still not be proved spurious.

As for the other "third factor" suggested—the degree of "sexual openness"—the recent study of Jaffee and Strauss (in press) measured the impact of the Sexual Liberalism Index on the Baron and Strauss formulae. While finding that sexual openness and tolerance is correlated, to a small but significant degree, with increases in reported rape rates, Jaffee and Strauss discovered the inclusion of the new index had no effect at all on the sex-magazine/rape association. While continuing to hold out hope—against all the evidence mentioned in the previous paragraph—that a relationship between "hypermasculine gender roles" and rape rates would render the sex-magazine correlation spurious, they felt compelled to conclude that their research "suggests that there may be more to the pornography-rape linkage than originally expected. That is, the type of material found in mass circulation sex-magazines may, as claimed by critics of such material, encourage or legitimate rape."[23]

Sex Offenders and Pornography. Somewhat less suggestive and useful, but nonetheless important, is correlational evidence exploring links between the use of sexually explicit material by sex offenders and their behavior. Dr. Gene Abel's (1985) study, in particular, is directly pertinent to the issues raised by Baron and Strauss: in treatment of 247 outpatient sex offenders (paraphiliacs), well over half admitted to use of adult men's magazines or similar material, and 56 percent of rapists stated that such materials "increased their deviant sexual interests." Comparison of those offenders who use "erotica" and those who do not produced only one statistically significant difference of direct relevance: users of "erotica" maintained their paraphilia far longer than nonusers. Between those whose deviant arousal was increased by "erotica" and those whose deviant arousal was not increased two statistically significant differences emerged: (1) the aroused-by-erotica subjects maintained their paraphilia longer; and (2) they had less "ability to control their behavior." On the whole, Dr. Abel concluded that "erotica . . . does not appear to affect significantly the behavior of sex offenders."[24]

---

23. Jaffee & Strauss (in press) p. 10. Rodney Stark, in *Demonstrating Sociology* (1985), has claimed to disprove the Baron and Strauss correlation, at least with respect to *Playboy*'s circulation rates. *Id.*, pp. 29–31. Because Stark's discussion of the issue is openly informal, and because the Baron and Strauss results have been replicated formally by others, Stark's view is not persuasive. *See*, Koss (1986) (in large sample of college students there existed a statistically significant relationship between prior consumption of pornography and self-reported sexual aggression).

24. Abel (1985), p. 5.

---

the problem lies in the prevalence of violence in the media, not on sex in the media." *Id.*, p. 13. Strauss' first statement is uncontestable: no correlation can, *by itself*, "demonstrate" causation. Strauss' concern about "misinterpretation" of his research seems somewhat bizarre in view of his published statement that his "findings suggest that the combination of a society that is characterized by a struggle to secure equal rights for women, *by a high readership of sex magazines* that depict women in ways that may legitimate violence, and by a context in which there is a high level of nonsexual violence, constitutes a mix of societal characteristics that precipitates rape." Baron & Strauss (1984), at 207. He then intimates that research suggests "social policies directed toward eliminating or mitigating the conditions that make rape more likely to occur." *Id.* It is Strauss, not the Commission, who has made suggestions of causal linkage based on correlational data alone. *See also* text to note 23.

With regard to his second observation, that violence in the media seems to be "the problem" rather than sex, the research is very far from "clearly" indicating any such thing. Thus it has been found that with regard to *same-sex* interactions, nonviolent but highly arousing erotic material facilitates aggression substantially more than "violent" material. Donnerstein (1983b). And when, angered males are shown a nonviolent, "erotic" film, then allowed a short *delay* before testing, their aggressive behavior toward women has been shown to increase dramatically, to levels far *higher* than for similarly treated subjects shown violent or neutral films. Donnerstein & Hallam (1978). The "delay" factor seems crucial, as measurements of aggression toward women taken immediately after film exposure tend to suggest that "erotic" material does not increase aggression. Donnerstein (1983b); Donnerstein & Berkowitz (1981). This "delayed reaction" effect is similar to that found by Zillman & Bryant (1982, 1984, 1985), in which "massive exposure" to nonviolent, degrading pornography over six weeks produced dramatic increases in subjects' acceptance of "rape myths" and "sex callousness." (By contrast Linz (1985) did not find such effects after a substantially shorter exposure period.) Obviously this experimental data is still at a primitive stage, but it hardly warrants the interpretation Strauss gives it.

Careful review of Dr. Abel's results and of his oral testimony, however, tends significantly to undercut that assertion. To begin with, the mean number of sex crimes committed by users of erotica was 29 percent higher than the mean for nonusers. Dr. Abel lists the difference as "not significant" but does not supply a "p value"; we thus cannot gauge what the actual probability is that the difference is explained only by chance.[25] The finding of no significance is particularly puzzling because, according to Dr. Abel's other findings, users of "erotica" commit the same number of sex crimes per month (actually 21 percent more, but once again the difference is listed as "not significant") and maintain their paraphilia for more total months. Mathematically this would seem to compel the conclusion (already suggested by the statistics on "mean number of sex crimes") that *by the end of their paraphilia*, the group using "erotica" will have committed more total sex crimes than nonusers. That indeed seemed to be the gist of his oral testimony, where he explained the "price" paid by sex offenders who use "erotica" to reduce their desire to commit sex crimes:

> . . . when you use the deviant fantasy in order to ejaculate, instead of attacking a kid or raping someone, it does transiently stop you from carrying out that behavior. In many cases, that is the case, but it's a transient phenomena. And in so using that tactic, the price you pay is maintenance of your arousal. That is your arousal stays strong and will get a little stronger. So over time you are more likely to maintain your arousal over a longer period of time, that means you can commit more acts.[26]

In view of these internal tensions, Dr. Abel's results are extremely difficult to use in their present form.[27] They seem clearly to indicate, and Dr. Abel said as much, that use of "erotica" by sex offenders (outside a treatment setting) is not "helpful."[28] On the other hand they do not seem to rule out, Dr. Abel's protests to the contrary notwithstanding, the possibility of some important statistical relationship between use of sexually explicit materials and commission of sex crimes by this population.

The possibility of such a relationship is clearly enhanced by several other relevant studies. Thus Dr. William Marshall (1985) found in an outpatient study that a far higher percentage of sex offenders currently use "hard-core" pornography than do a group of demographically similar "normals." Professor Diana Russell found high correlation in her study of 930 randomly selected adult women: a surprisingly high number of women victimized by wife rape and stranger rape who said pornography had played a substantial role in the event. A similar survey of 200 prostitutes by Silbert and Pines (1982) found that 24 percent of the large number who had been raped "mentioned allusions to pornographic material on the part of the rapist"—this without any questioning or prompting by the interviewer. Law enforcement witnesses we have heard have also consistently stated that pornographic materials are routinely found on the person of, or in the residence of arrested rapists. While all of this is, like Dr. Abel's evidence, "merely" correlational data, it suggests reason for further inquiry and research on the use of sexually explicit nonviolent materials by sex offenders.

Conclusions from Correlational Evidence An overview of "correlational" evidence available to us ultimately leads to only one firm conclusion. A highly significant, and not obviously spurious statistical relationship exists in the United States between state "adult magazine" circulation rates and sexual violence. That relationship may be explained by a causal connection or it may not; only careful attention to other forms of evidence can indicate which explanation is more plausible. Because "adult" magazines contain relatively little violence,[29] their connection (if one exists) to rape rates makes an excellent "test case" for considering the possible effects of the broader class of nonviolent but sexually explicit materials.

No clear statistical relationships exist, on the other hand, between cross-cultural measures of rape and sexually explicit materials, although such measures if anything tend slightly to support some relationship between the two. Nor is there *undisputed* evidence regarding the correlation of "erotica" use by

---

25. Dr. Abel has been asked to furnish the exact "p value" for this and other comparisons in his written testimony. For our purposes the appropriate level of "significance" in a matter such as this might be substantially different from that typically used in the social sciences. There a statistical difference between two groups is normally not described as "significant" unless there exists 95 percent probability that it did not occur by chance. The probability level appropriate for our use—which, after all, is only to determine whether a "substantial basis" for a finding exists—might be as low as 70 percent.

26. Houston Tr. 100. Earlier Dr. Abel has said the use of erotica by sex offenders "maintains their arousal over time, and therefore greater opportunities to commit further crimes occur." *Id.*, p. 88.

27. Because of his limitation of his study to the role of "hard-core pornography" (not including the typical "adult magazines" referred to by Dr. Abel in his study) Dr. Marshall's results are in no sense directly comparable to those of Dr. Abel. He does, however, find a pattern of pornography being used so integrally in preparation for and commission of sex offenses as to make his evidence highly pertinent.

28. *Id.*, pp. 97, 100.

29. Malamuth & Spinner (1979) (sexually violent content in *Playboy* and *Penthouse* from 1973 and 1977, amounted to less than 10 percent of total cartoon and pictorial content).

sex offenders and commission of sex crimes; it is at least strongly arguable, however, that such a relationship exists. Other sources of information may prove more informative in evaluating these ambiguities.

Experimental and Clinical Evidence A "causal" connection between circulation of adult material and sexual violence may only be inferred if one or more plausible explanations exist for how such "causation" could exist. Experimental evidence is particularly important in testing the likelihood of such causal links; as noted above, however, ethical and practical constraints insure that such evidence will always be open to charges of artificiality and obliqueness.[30] Simply put, actual rapes cannot be staged in the laboratory, nor can known rapists be subjected to testing which might provoke future violence. Retrospective "clinical" evidence, although it does generally relate to "real" rapes by "real" offenders, has the even more crippling handicap of relying on faulty, and self-serving, memory. Yet experimental and clinical evidence remain in this area the most effective tools for testing the "validity" of correlational data.

Searching the evidence for suggestions of a "cause-and-effect" pornography/rape connection inevitably leads down two different paths. The first observes the capacity of pornography to effect *arousal* in the viewer, and examines whether such arousal can be causally linked to sexual violence. The second, somewhat more indirect approach examines the effects of pornography consumption on viewer's *attitudes*, then considers whether such changes in attitudes could plausibly affect the incidence of rape.

Arousal One of the few undisputed properties of sexually explicit materials is their capacity to cause sexual arousal in many, if not most viewers.[31] One strand of experimental research has attempted to determine whether this arousal, alone or in combination with other factors, increases or decreases aggressive behavior in laboratory settings.

"Normals" With regard to "normal" subjects (usually college-age male volunteers), the results have been mixed, or at least highly complex. Thus highly arousing erotic materials, when combined with prior or subsequent anger, seem clearly to provoke heightened aggression by males against males.[32] But in a recent review of the research Professor Donnerstein made the following, more limited, statement about the effects of exposure to nonviolent pornography on male aggression toward women:

> . . . The question of whether or not nonaggressive pornography has an influence on aggression against women is not simple to answer. For one thing, there is not that much experimental research on the topic. Also, studies investigating this issue have differed in many ways. . . . These studies indicate that under certain conditions exposure to pornography can increase subsequent aggression against women. What seems to be required, however, is a lowering of aggressive inhibitions. This change in aggressive predisposition can come about in a number of ways. First, a higher level of anger, or frustration, than that exhibited in a laboratory setting could influence the effects of pornography on aggression against women. There is no question that such levels are present in the real world. Second, as mentioned earlier, drugs, alcohol, and other aggression disinhibitors very likely increase aggressive response to pornography. The main mediating factor, however appears to be the type of material viewed prior to an aggressive opportunity.[33]

While experimental findings are neither conclusive nor absolutely consistent, the bulk of research to date supports the conclusion: that where highly arousing nonviolent pornography is viewed in a context of anger or provocation, aggressive behavior against women increases. Outside the context of provocation, in Professor Donnerstein's view, nonviolent material which is "either mildly arousing or leads to a positive affective reaction" does not appear to increase subsequent aggressive behavior, while that which depicts "unequal power relationships with women" or "women as sexual objects" may provoke such behavior. As part of his belief that the issue warrants "much more investigation" he notes that the effects of nonaggressive pornography may not occur with only a single exposure,[34] which would explain varying results in experiments based on single exposure. Growing habituation to standard "pornography" over the years among likely experimental subjects may substantially affect the results of research.[35]

Sex Offenders Along slightly different lines, a certain amount of experimental and clinical evidence

30. Thus Gross (1983) has criticized the research of Zillman and Bryant (1982) because he suspects the subjects "were giving the researchers what they thought they wanted." *Id.* at 1ll. This, despite the elaborate efforts of the researchers to deceive the subjects into believing that they were most interested in aesthetic qualities of materials viewed, rather than their efforts on attitudes. Unfortunately Gross' criticism may be applicable to virtually any experiment in this area, or indeed in other areas of inquiry. And he is unable to suggest any way to surmount the artificiality inherent in laboratory experiments.

31. *See e.g.,* Donnerstein (1980); 1970 Commission Report pp. 198–241.

32. Donnerstein (1984); Donnerstein (1983b); Sapolsky (1984).

33. Donnerstein (1984), p. 62.

34. *Id. Compare* Check (1985) *with* Linz (1984). For further discussion of varying research results *see, supra* note 22.

35. *See,* Saplosky, (1984), p. 92; Wolchik, Braver & Jensen (1985).

suggests that rapists are aroused by nonviolent, sexually explicit materials, and that some consciously use such materials to prepare for and execute sexual violence. Thus rapists are normally as strongly aroused to consensual nonviolent pornography as nonrapists; they are, moreover, at least as aroused to images of mutually consenting sex as they are to those of rape.[36] Does this arousal to mutually-consenting imagery cause some of them to commit sex crimes which they might otherwise avoid? Evidence from at least Dr. William Marshall suggests that the answer may be yes: 33 percent of rapists interviewed for his study "had at least occasionally been incited to commit an offense by exposure to one or the other type of pornography specified in this study."[37] Of that group 75 percent reported that they had at least occasionally used 'consenting' pornography to elicit rape fantasies which in turn led to the commission of a rape (or an attempt at commiting a rape)."[38] A large number of other rapists in his sample used "consenting pornography" to "evoke rape fantasies" and consequent arousal. Indeed, fully 52 percent of the rapists in his sample (as compared to none of the "normals") used pornography "always" or "usually" during masturbation.[39]

Dr. Abel, while stating the belief that direct incitement to rape can be traced to sexually explicit depictions only in "exceedingly rare" cases, also found that a very high proportion of rapists use consenting "erotica" to elicit and maintain deviant arousal. Recent research has shown a high correlation between sexually deviant fantasies and deviant behavior,[40] and many treatment programs for rapists have been predicated on altering their deviant behavior through changing their fantasies and arousal patterns.[41] Dr. Abel and his colleagues at one point called for recognition of "fantasy as the pivotal process leading to deviant behavior."[42] To the extent that nonviolent, "consensual" pornography contributes to provoke or maintain deviant fantasy and arousal in rapists, it may be considered a "cause" of their deviant behavior.

General Population—Turning back to the general population—that is, both sex offenders *and* "normals"—it is important to note two significant theories concerning sexually aggressive behavior which are predicated on the biological forces of simple arousal. The first, called the "general emotional arousal theory," is described in one study as predicting that "by arousing either the sexual or aggressive drives in an individual, the overall general level of arousal would be increased, thereby making both sexual and aggressive responses more probable."[43] The second theory, which is more subtle and more flattering to the human will, adds an additional cognitive layer to the general-arousal theory:

> While evolutionary forces may have provided a biological basis for a link between sex and aggression, it is our contention that learning variables may accentuate or attenuate this relationship. We hypothesize that in human beings the biological link plays a relatively minor role and that to a large extent the relationship between sexual arousal and aggression is mediated by learned inhibitory and disinhibitory cues.[44]

Both theories associate arousal with aggression; the second merely adds the additional mediating factor of "learned inhibitory and disinhibitory cues." If this association is ultimately found valid, then a "casual" connection between circulation of highly arousing sexually explicit materials and the incidence of rape would be both clear and easy to explain: more sexual arousal in society (as a consequence of pornography) inevitably produces more sexual and more aggressive behavior, both of helpful and harmful varieties. If viewing sexually explicit materials cause Americans to have more sex, then some of that incremental sexual behavior will be of a sexually aggressive nature. The "rate" of rape as a percentage of all sexual intercourse will not change,[45] but the absolute number of rapes, and the number of people victimized by rape, will increase.[46]

---

36. Barbaree, Marshall & Lanthier, (1978); Abel, Recker & Skinner, (1980).

37. Marshall Statement p. 23.

38. *Id.*

39. *Id.*

40. Marshall (1984); Abel, Roulean and Cunningham-Rathmer (1985).

41. Abel, Blanchard & Jackson (1974); Marshall (1973); Marquis (1970); Davidson (1968).

42. Abel, Blanchard & Jackson (1974), p. 474.

43. Abel, Becker & Skinner (1980), p. 183. *See e.g.,* Saplosky (1984).

44. Malamuth, Feshback & Jaffe (1977); Donnerstein, Donnerstein & Evans (1975).

45. Rape statistics, of course, measure only the number of such acts, and the "rate" of such acts for a constant population group. They do not, and cannot, measure rape as a percentage of all sexual behavior.

46. Some general support for this hypothesis may be found in the fact that as rape dramatically increased in incidence in post-war America, so did sexual activity among the young—the age group most prone to sexual violence. Thus only about one-half of males 21 years of younger had engaged in sexual intercourse at the time of the first Kinsey study. A. Kinsey, *et al., Sexual Behavior in the Human Male* 316, while currently over 90 percent of boys appear to have begun such activity by age 17. R. Coles & Stokes, *Sex and the American Teenager* 73 (1985) (The Coles & Stokes sure is

The ability of sexually explicit materials to arouse those who view them may, therefore, be in itself a "cause" of sexually aggressive behavior—perhaps simply for rapists, or perhaps in a more general way. This evidence does not distinguish sexual material as being more culpable than, say, alcohol as a causal factor in rape—but it does suggest that the more highly arousing the material is, the greater will be its ultimate effect. Thus highly explicit sexual material will likely have more of an impact than material which is less sexually arousing. The evidence does not indicate, moreover, that "learned" cultural mores and social attitudes have no effect on preventing rape; rather, those factors may play a significant role in mediating the negative biological forces that push men toward rape.

Effects on Attitudes Toward Rape—"Disinhibition". If arousal to rape is mediated by learned attitudes, however, a change in those attitudes may in itself change the likelihood of rape occurring—may become a "cause" of sexual violence.[47]

Thus it is crucial to consider what the available experimental evidence shows about the effects of viewing nonviolent sexually explicit materials on attitudes toward women and toward rape. Although Professor Neil Malamuth and others have examined in some depth that question with regard to sexually *violent* materials, only very recently has substantial evidence emerged about materials which are similar to much of what is contained in the "adult magazines" examined by Baron and Strauss.

Despite some surface tension in the results, that evidence strongly suggests that such materials, when viewed in substantial quantities over extended periods of time, tend to increase callousness toward women and acceptance of "rape myths". Thus six hours of viewing "commonly available (nonviolent) pornography" over a six-week period caused men in several experiments to become more accepting of "gender dominance"[48] and "sex callousness"—to trivialize rape, and to discount the trauma suffered by its victims.[49] The careful and extensive study by Professor James Check found repeated exposure to the "most prevalent" form of nonviolent pornography currently available—that depicting the women subjects in a "dehumanized fashion"—had even stronger effects on subjects' "reported likelihood of rape" and "reported likelihood of forced sex acts," than sexually violent materials.[50] Both types of material had particularly profound effects, it is important to note, on those subjects with higher tendencies toward psychoticism.[51] Exposure to "nonviolent erotica"—described as being the type of depiction used in sex education and therapy materials—was found to have at best an ambivalent effect: likelihood-to-rape scores increased among those viewers to a level where they were not significantly different from either those in the "no exposure" or the "dehumanizing pornography" groups.[52]

Only one study currently extant seems to cast doubt on the tendency of viewing nonviolent pornography to increase "rape myth acceptance." In a recent doctoral dissertation Daniel Linz found that exposure of university psychology students to either two or five full-length X-rated nonviolent films over, respectively, a three- or ten-day period did not affect their attitudes toward a rapist or his victim in a simulated rape trial shown two days after exposure was completed.[53] Such attitudes were dramatically affected, by contrast, in a comparison group observing four extremely violent R-rated films with far less sexual content. Unfortunately, Linz' study is not directly comparable with previous ones in this area. First, Linz limited the time frame of exposure to less than two weeks.[54] Second, his study did not measure the subjects' scores on "likelihood-to-rape" or "likelihood-of-forced-sex-acts" scales similar to those used by Professor Check but rather studied subjects' reactions to a simulated rape trial. Reaction to the plight of a specific rape victim in a simulation is not as direct—and so at least arguably not as

47. *See generally,* Malamuth (1984).

48. Zillman & Bryant (1985b).

49. Check (1985), Zillman & Bryant (1982, 1984); Donnerstein (1984).

50. Check (1985), p. 49.

51. *Id.,* p. 53. Indeed, subjects with "low P" scores were not significantly affected by *any* of the sexually explicit materials, a finding which may call into question flat conclusions about the effects of pornography independent of the specific vulnerability of individual subjects, and which supports the role of a well-developed moral sense in mediating the effects of exposure.

52. *Id.* pp. 49, 53. It is notable that on the three measures of sexual violence in which no-exposure and "violent pornography" scores were significantly different, the "erotica" scores were slightly closer to those of the latter. Professor Check thus seems to have overstated the importance of his findings that "erotica" and "no exposure" scores were not "statistically significant".

53. Linz (1985).

54. Zillman and Bryant (1982, 1984, 1985), by contrast, used a six-week exposure model. Check (1985) used a time frame similar to Linz, but tested for *prior consumption* of pornography—finding that *only* those viewers with high *previous* consumption were affected by exposure to new materials. Thus the negative findings of Linz may well have to do with low prior exposure to pornography among his subjects—precluding, in the short time used, development of the effects of long-term exposure. *See, infra* text to note 57.

somewhat ambiguous on this point; in another table the percent of 18 year olds "having had intercourse" is listed at 46 percent. *Id.,* p. 73. In any case the trend toward earlier and greater sexual involvement is clear, for in Kinsey's survey only some 31 percent of all 18 year-old males had experienced sexual intercourse. Kinsey, *supra,* p. 316.

useful—a meassure as answers to questions about what the subject *himself* desires to do. Because his study did not include, as did Check's, comparisons based on his subjects' *prior* viewing habits, Linz' results must be treated with extreme caution. It is possible that the strong reaction to R-rated violent films was simply a function of low prior exposure to those films—the films may have their effects because of "shock value."[55] (College-age participants in studies of this nature are known, by contrast, to have previously seen large quantities of "commercialized erotica" and so would not likely have been as jarred by seeing more of it.)[56] The study did not measure the effects of X-rated *violent* films, which would have served to indicate the role of sexual explicitness in mediating the effects of viewing violence.

Despite its methodological limitations, the Linz dissertation does contribute one highly important finding to the data on nonviolent material. In a follow-up study of the participants in his experiment Linz conducted careful "debriefing" of all subjects with regard to the specific material each had seen, then measured their attitudes toward rape after a six-month period. For those subjects who had seen, then been "debriefed regarding R-rated violent and R-rated nonviolent materials, a dramatic reduction in "rape myth acceptance" occurred—with virtually no difference between those two groups in their final scores. "Debriefing" was thus seen as a success for both groups. Subjects who had seen X-rated nonviolent materials, by contrast, showed only the most minimal decline in "rape myth acceptance" after "debriefing" the lapse of six months—so that at the point of follow-up measurement they showed substantially higher toleration of rape than *either* of the R-rated groups.[57] The significance of this finding, not recognized by Linz himself, is its tendency to show long-term effects of "X-rated" material even in the face of positive efforts to "educate" viewers. In the "real world", as opposed to the laboratory, viewers of sexually explicit materials normally receive messages—"inhibitory cues"—contradicting those in the materials they watch. The Linz study provides tentative evidence that for sexual materials with a high degree of explicitness, such real-life "debriefing" may be unsuccessful.

The overall results of work on "long-term" exposure to standard, nonviolent pornography was confirmed and summarized in a statement by Professor Donnerstein in 1983:

> Let me end up talking in the last couple of minutes, about the long term research. Researchers like myself and Neil Malamuth at UCLA are looking at massive long term exposure to this material. Some interesting things occur. If you expose male subjects to six weeks' worth of standard hard-core pornography which does not contain overtly physical violence in it, you find changes in attitudes toward women. They become more calloused towards women. You find a trivialization towards rape which means after six weeks of exposure, male subjects are less likely to convict for a rape, less likely to give a harsh sentence to a rapist if in fact convicted.[58]

Professor Donnerstein went on to say:

> In our own research we are looking at the same thing. Let me point out one thing. We use in our research very normal people. I keep stressing that because it is very, very important. What we are doing is exposing hundreds and hundreds of males and now females to a six-week diet of sexually violent films, R-rated or X-rated or explicit X-rated films. We preselect these people on a number of tests to make sure they are not hostile, anxious or psychotic.
>
> Let me point out the National Institute of Mental Health and the National Science Foundation and our own subjects committee will not allow us to take hostile males and expose them to this type of material because of the risk to the community. They obviously know something some of us do not.[59]

Although Professor Donnerstein himself has recently emphasized most the harmful effects of *violent* depictions, the research strongly seems to support the proposition that longer-term, substantial exposure to "standard" nonviolent, sexually explicit materials acts as a "disinhibiting cue" for rape.

Overall Evidence for "Causation". No experiment has, for the reasons suggested by Professor Donnerstein, tested the effects of nonviolent, sexually explicit material on the aggressive behavior of known sex offenders or, indeed, those with even a tendency toward psychoticism. Experiments with "normal" subjects, however, have suggested two separate, but quite possibly interdependent means by which such

---

55. *See,* Zillman, Bryant & Carveth (1981) (viewing bestiality increased aggression due to "annoyance summation"). The shock value explanation for the Linz data is strengthened by the fact that later "debriefing" treatments over a six-month period seemed completely to reverse the effects of viewing these materials. Linz, p. 96.

56. Wolchik, Beaver & Jensen (1983).

57. Linz (1985), pp. 96–98.

58. *Public hrgs. on Ordinances to Add Pornography as Discrimination Against Women,* Minneapolis City Council, Sess. I, p. 31 (Dec. 12, 1983).

59. *Id.* at 32.

material could heighten the probability of sexual violence. The simple capacity of nonviolent material to produce strong *arousal* in both offenders and the general population may in and of itself produce higher levels of sexual violence. Of equal importance, "standard" commercial pornography may over time and with significant exposure work to undermine "learned" inhibitions against sexual violence. While "adult men's magazines" have not been the normal focus of experimental investigation, the material they contain is sufficiently arousing, and sufficiently tied to views of women only as "sexual objects," as to make the reasonable inference that these findings are applicable to them as a class. Thus the Badgley Committee in Canada found that in a group of "adult" magazines essentially the same as those studied by Baron and Strauss, photographic depictions of sexual bondage were three times as frequent as oral-genital contact, five times as frequent as vaginal penetration with penis or finger, and ten percent more frequent even than any form of kissing.[60] While further research is clearly indicated to determine the effects of this extremely common material, at present it may fairly be seen as falling within the range of materials as to which current experimental and clinical evidence is highly relevant.[61]

Evidence Against Causation. Studies of both arousal and attitudinal effects of viewing nonviolent materials thus provide several suggestive "causal" links between such viewing and sexual violence. What is the evidence *against* such a connection? If substantial enough, such data might preclude forming any opinion about the plausibility of the causal link suggested by the correlational data, in combination with indirect experimental and clinical data.

Unfortunately evidence which contraindicates the existence of a cause-and-effect relationship between nonviolent materials and sexual violence is slim. Short-term exposure of *normal* subjects to "mild erotica" has been shown to have negligible (and in some cases positive) effects on aggressive responses toward women in the laboratory.[62] As discussed above, results of short-term exposure to highly arousing material have been to the contrary, with enhancement of aggression occurring in cases with "prior anger."[63] Long-term exposure, however, which seems the condition most likely to resemble actual behavior, seems clearly to disinhibit subjects regarding sexual violence. And of course, the reaction of paraphiliacs even to brief exposure to "mild erotica" is far from clearly negligible; if anything, the studies point toward some use of such material by sex offenders to initiate and maintain the deviant fantasies which help push them toward more offending behavior.[64]

Nor is there substantial evidence showing *beneficial* effects of "standard" nonviolent pornography. It is crucial to note that when asked whether exposure to pornographic materials can ever reduce commission of sex crimes by paraphiliacs over the long term, Dr. Abel responded with a flat denial.[65] The Fraser Committee found, on a more general level, "there is no research documenting the beneficial effects of pornography," a proposition that is somewhat misleading but generally true. In sex therapy and sex education settings, research by Dr. Abel[66] and others suggest that such material may be useful, and the work of Professor Check, discussed above, indicates that materials which are overtly educational or therapeutic may be substantially "harmless" even when viewed outside a controlled environment. Studies for the 1970 Commission found that some sexual materials helped ease sexual tension and promote "liberal" attitudes toward sexuality—a result that may be seen as "beneficial" according to one's basic assumptions regarding sexual morality. Yet with regard to strongly arousing, nonviolent materials, both Dr. Abel's judgment concerning sex offenders and the Fraser Committee's findings about the general population seem well founded.

Conclusion

Ultimately the empirical evidence suggests the following conclusions: viewing nonviolent, sexually explicit material similar to widely circulated "adult magazines" is statistically related to a higher probability of rape. (Thus, for example, Wyoming has a "sex-magazine circulation rate" 45 percent higher than Montana's, with a rape rate 57 percent higher. Baron & Strauss (1985).) That relationship is not only highly significant, and constant from year to year, but it is not "spurious" when other potential "third factors" are considered. Evidence from both experimental and clinical studies demonstrates at least two possible ways in which that correlation might be explained by "causation": (1) through the simple

---

60. Badgley Report p. 1223. Of course graphic depictions of genitalia of nude models in such magazines—often with pubic hair shaved—serves as well to reduce those shown to the status of "sexual objects". This *general* description of magazines evaluated by Baron and Strauss and others should not be taken as specific to any *one* of them. Individual differences in format, and style and content may be crucial.

61. Thus Abel (1985) focused on such material in his study of sex offenders. As discussed above, *supra* text to notes 21–23, Dr. Abel's findings are ambivalent but troubling.

62. See Donnerstein (1984, 1980A).

63. Donnerstein & Hallam (1978).

64. For a discussion of the evidence on sex offenders presented by Dr. Abel and Dr. Marshall, *see*, *supra* text to notes 21–24, 34–40.

65. Houston Tr., p. 100.

66. Fraser Report p. 98.

arousal properties of such materials, and (2) through their disinhibiting qualities, their capacity to change attitudes regarding sexual aggression. The evidence is nonetheless far from conclusive, and points toward the need for substantially more, and better-focused research. At this point, little or no evidence exists which shows any beneficial effects of such materials.

It is useful to consider the weight of this data against that which supports our previous finding that *sexually violent* material is causally related to sexual violence. For that conclusion we had *no* correlational evidence demonstrating a "real-world" statistical relationship between the material and the behavior. By contrast, the experimental evidence was somewhat stronger—showing, for example, "negative effects" from short-term as well as long-term exposure. Sexually violent material is no more *arousing* to viewers (even to known rapists) than is "standard" nonviolent material (Abel, Barlow, Blanchard & Guild (1977). In the one study which directly attempted to compare the effects on *attitudes* of sexually violent material with effects from "dehumanizing" material and "erotica," the results showed no significant difference in the most crucial areas.[67] Only a well-founded intuition that direct depictions of sexual violence are more likely to produce such violence allows us to conclude that they are more "harmful" than nonviolent materials; the evidence from social science is at best ambivalent on the issue.[68] Our task is not an easy one, because with widely different backgrounds and substantially different ideas about what constitutes "proof" of a given fact, we are highly unlikely to reach consensus on highly disputed questions. With regard to the relationship between sexually explicit materials and sexual violence we will each carry away different levels of skepticism about the state of currently available evidence. And we will know, too, that our stated conclusions may be swept away by new research. Yet that does not relieve us of the obligation to state, not as scientists proclaiming "fact" but as policymakers confronting risk and probability, that wide circulation and consumption of materials similar to "adult men's magazines" must be a matter of concern among those seeking to combat sexual violence. There is at least a substantial basis, if not a preponderance of the evidence, to believe that such materials are a *part* (if only a small part) of the explanation for that cruel plague.

Acknowledgement. I am deeply grateful to Dr. Edna Einsiedel, The Commission's staff social scientist, for her review of, and comments on, the preliminary versions of this statement. The foregoing represents, however, only my own views and not necessarily hers.

NOTE: All references in the text and notes are to studies cited in the Report on Social Services of the Commission, except where a full citation is given.

PERSONAL STATEMENT OF COMMISSIONER FREDERICK SCHAUER

Pornography, in its most explicit and offensive forms, commands our attention in a way that few other things do. It is there, before our eyes, and in our minds thereafter, and its very thereness makes it hard to ignore it and hard to be dispassionate about it. Most importantly, the way in which the pornographic item demands our attention makes it hard to

67. Check (1985). Indeed, Check found that on many measures sexually violent materials produced less "negative effects" than "dehumanizing pornography"—although not by "significant" margins. "Erotica," of course, was also found not to be "significantly" different in its effects than "no exposure." See, supra note 52.

68. It is useful, as well, to compare the strength of our conclusions in this area with those of the Advisory Committee to the Surgeon General in an area which was at the time similarly contentious and difficult—the health risks of cigarette smoking. The evidence relied on for the Committee's conclusion was overwhelmingly correlational—showing higher death and illness rates among smokers than in non-smokers. The Committee recognized fully that correlational evidence did not show causality and looked to animal experiments, clinical data, and "population studies" (i.e., retrospective studies of smokers vs. control groups). Surg. Gen'l of the Pub. Health Serv., U.S. Dept. of H.E.W., (1964), pp. 26–27. With regard to lung cancer, those additional forms of evidence were sufficiently supportive of the correlational data to allow the Committee to conclude that "cigarette smoking is causally related to lung cancer in men"; with regard to women the data allowed the lesser conclusion that the data "point in the same direction." Id. p. 31. As for heart diseases, the Committee found that there existed a strong correlation between coronary disease and smoking, but found that the current explanations for causation from experimental and other evidence "do not account well for the observed association". Id. p. 327. Instead of throwing up its hands in the face of difficult and conflicting evidence the Committee said simply: "It is . . . more prudent to assume that the established association between cigarette smoking and coronary disease has causative meaning than to suspend judgement until no uncertainty remains." Id.

It would be presumptuous to compare the quantity of evidence before us with that reviewed by the Surgeon General's Committee; research on "pornography" is still in its infancy. But our responsibility to be as prudent as possible is the same, and the correlational evidence before us combined with at least a substantial strain of experimental and clinical data make it *prudent* to advise the public of the risks of the materials for which statistical data do exist.

generate that level of detachment that, however personally difficult, is an essential prerequisite of open-minded and intellectually honest inquiry. The eleven of us find ourselves on this Commission for different reasons. Although I consider myself as moral as the next person, and more moral than most, I do not deceive myself into thinking that my appointment to this task was a function either of my own morality or of my ability to identify, to reflect, or to speak for the moral values of others. These are important functions, and I am gratified that they have been represented on this Commission, but I have seen my own role differently.

As a teacher in a university, as an academic, and as a scholar, I have been asked to bring to our work some degree of knowledge about constitutional law in general and the law of free speech in particular, as well as some knowledge about the law of obscenity. But to be an academic is not to know about certain things, or even to have certain talents of intelligence, analysis, or creativity. Nor is it to hold an appointment in a university, for it is more than that. It is to be willing to pursue an inquiry in the most intellectually honest way possible, to be open to new ideas and to challenges, to follow the inquiry where it leads regardless of personal views, to be free to reach conclusions without having to serve an external constituency, to be able to make the best case for the opposing view and then confront that best case rather than the worst case, and to be willing to consider today that what one believed yesterday might be wrong.

This is an ideal, and it is an ideal that none of us reach. But it is the ideal that I take to have guided my aspirations for the work of this Commission, and especially to have guided my aspirations for my own role among the Commissioners. As I look back on what we have done, I am pleased with the way that our final product measures up against this standard. We have dealt with issues that have divided us, and that divide society, yet we have been able to agree on a great deal, we have been able to talk even where we have been unable to agree, and we have been able to put together a final report that explains rather than suppresses disagreement.

In their own statements the other Commissioners have concentrated largely on the issue of pornography, and on their reactions to it. I believe these issues are important, or else I would not have agreed to serve on this Commission, but for me what is even more important is the nature of the inquiry and the nature of the product, and what it says about the style and level of public discourse. It is not a necessary truth that the world has to be divided into liberals and conservatives, good guys and bad guys, reactionaries and radicals. Nor is a necessary truth that adjectives must substitute for analysis, that all that matters is what can be summarized in a headline or a three minute news segment, and that one good quote is better than a hundred pages of careful thought. To me our process and our product is a rejection of much that is worst about the nature of public discourse. It trusts the public to understand difficult issues if the various positions can be explained. It trusts the public to read and to understand a large amount of factual information. It records agreement where it exists without exacerbating minor differences, and it records disagreement where it exists without feeling compelled to reduce every serious disagreement to who won and who lost. It is a report that is designed to be read rather than summarized, to be thought about rather than used as rallying cry or flag of battle, and to be as much the beginning of serious discussion and debate rather than the end of it.

None of us can be expected to agree with every word, every line, every fact, and every recommendation contained in these pages. Discussion has resolved many of our differences, just as it has created new ones. Yet we expect to continue thinking about this issue, just as we expect others to. We deal here with an issue that involves sex, physical harm, privacy, morals, the environment of a community, the idea of community itself, the status of women, sexual preference, and a host of other issues that divide this and other societies. Faced with these divisions, we could have yelled at each other, chosen up sides, and looked for further reasons to disagree. But the world has no shortage of people who are looking to create or to accentuate divisions. It does need people who are willing to try to heal them, not by trying to persuade other people to adopt your point of view, but instead by reaching out and trying to understand theirs. We have tried to do this, and we have succeeded more than most. This Report contains a great deal on the issue of pornography, and there seems little point in adding to that here. But in thinking about pornography, this Report also says something about thinking, and I hope that part of our mission and our product will not be neglected.

STATEMENT OF DEANNE TILTON-DURFEE

My entire adult life has been spent in the field of child welfare and child protective services. As a result, my perspectives on the effects of pornography have been primarily focused on how these materials affect children and their families. However, in the course of the past year, it has become necessary to expand the boundaries of my concerns to include co-related issues such as adult victimization in the production, behavioral effects from the consumption, and crimes related to the production and consumption of pornography. Moreover, because a credible analysis must be a balanced one, I have found a critical need to weigh carefully the impact of any recommendation that might threaten the integrity of the First Amendment or unnecessarily limit choices available to the American public.

I have no doubt that there is very real harm resulting from the production, distribution and consumption of some pornography. Quite understandably, the nature and degree of the harm has been difficult to define. It is possible that establishment of a cause and effect relationship has and always will be an impossible task, given the human variables involved. In any case, it is clear that harms or benefits from consumption cannot be generalized accurately in that reactions to explicit materials will depend on the basic attitudes, situations, self-concepts, mental health, support services, and personal and sexual opportunities available to each individual consumer. Certainly, mere exposure to pornographic materials does not create criminal behavior. More than one observer of our Commission's work has noted that such a connection would render each Commissioner a potential sexual deviant.

It is therefore important to acknowledge that we cannot scientifically show that exposure to sexually explicit materials affects the behavior of most consumers. It is also important to acknowledge that we have no business regulating any expression in words or pictures without good cause. We do, however, have an obligation to protect those who are vulnerable to victimization, to prevent and deter crimes committed in the production or distribution of pornography, and to provide methods by which communities can preserve the quality of their neighborhoods.

CHILD VICTIMS

I wish to focus on the victimization of children for several reasons. First, because this is my area of expertise, second, because I believe children are often given patronizing support but little genuine respect as valuable members of our society, and third, because children are clearly the most vulnerable of all who may be affected by pornography. This is not only because of their developmental limitations, but because there is an assumption that parents or other trusted caretakers can and will protect them. Moreover, I believe that the roots of so much of the demand for pornography and the exploitations in the production and forced consumption of pornography lie in the childhoods of those involved.

Because children are such defenseless and quiet victims, and because those who exploit them seem rarely to meet the public stereotype of the "child molester," the very existence of child sexual exploitation has been the very slowest of all offenses to emerge. There is a profound reluctance on the part of the American public to respond to this tragic dilemma. This relates to a disbelief that this kind of thing could happen, a lack of confidence in resources available within the various social and legal service systems, and the suppression of painful memories on the part of adults who themselves suffered as child victims and who were neither believed nor rescued.

As our social and legal systems have responded to the emerging revelations regarding sexual exploitation of children, a common trend has been that the ages of the victims have become younger and younger. Although we had begun to acknowledge the reality of the exploitation of adolescents in the production of pornography, we found that pictures of pre-pubescent children, toddlers, and even infants in sexually explicit depictions became increasingly prevalent. This trend toward the inclusion of very young children in pornography correlates with an identical trend in the physical abuse and sexual exploitation of children throughout the country.

Recently, communities throughout the United States have been shaken by disclosures of major multi-victim and multi-perpetrator child sexual molestations within preschool settings. From one end of the country to the other, children are coming forward as young as three and four years of age to relate stories strikingly and frighteningly similar regarding the most cruel and perverted sexual abuses imaginable, perpetrated by trusted caretakers and responsible members of the community.[1] Each time one of these cases emerges, the local community and its social and legal systems are so overwhelmingly shocked and incredulous of what they are hearing from these tiny youngsters, the process of intervention and prosecution is awkward, and usually unsuccessful.

One common theme that emerges repeatedly is the statement by the children that their pictures have been taken in sexually explicit poses while involved in perverted sexual activities. Other children have spoken of boxes of pictures being carried away just prior to police searches. In my opinion, there is little doubt that there is a connection between the ritualistic molestation of the children involved in the many alleged preschool multi-victim, multi-perpetrator molestation cases, and a child pornography market. However, since we have failed to discover pictures to substantiate this belief, the existence, nature, extent and those responsible for this market have not been determined. The recommendation for a national task force to study possible relations between these preschool sexual rings and an organized child pornography market is what I consider one of the most significant recommendations in this report.

Many other recommendations included in the Child Pornography section are particularly encouraging including those which strengthen support services for the child victims, sensitize and improve the effectiveness of legal/judicial procedures to accommodate the child victim, and those which provide children with information and skills to protect themselves against those who might exploit them, whether or not the perpetrator is a stranger, trusted adult or a parent.

FAMILY LIFE EDUCATION

I truly believe that a significant measure in the protection of children and subsequent generations against exploitation lies in the incorporation of family life preparation programs within school systems. This is a concept which was opposed by some of my fellow Commissioners, and certainly by many parents in the general public. However, the challenge of raising healthy children is perhaps the most significant task that will be faced by the largest number of students in American schools. A large percentage of children who become involved in pornography and prostitution have run away from violent or exploitive homes.[2] Most reported child molestation is perpetrated by a family member.[3] In other words, if we depend completely on parental guidance, many children will never receive the benefit of information regarding their rights and responsibilities in making personal choices and the requirements of healthy parenting. Other children's own healthy experiences at home can be enhanced by age appropriate curriculum which clearly must respect the role of parents in determining life styles, cultural practices, and religious preferences. It seems incredible to me that we are unwilling to focus concern and educational resources on promoting healthy parenting and inter-personal skills at a level commensurate with our commitment to other curricula which may be of far less importance in the lives of future generations.

I would hope that educational systems throughout the country will follow the examples set by many school systems, including Los Angeles County, in responding to this major investment in our Country's future.

EXPOSURE OF CHILDREN TO EXPLICIT AND VIOLENT MATERIALS

The question has arisen regarding the effects of adult pornography on children. Children at various ages process information differently, and the psychological sense that something has an erotic meaning comes biologically and culturally with age. (Compare the reaction of a 17 year old and the reaction of his infant brother to the sight of a woman's breasts.) There are variations in how individual children develop intellectually and physically, and there are changes in children's vulnerability at critical stages. Moreover, a particular child's reaction to sexually explicit stimuli will depend to a great degree on that child's personal strengths and familial and social structures.

For obvious ethical reasons, we cannot condone large scale studies of the effects of exposure to pornography on various age groups of children. However, one can surmise from the availability of information we have regarding

---

1. Roland Summit, M.D. *Too Terrible to Hear*, November 20, 1985.
2. UCLA Bush Foundation Report. *Status Offenders in Los Angeles County, Focus on Runaway and Homeless Youth* (1985).
3. Child Welfare League of America. *Too Young to Run and the Status of Child Abuse in America* (1986).

developmental age vulnerabilities of children that those in the early adolescent age group might be the most susceptible and the least capable of managing social and psychological dilemma produced by exposure to pornography.[4]

Whatever the actual impact may be on children at any age, and given our inability to be scientifically exact on that issue, it seems clear that we have a responsibility to protect children against whatever potential harm may result from such exposure. For this reason, I strongly support laws which prohibit the sale of pornographic materials to children and prohibit children's entry into establishments which specialize in "Adults Only" materials. I am also pleased with the voluntary actions taken by many businesses to limit children's access to sexually explicit materials.

In my opinion, violent materials, sexual or non-sexual, are cause for the most serious concern regarding potential negative effects on children's attitudes and behavior. These materials have become increasingly pervasive in our culture. There is a critical need to seriously consider how we can effectively discourage proliferation of these destructive messages which reach out to children on television, in theatres and even by way of their toys and comic books.

There are some who believe that restrictions placed upon the adult consumption of pornography should be as strong as restrictions on children's consumption of pornography. The rationale given is that anything available to adults will eventually fall into the hands of chidren. Although there is little doubt that childhood curiosity will creatively find access to "forbidden" materials, I do not believe the "equal restriction" perspective is realistic or an avenue of choice. The laws of our society currently place many differentiated restrictions on adults and children. Certainly, the negative effects of alcohol consumption on children who access their parent's liquor cabinets is clearly established. We recommend closer parental supervision and either removal of the alcohol from the home or locking the doors of the liquor cabinet. When children become alcoholics, a growing national concern, recommendations include individual and family counseling, or Alcoholics Anonymous.

We can develop parallel responses in relation to children accessing their parent's pornography—closer parental supervision, use of lock boxes on televisions with cable programming, and mental health or other services for children exhibiting inappropriate or anti-social behavior following the consumption of pornography. Again, while we should not deny the potential harm that pornography may inflict on children who view it, it is extremely important to keep sight of other possible causes of what we consider to be negative behavioral effects. If a child who has been exposed to pornography begins exhibiting inappropriate sexual behavior, we must be extremely careful not to focus solely on the pornography, denying the possibility that the child may have been molested or, on the other hand, denied warm loving relationships within the family unit.

Children who have a well-integrated and reinforced positive sense of self are less apt to accept violent, callous, impersonal images of other people as part of their personal concept of life. Children who have healthy age-appropriate images of affectionate behaviors are less apt to accept perverse or violent destructive images as part of their own internal or external self. They do need social support systems to absorb confusion when it is present and to provide structures that allow them to explore their own responses to such stimuli.

PRIORITIZATION OF RESPONSE

The Commission's majority vote to encourage allocation of obscenity intervention resources in a prioritized manner has caused some concern on the part of those who believe all categories of pornography to be equally damaging. It is clear that current law enforcement resources are inadequate to respond effectively and appropriately to all types of pornography at all times. The prioritization should assist in focusing attention on those violent, degrading and dehumanizing materials that have gradually emerged, with impunity, as a major market. This does not preclude pursuing action against other material. However, it is the violent and degrading materials that reflect the changing nature of pornography in America, a major impetus for the creation of our Commission. We saw these materials, we were shocked by them, and our

---

4. Michael Durfee, M.D. *A Child Developmental Perspective to Conceptualize Possible Effects of Pornography on Children* (March 11, 1986).

reactions and concerns about them should be and were reflected in the decision to give them first priority in the allocation of law enforcement resources.

A WORD ABOUT WORDS

It was the majority opinion of the Commission that law enforcement agencies should not be encouraged to commit resources to the prosecution of the non-illustrated pornographic written word, unless the message is directed to children or involves child pornography. Again, there has been a great deal of concern regarding the possible proliferation of obscene books which encourage sexual perversions and other crimes. While I agree that passages in certain paperback books sold in adult book stores represent the most vile and offensive messages imaginable, I do not believe it is realistic or constructive to presume that obscenity prosecutions can be initiated or will be effective in protecting the public from any possible negative effects from the materials. I do, however, believe that the fear of censorship expressed by librarians and others concerned for the protection of literature which may contain "explicit" passages, is an extremely important consideration. Our Commission's respect for the special place of the written word was more a statement of support for freedom of speech than an action which was meant to, or will, change existing practices in the enforcement of obscenity laws.

TIME AND STRUCTURE

The time and structual constraints placed upon our Commission's work were extremely problematic, causing concern regarding compromise made in the final editing process. The workload has been unmanageable throughout the year. The ultimate task of reviewing over two thousand pages of final draft in three days time to meet our print deadline was totally unrealistic. In addition, the critical job of consolidating and clearing all the Commissioner's last minute corrections was an unreasonable expectation of the already exhausted Staff, who have reportedly worked into every night of the last several weeks. If the Commission had more resources to pursue additional study, more opportunity to meet in sub-committees, and more time to review the final product, I believe a more thoughtful and confident consensus would have resulted. However, given the Commission's limitations, the final report is a docu-

ment which raises issues that are relevant and worthy of a considerable investment of time and energy made by each Commissioner and the Staff. There are two specific recommendations about which I wish to express concern.

1. *RECOMMENDATION NUMBER 8: State Legislatures should amend, if necessary obscenity statutes to eliminate misdemeanor status for second offenses and make any second offense punishable as felony.*

The arbitrary imposition of a felony status for second offenders could possibly discourage any actions on some second offenses by Prosecutors denied room for negotiation.

2. *RECOMMENDATION NUMBER 88: Legislatures should conduct hearings and consider legislation recognizing a civil remedy for harms attributable to pornography.*

While I support the concept of civil rights actions on behalf of victims, a rewriting of the substantiation for this recommendation was not available for review by Commissioners at the time of the deadline for this statement.

It is also of considerable concern that the Commission members were never able to agree on the types of materials that fall within the framework for classes I, II, and III materials. In the absence of such clarity, and without a comprehensive survey of materials available in bookstores, theatres, video outlets, and other vendors, it is only conjecture to presume that the "predominance" of obscene materials portray degradation.

SUMMARY

The issues surrounding pornography defy simplification, challenge objectivity, and create passionate responses from opposing extremes of a multitude of political, religious, and philosophical spectrums.

It is my sincere hope that our focus on these confounding and controversial issues will assist the American people to develop a knowledgeable concern regarding the potential impact of pornography on their children and their communities, an understanding of the personal choices and public policy alternatives available to them, and the realization that pornography is the product of a demand resulting from a host of motivations we have only begun to identify.

It has occurred to me, throughout our Commission's hearings, that the subject of our inquiry, whether relating to adult or child pornography, has a very significant and direct connection to many issues surrounding the abuses and exploitation of children. I saw the clear characteristics of a helpless child in each adult victim testifying before us, and this helped me to understand how and why they tolerated the abuses about which so many are skeptical. I saw the angry and inadequate adult reenacting his or her own childhood abuses in much of the sado-masochistic materials. Perhaps most significantly, I saw the sad, lonely and desperate

search for intimacy denied in childhood on the faces of those who stood haplessly in the adult bookstores and those who told us of their addictions to obscene materials. It occurred to me, over and over again, that the real issue might be the effects of American family life on the consumption of pornography, rather than the reverse.

STATEMENT OF JUDITH BECKER, ELLEN LEVINE AND DEANNE TILTON-DURFEE

We are three women, who have, in varied ways, devoted our lives to the welfare of children and families: one as a specialist in the treatment of those who sexually abuse women and children, another as a journalist covering the diverse issues facing contemporary American women and the third as a specialist in the prevention and treatment of child abuse, neglect and molestation.

We share a deep concern about the effects of pornography on American women. Nevertheless, we found these issues troublesome because those women who testified before us were so deeply divided. Many condemned pornography as an ultimate offense against women, others opposed censorship categorically and defended women's rights to consume and perform in pornography. Although each of us has her own very strong negative, personal reactions to the various pornographic depictions, we believe our acceptance of service on this Commission carried with it the responsibility to enter this arena with an open mind, to weigh fairly the evidence presented to us and to set aside our personal biases in order to develop credible and balanced recommendations for the Federal Government regarding this extremely controversial subject.

We have, throughout the Commission's hearings, witnessed devastating testimony from women victimized in the production or forced consumption of pornography, and we have seen material that is offensive to the most permissive boundaries of our imaginations.

Much of this material violates the very fabric of our own ethical and moral standards.

We wish to express our strong personal objections to the offensive and totally inaccurate materials that portray women as eager victims of abuse or as beings of less competence or value to society than men. We disapprove equally of media depictions that discriminate unfairly against men, or against specific races, cultures or those with physical or mental disabilities. After consideration of the evidence presented, we conclude that those who exploit women's vulnerability in the production or consumption of pornography are inflicting harm that profoundly violates the rights of women, damages the integrity of the American family and threatens the quality of life for all men and women.

We abhor the exploitation of vulnerable people and condemn those who profit from it. We respect, however, the rights of all citizens to participate in legal activities if their participation is truly voluntary. We reject any judgmental and condescending efforts to speak on women's behalf as though they were helpless, mindless children.

Our most profound desire is that the women of America be provided an environment that encourages their sense of self-worth, self-respect and their ability to make genuine choices. We consider both the limitation of choices and sexual exploitation to be degrading attacks on the basic value and dignity of women.

STATEMENT OF DR. JUDITH BECKER AND ELLEN LEVINE

In accepting appointments to the Attorney General's Commission on Pornography, we both believed that stimulation of a national dialogue and debate on this very controversial subject was well within the purview of the government and in the best interests of the country. To this challenging commitment we bring very different personal and professional expertise. Dr. Judith Becker is a behavioral scientist whose career has been devoted to evaluating and treating victims and perpetrators of sexual crimes. Mrs. Ellen Levine is a journalist and editor who has focused on women's news. Although our backgrounds are different, we have found throughout the hearings and Commission meetings that we share similar views about the nature of the testimony presented and alternative ways in which the issue of obscenity might be approached. We have, therefore, decided to submit this joint statement.

THE PROCESS

During its public hearings, the Commission has accomplished much, garnered some press attention, and, as anticipated, created a certain amount of controversy. Our hope is that the past year's work will not end with the publication of this report, but will begin a process of discovery and disciplined study of the complicated problems associated with this subject.

We would be remiss, however, if we did not point out the limitations inherent in the investigative process we have just finished, because in some serious ways, the Commission's methods themselves have hindered the adequate pursuit of information.

The Limitation of the Public Forum

All meetings and hearings have been held as public forums, according to law, and although we do not suggest that it should have been otherwise, we must emphasize that such an open forum naturally inhibits a frank and full discussion of a subject as personal, private and emotionally volatile as the consumption of pornography. In collecting the testimony of victims, it was difficult enough to find witnesses willing to speak out about their intimate negative experiences with pornography. To find people willing to acknowledge their personal consumption of erotic and pornographic materials and comment favorably in public about their use has been nearly impossible. Since such material is selling to millions of apparently satisfied consumers, it seems obvious that the data gathered is not well balanced.

The Constraints of Time and Money

A number of factors directly affecting the Commission complicated its work and strained its abilities to work as thoroughly and effectively as it might have. Both the time and the money needed to work through these complications was lacking and hence they were largely unsolved.

1. The very word pornography, with its negative connotation, imposes impediments to an open-minded and objective investigation. Every member of the group brought suitcases full of prior bias, including previous personal exposure, religious, ethical, social, and even professional beliefs. To some a discussion of pornography raises concerns of sincerely and deeply felt moral imperatives; to others it is a feminist issue of violence against women; and to still others, it is a lightning rod attracting debates about First Amendment guarantees with the threat of censorship seen as the overriding danger. Full airing of the differences of the members of the Commission and establishment of a wide and firm common ground was not possible in the time and with the funds allotted.

2. The issue of pornography has confounded people for centuries and has long been a subject of sincere disagreement among decent people. Pornography has religious, ethical, social, psychological and legal ramifications. The idea that eleven individuals studying in their spare time could complete a comprehensive report on so complex a matter in so constricted a time frame is simply unrealistic. No self-respecting investigator would accept conclusions based on such a study, and unfortunately the document produced reflects these inadequacies.

3. The variety of pornography, in its forms, qualities, and intensities of expression is vast. The Commission concentrated almost exclusively on formulating recommendations aimed at law enforcement. While that fulfills the Commission's mandate, we believe that the core issues involving pornography and its prevalence are more usefully viewed as health and welfare concerns. As such, they would properly be matters for research by committees established by the National Institute of Mental Health.

Given the varied backgrounds of the commissioners, the depth and complications of the subject historically, and the variety of the materials available today, the Commission's most severe limitation was imposed by a lack of time and money to complete a thorough study.

Because it has been sixteen years since the last Commission on this topic met and it is likely to be years before another government group tangles with these questions, we believe it would have been reasonable to grant the group, if not more money, at least more time, as requested.

THE MANDATE

1. The first element of the Commission's mandate was the assessment of the problem's dimensions. While there is little doubt about the proliferation of pornography since 1970, no serious effort has been made to quantify the increase, either in general or specifically as to the various types of pornography sold. We do not even know whether or not what the Commission viewed during the course of the year reflected the nature of most of the pornographic and obscene material in the market; nor do we know if the materials shown us mirror the taste of the majority of consumers of pornography. The visuals, both print and video, were skewed to the very violent and extremely degrading. While one does not deny the existence of this material, the fact that it dominated the materials presented at our hearings may have distorted the Commission's judgment about the proportion of such violent material in relation to the total pornographic material in distribution. The Commission's investigations did reveal that technological innovations have created a new delivery system for the consumption of pornographic and erotic material (notably via home video and cable). Since the home video industry is still young, it is reasonable to assume that the supply and public demand for pornographic materials may increase. Some recent industry figures actually show video purchases and rentals of pornography on the increase. There is, however, a significant corresponding decrease in both the number of adult theaters in this country and the circulation figures of

the so-called skin magazines. This may indicate that although there is a change in the way in which pornography is purchased, there is actually a stable (nongrowth) market for it. We simply do not know.

Because of the stunning change in the way in which people now receive erotic stimuli (a shift from print to video), we suggest that research be conducted to discover whether and to what extent video makes a greater or stronger impression on the vulnerable users, particularly children and adolescents, than does print.

2. One critical concern of this Commission was to measure and assess pornography's role in causing anti-social behavior; but although the Commission struggled mightily to agree on definitions of such basic terms as pornography and erotica, it never did so. This failure to establish definitions acceptable to all members severely limited our ability to come to grips with the question of impact. Only the term "obscenity," which has a legal meaning, became a category we all understood. In fact, the commission failed to carve out a mutually satisfactory definition of antisocial behavior. In this statement, it should be noted, therefore, we use the phrase "antisocial behavior" to describe forced sexual acts: acts involving coercion of any kind or lack of consent. We do not include (as certain commissioners desired) such private sexual practices as masturbation, homosexuality between consenting adults or premarital sex, practices that are not the province of government to regulate.

3. The final responsibility of the Commission was to recommend to the Attorney General specific measures to limit the spread of pornography. While much of the Commission's time was spent on these proposals, only the child pornography recommendations received thorough discussion. Accordingly we strongly endorse those proposals.

We reiterate our strong belief that the paucity of certain types of testimony, including dissenting expert opinion and the haste and absence of significant debate with which other recommendations and their supporting arguments were prepared did not leave adequate time for full and fair discussions of many of the more restrictive and controversial proposals. Consequently, while we endorse many of these recommendations, we dissent on some, for reasons of critical policy differences, lack of clarity and more importantly, because evidence essential to a considered evaluation of the proposals was not presented.

For example, the concept of mandatory sentencing supported in several recommendations is a theory hotly debated by both law enforcement personnel and experts specializing in penal reform. Little testimony was heard on the merits or liabilities of this concept with the exception of pleas from understandably frustrated prosecutors discouraged by light sentencing. Without reasoned assessment of this problem, we cannot support the proposal for mandatory sentencing. Other specific recommendations with which we disagree will follow here.

Congress should enact a forfeiture statute to reach the proceeds and instruments of any offense commited in violation of the Federal obscenity laws.

Congress should amend the Federal laws to eliminate the necessity of proving transportation in interstate commerce. The laws should be enacted to only require proof that the distribution of the obscene material "affects" interstate commerce.

Congress should enact legislation making it an unfair business practice and an unfair labor practice for any employer to hire individuals to participate in commercial sexual performances.

State legislatures should amend, if necessary, obscenity statutes to eliminate misdemeanor status for second offenses and make any second offense punishable as a felony.

State legislatures should enact, if necessary, forfeiture provisions as part of the state obscenity laws.

The President's Commission on Uniform Sentencing should consider a provision for a minimum of one year imprisonment for any second or subsequent violation of Federal law involving obscene material that depicts adults.

Legislatures should conduct hearings and consider legislation recognizing a civil remedy for harms attributable to pornography.

Any form of indecent act by or among "adults only" pornographic outlet patrons should be unlawful.

TESTIMONY ON SOCIAL SCIENCE DATA

We have limited our comments here to the relatively bias-free testimony and social-science data.

Our interpretation of the material presented is, consequently, somewhat different from that of other Commission members. It has led us to a different emphasis in priorities and recommendations.

The Commission sought to break down pornography into the various types of sexually explicit material available in our society. Unfortunately, social science research to date has not uniformly followed any such categorization (although we certainly suggest that future researchers consider this option), and the attempt to force the available social science data to fit the Commission's categories is fruitless. That is why in this statement the conclusions and interpretations of what the social science data *says* and *does not say* follow the research, not the Commission, categories.

First, it is essential to state that the social science research has not been designed to evaluate the relationship between exposure to pornography and the commission of sexual crimes; therefore efforts to tease the current data into proof of a causal link between these acts simply cannot be accepted. Furthermore, social science does not speak to harm, on which this Commission report focuses. Social science research speaks of a relationship among variables or effects that can be positive or negative.

Research has evaluated adults rather than children, and it is the latter who are most likely to be influenced by pornography. Studies have relied almost exclusively on male college student volunteers, which means that the "generalizability" of this data is extremely limited. The only other category studied in depth is sex offenders. Information from the sex-offender population must be interpreted with care because it may be self-serving. The research conducted to date has been correlational and experimental. Despite these limitations, the research data can be interpreted to indicate the following:

1. In a laboratory setting, exposure to sex-

ually violent stimuli has a negative effect on research subjects as measured by acceptance of rape myth and aggression and callousness toward women. We do not know, however, how long this attitudinal change is sustained without further stimulation; more importantly, we do not know whether and why such an attitudinal change might transfer into a behavioral change. There is reason for concern about these findings because we do know that experience with sex offenders indicates they harbor belief systems and attitudes consistent with deviant sexual practices (e.g. "women enjoy being raped" or "sexual acts with a child are a way of showing love and affection to that child"). We know further that such attitudes appear to be a precursor and maintainer of actual deviant behavior in an offender population. Although we believe the potential exists for attitudinal changes to translate into behavioral changes in some circumstances, this possibility needs considerable additional investigation.

2. Very little social-science research has been conducted evaluating the impact of non-violent degrading material on the average adult. Furthermore, there is a problem of definition about what constitutes "degrading material." We strongly encourage further research to define and evaluate the impact of such material.

3. Although research findings are far from conclusive, the preponderance of existing data indicates that non-violent and non-degrading sexually explicit materials does not have a negative effect on adults.

4. In documents attached to the main report mention has been made of a possible relationship between circulation rates of pornographic magazines and sex crime rates. One of the authors of the study on which the Commission has based its conclusion, Murray Straus, has written to explain his own research, which he suggested was being misinterpreted. "I do not believe that this research demonstrates that pornography causes rape. . . . In general the scientific evidence clearly indicates that if one is concerned with the effects of media on rape, the problem lies in the prevalence

of violence in the media, not on sex in the media."

5. To date there is no single comprehensive theory that is agreed upon to explain the development of paraphilic behavior. Human behavior is complex and multi-causal. To say that exposure to pornography in and of itself causes an individual to commit a sexual crime is simplistic, not supported by the social science data, and overlooks many of the other variables that may be contributing causes. Research must be conducted on the development of sexual interest patterns if we are to understand and control paraphilic behavior.

6. Unfortunately little is known about the impact of sexually explicit material on children. Ethically and morally one could not and would not conduct experiments to examine such a relationship. We do know that adolescents and young adults are large consumers of these materials, and little is yet known about its impact on this population. We underscore the statement made in the main body of the Commission's report regarding social science research: "In many respects, research is still at a fairly rudimentary stage, and with few attempts to standardize categories of analysis, self-reporting questionnaires, types of stimulus materials, description of stimulus materials, measurement of effects and related problems. We recommend that moneys be made available to fund further research on this topic."

ENFORCEMENT PRIORITIES

We have been encouraged by testimony from federal, state, and local officials that those involved in the heinous crime of child pornography are being prosecuted vigorously and that this effort is a national priority. We applaud that action and believe that this prosecution should continue to be a number one priority in law enforcement resource allotments.

On the other hand, we have heard frequently that there is virtually no enforcement of adult obscenity laws. Our analysis of the data leads us to believe that the sexually violent material that is unquestionably obscene and described in the main report is of sufficient concern to warrant intensified prosecution. We are concerned about such material because the violence and the eroticization of that violence may indeed be a potentially explosive mix. Even in this category, however, social science research does not claim a casual link.

The social science data, however, provides even less basis for the claim of a causal link between non-violent degrading and humiliating pornography and sexual violence. One might assume that this material may teach offensive, though not necessarily criminal, behavior to certain vulnerable consumers.

Accordingly, in communities where standards so dictate, prosecution of non-violent degrading obscene materials may assume a lesser priority. It is in this area of non-violent degrading and humiliating pornographic images that the most controversy may arise. What is seen as degrading by one viewer may in fact not be so seen by another, much in the same way that one person's erotica is another's pornography. But this is one of the categories about which much needs to be learned. Perhaps there is a distinct difference between what men see as degrading to women and what women consider to be degrading.

As vital as this category of non-violent degrading material may be to the ultimate understanding of the effects of pornographic material in society, we caution against an overinclusive interpretation of it. The Report suggests that most of the pornographic material in circulation now belongs in this category. We have not been able to draw this conclusion based on evidence presented. As stated earlier, attempts to quantify the materials in circulation and the particular character of the content of that material remain only "guesstimates."

WHAT OF OUR CHILDREN?

The most disturbing issue facing the panel this year was the concern about children and their exposure to child and adult pornography. Adolescents are acknowledged as an enormous market for pornographic materials, and despite legislative efforts to restrict access, this material remains easily available to youngsters.

In fact, from an early age American children are bombarded by very stimulating sexual messages, most of which are not pornographic but certainly are frightening. This year, for example, the AIDS epidemic has prompted health officials to broadcast urgent radio and television warnings against homosexual anal intercourse and group sex and pleas for the use of condoms.

Because children may have trouble with these very public messages, and because too many young people get too much of their sex education from pornographic magazines and films, we strongly support relevant school sex education programs. Appropriate and accurate information about loving sexual experiences can help inoculate children against the potential damage from early exposure to negative images. Furthermore, we urge parents to monitor carefully their own children's exposure to these materials.

There cannot be enough done to protect our children—both from people who would abuse and seduce them into the abhorrent world of child pornography and from the unwelcome intrusion of too many sexual messages. And we urge that child pornography prosecutions be given priority over all other forms of obscenity violations.

CONCLUSION

Why does pornography thrive and proliferate today? Is the demand for pornography a mirror or a beacon? Why do consumers support a multi-million dollar market for such a variety of products? Is lack of vigorous law enforcement to blame? Is society more tolerant of pornography than ever before? Is society's perception of what constitutes pornography changing? Do the production and increasing sophistication of sexually explicit materials in themselves stimulate more interest in pornographic magazines, films and videos? Or vice-versa? Or are other social forces chiefly to blame?

The most knowledgeable observers suggest that these are complex and difficult questions, ones that cannot be easily answered and which in our opinions this Commission did not adequately address.

Consider what has occurred during the past two decades. The birth control pill has become widely used, with an associated increase in sexual activity. The mobility of the population continues to increase, with a subsequent breakdown in community attachments for more and more people. The divorce rate has skyrocketed. We have a national drug abuse problem. The Vietnam war has taken its toll on the national psyche. Twenty-five million additional women have joined the work force. The so-called Sexual Revolution has come and gone (Time magazine on April 9, 1984, announced its demise). Has not each of these factors and others had a role to play in the growth of pornography?

After a year of forums and deliberations, it is tempting to join in offering simple solutions to complex problems, in the form of the Commission's Recommendations. But we are not persuaded to do so. We believe it would be seriously misleading to read this report and see a green light for prosecuting all pornographers. We still know too little about why many men and some women use and enjoy pornography; if and why women's and men's sexual arousal response patterns to pornography differ. We still have more questions than answers, and we stress the need for both non-governmental solutions and tolerance for the views of others.

The commission of sexual crimes, the degradation of women, and the abuse and mistreatment of children are terrible and pressing problems that concern us urgently. As we face up to the extensive public consumption even of certain types of extreme pornographic materials, a need for massive public re-education about potential problems associated with them seems strongly indicated. We cannot tolerate messages of sexual humiliation directed to any group. But to make all pornography the scapegoat is not constructive. In the absence of significant social sanctions against pornography, the possibility of halting its use seems as slim as was the chance of halting the sales of liquor during Prohibition. In conclusion we repeat that we face a complex social and legal problem that requires extensive study before realistic remedies can be recommended.

PART

5

Reference Material

Bibliography

The following bibliography provides a listing of the resources relied upon by the Commission in drafting and formulating this Report. The Commission acknowledges that it lacks completeness and does not include all footnote or endnote references. Specific source citations accompany the text.

REGULATION OF PORNOGRAPHY—A HISTORICAL PERSPECTIVE

Cases

Federal
Bulter v. Michigan, 352 U.S. 380 (1957).
Chaplinsky v. New Hampshire, 315 U.S. 568 (1942).
Hudnut v. American Booksellers Assn., No. 85–1090 slip op. (Feb. 24, 1986).
Memoirs v. Massachusetts, 383 U.S. 413 (1965).
Miller v. California, 413 U.S. 15 (1973).
Paris Adult Theatre I v. Slaton, 413 U.S. 49 (1973).
Roth v. United States, 354 U.S. 476 (1957).
Smith v. United States, 431 U.S. 291 (1977).
Stanley v. Georgia, 394 U.S. 557 (1969).
United States v. One Book Entitled Ulysses, 72 F. 2d 705 (2d Cir. 1934).
American Booksellers Assn. v. Hudnut, 598 F. Supp. 1316 (S.D. Ind. 1984).
United States v. Bennett, 24 F. Cas. 1093 (C.C.S.D.N.Y.) (1879).
United States v. Two Obscene Books, 99 F. Supp. 760 (N.D. Col. 1951).

State
Attorney General v. Book Named "God's Little Acre", 326 Mass. 281, 93 N.E. 2d 819 (1950).
Commonwealth v. Friede, 271 Mass. 318, 171 N.E. 472 (1930).
Commonwealth v. Gordon, 66 Pa. D.C. 101 (Phila. 1949).
Commonwealth v. Homes, 17 Mass. 336 (1821).
Commonwealth v. Sharpless, 2 Serg. & Rawle 91 (1815).
People v. Friede, 223 N.Y.S. 565 (1929).

Other
Dominus Rex v. Curll, 2 Str. 789, 93 Eng. Rep. 849 (1727).
King v. Sedley, 1 Keble 620 (K.B.), 83 Eng. Rep. 1146 (1663) and 1 Sid. 168, 82 Eng. Rep. 1036 (1663).
Queen v. Read, 11 Mod. Rep. 142, 88 Eng. Rep. 953 (1708) and Fobescu's Reports 98, 91 Eng. Rep. 777 (1708).
Regina v. Hicklin, L.R. 3 Q.B. 360 (1868).

Statutes

5 Stat. 556 S28.
18 U.S.C. S1461.
Ancient Charter, Colony Laws and Province Laws of Massachusetts Bay (1814).
Indianapolis and Marion County, Ind., Ordinance (May 3, 1984) amended by Indianapolis and Marion County, Ind., Ordinance (June 15, 1984).
Laws of Vermont, 1824, Ch. XXIII, no. 1,523.
Mass. Rev. Stat. Ch. 310 S10.

Books

Bland, *A History of Book Illustrations* (1958).
Technical Report of the Commission on Obscenity and Pornography (1970).
Tribe., L., *American Constitutional Law* (1978).

PRODUCTION, DISTRIBUTION, AND TECHNOLOGY OF SEXUALLY EXPLICIT MATERIALS

Cases

Federal
Enslin v. Fulham, No. 83–137. Cir. -4 (E.D.N.C. 1984).
Hustler v. Gsell, Cir. Action No. R-74–1482 ( ).

State
Trans-Lux Theater v. People ex. rel. Sweeton, 366 So. 2d No. (Ala. 1979).

Statutes

47 U.S.C. S 521.
47 U.S.C. S 544.

Books

American Psychiatric Association, *Diagnostic and Statistical Manual of Mental Disorders* (3d ed. 1983).
Army and Air Force Exchange Service Manual (Jan. 1985).
Committee on Sexual Offenses Against Children and Youths, *Sexual Offenses Against Children* (1984).
Film World, *X-Rated Movie Handbook* (1986).
The Report of the Commission on Obscenity and Pornography (1970).
Trained Slave and Over Daddy's Knee (1984).

Periodicals

Audit Bureau of Circulation, *1985 Membership Roster*.
Audit Bureau of Circulation, *This is the ABC*.
Bane, *X-Rated Computers*, Genesis.
Carr, *Type Dirty to Me*, Playboy.
Citizens for Decency Through Law, *Cable Pornography: Problems and Solutions* (Jan. 1985).
Cook, J., *The "X"-Rated Economy*, Forbes (Sept. 18, 1978).
Dominatrix Domain, No. 17.
Engle M., *Sex and Your Telephone*, Wash. Post, Mar. 9, 1986, p. C.1.
Flesh Fantasy Newspaper, Vol. XIII, No. 23, Aug. 9, 1985.
Fundgeon Times, Vol. I, No. 4.
Getting User Friendly with Computer Sex, High Society (July 1985).
Rowe, *1985 Retailers Survey*, Video Store (Aug. 1985).
SEXTEX Brochure (Feb. 12, 1986).
Stricharchuk, *Selling Skin: "Porn King" Raiker Sherman Expands His Empire With the Help of a Businessman's Skills*, Wall St. J., May 8, 1985, p. 24, Col. 1.
The Abernathy/MacGregor Group, Press Release.
The Home Video Market: Times of Turbulence and Transition (Jan. 6, 1986).
The War Against Pornography, Newsweek 62 (Mar. 18, 1986).
VCRs: Coming on Strong, Time (Dec. 24, 1984).
Video Software Dealers Assn., *1984 VSDA Annual Survey*.
X-Rated: The Joys of CompuSex, Time (May 14, 1984).

Testimony

Chicago Hearing, Vol. I. Diann.
Chicago Hearing, Vol. I, Peter Petruzzellis.
Chicago Hearing, Vol. II, Frederick Scullin.
Chicago Hearing, Vol. I, Donald Smith.
Houston Hearing, Vol. I, W.D. Brown,
Los Angles Hearing, Vol. I, Les Baker.
———————————————————— Vol. I, James Clancy.
———————————————————— Vol. II, Charles Dawson.
———————————————————— Vol. II, Brian Cid.

———————————————— Vol. II, Caryl Cid.
———————————————— Vol. I, James Docherty.
———————————————— Vol. I, William Dunkle.
———————————————— Vol. I, Brenda Fox.
———————————————— Vol. II, Al Goldstein.
———————————————— Vol. I, Teresa Hillman.
———————————————— Vol. I, Loretta Haroian.
———————————————— Vol. I, Ted McIlvenna.
———————————————— Vol. I, Robert Peters.
———————————————— Vol. I, William Roberts.
———————————————— Vol. II, Dennis Solvin.
———————————————— Vol. II, Charles Sullivan.
———————————————— Vol. I, Judith Trevillian.
———————————————— Vol. II, Jack Valenti.
———————————————— Vol. I, Brent Ward.
———————————————— Vol. II, John Weston.
Miami Hearing, Vol. I, Mike Berish.
———————————————— Vol. I. Paul Hartman.
New York Hearing, Vol. I, Bookstore Operator.
———————————————— Vol. I, Ledra Brady.
———————————————— Vol. II, Sam Currin.
———————————————— Vol. I, William Kelly.
———————————————— Vol. I, Gerald Piazza.
———————————————— Vol. I, Carl Shoffler.
———————————————— Vol. I, Bruce Taylor.
Washington, D.C. Hearing, Vol. II, Dennis DeBord.
———————————————— Vol.II, Kenneth Lanning.
———————————————— Vol. I, Sarah ✂ .

Other Sources

Interview with Phil Alsup, Army and Air Force Exchange Service in Washington, D.C. (Mar. 7, 1986).
Interview with CompuServe and The Source sales representatives (Mar. 6, 1986).
Interview with Brenda Fox, General Counsel, National Cable Television Association, Feb. 21, 1986.
Interview with Detective Joseph Haggerty, Washington, D.C., Metropolitan Police Department, Feb. 21, 1986.
Interview with Jackie Kiel, Audit Bureau of Circulation, Feb. 10, 1986.
Interview with Ted McIlvenna, President, Institute for the Advanced Study of Human Sexuality, Feb. 28, 1986.
Interview with Charles Ruttenburg, Counsel, Video Software Dealers Assn., Mar. 7, 1986.
Interview with Estelle Shenkler, Counsel, Navy Resale Services Support Office (Mar. 6, 1986).
Interview with Ronald Siegel, Mar. 6, 1986.
Interview with Donald Smith, Los Angeles, California, Police Department, Mar. 9, 1986.
Interview with Dennis Sobin, President, First Amendment Consumer and Trade Society (FACTS), Apr. 11, 1986.
Interview with John Weston, Counsel, Adult Film Association of America, Mar. 8, 1986.
Letter from Ralph O. Dawson, Chairman of the Board, Time, Inc., to Alan Sears, Executive Director, Attorney General's Commission on Pornography (Mar. 14, 1986).

CHILD PORNOGRAPHY

Cases

Federal

Central Hudson Gas & Electric Corp. v. Public Utility Service Commission of New York, 447 U.S. 557 (1980).
Miller v. California, 413 U.S., (1973), p. 15.
New York v. Ferber, 458 U.S., (1982), p. 758.
Roth v. United States, 354 U.S., (1957), p. 476.
Stanley v. Georgia, 394 U.S., (1969), p. 557.
Wood v. Hustler Magazine, Inc., 736 F. 2d 1084 (5th cir. 1984).

State

Ohio v. Meadows, No. 84 CRB 25585, Slip. op. (1st Dist. Dec. 18, 1985).

Statutes and Rules

Federal
7 U.S.C. S126n.
7 U.S.C. S1361.
18 U.S.C. S2251.
18 U.S.C. S2252.
18 U.S.C. S2255.
42 U.S.C. S3002.
42 U.S.C. S3003.
42 U.S.C. S3004.

Books

Alan Guttmacher Institute, *Teenage Pregnancy: The Problem That Hasn't Gone Away* (1981).
Bolton, F., *The Pregnant Adolescent: Problems of Premature Parenthood,* (1980).
Centers for Disease Control, *Abortion Surveillance* (1985).
Committee on Sexual Offenses Against Children and Youth, 2 *Sexual Offenses Against Children,* (1984).
Diagnostic and Statistic Manual for Mental Disorders (American Psychiatric Assn. 3d ed. [1980]).
Enablers, Inc., *Juvenile Prostitution in Minnesota,* (1978).
✂ , C., *Male Model* (1979).
Lanning, K., *Collectors in Child Pornography and Sex Rings* (A. Wolbert Burgess ed. 1984).
Lederer, *Then and Now—An Interview with a Former Pornography Model* in *Take Back the Night: Women On Pornography* (1980).
U.S. Department of Justice, Federal Bureau of Investigation, *Child Molesting: A Behavioral Analysis for Law Enforcement* (1986).
Weisberg, D. K., *Children in the Night* (1985).

Articles

Lolita, No. 48.
Playgirl (Oct 1985).
Schoettle, U., *Child Exploitation: A Study of Child Pornography,* J. Am, Acad. Child Psych., (1980), p. 289.
Seminary Graduate Charged in Porno Computer Network, Fayetteville Times, Feb. 7, 1986.
Silbert & Pines, A., *Occupational Hazards of Street Prostitutes,* Comm. Just. & Behavior., (1981), p. 395.
Swing, No. 45 (1982).
Wonderland: Newsletter of the Lewis Carroll Collectors Guild (1984).

Testimony

Chicago Hearing, Vol. II, James S. Reynolds
―――――――――――――――――――――――― Vol. II, Frederick Scullin
―――――――――――――――――――――――― Vol. I, Joan Weber
Los Angeles Hearing, Vol. I, Miki   ✂
―――――――――――――――――――――――― Vol. I, George
Miami Hearing, Vol. I, Laura   ✂
―――――――――――――――――――――――― Vol. II, William Cassidy
―――――――――――――――――――――――― Vol. II, Alfred Danna
―――――――――――――――――――――――― Vol. II, Paul Der Ohannesian
―――――――――――――――――――――――― Vol. I, William Dworin
―――――――――――――――――――――――― Vol. II, Kenneth Elsesser
―――――――――――――――――――――――― Vol. II, Seth Goldstein
―――――――――――――――――――――――― Vol. I, Paul Hartman
―――――――――――――――――――――――― Vol. I, Kenneth Hermann
―――――――――――――――――――――――― Vol. II, Joyce Karlin
―――――――――――――――――――――――― Vol. I, Kenneth Lanning
―――――――――――――――――――――――― Vol. I, Robert Northrup
―――――――――――――――――――――――― Vol. II, Dennis Shaw
―――――――――――――――――――――――― Vol. II, Ulrich Schoettle
―――――――――――――――――――――――― Vol. II, Roland Summitt
―――――――――――――――――――――――― Vol. I, Toby Tyler
New York Hearing, Vol. II, Alan Dershowitz
―――――――――――――――――――――――― Vol. I, Carl Shoffler
Washington, D.C., Hearing, Vol. I, Charles Clauson
―――――――――――――――――――――――― Vol. I, David

_____ Vol. II, John Forbes
_____ Vol. I, Daniel Harrington
_____ Vol. I, Jeff
_____ Vol. II, John
_____ Vol. I, Lisa
_____ Vol. I, Daniel Mihalko
_____ Vol. II, Robert Prentke
_____ Vol. I, Jack Swagerty

Miscellaneous References

Cal. B. 141
Hearings Before the Senate Judiciary Committee, Subcommittee on Juvenile Justice (Oct. 1, 1985).
Letter from Joyce A. Karlin to Henry E. Hudson (Dec. 20, 1985).
Rothema, J. & David, T., Status Offenders in Los Angeles County, Focus on Runaway and Homeless Youth: A Study and Policy Recommendations (unpublished study).
S.B. 1305
S.B. 140

SOCIAL AND BEHAVIORAL SCIENCE

Abel, G., (1985). Testimony Before the Attorney General Commission on Pornography, Houston, Texas, September 13.
Abel, G., J. Becker and L. Skinner (1985) Aggressive behavior and sex. Unpublished Paper
Abel, G., M. Mittelman and J. Becker (1985). Sexual offenders: results of assessment and recommendations for treatment. In M.H. Ben-Aron, S.J. Hucker, and C.D. Webster (eds.). Clinical criminology: the assessment and treatment of criminal behavior. Toronto.
Abel, G., J. Rouleau and J. Cunningham-Rathner (1985). Sexually aggressive behavior. In W. Curran, A. McGarry and S. Shah (eds.). Modern legal psychiatry and psychology. Philadelphia: F.A. Davis Co.
Abel, G., M. Mittelman, and J. Becker (Unpublished Paper). The effects of erotica on paraphiliacs' behavior. Atlanta, Georgia.
Abel, G., Becker, J., Murphey, W. and Flanigan, B. (1981). Identifying dangerous child molesters. In R. Stuart (ed.), Violent behavior: social learning approaches to prediction, management and treatment. New York: Bruner/Mazel.
Abel, G., Becker, J. and Skinner, L. (1980). Aggressive behavior and sex. Psychiatric clinics of North America, 3:133–151.
Abel. G.G., Barlow, D.H., Blanchard, E. & Guild, D. (1977). The components of rapists' sexual arousal. Archives of general psychiatry, 34, 895–903.
Abel, G., Blanchard, E. & Becker, J. V. (1976). Psychological treatment of rapists. In M. Walker & S. Brodsky (eds.), Sexual assault: the victim and the rapist. Lexington, MA. Lexington Books.
Abel, G. & Blanchard, E. (1974). The role of fantasy in the treatment of sexual deviation. Archives of general psychiatry, 30, 467–75.
Abelson, H., R. Cohen, E. Heaton, and C. Suder (1970). National survey of public attitudes toward and experience with erotic materials. Technical report of the Commission on Obscenity and Pornography, vol. 6. Washington, D.C.: Gov't. Printing Office. 1–255.
Abramson, P. and Hayashi, H. (1984). Pornography in Japan: cross-cultural and theoretical considerations. In Malamuth, N.M. and Donnerstein, E. (eds.), Pornography and sexual aggression. Orlando, Florida: Academic Press.
Abramson, P., L. Perry, T. Seeley, D. Seeley, and A. Rothblatt (1981). Thermographic measurement of sexual arousal: a discriminant validity analysis. Archives of sexual behavior, 10:2; 175–176.
Amoroso, D.M., M. Brown, M. Pruesse, E. Ware and D. Pilkey (1970). An investigation of behavioral, psychological, and physiological reactions to pornographic stimuli. Technical report of the Commission on Obscenity and Pornography, vol. 8. Washington, D.C.: Gov't. Printing Office. 1–40.
Bachy, V. (1976). Danish "permissiveness" revisited. Journ. of Comm., 26:40–43.
Bandura, A. (1977). Social learning theory. New Jersey: Prentice Hall.
Bandura, A. (1973). Aggression: A social learning analysis. New York: Prentice-Hall.
Bandura, A. (1965). Influence of model's reinforcement contingency conditions on the acquisition of imitative responses. Journal of personality and social psychology, 1, 589–95.
Bandura, A., Blanchard, E., & Ritter, B. (1969). Relative efficacy of desensitization and modeling approaches for inducing behavioral, affective, and attitudinal changes. Journal of personality and social psychology, 13, 173–199.
Bandura, A., Ross, D. & Ross, S. (1963). Vicarious reinforcement and imitative learning. Journal of abnormal and social psychology, 67, 601–607.

Bandura, A., W. Underwood and M. Fromson (1975). Disinhibition of aggression through diffusion of responsibility and dehumanization of victims. *Journal of research in personality*, 9: 253–269.

Barlow, D.H. (1977). Assessment of sexual behavior. In A. Ciminero, K. Calhoun, & H. Adams ds.), *Handbook of behavioral assessment*, New York: John Wiley, 461–548.

Barnes, G.E., Malamuth, N.M. and Check, J.V.P. (1984a). Psychoticism and sexual arousal to rape depictions. *Pers. and Ind. Diff.*, 5:273–279.

Barnes, G.E., Malamuth, N.M. and Check, J.V.P. (1984b). Personality and sexuality. *Pers. and Ind. Diff.*, 5:159–172.

Baron, L. and M. Straus (1986). Rape and its relation to social disorganization, pornography, and sexual inequality. Paper presented at the International Congress on Rape, Israel, April, 1986.

Baron, L. and Straus, M. (1985). Legitimate violence and rape: a test of the cultural spillover theory. Paper presented at the Eastern Sociological Society meeting, Philadelphia, Pa.

Baron, L. and M. Straus (1984). Sexual stratification, pornography and rape. In N. Malamuth and E. Donnerstein (eds.), *Pornography and sexual aggression*, New York: Academic Press.

Baron, R.A. (1977). *Human aggression*. New York: Plenum Press.

Baron, R. A. (1974a). Aggression as a function of victim's pain cues, level of prior anger arousal, and exposure to an aggressive model. *Journal of personality and social psychology*, 29:117–124.

Baron, R.A. (1974b). The aggression-inhibiting influence of heightened sexual arousal. *Journal of personality and social psychology*, 30:318–322.

Baron, R.A. and Bell, P.A. (1977). Sexual arousal and aggression by males: effects of type of erotic stimuli and prior provocation. *Journal of personality and social psychology*, 35:79–87.

Ben-Veniste, Richard (1970). Pornography and sex crime: the Danish experience. *Technical report of the Commission on Obscenity and Pornography*, vol. 7. Washington, D.C.: Gov't. Printing Office. 245–262.

Berkowitz, L. (1971). Sex and violence: we can't have it both ways. *Psychology today*, May, 14–23.

Berkowitz, L. (1974). Some determinants of impulsive aggression: role of mediated associations with reinforcements for aggression. *Psychological review*. 81, 165–76.

Berkowitz, L. (1984). Some effects of thoughts on anti- and pro-social influences of media events: a cognitive-neoassociation analysis. *Psychological bulletin*. 95, 410–427.

Berkowitz, L. & Donnerstein, E. (1982). External validity is more than skin deep: some answers to criticisms of laboratory experiments (with special reference to research on aggression). *American psychologist*, 37, 245–257.

Berlin, F. (1983). Sex offenders: a biomedical perspective and a status report on biomedical treatment. In Greer, J. and Stuart, I. (eds.), *The sexual aggressor: current perspectives on treatment*. New York: Van Nostrand Reinhold Co.

Blader, J. and Marshall, W. (1984). The relationship between cognitive and erectile measures of sexual arousal in nonrapist males as a function of depicted aggression. *Beh. Res. and Ther.*, 17:215–222.

Bohmer, C. (1983). Legal and ethical issues in mandatory treatment: the patient's rights versus society's rights. In Greer, J. and Stuart, I. (eds.), *The sexual aggressor: current perspectives on treatment*. New York: Van Nostrand Reinhold Co.

Bramel, D. (1969). The arousal and reduction of hostility. In Mills, J. (ed.), *Experimental Social Psychology*. New York: Macmillan.

Briere, J. & Malamuth, N. M. (1983). Self-reported likelihood of sexually aggressive behavior: attitudinal vs. sexual explanations. *Journal of research in personality*, 17, 315–323.

Brody, S. (1977). Screen violence and film censorship: a review of research. *Home Office Research Study No. 40*. London: Her Majesty's Stationery Office.

Burgess, A. (1985). *Rape and sexual assault*. New York: Garland Press.

Burt, Martha R. (1980). Cultural myths and support for rape. *Journal of personality and social psychology*, 38, 217–230.

Byrne, D. and Sheffield, J. (1965). Response to sexually arousing stimuli as a function of repressing and sensitizing defenses. *Journal of abnormal psychology*, 70, 114–118.

Byrne, D. (1977). The imagery of sex. In J. Money and H. Musaph (eds.), *Handbook of sexology*, Amsterdam: Excerpta Media. pp. 327–350.

Byrne, D. and Byrne, L.A. (eds.) (1977). *Exploring human sexuality*. New York: Harper and Row.

Byrne, D. and J. Lamberth (1970), The effect of erotic stimuli on sex arousal, evaluative responses, and subsequent behavior. In *Technical Report of the Commission on Obscenity and Pornography*, vol. 8, Washington, D.C.: Gov't. Printing Office, pp. 41–67.

Caird, W. and Wincze, J.P. (1977), *Sex therapy: a behavioral approach*. New York: Harper and Row.

Cairns, R. B., Paul, J. C. N., & Wishner, J. (1962). Sex censorship: the assumptions of anti-obscenity laws and the empirical evidence. *Minnesota Law review*, 46, 1009–1041.

Cairns, R.B., J.C. Paul and J. Wishner (1970). Psychological assumptions in sex censorship: an evaluation review of recent research (1961–1968). In *Technical report of the Commission on Obscenity and Pornography*, vol. 1. Washington D.C.: U.S. Gov't. Printing Office.

Cantor, J.R., Zillmann, D. and Einsiedel, E.F. (1978). Female responses to provocation after exposure to aggressive and erotic films. *Communication research*, 5:4, 395–411.

Carter, D.L., Prentky, R., Knight, R., Vanderveer, P. and Boucher,R. (1985). Use of pornography in the criminal and developmental histories of sexual offenders. Report to the National Institute of Justice and National Institute of Mental Health.

Ceniti, J. & Malamuth, N. M. (1985). Effects of repeated exposure to sexually violent or sexually nonviolent stimuli on sexual arousal to rape and nonrape depictions. *Behavior research and therapy*.

Check. J.V.P. (1985). A survey of Canadians' attitudes regarding sexual content in media. Report to the Lamarsh Research Programme on Violence and Conflict Resolution and the Canadian Broadcasting Corporation. Toronto, Ontario.

Check. J.V.P. (1985). The effects of violent and nonviolent pornography. Report to the Dept. of Justice, Ottawa, Canada.

Check. J.V.P. and Malamuth, N.M. (1985, Pornography and sexual aggression: a social learning theory analysis. In M.L. McLaughlin (ed.), *Communication yearbook*, v. 9. Beverly Hills, CA: Sage Publications.

Check. J. V. P. & Malamuth, N.M. (1983). Sex-role stereotyping and reactions to stranger versus acquaintance rape. *Journal of personality and social psychology*, 45, 344–356.

Cline, V. B. (1974). *Where do you draw the line?* Provo, Utah: Brigham Young University Press.

Cochrane, P. (1978). Sex crimes and pornography revisited. *International journal of criminology and penology*, 6:307–17.

Commission on Obscenity and Pornography. (1970). *The Report of the Commission on Obscenity and Pornography*. Washington, D.C.: U.S. Gov't. Printing Office.

Comstock. G.C. (in press). Television and Film Violence. In S.J. Apter and A.P. Goldstein (eds.), *Youth violence: programs and prospects*. New York: Pergamon Press.

Cook, R. and R. Fosen (1970). Pornography and the sex offender: patterns of exposure and immediate arousal effects of pornographic stimuli. *Technical report of the Commission on Obscenity and Pornography*, vol. 7, Washington, D.C.: Gov't. Printing Office.

Court, J.H. (1984). Sex and violence: a ripple effect. In N. Malamuth and E. Donnerstein (eds.) *Pornography and sexual aggression*. New York: Academic Press.

Court, J.H. (1982). Rape trends in New South Wales: a discussion of conflicting evidence. *Australian journal of social issues*. 17:3, 202–206.

Court, J.H. (1981). Pornography update. *British journal of sexual medicine*. May. 28–30.

Court, J.H. (1977). Pornography and sex crimes: a reevaluation in light of recent trends around the world. *International journal of criminology and penology*, 5:129–157.

Davis, K. E. and Braught, G. N. (1970). Exposure to pornography, character, and sexual deviance: a retrospective survey. *Technical report of the Commission on Obscenity and Pornography*, vol. 7. Washington, D.C.: Gov't. Printing Office.

Dermer, M. and Pysczcynski, T.A. (1978). Effects of erotica on men's loving and liking responses for women they love. *Journal of personality and social psychology*, 36:1302–1310.

Dienstbier, R.A. (1977). Sex and violence: can research have it both ways? *Journal of Communication*, 27, 176–188.

Dietz, P.E. (1978) Social factors in rapists' behavior. In Rada, R. J. (ed.), *Clinical aspects of the rapist*. New York: Grune and Stratton.

Dietz, P.E. & Evans, B. (1982). Pornographic imagery and prevalence of paraphilia. *American journal of psychiatry*, 139, 1493–1495.

Dietz, P. E., Harry, B., and Hazelwood, R. R. (1986). Detective magazines: pornography for the sexual sadist? *Journal of Forensic Science*, 31:197–211.

Donnerstein, E. (1983a). Aggressive pornography: can it influence aggression against women? in G. Albee, S. Gordon, and H. Leitenberg (eds.), *Promoting sexual responsibility and preventing sexual problems*. Hanover, New Hampshire: University of New England Press.

Donnerstein, E. (1983b). Erotica and human aggression. In R. Geen and E. Donnerstein (eds.). *Aggression: theoretical and empirical reviews* (vol. 2). New York: Academic Press.

Donnerstein, E. (1980a). Aggressive erotica and violence against women. *Journal of personality and social psychology*, 39, 269–277.

Donnerstein, E. (1980b). Pornography and violence against women. *Annals of the New York Academy of Sciences* 347, 277–288.

Donnerstein, E. and Linz, D. (1984). Sexual violence in the media: a warning. *Psychology today*, January, 14–15.

Donnerstein, E. and Berkowitz, L. (1981). Victim reactions in aggressive-erotic films as a factor in violence against women. *Journal of personality and social psychology*, 41:710–724.

Donnerstein, E. and Hallam, J. (1978). The facilitating effects of erotica on aggression towards females. *Journal of personality and social psychology*, 36, 1270–1277.

Donnerstein, E. & Barrett, G. (1978). The effects of erotic stimuli on male aggression toward females. *Journal of personality and social psychology*, 36, 180–188.

Donnerstein, E., Donnerstein, M. & Evans, R. (1975). Erotic stimuli and aggression: facilitation or inhibition. *Journal of personality and social psychology*, 32: 237–244.

Eron, L. D. (1980). Prescription for the reduction of aggression, *American psychologist*, 35, 244–52.

Evans, D.R. (1968) Masturbatory fantasy and sexual deviation. *Behavioral research and therapy*, 6:17.

Eysenck, H.J. (1984). Afterword: sex, violence and the media. In Malamuth, N.M. and Donnerstein, E. (eds.), *Pornography and sexual aggression*. Orlando, Florida: Academic Press.

Eysenck, H.J. and Eysenck, S.B.G. (1976). *Psychoticism as a dimension of personality*. London: Hodder and Stoughton.

Eysenck, H. J. and Nias, D. K. (1978). *Sex, violence and the media*. New York: Harper and Row.

Farkas, G.M., Sine, L.F., and Evans, I.M. (1978). Personality, sexuality, and demographic differences between volunteers and nonvolunteers for a laboratory study of male sexual behavior. *Arch. of Sex. Beh.*, 7:513–520.

Finkelhor, D. (1984). *Child Sexual Abuse*. New York: The Press.

Fisher, W. A., and Byrne, D. (1978a). Individual differences in affective, evaluative, and behavioral responses to an erotic film. *Journal of applied social psychology*, 8, 355–365.

Fisher, W. A. and Byrne, D. (1978b). Sex differences in response to erotica: love versus lust. *Journal of personality and social psychology*, 36, 119–125.

Fisher, G. & Rivlin, E. (1971). Psychological needs of rapists. *British journal of criminology*. 11, 182–185.

Frodi, A. (1977). Sexual arousal, situational restrictiveness, and aggressive behavior. *Journal of research in personality*, 11, 48–58.

Gebhard. P. (1977). The acquisition of basic sex information. *Journ. Sex Res.*, 13:148–169.

Gebhard, P., Gagnon, J., Pomeroy, W. and Christenson, C. (1965). *Sex offenders: an analysis of types*. New York: Harper and Row.

Geen, R. and Quanty, M.B. (1977). The catharsis of aggression: an evaluation of a hypothesis. In L. Berkowitz (ed.), *Advances in experimental social psychology*, vol. 10., New York: Academic Press.

Gerbner, G., Gross, L., Eleey, M.F., Jackson-Beeck, M., Jeffries-Fox, S. & Signorelli, N. (1977). TV violence profile No. 8: the highlights. *Journal of Communications*, 32, 100–126.

Gerbner, G. (1980). Sex on television and what viewers learn from it. Paper presented at the annual conference of the National Association of Television Program Executives. San Francisco, February.

Gerbner, G., Gross, L., Morgan, M. & Signorelli, N. (1980). The mainstreaming of America: Violence profile No. 11. *Journal of communications*, 30:3, 10–29.

Glassman, M.B. (1978). Community standards of patent offensiveness: public opinion data and obscenity law. *Pub. Op. Res.*, 161–170.

Goldstein, M.J., Kant, H.S., and Hartman, J.J. (1974). *Pornography and sexual deviance*. Berkeley: Univ. of California Press.

Goldstein, M.J., H. Kant, L. Judd, C. Rice, and R. Green (1970). Exposure to pornography and sexual behavior in deviant and normal groups. *Technical report of the Commission on Obscenity and Pornography*, vol. 7. Washington, D.C.: Gov't. Printing Office. 1–90.

Goldstein, S. and Ibaraki, T. (1978). Japan: Aggression and aggression control in Japanese society. In Goldstein, A. and Segall, M. (eds.), *Aggression in global perspective*. New York: Pergamon Press.

Green, S.E. and Mosher, D.L. (1985). A causal model of sexual arousal to erotic fantasies. *Journal of sex research*, 21:1–23.

Griffitt, W. (1978). Affect, sex guilt, gender, and the rewarding-punishing effects of erotic stimuli. *Journal of personality and social psychology*, 36, 850–58.

Griffitt, W. (1975). Sexual experience and sexual responsiveness: sex differences. *Archives of sexual behavior*, 4, 529–540.

Griffitt, W. (1973). Response to erotica and the projection of response to erotica in the opposite sex. *Journal of experimental research in personality*, 6, 330–338.

Griffitt, W. and Kaiser, D.L. (1978). Affect, sex guilt, gender and the reward-punishing effects of erotic stimuli. *Journal of personality and social psychology*, 36:850–858.

Griffitt, W. and Jackson, T. (1970). Context effects in impression formation as a function of context source. *Psychon. Sci.*, 20:321–322.

Gutierres, S., D.T. Kenrick, & L. Goldberg (1985). Adverse influence on exposure to popular erotica: effects on judgments of others and judgments of one's spouse. Paper presented at the annual meeting of the Midwestern Psychological Association, Chicago, Illinois.

Heiby, E. & Becker, J. D. (1980). Effect of filmed modeling on the self-reported frequency of masturbation. *Archives of sexual behavior*, 9, 115–121.

Heiman, J. (1977). A psychophysiological exploration of sexual arousal patterns in females and males. *Psychophysiological*, 14: 266–274.

Heiman, J., LoPiccolo, L. and LoPiccolo, J. (1976). *Becoming orgasmic: a sexual growth program for women*. Englewood Cliffs, New Jersey: Prentice-Hall.

Howard, J., C. Reifler, and M. Liptzin (1970). Effects of exposure to pornography. *Technical report of the Commission on Obscenity and Pornography*, vol. 8. Washington, D.C.: Gov't. Printing Office, 97–132.

Howard, J.L., M. Liptzin, & C. Reifler (1973). Is pornography a problem? *Journal of social issues*, 29:163–81.

Howard, J.L., C. Reifler, and M. Liptzin (1971). Effects of exposure to pornography. In *Technical report of the Commission on Obscenity and Pornography*, vol. 8. Washington D.C.: U.S. Gov't. Printing Office.

Jaffe, Y., Malamuth, NM, Feingold, J. and Feshbach, S. (1974). Sexual arousal and behavioral aggression. *Journal of personality and social psychology*. 30:259–764.

Johnson, P. & Goodchilds, J. (1973). Pornography, sexuality, and social psychology. *Journal of Social Issues*, 29, 231–238.

Johnson, W., L. Kupperstein, and J. Peters (1970). Sex offenders' experience with erotica. *Technical report of the Commission on Obscenity and Pornography*, vol. 7. Washington, D.C.: Gov't Printing Office. 163–172.

Johnston, J. and Ettema, J.S. (1982). *Positive images: breaking stereotypes with children's television*. Beverly Hills, CA: Sage Publications.

Kelley, K. (in press). Variety is the spice of erotica: repeated exposure, novelty, sex, and sexual attitudes. *Archives of sexual behavior*.

Kelley, K. (in press). Sexual attitudes as determinants of the motivational properties of exposure to erotica. *Personality and individual differences*.

Kelley, K. (1985). Sex, sex guilt, and authoritarian differences in responses to explicit heterosexual and masturbatory slides. *Journal of sex research*, 21:68–85.

Kelley K. and D. Byrne (1983). Assessment of sexual responding: arousal, affect and behavior. In J. Cacioppo and R. Petty (eds.), *Social pscyhophysiology*. New York: Guilford, 467–490.

Kinsey, A., Pomeroy, W., Martin, C., and Gebhard, P. (1953). *Sexual behavior in the human female*. Philadelphia: W.B. Sanders.

Koss, M. (1986). Hidden rape: survey of psychopathological consequences. Report to the National Institute of Mental Health.

Koss, Mary (in press), Nonstranger sexual aggression: a discriminant analysis of the psychological characteristics of undetected offenders. *Sex Roles*.

Koss, Mary (in press), The hidden rape victim: personality, attitudinal and situational characteristics. *Psychology of women quarterly*.

Krafka, C.L. (1985). Sexually explicit, sexually violent, and violent media: effects of multiple naturalistic exposures and debriefing on female viewers. Unpublished Ph.D. dissertation, University of Wisconsin, Madison, Wisconsin.

Kruylanski, A.W. (1975). The human subject in the psychology experiment: fact and artifact. In Berhowitz, L. (ed.). *Advances in experimental social psychology*, vol. 8. New York: Academic Press.

Kupperstein, L. and W.C. Wilson (1970). Erotica and anti-social behavior: an analysis of selected social indicator statistics. *Technical report of the Commission on Obscenity and Pornography*, vol. 7. Washington, D. C.: Gov't. Printing Office. 311–324.

Kutchinsky, B. (1985). In Tomasson, R.F. (ed.), *Comparative social research*, v. 8. Connecticut: Jai Press.

Kutchinsky, B. (1973). The effect of easy availability of pornography on the incidence of sex crimes: the Danish experience. *Journal of social issues*, 29:3 163–181.

Kutchinsky, B. (1970a). Towards an explanation of the decrease in registered sex crimes in Copenhagen. *Technical report of the Commission on Obscenity and Pornography*. vol. 7. Washington, D.C.: Gov't. Printing Office. 263–310.

Kutchinsky, B. (1970b). The effect of pornography: a pilot experiment on perception, behavior, and attitudes. *Technical report of the Commission on Obscenity and Pornography*, vol. 8. Washington, D.C.: Gov't. Printing Office 133–169.

Lederer, L. (ed.) (1980). *Take back the night: women on pornography*. New York: William Morrow.

Liebert, R. and N.S. Schwartzberg (1977). Effects of mass media. *Annual review of psychology*, 28:141–173.

Linz, D. (1985). *Sexual violence in the mass media: effects on male viewers and implications for society*. Unpublished doctoral dissertation. Madison, Wisconsin: University of Wisconsin.

Lettman, R. (1961). Psychology: the socially indifferent science. *American Psychologist*, 16:232–236.

Malamuth, N.M. (in press). Predictors of naturalistic sexual aggression. *Journ. Pers. Soc. Psych.*, 50.

Malamuth, N.M. (1984a). Aggression against women: cultural and individual causes. In Malamuth, N.M. and Donnerstein, E. (eds.). *Pornography and sexual aggression*. New York: Academic Press.

Malamuth, N.M. (1984). The mass media and aggression against women: research findings and prevention. In A. Burgess (ed.), *Handbook of Research on Pornography and Sexual Assault*. New York: Garland Publishers.

Malamuth, N.M. (1983). Factors associated with rape as predictors of laboratory aggression against women. *Journal of Personality and Social Psychology*, 45, 432–442.

Malamuth, N.M. (1981a). Rape fantasies as a function of exposure to violent sexual stimuli. *Archives of Sexual Behavior*, 10, 33–47.

Malamuth, N.M. (1981b). Rape proclivity among males. *Journal of social issues*, 37, 138–157.

Malamuth, N.M. and Billings, V. (1986). The functions and effects of pornography: sexual communication versus the feminist models in light of research findings. In Bryant, J, and Zillmann, D. (ed.), *Perspectives on media effects*. Hillsdale, New Jersey: Lawrence Erlbaum.

Malamuth, N.M. and Briere, J. (In press). Sexually violent media: indirect effects on aggression against women. *Journ. of Soc. Issues*.

Malamuth, N.M., Check, J.V.P. and Briere, J. (1986). Sexual arousal in response to aggression: ideological, aggressive and sexual correlates. *Journ. Pers. Soc. Psych.*, 50:330–340.

Malamuth, N.M. and Check, J.V.P. (1985). The effects of aggressive pornography on beliefs in rape myths: individual differences. *Journ. Res. in Pers.*, 19:299–320.

Malamuth, N.M. and Check, J.V.P. (1983). Sexual arousal to rape depictions: individual differences. *Journal of Abnormal Psychology*, 92, 55–67.

Malamuth, N.M. and Check, J.V.P. (1981). The effects of mass media exposure on acceptance of violence against women: a field experiment. *Journal of Research in Personality*, 15, 436–446.

Malamuth, N.M. and Check, J. V. P. (1980a). Penile tumescence and perceptual responses to rape as a function of victim's perceived reactions. *Journal of Applied Social Psychology*, 10:6, 528–547.

Malamuth, N.M. and Check, J.V.P. (1980b). Sexual arousal to rape and consenting depictions: the importance of the woman's arousal. *Journal of Abnormal Psychology*, 89, 763–766.

Malamuth, N.M. & Donnerstein, E. (1982). The effects of aggressive-pornographic mass media stimuli. In L. Berkowitz (ed.), *Advances in experimental social psychology*, vol. 15 (103–136). New York: Academic Press.

Malamuth, N.M., Haber, S. & Feshbach, S. (1980). Testing hypotheses regarding rape: exposure to sexual violence, sex differences, and the "normality" of rapists. *Journal of Research in Personality*, 14, 121–137.

Malamuth, N.M., Heim, M., & Feshbach, S. (1980). Sexual responsiveness of college students to rape depictions: inhibitory and disinhibitory effects. *Journal of Personality and Social Psychology*, 38, 399–408.

Malamuth, N.M., Reisin, I. & Spinner, B. (1979). "Exposure to pornography and reactions to rape". Paper presented to the 86th annual convention of the American Psychological Association, New York.

Malamuth, N.M. & Spinner, B. (1980). A longitudinal content analysis of sexual violence in the best-selling erotic magazines, *The Journal of Sex Research*, 16:3, 226–237.

Mann, J., Berkowitz, L., Sidman, J., Starr, S., & West, S. (1974). Satiation of the transient stimulating effect of erotic films. *Journal of personality and social psychology*, 30, 729–735.

Mann, J., Sidman, J. & Starr, S. (1973). Evaluating social consequences of erotic films: an experimental approach. *Journal of Social Issues*, 29, 113–131.

Mann, J., Sidman, J. and Starr, S. (1970). Effects of erotic films on the sexual behavior of married couples. *Technical report of the Commission on Obscenity and Pornography*, vol. 8. Washington, D.C.: Gov't. Printing Office. 170–254.

Marshall, W. (1973). The modification of sexual fantasies: a combined treatment approach to the reduction of deviant sexual behavior. *Behavior research and therapy*, 11:557–564.

Marshall, W. (1985). Use of pornography by sexual offenders. Unpublished paper.

Marshall, W. (1984). Report on the use of pornography by sexual offenders. *Report to the Federal Department of Justice*. Ottawa, Canada.

Marshall, W. and Barbaree, H. (1984). Disorders of personality, impulse and adjustment. In Tuiner, S. and M. Herson (eds.), *Adult psychopathology: a behavioral perspective*. New York: Academic Press.

Marshall, W. and H. E. Barbaree (1978). The reduction of deviant arousal: satiation treatment for sexual aggressors. *Criminal justice behavior*, 5:294–303.

Marshall, W. and Christie, M. (1981). Pedophilia and aggression. *Criminal justice and behavior*, 8, 145–158.

Marshall, W., Earls, C., Segal, Z., and Darke, J. (1983). A behavioral program for the assessment and treatment of sexual aggressors. In K. Craig and R. McMahon (eds.). *Advances in clinical behavior therapy*. New York: Brunner/Mazel.

McKay, H.B. and Dolff, D.J. (1985). The impact of pornography: an analysis of research and summary of findings. *Working papers on pornography and prostitution*, Report No. 13. Ottawa, Canada: Ministry of Supply and Services.

Melamed, L. and Moss, M. (1975). Effect of context on ratings of attractiveness of photographs. *Jour. Psych.*, 90:129–136.

Merritt, C. G., Gerstl, J. E., & Lo Sciuto, L. A. (1975). Age and perceived effects of erotica-pornography: a national sample study. *Archives of sexual behavior*, 4, 605–621.

Meyer, T.P. (1972). The effects of sexually arousing and violent films on aggressive behavior. *Journal of Sex Research*, 8, 324–333.

Money, John (1985). The conceptual neutering of gender and the criminalization of sex. *Archives of sexual behavior*, 14:279–89.

Money, J. (1982). Sexosophy and sexology, philosophy and science: two halves, one whole. In Z. Hoch & H. I. Lief (eds.), *Sexology: sexual biology, behavior and therapy*. Amsterdam: Excerpta Medica.

Money, J. (1981). The development of sexuality and eroticism in humankind. *Quarterly review of biology*, 56:379–404, December.

Money, J. (1979). Sexual dictatorship, dissidence and democracy. *International journal of medicine and law*, 1:11–20.

Money, J. (1972). Pornography in the home. In J. Zubin & J. Money (eds.), *Contemporary sexual behavior: critical issues in the 1970s*. Baltimore: Johns Hopkins University Press.

Moreland, R. L. & Zajonc, R. B. (1976). A strong test of exposure effects. *Journal of experimental social psychology*, 12, 170–179.

Mosher, D. L. & O'Grady, K. E. (1979). Sex guilt, trait anxiety, and females' subjective sexual arousal to erotica. *Motivation and emotion*, 3, 235–249.

Mosher, D. (1970). Sex callousness toward women. *Technical Report of the Commission on Obscenity and Pornography*, vol. 8. Washington, D.C.: Gov't. Printing Office. 313–325.

Mosher, D. (1970). Psychological reactions to pornographic films. *Technical Report of the Commission on Obscenity and Pornography*, vol. 8. Washington, D.C.: Gov't. Printing Office. 255–312.

Mosher, D. (1970). Pornographic films, male verbal aggression against women, and guilt. *Technical report of the Commission on Obscenity and Pornography*, vol. 8. Washington, D.C.: Gov't. Printing Office, 357–379.

National Institute of Mental Health (1982). *Television and behavior: ten years of scientific progress and implications for the eighties*. J. 1 and 2. Bethesda, Maryland.

Nelson, E. (1982). *The influence of pornography on behavior*. London: Academic Press.

Newsweek (1985), March.

Propper, M. (1970). Exposure to sexually oriented materials among young male prison offenders. In *Technical Report of the Commission on Obscenity and Pornography*, vol. 9, Washington, D.C.: Gov't. Printing Office, 313–404.

Quinsey, V. L. (1984). Sexual aggression: studies of offenders against women. In D. Weisstub (ed.), *Law and mental health: international perspectives*, vol. 1. New York: Pergamon Press.

Quinsey, V.L. (1983). Prediction of recidivism and the evaluation of treatment programs for sex offenders. In S.N. Verdun-Jones and A.A. Keltner (eds.), *Sexual aggression and the law*. Criminology Research Center, Simon Fraser University.

Quinsey, V.L., Chaplin, T.C. and Upfold, D. (1984). Sexual arousal to nonsexual violence and sadomasochistic themes among rapists and non-sexual offenders. *Journal of consulting and clinical psychology*, 52: 651–657.

Quinsey, V.L., and T.C. Chaplin (1984). Stimulus control of rapists' and non-sex offenders' sexual arousal. *Behavioral assessment*, 6:169–176.

Quinsey, V.L. and T.C. Chaplin (1982). Penile responses to nonsexual violence among rapists. *Criminal justice and behavior*, 9:372–381, September.

Quinsey, V.L., Chaplin, T. and Carrigan, W. (1980). Biofeedback and signalled punishment in the modification of inappropriate sexual age preferences. *Beh. Ther.*, 11:567–576.

Quinsey, V.L., Chaplin, T. and G. Varney (1981). A comparison of rapists' and nonsex offenders sexual preferences for mutually consenting sex, rape, and physical abuse of women. *Behavioral assessment*, 3:127–135.

Quinsey, V.L. and Marshall, W. (1983). Procedures for reducing inappropriate sexual arousal: an evaluation review. In Greer, J.G. and Stuart, I. (eds.). *The sexual aggressor: current perspectives on treatment*. New York: Van Nostrand Reinhold Co.

Quinsey, V.L., C.M. Steinman, S.G. Bergersen, and T. Holmes (1975). Penile circumference, skin conductance, and ranking responses of child molesters and "normals" to sexual and nonsexual visual stimuli. *Behavior therapy*, 6:213–219.

Rada, R. T. (1978). Psychological factors in rapist behavior. In R.T. Rada (ed.), *Clinical aspects of the rapists*. New York: Grune and Stratton.

Reifler, C.B., Howard, J., Lipton, M.A., Liptzin, M.B. and Widman, D.E. (1971). Pornography: an experimental study of effects. *American journal of psychiatry*, 128:575–582.

Report of the Special Committee on Pornography and Prostitution, vol. 1 (1985). Ottawa: Minister of Supply and Services.

Rosenthal, R. and Rosnow, R. (1969). Artifact in behavioral research. New York: Academic Press.

Rubinstein, E. and Brown, J. (1985). *The media, social science, and social policy for children.* New Jersey: Ablex Corp.

Russell, D. (1975). *The politics of rape.* New York: Stein and Day.

Russell, D. (1980). Pornography and the women's liberation movement. In L. Lederer (ed.), *Take back the night: women on pornography.* New York: William Morrow.

Sapolsky, B.S. & Zillmann, D. (1981). The effect of soft-core and hard-core erotica on provoked and unprovoked hostile behavior. *Journal of Sex Research,* 17, 319–343.

Schill, T., Van Tuinen, M. and Doty, D. (1980). Repeated exposure to pornography and arousal levels of subjects varying in guilt. *Psychological reports,* 46:2 467–471.

Schmidt, G. (1975). Male-female differences in sexual arousal and behavior during and after exposure to sexually explicit stimuli. *Archives of sexual behavior,* 4, 353–364.

Schmidt, G. and Sigusch, V. (1973). Women's sexual arousal. In Zubin, J. and Money, J. (eds.). *Contemporary sexual behavior: critical issues in the 1970s.* Baltimore: Johns Hopkins University Press.

Scott, J. E. (1972). The changing nature of sex references in mass circulation magazines. *Public Opinion quarterly,* 36:80–86.

Scott, J.E. (1973). Sex references in the mass media. *Journal of sex research,* 9:196–209. August.

Scott, J.E. (1974). A reexamination of the public's perception of sexual deviance. *Western sociological review,* 5:82–86, Summer.

Scott, J.E. (In press). A longitudinal content analysis of sex references in mass circulation magazines. *Journal of sex research.*

Scott, J.E. (1985). Rape rates and the circulation rates of adult magazines. Paper presented to the annual meeting of the American Association for the Advancement of Science, Los Angeles.

Scully, D. and J. Marolla (1985). Riding the bull at Gilley's: rapists describe the rewards of rape. *Social problems,* February.

Scully, D. and J. Marolla (1984). Convicted rapists' vocabulary of motive: excuses and justifications, *Social problems,* 31:531–44.

Scully, D. and J. Marolla (1983). Convicted rapists: exploring a sociological model. *Final Report to the National Institute of Mental Health.* August.

Senn, C. H. (1985). A comparison of women's reactions to non-violent pornography, violent pornography, and erotica. Unpublished master's thesis, Dept. of Psychology, University of Calgary, Alberta, Canada.

Silbert, Mimi (1980). *Sexual assault of prostitutes.* National Center for the Prevention and Control of Rape. NIMH. November.

Sintchak, G. and Geer, J. (1975). A vaginal plethysmograph system. *Pscyhophysiology,* 12:113–115.

Simpson, M. and Schill, T. (1977). Patrons of massage parlors: some facts and figures. *Archives of sexual behavior.* 6:521–525.

Smith, D.G. (1976). The social content of pornography. *Journal of Communication,* 26, 16–33.

Special Committee on Pornography and Prostitution (1985). *Pornography and prostitution in Canada.* Ottawa: Ministry of Supply and Services.

Steinem, G. (1980). Erotica and pornography: a clear and present difference. In L. Lederer (ed.), *Take back the night:. women on pornography.* New York: Morrow.

Stock, W. (1983). The effects of violent pornography on women. Paper presented at the American Psychological Association meeting, Anaheim, CA.

Surgeon General's Scientific Advisory Committee on Television and Social Behavior (1972). *Television and growing up: the impact of televised violence.* Report to the Surgeon General, U.S. Public Health Service. Washington, D.C.: Gov't Printing Office.

Swart, C. and Berkowitz, L. (1976). Effects of a stimulus associated with a victim's pain on later aggression. *Journal of personality and social psychology,* 33:623–631.

Tannenbaum, P.H. (1970). Emotional arousal as a mediator of erotic communication effects. *Technical Report of the Commission on Obscenity and Pornography,*, vol. 8. Washington, D.C.: Gov't Printing Office. 326–356.

Tieger, T. (1981). Self-reported likelihood of raping and the social perception of rape. *Journal of Research in Personality,* 15, 147–158.

Tversky, A. & Kahneman, D. (1973). Availability: a heuristic for judging frequency and probability. *Cognitive Psychology,* 5, 207–232.

Wallace, D. H. (1973). Obscenity and contemporary community standards: a survey. *Journal of social issues,* 29, 53–68.

Walker, C.E. (1970). Erotic stimuli and the aggressive sexual offender. In *Technical Reports of the Commision on Obscenity and Pornography,* Washington, D.C.: Gov't. Printing Office, 7:91–147.

Washington Post (1986). March 24.

Weaver, J. B., Masland, J., and Zillmann, D. (1984). Effects of erotica on young men's aesthetic perception of their female sexual partners. *Per. & Motor Skills,* 58:929–930.

Weiss, W. (1969). Effects of the mass media on communication. In Lindzey, G. and Aronson, E. (eds.). *Handbook of Social Psychology*, V.S. Reading, Mass.: Addison-Wesley.

White, L.A. (1979). Erotica and aggression: the influence of sexual arousal, positive effect, and negative effect on aggressive behavior. *Journal of Personality and Social Psychology*, 37, 591–601.

Whitman, W. and Quinsey, V. L. (1981). Heterosocial skills training for institutionalized rapists and child molesters. *Can. Jour. of Beh. Sci.*, 13:105–114.

Williams, B. (1981). *Obscenity and film censorship: an abridgement of the Williams Report*. Cambridge: Cambridge University Press.

Wilson, W.C. (1978). Can pornography contribute to the prevention of sexual problems? In Qualls, C.B., J.P. Wincze, and D.H. Barlow (eds.). *The Prevention of Sexual Disorders: issues and approaches*. New York: Plenum Press.

Wilson, W. C. & Abelson, H. I. (1973). Experience with and attitudes toward explicit sexual materials. *Journal of social issues*, 29:3, 19–39.

Wolchik, S.A., Braver, S.L., and Jensen, K. (1985). Volunteer bias in erotica research: effects of intrusiveness of measure and sexual background. *Arch. of Sex. Beh.*, 14:93–107.

Wolchik, S.A., Spencer, S.L., and Lisi, I. (1983). Volunteer bias in research employing vaginal measures of sexual arousal: demographic, sexual and personality characteristics. *Arch. of Sex. Beh.*, 12:339–408.

Yaffe, M. and Nelson, E. (eds). *The influence of pornography on behavior*. New York: Academic Press.

Zajonc, R. B. (1968). Attitudinal effects of mere exposure. *Journal of personality and social psychology monograph supplement*, 9, 1–27.

Zajonc, R. B. & Rajecki, D. W. (1969). Exposure and affect: a field experiment. *Psychonomic science*, 17, 216–217.

Zillmann, D. (1984). *Connections between sex and aggression*. Hillsdale, New Jersey: Lawrence Erlbaum.

Zillmann, D. (1982). Television viewing and arousal. In Pearl, D., Bouthilet, L., and Lazar, J., *Television and behavior: ten years of scientific progress and implications for the eighties*. v. 2. Bethesda, Md.: National Institute of Mental Health.

Zillmann, D. (1979). *Hostility and aggression*. Hillsdale, New Jersey: Erlbaum.

Zillmann, D. and Bryant, J. (In press) Shifting preferences in pornography consumption. *Comm. Research*.

Zillmann, D. and Bryant, J. (1986a). Pornography's impact on sexual satisfaction. Unpublished Paper.

Zillmann, D. and Bryant J. (1986b). Effects of pornography consumption on family values: Unpublished paper.

Zillmann, D. & Bryant, J. (1982). Pornography, sexual callousness, and the trivialization of rape. *Journal of Communication*, 32:4, 10–21.

Zillmann, D., Bryant, J., & Carveth, R.A. (1981). The effect of erotica featuring sadomasochism and bestiality on motivated intermale aggression. *Personality and Social Psychology Bulletin*, 7, 153–159.

Zillmann, D., Bryant, J., Comisky, P.W. & Medoff, N.J. (1981). Excitation and hedonic valence in the effect of erotica on motivated intermale aggression. *European Journal of Social Psychology*, 11, 233–252.

Zillmann, D., Hoyt, J.L. & Day, K.D. (1974). Strength and duration of the effect of aggressive, violent, and erotic communications on subsequent aggressive behavior. *Communication Research*, 1, 286–306.

Zillmann, D. & Sapolsky, B.S. (1977). What mediates the effect of mild erotica on annoyance and hostile behavior in males? *Journal of Personality and Social Psychology*, 35, 587–596.

Zuckerman, M. (1971). Physiological measures of sexual arousal in the human. *Pych. Bull.*, 75:297–328.

LAW ENFORCEMENT

Cases

Federal

Carlin Communications, Inc. v. FCC, 749 F. 2d 113 (2d Cir. 1984).

CBS v. FCC, 435 U.S. 367 (1981).

Community Communication Co. v. City of Boulder, 660 F. 2d 1370 (10th circ. 1981), Cert. den. 457 U.S. 1105 (1982).

Community Television of Utah v. Roy City, 555 F. Supp. 1164 (D. Utah 1982).

FCC v. Pacifica Foundation, 438 U.S. 726 (1978).

Gulf Oil Corp. v. Copp Pawing Co., Inc., 419 U.S. 186 (1974).

HBO, Inc. v. Wilkinson, 531 F. Supp 987 (D. Utah 1982).

Kaplan v. California, 413 U.S. 15 (1973).

McLain v. Real Estate Board of New Orleans, 444 U.S. 232 (1978).

Memoirs v. Massachusetts, 383 U.S. 413 (1966).
Miller v. California, 413 U.S. 15 (1973).
National Broadcasting Co. v. United States, 319 U.S. 190 (1943).
Paris Adult Theatre I v. Staton, 413 U.S. 49 (1973).
Roth v. United States, 354 U.S. 476 (1957).
Stanley v. Georgia, 394 U.S. 557 (1969).
Turf Paradise, Inc, v. Arizona Downs, 670 F. 2d 813 (9th Cir. 1982).
United States v. American Building Maintenance Industries, 422 U.S. 271 (1975).
United States v. Reidel, 402 U.S. 351 (1971).
United States v. Roede, 526 F. 2d 736 (10th Cir. 1975), cert. den. 462 U.S. 905.
United States v. 37 Photographs, 402 U.S. 363 (1971).
United States v. Wrightwood Dairy Co., 315 U.S. 110 (1942).
Wickard v. Filburn, 317 U.S. 111 (1942).

States
Commonwealth v. Dufresne, C-19608 (Arlington Co., VA).
Commonwealth v. Kind, C-19168 (Arlington Co., VA).
Commonwealth v. Martin, C-19568 (Cir. Ct. Arlington Co. VA).
People v. Fixle, 56 Cal. App. 31, 128 Cal. Rpt. 363 (1976).
Trans-Lux Theatre v. People ex. rel. Sweeton, 366 So.
    2d 710 (Ala. 1979).

Other
In re WUHY-FM, 24 FCC 2d 408 (1970).

Constitution and Statutes

Federal

U.S. Const. art. I, S8, cl. 3.
11 U.S.C. S303 (Supp. II, 1984).
18 U.S.C. S492.
18 U.S.C. S844.
18 U.S.C. S881.
18 U.S.C. S924.
18 U.S.C. S1202.
18 U.S.C. S1462.
18 U.S.C. S1464.
18 U.S.C. S1465.
18 U.S.C. S1955.
18 U.S.C. S1961.
18 U.S.C. S1962 (West Supp. 1985).
18 U.S.C. S1963 (West Supp. 1985).
18 U.S.C. S2251.
18 U.S.C. S2252.
18 U.S.C. S2253.
18 U.S.C. S2254.
18 U.S.C. S2255.
18 U.S.C. S2318.
18 U.S.C. S2344.
18 U.S.C. S2421.
18 U.S.C. S2531.
47 U.S.C. S223.
47 U.S.C. S544.
47 U.S.C. S559.

States
Col. Penal Code S311 (West).

Books

Gilder, G., *The Spirit of Enterprise* (1984).

Articles

An Empirical Inquiry Into the Effects of Miller v. California on the Control of Obscenity, 52 N.Y.U.L. Rev. 810 (1977).
The Daily Sentinel (Aug. 13, 1984).
Hollywood Press (Aug. 9, 1985).
Morality in Media Newsletter (Nov. 1985).
National Decency Reporter (May—June 1985).
Tampa Tribune (Nov. 8, 1985).

Testimony

Chicago Hearing, Vol. I, Thomas Bohling.
_____, Vol. II, John Dugan.
_____, Vol. II, Hinson McAuliffe.
_____, Vol. II, Duncan McDonald.
_____, Vol. I, Paul McGready.
_____, Vol. I, Harold Mills.
_____, Vol. I, Jack O'Malley.
_____, Vol. II, Larry Parrish.
_____, Vol. II, James S. Reynolds.
_____, Vol. II, John Ruberti.
_____, Vol. II, Frederick Scullin.
_____, Vol. I, Donald Smith.
Houston Hearing, Vol. II, W.D. Brown.
Los Angeles Hearing, Vol. II, Brian Cid.
_____, Vol. II, James J. Clancy.
_____, Vol. I, James Docherty.
_____, Vol. I, William Dunkle.
_____, Vol. I, Brenda Fox.
_____, Vol. I, Ken Gillingham.
_____, Vol. I, Thomas Herwitz.
_____, Vol. II, Teresa Hillman.
_____, Vol. II, Charles Sullivan.
_____, Vol. I, Judith Trevillian.
_____, Vol. II, Jack Valenti.
_____, Vol. I, Brent Ward.
Miami Hearing, Vol. I, Mike Berish.
_____, Vol. II, Barbara Hattemer.
New York Hearing, Vol. II, Marcella Cohen.
_____, Vol. II, Sam Currin.
_____, Vol. II, William Johnson.
_____, Vol. I, William Kelly.
_____, Linda ✂ .
_____, Vol. I, Christopher J. Mega.
_____, Vol. II, Larry Schuchman.
_____, Vol. I, Carl Shoffler.
_____, Vol. II, Robert Showers.
Washington, D.C., Hearing, Vol. I, Charles Clauson.
_____, Vol. I, Mitch McConnell.
_____, Vol. I, Daniel Mihalko.
_____, Vol. I, Jack Swagerty.
_____, Vol. II, William Webster.

Miscellaneous References

Addendum to Brief for Appellant, FCC v. Pacifica Foundation, 438 U.S. 726 (1978).
Administrative Offices of the United States District Courts, United States District Courts Sentences Imposed Charts.
Brief for Appellant, FCC v. Pacifica Foundation, 438 U.S. 726 (1978).
Citizens for Decency Through Law, Cable Pornography: Problem and Solution (Jan. 1985).
Contract Between New Jersey Bell and Sundial Productions.
FCC News Release, General Docket, No. 83–989 (Oct. 16, 1985).
49 F.R. 24, 996 (June 4, 1984).
50 F.R. 42, 699 (Oct. 22, 1985).

Letter from Donald B. Nicholson to Alan E. Sears (Feb. 28, 1986).
New York Assembly Bill 8563-A. S.B. 1090
United States Department of Justice, *United States Attorney's Manual* (1981).

FIRST AMENDMENT CONSIDERATIONS

Cases

Federal

Aday v. United States, 388 U.S. 447 (1967) reversing 357 F. 2d 855 (6th Cir. 1966).
Bigilow v. Virginia, 421 U.S. 809 (1975).
Books, Inc. v. United States, 388 U.S. 449 (1967), reversing 358 F. 2d 935 (1 Cir. 1966).
Brandenburg v. Ohio, 359 U.S. 444 (1969).
Brockett v. Spokane Arcades, Inc., 105 S.Ct. 2794 (1985).
Chaplinsky v. New Hampshire, 315 U.S. 568 (1942).
Childs v. Oregon, 401 U.S. 1006 (1971) reversing per curium 431 F. 2d 272 (9th Cir. 1970).
Cohen v. California, 403 U.S. 15.
Erzoznik v. City of Jacksonville, 422 U.S. 205 (1975).
Gelling v. Texas, 343 U.S. 960 (1952).
Ginsberg v. New York, 390 U.S. 629 (1968).
Ginzberg v. United States, 383 U.S. 463 (1966).
Hamling v. United States, 418 U.S. 87 (1974).
Hess v. Indiana, 414 U.S. 105 (1973).
Jacobellis v. Ohio, 378 U.S. 184 (1964).
Jenkins v. Georgia, 418 U.S. 153 (1974).
Joseph Burstyn, Inc. v. Wilson, 343 U.S. 495 (1952).
Kingsley International Pictures Corp. v. Regents, 352 U.S. 380 (1957).
Kois v. Wisconsin, 408 U.S. 229 (1972).
Miller v. California, 413 U.S. 15 (1973).
Mishkin v. New York, 383 U.S. 502 (1965).
New York v. Ferber, 458 U.S. 747 (1982).
New York Times v. Sullivan, 376 U.S. 254 (1964).
Paris Adult Theater I v. Slaton, 413 U.S. 49 (1973).
Pinkus v. United States, 436 U.S. 293 (1978).
Potomac News Co. v. United States, 389 U.S. 47 (1967) reversing 373 F. 2d 635 (4th Cir. 1967).
Redrup v. New York, U.S. 767 (1967).
Renton v. Paytime Theatres, Ship. op. No. 89–1360 (Feb. 25, 1986).
Rosen v. United States, 161 U.S. 29 (1896).
Roth v. United States, 354 U.S. 476 (1957).
Smith v. United States, 431 U.S. 291 (1977).
Ward v. Illinois, 431 U.S. 767 (1977).
Winter v. New York, 333 U.S. 507 (1948).
Young v. American Mini-Theatres, 427 U.S. 50 (1976).
Childs v. Oregon, 431 F. 2d 272 (9th Cir. 1970.).
Eastman Kodak Co. v. Hendricks, 262 F. 2d 393 (9th Cir. 1958).
Flying Eagles Publications v. United States, 273 F. 2d 799 (1st. Cir. 1960).
Hunt v. Keriakos, 428 F. 2d 606 (1st. Cir. 1970). Cert. den. 400 U.S. 929.
J.R. Distributors Inc. v. Eskenberry, 725 F. 2d 482 (9th Cir. 1984).
Luros v. United States, 389 F. 2d 200 (8th Cir. 1968).
Miller v. United States, 431 F. 2d 655 (9th Cir. 1970).
Miller v. United States, 507 F. 2d 1100 (9th Cir. 1974). Cert. den. 95 S.Ct. 2620 (1975).
Penthouse International Ltd. v. McAuliffe, 610 F. 2d 1553 (5th Cir. 1980).
Randy Studebaker v. Nissan, 533 F. 2d 510 (10th Cir. 1976).
United States v. Alexander, 498 F. 2d 934 (2d Cir. 1974).
United States v. American Theater Corp., 526 F. 2d 48 (8th Cir. 1975).
United States v. Bananov, 418 F. 2d 1051 (9th Cir. 1969).
United States v. Bagnell, 674 F. 2d 826 (11th Cir. 1982). Cert. den. 103 S.Ct. 1449.
United States v. Battishi, 464 F. 2d 237 (6th Cir. 1981).
United States v. Bettork, 646 F. 2d 237 (6th Cir. 1981).
United States v. Bush, 582 F. 2d 1016 (5th Cir. 1978).
United States v. Central Magazine Sales Limited, 381 F. 2d 821 (4th Cir. 1967).
United States v. Danley, 523 F. 2d 364 (9th Cir. 1975).
United States v. Dochsteiner, 518 F. 2d 20 (9th Cir. 1975).

United States v. Dost, 575 F. 2d 1303 (10th Cir. 1978).
United States v. Friedman, 506 F. 2d 511 (8th Cir. 1974).
United States v. Gower, 503 F. 2d 189 (D.C. Cir. 1974).
United States v. Hoffman, 502 F. 2d 419 (D.C. Cir. 1974).
United States v. Keller, 259 F. 2d 54 (3d Cir. 1958).
United States v. Langford, 688 F. 2d 1088 (7th Cir. 1982).
United States v. Manerith, 448 F. 2d 583 (2d Cir. 1971).
United States v. Merrill, 746 F. 2d 458 (9th Cir. 1984).
United States v. Miller, 455 F. 2d 899, 505 F. 2d 1247 (9th Cir. 1972, 1974).
United States v. Obscene Film, Cards, & Magazines, 541 F. 2d 810 (9th Cir. 1976).
United States v. One Reel of Film, 481 F. 2d 206 (1st Cir. 1973).
United States v. Palladino, 475 F. 2d 65 (1st Cir. 1973).
United States v. Pelleznno, 467 F. 2d 41 (9th Cir. 1972).
United States v. Petrov, 747 F. 2d 824 (2d Cir. 1984).
United States v. Pryba, 502 F. 2d 391 (D.C. Cir. 1974). Cert. den. 95 S.Ct. 815 (1975).
United States v. Ratner, 502 F. 2d 1300 (5th Cir. 1974).
United States v. Sandy, 605 F. 2d 210 (6th Cir. 1979).
United States v. Themis, 484 F. 2d 1149 (5th Cir. 1973).
United States v. 35 mm Motion Picture Film, F. 2d (2d Cir. 1970).
United States v. Thomas, 613 F. 2d 787 (10th Cir. 1980).
United States v. 2200 Paperback Books, 565 F. 2d 556 (9th Cir. 1977).
United States v. Various Articles, 709 F. 2d 132 (2d Cir. 1983).
United States v. Various Articles, 750 F. 2d 296 (7th Cir. 1984).
United States v. Womack, 509 F.2d 368 (D.C. Cir. 1974). Cert. den. 95 S.Ct. 2644 (1975).
Henley v. Wise, 303 F. Supp. 62 (N.D. Ind. 1969).
McKenzie v. Butler, 398 F. Supp. 1319 (W.D. Tex. 1975).
Penthouse International v. Webb, 594 F. Supp. 1186 (N.D. Ga. 1984).
Right to Read Committee v. School Committee, 454 F. Supp. 703 (D. Mass. 1978).
Salvail v. Nashua Board of Education, 469 F. Supp. 69 (D.N.H. 1979).
United States v. Geadwell, 373 F. Supp. 247 (N.D. Ohio 1974).
United States v. Gundlack, 345 F. Supp. 709 (W.D. Pa. 1972).
United States v. Marks, 364 F. Supp. 1022 (E.D. Ky. 1973) *aff'd* 520 F.2d 913 (6th Cir. 1975) *rev'd on other grounds,* 430 U.S. 188 (1977).
United States v. Stewart, 377 F. Supp. 299 (E.D. Pa. 1971).
Weissbaum v. Hammon, 439 F. Supp. 873 (N.D. Ill, 1977).
Zippo v. Rogers, 216 F. Supp. 670 (S.D.N.Y. 1963).

State
Andrews v. State, 639 S.W. 2d 4 (Tex. App. 1982).
Attorney General v. Book Named John Cleland's Memoirs of a Woman of Pleasure, 349 Mass. 69, 206 N.F.2d 403, *rev'd on other grounds,* 383 U.S. 413 (1966).
Beir v. State, 681 S.W.2d 124 (Tex. Cr. App. 1984).
Brazelton v. State, 282 So.2d 342 (Ala. Ct. Cr. App. 1973).
Burns v. State, 512 S.W. 2d 928 (Ark. 1974).
Carlock v. Texas, 604 S.W.2d 787 (Crm. App. 1980).
City of Belleville v. Morgan, 376 N.E.2d 704 (Ill. 1974).
City of Chicago v. Universal Publishing and Dist. Corp., 34 Ill.2d 250, 215 N.E.2d 251 (1966).
City of Phoenix v. Tne., 4 Ariz. App. 303, 420 P.2d 26 (1966).
City of Rochester v. Carlson, 202 N.W.2d 632 (Minn. 1972).
Commonwealth v. Croll, 480 A.2d 266 (Pa. 1984).
Commonwealth v. 767 Main Corp., 357 N.E.2d 753 (Mass. 1976).
Commonwealth v. 707 Main Corp., 357 N.E.2d 753 (Mass. 1976).
Commonwealth v. Trainer, 374 N.E.2d 1216 (Mass. 1978).
Dawson v. State, 288 So.2d 483 (Fla. 1973).
Dixon v. Minn. Ct. of San Francisco, 267 Cal. App. 2d 784, 73 Cal. Rptr. 587.
Dyke v. Georgia, 209 S.E. 2d 166 (1974).
Garcia v. State, 663 S.W. 2d 611 (Tex. App. 1982).
Harlow v. City of Birmingham, 296 So. 2d 202 (Ala. Ct. Cr. App. 1974).
Herman v. Arkansas, 512 S.W.2d 923 (Ark. 1974).
Hewitt v. State Bd. of Censors, 254 A.2d 203 (Md. 1969).
Illinois v. Ridens, 282 N.E. 2d 691 (1972). Cert. den. 95 S.Ct. 2000 (1975).
Kaplan v. United States, 311 A. 2d 506 (D.C. App. 1973).
LaRue v. State, 611 S.W. 2d 63 (Tex. Cir. App. 1980).

Louisiana v. Short, 368 So. 2d 1078 (La. 1974).
McKinney v. City of Birmingham, 296 So. 2d 197 (Ala. 1973).
New Riviera Arts Theatre v. State, 412 S.W. 2d 890 (1967).
New York v. Buckley, 307 N.E. 2d 805 (1973).
North Carolina v. Bryant, 203 S.E. 2d 36 (N.C. 1974). Cert. den. 95 S. Ct. 238.
North Carolina v. Hara, 203 S.E. 2d 27 (N.C. 1974). Cert. den. 95 S. Ct. 238.
Orito v. State, 191 N.W. 2d 763 (Wisc. 1972).
People v. Better, 337 N.E. 2d 272 (Ill. 1975).
People v. Bloss, 201 N.W. 2d 806 (March 1972).
People v. Colgud, Inc., 402 N.E. 2d 1140 (N.Y. 1980).
People v. Crampa, 394 N.V.S. 2d 727 (1977).
People v. Enskat, 109 col. Rptr, 433 Cal. 3d 900 (1973). Cert. den. 418 U.S. 937.
People v. Fenkelstein, 9 N.Y. 2d 342, 174 N.E. 2d 470 (1961).
People v. Mature Enterprises, Inc., 343 N.Y.S. 2d 911 (1973).
People v. Nelson, 410 N.E. 2d 476 (N.E. 1980).
People v. Ridens, 321 N.E. 2d 264 (N.E. 1974). Cert. den. 421 U.S. 993.
People v. Rode, 57 Ill. App. 3d 649, 373 N.E. 2d 605 (1968).
People v. Sarnblad, 26 Cal App. 3d 801, 103 Cal. Rptr. 211 (1972).
People v. Speer, 52 Ill. App. 203, 367 N.E. 2d 372 (1977).
People v. Tannahill, 38 Ill. App. 3d 767, 348 N.E. 2d 84.
People v. Thomas, 346 N.E. 2d 190 (Ill. 1976).
Peters v. State, 449 N.E. 2d 311 (Ind. App. 1983).
Pierce v. State, 244 S.E. 2d 589 (Ga).
Pierce v. State, 296 So. 2d 218 (Ala.).
Price v. Commonwealth, 201 S.E. 2d 798 (Na. 1974). Cert. den. 419 U.S. 902.
Sanza v. State Bd. of Censors, 226 A. 2d 317 (Md. 1967).
Sedelbawer v. Indiana, 428 N.E. 2d 206 (Md. 1981). Cert. den. 455 U.S. 1035.
Slaton v. Paris Adult Theater I, 201 S.E. 2d 456 (Ga.).
Spry v. State, 156 Ga. App. 74, 274 S.E. 2d 2 (1983).
State v. American Theater Corp, 230 N.W. 2d 209 (Web. 1976).
State v. Benett, 292 S.E. 2d 590 (1982).
State v. Boyd, 300 N.E. 2d 752 (Ohio App. 1972).
State v. Burgun, 384 N.E. 2d 255 (Ohio 1978).
State v. Cardwell, 339 P. 2d 169 (Or. App.).
State v. DePiano, 375 A. 2d 1169 (N.J. 1977).
State v. Great American Theater Co., 608 P. 2d 951 (1980).
State v. Hull, 86 Wash. 2d 527, 546 P. 2d 912.
State v. Lebovitz, 202 N.W. 2d 648 (Minn. 1972).
State v. Lewitt, 222 A. 2d 579 (Ct. App. Conn. 1966).
State v. Little AA Corp., 191 Neb. 448, 215 N.W. 2d 853 (1974).
State v. Motion Picture, 547 P. 2d 760 (Kan.).
State v. Walden Book Co., 386 So. 2d 342 (La. 1980).
Trans-Lux Corp. v. Start ex rel. Sweeton, 366 So. 2d 710 (1979).
Velag Books, Inc. v. State's Attorney, 282 A. 2d 124 (Md. 1971).
Volkland v. State, 510 S.W. 2d 585 (Tex.).
Washington v. J-R Distributors, Inc., 512 P. 2d 1049 (1973). Cert. den. 418 U.S. 949 (1974).

Constitutions

Statutes
U.S. Const. Amend. I.
Wash. Rev. Code S7 48A 010.

Books

Schauer, F., *The Law of Obscenity* (1976).

Articles

Bork R., *Neutral Principles and Some First Amendment Problems*, 47 Md. L. Rev. 1 (1971).
Lokhart and McClure, *Literature, the Law of Obscenity, and the Constitution*, 38 Minn. L. Rev. 295
    (1954).
Chicago Hearing, Vol. I, Jane Wicher, p. 222.
Washington, D.C., Hearing, Vol. II, Lillian BeVier, p. 213.
_____, Vol. II, Barry Lynn, p. 746.

ORGANIZED CRIME

Cases

Federal
United States v. Guarino, 83–736, CV ESP-3P (Fla.).
United States v. Sovereign News Co., (W.D. Ky.).
United States v. Sturman, CR 85–133 (N.D. Ohio).
United States v. Thevis, 655 F. 2d 616 (5th Cir. 1983).

Articles

The Annual Report to the Legislature, *Organized Crime in California* (1984).
Federal Bureau of Investigation, *The Extent of Organized Crime Involvement in Pornography* (1978).
Investigative Report submitted by the Attorney General of California.
Investigative Services Division, Washington, D.C., Metropolitan Police Department, *Organized Crime's Involvement in the Pornography Industry* (1978).
Reagan, R., *Declaring War on Organized Crime*, The New York Times Magazine, Jan. 12, 1986.
The Report of the Commission on Obscenity and Pornography (1970).
Whalen, E., *Prince of Porn*, Cleveland (Aug. 1985).

Testimony

Los Angeles Hearing, Vol. II, Caryl Cid.
——————————————————, Vol. II, Brian Cid.
——————————————————, Vol. I, James Docherty.
——————————————————, Vol. I, Robert Peters.
——————————————————, Vol. II, Charles Sullivan.
Miami Hearing, Vol. II, Dennis Shaw.
New York Hearing, Vol. I, Thomas Bohling.
——————————————————, Vol. I, Bookstore Operator Interview with Edward Chapman.
——————————————————, Vol. II, Marcella Cohen.
——————————————————, Vol. I, Fratianno Interview with Edward Chapman.
——————————————————, Vol. I, James D. Harmon.
——————————————————, Vol. II, William Johnson.
——————————————————, Vol. I, William P. Kelly.
——————————————————, Vol. I, Linda ✂ .
——————————————————, Vol. II, Christopher J. Mega.
——————————————————, Vol. I, Carl Shoffler.
——————————————————, Vol. II, Robert Showers.
——————————————————, Vol. I, Marilyn Sommers.
——————————————————, Vol. IV, W.H.I.S.P.E.R..
——————————————————, Vol. I, Homer Young.
Washington, D.C., Hearing, Vol. I, Valerie ✂ .
——————————————————, Vol. II, William Webster.
——————————————————, Vol. I, Sarah ✂ .

Miscellaneous References

Cong. Rec. S433 (daily ed. Jan. 30, 1984) (Statement of Sen. Jesse Helms).
Letter from Marcella Cohen to Alan Sears (March 4, 1986).
Letter from William H. Webster to Henry Hudson.
President's Commission on Organized Crime (1986) (Testimony of Martin Light).

COMMUNITY, CITIZEN, AND CORPORATE ACTION AND RESPONSIBILITY

Cases

Federal
Miller v. California, 413 U.S. 15 (1973).
NAACP v. Claibourne Hardware Co., 458 U.S. 886 (1982).
Renton v. Playtime Theatres, Inc., No. 84–1360, ship op. (Feb. 25, 1986).
Missouri v. National Organization for Women, 670 F. 2d 1301 (8th Cr. 1980).

Testimony

Washington, D.C., Vol. I, Kandy Stroud, p. 243.

C H A P T E R • 3 3

Additional Suggested Reading Materials

Criminal Prosecutions

18. Am. Jur. Proof of Facts, *Obscenity—Motion Pictures,* 465 (1971).

Bates, F., *Pornography and The Expert Witness,* 20 Crim. L.Q. 250 (1978).

Beckett and Bell, *Community Standards: Admitting a Public Opinion Poll Into Evidence in an Obscenity Case,* 84, Case and Comment 18 (1979).

Binding Advisory Jury in Missouri Obscenity Cases, 45 U.M.K.C. L. Rev. 159 (1976).

Brigman, *The Controversial Role of the Expert in Obscenity Litigation,* 7 Cap. U. L. Rev. 519 (1978).

Cohen, F., *Obscenity Cases: Anatomy of a Winning Defense,* 14 Crim. L. Bull. 225 (1978).

Comment, *Expert Testimony in Obscenity Cases,* 18 Hastings, L. J. 161 (1966).

Community Standards in Obscenity Adjudication, 66 Cal. L. Rev. 1277 (1978).

The Constitutionality of Admitting the Video Tape Testimony at Trial of Sexually Abused Children, 7 Whittier L. Rev. 639 (1985).

Dewitt E. and Blackmar, C., *Federal Jury Practice and Instructions* (1970).

Evidentiary and Procedural Trends in State Legislation and Other Emerging Issues in Child Sexual Abuse Cases, 89 Dick. L. Rev. 645 (1985).

Frank, *Obscenity: Some Problems of Values and the Use of Experts,* 41 Was. L. Rev. 631 (1966).

George, B.S., Jr., *Obscenity Litigation: An Overview of Current Legal Controversies, National Journal of Criminal Defense.* 189 (1977).

Jury's Role in Criminal Obscenity Cases—A Closer Look, 28 Kan. L. Rev. 111 (1974).

Kutz, E., *Regulating Obscenity,* 5 Whitt, L. Rev. 1 (1983).

Lefcourt, G., et al., *Obscenity Law* (Practicing Law Institute Outline, 1974).

Linz, D., *Assessing Courtroom Performance from the Perspective of the Social Science Observer, The Trial Practice Attorney, and The "Jury Box".* Annual Meeting of the Law and Society Association, Toronto, June, 1982.

Linz, D., Penrod, S., Coates, D., Atkinson, M., Heuer, L., Herzberg, S., *The Use of Experts in the Courtroom: Attorney Judgments of Expert Witness Credibility.* Annual Meeting, Academy of Criminal Justice Science, March 1982.

Mann, J., *Fahringer Plays to a Hostile Court,* 4 Am. Law 39 (Aug. 1982).

Mayer, M.F., *New Approach to Obscenity—The Conspiracy Doctrine,* 21 St. Louis. U.L.J. 366 (1977).

McCommon, P., Bull, B., Taylor, B., *Preparation and Trial of an Obscenity Case: A Guide for Prosecuting Attorney,* (1985).

McGaffey, *A Realistic Look at Expert Witnesses in Obscenity Cases,* 69 N.W.U.L. Rev. 218 (1974).

Munson Lentz, M., *Comparison Evidence in Obscenity Trials,* 15 U. Mich. J.L. Ref. 45 (1981).

Note, *Constitutional Law—Appellate Procedure in Obscenity,* 52 U. Cin. L. Rev. 1131 (1983).

Note, *The Use of Expert Testimony in Obscenity Litigation,* 1965 Wisc. L. Rev. 113 (1965).

Pattern Jury Change, U.S. Fifth Circuit District Judge Association (1983).

Penrod, S., Linz, D., Coates, D., Heur, L., Atkinson, M., Herzberg, S., *First Impressions in the Courtroom: Juror Impressions of Prosecuting and Defense Attorneys in Voir Dire and Opening Statements.* Annual Meeting, Academy of Criminal Justice Science, March, 1982.

Prior Adversary Hearings on the Question of Obscenity, Colum. L. Rev. 1403 (1970).

Prior Adversary Hearing: Solution to Procedural Due Process Problems in Obscenity Seizures, 46 N.Y.U. L. Rev. 80 (1971).

Procedural Problems in the Seizure of Obscenity, 37 Albany L. Rev. 203 (1972).

Requirement and Techniques for Holding an Adversary Hearing Prior to Seizure of Obscene Material, 48 N.C. L. Rev. 830 (1970).

Rogge, *Obscenity Litigation*, 10 Am. Jur. Trials S50 (1965).

Schauer, F., *The Law of Obscenity* (1976). (See specifically Chapters 13 and 17).

Stern, *Toward a Rationale for the Use of Expert Testimony in Obscenity Litigation*, 20 Case West. Res. L. Rev. 527 (1969).

Stevens, P., *Community Standards and Federal Obscenity Prosecutions*, 55 S. Cal. L. Rev. 693 (1982).

Stoddart, C., *Corporate Responsibility for Common Law Crime*, 45 Crim. C. 35 (Feb. 1981).

Stone, R., *Obscenity Law Reform: Some Practical Problems*, 130 New L. J. 872 (1980).

Tuling, D., *Defense of "Public Good"*, 129 New L. J. 299 (1979).

Weaver, G., *Handbook on the Prosecution of Obscenity Cases* (1985).

Waples, G.L., White, M.J., *Choice of Community Standards in Federal Obscenity Proceedings: The Role of the Constitution and the Common Law*, 64 Va. L. Rev. 399 (1978).

Weinberg, R., *The Right to a Jury Trial in Obscenity Prosecution: A Sixth Amendment Analysis for a First Amendment Problem*, 50 Fordham L. Rev. 1311 (1982).

Young, R., *Right to Counsel . . . Conflict of Interests*, A.B.A.J. 636 (May 1981).

Civil Actions

Albaugh, K., *Regulation of Obscenity Through Nuisance Statute and Injunctive Remedies—the Prior Restraint Dilemma*, 19 Wake Forest L. Rev. 7 (1983).

Allen, P., *Public Nuisances, Private Lawyers*, 5 Cal. Law, 10 (Jul 1985).

Annot., *Pornoshops or Similar Places Disseminating Obscene Materials as Nuisance*, 55 A.L.R. 3d 1134 (1974).

Bodensteiner, I. and R. Berg Levinson, *Civil Liberties: Adherence to Established Principles*, 58 Chi-Kent L. Rev. 269 (1982).

Forkosch, *Obscenity, Copyright, and the Arts*, 10 New. Eng. L. Rev. 1 (1974).

Gorman, R., *The Demise of Civil Nuisance Action in Obscenity Control*, 14 Loy. U. Chi L. J. 31 (1982).

Green, R., *The Obscenity Defense to Copyright*, 69 Ky. L. J. 161 (1980).

Mayo, T., *Land Use Control*, 33 Syracuse L. Rev. 401 (1982).

McWalters, T., *An Attempt to Regulate Pornography Through Civil Rights Legislation: Is It Constitutional?*, 16 U. Tol. L. Rev. 231 (1984).

Nickerson, S. *Injunctions Pursuant to Public Nuisance Obscenity Statutes and the Doctrine of Prior Restraint*, 61 Wash. U. L.O. 775 (1983).

Note, *Community Standards, Class Actions, and Obscenity Under Miller v. California*, 88 Harv. L. Rev. 1838 (1975).

Note, *Immorality, Obscenity and the Law of Copyright*, 60 S. Dak. L. Rev. 109 (1961).

Note, *Private Ratings of Motion Pictures as a Basis for State Regulation*, 59 Geo. L.J. 1205 (1971).

Obscenity Not a Defense in Copyrght Infringement Action, 5 Art. b L. 68 (Spr. 1980).

Palumbo, N. Jr., *Obscenity and Copyright: An Illustrious Past and Future?*, 22 S. Tex. L.J. 87 (Wtr. 1982).

Schneider, *Authority of the Register of Copyrights to Deny Registration of a Claim to Copyright on the Ground of Obscenity*, 51 Chi-Kent L. Rev. 691 (1975).

Trachtman, J., *Pornography, Padlocks, and Prior Restraints: the Constitutional Limits of the Nuisance Power*, 58 N.Y.U. L. Rev. 1478 (1983).

Trollope, A., *Proceeding Against Defendant in Respect of Allegedly Obscene Film Where Trial of Same Issue Against Different Defendant Had Resulted in Acquittal—All Proceedings Capable of Being Brought Together Before Same Court—Whether Abuse of Process*, Crim. L. Rev. 350 (June 1984).

Statutes

18 U.S.C. S1461	18 U.S.C. S1736	19 U.S.C. S1305	18 U.S.C. S1963
18 U.S.C. S1462	18 U.S.C. S1737	39 U.S.C. S3008	18 U.S.C. S1964
18 U.S.C. S1463	18 U.S.C. S2251	39 U.S.C. S3011	18 U.S.C. S1965
18 U.S.C. S1464	18 U.S.C. S2252	47 U.S.C. S223	18 U.S.C. S1966
18 U.S.C. S1465	18 U.S.C. S2253	18 U.S.C. S1961	18 U.S.C. S1967
18 U.S.C. S1735	18 U.S.C. S2254	18 U.S.C. S1962	18 U.S.C. S1968

ORGANIZATIONS

National

Department of Justice
Criminal Division
Room 2107
Washington, D.C. 20530
(202) 633-2601

National Association of Attorneys General
444 North Capital Street
Washington, D.C.
(202) 628-0435

American Bar Association
750 North Lakeshore Drive
Chicago, Illinois
(312) 988-5000

Citizens for Decency Through Law, Inc.
11000 North Scottsdale Road
Suite 210
Scottsdale, Arizona 85254
(602) 483-8787

The American Civil Liberties Union
122 Maryland Avenue, N.E.
Washington, D.C. 20002
Barry W. Lynn
(202) 544-1681

National Federation For Decency
P.O. Drawer 2440
Tupelo, Mississippi 38803
Don Wildmon, Director

Feminists Anti-Censorship Task Force
Box 135
660 Amsterdam Avenue
New York, New York 10025
Nan D. Hunter

Rene Guyon Society
256 S. Robertson Blvd.
Beverly Hills, California 90213
Tim O'Hara

National Coalition Against Pornography, Inc. 800
Compton Road
Suite 9248
Cincinnati, Ohio 45231

Morality in Media
475 Riverside Drive
New York, New York 10115

State

State Attorney General
(located in particular state capital)

State Bar Association
(in particular state)

Staff Listing

PROFESSIONAL STAFF

David Cayer
J.D. American University

Peggy Coleman
J.D. University of Akron

Genevieve McSweeney Ryan
J.D. University of Michigan

Edna Einsiedel
Ph.D. Indiana University

MEDIA CONSULTANT

Richard Kimberly

FULL TIME INVESTIGATIVE STAFF

Detective Edward Chapman
Arlington County, Virginia, Police
  Department

Detective Joseph Haggerty
Metropolitan Police Department,
  Washington, D.C.

Inspector Daniel Mihalko
United States Postal Inspection Service

ADDITIONAL INVESTIGATIVE ASSISTANCE

Special Agent David Borden
United States Customs Service

Special Agent Sterling Epps
United States Customs Service

Special Agent Ramon Martinez
United States Customs Service

Special Agent William Ramey
United States Customs Service

Supervisory Special Agent Kenneth
  Lanning
Federal Bureau of Investigation

STAFF INTERNS

Jessica Feder   Laureen Buckert
Lois Ulm   Frenchette Chatman

Great appreciation is expressed to the many persons who served with the staff to make the completion of this project possible. Special appreciation and recognition goes to Jessica Feder who devoted hundreds of volunteer hours while she attended law school. The Commission expresses special appreciation to David Cayer who spent countless hours insuring that appropriate legal work was included within this Report and to Peggy Coleman for her work and editing. The Commission also specially recognizes the investigators who kept us in touch with the real world and its concerns.